The Paranoid Process

W.W. Meissner, S.J., M.D.

NEW YORK • JASON ARONSON • LONDON

to my parents, who gave life and love:
and to all the others who have helped me
grow in both

Classical Psychoanalysis and Its Applications

A SERIES OF BOOKS EDITED BY ROBERT LANGS, M.D.

Robert Langs
THE TECHNIQUE OF
  PSYCHOANALYTIC
  PSYCHOTHERAPY, VOLS. I AND II

THE THERAPEUTIC INTERACTION,
  TWO-VOLUME SET

THE BIPERSONAL FIELD

THE THERAPEUTIC INTERACTION:
  A SYNTHESIS

Judith Kestenberg
CHILDREN AND PARENTS:
  PSYCHOANALYTIC STUDIES IN
  DEVELOPMENT

Melitta Sperling
THE MAJOR NEUROSES AND
  BEHAVIOR DISORDERS IN
  CHILDREN

Peter L. Giovacchini
PSYCHOANALYSIS OF CHARACTER
  DISORDERS

PSYCHOTHERAPY OF PRIMITIVE
  MENTAL STATES

Otto Kernberg
BORDERLINE CONDITIONS AND
  PATHOLOGICAL NARCISSISM

OBJECT-RELATIONS THEORY AND
  CLINICAL PSYCHOANALYSIS

William A. Console
Richard D. Simons
Mark Rubinstein
THE FIRST ENCOUNTER

Humberto Nagera
FEMALE SEXUALITY AND THE
  OEDIPUS COMPLEX

OBSESSIONAL NEUROSES:
  DEVELOPMENTAL
  PSYCHOPATHOLOGY

Willi Hoffer
THE EARLY DEVELOPMENT AND
  EDUCATION OF THE CHILD

William Meissner
THE PARANOID PROCESS

Mardi Horowitz
STRESS RESPONSE SYNDROMES

HYSTERICAL PERSONALITY

Victor Rosen
STYLE, CHARACTER AND LANGUAGE

Charles Sarnoff
LATENCY

Heinz Lichtenstein
THE DILEMMA OF HUMAN IDENTITY

Simon Grolnick,
Leonard Barkin, Editors
in collaboration with
Werner Muensterberger,
BETWEEN FANTASY AND REALITY:
  TRANSITIONAL OBJECTS AND
  PHENOMENA

ARONSON

SERIES INTRODUCTION

In a span of some fifteen years of research, teaching, and writing, William Meissner has established himself as one of the most widely versed and productive of the current generation of psychoanalysts. His publications reflect his versatility and the breadth of his concerns and insights. They range from studies of a variety of problems in religion to investigations in neurophysiology and psychosomatics, and include explorations of family dynamics, dreaming, identification, values, problems in adolescents, and the schizophrenic process. In addition to his many fine papers, he has written books on religious life, the psychology of grace, the assault on authority, and basic concepts in psychoanalytic psychiatry (with Elizabeth Zetzel).

In this volume Meissner utilizes his broad background to develop an in-depth study of paranoid syndromes and processes. While this investigation is undertaken within the framework of classical psychoanalysis, it is supplemented by considerations drawn from a wide variety of sources, including psychological investigations, sociological studies, and explorations of family dynamics. The resultant comprehensive review of the literature and detailed presentation of his own clinical investigations are unmatched for their clarity, perceptiveness, and clinical usefulness. Once the reader comes to recognize that paranoid processes are on a continuum with daily, nonpathological human functioning, and that paranoid mechanisms are utilized by everyone, he comes to appreciate the extraordinary relevance of Meissner's presentation. There is, in addition, considerable clinical utility to his formulations and to his discussions of a variety of therapeutic techniques to be utilized with such patients. In all, this book is an unusual and worthy addition to this series, and testifies once again to the ever widening scope of classical psychoanalysis and its applications.

Robert Langs, M.D.

PREFACE

My interest in paranoia began in the confrontation with a series of severely disturbed paranoid patients. As I became increasingly familiar with their inner worlds and with the nature and content and form of their psychopathology, I became increasingly dissatisfied with the explanations and theoretical formulations that were typically and repeatedly brought to bear in my own and others' attempts to conceptualize and understand what we were experiencing with these patients. The more I looked, the more I listened, the more I tried to feel my way into the inner world of my patients, the more I became aware that what I was dealing with was of far greater breadth and relevance than simply the deviance and pathology that was so apparent in the behavior and thought processes of these patients.

With these questions and musings stirring in my head, I began the experience of a much more intense and detailed participation in the psychoanalytic process, which brought me ever more closely and intimately into the context and content of human thought processes. I began to see in the course of this experience that much that had manifested itself to me in the psychotic processes of much more primitive and disturbed patients was also identifiable in relatively healthy and far less maladapted human beings.

I began then, too, to think of my own experience, my own awareness of myself and how I fit into the world around me. I saw that my patients and I were dealing with similar problems, utilizing our common human resources in attempts to define and resolve basic problems of human experience and existence from which none of us could escape. Little by little, common mechanisms which linked these levels of organization and performance began to articulate themselves in my mind, and as I looked further in the clinical material they seemed to take shape and begin to emerge with a vividness and forcefulness that gave my inquiry a telling excitement and seemed to make it reverberate with meaning and motive.

The essential insight I have tried to articulate and substantiate, both by careful study of more traditional views about paranoia and by careful examination of pathological expressions of the syndrome, is that the basic mechanisms, which play themselves out in distorted and exaggerated forms in the pathology, are in fact the same basic mechanisms endemic to the human developmental process. These mechanisms contribute meaningfully and in profoundly important ways to the building up of human personality, to the establishment and sustaining of human identity, and to the elaboration and maintenance of the social and cultural structures within which such identities take shape and find their ultimate expression and cohesion. The consequence of this perspective is that paranoia, as a form of psychopathology, cannot be simply dissociated from the positive forces and processes which serve to build up and maintain meaningful and constructive areas of human growth and experience. The question remains ultimately to what degree the deviance and impairment of paranoid forms of pathology are indeed the price we pay for the constructive achievements and attainments that characterize human society and culture.

There is a further significant issue—the opposite side of the coin, in a sense—that is brought into focus by this consideration. I refer specifically to the question of the extent to which social forms of organization and functioning, based on and derived from the inner workings of the paranoid process—as it is described and discussed in this study—do not, in fact, create the context and the circumstances which contribute to the genesis of paranoia. This is perhaps most clearly focused on the level of family process and family interaction. The level of family pathology is not in the central focus of the present study, but it provides a significant context within which the mechanisms under consideration here articulate themselves and take their characteristic forms of expression. In all of the cases we have studied here, an important observation which demands further study and further understanding is that paranoia manifested in the individual patient comes out of a background in the family context in which paranoid elements are identifiable and effectively at work. The meaning of these observations and their importance for the understanding of the paranoid process in general is an area of further exploration that must wait another day.

The further step to a broader and more general understanding of the implementation of paranoid manifestations and processes on the level of social and cultural organization and functioning provides another context within which useful reflection and study is called for. At the present time we can do no more than to sketch in broad stretches the areas within which the paranoid process seems to come into play at such levels of social organization. The reflection at this level is important and constitutes an area in which basically psychoanalytic insight, derived from the study of intrapsychic processes, may be usefully extrapolated to the understanding of broader social structures and processes. Obviously, the extrapolation is not simple, and it is one that calls for serious consideration and further study. But it is my feeling at this juncture that the clinical and theoretical bases articulated in the present study may provide a foundation in terms of which the lines of continuity between intrapsychic processes, denominated here under the rubric of the "paranoid process," and social and cultural processes can be meaningfully established and articulated. That work too must wait for another day.

In any case, the excitement and personal interest that were generated for me in pursuing these ideas could not have been realized without the assistance, cooperation, and encouragement of countless individuals over the course of several years. It is impossible here to recall the countless exchanges of information and ideas, the numberless stimulating discussions with fellow clinicians, teachers, students, and others with whom my professional work and interest brought me into contact. Nonetheless, the contributions of certain individuals stand out in my mind and to them I wish to express my appreciation and deepest gratitude.

My appreciation goes, first of all, to Miss Rita Doucet for her helpfulness and cooperation in assisting with certain parts of the production of the manuscript; to Miss Betty Grove for her work in phases of secretarial preparation of the manuscript; and to Mrs. Melinda Hanson for her enthusiastic and indefatigable help in many phases of preparation—in typing, correcting, proofreading, and criticizing various parts.

My particular thanks go to Drs. Robert Eisendrath, Henry Grunebaum, Lee Hasenbush, Paul Myerson, Avery Weisman, and the late Elizabeth Zetzel, whose counsel, support, and encouragement helped me to learn a considerable amount in my initial and continuing struggle to understand and deal with the complex and difficult manifestations of the paranoid process which I encountered in my patients.

Thanks also go to Dr. Leonard Solomon for his critical evaluation of portions of the manuscript and his assistance in putting me in touch with certain portions of the material. I am grateful also to Dr. Nicholas Avery for his critical reading and appraisal of some of the theoretical portions of the manuscript. But, perhaps most centrally and significantly, my gratitude goes to Dr. Gregory Rochlin for his careful reading and criticizing of large portions of the manuscript and for his stimulating comments which have provided me with some of the basic insights and orientations which have come to fruition in this study.

I sincerely hope that the present work proves commensurate with the quality of the interest and contributions of these many friends. I also profoundly hope that what is contained in the following pages will contribute meaningfully and usefully to the understanding and alleviation of human suffering not merely in patients who have acquired one of the labels of paranoid psychopathology, but in the broader mass of humankind.

W. W. MEISSNER, S.J., M.D.

Cambridge, Massachusetts

CONTENTS

Part III
TOWARD A CLINICAL THEORY
OF THE PARANOID PROCESS

Contents

PART I

THE STRUCTURE AND FUNCTION OF PARANOID IDEATION

CHAPTER 1

The Development of
Theoretical Perspectives

The concept of paranoia was bequeathed to modern psychiatry in its Kraepelinian form. Kraepelin tried to distinguish paranoia from paraphrenia and paranoid dementia praecox. He described it as an insidiously developing, relatively unchanging delusional system which involved no hallucinations and could exist side by side with clear and orderly thinking. One of the basic problems in dealing with paranoia is that it usually is compounded with schizophrenic manifestations. Freud himself recognized this and still felt that there were grounds for distinguishing paranoia on dynamic bases. The specificity that he wished to retain seemed to have been based on the specific psychodynamic ideology that he defined in the now famous Schreber case. Sullivan on the other hand imagined them as imaginary poles of a clinical continuum. The imaginary poles stood apart and were rarely, if ever, in fact realized. He felt that every schizophrenic has some paranoid feelings and can be led to express them from time to time, and that conversely, every paranoid person also has some period of schizophrenic adjustment in his history (Sullivan, 1956).

The trend, however, has been in the direction of using the concept of paranoia with greater flexibility and with greater applicability. It is used not only as a diagnostic category but also as a descriptive personality trait which is characterized by isolation, hypersensitivity, guardedness, suspiciousness, and the use of projection as a defense. It has also been extended to include concepts of paranoid traits, or a paranoid attitude or outlook (Schwartz, 1963). In the present review we will be using the concept "paranoia" in its broader meaning as applying both to paranoid traits, paranoid mechanisms, or paranoid styles of life that can apply with varying degrees of intensity and pathology from severely disturbed psychotic states to relatively innocuous and more or less adaptive life-styles in relatively normal individuals and cultural institutions.

FREUD

Early Views
It was Freud, of course, who provided the decisive influence on contemporary thinking about paranoia. He defined paranoia as the

characteristic mechanism and related the paranoid state to basic conflicts over homosexual impulses. Although these elements are considered to be the mainstays of Freud's formulation, his ideas on the subject were considerably more complex and underwent a definite developmental progression.

In his earliest writing on the subject, the unpublished Draft H which he sent to Fliess in 1895, Freud places paranoia alongside obsessional ideas as an intellectual disorder and calls it an intellectual psychosis. He emphasizes the analogy between hysteria and obsessive states on one hand, and paranoia on the other, as pathological modes of defense (Freud, 1950 [1892-99], pp. 206-207). He says very simply, "People become paranoiac over things that they cannot put up with, provided that they possess the peculiar psychical disposition for it" (Freud, 1950 [1892-99], p. 207). The patient he describes spared herself the reproach of being a bad woman by projecting it outside. Whereas she would have had to accept the judgment pronounced from within, she could now reject one that was directed at her from the outside.

Paranoia was visualized as a defense against self-reproach, and the model Freud used was one he had developed from his study of hysteria, namely, that of repression of a painful idea which then was allowed to return in a modified form. Freud adds that the mechanism of projection is very commonly employed in normal life. It arises, he says, as a result of a normal tendency to presume that internal changes are due to external causes. The process is normal as long as we remain aware of the internal changes, but it becomes abnormal when we lose sight of the internal change. Paranoid projection, therefore, is really an abuse of a mechanism of projection for the purposes of defense (Freud, 1950, [1892-99], p. 209). Later, in Draft K, he describes paranoia as a pathological aberration of the relatively normal affective state of mortification. The painful affect is handled by projection onto the patient's fellowmen. The primary symptom is distrust or an excessive sensitiveness to other people. The determining element is thought to be the mechanism of projection which involves the refusal of belief in self-reproach. The partial failure of the defense and the return of the repressed in its distorted form produces secondary alterations of the ego which can take the form of either melancholia, that is, a sense of the ego's littleness or worthlessness, or can take the form of the more serious protective delusions of megalomania in which the ego is completely remodeled (Freud, 1950 [1892-99]).

In the section on paranoia in the paper "The Neuropsychoses of Defense" (1896), Freud discusses the case of a young mother who developed paranoid symptoms about six months postpartum. He emphasized the defensive nature of the symptoms and related them to the repression of distressing memories. The burden of an intolerable idea is relieved by means of

[handwritten marginalia at top: In paranoia — the burden of an intolerable idea is relieved by projection.]

projection. The patient guarded herself against the self-reproach and guilt related to infantile sexual experiences which returned in the form of accusations from hallucinated voices. In obsessional neurosis the initial self-reproach is repressed by the formation of a primary defense of self-distrust; but in paranoia the self-reproach is repressed in a projective manner by the defensive symptom of distrust of other people. The return of the repressed, however, in the form of delusional ideas, demands acceptance without contradiction from the ego. The preservation of defense demands that the ego adapt itself to them, so that interpretive delusions end in an alteration of the ego which provides a secondary stage of defense (Freud, 1896, p. 185).

In the years between the early papers and the publication of the Schreber case, Freud added several important observations. He noted the characteristic transformation of affectionate impulses into hostile impulses or the transformation of love into hate that is so characteristic of the paranoid mechanism (Freud, 1905b, p. 167). He also noted that the delusions of the paranoid represent fantasies which are basically sadomasochistic in composition (Freud, 1908, p. 162). These early papers bring us to the threshold of Freud's treatment of the Schreber case, except for the essential element, namely, the relationship to homosexuality. Beside some cryptic suggestions in a letter to Fliess in 1899, in which he suggested that paranoia involved a return to early levels of autoeroticism (Freud, 1887-1902, letter 125), there is hardly any mention of paranoia in Freud's writings. According to Jones he presented a paper on female paranoia to the Vienna Society in 1906, still without mention of the connection to homosexuality (Jones, 1955, p. 281). A little over a year later he proposed the hypothesis to Jung and Ferenzi (Freud, 1911, pp. 4-5). In these letters Freud hints that the suggestion had come originally from Fliess. There is also an unpublished memorandum sent by Freud to Jung, presumably early in 1907, on the subject of paranoia which has no hint of its connection to homosexuality (Freud, 1950 [1892-99], pp. 206-207). With these additional straws in the wind, then, Freud was ready to provide a more extensive analysis of paranoia and to express his more complete views on the subject. Thus the elements were at hand which Freud assembled into his analysis of the famous Schreber case.

[handwritten marginalia right margin: transformation of love into hate; delusions are sado-masochistic in nature]

The Schreber Case

Daniel Paul Schreber was a distinguished jurist who was born in 1842 and had a distinguished political career. He stood as a candidate for the Reichstag in the autumn of 1884, and quite soon after that was hospitalized for the first time. He was discharged in June of the following year and took up an appointment in the Leipzig Landgericht in 1886. He was able to carry on his official duties and functioned quite adequately until 1893, when he received an appointment to the court of appeals and was appointed the presiding judge in October of that year. In the following November, he was readmitted to the hospital and subsequently transferred to the Lindenhof Asylum, and soon after that back to Sonnenstein where he had originally been. He remained in the hospital for these years and wrote the *Memoirs* (Schreber, 1955) in the years of 1900-1902 and finally took legal action for his discharge from the hospital. The judgment was rendered in July of 1902, and he was discharged in the following December. The *Memoirs* were finally published in 1903. The *Memoirs* are an unusual document and provide an extraordinary opportunity for studying the content and thought processes of a paranoid psychosis. It wasn't until 1910, however, that the *Memoirs* came to Freud's attention and his analysis of the case was published in 1911 just after the death of Schreber (Freud, 1911).

Schreber's Delusions

Schreber's delusions were bizarre and elaborate. His original physician at the Leipzig clinic had been the famous neuropsychiatrist, Flechsig, whom Schreber had originally admired and regarded highly. But later on he felt that Flechsig was performing "soul murder" on him, the nature of which was never explained. Freud regarded the powerful persecutor as being a substitute for an important figure in the patient's emotional life prior to his illness. The person who was once loved and honored now becomes a hated and feared persecutor. Freud felt that the reason for this paranoid delusion was the fear of sexual abuse by Flechsig and that the exciting cause of the illness was then an outburst of homosexual libido. One of the persistent delusions of Schreber's illness was that he was being transformed into a woman by the power of God, that his genitalia were changing into a woman's genitalia, and that he was growing breasts.

The place of divinity in these delusions was very special. Schreber thought that divine influences were being exercised on his body by means of changes in his nerves. God himself was regarded as nothing but nerve, whereas men consisted of bodies and nerves. The nerves of God had a creative capacity in that they possessed all the properties of human nerves to a greatly intensified degree. They had the power of turning themselves into any kind of object in the created world in the form of rays that emanated from the deity. After the work of creation was finished, God had withdrawn to an immense distance and left the world to its own devices. His activity was restricted to drawing to himself the souls of the dead. Schreber felt that his sexual feelings were the feelings of a woman and described the nerves absorbed by him as having the character of female "nerves of voluptuousness" which thus transformed his body into a more female mode. Schreber in time began to reconcile himself to this sexual transformation and was able to bring it into harmony with the higher purposes of God. God himself was demanding femaleness from him. This transformation and his special relatedness to God were connected with his special mission in the world in which he was the special agent of God, to save and redeem God's creation. Schreber developed an elaborate theocosmology in which he elaborated God's special relationship to the world, the complex relationships within the divinity itself, and his special relationship to God.

Freud points out that the persecutor is divided into Flechsig and God, and that this represents a paranoid reaction to a previously established identification of the two figures. Just as hysteria condenses and identifies elements in the unconscious, it is characteristic of paranoia that it decomposes these condensations and identifications once again and projects them as separate entities in the external world. Freud speculates that God stands for the patient's distinguished father, and that the figure of Flechsig stands for the patient's older brother, who was three years his senior and who had died in 1877.

Freud comments that Schreber's relationship to God exhibited several curious features, which included a mixture of blasphemous criticism and mutinous insubordination on the one hand, and of reverent devotion on the other. God according to him was incapable of learning anything by experience, and did not understand living men because He only knew how to deal with corpses. Schreber also identified the sun directly with God, either the lower god (Ahriman), or sometimes the upper god (Ormuze). Thus Freud saw the sun and its rays that reached out to touch the world as being a symbol of the father, so that the conflict with God was construed as representing the infantile conflict with the father whom the patient loved and to whom he submitted himself. Thus the most dreaded threat of the father, that of castration, provided the material for Schreber's wishful fantasy of transformation into a woman.

Basic Conflict

Thus Freud regarded the basic conflict in paranoia as being the conflict over homosexual impulses. He applied the model of symptom formation that he had developed in the study of psychoneuroses, namely that of fixation, repression, and subsequent return of the repressed in formation of symptoms. Fixation in paranoia was at an early narcissistic level, intermediate between the primitive autoeroticism, in which one's own body was chosen as an object, and object love, in which the love object was of a heterosexual nature. The homosexual object choice and the conflict over it were repressed. The subsequent failure of the repression allowed for a return of the impulses which then had to be handled by the characteristic mechanisms of paranoia. The return of the partially repressed object could be dealt with in a variety of ways, for instance, by delusions of persecution, in which the once-loved object is turned into a persecutor, and the repressed love is transformed into conscious hate. Other forms of the return of the repressed were erotomania, or a flight to a heterosexual love object, or delusions of jealousy in which the feelings of love for a homosexual object are transferred to a woman, or finally megalomania, in which the love of any kind of object is rejected and the sexual overevaluation of a homosexual object is translated into overevaluation of the ego.

Projection

The fundamental mechanism of paranoia was the process of projection, in which an internal perception is repressed and reenters consciousness in a distorted form as an external perception. Freud reminds us, however, that projection does not play the same part in all forms of paranoia and, moreover, can be regarded as a much more general and relatively normal process. Whenever we refer the causes of internal sensations to external events rather than looking for internal causes, we are indulging in projection.

Schreber also had a conviction of the imminent destruction of the world. Freud saw this conviction in terms of the withdrawal of cathexis from the environment, so that the end of the world becomes a projection of the patient's inner catastrophe, the end of his subjective world due to the withdrawal of love. The delusional formation becomes, therefore, an attempt at recovery, a process of reconstruction in which the patient attempts to recapture his relationship to people and things. The repression which took the form of detachment of libido from external objects is undone in the process of recovery, which is carried out through projection. In paranoia, the libido that has been liberated by detachment becomes attached to the ego in the form of self-aggrandizement and megalomania. Thus there is a regression from sublimated homosexuality to narcissism which reflects the developmental fixation at the level of narcissistic object choice.

There are several cautionary notes that Freud adds to his treatment of the Schreber case. He laments the peculiar omission of chapter three of the *Memoirs*, in which the relationship of Schreber's experiences in his family were connected with his delusional convictions. Such material would be of the utmost importance in understanding the genesis of Schreber's paranoia, but we are able to reconstruct it only indirectly and partially from other sources, as we shall see. Freud also notes that social humiliations and slights often seem to have a role in the causation of paranoia, but discounts this as being secondary to and incidental to the underlying homosexual conflict. Despite his emphasis on the underlying homosexual conflict Freud makes an important qualification:

> In taking this view, then, that what lies at the core of the conflict in cases of paranoia among males is a homosexual wishful fantasy of *loving a man*, we shall certainly not forget that the confirmation of such an important

hypothesis can only follow upon the investigation of a large number of instances of every variety of paranoiac disorder. We must therefore be prepared, if need be, to limit our assertion to a single type of paranoia (1911, pp. 62-63).

Later Views

Freud did not significantly alter the content of his theory of paranoia in succeeding years, but he did add some significant modifications under the influence of his evolving ideas on narcissism and the gradual emergence of the structural theory. In the germinal paper on narcissism (1914), Freud spoke of a special psychic agency which performed the task of seeing to it that the satisfaction from the ego ideal was insured and which thus constantly watches the ego and measures it according to the ego ideal. He related this self-critical function to paranoid delusions of being watched. The delusion was a projection of the supervisory function of the internal criticizing agency, which thus re-created the situation in which the ego ideal and the critical agency of conscience were produced, namely, from the critical influence of the parents (Freud, 1914, pp. 95-96). The same ideas on the projection of conscience were presented substantially unchanged in the third part of *The Introductory Lectures* (Freud, 1916-17, pp. 248-249).

In 1923 Freud published another important treatment of the problem of paranoia in the form of an analysis of the demonic possession of a seventeenth-century painter, Christoph Haizmann (1923). Freud's account is of considerable interest from the point of view of the questions it raises for a psychoanalytic theory of psychosis. However, there is no indication that Freud's understanding of paranoid delusions had advanced much further than the lines laid down in his Schreber account (1911). In fact, it seems that he more or less intended it as a confirmation of the position he had formulated in his analysis of the Schreber *Memoirs*, namely, the derivation of paranoid pathology from unconscious homosexual wishes based on a frustrated longing for the father.[1]

The next important addition to the theory of paranoia came in his paper on "The Neurotic Mechanisms in Jealousy, Paranoia, and Homosexuality" (Freud, 1922). In pathological forms of jealousy, for example, there is a projection of impulses to infidelity onto the partner and this has a delusional quality about it. The use of projection and the implicit denial of repressed homosexual wishes make delusional jealousy one of the classic forms of paranoia. But the delusion is supported not merely by projection, but by a perception by the patient of the impulses to infidelity in his partner,

[1] A useful and critical review of the development of Freud's views on psychosis—particularly paranoia—together with an analysis of the Schreber and Haizmann cases is provided in MacAlpine and Hunter (1956). The Haizmann manuscript and related documents are also reproduced in translation.

even though these impulses are often quite unconscious. Similarly, paranoid people cannot regard anything as indifferent in the behavior and attitudes of people around them; they are often responding to the unconscious impulses of hostility in other people. ← introjection or projection

This addition to the theory was important because it acknowledged that more may be at work in producing the paranoid symptoms than simply projection, and secondly, that the role of hostility was perhaps more important than Freud had until this time allowed. Very early in his thinking about paranoia Freud had acknowledged the importance of hostile impulses (Freud, 1950, [1892-99], p. 254). The role of hostility had been overridden by Freud's interest in libidinal aspects of the neuroses and of paranoia. In this connection he commented that, in the genesis of paranoia in females, an important influence was the surprisingly regular fear of being killed or devoured by the mother, stemming from preoedipal levels of dependent attachment to her. A little girl's oral, aggressive, and sadistic wishes are presented in repressed form as fear of being killed by the mother, and Freud only offers the speculation that this fear may in part reflect the child's sensing of the unconscious hostility on the mother's part (Freud, 1931, pp. 227-237; 1933 [1932], p. 120). These latter considerations open the way to later formulations on the role of aggression in the genesis of paranoia.

Criticism

Freud's formulations form the substantial basis for our modern conceptions of paranoia. Nonetheless they are subject to criticism on several grounds. First, there is no good evidence that Freud had any extensive experience with paranoid psychoses. His theories are based on written accounts of patients whom he never saw personally, or on several cases in which his contact with the patient was superficial at best. Second, the formulation of his views took the form rather of an adaptation and application of his theory of symptom formation based on the study of psychoneuroses, in particular of hysteria. This procedure was counter to his normal methodological conviction (Meissner, 1971a) and seems to have been an exception to his normal pattern of clinical investigation. Third, the role of aggression in Freud's theory remained inchoate. He recognized the role of hostility in his early treatments of paranoia, but then any consideration of hostility seems to have been overwhelmed by his libidinal preoccupations. This is particularly true by the time of the writing of the Schreber case, in which hostility receives little or no mention. From our contemporary vantage point, it strikes us as strange that delusions of he end of the world could be analyzed in terms of withdrawal of libido without any mention of the obvious underlying hostility. Some hints occur as to the role of hostility in Freud's treatment of superego projections in his later writings. But these are only passing references. Freud's preoccupation throughout was with the supposed transformation of love into hate. Basing his thinking on this fixation point really forces him to the consideration of hate as a defense against libidinal involvements. It is easy to see how his theory of paranoia as a defense against repressed homosexuality fits this pattern quite well. It overlooks, however, that the basic problem to begin with may be in the management of hostility.

POST-FREUDIAN DEVELOPMENTS

The Kleinian Contribution: Paranoid and Depressive Positions

One of the most significant developments in the post-Freudian considerations of paranoia was the contribution of Melanie Klein (Klein, 1932, 1964). Following Abraham's formulation of paranoia as a regression to the earlier phase of anal sadism and as involving a partial introjection of the love object (Abraham, 1954, p. 490), Klein studied paranoid manifestations in young children. On the basis of her extensive clinical experience, Klein agreed with Abraham's basic position and felt that the period of maximal sadism in infantile development took its origin in the oral sadistic phase of libidinal development and extended through the period of early anal sadism. She felt that fixation at this point of maximal sadism provided the fixation point for the later development of paranoia.

The child's sadism is translated into fears of attacks upon itself from the part of both introjected and external objects. To the excreta are attributed, in fantasy, a poisonous and dangerous quality and a power of destruction, which arouses tremendous anxiety in the child and is defended against by delusions of reference and persecution. Klein felt that behind the homosexual love, which is regarded as transformed into hatred of the parent of the same sex, there was a deeper hatred and destructive wish. The child fantasies attacking the mother's breast and body and destroying them by means of his own dangerous and destructive feces. Klein regarded the homosexuality as a defense in the service of neutralizing the intense sadistic wishes to destroy the feared and hated parent.

Freud had hinted at the child's hostility to the mother and the fear of being devoured by the mother. Klein makes it clear in her formulation that this fear itself is due to the projection of sadistic impulses on the part of the child. Klein emphasizes that the sadistic fantasies of the omnipotent destructiveness of both bladder and bowels is closely connected with paranoid mechanisms. As Klein sees the process, the child projects its aggressive impulses onto the frustrating breast of the mother. The mother's breast thus becomes a persecuting object which is incorporated and thus becomes an internal persecutor. The ego struggles to defend itself against these internalized persecutors by processes of expulsion and projection. The resultant anxiety and the defense mechanisms associated with it form the basis of paranoia.

[Paranoia, Obsessional states, & Depression are linked]

Abraham had commented on the close association between depression and obsessional states. Klein also notes the close association between paranoia and the more severe forms of obsessional neurosis. Paranoia derives from the earlier anal sadistic phase through which the individual must pass. These rudimentary paranoid states are normally overcome in the subsequent secondary stage of anal sadism from which obsessional mechanisms derive. The severity of the obsessional illness will depend on the severity of the preceding paranoid disturbance, so that later on, if obsessional mechanisms cannot adequately overcome the paranoid fixation, the obsessional traits may give way to a frank paranoia. More significant, however, is Klein's view of the relationship between the paranoid and depressive states. They are closely associated but can be distinguished in terms of the direction of the persecution anxiety. In the paranoid the anxiety is primarily related to the preservation of the ego, but in the depressive it is primarily related to the preservation of the good internalized objects with which the ego is identified as a whole. The anxiety lest the good objects, and with them the ego, should be destroyed is associated with continuous efforts to save the good objects both internal and external.

In the earliest phase of the child's development, the persecuting object and the good objects are kept widely separated. However, when the child moves from the phase of the introjection of partial objects to the introjection of whole and real objects, these aspects must be brought closer together. This is a major developmental step to bring the bad and good objects into conjunction, and the child's ego must resort over and over again to the splitting of its objects into loved and hated, good and dangerous ones. If the child is able to gain more trust and confidence in its real objects and consequently in its introjected objects, the capacity for the tolerance of ambivalence, the capacity to relate to real objects develops. Klein writes as follows:

> It seems that at this stage of development the unification of external and internal, the loved and hated, real and imaginary objects is carried out in a way that each step in the unification leads again to a renewed splitting of the imagos. But as the adaptation to the external world increases, this splitting is carried out on planes that gradually come increasingly nearer and nearer to reality. This goes on until love for the real and the internalized objects and trust in them are well established. Then ambivalence, which is partly a safeguard against one's own hate and against the hated and terrifying objects, will in normal development again diminish in varying degrees (1964, p. 317).

The capacity for the child to move developmentally from the paranoid to the depressive position implies, therefore, the capacity to tolerate ambivalence and also the capacity to achieve full identification with the good objects. Along with the capacity for love of and identification with a good object—at first the breast and then the whole person, particularly of the mother—there goes hand in hand an anxiety for its destruction and disintegration, as well as feelings of guilt and remorse and a sense of responsibility for preserving it against persecutors. Associated with this there is the sadness related to expectation of impending loss of the good object. It is the unconscious knowledge of the hate resident in ambivalence that exists alongside the love and may at any point gain the upper hand and so destroy the loved object, which brings about the feelings of sorrow, guilt, and despair which underlie the depression.

The paranoid, according to Klein, cannot allow himself this fullness of identification. The reasons are multiple. The persecution anxiety is too great; the way to a full and stable introjection of a good object is blocked by multiple suspicions and fantastic anxieties, which quickly turn the loved object once again into a persecutor. The paranoid cannot get beyond his early relationship to internalized part objects and their sadistic accompaniments. Klein comments:

> Where the persecution anxiety for the ego is in the ascendant, a full and stable identification with another object, in the sense of looking at it and understanding it as it really is, and a full capacity for love, are not possible (1964, p. 291).

The paranoid is unable to tolerate the guilt and remorse which are implicit in the depressive position. Moreover, to move into the depressive position is threatening because it limits his capacity to use projection. Projection carries with it the fear of expelling the good objects and thus carries with it the threat of losing them. But, at the same time, if he expels what is evil from within himself he runs the risk of injuring and destroying the good external objects. Thus Klein proposes, as a basic component of her position and as a fundamental insight, that paranoid fears and suspicions operate as a defense against the intolerable anxiety and ambivalence of the depressive state.

Mrs. Klein's views have been controversial and have raised a number of basic problems from both methodological and conceptual points of view (Zetzel, 1956; Kernberg, 1969). Without accepting her theoretical suppositions, her descriptions of paranoia and depression have considerable clinical relevance and form important contributions to the study of these conditions. Her views have been of the greatest utility in refocusing our concerns toward the issues of aggression and hostility in the genesis of paranoia, and have also redirected our attention to the child's early life experiences as having considerable impact on the development of later pathological states. Whether her descriptions of paranoid and depressive concerns are capable of being validated in one- and two-year-old infants remains a moot question, but there can be little doubt that paranoid and depressive concerns can be identified in older children, and that in adult patients these same factors are of considerable significance in the elaboration of their illness.

Role of Aggression

Following Melanie Klein's lead, the emphasis shifted from libidinal to aggressive aspects of paranoia. Schmidebert (1931) presented two cases in which she felt that the paranoid idea arose out of aggressive impulses and formed an exact mirror image of sadistic fantasies. Aggression was directed primarily against the copulating parents in the primal scene, and was aroused by both homosexual and heterosexual wishes. She felt that the projection of sadism from both attitudes could produce paranoid delusions. Her emphasis was on the instinctual or aggressive derivation of the paranoid content, even though in both cases she remarks on the severe, harsh, and sadistic treatment meted out to these patients as children. The punitive attitude of the parents left the children in the position of feeling at all points that they could never do anything right. The combination of factors intensified the feelings of hate, anxiety and guilt and thus deprived these children of a normal outlet for their sadistic impulses and prevented their testing out of fantasies in reality. The aggression which was repressed and dammed up overflowed into the paranoid symptomatology.

Fenichel (1945) substantially agrees with Freud's formulation, but adds some comments on the role of the superego in paranoid delusions. He feels that these cannot be derived from a homosexual basis but may represent a relief by way of projection from the aggression which has been turned inward in the form of shame, guilt, or feelings of inadequacy. Similarly Knight (1940) discusses the element of intense unconscious hate in the paranoid by pointing out that the paranoid is caught up in an ever-present excessive need for love in order to neutralize the intense unconscious hate. More recently Hesselbach (1962) has emphasized the regression of the superego in delusion formation in paranoia. The original severity in the superego is determined by the severity of parental authority, by the projection of the patient's own aggressive impulses, and by the hostility resulting from repeated disappointment in them. In the regression there is a reemergence of certain archaic introjects which previously had constituted the ego ideal; these are then projected onto external objects which then become endowed with all the aggression and sadism with which the superego was once endowed. The delusional persecutors thereby take on the terrifying, sadistic, devouring, and phallic qualities of the original parental introjects. The function of the delusion of persecution is that it permits the unbearably guilt-ridden person to become righteously indignant and to struggle against sadistic impulses in the legitimate form of self-defense. While there were some progressive shifts in the development of thinking about paranoia and an increasing emphasis on the vicissitudes of aggression, as we have seen, the situation was still such that MacAlpine and Hunter (1953) could complain that the literature was concerned with confirming Freud's formulations and that no open criticism of his interpretation was to be found.

Delusions of Persecution → permit guilt-ridden person to become righteously indignant and to defend against the projected sadism in others rather than dealing w/ it in the self.

CONTRA SCHREBER

Reevaluation of the Schreber Case

One of the significant developments in more contemporary efforts to understand the problem of paranoia has been the effort to critically reevaluate Freud's formulations. This has in part taken the form of carefully reevaluating the Schreber case in the light of more extensive evidence that is now available to us (McCawley, 1971). As we have seen, there were some straws in the wind suggesting that the derivation of paranoia from homosexuality was not altogether adequate, but these impressions lacked any solid footing until the text of the *Memoirs* was made more generally available.

This was accomplished by the publication of the English translation of the *Memoirs* by MacAlpine and Hunter (Schreber, 1955). Surveying the literature at that time, they concluded that by and large the literature on paranoia had tended to carry along and uncritically endorse Freud's formulations. Basing their own analysis of the case on the full text of the *Memoirs* and its associated documents rather than on the extracts provided by Freud, MacAlpine and Hunter came to the conclusion:

> We have interpreted Schreber's psychosis as a reactivation of unconscious, archaic procreation fantasies concerning life, death, immortality, rebirth, creation, including self-impregnation, and accompanied by absolute ambisexuality expressed in doubt and uncertainty about his sex. Homosexual anxieties were secondary to the primary fantasy of having to be transformed into a woman to be able to procreate (Schreber, 1955, p. 395).

They felt that the confusion and ambiguity in sexual identity should be clearly differentiated from the passive homosexual wishes implied in Freud's use of the term.

Since then the Schreber case has come in for searching reevaluation and reformulation. Niederland pointed out that both of Schreber's illnesses were precipitated by his being elevated to a position of power and influence, and he felt that this was indicative of Schreber's dread of taking the father's position. The father was a primary figure in Schreber's psychosis and the frustrated needs were primarily dependent ones (Niederland, 1951). Schreber's delusional language was anal-sadistic in its origin, reflecting, rather than castration fears, the earlier pregenital fears centering around loss of the love object through the subject's own destructive rage. This reflected the intense ambivalence of the early libidinal object relationship and it was this ambivalence that was defended against by projection. The projection involved a symbolization and condensation in which previous libidinal ties were condensed into the concept of God, and thus lost libidinal objects were replaced by a verbal abstraction which restored the primary dependent relationship in a less threatening form, but at the same time at the sacrifice of reality. The *Memoirs* themselves represent a restitutive attempt to establish reality contact, and this was evidently successful until the death of Schreber's mother and the illness of his wife, at which point he again relapsed and died in the insane asylum four years later.

Schreber's Father

Niederland has also contributed a significant amount of imformation about Schreber's relationship to his father which has important implications for the genesis of paranoia. The father was Dr. Daniel Gottlieb Moritz Schreber, who was a physician, lecturer, writer, and clinical instructor in the medical school at Leipzig. He had specialized in orthopedics and had written and lectured widely on the upbringing of children and physical culture through the use of what he called "therapeutic gymnastics." This comprised an elaborate series of compulsive and rigid ritualizations which were calculated to break the will of the child and subject him to an inexorable discipline. Severe corporal punishment was indicated at the slightest infringement of any of these elaborate rules even from the earliest age, because the rebellious and disruptive acts of the child's crude nature had to be weakened and brought under control through the greatest strictness.

The father applied these educative methods rigorously to his own children, and undoubtedly the infant Schreber was therefore subjected to a relentless mental and physical torment under the guise of medical and educational principles. The elder Schreber was thus pathologically concerned with the control of both masturbatory and aggressive practices in children, but he disguised this compulsive sadism and rationalized it within the context of his almost missionary crusade for improved methods of physical culture and moral formation of children. Practices in child-rearing, given in some detail by Niederland, could be interpreted as compulsive-sadistic-projective experiences in self-control (Niederland, 1959).

This radical crushing of the child's crude nature was accomplished from the earliest age by suppression of all strivings for independence and lack of obedience to the elaborate rules required by the system. All indications of passions and bad habits had to be dealt with immediately and drastically by admonishments and mechanical restraints administered with bodily punishment. The elder Schreber maintained that properly administered, a state of complete submissiveness could be imposed on the child by the age of five or six years.

The father suffered a head injury and fell ill with a mental illness in about his fifty-first year. After the injury the father lived in partial seclusion and withdrew from many of his activities, as well as from personal contact with his children. He had violent outbursts of rage and fury and often tolerated only the presence of his wife. He died in 1861 at age fifty-three. It is striking, therefore, that the son became ill for the first time at the age of fifty-one and that his chief symptoms centered about complaints about his head, about a softening of the brain, and fears that he would die soon. Soon after that he was admitted to the Leipzig clinic where he made a suicidal attempt. Two years later when he reached the age of fifty-three, he recorded a marked deterioration of his condition which was marked by the signs of transformation into a woman that so characterized the course of his subsequent psychosis.

This material begins to shed considerable light on the kernel of truth that may have lain behind the psychosis. We can begin to understand the son's helpless longings for the father and his grievances when "God retired to an enormous distance." The complaint that God does not really understand living man is a reproach against the father whose books were filled with lifeless drawings of anatomical representation. It also is a reproach against that same Dr. Flechsig, whose scientific work with corpses and whose therapeutic interest in castration were undoubtedly well known to the patient (Niederland, 1959, 1968). Schreber's "little men" may very well refer to the drawings in his father's books, and the anatomical delusions that he entertained may also have referred to the illustrations of dissections in the same book, and undoubtedly were related to castration anxiety and sadomasochistic fantasies stemming from his childhood.

Other Views

MacAlpine and Hunter (1956, 1953) also pointed out the strong feminine aspect of Schreber's delusional system, particularly his calling the sun a "whore," which was not consistent with Freud's view that the sun was a symbolic representation of the father. However, Schreber's mother was very closely associated with the father's works and helped him carry them out, even assisting him in the writing, so that she became a participant in the father's compulsive sadistic practices. The controlling and omnipotent figure of the deified power that controlled Schreber's life was undoubtedly a fusion of both maternal and paternal images. In addition, Schreber's father had elaborate ideas about attraction and repulsion as governing principles of the universe and of the relationship of God to the universe and His control over it, which may well have formed a contributing aspect of Schreber's elaborate delusional cosmology (Niederland, 1963).

Katan (1950a, 1950b, 1952) follows Freud's basic view that the fundamental conflict in paranoia is the homosexual conflict. Schreber's hallucinations were a means of coping with unbearable homosexual urges, and thus formed a way of discharging libidinal energies by projection to God and the figure of Flechsig. Nunberg (1952) points out that Schreber's denial of Flechsig's real existence corresponds to his helplessness in mastering the attachment to the father that was reactivated in his transference relationship to Flechsig and had to be replaced by denial and the representation of Flechsig and the father in hallucinatory form. Nunberg also points to the role of superego projections in the construction of the hallucinations. The superego develops primarily through identification with the father figure, and by projection of the inner voices of conscience the father figure was replaced in the external world where he had originally belonged (Nunberg, 1952).

White's (1963) approach to the Schreber case is more in terms of Eriksonian categories. He suggests that the primitive, destructive, and dependent oral impulses toward the mother were of the most crucial importance and central to the pathology of the *Memoirs* (White, 1961). The methods of child-rearing employed by his parents produced the response of rage, mistrust, and unresolved oral destructive and dependent needs, and these could only be relinquished through identification with her, but also had to be defended against by a more superficial identification with the father, in which Schreber became competent and compulsively conscientious. This enabled him to weather the storms of puberty by way of intense identification with the compulsive and rigidly restrictive father. This helped him to manage the instinctual conflicts associated with childhood and adolescence, but left him quite vulnerable to the conflicts of intimacy and isolation on an adult level of adjustment. The emergence of hypochondriasis and subsequent paranoia represented a response to a generativity crisis which developed in the context of political defeat and his stillborn children. Beneath the facade of compulsive masculine identification, he remained secretly the infant who wishes to be the sole possessor of the wife-mother, and the delusional transformation into a woman may have been a psychotic way of symbolically merging with the mother. For an infant to destroy the mother is in fact to destroy the world, so that Schreber's world destruction fantasies may stem from primitive oral destructive impulses.

Carr (1963) comments that homosexual conflict does not seem to play a very considerable role in many cases, and that even though patients may engage in overt homosexual practices, they may also need psychotic defenses against an underlying unconscious and unacceptable sadistic incorporative impulse. He feels that the role of hostility is a central difficulty in all theories of paranoia. Paranoia along with homosexuality may both serve as defenses against hostility. Schreber's world destruction fantasies may thus be seen as a displacement of murderous wishes. Freud's handling of the Schreber case, therefore, has been criticized on both methodological and conceptual grounds (MacAlpine and Hunter, 1953; Walters, 1955).

Paranoia and Sexuality

Homosexuality

There has been a shift away from a primarily libidinal interpretation toward an interpretation in broader terms to include the vicissitudes of hostility, as well as other more complex pregenital issues and developmental concerns. There has been less emphasis on intrapsychic conflicts as bearing the etiological burden, and increasing awareness of the role of interpersonal and psychosocial complexities and their interplay with intrapsychic factors. The role of homosexuality particularly has come under criticism and more rigorous evaluation. Gardner (1931) found evidence of repressed homosexuality in 45 percent of a sample of 40 unselected cases of paranoid schizophrenia and 80 conditions of paranoid condition. Miller (1941) on the other hand was able to find indications of homosexuality as the basis of paranoia in only 12 of 400 cases. Similarly Klein and Horwitz (1949) reported preoccupations of homosexuality in only 1 out of 5 of a group of 80 cases. More recently Klaf and Davis (1960) reported findings on a large group of paranoid patients and found that homosexual preoccupations, previous homosexual experiences, and same-sex persecutors were found in a significantly higher degree in the paranoid group as opposed to the control group. Planansky and Johnston (1962), however, were unable to establish any clear-cut relationship between paranoia and homosexual concerns and felt that their data would better support a view of these two factors as developmentally independent. They also felt that difficulties and concerns in heterosexual and homosexual areas appeared to be equally distributed among the types of schizophrenia. Likewise De Busscher (1963) finds latent or manifest homosexual desires present in both paranoid and nonparanoid schizophrenics, but has been more impressed with the incest theme in cases of paranoia, particularly in the form of delusions of marital jealousy. Aronson's (1964) study of Rorschach data in paranoia lends some support to the homosexual hypothesis, since it finds an overwhelmingly greater number of homosexual signs in paranoid patients than in either nonparanoid psychotics or normals.

Thus the empirical studies that have attempted to assess the degree of homosexual content, either latent or manifest, in paranoid patients have proven neither to be so overwhelming nor so convincing that they can be accepted as directly supporting Freud's hypothesis. They point, however, to the role of homosexual content as a significant aspect of the symptomatology of paranoid states. Overall the evidence does not permit any conclusion as to the etiological role of homosexual conflicts, but suggests rather that homosexuality may be a significant aspect of the symptomatology in all states of schizophrenic regression, rather than specific to paranoia as such.

Pseudohomosexuality

An attempt to put the homosexual question into perspective has been made by Ovesey in his formulation of the concept of pseudohomosexuality (Ovesey, 1954, 1955a, 1955b). He maintains that what often passes for homosexual anxieties can be broken down into three separate motivational components, namely, the sexual component, a dependency component, and a power component. Only the sexual component seeks homosexual gratification and generates homosexual anxiety. The dependency and power components seek nonsexual goals, although they may make use of the genital organs to achieve them. These later components are pseudohomosexual ones in that the anxiety associated with their operation may be misinterpreted by the patient as true homosexual anxiety.

The pseudohomosexual conflict can develop in men who fail to meet the standards of society for masculine performance. The failure is related to inhibitions of assertion which originated in power struggles between the growing child and his parents or siblings. The struggles are perceived unconsciously in terms of symbolic murder, in which each of the adversaries seeks to kill the other. Aggressive moves on the part of the child carry the risk of lethal retaliation, and inhibition of aggression is the logical outcome. The equation of failure with castration, feminine inadequacy, and homosexuality underlies the pseudohomosexual conflict. The weaker male is forced to submit to castration by the stronger and thus is forced to submit to him as a woman. The patient tries to overcome the inadequacy by a compensatory show of strength, but this is doomed to failure because of the overwhelming conviction of inadequacy. The resort to a dependent stance through seeking magical protection of the omnipotent father-substitute fares little better. The dependent pseudohomosexual male tries to repair his castration through a magical fantasy of oral or anal incorporation of the stronger man's penis. Not only is he disappointed in his failure to attain the other's strength, but his position is interpreted as homosexual in motivation, so that the pseudohomosexual anxiety is intensified.

The pseudohomosexual conflict can be integrated on either a psychotic or neurotic level, but its psychotic integration is characteristically found in paranoia with or without the concomitant presence of true latent homosexuality. In this view the homosexual motivation becomes a special case which is neither a constant nor exclusive feature of paranoia. Ovesey feels that the power motivation as an elaboration of aggressive impulses, even without the elaboration of pseudohomosexual anxiety, is the constant feature in paranoid phenomena. Pseudohomosexual motivations occur with far greater frequency in paranoia than do the purely homosexual. The delusional forms of paranoia can thus be seen as attempts to deny and compensate for the pseudohomosexual conviction of inadequacy and weakness, and provide an adaptive channel for the recapturing of a measure of self-esteem and a sense of adequacy (Ovesey, 1955b).

In the light of these studies, it seems more viable to try to understand the paranoid dynamics as related to underlying developmental patterns which may share a common background or foundation with homosexual syndromes. Recent studies of homosexuality converge on a constellation of factors including a dominant, close-binding, and intimate mother; poor relationship ith the family; a position as youngest member or "baby" of the family; a childhood image of weakness, poor health, timorousness, vulnerability; along with early homosexual exposure and experience. As van den Aardweg (1972) has suggested, homosexuality seems best correlated with a self-image of one who is "inferior-pitiable."

The homosexual develops in his childhood a self-image of the weakling—an image which creates self-pity and elicits pity from others. This self-directed attitude may be repressed and thus become unconscious—persisting throughout life in the form of an internal self-pitying child who lives within the adult personality. Thus happiness becomes a role to be sought and never found—and success and satisfaction must be strongly resisted. We shall have occasion to document such self-attitudes in the genesis of paranoid ideation.

Perhaps the congruence between paranoid and homosexual processes can be seen most clearly in terms of the formation of a negative identity (Gonen, 1971). In the development of both the paranoid and the homosexual, the normal process of identity formation through the mutual and reciprocal interaction between the ego and social organization and processes is disrupted. The negative identity develops as a form of protest and negation of a set of established rules, standards, and values which are formed by society and enforced by authority figures. The difficulty of maintaining a negative identity in the face of social organizations, regulations, and institutions which suppress the behaviors and norms congruent with the negative identity leads such individuals to frequently develop rigid ideologies as a means of sustaining the negative identity. The strong rebellion and opposition also involve significant elements of self-negation and self-denial, so that there is a determinant tendency to cling to totalistic ideologies resulting in considerable rigidity and negative conformity. Such a pattern can be identified both in homosexual subjects and in the operation of the paranoid process. In both cases the formation and sustaining of a negative identity can be seen to be based on the pseudohomosexual anxiety and the conviction of vulnerability and powerlessness which Ovesey (1955a, 1955b) has described.

Transsexuality

I would like to mention briefly another syndrome in which the paranoid process seems to play a central role, namely, transsexualism. There is considerable controversy—often more emotional than enlightening—surrounding this entity and the current application of surgical approaches in dealing with it (Baker, 1969; Pauly, 1965). The syndrome has been carefully studied and discussed by Stoller (1968). The delusional quali-

ty of the patient's belief that he or she belongs to the opposite sex than that
indicated by genital anatomy has been variously noted (Northrup, 1959;
Worden and Marsh, 1955; Socarides, 1969). My purpose here is only to indicate that the syndrome focuses on a belief that is rigidly maintained in the
face of conflicting evidences and is apparently sustained by inner needs and
pressures. The paranoid process would consequently seem to play a significant role. There is also evidence to suggest that effective intervention early
enough—preadolescent or before—can modify gender role preference
(Green et al., 1972).

BROADENING PERSPECTIVES ON PARANOIA

Inferiority Feelings
     The shift in thinking about paranoia in terms of defense against, and
compensation for, feelings of inadequacy and inferiority was anticipated by
Sullivan. He regarded paranoid ideas of persecution and grandeur as complex processes which were intended to overcome or obliterate the
irremediable sense of inferiority, unworthiness, and the incapacity to
awaken positive attitudes in others. He describes a process in which inadequate approbation in the child's early experience produces a prevailing
negative self. This negative attitude interferes with subsequent securing of
interpersonal satisfactions. Feelings of personal inferiority, unworthiness,
and often loneliness are at times intolerable. The conviction evolves that the
individual is not capable of being fully human, and this creates an intolerable insecurity which makes it impossible to sustain any kind of adaptive effort (Sullivan, 1953a).
     Security and satisfaction are obtained by the paranoid projection in
which the inferior person is turned into a victim of persecution. The feeling
of worth is protected by the paranoid transference of blame onto other individuals. Thus the paranoid's security rests on his being persecuted. The
transfer of blame, however, covers an intolerable weakness, so that the
paranoid's self-system must continually draw into the projective system
anybody who would be critical or with whom one might be exposed to
criticism. The danger flags are continually flying and relationships can be
permitted only with people who do not represent danger in the sense of
reminding the paranoid of what it is that really ails him (Sullivan, 1956). The
awareness of inferiority creates an intolerable anxiety which represents a
fatal deficiency of the self-system, which is unable to disguise or exclude the
underlying sense of inferiority and consequent rejection and insecurity.

Masochism
     Following Freud's (1908) lead, Bak (1946) focused on the sadomaso-
chistic trends in paranoia. He sees the paranoid reaction as a delusional

masochism in which the regression to masochism is accompanied by withdrawal of libido along with increased hostility toward the previous love object and sadistic fantasies. When mastery over the hostility fails, sadism is projected as a delusional restitution which enables the masochism to be reinstituted in relation to the delusions of mistreatment and persecution.

The link between paranoia and masochism, however, has been strongly emphasized by Nydes (1963). He formulates the polarity between the masochistic and the paranoid character in the following terms: "The masochistic character appears to renounce 'power' for the sake of 'love'; and the paranoid character appears to renounce 'love' for the sake of 'power' " (p. 216). Thus, in the megalomaniac phase of delusional paranoia, the patient renounces love and adopts the position of the powerful figure of God or one who is equated with God. The masochist projects his wishes for power onto another person and renounces his own power for the sake of the love of the powerful figure. Nydes contrasts the paranoid orientation with the sadistic orientation and feels that they must be distinguished, even though they often overlap. The paranoid orientation is essentially defensive against the inner feeling of guilt. It involves identification with the victim, the one who is being persecuted, rather than identification with the aggressor, which is more characteristic of a sadistic orientation.

The power operation in paranoia is a kind of counterattack against an assumed accuser. The frequent effect of this is to provoke the punishment in reality against which he was supposedly defending himself. The paranoid is totally unaware of his own provocation, and the subsequent negative reaction simply affords a confirmation of his feelings that he is being persecuted. The paranoid equates power with invulnerability. He despises weakness in any form and will often endure excruciating pain. As Nydes points out, "to wish for love is to admit weakness, and to accept subjugation. It means yielding to castration, and to homosexual degradation" (1963, p. 223). He sees Schreber's submission to God as a humiliating emasculation, a form of masochistic regression which allows him some degree of safety and protection.

Nydes' position therefore comes very close to that of Ovesey, but whereas Ovesey stresses the patient's failure to meet the demands of society, Nydes stresses the paranoid's selection of negative features of an otherwise positive social response by reason of his punitive and infantile superego. The paranoid character expects to be punished for success rather than rewarded, as is the normal experience. Paranoid-masochistic trends may have adaptive aspects, but they are basically motivated by the need to resolve underlying intrapsychic conflicts. Thus both paranoid and masochistic types of characters have failed to achieve a healthy identification with the same-sex parent, who is unconsciously regarded as omnipotent. They wish to replace that parent and at the same time dread retaliation in the form of annihilation or castration.

Any form of self-assertion or real success is seen unconsciously as a defiance of, and a transgression against, the all-powerful authority figure. Success is played out in terms of the unconscious Oedipal drama of incest with the parent of the opposite sex, as well as murder of the parent of the same sex. Competition is particularly threatening since it implies a desperate combat with the projected infantile superego figure, so that the paranoid individual must resort to a delusional form of magical control in which the behavior, thoughts, and wishes of others are secretly directed and controlled. Any independence of others, however benign and apparently innocuous, ecomes a threat to the paranoid.

Relation to Depression

Closely related to this formulation is Schwartz's view of the paranoid-depressive continuum (1963, 1964). A notion basic to the continuum is that of responsibility, the depressive side characterized by self-reference in regard to responsibility, and the paranoid side by object-reference. He suggests that along with the Kleinian view of the introjection of good and bad objects, there is also an introjection of feelings of blame or responsiblity. The child may experience deprivation as related either to himself, to the mother, or to both. Insofar as he assumes the responsibility for his own deprivation, he develops the rudiments of the depressive orientation. If the deprivation is experienced as deriving from an external source over which the child has no control and for which he is not responsible, he develops the basis for a paranoid orientation. Klein's view of depression involves the guilt and remorse over destructive feelings directed to the bad mother insofar as they also injure the good mother. The notion of responsibility is implicit in this formulation, in that guilt and remorse imply it. In the paranoid position, however, there is no concept responsibility, guilt, remorse, or anything except feelings referred to external objects.

Schwartz substantially follows the point of view laid down by Sullivan, namely, that the paranoid person is faced with his own lack and his own unimportance or insignificance. His delusion is a denial of this intolerable idea and an attempt at compensation. Deprivation is interpreted as meaning that he does not matter to other people. His insignificance is not due to something that he has done or something for which he is responsible, but rather is due to the fact that there is nothing about him which has any value to others. The sense of inferiority and lack of worth is based on a narcissistic fixation which is related to a narcissistic wound suffered in early infancy. Schwartz comments as follows:

> Generally speaking, the hurt of infancy can be of two kinds: hurts of commission convey parental displeasure, while hurts of omission convey parental

abandonment. The relationship of these hurts to the constructs of "badness" and "insignificance" respectively are evident. Badness is a concept which is introjectible in terms of self-reference; the child can come to think of himself as bad. But meaninglessness and insignificance are not introjectible in self-referential terms, since the self is tautologically meaningful and significant to the self. Thus the internalization of feelings of insignificance must be in terms of object-reference. The denial of such feelings can only come from others. Hence the intense need for importance in the eyes of others, the willingness to settle for persecutory attention, and the preferential use of projection as a defensive technique (1963, pp. 352-353).

The patient thus needs to secure recognition from others, and this need makes him exceedingly hypersensitive to the responses of others, and also extremely vulnerable to them. Because his ability to form relationships to other people in the real community is impaired, the paranoid forms what Cameron (1959) has described as a "paranoid pseudocommunity." The paranoid pseudocommunity has relevance and significance by reason of its relationship to him as the central figure; the pseudocommunity has the specific function of affirming the patient's significance and relevance to other people. Unlike the autistic schizophrenic who denies the meaningful existence of others, the paranoid in fact creates others in a meaningful context in which they have a special relationship to him. As long as the paranoid delusional system is functioning adequately the patient is able to carry on without undue impairment. But as the vulnerability to challenge in the delusional system is increased, the patient becomes more distrusting, suspicious, guarded and even angry.

Closely related to this view is Salzman's view of paranoia, in which he sees the denial of low self-esteem as being central to the syndrome (Salzman, 1960). He sees the primary development in the denial of low self-esteem as the grandiosity of the paranoid, which then secondarily produces rebuffs from the environment. The projective transfer of blame through the delusional structure is then organized in a defensive manner to deal with this threat ot the primary grandiosity. It is not always clear that grandiosity plays such a primary role in all cases. However, the effort to compensate for the sense of inferiority or the loss of self-esteem seems to be a relatively constant feature.

In Modlin's (1963) study of paranoid states in women, he found that in those with adequate life adjustment and satisfactory marital relationships, a specific stress precipitated the patient into a phase of depression which was expressed in the sense of loss and reduction of self-esteem. This was accompanied by significant alterations in the husband-wife relationship, and an actual reduction in the frequency, or complete cessation of, sexual intercourse. Regression followed on the loss of self-esteem and projective delusional mechanisms appeared. Successful treatment of these women focused on the reassertion of the woman's feminine social role, on the regaining of her lost self-esteem, and finally on the reestablishment of the marital relationship.

The relationship between depression and paranoia has also been stressed by Allen (1967). These two states may substitute for one another, and in the treatment of a paranoid patient one frequently finds an underlying depression. The depression is primary and the paranoia is an attempt to deal with the implicit suicidal impulse. The paranoid patient is extremely sensitive to the suicidal impulse, and can deal with it only by projecting it. When the impulse becomes too strong to be handled by mechanisms of denial and projection, a serious suicide attempt may be made. Thus the paranoid defenses take their place alongside the manic defenses as major strategies to avoid and diminish the pain of depression and lowered self-esteem. The paranoid resorts to mechanisms of denial and projection, while the manic resorts to mechanisms of denial and flight into activity. At their pathological extremes, the paranoid psychosis and the manic-depressive psychosis are often difficult to differentiate.

In discussing the sources of anxiety in paranoid schizophrenics, Searles (1965) has pointed out that the paranoid sees his world as filled with sinister meanings and with malevolent intentions toward himself. He cannot ignore the persecuting figures because they actually represent the projection of his own unconscious feelings and attitudes, and if he renounces his concern over them, he is in fact renouncing part of himself. Yet he cannot come to terms with them because he cannot accept the abhorrent qualities that he has projected onto them. The alternatives are desperate because the price is cast in terms of loss of identity and disintegration of the self. The psychotic person seeks safety and protection by placing his self outside all experience and activity. It thus becomes an empty vacuum which is constantly threatened with being overwhelmed by the malevolent reality outside. Alongside the dread, however, there is an intense longing for participation in the world. Thus the deepest longing of the self becomes its greatest weakness and the source of its greatest dread, since to participate in reality is to run the risk of obliteration, of what Laing has called "engulfment" (Laing, 1965a).

Thus the basic issues of paranoia and depression lie very close together and in fact, we might think, share some of the same genetic roots. On the clinical front, the therapist is constantly faced with the problem of helping the paranoid patient to surrender his delusions, to face and to bear and hopefully to resolve the underlying depression which is threatening and which involves the loss of self and of all personal value. Often the expression of what Laing calls the "false self" is apparently normal—the obedient child, the ideal husband, the industrious worker. But in this compliance the individual does not have a sense of his own autonomy, and thus is unable to experience his separateness on the one hand, or his relatedness on the other, in a normal way. The sense of reality of his own selfhood is bound up in the other, and he is thus placed in a position of ontological dependency on the other. That dependency on the other for one's very existence becomes threatening indeed, so that the slightest indication of hostility or rejection from the other becomes a threat to the very existence of one's self. The alternatives are utter detachment and isolation, and the struggle becomes a struggle for one's lifeblood, for one's very survival. And Laing adds:

> Hatred is also necessarily present, for what else is the adequate object of hatred except that which endangers one's self? However, the anxiety to which the self is subject precludes the possiblity of a direct revelation of its hatred, except, as we shall see later, in psychosis. Indeed, what is called psychosis is sometimes simply the sudden removal of the veil of the false self, which had been serving to maintain an outer behavioral normality that may, long ago, have failed to be any reflection of the state of affairs in the secret self. Then the self will pour out accusations of persecution at the hands of that person with whom the false self has been complying for years (1965a, pp. 99-100).

EXPERIMENTAL STUDIES

Projective Studies

A considerable amount of evidence has been gathered employing more experimentally based types of research investigation into the problem of paranoia (Wolowitz, 1971). These studies cover a wide variety of research approaches to the problem and shed a considerable amount of light, both on the characteristics of the syndrome and on possible influences involved in its genesis. We have mentioned Aronson's (1964) study of Rorschach signs in paranoia in which he found that paranoid patients produced a higher frequency of homosexual signs than did nonparanoids, psychotics, or normals. However, Grauer (1954), using the same signs as Aronson, was unable to confirm his findings in a group of paranoid schizophrenics. Another study by McKeton et al. (1962) compared a group of hospitalized paranoid schizophrenics with neurotics and alcoholics using Rorschach signs of suppressed or repressed homosexuality, and found supporting evidence for a connection with homosexuality. Other studies of the relationship between homosexuality and paranoia have been reviewed above, and, as noted there, the conclusion as to the validity of the basically Freudian hypothesis remains very much in question and lacks convincing support.

An attempt was made by Beitner (1961) to assess identification processes in paranoid patients. He studied the differences between hospitalized paranoid-schizophrenic subjects and neurotic subjects in comparison with control groups by using a form of the semantic differential. On this measure, both the paranoid group and the anxiety-neurotic group showed defective identification with both parental figures. A confusion in sexual identification was not apparent in the paranoid group, although there was some evidence to support this in the neurotic group. Also of interest is

Caine's (1960) study of hostility and guilt in melancholic and paranoid patients. He employed both overt and covert measures of attitude to study these feelings in female patients. He found that paranoid patients did not act out their hostility, as measured by the MMPI scales and sentence-building tests, to the same degree as depressive patients, but their TAT stories expressed their hostility in stories involving murder, rape, violence, etc. His findings suggested that paranoids and depressives differed not so much in the intensity of their hostility but in the manner and direction in which they expressed it.

Other investigators have studied person-perception and self-perception in paranoid subjects. Daston, King, and Armitage (1953) found that paranoid schizophrenics showed significantly greater distortion of the descriptions of hypothetical people presented in short stories than did a normal group. Izard (1959), basing his study on the relationship between needs, motives, and perceptions, and using photographed faces to test perceptions of paranoid subjects, found that paranoids tend to perceive such faces as tense, suspicious, hostile, and threatening, whereas normal subjects do not. The findings with regard to self-perception, on the other hand, have not been altogether consistent. Friedman (1957) found no significant difference between his paranoid subjects and the normal controls with regard to congruence of their self and ideal-self concepts. However, Rogers, studying the same aspects of personality, found that his group of paranoid-schizophrenic subjects exhibited less self-ideal self discrepancy than did a control group. Havener and Izard's (1962) study of paranoid self-rating, using the Lorr scale for rating psychiatric patients, found that paranoids tended to overrate themselves in comparison with nonparanoid schizophrenics. They concluded that this was evidence of an unrealistic self-enhancement as a defense against loss of genuinely positive self-related affect and of satisfying interpersonal relationships.

Several groups have utilized the TAT effectively to study self-concepts in paranoid subjects. Friedman (1957) used an eighty-statement Q-sort to characterize the TAT hero of each subject, and then compared these with statements of the patient's ideal self-concepts. He found that the TAT heroes of normal subjects correlated more highly with their ideal self-concept than did either neurotic or paranoid TAT heroes. He also found that the paranoid's TAT hero reflected much greater degrees of feelings of inadequacy, dissatisfaction and pessimism, as well as more stressful interpersonal relationships.

Similarly, May (1970) studied TAT responses in paranoid and non-paranoid schizophrenics and normal controls of both sexes. Only male paranoids showed significant reactions to scenes of power and aggressive assertion—suggesting a high degree of anxiety and defensiveness over power issues. These conflicts were not found in female paranoids. This suggests that power anxiety may be sex-related. May also observes that "field-independence" as a cognitive style is characteristic both of males and paranoid schizophrenics (Witkin, H., 1965).

Wolowitz (1965) had hypothesized an approach-avoidance conflict in male paranoids with regard to "powerful appearing" men. In the approach aspect of the conflict, the paranoid wishes to be dependent on these powerful men and to appropriate their power through magical sexual-aggressive means. In the avoidance aspect, on the other hand, the paranoid anticipates and fears retaliation and destruction from more powerful and threatening male figures. This hypothesis substantially follows Nunberg's view that the paranoid is conflicted by his desire to magically absorb another male's power through homosexual contact, and by his fear of retaliation and destruction. Following up this hypothesis, Wolowitz and Shorkey (1966) studied the power themes of paranoid patients using the TAT. They took power concerns to mean any deficits or surpluses of personal resources which seemed to be related to masculine self-esteem, as for example, physical strength, social influence, etc. They found that paranoid schizophrenics expressed a significantly greater number of power themes in TAT stories than did subjects with a variety of other diagnoses.

In a later study, the same authors attempted to determine whether the power preoccupation in paranoid patients was the result of long-standing paranoid orientation or part of the cause of the disorder. To test this they studied the TAT stories of young children who had been diagnosed as paranoid-schizophrenic. They reasoned that the younger subject's paranoid condition would have had little time to affect their thinking processes, and that any indications of power motifs would more likely have a causal relationship to the disorder. They studied TAT stories from seventy young boys, ages ten to eleven, and found a similar preoccupation with power motifs. They interpreted the results as consistent with the hypothesis that power conflicts play a causative role in the etiology of paranoid disorders (Wolowitz and Shorkey, 1969).

Cognitive Studies

Some recent studies have focused on cognitive aspects of paranoid performance, particularly with regard to the progression from information input to hypothesis formation. One of the enigmas of paranoia is how it is that individuals whose intellectual and perceptual apparatuses are relatively intact can maintain delusional or false beliefs. Thus Sarvis (1962) suggested that one of the causes of paranoid reactions may lie in the area of perceptual distortion. She pointed out that sensory deprivation, sensory overload, or sensory distortion, as in delayed-feedback experiments, all tended to produce disorganization of secondary thought processes and produced marked anxiety. If perceptual deprivation, overload or distortion were maintained for a sufficient length of time or with sufficient severity, it would drive the subject into greater disorganization and specifically in the direction of a paranoid reaction.

This raises the question of whether the problem is to be seen as the level of sensory input, or at a subsequent level of information processing. Mc-Reynolds (1960) has proposed that the assimiliation of percepts is a critical aspect of normal cognitive functioning, and that anxiety may be thought of as the function of the quantity of percepts which the subject is unable to assimilate. The major detriment in such assimilation is the incongruencies among conceptual patterns according to which assimilation would occur. Thus he relates the characteristics of schizophrenia, including avoidance, withdrawal, apathy, and hallucinations, as in part attempts to deal with a high level of unassimilated percepts. Delusional beliefs thereby become attempts to bring about assimilation of otherwise unassimilable percepts.

Following this line of thinking, Abroms, Taintor, and Lhamon (1966) hypothesized that a task in which a judgment process must be based on incomplete amounts of data would cause paranoid subjects to form more atypical and incorrect judgments rather than not forming any judgments at all. Paranoid subjects, they felt, would tend to try to assimilate unassimilated percepts rather than suspending judgment, even at the price of accuracy. They also felt that this assimilation tendency would be more pronounced with the increasing severity of the paranoid symptomatology. Using a modification of the MMPI and results from gestalt completion figure tests, they found that the number of incorrect responses on the test increases with the severity of paranoid trait, and consequently that their hypotheses were substantiated. These findings are of great significance for the understanding of the genesis of paranoia.

Games Strategies

One of the most interesting developments in recent years has been the application of a two-person bargaining game to the study of paranoid processes. Deutsch (1958, 1962) had used this technique for study of personal and situational determinants of interpersonal trust and suspicion, Klein and Solomon (1966) studied the responses of schizophrenic patients in a two-person bargaining game in which the experimental confederate had assumed an exploitative strategy for the initial trials, and then subsequently adopted a conditionally cooperative strategy. Paranoid patients were found to maintain their noncooperative stance for a longer period after the confederate's reform. The authors question whether the paranoid rigidity was a result of the sinning confederate's initial exploitation, which might have reinforced the paranoid's suspicion, or whether it reflected a cognitive inability to adapt.

To study this, they set up a game situation in which the confederate's strategy shifted from unconditional to conditional cooperation (called the "lapsed saint" strategy), and also would shift from an unconditional non-cooperation to conditional cooperation (this strategy they referred to as "reformed sinner"). Comparing groups of paranoid and nonparanoid schizophrenics with a group of normal controls, the results indicate that the lapsed saint strategy produced higher levels of cooperation in the paranoids than in nonparanoid subjects. The reformed sinner strategy produced lower levels of exploitation in the paranoids as compared with nonparanoid subjects. The authors feel that their results are consistent with the power conflict view of paranoia as proposed by Ovesey (1955b). They write:

> Perhaps the major issue at stake for the paranoid-schizophrenics in the present experimental situation is not when and whom to trust, but rather a concern with the balance of power . . . . The paranoid's strategy is designed to test and redefine the existing balance of power. Thus, when the sinner is punitive and tough, the paranoid is docile and cooperative; with the sinner's abrupt shift to a soft unconditional benevolence, the paranoids react by shifting in the direction of an exploitative and dominating strategy. With the saint the reverse is true. The paranoids are initially exploitative, but when the saint shifts to a strategy of punishing noncooperation, the paranoids rapidly shift to a cooperative pattern (Hartford and Solomon, 1969, p. 502).

Thus the paranoid's stance is not indiscriminate but can be varied in accordance with the strategy of the other. These findings highlight the importance of the issues of power relations and control in the dynamics of paranoia.

There are methodological difficulties, however, in the study of trust and suspicion in such game strategies. As Kee and Knox (1970) have pointed out, the degree of manifest trust in such situations is related to the subject's subjective estimate that the other players will be trustworthy or not. It is thus necessary to distinguish in both trust and suspicion two related components—the observable choice behavior and a subjective state which underlies the manifest choice behavior. It would be important, therefore, to know the threshold at which subjective trust can become manifest as behavioral trust—the degree to which the subject feels that he can trust the other before he will in fact make a trusting decision. Such thresholds are undoubtedly determined by a variety of situational, structural, and internal dispositional factors.

Family Studies

One of the most interesting and fruitful areas of study, which has shed considerable light on the mechanisms and genesis of mental disease, has been studies in family dynamics. However, the major focus in such studies has been on the role of family relationships and patterns of interaction in the production of schizophrenia. These studies have been exhaustively reviewed and criticized elsewhere (Meissner, 1964; Mishler and Waxler, 1966; Lidz, Fleck, and Cornelison, 1965; and Boszormenyi-Nagy and Framo, 1965).

Few of these studies, unfortunately, have distinguished the paranoid dynamics within the broader focus of schizophrenia. In an attempt to describe the sociological aspects of the background of paranoia, Bonner (1960) describes the strictness, harshness, and domination of the patient's early pattern of family life. He remarks that the paranoid's opportunities for mastering the world around him or for promoting his own growth to maturity are often either reduced or eliminated, and that ultimately, the paranoid finds himself both despising the world and being despised by it. Goodman's (1968) study of the influence of parental figures found that paternal figures are more valent than maternal figures for paranoid schizophrenics but that the relationship was reversed for nonparanoid schizophrenics. Paranoids responded more quickly on the response latency measure when they were influenced by father figures, and correspondingly nonparanoids responded more quickly when influenced by maternal figures. Sletten and Ballous (1967) investigated the paranoid delusional system to try to determine which parent was the most fear-inspiring for the patient. They found that when the father was the most fear-inspiring parent, the subject had delusional ideas which concerned men only. But when the mother was the most fear-inspiring parent, the subjects tended to have delusions which involved both men and women, but in which women predominated. Thus they felt that the content of persecutory delusions was related to premorbid fears that were primarily influenced by the most threatening parent.

While such family studies have shed a great deal of light on our understanding of schizophrenia, they have not contributed a great deal to the understanding of paranoia beyond the indication of the importance of the child's relationship to the parents and the management of hostility in that relationship. It must be remembered, however, that investigation of schizophrenia is an exploration into a level of life adjustment or the development of the internal structure and personality functioning. Paranoia, however, is related more to questions of style of adaptation and living. The paranoid style of adaptation can be found at all levels of personality development and at all degrees of psychopathology, from the minimally neurotic to the intensely psychotic.

Studies in this area have not been greatly rewarding. Goldstein and Carr (1956) tried to study maternal attitudes toward child behavior of mothers of schizophrenics. Their effort was directed at testing out Arieti's suggestion that catatonics had been criticized for their actions as children while paranoids were criticized for their intentions. Their findings did not support this suggestion. Studies of patterns of interaction within families, which have focused primarily on schizophrenia as an entity have shown that generalized styles of interaction and generalized family norms appear to be more dominant than role differentials within family structure. Family resemblances have been found in psychological and biological traits, cognitive styles, value systems, and even political views. Investigators have found a strain toward consistency which requires and supports certain behaviors within the family and which creates an apparent similarity in styles of interaction within it.

This raises a question about the role of family styles and patterns of interaction in the generation of the paranoid style or the paranoid strategy. Wallace and Fogelson (1965), for example, have described two basic strategies which take place in schizophrenic families in which the schizophrenic, struggling to attain a total identity, strives to reduce the dissonance that he senses between his own real identity and the ideal identity. The strategies available for reducing the dissonance require either reducing the value of the ideal identity, or increasing the value of the real identity. They label these respective strategies as the withdrawal strategy and the paranoid strategy. In the withdrawal strategy, the victim sees himself as helpless, worthless, and incompetent. He feels there is no point in aspiring to anything more in life, and asks only that he be left alone. The paranoid strategy, on the other hand, allows the victim to absolve himself of blame and to feel that it is someone else who is worthless, incompetent, and even evil. The victim himself is good and competent, and well able to take care of himself. Thus his claimed identity becomes his ideal identity, and the real identity is denied and projected onto others through the paranoid defense.

The Mishler and Waxler (1968) study of patterns of interaction in schizophrenic families has provided some information about control strategies in family processes. In the context of an emphasis on power conflicts in paranoia, their findings on control strategies in schizophrenic families are of considerable interest. Strategies of attention control in normal families found clear patterns of role differentiation and a hierarchy of power and authority, without showing at the same time patterns of authoritarian or coercive control. In normal families the strategies of person-control and direct attempts at interpersonal influence are found in all members of these families, including the low-status children, and this pattern of interaction is strikingly different from that found in schizophrenic families. In male schizophrenic families, for example, they found a reversal of generational roles between fathers and sons, the patient and his mother thus holding relatively high power positions, with the father exerting little or no influence on the family system. In female schizophrenic families, the daughter is given little attention or respect and on her own part makes few attempts to influence the family proceedings.

Power was exercised in various forms of control strategy in an impersonal and rather indirect manner. Moreover, the evidence suggested that

these divergencies from normal power relations and control strategies within the family were more marked in situations where the schizophrenic
patient was present than in situations where the patient was not. The
authors comment that the dimension of power, of who has it and of how it is
used, is particularly sensitive to the presence of the patient. It is unfortunate
that these studies do not focus on the issue of paranoid versus nonparanoid
strategies in the schizophrenic syndrome, but their findings question the extent to which such deviations from normal power interactions influence the
generation of the paranoid style of thinking. It is not clear, by any means, to
what extent such strategies within the family have to do with the level of personality development and integration on the one hand (the schizophrenic
question), and on the other, to what extent they are concerned with styles of
interpersonal interaction and defense (the paranoid question).

CHAPTER 2

Paranoid States

PARANOID ELEMENTS

We have been discussing paranoia less in terms of its characteristics as a pathological state of mind and more in terms of its being a style of life experience and adaptation. It is a style of life experience which spans a wide spectrum of pathological states of mind of varying degrees of severity and distortion. The paranoid style represents a manner of construction of life experience and organization of reality which, from one point of view, permits a partial testing and validation of reality, but from another involves a distortion of reality testing.

From an adaptational perspective a paranoid state of mind can be looked on in terms of the organization of a system of coherent beliefs, which allows the patient to interpret his reality and organize it in such a way that it serves certain adaptive needs. We can examine, therefore, some of the elements of the paranoid style and examine the relationship between this manner of organizing one's interpretation of reality with other similar states of mental organization which serve both pathological and relatively normal needs.

The paranoid style, as we have seen, serves certain definite defensive purposes. Clinically, paranoid patients do not manifest any overt anxiety as such, or it is perhaps better to say that they manifest anxiety only when the paranoid defense begins to crumble. Searles has commented on this as follows:

> One point I wish to make at the outset is that the paranoid individual seems rarely, if ever—except in states of panic—to feel anxiety as such. I have come to believe it pathognomonic of him that he experiences, instead, an awareness of various ingredients of his surroundings—or, less often, of things within his body—as being charged with sinister meanings, charged with malevolence toward himself (1965, p. 465).

Paranoid defenses, therefore, can be seen as defending against anxiety or, as we have seen in our previous discussion of the relationship between paranoia and depression, against depression. Thus the paranoid style and the elements that contribute to it can be conceptualized as operating in the service of specific defenses.

Displacement of Responsibility

One of the most characteristic features of the paranoid style is that it tends to displace responsibility from the self, and to place it on others. Thus the paranoid sees difficulties that he encounters, not in terms of internal conflicts or of inadequacies of his own person, but rather in terms of forces and influences that surround him. Instead of blaming himself, as the depressive patient might, the paranoid blames others for his unhappiness. This projective aspect of the paranoid style also has a defensive purpose in that it avoids self-blame, which is so painful and threatening to the paranoid personality; but it also serves adaptive ends, in that it avoids self-reproach and allows the patient to maintain a measure of self-esteem, and provides for his continuing self-justification.

The paranoid can thus absolve himself of feelings of guilt or inadequacy, and place the responsibility for pain, evil, or weakness on some other person or group of persons. While the elements of denial and projection are easily recognized in this maneuver, there is also the element of self-assurance that the way one behaves, the way one feels, the way one believes, is indeed the right, true, and good course that ultimately carries with it the assurances of rightness and truth.

Suspiciousness

The element of paranoid suspiciousness has often been commented on (Cameron, 1959; Searles, 1965). The underlying uncertainties of paranoid conditions will not allow any exceptions or deviations from the paranoid construction. The suspicious guardedness of the paranoid, therefore, serves an important self-protective function and serves an important function in the preservation of rightness in the paranoid construction. The paranoid construction requires a certainty, consistency, and coherence which demands that the construction be tested out against the available data from the environment at all points.

Paranoid suspiciousness, therefore, is almost scientific in its interest in assimilating the available data of reality to the paranoid construction. If the data do not fit the theoretical construction, however, the paranoid runs the risk not merely of the destruction of a theory, but of something more devastating and more personally threatening. The paranoid interest, therefore, in assimilating data to the construction is not merely one of curiosity, but one of suspiciousness that is consistent with the implicit threat. Moreover, the projection of hostility carries with it the implication that other sources of influence on the paranoid subject have a hostile intent which is not always manifest, but which in the paranoid view must always be anticipated. Thus the paranoid patient is exquisitely sensitive to even the slightest indication of hostility, even when that hostility is quite latent or even unconscious in those with whom he is involved.

The overwhelming emphasis and the pressing need in the paranoid, in his constant testing of his construction of reality, is the preservation of that construction. Thus there is a constant pressure to reinterpret, to modify, and even to distort data that do not seem consistent with it. In this light the paranoid's suspiciousness can be seen as a constant effort to evaluate new evidences which are ambiguous, and to assess them in a manner which brings them into a consistent relation to the paranoid construction.

Grandiosity

The grandiosity of paranoid states is a characteristic that is a more or less constant feature of the syndrome, but whose intensity undergoes considerable degrees of variability. Freud had noted its recuperative and reparative aspects and the role that it plays in preservation of self-esteem, and the denial of weakness and dependency has often been commented on. In relationship to the paranoid construction, however, it can be seen as insistence upon the rightness of the construction and the goodness of its formulation. The retreat to grandiosity, therefore, not only involves a denial and a compensation, but it also involves an assertion of the conviction of rightness.

The intensity of the grandiosity is obviously a function of the need to deny the underlying weakness and inadequacy that the patient senses. This can, and often does, reach delusional proportions. Schreber's messianic delusions of an alliance with God can be seen not only as salvaging self-esteem and as a denial of his inner feelings of weakness and inadequacy, but also as an attempt to reconstitute meaningfulness and significance in his existence. If the paranoid construction is viewed as aimed at a coherent system of beliefs which give consistency, meaning, and rightness to the patient's life experience, then the role of grandiosity in supporting and sustaining this conviction can be more easily appreciated.

Delusional Fixity

The element of delusional fixity and conviction of the reality of the delusion has long been recognized as part of the paranoid syndrome. Freud (1940 [1938]) saw the basis for this in the persistence of a kernel of historical truth within the content of the delusion. The delusion, he felt, formed itself around fragments of experience derived from childhood. Thus a repressed fragment derived from preverbal levels of experience forces its way into consciousness in a distorted and displaced way. The belief attached to such delusions was thus derived from infantile sources, but was based upon an historical kernel of truth.

Moreover, the paranoid's projection does not occur in a vacuum. He is highly perceptive of, and sensitive to, the hostility that exists in the persecutor and reflects his own inner impulses. Thus the delusional system is not often without its reality elements (Freud, 1922). In his reconsideration of paranoid ideas, Waelder (1951) takes his point of departure in Kraepelin's definition of delusions as "erroneous judgments not subject to correction by experience." Thus the paranoid is unable to modify his beliefs under the impact of experience. Waelder, however, explains the paranoid inaccessibility to influence by appeal to Freud's hypothesis that adherence to delusional ideas reflects an intrinsic, although distorted, content of truth.

Frosch (1967) has contributed several important elements to the understanding of this sense of conviction and fixity. He points out the fixity and the compelling quality of neurotic symptoms. The neurotic may still be able to question the reality of his fear; that is to say, he has not lost his capacity to test reality, but he maintains a feeling of conviction about impending danger which provokes his anxiety. In addition to the kernel of historical truth, which can lend support and conviction to a delusional belief, Frosch points out that there are other pressures at work which operate in the direction of maintaining and reinforcing the delusional conviction. His patient, who maintained the delusional belief that the day was Friday rather than Saturday, finally was able to say that for her to admit the wrongness of her belief would have raised severe questions in her own mind about her sanity and mental intactness. Not to maintain her conviction would have meant that she was crazy, and for her to be crazy would have meant the loss of control, disintegration, and a complete negation of herself.

Frosch concludes that the problem of danger must be viewed hierarchically. The most basic and primitive fears operate at a biological level and involve the problem of survival. These fears are represented psychically by fears of disintegration and dissolution of self. Other fears and dangers are phase-related in terms of levels of psychic development, and assume forms relevant to the level of development of object-relations of ego structure and reality contact. The regression of psychotic states is associated with de-differentiation and the consequent fusion of self and object brings along with it the possibility of unconditional omnipotence. However, it may also bring the possibility of engulfment and absorption by the object with the consequent disappearance of the self. Frosch comments:

> It is the possibility that de-differentiation might eventuate in ultimate loss and dissolution of self that makes this phenomenon so frightening to the psychotic or borderline psychotic. Furthermore, the threat of de-differentiation with the ultimate eventuality of dissolution of self may be especially frightening to the psychotic because the possibility of reversal is minimal. In the normal and in the neurotic, blurring of ego boundaries and de-differentiation may be tolerated in the belief that ultimately the ego boundaries can be

reestablished intact . . . . In the psychotic, since the chance of reversal is less, the process of de-differentiation may really eventuate in dissolution of self. It is for this reason that in the psychotic de-differentiation is an ever-present and real danger (Frosch, 1967, p. 487).

Laing (1965) has discussed this same psychotic fear of dissolution and loss of self in terms of the fear of engulfment.

Thus the paranoid sense of conviction can be related to an historical kernel of truth on the one hand, and on the other hand to a set of psychological pressures which make the admission of error in the delusion threatening or painful. To admit error or inadequacy in one's theoretical formulation means that one must also in some sense admit personal defect. The threat to the self may extend all the way from relatively innocuous self-accusations, such as ignorance, stupidity, lack of intellectual capacity and understanding, or they may extend to psychotic levels of intensity in which dissolution and utter loss of self are implied and in which the individual faces engulfment or psychic death. The paranoid conviction of rightness, therefore, can be seen in terms of its function in maintaining self-esteem at one level, or in the maintaining of psychic integrity at another.

In these terms, then, paranoia can be fitted into a continuum of cognitive states in which available experiential data are integrated and interpreted in terms of a theoretical system of some sort. This applies to the formation of scientific theories and to the development of systems of religious belief. In this connection, we need only remind ourselves that the history of science is replete with examples of the conviction of theoretical rightness being unwilling to yield in the face of newly acquired evidences. Similarly, systems of religious belief are often maintained, if not in the face of contradictory evidence, at least in the face of lack of evidence. We shall return to this point below. But it seems safe to observe at this point that the need for conviction of rightness and the denial of uncertainty is a quality of human thinking that has broader application than merely to paranoia or related pathological conditions. Rather it spans a wide spectrum of adaptive and socially valuable human cognitive processes.

Paranoid Pseudocommunity

The last element that I would like to consider is the "paranoid pseudocommunity." As the paranoid delusion evolves, the patient gradually builds up a delusional reconstruction in which his projections become organized into a stable picture of external reality. Ideas of reference or persecution that are referred to nonspecific groups or isolated individuals gradually become organized into a unified group which has a definite plot aimed at the patient as the intended victim. This unified and organized group is constructed out of the patients' projections and forms of the pseudocommunity, which Cameron defines as follows: "The paranoid pseudocommunity is an imaginary organization, composed of real and imagined persons, whom the patient represents as united for the purpose of carrying out some action upon him" (1959, pp. 518-19). The formation of the pseudocommunity marks a phase of final crystallization and organization in the restitutional process of the psychosis. This has considerable advantage for the patient, since a known and organized source of danger is easier to tolerate and deal with than an unknown and diffuse source.

Interpretive System

This final organization of the delusional system reflects a strain toward consistency and completeness of explanation in the interpretive aspect of the delusion. Cognitive processes are structured in such a way as to form a meaningful interpretive system which can serve as the basis for clarification, explanation, and understanding. Once this organized interpretive schema is elaborated, any new cognitive input tends to be assimilated to the system and organized according to drive-determined principles. Real events are distorted and reinterpreted to fit the overall picture provided by the schema; nonspecific and trivial happenings are endowed with important and relevant significances; contradictory evidences are either rejected or ignored, or transformed to fit the overriding implications of the system. Further crystallization and fixation of this system of interpretations and beliefs leads to the picture of classic paranoia.

The paranoid puts a considerable amount of intellectual energy into the construction and interpretation of his view of reality. Freud (1914) had noted the tendency of paranoids to construct speculative systems, and attributed this to the externalization of the critical agency or conscience which he felt provided the inner resources for philosophical speculation. The classic example of this kind of speculative elaboration was the involved cosmological system evolved by Schreber (Freud, 1911). Such elaborate speculative systemization and organization of forces in external reality provides the paranoid with a consistent and coherent world view which supports his need for conviction of rightness, and erases the last semblances of uncertainty in his delusional beliefs. His tolerance for uncertainty or ambiguity is minimal, since it is precisely such uncertainty that poses a threat to his existence whose severity parallels the degree of his pathology. Furthermore, the elaboration of the pseudocommunity provides the paranoid with a meaningful context of object-relations, distorted and threatening though they may be, and serves to provide a meaningfulness for his personal existence which otherwise he would lack. It provides him with a context within which he carries out his life and fixes his place in a determinate fashion.

We can reemphasize at this point, at the risk of repetitiousness, that the paranoid need to eliminate ambiguity, to establish a consistent and coherent view of reality, and to formulate a belief system which enunciates in some determinate fashion one's place in life and one's relation to the structure of the world around one, is a basic human need which is shared by other forms of interpretive thinking and is not exclusively restricted to paranoia. I have undertaken this reevaluation of the elements of paranoia not to minimize the pathological distortion involved, but rather to emphasize the continuity between the elements, paranoia and what passes for less pathological and even normal states of mind. It is important for our understanding of the mechansms by which paranoia emerges as a distinctive pathological condition to understand how closely it is related to other states of mind which are more socially viable. It suggests furthermore that the genetic processes which underlie paranoid states may not be deviant elements in personal and social development, but may in fact be necessary components of normal and relatively healthy personal and social growth. With these rather nonspecific indications of the relationship between paranoia and related states, I would like to pass on to more specific consideration of both pathological and non-pathological conditions which share in varying degrees the elements of paranoid states.

PARANOID SYNDROMES

Paranoid States: Diagnostic Categorization
The traditional approach to paranoia, deriving from the influence of Kraepelin and Bleuler, has focused on a small number of paranoid states and has tried to establish these as diagnostic categories—even though the diagnostic stability of the categories has been quite variable (Lewis, 1970). The focus in the present study is not on the problems of diagnosis and the establishment of illness categories. My emphasis here is on process—and in this sense the paranoid dynamics can be found in all of the paranoid states which will be described. They vary considerably in the degree, intensity, and extent to which the paranoid process is operative.

The process point of view has validity not only in the specifically paranoid states, but also for the related toxic and organic states that produce paranoid symptoms. The description of these paranoid conditions offers a better sense of the variety and complexity of pathological forms through which the paranoid process expresses itself. It also makes it apparent, in the consideration of organic states in which paranoid symptoms are observed, that the function of the paranoid process bears a complex relationship to the integral functioning of the total organism. While the paranoid process does not depend on such organic factors for its operation, it is in no sense isolated from their influence. But we shall see more of this later.

Leading the parade of paranoid states is the so-called *true* or *classic paranoia*. It can be questioned whether this diagnostic entity ever really occurs. The *Diagnostic and Statistical Manual* (1968) labels it "an extremely rare condition." The constellation of symptoms involved in paranoia was one of the first to emerge from the diagnostic preoccupation of Kraepelin. Blueler, writing in 1911, offers the following description:

> The construction, from false premises, of a logically developed and in its various parts logically connected, unshakeable delusional system without any demonstrable disturbance affecting any of the other mental functions and, therefore, also without any symptoms of "deterioration" if one ignores the paranoiac's complete lack of insight into his own delusional system (Blueler, 1950).

While it remains possible that such an isolated and sequestered delusional system can function in the context of an otherwise integral personality, my own experience has not found this to be the case. Usually—even in patients who present an apparently isolated delusional system, without other apparent personality impairments—on more careful examination they prove to be schizophrenic. There is sufficient diagnostic variability to make the status of classic paranoia a moot question, but I suspect that most contemporary clinicians would tend to diagnose such patients as paranoid schizophrenics.

Paranoid schizophrenia is perhaps the most serious of the paranoid disorders. The paranoid schizophrenic demonstrates the characteristics of the paranoid process as we have described them above—but these characteristics are imbedded in a personality structure which is quite primitive and disorganized. Paranoid characteristics are frequently seen in schizophrenic disorders, both in acute episodes and in chronic cases. The delusional system in such cases tends to be bizarre and somewhat disorganized, with a considerable element of grandiosity. The delusions are often persecutory, and auditory hallucinations are often incorporated as part of or an expression of the delusional content.

The paranoid aspects of schizophrenic breakdowns are not often apparent, although by far the great majority of acute schizophrenic episodes have a strong paranoid flavor. Consequently the large majority of initial diagnoses of the schizophrenic process take the form of paranoid schizophrenia. Again based on my own clinical experience, the overlap between paranoid and schizophrenic manifestations is considerable, and in fact it is a rare schizophrenic patient who does not manifest some paranoid content. This may be flagrant or it may be deeply embedded in the patient's psyche, and it may form an aspect of his illness which he keeps well hidden. Frequently patients who have carried a label of chronic undifferentiated schizophrenia over the course of many years prove on deeper probing to have a latent paranoid core.

I have a suspicion, in reading many of the attempts to attain diagnostic clarity in dealing with these states, that distinctions are often made on the basis of degree, rather than of any significant qualitative difference between categories of patients. It is also quite possible that the historical differentiation of these categories may have been a function of the manner, depth, and sophistication of psychological investigation. In the large custodial institutions of the early part of this and the preceding century, there was little opportunity for careful and time-consuming diagnostic evaluation.

A term that has caused considerable confusion—a confusion that was not helped by its use in the DSM II—is the term *paraphrenia*. Kraepelin's original use of the term was meant to imply that the delusional content was not as rigidly systematized as in full-blown paranoia. Freud, however, used the term as roughly equivalent to our meaning of paranoid schizophrenia, particularly in his discussion of the Schreber case. The term probably does not have much diagnostic utility—particularly in attempts to distinguish it from paranoid schizophrenia. It would seem to represent a group of less disorganized and decompensated paranoid schizophrenics. Despite recent attempts to shore up the distinction (Frost, 1969), the usefulness of the distinction is not readily apparent.

The next important category is that of the *involutional paranoid state*. This is a counterpart to the more frequent involutional depressive condition. The onset is usually gradual, coming on in the involutional period late in life and often without any apparent precipitating stress. The delusional system usually presages death, along with a fear of abandonment. The fear of death may often be somewhat diffuse and vague, making a diagnostic discrimination between involutional paranoia and involutional depression somewhat difficult at times. The concerns of such patients often focus around the loss of physical capacity, the approaching end of active and useful life and career, and the encroachment of physical disability and increasing loss of function. Often the delusional content will be markedly hypochondriacal. As with involutional melancholia, agitation may be a marked aspect.

The preceding categories of paranoid states are psychotic in their level of functioning. But there is one major paranoid category which involves a more basically characterological personality distortion. The *paranoid personality* is characteristically hypersensitive, argumentative, suspicious —constantly maintaining a guarded and defensive attitude toward other people in his environment and the world around him. He is constantly on guard against being taken advantage of, constantly expecting attacks and injury from those around him. He may be quite tense or hostile, but often enough is quiet and receding—in either case maintaining a rigid guarded-ness and control of his environment and his relationships.

The rigidity and suspiciousness of these personalities make their per-sonal relationships extremely difficult and trying, particularly on people around them. They avoid close involvement and are quite prone to jealousy and angry outbursts. When their intelligence is high and their reality testing intact, they use these capacities in a strenuous and inflexible attempt to con-trol things and people around them. A frequent presentation of such cases in my own experience has been through a somewhat masochistic and depressed wife who comes seeking treatment because of her inability to tolerate the strain of what is happening at home. As it turns out, the husband is a rather paranoid individual who makes the home situation extremely difficult, full of tension, and makes difficult and troublesome demands on the wife as a means of bolstering and supporting his paranoid fears. Such paranoid husbands are almost universally resistant to any suggestion of treatment. I would see the paranoid personality, then, as one in which the paranoid process has become highly structuralized and embedded in the organization of the personality, so that it dominates the inner workings of the personality without necessarily impeding the structural and functional organization of the personality. While it is thus clear that the paranoid process can dominate personality organization without necessarily leading to psychotic disorganization, it is also quite clear that that process can be incorporated into personality organization with varying degrees and in varying ways. This sometimes gives rise to diagnostic difficulties. But we shall see more of this later.

Violence and the Paranoid Process

The problem of violence in paranoid patients is of particular interest, since it involves such a high degree of destructiveness and potential danger. The destructive potential is high in the paranoid syndromes that we have discussed—particularly in those which show a psychotic level of functioning or have a capacity for psychotic decompensation. It is readily understand-able that the persecutory delusions would lead the patient to defend himself by destructive counterattacks. This is particularly true insofar as the patient's underlying sense of vulnerability and helplessness may create acute levels of rather intense persecutory anxiety. The destructive counterattack is a way of relieving this anxiety. The patient's delusions may also allow for a rationalization or justification of the destructive activity. This is particularly true where paranoid grandiosity comes into play.

One of the important points that needs to be made in this connection is that the expression of violence is not limited to paranoid syndromes as such. Nonetheless, a cogent case can be made that, where violence is found as a part of the clinical picture, it is very likely to serve as an expression of underlying paranoid dynamics. This can be seen, for example, in violent patients who present themselves as the psychiatric emergency room (Lion et al., 1969). Such patients often presented with fears of loss of control or sudden destructive impulsivity, running "amok"—often with diffuse anxiety states and paniclike reactions. The breakthrough of destructive impulses was often without any clear-cut precipitant. Low frustration tolerance and poor work and marital histories were characteristic, along with superimposed paranoid elements. Self-esteem was low, and any narcissistic injury was dealt with by projection and an outburst of rage. Past histories often reflected a triat of enuresis, pyromania, or sadistic behavior to animals—a sadistic triad which has been found to be related to adult criminality (Hellman and Blackman, 1966).

Even when the violent impulses were directed toward particular objects, the violence was a form of reaction to dependency conflicts, and against the threat of diminished masculinity or physical weakness. The most frequent object of attack for these men was the wife. Such men seemed quite threatened by their dependency on their wives and their unconscious need for support from them—while the wives often manifested a masochistic need for punishment which responded to the husband's sadism. Some of these patients also had associated temporary lobe pathology or alcoholic pathology. (The association between these states and the paranoid process will be discussed in a later section.)

Homicide

The overlap between paranoid symptomatology and homicidal threats is considerable. In Macdonald's (1963) study of one hundred patients admitted to the hospital specifically for homicidal threats, paranoid delusions were present in thirty-five. Some of these showed considerable sadism in their histories, and even boasted of sadistic exploits, taking pleasure in such triumphs. Private armories with lethal weapons, including revolvers, pistols, shotguns, etc. were not infrequent. Such patients were often hypersensitive and easily provoked to angry outbursts. Even more passive-aggressive or passive-dependent personalities would experience outbursts of violent impulses—impulses such as were characteristically defended against. Pathological jealousy was a significant contributing factor to homicidal threats. Suspicions of marital infidelity often reached delusional proportions. Paranoid husbands with latent homosexual conflicts would often directly or indirectly encourage their wives to have affairs—and then react with great outrage. The victims in this series as well were family members—predominantly wives and husbands. The homicidal threats usually came in the context of intense sadomasochistic relationships. Macdonald remarks on the extraordinary reluctance on the part of relatives to seek advice or protection against the imminent threat of harm. Despite obvious signs of homicidal inclincations and preoccupations, relatives would often do nothing to effectively protect themselves or intervene in the process until forced to by physical assault or third-party interventions.

The study of homicidal adolescents suggests that the threat to kill the parents or the actual killing of the parents has a significant relationship to the degree of parent brutality (Duncan and Duncan, 1971). Similar patterns of parental brutality have also been identified in adult murderers (Duncan et al., 1958; Satten et al., 1960). There is some evidence also to suggest that similar dynamics are operative in cases of child abuse—suggesting that violence breeds violence (Silver et al., 1969). Part of the mechanism operating in such cases unquestionably involves identification with the aggressor—but it is clear from our own study of paranoid dynamics that the aggression need not be in the form of physical assault or brutality.

The incidence of homicide in relationship to paranoia is not at all unusual. A recent newspaper account came to my attention describing a fifty-eight-year-old man who had been waging a long battle with city authorities over the cluttering of his yard. The man lived alone and had few friends. He kept the yard of his home cluttered with junk and garbage which was quite unsightly and disturbing to the neighbors. For eighteen months he waged a battle with officials, who finally obtained a court order allowing them to clean up his yard as being a public nuisance. When the sanitation department workers arrived and began cleaning the yard, the owner, armed with a twelve-gauge shotgun, killed two of them. The police arrived and a gun battle ensued, during which this rather disturbed man shot himself with his own gun. A handwritten note was found in the grass beside his body. It read: "How can they abuse me anymore?"

The Wagner Case. Another fascinating example—the Wagner case—has been reported by Hilde Bruch (1967). On the night of September 4, 1913, a series of fires awakened the people of Mulhausen, then in southwest Germany. They ran into the street and there were confronted by a man whose face was covered by a black veil and who carried two pistols. He began firing and in a few minutes had killed eight men and one girl and had severely wounded twelve more people. He was then overpowered and found to be a man who had been a schoolteacher in the village more than ten years ago. He then confessed that on the preceding night he had quietly killed his wife and four children. He said that he had come to the town to take revenge on the men of the town for their scorn and disdain of him. On the day of the murders he had mailed a series of letters to the largest newspaper in Stuttgart completely confessing all of his crimes.

The amazement at this destructive outburst was increased by the fact that, prior to it, Wagner had been an exemplary man. He was described as an admirable citizen, dignified, quiet. The contrast to the horrible, carefully and deliberately calculated mass murder was overwhelming. The fateful chain of events began with a sodomistic act that had occurred in the summer of 1901. He shrouded this experience in strong and persistent secretiveness, and thus the suspicion existed that these experiences were not real but delusional. In any case his sexual and masturbatory urges stood in irrevocable opposition to his high and rather rigid moral standards and ethical concepts. He had a deep sense of guilt over these impulses.

He soon began to hear slanderous remarks about himself and became unshakably convinced that his crime was known to the people of the town. He felt that he was being watched and mocked and ridiculed, and lived in a constant dread of being arrested for his crime. He then took to carrying a loaded pistol—even when he took his final examination as a teacher in 1902, and also on his wedding day in 1903. He regarded his wife as more of a servant than a wife. He was unhappy about the birth of his children, but he was unusually indulgent with them—even extravagant. He explained this later as due to the fact that he knew that they only had a short time to live.

His mood was generally depressed and pessimistic, with many hypochondriacal complaints. He would occasionally experience suicidal impulses, wanting to drown himself. He lived in constant dread of public humiliation. At times he tried to accuse his persecutors, but when his accusations were denied he felt utterly helpless and had to hide his rage and shame from them. Gradually he evolved his plan for destruction and murder. He collected and hid weapons and other things needed for his plan—even practiced sharpshooting in the remote parts of the woods. He worked on his plans in elaborate detail, but again and again shrank from the actual execution of them.

He had been a devoted student of literature and developed an interest in drama. He wrote dramas of his own which he tried to get published. When he couldn't find a publisher for his plays he would have them printed at his own expense. On occasions when he would drink too much beer, his friends noted that he seemed to change his personality and became quite moody and morose, or quite grandiose and talkative. He would talk passionately about his favorite topics—God and religion, or free love, which he advocated with caustic cynicism, and his great dramas. His wife had been dissatisfying to him. He was not happy with his teaching and commented from time to time that one day he would become a famous man and would do deeds that would astound the world. His father was a peasant who had been an alcoholic and probably paranoid. His father had died when he was two years old and left his mother with nothing but debts. His mother had been promiscuous, and he was known in the village as the "widow's boy." He suffered then from depression, suicidal thoughts, and nightmares.

The last twenty-five years of his life were spent in an asylum. For several years he worked studiously on a drama which he called *Wahn* ("Delusion"). It was based on the life of Ludwig II of Bavaria. He was bitterly disappointed when this work, which he considered a masterpiece, was not produced. About the same time, a drama dealing with mental illness was produced by Franz Werfel in Stuttgart. Wagner became convinced that Werfel had stolen it from him, or that he had based it on his life. He became preoccupied with concerns of dramatic work of his having been stolen by other successful writers. He became gradually convinced that there was a Jewish conspiracy to deprive him of the rewards of his dramatic labors.

About this time political events in Germany began to catch up with him. He joined the Nazi Party in 1929, and was proud of the fact that he had been the first inmate in the hospital to do so. He followed with great enthusiasm the racial policies and persecutions of the Nazi regime, regarding them as justification for his own delusional thoughts. Wagner died finally an embittered man—embittered not because of any remorse for his murders, but because his persecutors had declared him insane and he had thus failed to find the fame that he sought as a literary figure. The Wagner case is a classic one and it illustrates, I think, the difficulty in identifying the potentially homicidal paranoid patient. The secretiveness and intelligence of the paranoid individual make it possible for him to conceal his intentions to a considerable degree.

Homicidal Intent. At times however—just as in the case of suicidal intents—homicidal threats are communicated before the fatal act is undertaken. Macdonald's (1967) follow-up study of patients who had made homicidal threats indicates a number of factors related to such threats, including parental brutality, parental seduction, fire-setting, sadistic and cruel treatment of animals, previous police arrests, particularly for assault, alcoholism, and attempted suicide. However the absence of suicide attempts suggests an even greater risk of homicide. The relationship between murder and paranoid tendencies is also underlined by Lanzkron's (1963) study of 150 cases of mental patients committed to a hospital who were charged with or indicted for murder. In approximately 40 percent of this group, the homicide was directly related to, or derived from, paranoid delusions. In an additional 32.6 percent, the insane paroxysmal, homicidal outburst was associated with motives which included anger, revenge, jealousy, etc. In another 27 percent, the insanity seemed to have developed after the homicide, but the motives again included such apparently paranoid motivations as morbid jealousy, revenge, cuckolding-reaction, etc. Thus in 40 percent of the cases the paranoid process is explicit enough to warrant a labeling as one of the recognizable paranoid syndromes. In an additional 50 or more percent of the cases, a detectable element of paranoia is recognizable. The same author has reported a number of cases of involutional paranoia in which delusions of infidelity or delusions of persecution led to murder (Lanzkron, 1961). These cases seem to suggest that, when the paranoid process is operating, homicidal tendencies are operative over prolonged periods of time, since forebodings and forewarnings of homicidal intent are retrospectively identifiable for considerable periods. It is also noteworthy that such paranoid delusions and homicidal intent are usually found in males more frequently than in females—Lanzkron cites a ratio of four to one.

Premonitory signs are frequently available—for those who are able or willing to read them. Malmquist (1971) has studied such prodromal signs in young adolescent murderers. Behavioral and mood changes were frequent—especially self-hate and pessimism. Efforts to gain help may occur but often are met with denial, particularly from close relatives. Object losses were frequent precipitants. Threats to masculinity often came in the form of provocations to fight—often from teenage girls—usually in sadomasochistic contexts. Somatic and hypochondriacal symptoms or delusions were found. Homosexual threats seemed to raise the homicidal index.

The feeling of helplessness and hopelessness is a strong predisposing factor to acts of violence (Halleck, 1967). An acute state of loss or mourning may plunge the adolescent beyond the point of no return. As we shall see, the dynamics of depression and paranoia are closely linked. In these cases of destructive and homicidal violence, it seems that the acute and intolerable exacerbation of depression precipitates the paranoid defense and its attendant solution—a paroxysmal attempt at survival and self-preservation in the face of desperate self-disintegration (Malmquist, 1971; Dalman, 1955). Despite the determinable role of paranoid dynamics in criminal violence, a diagnosis of paranoia has little predictive validity. The risks of prediction of criminal violence in a medicolegal framework have recently been discussed by Rubin (1972).

Criminal Violence

The detailed study of extremely violent prisoners suggests that, among such criminals, whose police records boast multiple assaults and frequent homicides, violence was frequently elicited with little or no provocation. These persons seemed to demonstrate a high degree of sensitivity to personal insult and a high degree of personal vulnerability—even to the point of carrying a weapon for protection over prolonged periods of time. These men felt that they had to be violent in the interest of self-defense, and frequently lacked a sense of moderation or restraint in their attacks on others—tending toward murderous violence rather than restrained anger. Memories of parental violence is common, but memories of brutal beatings surprisingly rare.

Studies of the body-buffer zones show that violent prisoners usually have zones almost four times larger than the body-buffer zones of nonviolent prisoners. Also the rear zones in the violent prisoners were larger than the front zones—the reverse being the case in nonviolent prisoners. The normal group showed a greater tendency to sensitivity to approach from the front rather than from the rear. These findings suggest that violent subjects perceive the rear surface of their bodies as an area of vulnerability, rather than as a protective barrier as in normal subjects. The combination of this hypersensitivity to approach from the rear with tendencies to perceive passive intrusion as homosexual provocation, along with frequent histories of homosexual contact and homosexual denial, strongly suggest a high level of homosexual anxiety (Kinzel, 1970). It also seems that this pattern of increased hypersensitivity to approach would indicate a higher degree of vulnerability and fear of attack from the outside. This, it seems to me, would be quite consistent with paranoid dynamics.

Political Assassination

One of the most interesting—if unusual—varieties of paranoid violence is manifested in the pathology of the assassin. Political assassination has been a commonplace in human history, but we can limit our consideration to the area of political assassination in the United States. Such assassinations have never been a part of the process of organized redistribution of political power. They were the actions of disturbed individuals who had no political status and whose motivations reflected paranoid suspiciousness, bitterness, grandiosity—elements that we have come to recognize as reflecting not merely the operation of the paranoid process, but of severe paranoid psychopathology. By the act of assailing an American President, each of these individuals has achieved a position of historical prominence that answers somehow to the grandiosity of his act. To assume the prerogative of terminating the career of an American President, and to thus force a great country to modify and change the course of its history, is an act of assumed power which provides the rationale and motivation for his act of political assassination.

The most recent of these political assailants is Arthur Bremer, who struck down George Wallace during the preconvention campaigns for the presidential nomination. Bremer shares certain marked characteristics with the list of other presidential assailants. Political assassins in American history have always been personal failures, isolated human beings who seemed incapable of any genuine human relationships and who were possessed with extraordinary ambitions quite beyond the limits of their own personal capacities and assets. Family life, in many of these cases, seems to have been severely disturbed and unstable, particularly during critical periods of emotional development. Bremer was a loner with no close friends. He remained quite isolated and unable to trust people. His life was a saga of repeated failures—particularly when measured against the vast ambitions that are reflected in his notebooks. He thought that he would become a great writer or photographer, but in fact the only jobs he was able to get were those of janitor and busboy.

The list of assassinations or attempts on the lives of Presidents in the United States is impressive. Richard Lawrence tried unsuccessfully to shoot Andrew Jackson. Lawrence was very likely a paranoid schizophrenic—indulging himself in the delusion that he was Richard III, king of England. His friends called him "King Dick." He is said to have believed that steamship interests in the United States were conspiring against him, and once tried to shoot a woman whom he thought was laughing at him. He developed the delusional belief that President Jackson had been the enemy of the Lawrence family and was somehow responsible for his father's insanity and death. He insisted after the attempt that his act would have been a great benefit to all the workingmen of the country, a belief that was supported by political dissidents who often accused Jackson of undermining the laboring class in the country.

John Wilkes Booth was the man who killed Abraham Lincoln. He was a rather temperamental, abusive, and frequently psychotic individual who drank to excess. His psychotic symptoms were often brought to the fore under the influence of alcohol. He had a relatively successful career as an actor and was particularly successful in the South, where he championed the cause of slavery. At about age twenty-four his career began to be jeopardized by a condition of chronic laryngitis. At this time he began to think of the possibility of killing Abraham Lincoln. He was convinced that Lincoln was trying to become the unlimited and absolute monarch of the United States. He finally killed himself before he was tracked down and captured. He presumably suffered from a paranoid psychosis.

Charles Guiteau shot President James Garfield. His father had been a religious fanatic with the delusional belief that he would live forever. Even as a child Guiteau had assumed his father's belief in divine inspiration. Guiteau had an erratic work record and indulged in considerable swindling and theft to support himself. After his divorce his psychosis became increasingly evident, and he became more nomadic and isolated and friendless in his pattern of living. He entertained political fantasies that he dreamed would bring him to great power and influence. He wrote in a note, "Garfield has wrecked the once grand Republican Party and for this he dies." After he had shot the President, a note was found in his pocket saying, "The President's removal is an act of God."

President McKinley was assassinated by Leon Czolgosz. Czolgosz was a distant and isolated man who never seemed to enjoy anything. He was unable to hold a job. He was never married and was never known to have a girl friend. He often thought people were trying to poison his food. He was fascinated by anarchism and declared at one point that he was against all religion, marriage, and government. He wrote the following confession: "I killed President McKinley because I done my duty. I don't believe one man should have so much service and another man should have none."

Teddy Roosevelt was wounded while a presidential candidate by John Schrank. Schrank was a quiet, neat, and well-mannered young man. He had no close relationships and he never married. He had hallucinatory experiences telling him that Roosevelt was responsible for McKinley's death, and concluded that it was his sacred mission to prevent Roosevelt from obtaining a third term. Prior to his attack Schrank had written: "Let every third termer be regarded as a traitor . . . . I am willing to die for my country. God has called me to be an instrument so help me God. Theodore Roosevelt is in a conspiracy with European monarchs to overthrow our Republic. We want no king. We want no murderer. We will not yield to Rome." His attack on Roosevelt was not fatal because the bullet struck a thick manuscript over the President's heart. Schrank was a paranoid schizophrenic who spent the rest of his life in a state hospital. When Franklin Roosevelt began to run for a third term, Schrank once again felt he was called on to save the nation.

In 1933 Giuseppe Zangara fired a shot at President-elect F.D.R., but missed him and killed Mayor Cermak of Chicago. Zangara hated his father and blamed the latter for all the troubles of his own life, including a variety of psychosomatic ailments. After coming to the United States, Zangara's hatred for all authority figures increased. He believed that the ruling class was keeping the poor under its heel and that the world would benefit if rulers were eliminated. He felt that kings, rulers, and capitalists kept money from the poor people like himself. Eleven years before his attempt on F.D.R.'s life, he had tried to kill King Victor Emmanuel of Italy. He suffered from a paranoid psychosis.

The Puerto Ricans who made an attempt on Harry Truman's life in 1950 were advocates of Puerto Rican independence. They and their accomplices believed that Truman was responsible for Puerto Rican suppression. There is no evidence that these men were psychotic, but the belief that Truman was somehow responsible for their misfortunes and the near-delusional belief that by an attack on the President's life they would be able to achieve some reasonable goal would indicate that, even if they were not psychotic, nonetheless the paranoid process would seem to have been at work. One of the basic contentions of the present study is that political fanaticism is a major expression of the paranoid process.

In recent years the Kennedy assassinations have been seared into the memories of Americans. Lee Harvey Oswald shot and killed John Kennedy on November 22, 1963. Oswald's own early life was unhappy. His father had died even before his birth and his mother was a rather suspicious and grandiose woman—probably paranoid. He underwent psychiatric evaluation at about age thirteen and at this time was found to be a rather schizoid individual with severe aggressive impulses and poor impulse control. He often had daydreams of killing people. When he was sixteen he had wanted to kill Eisenhower because he was "exploiting the working class." In the military he was defiant, a constant complainer, a loner, and a heavy drinker. He was court-martialed for illegal possession of a pistol. He was court-martialed again for provoking an officer. He spent nearly three years living in Russia and once attempted suicide when told he had to leave the country, because he did not want to return to America. He was later transported to the United States at government expense. In April 1963, he attempted the assassination of General Edmund Walker, but his shots missed the target. He justified this murder attempt by maintaining that Walker was a fascist and that his death might save the world. Oswald also wanted to kill Richard Nixon but never carried out the attempt. The assassination attempt and subsequent murder of Oswald by Jack Ruby were well-known contemporary events. Oswald was very likely a paranoid schizophrenic—and it is not unlikely that he may have sustained this diagnosis even at the time of his early psychiatric evaluation.

John Kennedy's younger brother, Robert, was shot and killed while campaigning for the presidential nomination on June 5, 1968. His assassin was Sirhan Sirhan. Sirhan's father revealed his set of mind to the world after the assassination when he admitted that his son had killed Kennedy, but tried to put the blame on the senator. "He provoked my son by threatening to supply arms to the Middle East . . . . My son did well . . . . Kennedy made trouble, not Sirhan." The father also swore vengeance on American political leaders after he received the news of his son's conviction for murder. Sirhan was a serious, studious, and rather isolated young man with no close friends. He shunned women. He had once been thrown from a horse, and following this, he felt suspicious and guarded about his medical care, feeling that he had been mistreated. He continued to have physical complaints without having any physical findings. Sirhan was vehemently anti-Jewish and was enraged by Robert Kennedy's pro-Israeli political statements. He had written a note before the attempt saying, "Robert Kennedy must die by June 5." And again, "The rich people step all over the poor." The psychiatric and psychological testimony presented during Sirhan's hearing to establish legal responsibility was quite conflicting. But in general there was agreement that he suffered from a paranoid disorder.

The Role of the Victim. The pattern of political fanaticism and the paranoid dynamics are fairly clear-cut in these cases. Yet one of the fascinating aspects of the events producing the final outcome of political assassinations is the role of the victim. The whole question involves the largely problematic area of psychology of political leadership and its complex relations to what we have been describing as the paranoid process. We can only note the relationship here in passing. Political personages are often highly ambitious, narcissistic, in many ways aggressive, and in many ways charismatic individuals. They are prone to make extreme authoritarian, dogmatic, or even inflammatory statements. The political process, and particularly political rhetoric, embraces and builds on basically paranoid dynamics in the population at large.

Moreover it is striking that many political leaders—and this is particularly true of Presidents of the United States—seem to expose themselves to obvious dangers quite unnecessarily and resist the cautions and precautions of concerned followers and friends. Lincoln was often the target of assassination attempts and threats. Despite pleas from friends and subordinates he continued to lead an unguarded life and to walk through the streets of Washington without protection. On one occasion his hat was shot off—on another an official next to him was gunned down—and yet Lincoln seemed to almost deliberately expose himself to such attacks. On the night of his assassination, he insisted that his box remain unguarded at the theater. John Kennedy frequently created difficulties for the Secret Service men assigned to protect him. And Robert Kennedy repeatedly flouted and tested death not only in his political life, but even in his pattern of daredevil recreation. We can only raise the question here—an extremely important and in many ways perplexing question—of the relationship between the paranoid process, as we are considering it here in a clinical framework, and the broader issues of political process and the implementation of extreme attitudes and actions which seem so indigenous to American political life.

Projective Aspects

The mechanisms of externalization and projection—particularly superego projections—have been carefully documented (Tuovinen, 1970). Prior to the activation of homicidal impulses and the acting out of the impulses, there is a regressive process in which oedipal murderous impulses are reactivated, and there is a form of superego regression to identification with the aggressor. Threats to the ego, usually stemming from the superego, are projected to the outside world and can there be attacked and destroyed. When the hated and feared object has been destroyed, the homicidal ego then returns to the same depressive state involving diffuse murderous rage and persecutory guilt which exercises its destructive effect within, and which it attempted to escape by the original projection. The projection is not limited, however, to the homicidal episode—it nonetheless forms a characteristic pattern of defense for such personalities. Projection usually takes the form of a readiness to see injustice, of which the criminal feels himself the victim. Nonetheless the acute and intense projection which accompanies the homicidal attempt can be seen as an attempt to salvage the integrity of the personality which is so severely threatened from within.

Assaultive Patients

On a lesser scale—but nonetheless significant in the management of hospital patients—the paranoid process also is related to the tendency for patients in the hospital to become assaultive. Such assaults may be deliberate, often retaliatory, but they may also be impulsive and occur in the context of loss of control. Sudden and uncontrolled explosions of rage and assaultive behavior may be quite unrelated to any identifiable provocation. Such patients are almost inevitably paranoid to one or another degree. Assaults may be provoked by the behavior of other patients or even in unconscious ways by the behavior of the hospital staff. Patients may have the feeling of helplessness in the face of staff members whom they see as powerful authority figures.

In my own experience, it has generally been paranoid patients who create disturbances on the hospital wards and who become assaultive either to other patients or to the staff. Usually such patients are also psychotic—although assaultive behavior is not infrequently seen in other diagnostic categories. The most frequent exception has been acutely manic patients, for whom the expression of anger and aggressive impulses is not infrequent (Kalogerakis, 1971).

The patient's impulse to violent acting-out also creates a difficulty in psychotherapy. The factors prompting such violent expression are complex and can play themselves out in a variety of ways. Frequently enough, particularly in men, the violence represents an aggressive attempt at defense against the intolerable psychic pain which may be related to the crisis of self-esteem involved in the underlying conflicts of dependency and power which are embedded in the therapeutic relationship. These conflicts may be related to homosexual issues, but frequently enough have more to do with power conflicts in the sense of pseudohomosexual conflicts.

Often such patients reveal a fragile sense of masculine identity with a history of many failures in self-assertion, particularly in conflicts with other men. They have painful and shameful feelings about submission and passivity. The basic conflicts of power and dependency are elaborated within the transference, and thus form a threat to masculine pride and narcissism. The therapeutic intervention is regarded as a humiliating surrender. Such patients often have fairly strong paranoid dynamics: however, it is usually only in cases of frank psychosis that the threat is generally responded to by overt destructive activity. The importance of distinguishing the issues of power and dependence from true homosexuality are central to the handling of such violent crises. Any interpretations made to such patients on the basis of latent homosexuality would only serve to escalate the threat and increase the anxiety—sometimes to the point of panic (Woods, 1972).

Toxic Influences

Paranoid symptomatology may be seen in any one of a number of conditions associated with the influence of toxic substances. There are a large number of such toxic substances which have been known to produce paranoid symptomatology, probably merely on the common basis of an alteration in central nervous system metabolism and functioning.

The accompanying change in states of consciousness may serve to exacerbate or activate latent paranoid tendencies in such individuals. However, the additional question remains largely unsolved—namely, whether the paranoid manifestations are directly related to the toxic effects of centrally active substances. It is more than likely in most of these cases that the effects are multiply determined—that is to say, that they are the combined result of an interaction of predisposing factors in the individual personality together with toxic effects of the drugs in question, and possibly additionally in conjunction with certain susceptibilities to toxic influence of central nervous system structures. I would like to stress here briefly some of the more common toxic states which are related to paranoid manifestations of this kind.

Alcohol

Interaction. It has long been recognized that there is an interaction between alcohol and paranoid mechanisms, but the nature and quality of the interaction remains unknown. There is no question that alcohol is used by some paranoid patients to relieve the tension associated with the paranoid condition. The patient is usually prevented by his suspiciousness and fears of contact and closeness from obtaining any of the usual gratifications in his relationships with other people. Nonetheless, there is evidence to suggest that the anxiety-reduction model for the use of alcohol is not very adequate. Tamerin and Mendelson (1969) in an experimental setting have shown that somewhat depressed and inhibited alcoholics experience a considerable increase in their aggressiveness and self-assertiveness—along with indications of irritability, childishness, and a provocative hypermasculine sort of contentiousness which is quite different in quality from their normal personality functioning. This form of pathological aggressiveness and assertiveness may well have been a defense against passive homosexual wishes, which became more active under the release of alcohol. However, we can also suggest that, under the influence of alcohol, preexisting paranoid tendencies are activated. The partial release from superego restraints and self-denigration may easily take the form of externalizations which permit greater degrees of external attack.

Consequently, we must conclude that if alcohol can in some cases serve to relieve the tension of paranoid symptoms, there are also other cases in which it is clear that its use can activate or expose previously latent paranoid tendencies. Thus the influences of the drug must be set in a context of the personality organization and function. This is also true in cases of frank paranoia—even on a psychotic level. Some patients will become more argumentative and aggressive, thus triggering responsive anger in those around them and increasing paranoid suspiciousness and defensiveness. Symptoms of paranoia may thus become more severe and ideas of reference and other delusions may be exacerbated.

However, even psychotic patients may find some diminution in the impact of persecutory delusions and hallucinations through the use of alcohol. This usually is the case when patients have consumed enough of the drug to diminish their usual degree of hyperalertness and attention concentration. Here too, it is noteworthy that some patients are very wary of the use of alcohol or even other drugs on the grounds that it will diminish their defensive alertness and hyperacuteness—thus leaving them vulnerable to attack. This pattern of thinking is often seen in paranoid patients who refuse to take medications recommended by the physician—or if they do not refuse the medications, will simply neglect to take them. Management of medications, where indicated in paranoid patients, is usually a difficult process. It is worth noting that acute paranoid symptoms may be exacerbated in susceptible persons with only a small quantity of alcohol consumption.

Pathological States. There are several toxic states that are associated with the use of alcohol. The first of these is *delirium tremens*, which may be due to direct toxic effects of the alcohol in the metabolism of the central nervous system, but is usually regarded clinically as an acute withdrawal syndrome. It usually follows the end of a bout of alcoholic drinking by several days and is rather sudden in onset. The delirium is accompanied by impairment of intellectual and perceptual functions. There is generally partial amnesia with confusion, disorientation, and impairments of attention, perception, and comprehension. The patient may be able to carry on a discussion with his physician, but consciousness is generally partially impaired. Hallucinations are frequent accompaniments of the syndrome—usually visual, but may also be auditory. These are generally vivid and may be frightening to the patient. The hallucinations may be amusing or entertaining, but often have a bizarre and extremely frightening quality—the patient may see monsters or spiders or scorpions or snakes, or other frightening things. The patient may feel that his life is threatened and in panic try to escape from these horribly threatening things.

There is also a specific paranoid state which is related to the use of alcohol, *alcoholic paranoia*, but this is generally regarded as a basically paranoid condition which is simply unveiled by the use of alcohol. The defenses against the paranoid process are probably weakened and the paranoid symptomatology then becomes more manifest. Such individuals usually show a lifelong pattern of personality disturbance. Usually the paranoid characteristics are relatively well compensated and latent, but under the influence of alcohol, the patient undergoes a psychotic decompensation and the paranoid traits become more florid and delusional (Thompson, 1959).

Another syndrome which is characteristically related to the use of alcohol is the so-called *alcoholic hallucinosis*. This syndrome is usually more severe and frequently more markedly paranoid as to its symptomatology than states of pathological intoxication. Such patients are usually felt to be basically schizophrenic, with the symptomatology being exacerbated by the toxic effects of alcohol. The alcoholic hallucinosis is usually accompanied by terrifying auditory hallucination, while the patient maintains a relatively clear sensorium. This contrasts the syndrome to delirium tremens in which the patient experiences primarily visual hallucinations together with a clouded state of consciousness. The hallucinations often take the form of superego accusations against the patient—often of a sexual nature.

It is interesting to note that patients who are afflicted by alcoholic hallucinosis rarely merge into what is known as the Korsakoff syndrome. While Korsakoff patients often go through states of severe agitation and delirium in the early acute phase, in the "burnt-out" phase, there is no indication of psychotic symptoms, such as hallucinations or delusions. In the advanced stages of Korsakoff syndrome, the patient will confabulate—that is, he will make up a story or recount imaginary events as a way of filling in the extensive memory gaps that are part of the syndrome; but these confabulations do not have the same quality as psychotic delusions. Thus, while the Korsakoff syndrome is often referred to as a "psychosis," it is clear that it is a condition that is secondary to the deterioration of cognitive—specifically memory—functions and it is not a psychosis in the usual sense. Moreover, Korsakoff patients rarely show signs of paranoia. Cases in which confabulation is associated with paranoid ideation in the invented material seem to represent the expression of premorbid paranoid personality organization (Berlyne, 1972). Consequently the hallucinosis is probably more correctly regarded as a symptomatology based on a schizophrenic process which is exacerbated or unveiled by the effects of alcohol on the central nervous system, rather than as a specific syndrome caused by the toxic effects of alcohol or its withdrawal.

Finally it should be noted that alcohol has a definite effect on the activation of certain epileptic syndromes (Ervin, 1967). This is true of a variety of epileptic disorders, but is particularly associated with psychomotorlike seizures. Such patients often are susceptible to alcoholic blackouts and the unleashing of violent behavior under the influence of epileptic discharges activated by the influence of alcohol.

Amphetamines

Amphetamine Psychosis. There are probably no other toxic substances which are as frequently linked with paranoid manifestations as the amphetamines. It has been well known for some years now that high doses or chronic use of them (or even in some cases as small an amount as 50 mg of dextroamphetamine) can produce a psychotic state with marked paranoid characteristics. Early reports had presumed that the action of amphetamines was to induce "a state of distractible alertness, facilitate feelings of personal reference from the environment, and thus precipitate paranoid episodes in emotionally predisposed persons; whether the episode is transitory or becomes chronic would depend on the severity of the pre-psychotic tendency toward paranoid, projective processes" (Chapman, 1954). More recent studies, however, have emphasized more specifically pharmacological effects. As in the case in all of these toxic states, the actual situation is more complex and involves the interactions between personality and contextual and drug effects.

The psychosis produced by acute or chronic abuse of amphetamines—as a toxic effect—has a relatively characteristic and predictable pattern which is much like paranoid schizophrenia (Rylander, 1972). Opinion is divided, as might be expected, as to the extent to which the toxic psychosis serves as a model psychosis for paranoid schizophrenia—but there is no question that the similarity is strong. Amphetamine psychotics are often delusional, and suffer from tactile hallucinations similar to those observed in cocaine psychosis—a form of hallucinatory parasitosis or formication. Amphetamine psychotics are often fascinated with tiny details of objects in their environment, and often spend hours contemplating some trivial thing.

In Ellinwood's study (1969) on the influence of amphetamines on cats, he observed compulsive grooming reminiscent of the delusional parasitosis, compulsive sniffing of a tiny area, often for hours at a time, and hyperattentiveness to movements and sounds in the environment. Aggressive cats tended to show hyperaggressivity under the influence of the drugs, while less aggressive cats showed an increase of fear and suspicious behavior. Ellinwood speculates that the intoxication with amphetamines stimulates the CNS components, which produce attending responses with subsequent emotional arousal when they are electrically stimulated. Thus stimulation of the amygdalae in normal animals produces many of the same type of responses as are observed under the influence of amphetamines. The amphetamine brings on a spiking activity in the amygdalae and results in catecholamine depletion. Similar effects are seen in the mesencephalic reticular activating system and in areas of the brain stem which coordinate eye movements with postural and vestibular mechanisms. Also it seems that the temporal cortex and the anterior limbic systems are involved. The activation of these areas may be related to the heightening and distortion of emotional interpretation of current experience and memory contents.

A later study by the same author (Ellinwood, 1971) indicates the relationship between amphetamine-induced paranoid states and homicidal acts. The causality is not linear, but must be taken in the context of predisposing personality factors and environmental circumstances which trigger the outbreak of violence. The use of amphetamines produces a paranoid state in which the increased suspiciousness and delusional distortion are accompanied by intense fear and panic, and a tendency to impulsive behavior. In this context an environmental stimulus which is misinterpreted—a relatively minor incident, perhaps—can act as a stimulus to violent response. In most of these cases, due to the suspiciousness and fear of attack, the patients at the time of the homicidal attempt were carrying a concealed weapon. The relationship of paranoid states to a tendency toward violent and often homicidal or suicidal behavior presents a serious consideration in the broad context of the increased availability and use of amphetamines.

It is likely that the amphetamine psychosis is very closely associated with paranoid psychosis. In any case the differentiation is difficult. The clinical cases that are available are often complicated by the use of other drugs and alcohol. Patients who develop amphetamine psychosis may show a preschizoid or preschizophrenic pattern of character pathology prior to the development of the psychosis, but they frequently show lack of any family history of schizophrenia, and the psychotic episode is usually of brief duration. They often also do not show the characteristic looseness of associations or deficit in reality testing which is so characteristic of the schizophrenic population (Lynn, 1971).

Clinical Studies. However, under experimental conditions, it is not difficult to produce the amphetamine psychosis. In the study reported by Griffith et al. (1972), psychosis developed in eight out of nine subjects under the administration of amphetamines, although the nine subjects were individuals with previous experience of self-administered amphetamine. The subjects became quite depressed, then hypochondriacal, irritable, faultfinding, and anorexic. In this particular study, predrug personality did not seem to be an important variable, since the subjects were not considered to be psychotic, or even borderline. The authors regard the effects as due to the psychotomimetic properties of the drug itself. They propose that the psychotic effects may be due to depletion of CNS catecholamine stores as a pharmacological effect of dextroamphetamine or one of its metabolites.

The abuse of amphetamines usually begins with oral ingestion, but the amount ingested must be rapidly increased due to the rapid buildup of tolerance to the drug effect. Many amphetamine users then turn to the intravenous use of the drug at increasingly high levels. Sooner or later, paranoid symptoms inevitably develop. Kramer et al. (1967) report in their group of amphetamine abusers that the delusional quality of the experiences in the toxic psychosis was available to the evaluation of the subjects. They would feel, for example, that strangers were watching them, that their friends had been informing on them, that their apartments were bugged by the police, or that shadows and trees in the street were actually disguised detectives, etc. But these persecutory fantasies and illusions were always recognized as delusional. The subjects knew that their feelings and thoughts were paranoid, but apparently were not seriously disturbed by it—often making a game out of the feelings.

Gradually very high tolerance levels are developed so that commercial preparations of amphetamines are unable to produce any effect. The sudden withdrawal of the drug often unmasks a degree of chronic fatigue that is built up over the sleepless days that have preceded. Often subjects are plunged into an intense depression which may be suicidal in its intensity. There is a distant abstinence syndrome which is associated with this pattern of withdrawal. The authors underlined the addictive potential of the use of amphetamines. The addictive potential is an aspect of the use of amphetamines that has only recently come into appreciation (Grinspoon and Hedblom, 1972).

Amphetamines as a family of drugs have been used for some years now for a variety of medical conditions. These conditions include the treatment of narcolepsy, the control of hyperkinetic behavioral disorders in children, the relief of fatigue and deterioration in psychomotor performance, the treatment of mild depression, appetite control, and for counteracting fatigue in persons who are required to perform tasks requiring strong mental or physical application over long periods of time. There is little question that the potential for abuse in such usages is great, particularly when it is appreciated that the effectiveness of amphetamines in a number of these more general usages is not very high. Self-medication is a particular danger in the use of these drugs (Committee on Alcoholism and Addiction, 1966).

In addition to the more common psychotic paranoid state produced as a toxic effect of the amphetamines, there has also been described an amphetamine abstinence psychosis, which is the most terrifying and dramatic sequel to wihdrawal of the drug after it has been used more or less chronically at toxic levels. Rather than seeming a toxic effect, it appears to be functional psychosis precipitated by amphetamine withdrawal. There is an interval between the stopping of amphetamine use and the onset of psychotic symptoms which may last a variable length of time, from a few days to as long as two months. The dependence on the drug is apparently physical and affects a number of body systems, particularly the suppression of REM sleep. After withdrawal of the drug there is a marked rebound and overcompensation in REM time, as well as a decrease in REM latency. Similar suppression and rebound phenomena of REM sleep have been observed in cases of other drugs of high addictive potential, such as heroin, morphine, alcohol, barbiturates etc. It has even been suggested that delirium tremens following prolonged alcohol consumption may represent a state of acute REM rebound from a chemically induced REM deprivation (Greenberg and Pearlman, 1967). Also Connel (1958) has suggested certain parallels between amphetamine addiction and alcoholism.

Recently the utility of amphetamine-induced psychosis as an experimental model for paranoid states has been carefully reviewed, and the data which emphasized similarities as well as the differences between amphetamine-induced psychosis and the clinically familiar and paranoid schizophrenia have been summarized by Snyder (1972, 1973). He quotes the Griffith et al. (1970, 1972) study in which a paranoidlike psychosis was induced by the administration of amphetamines in subjects without any prior history of amphetamine psychosis or any indication of schizoid or schizophrenic tendencies. The psychosis produced resembles paranoid schizophrenia and includes a number of behavioral effects such as hypervigilance, sleeplessness, and stereotypical behavior. Because of the subtlety and frequent difficulty of eliciting paranoid mechanisms, it would not seem that the possibility of predrug paranoid traits has been completely eliminated, even in these subjects.

Mechanisms. In any case—despite the obvious discrimination between the amphetamine psychosis and the paranoid psychosis—the effects of the drug seem to be unequivocal. The extent to which paranoid trends are embedded in the preexisting personality structure remains a moot question; but there is no question that the amphetamine effect is clearly in the direction of either exacerbating or producing paranoid tendencies. Both the amphetamine psychosis and the cocaine psychosis, both of which are produced by mechanisms which apparently involve the metabolism of brain catecholamines, provide the clearest models of drug-induced paranoid states (Ellinwood et al., 1973). Snyder discusses the differential effects of the amphetamines on catecholamine pathways, particularly those dealing with dopamine and norepinephrine. The more schizophrenic manifestations seem to be related to the effect on dopamine mediating tracts, while the more paranoid manifestations may relate to the norepinephrine mediated systems which relate to alerting mechanisms. Snyder writes:

> Besides their psychotogenic effects, amphetamines produce a wide spectrum of other effects. Perhaps, were amphetamines to act solely on selected dopamine tracts, the psychosis they precipitate would be a more faithful model of an undifferentiated form of schizophrenia or one whose characteristics were determined primarily by the previous personality of the patient. Conceivably, other amphetamine effects transform the "model schizophrenia" into a predominately paranoid psychosis. One possible candidate for a "contaminating" action would be the nonrepinephrine-mediated alerting effect of amphetamines. One might speculate that this alerting action forces the patient to strive for an intellectual framework in which to focus all the strange feelings that are coming over him as the psychosis develops (1972, p. 177).

The process of establishing meaning and discovering it in a system of delusions is what we have referred to equivalently as the "paranoid construction."

The paranoid construction together with the state of alertness and hypervigilance may be mediated by norepinephrine systems and may also facilitate preexisting trends in the personality. It is also possible with these patients that the paranoid dynamics may serve a protective or covering action in the face of the disruptive disorganization experienced in the schizophrenic effects produced by the drug. I only wish to note in passing that the dorsal norepinephrine system, which involves inputs to the medial forebrain bundle and septum, which subsequently exercise important neurophysiological influences on central structures involved in the processing of affective and cognitive inputs—including the hippocampus and related limbic system circuits (Meissner, 1966)—provides an important neurophysiological link which may also be involved in other toxic and organic states which produce paranoid manifestations.

LSD

The upsurge in the interest in, and use of, LSD in recent years needs little commentary. The patterns of use vary all the way from relatively innocuous and infrequent experimentation to heavy and frequent usage characteristic of the so-called "acid heads." For the latter types of individual, the use of acid becomes a motif around which the entire patterning of their lives is structured. The use of the drug becomes woven into a counterculture associated with the rebellion against society among middle-class and usually white youths.

LSD generally produces vegetative autonomic alterations which are followed by anxiety and even paranoid, depressive, or euphoric states (Hoch, 1959). With increasing doses, illusions can develop—and even delusions, which are often grandiose. The individual may feel omnipotent or may feel omniscient. Such feelings may lead to attempts to take exceedingly risky chances under dangerous circumstances, such as walking close to the edge of high cliffs, or putting oneself in needless danger. When anxiety feelings become exacerbated, apprehension can be a prominent feature, at which point paranoid delusions may take on a distinct persecutory character.

Prolonged delusional states with definite paranoid characteristics have been described by a number of investigators—and frequently are seen in a significant percentage of cases. Most of the studies of LSD effects indicate that, in patients in whom psychotic effects were produced by the drug, a fairly high percentage showed no manifestations of psychotic or schizoid personality structure prior to the taking of the drug. This would seem to indicate a direct pharmacological effect; however the same reservation that applies to the evaluation of amphetamine takers applies here as well—namely, that the evaluation of latent or hidden paranoid trends is difficult to accomplish and remains a possible contributing factor to the observed pathology.

Particularly disturbing is the so-called "flashback" phenomenon in which recurrent symptoms of depersonalization, delusional episodes, and often terrifying outright delusions can occur spontaneously, considerably after drug intake has ceased. These delusional flashback experiences can occur weeks to months after ingestion of LSD. The mechanism of the flashback is poorly understood, but it usually occurs more frequently in individuals who have taken the drug more frequently, and in whom the flashback experience occurred in relationship to situations of significant stress. Attention has also been called to the incidents of suicide and homicide in connection with LSD usage. The connection of these forms of violence with paranoid states of mind has already been discussed.

In a previous study of the functioning of the hippocampus and related limbic structures in cognitive processing, I discussed the disruptive effects of LSD on these structures. These effects may have to do with interruption of the internal circuitry of the hippocampus, or they may also relate to the production of seizure episodes in hippocampus and limbic structures. Hallucinogenic effects would thus correspond to seizurelike discharges which disrupt hippocampal function and integration of cognitive and affective experience (Meissner, 1966). It can be suggested that the paranoid manifestations of both amphetamine psychosis and the LSD psychosis may be related to disruptive effects of these agents on limbic system functioning which either directly produce paranoid distortions, usually of a delusional nature, or trigger a compensatory paranoid protective response. This formulation is speculative, but allows us to link the observations related to drug-induced paranoid states to the more psychological formulations that relate to the clinical observations which form the substance of the present study. It must be kept in mind, however, in evaluating the relationship between such drug effects and the occurrence of paranoid symptomatology, that, by and large, in uncontrolled and social usages, such drugs are frequently implemented within a counterculture which has been described popularly as the "drug culture." The thesis that I would advance is that the development of such a counterculture involves the implementation and expression of paranoid mechanisms which in part motivate, in part intensify, and enter into, complex interaction with drug effects.

Marijuana

Much the same situation obtains in the discussion of the relationship between marijuana and paranoid symptoms. However, in the case of marijuana, the intensity and the incidence of symptoms seem to be considerably reduced. There seems little doubt that marijuana has become a counterculture symbol, but that its use is considerably more benign and less destructive than the more severely toxic drugs like amphetamines and LSD (Pillard, 1970; Hollister, 1971). However, at greater doses marijuana also has hallucinogenic effects, and in a small percentage of cases produces a psychotic state.

The symptomatology of cannabis-induced psychosis is subject to considerable variability (Bernhardson and Gunne, 1972), but paranoid manifestations are relatively frequent (Keup, 1970; Talbott and Teague, 1969). In a series of twelve soldiers reported by Talbott and Teague (1969), ten of these men showed distinctly paranoid symptoms, including suspiciousness, referentiality, and delusions or hallucinations. They conclude that cannabis intoxication, as a causal or precipitating agent, should be considered in any case in which a young person presents with an acute toxic psychosis with paranoid features. The use of marijuana must generally be regarded as benign (Weil et al., 1968), but it must be remembered that a significant percentage of marijuana smokers tend to experiment with other psychedelic drugs, and a small percentage have also been found to use addicting drugs such as heroin (Carlin and Post, 1971; Siegel, 1971). A distinction must be made between people who use only marijuana, and those who expose themselves to multiple drug use. The latter category tend to reveal significant psychiatric impairments; however, it is quite possible that personality variables predispose to the use of marijuana. Young people who use marijuana are likely to be moody, anxious, impulsive, and rebellious (Robbins et al., 1970; Harmatz et al., 1972). When psychotic symptoms are associated with the use of marijuana, frequently enough they have a paranoid flavor to them. There may be both visual and auditory hallucinations with hypersensitivity to sound, often associated to marked suspiciousness and ideas of reference (Kolansky and Moore, 1971). The cabnabis effect, however, is nowhere nearly as specific as other drugs we have considered.

Exotic Syndromes

There are a number of rather unusual and rare conditions—at least in our own cultural setting—which have a paranoid flavor, but in which the paranoid mechanisms display themselves in unusual settings or in an unusual manner. These syndromes have been reviewed extensively elsewhere (Swanson et al., 1970; Arieti and Meth, 1959), so that they need not be discussed extensively here.

The first syndrome of interest is *Cotard's syndrome*—a syndrome which is known also as "the illusion of doubles." This phenomenon consists of the delusion that some other person in the patient's life is a double or an impostor who is impersonating someone. Thus the patient may feel that the person who presents himself as a doctor, and whose intentions are supposedly helpful, is in fact an impostor who really intends to do the patient harm. Arieti and Meth (1959) explain the syndrome psychodynamically—the patient cannot admit ambivalent feelings about an acquaintance and he therefore splits the friend's attributes and assigns the bad characteristics to the impostor, while retaining the good characteristics for the acquaintance. The projective aspects of this psychic mechanism would be consistent with the paranoid process.

Cotard's syndrome is also known as a "chronic delusional state of negation." This condition is usually linked to involutional states, and is often found in women. It involves a massive delusion in which the patient feels that nothing, including the patient's self, exists. There is some controversy as to whether the syndrome actually exists as such and, if it does exist, whether it might be better described as a form of psychotic depression. The converse of the Cotard phenomenon is the *autoscopic phenomena*—although it too cannot be considered as specifically paranoid in nature. In this condition the subject experiences an hallucination in which he has a sensation that his own body is somehow seen outside of himself. This phenomenon has been reported in patients who also suffer from epilepsy or migraine, but it may also be seen in schizophrenics or severe depressives. One of the most fascinating and intriguing descriptions of the autoscopic phenomena, placed in a system of paranoid delusions, is the narrative of the unfortunate clerk Golyodkin which is provided in Dostoevsky's "*The Double*."

Another interesting phenomenon is *Clerambault's syndrome*. In this the patient is usually a female, and is convinced that a certain man is in love with her. The man is usually a well-known public figure—an actor or a political personage. The syndrome consists of a variety of paranoid disorder with grandiose delusions that have a decidedly erotic tinge. The patient usually is diagnostically a paranoid schizophrenic.

Another characteristic syndrome, seen predominantly in Malayan men, is the *amok syndrome*. The amok syndrome involves a rampage of destructive violence in patients who are either chronically delusional or acutely confused—often in connection with some form of toxic syndrome. This syndrome is similar to the outbreaks of violence in toxic psychosis. Usually the patient is someone withdrawn and schizoid, and may appear to be brooding for a period of time; then suddenly without warning he grabs a weapon—usually a knife or rock or other lethal instrument—and begins to run around wildly slashing at anyone in sight. These episodes usually terminate only in death, either when the patient is killed or manages to kill himself. If he does survive the episode, there is usually total amnesia. Among Malayans, the episode is usually associated with possession by the devil; in more developed Western cultures, there may be voices that impel the patient to his outbursts. An interesting observation is that, as the level of education among the Malayan people has risen, the amok syndrome has become increasingly rare.

Recent evaluations of the amok syndrome have emphasized the importance of sociopsychological variables in the precipitation of the outbreak. External factors that seem to play a significant role are younger age, role crises of various kinds, recent losses, and drunkenness (Westermeyer, 1972). The effects of such precipitants can be related to assaults on self-esteem which precipitate a violent response. The usual period of withdrawal and brooding over real or imagined wrongs preceding the attack suggests the narcissistic withdrawal and narcissistic licking of wounds. The fury of the attack is directed without discrimination. This suggests that the persecutory delusion is generalized so that the destructive wish is quite diffuse. Since the advent of court proceedings or commitment to insane asylums, the incidence of amok in certain areas of the world has decreased. There are still occasional accounts of such outbreaks in areas of Malaya, but the overall incidence has diminished. There are similar accounts of outbreaks of senseless killing in all countries and cultures with a frequency not far from that of reports of amok (Teoh, 1972). Thus the amok phenomenon may not be at all culture-bound and may represent a variety of paranoid violence. In cases of apparently senseless and indiscriminate violence, as we have seen, the dynamics are usually specifically paranoid. Specific elements related to paranoid dynamics are the narcissistic injury (often seemingly trivial), the shameful affect, and persecutory fears related to supernatural powers or malevolent sorcerers. The behavior, although bizarre, serves to permit the affected individual to maintain a culturally determined role (Weidman and Sussex, 1971).

The *Whitico (Windigo) psychosis* is limited to certain Eskimo and Indian tribes. It is a form of possession syndrome in which the patient begins to brood and fear that he will turn into a Whitico—a giant figure made of ice who devours human beings. The patient gradually becomes increasingly delusional and begins to think that he has become a Whitico. He may in fact become murderous and cannibalistic. This is clearly a psychotic delusional state—an unusual variant of paranoid psychosis.

Voodoo death is a variant of the typical paranoid fear that someone is trying to kill the patient. In Voodoo death, in fact, the patient does die—apparently as an effect of his delusional fear. A similar syndrome is the so-called *Susto syndrome* in which the patient is violently frightened and shows marked anxiety along with hyperexcitability and severe depression and weight loss. The patient suffers from the delusion that his soul has been absorbed by the earth and is no longer present in his body. It is a variety of persecutory delusion. Another syndrome that has received some attention is the so-called *Puerto Rican syndrome* which is marked by a combination of panic, violent agitation, and violence—including self-mutilation. Paranoid symptoms have been described, including paranoid jealousy and ideas of infidelity and rather bizarre delusions. Doubt was cast on the existence of the syndrome by Mehlman, who analyzed several patients given this diagnosis. Patients could be described more aptly by a variety of other psychiatric diagnoses, so that it was not felt useful to designate the syndrome as a separate entity. These patients sometimes showed delusional and paranoid characteristics (Mehlman, 1961).

Organic Syndromes and Psychological Factors

Paranoid symptoms have been manifested in a wide variety of organic syndromes in which psychological disturbances have been attendant on the evolution of the organic condition. The emergence of such paranoid symptoms may well be a concomitant of a rather nonspecific nature to the physical deterioration and debility associated with the organic pathology. The anatomical or physiological deficits play a role in an already developed personality constellation, and influence the adjustment of the organism which is derived from specific patterns of integration of premorbid personality functioning.

In cases in which paranoid symptomatology appears in association with an advancing physical pathology, it is reasonable to suppose that the disease process is taking effect in a personality structure which is already disposed toward a paranoid pattern of responsiveness. Other patients respond with diverse patterns of psychological disturbance—depression being one of the major patterns of response to such physical insult. Thus paranoid and often psychotic symptoms can be seen in a wide variety of endocrinological and metabolic disorders. All of the hormonal imbalance syndromes, as well as the metabolic disorders—including uremia and pernicious anemia and porphyria—as well as other systematic disorders, particularly those affecting the circulatory system, such as systematic lupus or hypertension or cardiovascular impairments of various kinds, can produce these kinds of symptoms.

Infectious States

Infectious disease states are particularly interesting. Ebaugh and Tiffany (1959) have suggested that the types of psychosis associated with infectious states can be divided into four distinct types: paranoid syndromes in which the paranoid delusional state is a dominant feature of the syndrome, functional psychoses which are secondary to organic pathology, acute deliriums, and finally organic defect syndromes which can be attributed to specific CNS lesions. A typical pattern in infection-based disorders is that of an initial delirium with impairments of consciousness, confusion, disorientation, and memory defect, followed as the delirium deepens by the development of delusions which are usually persecutory or phobic in quality.

Of particular note is the syndrome of general paresis associated with syphilitic infection. This syndrome was more frequently seen in a period when the treatment of syphilitic infections was less effective and general paresis was a common manifestation of tertiary syphilis. The central deficit is a dementia with intellectual deterioration and impairment of memory function. A significant number of general paretics show a pattern of paranoid symptomatology which is expansive and grandiose. Although grandiose delusions are a prominent feature—often associated with a psychotic identification, as some famous or powerful figure—persecutory delusions are also seen frequently enough and can on occasion result in outbreaks of violent and destructive behavior.

Epileptic States

Particularly interesting under the heading of organic syndromes is the interaction between epileptic states and paranoid manifestations. From one point of view, one can point to significant psychogenic factors which might link epileptic states with paranoid manifestations. The child who suffers from convulsions is somehow regarded as different by his age-mates and by other significant figures in his environment. He may be treated in a special, careful or fragile manner. He comes to view himself consequently as different, and experience himself in terms of vulnerability and lack of control. Psychodynamic factors involving the guilt of parents and projective mechanisms, which we have described elsewhere in this study, can force on the epileptic child an introjected self-image of one who is somehow vulnerable, weak, and defective, and the object of hostile and demeaning treatment from important figures around him.

Psychomotor Epilepsy. Viewing the syndrome in this context establishes some continuity with the dynamics of the paranoid process as we have come to know it in the course of this study. But the further question which lurks in the background in cases of psychomotor epilepsy particularly, and which remains substantially unanswered, is the question as to whether the disorganization associated with psychomotor states contributes in some direct and/or casual manner to paranoid manifestations.

The frequency of paranoid manifestations in psychomotor epileptics has been frequently noted (Ervin, 1967). In a study. specifically of psychotic episodes occurring in known epileptic subjects, Dongier (1959) studied 516 epileptics with interseizure psychoses. He concluded that 44 percent of the psychotic occurrences took place in patients with psychomotor epilepsy—indicating a strong disposition for temporal lobe pathology to manifest itself in psychotic behavior. The characteristics of these psychotic episodes were described as including marked paranoid ideation along with anxiety and depression. By way of contrast, centrencephalic or generalized epilepsy seemed to show a more confused psychotic state with more consistently abnormal EEG patterns.

In reviewing the disruption in limbic system functioning that takes place in temporal lobe seizures, the disruption of the integration between experiencing and recording mechanisms was a central aspect of the temporal lobe syndrome (Meissner, 1966). In addition to the frequently observed overlap of temporal lobe epilepsy with personality disorders and even psychosis, one must add the important observations of EEG abnormalities affecting the septal, hippocampal, and amygdaloid regions in certain types of schizophrenic patients during active psychotic episodes. In both conditions—temporal lobe epilepsy and schizophrenia—abnormal activity in limbic structures is associated with disturbances of consciousness and effective psychological functioning. This reflects the central role of these CNS structures in the integration of higher functions. It has been observed in addition that nonictal psychiatric symptoms often are exacerbated when psychomotor seizures are reduced by medical means—but that both seem to be eliminated after temporal lobe resection. Conversely, it has been observed in some cases that psychosis appeared in cases of psychomotor epilepsy with the diminution of seizures—a striking relationship in view of the fact that seizure activity and psychotic behavior are often correlated.

On the opposite side of the coin, the association of personality disorder with psychomotor epilepsy is not accepted on all fronts. A comparison of matched groups of patients with focal temporal and frontal epilepsy with patients with nonfocal seizures indicates that nonfocal epileptics perform less well on tests of attention, but that they show no significant differences on tests of memory. Similar comparison of psychomotor against other forms of epilepsy has failed to demonstrate any significant differences on a variety of psychological and psychiatric measures. The argument has thus been presented by Stevens (1966), who argues that the psychomotor-temporal form of epilepsy is unique in that it also shows an age prevalence paralleling that of hospitalized psychosis in the general population. She suggests that the failure to control for this aspect accounts for the apparently increased incidence of the psychomotor syndrome in psychiatric populations, and conversely the high incidence of personality disorder in psychomotor epileptics.

One can suggest that the implication that temporal lobe disorder or psychomotor seizures have a causal influence in the production of paranoid symptomatology needs considerable proving. One distinct possibility that must be kept in mind is that subtle disruptions of the organization of internal experience, which might be associated with temporal lobe pathology, may serve as the precipitating basis for the organization of paranoid defenses. It has been observed, for example, that paranoid symptoms often precede or occur in the apparent absence of recognizable signs of an organic brain syndrome. It is possible in such cases that the paranoid behavior is an early indicator of organic difficulties, appearing in response to insidious or quite subtle organic disruptions, before any frank neurological impairment in memory functions or in the form of disorientation, delirium, or confusion might make itself known. Such impairments might serve to increase the subject's feelings of loss of control, of vulnerability and susceptibility, and thus increase fears of external threat or attack. The incipient organic deterioration may then serve to trigger previously existing paranoid trends or capacities.

The best evidence for anatomical and specifically neurological links between paranoid manifestations and physiological substrates is seen in the effects of the amphetamines and in lesions—either organic or epileptic—of the limbic system. This association, however, is by no means universal, and is certainly not exclusive. The disorders most commonly associated with paranoid manifestations are those involving distortion or disruption of perception and memory. If our analysis of the paranoid dynamics is correct, we can suggest that the deficit in these particular functions would be particularly closely linked to a need to reconstitute the realm of experience by the employment of paranoid mechanisms.

One aspect of the overall problem of the relationship between temporal lobe seizures and the production of apparent functional pathology is that the limbic system structures in general are known to have an extremely low threshold of seizure discharge. Consequently epileptic focuses can produce seizure discharge in limbic structures without any apparent alteration in the surface EEG recordings. A number of cases of spiking discharges from limbic structures in a context of negative surface EEG findings have been documented. This raises the interesting possibility that a certain percentage of cases might be suffering from undetected limbic system disorganization which may serve as the triggering condition for eliciting psychotic or paranoid manuifestations without detectable or identifiable organic findings using conventional techniques.

Epilepsy and Violence. The whole question of violence—which we have discussed above—and the problem of the interaction of epileptic and paranoid phenomena fall together at this point. The question arises of the extent to which patients who manifest violent behavior may suffer concurrently from paranoid and epileptic disorders. A recent study of so-called episodic dyscontrol (Bach-y-Rita et al., 1971) carefully evaluated a sizeable group of 130 patients who presented with the complaint of explosive violent behavior. The patients were categorized into the following groups: those with temporal lobe epilepsy, those with seizurelike outbursts, those with diffuse patterns of violence, those suffering from pathological intoxication (see discussion under effects of alcohol), and finally, those patients with repetitive violence directed at specific individuals in their environments.

Psychosocial histories revealed a fair amount of childhood deprivation and social maladjustment—including work and family instability. The patients seemed to demonstrate a chronic lack of control resulting in innumerable life difficulties, including job loss, family disruption, and brushes with the law. There was a high incidence of abnormal EEG findings and episodes of unconsciousness and seizures, suggesting that the difficulties experienced by many of these patients were the effects of minimal brain dysfunction (MBD). Psychodynamically these patients are described as rather dependent men—usually dependent on a strong mothering female figure—and as men with a poor sense of masculine identity. They tended to be outwardly hypermasculine and extremely intent on defending their masculinity against any questioning or insult. They shared a sense of uselessness, impotence and inability to change the environment which they confronted. In individual episodes of violence, there was a total breakdown of ego functioning and a disorganization of thought processes accompanied by an outpouring of primary process thought. The striking thing about this group of patients and their description is that they seem to reveal a high incidence of paranoid dynamics, including displacement, denial, and projection as prominent defense mechanisms. And we can also ask the question, even though a minority of these patients had identifiable temporal lobe pathology, whether in fact the acute episodes of violence might not have been linked with limbic system pathology which created an episode of acute vulnerabilty and psychic decompensation in individuals with paranoid predispositions. At this point these questions as to the interlocking of organic and psychopathological phenomena must remain no more than intriguing speculations.

CHAPTER 3

Pathological States
Related to Paranoia

ENVY AND JEALOUSY

Dynamic Aspects

The first set of pathological states to be considered are the closely related states of jealousy and envy. Freud had touched on the question of pathological jealousy in the Schreber case, but had presented his more developed views on the subject in his now classic paper on "Some Neurotic Mechanisms in Jealousy, Paranoia, and Homosexuality" (Freud, 1922). He distinguished between projected jealousy, which was derived from actual infidelity or impulses to infidelity, and delusional jealousies, which he related to repressed homosexual wishes. This classic formulation has been generally followed by psychoanalytic writers since Freud's time. However, Freud had also observed that states of jealousy were compounded of elements of grief, of a narcissistic wound, of feelings of enmity against the rival, and of a certain amount of self-criticism which held the subject accountable for his loss.

Jones (1929) followed up Freud's formulation by relating feelings of jealousy to an inner sense of deficiency which was connected with a sense of self-dissatisfaction and self-criticism. This was felt to be related to unconscious guilt feelings which derived from Oedipal conflicts. The unconscious guilt created a deficit in self-love, in self-esteem and self-respect, and left the jealous person extremely sensitive to criticism and with an excessive need for approval or recognition. Fenichel's (1945) treatment of jealousy also follows basically Freudian lines, but he too points to the element of ambivalence in the object-relations of jealous persons and underlines the components of depression, aggressiveness, and envy which reveal the jealous person's peculiar intolerance for loss of love. He comments that the fear of loss of love is extremely intense in personalities for whom such a loss means a diminution of self-esteem. A similar drift was identifiable in Riviere's (1932) analysis of a case of morbid jealousy in which she felt that the projection of infidelity was not sufficient to explain the patient's symptoms. The symptoms of flirtation and jealousy were rather related to oral-erotic and oral-sadistic fantasies of robbery and spoliation.

What passed for infidelity and jealousy according to Riviere were really attempts to rationalize the unconsious fantasies by genitalizing them.

Early attempts were made to link envy as a character trait with instinctual development. Abraham (1954) had pointed out the relation between envy and aggression. Envy involved hostility against the envied person along with an impulse to deprive him of the envied possession. Envy is closely related to character traits which involve attitudes of possessiveness and proprietorship. Glover (1956) linked envy with impatience and ambition as oral traits. He contrasted the optimism derived from oral gratification with the pessimism derived from oral frustration. The latter individuals show extreme hostility in response to neglect together with the tendency to carry a grudge. Tied to these feelings there is a sense of injustice, competitiveness, an unwillingness to share, and feelings of acute envy. He was careful to add, however, that the oral aspects of such characteristics are caught up in broader issues of giving, keeping and getting that involve overlapping levels of psychosexual development.

The view of envy and jealousy that has had a very considerable influence on psychoanalytic thinking has been that of Melanie Klein. In her work on *Envy and Gratitude* (1957), she more or less equated envy with basically sadistic impulses which she saw as operative from the very beginning of life. She described envy as an angry feeling that another person possesses and enjoys something desired—the envious impulse being to take it away or spoil it. She regards envy not as a feeling state or as a character trait that undergoes a course of development, but rather as a given motivating force in human behavior. She makes it the motive force for the infant's sadistic wishes and fantasies, and destructive impulses against the mother's breast in the first months of life. While Klein's formulations have had considerable impact, they have served as a stimulus to closer examination of envy and jealousy as affective states, rather than as accepted theoretical positions. As Joffe (1969) has recently pointed out, the Kleinian view bypasses the essential process of development and ignores the fact that envy and jealousy are object-directed affects or attitudes which require a more or less constant and reasonably well-established self-object differentiation before they can acquire any of their enduring characteristics.

More recently, Pao (1969) has related the development of the jealous state to recurrent losses, which serve as cumulative traumata with the development of inner conflicts of regression with which the patient was unable to deal. The patient exploited the primitive defenses of projection and denial to avoid the experience of grief and aggressivity. While there were homosexual elements present in the case, the author notes that the symptom of pathological jealousy could not be related to the intensification of homosexual impulses but rather seemed to be related to conflicts involving aggression and narcissism. He concludes that:

Pathological jealousy could best be understood as a persistent ego state, capable of being instituted by conflicts over homosexual and oral-sadistic impulses, and by other conflicts as well, including those surrounding grief and narcissism. From this point of view, divergent explanations of pathological jealousy, as expressed in the literature, became complementary (1969, p. 637).

The general shift in the literature from Oedipal to pre-Oedipal considerations and from sexual to aggressive and narcissistic issues was influenced to a considerable degree by the contributions of Sullivan. While envy and jealousy are obviously closely related states, Sullivan insisted on their differentiation. He felt that they were not only different affective states, but he related envy to a context involving two persons, while jealousy was related to contexts involving three or more persons (Sullivan, 1953b).

Sullivan felt that the envious personality was marked by a deficiency in what he called the self-system. He commented that the person who is successful in achieving security is not made uncomfortable by the discovery that other people have greater marks of prestige or ability than his own. But the envious person has a need to have more than he has, or more than someone else has. Sullivan felt that such individuals have learned to appraise themselves as unsatisfactory and as inadequate human beings. He pointed out that in the history of an envious person, in all cases, either the parental attitude had reinforced the impression that the patient simply did not rate or the parents had set excessively high goals which the patient was never able to attain. Thus he is always caught in the position of having to prove his adequacy.

Jealousy, however, is a matter of the inability to obtain complete intimacy with another human being. The insecurities based on unfortunate early life experiences make the jealous person incapable of intimacy, and when two other persons who are involved with himself, become more intimately involved with each other, the dynamism of jealousy can take over. This incapacity in the jealous person is related to a defect in the self, which Sullivan describes by saying that "the person has grown into his present position in life with a deep, however unwelcome, conviction of relative unworthiness" (Sullivan, 1956, p. 141).

Relation to Paranoia

The continuity between jealousy and envy and the paranoid states becomes more apparent. Not only are mechanisms of denial and projection in operation, but there is a sense of wounded narcissistic expectation and injustice, which serves to displace the blame for the individual's lack or loss to another person or persons or even to impersonal forces in the social environment. The envious person begins to feel not only that he has a right to the possession or state of well-being that he desires, but that another person's possessing it is a form of injustice that has been worked upon himself. As Spielman (1971) has commented in describing jealousy:

> In jealousy one experiences apprehension, anxiety, suspicion or mistrust concerning the loss of a highly valued possession, or the divergence to another, a third person, of affection and love. It is often associated with an attitude of vigilant guarding against the threatened loss and an effort to preserve the status quo—to maintain possession. In sexual love this might involve an attempt to exact exclusive devotion from the love object. . . . Rivalry with a third person is typically involved and highlights a crucial aspect of jealousy; it occurs in a three person situation in which the jealous person fears a third person will intrude upon a two-person relationship and take possession (pp. 62-63).

Consistent with Sullivan's views on the development of the self-system and its correlative self-esteem, Joffe (1969) has pointed out that relatively early disturbances in regulation of well-being can promote the excessive turning of aggression against the self. This may lead to depressive, self-destructive, and masochistic predispositions and associated superego impairments. The capacity to tolerate internal conflicts may be correspondingly limited, with the result that there is a tendency toward massive externalization and reliance on external sources of self-esteem. Such individuals harbor a deep sense of fantasied disability and inadequacy which constantly stimulates and reinforces envious feelings. Envy, then, as Abraham had earlier observed, is intimately related to the vicissitudes of narcissism. Such individuals are continually caught up in a process of conscious and/or unconscious comparison between themselves and the envied object in which their own feelings of self-devaluation and inadequacy are repeatedly reinforced by comparison with an admired and idealized object.

Thus, over against the Kleinian approach, Joffe (1969) insists that envy is a complex object-related attitude or tendency that is based on a number of component elements and requires a certain level of ego-development. Envy must include an id-derived motivating force, but it requires in addition the development of the capacity to distinguish between self and object. But even further, the child cannot envy without having the capacity for fantasy a desired end state as well as the ability to distinguish between such real fantasied wish fulfillment and the inner state of hallucinatory gratification. The ego must also have the resources to sustain a more or less enduring feeling state with more or less overt conscious aspects. Some degree of secondary process functioning and organization would undoubtedly be involved in this mechanism. Joffe comments:

> It should always be remembered that possessiveness and associated envious feelings are complex social responses rooted in the development of ego functions and reality object relations, and should never be reduced to instinctual sources alone (1969, p. 542).

Consequently, from the point of view of the ego and its development, envy can be seen as a painful ego-state which is related to the loss of self-esteem and self-respect. The envious response can be triggered by any of the sources that undermine self-esteem—whether that be in terms of instinctual disappointments or frustrations, superego attacks, disparity between real and ideal self-images, or even environmental influences. These influences come to bear on the discrepancy between the self-representation and the ideal self-representation which is invested with the individual's narcissism. The response to such discrepancy can take the form of depression, but envy can also emerge as a distinctly different ego-state. It involves the mobilization of aggression, and has embedded in it elements of admiration and hopefulness. The envious person does not accept or resign himself to the loss or deprivation that he feels. He covets and desires what he does not possess—whatever that may be—so that his enviousness is a defense against the threat of loss and acts to restore or sustain his injured or threatened narcissism. The feelings of resentment and injured deprivation can easily take a blaming course—and bridge over into a paranoid position. A paranoid element is not infrequently seen in states of relatively intense envy. In this sense envy is dynamically related to the paranoid position, but it may also serve as a prophylactic against the development of a paranoid response. It may serve as a manageable state of the ego which at once defends against depression, preserves narcissism and self-esteem, and avoids the excessive reaction of the paranoid position. Envy can thus be seen as having a coping aspect which may serve adaptive ends.

Differentiation

In a recent comparative study of the affective states of envy and jealousy, Spielman (1971) has described the elements common to the two states and some of the essential points which distinguish them. Envy is compounded by several elements. The first is emulation—a feeling based on a perception of excellence or admiration of the other person, along with the wish to equal or surpass that person with regard to the admired quality. It implies rivalry, but can also serve as a stimulus to development and/or defensive or adaptive management of feelings of anger and narcissistic injury. There is also in envy a narcissistic wound which is perhaps its most crucial aspect. The sense of lacking something is connected with feelings of inferiority, smallness, or diminished self-esteem. It may be associated with feelings of disappointment, mortification, or humiliation. There is also a longing for the desired possession or quality along with a feeling of anger at the possessor of it. In its mildest forms this may be experienced as discontent or disappointment, but may be manifested as resentment or even, at more intense levels, as maliciousness, malevolence, hatred or a wish to harm the possessor.

With regard to jealousy, however, envy can be viewed as a partial component—so that most of the components of envy will also be found in jealousy. They will have a somewhat variable significance, nonetheless. Emulation will be relatively inconspicuous or absent in jealousy. The narcissistic wound is usually much the same, but anger is a much more consistent and often more intense component of jealousy than of envy. A frequent component of jealous states, that is not found in simple envy, is tension due to unconscious homosexuality. This is typically the case in situations of sexual jealousy, whereas homosexual fears may often be activated when heterosexual striving is somehow frustrated. The homosexual and heterosexual impulses are thus brought into conflict—with the homosexual impulse usually relatively unconscious.

The other aspect of states of jealousy not found in envy is a certain suspicion or mistrust, a paranoid trend which may be experienced on a broad continuum ranging from vague apprehensions, doubts, or feelings of uncertainty about the motivations of others to a level of intensity which may reach delusional proportions, involving strong convictions about the evil intent of other individuals. It is at this level that the continuity of states of envy, and particularly jealousy, with paranoid process becomes most obvious.

Vengeance

It is interesting to note the close relationship between the affective states of envy and jealousy with the psychodynamics of grudges. The holding of grudges or the seeking of vengeance has been little studied by psychoanalysts, but a recent paper by Wixen (1971) has examined the subject. A grudge is a state of resentment or ill will that has certain consistent characteristics—there is often a close positive relationship between the persons involved. The intense degree of hatred or resentment generated is often out of proportion to the wrong committed or thought to have been committed. The individual who holds a grudge often feels pressured to defend or publicize or even elaborate the misdeed. The thought content is often of a distinctly paranoid quality—along with a tendency to phobically avoid any object of the grudge. Moreover the grudge holder seems to often have a rigid ego-ideal and a strong need for external narcissistic gratifications. In the content of the grudge there is often the feeling that a narcissistic injury has been sustained. The injury, whether real or imagined, is an injury to self-esteem and is often interpreted as a humiliation. The intense cathexis involved in "nursing a grudge" usually can be seen as derived from hidden libidinal elements related to a past history of close friendship with the object of the grudge.

On a more intense, and often more destructive, level, the psychology of vengeance seems to be continuous with the psychodynamics of grudges and affective states of envy and jealousy. Vengeance is a complex state which may be associated with pain and rage secondary to loss—and can be regarded as a response to an underlying depressive state. The psychology of vengeance has been discussed with considerable insight by Socarides (1966). The vengeful person is unforgiving, remorseless, ruthless, and inflexible. His revenge is single-minded and unswerving. He lives with a single-minded desire to "get even." He seeks revenge against all odds and no matter what the cost—and he experiences no guilt, no concern for the possible moral or other consequences of his contemplated revenge.

The individual may imagine that many wrongs are being worked against him and his thinking may have a definite paranoid coloring. He screens all incoming stimuli which might contradict or alter his state of mind. He often feeds his vengefulness by imaginings or fantasies of previous injuries which have been directed against him. Vengeful individuals very often identify with powerful or creative figures; these figures are also deeply envied. Often a superego figure, on whom strong feelings of envy have been projected, becomes the likely choice for vengeful urges: the figure is seen as particularly persecutory, as one who interferes with or tries to direct or control the patient's thought processes, who undercuts nd destroys his sense of well-being and sense of self-adequacy.

Socarides speculates that this aspect of the vengeance syndrome may underlie the apparently enigmatic assassination of important or powerful political figures. The aim of vengeance is to destroy the envied and feared superego figure which is seen unconsciously as a depriving and persecutory force. Similarly the violent outbursts and homicidal acts are often associated with motives of vengeance—the incidence of intolerable vengeful feelings, secondary to feelings of morbid jealousy or fear of infidelity, as concomitants to homicidal outbursts has already been noted.

The resort of the threatened ego to vengeful feelings reflects the underlying unconscious infantile fears, and the feelings of inferiority, weakness, and smallness. Typically vengeful individuals tend to screen out the fear aspect of the underlying affective state and compensate with fantasies or attempts to demonstrate capacity and strength. In these cases the absence of any conscious restraint or the absence of any guilt is a striking aspect of the phenomenon. This allows the expression of instinctual aims, particularly those of aggression. Superego demands may be partially met by the punishment of someone beyond the subject, namely the imagined offender. On the unconscious level, however, the intense guilt feelings remain, and must remain repressed or the individual is subject to severe depression. At the deepest levels there remains the guiltful conviction that relates to destructive impulses toward the good and loving objects involved in primitive impulses of envy.

The similarities between vengeance and paranoid conditions are also striking. Under both circumstances there is a marked superego regression (Hesselbach, 1962) with the concomitant projection of guilt. The characteristics of the vengeful state are remarkably similar to those we have been able to describe in conjunction with the paranoid process. It is note-worthy that in Socarides' attempts to differentiate these respective states, the points of differentiation which he offers are between states of vengefulness and psychotic states of paranoia. The point of our argument here, of course, is that the paranoid process can operate in a wide range of less than psychotic, and even normal, states.

Distribution

What needs to be remembered is that envy and jealousy, particularly envy, are almost universal phenomena—and this is particularly so in our own highly competitive, status-conscious and materially oriented society. We are continually being presented with indices of status and personal worth, so that the challenge to inner security and self-esteem is a constant and recurrent one. It is rare that people accept the responsibility for what they are and where they fit in the social schema. One is much more likely to hear complaints about the convergence of circumstances, social conditions, a lack of the "breaks," or any other set of external circumstances which allow a person to absolve himself of the responsibility for his state and con-dition in life. This is readily understandable in that if one is dissatisfied with one's self and one's state in life, not to utilize blaming mechanisms is to leave oneself saddled with the burden of responsibility for one's own dis-satisfaction—and this is an intolerable position.

Several points can be made about states of jealousy and envy. It is ob-vious that they are widespread in the population and, therefore, one pre-judices their consideration by calling them pathological. They range in in-tensity from the common and everyday varieties that are often experienced in interpersonal relationships to the extremely distorted and intense varieties found in pathological states. They encompass the spectrum, therefore, from adaptive coping forms of mental process to more maladaptive and distorted processes in which reality testing is severely impaired. It should also be noted that there is usually an element of historical truth in the content of such convictions. The rationalizations of the envious or jealous person may enunciate a fact of life. In every life its patterning is determined by social, economic, and historical forces which are beyond the individual's control. But the states of mind we are describing evolve when the individual dis-places responsibility from himself to these extrinsic forces, and thereby denies his own appropriate responsibility. Despite the fact that these phenomena are widely spread and that at more normal levels of operation they serve a relative coping function, they nonetheless carry the stamp of the pathological in that they involve a distortion of reality and reflect underly-ing narcissistic and aggressive conflicts which cannot be tolerated as such.

PREJUDICE

In taking up the consideration of prejudice, we are dealing with a state of mind that has close affinities to paranoid states and which bears the stamp of the pathological, but at the same time seems to be so widespread that it defies any easy classification as pathological. We have become aware only in the last few years, by reason of the growing concern over civil rights and more recently the pressures created by the Black Power movement, of the extent and intensity of prejudicial attitudes in contemporary society. Allport (1958) has given us a comprehensive discussion of the problem of prejudice, which traces the many complex facets of the problem and underlines the fact that prejudice is an extremely complicated phenomenon which has its root in intrapsychic conflicts, in processes of group interaction and related processes that take place at the social and cultural levels. The generation, patterning, and maintenance of prejudice are functions of the complex interplay of these many aspects of the problem.

The Nature of Prejudice

Allport defines prejudice as "an antipathy based upon a faulty and inflexible generalization. It may be felt or expressed. It may be directed toward a group as a whole, or toward an individual because he is a member of that group" (1958, p. 10). The definition condenses a number of important elements of prejudice which underline its relationship to paranoid states. First of all, it is an antipathy, suggesting that it is impregnated with fear and anger and that the hostility and rejection that it generates are being used in the service of unconscious defensive needs. The degree of antipathy and its expression in meaningful action can be quite varied. The expression of prejudicial attitudes and beliefs is perhaps the least harmful and most common expression of prejudice. If an individual's prejudice is more intense, he may actively avoid members of the group against which his prejudice is directed. At a more active level the prejudiced person may undertake acts of discrimination of various sorts—whether it be in relationship to employment, restriction from residential housing, limitation of political rights, discrimination in education and recreational opportunities, or exclusion of the prejudged group from other forms of social privilege.

Segregation in the United States has been a politically sanctioned and institutionalized form of discrimination which has been frequently enforced either legally or by local custom. The antipathy and prejudice can even lead to acts of violence. The number of examples of this in the United States has been steadily increasing. And finally, at the most appalling and sickening extreme, prejudicial attitudes can lead to wholesale extermination of groups of people against which the prejudice is directed—the historical record of pogroms and massacres and the hideous episode of Nazi concentration camps and extermination of the Jews come readily to mind.

The antipathy, moreover, is based upon faulty judgment which has been strongly influenced by psychological factors. Such judgments can be either judgments of fact or of value. One can entertain the belief, for example, that blacks are lazy and stupid, and one can attach to this a negative evaluation of these characteristics. Thus psychological factors can create a distorted picture of the object of prejudice, or it can alter the subject's evaluation of the qualities that he sees in the disliked object. Such prejudicial devaluations often are based upon underlying projections in which attributes of the subject's own personality are denied and projected onto the object of prejudice. Money-Kyrle (1960) has pointed out that the probable nature of such prejudices can be inferred from the nature of the subject's superego and ego-ideal. Individuals, for example, who hold intelligence as part of their ideal may tend to look on blacks as stupid in an unconscious attempt to minimize their own feelings of intellectual inadequacy and bolster the ideal.

Stereotypical Thinking

Prejudicial thinking is characterized by certain specific qualities. The stereotype is an oversimplified attitude or belief about some category of experience which allows us to justify our action in respect to that category. The utility of stereotypes is that they simplify the thought process involved in dealing with strange, different, or little understood aspects of reality, and provide a means of rationalization for felt emotional responses. Closely linked to stereotypical thinking is a tendency toward classification on the basis of insufficient evidence. It should be noted that this is not an exclusive character of prejudicial thinking, since the tendency to organize our experience and to group it in various classifications, particularly evaluative classifications of good and bad objects, on the basis of minimal amounts of information, is not altogether uncommon (Brigham, 1971; Cauthen et al., 1971).

The effort to assure one's self of adequacy of evidence, to assess the quality of evidence, to verify and validate the applicability and veracity of forms of classification, is a work that is carried on by scholars and scientists, not by common people. The human mind is quick to judge and classify objects of its experience, particularly when practical demands for decision and action are exerting an influence. Even scientific knowledge, when it is pressed into application, must often be applied without sufficient evidence. The art and practice of medicine is such an application. The physician is often in the position of having to decide upon a course of action or treatment without sufficient evidence to guarantee the presumptive diagnosis.

The process of stereotypical thinking has been analyzed into cognitive operations of categorization, assimilation, and search for coherence (Tajfel, 1969). Discrete categorizations of continuous dimensions—particularly in complex judgments of social realities—introduce simplifications and exaggerations which are resistant to contrary evidence. Assimilation refers to the complex process by which the content of the categories, to which individuals are assigned by reason of their social identity within a culture, is generated. Assimilation of social values and norms provides the content of intergroup attitudes—both within the group and toward outgroups. To these cognitive processes is added the search for coherence which brings organization to the understanding of social flux. Tajfel writes:

> If the individual is to adjust to the flux of social changes, he must attempt to understand it. In other words in order to deal with change an individual must make constant causal attributions about the processes responsible for it, and these attributions must fulfill at least two criteria: they must equip him to deal with new situations in a manner which appears consistent to him, and they must do this in a way which will preserve, as far as possible, his self-image or integrity. . . . One of the most important classes of events within the stream of constant social change arises directly from the fact that an individual is a member of numerous social groups that interact with other groups. Theoretically, two types of change (and consequently, of the need for cognitive adjustment to change) can be distinguished: intragroup and intergroup. The former consists of the individual's changing circumstances within the group or groups to which he belongs; the latter, of those aspects of the changing relations of his group with other groups which affect directly some important aspects of his life. In both cases, he needs to build a cognitive structure which provides him with a satisfactory explanation of the causes of change. A "satisfactory" explanation will manage to preserve personal integrity while at the same time—for reasons of cognitive economy—it will tend towards as much simplification as the situation allows for.

As we shall see later in this study, when we consider aspects of the mechanisms employed in the paranoid process, these cognitive operations of categorization, assimilation, and the tendency toward coherence form part of the cognitive process which we shall refer to as the paranoid construction. It is important at this point to note that the paranoid construction is intimately related to the cognitive organization of prejudicial attitudes as well as to the integration of an understanding of group coherence—and, not incidentally, to the cognitive integration of personal identity.

The prejudiced mind, however, employs stereotypes and tends toward biased classification as a result of inner emotional needs and pressures. Consequently its thinking is marked by a premature closure, which functions not merely in the face of an absence of evidence, but which reaches overly simplified and premature conclusions in the face of available evidences to the contrary. The pressure to categorize prematurely thus seems to be unconsciously motivated and seems to serve defensive functions.

As a result of this premature classification and premature closure, prejudicial thinking is marked by overgeneralization. Isolated pieces of evidence, which would support the formulation of the prejudice, are taken as having general validity and are presented as a basis for general conclusions about the object of prejudice. Other pieces of evidence, which would counterbalance the prejudice, are rejected as irrelevant or unimportant. Thus there is a radical selectivity which assimilates to the prejudicial category any evidence that would be consistent or supportive of it and eliminates from consideration any evidence that would be contrary.

Intolerance of Ambiguity

The pressure toward premature formulation of attitudes and drawing of conclusions rests upon an underlying intolerance of ambiguity. The prejudiced mind has a strong need for clear-cut and unambiguous categories, for a clear separation of categories of good and bad, and a clear-cut organization of the structure of reality in terms of these dichotomous categories. It seeks to eliminate all ambiguity and ambivalence, so that its possessor's own inner self-doubt and insecurity can be resolved by his affiliation to the unequivocally good aspects and groupings of his environment.

It should be noted finally that premature judgment and classification do not of themselves constitute prejudice, since almost all human thinking in some degree or other is marked by a degree of probability and uncertainty. But the element of premature judgment does become a prejudice when it shows itself to be irreversible in the face of new evidence and by its clinging to premature formulations. This aspect of prejudicial thinking best reflects the underlying pressure of unconscious motivations and marks the closest point of contact between prejudicial thinking and paranoid thinking. Both the paranoid and the prejudiced person have a strong investment in preserving their distorted beliefs and in maintaining them against the erosion of information or contradictory evidence.

Prejudice and Group Values

One of the important aspects of prejudicial thinking is its role in establishing and maintaining a psychological sense of group membership. The importance of the individual's social and cultural interaction and his participation in and membership in a variety of social groups and institutions has been underlined as having considerable significance for the development of the individual's sense of social identification and his development of and maintenance of a sense of identity. Erikson's (1963) work particularly has brought many aspects of this developmental interface into focus. The individual identifies himself by reason of his relationships to

various group structures and in turn receives a sense of his own social existence by reason of the group's recognition and response. Membership in
the ingroup provides an individual with a sense of belonging, of sharing, of
having a generational and individual history which establishes and secures
his identity. Allport writes:

> There is one law—universal in all human societies—that assists us in making
> an important prediction. In every society on earth the child is regarded as a
> member of his parents' groups. He belongs to the same race, stock, family
> tradition, religion, caste, and occupational status. To be sure, in our society
> he may when he grows older escape certain of these memberships, but not all.
> The child is ordinarily expected to acquire his parents' loyalties and pre-
> judices; and if the parent because of his group membership is an object of
> prejudice, the child too is automatically victimized (1958, p. 30).

Placing a high premium, therefore, on ingroup standards and behavior
is of considerable value and importance in psychological adjustment. The
prejudicial attitude maintains that valuation of the ingroup by a devaluation
and a rejection of the outgroup. His ingroup membership, adopting the
group and its values as a main anchorage in the regulation of his experience
and behavior, is reinforced by creating an attitude of hostility and suspicion
toward outgroups. Such a hostile attitude toward groups in which the individual does not hold membership and with which he has no sense of affiliation tends to intensify his sense of cohesion to his own ingroup constellation. Hence prejudice, from the point of view of the interaction
between groups, must be seen as divisive, destructive, and exclusive; nonetheless when seen from the perspective of the ingroup cohesion and solidarity, prejudice can have a constructive and socially reinforcing dimension.

Often ingroup valuation and solidarity and sense of belonging are reinforced in a paranoidlike fashion by the use of projective mechanisms, by
reason of which hostile and devaluing qualities are ascribed to outgroups,
and outgroup members. If the distortions and hostile qualities ascribed to
outgroups were of any validity, the individual's membership in the ingroup
would necessarily achieve added importance for the security and stability of
the ingroup member.

Allport (1958) notes in passing that an important aspect of group
membership is sharing in the values of the group. Personal values are indeed
intimate and important aspects of personality functioning, since they are the
guidelines by reason of which we carry out our lives. The necessity to sustain
and support such values can often lead to the development of prejudices.
The maintenance of personal values is subjected to the same pressures as the
maintenance of group membership. We shall return to the question of
values later on.

The phenomenon of prejudice obviously has large and important social
implications. Prejudice has undoubtedly had an extremely important role in

contributing to many aspects of the structure of contemporary society and to the creation of many of the most significant social problems of our contemporary era. The organization and structure of society are significantly influenced by mechanisms of introjection of, and identification with, ingroup elements, and the corresponding projection which leads to division and exclusion, pertaining to outgroups. The operation of prejudicial and paranoid mechanisms and the pressures toward ingroup valuation and the corresponding devaluation and rejection of outgroups has been traced by Pinderhughes (1969) in reference to racial segregation and the civil rights movement. He writes:

> Since repressed impulses are those which tend to be projected, and since all groups encourage in their members repression of impulses which threaten the group, these group-threatening motivations are commonly projected upon other groups. It is predictable, therefore, that members of different groups will impute to one another the same or similar threatening motivations. These group-related paranoid processes have not been considered pathological by psychiatrists. However, they are responsible for such extensive intrapsychic, interpersonal, and intergroup conflict, for so many misunderstandings, acts of violence, and deaths on a massive scale that psychiatrists may come to identify them as the most serious pathogenic factors in our era (pp. 1553-1554).

There is no doubt that the complex of factors which determine and maintain prejudicial attitudes is complex and difficult. It involves not only psychological but social, cultural, economic, religious, and many other factors. It also cannot be denied that the maintenance of group structures and the variety and variation among groups of different cultural, racial, national, and ethnic origins is not only deeply and historically embedded in the fabric of our society, but it also serves many positive, constructive functions in the stabilization of social order. Group differences, therefore, are not only embedded in the structure of society but they serve important constructive and stabilizing functions. The ultimate question that needs to be answered in approaching the problems of prejudice is whether ingroup membership and ingroup support can be maintained without the necessity of outgroup devaluation and exclusion with their accompaniments of hostile projection and phobic defenses. This may in fact be merely restating at a level of social process the basic therapeutic problem of paranoia.

THE AUTHORITARIAN PERSONALITY

Origin

The authoritarian personality is one of those characterological classifications which enjoys widespread occurrence, and can only be called pathological at the risk of diluting the significance of that term. It also lies very close to prejudice, both in its conceptual origins and in its practice. One of the roots of the concept of the authoritarian personality was Jaensch's (1938) study of anti-Semitism in the Nazi era.

After the war, this line of work was extended in the massive study at the University of California (Adorno et al., 1950), which based the concept of the authoritarian personality on the covariance of a wide variety of test data. These studies evolved a single test measure to identify the constellation of characteristics, which seemed to correspond to the authoritarian personality—this measure is now known as the F-scale (F for "fascism").

These studies characterize the authoritarian personality as tending to be conventional, that is, rigidly adhering to conventional middle-class values; as tending to have a submissive, uncritical attitude toward idealized moral authorities in the group; as tending to be extremely sensitive to those who violate conventional values; and as adopting excessively punitive responses toward such violations; as tending to be less subjectively or imaginatively oriented; as tending to believe in somewhat mystical determinance of individual fate and of thinking in more or less rigid categories—an overall tendency toward superstition and stereotypical thinking; as being preoccupied with issues of control, power-submission, strength-weakness, and as having a strong tendency to identify with figures who are seen as powerful and influential. These people are also seen as having a generalized hostile attitude of destructiveness and cynicism, and as tending to depend strongly on the use of projection as a mechanism of defense. Thus they constantly deal with the environment as though it were hostile and threatening, and maintain the belief that unless control and rigid organization are maintained, dreadful or destructive consequences would ensue.

The other major root of the consideration of the authoritarian personality is the work of Erich Fromm, which also derived from the Nazi experience (Fromm, 1941). Fromm stressed the sadomasochistic aspects of the authoritarian character and pointed out that the authoritarian tended to place himself in a position of dependence on powers outside of himself, whether the source of power be other people, institutions, or even the powers of nature. Along with masochistic tendencies, there were also more sadistic tendencies which strove to make others dependent on oneself, to have absolute power and control over others, and to rule them in such a way as to exploit them for one's own interest. Fromm characterized this attitude as "I rule you because I know what is best for you." This apparent strength or power can be maintained only by reason of the submission of weak persons around it. Such a balance of domination and submission often wears the face of love, but such love does not dominate the lives of others out of concern and care of them, but rather it has concern only because it can dominate them. The authoritarian need for power, therefore, is paradoxically rooted not in strength but in weakness.

Power

This formulation is strikingly close to Nydes' characterization of the paranoid character, who renounces love for the sake of power (Nydes, 1963). Conflicts over power are at the center of the authoritarian attitude. Fromm puts this very graphically:

> For the authoritarian character there exist, so to speak, two sexes: the powerful ones and the powerless ones. His love, admiration and readiness for submission are automatically aroused by power, whether of a person or of an institution. Power fascinates him not for any values for which a specific power may stand, but just because it is power. Just as his "love" is automatically aroused by power, so powerless people or institutions automatically arouse his contempt (1941, pp. 190-191).

Thus the authoritarian character admires authority as a source of power and tends to submit to it—simultaneously, however, wishing to be an authority himself and to have others submit to him.

Because of the authoritarian's concern and sensitivity to issues of control and power, he maintains an attitude of suspicion, generalized hostility, lack of trust, and critical cynicism. Projection of such impulses colors the environment with a variety of dangers and hostile threats, and makes the necessity for clinging to positions and control all the more pressing. The continual projection of aggressive and hostile impulses and the reaction to other individuals as threatening, hurtful, dangerous, or untrustworthy brings the authoritarian character very close on the pathological spectrum to the paranoid character.

The implications of such attitudes on many levels of social interaction and for the functioning of social structures in general are very rich and have been discussed elsewhere (Meissner, 1970a). I would only point out in a very general fashion that the authoritarian attitude represents one of the significant polarities in some of the most significant dichotomies and conflicts that have marked human history. If we juxtapose the authoritarian insistence on power, organization, control, and structure to the contrary parameters of spontaneity, flexibility, and freedom, we can immediately recognize that these parameters have been operative and influential in almost all areas of human endeavor. They represent what Nietzsche called the Apollonian and the Dionysian. From the political point of view, they represent the dichotomy of the totalitarian vs. the democratic. In religious matters, they represent the dichotomy between dogmatic rigidity and insistence on unchanging truth, which demands the submission of the faithful, on one hand, and the openness to religious understanding and historical consciousness, on the other, in which faith is a search for truth rather than a submission to it. Authoritarian attitudes are thus part of the warp and woof of human thought and experience.

The Open or Closed Mind

Closely related to considerations of the authoritarian attitude is the work of Rokeach (1960) on the organization of belief systems and their relation to what he calls the "open" or the "closed" mind. He defines a belief system as representing "all the beliefs, sets, expectancies, or hypotheses, conscious and unconscious, that a person at a given time accepts as true of the world he lives in " (p. 33). Similarly a disbelief system "contains all the disbeliefs, sets, expectancies, conscious and unconscious, that, to one degree or another, a person at a given time rejects as false" *(ibid.)*. This constellation of beliefs and disbeliefs, the belief-disbelief system, can be characterized for any individual as open or closed.

The open system is characterized by the following elements:

1. The degree of rejection of disbelief subsystems is relatively low at each point along the belief-disbelief continuum.

2. There is communication within parts of respective systems and between belief and disbelief systems.

3. The degree of differentiation between belief and disbelief systems shows relatively little discrepancy.

4. The specific content of central beliefs is to the effect that the world, or the immediate situation one is in, is a friendly one.

5. The formal content of beliefs about authority and those holding to it is that authority is not absolute and that people are not to be evaluated, if at all, in terms of their agreement or disagreement with authority.

6. The time perspective is relatively broad.

The closed system has the following characteristics:

1. The degree of rejection of disbelief subsystems at each point along the belief-disbelief continuum is relatively high.

2. There is an isolation of parts within and between systems.

3. The degree of differentiation between belief and disbelief systems shows a high degree of discrepancy.

4. There is relatively little differentiation within the disbelief system.

5. The world or the immediate situation tends to seem threatening.

6. The formal content of beliefs about authority is that authority is absolute and that people are to be accepted or rejected according to their agreement or disagreement with authority.

7. The time perspective is relatively narrow and future oriented (Rokeach, 1960, pp. 55-56).

The closed belief system shows remarkable consistency with the characteristics of the authoritarian attitude—particularly in respect to attitudes toward authority and in projective attitudes toward the environment. The need to deal with and compensate for feelings of inadequacy and self-hate by excessive concerns over power and status makes the individual susceptible to a cognitive confusion between information and the source of the information, and consequently fosters a tendency to closed systems of thought and belief. Overidentification with an absolute authority serves to defend against feelings of loneliness and isolation. Rokeach also points to a positive dimension in such an attitude:

> ... closed belief systems provide a systematic cognitive framework for rationalizing and justifying egocentric self-righteousness and the moral condemnation of others. Thus, the more closed the belief-disbelief system, the more do we conceive it to represent, in its totality, a tightly woven network of cognitive defenses against anxiety. Such psychoanalytic defense mechanisms as repression, rationalization, denial, projection, reaction formation and overidentification may all be seen to have their representation in the belief-disbelief system in the form of some belief or in the form of some structural relation among beliefs. Indeed, we suggest that, in the extreme, the closed system is nothing more than the total network of psychoanalytic defense mechanisms organized together to form a cognitive system and designed to shield a vulnerable mind (1960, pp. 69-70).

This view of the closed mind helps to fill out the portrait of the authoritarian personality, although its extension and implications are broader than the diagnostic issues. The continuity between these more characterological and relatively normal configurations of adaptation to the stress of the environment are apparent and deserve to be underlined. There is a spectrum of states of mind, stretching from psychotic paranoid delusions to the relatively normal attitudes of the closed mind, which rests upon a community of attitudes and mechanisms. The differentiation of degrees of pathogenicity in this continuum is a matter of degrees of intensity and relative adaptiveness to a social-cultural context. We have treated these states under the rubric of "pathological," but our considerations have led us into an ill-defined area between the pathological and the normal, if not frankly into the normal area. I would now like to turn to some unequivocally normal states of mind which are closely related to the preceding considerations and which extend the continuum of paranoidlike states even further.

NONPATHOLOGICAL STATES RELATED TO PARANOIA

Belief Systems

Characteristics
I would like at this point to briefly consider some of the characteristics of belief systems and the role that they play in psychic economy. Belief systems are general social phenomena which constitute a significant and central aspect of culture. Society directs a considerable amount of its energy

to the maintenance and support of institutions and structures which represent and stabilize its common beliefs. Belief systems are important for the
organization and vitality of the group. They are also important for young
people growing up into the society, becoming participating members of the
group and sharing in its culture. Answering to this continuing need in social
structures, there is an emergent need in young people for ideological commitment which is born out of the uneasiness of vague inner states and the
conflicts of emergent but unresolved identity. Thus society provides belief
systems, or what Erikson calls "ideologies," in response to the inner need of
youth for ideological commitment. Erikson, (1962, 1959) has described the
importance of the role of ideology in the shaping of the identity and in the
structuring of social institutions.

Belief systems refer to a variety of contents—whether these be religious,
political, scientific, or others. One tends to think primarily in terms of
religious systems of belief since religious belief is the prime analogue of this
type of cognitive process. But from a formal perspective, prescinding from
content, the belief system organizes the understanding of some aspect of
reality in terms of a coherent explanation. The explanation is not supported
scientifically at all points by explicit evidence—but adherence to the explanation is urged on other grounds. It is this aspect of the cognitive
organization that distinguishes belief systems from scientific theories—or,
correlatively, belief from knowledge. The belief system, therefore, requires
assent from those who accept it, not on the basis of evidence which
demonstrates its validity, but on the basis of inner needs which the belief
system satisfies and responds to. Most characteristic in this regard are
religious belief systems, precisely in that they answer to some of the most
basic and fundamental needs and insecurities in man. Religious beliefs respond to man's insecurities about the meaning of life and the confrontation
with death. The questions are met with a vacuum of evidence and lie beyond
the reach of scientific method. The religious belief system supplies an
answer, but an answer that is accepted on emotional grounds and in
response to inner needs.

Rokeach (1960) has made it clear that such belief systems can be
characterized by varying degrees of closedness or openness. The more closed
the belief system, the more one sees a rigidity in adherence to it, the greater
becomes the insistence on maintaining the totality of the belief system with
all its parts, the greater the degree of intolerance to other beliefs. In the same
work, Rokeach has distinguished rigidity from dogmatism, the former having to do with the resistance to change in single beliefs, the latter referring to
resistance to change in the belief system as such. He points out, however,
that the more dogmatic a person is, the more at risk is the total belief system
rather than single beliefs. The degree of dogmatism or of closedness is
associated with a need to adhere to the belief system as a whole whose

respective parts are interdependent. No single part of the whole can be challenged or questioned without posing a threat to the whole system. This attitude is based on the intensity of the inner needs which generate and sustain the belief system. The underlying intensity of need and insecurity can be very great indeed, and to this extent the individual needs the support and security of a complete, totally integrated, unshakeable and unquestionable view of his world and its meaning. If doubt is cast on any portion of the belief system, this means that doubt can be cast on any other portion, and this threatens the individual's inner stability. This threat can reach psychotic proportions, as we have seen, in which it is equivalently a threat of inner disintegration, loss of self, and psychic death.

Religious Belief Systems

From this point of view, one can begin to understand the paranoid necessity to complete and stabilize the person's delusional system. We can also understand his need to bring all data into congruence with his delusion and his need to maintain it in the face of contradictory evidence. There is thus an analogy between the paranoid delusional system and belief systems, particularly religious belief systems in which such basic and fundamental needs are involved. It is not surprising, considering the nature of the motivational issues, that in this area more than others one finds a greater degree of rigidity and dogmatism. But in the interest of clarifying our understanding, we must ask what it is that distinguishes systems of religious belief from paranoid delusions.

Religious belief systems are complex cognitive organizations which explain in a coherent fashion complex and difficult questions involving the origin of the universe, the relationship between the universe and the deity, the meaning of human existence, and the conditions of salvation. If one looks at the Judeo-Christian tradition, it represents a continuing and historically embedded effort to conceptualize and understand these and related questions. The earlier parts of the tradition were more of a retelling of the story of God's salvific action in Israelite history with only minimal attempts to theologize this history. Later parts of the tradition took the form of prophetic reflections on the history of divine intervention, particularly on the exodus and the subsequent desert experience which formed a central aspect of the Jewish historical and religious experience. The prophetic reflection was interpretive and more explicitly theological. Freud referred to such religious ideas as "illusions," stressing the role of human wishes in generating and maintaining such ideas. He offered a distinction, however, between such illusions and delusions.

> What is characteristic of illusions is that they are derived from human wishes. In this respect they come near to psychiatric delusions. But they differ from

them, too, apart from the more complicated structure of delusions. In the case of delusions, we emphasize as essential their being in contradiction with reality. Illusions need not necessarily be false—that is to say, unrealizable or in contradiction to reality. . . . Thus we call a belief an illusion when a wish-fulfillment is a prominent factor in its motivation, and in doing so we disregard its relations to reality, just as the illusion itself sets no store by verification (1927, p. 31).

The distinction between illusions and delusions is slippery, however, since delusions are not without their kernel of historical truth. Waelder (1951) has referred to the Hebrew belief that they were the chosen people as a collective delusion. And in addition it is not altogether certain that religious illusions have not been maintained in the face of contradictory reality. Religious belief systems are formed in some degree in response to basic human needs—Freud's illusions—but the degree of closedness and resistance to change by experience is a function of the degree to which the belief system serves a defensive function in preserving the believer from inner psychic insecurity and dread. Where that underlying anxiety is more intense, there is a tendency for those who adhere to the belief system to regard the system as a whole without differentiation of its parts and to feel that preservation of the parts is essential to the preservation of the whole. This is reflected in an increased rigidity and dogmatism and a reluctance to even question any part of the complex of moral and speculative positions which compose the system. In the current reexamination and reconsideration of basic moral positions among religious groups, particularly the sensitive area of sexual morality and contraception, part of the problem has to do with this form of pressure toward closedness and rigidity. The problem is complicated by the more general shift from a climate of belief which demands adherence to established doctrine (closed) to a greater emphasis on personal realization and grasp of religious truth in its historical and emergent dimensions (open).

How, then, does one draw a line between the theocosmological delusions of Schreber and the belief system of religious men? Schreber's *Memoirs* read in part like an elaborate theological tract. His delusional system is a highly evolved and systematized attempt to organize and understand his experience in terms of a coherent theory. Organized doctrine represents a similar attempt to interpret human experience and give it meaning in terms of a divinely instituted plan and guidance. Both delusional and belief systems reach certain untestable conclusions which cannot be contradicted by available evidences. How in fact would one go about disproving Schreber's delusion that he was being transformed into a woman? How would one disprove the Christian assertion of the real presence in the Eucharistic sacrifice? We can recognize that a delusional system is in conflict with reality as we interpret it, but how does one go about proving that our interpretation is sane and that the delusional one is insane and in contradiction to reality? Ultimately we cannot. We can resort to an appeal to consensus or to practical and adaptive exigencies that are consequent on our interpretation rather than the delusional one—but these are not matters of evidence. The delusional system as well as the belief system is maintained on the basis of a prior emotional commitment, not on the basis of evidences. The illusion sets no store by verification.

The apologetic argument which supports a given religious belief system appeals to Biblical accounts as part of the base of evidence, but this is an appeal to an historically antecedent belief system. Apologetics must ultimately appeal to an acceptance through faith which lies beyond the reach of reason. But this brings us closer to the element or elements that distinguish delusional from belief systems. The delusional system is created anew by the psychotic in response to inner idiosyncratic needs and serves to isolate him from communal participation in inverse proportion to the degree of development of his pseudocommunity. The religious belief system, however, is not created anew, but is the product of a tradition which is in some degree institutionalized and has a significant history. The content of the system, therefore, is not idiosyncratic but answers to common needs and shared concerns of the community. Contrary to the effect of a delusional system, the belief system serves to unite the believer with a community of believers and this in direct proportion to the degree that he shares in the shared beliefs of the community. The belief system fosters integration with and membership in a community of believers, and this social interaction, as Erikson has pointed out, is an important component of the support that the community offers to the emerging sense of identity.

Thus while the paranoid delusional system is divisive, exclusive, and is built out of the fabric of distrust, the belief system rests on shared conviction, mutual support, and trust. Some of Erikson's comments are very much to the point:

> The psychological observer must ask whether or not in any area under observation religion and tradition are living psychological forces creating the kind of faith or conviction which permeates a parent's personality and thus reinforces the child's basic trust ... in the world's trustworthiness. ... All religions have in common the periodical childlike surrender to a Provider or providers who can dispense earthly fortune as well as spiritual health ... the need for clearer self-delineation and self-restriction; and finally, the insight that individual trust must become a common faith, individual mistrust a commonly formulated evil, while the individual's need for restoration must become part of the ritual practice of many, and must become a sign of the trustworthiness of the community (1959, pp. 64-65).

Putting it in these terms makes it clear that one cannot discriminate delusional from belief systems on the grounds of underlying needs, inner structure, relation to reality, or—a point which deserves emphasis—on the grounds of underlying mechanisms. The mechanisms of introjection, projection, and cognitive construction are detectable in both contexts. One need only recall the Christian doctrine of hell and diabolic influence to appreciate that Christian theology provides ample opportunity for the projection of hostile impulses—whether this belief be regarded as a total projection closer to delusion, or whether one regards the doctrine as enouncing a kernel of truth. But even here the projection serves to underline a common peril and reinforces the ties to the community. The mechanisms of belief tend to support the individual's participation and membership in the community, whereas the mechanisms of paranoia tend to isolate and exclude the individual from the real community of objects—the delusional network of suspicious and hostile interactions in a paranoid pseudocommunity is a far cry from meaningful sharing in the community of one's fellows.

Value Systems

Closely related to belief systems are value systems. While beliefs pertain more to the cognitive organization and interpretation of the world and reality in which one exists, values pertain more to the actual standards and norms that people use in determining the direction and pattern of their activity. Allport (1958) has pointed out that values often form the basis of prejudice in that we tend to highly esteem attitudes with which we are narcissistically identified, and correspondingly we tend to devalue or regard hostilely any divergent attitudes. Values also represent critical aspects of personal involvement in community life. Individuals become incorporated into the community and acknowledged as members of the community in the degree to which they have internalized the shared values which the community holds as properly and characteristically its own. The community likewise recognizes its members by the degree to which they reflect and express these values. Where membership in such a psychological community is important for the stability and self-esteem of the individual, his adherence to the value system of the community is liable to be intensified and his tolerance for divergent values more limited. In this sense values can also take on the characteristics of closed or open systems—showing relative degrees of rigidity and resistance to change.

The psychology of values is extremely complex (Meissner, 1970c, 1970d, 1971) and beyond our present focus. It involves questions of the respective functions and interplay of ego and superego, the role of the ego ideal and its relation to both ego and superego, the development of conscience, and the vicissitudes of narcissism—to touch a few of the main headings. The development of a mature and realistic value system is a vital aspect of personality integration. As Jacobson (1964) and others have pointed out, the failure of developmental processes leading to mature value orientations creates difficulties in ego and superego identifications, in the establishing and maintenance of mature object relations, in defining and sustaining a coherent sense of identity, and in defining one's personal roles and functions in the context of the larger social community. Values are correlative to, and reinforce, the individual's pattern of meaningful identifications, and consequently provide one of the most significant parameters of mature personality integration.

The question of the role of values in personality functioning raises interesting questions about paranoid conditions. The central issue that it raises is that of narcissism. The paranoid system is invested with a quantity of narcissistic cathexis which is proportional to the intensity of the need to preserve the subject's self-esteem. The value system correspondingly distills a considerable amount of secondary narcissism into its organization, again in the interest of maintaining self-esteem. The paranoid system thus has a valuative aspect and serves similar restitutive functions for the paranoid that the normal value system serves for the normal personality. The paranoid system provides a sense of self-definition, establishes the patient in a meaningful relationship with the world of his experience, defines his place within that context, and provides a context of meaning within which he is able to determine his course of action and the pattern of his life.

The Paranoid Spectrum

The suggestion that we have been advancing here is not only that paranoid conditions can range over a wide spectrum of intensities, but also that the mechanisms and functions that characterize paranoid conditions are also identifiable in other relatively common, less pathological, and even normal aspects of human adaptation. This approach helps to clarify some aspects of paranoia and places it in a context in which psychotically distorting mechanisms can be seen to be strikingly similar to mechanisms that in normal personalities serve adaptive and developmental ends. Consideration of the genesis of paranoia and an understanding of its mechanisms must take this context into account.

This consideration also raises other related concerns. From an intrapsychic perspective the paranoid organization may be indistinguishable from the organization of relatively normal belief systems. Adherence to belief systems, however, can become fanatic with the generation of considerable hate and projective hostility toward adherents to divergent belief systems. Expanding the consideration to include more social aspects of such adherence, strong adherence to a belief system or to a value system shared within a group increases the coherence and solidarity within the group. This increases the sense of mutual sharing and support within the group and thus serves important psychological and social needs. The exclusive adherence to such ingroup ideologies tends to create a situation in which adherence is reinforced by rejection and devaluation of competing ideologies. Adherence to a set of ideas or beliefs, which give meaning to individual experience and upon which the individual places high value and personal significance, takes place through mechanisms of introjection and identification. The development of a personal value system and the consolidation of self-esteem are closely related to such group involvement and adherence. Other belief and value systems and the groups maintaining them must be seen as wrong, inadequate, evil, and to be rejected. The high valuation of one's own beliefs and values requires the expulsion of all elements that would tend to decrease its high estimation, and this is accomplished by projection. Thus undesirable elements are denied in one's own value system and are ascribed by projection to other value or belief systems. Thus the relationships are structured so as to permit prejudicial or even paranoid attitudes to control the relations between groups. Of such stuff are prejudice, persecution, riots, and wars made.

Thus strongly held ingroup beliefs can become the basis of paranoid attitudes that obtain between groups. This has not infrequently been the case in the history of religions, and currently is the case in the conflict between the black and white races in the contemporary setting. Ingroup beliefs and values, then, can become a form of group paranoia. The tendency to paranoid distortion on this level is proportional to the intensity of the need to adhere to ingroup ideology. This is again conditioned by the degree of inner insecurity and inadequacy that the ideology answers to from the inner aspect, and on the degree to which such adherence is threatened by external social forces from the outer aspect.

The point that I wish to emphasize is that mechanisms which serve to support constructive and adaptive belief and value systems, and which reinforce group membership and commitment, are from another perspective seen to be the basis of paranoid and paranoidlike attitudes. Belief and value mechanisms by reason of a changing context can become prejudiced or paranoid. Thus the same mechanisms underlie relatively normal as well as severely pathological states of mind. If Schreber's theological delusions and cosmological rationalizations were adhered to and affirmed by a large group of people as a theological belief system we would hesitate to call it delusional, just as we might hesitate to call the belief system involved in the mythical theogony of ancient Egypt a delusional system.

A dividing line is difficult to draw. Certainly we are more likely to attach the label of paranoia where the manifestations occur in a socially deviant context or in association with other forms of pathology—e.g., schizophrenic decompensation is the commonest example. But the mechanisms can be in operation across a broad spectrum of states of mind of varying degrees of adaptation. Our understanding of paranoid mechanisms and of the genesis of paranoid states must take into consideration that the genetic roots of paranoid states are probably widespread in the social matrix and in fact involve important constructive dimensions of social and personal integration. The same mechanisms that serve the ends of development and adaptation also serve from another perspective as the basis of paranoid forms of adjustment. The pathological distortion is very likely, then, a matter of quantitative variation rather than qualitative difference.

On the level of the psychopathology of everyday life, paranoid responses may have a realistic social context. Artiss and Bullard (1966) have pointed out that some patients harbor secrets which in fact have had real foundation and revelation of which was associated with threat of harm to the patient or others close to him. Often the secret has to do with expectations of advantage or advancement. In the face of disappointment there is a response of depressive anxiety which is followed by an outburst of paranoid thoughts—the "paranoid spike." The disillusionment provokes a defensive response which avoids acknowledgment of feelings of inadequacy and weakness. The authors comment that paranoid thinking and the distortion it produces seem to be a weapon of the weak. In fact, in all its manifestations and contexts, paranoid thinking fixes the individual in relation to others and creates an involvement with objects—an illusory distortion of, and substitute for, the kind of relationship wished for and desired but unobtainable.

Paranoid thinking is thus widespread and relatively common. It is one pattern of dealing with feelings of insecurity and inadequacy, or of protecting oneself from such feelings. It permeates individual patterns of adjustment and establishes itself on larger levels of social organization and interaction. Our understanding of such phenomena must rest on more than inner psychic dynamics, although these are central to its genesis. We need also to understand the social and cultural processes which bring it about that types of responses which are adaptive in one context can become distortive and maladaptive in another context.

CHAPTER 4

Paranoid Mechanisms

We have been considering the origins of contemporary views of paranoia in Freud's formulation of the libidinal and dynamic aspects of the syndrome. We then considered the development of those concepts and the gradual shift in emphasis from the libidinal aspects to questions of the economy of aggression. Concern over homosexuality has faded somewhat, and concerns over power relations and power conflicts have assumed increasing importance. The relationship of paranoid defenses to issues of depression, personal inadequacy, and diminished self-esteem have received increasing emphasis and have become central issues in the understanding and treatment of paranoid disorders. We have also undertaken to relate paranoid conditions and paranoid mechanisms to a spectrum of states of mind, which reach from the grossly pathological and distorted extreme of paranoid delusional systems to the more adaptive and developmentally relevant aspects of group affiliation, beliefs, and values.

Our objective in the immediately present undertaking is not so much to focus specifically on the problems related to understanding the mechanisms themselves, but to clarify their functioning and relation to clinical and related states. This seems to suggest itself as an important intermediary step in approaching an understanding of how such mechanisms are developed. The present consideration, therefore, is aimed at the further examination of the processes which underlie the genesis of paranoid and related conditions. The mechanisms that we shall focus on are projection and introjection, denial, and what I shall refer to as paranoid construction.

PROJECTION-INTROJECTION

Reciprocal Interrelation

It is generally agreed that projection is the characteristic and basic defense mechanism employed in paranoid states. It is quite obvious clinically that projection is found quite consistently in a variety of other clinical conditions (Jaffe, 1968), so that we cannot regard it as a defining or pathognomonic aspect of paranoid states. Freud put considerable emphasis on projection in trying to illumine the psychodynamics of paranoid delusions. The paranoid deals with painful or intolerable inner impulses by projecting them onto external objects. The process is rationalizable in terms of the economic principle that it is easier to flee from a threatening external source of pain than to avoid an internal source of pain (Nunberg, 1955). But it is not immediately evident why such should be the case.

The mechanism of projection can only be considered meaningfully in the context of its correlative intrapsychic process—introjection. The two processes are intimately related in the psychic economy. I have discussed the terminological and metapsychological aspects of projective and introjective processes elsewhere (Meissner, 1971b), and they need not be rehearsed here. While psychoanalysts, following Freud, have focused primarily on the role of projection in paranoia, there has been a tendency to overlook and underplay the equally important, although less apparent, role of introjective mechanisms. The importance of this consideration, from the point of view of understanding paranoid mechanisms as well as from the point of view of clinical intervention, has been underlined by Searles. On the basis of extensive clinical experience, he comments:

> Conspicuous as the defense mechanism of projection is in paranoid schizophrenia, I have come to believe that the complementary defense, introjection, while less easily detectable, is hardly less important. The patient lives chronically under the threat, that is, not only of persecutory figures experienced as part of the *outer* world, but also under that of *introjects* which he carries about, largely unknown to himself, within him. These are distorted representations of people which belong, properly speaking, to the world outside the confines of his ego, but which he experiences—in so far as he becomes aware of their presence—as having invaded his self. These, existing as foreign bodies in his personality, infringe upon and diminish the area of what might be thought of as his own self—an area being kept small, also, by the draining off into the outer world, through projection, of much affect and ideation which belongs to his self (1965, p. 467).

Projection and introjection are reciprocally related processes which regulate the individual's interaction with external objects. They become operative very early in the organism's experience and remain an operative feature in varying degrees for the rest of his life.

Role in Development

It is difficult to indicate starting points for the operation of projection and introjection, but they must begin extremely early in life. Klein has specified these processes in the first few months of life. She is undoubtedly correct in pointing to the operation of these mechanisms, but whether they operate in the manner she describes is a matter of controversy. The operation of projective and introjective mechanisms requires a certain degree of differentiation in intrapsychic structure—certainly enough to support a minimal degree of differentiation between self- and object-representations. Projection involves an attribution of parts of the self-representation to an object-representation; introjection involves a reciprocal attribution of parts of object-representations to the self-representations. At the same time pro-

jection and introjection are in part responsible for the emerging differentiation between self and object.

At their most primitive level these processes are relatively unstructured
and undifferentiated. It is impossible to know what the content of such neonatal processes might be, or what degree of awareness they might include.
Freud's speculation that projection has primarily to do with the operation
of the pleasure principle and that the organism responds to maintain an inner pleasurable state—the purified pleasure ego—is probably near the mark.
It is difficult to know whether at this primitive level the processes involved
are defensive or not. Klein insists that they are, but they may be serving the
interests of differentiation and development primarily, and only subsequently are brought to the uses of defense. At this level, internalizing and externalizing processes are differentiating rather than defensive processes, and
they are directed to the formation and establishment of boundaries between
the inner and the outer worlds, between self and object. They are fundamental processes through which internality and externality are constituted. Once
these fundamental differentiations are established, the same operations are
caught up in the commerce between the internal and the external.

The structuring of the inner world begins from the very first. Incorporative aspects of the infant's global and undifferentiated experience precede
the capacity to distinguish between self and object, but contribute a qualitative modification to the global experience. The experience is good or bad or
perhaps both, and, to the degree that it is unpleasurable, leads to primary
attempts at externalization which organize the emerging lines of differentiation. As these lines begin to form, introjection becomes possible and the
continuing structuralization of the inner world takes place through introjective mechanisms. The quality of introjects is derivative from, and constituted by, elements derived from both the inner and outer worlds. What is
introjected is qualitatively determined by the characteristics of the real object in conjunction with the elements attributed to it which derive from the
inner world. The introject, as we have discussed elsewhere (Meissner,
1971b), functions after the manner of a transitional object—it represents a
combination of derivatives from the inner and outer worlds which are
assimilated to the inner world.

What is internalized through introjection is a function of an interaction between the real qualities of the object, and the qualities which are attributed to it and which derive from the subject's inner world. This attribution of qualities, drawn from the inner world and attached to objects in the
outer world, is projection The quality of introjects, then, depends in part on
the qualities projected from the inner world of drives and instincts. To the
extent that hostile and destructive instincts are projected on the object, the
object becomes a bad, threatening object so that introjection of the object
creates a bad, threatening introject. Similarly projection of good, loving im-

pulses can help to provide good and loving introjections. The quality of the introject, however, is mitigated by the response of the object. A good and loving object can absorb significant amounts of aggressive projective affect and in a sense neutralize it, so that the introject is modified in the direction of ambivalence. Aggressive impulses thus become less threatening and the infant's capacity to tolerate rage is increased. A hostile, rejecting object, however, can intensify the destructive and threatening quality of the introject so that the internally destructive aspects of aggression are intensified.

The interplay of introjective and projective mechanisms weaves a pattern of relatedness to the world of objects and provides the fabric out of which the individual fashions his own self-image. Out of this interplay also develops his capacity to relate and identify with the objects in his environment. It also determines the quality of his object-relations. Projection and introjection must be seen in a developmental and differentiating perspective, which does not merely reduce them to defense mechanisms. Introjection and projection serve important functions, particularly in the early course of development. They are intimately involved in the gradual emergence of self- and object-differentiation. They are also intimately involved in determining the quality of one's own self-image and self-perception as well as the quality of one's object-relations. Jacobson has described this aspect of these mechanisms in these terms:

> During the preoedipal-narcissistic stage, gross primitive introjective and projective mechanisms, in conjunction with pleasure-unpleasure and perceptive experiences, participate in the constitution of self and object images and, hence, of object relations. The small child's limited capacity to distinguish between the external and internal world, which is responsible for the weakness of the boundaries between self and object images and the drastic cathectic shifts between them, promotes the continuous operation of introjective and projective processes. Thus, it is quite true that during the first years of life the child's self and object images still have more or less introjective and projective qualities (1964, pp. 46-47).

The developmental and defensive aspects of introjection and projection are intertwined. As development progresses, however, differentiation intrapsychically as well as between subject and object reaches a point at which further developmental progression depends on the emergence of other more highly integrated and less drive-dependent types of process. The persistence of projection and introjection beyond this point suggests that they are being employed in the service of defensive needs, rather than facilitating the interaction between subject and object which serves both to build the structure of the inner world through internalization and to qualify the experience of the outer world through projection. The persistence of introjective and projective mechanisms in the work of development extends at least through the resolution of the Oedipal situation, since introjection and projection are involved in the formation of the superego and the ego ideal.

It is difficult to say when their developmental function ceases. They may play a role in the reworking of previous developmental crises in adolescence. But beyond that they are primarily defensive in nature. Introjective responses to loss, while they provide the matrix for adaptive change and personal growth in the course of the life cycle, are primarily defensive responses. It is perhaps most accurate to say that the balance of developmental and defensive aspects of introjection and projection shift in the course of the life cycle and that the mechanisms to that extent undergo a change in function. They are continually at work adjusting the balance of instinctual pressures between the inner and outer worlds. The process is always in some degree defensive and in some degree developmental, in that its effects involve structuralizing intrapsychic aspects.

It is important to realize that introjection and projection are correlative. When we come to speak of projective mechanisms in paranoid states, we must remember that we are also speaking of correlative introjects. What is projected is derived from inner introjects. Beyond the level of the most primitive primary projections by which self-object differentiation is established, projection is a process of reexternalizing what has been internalized by introjection and internally modified by the influence of drive derivatives. Thus the understanding of projection requires an understanding of the operation of introjective mechanisms which have been involved in developmental processes. To understand what comes from the inner world we must try to understand what composes the inner world and how it got there.

Projection

Looking at projection in its broadest terms, Rapaport (1952) has described it as the structuring of the world in subjective terms according to an organizing principle inherent in the individual personality which seeks to diminish internal stress. This encompasses a variety of subtypes: (1) infantile projection, by which whatever is painful is externalized; (2) transference processes, which may include projective elements; (3) defensive projection (paranoid) of inner impulses; and finally (4) the structuring of the inner world as reflected in projective testing (Rapaport, 1944). The subjective structuring has to do with the internalization of introjects, which are then projected and help the infant to structure his world and to define the limits of self and the boundaries between what is within and what is without. The complex interplay of introjection and projection in structuring the inner and outer worlds is modified by the structuralizing effects of identificatory processes and the resulting emergence of a stable self. As the self becomes organized and stabilized, there is a corresponding definition of the structure, limits, and inherent stability of objects. Perception of the world becomes less drive-dependent, less organized in terms of defensive needs. The capacity for reality testing and tolerance for the distinctness and difference of objects matures.

One way of looking at projection is that it involves a partial de-differentiation or fusion of self- and object-representations (Jacobson, 1964). The infantile interplay between introjection and projection is involved in efforts to define and establish the boundary between self and object, and such fusion and confusion are undoubtedly part of the problem. In later defensive projections, however, such confusions are not apparent and patients seem to be hypersensitive to differences between themselves and others, particularly the objects of their projections. Attribution to the object of characteristics which derive from aspects of the self do not necessarily connote fusion of representations. Rather in the defensive use of projection the distinction between self and object is amplified in the interest of putting greater distance between the self and what it seeks to reject.

Projection does not involve a withdrawal of cathexis and does not imply a breakdown in cognitive functioning. It implies a careful attention to reality and to the object of the projection. The distortion of reality which it introduces is not a perceptual distortion. The distortion has rather to do with what the perception means. One attaches a significance to what one perceives, which derives from one's inner convictions and needs. Thus, the paranoid can agree with others as to what is observed, but he cannot share the same meanings with them. Projection, therefore, does not distort apparent reality, but it does distort the significance of the apparent reality. Projection is a form of interpretive distortion of external reality (Shapiro, 1965). This projection, as we shall see, plays an important role in relation to the paranoid construction.

The defensive use of projection can take a variety of forms. An attribute or quality that lies wholly in the subject and not at all in the object is perceived as a quality of the object and not as a quality of the subject. Conflict is resolved by ascribing to the other person or group the emotions, attitudes, or motives that actually belong to the subject, person or group. This use of projection involves a considerable degree of denial and involves a severe degree of distortion in the perception of external reality. Projection may also take the form of an exaggeration or emphasis of qualities in the other which the subject also possesses. The degree to which the subject is able to acknowledge the quality in himself varies, but the projection characteristically involves an accentuation of it in the other. Allport (1958) calls this "mote-beam" projection. Freud (1922) had pointed out that projection of this kind was often involved in jealousy, in which one partner might minimize his own impulses to infidelity while accentuating the impulses of the other partner. He assumes the presence of impulses to infidelity in both partners, even though unconscious. The projection takes the form of an exaggeration and accentuation of the quality detected in the other. Projection, however, need not take the form of either creating or exaggerating qualities in the other. It may simply take the form of providing an explanation and a justification for an inner state of mind by an appeal to external influences or the imagined intentions and motives of others.

It is important to keep the understanding of projection clear from related usages. We have been discussing the developmental and defensive forms of projection which share certain characteristics and are closely related. Such projections are correlative with introjection, and are thus pertinent to the forming of the self-image and the organization of object-relations. Projection should be carefully distinguished from transference phenomena which involve displacements from object to object rather than subject to object (Jacobson, 1964; Greenson, 1967). It should also be clear that phobic projections are only analogously projections and are better described as externalizations.

Projection is a defense that pertains primarily to object-relations. The content of projection derives from introjects which are in turn derived from object-relations. Moreover, projection is immediately caught up in the effectual involvement in object-relations. Jaffe (1968) has pointed to the dualistic and conflictual role of projection in involving the self in a persistent mode of ambivalence in dealing with objects. At one pole annihilation of the object is sought, whereas at the opposite pole identification with, and preservation of, the object is desired. There is a basic conflict between the impulse to destroy the object, to which some threatening subjective impulse has been ascribed, and the wish to protect the object, with which the subject has identified and is thus invested with narcissistic cathexis. The ego is faced with a need to maintain inner stability in the face of structural regression with its attendant threat of loss of control and instinctual discharge. It is interesting in this regard that paranoid patients are terribly threatened by any attempt to confront them with their rage and disappointment against significant and particularly primary objects. The paranoid position often seems to be calculated to preserve these objects and to preserve the object-relation. The ambivalence in the relationship is too difficult to tolerate and the rage against the object cannot be faced. These relationships are often the important source of introjects, and the projection to other objects provides a way of preserving the good aspects of the object-relationship. On another level, projection onto such important introjective objects provides a way of preserving the relation, even if on desperate terms.

Preservation of Self

The duality of preserving and annihilating, of introjecting and projecting, is inherent in the full spectrum of paranoid states. What seems most significant in the operation of these mechanisms is that there seems to be a close relation to situations or circumstances in which the ego has suffered or is about to suffer a significant loss. At such points the ego is confronted with its own inner sense of inadequacy and weakness. The mechanisms operate in the direction of preserving the inner elements that support self-esteem and its related narcissism. The complex of projection/introjection operates to re-work the object-relations involved so as to preserve the self in a meaningful context of relatedness. The analogue is the interplay of infantile projection/introjection in establishing the self and building its relatedness to objects. Consequently, the operation of these mechanisms cannot be regarded in isolation as a result of intrapsychic dynamisms alone, but must be seen in the larger context of the subject's relatedness to objects and his embeddedness in a social context.

While the defenses are operating in an attempt to preserve the self, it is apparent that their capacity to do so is limited. The paranoid patient is under duress from within and from without. His defensive struggle is aimed at rejecting the painful and evil parts of his self and locating them outside (projection) and affiliating unto himself the fragments of relationship which can enhance his own sense of self and his relatedness to the world of objects around him (introjection). But the attempt proves abortive since both projection and introjection operate in part to diminish the sense of self. Projection preserves a relation of a certain distorted quality to the object, but at the expense of loss of the projected parts of the self and compromise of the capacity to relate in ways which facilitate the growth and integration of self.

Introjection preserves the relation to the object within the ego, but in so doing creates an internalized presence which is subject to primary process influences and which preserves its derivative character. The cost to the self is the persistent infringement on its internal consistency and the reduction in its capacity to relate to objects more maturely. The defensive operation of introjection, therefore, attains some self-preservative compromise, but it interferes with the ego's capacity to integrate itself less in drive-derivative terms and more in terms of mature object-relatedness. Introjection in its early developmental aspects allows the emerging ego to work through primary process types of structural organization, but in its defensive aspects tends to fix processes of internal structural formation in drive-derivative primary process types of organization and thus prevents the emergence of more autonomous secondary process forms of ego integration (Meissner, 1971b).

The struggle to maintain object-relations or their equivalent and the correlative effort to preserve a sense of self can be seen in states related to paranoia. Often paranoid mechanisms come into play in the face of loss, grief, depression, or of a narcissistic wound. The jealous person has to struggle to maintain his relation with the object of his love in the face of narcissistic loss and jealous rage. Jones (1929) closes his classic paper on jealousy with the comment that ". . . jealousy is a sign of weakness in love, not of strength; it takes its source in fear, guilt, and hate rather than in love"

(p. 340). The weakness is one in the self which relates itself in narcissistic dependence to the object. The threat of loss of the object is a direct threat to inner stability and security of the self.

The situation in the operation of prejudice is similar. One can say that the hatred of others displayed in prejudicial attitudes is a reflection of the inner hatred of self. Prejudice is the vehicle of guilt, anxiety, and hatred. If a man has no esteem for himself, he will have no esteem for others. Prejudice is never simply a rejection and devaluation of another person or group, but it always involves the correlative adherence to, and enhancement of, an ingroup. Ingroup affiliation serves to bolster the sense of self and by identification with the group and its values tends to support the individual's sense of identity and belonging. In proportion to the extent that the enhancement of self derives from the valuation of the group, the individual is driven to reinforce the importance and value of the group. He can do this by the comparative devaluation of outgroups and their respective values. The necessity to treat outgroups and outgroup members prejudicially is a reflection of the individual's sense of inner insecurity and his uncertainty about the value of the ingroup. A similar observation can be made about adherence to belief systems which frequently are institutionalized and represent one aspect of adherence to the group holding the beliefs. Such adherence, then, is predicated on the basis of primary process needs rather than on the basis of more autonomous secondary process decision and commitment. The internalization of group values on such terms is analogously at least introjective, and seems to rest less on genuine identificatory processes.

Threat to Autonomy

One of the striking clinical aspects of paranoid conditions relates to the issue of autonomy. The paranoid patient lives in a state of continually threatened autonomy. He is constantly preoccupied with issues of control and domination. He may feel in an acute delusional condition that his thoughts are being controlled. Events and relationships are cast in the mold of an impending need to submit. Simple requests or directives from others become a demand for submission to the will of the other. Paranoid cooperation or obedience becomes a groveling prostration of self, in which the patient feels his weakness and impotence and hates it. Such patients cannot give in to another person or accede to the will of another without such compliance taking on the proportions of a total or near-total surrender of any sense of personal autonomy or independence.

The issue of autonomy in paranoid states has rarely been commented on, but it seems to play a central role in all of the paranoid patients I have known. Attention has been drawn to this aspect of paranoid functioning by Shapiro (1965). He feels that the paranoid's most characteristic concerns are related to the issue of autonomy. He comments:

> Where, for the normal person, autonomy brings a sense of competency, pride, and self-respect, the paranoid person, instead, is either arrogant and pseudo-competent or furtive and ashamed or, perhaps most often, both (p. 81).

The paranoid is continually taken up in the struggle over personal autonomy, continually confronted wiht the threat of external control and subjection.

A mature and stable sense of autonomy can allow room for a relaxation of inner controls so as to permit a certain degree of spontaneity or even of regression for adaptive or creative purposes—regression in the service of the ego. It can also allow itself to be open to the suggestion or influence of others, or can even submit itself to their will. It is capable of recognizing and respecting the autonomy of others and allowing them their measure of self-determination and independence. It can do these things without a sense of shame or humiliation, without any loss of self-esteem or self-respect. The autonomous person can give in without giving up, without surrendering himself to another's control and prostrating himself in humiliating abjection.

The paranoid can do none of these things. His sense of autonomy is rigid and fragile and unstable. He cannot tolerate giving in to external control or authority. He is acutely sensitive to any such influence, whether external or internal. The subjective world of the paranoid is marked by constant tension over the threat of giving in to external domination or to internal pressures—since both threaten the sense of autonomy. The relationship between this aspect of paranoid functioning and the issues of power and control is central to the understanding of the paranoid style. It also serves to clarify the relation between the paranoid style and the authoritarian attitude. Both are preoccupied with basic issues of autonomy.

The threat to autonomy can assume a variety of forms. The patient may see any request or demand as implying submission to another's will, such that to comply represents surrender of all rights of personal decision and independent judgment. The patient may feel that any authority-based directives which are not concerned with his immediate welfare and interest are an attack upon his individuality and an implicit disregard for him personally. This is equivalently a threat to his sense of self, which is placed in jeopardy by such distancing and group-based decisions of impersonal administration. Other patients may keep themselves in a state of constant vigilance, scanning the environment assiduously to detect any statement, any happening, any event, which raises the possibility of an infringement of their personal rights and autonomy as an individual.

It has been my clinical experience that such patients invariably are precipitated into their paranoid thinking and guardedness by the least suggestion that someone or some institution or process has power to control, manipulate, direct, influence, or in other ways determine the course of their activity or lives. Often patients are driven to extreme alternatives of submission and self-effacement and react to the least slight or imposition on their sense of autonomy by violent rebellion and outraged counterattack. This is often difficult for persons around them to understand, since it is not always apparent that the real issue for the patient is a threat to his autonomy. It often seems that he has become intensely enraged over an apparently trivial issue.

The threat to autonomy to which these patients are so sensitive derives from both the inner and the outer worlds. It is of course immediately apparent that social interaction takes place in an elaborate social network, in which a wide spectrum of external influences and expectations are generated, and to which every individual in the society is expected to conform. Social structures are permeated by the functions of authority which organize and direct the activity of individuals. Such social influence is seen by the paranoid as intrusion, controlling infringement, and an invasion of self which restrict his free self-direction and deprives him of the right to self-determination, which has become essential to the preservation of his sense of self. The sources of infringement often are integrated in the paranoid delusion on the basis of their common involvement in undermining the patient's sense of autonomy. The projective distortion plays a role in bringing suspect objects into line with the threat to autonomy. In one female patient, decompensation required hospitalization and subsequently any person, group, or institution even remotely or possibly related to the process of hospitalization was linked in a system of projective distortions. This included the doctor (or any doctor who might be involved in committal), her parents who permitted it, the hospital (or any hospital that might commit patients), the police who brought her there, the government which allowed such proceedings, etc. The issue was that they all constituted a threat to her autonomy, since the same agents that once conspired to put her in a hospital against her will could undoubtedly do so again. The role and function of each of these respective social and personal agents were distorted by massive projections of malignant intent in her regard.

The threat to autonomy is not merely external but derives from the patient's own inner world. It is perhaps not unreasonable to expect that the external threat to personal autonomy is intensified to the extent that the inner capacity for autonomy is compromised. The sense of autonomy rests on a complex of factors, but an important aspect of it has to do with the inner structure of the self. The sense of autonomy rests on the individual's real capacity for ego autonomy. The integration of an autonomous ego depends on a capacity for object-relatedness and on a capacity for meaningful identifications which contribute to inner structure formation in the ego. Introjects can contribute to structure formation in the ego, but only indirectly by reason of consequent identificatory processes (Meissner, 1971b). As long as introjects remain in a quasi-autonomous state and operate in terms of drive-dependent processes, they compromise the inner autonomy of the ego. The paranoid introjects consequently put the patient under constant threat, in that his autonomy is perceived as precarious and susceptible. In relation to this threat to autonomy, his sense of personal integrity and self-esteem are endangered. The genesis of such introjects is an important part of the understanding of paranoia.

Superego Projections

We might add a word about superego projections, since they form a considerable proportion of typically paranoid projections. Such projections are significant, for it was on the basis of paranoid delusions of being watched or observed that Freud was led to formulate his teaching concerning a self-observing and self-critical agency in the human psyche. This agency was conceptualized as the superego (Freud, 1914, 1916-17). The projective delusion of being watched, or feeling that thoughts and feelings can be detected by others, is one of the commonest paranoid delusions. In psychotic states, it is not uncommon for patients to experience auditory hallucinations of voices criticizing them or castigating them in derogatory terms. Such projections represent a relatively harsh and archaic superego which carries out its self-critical and devaluing function in this projected form.

The superego is constituted in large part by introjects which, as we have suggested, are closely related and susceptible to instinctual influences. Such introjects aggregate to themselves significant amounts of instinctual energy, particularly aggression. This pattern of superego formation is influenced strongly not only by harsh parental figures (identification with the aggressor), but also by assimilation of unneutralized intrapsychic hostility which intensifies the harsh and archaic morality of the superego and increases its hostile destructiveness. This process has been referred to (inaccurately I think) as an intrapsychic projection of aggression from the ego to the superego—a form of "intrapsychic paranoia" (Money-Kyrle, 1968). In any case, the superego introjects tend to assimilate the unfused aggression, thus interfering with more adaptive and healthy intrapsychic integration of these introjects. They retain a primitive and archaic quality and distort the inner reality of the individual's sense of identity and integrity. They maintain a certain level of pathogenic inner division and fragmentation, undermine the sense of well-being, self-esteem, and inner autonomy which derives from the integration of psychic structure, and by projection distort the individual's experience of his world and his place in it.

It is my impression that superego projections are closely linked with the issue of autonomy. The autonomy of the paranoid personality is threatened both internally and externally. The internal threat derives from introjects, the most important of which are the superego ones. The inner diminution of a sense of autonomy is closely tied to other effects of superego aggression. It calls forth feelings of inadequacy, diminished self-esteem, worthlessness, shame, and guilt. Projection serves to release some of this superego pressure. The paranoid projection can serve as a defense against the feelings of inner loss and futility that are associated with the internal threat to autonomy. If autonomy is threatened externally, at least the inner futility can be lessened and the external threat can be contested. Even if it cannot be avoided or overcome, one can preserve a false sense of rebellious autonomy in the face of an external threat. One cannot in the face of an internal threat. Superego projection is really a special case of the overall problem of projection/introjection in paranoid states.

DENIAL

The mechanism of denial undoubtedly plays a role in paranoid distortion, but it is not altogether clear that it is a distinct mechanism for projection, or whether it forms a component part of the projective mechanism. In Waelder's (1951) reconsideration of the structure of paranoid ideas, he places denial at the heart of the process. The essential aspect of delusional ideas, he feels is their resistance to correction by experience. Any excessive concentration of instinctual derivatives on an object, whether aggressive or libidinal, and whether the object is external or has been internalized, distorts the ego's sense of reality. He sees paranoid ideas as resting on an unsuccessful denial.

Freud (1911) has indicated the role of denial in his formulation of the four classic forms of paranoia. Each formula began with the statement of denial; "I do not love him." The statement of denial is then followed by a contradictory claim characteristic of the respective forms. Denial is thus a way of dealing not only with external events of a threatening or painful nature, but also with internal instinctual derivatives. The frustrating event or instinctual drive is denied, but what has been so denied can return in a distorted form. What is disclaimed may then return in the form of a claim or an assertion. The knowledge of the essential truth of the statement may account for its inaccessibility to influence. Waelder appeals to an isomorphism of symptom and defense: if the defense is denial, the return of the denied takes the form of a claim. The model is that of neurotic repression and the return of the repressed.

In a similar vein, Rycroft's (1960) attempt to establish contradiction as the basic mechanism of paranoia does not effectively establish contradiction as a separate mechanism. He describes a paranoid patient with many hysterical features whose defenses were organized around massive contradiction of wishes and fears. The notion of contradiction, as he develops it, implies construction of an organized pattern of behavior and thinking which is based on a number of defense mechanisms including denial and projection. It is not clear that contradiction is a mechanism, so much as a complex ego state or position, which derives from defense mechanisms like denial. Defense mechanisms operate at an unconscious level and should not be confused with conscious derivatives.

Denial, along with projection, is one of the primitive narcissistic defenses of the ego. Denial constitutes a basic unconscious unwillingness to perceive. It is a primitive technique for avoidance of what is painful or intolerable. While projection can operate at many levels of psychic integration and can even, as we have seen, function in the service of adaptive and self-sustaining needs, denial remains limited to primitive levels of defense. I would think it preferable here to follow Waelder and regard denial as closely linked to psychotic distortion. In some sense every defense involves an element of denial and distortion of reality, but to use the terms in that context seems only to dilute them to a point of reducing their usefulness. Similarly, to describe the common phenomenon of not acting in response to significant and acknowledged realities—e.g., traveling by airplane even though planes can and do crash (Moore and Fine, 1967)—as a form of denial, is to violate the meaning of defense mechanisms. Reality can be ignored without its being denied. Traveling by airplane reflects a realistic evaluation of comparative risks and need not in any sense involve a denial of reality. Denial, in the sense we are using it here, involves an unconscious avoidance of reality in which the reality is not acknowledged as existing at all.

Denial in paranoid states is seen in its grossest and most primitive form in acute delusional states and particularly in paranoid grandiosity. The use of denial, however, shades off into a spectrum of less apparent and less intense usages which often escape notice. Paranoid states, in which the distortion is not of the magnitude or intensity of psychosis, are frequently marked by selectivity of attention. Events or bits of information, which do not fit the paranoid preconception or which cannot easily be reconciled with it, are ignored and treated as if they are nonexistent. Assiduous attention is paid to other aspects of the patient's environment, but elements which fly in the face of his paranoid system drop out of consideration. It is difficult to discriminate in such cases whether in fact the patient is unable to acknowledge the existence of the reality (denial), or whether he can acknowledge its facticity but is unwilling for defensive reasons to take it into his reconstruction or interpretation of reality. Both are possible, but the latter strategy is less primitive and in fact is often observed in normal thought processes.

The paranoid patient's hyperalert and suspicious scrutiny of reality is pressured by the underlying need to integrate available data into a consistent system which answers to self-defensive and self-preservative ends. This pressured search for inner meaning thus can easily miss what is most obvious and most apparent to the normal mind. Suspicion will not permit anything that is obvious to be accepted at face value, until it can be reconciled with prior convictions. Thus, while the paranoid style can be acutely aware of concrete and often complex realities, it can also remain completely unaware of less complex and rather obvious aspects of situations, particularly social situations (Shapiro, 1965). This selective inattention to the obvious may be one important form of denial—or, where the fact is recognized but not accepted, may pass for denial.

Denial is closely linked with other mechanisms and thus poses some difficult problems, both theoretically and clinically. As Jacobson has pointed out (1957), denial and repression are closely related. Denial is the more primitive mechanism and is seen much more prominently in borderline and psychotic patients. The resort to denial is due to a relative deficiency in the repressive capacity of the ego. Repression represents a much more highly organized and controlling defense which reflects a much higher degree of integration within the ego and a much more developed capacity to direct specific countercathexes in the interest of defense. Repression involves the mobilization of countercathectic energies against the expression of id impulses and id derivatives. The ego consequently has a much greater degree of toleration for such impulse derivatives than would be suggested in denial. Denial is more of a simple withdrawal of cathexis from such id impulses. The ego is considerably less able to tolerate them and has fewer resources to direct against them. Its reaction is one of flight, not fight. It can offer no resistance and must resort to avoidance mechanisms.

Thus, while denial is a more primitive type of defense, it is often found operating at more neurotic levels. As Freud (1940 [1938]) suggested, denial has to do with the withdrawal of cathexis from perceptions, where the perceptions may be either external or internal. Repression has the effect of making ideas unconscious, but denial can only erect a protective screen between the preconscious and the conscious, so that ideas which have reached the preconscious level are prevented from becoming conscious. Thus both repression and denial deal with contradictory ideas; in repression one is in consciousness but the other is in the unconscious, whereas in denial both ideas have their place in the ego. This produces a split in the ego and the perceived reality is correspondingly distorted under the influence of instinctual conflicts (Jacobson, 1957). This results in a tendency for the ego to distort reality by a wish-fulfilling fantasy as a defense against an opposite, painful idea which also distorts reality.

Denial in paranoid states is not a characteristic defense, but it is one that is frequently identifiable. Paranoid suspiciousness and guardedness tend to keep the paranoid well tuned in on his perceptual environment. The paranoid style lies not so much in denying reality as reinterpreting it in terms of the victim's own inner system. However, when projective and reinterpretive devices cannot adequately handle the challenge presented by contradictory data, the paranoid readily resorts to denial. Often it serves the interest of maintaining the paranoid system to deny one aspect of a part of the patient's experience and to modify other aspects of it by projection. Thus these mechanisms may and often do operate in conjunction. Where the paranoid distortion has reached psychotic proportions, denial seems to be an important part of the process.

It is important to keep in perspective that denial, however primitive and distorting of reality, is not essentially a psychotic mechanism. It is often seen in the operation of belief systems, where individuals may resort to denial (not merely negation) in the service of preserving the belief system intact. It is seen in the operation of prejudice where good and constructive aspects of the object of prejudice are not only distorted by projection but actually treated as nonexistent. In all such cases, one is confronted with a basic capacity of the human mind to rely on the security of its inner constructions and to accept only that reality which can be brought into compromise with that inner vision. This brings us to the last consideration of the mechanisms that constitute paranoid states.

PARANOID CONSTRUCTION

In the preceding sections we have been discussing defense mechanisms involved in paranoid conditions. Projection, introjection, and denial are defense mechanisms in the strict sense that they are processes which the ego employs unconsciously to defend itself against painful or undesirable wishes and impulses. The present consideration, however, takes up an aspect of paranoid functioning which may not fall under the category of defense mechanism, but which does in fact serve defensive purposes. In referring to the paranoid construction, we are referring to a specifically cognitive aspect of the paranoid style. The paranoid style includes specific ways of thinking and perceiving, ways of experiencing emotion, and modes of subjective experience and activity (Shapiro, 1965). We are not dealing with a cognitive style in the sense of a clustering of consistencies of cognitive behavior (Gardner et al., 1959), but rather with a cognitive disposition which contributes an important dimension to the paranoid style.

Paranoid Cognition

One of the dominating characteristics of paranoid cognitive behavior is the intensity of attention that paranoids bring to perceptual activity. They seem to be always actively and intensely searching the environment, scanning like a radar warning system. It involves a supicious, rigid, and tensely directed attention. Shapiro (1965) has described this mode of attention as "rigidly intentional." In part the paranoid is actively scanning his environment to pick up bits of information or data which will lend credence to his inner system. The rigidity of his perceptual anticipations, driven from within by the pressure of drive derivatives and drive-dependent processes, fosters a tendency to selectivity in attention and allows him to discredit or reinterpret incoming data in terms of inner frames of reference. This may set the stage for processes of denial as well, as we have seen. In any case, it introduces, whether by denial or interpretive distortion, a highly selective view of the world which supports and confirms the inner apperception which gives meaning and coherence to the patient's experience. The patient's intellectual resources, his native intelligence, his acuteness, his attentiveness, are mobilized not in the service of reality testing but in the service of reality distortion. Attention becomes rigidly narrowed in focus and perceptual activity becomes a suspicious search for confirming evidence of an underlying bias. Shapiro (1965) refers to such evidence as a "clue"—that piece of confirming evidence which may seem insignificant to others, but which the investigator can seize on as providing convincing proof of his inner conviction. The Sherlock Holmes model expresses this aspect of the paranoid attitude quite well, but Holmes' clues were consistent with the full body of available evidence and could be accepted by consensus of even Watson. But the paranoid clue disregards other modifying or corrective aspects of reality, and its significance is acceptable only to the patient—consensus is not possible.

The paranoid construction is a form of interpretive thinking. It is the essential cognitive constituent which lies behind the formation and persistence of delusions. The whole problem of reality testing and judgment of reality is closely related to the matter of the paranoid construction, but we can do no more here than indicate the significance of the relation. Knowledge of reality does not rest on simple perceptions alone, but involves a judgment of some sort. This is true even at the level of asserting the reality of concrete objects. It becomes even more applicable at more complex levels of reality testing, when complex interpersonal or social variables are involved. Knowledge of reality always involves an interpretive judgment, but when the matter of judgment becomes more distanced from the level of simple physical perception, reality becomes increasingly a function of judgment rather than perception. Such judgment is interpretive in that it is never a matter of simple mechanical reaction to the impression of stimuli. Reality is grasped and acknowledged in reference to meanings, which are at once resident in the structure of reality but which are constituted subjectively by interpretive and symbolic processes in the mind. The data of experience must be organized and integrated into a coherent and meaningful context before they can be used as the basis for decision and action. The answer to the question "Is it real?" rests in part on the extent to which that part of experience can be integrated with the rest of the subject's inner frame of reference.

That context of meaning is normally developed through a gradual assimilation of interpretive norms in the course of development and a continual process of consensual validation with other humans, who face the same realities and can correct their interpretive judgments by continual feedback and comparison with other sets of perceptions and judgments. The paranoid is not altogether in that position. The inner necessities which drive him to a suspicious guardedness not only force his attention to a rigid intentionality and directedness but also make it impossible for him to entertain that degree of mutual communication of his inner convictions which would allow some degree of consensual validation. His judgments, therefore, are made without the benefit of such socially derived cognitive correctives. The constant threat that is posed to his sense of autonomy and self-esteem makes the inner system and his conviction of it terribly important, so that his efforts are directed to the preservation, reinforcement, and enlargment of that system. The primacy of the system, together with the disengagement from validating mechanisms, gives rise to the paranoid construction.

By the "paranoid construction" I am specifically designating that cognitive process by which incoming impressions are organized into a pattern of meaning which is primarily validated by reference to subjective needs rather than objective evidence or consensual agreement. That inner pattern of meaning receives the primary cathexis of narcissistic libido, so that its preservation and reinforcement are closely affiliated with the subject's preservation of self and self-esteem. The pressure to maintain this inner perspective forces the individual to adopt a suspicious attitude toward all fresh input. New information is always a danger to the system, in that it offers the threat of contradiction or refutation. It must be treated in such fashion as to allow the inner system to persist without challenge or confrontation. Incoming input may thus be handled by mechanisms of selection, distortion, or denial as we have indicated, insofar as that is required to bring the input into congruence with the inner pattern, or to discredit or avoid its lack of congruence. There is a striving for coherency of experience, in which the criteria of meaning and receptivity derive from the subjectively apprehended pole of experience. The inner meanings, which are thus constructed and defended, are at once a derivative and an answer to inner emotional needs—consequently the process of testing and validation does not follow the usual accepted canons for scientific evaluation and interpretation of evidence. The distortion and divergence from reality that this process introduces is most apparent in psychotic delusions in which the processes of selection, distortion, and denial are most apparently operative.

Paranoid Construction and Nonpathological Human Cognition

As I have suggested, however, in discussing normal states related to paranoia, the paranoid construction enjoys a much wider occurrence in the organization of human thought processes. Every human being has to deal with the basic cognitive problem of integrating his perceptual experience into meaningful patterns. The integration of the experience of objects into the experience of whole objects is often a difficulty for the fragmented schizophrenic ego, but it is not the problem we are dealing with here, nor is it typically the paranoid problem. We are dealing rather with the overall integration of objects and events into a pattern which not only relates them in a meaningful way and makes sense out of their occurrence, but also situates the current of events in a meaningful way in relation to the subject who experiences them. Every human being gains some perception of his world and how it relates to him. He fits the significant figures in his environment to a pattern which expresses the quality and nature of his relationship to them. He fits himself into a pattern which embraces the larger perspectives of social structures and groups. He must come to see himself in these multiple and overlapping contexts, and fit himself into them in ways which are meaningful and, in the normal course of things, at the same time give meaning to his life and activity.

The problem is that the data that reality provides are never so complete, so unambiguous, or so definite that such patterns of meaning are forced upon the human mind. The evidences are often unavailable, thus leaving a certain discontinuity in experience. The evidences that are available are often of varying degrees of clarity and certainty, and involve elements that can only be inferred or conjectured—the thoughts and intentions of other people for example. Man is forced to integrate and respond to his world in terms of something that he creates within himself which completes the picture, in a sense, and gives him a framework for interpreting what he experiences and a presumptive basis for decision and action. Such patterns of meaning are often provided by belief systems and ideologies, insofar as the individual is able to accept and affiliate himself to such prefabricated interpretations. This requires that the individual must share his belief system with others and must accept the shared perspective as properly his own. To this extent, belief systems diverge from the paranoid construction, since the criterion of validity becomes more social consensus rather than subjective need. The dichotomy obviously is not absolute, since belief systems are accepted in the degree that they answer to subjective needs, but the paranoid construction characteristically does not involve social consensus.

I would like to emphasize that the cognitive process that is involved in the paranoid construction is a basic characteristic of human cognition. Normally the construction that human beings make is flexible and open to correction in terms of new experience and in terms of the continual process of consensual validation with other persons and the community. But the paranoid construction resists this corrective. The point is that the same cognitive process, common in human thinking, can be diverted in the paranoid direction, insofar as subjective needs become the determining element rather than objective evidence or consensual agreement. The analogous problem arises wherever thought processes are involved in the interpretation or organization of data. Even in scientific thinking, the theory is a construction which organizes and interprets a certain set of data so that they are explainable in terms of a meaningful and coherent understanding.

The scientific mind is subject to correctives which control and lend validity to the theory. Validation must take place by finding confirming evidence and by reconciling the theory with apparently divergent evidence. The theory is also bolstered by the consensus of the scientific community and the continued willingness of knowledgeable scientists to accept the theory as a basis for understanding and activity. The history of science is not without examples in which the scientific mind deviated from its own canons of validation and confirmation. When a theory becomes rigid, when it is presumed rather than tested against new evidence, when a scientist becomes more concerned with defending theory than evaluating it, then we are dealing not with authentic science, but with something more akin to the paranoid construction. One of the charges made against analysts at one point in the history of psychoanalysis is that they were more interested in preserving Freud's theories than they were in developing or changing them in the face of new evidence. Whether the charge was justified or not, it is conceivable that subjective needs and concerns can invade a more scientific attitude, so that they become the criterion of validity and acceptance in the place of more objective norms.

In this regard it is also clear that an analogous pattern can develop in groups. The history of religion is rich with examples of belief systems which were maintained with intense and even violent force by those who adhered to them. These events suggest an unwillingness to question, explore, reformulate, rethink, and reevaluate the belief system. There was a need to cling to and defend the belief system born out of inner subjective needs, adherence to which provided for each individual and for the group a source of security and support. Similar mechanisms, as we have observed, can be identified in many forms of group adherence and intergroup conflict. Schools of scientific thought fall into the same difficulties. The prejudicial attitudes that develop between various groups, whether religious, racial, or socioeconomic, manifest similar processes by which objective processes of interpretation and validation are invaded by subjective needs, and those needs become the controlling element.

I would like to specify the relation between the paranoid construction and projection. Projection typically takes place at those points in the pattern which lack clarity or at which the evidence is ambiguous. Projection does not deal with what is actual and apparent. It deals with what is hidden and unavailable as direct evidence—the thoughts, feelings, intentions, and motives of others, for example. Projection, therefore, enters in to fill in the gaps in the information input. It is precisely such filling-in and making-whole to which the constructive aspect of cognition pertains. In the paranoid construction, the filling-in derives from inner subjective needs and is accomplished specifically by projection. What is projected, correspondingly, derives from the inner world of the subject and is based on introjective elements. Thus the paranoid construction, insofar as it diverges from normal patterns of cognitive construction which rest on real evidence and consensual agreement, begins to function in terms of mechanisms of projection and introjection. The operation of projective and introjective mechanisms in belief systems and prejudices has already been discussed.

Mythic Function

Taken in this context, it can be seen that the paranoid construction has certain affinities with mythical thinking. Myths are after all story forms which carry with them an emotional appeal for their own justification. The appeal is made not on the basis of the reality of the story, but on the basis of a truth inherent in the myth which is believed. Myth accomplishes for the primitive community what paranoid construction accomplishes for the individual. It was Malinowski (1955) who emphasized the sociological function of myths. The myth is not merely a story told, but it is a lived reality. It is an expression and a codification of beliefs. The sociological function overrides the historical function. Whatever the reality of historical events, the myth brings consistency of belief to past events rather than merely recording them. The myth was not history or an explanation of past events—it was a lived reality in the present life of the community. The paranoid construction is not merely a cognitive explanation of the individual's experience or memories—it is a lived present conviction and active reality.

The myth is in effect an embodiment of beliefs which reflect the values, attitudes, and convictions of the community. Behind the myth, there are a mentality and a form of thinking. Mythical thoughts cannot be regarded as mere invention, even though they are creative elaborations of mythical consciousness. The significance of the myth lies not in its content, but rather in the intensity and conviction with which it is experienced and believed. The analogous problem in the paranoid construction is not so much the content of what it asserts, but rather the intensity and conviction that lie behind it. It bears the stamp of necessity, which reflects the intensity of the inner subjective needs that it expresses and from which it derives. As Cassirer (1955) views mythic expressions, they are creative elaborations which express a tension of the subjective and objective, of the inside and the outside, which is resolved in terms of an intermediary form. The myth is not freely creative, but reflects an underlying necessity for the world of signs, the intermediary realm, to appear to consciousness as objective reality.

Mythical thinking is not a form of passive contemplation. It is rather an active creative elaboration of a view of reality that derives from a rich matrix of attitudes, emotions and purposes. It becomes a channel for the expression of dynamic forces at work, even unconsciously, in the community. Cassirer has observed:

> Insofar as myth condenses into lasting configuration, insofar as it sets before us the stable outlines of an objective world of forms, the significance of this world becomes intelligible to us only if behind it we can feel the dynamic of the life feeling from which it originally grew (1955, p. 69).

These comments are applicable in an analogous fashion to the paranoid construction. The paranoid construction demonstrates and bears the stamp of necessity which reflects the intensity of inner subjective needs. It weaves a tapestry of subjective and objective elements, so that what it experiences becomes a sign. In Cassirer's words: "Every beginning of myth, particularly every magical view of the world, is permeated by this belief in the objective character and objective force of the sign."

The paranoid construction is, therefore, a lived reality which expresses and grows out of an inner dynamic life feeling. That inner conviction is what gives meaning to the individual's experience. We cannot gain any entrance to the significance of his construction until we can feel the dynamic force that lies behind it and gives it life.

PERSPECTIVE ON PARANOID MECHANISMS

The mechanisms of projection/introjection, denial, and paranoid construction, which we have been discussing, are seen in their most extreme form in psychotic states in which the distortion and loss of reality are most apparent. These mechanisms are driven to their most extreme form by the intensity of underlying subjective needs, and in the extremities of psychosis the dominant subjective need is as intense as the radical need to preserve the self from engulfment and annihilation. The same mechanisms, however, operate in less intense and less extreme ways in response to more neurotic inner needs related to issues of castration and self-esteem. Thus individuals can function with basically neurotic styles which are fundamentally paranoid in character but not psychotic. The paranoid characteristics span a spectrum of psychopathologies from the minimally neurotic to the intensely psychotic.

The same mechanisms demonstrate, even in their most distorted forms, an adaptive function which serve to preserve object-relations and defend the self from narcissistic injury. This adaptive aspect of the paranoid mechanisms extends beyond the reach of psychopathology to the level of normal and culturally induced adaptive patterns of action and interaction. The same mechanisms can be socially and culturally reinforcing and supportive in one context, or can be distortive and maladaptive in another. Any theory of the genesis of paranoia must keep both aspects in perspective, and must bring those forces into focus which determine when the identical mechanisms are either adaptive or pathological.

CHAPTER 5

The Genesis of Paranoid Style

FROM SYMPTOM TO STYLE

We have been dealing with paranoid phenomena, both in their pathological deviations and in their more adaptive functions. Implicit in this consideration has been a shift from a focus on paranoid phenomena as symptoms to a focus on these same phenomena as a style of cognitive and affective functioning. Refocusing the consideration of paranoid ideation in this manner makes it possible to see that such phenomena can be elaborated across a broad spectrum of levels of personality functioning. It also sharpens the apperception that the same mechanisms can operate under conditions of severe pathological deviation and in mental states which are not merely socially acceptable, but are important aspects of developmental processes.

The shift of focus from a symptom-oriented view of paranoid phenomena to a stylistic view likewise shifts the orientation of an approach to the genesis of paranoid conditions. We can no longer merely concern ourselves with those factors which contribute to the formation of paranoid symptoms. The symptom is by definition a component of an illness and represents a form of deviation from accepted standards of normality. If the question regarding the genesis of paranoid states and ideas is cast in terms of a conceptual framework based on the approach to symptoms, then the answers must similarly be cast in terms of those factors which underlie the deviation of certain forms of thought and behavior from normal patterns. The symptom approach concerns itself, then, with a stratified segment of the factors which are involved in the genesis of the paranoid patterns of behavior. The approach must focus on those factors which bring the individual's patterns of functioning to a point of deviance. That approach leaves out of consideration those factors which underlie those patterns of thought and experience which serve adaptive functions, before they are turned into less adaptive and more deviant channels.

The approach to paranoid phenomena in terms of style, therefore, serves to broaden the base of questioning about genetic factors. The realization that paranoid delusions of persecution, jealousy, envy, prejudice, authoritarian attitudes, and beliefs and values share certain mechanisms which link them in a continuum of more or less adaptive states, forces us to broaden our consideration so as to include the significant factors that contribute to the formation of those mechanisms and processes which are common to these various states of mind. It raises the reflection that similar genetic conditions can serve in one context for the development of adaptive and developmentally healthy religious beliefs, but may also serve in another context for the formation of severely pathological and developmentally constricting paranoid ideas. Those factors are no less significant in the understanding of the genesis of the paranoid ideas than the other factors which are more immediately related to their deviation from normal.

Consequently, in turning at this point to consider the genesis of paranoid conditions, we are focusing on paranoia as a style of life and experience whose manifestations may or may not be pathological. Our view of paranoia is considerably broadened so that we can begin to recognize the presence of paranoidlike states of mind in attenuated and adaptive forms as having much greater distribution in the human environment out of which more pathological forms of paranoid thinking arise. Any genetic formulations pertaining to paranoia as such must take in the broader perspective that is implied in these much more widely occurring and general conditions.

The shift from symptoms to styles also carries with it a change in perspective from a concern with content and unconscious symbolic meaning to a concern with more formal characteristics in the organization and patterning of thought processes, affective responsivity, subjective experience and objective behaviors. The psychoanalytic approach took its origin from the startling revelation that symptoms have meaning, and the approach that Freud elaborated in his *Interpretation of Dreams* (1900) has served as the basis for nearly all of the subsequent analytic investigation of mental processes. The focus has been on the mental content, and psychoanalytic investigation has been a matter of unveiling by the combined techniques of free association and transference the inner unconscious meaning which ties the symptom to levels of infantile functioning and permits some understanding of the symptom in the patient's life and experience. The value of this approach is unquestioned and its importance is undiminished.

With the emergence of a more elaborate and sophisticated ego psychology, however, and with an increasing tendency for analysts to treat patients with problems less of a symptomatic nature and more of a characterological nature—or at least to undertake analysis more extensively on a characterological level—there has been a greater concomitant emphasis on process, formal aspects of the organization and patterning of thought processes, affects and experience, and generally on stylistic aspects of ego functioning. It has become apparent that there is more that is unconscious and pathogenic in the organization of personalities than the id-derived symbolic content and meaning. There are also ways in which the individual's thought patterns and patterns of affective response are organized, which are part and parcel of his pathology, which are for the most part inadvertent—and thus in part preconscious and in part unconscious—and which must be recognized as a significant aspect of his ego functioning. Such stylistic aspects of ego organization contribute to the patient's neurotic difficulties and are not less deserving of analytic attention in the therapeutic setting.

Thus, the shift from a symptomatic to a stylistic orientation carries with it significant implications for an inquiry into the genesis of the elements involved. The stylistic approach broadens the base of the inquiry simply because the stylistic elements that are involved have a wider incidence in the general population than the symptomatic elements that usually form the substance of psychopathology. There are also important shifts in what one looks at in searching out the determining influences in the patient's life history and experience. The relevant influences stem from all levels of human interaction, from the intimacy of the mother-child interface to the broadest levels of cultural and social integration.

While our attention in this consideration will be directed primarily toward stylistic concerns, the caution needs to be added that such concerns cannot be isolated and treated in a kind of investigative vacuum. The stylistic aspects of personality organization and fuctioning cannot simply be divorced from considerations of content. The respective approaches are intertwined and interrelated, both in the life and experience of the patient and in the complexities of psychoanalytic theory. One need only think of the problem of the relation between defenses and personality styles to be reminded of the relativity of these approaches.

THE RELATIONSHIP OF PARANOIA
AND DEPRESSION

Paranoia and depression are closely related states, both clinically and theoretically. It has been my experience clinically that paranoid patients can only relinquish their paranoid stance at the risk of encountering a severe depression. Part of the therapeutic difficulty in treating such patients is that one must help them to face their underlying depression and help them to bear it. Consequently, our thinking about the genesis of paranoia must take into account the relation between paranoid conditions and an underlying depressive stratum in the patient's personality structure.

Klein

The relationship between paranoia and depression had been noted by Freud in his early treatments of paranoia. He regarded paranoia as a defense against feelings of self-reproach, but he never developed this idea further in his later writings on the subject. It was not until Melanie Klein's contributions that the relation between paranoia and depression became a central concern of psychoanalytic thinking. She based her consideration on the vicissitudes of infantile sadism. The infant's sadism is initially directed against the mother's breast and body, wishing to bite, devour, and destroy them. The mother's breast is a prototype of the good and bad objects which the infant introjects from the beginning. The breast is good when he has it and it satisfies him; it is bad when it fails him. The breast is bad not only because it frustrates the child's wishes, but also because the child projects his own aggressive impulses onto it—with the result that breast becomes "bad" and objects become persecuting. The persecuting objects are feared as threatening to destroy him even as he wished to destroy the mother's breast. The sadism has thus become projected and redirected against the self. By the operation of projection and introjection, these persecutors are internalized and must be again defended against by projection and expulsion.

The ego also gains a loving relation to good objects together with a feeling of guilt for sadistic impulses. There is a need to try to preserve the good object against persecutors and a sadness related to the expectation of loss. The ego's unconscious knowledge of the presence of hate along with love, as well as the anxiety that the hate might gain the upper hand and so destroy the loved object, gives rise to the feelings of guilt and sorrow which underlie depression. As long as the ego can deal with part objects, the hate for bad objects and the love for good objects can be kept separate. But when the ego is able to integrate its experience to the level of dealing with whole objects, the same object becomes the object of both hate and love—and this ambivalence is central to the depressive position. The paranoid in Klein's view is unable to introject a good object or, if he does, cannot maintain it since the inherent sadism will turn it into a persecutor. The whole relation to objects is colored by the early experience of part objects as persecutors, which prevents his relating to real, whole objects.

The paranoid cannot bear the additional anxieties for a loved object or the guilt and remorse of the depression. The availability of projection is also limited in the depressive position since he runs the double risk of expelling good objects and of injuring good external objects by the projection. Thus the paranoid retreats from depression—even though, and, in a sense, to the extent that, the potentiality for depression remains. Klein writes:

> Thus we see that the sufferings connected with the depressive position thrust him back to the paranoiac position. Nevertheless, though he has retreated from it, the depressive position has been reached and therefore the liability to depression is always there. This accounts, in my opinion, for the fact that we frequently meet depression along with severe paranoia as well as in milder cases (1964, p. 292).

Whether or not one accepts Klein's formulation of the infantile development of the paranoid and depressive states, it seems clear that the dynamics of paranoia and depression are closely connected in adult patients. While there are many difficulties with her views on infantile sadism, there can be little doubt that these issues are quite relevant to the dynamics of adult paranoia. Paranoia serves as an important defense against depression. When paranoid patients can be induced to give up their paranoid stance, they do so only at the risk of clinical depression. Klein has also pointed to the important interplay of projection and introjection in both these states.

Relation of Paranoia and Depression to Aggression

Both depression and paranoia involve a partial regression and de-differentiation. The depressed patient and the paranoid are both dealing with the management of aggressive impulses. The depressed patient wards off aggressive impulses toward the loved object and translates them into an intensification of superego aggression. It is as if the ego protects itself from expressing aggression and destroying the loved object by projecting the aggression onto an internal persecutor—a sort of intrapsychic projection or externalization (Meissner, 1971b). The paranoid projection places the aggression in an external object instead of an internal object (introject). The depressive position represents a higher level of functioning, since it implies greater mastery of, and tolerance for, the aggression. But the regressive stance does not allow the ego to master the internalized conflict. The inner-directed hostility remains destructive, however, and the ego runs the risk of further regression toward an undifferentiated state. The aggressive conflict which was decathected externally is recathected internally in the conflict between superego and ego. Thus the depressive position internalizes the aggressive conflict which the paranoid position deals with by externalization (Katan, 1969).

There have been a number of attempts in the literature to deal with the relationship between paranoid and depressive states. Salzman's (1960) treatment of paranoia is of interest in this regard in that it deals with it primarily as a response to an underlying depression. He sees it as a delusional attempt to secure certain and universal acceptance. The primary step in the paranoid process is the development of a grandiose, if not messianic, self-concept, which is a direct attempt to deny and compensate for the underlying impoverishment of self and the depressive diminution of self-esteem. The primary grandiosity and its attendant narcissism produce rebuffs from the environment. The consequent threat to self-esteem is dealt with by secondary defensive externalizations, projections, and transfer of blame to external agents. Paranoia appears in this light as an alternate solution to the manic defense.

In this formulation the grandiosity is the primary paranoid response and other defensive maneuvers are secondary. It is not always so clear, however, that paranoid grandiosity is so primary that the other manifestations of the syndrome must be regarded as consequent on it. It seems overly simple to regard the patient's projective defenses as serving only to protect his grandiosity. Moreover, while grandiosity is part of the classic paranoid profile, it frequently enough plays a minimal, if not negligible, part in the patient's clinical picture. However, even if one qualifies the central role of paranoid grandiosity, the role of self-devaluation and low self-esteem in the development of paranoia must be taken into account. Even where the patient does not resort to the restitutive resource of paranoid grandiosity, his defensive stance may be seen as an attempt to salvage self-esteem. The essential technique is that of blaming, by which the patient absolves himself of responsibility for his deficiencies.

It has commonly been observed that paranoid and depressive states substitute for each other, and that they are found in different phases of the course of the same patient. Allen (1967) has pointed out that paranoia and depression, moreover, are two sides of the same coin. He sees depression as primary and the paranoid position as a defense. He feels that every depression involves a suicidal impulse, however repressed or latent. Paranoia, then, is an attempt to deal with the suicidal impulse by projecting it onto the environment and dealing with it as an external threat. He feels that paranoids are extremely sensitive to the suicidal aspect of depression, and that when the impulse becomes too strong for mechanisms of denial and projection to handle, then a suicide attempt may be made. The degree of intensity of the underlying suicidal impulse can be gauged frequently by the degree of elaboration and systematization in the paranoid destruction. Schreber's elaborate systematizations and fantasies of world destruction are a case in point. Without feeling it necessary to think of depression always at a level of suicidal intensity, paranoia can be seen as an attempt to deal with self-destructive aggression. There is no reason to doubt that, where the restorative process reaches psychotic proportions, the underlying self-destructive impulses are suicidal in intensity. Paranoid mechanisms may, however, also come into play at less intense levels of self-preservation, where the issues are more in terms of preserving self-esteem. Suicidal issues are more psychotic than neurotic issues, as Frosch (1967) has suggested. We must also keep in mind that paranoid mechanisms and paranoid defenses can be operative in relatively normal, adaptive, or developmental contexts in which suicidal issues are negligible.

In his reconsideration of the paranoid concept, Schwartz (1963, 1964) focuses on what he calls the "paranoid-depressive existential continuum." The central notion to the continuum is that of responsibility. The depressive pole of the continuum is that in which the subject refers the responsibility for his discomfort to himself; the paranoid pole is that in which the subject refers his discomfort to an object. The paranoid position in this conception is akin to Klein's formulation in which the internal experience, whether pleasurable or unpleasurable, is referred to objects. Internal pleasure is referred to a good object and internal lack of pleasure to a bad one. The paranoid position, therefore, recognizes no concept of responsibility, or guilt, or remorse, but only feelings referred to the good or bad qualities of external objects or part objects.

The paranoid is faced with his own inferiority and lack. He denies the intolerable idea of his own insignificance and shifts the responsibility for this elsewhere. He sees his deprivation as meaning that he does not matter to others because there is nothing in him that has any value to them. In this view, then, there is an underlying sense of inferiority and lack of worth—a form of narcissistic fixation and trauma—which the paranoid cannot internalize in self-referential terms, but only in terms of others. The denial of his significance comes from others. Thus, the essential aspects of the paranoid attitude include the underlying sense of worthlessness and insignificance, the inability to accept responsibility for these feelings, the incapacity to tolerate ambivalence and a consequent need to think in terms of absolutes. The paranoid maintains a constant need to find acceptance and recognition from others and is unable to accept himself as insignificant to them.

In her paper on manic-depressive states, Helene Deutsch (1965) reported on a lengthy analytic treatment of a woman who showed recurrent episodes of angry rebellion during the treatment. These passed directly into manic states without any noticeable depression. The patient's rebellious episodes were distinctly paranoid in character and the analyst was regarded as hostile, unloving, and persecuting. Deutsch remarks that this sort of paranoid element is present in all cases in which aggression appears as a constituent of the manic-depressive picture. The patient can fend off the guilt feelings associated with aggression by projecting the blame for this hatred onto the outside world. Thus the patient's own anger and hate can be considered as merely a response to ill treatment from others. The paranoia serves as a defense against the superego and the underlying depression. If the superego proved stronger than the defense, the patient would become depressed.

Another of Deutsch's patients became severely depressed following the death of her husband but then developed the delusional idea that her husband was not dead. Her delusional system developed around the idea that her husband was not dead, but that he had become a cruel persecutor trying to terrify her and do her harm. The patient was able to detoxify the malignant introject, which led her into a severe depression, by the projection of aggressive impulses onto the object. The transformation of the depressive position into a paranoid position served a defensive purpose in that it preserved the ego from the annihilative force of the fatal introject.

Ambivalence and Disillusionment

The depressive position is the more evolved and more difficult in that it implies at least a minimal capacity to tolerate ambivalence. The same object is both loved and hated. It is the presence of a loving relation within the ambivalence which makes the depressive position so difficult and which creates the regressive pressures for retreat to a paranoid stance. The depressive position is in this sense a healthier and developmentally more advanced position. Perhaps more than anyone else, Searles (1965) has pointed to the presence of loving ambivalence and its importance in many of the sicker patients. The basic feelings which structure the pathological relation between mother and child are feelings of fondness, adoration, compassion, solicitude, loving loyalty, and dedication. The illness is generated not merely out of mutual hatred and rejection, but out of a genuine love in the relation. The hostility serves as an unconscious and mutual denial of deeply repressed and loving feelings. Searles describes graphically how an outburst of murderous rage in a paranoid patient stemmed not only from the depression of murderous feelings, but from ambivalent feelings, both tender and solicitous as well as murderous, which derived from the patient's early relation to her mother (1965, p. 353). Love feelings are held as threatening and destructive and are repressed in a relatively primitive and poorly differentiated form. Love feelings are in fact poorly differentiated from primitive feelings of dependency and murderously destructive rage. This undifferentiated feeling complex occasionally breaks through repressive barriers in a frighteningly primitive form so that loving feelings must be avoided and repressed. The need is operative on both sides of the mother-child relation. The paranoid patient's libidinal impulses, therefore, both heterosexual as well as homosexual, carry with them these murderously ambivalent affects which threaten both the patient and his loved objects.

Searles points out that the paranoid position serves the function of masking and denying intense dependency needs which are devouring and destructive. The devouring quality of these needs leads the patient to feel that his loving dependency will destroy its object, or else that he will take in so much of the object that he will be engulfed himself. The paranoid surrounds himself with threatening and rejecting objects and thus circumvents the dangers of dependency and closeness. The paranoid mobilizes scorn, cynicism, hostility, and distrust in a constant effort to defend himself from these underlying positive affects. Searles describes a sense of disillusionment in these patients which is quite apt. Disillusion normally involves a series of steps—the object is first seen as wholly good, then with the emergence of undesirable characteristics as wholly bad, and these two sides are finally integrated into some more realistic appraisal of the person. The paranoid is more or less fixed at the second stage. For the paranoid, the disillusioning experiences came too early or with too great intensity for him to be able to integrate them. He could not work through the feelings of hurt and painful disappointment to reach that level of compassionate acceptance which allows integration of the object as a whole but ambivalent one. Instead the disillusioning object becomes split into disparate ones, and if the trauma occurs early enough these disparate percepts never become firmly integrated. The adult fixation on the object as bad is both a reaction to unresolved disillusioning traumata in the past and an unconscious defense against positive feelings and the threat of disillusionment in the present. The paranoid's struggles with his persecutors are in effect struggles with the unmanageably painful and therefore repressed disappointments and disillusionments he has suffered from them. For, as Freud indicated in his discussion of Schreber, the person who is hated and feared as a persecutor was once loved and honored.

These issues are profound and reach beyond pathology to the heart of human existence. It is not without reason that Schwartz (1963) could speak of paranoia and depression as an "existential" continuum. The difficulty of psychotherapy in paranoid states relates directly to this issue. The therapist must bring the patient face to face with his ambivalence and must help him to bear his depression and disillusionment—patient and therapist must move in the direction of what is most painful to each, not away from it. For many paranoid patients we cannot offer much more than human misery—without the murderous residues of infantile rage, hopefully. We hope for their capacity to love, to engage in the community of men—to share in human suffering without the torment of guilt, remorse, and hateful destructiveness. Speaking of the treatment of paranoid patients, Will has remarked:

> In this treatment procedure there is a reality that cannot be avoided, denied or talked away. There are losses that are not to be repaired; at best they can be acknowledged and the grief for them accepted. The great anxiety at separation, the haunting doubt of self, the ever-lurking fear of others, the living at the edge of loneliness—such are a part of one and may never be gone. Perhaps this is as it should be, no man being able without guilt to deny his being, or to divest himself entirely of that which has made him what he is. In psychotherapeutic work there is not a "recovery" of health, but only the gaining of strength to go on from what has been, into an unknown, with, perhaps, increased chance for both gain and loss, but with no clear prediction of the future. This courage to exist derives from some semblances of security in the past and must gain reinforcement in the present. There lies the task (1961a, p. 86).

PRECIPITATING FACTORS

While paranoia often runs an insidious and long drawn-out course of development, there are many cases in which a paranoid reaction, even of psychotic proportions, seems to be precipitated by an external event or series of events. The nature of such reactions and the influence of the precipitating events may shed some light on the genesis of the disposition to paranoia.

Threat to Life

Orbach and Bieber (1957) studied a group of patients who were confronted with the necessity of having a lifesaving operation. The patients were drawn from a nonpsychiatric population of cancer patients. They were faced with the reality of a potentially lethal disease and the prospect of mutilative surgery. These patients, in the face of this narcissistic assault, showed a variety of hypochondriacal, depressive, and paranoid responses. These reactions were accompanied by extensive denial in the face of the disruption of the individual's mechanisms for maintaining a sense of mastery and personal integrity. A critical factor was the need to maintain control over the threat posed by illness and injury. The assignment of blame for this loss of control determined whether the reaction took a depressive or a paranoid form. Attribution of blame to the self produced feelings of unworthiness, badness, and guilt. Attribution of blame to others brought feelings of anger over unjust injury and paranoid feelings. In the light of our preceding discussion, the depressive response can be seen as the primary response to threatened loss and narcissistic injury, and the paranoid pattern would emerge as a restitutive attempt to salvage self-esteem and a sense of worth.

Senility

A somewhat similar pattern can be detected in the emergence of paranoid symptoms in presenility and senility. The precipitants include the loss of physical function but also social isolation. Herbert and Jacobson (1967) studied a group of such patients over the age of sixty-five. Their premorbid personalities were generally schizoid or paranoid but they were precipitated into frank delusions by a background of disturbing factors which disrupted their capacity to cope. A lack of social contact was a prominent feature. Physical handicaps, particularly blindness and deafness, increased their isolation and intensified their personality difficulties, culminating in withdrawal to delusions and hallucinations. Here again the paranoid symptoms can be seen as an attempt to salvage some of the remnants of self from the ravages of loss and physical deterioration. The loneliness and isolation of these individuals undermined their self-esteem and sense of worth, and the paranoid construction enabled them to restore some measure of both. It also maintained some semblance of relatedness to objects (delusional relatedness is better than none) (Dias Cordeiro, J., 1970).

Social Isolation

In such cases, one is dealing with a combination of social isolation and physical impairments of sight and hearing. Social isolation itself, however, can be a significant precipitant. For example, the onset of paranoid symptoms were studied in a group of married women. To begin with, their husbands were older and rather socially isolated men who were reliable providers and were committed to maintaining the conventional appearances of marital role performance, but were virtually unable to express angry or sexual feelings directly. The marriages were stable but quite isolated from contacts with outsiders. The wife's psychosis emerged in the setting of the husband's withdrawal, along with cessation of intercourse. This deterioration continued until someone outside the family was involved; the wife was then hospitalized, and they then were able to reunite themselves and acted to once again exclude outsiders, including the hospital (DuPont and Grunebaum, 1968). The comparative isolation induced by the husband's withdrawal—especially in their already isolated situation—was sufficient to precipitate the frank psychosis.

The significance of social isolation should not be underestimated. The personality cannot maintain its normal functioning except in a matrix of social interaction. When disruptive events occur which isolate the individual from such interaction, normally adaptive patterns of response can no longer function adequately. Social isolation can frequently be found among the precipitants of paranoid reactions. But the concept of isolation has significance beyond the level of social contacts. Each individual shapes for himself a context of personal meaning and relevance which is embedded in a social matrix. The pattern of personal meaning is shaped by the multiple contexts of meaningful relatedness, and the overall meaning is continuous with, and in part derived from, the more general patterns of meaning which constitute the larger cultural matrix. There is a basic need for interaction with other individuals which is emotionally significant and meaningful to the subject. The terms in which such interpersonal contacts are felt to be meaningful are in part dictated by expectations which are culturally derived and internalized. The cultural matrix has considerable significance as a determining influence on what kinds of interactions are felt to be personally relevant and meaningful. When the susceptible individual is deprived of such a cultural matrix, his capacity to satisfy the expectations of others as well as to feel that his own expectations of others are in some sense fulfilled and reinforced is often severely impaired (Melon, J. 1970; Melon and Timsit, 1971). One can also think in terms of linguistic isolation as having parallel effects—"language shock" as well as "culture shock" (Steyn, 1972). The inability to respond meaningfully to others and the failure to receive meaningful responses from them throws the individual's sense of belonging out of kilter, with the result that self-esteem and the sense of personal worth are under attack. In individuals who lack a sense of security and identity and who thus must rely to a greater degree on the external supports for their sense of worth, cultural isolation can have a devastating effect. Prange (1959) has reported a dramatic case of an immigrant Chinese girl who developed acute features of delusional persecution and paranoia under these circumstances.

But even within the same culture—without the influence of cultural isolation—the effects of social isolation can be detected. In a sense, then, the effects of cultural isolation are mediated by social isolation, and the significant aspect is meaningful relatedness to other human beings. There is an interesting report of the development of paranoid pyschosis in a small group of Norwegian patients who had been Nazi collaborators during the war. After the war they were ostracized by their fellow countrymen. Even family and friends disowned them. The time lapse from liberation until the onset of symptoms ranged from 0 to 24 months, averaging 13 months. Apparently during the occupation they found a certain shared community among a small group of like collaborators, but with liberation this group was dispersed. They thus began to feel the full brunt of social isolation (Retterstol, 1968).

Loss of Function

As suggested above, the loss of significant functions can also serve to precipitate a paranoid reaction. Fitzgerald (1970) has reported on a series of recently acutely blinded adults. A major dysphoric reaction occurred in over 90 percent of these patients. A high percentage showed depressive affect, crying, withdrawal, lowered self-esteem, suicidal ideation, insomnia, guilt, shame, self-blame. A smaller percentage showed suspicion in some form or another, or they were found to foster some form of paranoid ideation. Depression is an easily understood response to the narcissistic trauma of loss of such an important function. The fact that a substantial minority of these patients showed a paranoid reaction to the acute loss suggests that the paranoia may be serving a defensive function in these patients as well.

In this regard, Rochlin (1965) has reported a case of an editor who was partially blinded as a result of an eye infection. The patient's initial reaction was depression—he felt deprived, impoverished, helpless and dependent. His dependence was all the more burdensome in the face of a family ethic that no one should receive more than any other and that all should share alike. His consequent low estimation of himself was a source of severe anguish. His hatred and resentment of his family was turned against himself in the form of self-destructive wishes. He became convinced that they hated him and always had. He developed the belief that they did not want him, were all against him, and that they were contemptuous of him because he was so useless. He became suspicious of their superficially good intentions toward him.

The loss of vision is a loss of a functionally important part of the self, and the significance of the loss is that it amounts to a narcissistic injury. The response is in the first instance and primarily a depressive one which undermines self-esteem and increases the sense of deprivation and narcissistic loss. The paranoid reaction comes as an attempt to redeem something of what has been lost. Behind the young editor's paranoid ideas, there was the conviction that he was cleverer than the rest of his family. His competence and attainments had served him both to bolster his inner insecurity and support his self-esteem, but also to channel his considerable competitiveness and aggression. His paranoid thoughts enabled him to serve both ends once more, but in a less productive manner.

The nature of the precipitants of the paranoid reaction varies, but they share a common element of producing a narcissistic injury. Narcissistic deprivation is followed by a depressive response which is marked by lowered self-esteem, feelings of worthlessness, a sense of inadequacy and inferiority. The paranoid response works to redeem some of the lost narcissism and recreates a meaningful pattern of relatedness in which self-esteem can survive. Consequently, the precipitants in no way determine the paranoid character of the individual's response, but they point to the intimate relationship between the dynamics of depression and those of paranoia. The genetic conditions which lie behind the paranoid pattern of response can be expected to share many elements in common with those which give rise to depressive states.

THE TRANSITION TO DELUSION

One of the critical phases of the process underlying the development of paranoia is the transitional phase in which the inner mental processes shift from a preparanoid organization to a more frankly paranoid form. Sullivan (1953) referred to the paranoid transformation of the personality: This transformation refers to the shifting of blame to others for what previously had to be maintained as a dissociated and intolerable aspect of one's own personality. The patient begins to elaborate personifications of specific evils. He can begin to ascribe to his enemies everything he has felt in himself to be a weakness, defect, or other inadequacy. He can rid himself of those impairments of his own personality from which he has suffered so long.

Sullivan describes a quality of illumination about this transformation. The patient gains the sudden insight which allows him suddenly to make sense out of it. The sense of inner defect is suddenly reversed and he begins to see that the others are really to blame. This transforming illumination is usually preceded by a suspicion and a sense of uncanniness which then flowers into the renovating realization—the cognitive reorganization which achieves the transfer of blame. The world becomes active, personified, blameworthy, malignant, and the patient is absolved of his weakness. Arieti (1961) describes the clearing of confusion and ambiguity and obscurity in terms of the dawning of a lucid realization. Things suddenly fall together and are assembled into a pattern that has meaning and relevance to the patient. The pieces of the jigsaw puzzle fit together in what Arieti calls a "psychotic insight." The psychotic insight establishes the paranoid psychosis. Will describes this process in the following terms:

> As communication fails isolation increases, and the sufferer finds himself caught in a nightmare, driven by a feeling of urgency to make sense of the incomprehensibles with which he is involved. He seeks a simple formula to make all clear, and if he is unfortunate he may elaborate the paranoid solution with its grandiosity, apportioning of blame, and chronic reformulation of the past and present to refine and protect a "system" that will reduce anxiety (1961b, p. 22).

The process has been described more in detail by Searles (1965). He suggests that the emergence of the paranoid delusion may represent the terminal point of a process in which the patient struggles to defend himself against his anxiety by a variety of mental states—perplexity, bafflement, uncertainty, confusion, and suspicion. Such defensive states develop an increasing intensity of pressure which seeks relief in the simplification of thought processes. The delusion provides such simplification and such relief. The process is analogous, according to Searles, to dream formation or development of a conversion symptom. Both involve complex determinants which are condensed into the conscious expression. The sense of intolerable complexity of thought from which relief is sought is in the subject's awareness.

As Searles sees him, the suspicious person is unable to tolerate, freely and spontaneously, in awareness the full intensity of his affective responses to both internal and external stimuli. Instead he delays and dilutes his response—anger in response to a provocative remark, for example—by focusing his attention in an intellectual way on the remark, searching for nuances and implications of what was meant, and why the remark was made. The inexorable flow of life will sweep more stimuli on him before any one has been processed. The normal person can allow himself to flow with the influx of stimuli and respond appropriately and proportionally to each. For the suspicious person the unavoidable influx of external stimuli and the constant pressure of internal stimuli become increasingly difficult, and the pressure involved in maintaining defenses against these emotions becomes increasingly intense and intolerable. He cannot bring himself to seek relief by admitting these affects into consciousness—they are simply too threatening.

The delusion brings relief from this increasing intensity and complexity. The delusion brings a reorganization of meaning which makes sense out of everything—or nearly so. It provides a focus for previously fragmented attention so that the influx of external and internal stimuli now can be related to this new formation. We have noted the characteristic selectivity of attention in paranoid states—stimuli that do not fit with the delusion are simply disregarded or discounted as irrelevant. The transformation is achieved by way of the paranoid construction. The increasing pressure which Searles describes has to do with the subject's inner needs and insecurity. The cognitive reorganization which is part of the paranoid construction is determined not so much by the logical force of available evidences, but by the inner subjective needs which the subject finds increasingly stressful and intolerable.

The paranoid transformation often serves as a resolution of an underlying process of schizophrenic disorganization. The perplexity, bafflement, uncertainty, confusion, and suspicion that Searles describes are frequently aspects of schizophrenic fragmentation and disintegration. Such aspects of depersonalization, however, can also occur at less pathological levels, but must always be seen as defensive operations. We can also add that the defenses are directed not to underlying feelings of anxiety alone, but also against underlying depressive affects. The shift from such unstable defensive patterns toward a paranoid resolution is an attempt to achieve cognitive closure and affective relief. To the extent that it achieves these objectives, the paranoid transformation becomes inflexible and relatively irreversible. To that extent the prospects for successful therapeutic intervention are diminished (Will, 1961a).

The emergence of clinical paranoia is an end stage of a developmental course which, at psychotic levels of severity, may extend back to the first year of life. The central theme of this development is the subversion of the child's will by a parent to believe that one's will can be unconditionally influenced by another person (Kovar, 1966). Through the years of childhood and adolescence, the patient may maintain himself in a prepsychotic state of uneasy equilibrium by avoiding situations in which the dictatorial parent or surrogate is not present. The presence of such a figure serves to organize and direct the preparanoid's life and activity. Kovar (1966) feels that, when such an authoritarian figure becomes unavailable, the delusional structure emerges. Its function is to provide the needed external influence. This observation is important, since it reemphasizes the fact that the paranoid defense is not only derived from inner uncertainties, disillusionments, and depressive anguish, but it has determinants which derive from the patient's environment as well. The inner dynamic determinants permit us to see the inner necessity of defense, but they do not help us to understand fully how it is that the pattern and style of defense becomes paranoid, rather than, for example, manic.

Some of the initial probing in this direction was done by Sullivan. He describes the paranoid transformation as passing from the feeling that one is the victim of one's own defects to the realization that one is the victim of a devilish environment. "It is not that *I* have something wrong with me, but that *he* does something to me." There is a passage from unhappy sanity to a relatively more comfortable paranoid psychosis. As he views the process, the self is built out of interactions—adjustments, expectations, compromises —with the culture. Our own inner security or insecurity is built on the recurrent evaluations of significant persons around us. We are blamed by others who may take out on us their sense of frustration with their own shortcomings. If we have a sense of this unfairness, we learn to blame them in turn for our own discomfort. The sources of our real discomfort date back to infancy and childhood and to our empathic ties to significant objects, before we could determine who was to blame for how bad we felt.

But the transfer of blame, while it saves us for the moment, is still open to question, and becomes even less secure when we subject it to consensual validation. In fact the real roots of feelings of insecurity and inadequacy are often hidden from us. To support his transference of blame, the paranoid provides an explanation, a context which gives meaning to, and substantiates, his blaming operation. The paranoid construction thus emerges in the service of completing, supporting, substantiating, and justifying the transference of blame which is the essential aspect of the paranoid transformation. The inner exigency to maintain the transfer of blame is the driving force behind the pressure to confirm the paranoid construction. The greater the insecurity, the more insistent the need to misinterpret or reinterpret every event to bring it into congruence with the basic construction. This delusional distortion may well reach schizophrenic proportions (Sullivan, 1956).

It is apparent that the transformation from preparanoid to paranoid thinking involves both a cognitive reorganization and a defensive realignment of the personality. Underlying both these aspects, there are genetic influences which determine the pattern of response and set the stage for the emergence of the paranoid defense. There are, therefore, genetic aspects of the problem which have to do with the painful aspects of the inner sense of inferiority, worthlessness, inadequacy, and a lack of a sense of autonomy and self-esteem—elements of the perception of oneself which are intolerable and require defensive maneuvers so that they can become bearable. There are also genetic aspects which have to do with the pattern and organization of defensive operations. Given the underlying need for defenses, what are the influences that mold the ego's resources to deal with such painful pressures in the direction of the paranoid defenses and mechanisms? When we talk about paranoid style, it is this cluster of influences that are most pertinent. However, we must not lose sight of the fact that the underlying necessities, to which the paranoid operation is a response, are also in their way determinants of the response. They are the irritants for which the paranoid position is a specific rejoinder. In this manner the several genetic currents interact and in a sense determine each other.

FACTORS UNDERLYING THE LACK OF A SENSE OF SELF-ESTEEM AND AUTONOMY

We are intent at this stage of our analysis on bringing into focus some of the influences which lie behind the feelings of inadequacy and worthlessness to which the paranoid reaction is a response. The general thesis that we are developing here is that the paranoid response is a more or less specific reaction to an underlying complex of depressive and autonomy-deprived self-impairments. The psychology behind such a deep sense of impairment cannot be adequately considered in the compass of what we are attempting here. But we can focus on some of the highlights of this inner state in order to help us to better understand the genesis of paranoia. It is our contention that part of the reason why the psychic response takes the form of paranoia lies in the nature of the underlying lack.

Restitutive Function

One of the important perspectives in this consideration is that paranoid states fit into a spectrum of patterns of response which share important characteristics with normal thinking processes. One aspect of this perspective is that paranoid processes share along with other mental states and activities the compelling human need to compensate for imagined or real deficiencies. As Rochlin has observed,

> Our efforts toward independence, autonomy and freedom (for instance, the skills that we master and the versatility that we show in adapting to and then influencing our environment), no less than the faiths we nurture, indicate how obliged we are to attempt to transcend our limits, to find reparations for our deficiencies, and thus to earn some relief from our frailties. It appears, therefore, that the development of character and behavior and their rewards may depend at least as much upon our failures and anguish as upon our satisfactions (1965, p. viii).

The same perspective applies analogously to paranoia—it redeems from deficiencies and frailties, but in a fashion that limits growth and deprives the self of more human satisfactions. Our question concerns itself with those aspects of the restitutive process in our patients which determine that the pattern of their response should take the form of paranoia rather than another more adaptive and liberating form.

Central to the whole consideration are the dread of abandonment and the basic conflicts over loss. Abandonment and loss are not merely traumata which cause pain and then pass. They have a profound effect which calls forth restitutive changes. The process of loss is always linked to its complementary process of restitution. The vicissitudes of the sense of personal worth and self-esteem are tied up with this cycle of loss and restitution.

The young child's narcissism and self-esteem are precarious and are subject to countless assaults from a series of inevitable experiences—parental disapproval, a shift of attention by the parents to a younger sibling, problems related to the loss of sphincter control, and a host of other experiences of childhood in which the self may feel devalued and self-esteem may be injured. An essential aspect of the development and maintenance of self-esteem is the continuance of meaningful relations between one's self and significant objects. One must have a sense of meaning something to others and of others meaning something to one's self in order to sustain a sense of inner value and esteem. When that meaningfulness is lost the satisfying image of one's self suffers. The essential narcissism on which self-esteem is based is prone to injury through the loss of objects. The more intense the underlying narcissism, the more prone the individual will be to experience loss of self-esteem in connection with object loss. Young children suffer loss but also demonstrate a readiness to accept substitute objects. In the progress of psychic development, when object libido has been established and the ego has been sufficiently altered by identificatory processes to exercise a self-critical function, object loss begins to be met with a lowering of self-esteem. Without this apparatus for self-devaluation, loss and abandonment are met with frustration, rage, and even hatred—but not with self-devalution.

The importance of the object in the process of forming and maintaining meaningful object-relations cannot be underestimated. When the object is threatened, object-relations are put in jeopardy. The threat can come from without—from the object or environmental factors that affect the object or the relationship; or it can come from within—when the object becomes the focus of the individual's aggression, he puts the object in jeopardy. In either case, the object-relation is endangered and the individual runs the risk of lowering his own self-esteem. The inner growth of the self is intimately linked to the quality of the individual's object-relationships. Without meaningful relations, the developmental and maturational processes underlying ego and instinctual growth are impaired, sometimes severely (Rochlin, 1965; Guntrip, 1969). The maturational process is more complex than this, but it cannot evolve in a reasonable fashion without a meaningful object outside of the self to which the self can relate and with which the self can interact. From the beginning of life, the ego depends on objects to complete the necessary conditions for development and adaptive functioning.

The psychology of depression is the psychology of disappointment and unfulfilled expectations. Disappointment evokes fury at those who frustrate the child's wishes and expectations, but when the frustrating object is also highly valued the frustrations come to represent abandonment. The wishes to destroy the object can be avoided only by turning the aggression against the self. On this point Rochlin comments:

> The tendency to direct the aggression against oneself comes about when the object has assumed an importance beyond its nurturing functions. As the object begins to have more value, the self has correspondingly less. The implications are significant because, as the narcissistic libido gives way to a measure of object libido, with emotional development, the fantasies of being left or abandoned become equated with being worthless. In other words, a sense of worthlessness occurs only when the object that may be lost is worthwhile. The loss of a worthless object is the loss of a trifle. It evokes neither aggression, a sense of devaluation, nor masochistic attacks (1965, pp. 16-17).

The ego has among its resources—increasingly as developmental progresses—ways of redeeming or minimizing its losses. The introjection of parental figures takes place relatively early in the development, as we have seen. These internalized figures become embedded in the character structure and thus minimize the impact of external loss. They also serve to divert hostility within, so that object losses in later stages of development tend to intensify internal aggression against the ego. Thus introjection serves important functions in preservation of objects, but it runs certain risks and dangers. The introjected object becomes part of the self and the destructive wishes and fantasies attached to it become a danger to the self. The introjected object becomes both a source of gratification, in that it preserves the essential tie to the object, and a source of menacing danger. The tension can be relieved in part by projection. The previously loved object is then perceived as directing criticism, reproach, and hate against the self. Internalization alone, then, is insufficient since, even though it preserves the object, it leads to isolation and withdrawal. Externalization becomes an important part of the process in that it reconstitutes the relation—and succeeds in both preserving the object and placating the inexorable and intensely destructive (suicidal) wishes of the superego.

Loss of Trust

While the dynamics of self-devaluation are attributable to somewhat more developed stages of psychic organization, the rudiments of it stem from the earliest strata of experience. The beginnings lie in the insecuriy of the infant in relation to the one who cares for him and who introduces him to the culture in which he will live. Will has noted that

> In his dependence upon mother, he develops the need and the ability to receive and to give tenderness and love, thus becoming inextricably bound—with anxiety, doubt, and fear, sorrow and delight—to the community of men (1961a, p. 74).

The issues here are very much those that have been delineated by Erikson—particularly in the earliest phases of development, which have to do with the development of a sense of basic trust and a sense of autonomy.

I will not attempt here to review Erikson's complex and rather well known analyses of these earliest stages of development. But I wish to highlight certain aspects and issues. The initial and primary issues related to the development of basic trust form the rudiments of later self-esteem and form an essential substratum on which a sense of autonomy can build. Erikson points out that

> The general state of trust . . . implies not only that one has learned to rely on the sameness and continuity of the outer providers, but also that one may trust oneself and the capacity of one's own organs to cope with urges; and that one is able to consider oneself trustworthy enough so that the providers will not need to be on guard lest they be nipped (Erikson, 1963, p. 248).

Two important points are involved. The first is that the state of trust is achieved by way of a mutual regulation between the mothering figure and the child. The second is that the process takes place within a matrix of objects. The two aspects play into each other in that the experience of mutual regulation between the child's own increasingly receptive capacity and the mother's techniques of satisfaction help to balance the homeostatic instability of the young organism causing discomfort. Such regulation must come from the interaction with an external object which becomes the source of comfort. The child must develop a sense of certainty and predictability about that object which will allow the mother to come and go without arousing inner anxiety and rage. She must become an inner certainty for the child, by which he achieves an inner sense of security and goodness. The human organism has a need for objects and a need for a sense of relatedness to objects which must be fulfilled in order for nonpathological development to take place.

Parental firmness must protect the child from the potential anarchy of his own undiscriminated impulses. The child must learn that angry wishes to have a choice, to assert his control, to manipulate demandingly, and to eliminate stubbornly will not jeopardize his basic sense of trust in himself and the others on whom he depends. If his environment encourages his self-assertion, it must also buffer him from meaningless and arbitrary experiences of shame and doubt. As Erikson points out, if the child is denied a well-guided experience of emerging autonomy and choice, he will turn the urges to control and manipulate against himself—the rudiments of precocious conscience and obsessive controls. The rage at frustrated wishes and needs must be turned away from the beloved and needed objects and can only be turned against the self in the form of shame and self-doubt. Erikson concludes:

> This stage, therefore, becomes decisive for the ratio of love and hate, coopera-tion and willfulness, freedom of self-expression and its suppression. From a sense of self-control without loss of self-esteem comes a lasting sense of good will and pride; from a sense of loss of self-control and of foreign overcontrol comes a lasting propensity for doubt and shame (1963, p. 254).

The derivatives of doubt, shame, and guilt can have disastrous conse-quences for later development. There is a presumption that the child de-serves or requires punishment, which mobilizes the underlying fear of loss and abandonment. He has a growing sense of resentment which both calls down further punishment and reinforces the sense of worthlessness and un-desirability. The groundwork is laid for a jaundiced view of life in which other persons are viewed as enemies and persecutors. These fears are inten-sified by the juvenile and adolescent need for acceptance which carries with it the fear of ostracism and rejection. Self-esteem suffers and one learns the techniques of disparagement and devaluation of others. The stage is set for the emergence of those defensive mechanisms which will support the tattered ego under this narcissistic assault (Sullivan, 1953).

The failure of these processes of mutual regulation and negotiation can be catastrophic. Mother and child become involved in a symbiotic relatedness out of which normal individuation takes place. If for some reason—fears of her own destructiveness or, more subtly, a breakdown in the process of mutual negotiation—the mother becomes psychologically aloof, the child's loving feelings for the mother cannot find adequate expres-sion and must be repressed. This leads to the introjection of the repressed aspects of the mother's personality and to the failure of the symbiotic rela-tion to be resolved in the course of development. Both mother and child fail to resolve the ambivalent phase of their developing relationship with the result that there is a clinging to their symbiosis. There is ambivalence in both mother and child which must be acknowledged, resolved and integrated into both mother and child's concept of themselves and each other before they can achieve real object-relatedness.

For the child, the failure to interact with the mother in meaningful re-latedness and to achieve a satisfying level of mutual negotiation and suc-cessful interchange carries with it a bitter disillusionment. The disillusion-ment is a response to the mother's incapacity to respond to the child's in-itiatives, so that she lets him down. Just at that point where he needs to perceive her as loving, trustworthy, and admirable, her own minimal self-esteem and fear of loving relatedness cause her to respond to his initiative toward closeness with an increase of anxiety and withdrawal.

The child is thus faced with an object for his identificatory strivings who is both low in self-esteem and somewhat ego-fragmented, and the child does identify with her, with disastrous results to his own developing ego. He emerges from this phase, naturally enough, not strengthened but profoundly weakened by his introjection of a mother-figure who is pervaded by a sense of worthlessness and whose ego-integration is precarious (Searles, 1965, p. 233).

It is interesting, in the light of these comments, to think of the Schreber case. White (1961) has pointed out that an often ignored, but central, feature of the *Memoirs* is the conflict with the mother. The mother conflict is represented in the figures of his wife, Flechsig, and God. The crucial elements were the primitive, destructive, dependent oral impulses toward the mother which formed the nucleus of his psychosis. These repressed and unresolved needs were channeled into the maternal introject, which was defended against at a more superficial level by identification with the aggressor—the competent and compulsively conscientious father. Beneath the compulsive masculine facade, there was the secret and repressed infant who wished to incorporate the mother. One can only wonder what fantasies of primitive destructiveness might have been triggered by his wife's recurrent miscarriages and their implications for the mystery of "soul-murder." His own infantile and repressed longings for the mother must have brought him at one level to hate his unborn children with whom he would have to share the mother. The destructive wishes were realized but could only be readmitted in projected form.

Loss of Power and Will

In the genesis of paranoia, these underlying psychotic issues are blended in varying degrees with the issues more specifically related to the development of autonomy. The impairments in a sense of autonomy, more than any other, relate to the development of a paranoid style. Schwartz (1964) has suggested that the adult capacity for free choice involves three elements—causality, power, and responsibility. The paranoid view involves a recognition of the fact that human beings can cause things to happen, but the paranoid lacks a sense of his own causal efficacy or power. The paranoid does not recognize in general that he has more power to influence his environment than he thinks he does. He has little sense of his effects on others. This is quite apparent clinically in paranoid patients who see themselves as victims without any sense of what they have done to elicit or provoke action against themselves. Schwartz points out that this style of adapting results from a pattern of parental interaction from which the child develops a view of himself as the passive target for other people's causal influence and as having no sense of power or responsibility for their activity.

Kovar (1966) has developed the same idea in terms of external influence—the central theme of the child's development is that the child's will is subverted by a parent who inculcates the belief that one person can unconditionally influence the actions of another. The future paranoid's development is characterized by avoidance of all situations in which the dictatorial parent or equivalent surrogate are not present to direct the patient's life and action. Such a controlling and invasive parent is a constant feature of the developmental contexts of paranoid patients. Frequently the pattern is related to early parent-child symbiotic relationships in which the child is fused with an omnipotent parent. The developmental alternatives are either submissive compliance or rebellious resistance. In the former case, an introjective resolution tends to predominate and the pattern of response tends to be more schizoid or depressed. Passive homosexuality may be a feature, but need not be (Ehrenwald, 1960). In the rebellious alternative, however, the resolution tends to be more paranoid. As we have observed frequently before, the latter alternative may serve as a defense against the former.

To add another comment on the Schreber case, we have discussed the deeper unresolved conflicts of dependency and destruction in his relationship to his mother. Those conflicts undermined the elements of basic trust in his development, and set the stage for the precarious resolution of issues of autonomy. We can also hypothesize that they left him with a deep inner sense of inferiority and inadequacy that was to take its toll in later years. But we would have little idea of the subsequent course of his growth in autonomy were it not for the efforts of Niederland (1951, 1960, 1959, 1963, 1968) in collecting the material concerning Schreber's father's teaching and disciplinary methods. It is plain from the *Memoirs* that Schreber's attempts to deal with the underlying conflicts—and we would suggest that symbiotic conflicts with the mother were active at the deepest level—took the form of an identification with his father. The mysteriously absent third chapter, however, only hints at a connection between the activities of some of the members of his family and the matter of "soul-murder." What Schreber had in mind may well have been crucial for our concerns here. But in the light of what we have learned about his father, the whole problem of "soul-murder" begins to take on meaning.

The father's rigid and sadistically punitive educational and training practices, which we know were practiced on the little Schreber, were calculated to break the child's will and bring him into complete submission. The regimen was a mental and physical assault on the child's nascent autonomy which relentlessly crushed any least sign of self-assertation or willfulness. Niederland (1959) is undoubtedly correct when he describes this procedure as an attempt on the father's part to projectively control his own impulses—sadistic and murderous and probably homosexual. His own impulses were projected onto the child, who had then to be relentlessly punished for them. The impact of these efforts on the psychic development of the young Schreber was catastrophic. The injuries to his sense of worth and self-esteem were irreparable, and the residues of self-doubt, shame, and guilt that he carried into his adult life could only be managed by paranoid and psychotic alternatives.

PART II

*CLINICAL PERSPECTIVES
ON THE
PARANOID PROCESS*

INTRODUCTION

We want to turn at this point to the clinical material upon which the present study is essentially based. In turning to this material, it may be well to pause for a moment of methodological reflection.

The psychoanalytic and clinical methodology is essentially one of naturalistic observation. It is based on the close observation and analysis of single case histories and the experience of the therapeutic encounter with individual patients, often extending over long periods of time. It is essentially this methodolgy which is employed in the present study.

Such an approach has its inherent limitations, but also carries within it certain specifiable advantages. The limitations are quite apparent, and Freud himself was quite aware of them. In commenting on the case of Dora, he wrote:

> It is, on the contrary, obvious that a single case history, even if it were complete and open to no doubt, cannot provide an answer to *all* the questions arising out of hysteria. It cannot give an insight into all the types of this disorder, into all the forms of internal structure of the neurosis, into all the possible kinds of relation between the mental and the somatic which are to be found in hysteria. It is not fair to expect from a single case more than it can offer. And anyone who has hitherto been unwilling to believe that a psychosexual aetiology holds good generally and without exception for hysteria is scarcely likely to be convinced of the fact by taking stock of a single case history. He would do better to suspend his judgment until his own work has earned him the right to a conviction (1905a, p. 13).

To this there can be added a methodological comment which Freud made a few years later regarding the way in which the analytic theorist uses case material. He commented:

> The cases of illness which come under a psycho-analyst's observation are of course of unequal value in adding to his knowledge. There are some in which he has to bring to bear all that he knows and from which he learns nothing; and there are others which show him what he already knows in a particularly clearly marked manner and in exceptionally revealing isolation, so that he is indebted to them not only for a confirmation but for an extension of his knowledge. We are justified in supposing that the psychical processes which we wish to study are no different in the first class of cases from what they are in the second, but we shall choose to describe them as they occur in the favorable and clear examples afforded by the latter. Similarly the theory of evolution assumes that in the animal kingdom, the segmentation of the egg proceeds in the same manner in those cases where a high degree of pigmentation is present and which are unfavorable for observation, as it does in those cases where the object of study is transparent and poorly pigmented and which are on that account selected for observation (1913a, p. 193).

Consequently our approach in the present study does not depend on the material or the analysis of any single case. Rather by a careful analysis of a series of cases and a comparative analysis of the patterns of development and defensive organization, we hope to elicit from each case in a differentiated manner certain aspects and dimensions of the paranoid process which are idiosyncratically expressed in the material of the respective case. To a certain extent the meaningful configuration within certain limits of variance can be identified in each of these cases, and consequently form a common core of paranoid dynamics which can be related specifically to the paranoid process. So there is differentiation and variation from case to case, which serves to flesh out and amplify our understanding of the paranoid process rather than reducing it simplistically to a core set of dynamics or inferences.

Consideration of a series of cases of varying degrees of psychological involvement, and from various strata of maturity of functioning and psychic organization, provides us with considerable enrichment of our understanding of the workings and functionings of the paranoid process rather than a reductively simplified and sterile appreciation. We are not seeking, therefore, a central core concept which reductively and simplistically provides an explanation for the identifiable patterns of paranoid pathology, but our concern is rather with the richness and variety of forms of expression of the paranoid process which reach a span that extends from the most disturbed levels of psychopathology to the limits of productive and creative human potentiality.

Moreover, as Freud has indicated in his comparison of the study of segmentation, we can expect to find that different aspects and different segments of the range of paranoid manifestations will be reflected in different ways in each of the different cases. This is a matter not merely of variation in the cases themselves, but also reflects the vicissitudes of obtaining clinical information which can vary so considerably from case to case. For some of these patients fairly extensive records were available, either from previous hospital admissions or from previous therapists who were able to provide more detailed impressions of the patient's history and pathology. Some of these patients have been involved in a therapeutic contact which has been considerably more extensive and deeper than others. Consequently like the egg of the sea urchin, our investigation cannot expect to learn the same things from all of them. It is only in their comparative study, with a sensitivity to the idiosyncratic variations that play themselves out from case to case, that we begin to grasp the manner in which the paranoid process has played itself out within the life experience of each of these individuals.

I would like also to offer a justification for presenting as detailed an analysis of these cases as I have made available here. From an analytic perspective there is no substitute for detailed case analysis. If one wishes to illustrate a point of theory or to explain a particular clinical finding or low-level clinical generalization, fragments of case histories are useful and often illustrative. But it is my conviction that in an attempt to study and formulate the workings of a process which is as extensive and central to human experience as the paranoid process, one cannot remain satisfied with bits and pieces. One must see the workings of the process in as great an extent as is feasible, not only in the current material which a patient brings to the therapeutic hour, but throughout the course of the patient's developmental history. A similar point has been made by Anna Freud in her foreword to Muriel Gardiner's volume on the Wolf-Man. Commenting on the dearth of adequately documented case histories, she observes:

> This failure in output where the practicing analyst's main preoccupation is concerned is not attributable to the fact that analysts know too little of their patients but to the opposite—that they know too much. The technical tools of analytic therapy such as free association, dream interpretation, resistance and transference interpretations produce a mass of data about the patient's life history, the healthy and the pathological sides of his nature, which, due to its bulk, is unwieldy and, if written up in undigested form, unreadable. To handle this raw material in a manner which produces, on the one hand, a vivid image of the individual person and, on the other hand, a detailed picture of a specific psychological disorder is no mean task and, as a literary achievement, far beyond the powers of most scientific authors. What is produced accordingly in our day are either snippets of clinical material used to illustrate some theoretical conception or, at best, one-sided clinical accounts which fail to acquaint the reader with the patient as a living personality (Freud, A., 1971, p. ix).

We can only hope, then, that in the case histories that follow we have been able to catch some of the living reality of the patient's experience as it reflects and expresses the underlying dimensions of the paranoid process.

CHAPTER 6

Miss Ann A.

THE PATIENT'S PROFILE

My first contact with Miss Ann A. came at a time when she was an inpatient in a large state mental hospital. She was living in a large ward which was primarily custodial in function. She was a plain, rather average and not terribly attractive girl. She was twenty-five years old and had been in the hospital for several months. As we shall see, it was only one of a number of hospitalizations. She was quiet and withdrawn on the ward. She initiated little or no contact with any of the ward personnel or with the other patients. She kept to herself, minded her own business and generally showed little interest or involvement with anything that was happening on the ward or in any of the hospital activities. Occasionally she would burst out in tears, but would resist any attempts to help her or to find out what was bothering her.

We began a course of psychotherapy that was to last over two years, and for most of that period she was seen at least once a week and sometimes more. She carried a diagnosis of chronic paranoid schizophrenia—the ward was one for patients who had been judged chronic and unresponsive to treatment. At that point in her career the paranoia was not very remarkable. She kept it quite hidden behind a facade of quiet passivity and compliance. It was only when she was stressed or when demands were put on her that she responded in terms of her feelings of persecution. At such times she would burst into tears and try to run away. When her anger and anxiety were really stirred, the paranoia became flagrant. Usually this expressed itself in delusions of a Communist plot against her.

The Family

To retreat to a point somewhere before the beginning, both of Ann's parents were Jewish in origin and background. Her father was a quiet and rather passive man. He was always quite close to his own family and particularly to his mother. He remained close to her even after his marriage and through the years was always very devoted to her—visiting her, doing things for her, taking her places. His relationship to her was close and dependent. He was a steady worker and was able to maintain a modest but adequate income through most of the years of his married life. For many years he drove a cab and finally rose to the position of manager of the cab company. For years he worked at night—thus making it necessary for him to sleep most of the day. This effectively minimized his contact with the family, particularly with his wife.

Ann's mother was four years younger than her husband. She was a blonde, obese, aggressive, and hostile woman. Her own relations with her family prior to her marriage had been difficult, if not chaotic. Her relationship with her mother was particularly poor. Her mother had been a bitter, critical, angry, hostile, depreciating woman. The relation to Ann's mother had always been one in which the mother had seen fit to criticize, pick on, devalue, and depreciate her daughter. The resentment was deep and pervasive in Ann's mother. She seemed unhappy with herself and with everything that surrounded her. This profound dissatisfaction extended to her family, her husband, her children, her home, her work—everything. Her relations with her family were governed by a domineering, intrusive, controlling, critical attitude that reflected her own inner dissatisfaction and resentment.

It is not surprising, therefore, that the family atmosphere from the beginning was riddled with anger, hostility, conflict, and bitter arguments and fighting between husband and wife. She was continually accusing him of being an inadequate provider and constantly confronting him with his deficiencies and shortcomings. She particularly resented his attachment to his mother. She also resented his maneuvers to stay out of the house—working nights, going out other times and leaving her with the children. Two constant focuses for their battles were the family financial situation and father's relative absence. It was never quite clear whether the mother was aware of the extent of the father's emotional withdrawal from her or not, but in fact for a period of nearly ten years prior to Ann's first hospital admission, the father carried on an affair. This was never explicitly talked about—or argued about—between them, but it can be presumed that the mother sensed something was up and probably resented it. In any case the degree of emotional separation between Ann's parents was severe—and their interaction was strikingly hostile and mutually destructive, particularly in the years of Ann's latency and adolescence.

The mother's relationship with everyone in the family was poor. There were two other siblings and her relation to both of them was hostile, critical, undercutting, domineering, intrusive, and controlling. Ann's older brother was her senior by three years. His relationship with the mother was also extremely argumentative, hostile, and conflictual. He and the mother were constantly at each other's throats. He was a quite stubborn and willful young man with an extremely low degree of frustration tolerance. His temper was explosive and he was given to enraged outbursts and had become physically violent with the mother.

The other sibling was Ann's younger sister, who was nine years her junior. This girl was extremely troubled and troublesome teenager. She was rather obese and this provided a constant focus for mother's critical and undercutting attacks. She had been doing poorly in school and in fact dropped out of high school in the second year. She had been a continual behavior problem both at home and at school, having been involved with a juvenile gang and in trouble with the law on several occasions. She had also been involved with drugs and developed a heroin addiction. She ran away from home on several occasions.

Thus it can be seen that this family system was riddled with psychopathology. The basic organization of the family system was provided by the pathological residues that each of the parents brought from his and her respective family of origin. The father brought his conflictual passive dependency and the mother her unresolved hostility and ambivalence. These provided the matrix within which the children interacted and assimilated the rudiments of deviant development. None of them escaped.

Ann's Development

It is within this unhappy, conflicted, difficult and hostile environment that we must situate our patient. Her early development was relatively unremarkable. Our knowledge of this early stage is limited by the fact that we are dependent on parental recollections. Parental recollections are noteworthy for their propensity to distortion, but even taking this into consideration we must recognize an extraordinary degree of masking and denial on the part of Ann's parents. They were both eager to put the blame on each other, but both were also strikingly oblivious to any difficulties that Ann may have had in her early childhood years.

Two significant facts jump out and provide a striking contrast to this uniformly pseudo-benign background. First, Ann was an habitual thumbsucker all through her childhood and did not give it up until she was almost twelve years old. Second, Ann had a persistent problem with enuresis until nearly the same age. Bed-wetting was a regular phenomenon and occurred almost nightly. This was a source of special concern to the mother, who picked on Ann for this and constantly ridiculed and shamed her for it. The patient, herself, in recalling this symptom felt that it usually happened when she was feeling anxious or frightened. One would have to conclude that anxiety and fright were a regular occurrence for little Ann.

The other striking aspect of this symptomatic material is that it was not volunteered by either parent. It came to light only under direct questioning and then was acknowledged only reluctantly. There was first an offhand admission that there had been some problems, but then only gradually and begrudgingly did the full extent of these problems become apparent. It was striking, the extent to which these parents were unwilling or unable to acknowledge deviance or difficulty in this child. This is particularly striking since these symptoms were so apparent and continued through so many years up through latency to the adolescent years. This in fact was a general pattern for these parents—an unwillingness to acknowledge difficulties and a tendency to denial. With Ann, the problem seemed to be more that the mother was so furious at Ann for not living up to her expectations and demands that she was totally unable to see it in terms of a problem for her daughter. She could only see it in terms of an attack on herself and an undercutting of her position as the good mother who raises her children properly. Any admission of a problem in her daughter, therefore, was equivalently an admission of defectiveness or failure on her own part—and she was strongly motivated to avoid this.

One can also suggest that the degree of denial suggests the extent to which these parents were unable to respond to Ann as a separate individual. They could see her only in terms of their own (primarily narcissistic) needs. Thus the pattern of projection and introjection was set in operation. The least tolerated and most hated aspects of the parents, particularly the mother, were projected onto little Ann, there to be rejected and denied.

Mother

Ann's mother manifested strikingly some of the elements of what Rickles (1971) has recently described as the "angry woman syndrome." These women come from families in which the mother was generally attractive, but often also alcoholic. They showed definitive preference for their male children and tended to devalue and denigrate their daughters—nearly to the point of open contempt. They constantly attack their husbands as inadequate—as providers and as lovers—and often accuse them of incestuous wishes toward their daughters. This is undoubtedly a projection of their own incestuous wishes for their fathers. Their life patterns are highly aggressive, sometimes with paranoid overtones. They are insecure in their own sexual role and identity as women and feel that all other women are lesbians. Their attitude toward their daughters is particularly undercutting and aggressively denigrating.

The history of Ann's relationship with her mother stands out as a particularly malignant one. Her mother—in the style of the angry woman —was constantly attacking Ann and undercutting her on every front. Ann was continually criticized, devalued, shamed, and held up for ridicule. The mother was intrusive and controlling. Everything that Ann did or attempted was subject to scrutiny and had to conform to the mother's judgment and evaluation. If Ann did not do it mother's way or in a way that mother approved, Ann was made to feel worthless, rebellious, and evil. Ann grew up with an abiding sense of inferiority and inadequacy. She had no sense of her own capacity or independence. What was attempted on her own was doomed to failure and bound to end in disaster.

Sexual and Social Life

The mother's intrusiveness and destructiveness were particularly marked in the sexual area. She resented deeply the more affectionate relationship between her husband and Ann. The way in which she spoke of this relationship and her feelings about it suggested that she conceived of it as a competitive sexual relationship between herself and her daughter. In addition, Ann's father maintained a more sympathetic but seductive relationship with her. This not only served to support the mother's fantasies but also served to keep her anger near the boiling point. The result was that mother's jealous attacks against Ann were continued and intensified —particularly as Ann grew into adolescence.

Ann was always a rather nervous, isolated, and withdrawn child. She did moderately well at school. She had average intelligence and was never forced to repeat a grade. As a child she had friends—mostly girls—and generally got along well with them. She belonged to several girls' cliques as a teenager. Her relationships were nearly all superficial and she was not really close to anyone. Her dating experience began at age thirteen. She dated boys almost exclusively on a steady basis—even if she went out with them only for a few weeks. She was very careful about dating only one boy at a time. Her fantasies about boys were highly eroticized. Her mother put constant pressure on her to go out, to date, to have a boyfriend. Much of Ann's fantasy life and her push toward heterosexual activity and steady dating was motivated by mother's insistence. Mother instilled the idea into her that any girl who did not have a special boyfriend was somehow inadequate or defective. At the same time, mother's attitude was inconsistent—as we might expect. Mother was constantly prying and questioning Ann about her dates and what went on. She intimated directly and indirectly that any girl who indulged in sexual feelings or practices was cheap, no good, a "whore," and would wind up without a man.

Ann's relationships with her peers were never very substantial or close. Her friends during childhood and latency years had been mostly girls. She did not have any really close friends. She was much preoccupied with the problem of being popular. This concern undoubtedly reflected mother's concerns about having popular children and her constant pressure on Ann to be popular and have friends.

It was in this context that Ann met her number one boyfriend—Bobby. She was fourteen and a half, and he was slightly older. She maintained a steady dating relationship with him until she was about eighteen. Ann regarded her relationship to Bobby as very special—something she would never forget. He was a hero to her, and she would spend hours daydreaming about him. During this period she did not go out with any other boys.

The pattern that can be discerned in these early years was ominous. Ann was becoming a withdrawn, isolated, quite schizoid girl who would not establish meaningful relations with her peers and who constantly carried the burden of her mother's expectations and her inadequacy in fulfilling them. The relation to Bobby was more one of fantasy than reality. It seems clear that Ann was becoming the bearer of the unsatisfied sexual impulses and feelings of sexual inadequacy—as well as the attitudes of sexual degradation—that were contained in her mother's projections.

Turning Point

Ann graduated from high school at eighteen. This marked a turning point in her life, the conjunction of several significant events which led to the precipitation of her illness. Within a short space of the time she graduated from high school, her family moved to a new neighborhood some distance from the old one, and Bobby broke off his relationship with her. There was thus a series of losses. She lost her school environment in which she had been able to maintain a fairly adequate level of adjustment, and thus had to surrender her more or less superficial relationships with schoolmates. She lost her ties to the old neighborhood and moved to a new one in which she knew no one and in which she felt that she was being watched and evaluated by the strangers who were her neighbors. There is a pathetic quality to this loss that seems remarkable. In later years, Ann would drive back to the old neighborhood and visit the places she knew as a child. There was a nostalgic longing in her voice when she talked about this old neighborhood. It seemed to have represented a part of her life when she was less troubled, more in touch with life and people around her, and more superficially adjusted. And finally, and perhaps most significantly, she lost Bobby.

It was as though Ann never really recovered from these losses— particularly the breakdown of her relationship with Bobby. She could never accept that loss and seemed to cling to that relationship and her fantasies about it in a desperate and forlorn way. Subsequent to that loss, in any case, she became increasingly isolated and withdrawn, and increasingly disturbed. She tried working, usually in a clerical or secretarial position, but was unable to keep any of her jobs for any extended period of time. In several of these jobs, she developed a crush on older men—usually men who were single or divorced. She would daydream about these men constantly and imagine herself going out with them, talking to them, etc.

In the meantime, the mother was putting more pressure on her to get a boyfriend and start dating. Mother found a boy who she thought would be good for Ann, and put pressure on her to go out with him and to marry him. Ann did not particularly like this boy and finally broke up with him. Mother, of course, was furious. She saw Ann's action as an attack on herself, as undermining her wishes, and as an attempt on Ann's part to undercut mother herself by not getting married. Mother saw the whole situation in highly narcissistic terms of what people might think of her as a mother if she had an unmarried daughter. She seemed incapable of thinking in terms of Ann's wishes or happiness.

The sexual area of Ann's life—while it had always been an area of confusion and uncertainty for her—became a central preoccupation and an area of conflict. Her sexual contacts had been generally quite limited. Even though she dated steadily with Bobby over several years, sexual activity was limited to kissing and occasional petting. She would not permit intercourse, although she acknowledged that she had wishes for it. She felt terribly conflicted over these wishes. She felt that the only way she could hold Bobby was by responding to his sexual interest—but her wishes and fantasies made her feel guilty and vile. Even a moderate degree of sexual activity made her feel cheap and dirty and worthless—the "whore" that her mother so frequently accused her of being. After the loss of Bobby, these feelings became increasingly intense. She felt more and more guilty about sexual feelings or thoughts. For several years she had bleached her hair, but even this began to make her feel cheap and dirty. Even when she walked past a group of boys and they made suggestive comments to her, she felt shamed, cheapened, and vile, as though their comments turned her into a prostitute or whore.

Over the course of several months following these losses and changes in her life. Ann became more and more withdrawn, isolated, and increasingly disturbed. Her behavior became more and more automatic and robotlike. She gradually lost interest in things around her, became more apathetic and depressed. She kept to herself more and more. She stopped dating and avoided any contacts with boys. If she was approached in any way or if a boy talked to her, she felt ashamed and guilty. She became more and more suspicious, feeling that people were insincere and deceitful. She felt that people at work or on the street or bus were talking about her, criticizing her, saying that she was a cheap whore and prostitute. The feelings of loss, abandonment, confusion, doubt, suspicion, and helpless vulnerability had crystallized into a frank paranoid psychosis.

The Emerging Psychosis

During this period she developed a variety of symptoms. She began to hear voices talking about her—when there was no one there. She began to have anxiety attacks, feeling cold, clammy, tense, and frightened. She described a number of visual illusions—everything seemed as though it were made out of gold, and things seemed smooth and round. Everything looked small and distant. Her desk at work looked like a miniature. The people around her looked stiff and lifeless—like stick figures. She also described several depersonalization phenomena. At times she felt that she was part of the desk—she would feel cold and lifeless, like an inanimate object. She felt at times that her arms and legs were not attached to her body and that they didn't belong to her. She began to feel that her body was turned inside out and that she could not stand up straight. Her thinking became increasingly disorganized and bizarre, and her capacity to function at work completely deteriorated. One night she ran away from home in a panic, and this precipitated her first hospital admission. She was just twenty years old.

During this hospitalization Ann began treatment with a new doctor. She continued to see this doctor for a period of over two years, and formed an intense and highly eroticized transference with him. The intensity of this relationship was evidenced by the fact that after several months of treatment the doctor had to cancel one appointment. In response Ann ingested a bottle of Excedrin tablets and had to be rehospitalized. For some time, her symptoms had been primarily depressive. She had been quite apathetic and somewhat disorganized, but otherwise functioning reasonably well. She impressed several interviewers during this period as being neither psychotic nor paranoid, but as a case of chronic and acute depression of a more neurotic sort. During the hospitalization following this ingestion, however, her behavior became increasingly bizarre and her thought patterns—while remaining quite depressed in content—became increasingly delusional. For example, she became somewhat friendly with an older male patient who subsequently died. Ann became quite depressed after this event, and complained that she could feel his coffin lying on top of her when she lay down. Then she began to feel that his coffin was inside her stomach.

The impression that she gave at this stage of her illness was one of severe depression—yet with occasional expressions of intense inner turmoil and distress. She was a sad and withdrawn figure on the ward. She complained of the fact that she was not going steady, that all of her friends were working or getting married and she could not, that she felt lifeless and hopeless and saw the world around her as inanimate. She was utterly confused about her own identity—not knowing who or what she was. She felt that there were no boundaries between herself and other people, or between herself and things near her. She continued to hear voices telling her she was no good, cheap, dirty, worthless. She talked about her fear of becoming a mental patient for the rest of her life, but felt helpless because she could do nothing about her mother who was always intruding in her life and trying to make her sick.

Her behavior at this time became quite regressed. She became quite withdrawn, spent most of her time in a fantasy world—much of which had to do with eroticized fantasies about her therapist. She was quiet and kept to herself most of the time, but whenever approached by the staff or asked to do anything, she would become quite tearful and regressed. This behavior served only to anger the staff, who felt that she was manipulating them by her regressive behavior. Any request, even for the most minor task, was met by weeping and crying and complaints of helplessness and hopelessness. The staff responded with anger and guilt feelings, fearing that their requests were making her sicker. If she were confronted in any way or if any pressure were put on her by the staff or by other patients, she would become quite angry and frankly paranoid. She would become quite upset and tearfully complain of a plot against her, that the staff wanted to hurt her and that they were part of the Communist plot to ruin her mind and damage her for life. In this context, she was finally transferred to the ward for chronic female patients. She remained on that service for over a year. Finally she went home for a visit and did not return to the hospital. She continued to see her therapist on a weekly basis as an outpatient.

She continued to live at home—but she remained quite withdrawn, staying in her room, talking little, doing nothing. She continued to meet with her therapist until he was drafted into the armed services. This brought the treatment to a close. This was very upsetting to Ann, and subsequently she became more and more morose and depressed, spending long hours crying and moaning, sleeping most of the day, and finally beginning to slowly decompensate again. The situation at home again became increasingly difficult until finally the mother had Ann sent back to the hospital. When Ann got to the hospital she was quite disorganized, delusional, and angry. She complained about the loss of her therapist, angrily talking about how he rejected and jilted her "for other women." She called herself a cheap, lousy whore. "Whatever I do, my life won't change . . . The same lousy people, people like you, are making me into a criminal, like that fourteen-year-old girl, lying on the floor in the hospital, playing with herself . . . You and the Communists and the rest of the cheap psychiatrists are interfering in my life, trying to hurt me, making accusations, making me feel like an animal until I die . . ."

Ann's state of mind at this point was delusionally psychotic and frankly paranoid. She saw herself as extremely vulnerable and easily hurt. She saw others around her as hard, cynical, cruel, and specifically as having ulterior motives in all that they did. These motives were directed against her—they intended to hurt her, trying to cheapen her into a sexually perverted animal, trying to ruin her mind and make her crazy. She saw herself a victim of malignant forces and persons around her from which she could not escape. Along with this strikingly paranoid core of her illness, there was an overwhelming sense of defeat and despair. She thought little of herself and harbored deep feelings of worthlessness, inadequacy, helplessness, hopelessness. It was striking that her self-accusations and self-devaluing followed a pattern set by her mother. Her accusations against herself were the accusations that her mother had always brought against her, and which the mother continued to cast in Ann's face.

It should be noted that the unexpected loss of her doctor was another traumatic abandonment which precipitated her into acute psychotic decompensation. The loss re-created the abandonment she had experienced when she lost Bobby. The transference aspects of these involvements were apparent, as we shall see.

Role of Parents

Ann was capable of recognizing and expressing some of her intense hatred for her mother. She rejected and reviled everything that her mother stood for. She struggled to make herself everything that the mother was not. Where mother was loud, pushy, aggressive, domineering, and intrusive, Ann strove to make herself quiet, unobtrusive, passive, inhibited, withdrawn. Her adopting this inept and passive position also served the important function of hiding and masking her murderous impulses—particularly against her mother. At the same time, Ann had accepted and in fact embodied her mother's critical and devalued perception of her. She lived out in her illness the distorted and deviant perception of herself that her mother had continually thrust on her.

The parents' responses to the efforts to treat Ann were interesting and characteristic. The father remained distant and relatively uninvolved. Whatever contacts there were found him to be quite guarded and distant. He was suspicious of hospitals and psychiatrists, and did not trust their motives. He was constantly busy intellectualizing about Ann's difficulties in a superficial way. He made it abundantly clear that he felt threatened by psychiatrists. He needed to absolve himself of any part of Ann's illness and responded to questions quite defensively, as though they were accusations of inadequacy on his part or of some responsibility of his own for her illness. He was quick to blame his wife whenever the opportunity arose.

Ann's mother was a source of difficulty all through the course of Ann's treatment, not only in these early stages but in the later stages as well. She would constantly write letters to involved hospital personnel, would make frequent telephone calls to doctors and social workers involved in the case, was continually making complaints about not being included in the treatment, about not knowing what was going on. This activity was quite undermining and threatening for Ann. It made the mother a constant threat to her treatment and a constant preoccupation. Ann could never quite reassure herself that the doctors were not in collusion with her mother. She repeatedly and endlessly questioned whether what she might say in therapy would be repeated to her mother. She repeatedly would ask whether any comment or suggestion of the therapist, or any administrative change, had been instigated by her mother. She was constantly preoccupied, consequently, over whether anything that was done for her by the therapist or hospital staff was motivated by the malignant wishes she attributed to her mother.

The pathological influence of the parents was unmistakable. Paranoid attitudes and projections played a prominent role in both parents. The father was guarded, suspicious, and engaged in frequent displacement of responsibility, particularly in his eagerness to cast blame on his wife. His attitude to Ann was seductively supportive and caring, but was clouded by his need to ally himself with her against his wife. Ann's mother was clearly the primary persecutor who was continually controlling, intruding, and pressuring Ann to submit to her demands and expectations. Her demanding intrusion was a constant threat to Ann's autonomy and to the viability of her therapy.

Therapy

It is at this point that I began my association with Ann. She had been in the hospital for several months and had not had any therapeutic contact since she had been forced to interrupt treatment almost two years before. She was happy to have a doctor again—particularly since it seemed to suggest that she was not altogether hopeless and that it might be possible for her to get out of the hospital. However, she obviously approached her relationship to me with mixed feeings. She could not be sure that I was to be trusted. Was I going to be like the other doctors who put her in the hospital and were trying to hurt her and ruin her mind—who somehow were in collusion with her mother and were carrying out her mother's malignant wishes against her? Or was I going to be like her favorite therapist who helped her and did so much for her?

Much of her talk was spent in musing about her former therapist. She obsessed again and again over things that he told her or things that he did. She was intensely preoccupied with what he might have meant, with what he thought about her, with what his actions and behavior toward her might have meant. It was terribly important to her that all these concerns could be interpreted in a positive light. Any suggestions of negative feelings or implications were very disturbing to her. Any suggestions that she might have had some positive feelings for him were met with vigorous denials and angry accusations of trying to make her out to be a cheap and dirty whore. This was often accompanied by tearful distress and a need to run out of the room.

The most difficult thing for her to integrate and talk about in that relationship was the fact that it ended. She felt it to be a rejection but was very confused about why it ended and whether the doctor did or did not want her as a patient. It represented a violation of the fantasy that she tried desperately to form and maintain—that she had a special and privileged relation to her therapist. It was very much as though the figure of Bobby and her doctor had somehow become fused and confused in her mind. Erotic feelings and fantasies stemming from her relation with Bobby were displaced into the relationship with her doctor. The disappointment in losing her relationship to Bobby and her inability to face and resolve that loss were transposed into her relation with her therapist. She clung to the fantasy and memory of that relation just as she did to the fantasy of her relationship with Bobby.

At a deeper level, both of these highly eroticized and delusional relationships served as a displacement for erotic and incestuous wishes for her father. The relation to her father was close and supportive. She felt that her father understood her, and wished her well—in contradistinction to her mother. She constantly turned to father for support and comfort. She confided in him, sought his advice, tried in a variety of ways to use him as a protective ally against her mother. The father's behavior toward her also had a rather seductive quality. In her own mind, Ann was quite unable to distinguish between sexual and erotic feelings and positive feelings she had toward her father. She generally avoided talking about her relationship with him and responded to any indication that she might have positive feelings for him as though it were an accusation of sexual longings that were frankly incestuous.

This perplexity in her own mind was reinforced both by the father's actually seductive response to her and by her mother's nearly delusional jealousy of the relation between father and daughter. The mother would angrily attack her husband and accuse him of wanting to sleep with Ann rather than with herself. And at the same time she would accuse Ann of having incestuous feelings for her father. Even as she was making these accusations, however, the mother also was pushing Ann on her father in subtle ways—making her more dependent on him and pushing her into closer physical contact with him.

Thus, it gradually became clear that much of Ann's confusion and difficulty in dealing with her relationship with both Bobby and her therapist was a reflection of deeper conflicts that stemmed from her libidinal involvement with her father. While this aspect of her difficulty was quite clear in the material, it was completely unavailable to her on any conscious level. The least approach to this material was incredibly threatening and would provoke severe paranoid anxiety and emotional turbulence.

The Attack

Ann's intense paranoid struggles with her mother continued through the course of treatment. Mother was constantly involved—intrusively telling Ann what she should do, criticizing her for not doing what the mother thought she should do. Ann interpreted her mother's intrusiveness as picking, as trying to hurt and destroy her, as trying to drive her crazy. Her struggle with the family came to a head soon before her second hospitalization. She started answering her mother back and the mother hit her. Ann started to hit back, and at that point the brother and father jumped in and restrained both the mother and daughter. Ann saw this as a militant attack on herself. She interpreted the intervention of her father and brother as their defending her mother. For her it represented proof that the whole family was against her and that they wanted to hurt her. She saw the intervention not as a preventing of further violence, but as an attack directly on her. We shall see similar critical events in the course of some of our other patients histories. An event occurs which gives substance to the patient's evolving belief, not only that the malicious member of the family is trying to hurt the patient, but that the rest of the family is in collusion against the patient. Such events are often taken by the patient as the critical bit of evidence which proves and clinches the paranoid delusion. They come to carry a burden of conviction far beyond their merit.

For Ann, this provided a critical focus for her belief that the family was trying to hurt her—as well as a verification of that belief. When we discussed this episode in therapy, I tried to point out that perhaps her father and brother were only trying to protect her from being hurt. She responded angrily to this suggestion—asking in great consternation how I could try to defend their action. They had so obviously tried to kill her, and I was trying to defend them. Her conclusion was that I must in some way be conspiring against her and that I also wanted to kill her.

Displacements

Along with these concerns about her family, Ann developed some interesting problems in the hospital. She got into a confrontation with the head nurse at one point over the performance of her ward work. Ann was omitting her ward job, and the head nurse of the ward consequently imposed some restrictions on her. Ann was furious, but characteristically expressed her anger in a paranoid manner. It so happened that the head nurse was black. Ann carried on a tirade against dirty "Niggers," saying that they were filthy, no good, cheap, and that they were all sex perverts. She carried on her tirade not only against the head nurse but also against the doctors and all the nurses, in fact the whole hospital. They were all out to get her. They were all in a plot against her. The head doctor in charge of the ward she accused of being a homosexual. They were all in the plot against her and were in league with the Communists. When questioned about her feelings about blacks, it became clear that the views Ann expressed in her paranoid rage were views her mother had often expressed.

Ann's rage and paranoid feelings about the head nurse continued for a considerable time. Her anger extended to me as well because I did not defend Ann. She felt that I was taking the nurse's side and therefore that I was against Ann. She cast the head nurse in the same light as her mother, and ascribed the same malignant intentions to her. Moreover, she felt that I was treating her as though she were of less value and lower than the nurse, who was a dirty, no good, sexually perverted "Nigger." Ann felt confused and angered that I would treat her as lower than such a person. How could I pretend to want to help her and still treat her like that? Similar questions would arise whenever Ann caught sight of any of my other patients—particularly the female patients. She would wonder whether I liked them more than I liked her, often being able to express fears that if I preferred them I might then want to get rid of her. She would often have to turn these feelings and doubts defensively around and express them in terms of her doubts about me and her wanting to stop treatment because I wasn't helping her enough. These attacks on me were usually very angry and bitter, and were accompanied by comparisons between me and her former therapist, who had helped her so much and whom she continually idealized.

Ann was able to gradually resolve some of her anger toward the head nurse during her hospital stay. As her relationship to the nurse improved, however, she became increasingly uncomfortable. She was afraid that if she should start liking blacks then she might be attracted sexually to black men. She was able at that point to admit that she had felt some attraction to black men in the past, but she feared that this meant that she was being dragged down to their low level. But in fact she felt that she was a good Jewish girl who would never do such a thing.

Another of the continual and overriding concerns that Ann had throughout the course of her treatment was the matter of privacy and confidentiality. She would repeatedly and constantly ask whether anything she confided to me would be private—whether anyone else would know about it. As she put it, she wanted to know if anyone else would ever "know her business." The question came up continually in regard to almost any contact that she had which bore the slightest relation to treatment. Nurses, attendants, other doctors, rehabilitation counselors, other patients, the people who ran a halfway house where she lived for a time, etc.—all were suspect, all became candidates for intruding on her life and her "business." The central person on whom this concern was focused, of course, was her mother. The mother's constant efforts at meddling in the treatment and intruding inevitably provoked this concern for Ann. But it was as though the mother's intrusiveness and evil intentions against her had been generalized to include anyone who might have the thinnest of concerns with her problems.

DISCUSSION

Mother-Child Interaction

The salient feature that emerges from this patient's history with considerable clarity is the destructive and undermining relationship between the patient and her mother. One is reminded inevitably of Searles' (1965) concepts of the destructive aspects of the mother-child symbiosis and what he calls the effort to drive the other person crazy, and their role in the etiology of schizophrenia. I would like to discuss some of these elements—not with a view to their role in the schizophrenic process, but in order to focus on some of the influence in the genesis of the paranoid process.

Searles points out that there are two important factors in the dynamics of the mothers of schizophrenic children. The first is the fear of her loving feelings, and the second is the mother's impaired sense of self-esteem. Both of these factors relate to an inadequate relationship of the mother with her own mother. The early life experience of not feeling loved and accepted by her own mother and the related need to repress her own loving feelings result in the feeling in adult life that she is unworthy of real love and devoid of a real capacity to love others, including her own children. This disposition in the mother prevents her from accepting the child's loving helpfulness and tends to undermine the latter's sense of worth. This impedes the important identifications with the mother that underlie ego development.

An additional factor, however, comes into play particularly and peculiarly in the relationship of the mother with the schizophrenic child. The mother is unable to see the child objectively as a unique and different individual, but responds to it in terms of unconscious perceptions which stem from her own unconscious and subjective needs. She sees the child as the embodiment of qualities and characteristics that represent the repressed aspects of herself. She tends to see the child as the lonely, isolated, hopelessly stupid, rejectable, or lustful self. We can see this aspect of the maternal projection clearly in Ann's relation to her mother. Her mother was constantly attacking Ann with these sorts of accusations—calling her stupid, worthless, a whore, dirty, a prostitute, etc.

But there is another side to the ambivalence. Along with this depreciating attitude, such mothers tend to react as though they were omnipotent mother-figures whose acceptance and approval their daughters constantly seek—without hope of ever attaining. Searles conceives of this aspect of the mother-child interaction as fostering the intense symbiosis which becomes a reflection of the symbiotic relatedness of the mother to her own mother. The mother thus transfers feelings and attitudes that were originally part of the symbiotic relationship between herself and her own mother when she was a child to the present relationship between herself and her daughter.

Thus, in Ann's relationship with her mother, some of the aspects of the intensely ambivalent and symbiotic relationship between her mother and the mother's own mother were reflected. The mother's relationship to her mother had been conflictual and destructive. The mother was caught up in an endless quest for approval from her mother which she never obtained. The quest for approval was shifted to little Ann—particularly in terms of the mother's need to have Ann endorse her mothering by performing as mother wished. Ann's failure to do this was interpreted by the mother as an attack which was intended to undercut and devalue her as she had been undercut and devalued by her own mother. The mother's perception of Ann was thus colored by the reprojection of her own introjected mother image onto Ann—with the result that Ann was seen as a malignant, evil, and destructive agent. Ann's introjection of this projection formed the nucleus of her pathology.

Pathological Introjection

The pathological introjection can have severe effects on the child's development. The positive and constructive ego-identifications require a context of loving admiration for the object of the identification—as well as the welcoming on the part of the parental object of the child's expressed wish to become like the parent. If this context does not obtain and persist, the process of psychic development comes to depend more on introjective mechanisms which more globally incorporate the parental images—including negative and destructive aspects—in the service of defense against the anxiety and ambivalence in the relationship (Meissner, 1971b). Thus the mother's low self-esteem and fear of loving relatedness frustrates the child's admiring wish to identify and forces the child to resort to more defensive introjections. The introjection can be crippling for the child. Searles comments:

> The child is thus faced with an object for his identificatory strivings who is both low in self-esteem and somewhat ego-fragmented, and the child does identify with her, with disastrous results to his own developing ego. He emerged from this phase, naturally enough, not strengthened but profoundly weakened by his introjection of a mother-figure who is pervaded by a sense of worthlessness and whose ego-integration is precarious (1965, p. 233).

The destructive maternal introject is again reprojected in the paranoid delusion. In Ann's case, the projection displaced the hostility and evil intentions derived from her mother onto the other important figures of her world and became enlarged at their most intense level to the dimensions of a Communist plot to destroy her mind and to drive her crazy.

Relation to Father

We shall return to this delusional thought, but we should first take into consideration Ann's relationship with her father. Searles comments that the histories of schizophrenic patients frequently present the father as the warmer and more accessible parent and the patient as more attached to the father than the distant and rejecting mother. The father is generally a rather infantile individual who responds to the child as a mother-figure. We have noted Ann's father's close and rather dependent relationship to his own mother. His caring solicitude for his mother seems to reflect his own dependent need for her and for her approval. This suggests that his relation with

Ann was influenced by his own needs for approval and for enacting a warm mothering role. His warmly mothering and seductive approach to Ann, therefore, seems to have been generated from deeper levels of his own inner conflict. He intervened in the relationship between Ann and her mother in part to fulfill these inner needs, and in part to have Ann for himself—as he wished to have his mother for himself. The conflict which this set up for Ann between her own wishes for loving dependence and affectionate gratification and the more sexual and seductively threatening aspects of the relationship with her father were clear.

The father's solicitude and affection for Ann were not simply that, but were caught up at the same time in the hostile context of his relationship with his wife. In part his relationship with Ann gave him a certain amount of satisfaction and affective reward. It also was a way for him to assuage his guilt over his own failure to intervene more effectively between Ann and the destructive assaults from her mother. At the same time, however, the attention he paid her served as a provocation and a counterirritant directed to his wife. It was his way of thumbing his nose at his wife and putting her in second place, with the result that his relation to Ann was continually kept in the focus of the angry process of attack and counterattack that went on between the two parents.

Maternal Hostility

We come now to the question of the intense hostility that Ann was subjected to, particularly from her mother. A number of authors have focused on the relation between the expression of parental hostility to the child and the determination of psychosis in the child. Searles (1965) has described the process in terms of an effort to drive the affected person crazy. In many cases there is a history of psychological assault by the parents on the child—an assault that is reflected in the patient's delusions. The effort to drive the patient crazy is equivalent to any form of interpersonal activity which creates or increases the psychological conflict in the patient.

There are a number of ways in which such inner conflict can be promoted that have relevance for the present case. If one person stimulates another sexually in circumstances in which expression of sexual needs or their gratification would be disastrous, conflict is created. In many schizophrenic histories, seductive behavior on the part of the patient tends to foster an intense conflict between aroused sexual impulses and the rigid and punitive superego taboos against incest. This was certainly a factor in Ann's relationship with her father.

The conflict can also arise in terms of the child's wishes to mature and assert its own individuality as opposed to regressive wishes to remain involved in an infantile symbiosis with the parent. In Ann's case this regressive pull was quite intense. One of the fascinating aspects of her course was the way in which she sabotaged any attempts to help her function more independently from her parents. She frustrated or derailed any efforts made to provide living arrangements which would allow her to separate from her family. She would cooperate in efforts to help her get involved in work situations which would allow her some degree of financial independence—but then would begin to function in inadequate ways that were clearly below her own level of current capability, making it necessary for her to retreat to a more passive and withdrawn situation in which her dependence and involvement with her parents were preserved and even intensified. While she was able to express her wishes to depend on her father and to have him take care of her, she was not able to deal on any conscious level with the fact that her regressive movement had the effect of drawing her closer to her mother. That closeness was intensely ambivalent and was in many ways a resubjection of herself to the mother's attacks, but it was an aspect of her involvement with her mother that Ann was inexorably drawn to, like a moth to the flame.

Searles has pointed out that similar conflicts can develop around the child's wishes to help the parent. Parents often make pleas for sympathy and understanding from the child, but then frustrate and reject the child's efforts to be helpful. The child's sympathy and wishes to help are thus compounded with guilt, rage, and a sense of personal helplessness and worthlessness. Ann's mother, as we have observed, was caught up in a lifelong and intense feeling of resentment and disappointment that affected most areas of her life. She was constantly appealing for sympathy and solace in her misery from most of the people she contacted. She had little to talk about except what she could complain of—her mother, her husband, her family, her deprivation of all the good things in life, etc. etc. She made this appeal for sympathy and help from all of the professional personnel with whom she had contact. Her interventions, or attempts at intervention, in Ann's treatment were driven by an obvious wish to be taken care of herself, and her enviousness of Ann because Ann was being taken care of in a way that she was not. Her continual complaint in the family was that no one cared about how she felt, or about her difficulties and problems, but everyone was concerned about Ann and her problems. The resentment for not caring was particularly directed at her husband, but also at Ann. At the same time, any efforts to respond to these appeals were angrily rejected—they might counter her resentful and deprived feelings to which she clung so tenaciously. The impact on Ann—as well as the rest of the family—was a continual sense of frustrated rage and guilt and impotence.

Ann's confusion and uncertainty were intensified by the welter of mixed messages that were communicated in the family, and by the distortion and denial that permeated most of the family interactions. In the face of the vicious and undercutting assaults toward Ann, the mother would blandly deny any hostility. Her actions were always prompted by the purest of motherly motives—that she was only thinking of Ann's good and that she was merely intent on seeing that Ann got ahead in life and was able to function more effectively. This often-repeated tactic on the mother's part drove Ann to a difficult position—whether to believe her own senses and the reality she experienced, or to believe the distortion and denial of her mother. She was being forced to surrender reality for the sake of a regressive symbiotic and destructive relatedness to her mother.

The process of intensifying and increasing the conflict in the sick family member has a definite function. The patient becomes the repository of the sickness in the family and the focus of their pathological reaction. Ann's mother harbored a psychotic core in her own personality that was both paranoid and depressive. This paranoid core was based on significant introjects which derived from her relationship with her own mother. This evil and malignant introject was again reprojected onto Ann, so that the mother responded to and interacted with Ann as though Ann were the bearer of the evil, malignant, hostile, destructive qualities that the mother had internalized from her own mother, but which remain repressed and unconscious in herself. It was this projected image that she worked to destroy and reject.

I would like to focus on the aspects of this pathological interaction which has to do with the paranoid development. One cannot escape—as the patient could not escape—the hostile and destructive milieu in which she was raised. The effect of this destructive atmosphere on Ann was predictable, if not unavoidable. She was presented with a chronic hostility which was simultaneously denied—and which she was also called on to deny. The hostile intrusiveness, particularly from he mother, with all its destructiveness and the malignant intent that Ann could grasp within it was a major factor in the development of her pathology. Her mother's intrusiveness and controlling of Ann's life and activity took the form of constant undercutting and critical devaluation. Ann experienced this as a constant attack. Her life and her thoughts were being intrusively controlled by her mother, and the control was one that the daughter could sense to be malignant and destructive. This inevitably issued in her fears and concerns that forces in her environment were trying to ruin her mind and to destroy her. The paranoid delusion was a reprojection of the destructive intrusiveness she experienced in relation to her own mother.

Symbiotic Ties

The process was complicated, however, by Ann's symbiotic ties to her mother. Despite the hostile and destructive aspects of this involvement, Ann could not draw away from it. Her primitive dependence and symbiotic need for involvement with her mother made separation from the mother—with its primitive fear of abandonment and annihilation—too threatening. Ann was left in the position, therefore, that any move in the direction of greater independence or autonomy on her part would have disastrous consequences—on one level for herself, but at another level for her mother. The symbiotic need lies in both directions—if Ann needed her mother, the mother also needed Ann. We have suggested that the symbiotic relatedness and the projection of the intolerable introject served an important function—that of preserving the fragile integration of the parent and of protecting the latter from insanity. The symbiotic union is a form of collusion in which the parental projection and the child's introjection are both put in the service of this objective. At an unconscious level, Ann's psychosis represented her need to protect the symbiotic mother from the threat of insanity. Breaking away from the symbiotic and dependent involvement would therefore come to represent the destruction—by death or insanity—of the mother. Ann was trapped—cut off by disastrous psychic consequences from any attempt at autonomy.

The symbiosis is thus prolonged, both in terms of the external circumstances of continued dependence and attachment, and also in terms of the internal clinging to the malignant introject. This is reflected in Ann's severe self-condemnatory and self-accusatory attitudes. She thought of herself as worthless, dirty, a whore, etc. These were all attitudes and devaluations which came originally from her mother, but were continued internally through the maternal introject. Thus Ann's capacity for inner growth was impaired both by external impediments and by internalization of a defective and destructive maternal introject. Any possibility of meaningful and constructive identifications was thereby subverted. Her capacity for positive and trusting human relationships was impaired by her experience and internalization of undermining destructiveness.

These developmental effects left her with a sense of internal worthlessness and helplessness which contributed to the predominantly depressive aspects of her pathology that were so evident in much of her clinical picture. The self-depreciation and devaluation was carried on internally much of the time. Often for long periods, she would present the picture of a severely depressed young woman. But the paranoid core persisted, and under conditions of stress would flare out. At these times the depreciation and devaluation and the malignant and destructive intent were situated in outside agents once again. She became once again the helpless victim of malignant forces which were bent on her destruction.

As we look back on little Ann's development, we are impressed by the intensity and destructive quality of her relationship with her parents. It was not simply that there was a highly ambivalent and destructive symbiosis with her mother, but also that the relationship with her father had a seductive and infantilizing quality. What was remarkable in both parents was the lack of sensitivity or responsiveness to Ann's inner needs and wants. Studies of early child development have made it clear that the mutual regulation and responsiveness between the mother and child from the earliest levels of their experience together—and particularly the mother's capacity to adapt her mothering activities to the cues which reflect the child's inner need states—are critical in the development of basic aspects of the ego. If we can project Ann's mother's persistent blindness and disregard of her daughter's inner states and feelings back to that early stratum in her development, the devastating consequences quickly become apparent.

Family Interaction

The parents' continuing denial of Ann's emotional difficulties remained a dominant aspect of the family's interaction, and characterized the interaction currently. The parents—both mother and father—were able to respond to Ann only in terms of their own inner needs and concerns. The strength of parental needs required that Ann respond to them rather than to her own needs. The result was a continual demand placed implicitly and explicitly on Ann to surrender her own interests in favor of the interests of her parents. This required a constant conforming to their expectations and demands without any acknowledgment of separate wishes and expectations of her own. This aspect of her relationship with her mother was particularly intense. She could only find acceptance and thereby preserve the symbiotic relatedness to her mother by compliance and conformity to her mother's demands. Any deviation from those demands was met with rejection, ridicule, and the threat of abandonment and loss of the needed relationship. Thus any move in the direction of self-expression or self-acknowledgment was extremely threatening. Ann had no room for inner growth, and the fragile sense of autonomy that was available to her was stunted and covered over with threats of destructive retribution.

Ann's preparanoid experience was consequently such as to leave her with a pervading sense of inner inadequacy and insecurity. Her inner psychic experience was dominated by destructive and evil introjects. Her childhood experience was one of continual threat, anxiety, and insecurity, always in precarious proximity to abandonment, always subjected to the devaluing and undermining influence of her mother's malignant attacks, and with no escape. She was shy, withdrawn, isolated, with no real allies to support her or respond to her emotional needs. As she approached adolescence, she felt the pressure of her mother's demands that she be sexually involved. Her relationship with Bobby enabled her to satisfy her mother's demand, at least in part. That relationship served as a partial buffer against the mother's undermining attack—partial in the sense that in defending herself from attack on one front she also opened herself to attack from another front in the form of mother's ridicule and devaluing of her sexual interests. It also served to satisfy mother's demands and thus preserve the symbiotic ties. When Ann lost that relationship—along with the other stabilizing relationships in the school and neighborhood settings—the effect was doubly devastating. It at once exposed her to her mother's undermining attacks and brought her face-to-face with her own inner insecurities and inadequacies. She needed desperately to find a defense against both—and the psychosis provided the needed defense.

Ann's gradual decompensation reflected her struggle with the malicious forces within her. The losses she suffered activated her rage, resentment, disappointment, and sorrow. She was unable to tolerate or contain her grief. She began to experience an inner disintegration which was reflected in her experience of distortion and disorganization of the world around her. The paranoid construction had an important restitutive dimension. It enabled her to reconstitute some degree of inner organization and avoid the frightening panic due to her inner fragmentation. It also enabled her to reorganize her experience in terms of malignant external forces which could be blamed for her position.

Paranoid Style

We have discussed the paranoid process as a style of cognition and experience. We would like to focus on the elements in Ann's experience which might have contributed to her development of the paranoid style. We have placed considerable emphasis on the aspects of Ann's development and experience within the family that impaired her sense of trust and autonomy. As we have suggested, the paranoid style has specific roots in these developmental impairments. But there were other elements in Ann's family milieu that might have played an important role. For one, there was a characteristic pattern of blaming that dominated the interactions in the family. The interaction between mother and father seemed to be one of a continual effort on the part of both parents to blame each other for their problems and resentments. The blaming was particularly intense on the part of Ann's mother. No one in this family was willing or able to accept any responsibility for his or her own unhappiness and inadequacy. The blaming on all sides was active, angry, vicious, and bitterly resentful.

The amount of prejudice that was reflected in parental attitudes is also worthy of note. The parents were solidly Jewish and adopted a somewhat ghettoish attitude toward all non-Jews. Non-Jews were regarded as outsiders. The racial prejudice against blacks was also particularly strong. Both parents shared this prejudice, but Ann's mother was most explicit and intense in the expression of her prejudice. She regarded blacks as lazy, filthy, immoral, sexually perverted and promiscuous, worthless, and something less than human. Ann's response to these prejudices was curious. She felt ambivalent about her own Jewishness—vacillating between wanting to deny her Jewish background and wanting to cling to it, between wanting to date

Jewish boys and finding them repulsive. Part of her attitude embraced a distinction between "nice Jews" and kikes. She saw herself and her family as nice Jews; this had to do with the fact they could count several doctors in her family's relations. This attitude was transparently her mother's. Her attitude toward blacks was also a reflection of her mother's prejudice. It was interesting, therefore, that Ann should compare herself with such lowly creatures—as if to ask whether she was a worthy object of her mother's hate and prejudice. The prejudice in Ann reflects the extent of her internalization of her mother's attitudes and values, not only about other people and social groups, but about herself as well.

Thus the human environment that provided the context for Ann's developmental experience not only brought certain influences to bear that impeded her inner growth, but also impressed on her a style of thinking and of organizing her experience. The elements of envy, jealousy, and prejudice that permeated the atmosphere of this family were efforts on the part of these individuals to redeem and restitute the sense of loss, deprivation, and inadequacy and wounded narcissism that each harbored within. The exercise of this pattern in the relationship between Ann and the other members of her family brought about the same inner inadequacy in her as well. The introjection that provides the basis for this inner sense of inadequacy also provided Ann with the mechanisms of defense against the painful affects connected with it. The process of this assimilation is one that we cannot determine in this material, but it undoubtedly embraces complex processes of learning, modeling, and imitative effects, as well as the important processes of internalization we have discussed. For Ann, the style of organizing her experience was brought into the service of defensive needs that responded to a primitive disorganization of her personality. The paranoid mechanisms were thereby organized into a psychotic defense, and issued into a frankly psychotic paranoid construction and paranoid delusion.

CHAPTER 7

Doctor Robert B.

THE PATIENT'S PROFILE

The case of Dr. Robert B. represents an example of a patient who led a premorbid life pattern that was not without its pathological indicators, but which seemed to fall within a relatively normal range of developmental and adjustment vicissitudes. It was not until he was beyond his thirtieth year that his pathology broke through in a most virulent form. One of the most difficult things for psychiatrists to understand is why certain patients seem to demonstrate a relatively adaptive life-style, but then seem to decompensate acutely in the face of often identifiable—but often, too, apparently unidentifiable—precipitants. As the present case suggests, often the precipitants are imposed on an underlying pathological process that can successfully conceal itself—or perhaps, can successfully be ignored or denied—until an acute and dramatic break with reality makes its presence undeniable.

Presenting Picture

Dr. B was brought to the hospital one quiet Sunday morning in a state of acute disorganization and turmoil. He was intermittently struggling violently, so that it required several hefty policemen to restrain him. When attempts were made to reassure him, he would lapse into a tense and constrained silence only to burst out screaming and struggling a few moments after. He would scream that he was God, that he didn't want to die. He repeatedly asked the doctor whether he was God, and when told the doctor was not God but a doctor, then asked whether he himself was going to die. At one point in all this turmoil, he broke away from the police and rushed over to a pretty young nurse. We all jumped, expecting violence, but instead he put his arms around her and asked, "Can I fuck you?" After these initial struggles, and with the aid of a moderate amount of phenothiazine, he stopped struggling and became quite compliant.

Within a few days the psychotic disorganization of the patient's thought processes began to abate, and little by little we began the long process of piecing together what had brought him to this state. The patient's recompensation at this point was remarkable. He seemed to be almost visibly struggling to pull himself together and to reengage himself with reality. In a relatively short time he was able to reconstitute himself and all marks of the psychosis had disappeared. This pattern was so noteworthy—the acuteness of his decompensation and the rapidity of his reconstitution—that the diagnostic issue was clouded. In many ways his behavior seemed to resemble the acute traumatic stress reactions so often seen in the military, in which acute disruption and disorganization take place in the face of battlefield stress, but then disappears with sedation in a brief period of time. These patients appear notoriously schizophrenic, but in fact are experiencing the effects of severe panic. Often they recover quickly and go back to the field of action and are able to function adequately.

Bob's pattern was quite similar to this—at least in its early stages. The signs of his psychosis disappeared quickly and he was released from the hospital within a few weeks and was able to return to his rather responsible and arduous duties. At the time he was completing a residency training in surgery. He was able to return to his service, and functioned adequately until the completion of his training. To flash ahead in the story, after the completion of his formal training he became increasingly apathetic and lethargic over a period of months. He became more and more deeply depressed, developed suicidal ideation, and finally after nearly six months out of the hospital had to be rehospitalized. He remained in a neurasthenic, and at times almost catatonic, state for almost a year—and then only slowly was he able to tolerate increasing periods out of the hospital. The acute pattern was by that time in progress of verging into a more chronic pattern. As we shall see, this clinical progression reflects the stage of an inner struggle Bob was waging to gain and preserve his sense of self against the powerful forces within.

Immediate History

At the time of his breakdown, Bob was nearing the completion of his residency in oral surgery. These had not been happy years for him. At the beginning of his program, he had been intent on proving that he was the best resident ever to go through it. He was intensely competitive, took every opportunity to show up his fellow residents, and was generally critical of the shortcomings of the program, of the caliber of the teachers, and particularly of the work of his immediate superiors. His attitude won him few friends, and he felt himself to be generally disliked and socially excluded by the other residents. At the same time he wanted desperately to be accepted and liked by them. The situation was difficult and unhappy for him.

His ambition and almost grandiose competitiveness also got him into difficult relationships with members of the teaching staff. He would sometimes challenge teachers in a hostile and critical manner, which tended to foster defensiveness and some antagonism. Several times his hostilely competitive attitude was pointed out to him by well-disposed teachers, but Bob resisted their interest, feeling that they were trying to put him down or shut him up. The quality of this competitiveness was reflected particularly in his relations with one of the senior staff surgeons who was generally regarded as the most distinguished of the teaching staff. Bob entered this relationship in an argumentative and challenging manner. On rounds, for example, he would challenge and criticize what the older man had said, and on several occasions gave the impression of treating the older man with casualness or disrespect. The senior man responded by putting Bob in his place. There was several public arguments and continuing conflict. The relationship deteriorated to the point that the older man refused to even speak with Bob and finally refused to allow Bob to enter the operating room with him.

Bob felt very badly about the way this relationship had developed. He wanted badly to have this distinguished teacher and surgeon recognize him and acknowledge him as knowing more than any other resident on the service. Bob himself felt that he in fact knew more than the other residents and was a more skillful surgeon than they were. He even felt that in many respects he knew as much or more than the senior men. He felt that he could learn a great deal from this particular man and wanted desperately to be acknowledged by him. He complained bitterly about his inability to communicate with this older man. He felt that he could not let him know how he really felt, and that so much of what did transpire between them was due to misunderstanding. He felt hurt, rejected and undercut by the older man's response. As we shall see, the qualities of this difficult relationship mirrored many aspects of Bob's relationship with his own father.

Bob had his difficulties other than personal in the residency program. From the beginning, he had admitted that becoming chief resident was his ambition. He set his sights on that goal, and regarded that position as his due, since he saw himself in highly narcissistic terms, as far superior to the other residents in knowledge and skill. A few months prior to his breakdown, the new chief resident was announced—and it was not Bob. He was bitterly disappointed, intensely critical and devaluing of the man who got the job, seeing him as inferior in skill and lacking in any real surgical capacity. Bob was particularly critical of the new chief's conservatism. He felt that the new man's surgical judgment was poor because he would never take any chances and always took the safest course. In his disappointment, Bob began to think that he was deprived of this coveted position by his superiors simply because they did not like him and wanted to get back at him. They were afraid to acknowledge that he did in fact know more than they did, and they had to keep him down because otherwise his real worth—as superior to themselves—would then have to be acknowledged. He saw the entire staff, including his fellow residents, as involved in a conspiracy to keep him in an inferior position and to prevent any acknowledgment of his ability.

Along with this disappointment, Bob was subject to increasing criticism because of the management of his cases and because of what was felt to be poor judgment. This dissatisfaction with his work came to a head in one incident. Soon after the chief resident had been appointed, Bob was operating on a child with a known bleeding disorder. Since the bleeding was greater than expected, Bob ordered a transfusion. When the chief resident saw the order for blood, he came into the operating room to investigate the reason for a transfusion. Since the operation was an elective minor procedure he told Bob to interrupt the procedure rather than give a transfusion. Bob disregarded the order and completed the procedure. Bob's response to the chief's order was that he had no "balls" and that in Bob's judgment the risk in stopping the procedure and reoperating at some later date would have been greater. Clearly, however, Bob was motivated by the wish to show up the new chief resident and to demonstrate his own superior surgical ability. He wanted to show that he could carry off surgical procedures that the chief resident didn't have the guts to attempt.

The upshot of this episode was that doubts were cast on his professional judgment, and he was told that the teaching staff had such doubts. He was told that his knowledge and surgical skills seemed satisfactory, but in view of the questions about his maturity of judgment, he would have to remain in the program for an additional period of time in order to allow the staff to decide about this aspect of his overall performance. Bob's disappointment and anger can be easily imagined. This development only served to reinforce his resentment and his feelings of conspiracy against himself on the part of the staff. Within a few days after receiving this announcement, the acute decompensation occurred. Behind these struggles and defensive competitiveness, we can sense Bob's injured narcissism, but also the sense of fragility and the anxious pressure for approval and accomplishment that would somehow reassure him that he was whole, that his existence was meaningful and purposeful, that he was not weak, defective and inadequate.

Decompensation and Delusion

The immediate setting for the acute decompensation was provided by a conference on hypnosis that was being conducted by an internationally renowned medical hypnotist. The conference was being held in a rather intensive fashion over a weekend. It should be explained that Bob had been interested in hypnotism for some time, and had trained himself to become quite skilled in the use of hypnosis in his clinical work. He had been using it with selected clinical patients in performing procedures, and had even once demonstrated it to his surgical colleagues as a technique in inducing deep anesthesia for an abdominal surgical procedure. It was apparent that Bob's interest in hypnosis was motivated by strong inner needs. He felt himself to be a very suggestible person, who could be easily swayed to accept any point of view. He felt himself to be thus vulnerable and weak. His interest and involvement in hypnosis thus had a decided counterphobic element—it provided a way in which Bob could suggest rather than be suggested to, influence rather than be influenced, and control rather than be controlled. It enabled him to deny his inner feelings of weakness and inadequacy, and provided a realizable channel for his wishes to be powerful and skillful, as well as a way of controlling and influencing others.

It was in the context of this intensive weekend conference that Bob began to decompensate. He began attending the conference, but after about a day he began to feel confused. He did not really know who or what he was. He felt himself perplexed, confused, befuddled. He described himself at this stage as phasing in and out of reality—at this point the delusional system began to assert itself. Bob began to think that he was in fact the famous Dr. X who was conducting the conference. He then began to think that he was having a homosexual affair with Dr. X. and that he was the special and favorite colleague and confidant of Dr. X. He was at first puzzled and perplexed by this belief, which seemed to come and go in brief delusional waves that became gradually established. He would return to reality between these delusional periods and wonder why he was having these thoughts and why he was believing them. Gradually his delusional beliefs became more and more elaborate and more stable. He began to think that he was a member of an extraterrestrial race of creatures who were gifted with godlike powers. They were immortal and would never die. They were the possessors of extraordinary powers. They could transpose themselves to any part of the universe and could enter or leave the solar system at will. They could also assume any identity just by willing it. Thus simply by willing it Bob could become the chief resident, or he could become the famous psychiatrist, Dr. X. He wondered to himself whether he should become a psychiatrist or not—whether he should follow the regular course of training of a psychiatrist or whether he should simply will it and become one in an instant. He might follow the regular course of training so no one would suspect his real powers and ability.

It was important for the members of this race to keep their real identity unknown. They had the special power to influence men's minds and to change the course of events. These powerful creatures entered the world to do good and help men straighten themselves out—just the sort of thing psychiatrists do. They were known only by other members of the same race, and if ordinary men knew who and what they were, they would be frightened and want to try to destroy them. Bob worried about dying during this period, but felt secure because in fact members of this race did not die. They didn't have to worry about sex, or about having to get married—since they were immortal. They didn't have to worry about God either, or about God punishing them for sins, since they were like gods themselves and very powerful.

In the midst of these delusional thoughts, Bob came to the conference that Sunday morning and walked up on the stage and presented himself as Dr. X. His bizarre behavior and disorganization were apparent, and he was brought directly to the hospital.

The Origin of Delusion

The course of the development of this paranoid delusion was gradual and progressive. We can immediately see that the content of the active delusional system was a form of restitutive defense against all of the patient's underlying concerns and feelings of weakness and vulnerability. His wish to become chief resident, for example, was translated into the delusional system and was satisfied by the delusional power to assume the identity of chief resident at will. We shall see that the other elements in the delusional content similarly reflected Bob's underlying fears and uncertainties and wishes.

The development of these acute symptoms presents an interesting course of emergence. The pattern is much like a deep root that is clearer and more defined near the surface, but becomes more widely spread and diffuse as it plunges deeper into the soil. We can thus trace Bob's illness and his symptoms back into his history, but as we so do they become all the more vague and diffuse—but, I think, still recognizable. At the beginning of his residency it was clear that his attitude was marked by intense competitiveness and phallic striving. He made it evident, even at that stage, that he felt that he had to prove something—something that he could not presume or feel comfortable in already possessing. Moreover, what he needed to prove could only be demonstrated by putting down his colleagues and proving that he was better than they were. Little by little a pattern of social exclusion, rivalry, jealousy, and gradually suspicions of a conspiratorial effort to undermine him became more evident. These feelings of jealous rivalry and suspiciousness came to a more marked intensity when Bob was denied the position as chief resident. His thinking at this point had a markedly paranoid flavor. The confrontation with the chief resident over the transfusion and the subsequent events which culminated in his having to extend his program provided a consummatory insult and injury to Bob's rather intense narcissism. His underlying feelings of inadequacy and inferiority were stirred and his defenses against those feelings were intensified.

The delusional system resolved his perplexity and confusion. It also served to allay and respond to his underlying fears and frustrated wishes. The emergence of the delusion, therefore, seemed to have followed a pattern of gradual emergence which could be traced back for several months and years. The elements were drawn together and intensified and crystallized in a relatively short time in the face of specific disappointments and losses. Further, the acute formation of the delusional content occurs in the context of an environmental stimulatory situation. If we try to look back further into Bob's history, we can begin to appreciate to what extent the delusion served a defensive function in responding to and countering his deepest anxieties.

The Family

Bob's family was middle-class and Jewish. He was the middle child of three—he had a sister four years older and one four years younger. His birth and early development were regarded as unremarkable. When Bob was born, the family lived in a blue-collar district in an eastern industrial city. His father was a self-made man who worked his way up from the ranks. The family's financial condition improved in later years, after Bob's father worked his way into a managerial position, but the early years were a struggle. Bob's early development was spent in this climate in which the family was struggling for upward mobility, socially and economically.

At home Bob was clearly his mother's favorite. He was her boy and in her eyes he could do no wrong. She was not a particularly attractive woman—rather plain and obese. Her major investment and interest in life was in her children and her home. She was rather possessive and domineering, controlling everything that went on in the home. She ran the house and did most of the disciplining of the children. Bob was quite close to his mother and very dependent on her. He was a sensitive and very obedient child. He rarely needed to be punished or disciplined, since he tried very hard to be a good boy. His dependence on his mother and maintaining her affection were of central importance for him. She was apparently quite affectionate with him, even into latency and early adolescent years. He recalls that she was always mothering him—that she would often embrace him. This would embarrass him, because he was aware of her heavy and pendulous breasts.

Bob was generally a shy and rather timid boy. He often played by himself. He did not get along well with children his own age in the neighborhood or in school. He felt that part of the reason for this was the fact that his family was Jewish, while the rest of the neighborhood was predominantly Catholic. The other children would often pick on him and call him a "dirty Jew." He was constantly getting into fights, but he would not defend himself. He would usually run away and cry. As a rule he would run to his mother, who would comfort and protect him. Bob was generally more comfortable playing with girls, but he was afraid that people would think that he was a sissy. These experiences tended to reinforce his feelings of inadequacy and vulnerability.

Bob's difficulties were complicated by the fact that he could not get along with his father. His father was a tough, ruthless, and aggressive man who was a physically minded and tough competitor when he was young. He grew up in the streets and had had to fight his way up. He despised and ridiculed his son's weakness and timidity. Bob always felt that his father was cold, harsh, and distant. He never felt that he could communicate with him. He wanted desperately to be able to talk with his father, to be close to him, to be liked by his father and to have his father be proud of him. But he never seemed to be able to gain his father's approval. He could never measure up to his father's expectations—and could certainly never measure up to his father's accomplishments. He reflected that, if he had been in his father's shoes, he could never have done what his father had done—he just wasn't strong enough or tough enough.

From as far back as he could remember, Bob lived in fear of his father. He recalled that his father would come home and would be irritable and short-tempered. His parents did not get along well at all, and he always felt that his inadequacy and weakness were the reasons. His father would be angry at him for not standing up like a man and fighting, while his mother would try to protect him. Bob remembered himself as very lonely and fearful as a child. He always felt the need to be close to someone—particularly his mother. His fantasies in this regard were of himself lying on one of his mother's huge breasts, fondling it, and feeling close and warm. This was the only way he felt he could escape fear and loneliness.

Phobic Childhood

Bob's early childhood was filled with phobic concerns and anxieties. He was constantly afraid of werewolves and goblins. He often had dreams in which werewolves and goblins of various types would attack him. When his father came home at night, he used to park the car in a garage and walk to the house along a dark, narrow sidewalk. After dinner it was Bob's job to empty the garbage. To do this he had to carry it out along this same dark sidewalk. He was constantly terrified that he would be attacked and killed by werewolves. This was transparently a displacement of his fear of his aggressive and feared father. Moreover, on one occasion, Bob was accosted on the bus by an older man, a derelict. Badly frightened by this experience, he was able to tell the school principal about it in his panic but was afraid to tell his parents—particularly out of fear of his father. These fears stayed with him over the years—on several occasions he reported nightmares of being attacked by werewolves. The similarity to Freud's famous case of the "Wolf-Man" springs readily to mind. In that case, as well, the homosexual longing for the father and the fear of castration were felt by Freud to play a central role in the generation of the child's anxiety. In Bob's case, his fears of his father—generated undoubtedly at an Oedipal level—were displaced into fearful imaginings and dreams of werewolves and into a fear of "dirty old men" who would accost him, presumably for homosexual purposes. The fears reflected Bob's inner concerns about his own passivity and vulnerability. They also mirrored the inner world of primitive and destructive objects that haunted his dreams and were projected into dark corners and alleyways.

Defectiveness

Bob's feelings of inadequacy were related to another source. He was born with a congenital hernia and one testicle had failed to descend. This was a source of constant concern—particularly to his mother. In her obsessive mothering, this became a focus of considerable anxiety and concern on her part. Bob's defectiveness was equivalently an assault on her own sense of adequacy. There were countless visits to doctors and special precautions to protect him from injury. Bob himself recalled that when he was playing the hernia would often swell and become somewhat painful. At these times he would become afraid of hurting himself. He felt that he couldn't play like the other kids and would often cry. This fear of being hurt played into his unwillingness and fear of fighting. His mother's obsessive concerns about his vulnerability and susceptibility to injury became part of his own attitude about himself. These fears and concerns—shared and communicated between mother and son—were contributing factors to Bob's feelings of inadequacy and his feeling unable to measure up to his father's tough standards. We can also see how the mother's protective concern and the father's contempt for such weakness would clash.

Bob recalled years of preoccupation with this condition. He remembered getting several series of hormone shots—none of which had any effect. Finally he was operated on when he was eleven years old. He recalled the operation vividly and remembered the rubber band running from his knee to his testicles. He remembered the embarrassment of this condition—especially in relation to the nurses and other patients in the hospital. It was a sign of his inferiority and the fact that his testicle had to be fixed. Bob's concern over his genitals had extended into his adult life. He was concerned that his penis was too small. He often asked the girls he had slept with whether his penis was big enough, whether it was as big as other men's, and whether it was big enough to satisfy them. He sought constant reassurance on this score. He also stubbornly clung to a belief that he was impotent—an astonishing fact in view of his sexual history. We can retrace the pertinent aspects of his sexual life at this point.

Sexuality

Bob's earliest memories of sexual interests related to his experiences in the family. When he was very young his mother used to bathe him with his sisters. He recalled his interest in his sisters' genitals and his embarrassment in showing them his own. He felt at such times that it was wrong for him to want to look at them and was afraid that his mother would catch him at it. His fear was that she would do something terrible to him if she knew that he was curious about his sister's sexual parts. He remembered that on frequent occasions, starting when he was about five or six years old, he would play with the girls in the neighborhood. They would go into the cellar and undress and play games with each other. He recalled that these games were exciting and he was always fearful of being caught. As he grew somewhat older he remembered thoughts and fantasies of having intercourse with his sister. He knew that these were "bad thoughts" and felt guilty about them, but also was afraid of what his parents would think of him or do to him if they knew that he had such evil ideas.

In his adolescent years Bob began to experiment sexually with many different girls. It was very important to him to have intercourse with as many of the girls he took out as possible. He had to prove that he could get them into bed and screw them; otherwise he was falling short of the performance that would be expected of a man. As time went on, through his college years and after, this pattern of intense sexuality persisted. He had a strong need for physical contact and a unique ability to draw women to him. With rare exceptions he was able to get them to go to bed with him. He described his feelings of warmth and closeness in the sexual embrace. He felt safe and secure with his penis in the woman's vagina, and anything short of that was fraught with anxiety and feelings of uncertainty and precariousness. He described the act of intercourse as "getting inside" a woman where you could finally feel safe and protected. The fantasy seemed to reflect an infantile wish to enter into the woman and find security and protection within her womb—a fantasy of return to the maternal matrix, the safe harbor of symbiosis.

Bob carried on an intense sexual life on multiple fronts. He always had several girl friends with whom he was actively sexually involved at any one time. By the time he came into treatment, he had women in nearly all parts of the country whom he would occasionally visit and sleep with. Some of these women were married and some not. In the course of his adventures, many of these women became pregnant. I say "many" because the exact number was never determined. In the course of therapy, the number kept increasing: Bob would casually mention another girl whom he got pregnant. The number mounted to the neighborhood of fifteen. Some of these women had abortions and some did not. Bob generally urged them to have abortions, but some of the women wanted to have their children—particularly the married women. On one occasion, Bob could not arrange for an abortionist and attempted the abortion himself. The abortion was successful, but the girl became very sick and had to be taken to a hospital. The event frightened Bob severely; he would often refer to this episode and accuse himself of nearly killing the girl.

The incredible fact was that despite this unusual record Bob persisted in the belief that he was impotent. He felt that he was impotent because of his defective testicle, even though he had been told differently after his successful surgery, and even though he knew better from his own medical knowledge. His denial in the face of such overwhelming evidence is striking. What is also very striking in all this is that Bob had adequate knowledge and adequate access to contraceptive means. Yet he made no effort in all these instances to utilize contraceptive precautions. In part this reflected his underlying conviction of his own impotence, but at a deeper level it reflected his unconscious sadistic wish to hurt and maim the women. These sadistic impulses found their expression indirectly and in a displaced manner in the impregnation and aborting of these many women. The guilt that Bob felt so deeply in relation to these episodes was related to the underlying unconscious sadistic and destructive impulses. We have already had occasion to observe how these same sadistic impulses were transposed into his activity as a surgeon.

Symbiotic Ambivalence. In working through these relationships, a primary issue was Bob's intense ambivalence in his relations with women. His yearning for closeness with them and his dependence on them had an infantile quality. He sought them out for protection, support, sympathy, warmth, and closeness. He needed them for the security, warmth, and protectiveness of their bodies. This was not simply a sexual yearning but was laden with much earlier—almost symbiotic—yearnings for closeness and protection and dependence on his mother. The descriptions and responses he gave of his sexual activity did not have a phallic quality at all, but rather the quality of a frightened little child cuddling close to his mother's warm body to shield himself from the cold buffeting and demands of the outside world. It was as though, behind the facade of phallic striving and narcissistic gratification in sexual conquests, there was a much more central core of infantile yearning and dependence on the woman that was satisfied in sexual union. It was as though Bob were reuniting himself with the maternal matrix in the act of intercourse—and wanted to fold himself in it and rest there safe from the demands of growing up and functioning as a big boy. His clinging to the belief in his impotence undoubtedly served the function of preserving the inner fantasy of infantile dependence—rather than the acceptance of mature phallic potency. It also served him to deny and repress the hostility and destructive urges that raged within against the bad, punitive mother.

Bob had successfully avoided marriage in all this activity. He talked much about the possibility in relation to his two current girl friends. He also recalled that once before he had felt that he was in love and wanted to marry. But the girls were all non-Jewish. He did not date Jewish girls and would never sleep with one. He recalled how he was always afraid of bringing his girl friends home to meet his mother, fearing that she would be angry because they were not Jewish. When he seriously considered marriage, the leading consideration in his mind was how deeply his mother would be hurt if he were to marry outside his religion. He had decided not to marry a Gentile girl because of the pain he felt it would cause his mother, and the same consideration entered into his ruminations about marrying either of the present girl friends—both of whom were non-Jewish. The Oedipal implications of this attitude were clear. He could not relinquish his symbiotic dependence on his mother—caught up in the deep ambivalence as it was. Nor could he date or sleep with Jewish girls, presumably because they were too much like mother and posed an incestuous threat. He was caught on both sides of the ambivalence: if he married a Jewish girl it would have carried the threat of incest; if he married a non-Jewish girl it would have carried the threat of an attack on mother and loss of her love. Bob could not resolve this ambivalence.

Religious and Authoritarian Conflicts

Related to this was the question of Bob's Jewishness. He regarded it as a stigma, something to be lived down. He worked very hard to deny it—he did not socialize with other Jews, did not date Jewish girls, did not observe any of the Jewish religious practices. All his life, he complained, he was told what good Jewish boys didn't do—particularly by his mother. Good Jewish boys didn't drink, they didn't have sex all over the place, they didn't fight, etc. His mother was strict in her religious observance, attending the synagogue regularly and praying. His father was just the opposite. He rarely went to the synagogue, and then only on his wife's pleading—and just for show. Bob felt that his father was a hypocrite, going to synagogue only on the high holy days and not really believing or living any of his religion in the rest of his life. Bob was made to go to synagogue school and learn Hebrew just to satisfy his father, who would brag about how well he knew Hebrew. Rebelling against the Jewish religion was a way of becoming more like father and at the same time of rejecting and hurting mother.

We have seen how Bob's relations with older figures who stood in some relation of authority to him were contaminated by competitive antagonism and hostility. He countered his underlying feelings of weakness and incapacity by continual attempts to compete, master, and prove himself. His early experience was one of constant pressure to perform—to measure up to a standard that he never felt he could meet. Whatever he did or accomplished was never good enough to satisfy either his mother or his father. He had to compete against his sisters, both of whom were bright students and good achievers. But they were not expected to achieve. Bob was the boy of the family; he was the object of mother's narcissistic investment and was expected to compete and achieve more than the girls. His inability to do this consistently was a constant source of dissastisfaction and disappointment for him and of criticism by his parents.

Thus, in reaction to his fears of inadequacy and his inner doubts about himself, he had a strong need to prove his superiority and ability at every turn. He found it necessary to gain approval from superior figures—teachers, supervisors, anyone whom he saw in a position superior to his own. This was also a factor in his relationship to me as his therapist. These relationships were contaminated by aspects of his relationship with his parents—particularly his father. The ambivalence was apparent. He had a strong need to be accepted and approved. He sought to be compliant and to do what he thought was expected of him. At the same time there was a strong impulse to compete and to prove himself as good as, or better than, the father substitute. He was caught in a difficult position: on one hand, he needed to be compliant in order to gain the approval he needed so badly; yet on the other hand, he wanted to compete and rebel in order to prove himself better. The dilemma of compliance versus rebellion is central in the paranoid conflict.

These elements entered into the transference relationship. He saw the psychiatrist as a powerful and influential figure from whom he had much to learn. The doctor was someone who could convey to him the secret of how to live in a healthy and successful manner—who could show him how to be the strong and successful man that he wished to become and felt he was not. We can recall that in his acute delusional state he thought that he had become a psychiatrist and that the role that he saw himself adopting as a member of his godlike race was that of psychiatrist—a position from which he could exercise control over men's minds and influence the course of human events. He saw his therapist very much in that light, and his expectations of therapy had a magic cast. He seemed to feel that all he had to do was to do the right thing, submit himself to the prescriptions of the psychiatrist and do what was asked of him, and he would automatically (magically) get better. This attitude reflected his childhood wishes to be accepted by his father and to gain strength and approval by pleasing the latter. Much of the early course of treatment was taken up with discussions of this area of his thinking. His attitude was that he would follow instructions to the letter, including talking about his history and thoughts and feelings in therapy; he would perform the "procedure" and get the job done—and then he would be healthy again and would leave all of this "bad dream" behind him. He wanted "to get in and get it over with." This was the set of mind with which he approached so many of the aspects of his life. He approached surgery in the same way, putting the emphasis on speed, precision of technique, and getting the job done. He found it difficult to resign himself to the slow, gradual, step-by-painful-step of the therapeutic process. From time to time he would voice his impatience and his disappointment that he hadn't done the job yet. Inevitably he tried to assign the blame to himself, taking his lack of ability to improve as proof of his inadequacy. As will become clearer, this very conformity with the demands of his professional role, as well as his cooperation with the expectations of therapy, formed the core of the "false self" that was fundamental to his pathology.

Compliance

Bob's increasing ambivalence created a problem for him in therapy. He felt that he needed and depended on the therapist but at the same time he felt that he could not express his anger at the latter. If he were to do that, he would run the risk of rejection and loss of the therapist, and then he would be lost. The repeated attempts of his father to interfere with his treatment, to transfer him from the hospital, to change his therapist were severely threatening to Bob from one point of view, but they also played into his ambivalence from another point of view. They also intensified Bob's rage at his father for running his life, something that Bob had always resented, even as he complied with his father's wishes out of his need to please and gain the parent's approval. The process became one of choosing between his father and his therapist. It was extremely difficult for him to follow the demands of therapy and to resist the pressure from his father. In the measure that he was able to do so and to thus remain in treatment, the threat of confronting the father and of expressing his rage at him drew closer and, as it did, Bob became all the more terrified of it.

Bob had always been extremely compliant to his parents' wishes, but as his therapy made clear, not without considerable resentment and bitterness toward them—and especially toward his father. There was only one exception to this that stood out in his history. When he went to college Bob followed a premed course with the intention of entering medical school. It was not clear that this was really Bob's wish—neither was it clear that it was not. What was clear was that his parents held this up to him from very early in his life as a desired goal and ambition. Toward the end of his college career, he applied to a number of medical schools but was not accepted. This was a severe disappointment to him. He reacted with anger toward his parents and bitterly renounced their demands and expectations. He described himself as wild, confused, and enraged. There was a family argument in which Bob bitterly rejected their demands—particularly their professional and religious demands. His father wanted him to be a doctor and his mother wanted him to be an observant (and good) Jewish boy. Bob stormed out of the house and went to New York—where he lived for a year and did a year of graduate work.

It is not at all clear what was going on in this episode. Bob's behavior was rather wild and disorganized, and one can wonder whether what was in process then was not a form of schizophrenic decompensation. In any case, the disruption was transient and there was a reconciliation with his parents. Bob himself did not know what he wanted to do, and it was in response to his father's suggestion that he applied for and was accepted in dental school. This factor became significant in his later course of treatment. Accepting father's suggestion and setting himself on the course of a dental career meant two important things to Bob. It meant first of all submission to his father's wishes, and at the same time, it meant an admission of his inadequacy, since he had to resign the goal of a career in medicine. Even in trying to satisfy his father's present wish, he was trying to satisfy a second-best wish. Even success in this new line, therefore, could not avoid the stigma of failure.

This became an important issue in Bob's treatment. After his acute break, he was able to finish his residency training. Then he was confronted with a decision whether to set up a practice in oral surgery or not. For a time he worked on a part-time basis in another surgeon's office, just enough to support himself. And he agonized over the decision. He was unable to make it—unable to commit himself to that course of action. He endlessly reviewed the possible alternatives, the difficulties, the locale, the opportunities—all in an obvious attempt to avoid coming to any conclusion. This process went on for months. As he was trying to make this decision—or trying not to make it—he became more and more depressed and withdrawn. Gradually he developed suicidal ideas which became sufficiently intense to warrant rehospitalization. He came back into the hospital and remained there for more than a year.

Bob's inability to make this important decision was multiply determined. It was from one point of view a decision to commit himself to a decisive life course—a career decision. That meant becoming adult, mature, taking responsibility. He felt himself unready, unprepared, incapable of accepting the responsibility for caring for patients, even though he had been able to perform professional duties in the supportive environment of the training program. He realized that he would have to make and take responsibility for important decisions regarding the care and treatment of his patients, and he did not feel himself man enough to do that. He made excuses of many kinds. One of the major ones was that he didn't know enough. With a sort of obsessional perfectionism he felt that he should know everything, and that if he didn't know everything he knew nothing. On occasions when he had to ask for a consult from the medical or other surgical services in the hospital, he felt inadequate because he didn't know as much about the consult's specialty as the consult. When the grandiosity and omnipotence of this extremely narcissistic position was pointed out to him, he responded that only when he knew everything could he feel secure about treating patients. He concluded that as long as he didn't know everything he was still inadequate. Moreover, he clung stubbornly to his conviction that his inability to learn everything was proof of his inadequacy and of his unsuitability for practicing oral surgery.

In addition, the choice of dentistry and oral surgery had been influenced by his father's wishes. This definitive compliance with father's wish was fraught with ambivalence. Bob saw his life as an endless process of striving to please his father and living up to father's expectations. Establishing himself as a practicing oral surgeon would be complying with his father's wishes in a definitive way. Further, becoming an oral surgeon was an admission of being second best—of not having been able to become what father really wanted, a doctor. And also—the career was father's choice, not Bob's. Bob envisioned the whole process by which he came to this point in his life as an endless chase, a treadmill that never stopped and which he hated and resented. His breakdown and hospitalization were equivalently stopping the treadmill, removing himself from the endless and fruitless effort. And he did not want to get back on. He wanted in some deep and final way to frustrate and disappoint his father's wish—to make himself a decisive failure and thus deliver a final blow at his father.

As we shall see, Bob's psychotic decompensation and his subsequent immobility represent a form of rebellion against his father, but also an attempt to abandon the facade of the competent, knowledgeable, capable, fearless, sexually hyperadequate, and counterphobically hyperactive professional man and entrepreneur. That facade was erected to meet the expectations of both parents—a compliance, a false self which he hated, and in his psychosis rejected and tried to destroy.

Phobic Dimension

There was another important element which entered into Bob's prolonged immobility. He was afraid of death. This was a constant preoccupation with him. You remember that one of the central elements in his delusion was that as a member of the godlike race he could not die. Neither did he have to fear the power of God since he was as powerful as God. Death in Bob's mind was linked with divine retribution. He feared that God would punish him for his many girl friends. When he would speak of these, he would often become tense and anxious, tremulous and tearful. He would moan, "How could I do such a thing!" He saw the abortions as hurtful and selfish—he persuaded the girls to have them not for their sakes, but to get himself off the hook and out of trouble. He felt that he would be punished for this.

Much of Bob's rejection of his Jewish faith and observance had to do with this issue. What he had done was clearly not what good Jewish boys do. His rejection of his parents' and particularly his mother's beliefs was a defense against his fears of punishment. Behind this anxiety and agony lay the Oedipal drama. The powerful father-god would punish him for his transgression against the mother-woman whom he had impregnated. His fear of his father was thus translated into and strongly determined his fears of death. But the fears were much more than the fears of castration due to an Oedipal transgression. The whole was suffused with preoedipal fears and destructiveness. The primitive sadistic urges were channeled into his wish to destroy the woman, the bad mother who had deprived and dominated him, yet to whom he was tied with such deep and symbiotic dependencies. The primitive aggression and destructiveness were also projected into the harsh, cold, and powerful father who could punish and destroy.

These fears paralyzed Bob. He placed himself in a safe and protected position, one in which there was no need for him to move at all. The hospital became a safe haven in which he escaped from the movement of life. To live, to commit himself to a course of action, to follow out the plans for his career meant on one level to emerge from the dependence and weakness of childhood into the activity of adult life. It meant to move from being a child to being an adult—to grow older—and thus to grow closer to death. This basic fear expressed itself in any step which suggested to him that he might move off his safe and regressive perch and progress toward greater capacity to function. He resisted every move toward improvement. Therapy became a slow and repetitive process in which there was negligible progress.

The whole process was complicated by the issue of compliance. Making progress in therapy became his father's wish, which Bob for these many reasons had to frustrate. It was directly his father's wish, for the father was continually putting pressure on him to get out of the hospital, pull himself together, start a practice, stop acting like a baby, stop costing father money. It also became an issue of transference, insofar as the therapist's wish for Bob to function more maturely became aligned with father's wish. The therapist became the substitute father who was pushing Bob to perform up to standard. This generated tremendous resistance to the treatment process. Bob's conflicts over compliance became a central issue in the treatment. The basic issue was centered on the fact that for him to remain compliant and passive and to submit himself to the wishes of the therapist was equivalently for him to remain sick. But for him to become noncompliant and to begin to take the first steps toward autonomy and self-assertion would be to allow his intense destructiveness to be unleashed.

Bob improved sufficiently to undertake weekend visits home. There he would spend most of the day in bed. His father could not restrain himself from attacking this behavior on Bob's part. He regarded it as being lazy, irresponsible, perverse, and suggestive of other bad things. Bob avoided any confrontation with his father over the sleeping, but he would return after such visits increasingly agitated and depressed. His complaint was that he could never satisfy his father and that he was really inadequate and sick. The events of the weekend had once again proven that. When the therapist suggested that if Bob wanted to sleep all weekend that was his business and not his father's, Bob found it very hard to accept. When I first observed that sleeping was all right if that's what he wanted to do, he looked at me incredulously, broke into a silly grin and said, "You can't mean that—that's just crazy!" For Bob, acting more healthily had become an act of compliance—a sacrifice of autonomy. Becoming more autonomous, even if it meant acting against his father's or my wishes, was seen as craziness.

Counterphobic Defenses

The curious thing about all this was that prior to his decompensation Bob had acted in quite a different manner. He had set out to prove himself in a variety of ways. He struggled to overcome all of his fears and doubts about himself. He overcame his fear of drowning by learning to swim and becoming an experienced scuba diver. He overcame his fear of heights by learning to fly an airplane and finally getting his own pilot's license. All of these efforts were strongly counterphobic and competitive. His efforts to overcome these fears were often marked by a willingness, if not an eagerness, to take chances, to take unnecessary risks, to test the limits of his skill and endurance, to prove that he had "guts" or "balls," to prove that he was a man and could face danger and "take it." This attitude extended to his work in surgery, as we have seen. He was willing to take risks, even when it was not necessary or was imprudent to do so, for the sake of demonstrating to himself and others that he could do it.

The countering defense, as might be expected, had a lot to do with his extreme and promiscuous sexual activity. Bob was afraid of his homosexuality. This had always been a concern for him. Part of his acute delusion was that he was having a homosexual affair with the famous Dr. X. He had also had one episode of homosexual activity with another boy when he was about seven or eight years old. This involved orogenital activity. Bob also had frequent homosexual fantasies about a man sucking his penis when he masturbated. These occurred when he was not getting enough sex from women. Thus his hypersexuality was equivalently a flight into heterosexuality—in part as a countering defense against his homosexual fears. There was no homosexual activity in his adult life, although he was able to admit occasional wishes in that direction. The flight to the woman and sexual activity with her was proof of his manhood, demonstrated his strength and power over women, and gave him continuing reassurance of life and strength.

Bob's Father

The problem for Bob in all of this was that the more successful he became in overcoming and defending himself against his inner fears in these ways, the more he became like his father. Bob hated and feared his father. He saw him as a tough, ruthless, selfish, and unprincipled man who would destroy anyone who got in his way. Father and mother had not gotten along at all well for years, and Bob's father had taken to consorting with other women. This was a source of continual conflict between father and mother, and a source of great anguish and pain to Bob's mother. Bob hated his father for this behavior, and yet strove to become more like his father. Becoming more like father was the best way of gaining father's approval and of being able to get close to him. Yet Bob hated what his father represented. Thus the conflict was drawn. Bob was trapped between two conflicting and constrasting parental identifications. To be strong and aggressive meant to become like his father—hard, cruel, sadistic, selfish, using women for one's own pleasure, being a tough "loner" and not being afraid of anything, being willing to do anything or to hurt anyone in order to get what one wanted. But not to be that was to become like mother—weak, dependent, easily hurt and sensitive, vulnerable, "gutless," "no balls," homosexual. Bob's solution of his dilemma was to find a safe middle ground where he could avoid either alternative, where he could withdraw himself from life and the ultimate threat of death, where he could hide from his destructive wishes and inner rage. It seemed that the configuration of counterphobic toughness and competitive competence that characterized Bob's false self was built around the central introjection of his father. Beneath this facade, however, there lay another image of himself, this time based on the pervasive and highly influential introjection of his victimized mother. It was through the internalization of these respective introjects that Bob found himself in such difficult straits. The course of his therapy required that he divest himself of, and work through, both of these pathogenic introjects.

If we look back in this story—a strange story in so many ways—we can begin to see how the acute delusional system, which Bob generated in the face of his accumulating losses and disappointments, answered to most of his inner fears and insecurities. To be a god, to have godlike powers, to be able to become what and who one wished at will, to be able to influence men's thoughts and to change the course of human events, to be immortal and to live forever, not to have to worry about sex or marriage, not to have to fear death and the divine wrath—the delusion was a solution for many deep and long-standing fears. We can also begin to see that the resolution

provided by the delusional system was an extreme fantasy, bizarre and unrealistic, but it was at the same time substantially an intensification and
delusional expression of thoughts and wishes that had been in Bob's head
for a long time. We can also see that the delusion answered not merely to
difficulties, uncertainties, and weaknesses that were current in Bob's life, but
that the origins and roots of these doubts reached back in his early
childhood experiences. We can trace an unbroken line of continuity from
earliest childhood memories which enunciates over and over again in multiple varieties and multiple modalities the theme of weakness and inadequacy.

DISCUSSION

Family Interaction

The factors and influences that lay behind Bob's pathology are multiple
and complex. Hopefully we can begin to tease some of these out of the
above clinical impressions. The first dimension of the story that emerges
with considerable force is the family constellation and patterns of interaction. Bob's father was seen by Bob as cold, hard, tough, demanding, harsh,
ruthless, and heartless. In part this must be taken as Bob's perception, with
its built-in distortions. But I can lend some support to this perception from
my own contacts with the father. He was an impatient and demanding
man—obviously used to getting his way and acting in a very hostile and
threatening manner when he didn't. He had formed a view of Bob's
problem, namely that Bob was weak and cowardly and that the solution to
Bob's problems lay in the direction of Bob getting off his ass and getting
busy. Any attempts to communicate any different perspective were completely ignored. The channels of communication were closed. One can easily
imagine the problem that Bob had to face all through the years in dealing
with this man—communication must, indeed, have been difficult for the
frightened and phobic little boy. The father blamed Bob's mother for all the
coddling and protectiveness she had showered on the boy. The split between
the parents was obvious and deep.

Bob's mother presented quite a contrasting picture. In most of our contacts with her, she was anxious and solicitous—willing to do anything so
that her poor boy would get better. Her conversation was larded with
statements of remorse and regret, wondering what she had done wrong, accusing herself of being a failure as a mother. The titer of guilt in this woman
was very high. One could see the intense preoccupation with doing the right
thing in the face of her inner doubts and uncertainty. These feelings had undoubtedly been intensified and focused to a great degree by Bob's illness,
but it would not be difficult to imagine that the same sorts of anxious concerns pervaded her mothering activities.

Developmental Matrix

The circumstances of Bob's early experience growing up in this family were determined by the combined pathologies of both parents, as well as by the fact that he was the only male child. His two sisters fared much better than he. They were both bright, attractive women who married well and were successfully engaged in the business of raising their respective families. Bob's relations with the older sister were more competitive than close. His relations with the younger girl were closer and more affectionate, although a certain amount of competitiveness was detectable there as well. Bob constantly felt himself being measured against both his sisters—more so with the older than with the younger. If he felt close to anyone in the family it was with his younger sister.

In any case, the burden of being the male child fell on him. His father wanted him to be a tough, scrappy kid who wouldn't let anybody push him around and who wouldn't back down from a fight. He wanted a son of whom he could be proud on his own terms—terms of toughness, aggressiveness, competitiveness, and physical prowess. Bob was none of these and thus he became a disappointment to his father. The father had no sympathy for his fears and unwillingness to fight. Bob was left with an intense desire to gain closeness and approval from the father, a desire that was to be continually and repeatedly frustrated.

The father became a feared—but intensely desired—object. The ambivalence in this relationship—from the very early times in Bob's experience—was intense. It is difficult to imagine this father ever being able to engage in loving and mutually satisfying play with Bob, even as a baby. In the years that Bob could remember there was never any time spent with his father, never any play, never any moments of mutual contact and enjoyment. His relation with his father was always one of trying to satisfy the father out of fear of the latter's disapproval—and never being able to do so. Bob's wish to become more like his father was contaminated by his ambivalence. The inner striving to become more like the parent—or derivatively to become more like he wanted him to be—was subverted. The possibilities for positive and ego-building identifications were minimized. The father could not be admired, loved, or imitated. He had also to be feared and hated in large measure. The striving to be like father had to take a defensive turn, as a protection against the threat of punitive destructiveness from the parent. If Bob could be more like father he could gain the latter's approval and avoid his punitive wrath and despising rejection.

The Paternal Introject

The increase of ambivalence in early object relations with the parents tends to shift the balance from positive and structuralizing ego-

identifications to more defensive introjections—the pattern of internalization which Anna Freud described as "identification with the aggressor."
The internalized aggression thus becomes part of the inner world of the
child and becomes available for projection to the world of objects. Thus
Bob reexternalized his fear of his father in a variety of phobic manifestations—fears of werewolves and goblins, frightening fantasies of evil-
intentioned old men who would hurt him, fears of the dark, phobic responses to any situations of danger or possible hurt. This pattern of response to the father set up an interaction of introjective and projective
defensive processes. The effect was to build up the danger and destructiveness in the world outside him and to concurrently repress and deny his
own inner destructiveness. Thus the world became a fearful place, and Bob
became more and more in terms of his own inner self-representations the
weak and vulnerable victim. Thus from the side of his relationship with his
father, what becomes internalized is the father's harsh and demanding attitude which demands that Bob be tough and strong, and despises and condemns him because he is not. The paternal introject, then, becomes the
nidus for a harsh and punitive superego which continually condemns and
criticizes Bob for his inadequacy and lack of manliness.

It is clear that Bob struggled with this introject throughout his life in so
many ways. His counterphobic activity, which permeated so many areas of
his life and work, from having to make the high school football team to having to be a "gutsy" surgeon, was an unrelenting attempt to counter, deny,
disprove, and invalidate this devalued perception of himself. His struggle
was never successful, regardless of his accomplishments and external
"proofs," because the counterphobic and counterdependent striving did not
affect the firmly planted introject within. It is also clear that he projected
this introjective attitude to others in the world around him. His fear was that
they would not regard him as a man—as having "guts" or "balls." He constantly had to work against that fear by proving on all sides that he was
better, unafraid, capable, the best resident, a good patient in psychotherapy,
an adequate lover with a big enough penis, etc. Even externalizing the introject and struggling with it out there did not enable him to resolve the conflict and the underlying ambivalence.

The Maternal Introject

Bob's relationship with his mother was also quite significant. She was a
rather anxious and insecure woman. She was insecure in her own inner
perception of herself as wife and mother. She was insecure in her relation
with her husband—unable to satisfy him sexually or emotionally. She was,
after all, five years his senior and not an attractive woman. She was quite
plain, and obese—a woman made for the home and kitchen. And it was
there that she invested herself. She gained some sense of security and self-

esteem from keeping up her house and providing good food for her family. She worked at being a good mother, and in a sense she must have been more than adequate. She provided a good home and a reasonably good model for her daughters. But her pathology focused more intensely in her relationship with Bob.

The reasons for this were several, as far as I can see. First of all, Bob was the only son. The Jewish tradition puts high value on sons, not on daughters. That, of course, raises problems for both daughters and sons. But it serves to put high expectations on sons. How one's sons turn out can be seen as the real test of how good and how successful the mother has been. And, as with so many mothers—whether Jewish or not—a son becomes the focus of much of their own repressed wishes to accomplish and compete, so that the son is expected to fulfill a role of achievement that they were denied. Much of this mother's narcissism became focused on Bob and invested in him. Second, there was his hernia and undescended testicle. He became to her the weak child who needed protection and special attention. He was vulnerable and had to be sheltered from physical, as well as from psychological, harm. In addition, this feeling brought the father and mother into direct conflict. The father could not tolerate the boy's weakness and attacked his wife's coddling and protectiveness. The mother in turn resented the father's attitude, seeing his attacks on Bob and his rejection as part of his rejecting and devaluing attitude to her. Arguments were frequent, and frequently enough centered on Bob and their differences regarding him.

Bob tried hard to be a good Jewish boy. But that meant being passive, compliant, obedient, religious, weak, and vulnerable. If Bob were to stand up for himself and to fight back, he would be violating the mother's code of what good Jewish boys did. Thus he was effectively caught between the conflicting expectations of his parents. To gain approval from father, he had to risk the loss of mother's love. But to keep close to mother and have her comfort and affection, he could not gain father's approval. Bob could no more reconcile these demands than his parents could reconcile their differences. Thus, not only was the conflict at large in the family, but it became an internal conflict for Bob.

Bob's view of himself as weak and defective and inadequate was an internalization of both parents' attitudes toward him, but it was also the product of his introjection and partial identification with the mother's own devalued self-representation. He in fact identified with the weak, vulnerable, victimized, and suffering woman. It was this inner representation of himself that he tried to deny and avoid all through his experience. The internalized representation of the mother was assimilated to his own self-image, and in a real sense he had thus internalized the conflict between his parents. His inner development and the inner drama of his life played itself out between these two conflicting and destructive introjects. He used the one to defend against the other. He could not resolve them—nor could he choose between them.

The inner configuration of Bob's pathology bears certain striking similarities to the pattern of Camus' hero of *The Fall*, particularly as this character has been analyzed by Barchilon (1971). Camus' hero, Jean Baptiste Clamence, like our own present hero, gives himself over to the achievement of prowess in many areas of physical activity—particularly the area of lovemaking. Barchilon (1971) comments on this aspect as follows:

> Something similar can be seen in Clamence's belated reaction against all his prowesses and successes, be it in sports, professionally, or with women. But this is the most superficial part of the mechanism at play. In our hero we can safely assume, from his dream of love, that sexual wishes toward the mother in the first years of his life had to be inhibited under penalty of death. Furthermore, the incest taboo was so powerful that not once in his life could he allow himself to fall [tomber] in love. Neither could he allow himself, even once, the fundamental satisfaction of procreating, in spite of an extreme narcissistic investment in his self. (Investments of this nature can often include one's children under the narcissistic mantle.) It is as if his sexuality, through an unending procession of women, was used to keep physical closeness and a semblance of intimacy with one woman only, the mother! And, for all the pleasure and coxcomb pride he took in it, *his penis was no more to him than an umbilical cord*, nor was he unaware of that fact since he kept calling sex: *His infirmity*! (p. 208)

Clamence's Don Juanism was effectively a direction of erotic and hostile wishes, fused together in a reflection of his underlying ambivalence outward, specifically toward women. His inaction in doing nothing to save the drowning woman was, therefore, an act of murder. The introjected object that had been the source of humiliation with him formed the feminine side of his own character which had to be projected to rid himself of it. Thus, for Clamence, the young woman must die in order to rid him of this feminine identification and to free him from the introjected mother. For Bob, his sexual prowess was an infantile reattachment through his penis-umbilicus—but it was the initiation of a sexual attack that was rooted in sadism and expressed finally in the repeatedly attempted abortions.

Pathogenic Relationships

The upshot of these interactions was that Bob was forced to introject the pathological aspects of both parents. His relations with neither parent were successful—and they left him with unfulfilled needs on both sides that he continually sought to satisfy and which were doomed to unfulfillment. He sought the mother and his once-treasured symbiotic closeness to her in his relationships with a procession of women, with none of whom he could establish a loving relationship and with none of whom he could accept the procreative responsibility. His near psychotic denial of his own potency and paternity in so many of these relationships bears testimony to his inability to accept this aspect of mature love relatedness. Moreover, in relationship to the authoritative males in his environment, he continually sought to create the relationship to the idealized father—strong, capable, knowledgeable, skilled, and respected—that he sought as a child and was always denied. The rehearsal of the Oedipal drama was, however, here too, inexorable. However much he sought the idealized father, he inevitably turned him into the rejecting, hostile, and devaluing father of his childhood. On both sides the parental introjects were projected into his outside relationships and there played out their inexorable and conflictual course.

The loser in this unresolvable struggle was Bob's ego. The need for these defensive and conflicting introjects—born on the one hand out of his symbiotic dependence on his mother and on the other hand out of his desperate longing for closeness to his father—deprived his ego of the necessary conditions for meaningful and constructive identifications which the development of the ego requires. Ego development, therefore, was impaired, and remained fixed at the level of the defensive organization of the introjects. Any further integration of ego and superego functions was short-circuited. Reflecting this inner impairment, the quality of his object-relations was similarly affected. He was unable to progress in his object-relations beyond a symbiotic clinging to a mother-substitute—despite the superficial hypersexuality—or beyond the anal-sadistic and fear-laden struggle with father-substitutes. His ambivalence on both sides was never resolved and the quality of his object-relations was highly contaminated by pregenital elements, even before the onset of his illness.

False Self-System

The inner fragmentation and division in Bob's psychic structure reflects the form of impaired psychic integration that was described originally by Winnicott (1960) as the "false self-system." Bob had in the course of his interaction with his parents developed a split-off portion of his personality which consisted primarily in his compliant false self. It was the superficial reflection of defensive structures which allowed him to approximate the idealized image projected by his mother—the "good Jewish boy." The intensity of his defensive needs created a significant split between this superficially functional false self and the inner structure of his personality. His parents—and the rest of the world as well—responded to and interacted with the false self and took it for the whole of Bob's psychic reality.

Laing's remarks on the compliance of the false self provide a telling description of the inner psychic condition of our patient.

> The actions of this false self are not necessarily imitations or copies of the other, though its actions may come to be largely impersonations or

caricatures of other personalities. The component we wish to separate off for
the moment is the initial compliance with the other person's intentions or expectations. This *usually* amounts to an excess of being "good," never doing
anything other than what one is told, never being "a trouble," never asserting
or even betraying any counterwill of one's own. Being good is not, however,
done out of any positive desire on the individual's own part to do the things
that are said by others to be good, but is a negative conformity to a standard
that is the other's standard and not one's own, and is prompted by the dread
of what might happen if one were to be oneself in actuality. The compliance is
partly, therefore, a betrayal of one's own true possibilities, but it is also a
technique of concealing and preserving one's own true possibilities, which
however, risk never becoming translated into actualities if they are entirely
concentrated in an inner self for whom all things are possible in imagination
but nothing is possible in fact (1965, p. 98).

Bob had functioned primarily in terms of this compliant and false self
system through most of the years of his childhood. His compliance was in
the service of preserving the symbiotic ties to the maternal matrix. Any
other course would have entailed—or so it seemed to him—the threat of loss
and abandonment. To have been himself would have entailed a loss of those
ties to the mother upon which he depended for survival.

Bob continued through the course of his career to function in terms of
this false self. He dealt with reality in terms of a facade—a defensive
organization—that he presented to the world and through which he interacted with the world. Even his defenses, however, were not really his own,
since they were impersonations of his father, rooted in his need to gain approval from the father and to comply with the latter's wishes. It was
fascinating during the course of his treatment to watch the fragmentation,
reemergence, and then further dissolution of the false self. After his first
break, Bob had rapid recourse to the false self system, as a set of behaviors
or attitudes that he could take up at will and parade before the eyes of the
onlookers. As he approached the ultimate compliance—the commitment to
a career in oral surgery which he saw as designated for him by his
father—the ambivalence which the false self concealed became more intense
and the false self was no longer adequate to carry the load. Through most of
the rest of his treatment, the question remained as to whether he would
resume the false self. We both recognized that he could take that course if he
so wished. His ambivalence and the intense and murderous hatred that lay
behind it prevent him from doing so.

Family Triangle

I wish to call attention to the pattern of involvement in Bob's relations
with his parents and in the family system. What emerges clearly out of the
clinical data is the impression that there was a clear triangular relationship
established within the family among the three leading characters of our
story. The drama of Bob's pathogenic relationships plays itself out with his

father and mother, and the two sisters seem to drop out of the picture, or at least seem to be involved in it only incidentally. Father, mother, and son function as a more or less undifferentiated unity, to which the other siblings are attached as minor appendages. The emotional relationships which we have been trying to focus on seem to embrace the participants in the triangle in an encompassing fashion that transcends the inner vicissitudes of each. There seems to take place a peculiar communication of feelings and affective states between Bob and his parents, so that Bob's inner feeling states seem somehow to blend into and participate in the feeling states of his parents. The feelings of both mother and father are responded to, sensed, shared in, and internally reflected in ways that make the discrimination of what feelings belong where and to whom rather difficult. Bob's inner feeling states did not seem to be his own, but rather they seemed to reflect the currents of emotion that flowed from each of his parents. The conflict that arose between them seemed to raise inner conflicting waves within Bob himself.

The triangle of mother, father, and Bob formed an emotional unit within the family structure. The emotional division and conflict between the parents were obvious and long-standing. The pattern was one that Bowen (1960) has called the "emotional divorce." The conflict between the parents focuses on Bob—rather than on his sisters. Thus Bob becomes involved in an emotional process that melds him into the emotional conflicts of his parents in special ways. The respective pathologies of his parents get projected onto him, with the result that both parents relate to him and respond to him in terms of the repressed and denied aspects of their own malfunctioning personalities. Bob became the weak and fearful child that embodies the inner uncertainty and vulnerability that father denies and fears in himself. Bob also becomes the embodiment of the inner anxiety and inadequacy of his mother. The result is his rejection by his father and his infantilization by his mother. Her inner anxiety becomes quickly communicated and reflected in Bob, who served as a physically separate yet emotionally fused part of herself. Her overly protective and sympathetic efforts are directed to dealing with the anxiety that she has externalized in her child—with the result that Bob becomes increasingly the infantilized and dependent child. He thus becomes more in need of her protective mothering and becomes likewise increasingly the object of his father's scorn and rejection. Thus Bob becomes the victim of parental pathologies. And both parents deal with their pathologies by projecting them on Bob—with devastating results.

In terms of our preceding analysis, the selection of the child to be involved in this projective process is highly specific and determined by a number of factors. It presumably operates differently in different families, depending on the respective contributing pathologies of the parents and circumstances of family structure and function at certain critical periods. The combination of factors that included both Bob being the only male child the family had, and the fact of his congenital defect, seemed to provide a sufficient stimulus to elicit the respective parental expectations and projections. He was the weak child who needed special care and protection—as well as the only son upon whom special expectations and demands were to be placed. Both these factors elicited particular responses and projections from both parents which derived from and reflected their individual needs. Thus Bob became involved in the family emotional system and became the participating victim of its pathogenic influence.

We have seen that his process set up the emotional conditions which acted to undermine the positive growth potential of Bob's ego. Bob's father remained almost completely unavailable to him as an object for real identification. His internalization of the father remained at the level of defensively colored introjection. Whatever identification he was able to achieve was fragile and highly contaminated with ambivalence. The only suggestion of identification was with the devalued and vulnerable figure of the mother, but this was so highly mitigated by symbiotic attachments and the ambivalent residues of her punitive possessiveness and infantilizing intrusiveness that one can speak of identification in only a shadowy and far from authentic sense. Bob's functioning personality—despite the fact that he was able to function in apparently healthier fashion well into his adult life—was a tissue of fragile introjects. The potentiality for regression was high, and when his obsessional and counterphobic defenses failed him in the face of critical disappointments and fundamental life decisions, the collapse and a severe regression to narcissistic state was the outcome.

Parental Attitude

While the undermining of developmental processes was having its ultimately devastating effect and was contributing to the basically schizophrenic process, it is central to our concern here to try to focus the elements that contributed to the paranoid pattern of Bob's illness. It is the fundamental working hypothesis in this study that certain basic processes are at work in the family structure which both reflect the impairment in the level of functioning of parental egos and also determine a pattern or style of family interaction which contributes to the emergence of certain patterns of defensive organization in the affected child. The tendency to assimilate this pattern of defense is linked to the relative susceptibility of the child in the family system. Insofar as the child remains an undifferentiated part of the family emotional system and is thus subject to the intense influence of the family projection process, he becomes liable to the assimilation of the unconscious (and sometimes conscious) patterns of defense that are generated in the family system.

What stands out in the history of this family are the relatively pathological attitudes which characterize the respective parents. The father's pervading set regarding the world in which he lives is one of hostility, guardedness, suspicion, distrustfulness, and ruthless competitiveness. He lives by the motto, "Do unto others before they do unto you!" *Homo homini lupus!* The father regards all other human beings as actual or potential competitors who are out to get him or hurt him in some way. He has no meaningful, rewarding, positive and loving human relationships. Even his relationship with his wife is filled with conflict and demeaning hostility. The only hint of positive feeling in his relationships is in relation to his daughters—and that is only a hint. There are undoubtedly historical antecedents and determinants of this set of mind in his own life experience. But an explanation in terms of hard times and the need to compete for economic survival carries us only part of the way. I would feel it necessary to think in terms of a hyperaggressive and hyperhostile defense against inner feelings of vulnerability and helplessness. These feelings are strongly repressed and denied, but the pattern of his life reflects the strength of his defenses, which answer to the intensity of the denied needs. He defends himself against the inner tender feelings which threaten him with dependency and vulnerability. Thus he needs to see the world and all of those in it as predators and sources of threat that must be attacked to preserve oneself.

If we turn to the mother's attitudes and defensive needs, we do not come off any better. The sense of inadequacy and vulnerability permeates her style of life and her window on the world. She felt inadequate as a wife and as a mother. She functioned more as a submissive body slave to her husband than as a wife. Yet in the same degree that she was submissive and compliant to him, she was controlling and demanding in relation to her children. It was as though she cloaked herself in her family in order to protect herself from the outside world. She had few friends, no outside interests—she wrapped herself in her family and made that the proving ground for her self-esteem and adequacy. Her investment in religion has important implications in this regard. Her adherence to orthodox Jewish beliefs and practices carries with it the overtones of her need for masochistic surrender. This was undoubtedly protective and supportive for her, since it allowed her to integrate her inner self-perception and her need to submit and suffer with a community of shared belief. However adaptive this may have been for her, it must only have served to reinforce the operation of the projective system in the family. It communicated from another direction the implicit assumption of the family existing in a position of precarious defenselessness as the objects of persecutory hostility from the surrounding community of non-Jews.

Thus the integration of the respective parental needs and defenses set a pattern that permeated the family system and was projected to the children, affecting the most involved child, Bob, most intensely. In terms of Bob's own inner psychic economy, he internalized—introjectively and defensively—the pattern that permeated the family system. This can be in part delineated in terms of introjective elements that derive from both parents. He makes the defensive conflicts of both parents part of his own inner psychic economy. If we can speak loosely of his identificatory pattern, we find that he has assimilated the weakness and vulnerability and dependency from both parents—more conscious in the mother than in the father, more defended against in the father than in the mother. In making this identification, he effectively introjects the weaknesses of both parents, rather than their strengths. Rather than building the strength of the ego, his introjections introduce fragmentation and conflict into his own inner economy. This unavoidably limits the potential for inner growth.

Impairment of Self-esteem

The effect on Bob's emerging sense of self and on his capacity for developing a positive sense of self-esteem were catastrophic. The developing sense of self formed around these weak and impaired introjects, with the result that his inner sense of self-esteem was severely compromised. The roots of depression were laid down within the context of the family projection system and the internalization processes which contributed to this impaired sense of self. The paranoid elements then served as a defense against the inner sense of devalued self and against the pangs of depression. Bob's life-style was generated around the struggle to deny these pathogenic introjects and their associated perception of himself. His attitude was generally in its inner core a paranoid attitude toward the world and toward the other people in his environment. The inner paranoia served as an alternative defense along with his intense hyperactivity and counterphobic and counterdependent striving. This had a definite manic flavor, with a strong element of denial.

From earliest childhood Bob's paranoid defense took shape. He saw himself as different from other children. He felt himself to be special and somehow superior to his playmates and schoolmates. He felt himself to be an "outsider," a "loner"—like his father. His latency and adolescent years were colored with highly narcissistic and omnipotent dreams of great accomplishments—of becoming a great man. His dreams of glory were cast in terms of fearless and courageous deeds, he would become a fearless hero—and later on the dreams took the form of ambitions to become a great scientist, a great doctor, and finally a great oral surgeon, a teacher, and a great researcher. These fantasies always had the implications of competitive striving, of winning out over others, of making others subservient, of gaining power and influence, of gaining the upper hand. These lifelong dreams of glory reached their apogee and most extreme expression in the acute and grandiosely omnipotent delusional ideas.

There is an element of inner superiority in all this, of contempt for all other human beings, and an inner drive to test the limits of what can be dared or challenged. He became a small-scale edition of Dostoevsky's self-willed man, a Raskolnikov, a hero who dared to reach beyond the limits of what was right and acceptable. He denied and rejected Jewish religious belief and morality. He dared and defied the Jewish God and the threat of His punishments. The drama he was acting out through most of his life was transparent. He was denying the maternal introject—as he struggled for and against the paternal introject. The struggle, as we have seen, was not authentic. The self-willed hero was a put-on, a false self which masked the compliance which doomed him even as it gave him the only sense of reality and power he could attain. It was a part of the massive denial which permeated his conscious life and functioning.

Paranoid Attitude

What was most characteristic of Bob's dealing with his repeated failures to achieve his narcissistic ambitions was his inability and unwillingness to accept responsibility for his own failure. His disappointments were always seen as due to circumstances, or due to the ill will and conspiratorial efforts of others against him. It became clear in this light that the paranoid attitude also served intense narcissistic needs. It served as a defense against the inner impairment of self-esteem and the devalued perception of himself. The projective aspect of this defense were clear, but Bob was consistently unable to perceive and understand not only the ways in which his projection operated, but also the ways in which he had provoked the hostile and antagonistic responses from his fellow residents—or for that matter from his most admired teachers. Even in discussing his relationships with his parents—during the course of his treatment—he was unable to grasp the ways in which he elicited and prolonged the hostility and dominating attacks of his father. The need to cling to his narcissistic expectations and to repress his destructive wishes was so intense that he was literally blinded to this aspect of his behavior. He persisted in wishing that his parents would treat him differently, saying that things would be better for him if only they would stop what they were doing, blaming them for trying to keep him a child, for not letting him sleep, etc.

As the course of Bob's treatment progressed, the manic defenses and the paranoid attitude became less and less available to him. The result was the intense and prolonged phase of neurasthenic depression. It was this depression that he had struggled against, and had tried in so many ways to hide from, throughout the course of his life. It was not merely a reversion of his murderous aggression against himself; although the intensity of his wish reached suicidal proportions and the depression did serve defense interests, it was in part dealing with his murderous rage against both parents. But it also formed at a deeper level an integral part of his inner self-representation and self-perception. It was the inner introject of weakness and destructiveness that he was at last permitting to come to consciousness.

Thus the paralysis of will and intention that overcame him as he confronted the final step of committing himself to a career was multiply determined. From one side it was induced by the loosening of his defensive structure as a result of the therapeutic process. From another side, however, the commitment to the career of his father's choosing represented the final compliance—a submission of himself that was loaded with intense ambivalence. His wish to please his father and gain his approval was countered and balanced by his intense resentment and murderous rage toward him. Accepting a career in oral surgery, once and for all, carried with it the implications of both the final gesture to gain his father's acceptance and approval, as well as a final surrender of the last vestige of his own autonomy.

What is underlined in this case in a unique way is that the pattern of Bob's illness and life experience form a meaningful whole. The entire complex of events and influences including his early life experiences, the course of his life and experience, the inner organization of needs and defenses, the patterning of family structure and influences, as well as the events surrounding his acute decompensation—and even the content of his delusional system—form an integral and understandable whole. The key and central defects in Bob's personality as they emerged in the course of his history and in the working out of his therapy focused around the issues of self-esteem and autonomy. The capacity for trust was also severely impaired. These issues became the central points of concentration in his treatment. We have seen the paradoxical ways in which these issues displayed themselves in the treatment relationship. Perhaps the most difficult issue was that of autonomy. The issues of trust and autonomy were intermingled in questions of health and sickness in ambiguous and confusing ways.

The course of therapeutic improvement had to lie in the direction of surrendering the intense sense of narcissistic expectation and omnipotence and in building the basic underpinnings of functional personality—trust and autonomy. Whether Bob will ever be able to accomplish this remains an open—and as yet unanswered—question.

CHAPTER 8

Miss Clare C.

The present case was one in which the outcome was much more optimistic than in the preceding cases. It was also a case that showed a
remarkable progression from severely impaired functioning to relatively
normal adaptation and a capacity for meaningful interpersonal
relationships. What the present case teaches us is that the therapy of
paranoid conditions is not altogether a dismal or hopeless prospect, and
that the relatively effective treatment of paranoid states can follow a predictable course in terms of the underlying pathogenic structure of the personality.

THE PATIENT'S PROFILE

Current Illness

It must be said that the beginnings of the treatment experience with
Miss C. were not particularly optimistic. She was transferred to our hospital
from a local general hospital where she had been treated for a near-fatal ingestion and for multiple lacerations. The acute episode had been building
for several weeks. She had been feeling increasingly depressed in the weeks
preceding this, and had taken some LSD. The trip was rather euphoric, but
as soon as she came off it she ingested a large enough amount of medication
to require emergency care at a hospital. During the following days there
were several more ingestions. Finally, she ingested an excess amount of barbiturates and was found by a boyfriend sitting on the toilet in her apartment, naked, drowsy, and trying to lacerate her abdomen with a razor
blade.

The series of events that required hospitalization had been building up
gradually. The patient was an attractive young woman in her mid-twenties.
Her life during the preceding few months had presented a peculiar study in
contrasts. She was living in a dirty and run-down apartment with several
other "hip" friends who were a few years younger than herself and who were
a very sick and marginally adjusted group. There were two males, both
homosexual, and two other girls, one of whom was schizophrenic. Clare was
the only one in the group who was making money. The rest of the group was
much involved in the drug scene, with a good deal of pot-smoking, LSD,
and some dabbling in narcotics. Clare resented the fact that these people
depended on her to support them and keep the apartment livable. She felt

that she was being taken advantage of, but felt unable to acknowledge or effectively deal with her anger. She later described her friends as "creeps, schizophrenics, and weirdos." In typical style she gradually and more intensely began to turn her destructive impulses against herself. The self-laceration was her preferred channel for expressing this self-destructive bent. When she was first seen, there were multiple lacerations over her lower abdomen, groin, thighs, and feet.

The striking contrast in her life pattern was presented by her functioning as a nurse. She was an R.N., and was working at the time in a very responsible and demanding position in the intensive care unit of a large general hospital. Her work there was outstandingly efficient and effective. She would set out each morning dressed in her crisp white uniform—adopting the role of the intelligent, capable, efficient, and hardworking nurse. When she returned to the apartment in the evening, the white uniform would come off, and in its place she would don dirty and sloppy dungarees. She would then immerse herself in the life-style and level of functioning that obtained in the rest of the group living with her. She felt as though this latter form of behavior represented her real self, and that the efficient nurse was a facade that she could put on to impress people and to deceive them into thinking she was something that she really was not.

While her work in the ICU was of high caliber, it took its toll on her. The ICU was a place where death was never far away. A high percentage of the patients she cared for died. If they did not die, they would get better and then be transferred out of the ICU back to the medical or surgical floors. One way or another people were always leaving. This situation was particularly stressful for Clare, for reasons that we shall see. She tried to keep her relationships in the ICU impersonal and professional. She kept herself distant from colleagues who worked with her. She tried to isolate herself emotionally from the patients. She became increasingly depressed. Also, she began to have disturbing and frightening dreams. She dreamt of people dying and of dead bodies lying beside her in the bed. She would awaken frightened and terribly anxious.

It should be noted at the beginning that the paranoid element in this case does not form a striking or predominant aspect of her pathology. It was an aspect of her illness that would erupt from time to time in situations of great stress and anxiety. It remained for the most part an element in the central core of her illness. It was a long time in the course of the development of a therapeutic relationship before she was able to tell me about her ideas of reference, her paranoid fears, persecutory anxieties—fears that people wanted to kill her or hurt her. The content of these paranoid fears sometimes seemed to reach delusional intensity, but most of the time she kept them under control and under wraps. However, they formed a central element in her pathology which she was constantly dealing with and which often motivated her behavior. It accounted in a primary way for her style of relating to other people and for her difficulties in establishing meaningful relationships. Her entire demeanor was permeated by a distrustfulness, an abiding suspiciousness, and an expectation of hurt or destruction. Ideas of reference and suspiciousness—as it turned out—were a constant feature of her experience. I came to know of these inner thoughts and feelings only through the course of several years of therapeutic contact. It was a hidden aspect of her experience that she kept concealed from even her closest friends and contacts. She had written about them to her former therapist:

> Now I see that those feelings are returning after a year of successfully squashing them, and after many years of trying to squash them. They brought on that siege of cutting when . . . . And I see them, since then, in tentative fantasies which I quickly push back into the cellar and slam the trapdoor over. They are biding quite quietly, waiting till someone arrives and my mental back is turned so that they may leap out of the black cellar and fasten tight on the person. Then I'll be forced to deal with them.

From our present perspective, Clare's words describe what we can recognize as expressions of the malignant introjects which constituted her inner world.

Psychiatric History

Clare first came into psychiatric treatment about four years prior to her last hospitalization and her coming into therapy with me. At the time she was a nursing student. The precipitating circumstances of her acute decompensation at that time involved her boyfriend, a rather unstable and probably schizophrenic young man whom Clare had known since childhood and dated episodically through the years. About this time she finally gave in to his wish to sleep with her, and she had intercourse with him on several occasions. She felt that she was being imposed upon, taken advantage of, and was infuriated and resentful at having to submit to the sexual play, but felt totally unable to express these feelings for fear of his rejecting her. The sexual activity was unsatisfactory and unrewarding both for her and for him, so that after this brief period of sexual involvement they more or less separated again. This had been the quality of her relationship to him for several years since they began dating in high school.

At this point Clare began to become increasingly depressed and withdrawn. Her appetite became quite poor and her periods irregular. Over the next six months she lost about thirty-five pounds and had only one menstrual period. During this time she began her student rotation on the psychiatric service. Her problem came to the immediate attention of her supervisor. She was quite depressed and was having difficulty in concentrating on her work, remembering simply nursing duties and performing routine tasks that she had mastered before. It was suggested that she take a leave of absence before undertaking the psychiatric rotation—so she left for a six weeks' break which she spent at her parent's home. At home she avoided contact with people as much as possible and spent most of her time alone, in her bedroom, reading and writing her thoughts in her diary. Her depression and extreme withdrawal did not abate.

She came back to the hospital and started her rotation. She was able to perform her duties admirably—despite the fact that she continued to be depressed. Her academic performance, as always, was excellent. She remained distant from her fellow students, however, and kept herself isolated and withdrawn. She would only talk to one or two of the girls and assiduously avoided the rest. She spent most of her time reading books about mental illness. She confided to one of her "talking" friends that she could see herself in the patients in the hospital. She was obsessively perfectionistic in her work and instituted a number of compulsive routines. Some of her behavior was rather bizarre. She decided to rearrange her room, so she piled all the rugs, drapes, furniture, and other belongings neatly in the closet and left only the bed, a chair, and the dresser in the room. These she would compulsively rearrange several times each day.

Despite these obsessional defenses the depression worsened. She became increasingly apathetic and withdrawn. She confided to one girl who had become a sort of confidant that she felt increasingly that she could not face each new day. Occasionally she would describe the details of dissections she had read about to the other nurses in a morbid fashion that tended to frighten the other girls. She would also talk about death and how morticians would prepare the corpse for burial.

After several months of a gradual and increasingly morbid picture, Clare began to feel impulses to cut herself. She began by scratching at her thighs with a pin. She had an unquenchable desire to see her own blood. She would scratch herself until she bled. During this time she was still functioning well as a student and kept her inner feelings very much to herself. Finally she confided to her friend some of her wishes to cut herself. Soon after she began cutting herself with razor blades. This was discovered one day when she had cut both of her thighs in several places, so that the blood was visibly soaking through her uniform while she was working on the ward. This bizarrely evolving picture and the encroachment of suicidal ideas made psychiatric referral imperative. Clare's self-laceration in her groin points to the important link between her self-hate and her own femininity. Her destructive impulses were directed against her own feminine self—that part of her that was rooted in the maternal introject.

Early Treatment

Clare was hospitalized at this point for the first time. She remained an inpatient for about four months, and during this time entered on a very meaningful and intensive course on psychotherapy. In retrospect, I would tend to regard the excellent progress she made therapeutically in later years as in part due to some of the solid work that was done during this first experience in treatment. At this time, however, Clare presented a very ominous picture. Some felt that she was a case of anorexia nervosa—probably associated with a schizophrenic process. Others felt that her pathology was deep and long-standing. She was repeatedly labeled in her hospital records from this period as suffering from an acute or possibly chronic undifferentiated schizophrenic reaction. Projective test data from this period seemed consistent with this overall impression. Her Rorschach contained many gory anatomical responses which were inappropriate and persevered from card to card. The focus was on pelvic and sexual anatomy. This picture was consistent with psychosis and severe conflict over sexuality. Moreover there was little to suggest any resources for strength or flexibility. Her capacity to tolerate emotional involvement was minimal. The theme of suicide following emotional loss was a prominent aspect of her TAT stories. The overall impression was that of an undifferentiated schizo-affective psychosis in a chronically fragile personality structure.

The treatment was difficult and arduous. Clare was extremely suspicious, guarded, cautious, and unwilling to enter into any close or emotionally involved relationship. Despite her caution, defensiveness, and resistance, Clare developed an intense and a generally positive transference for her doctor. She struggled against her feelings toward him. She would not admit to any positive feelings and could not tolerate any hostile or angry feelings. She refused to cry—even though she often felt like it—because that would be admitting that she was weak and helpless and that she needed his help. The work of the treatment was progressing nonetheless. She was able to finish her nursing training and performed academically on a high plane. She became much less depressed and during this entire period of two years there were no further episodes of cutting or other self-destructive pieces of acting out.

The crisis, however, came with the induction into the armed services of her doctor. This was a relatively precipitous event and somewhat unexpected on his part. For Clare it loomed as a sudden and major catastrophe. She had struggled for nearly two years with the issue of trust. At a point where she felt finally that she could begin to trust her doctor, she was losing him. At that point she began to realize how much the relationship meant to her and how much she depended on it. She felt desperate. Her sensitivity to loss and the feelings of rejection were intensified. She began to feel that he really did care for her—and even as she realized that, she had to lose him. She felt desperate and helpless, and unable to tolerate the rage that she felt at being abandoned. In their final meeting she cried for the first time.

In the face of this loss she decompensated, became severely self-destructive, cut herself again, and ingested a lethal dose of drugs. She was again hospitalized but had sufficiently recompensated within a few weeks to be discharged. Attempts were made to get her into therapy with another doctor, but the effort proved abortive.

The subsequent months were rocky ones. She was seen periodically at the emergency ward, usually for lacerations. On each occasion she would become acutely depressed and cut herself. This was usually in the context of a disappointment or of her rage at someone on whom she had become dependent and who had let her down. These episodes were marked by a severe tension and anxiety along with her depression, and experiences of depersonalization which were quite frightening to her. The cutting served as a release mechanism for the pent-up rage, and also served to reassure her of the fact that she was real and alive. It was a self-destructive mechanism for controlling and dealing with the rage that she felt within her and could not express in any other way. Her functioning throughout this period was adequate—she was able to work steadily—but her interpersonal relationships were sparse and very poor. Her reality testing remained intact and the general diagnostic impression of her doctors at this stage was that of a borderline personality. The paranoid elements in these repeated episodes went undetected, and the elements of thought disorder and autistic behavior that had been seen previously were no longer part of the clinical picture. Attempts were made all along this course to get her back into treatment, but they were resisted. She continued to live in this way, living an unstable and precarious existence until her final hospitalization.

The story thus far gives us a bizarre and tragic picture of a young woman of extraordinary gifts and intellectual abilities who was caught up in a process that had led to increasing isolation, withdrawal, and a pattern of self-destructive behavior that could only end in suicide unless it were somehow reversed. It is important to note that when she came to my attention at the point of her last hospitalization—despite the bizarre and quite disturbed quality of her behavior—there had been a definite shift in the structure of her pathology. By the time of my first contacts with her, one could not justify any diagnostic label that would indicate anything more pernicious than that of borderline personality. She was able to maintain areas of adequate ego-functioning in her life on a fairly steady basis. Her reality testing was intact. There was no indication of thought disorder, and the delusional elements of her paranoia were well controlled and concealed. The picture she presented, therefore, was an encouraging one, since it implied that she was capable of benefiting from treatment if the treatment process could meet and respond to the growth potential that was in her.

Before we begin to look at her therapeutic development, we need to look back in time at the original course of development. In order to begin to grasp some of the elements that contributed to her more current plight, we need to consider her early life experience and how it was patterned and influenced by the family environment in which she grew up. What was the family background out of which this tragically disturbed yet fascinating young woman emerged?

Family Background

Clare was the oldest of four siblings in her family. She was just four years old when her younger brother was born. He was followed a year later by another girl, Jenny. The youngest sibling was Ed, who was just ten years younger than Clare. The older brother was the one of her siblings that Clare felt closest to. She recalls that when they were playing as children, the alliance was always she and Fred aligned against her sister Jenny. She regarded him as a relatively calm and stable individual who had done reasonably well in school. She remarked, however, that he liked to draw horrible and gory pictures. She had a tendency to get very upset when he used marijuana or LSD, feeling that there was something self-destructive about it and not wanting him to mess himself up as she had.

Jenny was easily the most rebellious of the siblings. She had always had a conflictual relationship with her mother. Her adolescent years had been quite tumultuous, with a lot of smoking, drinking, and flirting with drugs and sex. Jenny demonstrated a strong capacity for self-destructive behavior. At one point her mother was after her to stop smoking and Jenny would burn her arms with the cigarette butts in defiance. She also attempted to scratch or cut her wrists on several occasions. Clare's relationship with Jenny was highly ambivalent—a mixture of sisterly affection and dependence as well as hostility and jealousy.

The youngest brother, Ed, was the baby of the family—and seemed to be on relatively good terms with everybody. Clare saw him as somehow different from the other siblings. She felt that he had been raised differently. Her father never punished or beat Ed, but talked to him and seemed to be more understanding in his regard. Clare herself took a very protective and caring—almost maternal—attitude toward him. She expressed strong feelings about his growing up normally and the need to protect him from the misery that afflicted her life.

Father

Clare's relationships with both her parents were fraught with difficulty and conflict. Her father was a relatively successful, but difficult man. In his youth he had been an angry young man. He had rebelled violently against any constraint, had espoused liberal—indeed radical—causes, angrily dropped out of college, had rebelled against his own parents and had moved away from home to be on his own when quite young and still in college. By dint of effort and intelligence, however, he had been able to make himself quite expert in certain areas. He worked as a consultant to industrial firms and was highly regarded in his area of expertise. He was a rather obsessive, controlling, demanding and perfectionistic man—and to a large extent projected these attributes into his relationship with the family. His control and rule over the family was tyrannical and at times violent. His word was law and he brooked no opposition. He laid down arbitrary and rigid rules for the governing of the family and dealt out swift and harsh punishment for any infringements of these rules. He would fly off the handle at the least provocation and was given to beating the children at the least displeasure. For Clare, this relationship was a most trying and difficult one. On the one hand she admired her father's intellectual interests and proficiency, his efficiency and his capacity to get things done. But at the same time she was terrified of him and repulsed by much of his behavior.

Clare saw herself and her older brother as the special targets of the father's hostility and violent attacks. She recalled repeated occasions when he would pump her with questions, and if she did not know the answers or didn't answer to his satisfaction, he would strike her angrily. She would often run in tears to her room and lock the door, terrified of her father's angry outbursts. One of the scenes that she recalled with particular vividness—a scene that was often repeated, apparently—was what took place at the dinner table. The father demanded that the children discuss interesting and intellectual subjects, and that they eat everything that was put before them. These scenes apparently became the focus for intense pitched battles. If Clare would balk at eating something, she would be sent to her room for fifteen minutes and then told to return to the table and eat all of the then cold food. If she refused, her father would fly into a rage, beat her viciously—even to the point of physical injury on occasion. She recalled times when she tried to avoid his blows by crawling under the table—at which times he would kick her in the head under the table. Clare would relate these episodes to me with a frightening intensity of feeling and hatred.

The father's general attitude toward Clare was critical and devaluing. Anything she did or accomplished was subject to little or no praise, but generous criticism. Nothing she did was ever right. Nothing she said or thought was correct—particularly when father held a different view. He was always right—he had to be right. He was continually holding her up to ridicule or devaluing criticism. This was particularly difficult for Clare, for her intelligence and perceptiveness were remarkable. It was father's view that women were not worth very much and were incapable of intellectual attainment of any worth. The father's attitude toward Clare's mother was much the same—constantly criticizing and undercutting. As far as he was concerned, women were good for only one thing, and he saw to it that they stayed where they belonged. Having Clare for his oldest daughter must have been difficult for him. She was very bright and very capable—much more so than any of the other children—and we can easily conjecture that he was no little threatened by Clare's obvious intelligence. This may also have been the case in his relation with his wife, since Clare felt that her mother might well have been as intelligent as her father. In any case, the father was pushed to constantly tear down and devalue whatever competence or capacity was manifested by the women in his life. It seems clear that the father became the persecutory object which served as the basis for Clare's paranoid pathology. His own style of relating to reality seems to have been decidedly paranoid.

Mother

The trouble with Clare's mother was that she adopted a submissive and nonchallenging role in relation to her husband. She never confronted her husband; she never intervened when he would go on his angry tirades or when he would beat the children so viciously. Clare's resentment at her mother for not protecting her against her father was deep and intense. The mother was in many ways a capable woman. She worked for many years as a psychiatric nurse, and for most of the time that Clare lived at home was the head nurse in a large psychiatric ward. At home, however, she kept her light under a bushel. She was apparently chronically depressed. Clare remembered her as never very warm or affectionate. She would often withdraw from the family and stay in her room for days on end, not eating, talking to no one. This would apparently happen particularly at times when she was enraged at her husband. She was a very conflicted women in regard to her own angry or hostile impulses, and would withdraw into a deep and sullen depression at such times.

These episodes of silent and sullen withdrawal were particularly difficult and perplexing to Clare. She could remember them as far back as her memory served her. She felt hurt and angered by them. She would wonder whether she was responsible for what was happening. At such times her mother was unavailable to her—in a sense, lost for a time. Clare felt hurt and abandoned, unable to understand why her mother would no longer talk to her, why she was so withdrawn and sad. These were times of real anguish and doubt for her, making her feel guilty for her hostile feelings toward her mother and her father, making her feel that she was somehow bad and evil and the cause of all the unhappiness in the family. It made her feel particularly that she was the evil power that drove her mother away from her.

The mother's illness became exacerbated on two occasions. The first took place when Clare was about eleven years old. The mother became severely depressed and suicidal. She had to be hospitalized and was given shock treatments. Clare remembered only that this time was full of severe disruptions and anxiety in the family. She recalled that her father was very worried, upset, and irritable. She could not understand what was happening, and remembered feeling responsible for her mother's plight and for her having to go to the hospital. Before she went to the hospital mother had been through a period of severe withdrawal, spending whole days in bed and communicating with no one. It was like one of mother's typical withdrawal episodes, except that it was on a larger and more intense scale.

The second occasion took place about five years prior to Clare's last hospitalization. The setting was the death of her mother's own mother. We shall have occasion to come back to this event because it proved to be a critical one for Clare as well. The grandmother had died of cancer of the breast. Her terminal course was long and drawn out. She became increasingly weak and emaciated and, in the final months of her life, required constant nursing care. Clare's mother undertook this responsibility. The difficulties surrounding this set of circumstances and the strain of caring for her mother in the face of an inevitable but slow death took its toll on Clare's mother. She began having increasing difficulties sleeping, and began taking Doriden. She took increasing doses, and just a few months after the grandmother died, the mother had to be hospitalized. She was suffering from what was thought to be chronic Doriden intoxication. Her behavior became bizarre and psychotic, with frank hallucinations. The exact nature of the decompensation remains obscure. Whether the psychotic symptoms were simply toxic in etiology, or whether there may have been any underlying schizophrenic process remains an open question. In any case she was hospitalized and treated for a rather long period on phenothiazines.

As the basic picture of the structure and pattern of interaction within this family emerges, we begin to see a pattern that we have already identified in our previous cases—and which we will meet again in subsequent cases. There is a basic imbalance in the parental relationship, one parent being relatively dominant and aggressive, while the other is relatively submissive and usually presents a more or less chronically depressed picture. We have also seen in our previous cases that one of the parents—usually the dominating, aggressive, and sadistic one—carries on an undercutting, devaluing, and critically disparaging attack on the patient. Clare was subject to this manner of treatment from her father, who would both criticize and devalue her for not meeting his high and exacting standards of performance, and yet would simultaneously work to impress on her that she was not able to measure up in any number of ways and for any number of reasons. The reasons were never specified but included the assumption that she couldn't live up to any standards of attainment or intellectual capacity simply because she was a girl; additional reasons could not be focused any more than in the impression left with Clare that she was worthless and inadequate in herself. The pattern of paranoid-depressive interaction which characterized the relationship between her parents set the terms for the introjective configuration within Clare herself.

Early Experience

Clare remembers very little of her early experience in the family. Her early years were apparently unremarkable, at least in so far as the data available to us would suggest. She was a healthy and apparently normal little girl. One of the significant events of her young years took place when the family moved to her grandmother's farm. The family lived there for over a year when Clare was about four years old, and then moved to the permanent family home in a nearby city where the father carried on his work. Clare remembered her relationship with her grandmother in very warm and special terms. Grandmother was a pleasant and affectionate woman and Clare had a special relation to her. She recalled her as someone who was warm, affectionate, loving, and pleasant—someone who was fun to be with—unlike her own mother and the rest of her family. Clare loved to spend vacations and holidays with her grandmother and recalled these occasions with her as the only times in her childhood that she felt happy and loved. Her relationship with her grandmother stands out in her early history as the only positive and warm attachment that she was able to have. As a consequence the loss of her grandmother was particularly difficult for Clare to integrate, but it may also have provided her with an important basis on which her later capacity for therapeutic improvement was able to build.

Clare grew up a shy and relatively withdrawn child. She kept to herself a great deal and had few childhood friends. She played almost exclusively with her brothers and sisters and made few friends at school. Academically her performance was quite superior: she was at the head of her class in grammar school and at the very top of her class in high school. She felt awkward and embarrassed about her intelligence, and undoubtedly she suffered many of the difficulties of bright girls. On one hand she was stimulated to compete with the bright boys in the school, but on the other she was too successful. She felt ostracized and isolated because of her intelligence. She was afraid that her schoolmates would not like her because she was too bright and won all the prizes. Her interests were not the same as other girls'. She never took any interest in play with her girl friends, never indulged in doll play or other girls' games, but was more interested in boys' games and in competing in sports, and developed early intellectual interests (probably from the pressures put on her from her father) in science and literature. She learned to read early and recalls spending most of her time as a child reading, and she read everything that she could get her hands on. She could never share her rather precocious interests with the other kids; the other girlds didn't know what she was talking about and cared less. The boys—some of them—might have afforded some outlet for communication, except for the fact that she felt so competitive with them and felt that they all avoided her because they didn't like smart girls—especially if the girl was smarter than they were. She developed the feeling that her intelligence was a liability, since because of it people disliked her and tried to put her down. She also developed the conviction that all the boys she knew—particularly the smarter ones whom she could admire and like—were out to show her up and take every opportunity to make her look stupid or inadequate. She could never appreciate the way in which this conviction paralleled the treatment she received at her father's hands.

Sexuality

I would like to focus at this point on Clare's sexual development, since it provided a significant vehicle for a considerable proportion of her pathology. It would be an underestimation to say that it was a conflicted development. It was the most difficult and problematic area of her life—as a child, as a growing adolescent, and as an adult. We must note at the very beginning that she grew up in a family context in which the female was severely devalued. Her mother provided her with a prime model of the weak and inadequate female—a woman with intellectual gifts and abilities who was devalued and continually undercut. The model of adult femininity that she provided for Clare was a highly depressive and masochistic one. Clare's emerging sense of feminine identity could not but have suffered and been severely impaired.

The sexual climate of the house was not a very positive one. The subject of sex was a prohibited and avoided area. There was no talk about sex at home, and Clare did not remember any attempts to teach herself or the other kids anything about it. The sexual life between her parents left something to be desired as well. Clare did not realize it at the time, but it turned out—something she only discovered during the course of her treatment with me—that her parents did not sleep together and stopped having intercourse altogether after her mother's severe (psychotic?) depression. This undoubtedly served to increase the level of sexual tension in the house at a time when Clare was entering her pubertal development.

Although talk about sex was prohibited, her mother's attitude toward sex gave Clare the impression that it was a dirty and evil business. Mother did not enjoy sex, and she avoided it and any reference to it. Father's attitude was quite different. In his liberalism and declared independence of any social conventions, he felt that the atmosphere toward sex in the house should be uninhibited and free. The split between the parents was wide, and their differences of opinion provided the battleground for many of their arguments. They differed particularly in the matter of how sexual matters should be handled in regard to the children. Father acted in a provocative manner. He used to walk around the house stark naked, appearing in front of the children casually in the nude. Clare—the oldest daughter—found this behavior extremely difficult and embarrassing. She remembered seeing her father's penis and feeling frightened of it—but at the same time fascinated by it. She particularly remembers his having an erection. She recalls vague dreams of her father approaching her sexually and feeling frightened and panicked.

The father continued this behavior for some years, even into Clare's adolescent years. He would come down to the kitchen at night, for example, completely naked and would never bother to check on who might be there. She recalled her embarrassment as a high school girl, and feared bringing anyone home because they might see her father. The father's behavior was strikingly seductive and his exhibitionism must have partially served his own sexual needs which were being frustrated in the sadomasochistic struggle with his wife. The documentation is obscure, but there is some suggestion that his seductiveness was particularly directed at Clare. She recalls episodes when the father came into her bedroom naked, terrifying her and stimulating her fantasies of brutal violation. She can recall only one occasion on which her father spoke to her about sexuality. He told her on that occasion that when men and women make love, it was really a sort of attack in which the man subdued the woman. He also told her that she could never trust any man because what each wanted from a girl was only one thing (the only thing to his mind females were good for!) and that was to attack her sexually. He added that the only man she could really trust was himself. The confusion and blending of sexual and aggressive themes in this message and in her relationship to her father are most striking.

Father's behavior was provocative (as well as exciting) to Clare in other ways as well. The family often spent vacation periods camping in the woods. They would frequently go on camping trips, an avocation of father's. At such times, when he had to urinate father would simply turn around. The family would joke about it, since everyone else would discreetly retire to a private place to urinate. Clare felt angry and resentful about this behavior of her father. She felt it was embarrassing, inconsiderate, and hypocritical. Her father would never relieve himself facing her but would always turn around. It was some time before Clare was able to acknowledge any wishes of her own that he would void facing her so that she could watch his penis. The wishes were present and active, but highly threatening and largely repressed. She recalled on occasion on one of these camping trips, when she retired to a secluded part of the woods to defecate. In the middle of this act father came upon her. She was terrified and frightened of him in the solitude of the woods. She was afraid that he would violate her, and felt shamed and vulnerable at his seeing her with her pants down defecating. She felt that there was something abnormal about her father's concern over and interest in excremental functions. She described his elaborate rituals surrounding elimination, and his flushing the toilet when he let go so that no one could hear it. She resented deeply his staring at her and making her feel ashamed. Her gratification, however, was deeply repressed.

Clare had heard about menstruation, but only in vague and general terms. Her menarche came as a shock and a bitter disappointment. She felt humiliated and debased. She felt that she was dirty and defiled by it, as though it were a mark of the evil and debased femininity that she reviled and hated. Her menstrual periods in her adolescent years and on into adult years

were difficult for her. She would have considerable premenstrual tension
and crampy pain with her periods. She would usually have to go to bed and
would often feel quite sick. She resented her periods bitterly, for they were
the mark of her worthless and filthy sex. She recalled several occasions in
high school when she would have an attack of menstrual cramps that were
so severe that she had to leave the classroom. On one or two occasions she
recalled fainting and having to be carried to the infirmary. She reflected her
bitterness and resentment over these episodes. She felt that all the boys and
the other girls in the class knew what was happening to her, and she felt embarrassed and shamed. These experiences reinforced her feelings that girls
were weak and worthless. Her resentment took the form of hatred for boys,
who didn't have to endure such things. She recalled with intense feelings of
frustrated rage and resentment how, on one occasion in high school, she was
taking a calculus final exam. The outcome of the exam would determine
whether she or one of the smart boys in the class would get the highest
grade. In the middle of the exam she had an attack of menstrual pain and
fainted. She was carried out of the classroom and could not finish the exam.
She complained that the boys had an unfair advantage over her just because
she was a girl, and her resentment in recalling this event was deep and bitter,
even a decade removed from the event.

Clare was extremely self-conscious of her sexuality. She recalled the occasion when her mother took her downtown to buy her first bra. When they
got home her father took it out and dangled it in front of her brothers and
made a joke of it. She felt hurt and angered and humiliated. She ran to her
room in tears, and never forgave him. As she was maturing, her mammary
development was exceptional. She was of slender and lean muscular build
otherwise, so that her breasts were a prominent endowment of her anatomy.
She took elaborate precautions to try to hide them. She wore heavy sweaters
and blouses. She adopted a slouched posture with shoulders hunched in an
attempt to minimize her breasts and make them less apparent. She hated
anything that smacked of femininity or feminine interests. Her mother forced her to get her hair curled once and she resisted bitterly, and hated the
curls vehemently. She never wanted to wear dresses or other girls' clothing.
She wore pants and heavy boys' shirts whenever she could.

Nonetheless sex remained an area of fascination for her. She would
read about it in sex manuals and books, and avidly read novels and stories
with sexual material in them. She remembered thinking time and again how
horrible and filthy sex was. She dated rarely—and she did not begin dating
until she was in high school and then only infrequently. Her dating activity
was infrequent even later on in college. When she was sixteen a boyfriend
kissed her and she remembered feeling dirty and defiled—feeling like a
cheap slut or whore.

College Years

Clare's college experience was not altogether a happy one. She attended a fashionable women's college. There were not many boys around and consequently dates were few. She maintained a tenuous relationship with the boy who had been an unsteady dating friend during high school years—this was the young man with whom she became sexually involved at the time of her first decompensation. The relationship was not very close however. Her relationships at the school were highly emotional and labile. She had few close friends, and, in the few relationships she had, the feelings were intense if extremely variable. She was sensitive to the least indication of hostile feelings from the other girls and was constantly testing her friends to see whether they still liked her or not. She became intensely jealous of friendships her friends might have with other girls. When she felt slighted or rejected—a prominent reaction on her part—she would become morose and depressed, have angry thoughts of destroying the dormitory or the school, or of terrible things happening to the people who were the present objects of her jealous rage and disappointment. She would withdraw from any contact with people, spending long hours in bed or in her room reading and immersing herself in fantasies.

Her relationships with her family at this time were not good. One of her reasons for going to school away from home was to get away from them and their influence. There was a rebelliousness and recalcitrance to her general behavior. She dressed sloppily and conducted herself in a manner so as to affront her parents' expectations. Her father was particularly angered and displeased by this behavior, or at least made his anger and displeasure more apparent. When she came home for visits there would be angry confrontations. While she was at school he would write angry and accusatory letters to her, scolding and berating her for her behavior, for her lackadaisical attitude, for her less than satisfactory academic performance, her friends, etc., etc. The letters would come and Clare would let them sit on her dresser for days, afraid to open them. She knew very well what they would contain, but she had difficulty in facing the angry and horrible feelings they stirred in her. She would usually wait until she felt in a somewhat better mood, and then open a letter with gritted teeth.

Grandmother's Death

In her third year of college, the aforementioned event of critical importance for Clare took place. Her grandmother, whose lingering illness had drawn out through the summer and part of the autumn, finally died. Clare was away at school at the time. During the summer months, she had spent most of her time with grandmother. She knew that grandmother was dying but couldn't face the fact. When she was alone during that summer, she wept bitterly over grandmother's approaching death. After she left for school, she felt sick at heart. She thought of writing to her grandmother, but could not bring herself to do it. Her parents, and particularly her mother, were angry at her for not writing in grandmother's last weeks. Mother finally wrote to her that if she didn't write, she would disown her and never let her set foot in her home again. Clare felt bitterly resentful about this attack. She felt that her parents never understood her feelings, and did not understand her feelings about grandmother and how deeply she felt her loss.

The death of her grandmother was a severe loss for Clare, and one that she could not deal with effectively at all. It became apparent that even five years later, when she dealt with the events surrounding grandmother's death in her therapy, she was still actively mourning her grandmother. The school year following was a depressed and unhappy one for Clare. The reverberations of grandmother's death were felt all through the family. Clare's mother particularly became increasingly depressed, a course that led to her hospitalization and acute (schizophrenic?) decompensation, as we have noted. Clare had been spending the summer vacations working as a waitress in a resort hotel. She became attached to a young man on whom she felt quite dependent, and with whom she engaged in considerable necking, kissing, and fondling, but no intercourse. The next summer, however, she became friendly with a black kitchen helper who was nearly forty. She confided to him her fears of intercourse, and he told her that he could show her how beautiful an experience it was. She allowed herself to have intercourse with this man, only to find the experience difficult and repulsive once again, and had intense feelings of worthlessness and filthiness. She felt that he had tricked and taken advantage of her.

After her graduation, she applied for nursing school. Her relationships with the other girls were much the same as they had been in college—intense, suspicious, jealous. She gained one close confidant in one of the other nursing students with whom she would share her fears and anxieties. As the friendship grew more intense, the two girls—both rather isolated and lonely girls—found their attraction with each other growing stronger and becoming more frankly sexual. There was one intimate experience in which they went to bed together and indulged in some fondling and touching. They were both frightened by the experience and by the intensity of their feelings, and decided that they would have to set limits on their intimacy. They were able to do this and remained friends without further physical contacts. It was soon after this that Clare began sleeping with her old high school boyfriend, and was soon plunged into her first decompensation and hospitalization.

The Therapeutic Experience

We have cast a backward look over the pattern of Clare's life which brought her to the hospital and into treatment. We can now turn to a more detailed look at the process of therapy itself. The course of Clare's improvement over several years of treatment offers us an opportunity to gain some understanding of the elements which constituted her basic pathology. Our objective will be to link these elements and their understanding to what we already know of her experience within the structure of her family and in relation to the experience she endured in relationship to her two rather disturbed parents.

When Clare came to our hospital and I first met her, she was a rather frightened and confused young woman. In my early contacts with her, she seemed moderately anxious but tried to present herself with a bland, almost casual, facade. It was almost as though in relating the events that brought her to the hospital, she was telling me about something interesting that had happened to someone else. Her manner was simplistic, even childlike, but she gave an unavoidable, if vague, impression of a deep underlying depression. She was obviously a bright and verbal person, and had a basic willingness to be involved and to communicate about herself. She had a unique ability to describe her feelings and inner processes—and a remarkable introspective bent. These qualities were to stand her in good stead in the years ahead.

She talked easily and readily about her early experiences and about her family. When she told me about her father's angry tirades and beatings, she smiled. I asked her why she smiled like that. She replied that she smiled when she felt angry and really felt like crying inside. She could allow herself to cry when she was alone, but not in front of anyone else. Her fear was that if she were to cry in front of me she would simply fall apart. She was able to talk about her feelings of loneliness and sadness and hurt. She felt this particularly in regard to her former therapist, whose loss she was still grieving. She wanted desperately to be loved by everyone. She was crying inside but couldn't let me see the tears. If she started to cry she felt that she would never be able to stop. She couldn't trust me, and didn't know if she ever could. She feared that if she started to cry it would hurt me in some way and would hurt the other patients in the hospital as well. She would feel guilty for doing such a thing.

After about three weeks in the hospital, there was an episode in which she broke a glass container and cut her wrist with the glass. The episode had been precipitated by one of the attendants leaving the hospital. Clare expressed her feelings of loneliness and anger—her feelings of unreality, anxiety, and depression. When she cut herself she could feel the pain and see the subcutaneous tissue below the skin. That made her feel that she must be real and that she was really in that tissue someplace. She referred to herself repeatedly as "an extension of the process C." She translated that into the unreal and dehumanized perception of herself as a machinelike extension of the impersonal and efficiently functioning "process" that she saw her father

226   The Paranoid Process

to be. The "process" functioned as a smoothly operating system that left no room for feelings. The "process" was not human—and Clare was the extension of that process.

Her perception of herself as hateful, destructive, loathsome, and evil was overwhelming. Her concern was to try to protect me from this powerful and magically destructive evil within her. Her attraction to me and her feelings for me were a danger because they raised the possibility that I might begin to care about her and thus be sucked in and destroyed by her evil poison. She labored to keep me at an emotional distance. She vacillated between anger at me and her fear of trusting me. She wanted to make our relationship nothing more than a strictly professional one—no personal interest or caring involved. She tried to maintain an image of me as simply doing my job—as she did as a nurse with her patients—no emotional involvement, just performing a professional function. I was someone she paid to perform that function. The payment of the fee became a sort of magical talisman which protected her from deeper feelings about me and insured that our relationship was a strictly contractual one. She talked about the anger and disgust she felt when her own patients became so dependent on her.

Clare's dreams served as an important element in the course of her treatment and reflected in a particularly impressive way the progress she was making. In the present instance, she was able in the context of the dream to being talking about her grandmother, how important and special that relationship had been for her, and was able to recount the painful events that surrounded her grandmother's death. In the course of this retelling, Clare was able to break down in tears. Her willingness to cry and weep in my presence was an index of the developing trust and understanding she felt with me. She was able to share with me her feelings of loneliness and despair, the feeling that she had lost the only person in the world who really loved and cared about her. I felt that something important was achieved at this stage of Clare's treatment. It seemed to establish a bond between us that had not been there before. Moreover, it was a situation in which she had showed me her hurt, and loneliness, and weakness, and vulnerability, and had come away without rejection, or loss, or destruction. I had not been overwhelmed or destroyed by the intensity of her feelings, and I had not run from them or withdrawn from her in any way.

Destructive Rage

Little by little she was able to express her anger and resentment against her parents. She felt that in her early years she had tried very hard to please them but never seemed able to. After she got to college, and especially after her grandmother died, her behavior became an attack on and rejection of her parents. She began messing herself up, wearing dirty and weird clothes, hanging around with weird people who were really strange and "fucked up" and whom she knew her parents disapproved of. She felt that she really wanted to hurt her parents, to show them how badly they had "fucked her up"—she wanted to destroy the "extension of the process C." that she felt herself to be. Her anger at her mother was intense for having permitted her father's sadistic attacks upon her and for not having intervened to protect her. At one point she saw a movie in which a soldier had a dog. The soldier became very apathetic and depressed. The troops had to be moved quickly to another place and they were loaded into a truck to be driven away. The soldier's dog could not be taken along. As the truck pulled away the dog ran after the truck barking after his adopted master. The sergeant who was sitting in the back of the truck pulled out his gun and shot the dog. The soldier did nothing to prevent it. Clare saw this episode as directly applicable to the situation with her parents. She complained that if the soldier had really loved the dog he would have prevented the shooting. The movie had presented an allegory of her childhood experience, and the rage, disappointment, and hurt that she felt was deep and nearly overwhelming.

Gradually she became aware of the extent and the ways in which she was like her parents. She began to realize how she was depressed and withdrawn like her mother, how when she was angry she would withdraw and close off communication with other people—that her mother was a nurse, too, and that her mother had been a mental patient as well. Her cutting had been largely focused in the area of her groin and thighs. She saw this as involving the feminine part of herself. She wanted to cut and attack the part of her that was most like her mother. She hated and reviled her body. She hated her breasts because they bounced and constantly reminded her of being a girl. She hated her periods because they were so dirty and shameful. She hated her body because it was so "bouncy and leaky"—and she repeatedly expressed her wish to cut and hurt and punish it. On one occasion she walked past a group of high school boys who made some obscene remarks and invited her to take off her clothes. She felt embarrassed, ashamed, guilty for arousing their interest in her body, furious and enraged and wanted to destroy them. She remembered her rage at her father for his sexual interest and provocations—for dangling her bra in front of her brothers.

As time went on, Clare was gradually and increasingly able to let me know about her anger toward me, and increasingly able to tolerate it and talk about it. When I had asked why she was making herself a mental patient, she had felt hurt and furious. She was afraid to tell me about these feelings; she feared that I would reject her and turn away from her as her mother used to do. She remarked that she had never really been able to get angry at her doctor before. But she was afraid of letting the anger out—not sure how far she could go, or what I would do if she did. She did not know whether I would withdraw from her and reject her as she felt her mother did, or whether I would turn on her in anger and attack her like her father did. Much later on in the treatment, there was a day during which the clinic was closed for a holiday and I had forgotten to remind her that we would omit our appointment that day. It turned out to be a cold, rainy, miserable day, and Clare had come to my office, to find it locked. She was furious with me. The next day she called me on the phone and leveled an angry blast at me—and then started crying. I told her we would discuss it at our next appointment. When we met she was still furious, but able to tell me what she was feeling and able to talk about her anger in a constructive way.

These experiences were multiplied in minor ways throughout the whole course of the treatment. Her fear was that if she let out her anger, she would destroy me or drive me away. Little by little she became more comfortable with her anger and was increasingly able to share it with me. As this capacity increased, her anger seemed to diminish in intensity. There was a magical quality to this aspect of her treatment which persisted for a long time. She saw me graphically as a strong and powerful sponge which was able to soak up the poison she exuded and to neutralize it. When I went on vacation during the first couple of years, she would voice her apprehensions in terms of her fear of what was going to happen when the powerful external control and neutralizing force was taken away from her. Would her evil power once again assert itself? Would her poison again work its magic on the world and the people around her?

Along with this, she became increasingly aware of the fact that her mind—her intelligence—was the strong, adequate, capable, and masculine part of herself. It was also the part that wanted to undercut, revile, degrade, despite, hurt, maim, and lacerate her feminine body. She saw that this part of herself was cast in the model of her father. She was like her father when she was critical, devaluing, and violating herself. She acted out in her own head the drama that she saw enacted so often between her parents. She turned her father's hostile and destructively devaluing attacks against herself, and made them her own. It served as a striking example of identification with the aggressor. She had to struggle with two difficult and opposing identifications. She identified with her mother as the weak, vulnerable, depressed, sensitive, hurt, victimized woman. She identified with her father as the cruel, evil, destructive, powerful, capable, intellectual, critical, demeaning masculine force. These identifications contended with each other within her.

As this material came to the fore in her therapy, there was a slow but detectable shift in the pattern of her handling of anger and destructive wishes outside of therapy. There were a number of occasions when someone had disappointed her or taken advantage of her and she became quite furious. Her pattern earlier in the therapy had been to deal with these feelings by being depressed, sullenly withdrawing, feeling that she was hateful and evil, wanting to punish and hurt herself, even to the point of wanting to commit suicide. More and more as time went on, her anger took a more outwardly directed—if cautiously guided—course. On one occasion her roommate, a rather depressed, angry, and provocative girl herself, had left a pile of dirty dishes in the sink. This culminated a series of episodes in which Clare felt that she was leaving the dirty work for Clare and taking advantage of her. Clare became furious, and proceeded to smash every plate in the apartment to smithereens. She felt proud of being able to do that rather than cutting herself (that impulse was also there!), but she still found it difficult to confront the other person directly with her anger.

Paranoid Core

During the major portions of the time Clare and I worked together, the paranoid elements in her pathology continued to assert themselves. She lived a guarded, suspicious, and mildly persecutory existence. She had constantly to struggle with ideas of reference, thoughts that people were staring at her, criticizing her, thinking evil thoughts about her, etc. The sexual area was a particularly difficult one in this regard. She would walk through the park on a summer day, and feel that the men there were staring at her, having sexual thoughts about her, that they would follow her and molest her. She would become anxious and fearful. On one occasion she was returning home from work and night and was followed for a short distance by a man. She went into a paroxysm of fear and anxiety and her imagination ran riot with fantasies of rape, sexual attack, and murder.

She visited her parents at one point during the treatment. When she returned, she reported several episodes when her fears of attack and of being killed were overwhelming. Driving one night with a boyfriend, she became terrified of his driving, feeling that he wanted to kill her. At the same time, she began having dreams about her father coming into her room and trying to kill her. One night in particular, she stayed up nearly the whole night paralyzed with the fear that he would come bursting through her bedroom door to beat and kill her. She even pushed the bed in front of the locked door, and spent the night sitting in a chair watching the door. Such beating fantasies are not without significance as we shall see.

Even when things were going well for her and she felt well, something could happen to plunge her into a spasm of paranoid anxieties. One of her friends was a young man who was given to taking acid. They were sharing an apartment with some other friends. Clare objected to his taking acid and to some of his other behavior. She told him to leave and there was an unpleasant exchange. Clare became quite upset, beset with fears that he would break into the apartment and try to kill her. She took a knife with her to bed as a protective measure. She felt so horrible that she wanted to cut herself again.

Inner Destructiveness

When circumstances provoked an angry response in her, Clare had a great deal of difficulty in managing the anger. Along with her paranoid fears of rape and murder, there was a strong tendency to feel herself responsible for the bad feelings. At such times, particularly, she thought of herself as evil and powerful. She felt that she possessed an evil and destructive power that could make other people around her feel and do things. She could make them like her and want to be with her—or she could make them have angry and destructive thoughts and wishes. She saw herself as emitting poisonous influences that corrupted and poisoned the thoughts of people around her. She felt that the evil thing should be destroyed. She would destroy it herself, or other people would want to destroy it. She tried to destroy it by cutting, by starving it to death, or by killing it. It was an evil, horrible, destructive, and powerful monster that had to be destroyed to protect other people from its evil influence. She could gradually recognize how important and powerful a person such fantasies made her. She also could recognize that such feelings were similar to those she had as a child, when she felt that she was responsible for her mother's depressive withdrawals. How powerful she must have felt to be able to exercise such significant control over her mother!

As might be expected from all this, the area of sexuality was quite problematical for Clare. She found it very difficult to enter into any relationships with men, and kept them at a well-guarded distance, despite the fact that she was an attractive young woman. She could relate in a very charming and pleasant manner, but when her sexual feelings were aroused or when the question of sexual activity and especially intercourse arose, she would become quite conflicted and would try to distance herself protectively. On occasion, in the midst of one of her self-destructive and self-punitive paroxysms, she would get herself screwed. It was quite clear that such activity was a substitute for cutting herself and served as an appropriate punishment for her feminine body and self.

On several such occasions she deliberately went to bed without taking contraceptive precautions, wanting to get herself pregnant. She reflected that getting pregnant would really get to her parents and upset them. Her father's sister had had to have an abortion once, and she recalled the huge stink that it caused in the family. Her self-destructive sexual behavior—as well as her other self-destructive behavior—was clearly an attack against her parents and an attempt to punish and disappoint them. Clare saw the sexual act as an act of brutality that men exercised on women, and pregnancy was the punishment dealt out to women. During intercourse, Clare described herself as feeling empty, as though she became nothing and completely lost any identity. She would feel as though she were being engulfed by the male and that all of the power and the force belonged to him. It became clear to her that the operative model for this fantasy was the relationship between her parents in which father was the powerful one who forced her mother into submission, and her mother was the weak, helpless, vulnerable, and pathetically passive female who had no recourse but submission.

This, incidentally, was her view of the therapeutic relationship. It was a view that changed only gradually and increasingly as time went on, and she came to see that our relationship was not one of dominance and submission, but of helpful support and cooperation. As these elements were gradually worked through, she came increasingly to be able to form real friendships with men and to feel herself a valued and significant person in the relationship. The issue for her with me—and with other men—was that she could not show them the evil and dreadful aspects of herself that lay within. She was afraid of letting her "dirty laundry" show, because that meant that people would be revolted and disgusted and turn away from her and abandon her. The "dirty laundry" was her hurt, vulnerable, depressed and lonely feelings that she associated with her femininity.

Allied with these incestuous wishes there were wishes to get rid of her mother. The rivalry with mother for father's penis and her wish to have her out of the way were complicated by her mother's depressive withdrawals and illness. Clare felt responsible for this effect on her mother—as though her hateful and competitive wishes that her mother would die or go away had in fact had this powerful and magical effect. But mother's retreat and withdrawal left Clare with a sense of omnipotence and served only to place her in greater jeopardy vis-a-vis her father. It raised the possibility that she could indeed take mother's place and have father's penis. The idea was threatening to her, but at the same time exciting. The fact that father made his penis so available to her served both to intensify her wishes and make the possibility of possessing his penis and getting rid of mother seem all the closer.

Termination

To complete the clinical picture of this patient and to close the story, let me say that her therapy was concluded by mutual agreement. She had done increasingly well and for some months had been quite symptom-free. She was leading a relatively normal and well-adjusted life. Finally she met a young man, became quite fond of him and decided to live with him. This required moving to another city. We terminated with the understanding that she might find it necessary or advisable to seek treatment in the future, but that her prospects for the moment seemed optimistic. She was happy at the turn of events in her life—felt confident in her ability to deal with her feelings, particularly her anger, and seemed hopeful that things had finally taken a positive turn for her. She saw clearly that the positive turn was within her power to accomplish and to continue.

DISCUSSION

The case of Clare C. offers us a rich complex of data which provides the basis for discussion of a number of important points. I would like to organize the discussion of this material around the following salient points. I would like to consider first the family pattern of interaction and its influence on her. Then I would like to consider the relationship between paranoid and depressive elements in Clare's own personality. In conjunction with this appraisal, I would like to consider the patterns of introjection and identification that the organization of her personality and functioning reflect.

Family Interaction

There are some striking features to the organization and functioning of Clare's family. The postures adopted by her parents leap to mind. Her father was harsh, critical, sadistic, punitive, vicious, demanding, perfectionistic, and brutal. Her mother was quiet, withdrawn, brooding, depressed, submissive and weak. The pattern fits that of a skewed family as described by Lidz (et al., 1965), in which one partner is dominating in the relationship and the other is dominated and submissive. In reference to this skewed pattern of family pathology, the relationship is described in these terms:

> In all, the rather serious psychopathology of one marital partner dominated the home. In some, the dissatisfaction and unhappiness of one spouse is apparent to the other and the children, but husband and wife manage to complement or support each other sufficiently to permit a degree of harmony . . . In all of these families, one partner who was extremely dependent or masochistic had married a spouse who had appeared to be a strong and protecting parental figure. The dependent partner would go along with or even support the weaknesses or psychopathological distortions of the parental partner because dependency or masochistic needs were met . . . . A striking feature in all cases was the psychopathology of the partner who appeared to be dominant, creating an abnormal environment which, being accepted by the "healthier" spouse, may have seemed to be a normal environment to the children. Considerable "masking" of potential sources of conflict occurred, creating an unreal atmosphere in which what was said and admitted differed from what was actually felt and done (Lidz et al., 1965, pp. 142-143).

In Clare's parents the psychopathology was generously distributed. The father's dominating and sadistic personality was complemented and responded to by the mother's depressive and masochistic submissiveness. It is important to note that this patterning of parental interactions creates an atmosphere of human relationships in which there is both a victim and a victimizer. In so far as the parents provide the meaningful models for the working through of human relationships, the basic pattern of victimization comes to permeate, and to add its peculiar quality to, all forms of relationship. Victimization becomes a basic premise in all forms of interaction. Particularly it becomes the basic premise for all forms of meaningful interaction between the sexes.

The emotional split between Clare's mother and father was profound—any real communication between them was short-circuited. There was a resulting gap in feedback processes and a consequent impairment of the relative reality testing on the part of both. Each of Clare's parents was operating in a sort of emotional vacuum in which each was responding more to his own emotional needs and fantasies than to the real qualities of the other. The mother's masochistic need to be victimized made it important for her to be able to see her husband as victimizing, and to have him actually victimize her. The father's need to be a victimizer made it important for him to see his wife as victimized, and to have her actually play out the role of being victimized. Each plays out the unexpressed expectations of the other, expectations that are generated on both sides by inner subjective needs.

The result is that a sort of emotional system is set up by the complementary and mutually reinforcing needs of the parents. The emotional interaction which constitutes the system, however, is set up on a relatively unconscious level and is elaborated out of the primarily repressed and unexpressed emotional needs and responsiveness of the parents. The parental pathologies thus intermingle and interact in such a way as to bring their combined pathogenic influence to bear on the children. The pathogenic impact is reinforced by the respective parental pathologies—by both the mother's masochistic submissiveness and the father's sadistic domination.

The interesting feature of this family interaction is that the pathogenic influence strikes at the female children more so than at the male children. A similar pattern has been identified in families with schizophrenic daughters, where the skewed pattern of family interaction was reflected in the father's constant undercutting and derogatory treatment of the mother. These mothers provided rather poor models of the feminine role both because of their own masochistic and depressive characters, and because of the constant contemptuous devaluation that came from the fathers. There seems little doubt that Clare's mother provided her with a poor model for identification and that this deficiency was complicated by her father's constantly demeaning and devaluing attack, not only on her mother, but also on herself.

Paranoid Elements

In such marriages—as Lidz' (1965) studies have suggested—the parents were often in open conflict, with each of the parents trying to undercut the worth of the other and each competing in a sense for the daughter's allegiance in the struggle. The mother's tendency for impoverished self-esteem and sense of inadequacy as woman and wife tends to be continually reinforced and intensified by the husband's derogation of her worth. She inevitably finds it impossible to maintain her position in the face of a dominating husband who may be quite grandiose—if not frankly paranoid—and who is often embittered because he does not receive the narcissistic gratification he requires from an admiring and submissive wife. The mother is thus thrust into an anxious and uncertain position in regard to her daughter. She is insecure about her capacity to function as a woman and mother, she is anxious about her capacity to raise her daughter, she often feels ill at ease with her daughter—possibly because of unexpressed homosexual concerns—and thus remains distant and aloof. As Lidz et al. (1965) point out, however, these mothers are not rejecting in the ordinary sense. They aspire to be good mothers, but their efforts are impeded by their anxiety, their unhappiness, and at times by their jealousy of their husbands' seductive interest in the daughter. The mother's aloofness impairs proper Oedipal attachments and distorts the identificatory processes between daughter and mother. Few of these mothers were psychotic, but rather tended toward a picture of resentful depression, perplexity, vagueness, and an imperviousness to the daughters' needs and feelings.

The fathers in these families were frequently paranoid or had clear-cut paranoid tendencies. They were highly narcissistic men who had strongly developed needs for admiration and approval. Often when they failed to get the obedience, loyalty, and admiration they demanded from their wives, they would turn to the daughter—many times in highly seductive ways bordering on incest—to gain what they needed from her. There was reasonably good evidence to suggest that Clare's father was rather paranoid. He was a suspicious and distrustful man, and his angry rages had a definite paranoid tinge to them. There was little doubt that he fitted the pattern often found in fathers of schizophrenic daughters. His behavior toward Clare was highly brutalizing and intensely seductive. His flaunting his genitals at her—to the point of naked parading—was highly sexualized for him and for her. Much of his behavior was directed toward gaining narcissistic gratification and admiration from her. He demanded constant compliance with his views, demanded and required that his opinion or view of things be accepted by her as the correct view—regardless of what her thoughts or opinions or feelings might have been—and he brooked no opposition and tolerated no divergent opinions. He also demanded total submission and acceptance of his authority. The incredible rigidity of these needs and the threatened authoritarian posture that is reflected in the episodes at the dinner table give us a valuable insight into the basically paranoid structure of his character.

Victimization

While the growth-limiting aspects of this involvement have often been described, I would like to focus here on the modality and patterning of it. In addition to impeding the child's opportunity for warm and meaningful relationships with both parents and distorting the patterns of identification which are so essential for psychological development, the pattern of interaction in Clare's family introduced other important parameters. Clare grew up in an atmosphere that taught her that human relationships were predicated on the interaction between victims and victimizers. She learned that the relationship between men and women was based on dominance and submission. As a woman it was therefore her lot to be victimized, taken advantage of, hurt, used, demeaned. Her only recourse was acceptance and submission—otherwise she became the victim of brutalizing attack. Her mother's constant message—lived out in the pattern of her own behavior and experience—was that women were inferior, inadequate, destined to be attacked, sexually abused, and victimized.

Thus there was an implicit style of relating and interacting that was founded on the underlying suppositions that in relating to other human beings one had to expect attack, hurt, victimization, and humiliation. This implicit message that was dictated in multiple facets of the family life and experience, and which was generated from the pattern of interacting pathologies in her parents, was also reinforced in the expressed attitudes of both parents. This had particular relevance to the area of heterosexual involvement: Clare's father taught her explicitly that men were out to get her and that they wanted nothing but to screw her. This approach left little room for an understanding of tender and loving feelings or for an appreciation and valuing of Clare's femininity as valued and appreciated.

The point I am emphasizing here is that there is an identifiably paranoid style that is promulgated within the family interaction that was both implicit in the pattern of interaction between the parents—as well as in the interaction between Clare and her father—and which became explicit in the communications made within the family. The explicit communication was found in Clare's family—particularly from her father—but often is not so explicit in other families. It is always an implicit part of the family interaction nonetheless.

Relation to Parents

The situation in the family interaction had severe implications for Clare's involvement in and resolution of her Oedipal relationships. Her preoedipal one-to-one relationships with both parents were disturbed and imbalanced, so that her involvement in the Oedipal situation was impaired from the beginning. The mother's aloofness and distance made it difficult for Clare to establish any warm and loving relation to her. Clare was left with an intense longing for closeness with her mother that was continually frustrated. The intensity of those homosexual longings was worrisome to Clare and frightened her, but they seemed to stem from the deep infantile longing for closeness with her mother that reflected the mother's relative un-availability at an earlier preoedipal level. At the same time Clare's wishes to do away with her mother as an Oedipal rival were complicated by the mother's depressive withdrawals. These left Clare with a sense of respon-sibility for her mother's hurt and increased her own sense of magical power—especially the power to hurt and control the feelings of others. Her wish to get rid of mother was realized and reinforced by mother's withdrawal.

Clare's relation to her father was also fraught with difficulty. The Oedipal wish to love him and be loved by him was complicated by his open seductiveness, which served to excite her sexual wishes to the point where they became threatening to her and highly conflicted. She felt shamed and guilty over the wishes stirred in her by his exposure to her—particularly her fascination with his penis. But this was all complicated again by his vicious and demeaning treatment of her. She hated and feared him at the same time. This aspect of her relationship with him was heavily overladen with pregenital elements. Her perception of him was highly contaminated by the projection of her own aggressive wishes and impulses onto him, so that the viciousness and sadism of his character was compounded in part of her own projected hostility and destructive wishes and in part of his own sadism and paranoid rage.

Beating Fantasies

The quality of this relationship was reflected best in Clare's paranoid fears of brutal assault from the father. We cannot easily escape a com-parison to Freud's discussions of beating fantasies in young children. In Freud's (1919) view, the beating fantasy was derived from Oedipal wishes which were regressively contaminated by anal-sadistic elements. The beating fantasies were thus related to the genesis of masochism. This view was con-firmed by Anna Freud, who was able to demonstrate in addition the in-fluence of such masochistic beating fantasies on daydreams and dreaming (A. Freud, 1923).

While the content of beating fantasies and wishes is derived from multi-ple developmental levels and carries varying implications, in Clare's case they must be situated in the context of severely pathological introjections which derived from the family context in which anal-sadistic components exercised a severely distorting and pathogenic influence on the course of Clare's development. Seen in a broader context, then, the fear of brutal assault—beating fantasy—would seem to reflect the extent of pregenital discoloration of relations in the family and the degree of masochistic-depressive pathology in relation to which the paranoid process operated. These sadistic fixations and regressions were reinforced differentially from both sides of the Oedipal triangle.

Ambivalence

On both sides of her Oedipal relationships, therefore, the ambivalence was intense. On both sides as well, her loving feelings were frustrated and were cast in a threatening mold. They were strongly contaminated as well by her anger and destructive wishes toward both parents. We have seen this as a predominant aspect of the parental involvements of all of our paranoid patients. The intensity of the ambivalence—derived from preoedipal levels—interferes in fundamental ways with the normal development of Oedipal involvements and consequently impairs the normal resolution of Oedipal relationships. The emerging pattern of identification is thus distorted and the developmental process resorts to more primitive and more highly defensive internalizing operations, particularly introjection, as we shall see. I would like to observe at this point, however, that the intensity of the ambivalence and the patterning of introjections reflects the interaction of parental pathologies which is reflected in, produced in part, and prolonged and intensified by, the pattern of familial interaction that obtains between them. The child who is affected is the child who becomes involved in the emotional interaction and conflict between the parents. Usually one child is more severely involved than any other—in this family Clare was most deeply involved, more so than her sister Jenny. The result is that the affected child becomes more intensely the victim of the combined parental pathologies and their interaction.

There were important saving elements in this complex of influences however. The most important of these—that one that stands out so starkly in her history—was Clare's relationship with her grandmother. This is the one relationship in Clare's early history that was affectionate and loving, that was not complicated by intense ambivalence, and that gave Clare the loving acceptance that she needed so desperately. It was on this ground that the girl was able in some degree to work out the vicissitudes of a meaningful therapeutic alliance derived from and built on the basic experience of a positive relationship that she had gotten from her grandmother. That relationship was a saving element in Clare's experience. It gave her some degree of protection from the pathological effects of her involvement with her parents, and it also provided the basis on which important and fundamental aspects of ego development were realized. The sustaining aspects of that relationship were given witness by the difficulties Clare began to experience after her grandmother's death. It was only as she was able to adequately mourn that loss that she was able to begin to mobilize some of the resources that she gained through that relationship.

Depression and Paranoia

We can turn to more specific consideration of the effect of these inter-actions in Clare. She demonstrated in a graphic manner the alternation between depression and paranoia that we have seen in other patients and will see again. She alternated between frankly paranoid fears and anxieties that she would be attacked or killed by some external agency and a severely depressed preoccupation with her own inner evilness and destructiveness. We have found this pattern in all of our paranoid patients. When the paranoid defensive position is given up, the patient becomes depressed—often the depression is severe. In Clare the location of the destructive and paranoid evil bounced back and forth. At times it was within her, and at other times it was located outside herself. Invariably she saw it located in some threatening male figure, never in a female, to my knowledge. This alternation between paranoid and depressive positions reflects the predominance of projective or introjective mechanisms in deal-ing with the intensity of her ambivalence and particularly the hostility and destructive wishes it involved. While projective mechanisms were predomi-nant, she tended to be more guarded, suspicious, and to experience paranoid fears and anxieties. As we shall see, an important aspect of her treatment was to allow the introjective elements to predominate and to then be able to work these through.

Introjective Configuration

It is useful in focusing our analysis of Clare's pathology to think in terms of the identificatory systems in terms of which her personality seemed to be structured. If we look in the first instance at the inner organization of her psychic life, there seemed to be two identifiable configurations of characteristics that dominated her inner experience. On the one hand, there was the perception of herself as worthless, valueless, undesirable, unlovable, weak, vulnerable, and somehow defective. The portrait of herself, drawn in these terms, was paralleled in many dimensions by her perception of her mother, who was the prototype of the devalued and vulnerable woman. Clare had internalized this representational configuration of her mother in a somewhat undifferentiated fashion, and it remained within her as a somewhat ego-alien part of her self. This aspect of her personality organiza-tion was given relatively exact location. It was localized—not sur-prisingly—in the more feminine parts of her body. Clare's intense self-hatred, which was directed toward this maternal introjection, was focused on her breasts and the area of her groin and thighs. She felt embarrassed and shamed because of these bodily signs of her femininity—and the areas she particularly lacerated were those surrounding her genitals. The cor-respondence in this aspect of her pathology with the dynamics found in self-wounding or self-mutilating adolescents is striking: the mutilation is an attack against the body as the source of regressive sexual and aggressive urgings, as well as the instrument of gratification of such impulses. In girls, this attack is specifically directed against the maternal introject (M. Freidman et al., 1972).

The other striking configuration of characteristics that formed the core of her self-representation was the view of herself as powerful, magically influential—able to shape and manipulate the minds of other people around her, making them pleased and happy, or making them unhappy and hurt and giving them evil and hateful thoughts—and seeing herself as somehow terribly destructive and poisonous to everyone with whom she came in contact. This view of herself was linked to a certain extent with her intellectual capacity, and was reinforced by her finding herself able to do so many things easily that other people found difficult. It was this powerful and intellectually capable part of Clare that directed the attack against her weak and vulnerable feminine self. This was the part of her that reviled and despised her own femininity. The powerful and destructive part of her self was that aspect which at times was located within her—associated at times with her head and at times, particularly in her dreams, in her intestines. It was also the aspect which she projected both in the content of dreams and in her paranoid anxieties more generally. This introjection was derived from her father, whom she both hated and feared; it was essentially a form of identification with the aggressor. Internally it functioned as a superego introject which directed its destructive power against the weak and defective feminine self. Externally, as a function of Clare's paranoid projection, it became the fearful source of power that intended to hurt, kill, or violate her.

This patterning of introjects offers an internalized version of the pattern of interaction that was in effect between Clare's parents. The external drama of victim and victimizer was rehearsed once again and played itself out on the inner stage of Clare's self. The inner organization of her self was derived not merely from each of her parents independently—nor was it derived from either one of them separately. It was derived from both parents interacting with each other in destructive and pathological ways. The pathological interaction is carried on within Clare with a resulting fragmentation and conflict-ridden division within herself. The constant inner struggle of these warring elements provided the basis of her pathology and directly impeded any resolution which might provide the basis for more constructive inner growth and development of her ego.

The presence of such introjects within her and the inner struggle between them posed a constant threat to Clare's ego. The threat was posed from both sides. From the side of the maternal introject, there was the threat of vulnerability and victimization. From the side of the parental introject, there was the threat of hurtful destructiveness. Either aspect was threatening and had to call forth its appropriate defenses. Clare's feelings of power and destructiveness were equivalently a defense against the feelings of weakness, vulnerability, and defectiveness. The paternal introject thus served as a partial defense against the maternal introject. Her feelings of weakness and vulnerability were a defense against the fearful harm and sense of destructive power that she felt. Thus, conversely, the maternal introject played a role as a defense against the destructiveness of the paternal introject. Clare vacillated between being the helpless victim and being the powerful destroyer.

The entire picture that we have is permeated with conflict and hostile aggression. The anal preoccupation is clear in Clare's father. The struggle was clearly joined. We are presented with a picture in which all levels of Clare's development were shot through with aggressive components. The intense ambivalence in these relationships and the fixation of aggressive growth processes were impeded. Clare's relationships with both parents were embedded with the need to defend herself from the aggressive threat each posed. In the face of this ambivalence, her deep longings for affection and acceptance and love were unanswered and frustrated. Her wishes or tendencies to become more like either parent were fraught with danger, and she had to resort to more defensive patterns of relating with them. Thus her internalization processes were directed into introjective channels in the interests of defense and a compromise adaptation that ensured some form of survival.

CHAPTER 9

Donald D.

The present case is one that came to our attention—like that of Bob B.—as a result of an acute decompensation. But the outcome in the present case has been considerably more optimistic than in Bob's case.

THE PATIENT'S PROFILE

Acute Decompensation

Don suffered only a single decompensation in the several years of our contact with him. At the time of his acute break he was just twenty years old. The break came in the midst of a conjunction of stressful events, each of which added its burden and seemed to have contributed to his breakdown. To begin with, in the months preceding his decompensation, he had been having difficulty with his studies. He was a student at a prominent eastern university where he had come to study only that year. He had started his college career at a university in his own hometown, but had not been satisfied with things there. He had originally matriculated there because of his father's wishes. His father wanted him to stay at home, since he was the last of the children to be there. Don had complied with this demand, but felt resentful and chafed somewhat under this restriction. He had cherished a wish to come to the present university since childhood and resented his father's blocking his ambition. Finally he decided to make the break from home and to make the transfer in the face of his father's wishes. Coming to the new university was a test of his academic capacity on one side, but even more significantly a test of his capacity to function on his own away from his family. This was the first time in his life that he had lived away from home. Consequently, his academic difficulties confronted him with his own fears of his inadequacy and dependence on home and family. For him not to make it in the big university was to fulfill his father's and his family's predictions of his downfall. And so he felt the pressure of his academic slippage acutely.

In addition, shortly before his decompensation, he had broken off his relationship with his girl friend. This was particularly traumatic since he had never had a real girl friend before this, and his relationship with her was held by him as a facet of his being able to "make it" on his own. He found the disruption of this relationship—a disruption initiated by the girl—as upsetting and disturbing. He felt that it was a sign of his lack of masculinity and of his immaturity. It was another signal of defeat for him.

A further factor was that shortly before the break Don had been elected president of his fraternity. He was well liked and rather popular among his fraternity brothers, but the election came to him as a surprise and a challenge. Not surprisingly, as we shall see, he felt that he was inadequate to handle the job and the responsibility that it imposed on him. These feelings were complicated by the fact that quite soon after he took office, Martin Luther King was murdered. Don was quite committed to liberal causes and had been actively involved in student activities for the improvement of civil rights, particularly for blacks. Martin Luther King had been one of his heroes, and Don was deeply affected by his death. He felt hurt, frustrated, angered, bitterly hateful, not only of whoever who had brought about King's death, but of all those who had opposed him and who stood in the way of all that King represented. He felt a sense of impotent rage and frustrated agony.

The response of the fraternity was to organize a daylong symposium at the university to consider the effects and implications of King's death on the civil rights movement. They wanted to organize it on a large scale and invite a number of prominent people to participate. The responsibility for organizing this program fell on Don's shoulders, and again typically he accepted this as a test of his abilities—particularly his ability to meet the responsibilities of his office. He plunged himself into this activity in a vigorous manner. He began working very hard, day and night, for several days. At this point he was on the brink of decompensation. His activity became more and more manic, he tried to do everything himself, making arrangements, setting up meetings, producing posters, running around from one thing to another in almost frantic style. His behavior became increasingly disorganized, frantic, and bizarre. His friends finally saw that his behavior was abnormal and increasingly disorganized, and thus brought him for psychiatric help.

There was one other contributing feature of this decompensation. This had to do with Don's father. Several weeks prior to the events surrounding the immediate decompensation, Don's father had suffered a fairly severe stroke. The onset of the stroke was particularly disturbing to Don in that his father had the stroke while Don was talking to him on the telephone. Don went home to visit his father shortly after, and the effects of the stroke had stabilized by that time. The father was left with a partial paresis and some slurring of speech. Don became quite concerned with his father's condition—his father was also diabetic and alcoholic—and felt quite concerned and conflicted with the imminent possibility of his father's death. He had many preoccupations about his responsibility for his father's stroke and many guilt feelings about it—as we shall see in more detail later.

When Don came to the hospital he was frankly psychotic. His behavior was disorganized and erratic. He was disoriented and unable to concentrate even on simple clinical tests. He was suffering from almost manic excitement. He was alternately agitated and fearful. He was incredibly anxious and tremulous. He was repeatedly distracted by auditory hallucinations which seemed quite threatening and frightening to him. The physician who examined him at this time was a woman, and his responses to her were highly sexualized and erotic. Any questions put to him were interpreted in a highly sexual fashion. His associations were loose and he babbled rather incoherently at times in a classic flight of ideas. His clothing was disheveled, and he kept trying to unzip his fly, and intermittently trying to remove his pants. He expressed in a highly disorganized fashion somatic delusions and paranoid preoccupations that people were out to get him or do him in. He was afraid that his friends, or the doctor, or the people in the hospital wanted to kill him. An initial diagnosis was made of acute schizophrenic episode with homosexual panic.

With phenothiazines and environmental restriction, this disorganized picture cleared remarkably quickly. Within hours the disorganized and bizarre quality of his behavior disappeared and the hallucinations ceased. For several days his paranoid preoccupations persisted. He was suspicious and guarded, thinking that people were out to get him. Ideas of reference were prominent. After a few days, however, even these residual symptoms had evaporated and he had apparently returned to a level of premorbid functioning.

Don was discharged from the hospital after a little more than two weeks. He then returned home, feeling uncertain about his future and not knowing what path to follow. His return home was obviously a defeat—a retreat from his failure. He had not been able to make it on his own, and his father's dire predictions had been verified by his breakdown. Once home, he began to get increasingly depressed. He did nothing—did not want to go to school, did not want to work. He just sat around and spent most of his time trying to piece together what had happened to him. He found little success in this effort and only became increasingly morose, withdrawn, and depressed. He began thinking of suicide and the idea grew on him with an intensity that frightened him. He finally came to the realization that he had reached the end of the road. He would either have to kill himself or try to get some help. He chose the latter course.

He began to see a private psychiatrist and was able to work through much of his depression. He was also able to make several important decisions about his future. He decided that he would leave home once again and pick up his academic work where he had left it. The effect of this phase of his therapy was that he had gained some measure of hope in himself, and a sufficient degree of confidence to permit him to try once more the path of his ambition that had once before led him to failure. He came back to the same university he had left when he decompensated and matriculated on a part-time basis. He also sought to continue the work of treatment that he had started so well at home. It was at this juncture that I undertook to continue Don's therapy.

Family Background

I would like to return to a consideration of Don's origins and background to try to trace some of the influences that contributed to his personality organization and ultimately to his illness. Our interest will be in the configuration and patterns of interaction that obtained in his family, for these seemed to have had a determinative role.

Don was the youngest of three children. His older sister was ten years his senior and his older brother was nine years older. He was never close to either of them. His relationship with his sister took on special qualities as we shall see, but he never felt any close ties or affection for her. The relation with the brother was distant and rather cold. Both siblings were married by the time of Don's illness and had not lived at home for several years. But apparently even in his childhood there had been little by way of meaningful relationship between Don and his brother and sister. He rarely produced any memories that involved them. They never played together, and apparently had as little to do with each other as possible.

There was a good reason for jealousy and resentment. Don arrived on the family scene nearly a decade after his siblings and he was clearly the baby of the family—in status as well as temporally. This special position was fostered and maintained by Don's mother. He was close to her and he held a particularly special relationship to her. As a child he spent a great deal of time with her, playing together and later on when he was a little older, helping her with her housework. She delighted in having him with her and there was a special bond between them. Later on, in his latency years, he preferred to spend his time after school at home with her, rather than going out to play with the other children. He recalled his feeling that she needed him around—that she needed something from him that only he could give her. This special relationship was an object of attack from other family members—especially his father. The father felt that he spent too much time hanging around home and that he should get out to play more. The mother, however, wanted to have him with her. This pattern of closeness and dependence on the mother is one that we have noted in several of these clinical cases. It serves to set the stage for introjection of the relatively devalued, depressed, and victimized mother figure.

Parental Interaction

The relationship between the parents was not a happy one. Don's father was a dentist, but a rather unsuccessful one. His practice was never flourishing. He was apparently a very irascible man with a violent temper. He was quick to explode in anger at patients. This inevitably meant that he never had many patients who were eager to come back to see him after a few visits. The family finances were shaky. They never seemed to have enough money to do things that they would have wanted to do. This was particularly irritating for Don's mother. She would criticize and badger her husband about money, and there were frequent arguments about this subject.

There were frequent arguments anyway. Don recalled that there was a major argument and confrontation almost every night. Both parents drank heavily. It is not clear that both were alcoholic, although Don stated unequivocally that such was the case. At any rate, they were both often drunk. By the time the end of the day came around, mother was frequently on the thin edge. She was given to tippling during the day, and apparently took more toward the end of the day in preparation for Don's father's arrival home. By the time he arrived, mother would be in a nasty and argumentative mood. Usually the argument started by mother launching an attack on Don's father. Sometimes Don's father would have had a few by the time he arrived home; even so, he would begin drinking and gradually get soused. Then the argument would rage, with lots of shouting and occasional physical abuse. Don's father had a mean temper anyway, and the mother would provoke him into physical violence without much difficulty.

These arguments were particularly wrenching for little Don. He would listen to his parents shouting at each other, and tremble fearfully. His fears were terrifying to his tender soul. He was afraid that one of his parents would be hurt in these fights—particularly his mother. He tended to see her as the vulnerable one in the relationship who was unjustly brutalized by his father. His sympathies definitely lay on her side then, and he saw his father as the unjust and brutal aggressor. Interestingly enough, during the course of his therapy he was able to see that his mother was not simply an innocent bystander, but that she was more often than not the *agent provocateur*. He was afraid, then, however, that his father would kill his mother. He knew that his father was a violent and quick-tempered man. He knew that his father kept a loaded gun in his bedroom drawer. These elements added to his fears and made him hate and fear his father. In addition, the argument would frequently take a turn and focus on him. His father would attack his mother in regard to her close relationship with him and would criticize her wanting to keep Don around her so much and keep him so close to her. Don often felt in these circumstances that his parents were really fighting about him. He felt responsible for their fighting and for the fact that they could never get along. He was afraid that he would be the cause of whatever dreadful outcomes he was imagining—whether that be a divorce and the breaking up of his family, or whether it be the murderous outcome that haunted his mind. In any case, the effect on him was dreadful.

Relationship to Mother

He recalled several instances when, after particularly violent arguments, his mother would come to his room, slobbering drunk. She would be crying. She would embrace him and fondle him—sobbing all the while how much she loved him and how much she needed him—asking whether he loved her and whether he would stay with her. These episodes were very discomforting to Don. He reflected on them that they seemed somehow abnormal. They embarrassed him and made him feel uneasy. He felt that her motives were apparent, and that there was something highly sexual and erotic about the procedure.

Don had always been very close to his mother. He grew up a rather shy and withdrawn child. He was bright and always did well in school, standing at the head of his class in grammar and high school. But he never got along well with his age-mates. He was small in stature and chubby in build. Because of his size and shyness, other kids tended to pick on him. He recalled that this was particularly painful for him in junior high school. He felt hurt and angry when kids picked on him—especially for his somewhat childlike, short and fat build. He remembered being very self-conscious. The boys would have to undress for gym class and Don was afraid of this. He was particularly afraid to expose his genitals, feeling embarrassed and ashamed. He felt that they were smaller than anyone else's and that if the other boys saw them he would be ridiculed and made fun of. He wanted only to escape from all this torment and stay at home with his mother—she was the only one who loved and understood him.

Relationship to Father

Don did not feel at all close to his father. Their relationship was a distant and difficult one through most of his childhood. He regarded his father—perhaps not inaccurately—as a violent man. He hated and feared him because of the way he treated his mother. Don felt a sense of smoldering anger and resentment against his father for as long as he could remember. His father was rather strict and rigid in his attitudes. He was quite conservative in his views and very authoritarian in his outlook. Don found this attitude of his father hard to take, and continually chafed against it. Even in later years there was constant friction between father and son over Don's wishes to follow his own inclinations. The conflict touched just about everything, including his dating activities, the college he went to, and the career he chose to follow. Father was generally restrictive and conservative, and any attempts on Don's part to break away or follow his own inclinations met with severe resistance and opposition from his father.

Don discovered when he was about eighteen that, in fact, his father had led a somewhat flamboyant and wild youth. Father had been a rather wild and rebellious—as well as angry—young man. He had eloped when he was a sophomore in college and had married his girl friend. The marriage lasted only a year and ended in divorce. It was only several years later that his father met his mother. Don reflected that his image of his father just didn't fit with his current attitudes as Don knew them. With considerable resentment, Don commented that the things his father did were several times as bad as anything Don had ever thought of doing—let alone actually done. Yet his father would give him hell for his minor infractions. Don could not see the justice in this.

Mother's Death

This pattern of life persisted in Don's family until he was about fourteen years old. At that point something happened to change the course of his life and the lives of his family in profound ways—Don's mother became ill. She had developed a cancer of the liver. No treatment was possible. The course of her illness was lingering and drawn out over several months. She gradually wasted away and finally died. Don was especially close to her in these last months of her life. He attended her in her illness. He spent most of his time with her. He remembered little of his feelings at that time. He did remember feeling guilty for his thoughts about her dying—his fantasying about all the sympathy he would get from people after her death.

She finally died, but at first Don did not feel her loss very deeply. He felt lonely for about a month, but felt that showing any feelings would have been a sign of weakness. In fact he felt somewhat relieved by her death. He was happy to have gotten rid of the constant fighting that was such a source of distress for him. It was apparent, however, as Don talked about these events surrounding his mother's death, that he was deeply affected by her loss. When he began to talk about her death, his eyes watered and his voice choked. The mourning process had not yet run its course, and he had not yet been able to resolve or come to terms with her death. This was one important area of work for his future therapy. The mark of her death was unmistakably on him. Not only was the pain of her loss still apparent, but the overall impression that he gave clinically was that somehow his development—however mitigated by the experiences prior to her death—had somehow stalled and remained at a plateau since her death. His appearance and manner were very much that of a young adolescent. Even his physical stature and appearance conveyed that impression, let alone the psychological issues he presented.

While the sense of loss and rage at his mother's death had been more or less repressed in Don's own response, the effects of his mother's death on the rest of the family were profound. His father took her death as a severe blow. He became increasingly morose and withdrawn. He kept to himself much of the time, and let his already slender practice more or less slip away from him. He began to stay home all day long and never went out. His social life deteriorated radically, and he would allow himself a rare and occasional dinner with old friends. The father erected a sort of shrine composed of pictures and favored objects associated with Don's mother. The father's depression and withdrawal lasted for a considerable length of time. Over the years he had become somewhat less withdrawn and depressed, but the effects were still evident. He, too, had been unable to adequately mourn his wife's passing. When he spoke of her it was to praise her, to say what a wonderful woman she was, what a good wife and mother she had been. Don reflected how different this was from what had passed between them when she had been alive. Further, the father became quite negligent of his own health. He was a fairly severe diabetic, to the point of having developed retinal complications that had affected his eyesight. He stopped following his diet, and often neglected his insulin. Don saw this behavior as self-destructive, and it worried and angered him, perhaps because this self-destructive behavior on his father's part came too close to fulfilling his own murderous wishes in his father's regard.

Struggle for Independence

The circumstances of Don's life changed radically after his mother's death. Things were unhappy for him at home. He could not get along with his authoritarian father, and there was little by way of positive affection that passed between them. If his father was not depressed and withdrawn, he was making demands on Don and setting restrictions against which Don felt he had to rebel and struggle. Don's relationship with his older sister also became considerably more difficult. She was a very domineering person and felt it her responsibility to take over where her mother had left off. She was much more of one mind with her father—very conservative and constricted in her approach—and felt that her mother had babied and catered to Don too much. She set about to rectify this deficiency in his upbringing. Don, in turn, was bitter, resentful, and hated and despised his sister, bitterly resenting her attempts to control and interfere in his life. There was a constant battle between them. Don had lost the protective haven that his mother had provided.

Soon after, however, the sister had married and moved out of the house. After the sister moved out, that left Don as the last of the children in the house. Despite their poor relationship, Don's father depended on him to a considerable degree. The father wanted to keep Don at home—out of motives of selfishness and dependence, it seems. The issue was particularly joined over the question of where Don should go to college. The father and sister insisted that he stay at home and attend a local institution that enjoyed a very good academic reputation. Don, however, cherished an ambition to attend a more prestigious institution away from home. It was also his ticket to freedom.

The argument raged intensely, but Don's argument and objections did not put much of a dent in his father's resolve. Then, too, Don could not quite master his own ambivalence. He wanted to leave his family—particularly his father. They did not get along and he hated the old man, particularly for the way he had treated Don's mother and all the misery he had caused her—as Don saw it. Part of him wanted nothing better than to get away from his father and his family—to get out from under their thumbs. But at the same time he felt guilty about these feelings and for the rage and hatred he felt toward his father. Moreover, he worried about his own capacity to function and be independent away from home. He had always lived at home—he had always been extremely dependent and protected especially by his mother. His ambivalence and his uncertainty kept him from making a break at that point, and he capitulated to their wishes. He stayed at home and went to the local school for two years.

By that time he had had enough. He overcame his ambivalence and worked up enough courage to confront his father's wishes and to make the break from home. His father gave in, but not without prognostications of Don's failure. His father predicted that he would not be able to make his own way away from home, and that he would not be able to meet the high academic standards of the school to which he wished to transfer. Thus, when Don came to our city to further his academic career, that action was laden with all the overtones of an act of rebellion, an expression of his rage and resentment against his father; an abandonment of the latter, who claimed that he needed him and clung to him possessively; an assertion of independence from father and family; and a challenge to his own sense of masculinity and personal adequacy and his capacity to master new challenges. As we can conjecture on the basis of this history—and as it turned out in fact—Don was vulnerable on any one and on all of these counts.

The Lure of Failure

If we reexamine in this light the circumstances surrounding his decompensation which seemed to have served as precipitating factors, we can see that his psychic reserves were under attack from many sides. His academic difficulties—the first time in his academic career that he had ever experienced any problems at all—were a signal of his inadequacy and a fulfillment of his father's prediction. His loss of his girl friend was an assault on his sense of masculine adequacy and served to undermine his sense of capacity to function away from his family. That loss may well also have revived the sense of loss from his mother's death that had never been resolved. Moreover, his father's stroke undoubtedly activated his feelings of guilt and responsibility for the illness and for the specter of impending death that it brought with it. His murderous and hateful wishes for his father's death stemmed from early levels of his child's mind, and these very wishes had made his departure from home and father all the more difficult.

Don felt that there was something self-destructive in the pattern of events that had led him to the hospital. It was as though something in him pushed him in the direction of fulfilling his father's dire predictions. It was as though some part of him wanted to prove once and for all that he was indeed a helpless, dependent, inadequate, vulnerable little child who couldn't make it on his own. It was as though his breakdown were a way of casting his failure in his father's face. It was a way of expressing all the hate and rage that he had felt for so long, but which he could never dare to bring himself to express. He could never express it because he felt it would destroy his father—kill him. He recalled bitterly how, when he first saw his sister after his hospitalization, she accosted him with the question, "How could you do this to your father?" He felt that in attacking his father he was only confirming and consolidating his own failure and inadequacy. The whole episode of his decompensation, his hospitalization, and his subsequent severe depression, which had led him to the brink of suicide, was a fitting punishment for his wishes to hurt, abandon, and destroy his father—wishes that had in part been acted out in his leaving home and coming to a different city.

Relationship to Women

At the point at which Don came into treatment with me, he was already set on a course of improvement. He had decided to come back to school and to try his luck once again.

As his schoolwork progressed he gradually convinced himself that he would be able to make the grade. He finally settled into an area of creative work which offered a wide scope for his talents and which he felt was sufficiently challenging and creative to satisfy him as a career. He became considerably more comfortable with this direction of his life and began to enjoy some significant successes. As he was making progress along these professional lines, he began to struggle with his sexuality. It was important in his mind that he make it with girls; this was a critical area for him for establishing and demonstrating his masculinity and adequacy. He acquired a girl friend—Judy—and gradually became more involved with her. He felt self-conscious and ill at ease with girls. He felt awkward and stupid in trying to meet them. Mixers were a torture for him. He was constantly haunted by the fear that if he tried to introduce himself to a girl she would laugh at him and reject him. As he put it, he would be "shot down or treated like shit."

As his relationship with Judy developed, he became increasingly fond of her. He was frightened of sexual activity, but wanted desperately to have it. He was afraid of getting "too physical," afraid of imposing something on her that she might not want, afraid of going to bed; he complained of how embarrassed and ashamed and self-conscious he felt about taking off his clothes in front of a girl. Little by little, however, he advanced toward a deeper and more involved relationship; first petting, then he went to bed with her without intercourse, then intercourse, then they decided to live together. This was a major step for him, because he felt that it involved a commitment on his part that he was afraid of making and uncertain as to whether he wanted to make it. Living with a girl seemed to be a terribly adult thing to do and he was not sure that he could handle it.

His feelings about intercourse were mixed. He was afraid of it because he felt it was an aggressive act. He was afraid of hurting Judy—but also afraid of being hurt. He gradually overcame these fears and increasingly the issues shifted from his concerns over the sexual act to his concerns over his relationship with Judy. She was talking marriage, but he was hesitant. He feared the commitment of a more permanent relationship. The idea of really loving her frightened him. It made him feel his vulnerability more intensely. If he allowed himself to love her, he could be hurt. Because he had had intercourse with her, he felt that he had some obligations to her—that he owed her something. He felt much closer and much more involved with Judy than with the previous girl friend, who had broken off their relationship before his breakdown. He had felt that loss intensely, judging that it was a terrible defeat for him, that it proved his inadequacy and impotency, proved that he couldn't make it with girls.

Discussion of these losses carried him back to the loss of his mother. Discussion of that critical loss formed an early focus of his therapy. He recounted her death and its aftermath in detail. At first there was a considerable amount of sad and remorseful affect, but this seemed to diminish the more we talked about it. This phase of his treatment seemed to provide an essential turning point. Gradually he was able to talk about his resentment against his mother—for overprotecting him, making him so dependent on her and finally for dying. He was able to explore his feelings of guilt and responsibility for her death. This seemed to offer him considerable relief and release. He began to function better and started making significant therapeutic progress. My impression had been that his inability to face some of his feelings about his mother and her death had placed a serious impediment to his emotional development. It seemed as though in the course of exploring and sharing these feelings a block had been removed—and the ensuing growth was striking.

Aggression and Self-Esteem

Another important area that this opened up was his concern over aggression and his inability to express it. Aggressive feelings frightened him. He recalled his parents' continual fighting and the fear and resentment he had had about it. He felt anger was of no use whatever, it only complicated things and produced hurt and rejection. It served no productive purpose at all, as far as he could see. Expressing his anger had always been a problem, even though he could recall many times and situations in which he had been enraged. These had particularly to do with his father and his sister. He had always kept his anger in and preferred to feel a smoldering resentment rather than let anyone know how angry and resentful he felt. He could recall only one episode in which he had lost his temper. On this occasion his aunt and uncle had come for dinner. The conversation had gotten around to the black problem. His uncle had made some derogatory remarks about blacks that Don found offensive and which made him angry. He got up to leave the table, and his father ordered him to sit down. He was furious and shouted an angry reply at his father. The force of his voice and the intensity of his feelings surprised and frightened him. That was the only time he had ever let out his anger and it scared him, although he could acknowledge in retrospect that it was a good feeling.

The issue of expressing anger was joined more directly with his family. During one Christmas vacation he planned to visit home. He had grown a beard and he could not decide whether to shave it off for the visit. He knew that if he wore it home there would be an angry confrontation with his sister over it. He was afraid to face this confrontation, but at the same time realized that he had to draw a line somewhere. He could not continue to capitulate and to try and avoid his anger. He decided to keep the beard. He went home and, predictably, the first night there was a showdown. He lost his temper—it was more of a calculated display than a loss of temper—and backed his sister down. He reported to me later that he was amazed at the response to his angry outburst. His sister backed off and didn't bother him during the rest of the visit. Everyone seemed to pull in their horns, and the rest of the visit was without incident. He even felt that the family was beginning to respect him for the first time.

Related to the issue was the question of self-esteem. Don's self-esteem was not very high. He felt himself inadequate, weak, vulnerable and described himself in many ways as helpless. There was a definite depressive tone to this regard for himself. He seemed in the beginning of treatment to regard this as his lot in life—as though the most he could expect from treatment was to be able to live with this burden. It soon became clear that this was a defensive pose. As Don put it, "If you don't expect anything, you won't get angry: and if you aren't worth anything, you can't expect anything!" The problem, of course, was that he did get angry, that he did have expectations—and that it was when these expectations were disappointed that he was most sensitive, hurt, and enraged.

This was a most difficult aspect of his problem for Don to put in perspective and to appreciate. He struggled to maintain his view of himself as inadequate and deprived. He insisted on trying to blame so many things in his background and history for his difficulties—his parents, their constant fighting, his sister, his mother's death, etc.—and he did not want to accept his own sense of entitlement as a part of his problem. But it was clear that his expectations were high. He expected people to like him and do things for him; he expected that his academic performance should be of high caliber, and that he should not have to work too hard to accomplish that; he expected girls to be attracted to him and to give him the sort of love and protection that he had had from his mother; and he expected that his family should accept his viewpoint and attitudes without question. When these expectations were not fulfilled, he felt resentful, hurt, disappointed, and angered.

Thus, keeping his self-esteem at a low level served a defensive function for him. It was a way to avoid and disqualify his anger, and the narcissistic entitlements and demands that lay behind it. Along with this there was a constant resentment at people interfering with his rights, forcing him to conform in school, at work, at home, etc. His talk about these matters—especially in the earlier phases of therapy—had a definite paranoid quality to it. He felt people were out to put him down, not give him a chance to show what he could do. Gradually as these issues were clarified and worked through, he began to adopt a less complaining and more optimistic demeanor. As it became clear how these expectations were distorting his perception of reality, he became more able to accept his own real potentialities, and began sounding and acting in a more hopeful manner.

Paranoid Aspects

I have not made much mention of the paranoid aspects of Don's clinical picture since they deserve to be seen against the backdrop of the more general picture. But they were a constant feature. In the early months of treatment he reported ideas of reference at almost every session. He felt people on the streets were staring at him. He felt people on streetcars were whispering about him. When I asked him what they were whispering he was vague in his reply, but the content of the whispering was generally hinted to be derogatory or critical. There were certain situations that provoked paranoid fears in him. There was a relatively dark passageway through which he had to pass to get to the entrance to his apartment building. Frequently, when he had to pass through this passage at night he would be overwhelmed by a feeling of panic—a dreadful fear and apprehension that there was someone waiting in the dark for him, ready to pounce on him, and kill and rob him. He entertained this fear even though the neighborhood in which he lived was comparatively safe and no one had ever been accosted or robbed—let alone killed—in that area.

There was also several episodes of severe paranoid anxiety that overtook him. On one such occasion, for example, he went into a lunch counter before one of his visits to me. He noticed a man sitting at the counter who seemed suspicious to him. He suddenly was overwhelmed with a terrible fear that the man would attack him and try to kill him. He suddenly had the idea that the man was a mental patient who had escaped from the hospital and who would suddenly go berserk and try to kill him. Don fled in a panic from the lunchroom, and came to my office trembling and frightened. He was able to test out the reality of his fear and the overwhelming anxiety, and able to see them as a projection, a projection of his own inner anger and destructiveness. In discussing this particular episode, he was able to relate it to his own fears of letting go of his aggression and killing and destroying. He referred to his fantasies of Judy's dying, being run over by a car, and of his attending the funeral, etc. He talked about his fantasies of the end of the world, of an atomic holocaust, and other destructive and overwhelming fantasies of death and destruction. He saw that the fantasies were his own creation, and that they were ways in which he frightened and scared the wits out of himself.

Therapy

As Don's therapy progressed, his attitude toward me became much more friendly—less guarded and less suspicious. For many months he kept a guarded distance in his relationship to me, obviously not trusting me to any great extent and feeling that treatment was bitter medicine that he had to take for his own good. He feared his dependency on me, or at least the possibility of that. It gradually became clear to him, however, that I was not going to engulf and trap him and keep him in a dependent position as his mother had done. It also became clear that I was not going to infringe his liberty and make authoritarian demands as his father had done. He found a different quality of relationship with me in which he could be unconstrained, independent, could exercise some degree of autonomy without fear of retribution or constraint. He assumed a comfortable distance in his relationship with me that allowed him to find a middle ground between dependency and abandonment. As he found that I respected his autonomy, he was better able to accept and respect his own autonomy.

Gradually the paranoid aspects of his behavior and experience faded into the background. Our focus on these paranoid features were limited to the explorations of the paranoid paroxysms—and these were few. My response to his reports of ideas of reference was limited to an incidental inquiry as to their content and an attempt to relate these to his feelings. His guardedness and suspiciousness gradually dissolved. The ideas of reference dropped out of the picture. The intensely paranoid episodes disappeared completely, and did not recur over the last half-year of treatment. Everything else in his life seemed to be progressing comfortably and satisfactorily. At his initiative we agreed to terminate. Don felt that he had accomplished what he had set out to do in therapy and I agreed. We decided that if ever he needed further help, he would come back. But it was his anticipation and hope—and mine—that he could carry on in what lay ahead of him with an assurance of his capacity to lead his own life and meet its challenges without feeling inadequate or incapable.

DISCUSSION

Family Interaction

If we turn our attention once again to the pattern of interaction in Don's family, we quickly become aware that there are some familiar elements at work. The interaction in this family was dominated by the poor relationship between Don's parents. The level of hostility and open conflict was comparatively high in the family. There was no clear pattern of dominance and submission in the interaction between his parents, rather a form of marital schism in which each partner was busy attacking and undermining the other.

It is important to note that Don and his parents formed an emotional triad of considerable intensity. Don was caught up in and emotionally involved in the emotional system that had been set up between his parents. The contribution of their respective individual pathologies and the interaction between them set the style and pattern of this complex system, and Don became involved in its influences and responsive to its pressures during the whole of his childhood. We have met this form of triadic involvement in our other cases.

We can wonder what particular chemistry may have been at work to set up this pathological pattern of relationship and interaction. We are groping in shadows because the data are obscure, but the questions are worth asking. We might wonder what emotional forces were at work to bring about the pregnancy—a decade after their other children and at a time when Don's mother was approaching the menopausal period. Was he the last fruit and proof of her femininity? Was his conception a last attempt to save a deteriorating marriage? We cannot be sure. What is quite clear is that the relationship between Don and his mother was close, affectionate, special, and mutually dependent—in a word, symbiotic. He was her special child—her *"Wunderkind."* The timing and circumstances of his birth, as well as the inner psychological needs of his mother, intertwined in such a way as to create a special bond between him and her that did not obtain with the other children. Her investment in him was deeper, more intense, much more special. He clung to her and she kept him close to her—even until her death.

In terms of this emotional involvement within the triad, it is no surprise that the arguments between the parents should often involve him—nor is it any surprise that the effect of these constant conflicts between the parents should have been so deep on him. The importance of the emotional involvement in this triad is that it creates the context in which Don became particularly susceptible to the pathological effect of the interaction between his parents. One aspect of this was a sort of emotional fusion or attachment between Don and his mother. As a result emotional currents and anxieties—even those unconscious to the mother herself—were communicated and shared in a sense by the child. The mother saw the child as an extension of herself and responded to the reflection of her own anxiety as she saw it in the child. Many such mothers maintain a closeness, protectiveness, and over-solicitiousness about the most involved child based on this extension mechanism.

Maternal Symbiosis

There is little doubt that Don's involvement with his mother was intense, close, and hence symbiotic. From his point of view the close ties to his mother made it difficult for him to establish the lines between himself and her. The continuing involvement made the adequate development differentiation between his own self and hers, between his own inner feelings and emotions and hers, difficult to establish and maintain. The closeness and dependency with his mother made them an emotional unit in a sense, and one important effect of this was not only that Don felt more sympathetic toward his mother in her emotional battles with the father, but that in some degree he experienced his own relationship with the father through the shared emotional closeness with the mother. Moreover, on the father's side of this interaction, his emotional perception and responsiveness to Don was cast in terms of his conscious and unconscious perception of Don and his mother *as a unit*. Consequently, not only did Don experience his relationship with his father partly in terms of the shared emotional oneness with his mother, but he was responded to in part by his father in terms of that same oneness.

The effects of Don's symbiotic attachment to his mother and her investment and attachment to him were profound. It seemed clear that the "identification" with her formed a large part of his functioning personality. The history gives us hints of this basic alignment in his passivity, his feminine interests, his liking to do housework and cooking—particularly when helping her at home. The quality of this pattern of behavior is almost that of mother's little girl, rather than that of a boy. But we also know that there was a certain lack of differentiation in this and an emotional closeness and dependency that suggests that separation from the mother and the surrender of his infantile dependence on her was impeded to some degree. In my view, the failure of such early separation processes sets up impediments to positive identification and individuation of the child's person. These early identifications are the processes which enable the child to adequately and increasingly achieve a differentiation between himself and others and to define his own emerging personality.

We also know clinically that such symbiotic attachments are burdened with considerable ambivalence. The symbiotic attachment increases the importance of the child's dependence on the mother. That dependence is magnified to the extent that any threat of separation or loss of the mother becomes devastating. A child's normal development allows him to gradually separate from the mother and to learn to function on his own without her protectiveness and presence. The persistence of a symbiotic attachment, however, does not allow this gradual separation, so that the growing child's dependence on the mother is intensified. Without her he is lost, and the threat of loss and abandonment becomes even more devastating and frightening. Where the mother's inner needs and gratifications are fulfilled by keeping the child in a dependent and symbiotic position, this process can be prolonged and extended—to the detriment of the child's developmental progression. Thus the mother's protectiveness and closeness can become an intrusiveness and an interference in the child's natural wishes to separate and to gain some measure of autonomy and initiative. The child's inner rage is stirred, but because of the essential dependence on the mother, this anger is itself terribly threatening. Its expression could drive away or destroy the central figure on which the child depends so intensely for survival.

The intensity of such ambivalence is often very great, and in more severe cases can reach cataclysmic proportions. Its resolution is essential for normal ego-structuring positive identifications to take place. If it is not so resolved, then the developing ego is forced into defensive postures and resorts to defensive mechanisms to deal with the threat posed by this ambivalence. Specifically introjective and projective mechanisms come to dominate the organization of the patient's inner world. For Don the introjection of aspects of both parents played an important role in his own pattern of pathology. The introjection and partial identification with his mother had assimilated the vulnerable and victimized aspects of her position in the family. In his closeness and dependency and emotional attachments to her he identified with her depressive, masochistically self-destructive and passive vulnerability.

Victim and Victimizer

In the midst of the family drama of victimization, Don tended to split the roles of victim and aggressive victimizer. He tended to see his mother as the unfortunate victim who was helplessly trapped in her hated position—and on the opposite side of his splitting process he tended to see his father as the brutal and aggressive victimizer. The elements of destructive aggressiveness were thus internally split off and projected onto his father. Don tended to describe his father as a violent, brutal, irascible and quick-tempered man. The father gave him plenty of evidence to support this perception. He kept a gun in his drawer. Don recalls several occasions when, during discussions about the black problem and civil rights, his father said that he wouldn't hesitate to shoot any blacks who would cause trouble. His father once said that if he ever found out that Don was taking drugs, he would kill him. In addition Don's father was a rather rigid, authoritarian, and highly prejudiced man. Don felt the pressure of his authoritarian domination as he grew older, and particularly surrounding his wishes to break away from home and be on his own.

Don's father was cast decisively in the role of the dangerous and destructive aggressor. The introjective process—following the pattern of an identification with the aggressor—assimilated this hostile destructiveness as a part of Don's own inner processes. The projection of these destructive wishes formed the basis of his paranoid fears and ideas. The picture was not this simple and straightforward by any means. Both parents were held as ambivalent objects—and both parents seemed to have shared in various ways in the process of undercutting and actively victimizing the other. There was some awareness of this in Don's mind, but it was a realization that he kept very much in the background. He tended to simplify and polarize the relative positions of his parents, in his own mind and in his recollections of their interaction. The fact of his mother's death tended to reinforce this pattern of perception. He not only felt guilt for his own hostile wishes toward his mother, but he saw his father as responsible for her death and held a bitter hatred for him on this account.

We can point out here again—as in other family interactions we have seen and will see—that the pattern of interaction and the collusive alignment of parental pathologies not only undermines the constructive aspects of inner psychological development in the child and forces internalization processes to function in more specifically defensive ways, but also generates a style of interaction within the family which can be characterized as paranoid. This derives at a fundamental level from the ambivalent victimization process that obtains in the parental interaction—it also derives from other aspects in the family process. In this family, we might wonder to what extent Don's father was really paranoid. We can document his authoritarian and highly prejudiced attitudes and beliefs. We can also document to a certain extent his own expectations of attack and destructive assault from outside. But we can also wonder about his angry attacks on his patients and others with whom he came in contact, and the increasing pattern of isolation and withdrawal that characterized his life-style. Projective mechanisms undoubtedly played a significant role in the father's experience—and there was a pattern of suspicious guardedness and withdrawal that might make us suspect some paranoid elements in him. We can wonder about Don's mother as well. She also led a rather withdrawn and isolated life. She had few friends, rarely went out, and stayed at home drinking: she seems to have had more chronically depressed periods than anything else. We really have less to go on than with Don's father. In any case there was a definite atmosphere in his family of isolation from the outside world, of hostility to outside influences, a family more or less closed in on itself and defensively withdrawn from the expectations of external threats. Don's father lived in a world of expected dangers and threats. His mother lived in a frightened isolation eased only by the oblivion of alcohol. In terms of his involvement in the pathology of his parents, Don was drawn into this vortex and shared in the fears and anxieties of his parents—fears and anxieties that were both partially expressed and also lived out in the style of the family existence. Don became a very shy, timid, withdrawn, fearful, child, who dreaded the outside world and clung to the protective closeness of home and mother.

Depression

The interplay of depressive and paranoid elements is a constant feature of all of these patients. When the predominance of paranoid defenses, and particularly projection, fails or is altered by therapy, the depressive aspects of the illness emerge—often with surprising intensity. Similar neurasthenic and depressive manifestations are clinically familiar in the usual course of patients with acute schizophrenic episodes (Roth, 1970). These patients often show a progression in phases of their illness. There is an initial phase of prepsychotic turmoil followed by the acute psychotic breakdown. This is followed, usually during hospitalization, by a phase of compensated transition which is relatively short, but which then passes into a more prolonged phase of depression and neurasthenia. The latter phase may last for months, and hopefully leads to a resolution of the depression and therapeutic improvement. The underlying mechanisms in these cases of postschizophrenic depression seem to bear some similarity to what is often observed in paranoid patients. There is some overlap, of course, in that the rate of conjunction between paranoid features and schizophrenia is high.

The schizophrenic's inner world can be seen not merely in terms of its relative disorganization and fragmentation, but also in terms of its organization around highly ambivalent and relatively fragmented introjections which are relatively undifferentiated—at least in the acute phase of the illness—and which are highly susceptible to regressive pulls. Introjects can function at nearly any level of psychic integration and organization—anywhere from the primitive levels of psychic dysfunction to highly structuralized levels of neurotic organization. The paranoid process can function anywhere along this continuum. The interplay of introjective and projective mechanisms is also found in paranoid patients—at whatever level of functioning—even as they are found in more severely disturbed schizophrenics. The differences have to do with the degree of regressive liability of the introjects and the extent of their de-differentiation.

The depression in these cases relates to a predominance of introjective mechanisms in the patient's defensive posture. His breakdown had signaled the failure of projective defenses. His capacity to externalize became mitigated and internalized aggression predominated. The destructive elements formed around the introjects that made up the basic structure of his personality and his inner world. He became both victim and victimizer—both helpless and vulnerable victim of destructive urges and at the same time the brutal and destructive aggressor. The drama of the interplay of these introjects would have played itself out in his own suicide—an internalization and an acting out of the fantasies of murderous destructiveness that he had experienced in relation to his parents. In suicide he would have intensified and completed his assimilation of both—he would become both murdered victim and murderous aggressor.

Homosexuality

It might be well to add a comment here about the question of homosexuality in relation to Don's pathology. Homosexuality was never an explicit problem, nor was it ever a focus of concern in psychotherapy. Don had never experienced homosexual wishes of any significant intensity and he had never had any homosexual experiences. He explicitly felt anxiety about his ability to relate to women—and particularly about his ability to satisfy them sexually. We can postulate a defensive element in this against underlying homosexual fears and doubts. But this anxiety was not cast in terms of homosexuality as such. The issue was much more in the line of what Ovesey (1954, 1955a, 1955b) has described in terms of pseudohomosexual conflicts. His concerns over his ability to "make it" with girls were much more in the line of proving to himself and his family—but primarily to himself—that he could function adequately in the business of being an independent and capable adult. The issue of independence and autonomous functioning, then, was compounded with homosexual anxiety, but not expressed explicitly as such a conflict. Both aspects of this complex conflict were rooted in his feminine identification, based on the introjection of the maternal image.

The Therapeutic Process

Don's ability to enter into the work of therapy was not immediate or without difficulty. He had first to assure himself that entering into a meaningful working relationship with me did not mean either that he would become passively engulfed and dependent on me as he had been on his mother, or that I would be rigid, demanding, and authoritarian as had been his father. My position was relatively neutral, objective, and dispassionate. I put no pressure on him for anything. I emphasized and consistently respected his independence and autonomy. My interest and focus of my questions and responses were simply to illuminate the inner meaning and purposes of his behavior. In the context of a good working relationship and with the maintenance of a consistent climate which neither pressured nor imposed anything on him. Don was able to mobilize and assert his own resources in the interest of treatment. Given a reassuring and supportive context for the therapeutic work, Don could begin to define and deal with the inner aspects of his own personality and its functioning.

We have discussed the organization of the crucial introjects already. They were reflected in his feelings of weakness and vulnerability and inadequacy on one hand, and in his fears of, and inability to express, anger on the other. His efforts to function autonomously and to effectively mobilize his initiatives had been compromised in varying degrees by these introjects. He struggled to assert and prove himself in many different areas of mastery—but always in the face of the risks involved in aggressive self-assertion and competitive strivings. Thus the introjects reinforced each other in his inner psychic economy; each was a defense against the other and each was needed as a defense against the threat of the other. The energies consumed in this inner struggle impeded the functioning of his ego and infringed severely on the areas of conflict-free functioning that were available to him. And as we have already seen, the projection of these introjective elements created eignificant difficulties in his adjustment to the outside world and in his ability to relate meaningfully to the people around him. Don functioned well and was relatively successful in establishing peer relationships—relationships in which his autonomy or independence was not questioned or threatened. He had considerable difficulty, however, in his relationships with superiors and authority figures, and in his relationships with women. In both these contexts the pattern of pathological interaction with his parents was revived. He saw authority figures largely as infringing on his autonomy and forcing him to do things he didn't want to do—or preventing him from doing things he wanted to do. And with women, of course, his sexual adequacy was challenged and called into question.

The process of dealing with those introjects in therapy was a gradual one. We had to determine the elements of his inner thoughts and feelings that gave some indication of the functioning of these introjects. Gradually the relationship between these inner patterns of thought and feeling and the respective relationship with each of his parents became clearer. The working through of these introjective elements took the form of correcting the imbalance in his perception of his parents. As we considered the quality of their relationship and the patterns of their interaction, it became increasingly clear to Don that his mother had not been in fact as helpless and victimized as he had tended to picture her in his mind's eye. It also became apparent that his father was not so much the brutal aggressor that he had always thought. Rather he began to see the helplessness and dependency in his father. He began to see ways in which the alignments he had always seen were not the only dimensions of the interaction between his parents. In some ways it became apparent that his mother had been the aggressor, the attacker, the instigator of fights, undercutting and demeaning his father. Correlatively, he could also begin to see the ways in which his father was a victim.

Parallel to this gradual clarification of the roles of his parents and their interaction, Don was also able to begin to adjust the respective introjective elements internally. He began to see that he was not as weak or vulnerable or inadequate as he thought. He also began to understand that his anger was neither so destructive nor so terrifying as he had felt. As his internal perception of himself was gradually modified, he was increasingly able to test out some of his new perceptions. With the continuing review and more objective framework of evaluation provided in therapy, he was able to test the reality of his perceptions. He learned with time that his introjectively determined perceptions were more of the order of fantasy distortions. He came increasingly to see that the inner reality of himself was something less than a destructive monster and something more than a helpless victim. As he became less monster and less victim, the area for potential inner growth of his ego was enlarged, and the scope for the autonomous exercise of ego-functions was systematically enlarged.

Resolution of Ambivalence

An important aspect of this development in therapy was its relationship to Don's ambivalence toward both parents. His basic inability to tolerate ambivalence had been responsible for the inner splitting and projecting that had structured his interaction with both parents and had contributed to the quality of the respective introjects. Don came slowly and reluctantly to see and understand his ambivalence toward his mother. He saw himself in terms of his dependent clinging to her as a loving and giving figure in his life. In the exploration of his prolonged and unfinished mourning of her death, however, it became increasingly clear that there was much in their relationship that he resented. He resented his dependence on her and her contributing to it by trying to keep him tied to her apron strings. He also resented her attacks on his father. This aspect of her behavior he had never been able to acknowledge to himself, and it was part of his need to see her as helpless and victimized. Similarly, in relation to his father, Don came to see that there was a strong bond between himself and his father, and that part of his anger and resentment against the old man was due to Don's more or less repressed wish to be close to his father and to be able to win a more secure place in his father's affection and respect. It came as a great revelation to him, for example, that after he blew up at his sister over his wearing a beard, his father began to treat him with greater deference and respect. The gradual clarification of these elements of his ambivalence went hand-in-hand with the clarification of his perceptions of both parents. His increasing ability to acknowledge ambivalence and to tolerate it contributed significantly to his therapeutic progress.

Modification of Narcissism

The upshot of these inner changes was that Don was able to see himself and the world around him in much more realistic and human terms. He began to see his own inner life more in terms of human feelings and potentialities, rather than in terms of omnipotent distortions or magical expectations. He was increasingly able to accept his own limitations along with his own potentialities. He began to set realistic goals and was able to modify his expectations to increasingly realistic terms. One of the more important aspects of treatment in these patients—one that we shall have occasion to focus on repeatedly in these cases—is the aspect of narcissism. One of the fundamental props of Don's therapeutic improvement was his being able to surrender his inner expectations—infantile and excessive as they were—and to be able to increasingly accept the reality of his own human person with its abilities and disabilities, strengths and weaknesses, hopes and disappointments. The point that can be made in reference to this case, however, is that the patient's ability to make the essential surrender of narcissism depends in vital ways on the working through of the introjective distortions, and a dissolution of the introjects themselves. In part the introjects serve as the defensive structuralizations in the inner psychic organization by which infantile narcissism is pathologically preserved and prolonged. We shall see more of this aspect of paranoid structure later.

CHAPTER 10

Miss Ellen E.

THE PATIENT'S PROFILE

The present case is of interest from the point of view of the patient's pattern of illness. When I first came to know her, she was about thirty. She had a long history of recurrent hospital admissions, extending over a period of about seven years. She carried a diagnosis of chronic paranoid schizophrenia, but her chronicity was by no means burnt out in any sense. Her episodes of decompensation were marked by intense anger and resentment which led her to readily and frequently lash out at her persecutors and physically attack them. Although her illness had extended over a period of several years, her interaction with her therapists and with others was full of lively feeling and responsiveness. The pattern of her illness was more one of recurrent episodes of relatively acute decompensation interspersed with periods of remission. Even during the periods of remission, however, her life was lived in continual suspiciousness, guardedness, and angry contentiousness with people she contacted.

First Contact

My first contacts with Ellen were memorable—although I later learned that the whole flavor of my experience with her were fairly typical of her manner of behaving and relating to other people. She was quite agitated and intensely angry. She acted in a manner to suggest total impatience and irritation with everything that was asked of her. She kept saying, "Let's get going and get this whole thing over with!" She was intensely suspicious of everything that was done or asked of her. During the first interview she would suddenly burst out into frightened tears that reflected her inner turmoil and distress. Then she would quickly turn from tears to an attitude of angry attack, shouting obscenities (she had developed a rich vocabulary that would make a truck driver blush) and venting her spleen on me or on the nurses or on a variety of other people who she felt were out to get her and were making things tough for her. The content of these outbursts were highly paranoid and was accompanied by extreme agitation and excitement.

Her behavior on admission to the hospital and for several days thereafter was extremely provocative and assaultive. Her general mode of behavior suggested a high degree of tension and inner turmoil. She would remain relatively quiet, keeping very much to herself and talking to no one, and then suddenly she would lash out at someone—usually one of the nurses who happened to be passing by, or occasionally one of the patients. Almost always the victim was a female. The suddenness and unpredictability of these apparently unprovoked attacks made it necessary to restrict her, and this move provoked additional attacks and angry accusations against the staff which had a highly paranoid cast.

But the admission procedure was particularly memorable for me! It was part of the admitting physician's responsibilities to complete a physical examination of the patient. After the initial interview with her, we went to the examining room. A nurse helped her to undress and prepare for the examination. Ellen's attitude was one of irritation and reluctant resentment, but she was nonetheless by and large cooperative. She continued the "let's get it over with" attitude here, too. The examination was unquestionably sexually stimulating for her. As it progressed she made several comments about how doctors got their kicks out of examining female patients, and expressed some of her resentment at such treatment. When we came to the pelvic examination, however, her anxiety reached a crescendo. She cooperated to a point—but only to a point. With some gentle reassurances from me and from the nurses standing by, we were able to proceed to the point of beginning to introduce some vaginal lubricant for the speculum examination. At this point Ellen began to writhe on the table, began screaming excitedly at the top of her voice that I was raping her. This outburst was so agitated and intense that I was really frightened by it, and decided that the physical examination was at that point finished. Discretion seemed to dictate an immediate retreat. Ellen calmed down as soon as I made my escape, and then proceeded to attack the nurse who was attending her. I confess that the whole episode had shaken me.

We can sense in these events the pugnacious and assaultive character of Ellen's paranoia. It is worth noting that our patients seem to vary between this aggressive "fight" stance against the threatening persecutors and a more phobic "flight" pattern of reaction in the face of mounting persecutory anxiety. The patterns may take characteristic forms, as in this case, or may vary from one circumstance to another.

Precipitants

The circumstances of Ellen's decompensation and admission to the hospital were of importance, particularly in that they give us the flavor of her illness and begin to point us in the direction of seeing some of the pathogenic influences in her history. Since her previous discharge from the hospital, Ellen had been living at home with her mother and was seeing her therapist on a weekly basis. During this period, she managed rather well. She was able to function relatively well and had completed a nursing refresher course at one of the local hospitals. She did quite well in this course and was able to get a nursing position at a large city hospital. However, about three weeks prior to her admission, her mother suffered a heart attack. The mother had had several such attacks in preceding years, and a fresh attack was a source of considerable threat to Ellen, as we shall see.

About the same time, her therapist brought up the subject of terminating their relationship. The circumstances had to do with his service-connected obligations which required that he reduce his patient load. Ellen was one of the patients to be reduced. This was a great disappointment to her, and stirred a considerable amount of anger and resentment. She felt that the doctor was just dumping her and that she was being pushed around from one doctor to another without any consideration of her wishes or preferences. She resented being shoved around—as she put it—and treated like any other patient. And indeed, there was some truth in this. She was being treated through the facilities of a state hospital, in which patient care is subject to the shifting complexities of resident turnover and the shifting of personnel from service to service. She in fact, had little to say about who her doctor was to be or how long she could remain in treatment with any one of them. Breaking off treatment with her present doctor, with whom she had been in therapy for nearly a year and a half, was a severe blow to her. She was obviously affected by the loss of the relationship.

In addition, Ellen had started to work about a week before her decompensation. She was apparently in the incipient stage of decompensation when she started the job and she had difficulty from the very beginning. She felt increasingly tense and anxious, became easily enraged, and her angry outbursts became more frequent. Her paranoid ideas became more prominent and intense and she became preoccupied with highly paranoid ideas about blacks and sexuality. She found it increasingly difficult to perform her duties at the hospital and became increasingly delusional. She finally reached the point where she was attending a black patient who was on intravenous fluids. She thought that this patient had wanted to assault her sexually, had pulled the needle out of his arm and had tried to stab her with it. She fled in terror from the hospital. She tried then to stay at home, but became increasingly disruptive and difficult to control.

The string of precipitants was revealing. The first was the mother's life-threatening heart attack. Ellen's relationship with her mother was difficult and highly ambivalent—as her history will suggest. She was strongly dependent on her mother, but her dependence was mixed with intense hostility. Their relationship was conflictual and strongly argumentative. Ellen resented her mother and hated her. Her murderous wishes were a constant feature of her relationship. The mother's attack put Ellen under severe stress and threat from at least two sides. She was confronted by tremendous guilt and remorse in relation to her murderous wishes against her mother in the face of mother's imminent death. She was also confronted by the impending loss of the object on which she was so intensely, if ambivalently, dependent. It should be noted that the mother exploited this aspect of Ellen's pathology. She played the role of the helpless cardiac cripple who was being tormented and brought to the brink of death by her daughter's anger and argumentativeness. Any of us, who had the opportunity to observe some of the interaction between mother and daughter, were impressed by the intense hatred of Ellen's mother for her—a hatred that was masked under a facade of self-sacrifice and self-martyrdom for the sake of her poor child.

The conjunction of the termination of her treatment with these events was a severe blow for Ellen. It served to reinforce her feelings of worthlessness, of being unwanted and rejected, of being treated as second-rate and as not counting for much. Her relationship with the therapist had been tempestuous, ambivalent, and difficult—as we might expect of any relationship in which Ellen was involved. Much of it was due to her need to test whether the therapist was really concerned for her welfare, whether he cared at all about her, whether she counted for him—and her doubts and fears were confirmed by the decision to terminate. The circumstances were indeed unfortunate, if unavoidable. The one prop that had enabled her to function in a healthier manner was torn out from under her. Her disappointment was intense, and her feelings of inner worthlessness and shame and her corresponding need for her paranoid defenses, were intensified. The stress of returning to nursing and the implicit challenge to her self-esteem only served as the appropriate setting in which her paranoid decompensation could play itself out. How did this relatively attractive young woman come to this state of incapacitating rage?

Family Background

In order to gain some purchase on this question, we shall return to the origins of Ellen's family and try to trace some of the elements in her background and development. The family was by origin and conviction Irish and Catholic—with strong adherence to both elements in its origins. Both parents had been born and raised in the old country. Ellen's mother was the third of four sisters. Her mother had died when she was quite young. Her father died when she was only fourteen. He had been a horse trainer and the family fortunes had never risen very high. After his death the sisters were without financial support, and they decided that they would come to America to find work. They came together in 1924; Ellen's mother was fifteen years old.

On her arrival, her mother's relatives were able to find employment for her as a maid in the house of a well-known and aristocratic New England Yankee family. Mrs. E. always spoke of this experience warmly and enthusiastically. She never described her position as that of a servant or maid, but regarded herself as one of the family. She seemed to feel that she somehow shared in the elegance and sophistication of her employers by way of her contact with them. They were socially involved with the foremost families of New England, and Mrs. E. would speak familiarly about these people as though they were her friends and acquaintances as well. She felt that she had acquired the taste and good breeding that she witnessed in her employment. She would comment, "When you work with people with blue blood, it stays in your own blood." One can note that the phrase is "work with" rather than "work for." Mrs. E. fantasized herself as the equal of her employers, and seems to have ambitioned and coveted their way of life as her own. She worked in this capacity for about five years.

About this time she met Mr. E. He was described as a big man, quiet, patient, gentle, and easygoing. He was working at the time as the streetcar conductor. These were the depression years. He had come to this country to find work in his early twenties, and before prohibition had worked in several speakeasies. After the repeal of prohibition and during the depression, he returned to the liquor business and was fairly successful. He and Ellen's mother were married in 1930—he was just twenty-eight and she was only twenty.

As was the fashion in those days, they had a fairly large family. The first child, a boy, was born in about ten or 11 months. They had seven children in all, the oldest boy being followed by a sequence of four girls. Ellen was the youngest of these, and she was followed in two years by another boy, who was followed in turn in the following year by still another boy. This left Ellen with an older brother—older by about eight years—and two younger brothers and three older sisters. Mrs. E. reports that all of the deliveries were without difficulty or complications, except for the first. She describes this labor as long and difficult and the delivery as very painful. It is interesting that this oldest boy became her favorite and was the fair-haired boy of the family. This was resented by the other siblings—particularly by Ellen. After the father's death the oldest brother took over the responsibility for Ellen's care. This, of course, only served to intensify and confirm Ellen's resentment.

Mrs. E. took great pride in her children and their success. They had all done relatively well with the exception of Ellen. All were married and had families, and all but the youngest boy had completed their college education. Mrs. E. would say, "My children are my whole life. Feeding them and seeing what they will become is my whole life." The view that she presented of life in the family was at once sanguine and idyllic. Everyone was happy and all the children were healthy and well cared for. Everyone was kind and helpful and loving. There were no financial problems. The children were always polite and clean and well-mannered. Mrs. E. recounted the good behavior of her children with pride and related it to her own experience of living with true "blue blood." She is continually anxious to emphasize and direct attention to the success that her children have had in life. When asked specifically about Ellen, Mrs. E. spoke sadly of her as "the crippled bird who just can't leave the nest." When pushed for specifics about her children, she was able to give only the vaguest of impressions. One had the distinct notion that her children were somehow perceived as extensions of herself, without clear differentiation or distinct personalities of their own—at least in her eyes.

Mrs. E. was an extremely neat and orderly housekeeper. She worked very hard to keep things in the best possible order, but she would become very upset and furious when the children would disturb things. She was the acting disciplinarian of the family. She would slap the children or beat them with a leather strap she kept for the purpose. She would fly into a rage easily and often over small matters, and have what are described as "temper tantrums." She would scream at the children and throw pots and dishes around during these eruptions. The family agreed that she had a violent and poorly controlled temper. The conflict, outbursts of temper, and angry confrontations between mother and children were fairly frequent. The father, for the most part, kept aside from all this. He managed to be out of the house most of the time. He worked long hours, laboring seven days a week, and would only return home late in the evening. He was a strong, quiet and easygoing man, but he could not tolerate the fighting at home. When he was home he played the role of peacemaker, but he was not often around to perform that function. His major tactic in dealing with the hostility in the family was to escape.

Along with this atmosphere of conflict and constant argument, there was little in the way of closeness and confiding. There was never any physical affection shown between either parent and any of the children. Nor was there ever any physical affection shown between the parents. There was little affection or sense of sharing between any of the siblings. Mrs. E. was described by the children as being like a Jewish mother. She was overly protective and intrusive. She was extremely sensitive to any negative response or rejection—real or imagined—from the children. If they did not submit to and accept her caring, she was hurt and offended. We shall have occasion to note this maternal solicitude—and its inherent destructiveness—for we shall meet it elsewhere in this study in various guises. From about the time of Ellen's first hospitalization, and particularly after her husband's death, Mrs. E. had considerable psychological difficulty. She had been chronically depressed. It had been necessary to hospitalize her on several occasions. In the subsequent years she received well over a hundred ECT treatments for her recurrent depressions. Ellen's mother emerges from this account as a rather obsessive woman who was highly conflicted over the issues of aggression and self-esteem—and who poured a considerable amount of her narcissistic investment into her mothering and housekeeping roles. Anything that reflected on her adequacy in these functions would trigger intense outbursts of poorly controlled rage. It seems that this aspect of her mother's own pathology had a considerable influence on the development of Ellen's own psychic troubles.

Early Years

We can focus our attention on Ellen and her own development. Of all the children, Ellen stands out as the one who gave the most trouble in raising. She was an active, aggressive, and mischievous child. She was constantly getting into fights with her siblings and with her age-mates in school and in the neighborhood. Much of her interaction with her own siblings was governed by an intense jealousy—a feeling that they were better loved and favored than she was. This feeling was particularly directed at her oldest brother whom she felt was favored by the mother. Although her mother staunchly denied any difficulties or problems in Ellen's childhood, there seem to have been many. From her earliest years there had been a continuing antagonism and conflict between Ellen and her mother. They could not seem to get along, and arguing and scolding seemed chronic. Mother saw Ellen as stubborn, willful, and vicious.

Again—in the face of mother's denials—Ellen seems to have been a persistent bed wetter from her earliest years through the school years until she was about twelve years old. This was a focus of intense concern on mother's part. Ellen was scolded and shamed for her wetting. Mother would give her Lysol baths in the morning before she went to school so that she would not smell badly in school. Ellen also on occasion would wet herself in school. She remembers her shame and embarrassment on this account and recalls that the wetting was related to her fear of asking the nuns for permission to go to the bathroom. Her whole school experience was colored by her fear of the nuns who taught her. For most of early school years she lived in terror of them, and as a result was a very obedient and submissive child. But there were unmistakable signs of her ornery disposition. Ellen had had special glasses prescribed for a mild strabismus and was supposed to wear the glasses at school. She refused to do this and repeatedly smashed several pairs of glasses. Her mother was, of course, enraged at this behavior, but Ellen stubbornly refused to wear the glasses. Finally her parents had to give up trying to force them on her.

Academically Ellen's school performance was adequate. Socially, however, it left much to be desired. She had few friends and seemed unable to get along with the other children. She was constantly getting into fights with the other students, and felt picked on and rejected by them. She could recall only one friend in all of grammar school—a girl who left the school because the nuns were too hard on her, according to Ellen. This pattern persisted until about the seventh or eighth grade. About this time, Ellen began to get into occasional trouble at school. She was resentful and resistive whenever the teachers told her to do something or demanded something from her that she was unwilling to do.

During these childhood years, Ellen was characterized by her quick temper and her relative lack of affection. There was little by way of affectionate exchange among the members of her family—but, even so, Ellen was less affectionate than the others. Her relationships with siblings, friends, and others were all characteristically antagonistic and stubbornly hostile. There was not very much of the tomboy in her, but she had a marked capacity for malicious mischief. Her jealousy of her oldest brother was a motivation for many of her pranks—and he became the special target, although the other siblings were also victims of her mischief. One such episode she recalled was her greasing the stairs with Crisco where she knew her brother would be coming. When he slipped and fell, she laughed maliciously.

She had few friends through all of her school years. In high school she dated very rarely, even though she was an attractive girl. Her attitude was one of hostile antagonism toward boys, but also toward girls. She would be critical in such relationships and ridicule anyone who tried to be friendly with her. She carried this attitude into her high school experience. Her father's business ventures had proven moderately successful and the family enjoyed a certain amount of affluence. It was possible to send the children to private schools. Ellen was sent to a fashionable Catholic high school for girls. Her antagonistic and suspicious attitude made it very difficult for her to make any friends among her fellow students. She felt that she was not as good as the other girls attending the school. She felt that her family was poorer and from a lower social class than theirs, and felt embarrassed and awkward about this. She regarded the other girls at the school as snobs. She made no friends. In her second year at this school, Ellen began getting into fights. She would attack other girls, thinking that they were talking about her or laughing at her. It seemed clear that her paranoid attitude was already established at this stage of her life.

During her high school years, she decided that she would like to become a nurse. The idea was not received favorably by the family. Her father particularly was opposed. He felt that with her temperament nursing would be too demanding and stressful for her. He thought she should aim at being a secretary or some other less stressful work.

First Decompensation

Finally she enrolled in a nursing school—against her parents' wishes. The experience was a difficult one. She did reasonably well in the course work and was able to graduate. She was under considerable stress during this period. She continued to have very few friends and dated only on rare occasions. She became increasingly temperamental, irritable and difficult to get along with at home. She would at times become physically abusive, striking out at members of the family and shouting obscenities at them. After her graduation from the school, she did not take the board of nursing examination and did not obtain her registration. She became extremely anxious and abusive, became violent and began to throw things at members of the family in excited outbursts; she was combative and delusional. This was her first acute decompensation and it occurred directly after her graduation from nursing school and her failure to obtain her nursing registration.

Ellen's first hospitalization lasted something over six months. On discharge she seemed to have recompensated quite effectively and seemed to have returned to a relatively good level of functioning. She got up enough courage to attempt the board examination and, despite her long absence from nursing, was able to pass it and received her registration in nursing. She worked for nearly a year in a nursing home and was able to function quite adequately. However, at this point, a series of events occurred which seemed to have had a decisive influence on her further course.

Father's Death

At this point Ellen's father developed acute diverticulitis. He remained at home for nearly a week and was finally taken to a hospital and operated on for a ruptured diverticulum. Ellen volunteered to perform the special nursing duties during his postoperative recuperation. On the third postoperative day, the father suffered a heart attack and died. The effect on Ellen was catastrophic. She began to decompensate again. Her outbursts of temper and angry attacks became more frequent. She became violent, hostile, and highly suspicious of her family and other people she came in contact with. She became increasingly difficult to control and her behavior was highly provocative and destructively hostile. As an example, the family decided to move out of the family house after the father's death. When her older brother started to load the furniture onto the car, he came back to find that Ellen had taken all the furniture off and had thrown it on the ground or smashed some of it against the car.

Her relationship with her mother became intensely hateful and mutually antagonistic. Ellen would criticize her mother and fly into angry tirades, cursing her and shouting obscenities. Occasionally she would fly at her and attack her physically as well. One of the family members commented that the two of them were like oil and fire—they just couldn't be allowed together. Finally, the family—in an effort to try to find some way of easing the situation—decided to take Ellen on a trip to the shore. While they were on their way, Ellen jumped out of the car and started to run away. One of the friends with them gave chase and tried to restrain her. When the police arrived, Ellen began to scream that the man was trying to rape her. Her rehospitalization could no longer be avoided and she was readmitted to the hospital at this time.

Mother's Psychosis

It is of considerable interest in the context of Ellen's recurrent decompensations to note what was happening to her mother. Soon after Ellen's first psychotic episode, while she was still in the hospital, her mother became psychotically depressed and also had to be admitted to the hospital. She felt responsible for Ellen's illness and blamed herself for what had happened to her. She responded quickly, however, to ECT and remained in the hospital for only a week. Again when her husband died, she became severely depressed and suicidal, wishing that she could die like her husband and be with him. Since that time, she had been more or less chronically depressed and had been treated countless times with ECT. In addition, soon after her husband's heart attack she began to suffer from cardiac symptoms. She developed pains in her chest and became obsessed with the fact that she might have heart disease. In fact in subsequent years she developed anginal pain on a physiological basis and suffered several heart attacks. She played the cardiac cripple to the hilt, however, and used her condition against Ellen in a rather sadistic and highly guilt-provoking manner. It seemed, then, that for both mother and daughter, the death of the father plunged them into chronic states of mental impairment. The mother's identification with the dead father seemed apparent.

Ellen and Her Mother

Ellen's history since the time of her father's death is one of recurrent hospitalizations, all of which seemed to follow a fairly typical pattern. She would create a scene, become abusive and assaultive, and would then be sent to the hospital. Once in the hospital, she would escape within a few days and return directly home. Usually the precipitant for her admission would be some form of disappointment or loss. On one occasion, her next younger brother got married. This was a disappointment to Ellen because she had been closer to him than to any of the other siblings. He had occasionally taken her along to parties with his friends and generally got along fairly well with her. His leaving home and getting married was a significant loss to Ellen. More often than not, however, the precipitating event for hospitalization had to do with something that would happen between Ellen and her mother. After an argument, for example, Ellen would set about making a scene. One of her favorite ways of making a scene was to go to one of the family's taverns and demand money from the barkeeper to pay for cab fare and something to eat. If the bartender didn't give her the money she would raise a terrible ruckus. The family was advised by Ellen's therapist not to cater to these whims of hers and the older brother asked the bartenders not to give her the money. The bartenders replied that they would rather quit their jobs than have to put up with the kind of disturbances that Ellen could kick up.

When Ellen returned home from her visits to the hospital, she would be quiet and restrained for several days, but then the situation would heat up and the chronic conflict and arguments with her mother would begin again. The quality of Ellen's interaction with her mother was central in understanding her pathology. The relationship was one of intense hostility and mutual dependence. They could not live with each other and they would not live without each other. Ellen's attitude toward her mother was one of constant criticism and sarcasm. Her sarcasm was particularly directed toward her mother's social pretensions—obviously one of the mother's points of vulnerability. She would also criticize her mother's housekeeping—another susceptible point. Her behavior was often demanding and provocative. When things did not go her way or she did not get what she wanted, she would fly into a rage and shout obscenities at her mother, and at times even attack her physically. Some of this behavior was tempered when there were other siblings around the house, but after the marriage of her youngest brother, Ellen and her mother were left together.

For the mother's part, she played the long-suffering and self-sacrificing martyr's role. Her treatment of Ellen, however, was essentially viciously undercutting. She would take every opportunity to make Ellen feel inadequate and inferior—reminding her of her inability to hold a job, or to get along with anyone, of not having any friends, particularly boyfriends, or being crippled and sick and inadequate. In indirect and insinuating ways, she would play on Ellen's guilt. She would make Ellen feel that she was responsible for her mother's depression and for her cardiac condition. She would even imply at times that Ellen was responsible for her father's death. Her mother often referred to her as "the crippled bird who can't leave the nest"—and the intonations of this expression as it came from the mother's lips were those of accusation, of a reminder to Ellen that she was sick and inadequate, of a hidden wish to make and keep Ellen the crippled bird. One had the sense that this mother almost took satisfaction from thinking of and having Ellen as her crippled bird.

Paranoid Psychosis

During the course of her many admissions, observers noted the intense feelings of insecurity, the intense dependency needs, and the threatening depressive feelings that lay beneath the surface—and against which Ellen defended herself by her belligerent attitude and hostile assaultiveness. Her attitude was always one of guarded suspiciousness. The content of her delusions were highly sexualized and often assaultive. At one point she had to be transferred from a state hospital to a private hospital because of her repeated escapes. She claimed that the state hospital was full of blacks and lesbians. She claimed that she had to continually fight them off, and was afraid that she would become a black or a lesbian herself. She believed that the doctors in the hospital were crawling into bed with her at night and having intercourse with her while she was asleep. She also thought that she had been forced to have intercourse with one of the blacks in the hospital.

She was also subject to auditory hallucinations during her more acute decompensations. The voices were of older women, sometimes men, and even children—but they all called her names, accused her of being a prostitute, or of having relations with blacks. Usually wherever she went, she could hear people talking about her, criticizing her, or saying that she was a prostitute. She felt that all these people had been taught by the nuns, priests, and doctors to dislike her and to call her these names. She also felt that there was a sort of master plan involving her mother, the nuns, priests, and doctors to put her away in the convent. On almost every admission, there were bitter and angry accusations against her mother for putting her away in the hospital. She also entertained the delusion of a boyfriend at one point who was a gangster and important racketeer, who would take her out and give her expensive presents and then have intercourse with her.

Ellen's delusional state was fairly constant. On one of her recent admissions, she was walking past a monument in a square near her home. She thought the people present were talking about her and laughing at her. It seemed that for more than a year she had felt that certain people whom she identified only as "the witches" had been talking about her and laughing at her in the same way. On this day, however, she heard them calling her a "dirty pig" and a "nigger." She became enraged and attacked the people sitting around the monument. The police were called and she was thus brought to the hospital. Her victims included a couple of young adolescents, an older woman, and an elderly man. Even in the hospital her voices continued to laugh at her, criticize her, call her a "nigger," accuse her of sleeping with blacks, or of being queer. It was not difficult to hear in these delusional accusations the echoes of her mother's voice.

Ellen's behavior in the hospital was extremely agitated and chaotic. Despite attempts to control her behavior and high doses of tranquilizing medications, she would burst out in angry tirades, shouting obscenities at nurses or patients. At times she would physically attack people and would have to be forcibly restrained. Escape attempts were frequent. Between her angry outbursts and attacking behavior, she would quiet down for a time and then suddenly dash for the ward door and try to run out of the hospital. This became a regular feature of her hospital routine. Frequently her attacks on other patients or the nursing staff were precipitated by her feeling that they were talking about her or accusing her of something. On a number of occasions her outbursts were related to her seeing elderly and demented female patients on the ward. Seeing these patients was very upsetting to her and she would "lose control."

Therapy

Attempts to conduct therapy with Ellen were difficult and chaotic. Her general attitude was one of hostile suspiciousness. Her moods were extremely labile. She would shift with startling quickness from angry accusations to tearful remorse. In moments of great distress, she would frequently begin talking with great feeling and remorse about her father and his death. At times she was able to weep bitterly about this event, but often her tears would turn to angry outbursts. It seemed clear that her paranoid outbursts were serving important defensive needs against the severe loss and intense feelings of depression that she could not tolerate. At such times her thinking would become quite obviously disorganized and loose, and she would become tremendously anxious. She would often feel that she was having a heart attack—feeling pain over her heart—having difficulty breathing, and feeling a tingling sense in her extremities.

Even in the best therapeutic relationship she was able to establish, it was plain that she could not tolerate any closeness and could not bring herself to trust her therapist. She was constantly testing, both in treatment sessions and in her behavior on the ward. When she succeeded in provoking a restrictive or repressive response from the staff, she took it as proof that they did not really care about her but were only out to do her in. Many of her escape attempts and provocative attacks also had this manipulative flavor. Unfortunately—but also almost unavoidably—she would succeed in making the staff angry at her, particularly by her frustration of their therapeutic intents and purposes. She was intent on re-creating in the therapeutic setting the pattern of interaction that she maintained at home with her mother.

DISCUSSION

In the Camp of the Enemy

The impression that Ellen gave and had given for most of her life was one of embattled defensiveness interrupted by hostile counterattacks. She lived in a stage of perpetual siege. She was always on guard, constantly keeping a watch out for an unexpected attack. Under the duress of these continual attacks, she lashed out at her enemy. Her capacity for sustaining the counterattack was one of the remarkable characteristics of Ellen's sickness. There was no capitulation before the enemy; instead she waged a continuing war. The analogy occurred to me of some of the embattled folk of Ellen's country of origin. There was no question for them of capitulation or compromise with the enemy; they will fight to death fanatically, no matter what the odds or the consequences. Ellen revealed some of that same spirit. She lived in the country of the enemy and her stubborn will gave no room for compromise or surrender. Hers was a fight to the last.

But what is most striking about her story from our point of view was that Ellen did indeed have an enemy. It was an enemy that she could not and perhaps did not want to rid herself of. Ellen's enemy was her mother. The relationship between them was intensely ambivalent, symbiotic, mutually hostile and destructive, mutually dependent. The disturbance of her relationship to her mother stemmed from the earliest levels of her childhood of which we have any knowledge.

Maternal Destructiveness

Ellen was apparently an affront to her mother's image of herself as a good, loving, caretaking, self-sacrificing, neat, orderly, capable, and effective mother. We must remember that this mother was also given to flying into towering rages when the children failed to keep the house orderly and clean. This rage was directed in a variety of ways against Ellen. We can recall at this point the hostile relationship that obtained between Ann A. and her mother. It is striking that in the two most severely disturbed female paranoid patients this pattern of maternal destructiveness was most apparent.

The disturbing quality of Ellen's relationship with her mother stood out in this family. While the mother's relations with the other children were not all that could be desired, they did not have this malignant, highly ambivalent, and destructive quality. We have no reliable information about the earliest aspects of this interaction. We can guess that Ellen may have been a more active or more irritable child and that her mother's inability to respond to this pattern of activity may have set the tone of their basic interaction. What seems clear is that Ellen emerged from those early years as a rather insecure and shy little girl, uncertain of her position in the life and affection of her family and tending to an antagonistic and hostile relationship with them. Her failure to meet her mother's exacting demands was met with ridicule and shaming. The Lysol baths, which lasted for some time, were repeated humiliations. Her wetting was a disgrace and a reflection on her mother. The blame was placed on Ellen, and she was made to feel inferior and inadequate and a source of shame to her mother and her family.

Much of Ellen's disturbed behavior can be seen as a continuing effort to ward off anticipated humiliation. Her response to the glasses for her strabismus was typical. She saw these glasses as a humiliation. The fact that her parents and particularly her mother tried to force them on her was proof enough that they constituted a humiliation and an embarrassment for her. She felt that the glasses were only a way of calling attention to her eyes, and that they only made her look worse. She felt that she had been robbed of her good looks and blamed her mother for the fact of her ocular abnormality.

Shame and Humiliation

Both the strabismus and, perhaps more importantly, the enuresis contributed to her sense of shame and humiliation. An important aspect of this experience in her early childhood years was the influence on the body image. The loss of sphincter control and the publicly apparent dysfunction of both her eyes and her urinary apparatus contributed to a devalued sense of her own body. She was left with the feeling that she had somehow been deprived of something—cheated out of something that would have made her whole and wholesome, rather than defective and shameful. We shall have the opportunity to return to this issue of the determinants of the body image and their impact on the developing personality later. But the sense of bodily defect and inability to control certain functions can serve as an important focus for an inner sense of shame and inferiority. The element of castration here is perhaps too obvious to comment on, but it should be noted that castration anxieties in both males and females tend to build on and incorporate deeper and more primitive fears of distrust, deprivation, and shameful inadequacy.

Along with this sense of shamefulness and inadequacy, Ellen possessed a considerable degree of very primitive narcissism. She expected in many ways to be taken care of, to be catered to, to be given attention and affection, to be treated in special and privileged ways. She thought of herself as a highborn person. This is interesting in view of the fact that it reflected her mother's almost delusional attitudes about social status and being in with the "blue bloods." In the hospital, Ellen would make very derogatory and uncomplimentary remarks about the other patients, making it very clear that she looked down on all of them and regarded them as socially inferior to herself and her family. Her attitude toward blacks was especially rich in contempt and disgust. This linked meaningfully to her delusional fears of having intercourse with blacks and becoming one of them. The delusional content referred back to and reflected the extremely prejudicial attitudes that permeated her family and which particularly characterized her mother. Along with her social ambition and high regard for the "blue bloods," Ellen's mother despised any race other than Anglo-Saxon or Irish. She despised any of the darker skinned people of Europe—Italians or people of Spanish descent—and regarded blacks as hardly human. Intercourse with a black in this context would be close to the lowest degree of human degradation and humiliation.

Parental Interaction

To the extent that we are able, we can try to focus the interaction that took place between Ellen and her parents. There can be little doubt that the interaction with the mother was of major pathogenic import. Early in the study of the genesis of the pathology of schizophrenia, the focus fell on the mother, so that the concept of the schizophrenogenic mother came into prominence. The essence of the concept retains its validity, although we have learned that the schizophrenogenic mother does not come to life and have her detrimental influence without a background of significant influences stemming from the rest of the family. In focusing on the genesis of the paranoid process, many of the same elements come into play. In a case like Ellen's the overlap of such familial influences is considerable.

The relationship between Ellen's parents was one of emotional divorce. There was little by way of affection that passed between them. They went their separate ways, coming together without affection. Intercourse was a form of mutual masturbation performed in the marriage bed. Ellen's mother was left in more or less complete domination of the home. She was in complete charge, her word and wish was law, she administered justice, meted out punishment, etc. Ellen's father became the titular head of the house *in absentia*. He spent as much time as possible out of the house, working all day and every day, and only coming home when things had quieted down and the children were in bed. His dealing with the problems at home was by way of withdrawal. The result was to leave the children with no one to turn to but their mother.

For Ellen, the consequences were catastrophic. Her mother, whose destructive sadism she was forced to struggle with, was thus the omnipotent power that determined the course and pattern of her life. She therefore had no recourse to her father—no source of alliance or support in the face of her mother's shaming and demeaning attacks. If her father became unavailable to his wife and the rest of the family, he also became unavailable to Ellen as well. In her position of vulnerability, the effects on her were severe. Ellen's attitude toward her father was one of idealized yearning. She idolized him and wanted to be with him. But he was never there. She felt that in some way she had been deprived of her father as well, and her blame fell, not unexpectedly, on her mother.

In this context, the circumstances of her father's death were particularly significant for Ellen. Her anger at him for leaving her, for staying away from her, and for leaving her vulnerable to her mother and not protecting her was intense. Yet she could not direct her anger at him because of the intensity of her longing for him. His death was a final leaving, a final disappointment, a final betrayal which left her with only her mother to turn to. Ellen could not tolerate or face her rage. In her moments of anxiety, she mimicked her father's fatal symptoms, and became hypochondriacally concerned that she might have a heart attack, as he did. A heart attack would provide the appropriate punishment for her murderous wishes born of her anger that her father might die. In her moments of decompensated distress, Ellen broke out in bitter self-accusation that she was responsible for her father's death. She still felt the anguish of guilt and the pain of his loss; she continued to mourn him in a decidedly pathological fashion. The mourning process crippled her psychologically for almost a decade.

Projections and Introjections

Ellen's auditory hallucinations, which were a relatively constant feature of her pathology, accused her of being a prostitute, of sleeping with blacks, and of being a lesbian. We have seen similar phenomena in other hallucinating patients. The accusations form the substance of demeaning and devaluing accusations—a form of superego projection in which the critical agency is located outside the subject. It seems immediately apparent that Ellen's critical and devaluing projections were related to the introjection of the bad, sadistic, and destructive mother.

Thus Ellen carried within her a source of inner conflict and turmoil. Her mother's blaming and shaming attitudes became her own and were directed inexorably against herself. Her inner world became shrouded in doubt and a sense of shame and blame. Her inner sense of self-possession and autonomy was precarious. She was pressured internally to defend herself by an arrogant attitude of pseudosuperiority and by violent attacks on those who she thought were looking down on her or thinking poorly of her. In doing this, she was adopting and adapting the modalities of defense she had seen so often on the part of her mother. Mother was given to demeaning others and giving herself airs of social superiority—thinking herself one of the "blue bloods"—in an attempt to defend against and protect herself from her own inner feelings of inferiority and poverty of position. It was mother also who would lash out in outbursts of temper, throwing things and attacking members of the family in enraged loss of control in the face of the frustration of her wishes or of failure on the part of others to support her feelings of self-importance and effectiveness. Ellen lived out in her own terms the model that she had continually before her.

The overwhelming influence of this relationship with her mother and the corresponding introjection reflects the intensity of Ellen's need to depend on her mother, as well as her intense inner wish to be loved by and close to her mother—the other side of her ambivalence. Ellen displayed in a graphic manner the inner duality of such introjects—the simultaneous wish to preserve and be close to the object, along with the intense wish to destroy and eliminate the hated object. This reflects and derives from the tremendous ambivalence that inheres in the relationship. It is nearly always a predominant feature of all symbiotic relationships. The symbiosis is intensified and prolonged by the intense ambivalence toward the object. To separate is to reject—and equivalently to destroy. In the face of such destructive wishes real separation becomes well-nigh impossible.

The threat to autonomy is inextricably bound up with this inner vicissitude of the symbiotic union. Not only does the ambivalence pose a destructive threat to the object, but it poses an inner threat as well, and the inner threat may often be the more catastrophic. The patient feels that to separate from the real object requires the surrender of the inner object as well. And if the inner object is destroyed and annihilated, there will be nothing left—the subject will be reduced to nothing, destroyed, annihilated. The hatred for the object becomes, through introjection, a hatred of the self, and the wish to annihilate the object poses the threat of annihilation of the self. The sense of inner autonomy becomes fragile and precarious. The result is that—as in Ellen's case—the patient's autonomy is threated both internally and externally. In this context, Ellen's severe decompensation in the face of her mother's life threatening condition becomes understandable.

CHAPTER 11

Fred F.

The present case is of considerable interest not only for the pattern of psychopathology that it presents, but also for the questions that it raises in a broader context. Because of the patient's life situation and involvements, his experience raises in a particularly forceful way the problem of the relationship between individual, intrapsychic pathology and the disruption of social processes and the distortion of social organization. The basic question to which we will have to address ourselves in approaching this particular case is: to what extent are the projective aspects of individual psychopathology verifiable or verified in the social structures and processes which provide the reality to which the projection is directed? It can be readily seen—and can be seen more at length in the following case material—that this consideration raises some perplexing and difficult questions regarding the sense of isolation and social alienation that many of our young people feel today.

THE PATIENT'S PROFILE

Initial Contact

I first came into contact with Fred when he was brought to the hospital for admission by the police. He was just twenty-two years old, a student at one of the local universities. The police had apprehended him the previous night, standing in the middle of a highway brandishing a crowbar at the passing cars in the road, thus obstructing traffic and causing a considerable disturbance. He was arrested, spent the night in jail, and then was sent by the judge to the hospital for psychiatric evaluation due to his obviously disorganized and bizarre behavior.

When I first spoke to Fred, he seemed somewhat tense, apprehensive, anxious, and rather agitated. He spoke readily and even eagerly, but with a certain degree of pressure behind his flow of speech. He seemed easily distractible and unable to follow a line of thought for very long. His mind would shoot off in tangential directions which gave the distinct impression of a loosening of his thought processes. He tried to affect a rather casual and self-assured facade, but at the same time gave the distinct impression of being inwardly uncertain, frightened, and insecure. His thoughts seemed almost obsessively preoccupied with questions of politics, human rights, freedom, individual expression, racial justice, social justice, etc. He would episodically break out into angry tirades about these subjects in a manner which reflected his intense rage and anger at the fact that unfortunate people in the world were taken advantage of and were powerless in the face of the heartless and cold, inhuman forces which controlled their lives.

From time to time he would refer to his own special powers and sensitivities which made him an extraordinarily valuable person. He felt that he had special powers which enabled him to read people's minds or which enabled him to make himself invisible. He felt that he had a special understanding of other cultures and other people which made it possible for him to be politically successful and astute. He expressed rather vague, yet definite, delusions of persecution. The identity of the persecutors was not very well defined—he spoke loudly of the government, or the university administration, or the FBI, or the "establishment," etc. It seemed that the purpose of all these forces was to thwart the patient and frustrate his ambitions of obtaining goals—such as financial success, or academic success, or success in the political area—that he felt he deserved. He even hinted vaguely at delusions of total world chaos and destruction, with hostile and powerful forces vying with each other and destroying each other in an attempt to take over the world.

Fred was at first fairly cooperative, despite his delusions and preoccupations. Even so, he would from time to time during the course of the examination make peremptory demands that questions of his be answered to his satisfaction. His attitude was one of suspicion and distrust. For example, he demanded to know what the function of the opthalmoscope was and why the doctor would want to look into his eyes with it. He was not satisfied and would not let the examination continue until the doctors had given him a rather lengthy explanation—even though he was obviously in no condition to absorb or appreciate the explanation given. As time wore on, however, despite increasing doses of phenothiazines, he became increasingly tense and agitated, and began to break out into angry shouting tirades. He also began to threaten other patients and staff with physical violence so that it became necessary to restrain him and restrict his activities. He seemed to quiet down on high doses of phenothiazines, but continued to have difficulty in restraining and controlling his angry impulses.

This was particularly true in the ward community meetings. In these meetings, it was the custom for matters of general concern to the patients to be discussed, but Fred seemed to respond to them as though they were political gatherings that he felt it necessary to harangue and exhort politically. On one such occasion, he jumped up in the middle of the meeting and interrupted the proceedings with an impassioned, intensely angry, and provocative tirade which had to do with the violation of patients' rights by the establishment and by the hospital, the staff and doctors, and an exhortation to the patients to revolt and take over the hospital. It was delivered in an intensely furious, angry, foot-stomping, shouting tirade that wound up with the patient throwing a chair on the floor and breaking it. This behavior was obviously very disruptive, and Fred had to be removed from the meeting—with, of course, a physical struggle to accomplish this. Gradually, as the medication took hold, he began to quiet down and to gain some better degree of control over his behavior, although the delusional content of his thought and the loosened and tangential quality of his thought processes remained disorganized for several weeks.

Prior Psychiatric History

It turned out that the present hospitalization was neither the first nor the last that Fred was to experience. I would like at this point in discussing his case to go back to the point of his first hospitalization and review the experiences which brought him to this second one. In the light of that more recent part of his history, we can then go back to his earlier life experience and family background to try to determine the influences which might have lain behind this illness and determined the pattern of its emergence.

Fred's first psychiatric hospitalization took place while he was serving in the armed services. We can pick up the story at the beginning of his college career. Fred's first year in college was not altogether a successful or encouraging one. At the university he quickly became involved in the drug scene and made friends mostly with other students who were also actively involved in taking drugs. He became a regular user of marijuana and also indulged in an occasional LSD trip. This routine became rather depressing for him. His grades were poor and he became rather distressed at his inability to perform well academically. He also wished to break away from the drug routine, which he felt was hurtful to himself. He felt that he was liable to be drafted anyway because of his poor marks, so he decided that he would enlist in the army.

His experience in the army was also an unhappy one. He was unable to develop any close friendships. He looked down on his fellow trainees as being less educated or less intelligent than himself. But most intensely of all he bitterly resented and hated the army discipline that was inflicted on him and to which he felt that he had to submit himself. He felt such discipline was a humiliation and an infringement on his rights. At the end of his basic training period, he was sent by the army to be trained as an electronics technician. By this time, of course, he had contacted some of his friends back in school and had received a shipment of LSD. By this time also his thinking was becoming increasingly disorganized and confused, and his capacity to control his anger and resentment increasingly impaired. He was becoming progressively suspicious and guarded and felt that the service was persecuting him. He felt that they were keeping him under surveillance.

He became confused, delusional, and frankly paranoid. He thought that his thought processes were being blocked by an electronic device, so that he couldn't remember things and could not think straight. He felt that the army was doing this to him and using this machine on him so that they could keep control over him and make him do what they wanted.

Fred's decompensation was, however, short-lived. He was hospitalized for a brief period and was then discharged from the hospital. He was given a medical discharge from the army and was mustered out. He decided to return to school and complete his studies. His performance academically continued to be rather mediocre. This was a severe blow to his narcissism. But his difficulties were more than merely academic. He tended to be shy and awkward, found it difficult to talk to people or to communicate with other students. He had constant ideas of reference. He felt that people were talking about him behind his back or that they were laughing at him. He recalled incidents when he would go to the school library to study, but was distinctly uncomfortable because he felt the other students were whispering about him or watching him. He desperately wanted to be able to reach people and gain their respect and admiration.

Political Involvement

Student politics offered him a ready-made channel by which he could both gain the respect of other students and achieve a degree of closeness with them, as well as a vehicle by which he could express his anger and resentment against society and its institutions. He became more and more involved in student politics in the university and developed a reputation as a student activist and radical. He threw himself into this activity with tremendous energy. He became quite facile in organizing and manipulating student groups and in mobilizing them in support of certain political causes on the campus. He organized and directed a number of demonstrations and campaigns in the university. Finally, toward the end of his third year, he ran as the vice-presidential candidate on the student radical ticket. He was riding high at that point. He was caught up in the election campaign in a manic fashion. He went about it with considerable energy—making speeches, organizing meetings, conducting the entire campaign himself. He poured out tremendous energy in trying to make it a success. He tried to make it a "campaign on the issues," as he put it—rather than a personality contest. His major opponent was a not-too-bright hockey player who had no real conception of what politics was all about, and Fred felt assured in his own mind that he was running a successful campaign and felt confident of his victory. However—he lost.

The election loss was a severe disappointment and a difficult narcissistic trauma. He had lost when he felt most assured of victory. The loss was a severe disappointment because it short-circuited his ambitions and hopes and plans for the future. His disappointment was intense, and he responded by plunging into a period of rather severe depression. Depite his depression, he managed to finish the school year. However, at the end of the school year came another disappointment which added another insult to his shaky self-image. During the year he had become quite involved with a girl in his class, and they had begun living together and sleeping together. This relationship persisted for several months. But at the end of the school year, the girl decided that her relationship to Fred was undesirable and that he was too unstable for any permanent sort of tie. She told him this and broke off the arrangement. Fred felt the loss and rejection severely. He became increasingly depressed. He tried to throw himself into a variety of activities to overcome the bitterness, resentment, and loneliness that he felt so acutely.

He threw himself into a furor of organizing activities. He began forming some of the students at the university into political groups, organized in a rather vague and nonspecific way for the defense of America. His description of the specific function and purpose of these groups was rather nebulous, but had some relationship to problems about military secrets, the war in Vietnam, government plots—in general, reflecting his intense concern at that time for the protection of the downtrodden student minorities from the influences of established institutions, both governmental and educational. There was a decidedly paranoid flavor to these organizing activities, but the paranoia was distilled into his political motivation.

His behavior at this point was extremely agitated and quite excitable, with all kinds of crazy thoughts running through his head in a disorganized and "hyper" fashion. He continued to use pot and acid with his friends. His obsessions with persecution, his flight of ideas, and his fear of losing his mind or of having others control his mind and his behavior increased over the ensuing weeks. Under the pressure and stress of these ideas he would become quite agitated, feeling angry and conceiving resentful ideas. One night he seized a crowbar and went out to a nearby highway. He felt incensed and infuriated at the cars on the highway, feeling that they were infringing on his constitutional rights and were preventing him from crossing the highway. He was determined to put a stop to this and to attack these machines that were so unfeeling and so uncaring of him and to destroy them. He placed himself in the middle of the road, brandishing the crowbar and threatening to hit the cars with it if they came near him. While he was doing this, he carried on an angry shouting tirade against the motorists in the cars. It was not long before the police showed up and took him into custody. From that point he made his way quickly to our hospital.

Fred seems to have reconstituted after this first decompensation but the degree of recompensation is questionable. It seems likely that he reconstituted to a level of paranoid adjustment in which the delusional process was present and active, but he was not out and out crazy. He was suspicious, guarded, and subject to ideas of reference, but the delusional content during this intermediate period seems to have been focused on the more general level of his feeling that he was the victim of corrupt social processes and evil social structures. His anger and resentment were directed against the "system"—and it was against this that he worked so actively and energetically in his political campaigns. The delusional system was thus effectively channeled into these political activities. The loss of the election was a blow and a disappointment—but one that was seen in specifically paranoid terms. In the face of his disappointment, Fred felt that the election had been rigged, and he was quite convinced that the university administration had engaged in some dirty-dealing and behind-the-back politicking which resulted in his loss. The loss of the election and the loss of his girl friend seemed to have been narcissistic affronts which he could not tolerate and which plunged him into a depressive position that he could not tolerate. The result was the subsequent exacerbation of his psychotic symptoms which evolved over a period of several weeks. And finally, of course, his psychotic rage erupted into the delusional outburst and agitation that we have described.

Family Background

Fred's family was comparatively isolated and one which exhibited a number of unusual and interesting features. The immediate family was composed of mother and father along with three sons. Fred was the oldest of the three boys; his next younger brother was two years his junior and the youngest boy, Tommy, about eight years younger than Fred. The family was from an upper-middle-class background on both sides. Fred's mother was a rather nervous and high-strung woman, with a long-standing, chronic drinking problem. She was a frail, tremulous woman, then in her mid-forties. She had been a chronic drinker throughout most of her married life and carried most of the physical stigmata of alcoholism. Even though she was only in her mid-forties, she gave the impression of a woman of considerably greater age.

Fred's father was a trim, lean, graying, and rather bland business executive. He was approaching fifty and looked somewhat younger than his years. He was two years older than his wife. Fred's father's mother had died when he was quite young and as a result the father was almost totally dependent on his father—Fred's paternal grandfather. The grandfather owned a resort hotel in the northeastern part of the country. He was a bitter, authoritarian, and tyrannical man. He ran his hotel in a rigid and authoritarian manner, and any employees who tried to differ with him or argue with him were summarily fired on the spot.

Fred's father worked for his father at the hotel and was treated by the old man as though he were just another employee. He had to adhere strictly to the old man's wishes or run the risk of getting thrown out. There was no warmth and no intimacy in their relationship. Fred's father respected and feared his father, and he was rigidly obedient to the latter's wishes, but there was no love and no warmth of any kind between them. Fred's father did reasonably well. He attended the better prep schools, and Ivy League college, and after graduation began work with a large business corporation as a sales and marketing executive. He attained a moderately good position in his firm and earned a respectable salary, but never seemed to be able to make it into the big time that he had always ambitioned and worked for. Many of his school friends and college chums had risen to positions of considerable eminence in their respective fields, and the father always felt somewhat remorseful and a little bitter about the fact he had been unable to make his mark in life and had been unable to achieve the eminence that he coveted. Even though he felt that he worked very hard for these goals and that he deserved them, they always seemed to elude him.

Parental Interaction

Fred described his father as a shy, reserved and secretive man. The father had very few friends or associates outside of his immediate business contacts and the family. In our contacts with him he was always pleasant and polite, reasonable and appropriate. But one could not avoid the impression of a certain guardedness—a shielding and protecting of himself that seemed to permeate all his relationships. We could almost describe the quality of this interaction with people as schizoid, except that it was subtle and in fact masked by a facade of easy sociability. Even in his warmest and most feelingful exchanges with Fred, there was this same quality of distance and guardedness that inserted itself. It became quite evident, in the interactions between father and son, the extent to which this posture of his father and the distance between them were sources of frustration for Fred that he was able to tolerate very poorly.

Fred's mother, on the other hand, was a somewhat warmer, although obviously considerably more infantile person than his father. Behind her ready facade of cocktail party pleasantry, one could sense a pervasive and rather chronic depression. She seemed to be a rather needy person, with a relatively available supply of affection and warmth, but that capacity for affection and warmth was not consistently available to her. She seemed to be an insecure and somewhat needy woman, who readily turned to her husband for support or for gratification of her own needs. At such times—when she turned to him for support or in a manner that expressed her needs and her expectation of response from him—it became apparent that Mr. F. was somewhat threatened by this and responded by even further withdrawal from her.

The marriage relationship had never been a good one. From the very beginning it had been filled with argument and conflict. The two of them seemed to disagree on a great many points. They seemed unable to resolve their differences. The usual pattern was that there would be a fight, and this would be followed by heavy drinking on the part of Mrs. F. and by an increased distancing and withdrawal on the part of Mr. F. As time went on, he arranged it so that he was obliged to spend more and more time away from home. They lived in the suburbs and he would leave in the early hours of the morning before Mrs. F. was out of bed and wouldn't return until the late evening hours. Weekends were hell. It was a rare weekend on which there was not a bitter argument and fight, and on which Mrs. F. did not get plastered stiff. Mr. F. also arranged in his capacity as a sales executive to take long trips to distant parts of the country and to foreign countries. This enabled him to be away from home and out of the stressful relationships with his wife and the rest of his family for even more extended periods of time. Inevitably, when he would go away on such trips, Mrs. F. would intensify her drinking and literally go on an extended binge during the period that her husband was away. While this pattern persisted from the earliest years, for a long time Mrs. F. kept her drinking for the most part a secret. She would hide the liquor so that her husband or the rest of the family would not discover it. She would also confine her heaviest drinking to periods in which her husband was absent.

What is most striking in all this is the quality of bland denial with which Fred's father treated the family problems. For many years, he refused to acknowledge that his wife had a drinking problem, even when confronted with unavoidable and irrefutable evidence that such was the case. In part her secretiveness was a contributing factor to this pattern, but it seems unavoidable that one also must acknowledge that Fred's father's unwillingness to face difficult emotional problems, together with his willingness to keep a safe emotional distance and to run from such problems when the opportunity presented itself, also played a significant part in the interaction between the couple.

The family experience was marked by considerable disorganization and disruption. In order to bolster the family finances, Fred's father took a position as a sales representative for his company in several foreign countries. He accepted his first foreign assignment when Fred was about six years old. The family had lived in a number of places in Fred's early years, moving every other year to a new location as Fred's father would be moved from one position to another in the company. The first foreign assignment was in Africa. The family lived there for the next eight years, but again the pattern of moving from place to place persisted. During the eight-year period they lived in ten different places. This was followed by a six-year stint in Greece.

Fred recalls all these moves with a great deal of bitterness. He regards himself as having been a lonely and isolated child. And he blames his parents for this because they were always moving from one place to another so that he never had a chance to develop any real friendships. He had to shift from school to school and he felt that this served only to disrupt his education and made it difficult for him to really accomplish anything. His resentment in this regard had to do with the fact that his parents always insisted that he do better schoolwork; yet they were the ones who made it impossible for him to do any better by their constant moving. Fred was not entirely convinced of his parents' blameworthiness, but made attempts to absolve them and cast the blame on the evil and malicious capitalistic and profiteering social system which made it necessary for his parents to have to do what they did. He complained bitterly, however, that all of this was done without any concern for or consultation about his own feelings and needs in the matter.

Interaction with Mother

Fred's relationship to his mother was particularly difficult. She doted on him and called him "her favorite." She would treat him with special affection—with a great deal of embracing and fondling. Fred reflected that she was just too loving for him. The seductive threat in this behavior is obvious—but it also provided a focus of jealousy between Fred and his younger brother. Fred's resentment about this in part had to do with his feeling that his mother's attention to him made his brother angry and destroyed the possibility of any real relationship with his sibling. Once again Fred blamed his parents for his difficulties.

Mother's affection, however, was very much a mixed blessing. Along with her seductive affectionateness, she also imposed rigid and strict demands on him for behavior and performance. When he did not fulfill her expectations exactly, she would punish him harshly. The discipline was apparently inconsistent and capricious. He would be punished severely at times when he did not expect it at all and when he had no idea what he had done that was wrong. He remembered her beating him for long periods until he was black and blue, and when he would cry she would become even more enraged and scream at him to stand up and take it like a man. He described one such episode vividly when he was only five or six years old. She was furious about something innocent that he had done and started to beat him. She kept knocking him down, then screamed at him to get up on his feet and take what was coming to him. Then she would knock him down again. She kept doing this to him for a considerable period of time and seemed unable to stop. These angry and capricious outbursts left an indelible impression on Fred.

Then too, she was constantly at him for one thing or another. She was always scolding him or criticizing his behavior. His manners were never right; he never seemed to be able to do anything right, to do anything to her satisfaction. If he did any chores around the house he never seemed to be able to do them in a way that satisfied his mother. He recalled that he worked very hard and wanted desperately to please her and do the right thing. But he never seemed to be able to measure up to her expectations. This applied to school as well. His marks were never good enough. He was in general a moderately good student. But no matter how hard he worked or how good his marks were, they did not please her. His performance was always deficient, always criticized, never measured up. He felt that he was in some way defective or inadequate.

The School Years—Exile

Fred recalls that as a young child he was quite fearful and isolated. He remembered terrible and frightening nightmares, although he could never recall the content of any of these dreams. As we shall see, nightmares were a feature of his later clinical pattern as well. He recalled awakening in the middle of the night terrified. He was afraid of animals as well. He remembered particularly having a fear of foxes. He recollected overhearing his parents talking about foxes carrying rabies. The family lived in a suburban area with a fair amount of wooded land in which Fred used to play. He became terrified of these woods, fearing that there would be foxes in them and that the animals might attack and bite him, and give him rabies that he would die from. He even remembered a fantasy that there were foxes hiding under his bed. He recalled that when he had to go to bed he was terrified. If he cried or put up a fuss, his parents would scold him or punish him and make him go to his room anyway. When he had to go to bed, he remembered running and leaping onto the bed over the footboard so that the foxes under the bed couldn't catch him and bite him.

When Fred was six years old, the family moved to Africa. This was exciting for him, and he recalled the early years there with pleasure. He remembered making friends with the native boys and being able to play with them. But the pattern of continued moving still made things difficult for him. When he was about ten years old, his parents decided to send him to England for schooling. The father's rationalization for this was severalfold. The first factor was that the schooling available in Africa was of very poor quality and he wanted Fred to have the advantage of good schools. Another factor was that he had spent most of his own young years in boarding schools and remembered that time as a good experience in his life. He thought it would be good if Fred could have something of the same experience. But the most important and pressing factor that motivated the decision was the quality of the relationship between Fred and his mother. The father recognized that this interaction was unhealthy and detrimental to Fred. He felt that things were getting worse instead of better, as he had hoped, and he saw no recourse in the living situation but to give Fred the chance to get away from his mother and thus give him an opportunity for survival.

On Fred's part, however, being sent away to school was an exile; he felt it to be a rejection and an abandonment. It was for him the certain sign of his disfavor and of his failure. He had failed to win his mother's approval, failed to satisfy her and measure up to her expectations. His banishment was particularly bitter in view of the fact that his younger brother was kept with the family. Fred had lost out in the intense rivalry with his brother as well. The banishment also intensified and further frustrated his wishes to get close to his father. In his crucial latency years, instead of gaining some sense of closeness and companionship with his father that he so desperately wanted, he was sent away to try to find his place among strangers.

Fred's resentment and bitterness ran deep. He was sent to an English boys' school and he hated it. He hated everything about it. He hated the other boys, he hated the teachers, he hated the restrictions and confinement, he hated the discipline, which was strict and often harsh. He could not make friends with the other boys. They taunted and picked on him because he was an American. They laughed at him because of the funny way he talked and expressed himself. He would respond with frustrated fury and rage. He was constantly getting into fights with the other boys. His attitude was sullen and rebellious and hostile. The other boys played tricks on him that made his life miserable, and their laughter hurt him and made him all the more furious.

His sense of isolation and abandonment grew through these years. His parents wrote to him infrequently. They never visited him—or at least he could never remember any such visits. They rarely ever sent him presents. Birthdays and holidays would often pass without a letter or a present. On each such occasion he was hurt and pained, and his sense of bitter resentment grew and deepened. He would plead to be able to come home for holidays, but the answer was always that it wouldn't be convenient, or that the family was going away, or that it would cost too much money for him to travel where they were. The expense incidentally was often the excuse for not being able to visit him at school. Fred remained in these English schools for several years. Because of his complaints and pleadings to be allowed to escape, he spent a year in school in Switzerland and another year in France. But these diversions were no matter. He was still lonely, still abandoned, and still could not make any friends to lighten the burden. The language barrier added to his difficulties.

Finally he was returned to the United States. His father had decided that he should attend a first-rate prep school—an experience his father thought would be in his best interests. Fred was enrolled in the prep school that his father had attended. The decision was made in the face of Fred's own complaints and protests. Father's mind was made up and that was that! The experience was again an unhappy and bitter one. His relationships with the other boys were intensely competitive and by and large hostile. He had few friends. He felt people were trying to put him down and keep him in an inferior place. He was quite rebellious and angry. He became a serious discipline problem and was always getting into hot water with the school authorities. He felt everyone was out to show him up and prevent him from showing his true abilities. His academic performance was barely passing. He felt the teachers were picking on him, were trying to make things difficult for him and were preventing him from showing his true ability and intelligence. He was intensely competitive in other areas. He felt that he showed more leadership ability than the other boys but that he was discriminated against and passed over because the administration and some of the boys were out to get him. When he was not elected to various class offices, he felt that he had been cheated and that the election had been rigged so that other fellows won and he didn't. He was able to unleash a considerable amount of anger and energy in athletics. He became known in the school as a fierce and ruthless competitor. His best game was soccer and, even though he was smaller in stature than most of the other kids, he managed to make the first team.

He made no friends in the school, either among the boys or among the faculty and administration. At the end of the year he was asked not to return to the school. Although his grades were passing, he was regarded as a disciplinary problem and the school did not want him back. Fred was hurt and angered by this. Once again he had failed, once again he was unable to measure up. He saw himself as a victim of circumstances and the ill will of others. He had too many things against him—not being able to live with his family, having to shift for himself, not having any friends or family to turn to, having everybody against him. How could anybody hope to succeed in the face of all that?

The Seduction

It was about this time that the family finally moved back to the United States and was reunited to some degree. However, Fred was not at home for any extended period of time. Here again the old pattern way played out. Father was absent most of the time. He would take off on long business trips leaving mother with the boys. Her drinking was carried on even more heavily. When the father was away, she would go on prolonged alcoholic sprees. This situation was difficult for Fred to handle. As oldest son, Fred felt that father was running away and dumping the responsibility for his mother in his lap. He felt angered at his father's failure to take his responsibility and his leaving Fred to deal with the problem. When mother would get soused,

Fred would feel helpless and inadequate, would feel that he had failed again and that he was useless and incompetent.

It was in this context that the single most significant event in Fred's history occurred. He was about sixteen at the time. His father was away on one of his extended trips. His mother had been drinking quite heavily. It was late at night and he was ready to go to bed. He had put his pajamas on and was preparing for bed. His mother called him into her room. She was lying on the bed, wearing nothing but a negligee. She made him lie down beside her and began to embrace and caress him. He felt terrified and helpless, as though he could do nothing but what she wished. She began to fondle his penis and he had an erection. They went on to have intercourse. She was inebriated almost to the point of incoherence.

The experience was devastating for Fred. He felt as though he were in a daze, as though it really wasn't happening. He couldn't believe that he was doing it. He remembered feeling aroused and excited, and particularly feeling that he wanted to hurt her, fix her for all that he had suffered at her hands. The next day his mother made no reference to it, except to allude that she had had a strange dream. A few nights later, within a week, the process was repeated again. The second experience was more deliberate on his part. He remembered having an orgasm—how good it felt—and that she had an orgasm too. The memory of these events stayed with him as a festering sore ever since. We will have more to say about it later. But it was clearly a focus for his most intense, ambivalent, and most destructive feelings.

The Clinical Picture

Fred was subsequently able to finish his high school requirements and be accepted in a large eastern university. We have already recounted his subsequent disappointments and the schizophrenic decompensations that brought him to our hospital and into therapy with me. I would like to turn at this point to my own experience working with him and to some of the material related to his treatment course. That material, placed against the background of his family problems and past experiences, raises some difficult and perplexing problems both for the treatment of paranoid patients in general, and for the understanding of the role of psychiatry vis-a-vis the patterns of social disorganization and disruption that swirl about us in contemporary society.

After his admission to the hospital, Fred began to slowly calm down and became increasingly less agitated, hostile, and assaultive. It took somewhat longer for his thought processes to become more organized. For several weeks his thought was rather tangential and he seemed to have difficulty holding a single line of thought for any length of time. He continued to have difficulty concentrating for a considerable period of time. Gradually he was able to become comfortable with the therapeutic situation and more and more able to recall parts of his history and to recount them to me. The substance of much of what was expressed in this early period of his treatment had to do with his intense disappointment and rage in relation to his parents. This would alternate with angry tirades against a wide spectrum of authority figures. The feeling connected with this material was intense. When he would get into these angry diatribes, it seemed that he had all he could do to keep the rage under control and to keep himself from simply exploding. He would clench his fists, pound on the desk furiously, twist his face into a tight, tense knot, shout out explicatives expressing his rage—and the furious intensity of it.

He was given a battery of tests at this point and the findings give us a fair representation of his inner turmoil. During the testing he was superficially friendly, but maintained a guarded and suspicious posture. During the intelligence test he became quite angry and defensive, and actually refused to continue the testing. He accused the psychologist of trying to control his mind, as he thought the other doctors were doing. After a lengthy discussion of his feelings about the testing and his illness, he agreed to continue the testing. But he remained quite guarded and would become very upset and defensive whenever he failed a test item. His performance was quite uneven: the full scale WAIS IQ was 99, but verbal was 108 and performance IQ 86. This reflected his reliance on verbal skills to cover his inadequacies and occasional inner confusion. I would like to quote from the psychologist's report:

> He made an effort to be quite intellectual in his responses, but his responses were quite empty and pretentious. He had markedly impaired comprehension, concentration, and attention. Besides being easily distracted, his associations were quite loose and the logic of some of his reasoning is quite odd. His abstracting ability is low. He tends to be either concrete or overly abstract. His general manner was suspicious and he readily projected responsibility and blame. Mr. F. clearly seems to have a thought disorder that interferes greatly with his ability to think clearly and to function at his appropriate level. He finds it very difficult to think on a secondary process level as he is quite vulnerable to the intrusion of primary process material. . . . He is under a great deal of instinctual push at this time. He feels quite anxious, agitated, and threatened. At times he feels as if he might lose control of his sexual and aggressive impulses. He feels that he is quite helpless and vulnerable to attack, especially at the hands of other males. Males are seen as being perpetually in conflict and quite aggressive. In the face of the aggression of male authority figures, he readily regresses to quite primitive levels of functioning. His own sexual identity is quite confused in that he sees himself as weak like a woman. His perception of women is that they are damaged and defective. He has partially identified with his mother yet feels rejected by her. Because of his mixed identity he vacillates between displacing the father and seeking his mother as a love object, and competing with her for the love and affection of his father. He feels that he has been unloved and neglected by his

parents and other adults, and sees himself as somewhat of a needy orphan child. His own dependency needs are reminders to him of his own vulnerability, and he finds them extremely frightening. The content of some of his Rorschach responses was interesting as well. He tended to see a variety of struggling and fighting male figures in the blots. He described a number of faces and skulls—with staring eyes and biting, tearing mouths and teeth and claws. On the fourth card he saw a giant monster looking down at him and threatening him. There were several other monsters as well—each seen as powerful and destructive. In seeing the monster on card IV he became quite anxious and laughed nervously. At one point he became rather disturbed and complained, "Wow! I'm getting sick. I don't know if I want to do any more of these. I'm really finding these incredible things in my subconscious. All these monsters and stuff! It makes me nervous and crazy—Wow! Like not being in your own head! You get into these things and you never know what you're going to find. It's ridiculous!" Again, after seeing a monster's head with a biting jaw on card VII, he commented, "Whoever made these up had a freaky mind. Mr. Rorschach had better be careful when he goes around making up these god-damned inkblots—if they came out of his head, then he had monsters in his head. It's like my nightmares—they make me nervous!"

The test data reflected the inner turmoil and disorganization that Fred was experiencing at the time. They also reflected his markedly paranoid posture and his tendency to resort to mechanisms of denial and projection in the face of failure or stressful anxiety. More importantly for our consideration, however, we were able to catch a glimpse of his inner world. It was flooded with destructive rage and hostile, aggressive impulses. His inner perception of himself was as a powerful, monstrous, and destructive force. He saw interpersonal contexts in terms of hostility, anger, destructive competitiveness, and vicious sadism. We were struck by the tearing, biting, primitive oral destructiveness that Fred felt to be within him. These are due to the destructive introjects that form the internal basis for his pathology. The primitive organization of these introjects is reflected in the susceptibility and vulnerability to instinctual pressures, as well as the resulting regressive pulls.

Therapeutic Experience

The same dynamics were observable in the therapeutic context as well. Fred was from time to time flooded with instinctual material that he seemed unable to control and channel effectively. This was particularly the case with his intense aggressive impulses. He would speak about his parents or their displacements and he would become increasingly angry, until finally he would be overwhelmed with such an intense rage that he had to struggle to maintain any semblance of control over. His constant preoccupation in the early months of treatment was with his inability to maintain control over these impulses and the fear the he would go crazy again. Along with this aspect, there was his sense of shame and depression at the fact that he had flipped out twice, and his fear that he was condemned to a life of marginal adjustment, instability, and repeated psychotic episodes. He saw himself in this regard as having been cheated by fate, as deprived and needy, as having been robbed by his parents and the society at large of a fair chance to make his way in the world and to grow up into an effective and mature adult.

Much of his anger was directed at social institutions and structures. He would focus these feelings in terms of flamboyant political arguments. He was skilled in proliferating arguments directed at the conclusion that society and its institutions were corrupt and degenerate. The rhetoric was heated and intense, and it would flow at a moment's notice from almost any content that had a minimal association with his resentment. These elaborate rhetorical demonstrations would intrude on his thought and his logical processes like a foreign element, but the intensity of feelings in relation to these concerns was so great that it seemed to overwhelm him and carry him away. Whole therapy hours were given over to these sorts of nonstop and unstoppable harangues.

Fred's harangues had a repetitious quality both in their undiminished intensity and the feelings of injured injustice and wronged privation that they generated. The repetition also extended to the content: he was constantly criticizing and attacking social institutions and their administrators. His chronic complaint was that they took advantage of helpless individuals, that they were organized for the advantage and profit of the powerful and for the exploitation of the downtrodden, that they operated in hidden and highly suspect ways which forced people to adhere to their demands and submit to their impositions whether they wished to or not, that they trampled on impotent individuals and forced them into patterns of life without any regard for their individuality or their own inclinations, that they operated with an inhumane indifference to people as people and treated them as insignificant ciphers to be manipulated and controlled, etc., etc.

He was caught up and highly reactive to all of the usual liberal causes. Whenever any reference to the Vietnam situation would come up, he would launch into a furious tirade against the American involvement there. Any form of conflict between young radicals and the establishment offered a focus for his rage. During this period, the Kent State tragedy occurred, as well as the Jackson episode. These events agonized him. He saw himself as one of the powerless and downtrodden minority that was being exploited and murdered by the establishment, an establishment that had all power and control over the lives of helpless victims like himself. He responded with a sense of impotent rage. He wanted to lash out at the establishment and all of its vile institutions, and to destroy them and kill the hated administrators who ran them.

His chronic rage was expressed in a highly inflammatory, provocative, leftist, and revolutionary rhetoric. He had read Marx and Lenin, and spouted references to them readily. He also quoted Chairman Mao enthusiastically. He rationalized any revolutionary action—no matter how destructive or violent—by an appeal to the criminal acts performed by the establishment in the name of society. If the government could blatantly exploit the poor downtrodden people of Vietnam, and could indiscriminately sentence thousands of young men to die for merely calloused and selfish and arbitrary ends, why couldn't the downtrodden take every advantage to redress the wrong, to balance the injustice and turn the weapons of the hated establishment against itself? In this manner he found riots, looting, murder of policemen and other civil servants, destruction of property belonging to schools and other public institutions, shoplifting ("ripping off"), cheating on exams, bilking large corporations like the telephone company, and an endless list of antisocial and criminal acts all justifiable and indeed courageous acts of defiance of an oppressive and unjust, evil system that crushed and destroyed so many helpless and unprivileged individuals.

Rage at Parents

These antisocial and revolutionary tirades were mingled with and alternated with his expressions of outrage and disappointment with his parents. His complaints were many, but the basic resentment was that they had treated him with such cold indifference, had callously abandoned and rejected him, victimized him without any concern for his wishes or needs, and had thus ruined his life. One of the important focuses of this rage had to do with money. Money was a chronic source of irritation and conflict between Fred and his parents. The lack of money had always been the excuse for not being able to do so many things, being unable to come home for visits, for the parents not being able to come visit him, for not being able to take him along with them on their foreign trips, for father's having to take the sort of positions that he did, etc. Money had also been a chronic focus of concern for Fred's father. He was always reminding the family of the scarcity of money and of the need to economize. For Fred this concern focused around his school expenses. Father was always impressing on him the sacrifices that they had to make in order to be able to send Fred away to private schools and later to college.

The money became a therapeutic issue, especially when Fred had to arrange for a fee for his treatment. We discussed his feelings about the money problem, particularly his rage at his father over it. In addition the father began to raise complaints over the length of Fred's hospital stay. He objected that it was costing too much and that Fred should do what he could to shorten it. Side by side with expressions of concern and sympathy for Fred's plight, the father would write letters chiding him for still being in the hospital and still costing money. Every communication would trigger an angry outburst from Fred. On each such occasion he would seem to deteriorate, getting increasingly psychotic, until we discovered that he had received another letter from father about the money and he was able to unleash some of his anger and resentment.

Money remained a focus of resentful interaction between father and son. It was difficult for Fred to acknowledge his anger over this issue, and it took some months before he was able to talk about it. I took up with him his father's complaints in detail. Gradually it became clear to Fred that the claims could not reflect the situation as the father presented it. His family was well off, lived in an expensive suburban area, was educating three sons, was able to take fairly expensive vacations each year, etc. Two points were crucial. One was that his father—in the midst of his complaints to Fred about spending too much money on hospitalization—bought a sailboat for several thousand dollars. The other factor of importance was that he began to realize the amount of money that was consumed by his mother's drinking. The sailboat brought into focus his father's irresponsibility and Fred's anger over it. The expense of the mother's drinking also brought to light Fred's anger and sense of frustration about it, and particularly his resentment at his father's inability to take any action to help her.

The Festering Wound

Along with the continuing theme of rage against his parents and their varied displacements, there ran a countertheme that came back recurrently in the course of therapy—and never seemed to achieve any resolution. It was some months before this material came out, and it would burst out again from time to time in periods of heightened disappointment or depression. I am referring to the cluster of events, memories, thoughts, and feelings that had to do with Fred's incestuous relations with his mother. He found it extremely difficult to think about or face the fact of what he had done. When it first came to the surface, it was in a paroxysm of guilt and self-degradation. Whenever he came back to the material, it was consistently with the same feelings of vileness, repugnance, and self-condemnation. He described it like a festering wound inside him. He agonized bitterly over his realization that he had certain talents and abilities, but he was unable to make any use of them because the horrible stuff that was stored up inside him made it impossible. He wanted desperately to be a leader, to do something meaningful in politics and accomplish important things, but "how could a 'lousy mother-fucker' do anything like that?"

He was constantly preoccupied with fears that people would find out about it. He was afraid that his friends would learn about it somehow, and when he walked down the street he imagined that people could look at him and tell what he had done. He saw himself as filthy, evil, and disgusting—and lived in constant fear that his terrible secret would be found out by others. He bemoaned the fact that such a terrible thing should have to happen to him. His anger and resentment lashed out at the terrible fate that had condemned him to such a crime. He raged against the culture that decreed incest to be such a horrible and degenerate thing. It was the worst crime—the one thing that was despised and condemned by our culture. Why did it have to happen to him? It was the worst possible sin and could not be forgiven.

Fred lived in constant dread that his father might find out about it. Almost every confrontation with his father was overladen with his fears and worry that father had somehow found out about what had happened. He wondered if perhaps his mother hadn't let it slip in one of her drunken stupors. Every restrictive or negative reaction from his father brought on a paroxysm of intensely paranoid fears that father had at last found out. This constant preoccupation served as another determinant of the conflicts that centered around the money issue. His father's accusations about money stirred up Fred's intense guilt feelings, not only about spending any money, but about being a terrible burden to his parents and an evil thing that deserved only punishment and retribution for his heinous crimes.

In this context Fred was gradually able to recognize the extent to which his rage was self-defeating and the extent to which it served his inner need to seek punishment and self-degradation. He also began to see that it was a vehicle for the expression of the tremendous rage that he felt against his parents. His failure was a way of asserting *their* failure: the effect was to punish them and make them feel guilty for all the wrongs they had perpetrated against him. His sickness was in that sense a way of getting back at them and punishing them. The rage stirred his guilt; he felt tremendously guilty and ashamed of his illness. He felt guilt not only for wanting to punish his parents but also for having been a failure. He felt he should never have gotten sick; having reasons for getting sick did not take away the stigma and weakness and crippled emotionality that go with it. He felt enraged at the thought that his resentment against his parents was running and ruining his life. Along with his sense of frustration and bitterness at what he regarded as an inexorable determinism in his life—with a resultant sense of frustrated helplessness and victimization—there was a stubborn clinging to his conviction that fate was against him and that the forces of parental problems, family circumstances, social pressures and demands of the "system," and cultural rigidities, had all conspired to his downfall. Whenever he came close to the incest, this complex of paranoid attitudes would rush to the surface and burst forth with characteristic intensity.

Sexual Relationships

There were other areas of continuing disappointment and frustration for him, in which he saw himself as, and became in fact, the sufferer. One of these important areas was that of his sexual activity. His relationships with girls were troublesome and troubled. He usually had several girls in which he was interested or who were interested in him. These relationships all had a quality of intense clinging dependency and a longing for intimacy. Fred felt almost desperately that he needed a woman for love and approval and warmth and comfort. It was terribly important to him that he be able to satisfy these girls sexually. He worried about his sexual potency and adequacy. He would have intercourse and then ask the girl whether his penis was big enough, whether it was bigger than the penises of other guys she had slept with, whether he had satisfied her as well as other guys, etc.

But these relationships were difficult for him, even when his wishes for closeness and warm responsiveness were being met. The closeness itself was threatening. He feared women, feared their demands on him, feared their manipulating and controlling him, feared his own dependency and his own wishes to be taken care of by them in a regressed and infantile way. He was able from time to time to relate these fears and concerns to his involvement with his mother. He feared and hated her control over his life, and he dreaded the control that any woman might exercise over him if he were to allow himself to become permanently attached to her. His anxieties were more than simple castration fears—although this was certain a detectible issue in his material—but his fear stemmed even more fundamentally from a much deeper and more primitive level of his psychic organization. The issue was one of engulfment, of being swallowed up and devoured by the powerful and all-consuming woman.

Along with this fundamental dread of the woman and her power, there was operative another perception of woman which saw them as defective and needy and damaged. His attitude to women in general was chauvinistic, regarding them as inferior to men in intelligence and general capacity for meaningful work or activity. This was interesting because these feelings were an affront to his liberal and revolutionary convictions, particularly in this era of women's liberation and equal rights. But in part his need to see women as defective was a protective screen against his fear of their hidden power, and a prop for his own inner feelings of weakness and inadequacy. As long as he could see them as weak and defective, he could both tolerate the exposure of his own weakness better and could allow himself to be more dependent with the concomitant threat of engulfment.

Behind this level of his concern was the further and deeper issue of his homosexual concerns. He had never indulged in homosexual practices and did not admit to or recognize any homosexual interests. But it remained a continual concern for him. In part it lay behind his compulsion to have a woman to sleep with, as a means of demonstrating his masculinity which was under continuous question and doubt internally. It determined his view of himself as weak and inadequate and as somehow defective and damaged. His fear of homosexuality was thus responsible to some extent for his rage and recrimination against his parents, against his father for not providing a strong and close alliance which could withstand the powerful subjugating and castrating mother, and against his mother for being so smothering and controlling. The only directly homosexual material that he produced in the course of his treatment was in the form of a dream. He dreamt that he was having intercourse with a beautiful girl and during the intercourse she turned into a boy. The patient was rather disturbed by this dream, wondering whether it meant that he was really homosexual after all. But he was able to laugh at it and then to talk about his attitudes toward homosexuality. He felt sorry for queers and wondered what it must be like to be queer. He admitted to curiosity about them but added that he had never felt any wishes to try it out. He felt that even though it was a deviant position he ought to try to understand their situation and be tolerant of it.

Counterdependency

Perhaps the clearest manifestation of this underlying homosexual concern lay in Fred's intense fears of dependency. He was threatened and terrified by any relationship in which he saw himself as passive and dependent. This obtained in his relationship to me even as it obtained in relation to his parents, the university administrators, professors, the United States government, the United States army—any context in which he was required to accept control and/or the influence of stronger and more powerful figures. He felt himself to be powerless, helpless, and victimized in relation to such figures. The sense of inner vulnerability was intolerable to him, and he strained every fiber of his being in a violent struggle to overcome and reduce it. He was in fact remarkable for the tenacity and intensity with which he carried on this struggle. I often found myself wondering how he managed to generate the seemingly endless reserves of psychic energy which he poured into this effort. It was the central focus and dynamic force in his life and experience.

This process was most apparent in his relationship to me. From the very beginning of our therapeutic experience together there was a subtle—and sometimes not so subtle—resistance. At first there was his anxiety to get out of the hospital, which was clearly related to his concerns over becoming dependent on the protective environment of the hospital, and his consequently becoming unable to cope effectively with the demands and stresses he expected in the outside world. I should point out immediately that his need to resist and counter the pull toward dependency was never unambiguous or without ambivalence. It was always counterbalanced and in conflict with his wish to be dependent and compliant. This struck me as a reflection of his childhood experience in which the gratification of his mother's seductive and loving affection was counterbalanced by the threat of subjugation and control at her hands. The price of loving closeness in that relationship had always been capitulation and subjugation.

Once out of the hospital, the resistance continued in a variety of forms. He would frequently miss appointments, more often than not come late. Exploration of his underlying fears of further involvement in therapy seemed to effect little change. After such discussions, he would seem to reproach himself and make a fresh resolution to the effect that therapy was good for him and he ought to do it right if he wanted to get better. He would come on time for the next hour, and then fall back into the familiar pattern. He also was reluctant to accept medication. In the hospital the nursing staff saw to it that he got and took his medication, but once out of the hospital the decision was in his hands. He did not like medication since it made him feel like a cripple, and he wanted to think that he could get along without it. Having to take medicine was a sign of his defectiveness and incompleteness, as well as a sign of his dependency on me.

Phobic Elements—Nightmares

A consistent feature of his clinical picture was the phobic elements in his pathology. These were frequently a problem for him, breaking out from time to time in a burst of phobic activity. By and large, however, he defended himself against these fears by a vigorously counterphobic attitude. He would complain that he was still haunted by the fears of his childhood, and would angrily deride himself for having these infantile fears. He insisted that he should be able to put them out of his mind and conduct his affairs in a more reasonable and adult manner. These phobic aspects of his personality also played a prominent role in his dream life. He would frequently have frightening and dreadful dreams in which people were beaten, burned, cut, and killed. These dreams would be populated with horrible monsters, and he would often awaken from them in a fit of terror. On occasion he would awaken screaming. These episodes were frightening to him, and he would fret that he was losing his mind and becoming crazy again. Occasionally he would dream of losing his mind and being put back into the hospital, with the fear that he would have to stay there for the rest of his life.

His dreams were sometimes a reflection of his waking concerns. One very striking instance of this was a dream he had in which he was a seal. He was caught on a beach where seal hunters were hitting the helpless seals over the head with heavy clubs, killing them and cutting them up with knives. The beach was covered with blood, and the air was rent with the terrified cries of helpless seals. He wanted to escape. He dove into the water and plunged deep to the bottom of the ocean and had to swim through a long dark tunnel. When he emerged he came upon a beach where there were no hunters. But there was a female seal there, and he began doing a "fire dance" which he described as a sort of mating dance. The dream expresses his usual feelings of helpless victimization, as a helpless seal subject to ruthless murder at the hands of the powerful hunters. He escapes into the protection of the female element—the darkness of the water's depths—and finds safety and consolation in the company of a female seal. The additional point of interest to this dream was the fact that it was dreamed during the period in which the trial of Bobby Seale—the militant Black Panther leader—was being featured in the headlines. This suggests Fred's further identification with the rebellious and disadvantaged groups, and that he saw himself in terms in which he envisioned Bobby Seale, as the helpless victim of the repressive and authoritarian elements of society. Fred felt strongly that Seale's trial was merely a thinly disguised attempt on the part of the authorities to "get" Seale. Seale's subsequent acquittal was a source of great glee for Fred.

Beside the severely disturbing anxiety dreams that Fred described, he also described a recurrent dream experience that was very frightening and distressing for him. He recalled having had severe nightmares for as long as he could remember. But even more disturbing than these dreadful and terrifying nightmares was the recurrent experience he had, an experience that tended to recur at times when he was particularly upset about something or particularly angry. He described a feeling of pressure on his chest that made it difficult for him to breathe. It was as though there were a heavy weight resting on his chest. It was a great weight crushing down on him and pressing the life out of him. He felt helpless and terribly frightened in these dreams. He described feeling totally paralyzed, unable to move or to get out from under the great crushing weight. The affect associated with this material was always one of terror and utter helplessness.

Tragic Course

Fred's depression was a prominent feature of his therapy. After his hospitalization and his relatively rapid emergence from his acute psychosis, he became increasingly depressed. He was apathetic and neurasthenic for a period of several weeks. He then seemed to mobilize himself and made struggling efforts to pull himself out of the doldrums and get himself moving. He could not altogether leave the depression behind. It clung to him and remained a more or less permanent feature of his pathology, interrupted only by angry outbursts of varying duration. In the depths of this depression, his feelings of hopelessness, guilt, shame, and self-devaluation were intense. He managed to relieve these intense feelings only by a manic immersion in external activities, particularly in the political and organizational activity related to student organizations and groups. This activity served to help him escape the depressive affects that tortured him so, and also gave him some basis for sustaining his faltering self-esteem. The paranoid thoughts, however, were never far away. When the sadness became too painful, he would begin to feel that people were looking at him, and that they could see that he was weird or crazy. How, he bemoaned, could he ever have any self-respect or self-esteem with such thoughts in his head? In such contexts—as we have already noted—the concerns about his incest, his associated feelings of worthlessness and guilt, and his paranoid fears that people would know about it would overwhelm him.

What I am describing in these pages is a tragic case. Fred was never able to unravel these tormenting elements. He clung stubbornly to his convictions, his resentments, his bitterness, and his anger. On countless occasions he made it clear that he would not forgive himself for the crimes of the past—particularly the incest with his mother—and moreover that he would not forgive his parents for what they had done to him. No less could he find any room for tempering his anger and resentment against the forces of evil that permeated his view of society and its institutions. He could recognize the elements of displacement from his parents and he could appreciate the intensity and infantility of his rage, but he could not give them up in any manner. He was severely distressed by the fact that these resentments played such a role in his life, but he could not surrender them. To do so in any degree was to him a betrayal of all that he had embraced and committed himself to: it meant to abandon his revolutionary convictions and his intense hatred of all authority in any of its forms. He saw himself as a revolutionary, and his continuing rage was essential to that posture—and, I believe, to the preservation of his own inner sense of identity. The therapeutic process never really had a chance.

The manner in which the treatment process and my association with this young man came to a close augured ominously for his future course. After almost three years of groping, stumbling, on-and-off, ambivalent therapy, Fred went to visit some friends in another part of the country. There he took some mescaline, in the face of the concern and opposition of his friends. He became disorganized and bizarre in his behavior. He was finally picked up again by the police and committed to the state hospital in that locality. He was at that point as agitated, uncontrolled, paranoid and psychotic as he had been as he had been when he had entered our hospital three years before.

DISCUSSION

Fred's case raises a number of interesting and difficult questions which, we will find, enjoy a certain amount of overlap with some of the succeeding cases, and which demand serious consideration in the attempt to understand the structure and functioning of paranoid processes. Among other elements in this case, a particularly important one is the interaction and interplay of individual psychopathological elements and the elements of social disorganization and dysfunction which surrounded the patient and had a profound influence on the shape and course of his illness. This particular issue is writ large in the consideration of paranoid problems and is a major aspect of the therapeutic approach to such patients.

The problems involved in this case were diffuse and touched on a widely separated range of important issues. In order to focus these issues more sharply, I would like to discuss some of the aspects of Fred's pathology which relate directly to the understanding of his own case, and then move to a consideration of some of the problems raised in his case for the disentanglement of the elements of social and individual pathology.

Marital Schism

Fred's family situation and the pattern of his early life experience were atypical—at least in external circumstances—although it may not be that his experience was all that atypical in relation to the experience of other paranoid patients. We can note that the pattern of interaction between his parents was typical of that described by Lidz and his group (1965) in terms of marital schism.

The effect of the continual schismatic undercutting that went on between Fred's parents was to continually widen the split between them. As a result Fred's father became more and more aloof and remote, not only from Fred's mother but from Fred himself. The effect of this aloofness was twofold: it undermined any basis for firm masculine identification with his father, and it left Fred exposed to the intensely ambivalent and destructive involvement with his mother. The deficiencies of Fred's father in supplying the important masculine model for his development arose not merely from his withdrawal and apparent indifference, but were also contributed to mightily by his mother's critical, hostile, and undercutting attitude to the father. Further, as Lidz (1965) has noted, mothers of schizophrenic sons are usually quite insecure in the performance of their marital and maternal roles. Their difficulties lead them to be oversolicitous and overprotective. They seem unable to differentiate their own feelings and anxieties from those of the child. They tend to be engulfing and often intensely seductive.

Pathogenic Interaction

Fred's mother was extremely inconstant and inconsistent in her mothering. She would at one point be overloving and hyperaffectionate—undoubtedly motivated by her own feelings of guilt and inadequacy in fulfilling her mothering role—and at another moment vindictive and highly punitive—this quite probably being related to her own inner narcissistic needs and the correspondingly high demands she placed on her favorite and firstborn son. With considerable intensity, she looked to Fred as a source of fulfillment and gratification that she was not receiving in her relationship with her husband, and at the same time striking out at him in a punitive and destructive fashion because he could not fulfill her expectations and needs. Fred was clearly the victim of her inner conflict and unresolved pathology, as well as of the unresolved tension inherent in the interaction between mother and father.

Fred's relationship to his father was difficult and disappointing, in the face of the father's distance and unavailability. Fred's view of his father was one that was filled with intense yearning and longing that was subject to recurrent frustration and disappointment. The sense of frustrated longing and the wish for closeness and acceptance became mingled with an equally frustrated sense of rage and abandonment. This provided a source of recurrent and cumulative trauma that was rehearsed again and again in Fred's experience. The first episodes were framed in the context of his childish longing for his father—the never available and always retreating object. But later episodes were framed in a larger context of extrusion from the family and exile and abandonment to foreign school-prisons. Each such removal, each such abandonment, each such implied and implicit rejection reopened the old wound and drove it deeper into Fred's scarred and sensitized psyche. Each recurrence of the same theme of abandonment and rejection revivified and reinforced the string of such abandonments that stretched back to the farthest and dimmest reaches of his memory, and beyond. The sense of hurt and disappointment and inner rage could not be unleashed, because it carried with it the threat of even greater rejection. As Fred himself wrote with simple eloquence: "Afraid to a degree that I was responsible for the trouble at home and afraid that I would be sent away again, I convinced myself I had absolutely no ill feelings toward you and mother. This led consequently to a deeper fear that I would lose what little love I was able to feel between us."

The sense of rejection and abandonment had a more or less inevitable consequence for Fred. He began to see himself in terms of his being unworthy of his parents', and particularly his father's love. He grew up under the sting of these cumulative traumata with an inner sense of being unloved and unlovable, of being unvalued and unvaluable. The sense of disappointment and rage could not be directed against his father on this account, and it issued in a pattern of self-devaluation. He was an unworthy object of his father's love and esteem. It is worth noting that this pattern of paternal distancing and lack of rewarding closeness is a recurrent theme in the histories of male paranoids. We have seen it clearly exemplified in the cases of Bob B. and Don D. and we shall have occasion to see it again in discussing the relationship of father and son in the remaining cases. In Fred's case it obtains a particular intensity and poignancy. It has in all these cases a particular impact on the young boy; it undermines his inner sense of self-worth and value, it mobilizes considerable amounts of inner rage and resentment that cannot find adequate discharge or sublimation, and it introduces a distorting factor into the identificatory processes that guide and underlie the course of normal psychic development.

Ambivalent Introjects

The result, of course, is that such identificatory processes are forced to evolve in a context of intense and relatively destructive ambivalence. The intensity of frustrated longing and love drives the internalizing processes in the direction of introjection. Such internalization takes place without the degree of adequate separation and individuation commensurate with healthier and ego-building identifications. The introjection assumes a necessary defensive function in the face of the intensely mobilized aggression and hate. The introjection becomes a wishful and magical clinging to the object to avoid the impact of destructive aggressive impulses toward the object. The introject thus takes in from the object in a relatively less discriminating and undifferentiated manner, so that the boundaries between self and object tend to become somewhat blurred and less solidly established. They are relatively susceptible, therefore, to regressive pulls, particularly under stress, and in Fred's case especially in the face of disappointed longing.

The introjective process has a number of significant consequences for the child's internal psychic development. In terms of the object, the relative distance creates a vacuum which is to a degree filled with the child's projected rage. The image of the parent becomes contaminated with the child's projected rage, and this image is consequently introjected as a much more malignant and potently destructive object than might be verifiable in the real parent. In addition, by that mysterious alchemy which is so incompletely understood, the frustrated and internalized rage is converted to superego aggressiveness, and thus becomes attached to the elements of the parental introjection which come to be involved in superego functions. This is Anna Freud's "identification with the aggressor." But the identification with the aggressor is only part of the picture. Fred's father assiduously portrayed himself as the helpless victim of forces beyond his control. He blamed wherever blame was possible—his wife, his job, economic circumstances, politics, etc. He was a victim, and Fred's identification with the victim became an important part of the introjective process. Fred himself became a victim—helpless, weak, impotent against the forces of power and control aligned against him. This became a central aspect of his paranoid pathology. It is the paranoid paradox—that Fred himself could become both the potentially and powerfully destructive monster, all the while retaining a meaningful view of himself as helpless and impotent victim. This involves a splitting of the introjective elements and their respective availability for reprojection. Fred himself was a victim and he saw others around him with whom he empathized projectively as victims. He was also a destructive and powerful figure and he saw figures to which he stood in some form of authority relation as powerful, controlling, and destructive forces.

Maternal Narcissism

Fred's relationship to his mother was also difficult, and its complex effects contributed significantly to the form of his pathology. As in other cases of mother-son relationship in this series, the ties between Fred and his mother were intense, highly ambivalent, and symbiotic. As the oldest son, Fred became his mother's special and favorite child. Her own highly narcissistic needs for reassurance and gratification in her mothering role led her to impose on Fred severe and demanding standards of performance. This demanding perfectionism extended to all aspects of his behavior. When he failed to meet these rigidly applied demands, he met with her rage and felt the intensity of her destructive wrath. Fred's failure to submit to and fulfill her demands was seen by her as an affront to her own narcissistic ideals, and thereby posed a serious threat to her own inner sense of inadequacy as a loving and capable mother.

In addition, in his position as favorite and first son, Fred became the object of many of his mother's frustrated affectional needs. The emotional divorce between his mother and father and the increasing distance between them left his mother emotionally starved and deprived. The intensity of her emotional involvement with her oldest son was thereby increased. The emotional closeness with Fred be an important source of satisfaction and gratification for her, as though the gratifications of complete mothering were in part substituted for the missing gratifications of womanly fulfillment and marital satisfaction. Thus the symbiotic closeness of mother and son was generated and intensified and the seductive quality of her affectional expression brought to bear in the relationship.

An important dimension of this interaction, however, was the apparent blurring of boundaries between mother and son. This was evident in her inability all through his childhood to respond in any meaningful way to his needs and expectations. She saw him in terms of a highly narcissistic perception as part of her self that demanded perfectibility and could not tolerate imperfection or limitation. There was in their relationship a combination of elements from the mother's side which had severe implications for Fred. There was an intensely and highly sexualized longing for closeness and affection. There was also an intense hatred and destructiveness toward any manifestations of his behavior or responsiveness that reflected his separateness and individuality. Searles (1966-67) has noted the fact that such maternal murderousness and destructiveness is often mobilized in the service of preserving the mother's fragilely precarious identity, an identity that is defensively symbiotic. The child's movements away from symbiotic involvement and dependence are seen by the mother as malicious and malevolent attempts by the child to destroy her omnipotent and pathologically symbiotic identity.

Incestuous Symbiosis

These currents came to a focus in the incest episode. On both sides of the relationship there was a regressive dissolution of ego boundaries and a flooding of instinctual material. The incestuous involvement answered to and derived from intense and highly ambivalent instinctual needs on the part of both mother and son. I would be persuaded that in the present case the incest was a manifestation of psychotic regression on both parts. It was in a sense a genital reaffirmation of the symbiotic union—with all of its intense longings for closeness, dependency, union—as well as with all of its intense murderousness, destructiveness, sadism, and fears of engulfment. From the mother's side it can be seen as motivated in part by intense needs to preserve her faltering sense of inner integrity and wholeness by embracing that part of herself that had become detached in him.

In thinking about the impact of this relationship on Fred, we can be sure that it contributed significantly and deeply to his pathology. The pathological symbiosis made it impossible for him to achieve any meaningful separation from his mother, so that any attempts to move in the direction of greater separateness or autonomy were met by her murderous and sadistic attacks. Built into these attacks was a blaming process that held him to be responsible in some sense for her own sense of inner frustration and emptiness. His sense of separateness and autonomy was jeopardized therefore externally. It was also jeopardized internally. The introjective process which derived from his need to cling to her as the symbiotic object and to preserve the slender and ambivalent ties to her resulted in the internalization of a highly pathogenic and destructive introject. The aggressive components that were derived from his mother's own murderous destructiveness and from his own internal murderous aggressiveness were amalgamated and fused in the inner introjects. These highly destructive elements remained poorly integrated and constituted fragments of his highly sadistic and destructive superego.

Victimization

But mother was also—as was his father—a victim. The introjective process internalized that aspect of her pathology as well, so that Fred became in part a reflection of her own helpless and victimized self. These elements are recognizable in Fred's perceptions of and interactions with women. He saw them in part as powerful, destructive, controlling and castrating agents; to involve oneself with them was to be victimized and controlled, to have to submit to their demands and be ruled by their whims—sexual and otherwise. But at the same time he saw them as defective, damaged, weak, and helplessly victimized creatures. On this side of his projections, he felt himself to be a monster who hurt and damaged the women who became closely involved with him. These elements were readily available for projective elaboration. These severely pathogenic introjects were likewise the basis for his sense of inner evil and worthlessness. Their fragility and fragmented propensity for regression left him with an impaired and fragmented sense of autonomy.

From one point of view, the introjection of these respective parental imagos had its implications for the organization of Fred's perception of himself and for the functioning of his personality. The structure of his rather fragmented self was organized around the respective introjects of both father and mother. We have pointed out the aspect of victimization which derived from both parents. There was also the aspect of destructive omnipotence. Both these elements were combined in Fred's inner psychic economy and structure and provided a focus for his pathology. Equally important, however, was the dimension of blaming and the shifting of responsibility that was evident in both parents. Each parent in subtle and not so subtle ways implicitly blamed Fred for a part of their own unhappiness and frustration. He became the victim, through blaming, of their respective inadequacy and failure. But in addition, the interaction between his father and mother was based on mutual blaming and accusation. Their relationship was mutually undercutting and destructive, and the predominant style of this mutually devastating interaction was one of blame and assignment of responsibility. Besides the dimensions of structural defect involved in the introjections of these pathological elements, there was built into Fred's functioning personality a style of defensiveness, a style which was based in part on the patterns of action and expression derived from these introjects, but also based in part on the assimilation and internalization of the patterns of interaction that constituted the family relationships.

Projective Aspects

The phobic aspects of Fred's personality functioning are also of importance and interest. His early childhood experience—apparently from the earliest strata of his memory—was highly phobic, and the phobic elements of his personality persisted into his pathology in later years. The early animal phobia—his morbid fear and anxiety particularly of rabid foxes—was an exquisite expression of his intense oral aggression and oral sadism. These same elements are reflected in his projective test material from the time of his decompensation. Phobic anxiety likewise remained a significant portion of his clinical picture through most of the time he was under treatment. We can note that phobic elements have been a frequent manifestation in these paranoid and paranoid-disposed patients. This raises the interesting question of the relation between phobic anxiety and the later development of paranoia.

Another important aspect of Fred's pathology was his recurrent nightmares. Recent research on the phenomenon of nightmares has suggested that this form of dream activity takes place in the stage of deep sleep (stage 4). The occurrence in this stage is somewhat paradoxical since dreaming activity has been thought to occur more typically in stages of REM activity (Broughton, R.J., 1968; Fisher et al., 1970). The stage 4 arousal nightmare is the most severe form observed and includes the night terrors of children ("pavor nocturnus") and the nightmares of adults. It also seems to include the nightmares that are associated with traumatic neuroses in adult life. These NREM forms of nightmare are distinguished from relatively severe REM anxiety dreams which are often described by subjects as "nightmares" (Fisher, C., et al., 1970 a,b; Hartman, 1970).

It seems likely that the nightmares that Fred describes as a frequent aspect of his childhood were of the "pavor nocturnus" variety. Moreover, nightmares remained a relatively constant feature of his adult experience. He would have nightmares often even before his decompensation, and they resumed again later in his treatment. The typical attack that he describes is that of the classic "incubus attack." He experienced the intense anxiety, the feeling of respiratory oppression and choking, the sense of paralysis and impending doom, and specifically the feeling of a great weight pressing down on his chest and crushing the life out of him. He would often awaken from these attacks screaming and feeling terrified and panicked. Fisher (1970) and others (Mack, 1969) have observed that in the nightmare the ego capacity for reality testing is lost. The nightmare, in fact, seems to represent a failure of defenses and a breakthrough of the psychosis which overwhelms and terrifies the fragmented ego.

We have discussed the projective aspects of Fred's pathology, but there remain the broader implications and complications of his projective pattern. Fred's view of the world was organized almost universally in terms of dichotomies of the strong vs. the weak, the victimizers vs. the victimized, the dominant vs. the submissive, the exploiters vs. the exploited, the manipulaters vs. the manipulated, the controllers vs. the controlled. He saw these patterns of relationship and interaction in almost every area of his interaction and in every aspect of social life and organization around him. He saw it in the lowest level of human exchange with the same intensity that he found it in the highest levels of social or political structure. In all of these contexts he viewed himself as the helpless victim of malevolent forces which were inhuman and uncaring. These inexorable and uncontrollable forces exercised their remorseless influence on his life, made decisions over which he had no control and nothing to say, exploited him for their selfish interests—all without any concern or interest in his needs and wishes and hopes. He saw himself—along with the countless other victims of society, the poor, the underprivileged, racial minorities, women, and any other underprivileged or deprived groups as the helpless victims of powerful and evil forces. He identified these forces as the government, the military-industrial complex, big corporations, the "system," the "establishment," the armed forces, the university and its administrators—any institution or individual who exercised authority or in any way made decisions that could conceivably affect him.

The projective aspects of this elaborate view of social reality were clear and obvious. It was also clear that he directed the same rage and sense of bitter frustration and disappointment against these agencies that he had felt and continued to feel toward his parents. His response on all these fronts amounted to an extensive projection of elements derived from the parental introjects. Just as he had seen the parents as powerful and unreachable and uninfluenceable figures, he also responded to the social forces and structures around him in the same manner. It was often clear to him and to me that the intensity of his rage was far out of proportion to the external situation that gave rise to it. The rage that was generated in these contemporary contexts of social interaction was a cumulation of the deeper and more intense rage that he had felt so often toward his parents.

These projective elements were elaborated into a paranoid construction that provided a complete context for his interaction with individuals and social groupings and structures that formed the fabric of his life. He saw himself as engaged in mortal struggle with these inexorable forces. He evolved a revolutionary rationale rooted in this overriding paranoid construction which dictated his attitudes and the patterning of his life and activity. There were self-defeating and self-destructive aspects to this attitude. He could not tolerate or adjust to army discipline or training. He had considerable difficulty in his educational endeavors simply because of his intolerance of discipline or requirements. Similarly, he refused to accept certain jobs that were available to him because they were with certain corporations that he hated for their exploitation of the workers or for their involvement in defense production, with the result that he had available to him only the most menial unskilled jobs. He could not therefore make very much money, and he was again bitter about the fact that a college graduate was reduced by society to such a state. He could not accept any responsibility of his own for the situation he found himself in.

The Paranoid Construction

In the course of my work with Fred, the paradoxical nature of his position came to impress me more and more. I struggled to understand why he clung so desperately to his elaborate paranoid construction. Time and again it was clear that he could only see his reality in terms of this construction. Any data that intruded on his perception that could not be integrated or reconciled with this view was ignored, denied, or reinterpreted—often with extreme distortions—so as to preserve the paranoid construction intact. I became increasingly aware of the internal necessity under which Fred's mind worked. The integrity of the paranoid construction was essential for the preservation of his own sense of inner integrity and identity. The paranoid construction was the only way in which Fred could make sense out of the cumulative data of his experience—and preserve some sense of the continuity of meaning in his life. His own inner sense of himself as a distinct and recognizable person was bound up with this construction.

Undoubtedly the construction served other important defensive needs. It provided a channel for his destructive aggressive impulses. It gave him an available and attackable external enemy against which he could direct his wrath without any of the risks that he had felt in his tormented relationship with his parents. It counterbalanced the inner sense of unimportance and worthlessness that determined his extremely low self-esteem and lay behind his complaints that the hated forces around him never responded to or gave any regard to his needs and wishes. It helped to generate a counterdepressive elevation of his self-esteem, in fact, by which he could become the courageous and intrepid hero of the downtrodden and underprivileged victims of the oppressive "system." The revolutionary fervor that he poured into his struggle against the forces of the hated establishment allowed him to legitimize his rage and to turn it into a reinforcing component of a positive ego-ideal, rather than to have it an undermining and self-destructive component of his own inner malignant self-perception (the bad introject).

The paranoid construction, therefore, gave Fred a consistent framework within which he could perceive and make consistent sense out of himself and the world around him. The clearest formulation of this understanding that I have seen is that provided by Searles (1966-67). He has suggested that one function of the sense of identity is to provide a sort of perceptual organ for grasping and integrating the complex aspects of the world around us. For Fred, the paranoid construction that he provided for himself not only made sense out of his bitter and frustrating life experience and provided him with a framework by which he could integrate his experience of the world around him. It provided him with the sensitivities and awarenesses that enabled him to formulate a world view which gave him a sense of purpose and direction and meaningfulness. Fred's commitment to radical politics and to a revolutionary credo was not merely an intellectual answer, but it shaped the pattern and meaning of his existence.

I would like to add a further note to this consideration of Fred's paranoid construction—one that I think has real significance in the consideration of paranoid patients. The paranoid construction was, in addition to the above features, an essential element in the maintenance of Fred's sense of autonomy. Paranoid autonomy is a fragile autonomy at best, really a pseudoautonomy. But the paranoid construction gives it some vitality and support. Autonomy is achieved only in terms of the oppositional defense against external forces. Autonomy is maintained in the struggle against the enemy—in fact maintains itself only in the struggle with the enemy. When the struggle ends autonomy ends. There is, therefore, an inner necessity to have and preserve an enemy against which one can struggle. Not to have an enemy is to lose autonomy (pseudoautonomy)—to lose a sense of oneself as an independent agent, an independent reality. It is to be swallowed up and become as nothing. In this light Fred's intense fear of being "co-opted" or aligned with the establishment enemy, and his intense need to fight against and strike out at every manifestation of the enemy can be seen as more readily understandable.

Belief Systems

It is at this point in our analysis of Fred's pathology that we begin to run into trouble. One important aspect of the paranoid construction is that it derives from and is generated by inner subjective needs. Inner subjective needs are by and large idiosyncratic, and are relatively immune to consensual validation. There is a continuum that stretches from the completely idiosyncratic and subjective, which we feel comfortable in labeling as "crazy," to the completely consensual or objective which we generally regard as "realistic." This gradation can be easily seen in belief systems of various kinds. A completely subjective and idiosyncratic religious belief system will be regarded as delusional, while a highly consensually validated religious belief system such as is found in any organized religion is accepted as normal.

The problem that Fred's paranoid construction raises is twofold: on one hand his construction is shared by large numbers of individuals in our society to varying degrees, and on the other hand there is a considerable amount of verification in reality for elements of the construction. The rhetoric and rationale that form a part of Fred's paranoid construction are standard stuff for large numbers of revolutionary-minded youth in our society—student radicals, SDS, the Weathermen, Negro militants, Black Panthers, etc. Consequently there is a considerable amount of consensual validation for Fred's construction. It forms a sort of paranoid construction of the left, and I do not intend to ignore the equally paranoid construction of the right that also contributes so significantly to current social problems and unrest.

Moreover, Fred's construction was not without verifying elements. Government policies have a tremendous impact on human lives, and they are made in a relative vacuum of influence from private citizens. Moreover, they are made in relation to large social units, never in terms of the subjective needs and hopes and desires of individuals. Young men are drafted against their wishes; they are sent to Vietnam and get killed. Society and its institutions do set rules and regulations that at times violate the individual, and in bureaucratic style fail to make reasonable exceptions to the rule. There was a burst of fire at Kent State and at Jackson State, and people were killed. The police are brutal at times, and they do beat and even sometimes kill individuals. There is racial injustice and prejudice, and underprivileged groups are in fact often caught in the grip of circumstances—economic and social—over which they have little or no control—helpless victims.

All of these aspects of reality were taken by Fred as verifications and justifications of his paranoid view. And the problem, of course, was that he was right! Up to a point. The problem is where to fix that point—and what to do about it—both in understanding what is involved and in attempts at dealing with it therapeutically. This raises a problem that is implicit in the paranoid delusion itself: to what extent and in what way is the paranoid construction a distortion or corruption of reality, and to what extent is it verifiable in reality? Understanding and treating the paranoid process require that these elements be disentangled.

Theoretically this question raises the issue of how intrapsychic, subjectively generated cognitive organizations like the paranoid construction are given a context and a basis for verification in various forms of social pathology. We will have occasion to return to this question in a variety of contexts, but it remains a fundamental one, and one which must be met in dealing with the problem of paranoia. It is also one which has profound implications for the understanding of social processes and social patterns of interaction. In Fred's case, it was necessary to draw a line between what was derived from his own pathology and what was derived from the pathology of the society around him. It was necessary to draw a line between the aspects of his rage which were derived from infantile frustrations and resentments and those which reflected his sincere outrage at the injustice and inhuman callousness he saw around him.

Idealism

Despite Fred's anger and the delusional aspects of his thinking, there remained an idealistic aspect of his outlook that could not be denied. His attitude was highly moralistic and severely condemnatory of the injustice and unfairness he saw. His ideals struck my middle-class mind as utopian and unrealistic. But as abstract notions of human conduct and social standards I found them to be noble and beautiful in large measure. I suspect that this aspect of young radicals and students is often picked up and elaborated by liberal-minded sympathizers of student unrest and radical politics, while other less idealistic aspects are soft-pedaled or ignored. Fred's moralism, however, was combined with a curious moral blindness or moral "double-think" which allowed him to condone and support the most blatant violence and destructiveness, as long as it was in support of his objectives or purposes. This same violence and use of force by the establishment enemy was bitterly denounced and condemned by him. He rationalized riots, destruction of property, looting, "ripping off," personal assault and violence, with an appeal to the perpetration of the same crimes by the establishment. If corporations exploit the masses and steal from them by making unjust profits, stealing from corporations is more than justified to redress the balance. If the government can kill people and destroy property in Vietnam, any destruction or injury perpetrated on the government or those who are in cahoots with it is amply justified. The real crime to him was not to steal and destroy, because in not stealing and destroying one was in fact contributing to the continuation of the crimes of the establishment.

The Revolutionary Dilemma

It seems to me that these are tricky issues. I am not sure how to resolve them. The revolutionary mentality in general is legitimated by real injustice and real oppression. It was clear to me that much of what Fred saw as injustice and oppression did not seem that way to me. There was much of what he complained about that I was able to accept as part of a viable, if imperfect, social structure, or as a necessary inconvenience or inefficiency of large and cumbersome social organizations. Even something as distasteful as the draft, for example, did not seem like a heinous plot on the part of cruel government machinators to enslave and kill the youth of the country. Given the complexities of contemporary international politics and the need for national defense, I could accept it as a relatively necessary evil. Fred could not. But even so, there was a great deal of what he complained about that I felt in partial or complete sympathy with. The real injustices should be eliminated.

But how? Fred's insistence was that violent overthrow and destruction was the only realizable way. The hated enemy—the authority figures and their institutions—must be destroyed. He found it very difficult to conceive of or accept any idea of working within the system to reform the system, of using the resources of the system to bring about the desired changes. He demanded instant and uncompromising change, a peremptory demand that would brook no opposition and no delay. This served as an excellent index of the extent to which his demand reflected more infantile and primary-process-dominated aspects of his position. The image of his wish to batter down the wall with his hand drew this aspect of the problem into clearer focus for him. He could see little by little that his more radical and revolutionary approach in fact did not succeed in knocking down the establishment wall—it only gave him a broken hand. He increasingly saw the degree and manner in which infantile residues contaminated and distorted his political radicalism, and this perception distressed him, because he realized its ineffectual and self-defeating parameters. He began to pose the question for himself as to what more realistic and effective means he might find to gain his cherished objectives.

As time went on and the material piled up, Fred became more and more aware of what was entailed in his reactions to things. His more infantile rage became more and more dystonic and distressing to him. As this aspect emerged, his political activity came to be more constructively channeled and less extreme. This, however, raised a problem for him, and he found himself in a difficult bind. Could he give up his infantile resentment and still remain a revolutionary, still committed to the ideals and values that he held so dear? In brief terms, he could not disentangle his underlying resentment from his radical and revolutionary perspective. To surrender the one meant to surrender the other. On this reef, I think, the therapy foundered. He could not maintain his revolutionary fervor and fanaticism without the infantile rage to drive it. In retrospect I feel that his ingestion of mescaline leading to rehospitalization and the disruption of his treatment with me reflects his recommitment to the basic rage.

Narcissism

The underlying issue in all this, and the one that emerged more and more clearly as therapy progressed, was his intense narcissism. He needed desperately to maintain an image of himself as a leader, as having a significant influence on the lives and thoughts of others, as becoming in some sense a special and important person. There was an omnipotent quality to these ideas; he worked to preserve a sense of his special capacities to produce dramatic and striking effects. He seemed to cling to a naive and almost simplisitic belief that his efforts would produce powerful effects and important changes in the social context around him. He cherished an inner belief that in some way he was gifted with special powers of persuasion that allowed him to influence the thoughts and feelings of people around him so that they would change their attitudes and political convictions. His repeated and constant failure to achieve his ambitious goals provided him with a constant source of bitter disappointment and resentment. His intense narcissistic investment in these ideals and ambitions was another facet of his need to preserve a sense of identity in the face of his inner fragility and fragmentation.

In this light Fred's utopian and revolutionary idealism emerged as an integral part of the syndrome. There is something tragic in this. The values and ideals to which Fred dedicates himself so intensely are unfortunately embedded in a narcissistic matrix. Fred's embrace is therefore driven by intense narcissistic needs. He clings to them and promotes them in a highly narcissistic manner. When these values and ideals are in question, they are overladen with high expectations, with a peremptoriness that cannot tolerate delay or opposition without intense disappointment and rage. The pressure of narcissistic needs drives him to a reliance on violent and destructive means of finding the satisfaction and fulfillment of his wishes. The tragedy is that these means are as destructive of his own wishes and objectives as they are of the forces he sees aligned against him—and perhaps even more so.

Paranoid Process and Values

An important point that emerges with particular poignancy in the present case is that the paranoid system has a unique relation to the formation and maintenance of value systems. In many cases this aspect of the paranoid problem remains muted, but in Fred's case the issue of values rises to the surface and presents itself with special intensity. Fred conceptualized and presented his divergence from society in terms of his rejection of the values and ideals of that society. From one point of view this became a relatively effective rationalization for his paranoid construction and the paranoid system. But from another point of view, the values that he adhered to so intently were an integral part of the identity that he had fashioned and which the paranoid construction was calculated to preserve. The problem that his case focuses is that these values are not totally idiosyncratic—as they might be in the case of a withdrawn and acutely psychotic paranoid—but they are shared at large by a significant proportion of the population, and they are relatively acceptable to reasonable men on realistic grounds. The value system allows him to mesh his deviant views with other like-minded individuals to achieve some sense of group solidarity, and to gain support and reinforcement for his own paranoid construction.

As our understanding of the structure of paranoid thought processes grows, it seems increasingly likely that the problem of value formation and value functioning must be considered as more central to the understanding of paranoia rather than peripheral. In Fred's case they played a complex role, both as a medium of expression of his paranoid construction, but also as a central dimension of that construction and as a motivating and integrating force in the corresponding preservation of Fred's fragile and faltering identity. Fred was able to define his identity around the central core of these values, a central core that he could defensively sustain and foster through the paranoid construction. It is this aspect of value formation and value functioning that directly and immediately focuses the socially disruptive and damaging aspects of this kind of paranoia. For there is no place in the economy of social growth and creativity that the integration of youthful energies with the traditions and institutions of society is more central than in the development, creation, progression, and integration of human values.

CHAPTER 12

Miss Gloria G.

The present case is in a variety of ways the most difficult and most chronic of the cases we have selected for this study. It is also one of the most studied cases in the series. We have a fair amount of data that deal directly with Gloria herself, and a considerable amount of data dealing with her family.

THE PATIENT'S PROFILE

Hospitalization

Our first contact with Gloria came on the day that she was brought by her parents for admission to the hospital. The situation at home had been deteriorating badly, to the point that the parents felt they could no longer tolerate the situation. Because of the deterioration in relationships at home, Gloria and her parents had begun seeing a private therapist about six months before. The doctor had been seeing Gloria once a week alone, and then seeing the parents in separate sessions. The therapy did not seem to improve matters much, and things became progressively worse. It had been Gloria's conviction—with some justification—that the basic problem was with her parents and that it was particularly her mother who needed psychiatric help. It turned out that her mother was the one who was pushing for hospitalization, but that her father had been resisting such a move for some time. The decision was precipitated by Gloria's demanding that the therapist do something about the situation—namely, that he have her mother committed to a mental hospital. The therapist recognized the deteriorating nature of the situation and the psychotic quality of Gloria's accusations. He persuaded the parents to allow Gloria to be hospitalized and made the arrangements.

The following day Gloria came to the hospital with her parents. It was her impression that they were coming to the hospital with the intention of committing her mother. In their anxiety over the situation and their ambivalence and guilt about it, the parents had left Gloria with this impression. When Gloria discovered that the doctors were going about admitting her, she became terrified, acutely paranoid, and began fighting desperately. She was frightened, angry, and confused. She could not understand why she was being railroaded into the hospital. She accused her parents of trying to solve their problems by putting her away. She finally capitulated and went to the ward to be admitted. But her attitude of resentful resistance was to become a marked aspect of her hospital experience, and was to continue to present a therapeutic problem through the rest of her treatment.

At the time of her admission she was a slender and rather plain young woman of twenty-one. She was neatly dressed, and wore her hair in plain long tresses hanging over her shoulders: she wore no makeup but gave a rather attractive appearance. She was obviously tense and anxious, intermittently tearful, but seemingly struggling to maintain some self-control. As she became more comfortable she would break out into angry tirades against her parents, expressing a good deal of anger and resentment at the parents' deceit in putting her into a mental hospital. Whenever we touched on something that related to her anger, she would become more confused and vague and would show considerable tendency to block. In talking about herself, she would make vague references to "problems," but was quite unable to specify what they were or what she felt about them. As we shall see later, this represented a defensive style that remained a feature of her therapy for several years.

Recent History

In the several months prior to these events, Gloria had run an increasingly deteriorating course, but the deterioration really extended over a period of at least two years. If we go back in her story to her senior year in high school we can trace some of the events involved in this pattern of deterioration. It was at that time that Gloria first met Peter. This was the first and only serious involvement with a boy that Gloria had experienced. He was somewhat older than she and was quite conflicted and troubled in his own right. Gloria met him through her younger sister, Gladys. Gladys thought he was somebody special and exciting, and Gloria seems to have followed along in her sister's perception of him. Gloria became quite attached to him. She went out with him frequently and they apparently spent a considerable amount of time together. She referred to this as "going steady," but it was not clear that Peter was not also seeing other girls—although Gloria only suspected this. It appears that the strongest tie in the relationship, in fact, was their talking about Peter's problems and conflicts. There was some necking and kissing, and toward the end of the relationship some pressure from Peter for intercourse.

The relationship was a difficult one for Gloria to handle. She had always been extremely shy and had a great deal of difficulty in relating to boys. The relationship with Peter was a different experience for her. It lasted until the end of her freshman year at college. At that point Peter went off on a summer vacation. After several weeks he called Gloria to tell her that he had married an older woman, a divorcee he had met on his vacation. The shock of this revelation was severe for Gloria. The relationship had become a serious one for her. She had been thinking of marriage, and trying to decide whether, when Peter returned, she would allow herself to have intercourse with him. All of these were trying decisions for her—but her hopes were dashed.

While this relationship was developing, Gloria was having considerable difficulty in other areas of her life. She had graduated from high school and enrolled at a large sidewalk university near her home. Her experience there was an extremely unhappy one. She became increasingly afraid to travel on the bus to school, afraid of being injured on the street, afraid that people were laughing at her, talking about her, thinking terrible things about her. She was totally unable to make any new friends at the university or to get to know her classmates. She avoided people, kept away from them, avoided talking to them. Her ideas of reference became more and more a disturbing part of her experience. She developed delusional ideas that people wanted to kill her or rape her. From time to time she had suicidal ideas and wanted to kill herself.

In the face of this decompensation and its isolating effects, she clung all the more desperately to Peter. When the news of his betrayal came, she was crushed. She became severely depressed and withdrawn. It became impossible for her to return to school, so she dropped out. It was amazing in the face of the accumulating difficulties that she was able to maintain a solid average grade standing, even though her ability to study was severely compromised. At this point she did nothing but sit around the house, staying in her room much of the time, sleeping long hours, and in general keeping herself quite withdrawn and isolated. It seems quite clear in retrospect that she was struggling with a paranoid psychosis at this point.

Finally at her parents' urging she got a job as a secretary. Her ability to work was apparently quite adequate and for a time she seemed to be doing well at her job. But she felt increasingly pressured, felt that the boss was making too many demands on her, and felt increasingly that she would not keep up the pace. Her relationships with her employer and fellow employees also gradually deteriorated. Finally she began to feel increasingly paranoid about the job, had a fight with the boss and quit. After a short interval she tried another job, which was less demanding. Again she did well for a short while, and then the difficulties developed. Finally, she quit her job and became severely withdrawn, staying in the house by herself, sleeping and staying in bed for days at a time.

Acute Decompensation

Concurrently with these events, the situation within the home became increasingly strained and difficult. The fights and arguments were frequent and increasingly intense. Gloria would engage in long and drawn-out discussions with her father. In these discussions she seemed unable to accept her father's point of view, but at the same time was unwilling to settle for anything else. She would keep the argument going by continuing to ply him with questions and by offering objections and counterarguments. The father—on his side—could not back away from the argument until he felt that Gloria had in fact accepted his point of view. The overall effect was to prolong the arguments almost interminably.

The most difficult relationship, however, was with her mother. Mrs. G.—as we shall see more in detail when we turn to the consideration of the family dynamics—was a rather depressed woman who felt very resentful when things did not go her way. This was particularly true when it came to the management of the household. She tended to be a somewhat sloppy housekeeper. Gloria would come out of her room from time to time and would do some bit of cleaning or other housework. Inevitably it was done in a manner that her mother did not approve of. Usually an argument would develop in which the mother would insist on Gloria's doing things her way or else minding her own business. Gloria in her turn would criticize her mother and constantly badger her about being lazy and not keeping the house as she should. It was clear that Gloria knew this to be a sensitive area for her mother and that her criticism and badgering had a provocative quality. Mrs. G. became increasingly exasperated with Gloria's behavior. She began pushing for Gloria to be hospitalized, but Mr. G. resisted this move. He could not bring himself to put his daughter in a hospital. The parents argued a fair amount over this issue.

The tension and level of conflict continued to rise. Finally, about a month before Gloria was to be admitted to the hospital, a rather critical episode occurred. I have found such episodes to play a significant part in the precipitation of the more acute phase of a paranoid process. It seems to represent an event that crystallizes the developing paranoid delusion and provides a sort of irrefutable proof to the validity of the paranoid claim. Patients will continually refer back to such an event in the course of subsequent therapy, as if making an appeal to a convincing *experimentum crucis* that verifies the paranoid delusion. Such indeed was the case with Gloria and this event. The details were a long time in emerging, but the events went something like this. Gloria was in her room cleaning around dinner time. Her mother had served the dinner and called Gloria to come to the table. Gloria did not come until several minutes later when the family was already seated at the table eating. When she walked into the dining room, her mother made a sarcastic remark about her coming to the table when she pleased rather than when the dinner was ready. Gloria became very angry at that point and launched into a verbal attack on her mother. The youngest sister, Glenda, who was just fourteen years old and who turned out to be a paranoid schizophrenic in her own right, became extremely upset at Gloria's attack on her mother. She leaped up and began to strike Gloria. Gloria fought back. The father and mother jumped up and tried to separate the struggling sisters. The father restrained Glenda while the mother tried to restrain Gloria. In the course of the struggle the mother slapped Gloria, apparently in an attempt to stop her hysterical screaming. The whole scene was an outbreak of violent and angry feelings, particularly on the part of the two sick daughters. The third daughter, Gladys, kept out of the fight.

Gloria was convinced from that moment on that her family was trying to kill her. She attributed this intention particularly to her mother. She would come back again and again to this episode and assert that the family had tried to kill her then. On each occasion that she would return to it, she would refer to it with obvious and intense anger. The episode was severely upsetting to the rest of the family as well. After it the second daughter, the twenty-year-old Gladys, decided to move out of the house. She gave as her reason that she could no longer tolerate the tension and conflict that Gloria was creating at home. The parents had the same feelings of growing intolerance of Gloria's more or less provocative and paranoid behavior. The deteriorating situation at home and finally the urging of the therapist made them determine to do something about the problem.

Gloria's complaint at the time of her hospitalization was that she was a being made the victim of her family's problems. Conversely, the family's complaint was that they were being made the victim of Gloria's problem. This pattern of dealing with problems by blaming was to prove significant in the understanding of Gloria's illness. But there was in fact an element of truth in both claims. Gloria was indeed victimized by her parents' problems to a significant degree, and it was also demonstrable that her illness had the effect of making them victims. It was an interlocking process of victimizing and being victimized.

Early Experience

It seems that Gloria started being a victim rather early in her career. Her pregnancy and delivery were uneventful, but problems were not long in coming. Early feeding was reported as difficult and full of tension for her mother. Gloria was breast-fed for about eight months, but apparently it was a difficult time for both mother and child. There is some question about the seriousness of the mother's impairment. There is one report to the effect that she suffered a postpartum depression. It is not clear how severe this may have been. She was not hospitalized, although she received some psychiatric treatment. There is little question, however, that she was markedly depressed during this period and that the demands of caring for her infant aroused considerable feelings of anxiety and inadequacy. She felt quite insecure of herself as a woman and as a mother, and her ministrations to little Gloria were laden with considerable anxiety and self-doubt.

Gloria's relationship with her mother was never very good. From a relatively bad start it pursued an uncertain course. From the reports that we can gather, Gloria seemed to have been an active child, and rather bright. She was continually getting into mischief. Mother was unable to cope effectively with this activity. She would respond with impatience and irritability. Her usual tactic was to threaten Gloria with some kind of abandonment. When Gloria would do something that her mother found herself unable to tolerate or cope with, mother would threaten to send Gloria away, even going so far as to pick up the telephone and place a simulated call to the orphanage. The threat of abandonment is perhaps the most terrifying to a young child, and Gloria's mother exploited it to the utmost. The experience made a deep impression on the child and carried the conviction that her mother did not really want her, and that if she had the chance she would get rid of her.

Sibling Rivalry

Things were made more difficult along the way by the birth of a second daughter when Gloria was about two years of age. Gladys' coming was inauspicious for several reasons. First of all, as we might anticipate, caring for the new infant was a difficult and anxiety-laden experience for Mrs. G. She was again quite depressed, although apparently less so than after Gloria's birth. The effect on Gloria was to deprive her of what little attention and affection she was able to attain from her mother. Moreover, the advent of little Gladys introduced a rival for the affection of her parents into Gloria's life.

It was a rivalry in which she always came off second best, or always felt that she came off second best. Gladys developed into a bright, active, and attractive child. She became outgoing, friendly, well-liked, had many friends all through her school years, was popular, was elected to a variety of school offices, had many dates—an apparently normal, healthy, involved, and active young girl and finally woman. Gloria, on the other hand, was reserved, shy, had few friends, involved herself in few activities, and was generally socially awkward and distanced. The prizes in the sibling rivalry clearly went to the younger sister, Gladys.

This was also clear in their respective relationships with the parents. Gladys—as time went by—got along better with her mother, was less of a problem for the parents to deal with, and was treated in more favorable ways by the father, or at least the relationship between the father and Gladys was seen in this light by Gloria. Father tended to bear out this perception by his feeling that Gladys was more mature and that he could talk to Gladys in ways that he could not to Gloria. Moreover, the two older girls were treated as though they were the same age—had the same privileges, the same responsibilities, the same bedtime, the same allowance, etc. Since Gloria was two years older she felt that she should have had some advantage over her younger sister, but they were treated exactly the same.

Gloria saw this as equivalently favoring the younger sister and resented it bitterly. As she put it, "I had all the responsibilities of being older, but none of the privileges!" This rigid equivalence between the two older sisters was maintained through their growing-up period. In high school they were allowed to date at the same time, had the same curfew, wore the same clothes, could use makeup at the same time, etc. All of this even though one sister was older by two years.

Growing Up Scared

In this general situation in which the stability and psychic health of Mrs. G. was so questionable and in which she was constantly and chronically depressed and irritable, Mr. G. exercised himself to support her and protect her and to fill in for her inadequacies. In the face of his wife's inability to cook, he did the cooking. In the face of her inept housekeeping, he did the cleaning and washing. In the face of her irritation and depression, he was constantly warning the children not to upset her, not to cause any trouble. His often repeated warning was that if the girls were not obedient and good, their mother might get sick. It seemed that Gloria took this warning to heart, and that Gladys did not take it very seriously at all. Gladys sought relief from the tension and difficulties at home by immersing herself in friendships and activities in school and elsewhere. Gloria, however, became more and more tied into the relationship with her parents. She tried desperately and seriously to be good and to please her mother, constantly hoping to gain her mother's appreciation and affection, but her attempts were never successful. She never felt that her mother approved of her or loved her. When her attempts were met with mother's irritation and scolding or with mother's depressive withdrawal, she felt confused and helpless. She began to feel somehow that she was responsible for her mother's poor moods and anger and that the reason that things were so bad at home was somehow due to her. She began to think of herself as evil and undesirable and hateful. These feelings were reinforced by her father's constant warnings and scoldings to the effect that she was hurting her mother by being naughty or uncooperative. These influences provided a continuing menace to Gloria's well-being and sense of self.

During these early Oedipal and latency years, Gloria developed a significant number of symptoms. Nightmares became a problem. She would frequently have terrifying dreams and would awaken from them feeling terribly frightened and helpless. She felt that there was no one to whom she could turn and nowhere she could get any help. She was frequently terribly frightened of going to bed because of the nightmares—but couldn't tell her mother or father. Another prominent symptom was phobic anxiety. This remained a more or less constant feature of her pathology from very early years. Phobic concerns were a significant part of her experience for as long as she could remember. Gloria was able to recall fears as a very young child that her father was going to die. She also remembered her fear that the family house was going to burn down. This was a continual preoccupation for her for a long period of time, and she was particularly concerned that the house would burn while she was asleep. In one of the early school grades she recalled hearing someone—probably her parents—talking about spinal meningitis. At the time one of her classmates was thought to have polio. This was still in the period before the polio vaccines had received wide acceptance and distribution. Gloria was terrified of getting spinal meningitis, and for a time refused to go to school.

Mother's Depression

When Gloria was seven years old, one of the critical events occurred that was significantly related to her illness. Her mother became pregnant with her youngest sister Glenda. As the pregnancy progressed, Mrs. G. became increasingly depressed. After the delivery she suffered a severe postpartum depression. The family was devastated. Mrs. G. had to be hospitalized, received shock treatments, and remained in the hospital for several months. The new baby had to be put out in a foster home for about a fourteen-month period. After her return home, Mrs. G. remained severely depressed and lethargic. She was unable to do anything, unable to care for the children, was extremely irritable and short-tempered.

The effect on Gloria was devastating. She could not understand her mother's illness. Her basic feeling was that her mother didn't love her. Her resentment and rage in response to that basic feeling brought with it intense feelings of guilt and worthlessness. When her mother became ill and went away to the hospital, Gloria felt terribly guilty and somehow responsible for the trouble. She recalled how desperately lonely and abandoned she felt at that time. She did not know what her mother's illness and absence meant. She was terrified that her mother might die.

When her mother finally returned, things were worse for Gloria than ever. Her mother spent most of her time moaning and crying and saying that she wished she were dead. She was quite irritable and impatient. Gloria seemed unable to do anything right. Even the slightest noise or disturbance or disobedience would set her mother off. Her father did not help matters for her very much. His anxiety and distress over his wife's illness were difficult for him to handle as well.

The picture that emerged from these early years was that of a sensitive, easily affected, delicate, shy, timorous, withdrawn, and terribly phobic and insecure little girl. Her experience was overburdened with feelings of shame and guilt. She burdened herself with feelings of evilness and felt herself to be the cause of the evil to those around her. She was caught up in extremely ambivalent relationships with the important figures in her life. It is difficult to find any figure with whom she was able to establish any sort of positive and rewarding and meaningful relationship. As she advanced into adolescence, her sexual conflicts became more intense. Her relationship to Peter was unstable and immature, based more on mutual weaknesses and immmaturities than on any strengths. By the time she got to college she was suffering from a full-blown paranoid psychosis, marked by ideas of reference, persecutory anxieties, suspiciousness, multiple projections, severe phobias, and hypochondriacal concerns, and from time to time with suicidal ideas. These symptoms and the severe dysphoric affects that accompanied them grew worse as time went on. The break with Peter turned the process from a progressively chronic one to a more acute process of decompensation. Gradually the paranoid process came to include the members of her family, to the accompaniment of increasing tension and conflict at home. Thus she found her way to our hospital.

In the Hospital

I would like to turn now to my own experience with Gloria, an experience which has stretched itself out over several years. It has been a varied experience, including the period of her hospitalization, which lasted over sixteen months, several more years of weekly psychotherapy, and a total of three years of weekly meetings with Gloria and her family. When I first met Gloria she was in a state of utter panic and terror. She had just learned that she was to be admitted to the hospital, and the prospect terrified her. It was my responsibility to see her through the admitting procedures and get her settled on the ward. In the face of her panic, I tried to be calm, patient, and firm. As soon as her parents had left, she seemed to respond to this approach and became more compliant and cooperative with the admission procedures. She balked at only one point in all the questioning and examining that was required, when I tried to examine her breasts as part of the physical examination. She refused to allow this part of the examination. She also refused a pelvic examination. I respected her wish and her fear.

On the ward she remained quiet and made little effort to communicate with other patients. Little by little, however, the picture began to change. Over the course of several weeks she became more and more uncooperative. My original hope was that a brief hospitalization would take enough pressure off Gloria and the family to allow a more effective treatment regimen to be set up, so that treatment could continue on an outpatient basis. The hope proved futile. Gloria increasingly engaged herself in struggles with the staff. She became increasingly uncooperative. She would not do anything that was requested of her, she would not do any of the ward jobs that were assigned to her, and she began to stay in bed in the mornings and sleep until almost noontime. She would not engage herself in any of the therapeutic activities offered by the staff. As this pattern of behavior developed, Gloria and I would discuss it in her therapy sessions. Her attitude was that she had been railroaded into the hospital and she would not cooperate in anything that went on. She expressed a great deal of anger at her parents for putting her in the hospital and a great deal of anger toward me for keeping her there. She also ventilated a considerable amount of ire at the staff for trying to make her do things that she didn't want to do.

Her behavior became increasingly provocative. She would deliberately flaunt ward regulations. The staff responded by imposing certain restrictive and punitive measures. It became clear that she was provoking these responses from the staff and that the whole process had an increasingly paranoid flavor to it. The inevitable escalation took place. She became disruptive and physically assaultive. The staff was forced to physically restrain her at times. Gloria saw this as an unprovoked assault on their part, and was unable to see her own role in provoking this sort of response.

An important area in which this sort of struggle took place was over her staying in bed long hours in the morning. One of the ward regulations was that patients were to rise by a certain hour in the morning. Gloria ignored this regulation. The staff tried urging, coaxing, persuasion, and a variety of other approaches. Other patients in the ward began to feel resentful and angry about Gloria's behavior. It was clear to the staff that Gloria was trying to re-create on the ward the kind of conflict and struggle that she had left behind her at home. Finally, in desperation one morning, the staff decided to roll her out of bed. The effect of this was to precipitate Gloria's rage and she became severely paranoid. She saw this action of the staff as a deliberate and malicious attack. She was minding her own business and not hurting anyone, and they came along and for no reason threw her out of bed. The whole episode was a rehearsal of the episode at the family dinner table in which she became convinced that the family was out to kill her. Gloria similarly became convinced that the ward staff was out to kill her.

I also decided that in view of her continuing and intensified paranoid symptoms medications were indicated. At first Gloria refused to take any medicines. I decided that any attempt to force the medication on her would only be playing into the same sort of game that we were anxious to avoid if possible. The nurses continued to offer her the medication on schedule, and Gloria continued to refuse it. Her reasons for doing so became a focus in therapy. She basically distrusted my medicine. She blamed me for the way she had been treated by the staff, and had to struggle with her paranoid concerns about me. She found it difficult to reconcile these with her more positive feeling toward me and with the fact that I treated her so kindly and patiently. She could not decide whether I was her benefactor or her enemy. Besides—and this played perhaps the dominant role in her thinking—if she took the medicine that would be to admit that she needed help, that she was indeed a patient, and that perhaps her parents had been right when they put her in the hospital. It took several months for these issues to be explored. From time to time Gloria would accept the medication from the nurses, but often when her ambivalence was high and her paranoid doubts activated she would refuse it. After several months she became more comfortable with the idea and began taking the medications regularly.

Depression

As these resistances were gradually worked through, Gloria's provocative struggles with the staff diminished. She became more cooperative and was able to settle into the ward routine in a relatively comfortable manner. As she relinquished her paranoid struggles, however, she entered into a deeper and deeper depression. Over the course of several months she became increasingly depressed. Whole therapy hours would be spent in anguished and tearful silence. She felt herself to be evil, degraded, worthless, and totally useless. She felt that she was completely unworthy of any love, that she was without value or any redeeming quality. She felt sad and quite anxious. She spoke repeatedly during this period of her sense of inner hopelessness and despair. She felt as though she were in a dark pit and that there was no way out of it. She was doomed to spend the whole of her life in it. There was no glimmer of hope. She began to have thoughts that her father and mother and sisters were going to die. She developed a delusional conviction that her father would have to die because—as she said—he was the only one in the family who had not suffered. After his death, she was convinced that the anguish that enveloped her and the torments that had plagued her family would come to an end. She saw it almost as an expiatory sacrifice to the gods.

As her depression deepened she became increasingly suicidal. She thought about it, talked about it increasingly in her therapy hours, and even dreamed about it. Her dreams—infrequently reported—were overloaded with themes of death, murderous attacks, violent accidents, and suicide. She seemed to walk in a world in which she was wrapped in a shroud of death. In the previous phase of her treatment, her provocative rage had challenged and confronted the staff and me. So too, her intense depression and despair challenged us once again, but in a more profound and difficult way. The staff made heroic efforts to maintain contact with her and to engage her in a variety of ways. This was extremely difficult since Gloria tended to isolate herself and withdraw from any contacts. It was difficult to talk with her since she was almost always tearful and morose. She was a painful person to be with, but the continuing effort to reach her and sustain communication was essential. Her suicidal preoccupations made it necessary also to keep ourselves as informed as possible of her state of mind. At several points the risk of suicide was felt to be very great and she had to be watched closely.

She came close to a suicidal attempt on several occasions—saving pills, hiding razor blades, etc.—but on none of these occasions did she actually come to the point of making the intended attempt.

Therapy with Gloria during this phase was difficult. She would come into my office, sit down, and start crying, sometimes for a whole hour. Sometimes she would seem lost in thought for long periods of time; she would sit with her head down or staring out the window, apparently oblivious to me and the world around her. My strategy was to allow her to bear the pain and the anguish—and to be simply there with her during the bearing of it. When she expressed her feelings of pain and anguish, I attempted nothing more than acknowledging her feelings, emphasizing only that they were feelings and that they must be very hard for her to bear. Actually her intense depression made the treatment difficult for me as well. The long silences, Gloria's lack of responsiveness, the marked blocking and retardation of her thought processes, and her own painful feelings made her therapy hours almost intolerable. During the long silences, I would occasionally offer her comments or leading questions or gentle attempts of many sorts to get the ball rolling a little bit. Sometimes she would respond to these initiatives, but often she would not. I found myself working very hard in the therapy to keep anything going. I also found myself resenting the fact that she made me work so hard.

I shared this feeling with her, and it came as a revelation to her that she could have that effect on me. The discussion of her own role in psychotherapy seemed helpful in that it became clearer to her that what was in question was not unquestioning submission to therapy, but that she was indeed an active participant and that if we were to get anywhere in her treatment it would require her working at it too. Somehow we passed through the deepest trough in her depression—or so it seemed—and little by little the intense depressive affect seemed to wane and recede. She seemed to gain slowly in energy and responsiveness. I was wary at this juncture and felt the need to be cautious about any suicidal intent. The frequency with which depressed patients commit suicide while apparently emerging from the deepest part of a depression is well known. But there were no mishaps; Gloria seemed to make steady progress in inching her way out of the pit of her depression.

As the depression faded, Gloria was increasingly able to spend more and more time outside the hospital. She began spending nights and then weekends at home. As her capacity to function progressed, it became apparent that she was less in need of the hospital. The question then arose as to where she would go when she left. This remained a focus of argument and conflict in the family for months; it was a question around which a number of significant family issues were activated (but the discussion of these issues is better left for our consideration of family dynamics).

Gloria finally resolved many of the questions by getting a job on her own initiative. She decided that she would live at home with her parents. The pros and cons and alternatives were discussed in a seemingly endless and repetitious fashion. The basic issue was one of dependency. For Gloria to go back home was equivalent to reestablishing and reasserting her dependence on her parents and her reluctance to stand on her own feet and face the world. Further, to be dependent on her parents meant to submit to them, to accept their standards and opinions, to live according to their desires and wishes, and more importantly to deny and stifle any wishes, desires, or inclinations of her own. It seemed in many respects a move toward greater infantilization, but it was not simply that, and there were compensating factors in other directions. Gloria was able to obtain a rather responsible job at a good salary. Under these terms she left the hospital and continued her therapy as an out-patient.

Therapy

Gloria's therapy dealt with a number of significant themes which repeated themselves again and again in seemingly endless variety. The basic issues were repeated and rehearsed countless times over the course of several years—to the extent that I often felt a sense of exasperation and frustration. When these issues were raised and discussed, it so often seemed that the previous discussions of the same matters had left no impression on Gloria whatsoever—the insights apparently gained seemed lost and obliterated. Yet I resolved early in her treatment that there was no recourse but to deal with each re-presentation of a given aspect of her experience as if it had arisen this time for the first time, as though she and I had never heard it before. Only after the matter had been explored again would I relate it to previous discussions, and then only to bring in material from previous discussions and relate it to the present focus rather than reminding Gloria that we had been over the same ground several times before. There was a strong need in her to deny the work of therapy and preserve the fragile status quo.

One of the primary issues that recurred in this fashion was Gloria's highly ambivalent relationships with her parents. Her ability to resolve the conflicting sides of this intense ambivalence was minimal. From session to session she would shift from one side of the ambivalence to the other, sometimes within a single session. At one point she would be enraged at and hate her mother and feel that her father was her only salvation, wishing to cling to him and totally reject her mother. At another time she would feel nothing but revulsion and hatred for her father and express her strong yearning for closeness and acceptance from her mother. She would vacillate between these extremes of love and hate for both parents.

Relation to Mother

There was a special quality about Gloria's relation with her mother. There was a strong and quite infantile yearning for a loving acceptance with her mother. This yearning was extremely primitive: I had the impression time and again while Gloria was talking about her mother that I was sitting with an infant who was crying for the warmth and protection of her mother's body and reaching desperately for for her mother's breast. Gloria expressed her wish for closeness with her mother in a manner that seemed to me highly regressive and primitive—the yearning of a helpless infant for the warmth and protection of the mother's arms. Along with this desperate and infantile longing, there was a sense of continual frustration and disappointment, as well as intense rage as the inevitable consequence of such intense wishes and their continual disappointment. This sense of profound and very primitive longing permeated everything that Gloria had to do or say about her mother. She complained often bitterly about the way in which her mother criticized and undercut her. She portrayed herself as trying as hard as she could to please her mother but never seeming able to satisfy her. But behind these complaints there was always a desperate longing for mother's love and affection that seemed bottomless and insatiable. Whatever she got from mother, it was not—and could not be—enough. Gloria complained again and again that she never got enough from mother, never got what she wanted, never got enough attention or affection. It took her a long time before we could begin to approach Gloria's rage at mother for continually disappointing her. Gloria felt from as far back in her life as she could remember that her mother did not want her and did not love her. She turned her rage into feelings of worthlessness and hatefulness, blaming herself for the fact that she felt unloved and unwanted.

Relation to Father

Gloria's relation with her father was also highly ambivalent and conflicted. In the face of her disappointment and frustration in her relation with her mother, Gloria turned to her father for love and support. He too disappointed her. Instead of protecting her from her mother and supporting her in her resentment of mother, he undercut her and only added to the burden of guilt that she carried. Her disappointment and anger at her father were also increased by her continually feeling that her father favored her younger sister more than herself. Gloria felt displaced from her father's affections by her sister Gladys. Consequently her longing for closeness and acceptance was repeatedly frustrated in relation to both parents.

Gloria's anger at her father took indirect forms of expression. She felt certain that her father was going to die or go crazy. She dreamed from time to time of her father's death; he would have a heart attack, or be hit by a car, and in the dream Gloria would be at the funeral, frightened and grief-stricken. These preoccupations with her father's death made her aware of how dependent she felt toward her father. She clung to him as if he were the sole support she had. She would ask him to do things for her, to go places with her, to take her out for coffee at the local coffeehouse, etc. Her longing and dependence on her father also had a primitive and infantile quality, although not as strongly as in relation to her mother. But Gloria had a special investment in relating to and interacting with her father. One important aspect of their relationship was the continual arguing between them. The arguments would continue for hours, and it was quite obvious that both father and daughter derived a considerable amount of gratification from these endless arguments. It was also obvious that both of them contributed to starting them and keeping them going. Neither of them could or would allow the argument to lapse, but they were both highly invested in keeping it going.

Gloria's attraction to her father was difficult for her to handle and caused her considerable conflict. She recalled that when she was about eight years old, her father was considering taking a job as a traveling salesman. The idea terrified Gloria. She would not accept the possibility of being left with her mother without her father's being there; she feared that her mother would hurt her or even kill her. This dependent clinging to father, however, had its difficult side for several reasons. One was the sexual aspect of their relationship. Her Oedipal wishes were too dangerous and difficult for her to handle. She was only able to admit her fears of sexual assault from her father after a long time.

It was also particularly difficult for Gloria to handle and express her angry feelings toward her father. She dreaded her own anger and felt that if she expressed it something dreadful would happen to him. On one occasion she did something nasty to him and he cried. Her mother scolded her on that occasion for being mean to her father. Gloria felt that if she expressed her feelings he would die or would go crazy, and inevitably that she would have to bear the responsibility for that dread outcome. It was with great difficulty and only slowly that she came more and more to recognize the fault lay not wholly in her. She came gradually to recognize that part of the problem had to do with her father, that he was overly sensitive and conflicted about his own feelings. Whenever she expressed any anger toward him he would respond by feeling hurt and unjustly mistreated. This would make Gloria feel guilty and reinforced her feeling worthless and evil. She was caught in a trap of ambivalence, with the result that in both directions, in relation to her mother and to her father, her wishes to be close and affectionate and her feelings of anger and resentment were cut off and became dangerous and difficult.

Dependence and Submission

Embedded in these ambivalent relationships, there was another issue that proved to be perhaps the most central and predominant theme in Gloria's treatment—and for that matter throughout the course of her illness. It was the theme of submission and the sacrifice of autonomy. Gloria would often undertake, for example, to help her mother with some of the housework. Her reasons—at one level—were to gain some approval from mother and to please her. But Gloria regarded mother as a sloppy and ineffective housekeeper. She wanted to do things in her way—whether it was dishes or laundry or cleaning or whatever. Mother would insist on having Gloria do things her way instead. There were frequent arguments over such matters, but it quickly became clear that the real issue was not how a particular bit of work was to be done. Rather the real issue was who was going to have their own way and who was going to submit. Although Gloria would argue with her mother, she never felt that in the last analysis there was any possibility of having her own way about things.

Father got into the act of course. When such argments arose, father would always impress upon Gloria that if she stood up to her mother and insisted on doing things her own way that mother would get sick again. This particularly dire threat was the most effective one which the father could find to keep Gloria in line. Gloria saw herself as much different in this regard from her younger sister Gladys. Gladys could do things she wanted and *could* stand up to mother. When I asked her why this was so, the inevitable reply was that her father let Gladys stand up to mother and let her get away with things, but for some unexplained reason he did not let Gloria do the same. Gloria explained this discrepancy by a presumed collusion between father and Gladys which was part of father's favoritism toward her. Gloria felt resentful and quite jealous over this. In the face of the threatened consequences of standing up to mother, Gloria felt that she was helpless; she had no recourse but to submit to her mother's wishes and to do everything as she wanted it done. If she did not try to be very good and do what mother wanted, she was faced with the constant threat of a recurrence of mother's illness and the loss of mother once again. The price of acceptance and closeness was complete and utter submission. The only alternative Gloria could see was that of complete and absolute rebellion, with the consequence of loss of love and catastrophic abandonment.

Gloria was caught in a similar bind in her relationship with her father, with an added element that intensified and complicated the problem. The added element was simply that her father played into this neurotic need on Gloria's part with his own neurotic needs to have her maintain her dependence on him and to remain submissive and accepting of his views and attitudes toward life and the world. On Gloria's part, she felt that she had to adhere to everything that her father said, had to accept his attitudes and views on matters of all kinds, had to do what he wanted her to do, etc. If she were not to follow this submissive pattern, dreadful things would happen. The dreadful things were usually misfortunes that would befall father—he would get sick, he would die, he would become crazy, or depressed, or suicidal. Any movement toward independence became translated in her mind into an attack on her father that would hurt, cripple, or kill him.

The intensity of these feelings was displaced in a variety of contexts. The chronic arguments between Gloria and her father were on her part motivated by the pressure she felt to submit to and to endorse his views. The argument was a reflection of her conflicts over such submission; she felt she had to submit but did not want to. Prolonging the argument was a way of compromise between these opposing aspects and, as we have seen, it was a means of involvement with her father which had considerable secondary gratification. Gloria went to college because her father said she should; she felt that she had no choice in the matter. She submitted to his wish but found a way of sabotaging his wish by getting sick and dropping out. She had argued about that too, feeling that if she could not win the argument and convince him of her point of view she would have to capitulate and completely accept his view of the matter. If she did not adhere to what he said, she felt terribly guilty, like a criminal who had committed some terrible crime and who had to be punished. She remembered such feelings for as long as her memory extended. There was both a desperate need to cling to this conviction—namely, to submit to and accept whatever her father said or else she would somehow lose him—and an underlying resentment and anger at having to submit and surrender her own thoughts and inclinations. This inner conflict provided a major focus of her treatment. She felt that she had to stay close to her father, because otherwise she would be hurt or somehow damaged.

It was quite clear that there was little or no room for compromise or give-and-take in Gloria's way of dealing with her family. The issue was total capitulation, either they were going to "give in" to her or she would have to "give in" to them. It had to be one way or the other, there was no room for flexibility or negotiation or for agreement without capitulation. As Gloria saw her position in the family, she had no alternatives but either to submit and surrender her views and wishes, or to fight for her views, to launch a counterattack that would have dangerous and dreadful consequences. She saw herself as having no rights, no right to have her own opinion, no right to think differently about things from her mother or father. If her opinion differed, then she must be in the wrong. There was no room in her head or in her family for people to have differing views and differing opinions. To have a different opinion was to attack the other person's opinion. More importantly, however, there was no room for Gloria to have an opinion of her own, or to make a decision of her own, especially if it were a a "wrong" decision or opinion. The definition of "wrong" came to be "differing from the opinions of others"—particularly the opinions of her father.

Submission in Therapy

The same attitude was generated in the transference. Gloria approached me with considerable wariness and fear. She saw me as someone with great power and knowledge. Her attitude was at first one of suspicion and distrust, but little by little that gave way to an attitude that said that I was the all-knowing and all-seeing doctor who understood the mysteries of why people behaved as they did and why people became mentally disturbed. She regarded her therapy as a process in which she came to my office and spent the allotted time with me, answered my questions, and then waited until I saw fit to tell her what the problem was and what she should do about it. She tried persistently and continually to shape the therapy in such a way that I would be put in the position of telling her what to do, so that she would be able to submit to my directives or wishes. Her wish to submit to my authority was overwhelming, but it also became increasingly clear that she knew no other way of carrying on a relationship with another human being. Again and again I pointed this out to her and frequently commented on the fact that she related to her father in just the same way. She at first denied any such parallel, but gradually came to accept its accuracy. When I tried to point out to her that she set up the relationship in the same way, she resisted the idea vigorously. She persisted in denying and rejecting any suggestion that she contributed in any way in making the relationship one of submission.

This conviction of hers and her persistent attitude were related to another crucial aspect of her treatment. A persistent issue in the treatment was whether and to what extent she was going to allow herself to become a patient. She had resisted hospitalization, blaming her parents for it and feeling that she had been unjustly and without reason railroaded into the hospital. She blamed me for permitting this to happen and for having participated in it. She had persistently resisted and rejected all aspects of her hospital program. The issue over and over again was whether she would accept the need and the reality of being a patient. She gradually came to terms with this partially during her hospital course, but *only* gradually and partially. She was able to accept some responsibilities in the hospital and to participate in some of the modalities of treatment offered. At each point, the same issue was rejoined and reworked. She always raised the issue in terms of whether she was going to be forced to submit to this or that treatment or regulation. She deeply resented the submitting because it was being forced on her, consistently refusing to accept it because she might need it or might be able to use it to her own benefit.

As time went on we continued to work our way up the treatment scale.

The issue was rejoined over medications. Was she going to submit to my wish for her to take certain medications or not? She would not accept my judgment that the medicines were necessary or useful for her. She continually questioned what the medicines were, why was she taking them, did she really need them, weren't there other medicines that would be better, etc. I made only moderate attempts to answer such questions. My answers would very likely not have satisfied her, and I felt that they were a cover for her real concerns, I related them directly to the question of whether she was going to be my patient and whether she was going to be able to trust me sufficiently to rely on my judgment about such things. She would never admit that she was gradually coming to accept me and trust me but continued to question and object, while at the same time she came around to taking the medication and in the long run very faithfully too. I felt quite sure that if I had not related the issue of taking medications to her concerns over having to submit and trusting me she would have sabotaged that as she had successfully sabotaged so many other things in her life.

The issue was also joined at another level within psychotherapy itself. From time to time, Gloria would make it quite clear that she had something on her mind that was causing her severe distress but she would not communicate to me. When I observed that I could not help her with her problems unless she shared them with me, she would reply that these were her own private thoughts and none of my business. She did not want to let me in on everything and had no intentions of telling me these private things. She had to keep something for herself. Such a stance by a paranoid patient puts the therapist in a difficult position. I was hopeful that she would share these "private" thoughts with me but I did not want to violate her emerging sense of autonomy. I chose a middle course. I indicated that I thought it was important for her to discuss such things and I was willing to help her with them, but that it was up to her to decide whether she wanted to talk about them or not. At times she would go on to talk about what was bothering her, but at other times, she would choose to keep the matter to herself.

Frequently the issue of whether she was going to be a patient was joined over her participation in the therapy process itself. Her attitude persistently was that her part of the bargain was to bring herself to my office at a given hour—no more. Time and again I pointed out that therapy was more than just bringing a warm body to my office. Her reluctance, however, persisted. In reply to my inquiries she would block, her memory would fail, she would present me with a blank mind without thoughts or feelings. The question here too was whether she was going to put herself to work in therapy, rather than making herself the passive and helpless victim of the process to which she had to submit herself. Her need to see herself as passive, powerless, helpless, and unable to take any action on her own behalf—even in therapy—was overwhelming.

Sexual Feelings

One of the areas that remained difficult for her to talk about was her sexual feelings. Her style typically when we drew near to any loaded or conflictual material was to become vague and general in her remarks and to block out any meaningful content. She would end up saying little more than "I don't know!" at such points. Any sexual thoughts or feelings were severely affected in this way. It was almost two years before she even admitted to any sexual feelings; this was remarkable in view of the fact that her sexual difficulties and her loss of the boyfriend Peter had been so closely involved with her decompensation. It was a well-guarded and defended area. Particularly guarded were any sexual feelings toward me. These came into focus gradually, at first through a discussion of her bodily sensations in the therapy sessions. She remarked first that she felt tense—the tension was located generally in her head and chest, but also in her stomach. From there we were gradually able to ease into talking about sexual feelings. Gloria was intensely ashamed and embarrassed by these feelings. She would not admit any sexual impulses toward me directly, but after some time was able to say that she felt warmly toward me and that she felt I was the only trustworthy person she knew. She would not admit that she might have such thoughts or wishes about me, but I would occasionally appear in her dreams and in one dream she came to the point of marrying me off to the sister of another patient.

The Wish to Regress

One of the persistent problems that had to be faced again and again in Gloria's treatment was her wish to regress. It was her wish to retreat from the world and from life and simply to be taken care of by her mother. She did not want to work, she did not want to be on her own. She did not want to grow up and function as an adult member of society. From time to time she was quite explicit about this infantile wish. Her resistance to therapy was in part motivated by a powerful wish not to surrender her infantile and highly narcissistic wish. My therapeutic efforts made inroads on that wish and posed a threat to it. At several points in her career, Gloria made serious bids to get herself back in the hospital. She stopped taking medications, developed increasingly severe phobias and paranoid anxieties, and became increasingly bizarre and disruptive in her behavior at home. When I made it clear to her that she would have to go to a rather forbidding state hospital near her home and that she could no longer be my patient, she gave up her regressive bid and returned to her usual pattern of behavior.

But the problem persisted. As therapy progressed the choice became more and more clearly defined for her. She had to choose between the regressive course and the course of increasing maturity and responsibility. The regressive course meant avoiding working in therapy, not gettting better, clinging to her symptoms—primarily phobias, anxieties, and paranoid ideas—and ultimately ending up a mental cripple for life. The progressive course meant working in therapy, giving up her fears and their incapacitating effects, taking charge of her life and starting to work to make it what she wanted. She had not been able to make any such decision; it is one that will be made, if at all, in the course of more years of therapy. But the issue is a primary one in her therapy.

Paranoid Anxieties

Her paranoid symptoms remained a persistent feature of her treatment. They became less of a problem as therapy progressed, and particularly after Gloria got out of the hospital. They never completely disappeared, and from time to time they would become more intense and paralyzing to her. It became clear in time that these symptoms were related to and in part in the service of her regressive infantile wishes. Her narcisssism generated expectations that were continually disappointed, and her rage and disappointment were dealt with by paranoid mechanisms.

At the beginning of her treatment, her paranoid ideas were quite severe and paralyzing. In her acute decompensation, she felt that the members of her family were trying to kill her and somewhat later she felt that the staff at the hospital was trying to kill her. She complained bitterly that she was being tortured by them and that as soon as she got out of the hospital she was going to sue them all and the hospital as well. These intense feelings and the distortions accompanying them dissipated somewhat, although Gloria never relinquished her feeling that the staff had mistreated her. This remained a problem for her because she knew that I was in agreement with the staff's accusations and she could not reconcile this with her growing trust in me as a kind, sympathetic, and helpful person. I made no attempt to help her resolve this dilemma, but simply tried to explore her feelings. Any attempt on my part to move her in one direction or the other would have been disastrous

Little by little these more general fears diminished, although they have remained a part of her clinical picture, ready to be revived and intensified at any moment. But gradually they seemed to lessen in intensity and Gloria seemed more and more able to deal with them on more realistic terms. She gradually became aware that these paranoid ideas and anxieties reflected her own inner feelings and were not based on any reality. She became increasingly aware that they were the product of her own projection. Little by little we were able to explore her fear and relate them to her own anger. She remained quite isolated and withdrawn however. She would complain that she was afraid of meeting people. She felt terribly embarrassed in being with other people and trying to carry on a conversation. She didn't know how to act or what to say. She was afraid of looking stupid or foolish. She was afraid that if she tried to relate to people, they would reject her. What gradually emerged, behind these fears and embarrassments that so paralyzed and plagued her, were Gloria's expectations that people should be nice to her, be interested in her, and even admire her. Her chronic and anticipated disappointments made her feel hostile and rejecting toward everyone she met. That her own hostility was in question rather than anyone else's she could recognize, but she could not appreciate that her own behavior brought about the reaction in others that she so resented and feared. It was a form of self-fulfilling prophecy.

Many of her fears were related to her concern that people would hate, reject, and revile her if they could see what she was really like. She felt that she was hateful and evil. She gradually came to recognize that she had so much anger and hatred stored up in her that if it ever came out people would want to reject her and get rid of her. She was a monster that would have to be destroyed. It turned out—by and large—that the "private thoughts" that Gloria was so reluctant to share with me were thoughts and feelings about how evil and hateful she was. Her fear was that if I knew about how bad she was I would want to get rid of her and would reject her.

Gloria is still in therapy. She is making slow and very unsteady progress. Much has changed in her relationship with her parents over the years. She has a much more realistic appraisal of their shortcomings and weaknesses. But the road ahead will be long and fraught with difficulty. Gloria has not yet made the choice between regression and progression. Her paranoid need to place the blame and the responsibility for her condition elsewhere is still strong and persistent. She still avoids and resists the commitment to the hard work of therapy, clinging to her wish for a magical solution. But the indices are more positive now than they were two or three years ago. How much further we can go remains a moot question. If the paranoid process in this young woman is or seems to be losing its sting, we cannot assure ourselves that it will not win out in the end. Time alone can tell.

DISCUSSION

Early Mother-Child Interaction

One of the first questions that the data in this case urge on us is the question of genetic influence. In most of the other cases we have been forced to surmise a pathogenic relationship between mother and child from later disturbances in the relationship. In Gloria's case, however, there seems to be good and clear-cut evidence that the relationship between Gloria and her mother was disturbed from the very beginning. The mother's postpartum depression and insecurity and inability to nurse and care for her child seem to have distorted the smooth regularity and mutuality that is so necessary for early development. In every case we have had to study, the relationship between a paranoid daughter and her mother was overloaded with ambivalence and hostility. In none of the cases is the evidence for this impairment in the mother-daughter relationship so clear or so early. As is so often the case, the evidence is provided not merely by the historical data but by the contemporary data provided by the patient's ongoing dynamics. Rarely in my experience have the pregenital elements behind the paranoid dynamics been so explicit. Gloria's yearning for love and affection from her mother, her tearful and anguished cry that her mother was lost to her, and that she could not reach out to her and embrace and be embraced by her as she wished, were infantile and regressive, primitive wishes of the infant to be held, cuddled, fed and warmed by the mother's body. In these tearful regressive episodes Gloria became the frustrated and wrathful infant who cannot reach the mother's breast. She seemed overwhelmed with a sense of deep loss and abandonment.

Freud had commented in his essay on female sexuality (1931) (1961):

> We find the little girl's aggressive oral and sadistic wishes in a form forced on them by early repression, as a fear of being killed by her mother—a fear which, in turn, justifies her death-wish against her mother, if that becomes conscious. It is impossible to say how often this fear of the mother is supported by an unconscious hostility on the mother's part which is sensed by the girl (p. 237).

For Gloria these primitive aggressive impulses were derived not merely from the usual run of frustrating and denying responses that are inevitably involved in any maternal ministrations. From the beginning Mrs. G.'s attempts at mothering had been permeated with anxiety and her own sense of insecurity in the performance of her mothering duties. We shall see more of this later, but we can recall at this point that Gloria's earliest experience with her mother was shrouded with a severe depression in the mother. Moreover the mother's difficulties with her mothering position were persistent, extending in fact into the period of Gloria's psychotic decompensation and treatment.

Gloria's desperate longing for closeness and affection from her mother and its continual frustration was one of the significant leitmotivs of her life and experience. We can suggest a number of important consequences of this basic dimension of her life, particularly in regard to her early life experience. The basic uncertainty and instability in the early mother-child interaction undermined the establishment of basic trust. Gloria was faced early in her experience with the equivalent of maternal loss or its threat. She was not provided with a stable, responsive, and constant mothering object. Her mother was conflicted, anxious, and depressed—psychologically withdrawn and unavailable in a variety of ways. Gloria did not have the opportunity for the experience of mutual regulation and responsiveness that lies at the root of basic trust.

Loss and Abandonment

The unavailability or threat of loss of her mother produces a situation in which the basic anxiety of loss is countered by the child's clinging excessively to the symbiotic tie with the mother. We have some indications from Mahler's careful studies that in the face of the mother's relative unavailability any movement toward separation is overburdened with the threat of loss and abandonment (Mahler, 1968). The child must cling to the mother and becomes excessively dependent on the mother's support and affection. Such a child becomes a victim. Gloria was trapped between the terrifying threat of loss and abandonment on one hand and the threat of her mother's hostility and rejection on the other. The basic issue for Gloria lay at a very primitive level of symbiotic attachment, an attachment that was continually frustrated and denied. At a very fundamental level her pathology was rooted in the issues of separation and individuation.

In the wake of this primitive and initial unavailability of her mother, the subsequent events which served to separate Gloria even further from her mother came as traumatic events in an already pathological relationship. Less than two years after Gloria's birth her younger sister was born. Once again Mrs. G. suffered an acute exacerbation of her more or less chronic depression. Added to the problems created by the coming of a second child—a rival for her mother's limited reserve of affection—there was the increased withdrawal created by her mother's postpartum depression. This only served to intensify Gloria's sense of loss. Then she was forced to share the limited and relatively unavailable store of affection with her sister.

We can imagine how all of this was complicated by Gloria's angry and resentful feelings. She must have felt that her hateful and resentful wishes toward her mother were driving her mother away from her. It was this very thought that Gloria often expressed in her therapy, that if people knew how horrible and evil she was they would reject her and turn away from her. She felt that her angry feelings drove people away; she had after all let Peter know some of her feelings and he had run away from her and rejected her. The pattern of self-blame reached an apogee when Gloria's mother became psychotically depressed after the birth of the third child, Glenda. Gloria was convinced that she was the responsible agent for her mother's sickness and unhappiness. She had lost her mother in a real sense, but, more than having lost her, she had driven her away. But the pain of loss reached back to a very primitive level of her experience when the threat of loss and abandonment colored her earliest experiences. Gloria remarked at one point in her therapy with considerable insight that she had lost her mother and it had taken her many years to weep over it.

Ambivalence to Father

As a result of this profound and continuing sense of loss, Gloria turned for support and affection to her father. For a variety of reasons this was less than satisfactory for her. Her father could not respond to her deep and overwhelming needs. He was a needy man himself, and to some degree sought the affection he needed from his daughters. He was a relatively warm and sympathetic person and tried to become both father and mother in the face of Mrs. G.'s sense of inadequacy. He sacrificed himself in the face of his wife's illness and incapacity and he tried to fill the gap and keep the family together. Gloria's relation to her father was complex and difficult. The interlocking of her need for affection and closeness and his need for affectionate approval made the relationship rather seductive and in this regard threatening for both father and daughter. This made it difficult for both to find the support they needed in their relationship. Gloria felt that she could not reach her father, could not get close to him. And as we have seen she felt that the father favored her younger sister. She resented this and resented her father's failure to support her and protect her from her mother's hostility.

The relationship was thus highly ambivalent. Gloria felt that the only way she could keep any relationship to her father was by conforming with his views and wishes. She had to keep herself dependent and submissive to him, or else she would be cast out and abandoned by him as well. Yet it is clear that her rage was stirred by this circumstance as well. She felt that she had to submit, and bitterly resented and struggled against it. It is particularly important to note that the rage which welled up in her was too dangerous and too destructive for Gloria to deal with. It was murderous rage and it threatened the loss or destruction of those objects on which she was also so dependent and to which she had to cling so desperately. The risk of expressing her rage was too high. It had to be repressed—and turned finally into paranoid and phobic channels.

Pathogenic Internalization

The highly ambivalent quality of her relationships with both parents inevitably had a severely pathogenic influence on Gloria's development. Internalization was disturbed from the very beginning. In the normal course of separation and individuation, the continuously supportive and relatively nonambivalent interaction with the parents—early in development particularly with the mother—enables the child to separate himself out of the parental matrix and become a distinct individual. The process is dependent internally on processes of introjection and identification. If the parents and the quality of the child's relation to the parents permit, then the child is able to form relatively stable and positive introjections of both parents, introjects that are not significantly contaminated by hostile and destructive elements. Such introjects are positive forces in healthy psychic development. They form the basis on which strong and positive ego-identifications can be made, and thus the child follows a path toward relative psychic health. But when the child's primary object relations are highly contaminated with ambivalence, the outcome is often less optimistic. Introjects are significantly more aggressively colored and become internal focuses of destructiveness. Identification processes are impeded and fragmentized. Identifications are highly contaminated by destructive introjective components and resist integration into harmonious ego-structures. The introjects tend to retain their susceptibility to primary process organization and remain relatively susceptible to regressive drive influences.

The internal drama for Gloria was dominated by the highly pathogenic and destructive introjects from both mother and father. In one facet of her inner psychic life she had become identified with the depressed, worthless, and victimized image of her mother. She had played out this role and clung to it insistently. Thus her stubborn clinging to her passivity and her insistence on the need to submit were in part a clinging to the maternal introject, or at least this aspect of it. There was also another aspect of her own inner experience of self that made Gloria feel that she was evil, hateful, repugnant and worth nothing more than to be thrown out and destroyed. These feelings had been her mother's when Gloria was very young, and they formed an indelible part of the maternal introject. The other aspect was her mother's more conscious attitudes of criticism and shaming. The mother directed these hostile attitudes not only toward herself, but also toward Gloria. Mother was constantly either criticizing or shaming Gloria. And Gloria's attempts to stem the tide and to gain some small measure of approval met only criticism or devaluation from her mother.

Gloria also suffered significantly from her paternal introject as well. As we have seen in other cases, the patterning of introjects tends to find reinforcement. The parental introjects tend to reinforce each other, thus confirming the patient's pathology. Gloria's father—as we shall see—was a rather paranoid man. We have seen the extent to which Gloria was driven to accept and make her own his views and attitudes, even though she was conflicted about it and struggled with him over such views and opinions. Submission and acceptance of his views as her own were for her the price of her relationship with him, a relationship that she needed so desperately. His paranoid views, in short, became her own. She once observed—very much to the point—that her father lived in a world of "creeps and weirdos" and that was also her world. His cautions, admonitions, and attitudes were internalized and formed the substance of her paranoid view of the world.

These introjective elements functioned internally as rather primitive and severe superego elements. Gloria's attitude toward herself was severely critical, undermining, devaluing, and destructive. She saw herself as worthless, inferior, evil, hateful, and as a highly malignant and destructive force. There was a high degree of internal distortion that gave these attitudes a magical and powerful quality. Where her father had told her that it was naughty to disobey her mother and make her mother sick, Gloria saw herself as a powerful and evilly malignant force that could make her mother ill and even destroy her. The transferral of Gloria's more repressed destructive and murderous wishes to these introjects served to magnify and enlarge their destructiveness.

Paranoid Mechanisms

These introjective elements served as the basis for Gloria's projections. The destructive elements were translated into evil intentions that threatened to harm or destroy her. The people around her in varying degree and at different times wanted to hurt her, reject her, put her down, make her appear stupid or useless, or even at the moments of more intense paranoia wanted to kill her. She clung to her picture of herself as a helpless, and passive victim of these external threats. It was easier and safer for her to regard herself as fearful and passive than for her to face the picture of herself as angry and destructive. The problem, of course, was that she could not accept any responsibility for her own anger and rage without at the same time facing her own inner perception of herself as evil, hateful, worthless, and powerfully destructive.

The alternation between paranoid fearfulness and depressive self-hate shaped Gloria's clinical course. As she retreated from her paranoid stance in the more acute phase of her illness, there emerged intense feelings of self-hate, self-blame, guilt, shame, intense sadness, and the anguish of loss and abandonment that we have described. It was clear that her paranoid stance was substantially a defense against these painful and tormenting feelings. The paranoid construction is born out of the need to avoid the ultimate condemnation of self. The alignment of the introjects makes it impossible for the paranoid patient to accept anger without accepting with it all the worst distortions and magical destructiveness of the internalized introjects. These must be discharged, disowned, dispelled—thrust out and completely dissociated from the self. The anal image of the discharge of evil and repugnant feces comes to life. The paranoid construction reorganizes the patient's perception and interpretation of reality in such a way as to account for the desperate circumstances he finds himself in, and to dissociate and absolve him from the ultimate condemnation that threatens him. The evil must be located elsewhere.

Narcissistic Substratum

It is important to realize that the paranoid process builds on a substratum. The substratum in this case—as in all the cases we are considering—is narcissism. It seems to me that an excessive and pathological narcissism is an unavoidable consequence and concomitant of the impairment of separation and individuation processes in early life. The child learns to relinquish primitive narcissism to the extent that he is able to develop independent and autonomous resources for gratification and self-satisfaction. If that is not possible or is thwarted for one or another reason—and in the face of the threatened loss and abandonment of the gratifying objects—narcissism remains a predominant aspect of the psychic economy and comes to exercise a pathological influence.

In Gloria's case we can recognize its influence in her continuing wish for and expectation of the gratification of affection and loving closeness from her parents. This expectation in regard to the primary objects became generalized as she grew older. She expected to be liked and sought after and courted by the people around her. The inevitable disappointment of these expectations underlay the continuing sense of rage that had to be managed by pathological mechanisms of introjection and projection. The pathological aspect of such narcissism is that the patient continues to entertain such excessive expectations, even when it is clear objectively and to the patient that they are doomed to frustration and disappointment. The effect of such narcissism is to draw the patient to cling to this continuing state of disappointment and rage. One often sees something similar in severely depressed patients, although as a rule in paranoid patients the narcissism is more primitive and rigidly maintained. Paranoid patients do not want to give up their sense of entitlement and their basic sense of outraged justice. They are reluctant to compromise their expectations. Instead of facing the reality of an ungiving mother whose resources for affection and loving responsiveness were severely limited, Gloria clung to her implicit belief that in some manner she could get from her mother what she wanted. She clung to that belief and its painful consequences, rather than find other sources of gratification and affection for herself.

Vicissitudes of Aggression

She was extremely sensitive to the slightest innuendos or feelings. This was particularly true of any anger or hostility in people around her. It was particularly true in the therapeutic relationship. She often provoked feelings of impatience, anger, frustration, and irritation in me. She responded to such feelings in me, sometimes even before I was aware of them myself. I found that the most productive way to deal with such feelings was to communicate them or admit them to her, and then try to discuss the reasons for my feeling as I did and what role she might have played in making me feel that way. This sort of sensitivity is substantially an extension of the usual paranoid hypersensitivity and hyperawareness. The paranoid defense requires constant vigilance and constant scanning of the environment to detect possible sources of hostility and harm.

Once again Gloria's experience calls our attention to the frequent occurrence of phobias and nightmares in paranoid patients. Most typically her fears had a decidedly paranoid cast—someone would kill her, or rape her, or, on a more moderate scale, people would criticize, ridicule, humiliate, or embarrass her. Such identifiably paranoid anxieties would often shade over into more generally phobic concerns, and the line was often difficult to draw between them. She would be terrified at the idea of riding on buses or streetcars. At times this was linked with her fear that someone might try to kill her, but often as not the fear could not be linked with anything more specific than that there might be an accident. She was afraid of streetcars particularly in that they went underground as part of their route and Gloria was frightened of being underground and frightened of being in the dark. Such phobic concerns formed the substance of her nightmares. In them she was time and again again threatened with death—men chasing her with knives to murder her (symbolic?), people trying to run her down with automobiles, etc., etc. These dreams were often more active during periods in which clinically her fears had diminished somewhat and she was functioning on a somewhat less impaired level. It seemed reasonable to me to assume that these anxiety dreams were functioning in some degree as substitute for her psychotic symptoms.

Trust and Autonomy

We have observed that the issues of basic trust and autonomy are primary in the psychopathology of paranoid states. It can be seen quite readily that these issues were central in the present case. Gloria's early mothering experience was defective on a number of counts. Her mother's depression diminished her availability and responsiveness to Gloria's needs. Moreover, her mothering activities were overburdened with her feelings of anxiety, insecurity, and inadequacy. Her mothering was consequently inconstant and conflicted. There was no opportunity and no sign of a secure and reassuring interaction between mother and child. The mutually rewarding and responsive relationship that offers the opportunity for the development of basic trust was lacking. The failure to achieve a sense of trust in the significant caretakers is unavoidably accompanied by a failure to achieve a sense of trust in oneself, in one's own trustworthiness. These deficits in self-esteem in turn impair severely the capacity for meaningful relations, as was evident in Gloria's therapeutic experience. Her relationship to me was shrouded in distrust and suspicion. It took literally years before even the glimmer of a capacity to trust appeared. Even then, the issue of trust remained a central one for the continuing course of therapy. It was the issue that was embedded in her chronic resistance to participating in and committing herself to the process of therapy and to the therapeutic relationship.

The impairment of trust developmentally undercuts the basis on which the child's emerging sense of autonomy can be erected. The child requires a trusting relationship particularly with the mother, which can allow him to undertake initiatives without fear of the loss of love and support. We have seen that this basis was not available to Gloria. Her whole relationship to her mother was overshadowed by the continuing threat of loss and abandonment. Any initiatives toward independent behavior on Gloria's part were taken at great risk. The difficulty in negotiating this developmental step toward diminishing dependence and emerging autonomy was magnified by Gloria's mother's incapacity to deal with Gloria's emerging self-will. As far as we know Mrs. G.'s own insecurities made it necessary for her to exercise more or less rigid and inflexible control over Gloria's behavior. Gloria's childish initiatives toward independent action were a threat to her. We know that the mother's demands on her daughter extended to feeding and to toilet training. Mother kept to a rather rigid feeding schedule, and tried to make Gloria feed even when she did not want it. Toilet training was done on schedule, and became an issue of control. We do not have a great deal of evidence to suggest that either of these typical interaction situations were productive of severe conflict, but it seems clear from the mother's attitude toward them and her manner of going about them that they turned out to be situations in which the infant Gloria was overcontrolled.

Gloria was never severely punished. She did not need to be. The usual tactic for keeping Gloria in line, and for mother to allay her own anxiety, was for Gloria to be threatened with abandonment. This controlling tactic was so frequently resorted to because it seemed to be so successful. But we can see that it was so precisely because it struck Gloria at the level of her greatest vulnerability. Unwittingly and unconsciously, Gloria's parents reinforced and intensified her most severe infantile trauma. It is worth noting that what was in question here was not merely a form of disciplinary practice, but that this practice and the means of maintaining parental control and authority were motivated by powerful anxieties in both parents. There was a real sense in which the impulses to independent and autonomous action on Gloria's part were a severe threat to both parents. Her autonomy had to be crushed in order to preserve the psychic integrity of the parents.

The picture is not all that simple, however. Gloria played a significant role in the interaction with her parents. She was an unconscious collaborator in the continuing frustration and impairment of her own autonomy. The many ways in which she drew those around her to violate her autonomy and exercise control over her, were quite apparent in the interaction with the staff of the hospital, in the repeated patterns of interaction between Gloria and her parents, and, particularly striking to me, in her interaction with me in therapy. After the therapeutic relationship had matured and after she had gained some moderate degree of trust, Gloria subjected me to a continual and unrelenting seduction to exercise control and direct her in one or another direction. It was an attempt to re-create within the transference the pattern of relationship that she had developed with her parents. We have glimpsed some of its origins and motivations. But suffice it to say that it provides a difficult therapeutic dilemma for the therapist and was one of the most difficult aspects of Gloria's therapy to deal with.

But Gloria was really no different than the other patients we have been considering. The issue of autonomy is central in every case. This is particularly difficult when movement in the therapy is so slow and inapparent, as it was with Gloria and with several other cases, especially Bob B. The therapist finds himself wanting to tell the patient what to do, wanting to get the therapy moving, wanting to become more active and directive, out of a sense of frustration and impotence. But the therapeutic task, it seems to me, is not to take away or violate the patient's autonomy as others around the patient have done for so long, but to allow the patient's autonomy to grow, to give it room to flourish, to enable the patient to find and realize it. It is precisely this course of therapeutic intent that the patient resists, and that is perhaps the best index of its therapeutic significance. It is also the striking point that makes the therapy of the paranoid process so difficult.

CHAPTER 13

Mr. Henry H.

The present case is that of a patient whom I saw rather intensively over a period of eight months, a relatively brief period of treatment in comparison to some of the other cases in this study. But Henry presents some interesting facets to his paranoia that provide additional understanding of the paranoid process.

THE PATIENT'S PROFILE

Hospitalization

My first contact with Henry came in the context of his most recent hospitalization. The circumstances surrounding the admission to the hospital were rather bizarre. He had arrived in the community quite recently and had contacted an old friend who was working as a resident in one of the local hospitals. This doctor had welcomed him, given him money, arranged for a room for Henry to sleep in at the hospital, and introduced him to several young nurses. Henry was coming off a recent hospitalization and was taking phenothiazines. The doctor friend took Henry to the psychiatric clinic so that his medications could be managed and treatment obtained if necessary.

Henry quickly became rather intensely involved with one of the nurses he had met. He dated this girl frequently for several weeks, and then decided that he was falling in love with her. He decided to ask her to marry him and determined that he would pour out his tale of misery and woe to her. It is not clear whether at this time he was in the incipient stages of decompensation, but certainly the subsequent events had a bizarre quality. Henry began by drinking heavily; the effect was very likely potentiated by the medication he was taking. He then went to the girl's apartment. He began to pour out his protestations of love and his desperate need to be close to her. The girl had no particularly strong romantic interest in him, however, and his wild appearance and manner frightened her. She tried to get him out of the apartment, but he wouldn't leave. Finally she ran out of the apartment to get away from him, but he ran out after her. By this time the excitement and screaming had aroused the neighbors and the police arrived. When the police came Henry ran back up to the apartment and locked himself in. The police had to batter the door down to get him out.

Psychiatric examination showed Henry to be quite excited and agitated.

The psychiatrist could not determine whether his behavior had been due to decompensation or to inebriation. When he spoke about his doctor friend who had introduced him to the nurse, Henry was quite vociferous in expressing his disappointment, his anger at the friend for not helping him more, for betraying him, for luring him to this city and treating him so poorly, introducing him to women who would lead him on and get him into such trouble, etc. The content was full of distortions and delusional material. The ideation was quite paranoid, and Henry could not recognize anything extraordinary or strange about his behavior. Because of the bizarre behavior, paranoid ideation, and the depressive content of his thinking it was felt that further evaluation was advisable.

When I first met him and began his evaluation, there was little that was remarkable about him. He was thirty-one years old, husky in build, somewhat balding, a moderately good-looking man. His mental functions were quite intact. The diagnostic points that stuck out, however, were his tremendous tension and anxiety. He sat with clenched fists, almost rigid, and with large drops of sweat standing on his forehead. Along with his obvious anxiety there was a strong degree of denial. Despite his tenseness and agitation he denied that he felt tense or anxious in any way. He tended to minimize or deny any significant difficulties in the past and resorted to elaborate intellectualized rationalizations to explain his behavior. He was able to express his feelings of bewilderment and disillusionment over the fact that the people he had counted on so much had all let him down.

Family Background

I would like to return at this point to review the family background and personal history, the odyssey of fact and circumstance that brought Henry to our attention. We can then turn to a consideration of our experience with him as a patient in the hospital. The material came forth with a considerable amount of rage at the important figures in his life. The material itself had a paranoid flavor but it also represented the patient's world of experience and objects as he lived them.

The dominant part of the family background for this patient has to do with his father's family. The father was the youngest son in a family of brothers. Little is known about his parents, except that his father was a well-to-do dentist and founded what was described by the patient as a "dental dynasty" in a large midwestern city. The father had two older brothers, Fred and Clement, both of whom followed in their father's footsteps. They became orthodontists and were both quite successful. They lived in large houses, had comfortable incomes, and could afford expensive cars and servants. They were in the first rank of local society. Henry's father had been the family black sheep. He rebelled against his father's attempts to force him to follow a career in dentistry. He had run away from home and married young, apparently in a burst of impulsive anger and rebellious defiance of his father. Financially he was less successful than his brothers. He worked for years as a salesman and never rose to any position of importance in his company. He was regarded in family terms as the problem son and the family failure, even though he was able to work steadily and earned a respectable income. His failure to follow dentistry put the stamp of failure on him in his family's eyes. He also had a drinking problem which persisted through the years.

When Henry's father married he more or less separated himself from his family. The circumstances of his marriage had not been propitious—and the marriage did not last long. He and his wife could not tolerate each other, they fought constantly, and they were soon separated and divorced. They had no children. Not long after, he met and married Henry's mother. She was from an undistinguished and poor family. Moreover she was a Catholic. On both counts she was resented and maligned by his family. She was from a lower social stratum and therefore not worthy to be a part of their family. Morever the family was basically Methodist in religious conviction, and her Catholicism was an affront and a challenge to them. In these circumstances the relationships between Henry's mother and his father's family were doomed to be acrimonious and bitter. Henry clearly saw his mother as the helpless victim of the prejudice and bitterness of his father's family.

The relationship between Henry's father and mother was not a happy one in its own right. The father was bitter, sarcastic, demanding, irritable, hostile, and at times sadistically brutal. He was extremely temperamental and often quickly aroused to anger at the least provocation. He would frequently drink to excess, and these drinking bouts would inevitably be accompanied by vicious outbursts and beatings. The mother was patient and long-suffering. They had two children, both boys. The older boy Larry was five years older than Henry. The boys were very close. They lived on the outskirts of a small eastern city and had few neighbors. There were no other children to play with where they lived, so that the brothers became constant playmates. Henry looked up to and idolized his older brother. They spent a great deal of time together, mostly Henry tagging along with his brother when he went fishing, or out in the woods. According to Henry's account, they got along well and never fought with each other. Henry was definitely the weaker little brother.

There was a significant interruption in this conflictual pattern of family life when Henry was about four years old. Pearl Harbor broke upon the nation and we were suddenly at war. Henry's father was taken into the service and remained away from home for several years. The situation with the father's family was intolerable. They were constantly interfering and trying to run his mother's life. Henry recalls that his father's mother was an incredibly dominating and controlling woman—a "real bitch"—as he put it.

Apparently when his father went into the armed service, the father's family tried to take charge of his family. He recalled that his mother was very unhappy at this time. In order to get away from the family, she took her two sons and moved to Florida, where they continued to live until the war was over and the family reunited. She worked during this time and raised her family. Henry saw this whole episode as a part of the overall picture of his mother as the helpless victim of the heartless and evil intentions of this father's family—as well as of his father.

Parental Conflict

The war years provided a hiatus, a period of relative quiet in the family process. But when the war was over and Henry's father back on the scene, things picked up again. The family atmosphere was one of constant turmoil, dominated by the completely unpredictable outbursts of anger from his father. For apparently no reason, he would explode in an angry tirade, usually directed against Henry's mother. When these outbursts would occur, they would often last for days at a time. His father would often beat his mother during these satanic releases. He would break furniture and literally lose control of himself. On occasion he would physically beat the boys. Often when these outbursts would occur, Henry and his brother would run away from the house and stay away until nightfall. Henry lived in perpetual fear of his father. He could not talk to him, he could not approach him, he could never ask the father for anything for fear of the father's breaking out into one of his rages.

Henry recalls one particularly traumatic episode in which his father went into one of his towering rages. His mother ran out of the house and was gone for several days. Finally his father left too. When he brought her back she was covered with bruises and had obviously been beaten, presumably by the father when he caught up with her. Henry recalled this episode with intense feeling and a sense of extreme bitterness and hatred for his father. He lived in fear of the latter. But his fear of and estrangement from his father were matched by his closeness and dependence on his mother. He was her baby, and she cared for and protected him, especially from his father.

He was closely involved with his mother. He saw her as a loving, self-sacrificing angel, who was as good and giving and caring as his father was evil, hateful, and selfish. They clung together in a mutually supporting and shared fear of his father. When his father would beat his mother, Henry recalled that his hatred of his father knew no bounds. He would gladly have killed him, or gladly seen him dead by any means. At such times he remembers wishing that he were big enough to beat his father to a pulp, to literally "kick the shit out of him!" He saw his mother and himself as the unfortunate victims of the cruelty and sadistic brutality of his father.

Mother's Death

In this highly conflicted and difficult setting, the one event that may have had more impact on Henry's pathology than any other took place. When he was twelve years old, his mother died of cancer of the breast. The loss was a severe one, a loss that in fact Henry never recovered from. He recalled that he was outside playing baseball one afternoon. The son of the local doctor came out and told him that his mother had died. He remembered feeling confused and bewildered. He could not remember crying, nor could he remember any of the details of what happened after she died. He remembered feeling resentful and deprived. He felt that his religious ideas were all confused at the time. He felt no one cared about him anymore. He felt that God could not care about him because He had taken his mother away.

Father's Desertion

Henry's mother's death signaled the dissolution of the family. His father took the two boys to live with his brother Clem and his wife. He literally turned the boys over to them to raise, and he disappeared. Henry felt abandoned and rejected by his father, and it did not seem unlikely that there was some reality to this impression. Henry's father was a severely disturbed man. His relationships with his family were intensely ambivalent. His tantrums and violent rages, so easily provoked and often inappropriate, as well as so explosive and destructive, seemed to have a psychotic quality about them. In any case he took the first opportunity to dump his sons. The effect on Henry was profound. He felt as though he were totally abandoned—he had lost both mother and father. In the loss of his mother he felt that he had taken away from him the one person in the whole world who cared anything about him. The rejection and abandonment by his father only intensified and completed the sense of loss. He recalled wistfully that his father cried when he left. But he added with a note of considerable regret and sadness that his father made the biggest mistake of his life when he left Henry and his brother with his aunt and uncle. Father would occasionally visit, and Henry always hoped desperately that he would take him away with him so that his family could be reunited. But he never did.

Not long after, Henry's father remarried. He had moved to another part of the country and started another family. This raised hopes in Henry's mind that perhaps his father would want to try to put the family together again. He begged to be able to rejoin his father. This possibility was resisted for a time, presumably because of his father's reluctance and resistance. Finally a visit was arranged. What Henry found was disappointing. His father was as brutal and tyrannical as ever. He was as harsh and mean to his new wife as he had been to Henry's mother. Larry visited at the time and he and Henry talked about their father. Larry observed that his father did not seem to have learned anything at all. He was cruel, difficult, and hateful as ever. Henry's disappointment was severe. He felt excluded, rejected, unloved by his father and unwanted. It seems reasonable to presume that these were indeed the father's sentiments. Henry held out a slender hope of reunion, however, until his stepmother got pregnant. That signaled the final exclusion. Father had a new family and Henry was not part of it.

The New Parents

Henry hated his aunt and uncle, particularly his aunt. His Uncle Clem was a relatively quiet and passive man who kept his mouth shut and thus kept himself out of trouble. He tended to his business and let Aunt Mary run the show at home. She was a strong-willed and dominating woman. They had never had any children of their own, a point that was significant since it was the one great disappointment of their lives. Mary welcomed the opportunity to take charge of Henry. She vowed to his father that she would make him perfect. She was rigid, demanding, and perfectionistic. Henry was sent to a fashionable private school where he felt too much was demanded from him. He had to work hard, and his aunt demanded that he spend long hours studying and doing his homework. She also forced him to work for an allowance. She made him work in the garden, cut the lawns, help in cleaning the house, and do other odd jobs. He complained that he was always so tired from working that he couldn't concentrate on his studies. He felt trapped, resentful, bitter, angry, lost, and helpless. The picture he painted was like something out of a Dickens novel. A helpless waif, orphaned and abandoned, thrust among unscrupulous and unfeeling people who took advantage of him and exercised their sadistic urges on him.

The picture he presented was one of unrelieved anguish and hurt. One could easily suspect that it was overdrawn for effect. There seems little doubt, however, that Henry and his aunt did not hit it off. There were frequent arguments and she would try to beat him. He recalled her ripping his shirt off in one fight. It seems likely that his deep resentment and bitterness were not kept within, but found their way into rebellious and resentful behavior. It was apparently because of such behavior and the difficulty his aunt and uncle had in managing him that they decided to send him to military school. The situation for Henry was all the more difficult because he lost his only ally early in the game. After a few months, Larry left the aunt and uncle to go to college. For Larry it was a welcome escape. For Henry it was a disaster. He lost his only source of support. He and Larry had clung together through the years in the face of their tyrannical father. Now Henry was left on his own. Henry was in touch with his feelings of loss and abandonment, and also with his feelings of resentment toward Larry for leaving him and letting him down. The theme of important figures on whom

Henry depended leaving him and letting him down came to be a major element in his life and experience.

Being sent to the military academy was another exile, another abandonment, another rejection. He recalled that life in the school was a horror. He was lonely, depressed, lost. He spent long hours there just crying and feeling very sorry for himself. He could not make any friends, and the regimen and discipline at the school were harsh and rigid—just the thing his aunt would approve of. He felt as though he had been condemned to a concentration camp. He saw the other kids there as pretty much in the same boat; they were all there because their families didn't want them and had gotten rid of them by exiling them to this school. Finally his father came to visit. Henry wept bitterly, told his father how unhappy he was and begged to be taken out of the school. The school was worse than life with his aunt and uncle.

So back he went. Life was unhappy but tolerable with them. He lived there for four years altogether. He went to a private prep school until it was time to go to college. He apparently did reasonably well in school and was able to be accepted by a prominent eastern university. Aunt Mary had become very possessive during this time. She wanted him to go to school near home. She was hurt by his wanting to go away to school. But it was finally decided that he should. She cried when he left. But Henry wanted little more than to get away. Life with his aunt and uncle had been a torment. There was little room in his mind for appreciation of their solicitude and care for him. There was too much resentment, too much of a sense of injustice and deprivation, too much a sense of what he had lost and did not have rather than what he did have or had gotten.

College Years

College years were perhaps the fullest and happiest in Henry's life. He was supported by his aunt and uncle but spent very little time with them. His grades were average, and he was socially active. Summers were spent working, usually at a resort hotel where he followed the routine for college boys, waiting on tables, doing odd jobs, teaching daughters of well-to-do clients how to sail or play tennis. Sexual contacts were frequent enough. Henry had a way of getting himself sexually involved with girls rather quickly, usually for only one or two night stands. He felt an intense need to be close to a woman and to be loved and taken care of by her. The sexual experience was one of the important ways in which he satisfied his need to feel close.

During his last year in college, Henry met his wife Sally. Sally was from an Italian Catholic family. She had led a rather sheltered life, had never lived anywhere but with her family, and was quite dependent on her parents. When he announced his intention of marrying her, there was a big flap from his aunt and uncle. They objected strongly to her Catholicism and raised all sorts of arguments about birth control. Even though the family felt strongly about it, Sally had no qualms about birth control. They finally married, but Henry's resentment and anger at his aunt and uncle were deep. They gave him plenty of bad advice, but little money or support. They remained critical of and hostile to Sally. Henry recalls that one day on the way to church his uncle made a crack to the effect that Sally's wearing a veil in church was hypocrisy. Henry was furious with his uncle, but felt that he couldn't say anything. At times his rage was so great that he just wanted to kill himself.

Graduate School and Marriage

Under pressure from Mary and Clem, it was agreed that Henry would go to dental school at a large midwestern university after his marriage. They agreed to pay for his tuition and give him an allowance to live on. The family investment in dentistry was high, and in face of Henry's lack of direction, his relatives had decided that this would be the obvious thing for him to do. Henry was compliant. But he nonetheless complained about many aspects of it. He argued that his aunt and uncle did not give him enough money; that they expected him to do nothing but study and work; that they did not give himself and Sally enough to live comfortably on or to afford any luxuries; that they kept checking up on him to see what he was doing with the money and whether he was performing up to their expectations. All of this galled and enraged him.

Things did not go well. Henry found the schoolwork demanding and difficult. He had to spend long hours studying and longer hours working in the laboratory. He found that he could not study at home, and so would spend most of his evening in the library. He began having increasing difficulties concentrating. He began to feel more and more depressed. He and his wife were living in a small apartment that was quite confining. It was all that they could afford on his allowance, however. Moreover, his uncle never stopped complaining about finances and how much the young man was spending.

Sally was very unhappy. She didn't like the apartment. She found it difficult to make friends with any of the neighbors. She felt that midwesterners were cold and distant people and that she could not relate to them. She felt alone and isolated. She was homesick and missed her family very much. She was alone most of the time, since Henry spent so much time away from her. He felt that she was too demanding sexually and that he could not satisfy her needs. He recalled one night when he had agreed to have some of his friends over to study for a bacteriology exam, Sally gave him a look, he remembered, that said she wanted him right then and there. He felt that she wanted him to tell his friends to get out and for him to take her to bed. The element of projection in this episode and the erotomania involved suggest the level of primitive defenses Henry was employing even at that time.

Another element was that Sally wanted badly to have a baby. The prospect of having children frightened Henry. He felt that it would only create more problems. It would cost money and his uncle was already complaining about finances and threatening to cut off the supply. But even more so, the thought of the responsibility was threatening to him. He saw a baby as something that Sally wanted for herself, and as something that would exclude him from her affection. He felt that she should only be concerned with helping him get through school, and not be selfishly wanting something that would gratify her and only create more problems for him. As a result he avoided her sexually more and more. When they did have sex, he insisted on using prophylactics. The issue of the baby became an area of contention and struggle. If he loved her, she felt that he would want to give her a child. But if she loved him, he felt that she would not want to have a child.

Finally things became so difficult that Sally decided that she would return east to spend some time with her parents. Her leaving, even though intended only as a visit, was traumatic for Henry. He became quite depressed, morose, unable to work or study. He felt that Sally had let him down. He felt angry and hurt by her leaving. If she really loved him, he reasoned, she would have stuck by him and supported him no matter what. He felt harassed and beleaguered, as if caught between two warring camps, one being Sally's family back east and the other his own family, particularly his aunt and uncle. They were complaining that he wasn't working hard enough, that he was not performing up to expectations, that he was spending too much money, etc. He felt abandoned and unloved. He felt that no one cared about him, that people were out to hurt him and do him in. It seemed obvious in retrospect that he was decompensating at this time and that his paranoid thinking was well established.

Gradual Decompensation

Sally returned only to find things more chaotic and difficult than ever. She quickly decided that she could not take any more of it. She told Henry that she did not love him anymore, that she could not continue to live under these conditions, and that she was going to divorce him. She left and returned to her family. After this Henry collapsed completely. He became severely depressed and suicidal, and had to be hospitalized. He reconstituted quickly and remained in the hospital only a month. He had to drop out of school. However, Sally went ahead with the divorce. Henry decided to stay where he was and get a job. He worked for a time, intending to return to school when he felt able to do so. He was bitter and resentful about his relationship to Sally and about the divorce. He blamed her fully for what had happened.

It was not long after these events that he met Edna. She was a schoolteacher. She had been twice married previously and twice divorced. In his typical style, Henry was feeling lonely, abandoned, and lost after his wife had divorced him. He turned to Edna with long-frustrated needs for affection and warmth. Edna responded amply. They quickly developed an intense and highly sexual relationship. Henry recalled this whole episode with a sense of wonder. He recalled, "I never knew that there were so many ways of doing sex. She really knew her way around!" He wondered whether Edna was really a nymphomaniac; they spent nearly all their time together in bed. He finally decided to move in with Edna and they lived together for about six months.

As he became increasingly involved with her, his yearnings for a close and enduring relationship grew. He decided that he wanted to marry Edna. When he announced this intention to the family, there was an expectable explosion. The family was violently opposed to marrying a woman who had been twice divorced. They regarded her as a prostitute. His Uncle Clem and Aunt Mary were adamant. He could choose between Edna and them. If he chose Edna they would cut off any support financially and wanted to have nothing to do with him ever again in the future.

Henry's rage was boundless. Once again his family had interfered in his life. Once again he had been made a helpless victim. They had tried to run his life ever since his mother died, and now they were doing it again. He became suicidal. He ran out and got a bottle of sleeping pills. Edna was frightened and called his doctor. When they reached him he had swallowed the pills and was comatose. He was felt to be psychotic at that point and was hospitalized again—this time for nearly a year. Henry recalled with particular bitterness that when it was decided to hospitalize him his father came and talked to the doctor. His father told the doctor. "This boy has had the best of everything!" He felt deeply resentful about his father's attitude. "I can't understand how they could be such pricks and bastards!" Henry exclaimed. He felt that his father and his family had never really cared anything about him.

There is little doubt that this was a severe regressive episode. There were no hallucinations or frank delusions, but his recollections and impressions were confused and disorganized. He was deeply depressed. The conditions at the hospital—a state institution in the Midwest—appalled and frightened him. He saw how unhappy other patients in the hospital were and how their lives were ruined. He feared that he would fall completely apart and end up a vegetable like so many others. He felt absolutely abandoned and alone. There was no one to whom he could turn. He felt that his father and his family had completely turned against him and abandoned him. Gradually his condition improved and his depression receded. When he was finally released from the hospital he had nowhere to go; there was nowhere that he felt he belonged. He stayed in that area for a while. He got a job and was able to support himself. But he felt isolated, he felt that he wasn't making it. He had difficulty making friends and finding a place for himself. He finally got the idea that he needed to get to another place, make a new life for himself, get a new job, and, above all, find some woman to whom he could get close, with whom he could have a warm and lasting relationship, whom he could love and who would love and take care of him. Thus he decided to come to Boston.

Therapy

Therapy with Henry turned out to be a fascinating experience, particularly, as we shall see, in that he re-created the cycle of intense sexual involvement, disappointment, and suicidal wishes that had plagued him so often in the past. The beginning of his therapy was primarily taken up with the telling of a story. He painted a broad picture of himself as deprived, unfortunate, ill-starred, rejected and abandoned, unloved and unwanted. Each episode of misfortune or rejection was recounted with generous amounts of self-pity and depressive affect. In short order he began to weep about his losses. For months every interview was given over to long periods of profuse weeping. The tears just seemed to well up from some inexhaustible inner fountain.

Gradually the tears and the self-pity were more and more accompanied by expressions of bitterness and hatred. His rage was directed at first toward his aunt and uncle who had treated him so badly, but increasingly toward his father. It was interesting that soon after his admission, I called his father by long distance. The father was irate at being called. He wanted nothing to do with Henry. He shouted into the phone that Henry had never lived up to his expectations, that he would never amount to anything, and that as far as he was concerned he no longer considered Henry his son. He made it quite clear that he did not want to hear from me again—no matter what! The degree of anger seemed quite inappropriate. But I could see what Henry had to deal with.

Henry was feeling very sorry for himself, feeling that he was an unfortunate and helpless victim, and blaming everyone in his life who had let him down and disappointed him. He complained that no one of them cared about him or loved him at all. Sally, Edna, his aunt and uncle, his father, they were all cold and callous. They didn't care about him in the least. The only one who had cared was his mother, and they had taken her away from him. He clearly saw his mother's death as due to the antagonism between herself and his father and father's family. They picked on her and cut her down mercilessly, until finally they killed her. And they picked on him, too, but he would not let them do it any more. He felt that he hated them all and that he would have nothing to do with them.

He confessed at one point that he felt badly about crying so much in his therapy sessions. He had never been able to cry like that before, but he felt humiliated by it. He also feared that I wouldn't be able to take it. If he poured out his worst feelings, he fantasized that it would damage me or hurt me in some way. He began to feel that I was the only one in his life who cared, the only one he could trust. The others could not be trusted, because they were only out to use him or get something out of him. But he began to see me as a strong, supportive, and caring figure—the good father he had always wanted and yearned for, but never got. He said at one point that he just wanted to come into my office, put his head in my lap and cry his heart out. His fantasy was that I would hold him and care for him.

It was clear in time what his copious tears were about. On one hand he was still deeply mourning his mother. His loss had affected him profoundly. He saw her death as part of a conspiracy involving the father and the father's family. They hated her because she was so good. They hated her Catholicism and they picked and beat her to death. He viewed the family conspiracy as evil and maliciously destructive. And they had turned their evil power against him because he was like her. His older brother had escaped because he looked like his father. But Henry became the victim because he looked like his mother and because he was her favorite. He was never able to get to any feelings of resentment directed toward his mother, however. She remained the pure, loving, giving, caring mother. Any resentment for her not protecting him from his father's rages and beatings, or for her dying and abandoning him, were strongly repressed.

One day, in one of our therapy sessions and without any preliminaries, Henry suddenly presented me with a list of literary works. He announced that the list contained the whole story of his problem. In response to my puzzlement and inquiries, he would reply that the whole story was right there and that if I read these works I would surely understand his problem.

The whole episode was a puzzling attempt to intellectualize and distance himself from the turmoil of distressing emotions that he was experiencing. While the lists amounted to a protective maneuver—both from his own inner experience and from my intrusion on his inner life—they were also expressive of his inner anguish and confusion. The literary world reflected in these works was one of inner anguish and inner destitution and emptiness. It reflected a constant search for meaning and wholeness that is repeatedly rebuffed and denied. It evoked a world in which the torment of the unbridgeable gap between souls, between man and woman, between man and man, was the basic human affliction. There was the eschatological preoccupation with meaning, with destiny, with death, and the yearning for the face of the ultimate parent who stood beyond all reality and all life. It is not without reason, then, that in the light of our patient's inner turmoil we find Durrell writing in the last pages of *Justine*, "Underneath all his preoccupations with sex, society, religion, etc. (all the staple abstractions which allow the forebrain to chatter) there is, quite simply, a man *tortured beyond endurance by the lack of tenderness in the world''* (italics supplied). Henry was ceaselessly seeking, like the starved and lost souls of Kafka's imaginary world and Durrell's exotic and erotic Alexandria, that ultimate tenderness and loving acceptance that had been denied him.

A Reenactment

It was at this juncture in Henry's treatment, after about six months in the hospital, that the next important development in his course occurred. He gradually became involved with a young married woman on the service. It was understandably difficult to keep such involvements unnoticed on an open hospital service, so that the matter was brought to my attention almost from the start. Needless to say, any sexual activity among patients was proscribed by hospital rules and frowned on by the administration. So the increasingly intense affair was a prominent focus of Henry's psychotherapy for a considerable period of time. The affair was of interest in that it provided another repetition of the same pattern that had led Henry to the brink of suicide so often before. My therapeutic effort was to try to help him explore what was happening in order to help him gain some insight into the motivations behind this severely self-defeating and self-destructive aspect of his life.

The affair started by Henry and this woman playing games together. He described playing Scrabble with her. As they played he said that certain words kept coming up that indicated to him that she wanted him. He claimed that he couldn't believe his eyes, couldn't believe that she was trying to seduce him. However, he could not be specific about what the words were or how he knew that she was seducing him. The factual data were impossible to determine. But Henry's rather consistent style was to portray himself as the passive victim in all his relationships with women. They were always the ones who seduced him, involved him sexually, roused his desires and passions and then rebuffed and rejected him. He was never able to acknowledge his own role in these relationships, and so it was in this one. He consistently maintained that he did not know what was going on, that he had been led on unwittingly and naively, and that he was helpless to stop his sexual involvement. It seems more likely that what actually happened was more a product of his erotomania than any actual seduction.

The intensity of the relationship was building. They started having intercourse. Henry continued to present his role in the relationship as passive and helpless. She was seducing him. She was the one who insisted on intercourse. He placed the entire responsibility for the relationship and for what happened in it on her shoulders. He absolved himself of any blame. He could not see that what was happening was detrimental in any way to her or to himself. If anyone was hurt by it, he felt it was certainly not her, but himself. He felt that if anyone was being taken advantage of, it was himself.

He drew the analogy between his affair and his relationship with his wife. She was the one who had enticed and come after him. She had seduced and involved him, gotten him to marry her, and then had turned against him and abandoned him.

As the relationship intensified he became more suicidal. It seemed that as he became more involved sexually his need to feel close and to merge with the object became increasingly intense. He could not get close enough. As his needs became more intense he felt increasingly frustrated and impatient. He complained repeatedly that what he wanted was a really close and permanent relationship. But no relationship seemed capable of satisfying this deep and primitive for total inclusion and total merging. The intensity of this need, its engulfing quality, and its uncompromising demandingness all frightened the woman. It stimulated her fears of being swallowed up and consumed by this passionate need.

Abandonment and Longing

The woman continued her sexual involvement with him for a time, but then began to think better of it. She started to pull back from the relationship. Henry's response was to become increasingly depressed and suicidal. Finally, one night after she had refused intercourse with him, Henry fled from the hospital threatening suicide. The whole process was a step-by-step repetition of the pattern of involvement he had experienced with his wife and with his several girl friends. He had become quickly immersed in the relationship to the point at which his intense needs for closeness were brought into operation. The impelling peremptoriness of his demands then acted to frighten the woman and to make the relationship more difficult and problematic than loving. As the object began to draw away, Henry would begin to feel the intense sense of abandonment and longing, as well as the intense rage that went along with it. The rage against the abandoning object was turned into depressive affect and suicidal ideation.

During his excursion from the hospital Henry called his father on the telephone. In his deep longing and in the face of his feelings of rejection and abandonment, he turned regressively to the earlier and ambivalently wished-for object. Once again the yearning was to be frustrated and rebuffed. His father was not in the least sympathetic with Henry's difficulties. He told his son angrily that psychiatry was a load of bunk and that the only trouble with Henry was that he was lazy. If he were to get off his ass and get a job, everything would be all right. He also refused to help Henry in any way. The son's response to this was not unlike that he had always had to his father—frustrated rage and pained disappointment. The experience revivified his feelings that his father had never wanted or cared about him, that he could never talk to his father, and that any contact with him was only going to be hurtful. His father told him never to call again until he had made a success of himself. This triggered off a series of intense outbursts of bitter resentment against the uncaring father who had given him nothing, had left him with rapacious and manipulating relatives, and who had done nothing to help him make his way in life. Henry bitterly blamed his father for the fact that he was a failure, that he could never be a success.

The hospital affair provided a template for the repetitious pattern of involvement, disappointment, and self-destructive wishes that had become a familiar theme in Henry's life. His inner needs for closeness and passive dependence led him into relationships with women that quickly and easily became too close and highly sexualized. Part of the impetus derived from his infantile wishes and needs, but part also derived from his homosexual wishes and fears. The desired closeness to the female served as a buffer and a defense against homosexual wishes, behind which, of course, lay the frustrated yearnings for closeness to the father. These impetuous needs seemed inevitably to draw him into inappropriate relationships, those in which any semblance of close and meaningful union was foredoomed. As the relationship heated up and became increasingly intimate, Henry's infantile wishes to merge with and totally encompass the object were swept into action. The frightening intensity of these wishes caused the woman to withdraw. The withdrawal was felt by Henry as a recrudescence and reenactment of the loss and abandonment he had felt when his mother died. The unresolved grief, the sense of loss and abandonment, of inner despair, of disappointment leading to frustrated rage, and the turning of rage into depressive channels, brought him to a paroxysm of self-destructive agony. His suicidal ideas and gestures were an attack against the frustrating and rejecting objects—at the most superficial level the immediate object, the woman who could not be totally possessed, and at a deeper level the lost mother and the unreachable father.

Then one day he suddenly disappeared from the hospital. He wrote several subsequent letters. He returned to the town where he had been a dental student. He returned to treatment with his former therapist, got a job, and was hoping to reenter dental school and finish his studies. I could not help but wonder whether the therapeutic process had generated enough insight to enable him to avoid the pitfalls of his remarkable repetition compulsion, or whether he had achieved a plateau from which he would once again stumble blindly and fall.

DISCUSSION

Depressive Aspect

It seems clear from the clinical material that we have presented that Henry's case is predominated more by depressive elements than by paranoid ones. The depressive reactions stand forth in center stage, while the paranoia forms a slender subplot that weaves more or less subtly through the acts of the drama. We have seen this delicate interplay and interweaving of depressive and paranoid themes in all of our patients, in each case striking a different balance and a different proportion. The ratio of paranoia and depression is an unstable one and shifts from time to time and from stage to stage of the patient's illness. The shifts can also be detected and followed through the course of the patient's therapy.

Blaming

Henry's paranoia expressed itself primarily in his reluctance to accept any responsibility for his condition and state of life and his consistent displacement of responsibility to objects around him. He blamed the women with whom he had been involved for the failure of his relationships with them. He blamed his aunt and uncle for their hardheartedness and callousness. Things went wrong because they put too much pressure on him, because they made impossible demands on him, because they refused to give him enough money, etc., etc. He blamed his father for not keeping the family together, for killing his mother, for abandoning him to his relatives, for not caring or loving him, etc. He blamed his wife for not loving him enough, for being too dependent on her parents, for making more demands on him than he could meet. Now here in all this is there any suggestion that he might have had a role in his disappointments and failures, or that things might have turned out differently had he been more resourceful or self-reliant. He could not see that his own expectations that other people should take responsibility and deliver him from his burdens was a major contributing factor to his problems.

The blaming mechanism was his ready resource. When his affair with the nurse turned to disappointment, he quickly cast the blame on his doctor friend—who got him into the mess by introducing him to the girl and who would not take care of him and protect him as Henry felt he should. In the hospital when the question was raised of his difficulties in relating to other patients and his inability to communicate to any of the people in his environment, the blame was put on them because they were so ungiving, so uncommunicative, so unresponsive, so uncaring, so withdrawn. The blaming mechanism reached its greatest intensity in Henry's delusional convictions that his relatives were trying to hurt him, to make him grovel and to see him writhe in pain and misery and suffering. In his most paranoid moments, he saw them as slowly and agonizingly trying to kill him, just as they tried to kill his mother.

Henry is a good example of what I would call the "unsuccessful paranoid." His use of denial and projection are not adequate to protect him from the depressive core of his illness. The depression and the paranoia become linked together. The paranoia does not succeed—as it so often does in paranoid patients—in relieving him of the burden of depression. The depression persists and at times seems exacerbated by his paranoid attitudes. The more intense his resentment and rage against these offending objects and the more bitter his blaming of them for what they have done to him, the more intensely does he feel himself to be the helpless victim and the deeper does he sink into self-destructive despair.

Identification with the Victim

Central to his pathology was his strong sense of identification with the victim-martyr mother. He saw himself as linked to her as the helpless victim of a conspiracy between his father and his father's family to humiliate, torment, and destroy himself and his mother. Time and again he expressed the utopian wish that by his suffering those hateful people would learn love. I can only conjecture that such sentiments were heard from his mother's lips. His identification gave him a strong element of passive and almost feminine dependency. He needed desperately to cling to objects, to be taken care of and protected. Linked to this was the latent homosexual wish to submit himself to the strong and brutal father, so that the price of love would be humiliation, subjection and submission, and complete subordination to the brutalizing object.

The identification with the victim-martyr mother formed the depressive core of his pathology. There was also a strong identification with the aggressor father. This pathological introjection was motivated by his intense longing and yearning for closeness to the father. That longing persisted through the whole course of his illness. The ambivalence toward the father was intense. The loving aspect and the yearning for father were repressed and became fused with the passive feminine longings for masochistic surrender. The hostile and destructive components were introjected and joined to a punitive and destructive superego. It was these elements that were susceptible to projection and formed the reactive core of his paranoia.

This is the only case we have in which the parental figure seems to have in fact been brutalizing and openly sadistic to any marked degree. The parental sadism has generally been more subtle and subdued. But Henry's case certainly mirrors the configuration that is identifiable in all of these male paranoids—a combination of identification based on the degraded and devalued victim mother and the distant, yearned-for, but unavailable father. The frank brutality of Henry's father only adds a terrifying dimension to the essential elements of rejection and parental unavailability. The impact of his father's brutalizing on Henry was to intensify his need to avoid and repress any aggressive impulses of his own. Aggression became linked for him with fantasies of destructiveness and hurtfulness, thus forcing him even more in the direction of a protective and unaggressive posture of passivity and masochistic victimhood. His father's hostility, in other words, drove him more intensely toward dependence on his mother and increasing identification with her.

Narcissism

One important factor that needs to be kept in perspective in this case is Henry's pathological narcissism. This element consistently eluded therapeutic exploration, but it formed a central dimension of his pathology. His narcissistic expectations and his sense of infantile entitlement were prominent in all of his pathological involvements. He felt that the world owed him a comfortable living, and he resented having to work for it or earn it. He felt that his family owed it to him to take care of him and provide for him, and that any demands on him to work for what he got or to have to meet certain standards of performance were unjust and a cruel denial of what he felt was owed to him. He felt that the women he was involved with should surrender everything for his sake, that they should hold nothing back. Whatever was held back was interpreted by him as withholding from him, as rejection and abandonment. The pattern of narcissistic expectations and entitlement, frustration and disappointment of these expectations, and the resultant rage has been described by Murray (1964).

The narcissism in our patient strikes at an even deeper level. What escaped our scrutiny and exploration in this patient was his ambivalence toward his mother. Positive and idealizing attitudes were kept in the forefront, while the negative and resentful attitudes were submerged. In the patient's unresolved grief and mourning over his mother's death, the rage at his mother's betrayal and departure, and the deeper narcissistically motivated wishes for her death were completely beyond the patient's reach. His destructive fantasies were repressed and the destructive wishes projected onto his father. Murray observes in regard to one of his patients that

> . . . the continuous repetition compulsion of his assumed role in mother's injury is stimulated by the occurrence of any phallic impulse. Reaction to this is intolerable guilt and regressive flight to the fantasies of her pregenital world, which serves to weaken his reality sense. The narcissism validates his defensive attitudes and allows him to use all love objects as a milieu for the focus of his explosive rage and projection devices. Magic control, omnipotence, power of the wish, and full entitlement are all at work. But there is also a tremendous insecurity, because if one of these pregenital functions fails, the all-or-none law works and his world falls apart (p. 495).

In the present case, we can presume that the activation of phallic libidinal as well as aggressive impulses activated the latent and unconscious fantasies of his destructive wishes against his mother and thrust him regressively into the ambivalent torment of desperate longing to be close and fantasies of destroying the love object by the very closeness. The narcissism and the sense of entitlement to mother's love or its equivalent served both to buffer these fantasies and to justify his magical expectations and projections.

The Paranoid Influence

We should not overlook in our consideration of Henry's pathology, the tremendous influence of his father. It was not merely the introjection of the aggressive father-image that contributed to his paranoia, but it seemed also that the father himself was severely paranoid, quite possibly psychotically paranoid. We have no way to document this influence, but we know that in other instances the paranoia of one or the other parent can come to dominate the unconscious as well as conscious attitudes within the family. The family constellation here of a paranoid father and a masochistically depressed mother has become quite familiar in the study of these cases, particularly in families with paranoid sons.

Henry's paranoia, therefore, was very likely a product of both pathological internalizations derived from both parents and learned attitudes and styles of thinking derived particularly from his father. The paranoia established a place for him, as well as a form of identity by which he could situate himself in relation to his family and others around him. Henry's position as the helpless victim and martyr established a pattern of relationships which defined a community to which he belonged and within which he had a certain role to play and certain functions to serve. Within this complex of pathological relatedness, it also provided him with a sense of identity which he otherwise lacked. This identity, however, was a pathological creation, a pseudoidentity that sustained its life by its continued involvement in the pathological interaction within the family system. In Henry's case, as in so many others, the internalization of the paternal and maternal introjects as component parts of the family interaction system formed the internal core of the paranoid pathology. The external drama of the family system is thus reenacted in the inner stage of the patient's psyche, and in the moments of frankly paranoid projection is rehearsed once more on the external stage of interpersonal relations.

CHAPTER 14

Mr. James J.

THE PATIENT'S PROFILE

Psychoanalytic Approach

The present case is one of the most central in this study. The material was gathered over the course of intensive psychoanalysis through a period of four years. The analysis was conducted on a five-session-per-week basis and was based throughout on more or less classic notions of psychoanalytic therapy. The patient was treated on the couch, and the method of free association and interpretation was employed. It must, therefore, be appreciated that this case is based on material that is both considerably more detailed and voluminous and in many respects qualitatively different from that of the preceding cases. These differences between a more traditionally psychoanalytic and a psychotherapeutic approach, however, offer us an opportunity to inquire into the paranoid process from a somewhat different perspective—one that lends considerable support to the impressions and tentative hypotheses that have emerged in our study to this point.

An important emphasis that the material from this patient provides—as well as the following patient, who was also treated in intensive psychoanalysis—is that the paranoid process operates in significant ways even in patients who are relatively healthy and who can be regarded as potentially good candidates for successful psychoanalysis. The personality structures of the previous patients in this series have all been borderline or psychotic. It was quite clear, however, that Jim possessed a well-established and solidly neurotic character structure. The study of his case, therefore, is particularly interesting in that the paranoid process here displays itself in a much better integrated picture of personality function than we have had opportunity to see to this point.

Presenting Complaints

In the beginning Jim did not present an unusual picture. He decided to seek treatment while he was still in his graduate studies. The precipitating event had been the disruption of a relationship with his girl friend, which proved to be somewhat traumatic for him. But this was superimposed on more chronic difficulties. His relationships with his family had been difficult and quite tense since he had come to graduate school. Moreover he suffered from long-standing difficulties in day-to-day living. He felt himself to be rather shy and insecure; he had difficulties in relating to people and to his friends, both male and female. He constantly felt tense and worried. His world was discolored by almost constant anxiety, and at times this was nearly incapacitating. This was particularly the case when he felt called on to perform—when he was called on in class, or when he wanted to ask a question, or when he had to make some form of presentation to his class or other group, or when he had to talk with any of his professors or his adviser. At such times he would literally shake with anxiety; he would sweat profusely and feel that he would surely bungle what he was doing or make a fool of himself. He would begin to stammer, could not organize his thoughts, forgot important things that he knew he otherwise had firmly in mind—and generally deteriorated in his level of functioning.

This was also very much the case in his relations to women. He felt awkward and embarrassed in asking girls for dates, feeling sure that they would turn him down, or that they thought him funny or ugly or repulsive. He could overcome his doubts and anxieties to a point, but when the relationship became somewhat closer, his difficulties increased. When he came to a point in the relationship at which sexual activity seemed possible, his anxiety markedly increased. He became obsessed with the idea that he could not perform sexually, and felt that he only wanted to plunge in and get it over. His major complaint was premature ejaculation; this was a fear that pervaded all of his thinking about sex and was proof to him of his sexual inferiority and inadequacy.

In the face of these anxieties and the incapacitation related to it, Jim decided to seek help. He was treated in psychotherapy for a brief period of a few months in a local clinic. He gradually came to realize that his problems were deep and long-standing. When the psychiatrist suggested that he seek more extensive treatment—psychoanalysis—he responded positively, if hesitantly, and was referred to me.

I saw him in several evaluative interviews vis-à-vis. He was in his early twenties, short in stature but stocky and well-built. His manner was at first noticeably tense and his speech produced with some pressure and was punctuated with nervous laughter. His level of anxiety was obviously high. During the course of the first interview he seemed to relax somewhat and his nervous movements seemed to disappear. He was able to relate with apparent warmth and spontaneity, expressed himself fluently and with some insight—and despite his anxiety left a rather good impression. There was no evidence of thought disorder or severe depression. Despite the incapacitation of his anxiety, he had managed to maintain a rather high level of achievement and performance in his academic pursuits. In the last interview he was able to show some humor and warmth, and generally seemed well able to accept and utilize my questions and a few trial interpretations. He seemed sincerely troubled and well motivated, and I felt that he would be a rather suitable candidate for analysis. My diagnostic impression was that he presented a symptomatic picture consistent with anxiety hysteria and that his personality was structured along the lines of male hysteria with an admixture of obsessive-compulsive features. I felt he would be an interesting patient.

Family Background

We can stop for a moment at this point to review briefly the essential data of the score or so of years that preceded his coming to analysis. Jim was born in a large midwestern city in the years following the World War II. He was the third of three sons born to his parents. His mother and father were both of Jewish extraction. His father owned his own business, a small manufacturing company. The family struggled along through difficult times financially, and it was not until after the war that the father's company took hold and became a relatively successful venture. Thus it was not until Jimmy was about five years old that the family moved from a relatively poor section of the city to a more comfortable middle-class neighborhood. There was a definite turning point in the family history from the hard times to the better times that followed the war. Consequently the family situation that Jimmy experienced when he was growing up had a quite different flavor from that experienced by his older brothers.

In the early years the family lived in a more-or-less ghetto atmosphere. They lived in an almost exclusively Jewish neighborhood. The family was closely surrounded by relatives. The grandparents—the mother's parents—lived nearby and an aunt and uncle lived in the flat upstairs.

The extended family group was provided by mother's family. Father's family had been disrupted early. His father had died when father was quite young and his mother had abandoned the family. Consequently father had little to do with his own family of origin. Jimmy's own family, however, provided a nucleus around which the other elements in the extended family seemed to cluster. The father was a shrewd businessman and through the years had been consistently able to provide his family with a steady if not comfortable standard of living. He was also the support and provider for the grandparents and in part for his wife's brother's family. He was generous in giving to them even through the hard times. When his business had begun to flourish, the father was able to provide a more comfortable standard of living.

The grandparents were a revered elderly couple. The grandmother was a gentle, sympathetic, and kindly old woman. Jimmy felt very close to her and recalled warm feelings toward her from his childhood. He regarded her as the real source of strength in the family. Grandfather was a reserved, stoical, revered elder of the community—white-bearded, quiet, patriarchal. Jimmy held his grandfather in awe. But he felt a great distance between himself and the revered old man. He struggled to find ways of relating to the imposing figure of his prophetlike grandfather but never with any great success.

While Jimmy's father was the major source of support for all these people, he was relatively passive and permissive at home. He left the management of the home to Jimmy's mother. Mother was the dominating and intrusively controlling Jewish mother. When Philip Roth's novel *Portnoy's Complaint* came out, Jimmy remarked any number of times on what a strong similarity there was between Portnoy's mother and his own. While Jimmy saw his father as weak, ineffectual, compliant, and as giving in to whatever demands were made on him and never having his own way in family matters, he saw his mother as a dominating, controlling, intrusive, undercutting, critical, devaluing. One of the constant enigmas for Jimmy was how his father could be so shrewd and successful in business and respected in the community when he was such a weak and ineffectual person at home.

Joe

Jimmy's oldest brother, Joe, was eleven when Jimmy was born. In his childhood years, Jimmy idolized Joe. He was the big brother who was admired, popular, who knew his way around and was successful with girls. Joe was the family playboy. He never studied, had many girl friends, was constantly dating and going to parties. Joe's frivolous ways were a source of anxiety for his parents, but for Jimmy they were the hallmark of the cool and smooth "operator" who knew how to get what he wanted and never failed in getting it. Joe was everything that his father was not in Jimmy's eyes. When Joe came into the room he was immediately the center of attention. When Joe went to a restaurant he knew how to get the best table. Joe was the slick manipulator who could get what he wanted out of people, particularly out of women. He could have any girl he wanted. Father was none of these things. Jimmy would tag after his older brother. He loved to be with him and recalled that on some occasions, Joe would take Jimmy out with him on his dates. They would share a fantasy game—namely, that Jimmy was Joe's son. Jimmy felt that he would much rather have had Joe for a father than his real father, who seemed so clumsy and weak.

The contrast between his childhood fantasy ideal and the reality of Joe's adult life was difficult for Jimmy to accept. Joe married a rather ordinary girl and settled down to a rather humdrum, ordinary, if moderately successful, business career. He became an ordinary Joe, an idol with clay feet. Jimmy's fantasy was that marriage and the influence of Joe's wife were the responsible causes of this reversal. This reflected his feelings about the relationship between his mother and father. Jim had always felt that his father could have made it in big business if only he had been willing to take the big gamble, the risky investment that would have spelled the difference between ordinary moderate success and the big time. As he saw it, father never did this because Jimmy's mother would not allow it—that mother was the cautious and conservative one who held father down because she could not tolerate the idea of his becoming too successful or powerful. Jimmy saw women generally as powerful and controlling, as exercising a limiting and repressive and demanding influence on men.

Harry

The other brother was Harry. Harry was a good seven years older than Jim, and in many ways was one of the most important figures in Jim's life, second only to his parents. Harry was the family genius. His scholastic performance was consistently brilliant. He provided a radical contrast to Joe whose interests were decidedly nonacademic. Harry was an intense and dedicated student. He poured his energies into schoolwork, to the detriment of all other interests. He had few friends and dated very little. The picture that emerges from Jimmy's accounts of him is that of a serious, withdrawn, angry, contemptuous, severely obsessional and highly intellectualized and moralistic adolescent.

Jimmy's relationship with Harry over the years was extremely difficult and highly ambivalent. In a way he also idolized Harry and greatly admired his intelligence and accomplishments. Harry set an incomparable standard for him. Jimmy wanted to emulate his brother and gain some of the recognition and acceptance he felt Harry received for himself. He also felt that it was an impossible task, that he never could match or even approach his brother's standards of performance. He also strove to be with his brother and gain a closer and friendlier relationship with him. This too seemed impossible. Harry did not seem to want to have much to do with his baby brother. In childhood games, Harry would play tricks on him so that Jimmy would be made to look or feel foolish or stupid. Sometimes Harry and his friends would trick Jimmy and run away, leaving him alone.

Harry went away to college. When he would come home, his arrival was awaited with great pleasure and anticipation by little Jimmy. He would look forward to Harry's homecoming and think about the exciting things that they could do together. Jimmy was usually disappointed. Harry would always have other things to do and never seemed to have much time for Jimmy. Jimmy's greatest delight was when he could get his brother to teach him something. At times he would try to get Harry to help him with his school assignments, but usually any help was accompanied by severe criticisms and comments that left Jimmy feeling that he was just too stupid and incapable of ever doing anything. Jimmy recalled, for example, that he showed Harry his Bar Mitzvah speech—one he had written himself—and asked Harry for help in improving it. Harry tore up the speech and wrote another, saying that Jimmy's effort was worthless and stupid. Harry was often hypercritical and sarcastic, and Jimmy felt this as a severe rebuff and rejection. We shall see that there was built into this relationship an intense sibling rivalry.

Early Dependence

Jimmy was clearly the baby of the family. His mother tended to be obsessively controlling, overly anxious in her mothering, overly solicitous and overly protective. He was toilet trained early, and this was apparently a matter of importance for mother, as well as a measure of her capacity and performance. In general he seems to have been rather close to her in these early years and quite dependent. He recalled an occasion in these years when his parents decided to go away for a brief vacation. They left without preparing him—obviously apprehensive over his response—and arrangements were made for him to stay in a nursery while they were away. As soon as he realized what was happening, he started screaming and sobbing incessantly. He struggled and resisted going to the nursery, screaming and sobbing all the while, until his parents had to abandon their plans and return home.

The Operation

The most significant single childhood event occurred when he was almost five years old. It had been discovered previously that he had a patent ductus arteriosus. This congenital anomaly became the focus for mother's obsessive doubts and guilt feelings and apparently served to intensify her anxieties and her obsessively overprotective mothering. The condition was treated as a shameful secret, a blot on the family and a mark against mother. Visits to the doctor were shrouded in secrecy and concealment; mother would go to elaborate efforts to conceal the fact of the ailment from relatives and friends. The reasons for the anxiety and concealment were kept from Jimmy, and, of course, his fantasies as to what was going on flourished. Finally the decision was made to operate and Jimmy was taken to the hospital. The operation came as a bolt from the blue for Jimmy. He had not expected it; in the parents' typical style they had avoided the subject and concealed it from him. Being taken to the hospital came upon him as a sudden, unexpected, terrifying, and traumatic event. It was an unprovoked and undeserved attack, and coming at the height of his Oedipal involvement, it gained all the overtones of a castration attack and a punishment for forbidden Oedipal wishes.

The operation provided an important focus for Jimmy's further development. He recalls his amazement at the huge scar that stretched across his chest. He expected it to fall apart any moment. He felt himself to be weak and defective, vulnerable, marked for life as impotent and worthless. These fantasies were reinforced by the fact that the family moved during his period in the hospital, and Jimmy came home to a new house and a new neighborhood. He felt that the change was because of the family's shame and need to conceal his defectiveness. The whole circumstance of the operation and its reverberations served to intensify his dependence and clinging to his mother. He became in her eyes and in his own the defective and weak child, who had to be taken care of and protected, who had to be given special consideration and who could not tolerate being subjected to the normal give-and-take of competition and effort in the harsh world. Effectively, Jimmy and his mother entered into a collusion to keep him a weak, defective, castrated, and impotent little boy.

The situation surrounding the operation was complicated by the fact that in the year preceding it Jimmy's mother developed a hyperthyroid goiter with exophthalmos. This condition must have contributed to her own level of anxiety and to her hyperactivity. In Jimmy's recollections, she became like a "mad woman." Since Jimmy's own congenital condition was discovered when he was just about two-and-a-half years old, it is quite likely that some of the symptoms associated with mother's hyperthyroidism grew apace with the anxiety over his condition. Jimmy could not avoid connecting his heart defect with his mother's illness, and drawing the deeper conclusion that somehow he was the defective child who had severely and permanently damaged his mother in being born.

The Baby

The image of his specialness and defectiveness was carried on into childhood. Around the house he was the "baby." His pranks were laughed at and his naughtiness excused as "cute." He continued to be close to and dependent on his mother. He dreaded spending any time away from her. When his parents would be planning an evening out of the house, he would raise a terrible fuss—crying and screaming—with the result that frequently they would alter their plans and either take him along or stay home. As a result he was often taken along to restaurants or nightclubs, adventures which he found stimulating and exciting. At other times when his parents had to stay home, he felt guilty and powerful in that he could make them do as he wished. Jimmy was unquestionably a very bright and precocious child, and he quickly mimicked adult mannerisms. He recalled wanting to dress like an adult, wanting a checking account of his own when he was seven, trying to order drinks in a restaurant, etc. These were all treated as "cute escapades" by the family.

Throughout most of his childhood until about the age of eleven, Jimmy was enuretic. He had been toilet trained early but the enuresis started when he was about three-and-a-half. It is interesting that this enuresis coincides in time both with the onset of mother's illness and with the mounting anxiety over his heart condition. The enuresis was a source of constant shame. It was a conclusive proof that he was defective and nothing more than a baby. The enuresis continued unabated during his latency years. The family tried every ruse and device to get him to stop. He and his older brother shared the same room. On one occasion Jimmy switched his beds around. His mother wasn't sure which bed was his, and identified it by smelling the sheets, Jimmy recalled the embarrassment he suffered on this account. Finally his mother got a machine that rang a bell every time he wet. The enuresis stopped in a few short weeks after they started using the machine. He was then twelve years old.

School Problems

School was also difficult for Jimmy to cope with. From the beginning he was reluctant to go. He looked down on the other children, and resented the fact that he had to be put into school with these little kids who didn't know anything. Jimmy found it difficult to accept the fact that he was a child. He found it disconcerting and embarrassing when he did not know everything that was being taught. He could not admit it when he didn't understand something or missed something in class. He missed a class in the first grade in which the vowels were taught. When he returned to school all the other kids seemed to know about this and he didn't. He struggled for months with his feelings of missing out, of falling behind, of not being able to match up to the other kids and of being a failure.

School was also a place of competition. Jimmy did his best to avoid this. He avoided doing too well in school. He learned readily but refused to study, or better to have to study. He always passed comfortably, but never did work commensurate with his abilities. He was afraid to try because trying meant running the risk of failing in the attempt to supersede others. His only moderately successful performance was cast in constant contrast to his older brother's remarkably successful scholastic record. Whatever Jimmy achieved, therefore, was not enough. It could not be enough. So there was little point in trying very hard to do better. He was foredoomed to be a failure.

Going to school produced an interesting morning scenario. Jimmy would almost invariably put off getting himself ready for school. He would get up late. He would find all sorts of ways of wasting time to avoid facing the inevitability of going to school. He was always anxious, apprehensive, and fearful of it. The inevitable outcome was that he would finally realize in a panic that he was going to be late if he tried to walk or run to school. So he cried to get his mother out of bed to drive him to school. Mother would rouse herself and plunge into his panic. She would become almost maniacal—leap out of bed, throw her coat over her nightgown, and frantically rush Jimmy to school in the car. It seems hard to come to terms with, but this scenario was rehearsed morning after morning with considerable regularity through the years of Jimmy's schooling. It served rather obvious purposes of both reinforcing his anxieties and sense of dependence on his mother and of confirming his own inability to deal with the demands of reality. It also displayed his mother's unique qualities of anxious concern and her inability to take a firm and disciplining stand on any given issue.

Stealing and Deception

Another interesting aspect of Jimmy's childhood experience was his stealing. When he was about seven or eight, he began filching dimes and quarters from his mother's purse. This continued for some time without apparent notice, but then also continued for a considerable time with little doubt that it must have been noticed. Little Jimmy, however, lived in dread that his crime would be discovered. He was given a small allowance, but it was obviously not enough. He felt that he was driven by an almost insatiable desire for things. He felt himself to be a miserable child. He kept searching for and trying to get that one thing more that he hoped would make him happy. He wanted more candy, one more yoyo, another toy, always something else from what he had or was given by his parents. He even occasionally stole things from the local stores. A little later in his career he started gambling on a small scale. When he lost he needed money to meet his debts. At one point he was forced to sell a rather extensive stamp collection that his brother Harry had had and had passed on to him. All of this surreptitious activity led to elaborate devices for concealing his activities and rather imaginative fabrications to explain the telltale indications noticed by his family. Deviousness and concealment became a leitmotif of his experience. It seemed impossible that his parents should not have been aware of some of this activity, and it was not clear whether they were somewhat amused by it or whether they simply chose to avoid the whole matter and the obvious problems that it reflected. Jimmy was trying desperately to fill the inner emptiness and defectiveness that he felt in himself; it was a hole that no amount of external possessions could fill.

The Outsider

Jimmy's primary and secondary schooling took place in schools near his home. These years were unhappy ones for him. He generally stayed close to home and particularly to his mother. His dread of school continued. When school was over he would not spend much time with friends in after-school activities—particularly sports—but would retreat to the safety and special security of home. He felt himself to be alien and different, an outsider. He was generally a loner and associated only minimally with his agemates. His forays into the outer world and his attempts to break out of this unhappy pattern was accompanied by fears and anxiety and were followed by an unavoidable sense of failure and defectiveness. He kept himself from joining in with other kids on the block in their childhood games. He kept himself an outsider and retreated to the specialness and protectiveness of his home. Rather than dealing effectively with this pattern, Jimmy's mother apparently found it gratifying and seemed to relish and encourage this closeness and clinging.

Jimmy was able to emerge somewhat into the life of his peers. He got his courage up enough to play some football, and found to his amazement that even though he was small in stature he could hold his own. He lived in constant dread of being injured but played in spite of his fear. Social life was difficult for him. Asking a girl for a date was a trial by fire. He dreaded the ordeal—often avoided it. Girls were threatening and terrifying for him—but his late latency and adolescent mind was filled with sexual fantasies and wishes. These too were terrifying and produced considerable anxiety in him. They also had to be kept secret and concealed with as much deviousness as he could muster, not only from his parents but also from the girls. If they knew what was on his mind they would be disgusted and horrified.

Away from Home

The decision to go to college away from home was a major one. It meant a step away from his dependence. He took it with reluctance, diffidence, and ambivalence. In college, away from the anxious protectiveness of home and mother, he blossomed to some extent. He became a good student, getting straight A's. He took up wrestling and wrestled on the school team. He became more involved with girls, even to the point of having his first sexual experience. These steps toward adulthood were taken with considerable anxiety and self-doubt. He constantly had to struggle with the wish to retreat to home and mother: he had to worry and become anxious over his fears of being too successful, of going too far, of overreaching himself and falling inevitably on his face. The specter of his defectiveness and of his unavoidable failure dogged his every step. Often he found ways of defeating himself and of proving to himself the inevitability of his failure. In wrestling he became moderately successful, yet always lost in the big match. He recalled one match in the finals of a big tournament when he felt that he clearly had victory in his grasp, but somehow managed to lose. He associated this with his competition with his brothers, particularly Harry. Harry was inept in any form of sports. When they played squash Jimmy would often be in the process of soundly trouncing his brother, but then would suddenly and inexplicably let up, and Harry's dogged determination would win out. Jimmy was once again the loser in the competition with Harry.

Jimmy graduated *magna cum laude* from college—an accomplishment he was forced to devalue and underrate. But it brought him to a choice point in his life. Should he go on for further schooling? There was no question but that he would. But doing what? He was interested in economics and desired rather strongly to pursue a doctorate in that field. His parents would have none of that. They insisted that he pursue one of the professions so that he could make some money and have a comfortable life. Jimmy was adamant. The battle lines were drawn. The family turned to Harry for counsel. Harry sided with the parents, and Jimmy was once again the loser. He bitterly resented this whole episode, seeing it as a telling example of how his parents interfered with and tried to control his life. He was particularly bitter about Harry's interference. He saw them as conspiring to ruin his life and to keep him in a less successful, unhappy, and subordinate position.

His subsequent applications for law school were carried out with his usual diffidence, procrastination, and delaying tactics. He characteristically couldn't decide on what schools he would apply to, and then sent his applications in late. Despite his efforts, he was accepted by one of the most prestigious schools in the country. His success was confounding, and it served only to thrust him into a situation of competitiveness and accomplishment at a high level. His basic conflicts over aggression, achievement, success, and maturity were stirred to new intensity, and thus precipitated his increased anxiety and his desperate need for help.

These are the broad lines of his history as he approached the analysis. We can already discern certain patterns and themes that predominated his neurosis and character. But these take on added meaning and depth in the light of the material that emerged only gradually from his analysis. We would like to turn to a more detailed examination of these multiple and overlapping themes, striving in their presentation and recounting to provide an impression of their evolution and modification in the course of his therapy. This will hopefully provide some sense of the manner in which the analysis was able to make some inroads on his paranoid convictions and on the dynamic and genetic roots of his paranoid process. Finally, we will want to try to focus the way in which these interlocking themes played into the process of the analysis and into the transference relationship as it developed in the analysis.

Mother

As the analysis progressed the first important figure to emerge was the patient's mother. There was little doubt that her influence on him was strong and decisive. He saw his own birth as a device to provide something to occupy his mother's later years. He was intended and conceived as her toy, her plaything, something that she could amuse herself with and derive gratification from. There was in him both an intense wish to fill this gratifying function for her, and at the same time an equally if not more intense bitterness and resentment that he was regarded by her and by the family as the "baby" and that his attempts to express or assert himself were met by amused smiles and laughter and comments that what he was doing was "cute." He resented the attempts to treat him as a child, even, or especially, when such treatment was entirely appropriate.

Jimmy's mothering experience was colored strongly by mother's anxiety and guilt-ridden hyperconcern. From the very beginning the level of anxiety was high and the pattern of mothering tense, obsessive, worrisome, and concerned. Jimmy's mother was a first-rate worrier, and very typically tended to think in terms of the worst and most dreadful possibilities. There was a preoccupation in her mind with the possibility of congenital defects. It is not clear from available information whether there was any family background or history to support such concern, but in any event when Jimmy's heart defect was discovered it brought all mother's worst fears to the fore.

The obsessive quality of her caretaking was a predominant feature. She insisted on regular feedings, by the clock, a doctrine she strongly urged on her sons' wives in the care of her grandchildren. The clearest manifestations of this obsessiveness with Jimmy, however, was in the toilet-training context. Jimmy was toilet-trained early. He was put on the potty at regular times and left there until he did his job. Performance on the potty was a performance for mother's pleasure. Insofar as this interaction can be reconstructed, it seems to have carried the elements of his own later and more articulated ambivalence. Pleasing her was gratifying but it carried with it the overtones of having to please and of submitting to her wishes. To encourage his urinating and defecating, mother would tickle his penis. The masturbatory and seductive aspects of this behavior are unmistakable. For Jimmy the price of gaining mother's approval and her affection was giving in and performing for her pleasure.

The dependence and closeness in their relationship was marked. He clung to her and as he grew older was beset by fears of losing her. When she would leave him for any time he would have terrifying fantasies of her being killed in an accident and never coming back. Such departures were always accompanied by his screaming and crying and carrying on. Mother was entirely incapable of dealing with this behavior realistically or effectively, but would respond with excessive concern and placating maneuvers. This quickly became a channel for his manipulating her. His childhood efforts were strongly directed to gaining her acceptance and approval and to building a close, protective, intimate, and special relationship to her. He effectively made himself her baby. Much of his attempts at "cute" behavior were directed to her. He would make up special secrets which he would tell only to her, with the specific objective of excluding his father and brothers from the special relation. They could not share the secrets which were privileged communications between himself and his mother. Her interest in the secrets was a special form of attention that she paid to him—related to the special attention he got on the potty.

Sexual Interest

As Jimmy grew older this special relationship with his mother grew into a mutually gratifying and rather seductive enterprise. His attachment to his mother was intense and highly sexualized. His interest in his mother's body was intense. He would bathe with his father, but he was not permitted to bathe with his mother. He felt rejected and excluded and his curiosity became actively involved in wondering about the difference between mother and father—what was being hidden that he should know about? He was convinced that mother also had a penis. On occasion mother would walk around in the house nude. This was extremely exciting for Jimmy. He would sneak a look at mother's body, but with great fear of getting caught looking and of having his wishes and thoughts discovered. He would feel guilty about these episodes, but the curiosity and excitement were too great to prevent him from looking. He was quick to notice that mother did not have a penis—or at least did not seem to have one. He fantasized that she must have one but that it was folded somehow between her legs. He experimented with his own penis, folding it between his legs so that he would look like mother. He decided that if he could get some idea of what it was like between mother's legs, he would understand what it was that was so secret and forbidden.

One factor that contributed significantly to these concerns was the fact that until the time of his operation—and for a while after—Jimmy slept in his parents' bedroom. His memories of this setting were exceptionally vivid. He remembers the frequent occasions when he could watch his parents performing intercourse. Particularly vivid were his memories of the times when mother was on top. There was something frightening and fascinating in it for him, and he fantasized that his mother was "wild" in bed with his father. He recalled his guilt and apprehension that his parents might catch him looking. His parents would often have sex in the morning, presumably before Jimmy would be awake. But he was often awake, and remembered his hesitation and uncertainty as to whether he could roll over in bed or start getting up even though he was awake, for fear of seeing his father and mother doing something he shouldn't see. He also recalled his feelings of resentment and rejection when his mother would tuck him in bed, kiss him good-night, and then get in bed with his father. Why wouldn't she go to bed with him? If there weren't something wrong with him, she would.

Jimmy also frequently slept with his parents in the same bed during these years. He recalls his fears of wetting and being scolded for it. He also recalled his wishes to examine his mother's body and to touch her breasts, and his fear of being discovered.

Later, of course, during his latency and early adolescent years, it was regularly mother's custom to come and say good-night to him. These were moments of special intimacy for Jimmy. Usually she would rub his back before going to sleep. This was exciting for him, and he would playfully try to get her to rub lower on his back over his buttocks—"below the belt" as he put it. There was a seductive quality to this interaction. Mother also seemed to derive a certain stimulation and gratification from this seductive interplay. He recalls his wishes for her to play with his testicles and fondle his penis, an obvious throwback to the potty seduction which had been stimulating for mother and son. Mother never gratified his wish, however, and would always call off the game just when he felt it was possible that she might do it this time. In time, he would reduce the tension after she left by masturbating, still wishing that she would do it to him. Her refusal to indulge his wishes and fantasies was taken as another proof that there was something wrong with him, something that repulsed her and turned her away from him and back to his father.

Maternal Involvement

Jimmy invested considerable effort in striving to gain his mother's affection and attention. All through his latency and early adolescent years, he would retreat from the anxious and uneasy world of his peers; he would come home from school, avoiding the insecure and dubious involvement with his peers, and retreat to the security and specialness of home and his relationship to his mother. He would try to engage her in conversation, telling her all the interesting things that happened to him, making up stories to keep her involved in the face of his own perception that adults were not very much interested in his child's world. He felt he could never compete with or be as interesting or worthwhile as his big brothers. He complained about these conversations with mother that he always seemed more involved and invested in them than she did. Often when the telephone would ring mother would interrupt the conversation to carry on a trivial and unimportant dialogue with a friend of hers. These interruptions would infuriate Jimmy, a resentment that was revived and reexperienced by the occasions when the telephone in my office would ring and I would interrupt a session to answer it.

There was always a secret specialness and an exclusivity to this relationship. Jimmy clung to it as a protective haven against the threats and inevitable defeats that awaited him in the outside world. The pattern extended itself even through his high school years. He recalled spending one summer about that time frequently going with his mother to visit art galleries and shows. They were interested at the time in buying a painting, and the enterprise became a special project between Jimmy and his mother. They shared a special knowledge and appreciation that the rest of the family was excluded from. It was an especially bitter pill to swallow when the final selection had to be subjected to his father's approval. It was a violation of the specialness that Jimmy had built around the whole project.

Ambivalence to Mother

While this dimension of the persistent striving for closeness and approving attention from mother was a predominant theme throughout Jimmy's development, there was also a countertheme that carried the opposite side of his powerful ambivalence. He came to regard his mother as inconsistent and unpredictable. He would tell her things that he thought amusing or interesting, and without apparent reason and without any warning she would become anxious and worried and upset. He began to see her as a powerful, intruding, destructive, overpowering, and overwhelming figure. She controlled his life; she intruded into every corner of it—she was possessive, demanding, castrating. Everything that was done was interpreted in terms of its effect on her; it was done either *for* her or *against* her. If Jimmy did not get a haircut, he did it to hurt her. If he did get a haircut, he did it for her sake. Everything that was not congruent with her wishes became an attack against her and a rejection of her. Everything that happened that was not exactly as she wished or expected became a calamity, a catastrophe. And there was no distinction between great calamities and small. They all elicited the same response of hurt, tormented self-pity, and outraged injustice; she was a helpless victim, tormented by the selfishness, lack of gratitude, carelessness, thoughtlessness, stupidity, stubbornness and willfulness of her children. When this reaction was turned against Jimmy, he writhed with guilt and anguished remorse. He felt himself to be evil and worthless. His underlying conviction that he was the evil and hurtful and defective child that had somehow damaged and burdened his mother by his birth received a measure of reinforcement and reintensification.

While his first report of his reponse to his mother's controlling and intrusive behavior was cast in terms of his frustration and sense of oppression and constraint, his continuing complaints about her gradually began to introduce a different note. While he bitterly complained about the way she intruded on and controlled his life, it became increasingly clear that he elicited and fostered this behavior in his interaction with her. This aspect of the interaction became clear in a particularly horrendous episode. He had returned home for a visit. On these visits he would defiantly flaunt his violations of his mother's standards: he refused for example to trim his shoulder-length locks on the grounds that it represented a surrender of his freedom and individuality. On this occasion he left a joint of pot where mother was sure to see it. She did, and this precipitated a horrendous scene when he came home one evening. Mother accused him of being a dope addict, wept bitterly, carried on histrionically as though he had been a hardened criminal and was lost forever. This hysterical argument raged for hours and ended by mother resolving that she would "sit shiva" for him. The episode was a paroxysmal expression of the more constant pattern of their relationship, but it was also quite clear, for the first time to Jim, that he brought about and encouraged such interactions with his mother.

Jimmy's later relationships with his mother were caught up intensely in the ambivalence that had permeated them from the beginning. He saw her as intruding, controlling, dominating, and particularly as inserting herself between himself and his father. Jimmy longed for a closer relationship and understanding between himself and his father, but it always seemed that his mother was interfering and keeping them apart. She would break into their conversations, she would change the subject when their conversation turned to subjects they could talk about, etc. He saw her more and more clearly in the course of his analysis as an extremely neurotic, anxious, and troubled woman. This was an important appreciation for him to attain, since he had formed an impression that placed the blame on himself as weak, defective, unlovable, and hurtful. He began to see that mother had problems of her own. His early visits home were destructive of any sense of distance and control that he had achieved in the analysis. He would regress to the same pattern of ambivalent interaction with her, to his own chagrin and disappointment. Gradually his ability to stand on his own grew and with it the ability to become less responsive and involved in her neurotic behavior.

The inescapable tension of involvement vs. noninvolvement formed a major dimension of his analysis, and displayed itself in disguised and displaced ways in other aspects of his experience—as we shall see. Involvement meant surrender to mother's obsessive and worrisome and guilt-provoking anxiety, but it also meant receiving her attention and a privileged and special involvement with her as the defective child, the helpless baby who needed to be protected and hovered over with anxious concern. But to be uninvolved meant rejection and isolation, being cut off from all contact and all affection. Jimmy was caught between these unhappy alternatives. He was able to recognize and face his fears. It was considerably more difficult for him to recognize the manner in which he clung to his mother as well as the extent to which her anxious and obsessive concerns about him were gratifying to him as well as to her. His weakness and defectiveness was *the* special secret that they shared between them and which no one else understood and accepted. Even more unavailable, however, was the intense rage and resentment that discolored his relationship to her, not merely the anger at her controlling and intrusiveness, but the deeper rage at her frustrating his Oedipal wishes and infantile longings.

Father

Jimmy's relationship to his father was less definite in its outline, and, in contrast to his feelings toward his mother, the material regarding his father was slow in taking shape and emerging during the analysis. In his childhood memories his father was a distant and remote figure. There are no memories of any close contact with father, Jimmy's complaint was that he never paid any attention to him and never spent any time playing with him. At this early level the father's role seems to have been defined in Jimmy's mind largely in relation to his mother. This role was complicated and confusing in Jimmy's mind from the beginning. His father was the sole source of support for the family. How he accomplished this and where father's money came from remained a source of mystery and wonder for Jimmy all through his childhood. But at home he clearly saw his father as a weak and ineffectual man who was controlled and dominated by Jimmy's mother. Mother ran the house and made the decisions, and father had no other choice but to comply with her wishes and to give in to her.

Mother and father would often argue. In these family fights, Jimmy rarely, if ever, saw his father coming out the victor. Mother always won, mother always had her way. She was the powerful, controlling, dominating one, who always got her way. Father was the weak, vulnerable, manipulable sucker who got taken and was pushed around by mother and the family, and who had no say of his own. This image of father was reinforced by Jimmy's fantasies about the parents' sexual activities. He saw his mother as wild and insatiable in bed, as attacking father and submitting him to her sexual wishes. The images of mother pulling down father's pants and of mother lying on top in sexual activity were tied in with this fantasy. True to his ambivalent view of father, however, this view was varied by his seeing father as demanding sex of the mother and forcing her to submit to him. Sex was seen as a battleground between the parents, in which the alternatives were victory or submission. In the battle, Jimmy could never be sure whether mother was attacking father, or father was attacking mother. There was no room in this consideration for tenderness or loving affection.

Jimmy saw his father as exceptionally susceptible to defeat and hurt. In part—as a reflection of his Oedipal wishes—he sought to inflict defeat on his father. The testing ground was his relationship with his mother. The closeness and secretive specialness of his interaction with her was also aimed at his father. If his father could take his mother off with him to bed, then little

Jimmy could take mother away from father through these confidences and special secrets. It was especially humiliating for him when mother would divulge these little secrets to father, treating them as "cute" and "amusing."

Alongside this wish to defeat and replace father, there was the fear of hurting him and putting him to shame. He felt guilty in exploiting and taking advantage of his father. Money was an important area in which this was played out. When Jimmy would try to get more money out of his father, an increase in his allowance, or money for something that he wanted to buy—stamps, toys, a yoyo, candy, etc.—he would feel that he was bilking his father and taking advantage of him. He would be caught between the fear of hurting his father and the desire to get what he felt he needed. To be successful and to obtain what he wanted for himself were identified in his mind with an attack on and defeat of his father.

His father's weakness was a constant disappointment to Jimmy. He wished desperately that his father were stronger and that he would control how things went at home. He wished that his father would stand up to his mother and not let her control everything. But his father never did. He always gave in and permitted mother to run the show. Jimmy's fantasy was that mother ran father's life too, as well as his own. He fantasied that father could really have made it big, become a powerful business tycoon, if it had not been for mother holding him down and preventing him from taking the big gamble, the one fantastic speculation that would have made him rich and powerful. He felt that mother kept father from this success because if father were rich and powerful her own influence and strength would be threatened. It was important, therefore, for mother to keep father under control, to keep him down.

Ambivalence to Father

Despite these wishes, he saw himself and his mother as allied against father in using and exploiting him. Jimmy felt embarrassed by the father's ignornace, his social ineptitude, his crude and homely mannerisms, his lack of cool and smoothness. He could never understand why people in their community liked and respected him, sought his advice, elected him to important posts in the synagogue, etc. The family belonged to a Jewish country club and the time spent there was by-and-large an embarrassment for Jimmy. He saw his father as crude, clumsy, and just not knowing his way around. Jimmy felt quite superior to his father in this regard. His father made his way through life by being compliant, agreeable, non-threatening—a nice guy. Jimmy would have none of that; he didn't want to be regarded as a "nice guy nothing." He wanted power, and the respect and influence that went with it.

While Jimmy felt angered by his father's inability to put mother in her place—and despised his father's weakness—he was also angered by his mother's continual interference and interruption of his relationship with his father. He had a strong yearning for greater closeness to his father. He felt his father was an enigma and that he could not understand him. The yearnings carried a homosexual component. Jimmy recalled occasions when friends would be visiting the family and Jimmy would have to sleep with his father. His fear was that his father would roll over on him in the morning and kiss him, just as he rolled over on mother. The fear was compounded of a wish and a reaction to the wish.

It was clear that in Jimmy's mind his regressive wishes to remain his mother's special dependent and defective baby were paralleled by his thinking of any moves toward greater maturity or independence in his thinking or action as attacks on his father calculated to defeat and humiliate him. Both of these currents in his thinking had to be thoroughly worked through in the course of his analysis. He gradually became more aware of these infantile wishes and fears, and came at one point to a showdown with both his parents. The confrontation was generated over his vacation plans to go on a long car trip with his girl friend. The family was horrified and mortified. The scandal of traveling unchaperoned with a girl was too much for mother. Mother launched another all-out attack. Jimmy saw her as the protagonist and the struggle that was launched as a last-ditch battle for survival. Everything was at stake. He saw his father's role in this as basically sympathetic to Jimmy's cause, but as manipulated and controlled by mother. Mother threatened to completely disown him if he went on the trip. Jimmy hung on desperately, thinking in his despair of calling me for advice and support, but was finally able to withstand the onslaught. When it was clear that he would not budge, his parents begrudgingly gave in. When the battle had been won, father capitulated, and immediately sat down and wrote several checks to provide funds for Jimmy's expenses on the trip. Jimmy was torn by his intense wishes to be on good terms with them, to give in to their wishes, to be their good little boy—and at the same time to free himself from their domination and control—especially his mother's. The risk was twofold. He ran the risk of losing his mother's affection and being rejected by her, and he ran the risk of defeating and humiliating his father. Father's writing out the checks was the terms of surrender, a humiliating defeat as Jimmy saw it.

There was little doubt that the whole relationship with his father was colored strongly by Oedipal concerns. We have seen the clear indications of Oedipal rivalry, but it was also clear that Jimmy saw his father as the powerful and threatening castrator. Father had in fact never once spanked Jimmy. On one occasion he had become angry at Jimmy and was going to spank him, but Jimmy ran away and his father couldn't catch him. The boy was incensed by this episode, particularly by the humiliation that would be involved in getting spanked—something that was applied to naughty children.

Jimmy in no way wanted to think of himself as a child. But even though father was generally a kind and generous man, there was plenty of room left for Jimmy's Oedipal fantasies to play themselves out, particularly in view of father's relative taciturnity and uncommunicativeness. In one dream he pictured father bringing him a box of cookies which turned into penises. He associated this with the time of his operation, when father had brought him a box of cookies. He also recalled his fear of the operation and the mutilation it incurred. His fantasy was that his father was unable to perform the operation-castration himself, so he hired the doctor to do it. Father was a powerful castrator who collected penises and who was the malign force behind the operation. We shall see more of this later.

The opposite side of this fear and the anxiety related to it was Jimmy's wish to gain his father's approval and to prove himself worthy of his father's affection. He fantasied himself becoming successful and making lots of money so that he could support and take care of his father in his old age. He would become the "good son" in relation to his father—just as he envisioned his father having been toward his grandfather—his mother's father. Father's own father had abandoned his family when father was still a child, and father had never really known his own father. But he treated the family patriarch with great deference and respect, as well as supporting the grandparents financially. While little Jimmy fantasied such a role for himself as a means of gaining his father's approval, he never seemed to be able to fill the bill. Such success seemed always beyond his grasp. He was always the weak child who could accomplish nothing significant and who could never do enough to make father proud of him. The standard of comparison, of course, was always his older brothers. He could not measure up to or match them: father could be proud of them but not of Jimmy. When it became clear, however, that father was quite proud of Jimmy's accomplishments—especially in his college and law school careers—this was very difficult for Jimmy to accept. The specter of becoming too good, too successful, too powerful and important dogged his heels—together with the fantasied defeat and humiliation of his father that it entailed.

Closely related to this wish to gain his father's approval, there lurked a deeper and less accessible fantasy. Jimmy felt that in having a child in their advanced years his parents had had enough of boys and that they had wished for a daughter. He attributed this wish particularly to his father, but also to his mother. His birth, then, had been a disappointment to his father. Jimmy felt inadequate to meet the standards set by his brothers, and cherished the fantasy that if he were only a girl he could then have found approval and affection in his father's eyes. To be a boy meant to have to compete with his brothers, on their terms. His older brother Joe had been the personality boy—the social success—and his brother Harry was the family genius. How could little Jimmy be expected to match their performance? He could find no separate and different way in which he could be a success on his own terms. If he had been a girl that different way might have been available to him. As it was he was nothing but a defective male child, doomed to inevitable failure.

The Nemesis

These same elements were at work in Jimmy's relationship with Harry but at a more intense, more ambivalent, and more conflicted pitch. The sibling rivalry was severe, and terribly threatening for Jimmy. His ambivalence was strong and highly conflictual. On the one hand he admired his brother and wanted to emulate him. But alliance with Harry meant subjugation and humiliation. If Jimmy asked Harry for help with homework or something he was trying to write, it meant subjugation to a brutal criticism and having to do the whole thing Harry's way. Jimmy would come away from such attempts feeling bruised, beaten, worthless, and humiliated. Harry's treatment obviously enraged him, but he was quite unable to tolerate or express that rage.

The anger found its own forms of expression. One channel was exploiting his closeness with mother, something that irked and galled Harry. Jimmy found other ways as well. He managed to mess up his brother's valued stamp collection, with the effect that Harry poured out even more vituperation and used the episode as further proof that Jimmy was nothing but a nuisance and annoyance. In getting back at his brother Jimmy was inevitably providing ammunition for Harry, and also reinforcing his own image of himself as a messy punk little kid who contaminated and befouled whatever he touched. On one occasion Jimmy struck back, by kicking his brother in the testicles. He was terrified by the fact that he could hurt his older brother, even though he secretly relished his brother's pain. On another occasion Harry got angry at him and chased him into the house. Jimmy slammed the screen door on Harry's finger, damaging it severely. His own angry wishes to harm and injure Harry were frightening to him. The translation into real pain and inflicted damage made the possibility of realizing his murderous wishes even more devastating.

Whatever the flavor of their childhood relationship, Jimmy projected the image of Harry as his childhood nemesis. Consistent with his inability to feel and express aggression it took a considerable amount of work in the analysis before Jimmy was in a position to deal effectively with this relationship. He gradually drew a portrait of his brother's rather sadistic and demeaning treatment of him. As might easily be imagined, it was only in the transference that much of these feelings came to light. We will see more of the transference development later, but an important part of it was Jimmy's feeling that I was out to get him, to criticize and put him down, that I would sooner or later use anything he told me against him, particularly any of his foibles, peccadilloes, or secret thoughts about his weakness and inadequacy. He was convinced that, no matter how kindly or considerately I treated him, one day without warning and without reason I was going to turn on him and tear him apart. These feelings went back at least in part to his relation with Harry. He came to realize that in large measure his anxieties that people were going to attack him or put him down or criticize him or demean him or make him look foolish or stupid—all palpable fears that dominated his life—had a recognizable source. His feelings about me were clearly related to the fact that Harry would often lead him on by asking him questions, and then unexpectedly spring the trap on him and ridicule his foolishness. Jim expected the same of me, and of others in his life. As we shall see this aspect of the transference was highly overdetermined.

A Child Forever

Thus Jimmy was surrounded by adults—people who knew more, could do more important and interesting things than he could, take initiatives that he could not, be allowed privileges and gratifications that he could not. He resented his lot—that of the baby of the family—and strove mightily to act in adult ways. These attempts were obviously inappropriate, and turned out to be merely attempts of a child to mimic and ape the antics of his elders. Inevitably they provided a source of amusement and condescending interest for the adults around him. He complained of feeling like a midget, as if he were the possessor of an adult mind that was by accident trapped in a child's body. He wanted desperately to be treated like an adult, but he was not.

There was a curious quality to this perception of himself. It was as though he felt himself forever doomed to being a child. He had no operative concept of development. There was no appreciation of himself as growing up and developing his capacities through time, and thus little by little becoming an adult. He absolutized the disparity between himself and his elders. He was small, weak, incapable, bumbling, ignorant, and defective, and there was no idea of ever being anything but that. *They* were strong, capable, effective, smart, and adult, and it seemed that they were always so.

This attitude carried over to Jimmy's life concerns; he could not envision himself becoming more proficient and capable in his professional work. It was as if in his mind he was unskilled and ineffective and others around him were knowledgeable, effective, and capable. There was little concept of his own ability to learn and to develop skills and capacities, and to become as proficient as the older and more experienced professionals who surrounded him. There was no concept of his being able to change and grow in the analysis either. He seemed to cling to the notion that he was defective and inadequate and that there was no possibility of changing this state of affairs. Any attempt to do so or any thoughts that such might actually be taking place were illusory.

The Operation as Castration

Unquestionably the most central event in Jimmy's childhood experience which contributed significantly to his pathology and which focused so many of the determinants was his heart operation. The event was undoubtedly traumatic. He remembered his mother's anxiety, the months of seemingly endless visits to doctors, the secrecy and concealment—all of which was unexplained to him. He had no inkling of any trouble, he remembered no symptoms or incapacitation that would have indicated to him that anything was wrong. Mother apparently anxiously ran from doctor to doctor trying desperately to escape the inevitability of an operation. Finally one cardiac surgeon was able to convince her of the necessity of the procedure. Jimmy recalled that he was like a great white god, and he and his mother were like worshiping natives at his feet.

Mother characteristically approached this whole anxiety-laden episode with deception and deceit. She kept the problem from Jimmy. Not surprisingly, one of Jimmy's major preoccupations was that things were being kept from him, that people were holding out on him and not telling him the truth. In the analysis, for example, he repeatedly and often accused me of holding out on him, of not telling him how hopeless and worthless he was, of not telling him the awful truth, of deceiving him and concealing things from him. If I made an interpretation he would often feel that I was holding back the real truth, or I was only telling him part of the story and that I was concealing the rest because he was just too weak to take it or be able to handle it.

The operation was severely traumatic. It came out of the blue—as an "unprovoked attack" as Jimmy put it. The memory of the operation was conflated with a previous episode that had taken place when Jimmy was about three. There was a severe polio epidemic and Jimmy took sick. Mother's anxiety skyrocketed. He developed some symptoms, and was immediately rushed to the hospital in a panic. In this atmosphere of panicked anxiety, it was decided in the emergency room to do a spinal tap to rule out polio. Jimmy was terrified. His mother was distraught, and kept insisting that the doctors perform more tests to make sure he did not have this or that. This only further intensified Jimmy's anguish and terror. He reflected in retrospect that it seemed as though she were wishing that something was wrong with him.

There was little doubt that Jimmy experienced the operation as a castration. He was terrified of the event, overwhelmed by the fear that there was something dreadfully wrong with him that would never be cured. He felt that the family wanted to get rid of him, as something shameful and embarrassing, a blot on the family reputation that had to be concealed and hidden from the eyes of others. His family was moving to a new neighborhood and he fantasied that they wanted to get rid of their secret shame. His associations led to the thought that his father did not want to get rid of him himself, so he hired the doctor to do the job. The doctor, who he admired and who seemed so wonderful and powerful, also turned out to be the one who cut him. The parallels to the analysis were quick to be drawn. Analysis was envisioned as "surgery with a dull knife." When the family would ridicule or make fun of him, Jimmy used to say, "If you're going to do surgery on somebody, you should at least use an anesthetic!" He saw me in terms of the powerful doctor who would cut him up and castrate him.

After the operation he recalled vividly sitting on the front steps of his new home, feeling very lonely and forlorn. He had no friends, he felt weak and scared, still wearing the bandages from the operation, afraid to move out of fear that the bandages would fall off and the great wound would come open and he would die. His preoccupation with the wound lasted for years. He would literally spend hours in front of the mirror, examining and testing the scar. He would examine the long track of the incision that ran from the front of his chest all the way around to the back. He was afraid to touch it—even years later—for fear that it would come open. He could not imagine how it could stay together. He imagined it falling open like a vagina; it was his castration, and it thus became the focus for all his castration anxieties, his fears, his conviction of defectiveness and vulnerability.

There was along with this conviction a curious persuasion that the operation had not been curative at all, that it had not in fact made him whole and healthy. He had been "fixed," but to his mind the connotation was threatening—"I'll fix you" or "I'll fix your wagon!" He felt that he had had a job done on him, and that the operation, instead of being a remedial procedure, had in fact been a castrating attack in which he had been "fixed" as a fitting punishment for his Oedpial wishes. The conviction that the operation had not been a cure was one that he stubbornly clung to in the face of all evidence to the contrary. It was also a conviction that his mother seemed to embrace as well. For both of them the operation became the conclusive evidence that he was the special, weak, defective child who needed special care and special treatment.

Secondary Gain

There was another side to the whole episode that also played an important role. After the terror of the operation, Jimmy became the object of considerable attention. The attention was extremely gratifying and came from all sides. The family members came to visit him in the hospital and brought him all sorts of gifts and good things. Even Harry was nice to him and treated him with kindness. Through the operation, then, Jimmy achieved the attention and special consideration that he had always wanted. The important aspect that lay behind this experience was that he gained such gratifying treatment by reason of his being castrated, weak, defective. This provided a model for much of his subsequent behavior. He continually and repeatedly sought to relate to important figures in his life by being weak and compliant, by presenting himself as inept and ineffectual and thus nonthreatening, by seeking help and protection from the strong figures around him—seeking that quality of special relationship in which he could feel nonthreatened and nonanxious, a relationship in which he was clearly the weak and nonthreatening inferior. He acted this role out in many of his relationships, particularly in relation to male figures, professors, administrators, doctors, etc. It played a considerable role in the analysis, as we shall see.

These motifs came together in the way that Jimmy used the operation material in the analysis. It was at first an important discovery, and he excitedly traced out the various influences and implications in his thinking and behavior. More and more, however, he used it as an explanation and inevitably as an excuse for many of his problems. He began to present his associations to events connected with the operation as though they were interesting pieces of confidence between himself and me. These were pieces of data that would interest and please me. He was in fact using the operation in the analysis in an analogous manner to the use he made of it with his mother. It was part of his attempt to gain a special and confidential relationship to me, so that I would not harm him because he was so vulnerable and weak. All of these aspects of his use of the operative experience had to be painfully and repeatedly worked through before any shift in his convictions regarding the operation became apparent.

Defectiveness

If there was any theme that dominated Jimmy's analysis from beginning to end it was the theme of his defectiveness. There was no area of his life and experience that it had not touched and within which it had not worked its malign and often devastating influence. As is clear from the material we have already considered, the theme of defectiveness dominated his early life. It was embedded in his relations with his mother and in his relations with his father and brothers as well. He and his mother shared the secret conviction that he was a defective and damaged child, that he was doomed to be inadequate, weak, dependent, without strength or power, that he could never grow up to be a man and stand on his own feet. This almost symbiotic conviction was given shape and substance by his heart defect and the circumstances of his operation. The operation was not a correction of his defect and a cure; it was rather a confirmation of their worst fears and the irrevocable proof of his inner defectiveness and impotence.

Jimmy tried desperately to find ways to compensate for these overriding and inexorable inner feelings of defectiveness and inadequacy. He tried to act like an adult, but he had little or no idea of what that was all about. His attempts amounted to nothing more than pantomimes and childish mimicry of adult ways of acting. The family's amused response only served to reinforce his feelings of inferiority, and also reinforced his feelings that they did not understand what was going on inside him, and what is more, they did not care about it. He tried to find ways of making himself more interesting or of making himself seem worthwhile. His conviction was that anything he had to offer was worthless and of little value to the adults around him. So he invented things. But it was difficult for Jimmy to keep the lines between fantasy and reality clear. He had to invent stories to support the credibility of other stories. It was not clear whether his mother could see through this confabulation or whether she actually believed his tales. In any case she encouraged the tale-telling all through his childhood.

Not only his storytelling, but also his stealing, were very much related to his underlying sense of defect. He felt that there was something lacking in himself that he tried to fill up with external things. As a child he felt that having more things would somehow make life better for him, and ease the burden of his unhappiness. He always seemed to feel that if he had that one more thing, then he would be able to make it, he would be able to be accepted by the other kids, be able to join in and not have to feel that he was different or that he was an outsider. He always wanted another toy, another cap pistol, another yoyo. When he entered the latency phase of collecting he had to have the biggest collection of stamps, he wanted to have all the comic books that were ever printed; he did not feel satisfied until he had assured himself that he had everything. His parents bought him a record player, and he wished for a record collection, and desperately felt that he had to have every record imaginable. This latter wish carried over into adult life. He kept a record collection, but always felt that it was worthless and inadequate, because it did not have every conceivable record in it. He would experience strong impulses to run out and buy up every record he could afford, just to make his collection less defective. He saw such possessions as mirroring himself; they were defective and inadequate, even as he was. The magical wish was that somehow by building them up and making them bigger and more complete, he could manage to build up his own inner sense of emptiness and incompleteness.

This need to fill up and compensate led to his stealing. He felt desperately that he needed more things than his parents were willing to give him, that they did not understand his need, and he could not explain it to them. He stole at first small amounts of money from his mother's purse. He bought candy or small toys with it. He would give the candy to his friends, a bribe for their acceptance. Then he began to steal from other places. He would shoplift items from local merchants. He could not explain his need, but he then had to explain how these things came into his possession. He quickly became involved in an incredible series of complicated subterfuges and involved lies. His life seemed to be built on deceit. Finally his parents found out about the shoplifting. Their response was shame and anger. He was suitably punished. But they made no attempt to understand what lay behind his behavior. He felt even more forlorn and lost, forced to face his emptiness and defectiveness without any means of redeeming it. During the analysis, there were several episodes of shoplifting—regressive expressions of his need to compensate for his inner lack that vividly revived these childhood feelings.

Failure

The projection from the inner to the outer world affected his whole experience. He could take care of nothing, could make no investment in preserving or maintaining things that he owned. His car was in a constant state of disrepair. His apartment was a mess. It was as though he put everything in a state of defective functioning or disarray, for it was only in that context that he felt comfortable. He constructed the world around him to fit the inner image of himself. His car would not start properly and was literally falling apart because it belonged to him—that was as much as he deserved or could expect. Anything valuable that he received was sure to be destroyed in his hands. His parents bought him an expensive stereo rig, and he was convinced that it was too good for him, that he would mess it up, that he would not be able to take proper care of it, that he would quickly break it and reduce it to a state of uselessness and defectiveness.

The same set of convictions permeated his work and professional activity. In school he was constantly convinced that he was going to flunk exams, fail courses, and that if he were called on in class to answer any questions he would blunder, if he spoke up in classes or seminars he would make a fool of himself and let everyone know how little he knew and how stupid he was. In his professional work he was nearly paralyzed at every step. If he had to make a telephone call, he would put it off and agonize over his fear of messing up the negotiation and making all sorts of foolish mistakes. If he had to write a letter he was convinced that he would be unable to do it, unable to say the right things, that he would mess things up, etc. It can easily be imagined that these preoccupations with failure and the conviction of messing up became even stronger in proportion to the importance or significance of what he was trying to do.

Presenting a case in court was a paradigmatic situation of assured failure. To begin with he had great difficulty in negotiating with other lawyers. His fears of making mistakes and appearing like a foolish little kid to them, and his concomitant anxiety, made this procedure very difficult for him. He felt that he was a little kid, interfering in adult business, messing around up to a point. Before that point they would be amused and condescending; after it they would be angry at him and would attack him in retaliation. In court he felt like a small child, playing an adult role for which he was not ready and not suited. Because of his short stature he had to look up at the other lawyers. Looking up at the judge was like looking up at some great and powerful figure. He constantly felt that the judge would see through him at any moment, see that he was ineffective, stupid, that he was carrying out a charade of being a lawyer, that he didn't deserve to be in court, and the judge would then throw him out of court, humiliate him and cast him out ignominiously. These feelings were directly related to similar feelings and fears that he had had in relation to his father. Standing before the judge was like an Oedpial child standing in fear before the powerful, castrating father of his fantasies.

Such humilitating discovery would finally reveal his worthlessness and defectiveness. Jimmy preserved a sense of deceit and subterfuge in all of this. He constantly felt that he was deceiving people, pulling the wool over their eyes, and that any moment he would be found out and unmasked. This feeling permeated all his relationships. He felt it in school when talking to his professors, when talking to other lawyers, in his relationships with women—and not surprisingly in his analysis. He persistently expressed the feeling that he was messing up the analysis, that he wasn't able to do it right, that the analysis was after all going to prove once and for all his defectiveness. His concern focused especially on free associating. He constantly complained that he couldn't do it, that he was just messing things up. When he experienced a relatively free flow of associative material, he would feel that it was wasting time, "bullshitting."

There were several interesting aspects to this inner sense of defectiveness. One was that Jimmy fantasied that the end results of his weakness and incompetence and impotence was to be suicide. There was no other way out; it seemed the inevitable and inexorable consequence, born out of irrefutable logic, that he should have to kill himself. He was doomed to failure, and it was simply mistaken and misguided to think otherwise. What was interesting was the invariant mode of suicide: he would stab himself in the heart. His fantasy was elaborated in relation to the analysis. He fantasied that one day I would turn on him and tell him the farce was over, that there was nothing left for him but suicide, and that I would then stab him in the heart and put an end to it all. The fantasy was clearly related to his association of the analysis with the heart operation: the doctor would once again stab him in the heart, and the procedure would not cure him. At best it could only put an end to his misery.

Fading Resistance

His resistance in this area was stubborn as rock. Only little by little did it wear away, under the persistent pressure of my interpretations and the analytic process. At first his attitude did not seem to budge in the analysis. But it gradually became more and more evident that in one or other area of his life he was beginning to function more adequately. He began to be able to speak up in class without embarrassment or undue anxiety. He was increasingly able to converse with and consult professors without a feeling of panic and predestined failure. He was slowly and by infinitesimal degrees able to function more effectively in his work. He became increasingly comfortable with the courtroom situation, and even began to enjoy it. As we shall see, his severe anxiety in sexual matters also began to diminish and finally disappear. Ever so slowly he began to accept the possibility that he could make the analysis a success too, that it need not turn out to be a failure. As he stuck to the analysis over time and began to make it work for him, the disparity between the reality and his fantasy became all the more marked and unavoidable. Such too was the case in relation to his extraanalytic experiences. The gap between the reality of his performance and the doubts and fears of his fantasies became irreconcilable. The fantasy had ceased to dominate and control his behavior, but it became all the more clear that he clung to it in neurotic and willfully stubborn ways.

Anality

The anal quality of this material is striking. We shall have the opportunity of seeing other material that suggests a strong anal preoccupation and fixation. There seems little doubt that Jimmy's sense of defectiveness and failure was strongly linked to anal issues. His mother's involvement in her approval of his performances was part of it. His performances on the potty were much involved in gaining her approval and attention. She would always check on what he had done. He recalled hearing about another child who had swallowed a penny, and the child's mother had searched through the feces until she found it. He immediately referred this image to his own mother and her intense preoccupation with his stool. He never felt that he had done it right, always felt that he had produced something rotten and evil. He could never stand the smell of his own excrement as a child, and mother had to keep an Airwick in the bathroom. She was always checking up on him in the bathroom.

Jimmy preserved an image of himself as a messy little kid. He related this to images of himself sitting in a corner having moved his bowels and made a mess. He had vague recollections of having to be washed because of such messing. He recalled that he had been bowel and bladder trained for some time before his mother's illness. The image of the messy little kid was thus regressively revived—the weak, little, messy, defective baby who could not control himself and who could not avoid making a mess—being a failure. The regression was apparently related to his mother's illness and operation for goiter, but then persisted as far as the enuresis was concerned into preadolescence. It was another convincing proof of Jimmy's inherent defectiveness and of the unavoidability of failure.

Hypochondriasis

Closely linked to Jimmy's conviction of defectiveness were a series of hypochondriacal concerns. He dreaded a severe and incapacitating illness. Every least symptom or ache or pain was immediately magnified into a dreaded disease. His favorite was cancer; every least ache or bruise or swelling was the first stage of a fatal malignancy. He would rush to the doctor, receive a thorough examination in which nothing would be found, receive reassurance from the doctor, and return home. On such occasions he had great difficulty trusting the doctor, feeling that the latter had not taken sufficient care with the examination, that he had not done the right tests, or if all these failed, feeling that the doctor was withholding the bitter truth from him. He would worry about this for days, until it was replaced by some other worry. Another favorite disease was diabetes; there was a family history and his father had a mild case. He would often ask doctors about it, and one doctor even told him that he should have a regular sugar test in view of his family history.

The other area of hypochondriacal concern was his penis. He felt it was too small, and even sometimes believed that it was shrinking and getting smaller. There was at times a definite delusional quality to this concern. At other times he would feel that there was something wrong with his penis—that it was bent, that it was somehow broken, that there were strange lumps on it, etc. Many of these fears were related to his concerns over masturbation. He was afraid that he had damaged his organ—another manifestation of his underlying conviction of defect and the inevitability of failure. Even masturbation carried with it the curse of damage, destruction and impotence. A recurrent association in this regard was Hemingway's *The Sun Also Rises* in which the hero is impotent.

For Jim impotence would have been the ultimate failure, the definitive proof of his failure and defectiveness. He saw himself as a cripple, deformed for life, and thus repulsive and undesirable. There was an interesting twist to this in his associations. He felt that his illness, his heart defect, and his fantasied fatal illness was somehow directed against his mother. He was thus her burden and she was angry at him for not being a girl, for not being perfectly healthy, for not being without defect. He fantasied telling her of his terminal illness, how she would take it, how she would devote herself to him and nurse him on his deathbed. He would be her cripple, and his terminal fantasy was that his chest would break open along the suture line that had scarred him for life. His fantasy intermingled the motif of his defectiveness, his wishes for special closeness with mother, his deeply ambivalent sadistic impulses toward her, and his fateful condemnation to the ultimate failure and death.

Dependence Conflicts

Throughout the analysis, he had to struggle with his wishes to be passive and dependent. These wishes formed in fact the other side of his preoccupations and fears that I would attack and hurt him. The opposite pole to his guarded suspiciousness and constant fear of attack was total submission and unquestioning subjugation. He could find little ground between these drastic alternatives. He felt himself becoming increasingly dependent on the analysis and increasingly involved in it. The only way he would envision this was in terms of complete surrender. This meant handing himself over to me to do with as I pleased. The alternative was attack, struggle, confrontation, my destroying him or his destroying me. It took many months for us to work through his paranoid anxieties. As his conviction that I would attack him and tear him apart receded, his wish to gain a close, friendly, loving, passive, and submissive relationship with me came into the focus of the analysis.

He recalled a particular occasion when he had been away from home for one summer at camp. He had been very unhappy at camp, unable to make any friends among the other boys, unable to join in their childish games and keeping himself more or less an outsider. At the end of camp, he was offered an opportunity to join some of the older boys and counselors on a canoe trip. He knew his mother would want him to come home. The canoe trip would have meant a step away from her, an adventure away from his childhood dependence, a more grown-up and independent undertaking. He could not accept it. He was frightened by it. He had to retreat to the safety of his clinging dependence on his mother.

The canoe trip became a sort of paradigm of his difficulty in the analysis. Was he going to be able to embark on the adventure that analysis offered him—the opportunity for greater independence and maturity and the capacity for adult functioning? Or would he cling to his self-appointed condition of defective dependence? He saw himself as desperately needing me to support him and help him. He felt intensely dependent on me, as he had felt fearfully dependent on his mother. He felt the need to feel me as his powerful protector to whom he could submit himself in loving subjugation.

He had recurrent dreams about the analytic situation, in which he and I would be talking face-to-face, not as doctor and patient, but as good and close friends. Or we would be lying on the couch embracing and fondling each other. The homosexual content in these dream fantasies and wishes was clear. So also was the threat in them, that of complete submission to my power which could then be capriciously and viciously used against him, and against which he had no defense.

Another important aspect of his concerns over dependency was his feeling that I might be dependent on him. I might depend on him to be co-operative, a good patient, one that didn't cause any trouble or didn't argue or resist in any way. The wish to have me dependent reflected his desires to be powerful himself, not to be in the position of submitting, but of having me submit to him and to obey his wishes. These wishes were highly erotized, and were associated with his parallel wishes for women to submit to him sexually, as well as to his latency and adolescent fantasies of having boys submit to him sexually. He feared that if he showed any independence or any will of his own in the analysis I would not be able to handle it. I would become anxious, or upset, or hurt and depressed. He tried assiduously to avoid any objection, or questioning, or confronting of any of my observations or interpretations. Behind this behavior there lurked the image of his father. Any moves on his part toward greater independence within the analysis were seen as against me, as putting me down, as putting my value and competence in question, as making me feel worthless and humiliated. The same issues pervaded his relationship with his mother. His response to me was cast in the same extreme form that it had been toward his mother and father: the alternatives were complete subjugation, which he hated and reviled, or destructive hostility, which he feared and avoided. It was extremely difficult to find a workable middle ground in which he could express himself and take his own independent position without attacking or destroying or humiliating or defeating me—or alternatively being attacked, defeated, and humiliated.

Sexual Conflicts

Perhaps more than any other area, the problem of sexuality served as a central focus for the analysis. It became a catchall area within which all the themes and preoccupations we have been describing were channeled, and to which we returned again and again in a continuing reworking and working through of the basic issues. When his feelings of inadequacy and his convictions about his weakness and defectiveness had been eroded in most of the other areas of his life, he remained stubbornly convinced that he was doomed to be a failure sexually.

From his first experience with girls, he had been hesitant and frightened. He felt awkward, unsure of himself, and could never understand how other guys got to know girls and got to take them out. He felt that he was an outsider here, too, unable to understand what it was all about. Asking a girl for a date was a "trial by fire"—he dreaded the refusal, the rejection, being told that he was no good, that he just couldn't hack it. The adolescent sexual talk about making girls excited him, but he had little idea of what that meant or how one did it. His attempts to touch girls or feel them up were met with rebuffs. He would become terribly anxious and his attempts were clumsy and awkward.

Alongside this timorous and inhibited experience, he maintained an active and quite different fantasy life. In his latency years, he had cherished an elaborate fantasy in which he was the master of a large school of boys. The boys were all absolutely submissive to his will. They were all naked in the school, and Jimmy lived in an apartment at the top of the school. He would bring the boys there and play with them sexually. They would completely submit to his sexual wishes. It was at this time that Piggy, the kid who lived next door, came into the picture. They started playing with each other, and Piggy passively accommodated himself to any of Jimmy's sexual wishes. The extent of the actual activity is uncertain—probably little more than mutual masturbation—but for Jimmy this was the realization in fact of his fantasy. The activity lasted for only a few months.

When Jimmy came into puberty, the fantasy did not disappear, but instead of only boys being in the school, there were also girls. Masturbation fantasies pertained to certain girls to whom he was attracted but whom he was afraid to approach. He would fantasy them without clothes and in the fantasies they would be completely submissive to his wishes. Most exciting were the fantasies of fellatio—getting a "blow job"—and anal intercourse. In the fantasy he was domineering and powerful. He could tell the girl to "strip and suck"—and she would be immediately submissive to his commands. Essential to the fantasy, however, was the idea that she would be forced to do it against her will, so powerful was he that she could not resist his wishes. Along with this there was a sadistic streak. He would imagine himself tying up these naked girls so that they were helpless, then beating them, whipping them, screwing them, and having them suck his penis.

The difficulty was that, however exciting and gratifying the fantasies, they intruded on his attempts to relate sexually. As he became increasingly intimate with a given date, he also became increasingly tense and anxious. He began to think of the real girl in terms of the slave-woman of his fantasies. Every conversation became a seduction. Every movement placed him on the threshold of rape. His mind was flooded with preoccupations—would she do it? Would she surrender herself to him? Would she "strip and suck"? The overpowering fear was that she would. His fantasies might become a reality, as they had with Piggy. He longed for and dreamed about a girl who would take Piggy's place, who would become his sexual

slave and fulfill his every whim. Every girl he met became an instant candidate for the position. At the same time, the prospect filled him with anxious dread. He was trapped between the fulfillment of his desires—so that he
would become the powerful and destructive phallic aggressor—and the fear
of failure—so that his weakness and defectiveness would be preserved and
confirmed. With every girl, and in every least contact with girls, he was
caught between his anxious wishes to sexualize and to desexualize, to
succeed or to fail, to play the man or the child.

He was convinced that there was something reprehensible and evil
about wanting sex. His parents would not approve of sleeping with girls. It
was something that he had to be devious about, something that he had to
cover up. He was afraid that girls would find out what he was thinking and
what he wanted to do to them: then they would know that he was perverted
and dangerous, and that he should be repulsed and avoided. He felt that if
he made any move in that direction, he would be found out, that he was
doomed to be a sexual failure as well. He felt he wanted to leap in and get
the whole thing over, but at the same time dreading his coming too soon,
ejaculating prematurely in his pants so that then the girl would know that he
was a weak and defective male and could not control himself.

Oedipal Determinants

As we worked on these problems in the analysis he became increasingly
able to relate to girls and then was able to enter a rather intense sexual
relationship with a girl named Janet. All of his sexual fears and concerns
were again focused in this relationship. He could not believe that she was
really interested in him and that she could care for him. He saw himself as
an outsider. He dreamed at one point that they were in a motel room. Janet
was in bed with another man, Jimmy was forced to sleep in a chair. He
sneaked over to the bed and watched while Janet and the man were lying
naked in the bed. The man was very good—"screwing and eating" her.
Janet looked up and saw Jimmy, but didn't stop. The man kept screwing for
the longest time, and Janet was having intense orgasms. Jimmy felt inadequate and lonely—left out. Then Janet came to him and tried to console
him. He was dejected and just wanted to cry. "How could they do this to
me?"

He recalled that the arrangement of furniture in the room was similar
to that in his parents' bedroom. He recalled his feelings of being left out and
lonely when his parents were in bed together. How could his mother go to
bed with his father and leave Jimmy alone? How could they leave him out of
it?

Jimmy learned to handle these anxieties and feelings of hurt and disappointment by elaborate devices. He kept himself on friendly terms with a

number of girls but assiduously avoided any sexual involvement with them. He tried to present himself as sexually nonthreatening. He cast himself in the role of confidant. Usually his contacts with girls were set in a three-person framework. He would get to know the girl through a friend of his who would be the girl's boyfriend. The girl would be sexually involved with the boyfriend, and Jimmy would fill in as the nonsexual but confidentially intimate third party. He recalled his hurt and resentful feelings when these girls would go off to bed with the other guys. The pattern and the details of its elaboration was clearly a re-creation of the Oedipal triad. Jimmy strove for a close and intimate association with the girls, but feared the intimacy of sexual contact, even as he strove to be close to his mother, but was threatened and frightened by his sexual desires for her.

In Jimmy's view sex was something that girls submitted to even though they didn't want it or like it. They had to be forced into it, or tricked into it. If a boy had relations with a girl, it was something that he got away with by being sneaky or devious. It did not take long to discover that this attitude was derived from his mother. She saw sex as something that men did to women, as something women had to accept as part of their burden in life, that in sex boys hurt girls, even if they don't know that they were. Mother and son shared the fantasy that sex was aggressive and hurtful and destructive. Jimmy's comment:

> She's a woman with a lot of anger. She's terrified of her emotions. When my grandfather died, she almost cracked up—she was still crying a year later. She took it harder than my grandmother. She sees everything as hurting her. I could never understand it. She can't let people live their own lives. She thinks her children grew up just to hurt her. That's just the way she puts it. My whole life is based on that. I grew up with the feeling that I could really do damage. The scariest line is "How could you do this to me?" She used it often—not just for special occasions. How could boys do such things to girls? And the grimmest part is that she never gives up. That was part of her sitting shiva—to grow up was to kill mother.

Jimmy's sexual life was dominated by his persistent attachment to his mother and by the image of the relationship between his parents. To allow oneself to love a woman was to become vulnerable and weak, to be taken advantage of and exploited and controlled and domineered. The only sexuality he could conceive of was the sexuality of brute force, sadistic subjugation, phallic aggression. The alternatives were to force the woman to submit or to be subjugated and controlled by her. His ambivalence was displayed on both sides of this dilemma. His aggressive and sadistic wishes to force women to become his sexual slaves were matched by his fears of hurting them by this form of hypermasculine attack. His wishes to be passive and dependent were matched by his intense fears of vulnerability and weakness. It was a trap out of which he could not find his way.

The relationship was shrouded in Jimmy's mind with clearly Oedpial concerns. He feared that Janet would control his life, would pull him down so that he could no longer be free and independent, that he would be trapped into having to please her and submit to her whims and her control, as he had so often seen his father having to give in to his mother. For a time he fended off his tender and loving feelings for Janet, but they were soon evident. He found them threatening. To allow oneself to feel and to admit love for a girl, was to put oneself in a vulnerable position. He wanted to keep himself in the position of being able to play at sex—without accepting any deeper or more meaningful commitments. Loving a girl meant marriage, restriction, responsibility, being trapped, and helpless, and vulnerable.

The fear and longing for his mother lie behind these concerns. At one point he dreamed that he and Janet were lying together naked. He moved his bowels, and Janet wiped his behind. She asked him if he wanted vasoline rubbed on his penis. He remembered that the night before Janet had been playing with his penis and had "beat him off." He had felt passive, as though she were just leading him around by the penis. The associations moved to the scenes with his mother, when she would rub his back, and he would want her to play with his buttocks and fondle his penis. Beyond that were the memories of sitting on the potty and of her stroking his penis. His mother had led him around by the penis, got him to do her bidding by playing with his penis. In relationship to Janet he felt like a helpless baby that she could play with and do with as she pleased. While this quality permeated all of his relations with women, it was also starkly enunciated in his relationship with another girl who was several inches taller than he was. He remarked that when he was lying on top of her he felt like a baby on its mother's stomach. He would often remark with both of these girls how much he liked to play with and suck on their breasts, and that their breasts reminded him of his mother's large breasts.

Castration and Impotence

The castration anxiety in all of this was a strong component of his fears. Not long after he had begun to sleep with Janet, he dreamed that he was sleeping with a huge black woman who had large sharp teeth in her vagina. He first recalled his first visit to a prostitute when he was about fifteen. He remembered that he was frightened, that he couldn't get an erection, that he wanted her to give him a "blow job." The woman had a large dog and Jimmy remembered his fear that the dog would bite off his penis. A second memory was of a time in college when a friend of his, whom he saw as a strong male figure, suggested that they get some women. Jimmy had not wanted this, but went along with it because he didn't want to seem afraid or weak in his friend's eyes. The two women arrived, one white and one black.

Jimmy got the black. He remembered that his friend had "laid" his girl and screwed her in a matter of a couple of minutes, but Jimmy didn't know what to do. He had trouble getting an erection. Then he couldn't penetrate, and then he came prematurely all over her belly. His friend and the other girl sat watching him, and his embarrassment and shame were mortifying. He felt like he was a little kid who had messed his pants, and everyone could see that he was a defective, messy baby who couldn't control his bowels or his penis.

Another association in this context, which had to do with premature ejaculation, was his feeling that intercourse was like running to the toilet when he had to go as a child. He felt that there was little sense of separation in his mind between bedroom and bathroom. As a child he would wait until he couldn't hold it any longer, then run for the bathroom, so that he could go quickly. Then his mother was pleased and proud of him. The problem, of course, was that he would sometimes wet his pants. The association with premature ejaculation was clear, as was also the conclusion that wetting his pants, like coming too soon, was proof of his defectiveness and inability to control himself.

Powerlessness

It can be seen that one of the central components of Jimmy's sexual experience was the issue of power, and so it was in most of the other areas of his experience. For him every relationship, every context in which he had to deal with other people, became a field in which the forces of power and submission played themselves out. The alternatives were clear-cut and decisive—either mastery and power or complete submission. The alternatives were cast in his fantasies as radical extremes. If he were not in possession of absolute and unchallengeable power, he was in danger of complete subjugation and vulnerability. He recalled as a child that he always felt that he was helplessly submitted to his parents' power, particularly that of his mother. But—to look at the opposite side of the coin—when his parents so frequently capitulated and gave in to his wishes (as, for example, his tantrums when they were about to go out for an evening), he felt a frightening sense of power over them and felt that he was bad and demanding to make them do something against their wills.

The power issue was carried over into all of his relations with authority figures. He saw them as powerful and dangerous, felt that they could turn against him at the least warning and hurt him in some unforeseen way. He was frightened of policemen, professors, judges in court, the landlord—anyone for whom there was any possibility of having a decision-making capacity that could affect Jimmy in any way. He saw others as powerful, and himself as powerless. Along with this concern with power, he was extremely sensitive to any infringement on his rights or freedom. The loss of freedom was a chronic complaint that he brought forth in multiple situations, not merely the sexual. He could not envision himself as an active agent with capacity and potency to set goals and accomplish them. The notion of cooperation or collaboration was completely foreign to his way of thinking. His was a master-slave morality of the first order.

The issue of power came to be a major focus of the analysis. Jimmy saw the analytic situation in terms of a power struggle. I was the powerful one, and he was the powerless and helpless victim. I was a dangerous opponent who was lying in wait, ready to pounce on him and destroy him. He was afraid of my "shooting him down" or "putting him down." The issue was raised in many contexts. I was the one who determined the appointment times, the days off, the vacation periods. Jimmy saw himself as having no say in these matters, as having the only recourse of accepting and submitting to my decision. Little by little we were able to explore his feelings about this sort of issue and to test some of the reality.

There was a long period during which his participation in the analysis was somewhat tenuous. He wanted to stop the analysis, to leave my office and never come back—that would be the only way he could gain control of the situation and assert his will, as against merely passively submitting to mine. Yet, at the same time, he would never miss an appointment and would anxiously arrive in my waiting room well ahead of the scheduled appointment time. His tactic was obviously to deal with his fears and anxieties, not by active mastery and counterphobic assertion, but by capitulation and by avoiding any behavior that would even suggest opposition or any counterwishes of his own. He felt that I demanded such slavish adherence to appointment schedules and that he had no recourse but to submit, in the meanwhile putting himself into paroxysms of anxiety when heavy traffic or other involvements might impinge on his time and put him in danger of arriving at my office a few minutes late.

The question of power in the analytic relationship was complicated by the implications of the relationship between doctor and patient. The patient was the one who submitted to the doctor. Jimmy's associations drew him back to the image of the powerful heart surgeon to whose will he had been forced to submit, without any say in the matter on his part. He was not even told about it. And the powerful doctor had cut him open, had left him with a great scar that wrapped itself around his chest and threatened to open up at any moment. He had been forced to submit, utterly helpless and vulnerable, and had been left scarred and maimed for life. Such was Jimmy's fantasy!

The question of power remained a live issue throughout the entire course of the analysis. It was extremely difficult for Jim to accept the idea that the analysis could be a cooperative venture in which he and I could work together toward a resolution of his difficulties, and in which he could take an active, responsible, and determining part. Only gradually, as this issue was worked through, did his obsessive anxiety diminish, so that he was able to make his own decisions about taking time away from the analysis—as his job sometimes required—or even feeling more comfortable when he arrived in my office a few minutes late. His tendency to erotize this aspect of his experience was unmistakable. He saw the power dichotomy in terms of winning me over and gaining the same sort of special, intimate, confidential relation he had with his mother. His term for losing out in the power struggle was being "fucked over." His often-repeated accusation against me was that I was "fucking him over."

What was most significant in his manner of dealing with the threat in our relationship was the fact that he placed himself—at least in fantasy terms—in the position of the helpless and weak submitter. This was consistent with the defensive style that he had evolved over the years. It was a posture that had been fixed for him at an early age. He could not run the risk of striving to gain what he wanted by active assertion, so he adopted the position of the passive and dependent child. The weak and defective baby was no threat to anyone, but he got his way by being helpless and weak. As a poor weak and defective baby he had to be protected and taken care of and given special consideration. Jimmy worked at re-creating the quality of special defectiveness and helplessness, that he had had in his relation with his mother, in the analytic situation. When it became clear to him that I was not going to respond as his mother had, he was both frustrated and angered—but also relieved. It was only at this point that the basis for a firm therapeutic contact could be laid down.

Conflicts over Aggression

Woven into the fabric of this analytic tapestry, like a constantly recurring leitmotif that permeated and colored every corner of the picture, was the theme of aggression. Jimmy's conflicts over aggression—the need to control it and suppress it and avoid any expression of it—were a major source of difficulty for him. We have already seen the manner in which the conflicts over aggression came to play such a significant role in the sexual sphere. He was driven on the one side by his intense phallic wishes and desires; yet on the other side he was inhibited and impeded in the expression of these sexual wishes by his fears and anxieties. The idea that sex was aggressive and hurtful derived from his mother. But it was not merely in the area of sexuality that she impressed on him his destructiveness and dangerousness. From the very beginning he had come to think of himself as the defective child who had injured and damaged his mother in being born. The onset of her hyperthyroid condition and the coincident exacerbation of her neurotic anxieties tended to reinforce this apperception. The turmoil of anxiety centering around his own heart defect and the operation were major ingredients of this neurotic brew.

Added to this underlying conviction, there was the fact that in true "Jewish mother" style every action on his part that deviated from his parents' wishes or that smacked of independence and self-assertion was interpreted as an attack on his parents, as calculated to hurt and disappoint them. Jimmy's mother also had a habit of charging that Jimmy's "bad" behavior would be the cause of his father's death. Jimmy's disobedience would give his father a heart attack, so that Jimmy would then be responsible for his father's death. Jimmy's young mind could not distinguish very well between fantasy and reality, as well as the fact that his mother's dire threats were readily conjoined to his solidly embedded, if unconscious, convictions of his own destructiveness.

Jimmy's defense against the threat of harmful destructiveness was to keep himself the weak, helpless baby, even though at the same time he bitterly resented and felt angered and hurt by being treated as such.

He continually saw himself and tried to portray himself as inadequate and defective. He recalled as a child his favorites were the Wizard of Oz stories. He thought of himself as being the Tin Woodsman or the Scarecrow. They were defective as he was—and they were doomed to failure too. Any accomplishments or attainments had to be kept hidden. Successful performance was "showing off." He could not think of himself as a capable adult; rather the image he clung to was that of the baby who only played at being an adult. When a baby did adult things, he was showing off, and his performance was only fit to be smiled at or laughed at and treated as "cute." In countless situations—court appearances, dealing with clients, arguing cases, making telephone calls, relating sexually to women, writing letters, anything in which adult performance was in play—Jimmy dreaded such "showing off." Successful performance was "too much," it was "going too far." The image was that of losing control and bringing about unexpected and unforeseeable consequences. In Jimmy's mind the consequences were inevitably disastrous.

In the throes of his neurosis, he set about defeating himself and preventing such successes. In court presentations he would stammer and stutter and forget his argument. In sex he would fail to get an erection or would ejaculate prematurely. In writing a paper he would procrastinate out of anxiety until he had to rush desperately to finish the assignment, with consequent deterioration in the quality of his work. Such behavior was clearly in the service of several closely linked objectives—avoiding destructive consequences, minimizing competition, and preserving the dominant fantasy of his defectiveness. He worked at making himself a failure. His flight from aggressive competition was tied tightly to the latent competition and rivalry with his brothers. As a child he had avoided such competition because he was certainly the loser. As an adult he continued to avoid it. To be better than Joe he would have to be a supersuccessful lover. To be better than Harry he would have to be supersmart. If he could not reach those exalted standards, there was nothing left but failure. It was again the logic of extremes—all or nothing.

The threat of aggression was demonstrated graphically in a dream. In the dream a tough-looking guy was in a building packing large amounts of money into boxes. He was carrying a gun. He had just robbed a bank and was packing the money for his getaway. Jim was standing outside with a gun in his hand. The man came out of the building and Jimmy was terrified. He thought that the guy would shoot him, so he threw away the gun and started running. The dream was a reflection of his waking experience. He was always throwing away his gun, denying and hiding any aggressiveness or assertiveness out of fear that someone would attack him in turn. Beyond that was the fear that if he did not throw away the gun that he might himself go too far and thus become the agent of destruction.

Paranoid Attitudes

All of these elements were channeled into and contributed to Jimmy's paranoid attitudes. He made his way through a world that was populated with enemies. All around him there were strong, powerful figures ready to pounce on him and do him in. He often felt people were criticizing him, or that they were laughing at him behind his back. Frequently in the course of his analysis—even remarkably late in the course of it—the feeling would burst upon him that I was snickering at him and laughing behind his back. He imagined that I thought what he was saying was inconsequential or boring or stupid or laughable. At every step he expected attack from the powerful forces that surrounded him, in the analysis and without. He felt that people were out to get him, that they were just looking for the first opportunity to put him down, to show him up, to make his weakness and defectiveness apparent. He was constantly in fear of being "shot down" as he put it.

These fears and expectations of attack would become more intense when his feelings of defectiveness were brought to the surface. Whenever he made any attempt to assert himself or to act independently, his behavior served as a putting-to-the-test of his basic hypothesis—that he was defective and worthless. Any assertion or independence was an invitation for others to attack him and destroy him. This was certainly the pattern that he had learned to expect in his childhood and in the family context. He had learned to trust no one. This was one of the most difficult aspects of his treatment. For him to trust me meant for him to put himself at my mercy. He had no assurance, and every expectation, that I would take advantage of his vulnerability and "put him down." Again and again in the course of the analysis, he would express his persistent fears that I would turn on him, tell him he was not worth any more trouble, that he would never be able to finish the analysis, and that we might as well throw in the towel. At home, to confide in either his mother or his brother meant to invite treatment as the baby, to be intruded on and controlled, to be criticized and ridiculed and attacked—never to be understood and accepted as he was and helped.

The world around him was hostile and aggressive and threatening and controlling. It was a world of mothers and brothers. He saw himself as a helpless victim, a pawn in others' hands. He felt himself to be ugly and repulsive. He had frequent dreams in which people were disgusted and repulsed by him. They would either treat him with contempt and disgust or else attack him and chase him. The police were always after him, a circumstance that was reinforced by his occasional fringe illegal activities, such as selling pot. Such devices were obviously calculated to give some real substance to the fears and anxieties of his fantasies. In his dream life he would look in the mirror and his face would be covered with repulsive bugs that he couldn't pull off. He even described occasions when he felt the same when he looked at his face in the mirror while awake, as though there were ugly and deforming growths and scabs. He felt he smelled bad, recalling he could never stand the smell of his own feces. He constantly worried about smelling badly in public and on dates too. He associated his bad smell with his tendency to perspire heavily, especially when he felt anxious.

Everywhere he looked he saw the looming potential for confrontation and conflict. I had opened a new office, but had not started seeing him there until after several months. His reaction was as follows:

> I wanted to move all year, but you turned me down. I felt tense about it. I wonder whether you gave in, like Janet giving in. Even if she doesn't see it that way. I think she might be. If you don't do what I want, then you're restricting my freedom. I won't give in—I feel angry but I hold it in. It's a confusion between disappointment and feeling fucked over. It makes me feel paranoid—it shows me you can't be trusted.

I wondered if his paranoid feelings came on when he didn't get what he wanted.

> Not so much now, but they did as a kid. I was quick to jump to conclusions. It seems alien now, but I can slip into it easily. I saw my parents as enemies. My mother was taking over my life, fitting me into patterns. It was related to my being so weak and vulnerable and being pushed around. I was always collecting data.

My question here focused on whether he collected all the data, or only that data that fit his view of things.

> Well it was easy to distort. That's the difference between writing a brief and writing a paper. In a brief you pick the hypothesis, then find the data to support it. The idea that I'm just a patient puts me in the position to be shat on. That runs through our whole family. It means I have to make a spiel to you—"Don't hurt me because I'm just a weak little kid!" That's noncompetitive. I won't fight, but I'll hurt if I don't get what I want. But I'd feel bad if you gave in. If I could get something out of you by arguing, I'd think you were weak—I could get away with anything.

I remarked that his view seemed to presume that giving in was a sign of weakness.

> That's the way I always saw my parents—as giving in. The only way to avoid it is by not wanting anything or not asking for anything.

It was clear that Jimmy saw the world in terms of hostile and armed confrontation. His was the Swiss defense—no one would ever attack a noncombatant who was worthless and defenseless. But unlike the Swiss, he had strong impulses to act aggressively himself. His own wishes, which he repressed and denied, were strongly hostile and were expressed in terms of fantasies of domination and forcing others to submit to his will—sexually and otherwise. The least act of assertion was redolent with the wishes and fantasies of such phallic, aggressive, and dominating impulses. He expected the attack from others that he wished to launch himself, but was too afraid to even attempt. It took several years of clarifications and interpretations and working through of these feelings in the analytic setting before he began to see that the grim and ominous colors with which he had painted his world came from his own brush. This realization was gained at first in his relationship to me, and then gradually in the other areas of his activity.

The logic of extremes played itself into this context too. If there was any slight disproportion in any of his relationships, he would view it as one of total domination and submission. If he was not completely in control of what was going on, he felt himself to be at the mercy of those around him and thereby vulnerable to their attacks. He thought in all-or-none terms. One was either on the top—or on the bottom. The image was rooted in his child's vision of his parents in bed, and the image of his mother on top of his father. The only way to assure himself that he was not on the bottom was to try to put someone else on the bottom. He felt people were always trying to do just that to him.

Only gradually could he see that in fact not only was there no evidence that anyone was trying to put him down, but in many instances the only one putting him down was himself. This was very clear in the analysis. On a number of occasions, he acted out attempts to get me to criticize or ridicule him, to be intrusive and controlling as his mother had been, and thus validate his expectations. When he saw what was afoot in these episodes, he began to realize that he had often done similar things, not only at home, but in his work and other parts of his life. By playing the weak and submissively compliant role, he had literally invited others around him to take advantage of him; he had maneuvered them into the dominating position. Then he could feel resentful and rebellious, angered and bitter at his lot in life as the worthless and defective underdog who could have no expectations of success, recognition, or reward. The prophecy was self-fulfilling!

The Specter of Narcissism

Behind these preoccupations and wishes and fears, there lurked the specter of narcissism. More than any other aspect of his dynamics, the element of narcissism seemed to evade the analytic process. It was well marked and well defended—from Jim himself and from me in the analysis. It was an elusive subject that always seemed to be hovering on the horizon, but which we were able to get hold of only with painful slowness, and then with great reluctance on Jim's part. But it was nonetheless unmistakable. It emerged first in the transference. In the face of his fears and severe persecutory anxiety as the analysis progressed, Jim began to express his wishes to have a special sort of relation to me. He wanted to feel close and intimate. As he said, "I want to make you mine." He had fantasies of what it would be like for me to call off the hour and we could both go out for a cup of coffee, and then we could really have a heart-to-heart talk. He wanted to be a special patient, so that I would be proud of him and happy with him. His dreams frequently represented the analytic situation in which the usual pattern was overthrown and he and I were engaged in some intimate and personal exchange—even at times frankly sexual. For a long time he was quite resistant to any interpretation of mine that had an analytic ring to it. When I would relate his feelings toward me back to his parents, he would complain that that was "textbook stuff" and that he didn't want to accept the idea that such ordinary stuff might apply to himself. He wanted to be different and therefore more interesting to me. He even wanted to be difficult, because then he could be something out of the ordinary. He hated the idea of being ordinary—like everyone else.

He recalled how important it had been at home for him to feel special and different. He had attained that by being mother's good little boy and by being the defective baby. He couldn't be special in any grown-up way: when he tried, they just laughed at him and said he was "cute." He couldn't match the level of performance set by his popular and sexy brother Joe, or his supersmart brother Harry—the family genius. There was nothing left for him. He could only be special by being weak, and helpless, and powerless, and defective. He had been able to do this with his mother. He could cling to her and run to her for protection, and she responded and played the game with him. He could be special for her. There was no need to try to make it in school or on the playground with other kids: he could retreat back home where he knew he was special. In the analysis he wanted to re-create that sort of nonchallenging, noncompetitive, safe, intimate, protective relationship. He wanted to be my baby, my special patient whom I would take care of and protect.

He felt that he just had to be special or there was no use carrying on, no use living. He would not face the possibility that he was just ordinary, like other people. That was the trouble in playing with other kids; he couldn't join in their childish games, because that would have meant that he was like them—just ordinary little kids. He had to be different, an outsider. He was raised to be superior. He was his mother's child. He had always felt that his family was superior to others. He reflected with great pride on his brothers, on what they could do and what they had accomplished.

At times he felt superior himself, but he always had to turn it around and make himself feel inferior and stupid. In his fantasies he was a superman—supersmart, superstrong, supersexual. He felt that he should be able to get things he wanted without having to work or struggle for them. He should have the girls he wanted without even having to try for them. They should want to sleep with him without any hassles. He should get all A's without bothering to study. When he sat down to write a paper, it should be a masterpiece. His colleagues and professors should have recognized his talent and applauded him for it. The difficulty, of course, was that when he tried to write or perform in the classroom or courtroom, his performance did not measure up to these standards of genius. In his mind they were thereby merely more evidence of his inadequacy and failure. If you can't be the best, you are doomed to be a failure. You were somebody special, or you were a failure.

There was a unique paradox concealed within this narcissistic logic. For Jim there was an investment in and a commitment to failure. His high narcissistic expectations set the stage for failure. When his work was not recognized and proclaimed as the work of a genius, he was proven once again to be a failure. The paradox for him was that to be a failure was his success. To be weak and defective was the basis of his specialness. The operation which had confirmed and demonstrated his defectiveness had also made him the special child who thereby was given special attention and consideration. The special attention and special treatment were continued and preserved by his maintaining himself in the position of the baby. He became the family prince. He commented: "Even if you lose, even if you are beaten, you're still the prince!" In this distorted logic, success and failure had become blurred and confused. Success had become failure, and failure had become success. Success had come to mean power, strength, hurtful destructiveness, cold hard egotism, loss of love, isolation, and attack from other hostile and powerful antagonists. Failure had come to mean safety, protection, loving care, specialness. Failure had become Jimmy's strength. It was his avenue to being babied, being allowed to get away with things, being given special privileges and special consideration.

Persecutory Anxiety

The course of Jim's analysis was by no means smooth and untroubled. From the beginning his anxiety was a prominent feature. He was evidently terribly frightened of the situation he had put himself in. He had delivered himself into the clutches of a powerful monster who could control him, turn on him, and destroy him, and all his fears of vulnerability and attack were raised to a pitch of intensity. He saw me as a Nazi stormtrooper who would delight sadistically in tormenting and bringing ruin upon my helpless Jewish victim. These thoughts dominated his fantasies and dreams. He talked of leaving the analysis, of wanting to bolt off the couch and run to safety, of wanting to get on his knees and beg me to be kind and merciful, of begging me not to hurt him. These fears were dramatic and dominated the early phase of his analysis. My presumption was that the intensity of these anxieties in the opening phase of the analysis was prepared by the interval of nearly two months which separated our initial evaluative interviews and the actual beginning of the analysis. He brought with him a transference readiness that had been tuned up to a high pitch of intensity.

It became quickly apparent that something had to be done or the analysis would be in imminent danger of foundering on the harsh rocks of Jimmy's acute persecutory anxiety. It was necessary to intervene somewhat actively and to make attempts to reinforce the therapeutic alliance. Jimmy needed an ally and support in order to gain some perspective on his neurotic fears and anxieties. I was able to point out the transference elements which loomed so large in this material. I suggested that the malignant thoughts and intentions that he attributed to me were his thoughts and not mine, that in fact he had no idea of what my thoughts really were. I was also able to suggest that he expected me to respond as his mother had, by being intrusive and controlling and by trying to run his life: but perhaps the analytic situation was quite different, in fact one such as he had never experienced before in any other context of his life. I also made the point that it seemed very difficult for him to think of the analysis in terms of a cooperative effort in which he and I might work together to understand his problems and help him to deal with them.

Exploration and rather extensive working through of the persecutory concerns related to his parents seemed to diminish his paranoid fears in the analysis, but did not eliminate them. It was gradually apparent that there were other determinants of these anxieties which had not been adequately dealt with. Little by little they came into focus. They had to do with Jimmy's older brother Harry. It turned out that the decision to undertake analysis was strongly influenced by Harry, who advised Jimmy throughout and supported the decision. In the ancient spirit of his resentment, Jimmy felt that being in analysis was another manifestation and instance of his brother's trying to push him around and run his life. In undertaking the analysis he was following Harry's wishes, not his own. The analysis was Harry's, not Jimmy's.

He felt resentment about this state of affairs, but in his typical style reinforced his submission to Harry's wishes and his supposed dependence on Harry by continually consulting the latter about what was happening in his analysis. As we explored his fears and doubts and questions, it soon became apparent that the thoughts he was expressing were in fair measure not his own, but they were ideas that he had picked up from conversations with his brother. Harry would tell him stories about how analysts dealt with patients, how they tricked them, how they manipulated patients by using certain techniques, how patients became dependent, etc.—all of which seemed to feed into and reinforce Jimmy's paranoid fears. There was obviously no way of knowing how much of this really came from his brother and how much of it was distortion on the part of Jimmy himself. The question that had to be settled was whether this was going to be his analysis or his brother's. He was clearly using his brother as a defense against his own deeper fears that, if he committed himself to the analysis, made it his own, and invested himself in the hard work that it entailed to make it a success, he might not be able to do it. He was clinging to the position of dependent little brother—the baby—afraid to take the risk of succeeding or failing on his own.

A side issue—although an important one—was Jimmy's persuasion that his analyst and his brother were in communication about his analysis, and that they were in cahoots in plotting to bring about his downfall. Again, these quasi-delusional fears were not responded to. They were simply heard and, where possible, related to his persecuting nemesis.

The focus of the analysis moved away from these anxieties. We turned instead to the myriad and multifaceted contexts in which Jim felt himself to be weak and defective and doomed to failure. The contexts were many—we have seen most of the important ones. His depressive feelings had to be worked through in each instance. This was by far the longest phase of his analysis. He increasingly came to see that the basis for his anxieties was not the reality that confronted him, but the elaborate fantasy that he carried in his head. The working through consisted in large measure in the defining and demonstrating of the operation and effects of this fantasy in so many contexts of his life and activity—sex, work, study, play, etc. The roots of the fantasy were clear and the working through brought us back again and again to the infantile basis of his convictions of defectiveness and helplessness and weakness.

As these issues were gradually worked through, the anxieties diminished in other areas of his experience as well. He slowly developed a rather firm and productive therapeutic relationship. He felt less and less of a distance and difference between himself and me, and more of a sense of his own capacity to do the work of the analysis—freer to advance his own interpretations, to offer his associations without fear of seeming foolish, or being laughed at. Free associating was no longer "bullshitting." The paranoid thoughts seemed to evaporate. They became increasingly rare, and were revived only in minor forms and as passing thoughts with less and less conviction or feeling in them. The paranoid concerns in the many other parts of his life faded and became remote in his experience as time went on.

Termination

I do not wish to extend this account of Jimmy's analysis any more than necessary; it is already rather lengthy. But the termination phase was significant. Not unexpectedly, many of his anxieties and fears were brought up again in the context of termination. They were verbalized as fears of regressing after the end of the analysis when he no longer had me and the analysis to fall back on. The fears did not have the same intensity or quality of concern as before. They were voiced more or less as thoughtful possibilities rather than experienced as anxieties. I responded to these fears as the last vestiges of his wish to be dependent and to avoid having to be responsible for himself and standing on his own feet. He was able to recognize that he had indeed accomplished a great deal during the course of the analysis, but was reluctant to accept the idea that he could go on from there and make a success of his life without the analysis. The basic question at that point, in terms of analysis, was whether the work that had been done in the past years was due to my efforts or whether the effects were due to the part that Jimmy himself had played in making them a reality. The realization that I had been on the sidelines coaching, but that he had been in there playing the game and that he himself was the responsible agent for his own therapeutic success, was an important stabilizing insight.

And so the analysis was ended—successfully I think.

DISCUSSION

The Depressive Component

The material provided by Jimmy's analysis, perhaps because of its detail and the peculiar quality of the analytic material, offers considerable reinforcement to the view of the paranoid process that we have been evolving in this study. But it also offers us a unique insight into the relationships and interplay of the various factors that lie behind the paranoid process. The primary fact that emerges from this clinical history with peculiar vividness and force is the conviction that Jimmy had of his own defectiveness. Around that central element the other disparate elements of his history and his experience cluster in such a way that they give the entire clinical picture a consistency and symbolic dimension that is often not grasped in less complete case material.

It is also immediately apparent that there is an intimate connection between this core of defectiveness and the central depressive component of Jimmy's pathology. One of the important things learned from the study of previous cases is that the depressive and paranoid elements go together, and that they play off and mutually reinforce each other. The link between Jimmy's depressive view of himself as weak and defective and the intensity of his paranoid anxieties was evident. We need have little hesitation in observing that the paranoid process operated as a defense against the painful depressive affects lying underneath them. It is also impressive, even in reasonably healthy personality structures, how deep and intense the depressive convictions can be embedded. In fact the major portion of the analytic work, extending over a number of years, had to do precisely with the stubborn resistance with which Jimmy clung to his idea of his defectiveness.

Family Reinforcement

Since the paranoid process can be seen so often as a defense against and a compensation for the underlying depressive core, it is important in attempting to understand the process for us to understand what it is that gives this depressive core of the illness such strength and resiliency. The answers to such an inquiry—however slender and partial they may be—are multiple and complex. To go back once more to Jimmy's family context, it is apparent that the notion of his defectiveness is reinforced from many angles. It seemed as though all the family members had formed a kind of collusive net in which the combined efforts of Jimmy's mother, his father, and both of his brothers were directed toward keeping Jimmy in the role of the family baby. There seems little doubt that Jimmy's heart defect played into his mother's pathology in very direct and very dramatic ways. It effectively mobilized her obsessive concern, and served as a basis for her protective obtrusiveness. It was also the foundation for the very special and secretive relationship that Jimmy had with his mother.

The pattern was established, and all of the family members worked to maintain it. This was true even of Jimmy's father, even though the latter seemed to have been a rather remote participant in the family interaction.

Nonetheless, his role seems to have been a significant one. The father failed in important ways to make up for the deficits that followed upon the pathological interaction between Jimmy and his mother. From his father, Jimmy took away a sense of disappointment, a feeling that his father was not interested in him, that he did not think much of him, and that somehow Jimmy was completely unable to behave in such a way that his father would finally take an interest in him and be proud of him. It seems quite likely from the details we know of the family life that Jimmy's father maintained his distance from the family interaction as a way of avoiding conflict and confrontation with his wife. His relatively passive and permissive attitude seems to have been calculated more to support his wife's insecurity and uncertainty than anything else. Jimmy, of course, interpreted his father's behavior as weakness, just as he also interpreted his father's remoteness and relative silence as rejection.

Enuresis

In this context, then, Jimmy's enuresis takes on particular importance and significance. It is significant not only because of its duration—Jimmy remained enuretic well into his preadolescent years—and because of the pattern of its recurrence, i.e., in close relation to his mother's thyroid condition and the subsequent operation, but also because of the connections it established with the core elements of his defectiveness. It was probable—and smellable— evidence of his weakness and inadequacy. There seems to be little doubt that the enuresis tied together a number of significant strands in Jimmy's experience. He was ashamed by the smell. His mother's smelling of the sheets was more embarrassing to him than any other aspect of his enuresis. And he related it to the bad smell of his feces which mother had to counter with Airwick. His constant adult fear was of smelling bad; in consequence he had to use a variety of colognes and deodorants. His inability to hold on to his semen in a sexual encounter was directly related to his inability to retain his water in the bed-wetting context. All of these elements led back to the basic context of loss of control, the inability to regulate one's sphincters, making a bad-smelling mess—all of which was clearly related to his concept of himself as a defective, repulsive, messy, little kid.

There is evidence to suggest that prolonged enuresis is significantly related to family problems. Enuretic families show patterns of parental conflict which are frequently severe enough to lead to separation and divorce. Such families show a pattern of poor sibling relationships and of preference for other siblings on the part of the parents, factors which seem to contribute to an overall pattern of rejection experienced by the enuretic child. Often mothers of enuretic children show a particular preoccupation with toilet training, with a greater concern and more negative emotions surrounding the toilet-training experience, (Umphress et al., 1970). Moreover, the degree to which nocturnal enuresis can be related to and involved with maternal pathology has been amply demonstrated (Blum, 1970).

There seems little doubt that Jimmy's enuresis was linked with his mother's anxieties and with her continuing solicitude and overprotectiveness. We can be less sure of the role that it played in maintaining the balance of psychic forces within the family system. The evidence suggests, however, that it played into and reinforced the more general pattern of family integration which was set up around Jimmy's position as the weak and defective family baby. It is clear that the symptoms reemerged in the context of increased anxiety and stress in relation to mother's thyroid condition. For Jimmy, however, it remained fixed as a symptomatic expression of the process that had been generated in the family. From his point of view the enuresis produced important by-products, since it elicited his mother's continual concern and involved attention. The enuresis thereby indirectly served to consolidate his position as the defective, dependent child who needed special care and concern.

Phobias

Another important area which looms large in Jimmy's early experience was his phobias. We know from later evidence that Jimmy was subject to a number of phobic anxieties. Among these, for example, was his fear of dogs. He always became very anxious and fearful when he got near any dogs because he felt they might be able to smell his bad and repulsive odor, and that they would consequently attack and bite him. It is not difficult to fit this type of phobia into the pattern of his other anxieties and preoccupations, particularly his marked castration fears.

However, he was troubled rather severely with hypochondriacal disease phobias—the principal one, of course, being cancerphobia. Such patients often demonstrate features of their psychopathology that are quite similar to those we have identified in Jimmy. They are often prone to inhibitions of anger, to excessive bodily concern and low self-esteem. As children they often have histories of being weak, sickly, and overprotected. There is also a tendency among such disease phobics to be the youngest sibling (Bianchi, 1971).

This basically phobic disposition was also a feature of Jimmy's childhood, as we have seen. He was often terrified that when his mother or father would go away for any length of time something would happen to them, that they would be killed and they would never come home again. This fear was, in fact, behind some of his childish tantrums when the parents would try to go away. And even when he was still quite young, he heard one day a report on the radio about a religious fanatic who was predicting the end of the world. The idea took hold of him and he lived in dread of this horrible event for weeks, not daring to tell anyone and feeling he could not discuss it with his parents or others because they would tell him it was foolish or childish.

Then there was the matter of his school phobia. It seems difficult to escape the conclusion, based on the manner in which the school phobia, prolonged over so many years, expressed itself—by hectically dragging mother out of bed at the last minute and getting her helplessly involved in the pell-mell rush for school—that the school phobia did serve similar ends and similar libidinal interests as the enuresis, and in fact the whole syndrome of Jimmy's defectiveness and his need to be babied and helped.

Jimmy's work phobia in later years seemed to serve a similar function in his adult living as the school phobia had served in his childhood period. They were unmistakably ways in which Jimmy clung to his defective and special status and thereby clung to his Oedipal involvement with his mother. It is interesting that Jimmy shared with other job phobics a number of significant characteristics. Such patients experience considerable difficulty in getting to work. They frequently have bouts of anxiety with depressive episodes and somatic complaints. They tend to be conscientious and perfectionistic, and hardworking. Job performance is usually exceptional, but does not come up to the levels of their own expectations. Their self-criticism usually causes them to feel that their position is constantly in jeopardy, and that they are continually in danger of being fired. The self-image is one that is closely associated with failure (Radin, 1972).

Family Mythology

Also impressive is the degree to which aggressive components permeate this family system. We have learned something in recent years of the manner in which aggression can affect family interaction patterns. The inability in such a family to share, communicate, and absorb, and thereby neutralize, aggression is a primary cause for the consequent expression of psychopathology. Those family members seem to be most intensely affected who are most intimately and deeply involved in the family emotional interaction. In Jimmy's family the conflicts over aggression seem to have been deep and abiding. The family atmosphere seems to have been permeated by a set of convictions—or perhaps one had better call it a mythology—about the consequences of the expression or acknowledgment of aggression.

Such a mythology forms a rather complicated and distorted system of beliefs based on conflicts over aggression, which determines and directs the patterns of interaction which are tolerated within the family context (Raybin, 1971). Jimmy's family seems to have been permeated by a set of attitudes, never directly formulated or expressed, but which seem to have

dominated the family milieu. Any expression of aggression was not tolerated and was anxiously avoided. There was a brooding sense of preoccupation with imminent disaster. Whatever happened the response was cast in
terms of the most dreadful and undesirable consequences. Problems or difficulties that people in the family might have could not be shared and talked
about, but rather had to be shunted into the background and denied or
avoided.

This mythology—if we can call it that—seemed to have been generated
(primarily) by Jimmy's mother. It should be noted, however, that such predominant family atmospheres are not generally sustained by a single individual in the family, but rather they require a collusive involvement of
most, if not all, of the family members. Given this family atmosphere, it
becomes easy to understand how the discovery of Jimmy's heart defect
played into, focused, and concretized a set of fears and anxiety-laden anticipations that already pervaded the family atmosphere.

The handling of the difficulties surrounding his heart defect and the
associated operation was unquestionably neurotic and highly maladaptive.
It gave room for play for mother's worst anticipations and anxieties and
preoccupations. This aspect of the situation is highlighted by the fact that
after the operation the level did not seem to significantly decrease. One
would have expected that a curative procedure that had repaired the congenital defect and had made Jimmy a whole and healthy young boy would
have caused an alleviation of the anxiety that was connected with the
procedure. But such was not the case. Counter to all claims of reality, both
Jimmy and his mother sustained their almost delusional belief that rather
than having cured Jimmy, the operation was a convincing proof of his inherent defectiveness and weakness. The conclusion seems inescapable that
the clinging on the part of both Jimmy and his mother to the belief in his
defectiveness and the collaboration of the rest of the family in continuing
and contributing to that belief was in some way symptomatic of a deeper
level of disturbance in the family system itself. The data at our disposal are
not sufficiently detailed or extensive to allow more specific documentation
of that conclusion. But it seems to be an essential ingredient behind the
pattern of childhood phobias and other symptoms which marked Jimmy's
early experience.

Family System

But I would like to focus at this point on the broader implications of
Jimmy's participation in the family context. If we put aside for a moment
the narcissistic considerations in this interaction, we can look at the family
interaction as a collaborative effort, which was calculated to define a place
and a role and a function for Jimmy within the family matrix. This definition of place and function in the family takes place at a quite unconscious

level. One can think of a multiplicity of levels of function and interaction within such families. There are levels of conscious, intentional, deliberate interaction in which patterns of interactions develop in relation to real needs and concerns of the family group. But there are also less conscious, less intentional levels of implicit interaction which are much more determined by patterns of emotional need and responsiveness within the family.

Thus each person in the family is ascribed a set of functions and expectations and limitations by which the unit defines him specifically as a member and by which it communicates to him the specific expectations it has for him. Thus from Jimmy's point of view, the family defined for him a position which he was to occupy, and which for him *not* to occupy carried with it the threat of dire consequences. That position was where he belonged. That position was what he *was* essentially in the eyes of the family and reciprocally in his own eyes. That position was defined to be the family "baby"—dependent, unreliable, irresponsible, unexceptional, the mediocre and incompetent family baby. For Jimmy to imagine anything but that role, or for him to attempt any behavior that was not consistent with such role was to incur the consequences vis-à-vis the rest of the family. Those consequences, which were implicitly punitive, would never be explicitly defined or stated. They were nonetheless operative. The implications they spelled out were a loss of love, a loss of his position within the family, the threat of retaliatory rejection, literally the threat of being cast into the outer darkness where he would wander alone and unloved, doomed to a fate worse than death.

The strength of these forces and their powerful influence on Jimmy could be measured by the fact that in countless ways, and with seemingly endless repetition during the course of this analysis, it was precisely these kinds of anxieties and concerns and preoccupations that he offered as his own, as part of his fantasy of the consequences of deviating from the established pattern. He was completely blind—at least in the beginning—to the fact that these threatening consequences had been generated by, and were continually being reinforced from, his family. Even in his adult life, for Jimmy not to be a weak, defective, dependent failure, meant that he would run the risk of being cut off from his family, of being rejected by them, of losing all meaningful emotional ties to them. When we add to this pattern of integration of the emotional system in the family the powerful claims of both obviously Oedipal gratifications as well as strong narcissistic ties, we can appreciate the intensity with which Jimmy clung to his affective position. It was these intense needs that underlay both the paranoid process as well as the stubbornness and resilience of Jimmy's resistance in the analysis. And it was against these very resistances that the analytic work had to be done.

Internalizations

The combined effect of these forces was to give Jimmy what we can call loosely a sense of identity, of belonging, of establishing a niche into which he fit and from which he could not stray without threat of severe retaliation or disaster. The complex processes and interactions that were taking place around Jimmy and which established a developmental matrix within his family were only one dimension of the problem. Another significant dimension had to do with the processes of internalization that somehow made these expectations and directives of the family system part of Jimmy's internal world. One of the important dimensions in understanding the paranoid process is precisely the manner in which the conjunction of family processes and intrapsychic internalizations contributes to the organization of personality structure in such a way as to support the paranoid process. As we have seen in the other cases in this study, the pattern of identifications seems to be rather complex, and in Jimmy's case the pattern seems to have been no less complex. The data here are more convincing, perhaps because of the amount of pertinent information that is available in Jimmy's case that could be only hinted at or surmised in other cases. Moreover, an additional and extremely significant dimension of these identificatory processes was manifested in the analytic situation, specifically in the transference neurosis. The historical impressions received a vital concretization and vivid realization that makes the interplay of identificatory processes all the more convincing.

Perhaps the most significant identification was that with his mother. Jimmy's defectiveness was not merely a special bond or privileged secret that he and his mother shared: it was the inner reality about himself and about her, as well as her inner reality and conviction about himself and her. Their symbiotic pact was based on more than shared attitudes and secrets. Jimmy saw his mother as defective, castrated. He saw himself in the same light. However much he fussed and worried and bitterly complained about his mother's anxious and concerned treatment of him, there was no escaping the fact that Jimmy treated himself with the same attitudes and concerns and anxieties. While Jimmy saw his mother as castrated and defective, it is nonetheless true that he saw her ambivalently also as powerful and intrusive and controlling. Prior to his analysis, Jimmy was never able to resolve these two aspects of his mother. He could not make up his mind whether *he* was weak or strong. If a part of him desired to be his mother's weak, castrated, dependent little girl, there was also a part of him that really felt he was a weak, dependent little girl. It was this aspect of himself that expressed itself in homosexual fantasies and wishes, particularly of being submissive and dependent on a strong, powerful male figure.

Jimmy's identification with his father was also strong and complex. In contrast to his identification with his mother, however, the identification

428 The Paranoid Process

with his father was more subtle and more enigmatic. Again it was fraught with ambiguity and ambivalence. Jimmy saw his father predominantly as a weak man who was controlled by his mother. He saw his father as a man who had been victimized by his family. Yet there was the other side of his father, the side that was somehow reinforced by his father's remoteness and uncommunicativeness. Here again the parameters of strength and weakness were confused and obliterated. Jimmy could not discern whether his father was indeed a weak, ineffective victim, or whether he was in fact a strong, competent, shrewd man of the world. His childhood picture was of the former, but as the years went on and Jimmy's awareness of the difficulty and complexity of his father's business and work and his role in the community grew, Jimmy came more and more to appreciate and understand his father.

For both parents, then, Jimmy's adult perception of them seemed to have turned to the opposite of the childhood perception he had held. Both of these parental introjections, it can be noted, were cast in terms of the confusion and ambiguity of victim and aggressor. Jimmy's relationships with both parents, as well as the identifications that derived from those relationships, were infused with sadomasochistic concerns.

The other extremely important relationship that had a significant impact on Jimmy's development was the relationship with his older brother Harry. Here again the relationship was colored with intense sibling rivalry, with powerful ambivalent feelings, and with strong influences of sadomasochism. It is not uncommon within the family context for sibling relationships to have significant modifying influences on the child's development. At times, such relationships can be constructive or contribute to positive identifications, particularly if the sibling object in question is uninvolved and unaffected by the family pathology. In Jimmy's case, however, the relationship and interaction with Harry was based on such intensely rivalrous and ambivalent elements that the introjections derived from it tended to reinforce the masochistic and victimized dimensions of Jimmy's character structure. For the best part of their relationship Harry was clearly the sadistic aggressor, except for those episodes in which Jimmy was able to lash back in anger. The masochistic reinforcement derived from this relationship, however, had the added benefit of reinforcing Jimmy's dependent and defective position—and therefore the specialness of the relationship with his mother.

Sadomasochistic Relationships

Particularly striking in the conjunction of these introjections is the aspect of what Anna Freud has called the "identification with the aggressor." In Jimmy's family relationship there was little room for tenderness, concern, empathy, or for a sense of autonomy or individuality of other persons. Object relationships on all sides were heavily contaminated by sadomasochistic elements, by predominant concerns over dominance and submission, by continual struggles over subjection and subjugation. It is little wonder that during his analysis Jimmy continually complained about the violation of his freedom, about his fears of intrusion and domination, about his concerns about being controlled and intruded upon and dominated during the analysis. These, after all, were the substance of his object relationships and of his experience of significant others from the very beginning.

He could not conceive of significant relationships with other human beings except in terms of sadomasochistic struggle or of conflicts over power. The sadomasochistic quality of the perduring relationships in Jimmy's family is eloquent testimony to the pathological effects of unresolved aggression within the family system. We might wonder what it is that contributes to and sustains such a pattern of pathological interaction within that system. The answer, it seems to me, must lie in the interlocking projections which individual members of the system contribute, projections which are somehow shared and reinforced by other members of the family system.

It seems clear that the matrix of the pathological interactions that Jimmy was caught up in was determined to a large extent by his mother's anxieties. Hers was a ghetto mentality. She feared the outside world. That world to her mind was hostile and destructive. She felt comfortable only with a narrow circle of relatives and close friends, and to venture outside of that narrow confine meant to court hostile and destructive retaliation. It is interesting to speculate to what extent these atttitudes of his mother were a reflection of her Jewish background, her ghetto upbringing, or any of her religious convictions. The data at our disposal are certainly not adequate to shed any considerable light on these connections, but we can only conclude that the elements of guarded isolation, of suspiciousness of the outside world, and of finding comfort, solace, and support in a narrow group of like-minded people was entirely in keeping with her paranoid attitudes. There was little question that these attitudes, however, permeated the family atmosphere and determined to a considerable extent the patterns of behavior, particularly the behavior patterns of Jimmy and his older brother Harry.

Pregenital Determinants

While it is clear that the Oedipal elements played a prominent and considerable role in Jimmy's character structure and psychopathology, it is also true that his pathology expresses and reflects a significant determination by pregenital elements. It was undoubtedly the perduring influence of these rather infantile and primitive, pregenital elements that made the course of his treatment more difficult and the strength of his resistance more rigid. Certainly the anal-erotic and the anal-sadistic components of his character were strongly marked. We have noted his preoccupation with anal intercourse, both actively and passively. He not only desired to perform anal intercourse with his girl friends, but in fantasies he often saw himself submitting passively to the anal assault of a strong, powerful male.

Part of this anal fixation had been imbedded in his character structure in the form of excessive perfectionism and his rather stubborn negativeness. Along with his characteristic obstinacy and wishes to be perfect and his wanting to stubbornly resist influence from outside, there was a characteristic preoccupation with messiness. He was often almost defiantly untidy, and kept his personal belongings in a state of messiness and disrepair. There was also the almost overwhelming ambivalence that characterized all of his interpersonal relationships. We have also had occasion to note the sadomasochistic elements that permeated his relationships within and outside of the analysis. These reflect a strong anal fixation, and undoubtedly relate back to the strong influence of his mother and her own rather strong anal preoccupation.

There seems little doubt that Jimmy's Oedipal involvements with his mother were colored by anal fixation. We can recall the somewhat seductive scenes of his wanting her to rub his buttocks during the nightly back-rubbing scenes, as well as the earlier infantile scenes on the potty. It is striking in this context that mother's attempts to seduce Jimmy into performance on the potty by tickling his penis in a sense joins a number of significant threads of Jimmy's underlying psychopathology. The strong fusion of anal and genital libido seemed to characterize and predominate his adult heterosexual relationships. It was clear that seduction by the woman was a giving-in, a passive pleasing of the woman, a defeat in the anal struggle for dominance or submission—being "led around by the penis"; it raised the threat of being controlled, of losing one's freedom of self-expression, of subjecting oneself to the power and the will of a woman.

This strong component of sadomasochism affected all of Jimmy's relationships, but particularly those of a sexual nature. Jimmy was unable to have a relationship with a woman in any way other than in terms of power, in which the sexual encounter was a struggle, in which the outcome could be seen only in terms of victory or loss, success or failure, mastery or enslavement. There was little doubt that Jimmy's strong wishes to beat and torment women, to tie them up and whip them, as part of the sexual performance, to force them to submit to humiliating and perverse sexual practices—all had their roots in the intense ambivalence that Jimmy still held toward his mother.

The other significant infantile component of Jimmy's personality was his orality. It was expressed, of course, in his sexuality, but also, and perhaps more significantly, in the addictive aspects of his personality, and in the pattern of clinging and rather infantile dependency that characterized so much of his behavior, both in and outside of the analysis. This aspect of Jimmy's personality is reflected in his feeling of inner defectiveness and emptiness, of a sense of needing to be filled up, of having to depend on things outside of himself to maintain a sense of his own reality and capacity.

The oral aspects of his sexuality combined a number of aspects of his instinctual life. These were focused most intensely in his wishes for and fantasies of fellatio. He wanted to have his penis sucked on, underlining the breast-penis equivalence and his own introjective identification with mother. Castration anxiety played a major role here. His anxiety dream of the classic "vagina dentata" and his paralyzing fear of the prostitute's dog who might bite his penis off were closely related. By putting his penis in a girl's mouth, he was putting himself in a vulnerable position, exposing himself to her castrating teeth and the dreaded and externalized oral sadism. There was a counterphobic element of "getting away with it."

But there was another aspect. In the fellatio there was not only a gratifying feminine identification, but identification with the aggressor. The woman was sadomasochistically forced to submit—to "strip and suck." Jimmy was expressing in these fantasies the aggressive dominating aspects of the maternal introject, as well as the sadistic aspects of his own intense ambivalence toward his mother. The humiliation and degradation of the woman was thus multiply determined.

Antisocial Tendencies

Closely related to these addictive and oral aspects of Jimmy's personality was the whole question of his antisocial tendencies. Even as a child, there was a decided pattern of lying and stealing and general deviousness which characterized his adjustment within the family. It was clear on the childhood level—as was the case in so many other aspects of his behavior that we have discussed—that much of this devious behavior was directed toward his mother. The lying and telling of stories was obviously calculated to increase her interest in him, and to maximize their mutual involvement. It was Jimmy's way of trying to prolong and extend the special nature of their relationship. It seems apparent also that the stealing was a form of communication directed at his mother, calculated to gain her attention and involvement, even as the enuresis had similarly been intended, and communicating in a sense his underlying feeling of helplessness and emptiness and the fear of losing his dependent, clinging, supportive relationship with her.

I would like at this point to recapitulate some of the comments of Winnicott (1958) on the dynamics underlying the antisocial tendency. The point that Winnicott makes clear is that the development of the antisocial tendency is closely related to the emergence and responsiveness to drives within the parent-child matrix. Stealing and lying lie at the heart of the tendency. When the child steals an object he is not looking for the object stolen, but rather he is seeking a form of parental involvement not otherwise available. Winnicott puts it in these words:

> When a child steals outside his own home he is still looking for his mother, but he is seeking with more sense of frustration, and increasingly needing to find at the same time the paternal authority that can and will put a limit to the actual effect of his impulsive behavior, and to the acting out of the ideas that come to him when he is in a state of excitement. . . . The strict father that the child evokes may also be loving, but he must first be strict and strong. Only when the strict and strong father figure is in evidence can the child regain his primitive love impulses, his sense of guilt, and his wish to mend. Unless he gets into trouble, the delinquent can only become more and more inhibited in love, and consequently more and more depressed and depersonalized, and eventually unable to feel the reality of things at all, except the reality of violence (1969, pp. 228-229).

It is possible to think then in terms of two trends—the stealing and destruction, and the object-seeking and object-clinging. The union of these trends in the antisocial tendency may in fact be a tendency toward self-cure, an attempt to fuse the instinctual trends that have previously been defused. The original deprivation may carry with it a fusion of the aggressive and libidinal trends in the child, so that the child then claims the mother by a mixture of stealing and hurting and messing. Winnicott emphasizes that the nuisance value of the antisocial child is an essential feature of his behavior, as well as a favorable indicator of the potentiality of recovery of the lost fusion of libidinal and aggressive drives. As Winnicott observes, the normal child has considerable disruptive and nuisance value. He writes:

> The normal child, if he has confidence in father and mother, pulls out all the stops. In the course of time he tries out his powers to disrupt, to destroy, to frighten, to wear down, to waste, to wangle, and to appropriate. . . . If the home can stand up to all the child can do to disrupt it, he settles down to play; but business first, the test must be made, especially if there is some doubt as to the stability of the parental set up and the home (by which I mean so much more than house). At first the child needs to be conscious of a framework if he is to feel free, and if he is to be able to play, to draw his own pictures, to be an irresponsible child (*ibid*., pp. 227).

It seems, therefore, that in the normal course of development ordinary wetting and messing have their own built-in nuisance value. These can be incorporated into the antisocial tendency. Thus the latter tendency can express itself in stealing and lying as well as incontinence and the making of a mess generally. Each such symptom has its specific value and implication, but a common factor is the nuisance value that they attain in relationship to the parents. That value is thus exploited by the child. An essential feature of this is that the infant has reached a capacity to perceive that the cause of the disaster lies in an environmental failure. This perception that such cause lies externally rather than internally is responsible for the personality distortion and the consequent urge to seek for a new cure by environmental supervision.

Antisocial children are constantly seeking out this cure by environmental supervision, but the external provision does not make up for the internal loss. Winnicott places the original deprivation at a point in development when the infant or small child is in the process of achieving some fusion of libidinal and aggressive drives. The experience of the emerging drive brings about a recognition in the child that what Winnicott called ruthlessness is about to become an aspect of his relating to the environment. The child thus stirs up the immediate environment in an effort to alert it to the imminent danger so that the environment may be organized to tolerate the nuisance involved. Winnicott observes:

> If the situation holds, the environment must be tested and retested in its capacity to stand the aggression, to prevent or repair the destruction, to tolerate the nuisance, to recognize the positive elements in the antisocial tendency, to provide and preserve the object that is to be sought and found. In a favorable case, when there is not too much madness or unconscious compulsion or paranoid organization, etc., the favorable conditions may in the course of time enable the child to find and love a person, instead of continuing the search by laying claims on substitute objects that had lost their symbolic value (1958, p. 314).

It is apparent that the favorable conditions that Winnicott speaks of did not obtain in Jimmy's family, and particularly in the relationship with his anxious, obsessively concerned, and perhaps somewhat paranoid mother to whom these antisocial strivings seemed to have been primarily directed.

The "Exception"

We have had occasion to observe the play of the elements of narcissism throughout Jimmy's neurosis. If we translate the special quality of his weakness and defectiveness into terms of his being an exception, we are drawn inexorably to the classic treatment of the "exceptions" first given by Freud (1916). Freud's comments find a peculiar aptness and applicability to what we know about Jimmy.

> Now it is no doubt that everyone would like to consider himself an exception and claim privileges over everyone else. Precisely because of this, there must be a particular reason, and one not universally present, if someone actually proclaims himself an exception and behaves as such. This reason may be of more than one kind; in the cases I investigated I succeeded in finding a common peculiarity in the earlier experiences of these patients' lives. Their neuroses were connected with some experience or suffering to which they had

been subjected in their earliest childhood, one in respect of which they knew themselves to be guiltless, and which they could look upon as an unjust disadvantage imposed upon them. The privileges that they claimed as a result of this injustice, and the rebelliousness it engendered, had contributed not a little to intensify the outbreak of their neurosis (1916, p. 313).

For Jimmy the experience of his childhood to which he had been unjustly and guiltlessly subjected was the rather severe trauma of his heart operation. It is clear, however, from all that we have said, that the heart operation served only as a symbolic focus for a whole complex of detrimental influences that combined to persistently reinforce Jimmy's position as the weak and defective child. The heart operation itself had been a severe trauma. One must nonetheless think in terms of a cumulative trauma, or a perduring situation of trauma which persisted throughout the course of Jimmy's development. It is tempting at this point to quote again the powerful tirade with which Shakespeare introduces his famous exception, the duke of Gloucester, Richard III. It is tempting because it so aptly demonstrates the essential characteristics of the exception, as well as the fact that Freud himself quotes this famous speech. But I shall not resist the temptation. In the words of Shakespeare's deformed prince there echoes a refrain I heard in countless utterances from the analytic couch during the course of Jimmy's analysis.

> But I, that am not shap'd for sportive tricks,
> Nor made to court an amorous looking-glass;
> I, that am rudely stamp'd, and warm love's majesty
> To strut before a wanton ambling nymph;
> I, that am curtail'd of this fair proportion,
> Cheated of feature by dissembling nature,
> Deform'd, unfinish'd, sent before my time
> Into this breathing world, scarce half made up,
> And that so lamely and unfashionable
> That dogs bark at me, as I halt by them;
> Why, I, in this weak piping time of peace,
> Have no delight to pass away the time,
> Unless to see my shadow in the sun
> And descant on mine own deformity:
> And therefore, since I can not prove a lover,
> To entertain these fair, well-spoken days,
> I am determined to prove a villain,
> And hate the idle pleasures of these days (1945, p. 596).

Thus did Jimmy view his own deformity and his own defectiveness. He too had determined upon being a villain; that is to say, a rebellious, troublesome nuisance, a failure in the eyes of the world. If he was able to find ways to achieve this in his child world, it was all the more difficult in the world of adult demands and responsibilities. Yet the rebellious, villainous, revengeful impulse continued to hold sway in his fantasy life. At the same time his conflicts over aggression, his intense fears of retaliation and harm, and his fears of the loss of love and of loss of the special quality of dependence that was his ultimate safeguard and protection prevented him from any meaningful expression of these powerful urges. He could be a Gloucester only in his fantasies. And his wish to become a Richard, with the power to command and subjugate and destroy, terrified and paralyzed him.

Narcissism and the Paranoid Process

Thus we can begin to appreciate that it was basically these narcissistic expectations—denied, disappointed, and unfulfilled—that underlay and gave motive power to much of Jimmy's pathology. We are faced here again with what Murray has called the "narcissistic triad" (1964)—narcissistic expectations go unsatisfied and unfulfilled and produce a response of disappointment and rage that does not meet and respond to the inner needs and privileged expectations the underlying narcissism requires. The rage against ambivalent objects, which are also the objects of primitive love and protective fulfillment, cannot be directly expressed without catastrophic effects. Consequently it must be displaced through projection, so that the unfulfilling and unresponsive outside world, which fails to meet and satisfy the intense narcissistic needs, becomes a hostile and destructive world of retaliatory attack and hostile intent.

These considerations draw us inevitably, once again, to the problem of separation and individuation (Mahler, 1968). It is evident from the material that we have presented that there was an intense degree of separation anxiety that characterized Jimmy's early childhood experience and which persisted through the major portion of his subsequent developmental years. His symbiotic and infantile dependence particularly on his mother produced certain inevitable impairments in his individuation. While these impairments and their consequences are easily traceable, they do not seem to have been on a level of pathological intensity which we have been able to identify in other of our patients. Nonetheless, we are once again confronted with the connections between difficulties in separation-individuation and the genesis of the paranoid process. Our understanding of the genesis of the paranoid process has to deal with a complex of interlocking and interacting factors which includes the separation-individuation process, problems of infantile dependence, narcissism, as well as antisocial and phobic tendencies.

CHAPTER 15

Miss Karen K.

THE PATIENT'S PROFILE

Presenting Complaint

The present case is that of a young woman in her mid-twenties who came seeking psychoanalysis primarily because of the difficulty she was having in heterosexual relationships. She was unmarried, and although she could claim other areas in her life in which there had been significant achievement, the area of heterosexual adjustment had been a most chaotic and unhappy one for her. As a result she found herself quite unhappy and depressed.

She had, it turned out, become quickly and rather intensely involved in relationships with men which turned out to be short-lived and most unsatisfactory. Her involvement in these relationships was always very competitive and basically sadomasochistic. The men in these relationships were almost exclusively unavailable, that is, they were either married or sufficiently immature to preclude even a remote possibility for a meaningful and perduring heterosexual involvement, let alone marriage.

Karen's decision to seek therapeutic help came as a result of a particularly intense, unusually disappointing, and extraordinarily sadomasochistic relationship, in which she and her boyfriend would alternate in attempts to undercut and devalue each other, even to the point of physical beatings and abuse. She found herself acutely depressed and confused after the breakup of this unhappy relationship. She was intelligent and resourceful enough, however, to recognize that there was a recurrent pattern in these relationships and that she had better think about doing something about it. She sought psychiatric consultation, and psychoanalysis was recommended.

When Karen first came to my office I found her to be a very impressive person. She was a tall, statuesque, platinum blonde, who was very attractive and obviously very bright. She handled herself with considerable poise and composure, even though it was detectable that she was covering a considerable degree of insecurity and anxiety. Over the course of several interviews, she told me something of the problems she faced and some of the general outlines of what her life had been like. There was little doubt in my mind that she was clinically depressed, but what impressed me perhaps more strongly than anything else was her remarkable resourcefulness and her capacity for mobilizing her energy and generally effective defenses in the service of dealing with her disappointments and anxieties.

In fact, she had been able to accomplish a considerable amount in her score or more of years. Despite considerable adversity, as we shall see, her academic career had been remarkably successful. She had always been at the top of her class through grade school and high school. She had graduated with high honors from a prominent eastern university and was elected a member of Phi Beta Kappa. She had continued on to postgraduate work, and at the time was just beginning the work on her doctoral dissertation.

Family Disorganization

The history she described to me was an unusual one, and I will recount it here only in the broadest details, leaving the specifics for later reconstruction in relation to the analytic material. Karen's parents were married before the onset of World War II. The family background was Jewish on both sides, although the mother's family was somewhat better off financially and socially than the father's. The father was a career army man, for most of his years in the service attached to army intelligence. Karen's mother was the youngest in her family, and her marriage to a career army officer seems to have been regarded in the upwardly mobile social atmosphere of her middle-class Jewish family as something of a family disgrace.

During the early years of their marriage, the young couple traveled extensively in connection with his reassignments in various parts of the country. Finally when World War II broke out, there was a rather lengthy separation for the duration of the war. During the war years the father served in army intelligence operations, working particularly in the Pacific area, and the mother returned to live with her own family. After the war, the couple was again reunited, and in due course Karen was born.

When she was only a few months old, her father was again reassigned and had to leave the family. He did not return again until she was about eighteen months old. The family history, from the beginning of Karen's experience in it, was defined in terms of the father's reassignments and the recurrent separations from him. Often enough, the family would move to the new location where the father had been assigned, at least whenever this was possible. But on frequent occasions it was either impractical or impossible for them to stay together, and as a consequence there were long periods, several times lasting for many months to years, when Karen's father was not with them. One particularly lengthy period was during the Korean War, when Karen was about six or seven, when the father was separated from his family for over two years.

The result of this state of affairs was that the family had to follow an extremely mobile pattern of life. They seemed to be moving from one place to another every few months, and certainly averaging more than once a year. At one point Karen added up something like nineteen different moves that her family had to make. As a result she never spent more than a year in any particular school. Again and again, she had to pick up and move with her parents, usually her mother, leave her friends and schoolmates, and move to a new place where she would have to make new friends and establish herself once again in a new school. She became expert in establishing herself on a secure academic footing in the new schools, and quickly precipitating herself into intense relationship with her peers. She described herself as always having the feeling that she had to get as much out of what was going on around her as possible. She could not afford to miss out on anything, because she never knew when the good things, the friends, and the security around her would be snatched away unexpectedly and seemingly without reason.

Frequently, especially when her father was assigned to overseas, she and her mother would move back to live with the mother's brother's family. They were apparently warmly and generously received, but Karen always felt that they were received as though they were "poor relatives." Moving back with her mother's family was a reminder of what she did not have, namely, the stability and security of a home that she and her family could call their own, and the financial and social status that the mother's family held. As we shall see later on, much of this resentment and disappointment was focused in her relationship to her cousin Ann, who was the same age and with whom she developed a rather intense sibling rivalry. As we shall see later, Karen's bitter and resentful attitude toward her mother's family formed an important part of her overall pathology.

Growing Up Without Father

Her childhood performance was in fact generally precocious. She recalled that she walked and talked at a very early age, and particularly that she was toilet trained by the time she was a year old. She remembered that there was a family story to the effect that when her father returned from his first absence, when she was only eighteen months of age, the family went out to a restaurant and she was able to sit at the table and eat with the adults. She regarded this precocity in her training a result of her mother's obsessional disposition. As a result, she regards herself as having been excessively neat and orderly and controlled even as a very young child.

She recalled that in the years of her growing up she was extremely sensitive to any criticism or any accusation. Whenever anyone would indicate displeasure with her or indicate that she had not in some way measured up to expectations, she would feel incredible guilt. Apparently her mother was particularly able to utilize this emerging aspect of her character as a way of keeping her under control. Later on in the higher grades in high school, this sensitiveness continued and she would become extremely upset and sometimes even hysterical when things would happen to disappoint her, or her peers would in one or other fashion reject her or cause her to feel inadequate. In these early years, she seemed to have been somewhat excessively dependent on her mother. Whenever something happened to frighten or upset her, she would run to her mother for consolation and protection. This pattern was probably reinforced by the absence of her father and the obsessive concern and solicitousness of her mother.

In high school the problems of popularity and attractiveness began to assert themselves. It was extremely important for her that she be well liked by her classmates and that she establish herself as one of the more popular girls. Anything which threw that status into question was extremely upsetting and troublesome for her. Increasingly she became aware of herself as an attractive female, but had difficulty with this in face of the rather repressive sexual attitudes of her parents, particularly her mother. Her mother would not allow her to dress in a more mature fashion or to wear lipstick or high heels until she was about sixteen. It was only then that she was allowed to date boys. Later on we will see more in detail some of the contradictory and inconsistent elements in the parents' sexual attitudes.

Sexual Rebellion

But in the face of these restrictions Karen had considerable difficulty. She found her parents' attitudes repressive and restrictive. During one year toward the end of her high school period, she lived with her family in the Philippines where the atmosphere was much more open and relaxed. She feels that during this time she went through a minor rebellion against her parents' restrictions, staying up late at night, smoking cigarettes, drinking rather heavily, and engaging in minor sexual episodes of kissing and petting. She was particularly resentful at having again to surrender this atmosphere in which she felt freer, as well as more accepted and popular among her peers.

By the time she had graduated from high school and had entered college, Karen seemed to have reached a significant turning point in her development. When she arrived at the private eastern university at which she had matriculated, she decided it was time for her to throw off the restraints and restrictions that had been imposed on her for so long by her mother. At that point, she had never had intercourse. She determined that she would lose her virginity, and set about accomplishing this with considerable vengeance. Her mother had said to her on repeated occasions that men do not marry women who smoke and who are not virgins. Consequently Karen set about a rather intense program of heavy drinking, smoking, and sexual activity. She was quite successful in these endeavors, and became known as an "easy lay." She had frequent sexual experiences with many different men, even being unofficially taken over by a whole fraternity. She took satisfaction, even relish, out of the idea that she could lead such a life of sexual indulgence, while at the same time she performed paradoxically in a highly credible manner academically. She literally wanted to be all things to all men. She broke college rules carelessly, and almost seemed to flaunt herself in the face of any authority. When the dorm mother tried to set some limits on her, she became angry and incensed and rebellious, throwing things and smashing windows to have her own way.

There had to be a reaction to this pattern of frenetic acting out. When it became clear to her that she had established a rather unsavory reputation for herself on campus, she felt bitterly resentful and betrayed. She felt that the liberal atmosphere that she had imbibed on campus was in part responsible for her throwing off of restraints and inhibitions. When the judgmental and somewhat condemnatory attitudes came back to her, she felt somehow betrayed and used. She became deeply resentful of all of the boys at the college who had taken advantage of her willingness to be sexually available to them. Consequently, when she went on to graduate school she spent a rather extended period of about a year-and-a-half in which she shunned any sexual contacts and kept her social life to a minimum. During this period she rather obsessively concentrated on her academic activity and threw herself wholeheartedly and devotedly into her doctoral studies.

The Sadomasochistic Pattern

The work and the study were rewarding in retrospect, but she looked back on that period as an emotional and social desert. She was able to sustain this pattern for a fairly long time, but increasingly she began to experience a more and more troublesome depression. Finally after two years of doctoral work she decided to interrupt her studies and went to New York, where she worked for a time in secretarial and similar jobs. She began dating again, but once again fell into this pattern of forming intense and rather sadomasochistic relationships in which she felt herself to be taken advantage of and sexually abused, and in which she defended herself by demeaning her male partners, and using her rapier sharp wit and intelligence to put down and undermine the men. This did not continue long, however, since she felt that her life was increasingly unsatisfactory, that she was getting nowhere, that her relationships were unrewarding and in fact self-destructive, and that she was only making herself available as an object for the sexual exploitation of the rapacious males around her—as she called it the "meat market."

At this juncture, she determined to return to academia and to focus on finishing her doctoral work. She took a job as an instructor at a local university and started to lay the ground for her work on her dissertation. In her new job the same pattern of sexual involvements developed. Most of the men in her department were married, but despite this she managed to make the rounds with nearly all of the men in the department within a relatively short time. Most of these relationships were rather intense and sexually active, but it quickly became clear that in none of these cases was there any promise of a meaningful relationship for her. In one or two cases there was talk of divorce and marriage, but in each case she was bitterly disappointed. When she had in this fashion run through the list of available men in the department, she became increasingly depressed and anxious, and began to think seriously of the possibility of therapy.

The First Hour

Karen's first hour on the couch was an illuminating one and enunciated many of the interlocking themes which will take up the bulk of our consideration. We can reconstruct this first hour here as a sort of prelude to the further exploration of her analytic material.

As she approached the couch, she asked whether I had an ashtray and whether it would be possible for her to smoke on the couch. I replied that perhaps that was something we could talk about. She lay down in a rigid position and for several minutes was silent. On the wall there was hanging a quite undistinguished and cheap painting of a country scene. She began by commenting on the painting, "I'm looking at that painting on the wall, and I'm not crazy about it. It looks sometimes like a van Gogh, but it's the worst I've even seen. I don't think I can get through this thing without smoking." I wondered what her thoughts were about not smoking. "I enjoy it. I like the taste, and I guess I smoke for all the possible reasons. I'd like to stop; at least I would have more money. But I feel hostile to anything like an order or demand. You said we could talk about it. That's not a demand. It's difficult when there is a block of time. I usually have a smoke before I go into the theater. The house on the right is just wrong for that print." There was a silence of several minutes. "I wonder if it's really a van Gogh. I guess that's not tactful—you must like it." I wondered at that point whether she was concerned about offending me. "Well I would have things in my home that I liked, and I would think it would be the same in your office. But I have the impression that you wouldn't invest much in this office or building." The comment reflected the dilapidated state of the hospital building.

> Let's get back to the cigarettes. I take cues from people. It's irritating not to be able to look at you. I made the mistake of watching Marcus Welby last night. It was the story of a suicidal woman, but she felt her life wasn't worth living. She could only be attracted to married men, since she felt they were safe. She went to an analyst, but he wasn't Freudian. It seems that they cured each other. I wonder if I'm looking for similarities or differences? I guess I'm being superficial. The shrink was dying from an amyotrophic laternal sclerosis. I guess it's a plight common enough to evoke identification, but it

wouldn't have much appeal. It's the difficulty of individual problems as against social patterns. What are the reasons why a career woman would get into that position? It seems like a conspiracy between the outside and the inside. The relationship I had this summer was one of the best I ever had. I still want a cigarette.

There was a long silence following this.

I wonder if I felt threatened? I didn't think of him as married, but I was able to accept the relationship and didn't have to feel so defensive. It was just a relationship of a victim and a victimizer. I wonder if it happened because I knew he was married, or did it just go right and did I relate to him as an eligible man? That may be unanswerable. I'm feeling verbal resistance, this whole thing feels intimidating.

I commented that this was a new experience for her. She replied, "It gives rise to the greatest resistance, but I try to make it sound good. I have a lot of self-pity over all the rotten things that have happened to me. Things have got to get better. This was not a pleasant year. Things are so close to the surface, but I'm afraid to let go." At this point she became tearful.

My parents never tell me anything. I remember when I got home and my mother rushed out of the house saying, "Now don't get upset, but . . ." That was when my father had his stroke. Fortunately it was minor, but when mother said that, I began to feel myself get cold and hard. The next time it was when my father had an accident. He was all cut up and in bad psychological shape. He lost his job with the government and then had an accident and ruined a new car. It was the first accident he had had in years, but the insurance company screwed him. He still thinks of me as a baby. He had his teeth pulled and he didn't like his job at all. His sixtieth birthday was so depressing, and I took a thousand dollars.

Here the tears began to flow copiously. Then in a somewhat resentful tone, she went on.

My mother wasn't a martyr, but why should I hate to take money? If I owe anybody anything I remember it for years. That should make you feel better.

The comment was prompted by a preceding discussion about the fee.

How can I pay for this? What if I got sick? Money always seems to be a problem. My mother's relatives are rich, but I hate them. My father always feels so inadequate. They never go traveling with her family because I take the money and they can't afford it. They invited the family to come to my graduation, and it made me feel like a pawn. I hate this comparative shit. But my father took them out to dinner, and that was nice.

There was a pause here again.

I felt like working again last night, starting to work on my thesis. I hope I can sell my adviser on the topic. I certainly have talked about a range of things today. There was a bomb scare at the university this morning. This whole thing is getting ridiculous—but I guess it's an effective political statement. It scares people but it doesn't hurt anybody. But the police seem so laconic. By the way is there a bathroom on this floor? I may need it. I'm going to read more about analysis, because I want to use Freud in my course. One of the major themes there is dehumanization which goes along with desexualization. Freud didn't invent the unconscious or sex. The whole idea of penis envy is so damn moralistic and smug. It says ladies have to "take things like a man." I guess you have to accept the conclusion if you accept the premises. I wonder about your silence—is it a companionable silence?

Themes

This first session revealed a considerable amount. She was obviously anxious, and in her anxiety many of her pervasive concerns were manifested. She was guarded and worried about the problem of having to submit in the analysis, but yet at the same time worried about offending me or hurting my feelings. The comment on the "van Gogh" print on my wall reflected her need to see the analysis as something special and valuable. Her references to the suicidal woman in the television program and the remarkable similarities to her own difficulties suggested the underlying depression with which she was struggling. It also enunciated themes which were to work themselves out through the course of the analysis, particularly the theme of individual difficulties as opposed to social and cultural expectations, as well as the parallel theme of internal conflicts as opposed to external forces. Karen was unsure whether she would have to accept the blame for her problems herself or whether she would cast the blame on circumstances and persons in her environment. Related to this she also enunciated the problems of being a career woman and what that might mean to her.

Also extremely important in her pathology was the theme of the victim and the victimizer, again a focus of considerable anxiety and difficulty for her. She portrayed herself as the disadvantaged victim of things that had happened around her. She was able to focus this particularly in relationship to her parents, focusing on her mother's role as the martyr in the family and on mother's capacity for eliciting guilt in her. She also made it clear that she was very upset about things that had happened to her father, and immediately placed these calamities in conjunction with her own taking money from her parents. This suggested the ease with which her guilt was mobilized and the importance it assumed in her pathology.

Finally, at the end of the session she began to refer more directly to the process of analysis and evinced her concerns about it. Particularly noteworthy was her resistance to the notion of the unconscious and to that of penis envy. She felt deeply concerned about any theoretical imposition which the analysis or the analyst might make upon her which would reduce her to some lesser common denominator. All of these themes were to be endlessly repeated and rehearsed throughout the course of her analysis.

Defensiveness and Coping

One of the early themes to emerge in the analysis and one which expressed and reflected Karen's rather rigid defensiveness had to do with her need to see herself as effectively coping. Her defense took the form of being hard on herself and demanding. She commented, "No one could be harder. That assumes that people will be hard on me and I expect them to be. I substitute somebody else's explanations for my own, and I expect a slap across the knuckles." The coping was intimately connected with her tendency to blame herself when things went wrong and to feel guilty. It was easier for her to accept the blame, because then she felt she could do something about it. "If life is shitty, then I can't handle it."

But assuming her own fault in things allowed her to mobilize her coping resources. She prepared herself for the worst and then would brace herself for the anticipated blow. She commented, "I only hurt myself. I can't block off my emotional responses. I turn the other cheek, but I can't roll with the punch. I seem to have foresight but no flexibility, so that I just take the blows in the worst possible way." I commented at this point that she seemed like a good soldier, and she replied, "I never enlisted. I was drafted. But a good soldier should know when to duck, but only on command." There seemed little doubt that this was closely related to her underlying fears of vulnerability.

The motif of coping played itself out even in the analytic situation and provided a major theme of resistance. She felt threatened by my interventions and wanted to "do it for myself." The paranoid quality of her fear was evident. She said,

> I feel so vulnerable, as if I am going to get hurt. If I'm strong I won't get hurt. But what's so good about being strong? People always back away from being needed, but being weak turns me off. I hate it when people get that puppydog look. I would shrink myself before you did. I would respond in advance, like Madame DeFarge watching my own head roll. I'd do it to myself before it was done to me.

I wondered at this point whether she felt my comments were hurtful to her. "You're Madame DeFarge," she said. "You're the observer, calloused, enjoying the spectacle for your entertainment, getting your kicks out of watching heads roll."

The coping was obviously a defense against her underlying depression. She felt that coping was less painful for her and it was something that she could count on. It was easier for her than allowing other people to see her suffering. In a sense she resented the necessity to cope, but the alternative was dependence, something that she dreaded and feared. She observed that she didn't want to have anybody who would desert her. After all she had been deserted by her father again and again. One of the hardest things for her to take was the idea of being left. The need to cope was indeed a defense against the underlying fear of dependency and the associated fear of being left and abandoned.

The coping part of herself was the strong, intellectual, and masculine part of herself which protected her from the weak, vulnerable, and feminine part of her. She felt herself to be precarious and fragile; if she leaned a little she would fall, so that even leaning a little was fraught with danger. Countless situations were turned into ones that threatened her and to which she needed to respond by coping. Referring to a friend who was also in analysis, she said, "Marge gets hopeless, but I get copeless." And again, "If I come on even slightly less than my strongest self, I feel vulnerable."

Control

Related to the issue of coping was that of control. This became very clear in the context of the analysis. In one of the earlier sessions Karen commented, "I feel that I'm fighting a helpless feeling, not knowing where I'm going." I replied that she wanted to put me in her position and herself in my own position. She replied, "It's a question of control, I'm afraid of losing control. I have a Faustian thing about knowledge and understanding. I can control something by putting it into words. It reminds me of my parents always telling me to control myself. I hated that. It gives me a Univac self-image, that I could work anything out rationally. I could rationalize my emotions, my bitterness and hostility."

The whole pattern of the loss of control carried with it certain definite dangers and risks. Karen felt that, if she lost the rigid control that she maintained over herself, she would become violent and destructive. She would start screaming and never stop. She would throw and smash things and become uncontrollably destructive. Moreover, if she lost control she could never get it back. She recalled the fights she had had with her boyfriend as episodes in which there was a total loss of control. She could not understand the violence that would come out in these fights, and was terribly frightened by it. Her concern extended not only to the vulnerability she felt when she relinquished control to others in her environment, but to anything that was inflicted on her over which she felt no control. This extended even to the ultimate vulnerability of death. She continually returned to her concerns over growing older and of getting closer to death. Death represented the ultimate violation over which she had no control.

In the analysis the issue of control was a primary one. The instrument of her control was her intelligence, so that any of my attempts to interpret to her were taken as attempts to control. She could not tolerate the idea of relinquishing control to me. She could not allow me to be in control of the analysis, since that would mean making herself vulnerable to attack. The fear of control was particularly related to the question of relinquishing control to a doctor. Her fearful attitude was highly overdetermined. When she had been quite young, she had been living with her family in Japan and had become sick. She had been taken to a Japanese hospital and had been quite terrified of the Japanese doctors. According to her recollection they had wanted to bleed her, but she had had to be rescued and taken to the United States military hospital instead.

On another occasion when she had been scheduled to have a tonsillectomy, the knowledge of the forthcoming operation had been kept from her due to her mother's protective anxieties. Her uncle, who was a physician, had taken her to the operating room with reassurances that nothing was going to happen to her. When the anesthesia mask was clamped over her face, she became panicked and terrified. She held this deception against her uncle with considerable bitterness and vehemence.

Moreover, this same uncle had been looking after her father when the father died. We will have to return more in detail later to the father's death, since it took place soon after the analysis began and played a significant part in the course of the analysis. But Karen held it against this uncle that he had not been more attentive and competent in taking care of her father's heart condition.

Her basic question in all of this concerned the competence of doctors and the uncertainties of medical diagnosis and treatment. Karen constantly complained that doctors never really knew what they were doing, and that patients were helpless and vulnerable because they had to put themselves in the doctor's hands and rely on their uncertain judgment. This necessity mobilized much of her underlying sense of vulnerability and her helpless rage at not being able to control the situation. The question also pervaded her relationship to me in the analysis. She wondered about my competence and continually questioned it, particularly when her resistance was high and when she felt threatened by any intervention I made. She repeatedly emphasized that the important thing to her was that I should be right, rather than that my intentions toward her should be good. Despite this demand for my competence in making interpretations, the equation of knowledge with power brought it about that the more correct my interpretations were, the more threatened she felt.

Submission

Consistent with her intense need to cope and control, Karen responded to any exercise of authority in a highly threatened and rebellious manner. She made a point of going against my conventions and making sure that she rebelled against what she called "rigid codes." Such codes had an inevitable leveling effect. She observed, "Everyone is subject to the same rules, treated like ciphers. I didn't like that, whether it was from the universe or from my family. I had to individualize myself. I can't function without feeling that I am an individual, that I am special and different, an army brat . . . doing other than expected." Such an attitude was an affront to her family's way of life, and as she looked at her married friends the submissiveness she saw in her former girl friends scared her. She felt that such relationships were restrictive and ordered. Marriage offered her the threat of being subjected to someone else's will, someone else's control.

In the analysis it was much the same, although she felt intrigued by the intellectual stimulation and subtlety of the analytic process. But she refused to submit herself to anything she felt was arbitrary. It stirred up in her a feeling of indignant, sickening anger. She wanted to say to me, "Who the hell do you think you are?" She hated and had nothing but contempt for that attitude in her parents that allowed them to submit themselves to the arbitrary decisions of the army, particularly when those decisions took her father away from her. She felt it was arbitrary and contemptible, and made her feel as if she was treated as though she didn't exist at all. Any acceptance of the directives of authority were seen by her as "ass kissing." The alternatives were clearly either angry and contemptuous rebellion or humiliating submission. Only gradually was she able to relate these feelings to the submission she had felt with her parents.

In the analysis the issue of authority and submission to authority was joined from the very first hour. Her initial question about smoking on the couch had in fact addressed itself to that issue. Was I going to be arbitrary and rigid, treating her in an authoritarian manner, or was I going to be flexible and allow her to have her own way?

Struggle with Authority Figures

It gradually became clear to her that part of what was at issue was her rebellion against her parents. She recalled that the drinking and smoking and sexual experimentation were a rebellion against her mother's injunctives, particularly the prohibitions about sex. When she got to college, she at last felt she was beyond her parents' control, but she felt that what was most irritating to her and what she most wanted to rebel against was the necessity for having to hide her activities or lying to her parents. She desperately wanted them to recognize her for what she was as an individual, and not as some figment of their imagination. She wanted her mother particularly to find out what she was doing, to hurt her, and to shock mother's sensibilities. On one occasion she left contraceptive devices in a place where it was quite likely that mother would discover them. On another occasion she called mother up from a boyfriend's apartment telling her that she was not coming home. On each of these occasions mother was properly shocked and upset and the inevitable battle of recriminations was set off. But it was clear that Karen not only set up these battles, but in a way relished them. Leaving things for mother to find was, she said, "A slap in the face." She wanted people to face up to it, to understand her, and most of all to accept her for her real self.

It was not difficult for her to link her struggle with authority figures with the figure of her father as well. In a very early hour she began talking about hating authority figures and their restrictions, and then almost in the same breath began talking about how attractive a man in uniform was to her. She immediately referred this to her father. Later she was able to express her concerns about people who make rules that impose something on others. Her fear of the chairman was based on the fact that he could enforce the rules in the department. He had the force of law behind him. Her life, she commented, was filled with "Thou shalt nots" which were imposed on her without any say on her part. With her father she never knew what the rules were and was only able to discover them when she had transgressed them. She felt that her father's rule-making and enforcing were so arbitrary, yet could relate this arbitrariness and authoritarian attitude on his part to his own feelings of insecurity. Being arbitrary and autocratic were his ways of maintaining control. She described anyone who made rules or exercised authority as a "fascist."

Competitiveness

In the light of these aspects of her character, it would not be surprising were we to discover a considerable amount of competitiveness in Karen's personality. There were aspects of her behavior that were phallic and aggressive. She owned a large male German shepherd and delighted in parading him around the neighborhood, particularly when she would meet male friends whose dogs were nowhere nearly as impressive as hers. She also owned a big, high-powered, sports-model car and prided herself on her ability to drive hard and fast, like a man. She referred to the automobile as "a car a girl should never drive," and was quite explicit about the ways in which she exploited the car and her driving ability to make her male friends feel inferior.

A particular area of her competitiveness, however, was in the area of her intellectual capacity. In relation to men with whom she felt clearly intellectually superior, she felt a certain contempt. A particular area in which her intellectual competitiveness revealed itself was in her teaching. She taught a section in conjunction with a male member of her department, and she carried on a running guerrilla warfare with him over who taught the better course. At certain times when his course was oversubscribed in comparison to her own, she felt bitterly resentful of this and accused him of using unfair tactics to solicit students to come to his course. She observed that she refused to prostitute herself in this manner. She felt at times that he was "shitting on her," and even expressing quite paranoid feelings about comments that some of the students made about not wanting to take the course from a woman. She observed that she should have "shat" on him first, and that it was the kind of crap that women in academia had to subject themselves to.

She saw things very much in either-or terms. If she was not being admired, she felt she was being ignored. As she put it, her drive was constantly to be a star. And if she didn't get the acknowledgement and attention she required, she began to feel ignored and devalued and easily fell into paranoid attitudes that people were out to get her or to do her in.

It is worth noting in passing the rather anal quality of the material she presented. She constantly referred to being "shat on," frequently used the expression "That shits!" Whatever she disagreed with was a "load of crap," and whenever anyone did anything that was to her disadvantage or her displeasure she would refer to it as "crapping" on her. Crapping on someone carried the implications of putting them down, hurting or demeaning them in some way. The anal imagery carried the implications of her hostility and competitive destructiveness.

Sexual Conflicts

In the light of these concerns, it should not come as much of a surprise that the area of sexuality was one that was highly conflicted for Karen. While she effected a strongly libertarian attitude toward sex, envisioning herself as the embodiment of the liberated woman—at the same time there was a certain embarrassment and hesitancy about sexual matters, as well as a rather pervasive if sometimes strongly denied sense of guilt about her sexual activities. There was a strong counterphobic element in all of this, however, as if she were somehow determined to prove to herself that she was not going to be sexually inhibited or constrained, as her mother was, or that she would not allow herself to feel any of the stirrings of guilt that were attendant on her sexual proclivity. There was a strong wish in her to deny any such guilt, and it was really only after several years of analysis that we were able to get to the point where she could acknowledge such guilt in herself. The critical issue, of course, in all of this was that the guilt feelings were allied with her identification with her mother, against which she found it so pressingly urgent to defend herself in so many ways. We will have the opportunity to suggest later on that many of the masochistic and depressive aspects of her character were related to this unconscious sense of guilt. Or, looking at it in another perspective, the sexual acting-out served as a countering defense against the inner sense of guilt. Stylistically this was quite parallel with her more general pattern of controlling and coping in the face of her underlying, although denied, sense of weakness and vulnerability.

Karen saw the sexual relationship primarily in sadomasochistic terms, in which the male was the strong, dominating, controlling, and powerful figure, while the female was seen as weak, subjugated, inferior, and passive. She felt powerfully conflicted about this and played out the various sides of her conflicts in her relationships with the various men she knew. Getting screwed for her was in a sense an act of subjugation and submission. In this aspect she responded with passivity in the sexual encounter and an emotional blocking which left her generally frigid, although it equivalently protected her from feeling any of the painfully subjugating emotions. In her sexual activity she resented bitterly the act she had to put on to convince her male partner that she had in fact had an orgasm, but any orgastic experience was by far the exception for her. She saw this faking of orgasms as essential for protecting and supporting the fragile sense of masculine competency. At the same time there was a part of her that was motivated to try to control and manipulate the sexual relationship. She often spoke of "screwing guys," and thrust herself into sexual encounters as a way of coping with and mastering her anxiety.

The significant part of this sexual attitude was her feeling about her own genitals. Her basic feelings about her own genital anatomy and function were kept well hidden and were long in coming into the open. She had an abiding sense of her own genital inferiority. She regarded her vagina as dirty, messy, dark, dank, foul-smelling, as a place where foul odors and substances were emitted. There seemed little question that the basic conception operating in this regard was fundamentally cloacal, and that the image of female genital functioning in her mind was contaminated by anal determinants. After the fashion of reaction formations, she found it necessary to institute a number of obsessional cleansing rituals surrounding her sexual activity. She would wash and douche and cleanse carefully her entire genital area before any sexual encounter. She would also perform a similar cleansing ritual after a sexual encounter.

In contrast to her attitude to her own genital, she regarded the penis as strong and clean.

One other aspect of her sexuality which bears comment is an aspect that did not come to light until a good two-and-a-half years of the analysis had passed. One day she casually mentioned that it was a custom in her home for her parents to walk around nude a good bit of the time. She recalls that this was the normal thing in the family in all the years she was growing up, until the time she left to go to college. She also remembered during that period frequently taking showers with her father. She tried to treat this matter as entirely casual and inconsequential. When I wondered why it was that she had never mentioned it during the long period of her analysis she denied it had any significance, and resisted any suggestion that it might have been something she might have avoided. However, I think it shed some light on the sexual conflicts that we have been able to identify. On the one hand we know that the attitudes of the parents toward sexuality, particularly the mother's attitudes, were quite repressive and restrictive, if not downright prudish. We know how stringently the mother restricted Karen's sexual activity, not allowing her to date boys until she was sixteen years old. Yet, at the same time, there was this persistent and rather high level of sexual excitation and in addition presumably, built-in seduction. The combination of excitation and repression gave a double message which served only to confuse and confound Karen's emerging view of sexuality, and more particularly her own sexuality.

Particularly conflictual for her were the more perverse and fetishistic practices. She had strong feelings about oral-genital sex even though in several of her relationships she had engaged in fellatio. Particularly in one relationship—the one which developed into such a mutually abusive sado-masochistic tango—fellatio became a constant feature of the sexual activity. She would use her mouth on him, but he would never reciprocate. As a result she felt demeaned and abused and her feelings that her own genitals were repulsive and dirty were confirmed by his refusal to use his mouth on her. Another partner had asked her to wear black nylon stockings and a garter belt while performing intercourse. This excited him and increased his satisfacton in intercourse and she went along with it as a way of pleasing him. But again she felt demeaned and devalued. She felt that she was not adequate in herself and again felt bitter and resentful about this kind of request.

The Victim and the Victimizers

Several elements in these relationships seemed pervasive. Inevitably Karen saw herself as abused, taken advantage of in a variety of ways, and victimized. The victimization seemed to come about by reason of the fact that men would put their needs ahead of hers. As she saw it, men were only able to keep themselves in a secure and superior position by keeping women down. Karen's narcissism found it difficult to tolerate this. When this situation arose Karen responded with bitter resentment and angry contempt. She would revile these men as weak, inadequate and stupid. She felt embittered and enraged by the fact that she was not able to get out of these men the kind of care, attention, solicitude, support, and affection that she sought. She desperately needed approval and seemed as though she expected the man to more or less subjugate his interests and needs to her own. Any deviation from this pattern was seen by her as withdrawal or weakness or inadequacy.

Her attitude toward men varied between two extremes. On the one extreme was the strong, capable, and powerful figure of the male who was also dominating and subjugating. These were the "brutes." At the other extreme, however, were the men who were impotent, inadequate, weak, who were unable to satisfy her sexually, who were threatened by any closeness or demands that she might make upon them. These were the "momma's boys," who were closely dependent and attached to their mothers. Karen saw herself as posing a threat to this symbiotic mother-tie. These latter men were referred to as the "puppydogs."

Once these extreme categories defined themselves, it became quickly apparent that, in Karen's view of men, if they were not being brutes they were inexorably categorized as puppydogs. Similarly if they were not clearly established as puppydogs, she tended to regard them as brutes. The categories played themselves out, inevitably, in the analysis. On any occasion when I would confront her or make an interpretation that challenged her defenses, Karen would react to me in a highly threatened and vulnerable manner, regarding me as an insensitive and calloused brute to whom she would have to submit and subjugate herself. When, however, my approach was gentle and tactful, she seemed to want to interpret this as a sign of weakness, so that any attempts on her part to argue with me or put me down, or to challenge my position as the invincible and invulnerable analyst, would be threatening or hurtful to me. In such phases she would regard me and react to me as though I were a puppydog.

In the closing months of her analysis, Karen formed another relationship with a young man who was a few years her junior and who had at one time been a student in one of her classes. There were a number of things that put Ted in an inferior position in the relationship, and thus made the relationship considerably less threatening for Karen. Despite his own inhibitions and depressive sense of his own inadequacy, he was able to establish a rather warm and mutually satisfying relationship with Karen. Moreover, the relationship was sexually gratifying and for perhaps the first time she began to find herself spontaneously responding in the sexual situation and feeling comfortable and relatively unthreatened in sexual relations. As far as Karen was concerned, she finally had been able to attain a warm, mutually supportive and gratifying relationship in which she found herself really caring about Ted, and feeling that he really cared about and was concerned about her. In the relationship she did not feel exploited or taken advantage of or subjugated. She honestly felt that for the first time in a relationship with a man the possibility was available to her of working out an egalitarian and mutually satisfying relationship.

The Femme Fatale

If Karen felt contempt for and despised the masculine inadequacy and impotence that were so easily threatened, she also saw herself as threatening and destructive to men. She referred to herself as a "femme fatale." She recounted that her father used to have a nutcracker that was made in the form of a woman, you cracked the nuts by putting the nuts between the woman's legs. While she recounted this with humor, it was not long after

The Paranoid Process

that she referred to herself as a "ball-buster." She struggled with her anxiety about having a cold, calculating appearance, even though she could recognize that men had to be insecure to pick that up in her. It was something that put them off and scared them, something that she didn't want to do.

But images were even more destructive and devouring. In talking about a series of old boyfriends, she commented at one point,

> I seem to be belching up old Jonahs. The images are so distressing—just dreams from undigested material. It means that I'm a whale, devouring and consuming. I guess I devoured Jim. I see the female genitals as devouring and mutilated—I think of snake imagery. There is a story about a woman watching a snake devouring a rat, and as she watches she begins to writhe like a snake. It sounds very phallic. A devouring woman, castrating—I guess I'm very much afraid of being like that.

Karen envisioned the male chauvinist attitude which she so despised as basically a defense against male feelings of inadequacy. She saw herself as threatening to such men insofar as she presented herself as a strong, capable, intelligent, and sexually demeaning woman. She felt that this approach made men feel impotent. She observed that she often sounded so opinionated and aggressive. That was the way *not* to get a man, but that was what she felt herself to be.

She felt that men were threatened because she was too bright and too attractive. I commented on the paradox that that seemed to present, since she saw as threatening to men what one might otherwise think attractive. She replied that when she got defensive she used her brains and her beauty as weapons, but that even so, insecure men were threatened. I wondered whether it was more than just a question of having beauty and brains, but rather a question of how she used them. Perhaps there was something in her that wanted to be threatening. She resisted such an interpretation, and insisted that it was not anything about the way she used her capacities that turned out to be so threatening to men; she insisted that it was the nature of the male beast to be threatened by a capable and intelligent, even though attractive, woman.

Very much later in her analysis she was able to put some of this into perspective. She knew she had good intelligence, but at the same time felt herself to be weak and vulnerable emotionally. But she had always had difficulty in recognizing that in herself, particularly in her relations with men. She felt it necessary to defend herself, but then she saw herself as castrating, something that she felt unhappy and guilty about. Still she could say that the men were "bastards." Perhaps they were, or perhaps they were not. But she could see them as bastards particularly because of the underlying threat that she was reacting to.

Intelligence vs. Femininity

Closely related to these fears of being castrating and devouring were Karen's attitudes toward herself as an intelligent professional woman. She stoutly maintained that any kind of professional career or intellectual competence in a woman had to stand in opposition to any possibility in gaining satisfaction and fulfillment in life as a woman. Intellectual competence and a career were thus placed in diametric opposition to sexual fulfillment and satisfaction, as well as in opposition to any possibility of marriage and a satisfactory family life.

These feelings were closely linked to Karen's underlying sentiments regarding her own femininity. She saw her difficulties with men specifically in terms of her academic credentials and her teaching position. Her intelligence was obvious because of her vocabulary and her capacity to think and criticize. But a woman was supposed to be silly, and stupid, and feminine, and she felt that anything else was a threat to men and made them nervous.

Karen tried stoutly to maintain the position that the issues involved in this matter were not something peculiar to her, but that they were issues that persisted at large in American society. She continually appealed to the feminist argument of exploitation and subjugation, holding out that that explained more than psychoanalysis could. If a woman was bright, she was considered aggressive. But clearly her own need to avoid any form of submission or dependence led her to employ her intelligence in an aggressive manner. She commented, "I want to avoid being thought of as a dumb-dumb. I am sufficiently attractive that men have sex on their mind—a dumb broad good for a lay. That raises my hackles. My cousin was a dumb broad, and they always played her off against me and set us at each other's throats, I wanted to be liked for myself, but that's risky." Further, if she were to admit there might be something defensive or aggressive about her use of her intelligence, that would let men off the hook. It would give them an excuse for being threatened, for being chauvinist.

Any suggestion that such extreme positions or defensive arguments might not bear the full weight of the truth created a staunch and immediate resistance in her.

The whole issue of being a professional woman and having an academic career was one that persisted throughout the whole of the analysis, and in fact, you will remember, was raised in the very first hour. Her defense was the externalizing defense of attributing to society and culture all of the responsibility for the difficulty she encountered. When I questioned her, she would become extremely defensive and argumentative. She insisted that being a career woman was a liability and that it imposed limits on her. She protested, "If you want to talk about using intelligence threateningly, OK, but don't try to deny reality."

It was difficult to weave a path which would acknowledge the reality of the complaint she made, namely, that there were chauvinistic attitudes and culturally embedded expectations with which she had to deal, and keeping open the exploration of her own attitudes and feelings and the ways in which her own need to defend herself exploited such cultural and social elements. It was only gradually, and really only toward the end of the analysis, that she was able to bring some of this into a more balanced perspective, recognizing that part of her wanted to blame chauvinistic attitudes for the difficulties she encountered, but that her own insecurities played a considerable role in embellishing and magnifying the difficulties.

The extent of the anger that was generated by these issues was reflected one day on her having walked past a construction site. She was wearing a miniskirt, and as she passed the construction site the workers began making comments to her and whistling at her. She was furious. She said, "They're just a bunch of animals. I don't see that as an analytic problem. It's real! The cure isn't analysis, it's genocide. And it's not my fantasy! I just don't understand what you mean by fantasy. I see it out there. It's the totalitarian prototype, subjugation, making lampshades out of people. Men have a right to use women as sexual objects."

I commented that she seemed to want to keep thinking about this problem in an either-or framework so that any analysis of it was precluded. I drew an analogy to the problem of black prejudice, namely, that there was indeed a social phenomenon of racial prejudice, but that one of the major difficulties in trying to deal with it was the fact that so many blacks tended to accept the prejudice and to see themselves as inferior. It was easy for them to see the external racial prejudice directed against them, but very hard indeed for them to recognize and accept and to do anything about their own inner prejudice. She saw the point, but found it very difficult to recognize and accept her own prejudice. She insisted on seeing her intelligence as threatening and refused to recognize that not all men would be threatened by an intelligent woman, and that there might be any possibility that her use of intelligence might itself be aggressive. She insisted that our culture accepted men as ambitious, but that it insisted on seeing women as aggressive.

The Martyr Complex

In the light of all this, although Karen complained bitterly about being "crapped on from all directions," being taken advantage of, and constantly feeling hurt and cheated, it quickly became apparent that she continually got herself into situations and relationships in which this turned out to be the case. It seemed as if she went out of her way to get hurt, as though she were seeking out suffering in some perverse way. She struggled not to show her hurt and disappointed feelings, but at the same time painted herself as exquisitely sensitive and suffering. The analogy to her mother came quickly to mind. As Karen put it, it was like being a geisha, serving someone else's needs, erasing someone else's pain. The picture was the picture of mother's silent suffering, particularly in the relationship with Karen's father. Karen was able grudgingly to admit that she seemed to be cut out of the same mold as her mother, that of the suffering victim.

But over and above this there was a need to punish herself. The punishment was an expiation to the gods, and she would rather do it herself than have someone else do it. She would rather be pained herself than to hurt someone else—just like her mother's martyr complex. She easily felt that she was in the wrong, that she had transgressed in some manner that she often could not define, or that she had to apologize for herself. The contexts for this were multiple, whether it be in sexual activity, in which she felt that she should apologize for not being sufficiently attractive or entertaining or responsive to her partner's needs, or in her teaching, where she vacillated uncertainly between apologizing to her students or berating them for their poor performance. If she made demands on her students or tried to set standards of performance which they failed to meet or resisted, she immediately felt apologetic, as though it were her fault that the students could not master the material, that she should have made the course easier, that it should not have been so demanding, that she had not been sufficiently entertaining, or that her teaching was not sufficiently clear or forceful. On all of these fronts she was constantly plagued with feelings of self-doubt and insecurity. She assumed often enough that she was the stronger individual in any situation, and that she could bear the hurt and disappointment, but that others could not. Consequently, it was better for her to feel hurt and disappointed rather than hurting someone else.

Her tendency to put herself in the position of disadvantage and suffering was exemplified in the fact that she chose the most difficult subject and the most demanding director in her department for her dissertation. She described him as the "biggest bastard around." She felt that he let her talk about her subject until she had managed to hang herself, a form of self-execution. She was just asking to be "shat on." But she observed that she seemed to function best when she was working with a bastard, and that if someone was being protective or kind to her, she felt that she was being condescended to. On the one hand she found herself caring deeply about people who were able to hurt her, and on the other hand she felt that if a man was capable of being a bastard, she would be the one to bring it out in him.

Subjugation in the Analysis

The obvious reference for many of these feelings was the analytic situation and particularly Karen's relation to me. With reference to the analysis, she observed, "I'm so afraid to be limited, I feel I have to fight back. I'm afraid of being made to feel I've done something wrong, of being boring, or just skimming, not being good enough. I just can't take the criticism." I commented that she seemed to feel that I would criticize her, and she replied,

How could you not? You have been informed of my wrongdoings, that I am disgusting—that's my mother's word. I want to please everybody, and I can't stand people thinking negatively about me. I wanted to be respected and liked, but compliments are embarrassing. I feel I maneuver people into giving them. But I didn't enjoy being told that I was disgusting—particularly for things I did on my own, especially for sex. I was proud of my liberated self, of being guiltless, of being as good as she (mother) thought, but for different reasons. But I have to submit myself to gain approval.

I wondered whether she felt she had to submit herself in the analysis. "No, I'm not submitting, but you're Madame DeFarge sitting there and enjoying the spectacle." I observed that she somehow presumed that she was a spectacle and that I enjoyed it. "I want to be a spectacle. I want to be noticed." And I agreed indeed that there was something in her that wanted to make a spectacle of herself, but at the same time, wanted to have a Madame DeFarge sitting and maliciously enjoying the spectacle. She bitterly observed, then, that she felt maligned and rejected, just a little girl looking to be "shat on," going to a shrink five times a week to make sure that she was maligned and ill-treated, playing perversely in the shit. She then added angrily, "I won't buy that it's all my fault, I'm not a raving paranoid." She referred to the analysis somewhat bitterly as "picking at myself." Later on she commented,

A lot of things are coming together here. I asked for help and it was denied, and I'll never ask again. Help is not going to come. I turn against the person I feel pulled toward. I've turned against the analysis and it's machination. I never thought childhood would elicit these responses. I was kicked and taught to say, "Thank you." Thanks for the obstacles, thanks for the difficulties, thanks for the pain. I take it as a putdown, if people make it easy or are nice to me.

And again,

I was listening to a doctor talk about his patients, and it made my skin crawl. Does psychoanalysis exist to service people, or do people exist to service psychoanalytic concepts? You just don't discard the patient if he doesn't fit the hypothesis. It's science against the individual, and the categories seem more important than the people . . . Doctors are not bound to preserve confidences but lawyers are. I would never tell my uncle anything. I think about doctors joking about patients—the more you know the more ways you can hurt me. And I just don't hand people weapons to hurt me.

Subjugation and Castration

But the problem of relating to men was more complicated. It was not merely a problem of resisting the advances of exploitive and manipulative men. What was more of a problem was that when Karen began to really care about someone, the very caring began to get her into difficulty. She commented, "It turns me off if they care more for me than I care for them. It scares me. It makes them into puppydogs, as though their life depends on me. It reminds me of my mother's look, so hurt, as if she couldn't fight back." I commented that she seemed to be in a bind, that if men cared more about her they became vulnerable, and, if she cared for them, she became vulnerable. She replied, "Every woman adores a fascist—the boot in the face, the brute. 'The man in black with a Mein Kampf look, with a love of the rack and the screw.' I'm just not very trusting. The pathological killer whose only pleasure is meanness." She summarized her sense of vulnerability and defensiveness and her fears of castrating the man in a telling phrase, "She cuts his prick off to spite her face. That's my mother's principle—but you only end up hurting yourself."

The motifs of castration and helpless subjugation were summed up and expressed in a very vivid dream. "I was beginning to masturbate and I could feel long hairs, stiff like wires, around my anus. Then I started cutting them off with a scissors, and I realized it was part of my spine, like a tail. I realized it was part of myself. I awoke with a numb feeling in my back." Her associations immediately led to the archetypal quality of the dream and the enunciation of the themes of mutilation, punishment, and castration. It gave her a scary, frightened feeling, as though she had destroyed herself. She commented,

> I'm so scared of physical harm to myself. My own death seems more possible now. The dream is obvious—women are more inhibited in talking about masturbation. But I'm afraid that maybe it's better than sex with a man. Women are not supposed to get horny. I block out masturbation or oral-genital sex, but I feel better about the actuality. I only really feel natural about straight intercourse, everything else is embarrassing. That's just a half-step past my mother. My mother is always in the closet. I'm really always compromising myself for somebody else's pleasure—I think of faking an orgasm. I can't make demands in bed. If I tell a guy he should do something else, it means that what he is doing is wrong, so I'm afraid I'm not going to please him, and I'm afraid of being slapped down for asking for anything.

The basic masochism which permeated her character structure was closely tied up with and derived from her sense of her own femininity as devalued, inferior, and weak. Femininity to her meant weakness, inferiority, submission, and helpless vulnerability. She struggled continually against what she saw as the basic psychoanalytic view of women as castrated and inferior. Women were supposed to be silly, and hysterical, and stupid, so our culture dictated and people's expectations demanded. But she refused to be that. She saw herself embattled in a society and a culture that sought only to subjugate and denigrate women; she refused to accede to or subjugate herself to such demeaning stereotypes.

To counter that she adopted a radical feminist posture and bitterly reviled the sad state of affairs that forced people to play roles. She saw society as prejudiced, biased, and sexist. The rivalry between the sexes was a form of power politics. She complained bitterly that her mother was mired in the feminine role. She bitterly decried the acting out of such roles. There was a young couple with whom she was quite friendly. The wife earned a higher salary than her husband, but turned the salary over to him so that he could manage the family finances. He in turn gave his wife an allowance every week. Thinking about this arrangement made Karen furious. Who the hell did he think he was? What could be more unfair than for a husband to give his wife a mere pittance as an allowance out of a salary that she had earned. That was the height of chauvinism and servile dominance. She bitterly derided female chauvinism—the attitude that said a woman had to defer to a male for help and support just because he was a man.

Vulnerability

But at a deeper level, a level that was deeply repressed and denied, there was a pervasive sense of feminine inadequacy and vulnerability. She felt herself to be contaminated and dirty, and had a deep sense of outrage at what she called her biological self. She complained of her genitals as dirty and messy. She saw herself as victimized, and maintained an abiding sense of outrage on account of it. As she saw it, women always got the brown end of the stick. It was their lot to be "shat on" and taken advantage of. She got into a bitter argument with her department vice-chairman about who would make a pot of coffee. She refused to make the coffee just because "that officious SOB chauvinist" thought making coffee was women's work. She struggled against anything that would suggest that women were in any way inferior, or for that matter even different.

The threat of vulnerability ran through all of her thinking about sex and its meaning in her life. When she was making love with a man, she regarded him as in control of the situation, so there was no other course for her but to be vulnerable and subjugated. But yet she found herself perversely attracted to such subjugation. She commented that she was attracted to men who treated her harshly and insensitively. She commented, "A brute is attractive. If he beats you over the head with a stiff penis and drags you to bed, you know he wants you." She felt in general that she allowed the man to be the center of the relationship, and saw herself as hovering on the periphery. What he wanted and needed in the relationship took precedence over what she wanted and needed, just as in her parents' relationship it seemed that her father was the center and her mother took a subordinate position. She felt there was no alternative in this paradigm, she could only be a Desdemona.

Her only recourse to deal with this situation was to turn off her feelings, so that she became isolated and frigid. She put it in terms of a particular reference for herself, commenting that the person who drives is always the one who is in the center. This related to her image of driving fast sports cars as a masculine activity. She even preferred a regulation stick-shift because that gave her a sense of power and control. The phallic reference was transparent.

In Karen's mind, the feminine was identified with the hysterical, weak, helpless, whimpering, and crying female. She made it quite clear that she would not allow herself to see herself in those terms. Yet she feared her weakness, her emotionality, and her sensitivity. She could admit that there was a lot that she might want to cry about, but crying was weakness. It meant exposure, nudity, a lack of control. She could recognize that she wasn't really as independent and self-sufficient as she tried to make people believe. But her parents had made her submit, and she felt weak and helpless with them. They said, "Do as I say." There was no way to fight back. To get anything she had to beg on her knees, and when she got anything on her own it wasn't worth anything because it was without their approval. To have a relationship to a man, she felt she had to be an incompetent nitwit. Any relationship had to be based on her being crippled. As she put it, "Being feminine in this society is being a cripple, and I just can't do that."

The prototype of feminine weakness was the character of Desdemona—the sweet, insipid, helpless female who needed to be protected by the strong, capable male. Karen protested, "That's what I'm not. I don't want to be protected and lied to. It implies weakness . . . you've got to be tough to gain respect."

The predominant element in her fears was the fear that if she allowed herself to be treated as a woman, then men would not treat her as anything else, that she would be reduced to a least common denominator. At times she felt desperate about meeting new men, and tried a variety of ways of accomplishing this, including enlisting herself in a computer dating program. But she felt this was prostituting herself. She thought it was like putting herself on display in a meat market, selling herself and consequently demeaning herself. She complained, "I have to be an individual. I hate the image of the Marlboro man, the protector of women—the man who defends a woman's chastity is a fink. I want to be different from the rest of women. I don't like what being a woman means. You turn them upside down and they're all the same. And I hate that!"

One significant area in which her feelings of being demeaned and reduced to a least common denominator were particularly provoked was that of having a pelvic examination. She commented that she felt exposed and helpless. It reminded her of the feeling of fright and vulnerability that she had when her tonsils were taken out. It was like being attacked from behind. She felt anxious and paranoid when she was not able to see what was behind her. Moreover, when a woman is on her back she gets screwed. In the examination, Karen felt as though she were being raped, as though it were an effacement, a reduction and violation of her individuality. It was an indignity, a humiliation, and it removed the aura of feminine mystery. She became just another body. She wanted to be treated as an individual, but she felt as though she were being treated as another block of meat. As we shall see later on, this attitude toward the internal examination was one that became quickly transferred to the analytic situation, where she was forced to lie down in a position of vulnerability, where she could be easily screwed, and where she had to fear the hidden attack from an unseen persecutor.

The Threat to Individuality

The reduction to a least common denominator, along with its attendant reduction in Karen's sense of self or her individuality or uniqueness, was a pervasive theme throughout the course of the analysis. Anything that brought pressure to bear on her sense of uniqueness and individuality posed a dire threat to her—the threat of loss of her "identity." She complained bitterly that her mother's family never treated her as an individual, but rather as merely her mother or father's daughter. She complained that her parents never saw her or treated her as an individual; it was as though she was constantly screaming at them "Look at me! Listen to me!"

It would not be at all surprising, in the light of all this, were we to find the same terror and threat in the loss of individuality permeating most of her analysis as well. And indeed such was the case. She complained that any interpretations did not do justice to the quality of her individual neurosis, that they were reductionist, that she felt "pinned to a board, like a specimen" and went on to talk about bringing a specimen to a doctor in a Skippy peanut butter jar. In the analysis she felt de-individualized, "like any other schizophrenic." She wanted the benefits of analysis, but without surrendering her individuality. She felt a fear of something being imposed on her and that such an imposition would reduce her to a stock theoretical explanation and thus drain any individuality out of her. She complained, "If you think something about me, then I become that. It's magical. But there is no bar of appeal, just like there was nothing that could change what my father thought of me. That image was me, like having to wear two left gloves—you start assuming you have two left hands."

In the face of any criticism she felt diminished, feeling that if she were not acknowledged and recognized in all of her individuality, then somehow she did not exist. Referring to her close friend Marge who had been through five years of analysis she observed, "I'm more self-aware now than she ever was. But I'm determined to be triumphant, even if psychoanalysis is a crock of shit." I wondered if her feelings were not related to her difficulty in admitting to herself that she might have an unconscious. After all, having an unconscious would somehow, as she saw it, reduce her individuality. She replied, "But I want it to be my unconscious, not Freud's. It's related to my feeling so vulnerable and feeling that I'm losing my identity. That's part of femininity—experience teaches me that there are a lot of people out there who want to try to use me as a vessel, who want to take advantage." But perhaps the bitterest pill for her to swallow was the realization that in her continual preoccupation and fear that she would respond as a weak, susceptible, vulnerable, and helpless female, it was she herself who did the greatest violence to her own individuality.

Victimization

If there was any motif that summarized and focused Karen's concerns and fears it was that of victimhood, or equivalently, martyrdom. This theme was enunciated in the very first hour as we have already seen. Her conviction of being a victim permeated her attitudes toward sexual involvement. She felt used and abused. She referred to herself as a "part time geisha," feeling that any form of sexual involvement was simply a form of prostitution in which she submitted herself to the sexual desires of her male companion. "All they ever want is my ass," was her constant complaint. The sexual encounter was constantly depicted in terms of the interaction between a victim and a victimizer. Every time her family moved it was another victimization—she was victimized by the army and victimized by her father. She felt victimized by the criticisms of her adviser and perhaps more particularly felt herself to be my victim in the analysis.

It was only with considerable difficulty and in the face of great resistance that she was able to gradually see that becoming a victim was something she did herself, that she cast herself in the victim's role. She continually got herself into situations in which it turned out that she was the one who was hurt, she was the one who became the martyr. She complained that you could not get anything in life without its being taken away, and that it was better not to get anything, that nothing was for free, everyone exacted their pound of flesh.

It very quickly became apparent that victimization had a very specific meaning for Karen. It meant not being special, not being acknowledged and approved of, not being accorded special recognition because of her uniqueness and individuality. More precisely, the feelings of martyrdom and victimization were generated in any situation in which her own sense of importance was overridden by the importance of someone else. In any situation in which she was not given the first accord, and in which someone else's views or sentiments or feelings took precedence over her, she immediately felt she was being "shat on," taken advantage of, forced to submit herself, feeling humiliated, victimized, and martyred. There was a flamboyant, almost histrionic quality to this reaction, a kind of wailing, dirgelike quality which lent her complaining a sense of urgency and melodrama. Along with these feelings, however, there was also a strong strain of outraged fury which burst out in the agonized cry, "Who in hell do they think they are?"

It was also abundantly clear that there was an identification in her mind between being a martyr and being a woman. When her father said to her mother "Don't be a martyr!" it really meant "Don't be a woman!" To be a woman meant equivalently to be a victim, to be a martyr, to be weak and full of hurt, depressed, to have sentimental emotionality. She could not understand how other people could be emotional without being weak. The model for this attitude was quite clearly Karen's mother. She spoke frequently about her mother's "martyr complex." Her mother bore the brunt of her father's frequent abuses and constantly complained to Karen about how disadvantaged and difficult she felt her life to be. Mother's martyrdom extended even to the bed, where she communicated the attitude that sex was not a matter of enjoyment for her, but that she had to submit herself to it simply because Karen's father wanted it. The unavoidable message, of course, was that the woman had to submit to the wishes of a man and to put herself at the demeaning service of his sexual pleasure.

Anti-Semitism

A particular subcategory of victimization was tied in with Karen's Jewishness. She recalled the first time she became aware of anti-Semitism, when a little boy she was playing with called her a "dirty Jew." She felt hurt and confused by this and somehow felt she was different and inferior because of it. The fact of her being Jewish was a source of considerable anxiety for Karen. She felt it was like being black—something over which she could exercise no control or no choice—something she could neither manipulate nor control and therefore something about which she could only feel helpless and vulnerable. She could only think of Auschwitz, and remind herself of the gas chamber showers at Dachau. She felt also conflicted and uneasy about the Jewish attitude that suffering makes one superior, since she could feel the same attitude within herself.

One day a police siren sounding outside of my office reminded her of the Gestapo, and the fact that when she had been in high school she had played the part of Anne Frank in a production of *The Diary of Anne Frank*. She commented,

> I hate sirens, they remind me of the Gestapo and Anne Frank—trucks coming to take those people away. I had a recurrent dream when I was young of being in an attack and hearing a train whistle—somehow I associate that with

> Germany. I remembered that when I played the part of Anne Frank I broke down crying in the middle of the play. It was a martyrdom—martyr-dummy. It was all so useless—the state as the fatherland—pro patria mori—that is an absolute crock.

I wondered if the martyr-dummy had anything to do with Karen's mother. "I spent my life avoiding what I have become—identified with my mother, persecuted by the fatherland, the United States government."

She remembered when she had visited Dachau with her parents they had found her family name enscribed on the wall of the gas chamber. She recalled how vulnerable she felt, how great a fear she felt of being a victim and a martyr. She went on to imagine how her father must have killed people in the war, wondering whether she identified with being a victim or victimizer. She then recalled scenes from the movie *The Godfather* and commented that recalling all that violence and mutilation made her want to cry. I commented on her fear of being hurt or mutilated. She replied, "I am afraid of feminine mutilation, but displaced to my head. I feel mutilated if I can't understand." What was striking about these associations was that in any number of situations that recurred throughout the course of the analysis, Karen would revert back to these series of associations that had to do with Dachau and Anne Frank. Her abiding concern seemed to be that the least expression of prejudice or anti-Semitism in particular would bring to mind these horrible scenes and the awful apprehension that something like that would happen to her, even here and now.

It was particularly striking, in the light of these inner feelings, that Karen felt a sense of repulsion and rage which she directed against things Jewish. This persisted through almost the whole of her analysis, and was not significantly modified until the very closing stages of the analysis. She reviled the teachings of rabbis, calling it "a crock of shit." She felt a sense of rage at the smug superiority of Jewish people she knew, a superiority that she felt was reprehensible. She scorned their regarding themselves as the "chosen people" and even went so far that she felt enraged at such people wishing that she could exterminate them. She felt contempt for Jewish clannishness, for the stereotypes that were attached to Jews. She referred to such stereotypes as "Jewy." The notion that she might be regarded as a little Jewish princess, or as a "castrating Jewish female," was frightening to her. These were all things, she felt, that made people point fingers at Jews, refer to them as "them."

She was particularly enraged by the Jewy attitudes and behaviors she found in her mother's family. She found such behavior and such smug self-satisfaction, such narrowness and clannishness in them to be most disgusting and reprehensible. It was only in the closing months of her analysis that she was able to soften her feelings of contempt and rage in this matter. She felt herself then more willing to accept her own Jewishness and her own

Jewish religious belief. She came to recognize that the violent rejection she had previously felt was connected with her own feelings of vulnerability. She even came to the point of wondering if she ever had a child what religious faith she would want to instill in the child, and her answer, surprising even to me, was that she wanted to raise the child as a Jew.

That sentiment surprised me because it told me more than anything else she had indicated that the abiding and deeply pervasive sense of vulnerability that penetrated almost every fiber of her psychological being had been finally reached and significantly modified.

Negative Transference

The place, of course, where these underlying feelings of vulnerability came to their most vivid focus and expression was in the analytic relationship. Karen saw the analytic situation as a trap, just as she saw any acceptance on her part of the analytic process or of my interpretation as submitting herself and making herself helpless and impotent. The threat of seeing me as omnipotent and controlling and herself as helpless and vulnerable, was exceedingly powerful, and she struggled violently against it, refusing to see herself as helpless or to see me as omnipotent. Yet there was a part of her that worked to bring out the bastard in me, so that the analytic encounter became a process of scoring points—she against me, and me against her.

The analytic relationship was essentially a power struggle, and she assumed I would use against her what I knew about her—that analysis, like life, was nothing but a scorecard. She felt I was judging her, judging that she was weak and evil and wrong. On the couch she felt as though she were on a dissecting table, and she felt terribly weak, and exposed, and vulnerable. She related this to the experience of a pelvic examination, where she felt humiliated and reduced to being just another body, just another block of meat. She played artfully on the work *shrink*, someone who reduces patients to a least common denominator, to the basest emotions, and eliminated any individuality or value in them. She referred to her fear that if she gave an inch in the analysis, she would be nailed to the wall. She called it a "doomsday machine in my head, a sense of terrible vulnerability."

Intelligence, Masculinity and Aggression

Opposed to this deep sense of feminine weakness and vulnerability, Karen regarded her mind as the strong, masculine part of herself. She spoke of the dichotomy between her physical self and her mental self, the dichotomy between her behind and her head. It was the weak, vulnerable, feminine part of herself that she placed in opposition to the strong, competitive, aggressive, and intellectual part. It was with her mind that she was able to defend herself, able to control and manipulate reality in the service of defense. Her mind was like the Univac machine—cold, unfeeling, efficient, and totally invulnerable. Feelings were dangerous because they involved a softening of control.

Intelligence was her weapon, her lifeblood, the unshakable resource that she needed for survival and self-protection. She literally lived by her wit, always needing a ready retort, having a quick answer, the last word. She constantly felt the need to take the opposite point of view and to refuse to accept someone else's point of view, particularly when it was expected of her. This attitude entered strongly into the analysis. She used her mind like a rapier to cut and thrust and put others on the defense. Her mind she felt was like a razor; the problem with the razor of course is that it can cut more than one way.

The strong, controlling, competent, intellectual, and castrating aspects of Karen's personality went along with her strong sense of aggression and hostility that displayed itself more generally. From time to time the rage would rush forth, and its destructive intensity was frightening to her. In her rage she felt the intense desire to hurt and wound, often reaching a blind, murderous intensity which she found terrifying. She felt the sickening urge to kill. On one occasion she had been driving on a throughway and found herself being raced by a guy in another car. She became so enraged at his cutting her off that she almost ran him into a guardrail. Whenever she felt put down or taken advantage of, she responded with intense rage. She commented, "I can't stand the anger, because I want to kill." She added poignantly, "If I said I wanted to kill my parents, it would make me feel guilty for the rest of my life." This destructive rage had to be tempered and controlled, rigidly and vigilantly. If it were allowed to be released, the consequences would be catastrophic. She said, "If anybody tells me what to do, or tries to tell me what's right, I feel a hot rage and fury, I just can't take orders." In the face of such reduction and submission, her anger burst forth and seemed to last longer than it should. Any prejudice made her rankle with resentment, particularly the sort of sexist and chauvinist prejudice which said to her that she was only a woman, only a sex object, without intelligence, strength, or individuality.

She acknowledged that she had a violent temper, and frequently, especially during drinking bouts, had experienced blackouts. She attributed the temper to the "Hungarian" in her. She thought of herself as a violent Hungarian, a redhead with a temper, and she described herself as a "seething hotbed of violence," literally a destructive monster that needed to be controlled and chained down. She saw this violent aspect of herself as related to her father. She saw him as a violent man, and remarked that he and she were the ones in the family with the "Hungarian tempers." And yet despite the intensity of her fears and the preoccupations with her repressed rage, there was a certain perverse gratification she took in expressing her aggression. This was particularly true in any competitive struggle she would engage in with men, whether it be arguments or competing with men in driving automobiles, or in sarcastic retorts, putting them down, besting them intellectually.

Guilt

The march of her defensiveness and aggressive hostility with its implicit destructiveness was followed inevitably by the shadow of guilt. That shadow cast itself over almost every aspect of her life. As she commented, "The world is divided into the guilty and the hostile. I always thought of myself as hostile, but I am continually blaming myself for everything." Any attempt on her part at self-assertion or self-regard was fragmented by the corrosion of self-doubt and guilt.

Very early in the course of the analysis, in one of the first hours, she recalled an incident that occurred when she was only six or seven years old. At the time they were living in her mother's sister's home, during one of her father's periodic absences. Her uncle had left in a dresser drawer a service revolver, which Karen found. She brought it to her mother and held it up, pointing it at her mother ostensibly to show it to her. The expression on her mother's face was one of terror and anger. She did not remember whether anything was said to her, but she felt she had done something horribly, terribly wrong. She ran crying to her room and locked herself in and remained there in utter disconsolation for hours. She wondered whether her uncle had put the gun there to trap her because he did not like her, or even that he might have wanted to kill her. The gun became the symbol of her wrongdoing. She returned to that scene repeatedly in the context of talking about her guilty feelings, the feeling that she had done something terribly wrong, a crime for which she deserved only punishment and rejection. It was also a symbol of her victimization, the terrible crime that was imposed on her, of which she was accused and judged guilty without any awareness on her part that she had committed the crime. It was only in the closing months of her analysis, when so much of the rage and ambivalence toward her mother had been worked through, that she was able to understand that what had terrified and frightened her in this episode must have been her own destructive impulses toward her mother, and it was these that caused her to feel so guilty and criminal. The insight came as a dawning realization that seemed to bring her considerable relief and served to relieve her in a striking manner of a considerable pattern of her burden of guilt.

But nonetheless the guilt was pervasive. Despite her protestations of sexual liberation, she felt guilt about her somewhat promiscuous sexual relations, saying she always felt her mother was looking over her shoulder. But then she added defiantly that she would continue to do what she had been doing, because she wanted her parents to know she was as good as they wanted her to be, but not for their reasons. She complained continually of her mother's apparent sexual naivete, recalling that when she was a teenager her father had given her an army manual on syphilis and gonorrhea. She and her father shared the sexual knowledge that mother avoided. She also felt guilty about masturbation, even though intellectually she knew there was nothing wrong with it.

She could not help but avoid the disparity between what she thought in her head and what she felt in her emotions. Clearly her intellectual self spoke with the voice of her father, while her emotional self, the vulnerable feminine part of her, spoke with the voice of her mother. Her mother's injunctions about sexual activity only made her feel guilty. She recalled that at one point her mother said to her when she was going out on a date, "I hope he keeps his hands off of you." The problem was of course that he hadn't, and consequently Karen felt guilty, evil, dirty, and felt that what she was doing was terribly wrong. The mother's other primary dictum was that "Men do not marry women who are not virgins and who smoke." Consequently Karen set about screwing and smoking with a vengeance. She referred to herself as leaving "trails of slime and sexual guilt."

She felt that if her mother knew about her sexual activity she would feel she was a slut, yet there was a strong impulse in her to defiantly rub her mother's nose in it. She saw herself as a bad girl who slept with too many men too many times. She felt herself to be a prostitute, certainly in terms of her parents' morality, and the inevitable consequence of her prostitution was that her mother's dictum would come true, namely, that men only marry virgins. The thought of punishing herself by becoming pregnant, had often come to mind, and particularly what it would do to her mother if she would become so.

If someone thought that she should do something different than her own intentions, she would begin to feel guilty that somehow she was doing something she should not. She castigated herself for any slightest imperfection or faux pas. Even when there was nothing specific that she could worry about, she would worry about what other people were thinking about her. Frequently enough she would blame herself for things that other people had not even noticed and were hardly concerned about. Her world view was permeated with motifs of blame and guilt. There was nothing that could happen without either blame or guilt or both. Similarly she stoutly resisted and refused to accept any notion that the universe was not dominated by concepts of right and wrong. Everything in the universe was either right or wrong, praiseworthy or blameworthy, susceptible of guilt and punishment. The sense of obligation and responsibility was omnipresent. She felt particularly responsible for her parents' unhappiness and frustration. She commented, "My mother even gave me a sense of obligation for having been born."

The Money Problem

An area in which these feelings of guilt and obligation were easily mobilized had to do with money. In the very first hour, she referred to her father's deteriorating health, and then wept that she had taken a thousand dollars from him, that she had felt guilty and reprehensible for this, and that if she ever owed anyone anything she would remember it for years. She could not ask her parents for money, because it seemed as though that was hurting them, putting a burden on them for which she then felt responsible. She saw herself as taking her parents' money so that her parents had to give up things and deprive themselves for her sake. Her mother had to work and go without the niceties or comforts of life. She could never take anything from her parents without her mother impressing on her how much she was depriving them, part of the mother's martyr act.

Karen inevitably felt guilty and burdened by anything she thereby received from her parents. Her father was also terribly insecure about money. He had supported Karen at college and had taken out a loan to do so. She always felt that her education had been a tremendous burden on her parents. It was difficult for her to take anything without a feeling of guilt, without a feeling she was taking it away from her parents and depriving them, that what was given her was not a gift but a sacrifice. Particularly painful for her was the money that came from her father's insurance estate after his death. She saw it as blood money; she felt as though to take and use that money was in a way to accept it in place of her father and as a substitute for him, as though somehow to take the money was to be responsible for his death.

A particularly delicate area of the analysis was the whole question of the fee. I had agreed with her in the initial negotiations to conduct the analysis at a significantly reduced fee, with the understanding that when her financial situation improved we would raise the fee—even though it remained at a reduced rate throughout the course of the analysis. Such an arrangement inevitably stirred all of the guilt-ladened concerns that focused on the matter of money. Her receiving the analysis at a fee that made it possible for her to support it raised the question of whether I was making a sacrifice for her benefit, for which she would have to feel guilty and obligated to me. She was obviously threatened by and conflicted about anything in the course of analysis that placed her in my debt or stirred any feelings of gratitude in her. Such sentiments only served to stir her feelings of vulnerability and susceptibility, as if gratitude or a sense of obligation equivalently placed her within someone else's power. The sexual analogy was close at hand; if a man took her out for an evening or took her to dinner, she felt inevitably that she would have to pay the price by surrendering her body to him. Her fears of being taken advantage of and of vulnerable susceptibility were thus mobilized around the issue of the fee and owing me money.

She saw herself as prostituting herself in the analysis, but that was somewhat paradoxical; there she had to pay to get screwed. A particularly graphic moment demonstrating her feelings about money and the analysis came at the point where she received a graduate fellowship which gave her a rather generous stipend. When I commented that she might want to give some consideration to changing her fee for the analysis, it became immediately evident that I had made a gross and horrendous blunder. She became immediately defensive, and angry, and hostile. I was like any other bastard. All I wanted was my slice of the pie. She immediately became the outraged, defenseless, helpless, and disadvantaged victim. She complained bitterly that she could never get anything in life without its being taken away. She immediately referred this feeling back to her father and how she felt "shitty" whenever she took anything from her parents. It was just better not to get anything; you didn't get anything in life for free, everyone took their pound of flesh. It was all right for people to take things from her and to leave her needy and deprived, but she could not take things from other people. She had wanted me to approve and congratulate her, not to intrude upon her with the demands of reality. Once again her expectations had been disappointed and she felt angry, hurt, and fearful. She saw me as grossly insensitive, inhumane, as taking advantage of her and abusing her. She felt my suggestion as an accusation that she was not living up to her obligations in the analysis. She saw what I said as a diabolical manipulation, just as her parents used to treat her. I had put her fellowship on the lowest common denominator, and equivalently had taken it away from her.

Depression

If the material we have presented thus far has not already sufficiently suggested it, we can take note here of a continuing preoccupation throughout the whole course of Karen's analysis, namely, with her depression. It was clear from the beginning that there was an underlying depression that lurked beneath her staunch and vigorous defensiveness. From time to time it would show its head sufficiently to be a focus of continuing concern, raising the important question of the extent to which her defenses could be usefully undermined or confronted without exposing her to the risk of an overwhelming depression.

She felt sad, helpless and lonely. She was infrequently able to express her sense of weakness, helplessness and deep hurt, but when she did so it only prompted a defensive reaction, since she saw those feelings as wrapped up in her weakness and vulnerability. She felt sick and alone and did not want to look at her loneliness or her sickness. She saw herself as a "lump of frustrated desire," but could not bring herself to speak of the feelings of pain and frustrated longing in her. Sometimes when she drank too much or smoked some pot, the depressive feeling would come out from under its coverings and sweep over her in a wave of melancholia.

At such times she would have a feeling of loathing for herself, seeing herself as vile and hateful and despicable. She felt herself to be rootless and aimless, with nothing in her life but things to complain about and disappointment. She complained, "Where has my youth gone? To be this young and so tied down by responsibilities and obligations is an obscenity." The facade of competence and intellectual superiority that she affected she felt was a sham, as though she were getting away with something, deceiving people, getting credit for something that she simply did not deserve. Underneath the sham facade she felt insecure, helpless, and hatefully corrupt. She felt she always had to be entertaining, and bright, and witty, or otherwise she would not be accepted, she would not be liked. For her it was a surprise when people responded positively to her and seemed to value her. "I keep trying to prove my value, but I simply remain unconvinced."

At times when her depression was more acute, references to suicide were prominent. In the very first hour she spoke of a suicidal woman who was so much like herself. She also identified with a young coed who was beaten to death and raped—she was so young and alone and vulnerable. She identified herself with an older friend who was chronically depressed and yet had spent so many years in analysis. She felt a sense of envy and outrage at women who attempted suicide to get what they wanted. She saw it as a means of getting attention, of crying that they were hurt and of getting people to respond to the hurt, to take care of them. While there was a part of her that wanted to cry out for help and complain of her hurt, at the same time she despised it as weak, and simpering, and feminine.

One of the more poignant areas in which these feelings were mobilized centered around her father's death, which occurred early in the analysis. His leaving her intensified her feelings of loss and loneliness and vulnerability. This was another example of how she had been victimized by fate. She complained, "Who am I to be so young and to be without a father." She felt hurt and angered and bitter and resentful. The tears she shed for her father became a vehicle for expressing the sense of outraged betrayal, of being cheated and deprived, of being left alone and weak and vulnerable, feeling a sense of outraged deprivation at having to face the difficulties of life.

A peculiar expression of her feelings of inner pain and of her depressive affect came to a focus in relation to her stomach. On frequent occasions her stomach would growl on the couch, and she became preoccupied with it as well as embarrassed by it. At one point she commented, "My stomach doesn't growl—it cries. It's all the tears I've swallowed through the years." She wondered if she wasn't getting an ulcer, feeling that if anyone lived as she was living, how could they avoid it. She observed, "I'm holding something in, it's seething in there. I'm having stomach cramps—it's pretty easy to get depressed. I'm holding in all the sorrow and frustration and unhappiness." And on one occasion she referred to the "primal scream" and then commented on her rumbling stomach. "It sounds like Dr. Frankenstein's laboratory—bubbling away. My sympathy is on the side of the monster, Dr. Frankenstein's child." When I asked her about the monster she replied with some chagrin, "I shouldn't have mentioned it. It was created and then ignored by Frankenstein. It is ugly—it's all just a bad dream. Frankenstein runs away and there is no one to reciprocate love—it's too ugly and too different. Little girl, do you feel ugly and ignored? Do you feel that you were created and then ignored? The creator just wouldn't make you a mate." It was difficult to avoid the distinct impression that much of Karen's sorrow and depression were related to the fact that indeed she had been created and that her creator had left her and ignored her.

Paranoid Manifestations

Against this sense of weakness and depressive emptiness, Karen erected a variety of defenses, some of which we have already considered. The most important constellation of defenses, however, clustered around a rather paranoid attitude which involved considerable externalization, projection, feelings of persecution, and displacement of blame. She saw herself in many contexts of life as disadvantaged, as cheated and deprived, as victimized by those around her. There was always something wrong with the people or institutions or social phenomena which constituted her environment. She saw these forces as working to undermine or deprive her, to take away from her what she felt was rightfully hers and what she had a right to expect from people and institutions.

It was in the analysis that her paranoid feelings were mobilized with their greatest intensity. The analysis threatened her considerably and she felt extremely vulnerable to my interpretations. She saw me as a judge and felt that there was no possibility that I might think well of her and be motivated only to help her. The intensity of her defensiveness was often paroxysmal. She was panicked, frightened, as though she were literally with her back to the wall fighting for her life. She saw me as some kind of malicious and destructive monster who was bent only on reducing her to submission and destroying her. She felt persecuted and attacked.

When I attempted to explore these feeling with her she stoutly insisted that the analysis could be no other way than as she saw it. She saw all relationships in terms of "shitters and shittees," those who took the crap and those who gave it out—the victims and the victimizers. What was surprising in the organization of these defenses was their intenseness and the degree of distortion that they could introduce into the analytic relationship. It was also abundantly clear in these frequently repeated contexts that what motivated these paranoid defenses was an intense fear and a sense of inner weakness and vulnerability that threatened her severely and made it necessary for her to erect such staunch defenses and resistance. It was only when the roots of this sense of vulnerability had been thoroughly analyzed that her "furies," as she called them, began to fade and disappear.

Disappointed Expectations

Implicit in much of this material is the unremitting dialectic of narcissistic expectation and disappointment, of hope and frustration, of entitlement and disillusionment. Karen set her standards high; she expected to do everything well, to do it right, to do it immediately, and to do it according to a high standard of performance. She saw herself as sacrificing herself to an ideal of perfection, a sort of romanticized, idealized self-portrait of the heroic woman struggling to overcome overwhelming odds. She felt a need to be spectacular in everything she did, either to impress people with her brilliance and capacity, or with her rebelliousness and stubbornness. She wanted to be the absolute best, totally right, and she felt according to the inexorable dictates of her narcissistic logic that if she were not this she was then nothing, a nobody.

Mere existence was not enough for her; she set high standards and dictated high expectations for herself and to change those expectations would mean for her to run the risk of contempt. She rebelled against being just a child, someone's daughter, just a girl, or even an ordinary analytic case. She complained that her parents expected her to be perfect, as though she were a god. "My parents raised me to be Jesus Christ," she said. Her expectations permeated her relationships with men, expecting them to make her feel important, cherished, needed, and desired. But her expectations were always disappointed, and the fulfillment always carried with it a disparity of anticipation. If her partners did not treat her in such a manner, she began to feel unspecial, began to feel disappointed, angered, and cheated. She could recall how disappointed and unspecial she felt whenever her father went away. She protected herself in such situations with anger and contempt. In the face of her disappointment and contemptuous rage she protested continually, "Somebody has got to be good enough for me."

An area of particular disappointment for Karen was her relationship with her mother. We shall see more of this shortly, but it seems that every contact with her mother renewed for Karen a sense of outraged disappointment and frustration. It was apparent that she carried into that relationship a set of expectations that demanded from her mother something that her mother was clearly incapable of providing. Behind the conflictual interaction and the angry tirades against her mother, there were the constantly abiding yearning and frustrating expectations that her mother would indeed recognize her and accept and love her for what she was, on her own terms, as the individual she defined herself to be, with her values and attitudes and behaviors. This expectation of acceptance and recognition from mother was continually denied and frustrated. It became a paradigm of Karen's relationship with other individuals on many fronts.

Karen prided herself on being special. She regarded herself as having been a spoiled brat, what she called the "only child syndrome." The spoiled brat was of course part of being an "army brat." She always found it relatively easy to get what she wanted, especially in school where she was always capable of gaining approval from teachers and schoolmates, both in terms of academic performance and popularity. Later on she took a great deal of satisfaction out of being able to get any guy she wanted, and particularly of being able to get them in bed. During her college years this had been a particular satisfaction to her.

Whatever she did had to be striking and impressive: she had to stand out above the crowd. She felt that if she was not being noticed, she didn't count at all. She felt that she had a greater right to live and be happy than other people. She declared that she was not a democrat, and that her view was arrogant and superior. But her expectations of what life should give her were constantly being disappointed and frustrated. She was raised, she felt, to believe in male dominance and female superiority. Her father was the dominant figure in the family, but they both thought mother was superior. She went on to observe she had always felt superior to the men she had known even though she might have wanted them to be dominant in the relationship. It was difficult for her to undermine her own superiority, especially when she was so afraid of not being seen at her full stature, of being overlooked or ignored. But her own superiority was one of the greatest sources of her continual disappointment. She was an elitist, and it left her feeling lonely and self-righteous. She was constantly disappointed because people could never measure up to her expectations and were constantly failing and frustrating her.

During one hour Karen reported that her mother had called her to ask why Karen had not sent a get-well card to her aunt who had a mastectomy. Her mother had said everyone else had sent a card or flowers, and wanted to know why Karen had not. Karen's response was to feel infuriated, full of rage and hate and guilt toward her mother. I wondered why she reacted in this way and her reply was as follows:

> It's running to my mother to have her fix the hurt. I remembered when that boy in Germany called me a "dirty Jew," or when I hurt my finger, and she eased the pain. And later in college though, she blamed me for causing the hurt and for upsetting her. I was always afraid of giving in or of making concessions, but I still want to be what my mother wants me to be. I remembered the story of the one-eyed man in the land of the blind. He is the only one who can see, and he begins to think himself very special and very powerful. He is the only one who can see reality for what it is. But finally he ends up wanting to put out his own eye.

I commented that was indeed her fear, and that her struggle for independence indicated she was still caught up in a web of dependence on her mother. She replied, "She was all I had when my father was away. I resented terribly our dependence on her family. We had no home, and we were always going to see what they had and what they did. I always had to be grateful for anything they gave me. I simply rebelled at the idea of any concession."

Karen's specialness was the specialness of the one-eyed man in the land of the blind. But, fortunately, it did not remain as such. Her conviction that her perception of herself and the reality around her was the correct one and that any other was distorted and blind, gradually gave way during the course of her analysis. It became less and less a matter of either-or, or of all-or-nothing perspectives for her. Toward the end of the analysis she was able to remark somewhat plaintively, "If I could only accept that 70 percent was enough, and that I already have 80 percent, then life could be all right for me." As we shall see it was this modulation of the all-or-nothing basis of her thinking, rooted as it was in the dynamics and vicissitudes of narcissism, that lay at the heart of her pathology. It gradually became less and less a matter of 100 percent or zero, and she was indeed able to accept that something less than specialness and its concomitant pressure of perfection was less intolerable, if not more desirable.

Father

There can be little question that Karen's Oedipal involvement with her father was quite intense. She quite frankly adored her father, and felt that he was the only one in the family who cared about her, loved her, and took pride in her and her accomplishments. After his death she spoke repeatedly and in terms of tender endearment about his mannerisms and peculiarities—how he would want her to talk to him and just enjoyed listening to her, how his face would break into a smile when she walked into the room, how he would fall asleep watching the television, etc. She spoke of how handsome he was, especially when he wore his uniform. In a special way he was the man in her life.

One of the hardest things for her to bear was her disappointment and frustration at his continual leavings. She commented at one point that she seemed to love most deeply what was beyond touch for her, that she found most appealing what was least possible. But when he would come home again, his coming was filled with anticipation. When he came it was like the coming of the Messiah, he was so handsome and so wonderful in her eyes. If he was gruff she loved him for his gruffness, and was able to relate this to her feeling that she could function best with a bastard for a director or an analyst. She observed at one point she wanted "a man of few words, all ill-chosen," and added that I was a man of few words, just like her father. But somehow that made what her father said, as well as what I said, seem all the more important.

The Oedipal motifs became quite explicit. She wanted to have her father without her mother, without any other women around. She wanted to have him and possess him totally. She felt if Daddy loved her she didn't need any other man. Her disappointment when he would leave her was intense. She felt disappointed and frustrated and felt as though she was no longer important to him.

She gradually was able to see that her relationship with her father formed a sort of paradigm for her relationships with other men. The repetition-compulsion took the particular form of bringing it about that with each new man she was disappointed and left. Her social life was a recurring rhythm of leaving and rejoining, and each new man was for her like a rejoining with her father—each new meeting was characterized by a need for instant intimacy, a need to get to know him and to get close quickly. She commented that army brats always do that because the relationship is over so soon; one had to get as much as one could out of it because it was only going to last for a short time. The paradigm for this of course was her father, and she commented, "But my father was so dominant. No man whistles for me but my father. I'm doomed to look for Daddy and not to find him. I always seem to be looking for a man who will be a brute, or who will be distant and unavailable."

There was a sense of comradeship and sharing between Karen and her father that was a source of great pride and consolation to her. She and her father formed a comradeship of sympathy and understanding that separated them from the rest of the world and stood them over against her mother and her mother's family, against the United States government, in fact against the world. They were both aloof and cautious. They both rebelled against the family, they both had different careers from the rest of the family, and different values.

She and her father would never give in or would never apologize, for that only meant you were wrong and weak. Even in physical attributes she saw herself as like her father in striking ways. She felt her hands were big like his, and that her hands and feet tended to be cold like his, since they both had "lousy circulation." There was an explicit phallic reference with respect to the hands, since at another point she remarked that a man's hands and the size of his penis were correlated, and that she liked men with big hands. She then went on to comment on the size of her own hands, and how her boyfriends often commented on how big they were. She also saw herself as walking like her father, with military bearing as if on parade. They both stood straight like ramrods, and she referred to herself as "walking like a soldier," or again as being a "good little soldier." Her father was strong, silent, and aloof. Karen prided herself on being tall, almost as tall as her father. She also liked tall men who stood straight and rigid. The phallic reference in all of this was quite clear. Her father was stony-faced, and never showed any emotion or weakness. It was just in these terms that Karen liked to think of herself, the opposite of the weak, emotional, and hysterical female.

Neither of them would ask for anything no matter how badly they wanted or needed it—it was a matter of pride. Like her father she saw herself as regimented, strict, quiet, and shut off and aloof within the family. She and her father were separate and apart, but together—he was the only one who was with her and who understood her and his loss was a great pain for her. With regard to the family she often said, "They can have my mother, but they'll never get me or my father." Her father was neat, efficient, organized, and in control of things. He was scrupulously honest, he did things the hard way, his own way, independently, and he would never ask anyone for help or let anyone help him. He would never take anything from anyone, would never depend on anyone, since to do so was to be weakened and emasculated. "Do it yourself, or don't do it!" was his basic philosophy.

One of the important areas they shared together was their interest in cars—an interest which was mutually satisfying to both Karen and her father and which effectively excluded her mother. Mother was the dumb-dumb woman who was completely ignorant and innocent of anything about automobiles. The knowledge of and interest in cars was a masculine thing that Karen shared with her father. It was only grudgingly that her father admitted she was an excellent driver. She felt it was like pulling teeth to get him to acknowledge her ability. She recalled an episode in which he was towing a U-haul and was very anxious and uncertain about it. Karen took over the wheel and he only reluctantly admitted she handled the car better than he. A part of Karen felt that her father had always wanted a son and that he had been disappointed when she turned out to be a girl. Sharing such common masculine interests with him seemed to make up for that, so she felt she became in a way the son he had always wanted. It was a source of great pride to her that at one point he could say to her that if she were only a boy she would have been at West Point. She sometimes described her relationship with her father in terms of "military camaraderie."

Identification with the Aggressor. If there was a side of Karen that adored and was attracted to her father, there was another side that was terrified and frightened of him. However, the negative side of her ambivalence was considerably less available to her. It was only after extensive analytic work that she was able to acknowledge and recognize her considerable ambivalence toward him. She was easily able to recognize that in fact he scared her, and that she often dreaded his anger, fearing that he would hurt or kill her. Even so she often did things to provoke his anger. When he was around, she felt terrified of him and would often hide from him, avoiding him for fear of the punishment he would deal out to her. Karen unquestionably saw herself as the victim of her father's potential destructiveness and violence. She commented any number of times on how they would yell at each other and fight, and if it hadn't been for her mother's presence as a peacemaker they would literally have torn each other apart. Their relationship was one of "submerged violence" and Karen described herself and her father—with some admixture of pride—as both having "Hungarian tempers." They were both possessed of a "sulking fury," the power to hurt and destroy, even to kill.

The overriding influence of Karen's identification with her aggressive and destructive father was meshed with Karen's adoring Oedipal wish to submit to her father's brutality. As she saw it, every woman adores a fascist, and her relationships with men were nothing but a seeking of an "Aryan-type bastard from the past." Unquestionably Karen's father was the fascist and the bastard with whom she constantly sought to create a relationship. It was a relationship in which she was inevitably forced to submit and become the suffering victim. He was the brutal fascist, who would give her nothing but a boot in the face; he was her "man in black, with a Mein Kampf look, with a love of the rack and the screw."

Ambivalence to Father. It was only little by little and over a long period of the analysis that Karen's anger at her father revealed itself. She felt that time and again he had betrayed her, and she focused this feeling particularly in relationship to money questions; as for example, his having taken a loan on his insurance to pay for her education. It was clear, however, that the motif of betrayal extended further than that and included his constant leaving.

She frequently had dreams about her father's dying, and when his death finally became a reality, her guilt feelings were powerful, even overwhelming. But she refused to acknowledge that the feeling was one of guilt; rather she resentfully saw herself as cheated and betrayed. She commented, "If a crime was committed, I was the victim!" She bitterly resented what she determined to be her father's arbitrary decisions. She also boiled with rage in the face of his apparently inconsistent decisions. She recalled how when she was learning to drive a car he had forbidden her to take the car out, but then allowed her cousin Ann to drive the car. Karen was furious. She commented, "No matter how people try they fuck up. My father let Ann drive the car when he wouldn't let me. I would have told him to fuck himself, but the response would have been murderous. I realized how stupid it all was later, but it just infuriated me. Father was the oppressor, the fascist."

Perhaps the most central focus for Karen's feelings of anger and betrayal was her father's constant leaving. She felt that her life was lived in a constant state of waiting for something to happen, waiting for sublime moments, the moments when her father would come back. Life was nothing but a series of tours of duty. For all the years of moving she felt she was missing something she wanted but somehow wasn't getting. Presumably her father's absence left an emptiness that Karen could not fill. Somehow she felt responsible for his leaving; she somehow assumed he didn't want to be with her. She remarked plaintively at one point that if you really wanted to be with someone you would find a way to do it.

She struggled vigorously against any Oedipal interpretation, as we shall see, but stoutly maintained she could not have Oedipal feelings since her father had never been there; and that is exactly what she expected from men, that they would not be there. She complained bitterly about the inconsiderateness, the insensitivity, the stupidity of men. Everyone else's life should revolve around theirs, and a poor helpless woman had to be subject to whatever they wanted. When I asked her whether her feelings had any relationship to my going away on vacation, she became extremely defensive. In her typical counterpoint style, Karen insisted that her feelings of anger at my going on vacation had nothing to do with her father, but then added, "If you allow yourself to be used, there is always somebody there to use you; they find each other." She resisted any sense of dependence on me. "I just don't get dependent on somebody who is not going to be around. That's a 'tic nerveuse,' it reminds me of my father. I guess I have a desire to be dependent, but I have no intention of letting myself. There is just no reliability in the universe. The good things go away for the stupidest reasons. There are so many people who just don't want to be depended on, so you just can't count on their being there.

Father's Death. Karen's mixed and highly conflicted feelings about her father came to a head as a result of his death. He died suddenly of a heart attack. The year or so prior to his death had seen a number of episodes that stirred Karen's guilt and made it all the more necessary for her to repress the negative side of her ambivalence toward her father. He had been retired from the Army and had suffered a mild stroke. Soon after that, he had been in an automobile accident, and subsequently had lost his job. His own sense of insecurity and inadequacy and, apparently, depression affected Karen severely.

When he died it became more difficult for her to acknowledge and face the negative aspects of her relationship with her father. But his loss came as the ultimate and definitive leaving. And all the feelings that were stirred in the previous multiple leavings that had pained and anguished her so much were once again revived. She felt betrayed and cheated and victimized. She tended to idealize her father and her relationship with him, and took a great deal of pride in the aspects of her character—no matter how painful to her—that seemed similar to his. It was only in the mourning of his definitive loss that she was able to tolerate some of the angry and murderous impulses that had for so long been repressed. In broader scope, however, accepting her father's death meant for Karen accepting her lot in a limited and cold, uncaring world, in which there were many frustrations and limitations and disappointments. Ultimately it meant surrendering her infantile narcissism.

The Masochistic Motif. There was an interesting motif that related closely to the material pertaining to Karen's relationship with her father and which played itself out in the course of the analysis. Frequently in the early parts of the analysis she referred to herself as being "slapped in the face," or as "turning the other cheek," "rolling with the punch," saying she always expected to get slapped down, and that she took it in the worst way possible. On several occasions in referring to free association, she commented that opening doors made her expect to get a slap in the face. The motif of getting slapped in the face seemed to lie very close in significance to the idea of being "shat on." It seemed that whatever she did she could only expect to get slapped in the face for it. She feared it, expected it, but yet always seemed to stick her chin out.

She related these feelings to an episode that happened when her father got his orders for Korea. Karen was only 14, but she became very upset when her mother seemed to accept the news so calmly. Karen began screaming at her mother, and her father became angry and started to chase her. Karen was scared to death and ran into her room, slammed the door behind her and locked it. Her father demanded that she open the door. She finally did so, and he slapped her in the face. She later commented that she felt there was no way out; she was trapped, helpless. If she stayed in the room, he would have killed her; and if she opened the door, he would have killed her. She then recalled another episode when he was driving with her some years later. The car behind them was honking its horn at her, and she exclaimed in response to the horn. "Oh shut up!" Without any warning and to her mind without any explanation, her father slapped her, apparently thinking she had addressed that comment to him. Again, she felt enraged, betrayed, victimized. On another occasion, when one of her boyfriends wanted to stay over at the house, her father would not permit it and she told him he had a "shitty" sense of hospitality. On that occasion also he slapped her. The masochistic quality of these memories was clear in the following comments:

> I was always afraid of punishment. My father would get furious but he never hit me much. I used to think of him as coming after me with his fists. He had beautiful hands—they were strong and masculine; none of his brothers have hands like that. I dislike men with the wrong kinds of hands. My father's hands were so attractive; I was slapped by them. That's so sick, masochistic! My feelings about my father comprise the most intense hatred and love. It

was the same with some of my friends, it was an agony and an ecstasy, and I couldn't have one without the other.

We can also recall, in connection with these associations, Karen's linking of hands with the male phallus.

Mother

If Karen's attitude toward her father was characterized by conscious admiration and adulation together with less than conscious resentment and hostility, her attitude toward her mother was quite the opposite. The conscious aspects of her relationship with her mother involved bitter resentment and hostility, while the more hidden aspects of their relationship carried within them the seeds of a continual yearning for closeness and acceptance from her mother, and a deep-seated identification with her.

One subject which was particularly painful for Karen was the whole question of marriage. Karen's mother continually put pressure on her to get married, and seemed to propose marriage in such a way as to make it seem a panacea that, at least in her eyes, would resolve all of Karen's problems. Karen had a continual sense of frustration about this, since it was an important area in which mother seemed to have decided that she was a failure, and which represented an important disappointment for Karen in that it represented a signal area in which her mother failed to understand her.

She felt that as a child she was overly punished and disciplined. The image of her father killing people was threatening to her, and she was terrified of the anger in her mother's face. Her mother's face was ugly and frightening. Her mother's voice had a ring of accusation in it that made her feel guilty, as though she had done something terribly wrong. She said, "She has a voice like an assault, like being slapped in the face, like striking you with words. It's frightening, hateful, her face gets distorted and ugly. I just didn't want to look at her and listen to her, shaking her finger at me like a witch." She remembered as a child feeling shaky and nauseated, terrified of the punishment that she expected from her mother. She went on to say, "Now I punish myself to expiate the gods. It hurts less if I do it myself. I punish myself, but it's my parents inside—my guilt, everything is right or wrong and there is no reward for getting angry. There is only disapproval, like the hatred in my mother's face."

Karen's anger and resentment of her mother was very close to the surface and returned as a constant motif of the analysis. She frequently had fantasies of her mother's dying, but was offended and pained at the thought that her mother would be buried in her father's grave. The attack on her mother covered considerable ground. As Karen saw it, her mother was intent on doing the right thing regardless of the cost—particularly regardless of what it cost Karen in terms of pain and hurt. She resented having to be left so often with her mother when her father would go away. She took out her resentment on her mother. If Karen said one thing, she knew her mother would say the opposite, so that Karen could then condemn her mother's position. If Karen did not do what her mother wished her to do, it was as though Karen was doing it to hurt her mother, doing it against her. Thus her going to graduate school was something she did against her mother, and similarly not being married was something Karen did to her mother.

Mother was constantly on the scene, picking on her, criticizing her, watching her, always hovering and intrusive. Karen commented, "The years of her criticizing my clothing come back to haunt me. She doesn't do it anymore, but I do it for myself. I get irritated about such trivia. It didn't seem trivial when I was getting picked on though. I would have to dress under my mother's eagle eye, and I wanted to put her through the wall. If I got up at night to go to the bathroom, she'd jump up and want to know what was the matter." When I commented that mother's attitude seemed to always presume there was something the matter, Karen replied that was indeed a family trait, and that every time the phone rang her father was being shipped out somewhere. Karen found her mother's questions and inquiries intrusive and oppressive. She felt her mother was trying to run her life. Karen complained bitterly that her mother seemed to think that being a mother gave her a *carte blanche* to ride roughshod over Karen's feelings.

In her anguish, Karen felt a strong urge to counterattack, to make her mother squirm and feel "shitty" as mother had so often made Karen feel by her accusations and criticisms. Particularly she wanted to rub her mother's nose in the sexual slime that Karen felt she was wallowing in. Referring to her arguments with her mother, Karen commented at one point:

> My mother just can't get out of her own narrow self to help me. She can't see that I don't mean to threaten her. The arguments are always either/or. If I'm right, she's wrong; and if she's right, I must be wrong. We both start from the wrong end. To establish me, I had to try to destroy whatever there was of her in me, including the middle-class morality, the bigotry, the Puritan morality, being the Desdemona, the judging and condemning, the priggishness etc. I set out to prove that I was right and she was wrong, I did everything a whore could do without becoming one. I was free of kids and other people's orders and demands, but somehow I felt wrong.

Identification with the Victim. Not only did Karen carry within her her mother's hypocritical standards and superego attitudes, but particularly in reference to her view of herself as the excessively vulnerable woman and the self-sacrificing, suffering martyr, Karen was strongly identified with the figure of her mother. As the lineaments of this introjection became increasingly clear during the course of the analysis, Karen found it increasingly necessary to struggle against it and to resist my attempts to clarify this aspect of her personality. An important piece of work in the analysis was accomplished in Karen's being able to see that her threatened, defensive, and vulnerable self was based on this image of her mother. It was only when she was able to free herself of her dependence on her mother that she began to be able to see that it was possible to change this pattern of introjection, and thus to see that she was not as vulnerable as she might have thought, and that it was not so urging and pressing a need for her to protect and defend herself on so many fronts.

But there was underlying this introjective pattern a tremendous and powerful need to seek approval and to gain acceptance from her mother. Only reluctantly was she able to admit that she constantly sought her mother's approval, and that she had a great need for her mother to understand and accept her. She wanted her mother to care for her as she really was, but she always felt her mother cared for her only in terms of what her mother wanted her to be. When her mother told her she was disgusting or criticized her for minor things, she experienced a strong sense of disappointment and hurt. Even when her mother did not know about her activity, Karen worried about what mother would think of her. If mother knew about her sexual activity, for example, her mother would think she was a slut. Karen wanted her mother to like and approve of her for what she was but she was convinced that if mother knew what she was, she would be disgusted and disapproving. Paradoxically, of course, Karen set out to provoke that disapproval and rejection from her mother that she simultaneously dreaded with such intensity.

An interesting aspect of Karen's relationship with her mother was expressed in terms of her relationships with her relatives. There was a decisive split between the two sides of the family. In Karen's eyes her father's family could do no wrong. They were sympathetic, understanding, and responsive. Her attitudes towards her mother's family were diametrically opposite. She set herself up in angry opposition to them and rejected everything they stood for. She saw them as selfish, insensitive, inconsiderate, uncaring and unresponsive, prejudiced, bigoted, snobbish, materialistic, etc. In setting herself in opposition to them, it was clear she invited their criticism and attack, but then felt embittered, deprived, betrayed, and victimized by this treatment.

As she saw it the only terms on which she could tolerate the family or be tolerated by them was complete conformity to their expectations and demands. This she staunchly and vigorously rejected. Their expectations were strikingly close to her mother's. They expected her to get married—preferably to a doctor, or at least a lawyer. They also expected her to fulfill the traditional role of the woman: the housekeeping, baby-making slave. Karen recounted with considerable anger and bitterness how her uncle had said to her on one occasion that she could give up this nonsense of getting a Ph. D. and go out and get herself an MRS.

It gradually became clear that the issues with mother's family and with mother were identical, and that Karen's difficulties in relating to men were in part caught up in the struggle against the expectations of mother and her family that she be the sort of woman that they expected her to be.

Transference Distortions

The themes which we have been surveying played themselves out with peculiar intensity in the transference. From the beginning of the analysis the transference elements were detectably at work, creating intense anxiety and prompting Karen to mobilize her defenses with a considerable amount of resistance. Gradually, however, as the transference neurosis deepened and intensified, her defensiveness became severe and reached frankly paranoid proportions. From the beginning of the analysis she was highly resistant, feeling a considerable amount of antipathy and hostility and stoutly resisting any directives from me. She made it clear that she did not like being told what to do. She was afraid of being pinned down and known.

She felt a good deal of uncertainty about me. She had no way of judging my competence and felt it would be useless for her to ask since she expected that any questions she might ask would not be answered. She was being asked to make a leap of faith, and her presumption was that I would be rigid, controlling, and that I would somehow make her suffer. She was afraid that I would pin her down, like a lepidopterist, categorizing her, pinning her to the couch. She saw herself as spending years in analysis "wedded to the couch," as she put it, figuratively a marriage in which the conflicts of masculine and feminine roles would be played out and in which she could only expect to get "shat on," to have to suffer, waiting with apprehension and anxiety for the bomb to drop.

She stoutly resisted this perception, insisting that she was not a simple case, that she was complex and difficult, and she refused to be easily dismissed or easily understood. She felt that she had to be different, stunning, and that she had to impress me or else she would feel violated and reduced, as if she didn't exist. From the very beginning of the analysis, any attempt on my part to interpret or offer observations was extremely threatening to her. She felt I was imposing categories that trapped and reduced her within some preconceived analytic schema. She saw herself as the victim of my need to maintain an analytic perspective. The problem was not in her: the problem was my defenses and my feeling threatened by anything that violated or could not be fitted into my analytic perspective. She gave me fair warning almost from the beginning: "I don't envy you, you have to deal with me. You had better be on your toes!"

She was constantly preoccupied with the fear that I would become angry at her and would take it out on her in some way, but that I would not show it. She felt frustrated and resentful at not knowing what I was thinking about her. She felt I was judging her and that my judgment was negative, that she was wrong and despicable. She felt that in the analysis it was like walking on cracked eggshells. She felt on the spot, that she was somehow at fault, and that being on the couch was like being on a dissecting table. I was a Madame DeFarge, sitting behind her and observing her, callously enjoying the spectacle of her suffering and agony. That suffering was an entertainment for me; I got my kicks out of watching heads roll.

One day she began talking about something she had heard about rodent exterminators with years of advanced training. She commented that it could apply to me, or to herself, or even to her father. Her father was in the business of killing people—vicious people, like rats. She went on to say, "It applies to both of us in terms of our advanced training. The rats are waiting to come out. But I wonder which one of us the couch serves. I have the image of Eve lying supine, with the serpent as an evil toad whispering in her ear."

Nonetheless there was a part of her that wanted me to be perfect and competent. Similarly there was a part of her that wanted to be dependent and taken care of. She speculated about her interest in medical programs on television. She felt a fascination with the medical world that seemed to have increased since she had started analysis. She speculated that perhaps she wanted to marry a doctor—certainly that had been drummed into her for years.

In a special way she thought of me as inaccessible, and complained about the limitation of a regimented relationship. In a way her father was inaccessible and distant; he was a man of few words even as I was a man of few words. But if he said little, his eyes could see right through her, could see she was being deceptive or phony. She went on to say that was what she hated most about the idea of psychoanalytic theories being imposed on her. It was as if they see right through you. She added, "I guess that's Daddy. Well, that's as much transference as you're going to get!"

If her father had been the stern, silent, and inaccessible man in her life, she felt all the more intently the challenge of gaining his approval and pleasing him. Clearly there was a part of her that sought my approval in the analysis, sought reassurance from me that she was doing the analysis well and that she was making progress, and that her productions on the couch were pleasing and acceptable to me. But along with the need to gain approval, there was the conviction that she had to submit herself to the analytic process and my demands in order to gain it. But submission to her meant being demeaned and reduced, losing her individuality and being treated as a common case.

One of the most threatening aspects of her transference involvement was the sexual connotations of it. Any indication or suggestion of this was stoutly resisted and denied even though the indications of it were liberally sprinkled throughout her material. Any attempt to bring it up was labeled as my problem and not hers. But at one point she was able to comment that any interest that a man might have in her could only be sexual.

She felt deep down that my interest in her was sexual, but her fear was that I would seduce her and then leave her. After all, all men were "insensitive schmucks." The erotic element, however, revealed itself in various ways, most particularly in terms of Karen's fear of submission and vulnerability, almost a direct translation of her fears and concerns in the sexual relationship. She commented on her tendency to avoid looking at me when coming into or leaving the office, and observed it was a way of keeping herself disengaged. She had no intention of developing any transference to me, of falling in love with her shrink. She commented on a friend of hers who was trying to get her shrink in bed, and felt threatened by that idea.

She felt threatened particularly by her own potential for dependence, but commented that she refused to allow herself to become dependent on someone who was not going to be around. The obvious reference, of course, was her father. The notion of transference was threatening to her because it meant that if she was to fall in love with her shrink, she would have to compromise her intelligence—something she refused to do. And if she refused to compromise her intelligence, that left her with the only alternative of being an intelligent woman who made men feel stupid and inadequate and consequently threatened them.

The stark threat of these transference alternatives was modified in time, but only slowly and gradually. The working through of these transference elements was in fact a crucial element in the analytic progression and provided the primary basis for Karen's analytic improvement. The first indication of a shift in the transference alignment came in the form of a dream—the only dream in which the analyst appeared explicitly, and the only dream in which a transference interpretation was possible. It occurred about a year prior to termination.

The scene was an apartment into which Karen was moving. It was dark and it was not quite like her present apartment. There were some students there helping her, and two girls were sitting and talking, quite oblivious of what was going on. I was there in the background as a supportive figure; but there was someone else there who was also Karen's analyst. Somehow she felt more emotionally involved with him than with me. Karen's mother was there saying unbelievably destructive and accusatory things about Karen. Karen became angry and started slapping her mother up and down the front of her body, but with apparently no affect. I was standing there listening. She then fell into a trance and fell asleep. When she woke up the argument with her mother started up all over again. But this time there was a low armchair there with no legs, and her father was in it. He was dead and blood was coming out of his mouth. She and her mother started fighting over him. Her mother was accusing her and Karen was anxious and upset, trying to tell her mother something was wrong with her father and that he was dead. I somehow got her out of there. She commented, "You were completely supportive. You were on my side. It was incredibly real, even with color."

She commented on the two analysts in the dream and on her feeling of being thrown back on the analysis for support. She related the dream to her ambivalence toward me—to her seeing me as supportive and helpful on the one hand, but also feeling that there was another part of me with which she was more emotionally involved. She commented that the other analyst seemed to be a cross between one of her boyfriends whom she felt to be insensitive and callous and an analyst whom she had heard discussing a paper and whose discussion she felt was nothing but an imposition of analytic interpretations with little or no evidence. This was exactly the complaint she had launched against me in the analysis. She found it difficult to determine whether I was the insensitive and unresponsive analyst who would impose interpretations on her, in calloused disconcern for her individuality and uniqueness, or whether I was a sympathetic and helpful figure with whom she could ally herself and from whom she could gain strength and support.

Trust

The basic issue in all of this was the issue of trust. Karen saw the analytic situation and her relationship to me specifically as requiring a leap of faith which left her exposed and vulnerable. Could she trust anyone beside herself? She called herself the "do-it-yourself-kid." She placed great stock in her own self-reliance; if she could not rely on herself who was there she could trust? She had trusted other men, made herself vulerable in other relationships, but had always been betrayed. The paradigm for this was her relationship with her father, where her expectations and hopes had always been frustrated and disappointed. She felt betrayed by his constant leaving, and the betrayal became the paradigm for other relationships.

Karen's history, as she recounted it, is a saga of continual and unremitting betrayal. Her reminiscences of childhood, for example, were accounts of betrayal—promises that her parents made and failed to keep, hopes that she was allowed to cherish and build upon that were frustrated and disappointed, expectations that were generated and consequently disappointed. There seemed to have been a characteristic deceitfulness that found its way into her mother's way of dealing with her. Her mother was unable to deny Karen something that she wished, and both she and her father seemed unable to simply confront Karen's wishes and in a straightforward way forbid her to do or have what she wanted. They resorted to indirect means of postponing or dallying with decisions and then in the final analysis preventing her from having what she had asked for or from doing what she had wanted to do.

This was a constantly recurring pattern by which the parents dealt with her in her childhood years. The result was that, without a firm refusal or denial or prior parental prohibition, Karen would build up her expectations and finally, when it was clear that she would not get what she wanted, her disappointment was all the more intense. Her parents would in a dilatory way say that maybe she could have what she wanted, or say that they would think about it later, or use a variety of other diversionary tactics. When the parents finally did say no under such circumstances, the prohibition came across to Karen as a betrayal.

We have noted other significant betrayals that she experienced, not the least of which were her father's repeated departures. True to the parents' style of avoidance, the father's departures were not treated in a straight-forward or planned manner. Rather they were painful and disappointing events, certainly to Karen's mother, and to Karen as well. Consequently they were events that were not talked about, were not planned, were not scheduled, so that there was never any opportunity to work through the issues of disappointment and loss. Rather the issue was always avoided, not discussed, even denied. The father would then spring his new orders on the family as a last-minute surprise, immediately before he took leave.

Again it was a process, so characteristic in Karen's family, of avoiding painful issues, allowing expectations to rise, and then cruelly and abruptly dashing them to the ground. Thus father's leavings were harsh, cruel, unfeeling betrayals that took the form of cruelly and arbitrarily imposing on Karen her parents' will, placing their needs and wishes before her own. It was a reenactment and re-creation of the paradigm that must have permeated most interactions with her parents from the very beginning of her life.

The issue of betrayal was also embedded in Karen's continuing relationship with her mother. Karen's unremitting expectation was that she should be accepted and recognized for herself, in short that she be given a sense of the trustworthiness of her own individuality by her mother. This expectation was constantly betrayed. Her mother's own needs intruded on the relationship and took unremitting precedence over Karen's needs, wishes, expectations, and hopes. The message that was continually broadcast from mother was her anxiety that Karen should do the right thing, act in an appropriate and approvable manner, respond in ways that would support mother's own expectations and needs for her to be the dutiful and conformingly observant daughter.

For Karen to trust meant to open herself to being hurt. She felt more cautious now, more suspicious, more guarded. Her attitude was more cynical now; she was not going to let herself get involved in such a relationship again.

If she could not trust anyone else, where was there for her to place her trust? The only thing she could trust was her own intelligence, her own brain, her own capacity to understand and analyze. Consequently, it was inevitable that anything in the analysis that brought into focus anything she had not already thought of and not already considered and analyzed, anything unexpected, anything hidden, anything that smacked of the unconscious was for her a source of threat and tremendous anxiety. If she could not know, if she could not understand and analyze, she felt vulnerable, helpless, and incredibly threatened

She felt the powerful pull of dependence on me, which made a demand on her to place her trust in me in the analytic relationship. This was one of the most difficult things for her to accomplish. It was also a powerful source of much of her resistance. She felt it necessary to match her intelligence against mine—to reassure herself against the feelings of vulnerability and helplessness by exercising her own analytic intelligence and demonstrating to herself that her understanding and her capacity to analyze were superior to mine.

Resistance

The major problem throughout the whole of the analysis was Karen's extreme defensiveness. At times this reached rather extreme degrees, and it often seemed as if the analysis itself was in jeopardy. Karen's defensiveness was not at all indirect. There was little of what could be termed acting-out, and except for certain points where she was deliberately retaliating, her coming to the analysis was generally punctual. Almost without exception she would appear in my office a few minutes before the scheduled meeting time. On the contrary, her resistance was explicit and direct. From the earliest hours she made it plain that she felt threatened and defensive, even though she was trying not to be so defensive in the analysis. She knew, she said, that when she came to the analysis she expected to feel threatened and defensive, expecting it to be painful and to have to suffer.

But she found herself struggling against a helpless feeling, not being able to control the situation and not knowing where it was going. She found herself using evasive tactics and feeling that somehow her defensiveness was something that she should be able to overcome and that her not doing so put her at fault. She commented at one point, "It pisses me off that I am fighting myself like this, but part of me is not about to give up any secrets without a fight." She described herself as having an inner core that was heavily guarded and that she could only take things so far and then felt she had to stop. She found herself wanting to turn the tables on me, defending herself, avoiding things and trying to control. She wanted to try to prove my stupidity and my insensitivity. She took a certain smug satisfaction from her ability to contend with me. And she stated, "It's hard for me to accept anything you say. Anybody not in love with me is stupid and insensitive, but I won't apply that to you. People are not stupid and insensitive who don't want to love. It's important to me to prove you wrong . . . . I need my defenses more than I need this analysis."

Even in the terminal phases of the analysis, when her defensiveness had become considerably softened and modified, the same motifs were in operation. At one point she began talking about a variety of superficial subjects, and I commented that she seemed to be avoiding the subject of termination. She replied she had no strong feelings about it, or rather that she blocked them. She saw me now as an equal, like other men who had been good friends and who had been supportive, but that the relationship was not an essential one for her. I wondered what would motivate her to see it in such terms. She replied she still felt a fear of being hurt. If she felt the relationship was not important to me, that made it unimportant to her. I commented that there had indeed been one very important relationship with a man in which he was terribly important to her, but she could not be sure how important she was to him. She replied that had been very painful for her, but why should she get into it at this point. There was too much hurt, and it was better to avoid it. At that point, however, in the advanced stage of the analysis, she could recognize how strong the urge in her to avoid the pain of separation from the analysis in fact was.

It was particularly the transference aspects of such feelings that caused her difficulty. She stoutly resisted the notion of transference and any suggestion that she might have a transference through the greater part of the analysis. In the beginning, she consistently avoided references to me or to her feelings about me, and I had to call these to her attention. Whenever I did so, she felt resistance and responded to it as a threat. The notion of transference was too clinical and too impersonal. She wanted to think that it was unimportant and that it had little relevance or significance for her problems. Later on in the course of the analysis when it was quite clear she had developed quite intense feelings for me, she still stoutly refused to admit that there was any transference involved. She cried out at one point, "I don't make you into anything." I pointed out at that juncture that she seemed to be making me into a judge. She replied, "Well you can call it transference, but I call it real."

Particularly poignant in this regard was the whole issue of abandonment. She stoutly resisted any feelings of loss or remorse at times when I went on vacation. Such periods in the analysis were inevitably periods of heightened defensiveness—presumably since the forthcoming vacation provoked her feelings of dependence and loss. Midway through the analysis, during the last session before my vacation, she commented that she felt very little about my going on vacation but remarked that this was the last day. I inquired about her feelings and she replied that of course she had none—or none she would allow herself. If it bothered her, she didn't want to know about it. She was totally resistant to what she called the "archetypal abandonment theme." I replied that she seemed to feel that people's leaving should not be important. She replied, "I'm just not hysterical about your leaving, I'm not going to feel anything until I just can't avoid it. I don't want to feel any pain."

The fear of regression and the vulnerability she associated with it and particularly the fear of slipping into the transference neurosis was paralyzing for her. To her mind it meant surrender, submission. She struggled against this, frightened and angry and totally resistant. At one point she commented:

> It's time to stop playing games. I assume this will take longer because my resistance is so high. I hate talking about how I don't want to be here. I see it as a game—love and hate your shrink, be dependent or not dependent, little rituals. Dr. Freud is Dr. Sig Heiler—it means fascism, the salute to the master, commitment to a set of beliefs. I can't credit it and I can't believe it. The alternative is to say that the method is valid and that you know what you are doing. For me to suspend judgment is to submit, to be ruled by something irrational, to let someone else do the thinking for me, to lose all control. . . . This could screw me up and I have to be wary of that. I don't know your competence and that's a lot to swallow. I wouldn't submit to surgery without knowing more about the surgeon. But you are asking me to submit to something I don't believe in, and that's an insult to my intelligence.

The analysis was a battleground, a battle of wits in which the issue was equality versus subservience. If she accepted my interpretations, she would be subservient to them and submissive to me.

Paranoid Defense

In the face of the analytic threat and the danger it posed, Karen launched a vigorous counterattack. It was cast in highly intellectualized and highly defensive terms. She created an elaborate rationalization—I will not use the stronger term delusion—which reflected a rather paranoid stance which emerged within the context of the analysis and which served obvious defensive purposes. Her stance said that the analysis was equivalently a process of imposing certain hypothetical suppositions on her which required that she be fitted into certain psychoanalytic categories. She further argued that the necessity underlying this was my need to be right, because if my intellectual understanding was not right then I would be threatened and be shown to be inadequate. The problem therefore was not in Karen, but in the analysis and in me. The difficulty was with my defenses and my inner conflicts, and not at all with her.

It was anathema to her to behave or to feel what an analytic patient was supposed to do or feel. She did not like fitting into what the books described, and she resisted totally the idea of becoming just another analytic case. She refused to allow herself to see herself as sick, as having human weaknesses. To be sick meant to be weak, dependent, and vulnerable, and the idea was terrifying to her. If she allowed herself to feel that, then something terrible would happen and there would be no one to protect her, no one to take care of her; consequently she could only rely on herself. She took a "cut the shit" attitude and clung tenaciously to her intellectualized convictions.

She objected vigorously to what she saw as the analytic methodology. Any attempts on my part to point to parallels in her experience, or to analogues between the past and the present, were met with staunch objection that such interpretations were plausible but also were wrong. I was incapable of seeing the limits of my methodology, and it was necessary for me to create something to analyze. She could admit the plausibility of the connections, but she stoutly maintained that she could not experience them and she refused to place her trust in something she did not experience. Any connections I pointed to were met with the objection that they were arbitrary and had no meaning or relevance for her.

The whole thing was the product of an entirely arbitrary process that had no relation to her, no empathy with her feelings, no respect for her individuality. My interpretations were preconceptions, hypotheses that were imposed on her. The analysis was thus a process of looking for fragments of data that would fit such preconceived notions. She could not credit the theory, she could not put any belief in the preconception, and she refused to submit herself to what she could not credit or believe. She wanted to rebel, to leave the analysis, to walk out. It would be her way of controlling, or putting her foot on my gut and making me squirm. She resented bitterly the tying up of loose ends, wrapping her up in a neat package, putting little Karen in a drawer, trapping her in categories and preconceptions. Imposing the Freudian categories made the helpless individual look dumb, as though blindly and unconsciously motivated. She rebelled against the idea of being thought dumb. She cried out in angry anguish,

> I refuse to be responsible for someone else's problem or for somebody else's paradigm. I feel I am being judged by decree, not by evidence; it's Freud, the United States Government, the United States Army, fascism. They all deny individual rights. I can't accept all of that as being reduced to a threatening picture of my father.

Clearly, the attraction to an intellectual debate was difficult to resist, and the more successful my interpretations and clarifications, the more threatened she became. The threat specifically was that my intelligence with the power of the analytic perspective might override her defenses and reach into the susceptible and vulnerable core that she so staunchly defended.

Therapeutic Crisis

The intensity of her feeling about this and her fear of the analytic reduction was exemplified strikingly in a perhaps inappropriate, or at least ill-
timed, intrepretation. She was discussing the process of writing and how she
enjoyed it even though it was terribly painful. She described it as like a flow,
that you had to let run its course. It was the pain of absolute concentration
and unified tension. But that when the tension was released there was a feeling of relaxation and satisfaction. I observed that her description of this
process made it sound like an orgasm. My blunder became immediately obvious. She responded with hurt and offended outrage. She became defensive
and angry and cried out that was typical of psychoanalysis, that I was not
listening to her, that I had no sympathy with her, and she ended by saying,
"Fuck you!"

The next day she returned and announced she was not going to stay in
analysis. She found it fruitless, expensive, futile, and destructive. I asked her
about her reaction to my comment on the previous day and she replied it
was a vile reduction, a dirty joke. Moreover, she refused to accede to my
superiority. I could think whatever I liked, she didn't care. She refused to
trust anyone more than herself and in analysis there was need for trust, but
she didn't have it and she wasn't going to get it. She went on to say it might
be reasonable for me to think she was being defensive, but that wasn't true.
The fact was that my remark was tasteless and deflating and demeaning.
Perhaps she expected too much, but then she should get the hell out. If it
wasn't helping her or making her happy, then the smart thing was to get out
while the getting was good. That would make her into the great martyr
female.

I could only point out at this juncture that she seemed to be making the
analytic situation into a self-fulfilling prophecy and that perhaps this was
part of the problem. But she was angry and hurt and quite resistant, and she
announced that she was not coming back for the rest of that week. After all,
it was her life and her analysis. And she was true to her word; she stayed
away from the analysis for the following three days. I use this episode here
as an example of her resistance, but in fact it turned out to be a crucial turning point in the analysis. What in fact it brought into focus was the basic
question of whether the analysis was a situation of conflict and submission,
or whether it was in fact a cooperative venture in which she and I were involved in a collaboration rather than a competition. Moreoever, the fact
that she could rebelliously and petulantly take herself out of the analysis
without any recrimination or hostility on my part demonstrated graphically
that she indeed had a measure of control and that she was not a helpless victim of the analytic process. More specifically, it demonstrated that she was
neither as weak nor as susceptible nor as vulnerable as her fantasies might
dictate.

In fact, Karen's defenses took a form which was predominated by a rather paranoid quality. Her defensive posture was highly rationalized and intellectualized, but it was based upon a fundamental attempt to externalize and displace the basic conflicts into the external world about her. At times her defensiveness took on a more precisely paranoid dimension. At such times, her defensive system was under particularly intense pressure and the persecutory anxiety became elevated to the point that her responses to me bordered on panic and were cast in a modality which saw me as the primary persecutor and nemesis of her existence.

Projective System

Within this paranoid framework and its attendant anxiety, Karen fell back on a fairly persistent line of defensive argument. The argument was essentially based on her projective system and her fundamentally externalizing defense. The motif was enunciated in the very first hour: the real difficulty was not personal and individual, that is to say intrapsychic problems, but rather social and cultural patterns which acted in such a way as to victimize the individual.

Given this attitude it was little surprise that she should be sympathetic with the Women's Liberation Movement. What the movement told her in effect was that the problem was not hers, but it was one generated on a social and cultural level and that it was essentially based on social and cultural prejudices. Intelligent women, especially women in a profession or who have a career, alienate and threaten men simply by being what they are. Women were in fact sexually repressed. She saw the family as a political system devised to maintain male dominance.

Rather than penis envy, the problem was power politics. Women were treated as inferior, as children, as if they had no voice and no rights. Moreover, if a woman had opinions and had thought about things and expressed her opinions, especially if she were intelligent, she was automatically labeled as aggressive and castrating. Even though it was abundantly clear that her defensiveness and aggressiveness was called into play to protect her fragile vulnerability, she staunchly refused to acknowledge that had anything to do with the way things were. Moreover, she insisted on the dichotomy. If the problems were internal, they could not be external; and conversely if they were external, she refused to admit that her own internal dynamics could have anything to do with them. In her better moments, however, when she felt secure and less threatened in the analysis, she would somewhat reluctantly admit that what was happening within her might have something to do with the way things turned out. She saw that the world was in complicity with her own inner prejudices. As she put it, "There's a good deal out there, but a good deal in me, too." And again much later in the course of the analysis, "I guess I'm halfway between seeing it as my problem and the world's problem. That the people who I meet are unavailable or married isn't my fault, but I seem to be in a rut lined with the best excuses."

An episode that seemed to make an impression on her took place during a plane ride in which she was returning from a short vacation. She met a young girl on the plane who was a college girl, was interested in the same professional field as Karen, and was also a Phi Beta Kappa. They got into a discussion of graduate schools and the young woman's attitude made a strong impression on Karen. She was highly critical, in fact condescending. None of the schools she considered—including some of the best in the country—seemed good enough. Karen found herself reacting with some irritation. She suggested to the young woman that the problem might not be in the universities but in her own attitude. Immediately the girl got defensive and started to rationalize why it couldn't be her own attitude but had to be something out there in reality. Karen commented that it was so pitifully easy to see through her defense, and that in it she saw a mirror of herself. She commented, "She was so insecure. Who else on that plane could have seen that what she was really saying was 'love me.' But it comes across as a defensive and condescending attitude. I couldn't have been that bad—but I guess the degree of defensiveness must be related to the degree of vulnerability."

Penis Envy

An interesting sidelight on this aspect of Karen's vulnerability, as well as a focus of some theoretical concern, was the whole issue of penis envy. In terms of the analytic process it provided a sort of touchstone against which Karen's modality of defense could be evaluated. She made it clear from the very beginning that the question was one of significant concern for her. She was concerned with how Freudian I was, and her concern carried in it a significant ambivalence. On the one hand she wanted me to be perfectly Freudian, in the sense that I would then be a perfect analyst, but on the other hand the application of basically Freudian notions such as penis envy posed a powerful threat to her.

Penis envy meant that women were somehow mutilated, wounded, inferior and vulnerable. Any suggestion of castration or penis envy raised her level of defensiveness to a high degree. However staunch her defenses, there was plenty of evidence to support a penis envy hypothesis. Particularly striking was her sense of vulnerability and particularly the feeling of being controlled in the sexual encounter. She saw her own female genitalia as dirty and somehow defective and linked this with her sense of loss of control in the sexual act. The male penis was somehow strong and clean and provided a man with a capacity for control over a woman.

She had a number of phallic substitutes, however, which filled up the deficit. One was her dog, a large, male German shepherd. Another was the car which she referred to as "a car a girl shouldn't drive." Last, although certainly not least, there was her brain, the penis-brain she could inflate to impress others and particularly to defend, put down, and place the male at a competitive disadvantage. If the competition was placed on the level of phallic power, she could make sure that hers was the bigger penis-brain. This in fact was a considerable source of anxiety for her in the analysis, since it was clear she was threatened by my control and my capacity to influence her insofar as my penis-brain might possibly be bigger than hers. The phallic reference in terms of automobiles was clear; she thought of herself as like a car, a complicated mechanism with a standard stick-shift, noting that a stick-shift gives greater control and a greater appearance of mastery. Moreover, cars were something she and her father shared together—an area in which she could prove she was as good as any boy, particularly as good as the son he might have had. The same principle applied to other interests she shared with her father from time to time: her tomboyishness, her eagerness to play baseball with her father, their liking for dogs and animals, etc.

Her equivalent for penis envy was the conflict between power and powerlessness—or as she termed it "power politics." Male dominance was thus penis power, and such power was politically denied to both women and children. She commented in regard to psychoanalysis with some cynicism that she thought penis envy had gone out of style in more sophisticated circles. After all, women's liberation has changed penis envy into penis contempt. But, however much she mouthed the rhetoric of penis, the contempt did not permeate her reality. She was convinced, for example, that the male orgasm was somehow superior—more gratifying, more fulfilling. She constantly questioned her boyfriend about this, finding it fascinating. Similarly, she was convinced that the orgasm would somehow be better if the male were not circumcised and observed that if she ever had a son she would not have him circumcised. To be circumcised (castrated) was somehow to make a Jew more like a woman, more inferior and more powerless. Her associations ran to horror movies and powerful monsters such as King Kong, the frightening embodiment of phallic power.

Some months before the termination of the analysis, there was an interesting piece of material that offered some commentary on the issues of power and control and castration. She had been buying a gift for her director and selected a card to go with it which showed a figure of Snoopy leaning on Charlie Brown and the caption said, "It's nice to have someone to lean on." She then commented that she had selected this card in preference to a second card which had attracted her. The second card had the figure of Charlie Brown on the face of it with a cut thumb. Inside there was a drawing of Snoopy, who was saying, "What is he complaining about? I don't even have a thumb."

It was really only in the closing months of the analysis that she was able to address herself to the issue of penis envy with any equanimity and balance, as well as with any degree of insight. She was able to say that the concept of penis envy was distasteful to her and she preferred to think of it in terms of powerlessness. She could recognize her own sense of deference to men, somehow thinking of them as stronger and protective—persons she could lean on and gain strength from. She related this to physical size, particularly to the size of the male penis. In sex she clearly felt that the man was in control of the activity, and that she herself was relatively passive.

Termination

Gradually things began to go better for her outside of the analysis. Her relationships with men began to be less conflictual and disappointing, and her professional work became increasingly effective and decreasingly caught up in contentious struggles and angry and destructive outbursts against authority figures of all kinds. In fact the major share of the analytic work and the productive working through of the analytic process was accomplished in that last year.

When it finally came time to terminate, the work of termination extended over a period of several months. The change in Karen's interaction with me was remarkable. She was expressive, reflective, and extremely productive within the analytic relationship. In very graphic ways she began to show more of the expectable reactions to the ending of the analysis. She became apprehensive as to whether the gains she had made would be lost. She worried whether she would be able to give up the analysis on which she felt she had become somewhat dependent. She was able to feel appropriately sad and somewhat depressed as the termination of the analysis approached. For a brief period of time, many of the symptoms she had experienced prior to the analysis and even in the early stages of the analysis seemed to recur.

Toward the end of the analysis the vulnerability, which had been such a striking aspect of her whole analytic picture, seemed to have largely evaporated. In the closing months of the analysis, there was little of the defensiveness and contentiousness that had been such a striking feature prior to that. Incredibly enough, she even came to the point of refurbishing her commitment to her own Jewish faith. In discussions with her boyfriend about the possibility of marriage, she felt that not only might she want to have children—something she had always violently rejected and reviled in the past—but that she might even want a little girl. Moreover, if she had children she would want to raise them in the Jewish faith. Toward the end of the analysis as well, her sexual experience became considerably enriched and more gratifying. She began to have orgasms regularly, something that had been denied her in the past.

Looking back on the analysis, she felt gratified by what she had experienced and felt she had discovered a new sense of freedom. I wondered if she had ever expected to be where she was here at the end of the analysis.

She replied that before getting into the analysis she had never realized how intense her feelings were for her mother, particularly her hatred for her mother. She had also never realized how poorly she had felt about herself. She had spent a lot of effort trying to avoid those feelings, and added rather musingly and amusingly that the last thing she would ever admit to were her feelings.

She added that she felt somewhat maudlin in this last hour, or that she might feel that way if she let herself. She also felt a sense of gratitude to me. I replied that her feelings were appropriate, and that we could not have accomplished what we had accomplished or bring the analysis to a close without some feeling of sadness. At this point it was apparent she was struggling to hold back her tears, trying to carry off the separation and termination without showing how deeply she felt. She commented that she was afraid of showing any weakness. She thanked me with as much feeling and a sense of gratitude as I had ever seen in her in all the years we had worked together. She left my office with her eyes filled with tears and her cheeks moistened.

DISCUSSION

In considering Karen's experience, and particularly in considering the remarkable transition from rigidly threatened defensiveness to a condition of tenderness and trust and even gratitude, we have a unique opportunity to focus the issues and problems related to the paranoid process. Nowhere in any of these cases is the inner dialectic between vulnerability and victimhood on the one hand and the institution of paranoid defenses on the other, more clearly or more succinctly articulated. Our purpose here is to articulate and focus the elements which contributed to this constellation of defenses.

Karen's pathology expresses, in very direct ways, the vicissitudes of the parental introjects which provided the developmental context out of which her characterological problems, as well as her characteristic defensiveness within the analysis, arose. In relationship to both parents, we can see played out the elements of her restrictive identification both with the aggressor and with the victim.

Separation and Abandonment

Her relationship with her father was largely conditioned by the circumstances of his career and the recurrent and inevitable comings and departings. For much of her young life, her father was an absent figure; and yet, even in his absence, the whole context of her experience was focused around him as a central and dominating figure. The circumstances of her life were determined by his comings and goings and dictated by his assignments, his career. This determined not only whether he was there, but where she and her mother lived, and under what circumstances, whether on this or that Army base, or with her mother's family, and for how long. Time and again, the whole fabric of Karen's life was disrupted and had to be reorganized due to the demands of her father's Army career.

The impact of such cycles of separation and reunion has been examined in similar cases (Crumley and Blumenthal, 1973). It constitutes a basic in terference with the needs and rights of the separated child, and precipitates severe crises which leave their scars on the emerging psychological structure. Early reactions are similar to reactions following loss of a parent by death. The reactions include rage over the desertion, denial of loss, an intense fantasy relationship with the absent parent, persistent efforts at reunion, arousal of irrational guilt and punishment needs, increased separation anxiety and fears of abandonment, splitting of ambivalence and redirection of hostility toward the self, a strong sense of narcissistic injury, and a variety of regressive symptoms.

During the father's absence in these cases, the remainder of the family tried to compensate for his absence by turning inward, as though nursing a wound. The child took over the father's personality traits in an exaggerated defensive identification. The emotional attachment to an idealized memory of the father also developed. The father's return seemed to reactivate the painful feelings associated with his leaving. Painful adjustments made during his absence had to be undone and new attachments formed.

This recurrent cycle of departure, absence, and return seemed to affect development in significant ways. Departure was often followed by disobedience, poor school performance, or antisocial behavior. The child often sought punishment, as though he were guilty of driving his father away. Aggressive behavior was often seen in an attempt to resist regressive pulls toward the mother. Less frequently the ambivalent anger and guilty fear of punishment resulted in an overly strict superego. The child would often be overly conscientious and compulsively neat. A number of these children became strikingly depressed with persistent themes of helplessness, powerlessness and impotence. The mother's depression was also frequently a prominent part of the picture. Finally, the child's relationship with the mother became regularly more difficult. The rage over the loss of the father was split off and directed toward the mother, making the relationship with her increasingly ambivalent and difficult.

Obviously, many of these findings are quite consistent with the pattern of development we have been able to trace in the present case. Indeed, we might well be able to add Karen to the list, since so many of the effects experienced by these "Army brats" were identifiable in her case equally well. The fact of the recurrent cycle of loss and reunion, therefore, has its determinable effects. But we must remind ourselves that it was not merely these external circumstances that carried the burden of her pathology—even though the evidence would suggest that the circumstances provided a highly influential context. More significant—and apparently intensified and reinforced by the circumstances—were the personalities of her respective parents as they played themselves out in this unstable and loss-riddled set of life circumstances.

Paternal Introject

It seems clear that the very fact of her father's absence intensified some important aspects of Karen's relating to him. He became the powerful and important figure with whom it was terribly important for her to establish a positive and accepting relationship. In her mind, he became an idealized figure: strong, silent, mysterious, powerful; that somehow destructive and potentially dangerous man in her life. She responded to him with a mixture of intense admiration and fear. She wondered about his comings and goings, about the cloak of mystery that surrounded his activity, about his mysterious silence, which would not permit him to talk about his work or what he did outside of the family. She was frightened by the mysterious men who came to visit him in the dark of the night and talked with him in subdued voices about strange and dreadful things. He was a man with the power to kill other men and he was involved in deadly enterprises of some unknown nature.

Moreover, in his relationship to her, he was an authoritarian dictator who arbitrarily enforced his will upon her and forced her to submit regardless of her will or her feelings. His relationship to her was in large measure based on his giving orders and his expectation that she should take them like a "good little soldier." On the one hand there was a strong need for her to please and submit to his wishes, but on the other hand, there was an intense fear and a need to rebel and struggle against his authority. They shared a certain stubborness and willfulness, part of what Karen referred to as the "Hungarian temper." He could not give in to the threat to his authority and fragile self-esteem, while she could not give in to her fear of subjugation and diminution. He was very clearly the man in her life, the brute, the fascist, the giver of arbitrary orders which demanded capitulation and subjugation and submission. He became for her the paradigm of all men.

Yet they were so much alike. What comes through with striking clarity is the strength of Karen's identification with the aggressor. The "Hungarian tempers," the stubborness, the profound sense of her own capacity to hurt and disappoint and destroy—all seem to be related to the aggressive aspects of the paternal introject. She was tall like her father and even took pride in walking in a military manner even as he did. The phallic and narcissistic aspects of this introjective alignment would be hard to ignore.

Yet the introjective configuration reached even further. If the father was the strong, demanding, authoritarian, fascist-brute, she also saw him as threatened and fragile and vulnerable. The parallel of their character in this regard is striking. If father's authority were threatened, he had all the more to insist on having his orders obeyed and on having Karen submit to his wishes. She was a precocious child and must not have missed the underlying flaws in his facade of strength. All the more striking that her own facade of capable coping and resourcefulness was built on an uncertain and fragile foundation of sand.

For both of them, strength was essentially defensive. This threatened and vulnerable aspect of her father came more clearly into focus after his retirement from the Army. He became increasingly insecure, dependent, even more paranoid. On her part, she became correspondingly afflicted with a sense of her own power and capacity to hurt and disappoint him. Her ambivalence played itself out within a stately waltz of interlocking pathologies. As long as he was the powerful fascist, she could be admiring and rebellious. But as he became the more dependent and susceptible puppydog, she became caught up in the conflicts of guilt and pity and contempt.

Particularly striking—if my reader will tolerate the pun—was the central role of Karen's recollections of being beaten, and specifically slapped in the face, by her father. Freud was the first to point out the link between beating fantasies and Oedipal wishes. In Karen's case we are dealing not so much with a fantasy in the technical sense as with a set of specific recollections, that is to say memories, which serve a screen function in part, in that they express the underlying wish. The memory thus serves an equivalent function to the fantasy with the added element that the wish attaches itself to a specific memory in order to express its function.

The connection in Karen's case was clearly established through her associations to the episodes in which she was slapped in the face by her father. She referred to his big hands, then associated big hands with big penises. She also observed how beautiful and strong her father's hands were. The whole complex of associations provides a strong indication of the basic function in Karen's pathology of the feminine masochistic wish. The association between her own big hands and her father's big hands further reflects her identification with his aggressive, beating, face-slapping and brutal aspects. And indeed part of her own masochism as we have seen, was aptly translated into beating herself in the paroxysms of guilt that she so often experienced.

Maternal Introject

If Karen's' relationship to her father can be said to have been riddled with ambivalence and conflict, no less must be said of her relationship with her mother. Moreover, if the recurrent drama of leaving and returning, of recurrent struggling for closeness and approval and abandonment, had provided the fabric of the intensity of Karen's involvement with her father, it is also true that the upshot of the drama of abandonment was that Karen was thrown with peculiar intensity onto a conflictful dependence on her mother. That mother was overly obsessive, compulsive, overly anxious and intrusive, constantly controlling, criticizing, accusing and berating.

There seems little doubt that the major parameters of Karen's superego derived directly from her mother. Mother's caretaking seemed to be an unending process of impingement, intrusion, and anxious controlling. Karen's own attitudes were intensely self-critical—criticizing her every behavior, her appearance, her dress, in an unending anxiety to obtain approval and acceptance, to be thought right, good, and praiseworthy. The parallel of these anxieties to what Karen could recognize and revile in her mother proved extremely distressing. She speaks of dressing under her mother's "eagle eye." The "eagle eye" had indeed become an internal possession: allseeing, omniscient, pervasive, the burden of a continual persecution of unending criticism and blame.

Then the introjection went beyond that. Mother's continual portrayal of herself was as a disadvantaged, unfortunate, abandoned, victimized, martyr-woman-mother. The maternal introject carried within it the motifs of victimized womanhood: she was the woman who was put down, "shat upon," slapped down, "screwed," and abandoned. The values and attitudes, which Karen's mother so insistently and continuously promulgated, thus became the rationalization for feminine victimization.

Karen of course—at least on one level—would have no part of it. But the bitter fact was that she indeed placed herself in the position of being victimized and constantly promulgated the view of her own victimization internally—even when the external situation might have lent itself to another perception or interpretation—and erected the fear of victimization and feminine subjugation as the leitmotif of her existence. Thus the maternal introject played itself out in terms of the complex ambivalences which seemed to color all of Karen's experience and indeed spelled out the dimensions of her inner world. There is both an aggressive and a victimized aspect of the introject. If her mother was the harsh, punitive, demeaning, critical and ever-watchful "eagle eye"—the eye that seemed to never sleep or close—she was also the abandoned, victimized, demeaned and vulnerable woman, condemned to live out her life in the shadow and under the power of the capriciousness and arbitrariness of Karen's father. She was, indeed, the Desdemona to his Othello.

But there were further readouts from this important introject. We have noted the strongly compulsive, anal quality of Karen's character, and there seems little doubt that this aspect of her character was not only induced by the quality of her early experiences in relationship to her mother, but also reflected some of the parameters of the underlying introject. There seems little reason to question the anality in mother's personality since her obsessive-compulsive qualities and the severe and punitive aspects of the superego seem well established. These aspects were also clearly evidenced in Karen's own personality. Not only was there a strong anal focus, but Karen's considerable ambivalence, her stubborn willfulness, and her capacity to engage in unremitting anal struggles within the analysis seemed clearly to enunciate this aspect of her personality. She had in fact strongly internalized her mother's preoccupations with neatness, cleanliness, and punctuality, along with the abiding preoccupations with organization and control. The operation of reaction formation loomed large in the many ramifications of Karen's life-style.

Karen was literally trapped between her intense need to gain approval and acceptance from her demanding and rigidly obsessional mother and her intense fear of the devalued and demeaned image of femininity and womanhood which she assimilated from that same mother. The fear of victimized and degraded femininity carried with it an overloading of anal elements. Karen's unconscious conception of her own genitals seems to have been more or less cloacal, seeing them as somehow dirty, wounded, unclean, and as emitting foul and disgusting odors and substances. She preoccupied herself in a rather excessive way with cleanliness, as we have noted, particularly with her genital area. She douched and washed and cleansed repeatedly and compulsively, constantly dreading that her male companions would be repulsed or disgusted by the sight or smell or contact with her genitals.

This attitude in part reflects that which we can identify in her mother, who regarded anything having to do with sexuality, and particularly feminine sexuality, as dirty and disgusting. Consequently, we can infer a strong coloration of anal-sadistic elements functioning as drive determinants of the respective introjects. Related to this, undoubtedly, were Karen's persecutory fears of destructive attack, her fears of attack from the rear—that direction in which she was blind and from which unexpected and unpredictable attacks could be launched—and her preoccupations with hurting others, which bear such a remarkably consistent and clear anal stamp. She was in effect, either "crapping on" someone else or in danger of being "crapped on" by someone else. Moreover, being "crapped on," put down, subjugated, slapped down, were all elements which played themselves out in the sexual arena.

Introjective Interaction

If we bring into focus at this point the introjective configuration that is identifiable in Karen's intrapsychic world, we can begin to see that it offers certain specific resemblances to the introjective pattern that we have become familiar with in the study of the paranoid process. To put it in terms of the Oedipal configuration, we can think in terms of the positive and the negative Oedipal situations. For Karen, it is the positive Oedipal relationship which lies closest to the surface. In these terms, she adores and idealizes her father, and hates and reviles and struggles against her mother. In these terms, she identifies with the strong aggressive controlling aspect of her father and tries to set a distance between her and mother.

But it is not this aspect of her intrapsychic economy which lies at the root of the difficulty. At a deeper level there is the negative Oedipal complex. At this level, Karen yearns for and constantly seeks approval and acceptance and closeness with her mother, while she rejects her father's authoritarian control and feels contempt for his pathetic insecurity and weakness. It is in these terms that Karen identifies with the vulnerable and victimized woman-mother and internalizes her mother's critical, accusatory, and punitive attitudes. This is also the source of her contempt for male inadequacy and dependency and her contemptuous hostility for the "puppydog."

What is impressive here—although by no means new—is the fact that the Oedipal involvement itself is less meaningful than the introjective prehistory which provides the substance out of which the Oedipal configuration is evolved. It is the patterning of these introjects, developed through the preoedipal developmental history and carrying with them pregenital determinants—in this case, and in many of the cases of paranoid manifestations, specifically the anal determinants—that gives shape to and determines the quality and the emphasis within the Oedipal configurations.

Part of the problem in dealing with Karen's pathology is that there is a certain splitting between these introjective organizations with a resulting alternation between one configuration and another. The splitting and the sequential emphasis and adoption of introjective positions serves rather intense defensive needs. Thus, for Karen, the adoption of the strong, controlling, coping, aggressive, mastering position, which reflects so directly her introjection of the more adequate aspects of her father's personality, serves as an important and indeed essential defense against the sense of weakness and vulnerability and victimized martyrhood which is involved in the maternal introject. Conversely, the adoption of the alternative position, that of susceptible, vulnerable and dependent female, serves important defensive needs in avoiding and protecting Karen from the intensity of destructive and hostile impulses involved in the introjection of the aggressor.

It is important to note there that the alternative introjective positions cannot simply be identified on any one-to-one basis with the respective parental figures. Rather, the complex introjective alignment is a result of the interplay and the interaction of introjective elements derived from both parents. Consequently, if we were to denominate one aspect of Karen's introjective economy in terms of identification with the aggressor, we would have to make reference to introjective elements derived from both parental figures involving, for example, father's authoritarian and mysteriously destructive aspects, as well as mother's punitive and harsh accusatory superego stance. Alternatively, if we focus on the victimized aspect of Karen's introjective alignment, we would similarly have to make reference not only to the pose of victimized and martyred femininity represented by the figure of the mother, but would also have to add to that the sense of inadequacy and vulnerability and pathetic susceptibility which Karen unquestionably could detect under her father's bluster and military facade, and which became quite apparent after his retirement from the Army and the onset of insecurities in connection with his job and the erosions of time and age.

Projective Elements

Another important dimension that we need to remind ourselves of in reference to the introjective vicissitudes is that these provide the fundament and the substance on the basis of which projective mechanisms function. In her pathological alternation between these introjective components, Karen inevitably would repress the alternate aspect of the introjective alignment. The repressed aspect of the introjective organization would become the substance of the projection. Consequently, when the introjective alignment was dominated by the aspects of victimization, the aggressive components were projected into the external objects. This projection took place in the analysis, whereby I became the insensitive brute whose only objective was to submit her to analytic categories and to make her dependent and vulnerable and susceptible to my interpretations.

The projection, however, also played itself out in much broader perspectives. In these terms, Karen was easily capable of painting the entire society and culture in which she lived in terms which cast it in the role of the brutal and insensitive, fascist agent of the suppression and debasement of women, and particularly a force which victimized and took advantage of Karen herself, depriving her of her sense of uniqueness and individuality and the specialness that formed such an important support for her inner security.

Similarly, when the strong, resourceful, coping and more aggressive aspects dominated the introjective economy, it was the victim aspect that became the basis for projection. Thus, within the analysis, her defensively derived need to counterattack and to undermine my methodology and challenge my analytic competence ran the risk of hurting and defeating me. It was this aspect of her projective effort which made me into a potential "puppydog" and which consequently cast upon her the burden of destructiveness and hurtfulness. It was this burden that inevitably called forth the unavoidable chastisement of guilt.

But she carried the same mechanism into her relationship with other men as well. The alternatives were clearly structured and stated: if a man was not relating to her as an insensitive brute, if he showed any weakness or insecurity or even loving dependence on her, this served only to elicit her contempt and her aggressive wish to put him down and treat him as a "puppydog." This too found its larger ramification and rationalization on the broad canvas of the outer world. She decried the social processes and mechanisms by which men were required to remain their mother's little boys, and thus became inadequate and too weak and insecure to deal with a strong-minded, intelligent, and professional woman such as herself. Thus, for Karen men were seen dichotomously as either strong, powerful, destructive, callous, insensitive brutes who victimized and took advantage of women, demeaning and subjugating them sexually and socially and intellectually; or they were weak, insecure, inadequate, impotent, and pathetically vulnerable creatures who could be destroyed by any woman who did not place herself in a demeaned, nonthreatening, and subjugated role. One of the very central and important aspects of the analytic process was the definition and testing out and working through of these introjective-projective complexes and a gradual erosion of the dichotomous logic which dictated that the universe had to be divided between these extreme polarities. The logic, of course, was derived from and expressed the dichotomized organization of Karen's internal world. The work of analysis was directed to the modification and erosion of that internal polarization.

Developmental Implications

An additional point can be made regarding the Oedipal configuration. Our consideration thus far has been primarily in terms of the impact of the introjective organization on the Oedipal alignment and the essential foundation which this implies for the subsequent projection through which the paranoid process is manifested. In fact, one of the primary indicators of the introjective influence in this situation is the susceptibility to projection as well as the regressive influence of drive derivatives. Clearly, the projective elements that we have been discussing in Karen's case reflect both of those dimensions. However, we can shift the emphasis for the moment and look at the Oedipal situation, not simply in terms of its reflection in paranoid mechanisms, but more specifically as an outcome of the operation of the paranoid process.

We are touching here upon a broader implication of the functioning of the paranoid process, not simply in terms of identifiable pathology, but more broadly in terms of its influence in the developmental process—even in the normal progression of psychological health. Conceived in broader terms, the paranoid process functions to define and establish and give coherent organization to the inner world, specifically in the organization and sustaining of a sense of self. Such an internal organization requires a correlative and parallel separation of self from the surrounding environment—physical and personal and social. Thus, while the paranoid process acts to maximize a sense of internal consistency, it does so only at the price of definition against and separation from the outside world.

The Oedipal configuration can thus be conceived in terms of a necessary evolution in this process of self-definition and separation. The child must somehow define himself not only in relation to but as separate from both parental figures. An important stage in this evolution of definition and separation takes place by reason of the definition of self through the adherence to one parental figure, thereby achieving a separation of self from the other parental figure. The defining and separating must go on in both directions, however, so that a similar process of defining adherence and separation must take place in the opposite direction.

The working of defining and separating is tied up with the mechanisms of introjection and projection. The inner definition takes place through introjection and the outer separation takes place through projection. Normally, this process works itself through to an increasingly stable and clear definition of self so that the defensive aspects of the process of introjection and projection become modified and minimized. The problem for Karen, in a sense, was that the junction of the paranoid process in achieving this sense of definition and separation was not able to move beyond the level of alternating between the ambivalent aspects of her involvement with the parental figures. This was in part due to the influence of pregenital determinants which contaminated the growth potential of these processes by activating defensive needs and accompanying ambivalence, the intensity of which Karen could not tolerate without resorting to defensive postures including the splitting of introjective elements.

The role of penis envy in this case prompts me to make a comment about it. We have had occasion in surveying the various aspects of the paranoid process to note the relationship of the process to the problem of envy and jealousy. Penis envy would seem to fall under this rubric as a special case of the working out of paranoid mechanisms within the developmental context. The paranoid process utilizes differences, no matter how minimal or otherwise inconsequential, in the interest of defining self through definition of differences. The focus on differences, of course, is utilized in the interest of separation of self as an integral aspect of the defining process.

The presence or the absence of the penis is a major difference which ultimately defines the difference between male and female. The difference between penis-possession and penis-lack thus must play a very central role in the emerging definition of the child's sexual identity. The developmental functions of definition and separation in tandem with the processes of identification and differentiation with the same and opposite sex parents respectively, constitute the normal process of healthy formation of sexual identity. The process employs the same basic mechanisms which we have identified as correlative with the paranoid process.

The distortion and the pathological corruption enter when the process of separation becomes contaminated with envy. The pathological distortion is rooted in narcissism; what is possessed by another and is not possessed by oneself is an index of the incompleteness and defectiveness of the self. Thus, the possession of another must be envied since the underlying dictate of the narcissistic premise is that one's self is omnipotently entitled to the possession of everything. On this narcissistic foundation, then, the whole concept of the lack of penis as conjoined with notions of inferiority and powerlessness takes its origin.

Thus, for Karen, lack of a penis meant deprivation, impotence, weakness, powerlessness, and vulnerability. Consequently, we can not only recognize these as the castration motifs but also identify their psychological origins in the postulates of pathological narcissism. One should not miss the critical issue in all this, as many do. In this context, it should be clear that penis envy is an almost unavoidable consequence of the residues of infantile narcissism in the baby girl, and that the resolution of penis envy involves important processes in the working through of injured narcissism leading to a more positive definition of sexual identity and an integration of the concept of self as inherently female.

Another aspect of the paranoid distortion in this particular case, and one which I suspect is shared to a greater or lesser degree by many women in contemporary society, is the translation of penis envy into penis contempt. The mechanism is transparently paranoid and defensive, calculated to salvage the primarily injured narcissism which is reflected in penis envy. The process follows the paradigm that we have already established whereby the projective defense serves as a compensation and salvaging maneuver to preserve and sustain the narcissistically injured self. Analysts are familiar with the narcissistic defense which involves a contempt for and a devaluing of the analyst as a means of preserving the threatened inner integrity which the patient feels in the face of the analytic regression. Certainly, in the present case, that form of defensiveness has been amply demonstrated. It is also clear that Karen's defensiveness and her attempts to devalue and place in contempt both the analyst and the analytic process—not to mention the whole of psychoanalysis and Freudian theory—were equivalently a form of penis contempt and constituted an elaborate narcissistic (paranoid) defense.

The Issue of Autonomy

We have pointed out in any number of these cases that the issue of imperiled autonomy is one that is characteristic of the paranoid forms of pathology. Karen's autonomy was a threatened and fragile autonomy. But there would seem to be room for some distinctions to be made in discussing the question of diminished autonomy in cases such as these. There were indeed many respects in which Karen's ego-functions were intact and operated with a considerable degree of autonomy. There is certainly room for a distinction between autonomy which has its reference to ego-capacities and ego-functions, and the autonomy which has its primary reference to the self. It is the latter form of autonomy that shows itself to be significantly threatened in the present instance, and which shows itself to be decisively threatened in all the cases we have considered in this study. It is also the form of autonomy that received its most pregnant description at the hands of Erik Erikson.

If the distinction between ego-autonomy and self-autonomy has a legitimate place, the complexities of their interrelationship would seem to demand theoretical clarification. Certainly in the more distorted forms of paranoid functioning, in which autonomy is most severely threatened, there would seem to be ample room for the consideration of both modalities of impoverished autonomy. However there are other cases, such as the present one, in which the distinction may have some validity and clinical import. It is not clear that the paranoid mechanisms represent a simple case of drive-derivative influences invading the functioning of ego-capacities. What predominates the clinical picture in the present case is Karen's sense of threatened autonomy, sense of threat to her self as an autonomously functioning self. It is this aspect of her inner functioning which is closely related to the motifs of vulnerability and victimization that played such a significant role in her psychopathology.

We do not have far to look in determining some of the sources of Karen's sense of threatened autonomy. An important influence was the continuing incursiveness and obsessive control exercised by her mother throughout the period of her development. The struggle that Karen engaged in with her mother was in its most central core dimension a struggle for autonomy. The struggle was joined from the very beginning and presumably reached a first level of intensity over the issues of anal control and regulation. Karen emerged in a development sense from that battle with an abiding sense of willfulness and stubbornness which serves as the hallmark of an imperiled autonomy. The campaign against her mother continued to be waged throughout aspects of her analysis. It was—simply put and in all essential aspects—a battle for the establishment and preservation of Karen's autonomy. Moreover, the battle was fought largely in anal terms. Anything that Karen did that stood in opposition to her mother's will had to be interpreted as an attack on mother. Thus when Karen decided to go to graduate school, or when she decided to live with her boyfriend and postponed her decision to marry, these were taken as having been done against her mother, rather than as autonomous and self-motivated decisions.

Narcissism

We have already considered the role of narcissism in Karen's defensiveness—particularly in relation to her need to be different, to stand out, not to conform to expectations or explanations—and the immense struggle that she entered into, not only in the analysis but through the course of her life, to preserve her "individuality." The saga of her narcissism likewise played itself out in her expectations that were continually frustrated and denied. It was these constantly rejuvenated expectations that left her in a state of continual disappointment. Her expectations reached out to her mother, from whom she always anticipated and looked for acceptance and approval, but never got it; to her father from whom she longed for a close and abiding relationship, but was continually denied this because of his remoteness and his continual abandonment; to her boyfriends from whom she expected tenderness and concern and a primary place in their affections, but in relation to whom she constantly felt herself to be subjected to their needs and their self-importance. We have also seen the depressive rage that grew out of this narcissistic embroilment. Karen lived under the curse of narcissism. It was essentially this narcissism that underlay her inner anguish and her embattled defensiveness. A question we might ask at this juncture is: What influences come to bear on a child like Karen which turn the course of narcissistic development from a pattern of gradually emerging self-esteem to these more pathological deviations?

The point of departure for this consideration lies in the interface between parental narcissism and infantile narcissism. If the child is to grow out of the cocoon of infantile narcissism, it must be by the emergence of a significant object-relatedness. There is a hunger for object involvement that is embedded in the instinctual life of every human infant. But the relationship to real objects must be worked out in the context of a developing mutuality. The child becomes able to relate to real objects in the measure to which he is responded to and met in the ongoing interaction with significant objects as a real object himself. In fact, the emerging context of mutuality requires that the parent be able to respond to the child as a distinct and separate and uniquely individualized object.

This basic acceptance and recognition of the child's emerging self by the significant objects in the environment serves as a basic contributing force to the shaping of developing self-esteem. To the extent that the child's emerging self is accepted, recognized, interacted with in meaningful ways and perhaps even more crucially, loved, the child is able to internalize this aspect of self-regard in an age-appropriate manner specific to the stages of his developmental progression. Such an occurrence, however, requires in the significant object to which the child is thus related, a capacity to relate to the child as a distinct and separate individual and to recognize and acknowledge what is intrinsic to the child as something that is valued, loved, esteemed, and cherished for its own sake.

What then interferes with this pattern of emerging narcissism which would otherwise result in a healthy and realistic sense of self-esteem? The proposition being advanced here is that it is specifically the parental narcissism that inhibits the capacity of the parents to respond to the emergent self of the child and which alters and distorts the internalizations which contribute to the healthier progression in the child's development in self-esteem.

In Karen's case, it seems clear that her mother's own sense of self-esteem was so delicately precarious and her narcissistic needs were so intense and readily mobilized that they interfered with her capacity to respond to the inner needs of her child. Such a recognition and acceptance from her mother is what Karen never received in the earliest stages of her developmental experience, and it is precisely what she continually sought and was continually denied. The denial was driven by the strength of her mother's own narcissistic fixations and needs. Consequently we can conclude that Karen was "loved" or "accepted" only to the degree that she was able to respond to and fulfill her mother's narcissistic demands. To an extent, Karen was able to do this—she became the neat and precociously self-possessed and studiously organized child that the mother demanded. This gained her a measure of mother's acceptance, but the price had to be paid.

What it effected was a split between the obedient, clean, punctual, responsible, studious and subjugated self that she presented to the external world to gain its acceptance and approval and the inner self that cloaked itself in rebelliousness and defensiveness and wallowed in its threatened vulnerability and resentful victimization. Thus Karen erected within her own inner world a false self which represented her conformity to her mother's demands but also represented an inner violation, a subjugation, a victimization, a rape and assault, a violence upon what she felt to be most authentically and centrally her true self.

The struggle to preserve that sense of authentic self was joined from the earliest levels of her recollection in the continuing combat with her mother. It was also rejoined with startling strength and precipitous clarity in the context of the analysis, where the basic issue that had to be joined was whether my narcissistic needs to reduce her to an analytic conception, and thus force her into a position of subjugated conformity and violation of her inner self, were to take precedence over allowing the authentic impulse to her own integrity to emerge. The question was equivalently: Whose narcissistic needs were to be served by the analysis, mine or hers? What had to be established was the possibility that it need not be a question of mine versus hers, but that it could perhaps be a question of both, or even neither.

Dialectic of Blame and Responsibility

That basic dichotomy was paralleled by and underlay a similar dichotomous polarization which had to do with the dialectic of blame and responsibility that Karen set up in the analysis. It was a dialectic and dichotomization that permeated not only her relationship with me, but the whole fabric of her existence. The alternatives were seen decisively by her either in terms of self-blame, and therefore self-deficiency and failure, or in terms of the externalized view, which cast the blame for her pain and disappointment and the responsibility for the narcissistic insult and trauma that she continually experienced on external agents—her mother, her father, her male friends, her director, her analyst, etc., etc.

The dichotomization of inside versus outside followed the typical pattern of either-or, all-or-nothing thinking which reflects so graphically the underlying narcissistic dynamics. The inner logic of her narcissistic position dictated that she should be omnipotently influential, and therefore responsible, so that she could become the totally responsible agent of her own pain and agony—or alternatively, she was to be the totally impotent and helpless victim of the omnipotent power of outside agencies. Clinicians are familiar with these coextensive polarizations of omnipotence and impotence in particular forms of narcissistic personalities. The polarities are frequently identifiable in more primitive personality organizations, significantly in borderline personalities, although the defective structural aspects are missing in the present case. The basis of Karen's dichotomous thinking was clearly the underlying narcissistic fixation.

Karen's clinging to these polarized and dichotomized alternatives served the intense interests of her defensive alignment. It proved exceedingly difficult to break through the logic of this schema. Again and again in the course of the analysis, when we reached the impasse created by this dichotomy, it was necessary to confront her insistence on the dichotomy and to point out the distortions it created. Clearly enough there was sufficient truth in the externalized accusations that she made. It was unavoidably true that in many instances specific figures in her environment had placed their own narcissistic interests ahead of hers. It was true and relatively unarguable that there were inherent in our culture a variety of attitudes which devalued and disadvantaged women. It was also relatively true that there were at loose certain prejudicial attitudes toward intelligent professional women, as Karen so bitterly complained.

The evidence and the attitudes regarding the cultural and psychological stereotypes dictating an inconsistency between the role of the educated and professionally competent woman and the prevailing cultural expectation for femininity and feminine behavior have been discussed by Horner (1970). She writes:

> As a whole, society has been unable to reconcile personal ambition, accomplishment, and success with femininity. The more successful or independent a woman becomes, the more afraid society is that she has lost her femininity and therefore must be a failure as a wife and mother. She is viewed as a hostile and destructive force within the society. On the other hand, the more successful a man is in his work (as reflected in his high status, salary, and administrative powers—all of which are in keeping with his masculinity), the more attractive he becomes as a spouse and father. Whereas men are unsexed by failure, women seem to be unsexed by success (p. 55).

But quite clearly in none of these defensive positions that Karen so strenuously adopted and defended were the points at issue to be misconstrued as the significant focuses of our analytic concern. I was constantly in the position of granting her the substance of her externalized complaint and having to work then to refocus the issue in terms of the threat or anxiety or feelings of vulnerability and victimization that formed such a significant component of her internal response to such external situations. In the face of her constant effort to force the analysis and me into superego positions, I had to work strenuously to maintain a position of neutrality, constantly trying to maintain a position in which my observations and interpretations were not to be taken as criticisms or accusations, but rather points of observation that she and I might jointly and collaboratively consider and investigate.

Once the rudiments of the therapeutic alliance had been established, it became relatively a simple matter to expand and consolidate the areas of alliance, and correspondingly the intense defensiveness and guardedness that had been so characteristic of the previous analytic course became minimized. It was only then that the significant analytic work could be done. Then clarifications and interpretations began to have a discriminable and significant therapeutic impact. More significantly, it was only then that the intensely defensive split that she maintained between the vulnerable, victimized, feminine aspects of her self, and the strong, coping, controlling and aggressively destructive aspects of her self could begin to be modified and ameliorated. Correlative to this modification of inner defensive postures and introjective alignments, there became available a significantly greater potential for positive and constructive identifications—particularly and specifically with the analyst.

PART III
TOWARD A CLINICAL THEORY
OF THE PARANOID PROCESS

INTRODUCTION

Our journey to this point has been a long one. We have surveyed a significant area of psychiatric history, and have made our way, somewhat laboriously, through the heavy thickets of the scientific study of paranoia. The many approaches are multiple and complex, and they each in their respective ways, offer us a fragment of a perception, a view of the total problem from one vantage point, a partial and a limited understanding.

We have also tried to look at a number of cases in which the paranoid process could be identified. In studying such case material, we are confronted with obvious differences. There are differences that stem from the uniqueness and individuality of each patient and his life experience. There are also significant differences that issue from the variations in levels of pathology. The material we have presented in the case studies ranges from severely sick, chronic paranoid schizophrenics, to a spectrum of intermediate levels of borderline pathology, to a level of relatively healthy, if neurotic, patients, even those who were appropriate and successful candidates for psychoanalysis.

Even though such divergences of personality and diagnosis are impressive, our purpose is nonetheless to discern and define those elements which they share, which somehow influence and direct the paranoid aspects of their inner life and behavior. It is our purpose at this point to turn our attention to this task. The diversity and complexity that we have seen in the study of the literature and in the analysis of individual cases leave us with an impression of multiplicity and diversity which must be brought together and focused to allow us a deeper understanding of the paranoid process, its genesis, its function, and its significant influences.

CHAPTER 16

Paranoia as Process

THE CONCEPT OF PROCESS

Our concern at this point in the development of the argument is to focus the problem of paranoia specifically in terms of the concept of "process." We are concerned even more specifically with formulating a concept of the paranoid process which will bear the weight of a series of implications which seem to be intimately attached to the nature of the paranoid process itself.

This shift in emphasis to a consideration of process would seem to be a consistent extension of identifiable trends in psychoanalytic thinking. Along one line of development, the emphasis in analytic conceptualization has moved from a concern with diagnosis as such to an emphasis on underlying mechanisms. In the history of the development of psychoanalysis this has usually taken the form of focusing on defense mechanisms, but in a contemporary framework the consideration is much broader. Under the stimulus provided by the conceptual development of a more consistent and sophisticated ego psychology, considerably greater emphasis has been placed on the study of ego functions and their operations, either as isolated psychological phenomena or as coordinated into meaningful patterns. Thus considerably greater emphasis in recent times has been placed on the study of perceptual and cognitive functions within a psychoanalytic framework.

Along another line of historical development, emphasis in psychoanalysis has shifted from a concern with a level of symptomatology—focusing on concerns of symptom formation and expression—to a level of greater interest in characterological variables. The emphasis shifts from the interpretation of specific conflicts and psychodynamic patterns to an emphasis on those factors which underlie the formation of character and which pertain more specifically to less intrapsychic and more extrapsychic concerns. This line of development therefore implicates another line of development which can be identified in the history of psychoanalysis. I am referring to the shift from the concern with more specifically instinctual and conflict-based levels of functioning and pathology to a concern with those aspects of the organization and functioning of the personality which are not only formed by, strongly influenced by, and continually interacting with the social and cultural environment within which the personality functions.

The emphasis in this area of psychoanalytic thinking falls upon object-relations, but the work of Erikson particularly has made it clear that the psychoanalytic reflection cannot stop simply at the level of object-relations. Object-relations theory, again, becomes a channel through which other important variables are expressed and must be understood. The individual is in a constant process of influence and interaction between himself and his environment. The society within which he lives and the culture which he assimilates and responds to have important and determinative influences on his own personality functioning, not merely in an interactional framework, but more specifically in internal, intrapsychic, and psychodynamic terms.

BROADER IMPLICATIONS

Thus the understanding of the paranoid process intends to embrace and express these various aspects of psychic functioning. We are attempting, in other words, to provide a formulation which will embrace these multiple facts in a meaningful, consistent, and unified manner. The concept, therefore, must have sufficient breadth and explanatory power to embrace the forms of pathology which we can identify as specifically paranoid. But if we were to restrict our considerations to merely the identifiable forms of pathology, we would be constraining ourselves within the limits set by an older and narrower set of concerns and interests. The material we have been considering makes it clear that paranoid mechanisms are at work in many other aspects of human experience than those which can be labeled simply as pathological.

Paranoid forms of thinking in fact seem to form a meaningful part of the fabric of human experience. We have discussed the continuity between more specifically paranoid forms of thinking and acting and more general psychological phenomena such as envy, prejudice, and jealousy. Even if one were to allow that these minor forms of psychopathology were identifiable at large in the general population, one might still feel that states of acute envy or jealousy might be regarded as transitional states of otherwise normally functioning personalities. If one stops, however, to consider the phenomena of prejudice, it becomes clear that we are dealing with something that cannot be considered in a limited fashion within the restrictive context of psychopathology. Prejudicial thinking is built into the very fabric of the organization of our society and our culture. If we can recognize prejudice as being neurotically motivated and can consider it as a form of psychopathology somehow operative within the range of normal functioning, then we begin to obliterate the concept of psychopathology itself.

But my intention here is to extend the function and the implications of the paranoid process even further. I will argue that the paranoid process is an important positive and constructive force in the organization of society and in the development of individual personality. The process is intimately involved in the forming and sustaining of social groupings, it expresses itself in a variety of ways in the structuring of social institutions, it is woven through the whole fabric and process of political organization of society, and it is a functional part of the fundamental orientation which underlies the organization and structuring of belief systems. This latter aspect of the implementation of the paranoid process is critical to the understanding of religious phenomena and the more general aspects of religious functioning. And finally the paranoid process is one of the major contributing forces to the organization of value systems, which are so deeply embedded in the workings of social structures and cultural forces.

On a more specifically psychological level, the contention being advanced in this study is that the paranoid process has important developmental aspects as well. The idea which we are developing, then, would suggest that the process has important contributions to make at critical points in individual development, and perhaps most strikingly at the level of adolescent development in the process of identity formation.

It is clear, then, that this formulation of the paranoid process is one which effectively disengages it from its roots in psychopathology and gives it a broader and more sweeping conceptualization. The paranoid process then embraces both pathological and nonpathological manifestations. If it is a source of deviation and distortion on one hand, it must also be seen as a force in the positive upbuilding of personality and society. The force of the argument that we are advancing is directed to the appreciation that one cannot understand the one without the other, that one cannot understand the pathological manifestations of the paranoid process without at the same time understanding its functions and effects in the more normal, nonpathological, and broader aspects of its implementation.

Our attempt in this theoretical consideration will be to define and explore the lines of continuity along the various manifestations of the paranoid process, so that its consistency and inner coherency become more specific and intelligible. The object of our study and consideration then is not specific manifestations of the paranoid process, but rather the process itself.

If such a consideration reaches beyond the limits of psychiatric concern, it cannot be said to reach beyond the limits of psychoanalytic concern. From its very beginnings, a general cultural interest has been an integral part of the focus of psychoanalytic concern, dating indeed from the interests of Freud himself in the dreaming processes and the vicissitudes of meaning in human psychological functioning. Freud's discoveries in *The Interpretations of Dreams* (1900) were intended to be part of his own inner compulsion to understand not only human psychopathology, but the inner workings of the human mind itself. As early as 1895, Freud wrote to Fliess:

> But the chief reason was this; a man like me cannot live without a hobby-horse, a consuming passion—in Schiller's words a tyrant. I have found my tyrant, and in his service I know no limits. My tyrant is psychology; it has always been my distant, beckoning goal, and now, since I have hit on the neurosis, it has come so much the nearer. I am plagued with two ambitions: to see how the theory of mental functioning takes shape if quantitative considerations, a sort of economics of nerve-force, are introduced into it; and secondly, to abstract from psychopathology what may be of benefit to normal psychology. Actually a satisfactory general theory of neuropsychotic disturbances is impossible if it cannot be brought into association with clear assumptions about normal mental processes (1887-1902, pp. 122-123).

The broader implications then of the study of psychopathology were apparent in the thinking of Freud—the culturalist and generalist—from almost the beginning of his scientific endeavors. But the extension of understanding from the level of psychopathology to broader cultural concerns—particularly when it is articulated in terms of specific functions and mechanisms—demands and requires the formulation of a broader conceptual framework.

In focusing on the notion of process, we are attempting to bring into clearer articulation a specific set of functions, operations, and intentions, which characterize the operation of the paranoid process in any of its multiple manifestations. The articulation of the functions, operations, and intentions of the paranoid process constitutes an essential definition of that process. In our attempt to theoretically describe and define these various aspects of the process, we will be in effect—to whatever degree possible—defining the process itself.

THE DIAGNOSTIC PROBLEM

Pathological vs. Nonpathological

If it might be claimed that, in the theoretical perspective of the paranoid process, diagnostic concerns fade somewhat into the background; it must also be emphasized that they lend the problem of diagnosis a new scope and a new subtlety. While it may be true that classificatory concerns focusing on issues of psychopathology and the definition of syndromes is less relevant, it is nonetheless extremely important that the signs of the functioning of the paranoid process be identifiable and recognizable. Within a limited perspective of the concern over psychiatric diagnosis, the emphasis must be on the identification of the deviant signs or manifestations of the process which provide the basis for psychiatric judgment and intervention.

Since considerable discussion has already been given over to the specifically diagnostic considerations (cf. sections on paranoid indications and mechanisms above), an exhaustive restatement of them would not be very useful at this point. However, a major emphasis of this study, which does demand consideration at this point, is that the paranoid process is not limited to definable forms of specifically paranoid pathology, but that it can be found embedded in a wide spectrum of clinical entities, as well as in normal functional states. The point that needs to be emphasized is that, frequently enough, paranoid manifestations are quite subtle and often form a relatively hidden and latent portion of the patient's personality, which may only emerge under special circumstances or after lengthy periods of treatment. We will discuss some of the patterns of interaction between the paranoid process and specific diagnostic entities, but it is apparent in our case studies that the paranoid process can manifest itself in severely distorted forms, but that it can also manifest itself in quite subtle and not often apparent ways in personalities which are fairly well organized and enjoy a high degree of integration and capacity for effective psychological functioning.

Paranoid Indices

It becomes relatively difficult, therefore, to think in terms of subtle and often very "soft" indicators which might reflect the operation of the paranoid process at rather minimal levels. The difficulty, of course, is that such minimal indicators shade over into levels of normal functioning—but that after all is one of the major points of significance of the present study. Such early indicators are extremely subtle, for the most part, and may often present themselves in quite muted forms in the organization of the patients' behavior. When patients present the clinician with relatively patent paranoid concerns—as for example a concern with secrecy and confidentiality, a guardedness and suspiciousness of manner, with identifiable ideas of references, etc.—clinical judgment and awareness is a simple and straightforward matter. But the case is not always so clear-cut. Moreover, we have a presumption and a right as clinicians to examine our patients in the light of potential psychopathology. However, when we approach the nonclinical sphere of broader social involvements and cultural manifestations, the question of paranoid manifestations becomes considerably more difficult and nuanced.

One manifestation of the paranoid process which enjoys a considerable spectrum of expression is what Bullard (1960) has referred to as "centrality." The notion of centrality expresses the patient's notion of somehow being in the center of interest or attention from other people. Such a state of mind can present itself in the most normal of ways, and may be taken for granted as a natural state of mind for one who has come into the focus of psychiatric interest—for whatever reason. But the feelings of centrality may also serve as a subtle expression of the patient's feelings of impingement by outside forces, of a sense of being a passive recipient of external influences to which he is somehow subjected and over which he may feel he has little or no control.

Hypersensitivity is another subtle indicator of an underlying paranoid process. The patient may seem to be more than unusually reactive to the comments or opinions of other people, may have a feeling of being slighted or wronged or mistreated. This again falls well within the spectrum of normal behaviors, and may indeed have considerable justification in reality; nonetheless, the astute clinician needs to be aware of the potentiality of early and minimal paranoid manifestations. Another curious manifestation is the facade of self-sufficiency which patients often present to the clinician. One can discern beneath such apparent self-sufficiency a sense of vulnerability and susceptibility which is countered by the "adequate" facade.

Another interesting manifestation that might be regarded as somewhat surprising, particularly in analytic patients, is a preoccupation with hidden meanings. This is particularly noteworthy in the context of exploratory psychotherapy or psychoanalysis, where the concern with hidden meanings is part of the therapeutic process. One can easily be misled into thinking that the patient is demonstrating a productive involvement in the treatment, when in fact the concern with hidden meanings or hidden motives may be a reflection of an underlying paranoid process.

Another subtle and pervasive concern that relates to the functioning of the paranoid process is the concern over autonomy. The variety and heterogeneity of the concerns over autonomy is considerable and may take extremely subtle forms indeed. When a patient expresses a fear of loss of control the issue is unequivocal, but often the patient's concerns may be expressed in a variety of resistances or avoidances, or even of unexpressed and silent inner reservations which are not specifically directed to the undoing of therapeutic efforts, but which are more directly concerned with preoccupations with autonomy and the underlying fears of violation of autonomy that are so closely linked with the paranoid style.

Another important and subtle manifestation is the tendency to blaming. This is closely related to tendencies to externalization, the disposition of the patient to formulate and understand his difficulties in terms of external circumstances, forces, events, persons, etc.

Another set of indicators has to do with feelings of inadequacy or deficiency. Here again the manifestation is such a common part of the clinical experience that one almost hesitates to suggest that there may be important connections with the operation of the paranoid process; nonetheless such concern over inadequacy may play an important role in paranoid dynamics. This may take the expression of complaints about being too short or being too tall, may take the form of concern over genital inadequacy, or may take a more diffuse and nonspecific form as concerns about being somehow different. Some patients express an idea of somehow being an outsider, of not being a part of the social or political or cultural context in which they carry out their lives. Often there may be a quite diffuse concern over values or purposes or beliefs which might lead one to think in terms of more descriptive categories such as "identity diffusion," but these concerns may also be seen in the context of a concern over difference and separation which may reflect a paranoid modality.

Another significant area is the whole question of authority relations, and this type of manifestation refers back to the concern over problems of power and powerlessness which are so closely related to paranoid concerns. We discussed some of these issues in relation to the authoritarian personality, but it must be noted here that they can serve as an area of particular expression of the paranoid process. Here again we can note the generality of such manifestations, particularly in younger segments of the population. Related to this is an area in which considerable confusion can arise, but which nonetheless may serve as an expression of paranoid concerns. I am referring to feelings of righteousness, of feelings of resentment about social injustice, of dedication to causes and campaigns, and a whole host of purposeful involvements which may pass for manifestations of social conscience or social sensitivity, or a variety of constructive and valuable emphases which may also reflect the operation of the paranoid process.

One can begin to sense the inherent difficulty in discussing diagnostic concerns in this whole area. The borderline between the pathological and the nonpathological becomes quickly blurred and obfuscated. The early indicators that we have suggested—while certainly not exhaustive or detailed—can be looked at in terms of the relationship to potential psychopathology in a specifically clinical context. As such they may be minimal indices of an underlying concealed paranoid process which is functioning in relatively pathological ways, so that the identification of such indicators can serve to raise the index of suspicion for a diagnosis of paranoia, or at least of paranoid mechanisms.

In the broader nonclinical context, however, these same indices are relatively human stuff. Who is there of us who at one time or other does not manifest one or another of these indicators of the paranoid process? One might conclude, therefore, that such indices were meaningless, or that they were of little relevance to any clinical concerns. However, one can take the opposite tack, as we are doing here, and say that such minimal indicators may indeed be reflectors of the operation of a paranoid process, and that such a process has broad implications for the understanding of human functioning and behavior even in a nonclinical and broader cultural context.

The argument however—it should be noted—does not rest on the identification or the generality of such minimal indicators of the paranoid process, but rests also and more specifically on the understanding of the functions of the paranoid process and its continuity with identifiably pathological forms. It is apparent, therefore, that a diagnostic concern can be quite misleading. One can easily be seduced into thinking that everyone is paranoid, or that social institutions and cultural processes are themselves pathological, but it seems to me that one could only reach this inference by reason of clinging to an older diagnostic frame of reference, rather than shifting the level of consideration to the understanding of the paranoid process.

CLINICAL CONTEXTS

I would like to address a comment briefly at this time to the operation of the paranoid process specifically in regard to certain clinical entities: the nature of the specifically pathological manifestations of paranoia in the context of other diagnostic entities. This is an important point since my presumption is that paranoid elements enjoy a wide distribution in the general population, and that if one looks carefully enough and with sufficient intensity one can find paranoid manifestations with few exclusions in most human beings.

But I am focusing for the moment on the question of the extent to which identifiable clinical paranoia can be found in conjunction with other diagnostic categories. The first diagnostic category that I would like to consider is that of homosexuality. The connection between homosexuality and paranoid dynamics is a classic one, and was enunciated clearly, as we have seen, by Freud. As we have also seen, the inference that homosexuality and paranoia are always linked is also a questionable one. However, the dynamics of homosexuality can be and often are associated with the dynamics of paranoia. This is particularly the case where homosexuality reflects a feminine identification. Where homosexuality comes to mean passivity, submission to the power of the strong father, identification with the weak, passive, victimized, and powerless mother, the dynamics underlying homosexuality come to lie very close to those we have seen in reference to the paranoid process.

If paranoia can be a defense against underlying homosexual conflicts, it seems equally true that homosexuality can serve as a defense against underlying paranoid conflicts. What seems to me useful to keep in perspective is that both homosexuality and paranoia may be a response to similar underlying concerns. Thus they may be seen to function in conjunction, or be linked in reciprocal defensiveness, or may follow disparate paths both defensively and developmentally. It seems to me that, frequently enough, the breakdown of paranoid defenses is what brings the homosexual into treatment. Moreover, frequently enough, the paranoid defenses are what makes the treatment of homosexuality so problematic and difficult.

Another important area in which the paranoid process can function is in relationship to phobias. We have had occasion to suggest that there may be some genetic relationship between childhood phobias and the development of paranoid personalities. Often it is difficult to draw the line between phobic states and more specifically paranoid processes. Both are forms of externalization. My experience is that paranoid patients tend to show phobic symptoms, often of a rather severe nature. It is difficult for example to draw the line between a severe agoraphobia and a frank paranoia. We will have occasion to discuss this question later on in our theoretical consideration, but in terms of diagnostic concerns it seems to me that phobic responses may often mask underlying paranoid concerns.

I recall one patient of mine who presented with a combination of phobic anxiety and depression that was relatively severe and resisted attempts at therapeutic intervention for a considerable period of time. It was only gradually that I became aware that the apparent agoraphobia, which became the focus for our therapeutic concerns, was covering a host of paranoid symptoms including ideas of reference and fears of attack and annihilation. It should be remembered that when Freud originally discussed the symptom of agoraphobia, he related it to identification with the prostitute in women and discussed the dynamics of the phobic condition in terms of the underlying wish to be violated. One can add at this point that in the same example there may also be a residual fear of vulnerability and violation which may underlie a specifically paranoid dynamic as well (Freud, 1887-1902, pp. 181-182).

Another important diagnostic category is that of so-called psychopathic or the sociopathic personality disturbance. The DSM II describes this form of disorder under the rubric of antisocial personality.

As Cleckley has pointed out (1959), the psychopath typically demonstrates superior intelligence and other assets, and is able to succeed brilliantly for short periods of time in work, or study, or other human relationships, but inevitably and repeatedly fails in almost all the contexts of his endeavor. He proves himself inadequate, defective, and a failure. The lack of anxiety in such personalities, the tendency to displace blame to external forces, the inability to accept responsibility, and the antisocial tendencies begin to suggest ramifications of the paranoid process. The antisocial or psychopathic personality would seem to be a masked form of underlying paranoid dynamics. The paranoid process works in such a way as to set off such an individual from the rest of society, to endow him with certain special and narcissistic qualities, and to place him in a position that is inevitably in opposition to the social fabric. The sociopath stands in continuity with neighboring areas of psychiatric concern, specifically delinquency and criminal behavior. These also may express underlying paranoid dynamics.

The conjunction of paranoid manifestations and obsessional syndromes is, in my experience, not infrequent. This tends to be more so the case in the more severe obsessional states. It may in fact be seen with considerable regularity in borderline patients. Goldberg (1965) has reported a small series of four cases in which obsessional and paranoid mechanisms have coexisted over a considerable length of time without emerging into frank psychosis. It seems to me, in general, that there is a greater tendency for paranoid manifestations to be associated with obsessional syndromes than with hysterical syndromes.

However, as clinicians are well aware these days, more and more in analytic practice there is a tendency not to see relatively clear-cut neurotic syndromes, but rather complex personality organizations in which obsessional and hysterical features are combined in various proportions. My patient Jim J. represents a striking case of this congeries of personality characteristics. He suffered severely from anxiety and presented initially as a rather striking case of male anxiety hysteria. It gradually became clear, however, in the course of his analysis that he had a strong obsessional element in his personality which he was in many ways able to mobilize effectively as a defense against his underlying anxieties. We have discussed the rather significant role of paranoid manifestations in his overall personality functioning as well.

It should be noted that in relatively severe states of hysterical anxiety paranoid preoccupations may play a role in the clinical picture. It is also clear that paranoid manifestations may occur in varying combinations with hysterical manifestations. I am reminded of the excellent case discussion of Rycroft (1968), and more strikingly in the description of a case of hysteria by Jaffe (1971 a, b). The question remains as to whether both these cases might not have been borderline. The association between hysterical personality configurations and preoccupations and conflicts over homosexuality are a well established clinical phenomenon. We can only take note at this point of the links between feelings of feminine vulnerability, passivity, and penis envy, and the linkages between such concerns and what we have been describing here as paranoid dynamics.

We might also note the relationship between the hysterical process and depression. A frequent linking of depressive dynamics with hysterical manifestations is a well-known clinical concern, one that raises specific problems for establishing criteria of analyzability. This general area of clinical concern was focused on by Zetzel (1968), who also provided a classificatory scheme of levels of hysterical organization in which one of the primary parameters was the depth of accompanying depression. It remains a moot question the extent to which paranoid mechanisms can be mobilized in the service of defending against such underlying depression, but at this point I can only suggest that the incidence of such paranoid responses may be more frequent than has otherwise been suspected.

A word should be said here about the so-called schizoid personality disorders. If the incidence of paranoid manifestations must be regarded as questionable in the obsessional and hysterical disorders, that question would seem to be resolved in reference to schizoid disorders. My experience with schizoid characters has been limited, but in almost every case that I have had the opportunity to become familiar with there has been an identifiable paranoid core to the disorder. One is reminded inevitably of the so-called schizoid-paranoid positions described by Melanie Klein, a conjunction that we had occasion to discuss in relationship to Klein's contributions to the understanding of development. Guntrip (1969) attempts to separate the paranoid-schizoid position into its respective components. If the "depressive position" is guilt-burdened, then the "paranoid position" must be regarded as fear-burdened. But Guntrip would regard the so-called schizoid position as lying still deeper than either the depressive or paranoid positions, thus representing a state in which the infantile ego has withdrawn from object-relations and seeks safety away from the anxieties of persecution or guilt. He writes:

> The paranoid individual faces physical persecution (as in dreams of being attacked by murderous figures) and the depressed individual faces moral persecution (as, for example, in feeling surrounded by accusing eyes and pointing fingers), so that Klein regards both positions as setting up a primary form of anxiety. In fact, most individuals prefer to face either depressive anxiety (guilt) or persecutory anxiety (amoral fear) or an oscillation between them, rather than face the extreme schizoid loss of everything, both objects and ego. *Both persecutory anxiety and depressive anxiety are object-relations experiences while the schizoid position cancels object-relations in the attempt to escape from anxiety of all kinds* (1969, p. 57).

What Guntrip describes is a relatively pure state of affairs relating to the dynamic configuration of infantile positions. However, clinically such pure positions are rarely seen in isolation. Klein's description may therefore be closer to the clinical basis. To my way of thinking the paranoid response may be seen as a defense against underlying depressive concerns, and the schizoid position may be envisioned as a defensive avoidance against both. My own clinical experience suggests that the schizoid and paranoid manifestations seem to be clinically closely linked. The moot question which remains is whether or not the typical state of schizoid withdrawal and isolation is not in fact a manifestation of paranoid processes and a defense against paranoid anxieties.

We have had occasion already to discuss the overlap between paranoid symptoms and schizophrenic manifestations. Flagrant paranoid delusions are most frequently seen in the context of the schizophrenic process. Our attempt in the present study was to focus the paranoid dynamics as discernible and independent of the schizophrenic process, even though the overlap in clinical presentation was quite strong, and even though both the schizophrenic and paranoid process seemed to share a number of common etiological influences. The paranoid process can then be seen as independent of, although in many cases secondary to, the schizophrenic process.

In any number of cases, the paranoid resolution seems to function as a defensive bulwark against further schizophrenic deterioration. We have been able to identify the interplay of these respective processes in a number of cases we have analyzed above. The schizophrenic process has built into it a sense of inherent vulnerability, victimization, weakness, loss of autonomy and trust, and other factors which might precipitate a paranoid response. The paranoia may be seen in terms of a restitutional response to the schizophrenic decompensation. Paranoid schizophrenics, then, may be seen as schizophrenics who have retained sufficient internal structure and capacity to mobilize their resources in a form of paranoid defense. Diagnostically, however, this particular group does not provide much difficulty, since the paranoid manifestations are usually of psychotic proportions and are therefore easily recognized.

The association of paranoia with hypochondriacal symptoms presents something of a problem. In a number of our case studies, the patients presented with hypochondriacal concerns. Without exception, when such concerns were in evidence, they could be seen to be related to the underlying self-image that was characterized by weakness, deficiency, inadequacy, and vulnerability. Hypochondriacal concerns, therefore, could be seen as linked to the underlying depressive core in the patient's personality. A study of the incidence of hypochondriacal manifestations in patients diagnosed with paranoid syndromes reveals that while the incidence of hypochondria in schizophrenic and depressive patients was relatively high, the incidence in cases of diagnosed paranoia was strikingly low (Stenback, 1964). One could argue, therefore, that the manifestation of hypochondriacal and/or depressive symptoms would be a function of the effectiveness of the paranoid defenses. In cases of frank, psychotic paranoia, one might therefore expect a minimal manifestation of accompanying depressive and/or hypochondriacal manifestations. In cases where the paranoia is combined with either schizophrenic deterioration or a loosening of the paranoid defenses, one might expect to see a higher incidence of both depressive and hypochondriacal manifestations. In our own patients, we have noted that the depressive aspects of their illness did not become apparent—and in all cases did not become a predominant part of their symptomatology—until the paranoid defenses had been undermined in the course of the treatment. In some patients, there is a marked vacillation back and forth between paranoid and depressive aspects.

THE RELATION TO MANIC DEFENSE

I would like to add a comment about manic states and the manic defense in general. Manic states are generally regarded as manifestations of manic-depressive psychosis, but they may be found in other pathological states such as schizophrenia or the schizoaffective disorders, as well as in organic states. Manic states are usually associated with either antecedent or consequent depressive states, but there are also manic states which may show a persistent or intermittent pattern without marked depressive accompaniments. Such patients may also suffer from persecutory delusions. The manic state is accompanied with psychomotor activity, elation of mood, ease of distractibility, and often delusions that have a marked omnipotent or omniscient quality to them. Manics often show an exaggerated sense of self-esteem and self-confidence and not infrequently try to act out the grandiose delusions which they develop.

The manic defense, like the paranoid defense, is regarded as a response to an underlying state of depression, usually related to a preoccupation with real or fantasized loss. Part of the manic defense involves a tendency for the underlying conflict to be externalized, so that aggressive drive derivatives may be attributed to external objects, thus allowing the patient to interact with the object in aggressive or competitive or destructive ways. It is noteworthy that in manic states the cathexis of object representations remains virtually intact. Freeman (1971) has drawn attention to some differences in the defensive organization of manic as opposed to schizophrenic states. He writes:

> Externalization is much more in evidence in mania than in schizophrenia. Projection, which you so frequently find in schizophrenia, is rare in mania. Projection, involving as it does a distortion of the drive with respect to its aim and object, results in a passive experience of the barred drive representation. The very essence of mania is overactivity and a passive experiencing of drive expression is quite foreign to the condition. . . . Patients suffering from mania only feel themselves to be persecuted when they are confined and prevented from carrying through their intentions. This may give the impression of a "persecutory" element in their thinking. The view taken here is that when the defense of projection operates, the corresponding phenomena (persecutory delusions, etc.) will only make an appearance in phases of illness that are not characterized by psychomotor overactivity, i.e., when the drive representations are blocked from an outlet to the external world. It is the cases which show psychomotor overactivity alternating with persecutory delusions that puzzle the clinical psychiatrist who then cannot decide whether he is confronted with a case of mania, schizophrenia, or paranoid psychosis (p. 485).

It should be noted that the manic defense shares with the paranoid defense the dimensions of grandiosity and the tendency to externalization of aggression. Freeman suggests that the externalizing of projective defenses form an alternative to hypermanic overactivity in serving defensive objectives. The suggestion is well taken and may reflect the availability of alternate routes of energy discharge, either through motoric hyperactivity or through channels of cognitive reconstruction. One can speculate here on genetic patterns which might influence the pathology in the direction of either manic or paranoid defenses. We have no clear purchase on the question, but it provides an intriguing speculation.

We can wonder, for example, whether in the family backgrounds of manic patients there might not have been a persistent pattern of defense against the depressive affect through the use of external activity rather than, as is so often the case in paranoid families, of the utilization of rationalizing and blaming processes as a way of defending against similar depressive affects. Our suggestion is that it is the family context which provides the matrix of learning of defensive patterns and the reinforcement of them by a variety of interactional and internalizing devices. We shall see more of this in reference to the genesis of paranoia, but the question as to the differential influences in the genesis of mania seem to this writer at least to be relevant.

In any case it seems that in cases of manic-depressive psychosis several factors are related to a relatively poor prognosis. A recent study suggests that the poor prognosis is associated with the female sex, and with the occurrence of either manic or paranoid manifestations. Prognosis is relatively good in patients who experience recurrent depressive episodes without associated manic attacks (Shobe and Brion, 1971). We might suggest in this conjunction that the paranoid defense is a viable alternative to manic defense, even in clearly diagnosed cases of manic-depressive psychosis. Carlson and Goodwin (1973) have recently demonstrated that the presence of paranoid symptomatology does not indicate the presence of a schizophrenic process and does not rule out a diagnosis of affective disorder.

If the alternation or substitution between manic and paranoid defenses is understandable on dynamic grounds—in terms of its relation to and defensive avoidance of underlying depressive elements—the relationship between manic and paranoid defenses may not be altogether indefensible on more strictly biological or biochemical grounds. A recent careful study of the "switching process" in manic-depressive illness by Bunney et al. (1972) has indicated that specific neurotransmitter catecholamines—specifically dopamine and/or norepinephrine—are functionally increased in specific brain areas prior to the switch from depression into mania. They speculate that the specific switching mechanisms which are involved include a genetically transmitted defect which involves specific mechanisms which must be activated, and that the activation process is somehow reversible.

The genetic abnormality is thought to affect a mechanism which regulates the amount of functional neurotransmitter—most probably norepinephrine—at the synaptic cleft, perhaps by interference with norepinephrine transport across neural membranes. The switching process can be activated by a number of chemically active agents, not only the tricyclic antidepressants but also the amphetamines. We are reminded here that considerations of amphetamine psychosis suggested that the effects of the amphetamines on the central nervous system were probably medicated by the effect of dopamine and norepinephrine on specific activating systems. It may be that the release of these specific neurotransmitter agents in the central nervous system, by whatever underlying genetic or pharmacologic agency this is achieved, increases the activity in central nervous system structures which may underlie and give rise to both manic and paranoid manifestations. The further question would seem to remain as yet indeterminate—that is, whether the choice of alternative, whether manic or paranoid, is a result of central nervous system effects (the activation of specific and alternate neuronal systems) or whether the alternative is a function of more specifically psychological determinants. These possibilities indeed need not be exclusive.

CHAPTER 17

Paranoid Mechanisms: Introjection

Our argument has advanced to the point where we can begin to articulate a theory of the paranoid process. It should be plain from a reading of what has preceded that the elements of a theory and fragments of its development have been scattered throughout the pages of this book. But at this point our intention and effort are directed to welding together these scattered fragments into a consistent and coherent theoretical statement.

We will formulate our concept of the paranoid process in progressive steps. The first step is to formulate that portion of the theory which has to do with the mechanisms of the paranoid process, specifically the mechanisms of introjection, projection, and what we have described as the paranoid construction. Our next step is to describe the functional aspects of the paranoid process, particularly those that serve defensive purposes in the organization of psychic functioning, as well as those that are more specifically related to the vicissitudes of the developmental process. Our emphasis all along during the course of this study has been on the positive and constructive aspects of the paranoid process, aspects that must stand alongside of and be integrated theoretically with more destructive and defensive functions.

The succeeding theoretical concern will focus on the adaptational aspects of the paranoid process, as an extension of both defensive and developmental functions. It is our contention that the process has specific adaptive functions to serve in reference to a broad spectrum of social, cultural, political, religious, and other cultural contexts where the workings of the process intermesh with the processes of formation of groups, the organization of institutions and social structures, as well as the integration of belief systems and value systems.

Paranoid Mechanisms

On the first level of our investigation, the attempt to explicate an understanding of the paranoid process approaches the process from the point of view of its constituent mechanisms. This is perhaps the first and most obvious level of intentionality involved in the paranoid process. The mechanical perspective approaches the process and formulates an understanding of it in terms of the operations, which are distinguishable and identifiable as essential elements of the process.

In discussing the paranoid mechanisms, our consideration is focused on the operation and characteristics of the mechanisms themselves. Our concern here is with the nature of the specific mechanisms and with their substantiation and manifestation in the clinical material. At another level of our consideration, we will have occasion to look more carefully at the genetic influences that shape and give rise to such mechanisms. But our present emphasis is on the functional consideration of the mechanisms themselves and their contributing role in the organization of the paranoid process.

Perhaps one of the most central considerations that emerges from the data we have been analyzing has to do with the role of introjects in the organization of the internal world of the paranoid patient. In fact, it can be said that the originating impulse of the present study was derived from a growing awareness of the importance of so-called identificatory processes in the understanding of paranoid patients.

The Concept of Introjection

The first order of business is to clarify the notion of introjection itself. In another place (Meissner, 1971b, 1972), I have attempted a clarification of the problems of internalization in a somewhat broader theoretical perspective, but the role of introjection in the understanding of internalization processes is a central one. This is particularly true since introjection functions over a relatively broad range of developmental events, and has considerable influence in the patterns of internal structuralization. Along with identification, introjection provides the basic roots by which object-relations are internalized and form the structural parameters for the up-building of ego and superego.

In my previous attempt to specify the concept of introjection, I put it in the following terms:

> Incorporation and introjection are . . . internalizing mechanisms which serve phase-specific developmental and defensive ends which are correlative with the level of internal structure formation and the degree of object relatedness. Introjection, together with its correlative mechanism of projection, is analyzed in terms of a transitional object model of object relatedness. Introjection is distinguished from identification by reason of its instinctual drive-dependence and derivation, its function in the economy of conflict and defense, the character of introjects as primary process presences (as quasi-autonomous sources of intra-psychic activity which maintains a relative distance from the subjective ego core), and by its susceptibility to projection and greater capacity for regression. Introjection, therefore, emerges as a metapsychologically distinct process which differs from identification, economically, dynamically, structurally, genetically, and adaptively (1971b, pp. 300-301).

Thus in speaking of the introjective aspects of the paranoid process, we are specifically addressing ourselves to the significant aspects of the internal structure of the personality. Clinically speaking, we might ask ourselves in what way introjective processes manifest themselves. According to the formulation just quoted, the critical elements which characteristically are reflected in the economy of introjects are their derivation from and dependence on instinctual derivatives, their role in internal conflict and defensive operations, their susceptibility to primary process influences, their regressive potential and finally their capacity for projection. It must be remembered in this context that introjects have to do with the organization and representation of the patient's self.

The concept of introjection was acquired by Freud from Ferenczi. The classic formulation of the mechanism of introjection was provided in Freud's *Mourning and Melancholia* (Freud, 1917). Freud described introjection as the mechanism by which the lost object was internalized so that it became a part of the organization of the ego. As he put it, "the shadow of the object fell on the ego." The mechanism was one which he labeled as narcissistic identification, and it was the basic mechanism that he applied to the development of the superego, as a result of the dissolution of the Oedipal situation.

Although the analysis of the superego provided a sort of template in Freud's thinking for the description of introjective processes, it seems clear that introjection is not limited to superego formulation. If we think of a continuum of internalization processes, introjection stands somewhere in between the more primitive mechanisms of incorporation, which functions at a relatively oral and highly narcissistic level, and the more autonomous and integrated processes which are characteristic of identification.

The Introject and Transitional Object Relation

One of the most important aspects of the process of introjection is the status of object representation. Introjection is based on the replacement of the relation to an external object by a relation to an internal object. In primitive incorporation, the internalization of the object is more global, so the object loses its characteristic as object and becomes totally part of the subject's inner world. Introjection, however, preserves some aspect of the objectivity of the object and its relevance to the external world.

In his discussion of the relationship between object relations and internal structure, Modell (1968) has suggested that the transitional human object is one that somehow stands midway between what is created by the inner world and what exists in the external world. The transitional object is, therefore, in the environment but its separateness from the self is only partially acknowledged. It is a created environment. The properties attributed to the transitional object are created by the subject and thus reflect the inner life of the subject. That transitional object itself is created out of the interplay of processes of introjection and projection, which create a state of fluid oscillation between what can be attributed to the object and what can be taken into the self. Thus Modell writes:

> The transitional object is not a part of the self—it is "something" in the environment. However, it is endowed with qualities that are created by the subject by the oscillation of introjection and projection. Therefore, the mode of transitional object relationships is one where the differences between the self and the object are minimized. The object is not acknowledged as separate from the self (1968, p. 36).

Thus it is important to observe that introjection and projection may be regarded as correlative mechanisms that serve the function of organizing the subject's inner world. The structure of that inner world, in consequence, is correlated with and derived from the quality of the subject's object relations.

My view of introjection, then, is that it is a form of internalization which pertains to transitional object relations. The parental objects must be regarded as transitional, that is, as objects that are colored by the child's projections from the inner world. The process of introjection creates a transitional internal object that replaces the external libidinal relation to the parent. The internalized object, or introject, retains its basically transitional character, even as it becomes a part of the subject's inner world.

In Freud's original formulation of the process of introjection, it specifically involved loss of the object. In the present view, the child's Oedipal relationship to his parents is a form of transitional object relation. The parents by reason of the introjection cease to serve as specifically transitional objects, but the transitional mode of relation to the object is preserved even as the latter is abandoned. The parents cease to serve as transitional objects due to the introjective process, but the creative aspect derived from the child's inner world is preserved in the introject. Thus the process of introjection has a very important role to play in the psychic economy. It is an important mechanism for the mastery of instinctual forces and is closely involved in instinctual vicissitudes. This is equally true for both aggressive and libidinal instincts. Ultimately the characteristics and quality of the child's emerging superego depend on the quality of instinctual elements which are at one point projected onto parental objects and then secondarily introjected.

The introjected object loses its object function as it becomes part of the inner world, but it retains its connections with the external world at the same time. It carries with it into the internal world the residues of object derivation. Like the transitional object itself, it participates in both worlds. It is thus never internalized to the same extent as ego identifications. Within the range of consciousness it is something objectified within the reality of the self. Introjection covers a wide range of internalizing mechanisms which may vary considerably with the transitional character of the object. Those that are more primitive and more intensely endowed with instinctual derivatives are more apparently introjective. But the contribution of the inner world may be considerably muted, and may thus be less apparent, so that the instinctual influences are minimized and the introjects come much closer to the identificatory pole. They are distinguished, even so, by their distance from the ego core, when conscious, and by their embodiment with instinctual energies, both libidinal and aggressive.

Introjects as Structure

Similarly introjection is a dynamic process. There is a progression in the organization of introjects from the more primitive and instinctually derived to the more integrated and composite fusions of introjects (Greenson, 1954). This patterning of the fusion of introjects takes the form of what Kernberg (1966) calls the active valence of introjects. Introjects of positive affective valence, i.e., libidinally gratifying, become organized into good internal objects. Conversely, negative introjects, i.e., those derived from destructive aggression, become organized into bad internal objects. As this organization proceeds, there is an evolution of inner structure by which the internal organization becomes more elaborate and more integrated. Each level of structuralization permits further evolution of structure formation and internalization. The introjects serve an important set of functions, both defensive and developmental, in the mastery of instinct and in the development of inner systems of regulation. It achieves a relative binding of significant amounts of instinctual energy in internal structural forms.

We cannot regard these modifications of the inner world in simply representational terms. Introjection has been described in terms of the assimilation of object representations to the self-representation. This is undoubtedly part of the effect of introjective processes, but it tends to leave out the structuralizing aspects of introjection. The structural perspective regards the introject as a source of intrapsychic influence and quasi-autonomous activity which can substitute for the object as a source of either narcissistic gratification or aggressive impulse. The introject is thus a center of functional organization that possesses its own relative autonomy in the economy of psychic functioning. Even so, they remain tied to instinctual derivatives and relatively susceptible to drive influences.

Schafer (1968a) has used the term "primary-process presence" to describe the subjective presentation of introjects. They represent fixation points of a more or less primitive level of organization within the psyche. That organization is more primitive when it reflects earlier levels of development, as well as reflecting a susceptibility to regressive pulls which is also increased at more primitive levels. Thus the introjection, functioning within the subject's inner world, reflects a primary process influence even after the transitional type of object representation has been internalized. Where the introjects function at a higher level of organization and are less intensely effected by specifically drive derivatives, further consolidation by identificatory processes is more likely and the susceptibility to regression is minimized.

Related to this aspect of the internal organization of introjects is the whole question of projection. We have observed that the processes of introjection and projection are correlative—and this aspect of their involvement will be taken up more specifically in the consideration of the mechanism of projection itself. But it can be pointed out here that the more primitive the level of organization, the more intense the relationship and influence of drive derivatives, the more susceptible are introjects to subsequent projection. To round off this attempt to define more specifically the nature of introjection and the introjected object, let me quote a somewhat lapidary formula from the previously cited study. The formulation is given there in the following terms:

> Introjection is a process of internalization through which transitional object relations are replaced by an internal modification of the self in the form of an introject. Introjects are thus primary process presences which enjoy a quasi-autonomous state within the self that permits them to substitute for the transitional object as sources of instinct-related and drive-dependent activity. (Ibid. p. 300).

While these considerations are unavoidably abstract and even abstruse, they do not in any sense rule out the important aspects of our consideration of introjection in relationship to the paranoid process. They provide a rather spare skeleton to which a considerable amount of meat must be added. As Shafer (1960) observed, Freud's original formulation of the notion of the superego was based particularly on his observations of melancholia, obsessional neurosis, and paranoia. The introjective pathology we are concerned with in the present study is not simply a superego pathology. Nonetheless the introjective aspects of it are a primary element. It is our assumption, and at this point in the evolution of this study, our conviction, that the understanding of the paranoid process has a great deal to teach us about the basic processes that are involved not merely in superego formation, but even more broadly in the wider latitude of personality formation.

Ambivalence

Focusing then on the introjective pathology in our patients, it becomes clear that in all of the patients we have studied, the patient's personality, the internal pattern of organization which constitutes the inner reality of his personality and of his self, is organized around identifiable introjects. The introjects are derived from object-relations which are overloaded with intense ambivalent affect. The introjects are patterned out of a combination of internalizations of relations to the significant figures in the child's environment, particularly the mother and father, but also other significant figures, particularly the siblings. Thus the introjective alignment that characterizes the inner world of any given patient will vary according to the patterning of these introjects.

The ambivalence is an extremely important aspect of introjective pathology, since it is the more or less destructive component of the ambivalence which fixates the process of internalization at the level of introjection. Where ambivalence is minimal, and where the destructive component doesn't interfere with the process of internalization, the introjective aspects of the individual's developmental structuring are minimized and the mechanisms of identification are thus able to play a more significant role in the developmental process. We will have more to say about this under the heading of genetic influences, but the point to be made here is that the quality of the introject derives from and reflects the quality of the object-relations with important figures.

More significantly these important relationships are highly ambivalent: it is this aspect of the relationship which provides the context for introjective mechanisms to come into play. Moreover, the more intense these ambivalent relations, the more is the internalized object the bearer of intense and conflicted emotions. The greater the intensity of ambivalence, therefore, the greater will be the susceptibility of the introject itself to the influence of drive derivatives, particularly the derivatives of aggressive drives.

Thus our patients acquire a presence within the inner world of their experience of themselves which is quasi-autonomous and which is the bearer of a burden of painful, anxiety-producing, and self-depreciating affects. In the most severely disturbed patients, who function at a more or less schizophrenic level—I am thinking now particularly of Ann, Bob, Clare, Ellen, Fred, Gloria, and Henry—the introject presents itself as a palpable presence within the self, a presence that at times almost seems to have an independent reality and life of its own. In these cases, the introject has fairly specific and consistent and identifiable characteristics. It reflects the introjective assimilation of a relation to both a destructive, aggressive, victimizing object, on one hand, and the introjective assimilation of the relation to a victimized object, on the other. These introjects operate in conjunction within the inner world of the patient, so that the latter feels at one time that he is a weak, helpless, dependent, and altogether ineffectual victim, but at other times will feel that he is in fact a powerful, destructive, monstrous, and dangerous individual who can only create destruction and harm in whatever he attempts.

Sadomasochism—Identification with the Victim

These aspects of the inner self of the paranoid patient reflect the dynamics at work in the world of significant objects which surrounds him. In all of these cases the patient's parents enact the drama of sadomasochism, with varying degrees of intensity and decisiveness, often varying the roles so that their relationship comes to be mutually victimizing, and perhaps victimizing in different areas, in different ways, to different degrees—with an almost endless capacity for variation and subtlety. It is this drama and mutual interaction of victim and victimizer that the paranoid patient has internalized. He carries it on within himself and carries it on against himself.

I think it is worth making a point that, while there may be a more or less generalizable pattern, what is more significant in the development of the pathology is that the parents are somehow or other caught up in a complex interaction which involves sadomasochistic components of victimizing and being victimized. From our previous discussion it would be clear that the quality of the introjects depends not so much on the separate introjections from parental figures as on the combination of introjective elements that derive in fact from the ambivalent quality of the patient's relationship to both parental figures.

The significance which this so-called "identification with the victim" can play in the dynamics of paranoia can readily be seen. It is precisely this introjected victimized object, which has been internalized and has been incorporated into the self, which the patient must struggle to defend and protect. It is this aspect of himself which the patient sees as weak, helpless, dependent, ineffectual, deficient, defective, and inadequate. For some patients the issue is weakness and defectiveness, but for others the issue is spelled out in more explicitly sadomasochistic terms of vulnerability. The defensive characteristics of the paranoid state which we have observed in so many of these patients wraps itself around this inner core of introjective deficit.

However, just as in ambivalence there is always another side, so too in the victimizing process there is another side. If there is a victim, there must be a victimizer. If the drama of victimization is internalized, there is also internalized a victimizer. It is this aspect of the patient's development which Anna Freud has described in terms of "identification with the aggressor" (A. Freud, 1936). It is this aspect of the introjective process which is usually thought of as more closely allied with the formation of superego precursors and finally of the superego itself. In our sicker patients, this victimizing introjective aspect of the inner organization of the psyche manifests itself in quite explicit terms: there is a powerful, destructive evil, and hurtful monster that lurks inside of them which is ready to leap out and unleash destruction on any and all objects around them. The description of this monster is most graphic and dramatic in Clare, but it is also seen in its own style in all of these patients. Here again the monstrousness and autonomy of the primary process presence is more predominant and well delineated in the more primitive patients.

It should be noted that the intensity of the destructive affect which gives the monster its evil, poisonous, and destructive potentiality is precisely what prevents the introjective assimilation from the object from being more generally metabolized and integrated with other psychic structures. The more primitive and intense the aggressive component of the ambivalence to the object, therefore, the more destructive, monstrous, and potentially hurtful is this aspect of the introject felt to be

This is the aspect of the paranoid pathology which is perhaps most difficult to elicit and define. This is the aspect of the patient which he is most anxious to keep in check, to keep out of view, to withhold from expression. It is that part of himself which he feels is not only most destructive and hurtful, but which is most despicable and hateful to others. It is his fear, for example, in therapy, that any inkling that he might give the therapist of this inner lurking evilness and monstrosity would drive the therapist away, would destroy his fragile relationship with the therapist, and would bring the therapy to a halt. The monstrous rage which such patients feel boiling inside them, which is somehow sensed without being in explicit awareness, is what inhibits them from the more productive and useful expression of aggression, even when it seems reasonable and appropriate. This is a fundamental therapeutic issue for all paranoid patients. In the treatment process, it is closely related to the issue of trust, for it is only on the basis of a well-developed and firm sense of trust in the therapist and to some extent in themselves that patients can begin to reveal this inner evilness and destructiveness.

Victimized Introject

Several comments are worth making about these respective introjects. It is clear for the most part that the victimized introject is the basis for the depressive pathology that is so often seen in these patients. From what we have already said, it becomes apparent that the depressive aspects are the parts of themselves which the patients are most in touch with, and are most able to share with the therapist. It is somehow more acceptable to be a victim than a victimizing monster. The sharing of the victimized self, however, is not altogether easy, since it involves an opening to another of their defective and vulnerable selves. The capacity to do this again depends on the achievement of a certain degree of trust in the therapist. The degree of trust must be sufficient to allow the patient to feel that he will not be attacked or taken advantage of should he reveal this aspect of himself.

The victimized introject, then, underlies the patient's depressive pathology. It is that aspect of himself that he devalues and denigrates. It is associated with often fairly painful affects—feelings of worthlessness and uselessness, helplessness, hopelessness, etc. But this depressive introject, however painful and loaded with discomfort it may be, is nonetheless more or less tolerable to the patient. Thus there is a tendency in these patients to allow themselves to function as, and see themselves in terms of, their status as victims, while the opposite state is one that is consistently avoided. Thus, when the delusional system evolves in schizophrenic patients particularly, the delusional system is felt to be directed against themselves as victims in some sense.

More intolerable, however, is the more aggressive and destructive introject that is overloaded with sadistic components, and which these patients cannot tolerate in themselves. Thus the projective delusions usually acquire a persecutory quality. It is as though the patient were saying "I am not a sadistic and destructive monster, but I am a victim of other forces which seek to persecute and destroy me." In all of our patients, consequently, the clinical picture is dominated to a large extent by the portrayal of themselves as in one way or another victimized, and it was often only with considerable therapeutic effort and over long periods of time that they were able to acknowledge any elements of sadistic aggressiveness in themselves. There is no question, however, as we have pointed out countless times, that the status of victim is an uncomfortable and painful one for the patients, and they exercise themselves in a variety of ways to escape from this painful condition.

One of the important emphases that must be understood in order to complete the understanding of the paranoid process, as well as to guide an effective therapeutic intervention, is that these introjects—both the victimized and victimizing ones—are correlative. They not only go together inevitably, but they feed off and reinforce each other. To this extent they rehearse the parental pathologies; the patterns of sadism and masochism are reciprocal and reinforcing. The more victimized, helpless, and defective the patient presents himself as being, the more we can assure ourselves that the accompanying introject of powerful aggressiveness is also a component of his intrapsychic organization. The powerlessness and dangerousness of the aggressive introject can be measured by the degree to which the patient feels himself also to be helpless, victimized, and inadequate.

It should also be noted that both of these introjective components are susceptible to projection. Paranoid patients are generally more prone to retain the depressive introject and deal with the aggressive introject by projection. However, there is almost always a projective component which is based on the depressive introject, so that the patient in one area or other of his experience feels himself to be harmful, dangerous, and as able to powerfully influence and hurtfully affect the lives of important individuals around him. A not uncommon feature in these patients is the tendency to assign themselves responsibility for the harmful or destructive events that occur around them. This is perfectly consistent with the depressive aspect of their pathology on the one hand, but also feeds into the view of themselves as powerfully destructive and hurtful.

The psychology of the introjects and their involvement in the alternative processes of projection and introjection forms the underpinning for the process of blaming which is so characteristic of patients with paranoid tendencies. The blaming process is caught up in the assignment of responsibilities. As we have noted previously in our discussion, the depressive position, on the other hand, is one in which the responsibility is assigned to an external agency.

It should be noted immediately that on either pole of the functioning of introjection or projection blaming is at issue. Paradoxically, in the depressive state, it is the aggressive introject which is retained and which forms the basis of the patient's self-blaming. Conversely in the paranoid condition, it is the depressive introject which is retained, and the aggressive component which is projected externally and which is then seen as the agency of blame.

I add this observation since I think it complements the usual view of the depressive condition as a form of superego attack upon the ego. We might be led to think that the basic dynamism of self-blaming or guilt was based solely on the victimized introject. But I think it is important to see that the process involves another dimension which may be clinically more significant. Thus in the depressive state the patient is both victim and victimizer, but in the paranoid state he is able to regard himself more purely as only a victim. Thus the potential threat of seeing one's self as aggressive and as victimizer is mitigated. This allows us to appreciate from a different point of view the utility of the paranoid defense.

Reflection of Parental Introjects

Although it is clear that the inner drama of the introjects to some degree reflects the parental pathologies and the patterns of interaction between the parents, it is nonetheless clear that the internal drama is drawn in much more stark and extreme lines than the external parental drama. This reflects the fact that the introject is not simply an internalization. It is an internalization which organizes and draws to itself specific drive derivatives. Those derivatives are both libidinal and aggressive. It is clear that while the libidinal components of the introjects have a function of fostering the union of introjective components into more integral good internalized objects and thus facilitating and inducing more autonomous patterns of identification, which allow the structuring of a more stable and integral ego, the aggressive components have an opposite and deleterious effect, in that they inhibit the capacity for such integration and tend to polarize the introjective components.

Thus in the introjective alignment in the patients we are considering, the separation of the sadistic and masochistic elements of the internalized objects tends to be radicalized and intensified rather than diminished and minimized. Moreover, the more primitive the organization of these introjects, the more susceptible they are to drive influences, particularly the influence of aggressive and destructive drives. They thus serve as a focal point within the psychic economy toward which these destructive instinctual components can be aggregated and compounded. Thus the aggressive aspects of the introjects tend to be more radical and extreme than one might expect simply on the basis of object internalization.

But there is another important aspect of this process that must be kept in mind. That is, what is internalized from the object relates more to the introjective structure of the inner world of the object than it does to the external characteristics or observable qualities of the behavior of the object. Thus, as Freud pointed out in his magnificent description of the development of the superego in *The Ego and the Id* (1923), the child incorporates not simply the parent as an object, but more specifically the parent's superego. Thus the patterning of introjects has more to do with the organization of introjects in the parents and the way in which they interact with and respond to each other, than it does to the actual behavioral interactions between the parents on a more extrinsic observational level. Consequently both of these aspects must be taken into consideration when we are dealing with the question of understanding the alignment of introjects that comes about in the patient.

Autonomy

We have already had occasion to examine the difficulties that paranoid patients have with the issue of autonomy. These patients feel themselves to be threatened continually by the inevitability of submission to forces and persons around them. This may take the form of frankly paranoid delusions, or it may take more subtle forms of feeling victimized, feeling that one is being taken advantage of, or of struggles with authority figures. The deficits in autonomy are closely related to the feeling of powerlessness and helplessness that is associated with the depressive introject. The sense of autonomy is more broadly undermined by both external and internal influences.

The paranoid patient is subject to external threats to his autonomy. We have seen this clearly in all of our cases. The patient in the childhood situation in relationship to the parents is thrust into a position in which compliance is exacted at the cost of either punishment or the loss of love. The parent demands compliance and submission from the child. The demands are often severe and rigid. The child is caught up in the pattern of sadomasochistic interaction which is characteristic of the relationship between his parents and more generally the relationship in the family itself. The child himself thereby becomes a victim.

Part of his experience then is in reality an experience of persecution, of a demand for submission and compliance, of a violation of his autonomous rights and capacity for autonomous functioning. This was most clear, for example, in Gloria's relationship to her parents, particularly her father. Neither Gloria nor her father could rest until a point had been reached at which she was completely accepting and compliant to his point of view and wishes. Bob was also caught up in a continual interaction with his parents, particularly his father, in which he was constantly striving to live up to his father's expectations, always however with the feeling that he was never able to do it, that he was never quite good enough.

It is interesting that in some of these patients the paranoid position takes the form of a rebellion against this enforcement of compliance. Ann complains that her mother is trying to kill her. Bob uses his psychosis as a way of taking himself off of the path towards success that his father had laid out for him. Ellen revolts violently against the pattern of submissive goodness which her mother continually tries to foist on her. Gloria becomes psychotically disturbed and feels that her parents are trying to kill her. From this point of view, the paranoid outbursts in these patients can be seen as an attempt to establish some individuality, to achieve some sense of independence.

What is interesting is that the ordinary channels for establishing such autonomy seem cut off from them. Even as they rebel against the pressure of external compliance and submission, they assign themselves another set of persecutors—even delusional persecutors—who threaten their autonomy and independence on a new level. It is as though the fragile sense of autonomy saves itself by finding enemies against which it can struggle on some new level. Fred, for example, avoids the threat to his autonomy, which is related to his involvement with his parents, by rebelling against and rejecting their wishes and engaging himself in a new struggle in which the controlling and persecuting forces are cast in the larger framework of university and society. Yet the paradox is that, in so struggling to gain some inner sense of autonomous capacity, these patients prolong and extend the identical threat to autonomy by the projection of persecutory forces. Thus the threat to autonomy is initially introjected and carried from the external demands of the parents to the internal demands of the introjected parental objects, but then reprojected to re-create the threat to autonomy in the external sphere.

But the threat to autonomy is also internal. I do not mean merely in this sense that the threatening and limiting objects are internalized—although this is a significant aspect of the internal economy of the introjects—but that the introjects themselves, by reason of their regressive potential and instability and by reason of their susceptibility to drive-dependent influences, serve to undermine the patient's sense of inner autonomy. Thus the inner sense of helplessness and powerlessness is reinforced considerably. The instability and fragility of the introjects are a primary consideration in the attempts to effectively treat such patients.

Patients will often complain of feelings of loss of identity, or a feeling of losing themselves in the face of external pressures and demands, or a feeling that they have no reality except in terms of their capacity to respond to the initiatives of other people. All of this is a reflection of an inner sense of impairment and susceptibility of their own inner autonomy. This is, of course, a matter of degree. In the more severely psychotic patients, where the status of the introjects is more fragmented and reflects a considerably greater regressive potential, the sense of autonomy is most severely compromised. For such patients the fear of loss of autonomy reaches cataclysmic proportions, and it often reflects itself in a paralyzing fear of death, as in the case of Bob, or in a fear of total annihilation, as was the case for Ann and Henry.

But even in our healthier patients who are able to mobilize relatively effective defenses against this feeling, there is still a sense of susceptibility or capacity to be influenced excessively, a fear of falling into positions of dependence and vulnerability, of being in control of other powerful figures which is often quite threatening to them. Thus it is often quite difficult to draw a line effectively between the instinctual dimensions of depressive or masochistic tendencies and the more ego-based issued of threats to autonomy. Both are relevant and these clinical phenomena undoubtedly reflect varying proportions of these respective influences.

It is worth noting in this connection that the extremes of both powerlessness and powerfulness are both in their own way distortions of basic autonomy. Autonomy carries within it the connotation not only of having a sense of one's own independence and capacity, but also a capacity for accepting and recognizing the independence and individuality of other selves around one. If a sense of powerlessness undermines autonomy, from the point of view of denying the inner capacity of self, the sense of excessive powerfulness undermines the autonomy from the point of view of denying the independent capacity and autonomy of the other. Consequently, whether the paranoid patient sees himself as a threatened and helpless victim who is victimized by external persecuting forces, or whether he sees himself as a powerful, evil, and dangerously destructive monster who can victimize and hurt and destroy those around him—in either case this reflects a distortion of autonomy.

Superego

I would like to direct attention at this point to the whole question of the introjective pathology and its relationship to the superego. In Freud's original view of paranoia, the projected elements were regarded as specifically superego elements—particularly in the context of external persecutory forces being directed against the ego, or in the frequent paranoid delusion of being watched. The external persecutor, the watchful parent who kept his eyes on the patient and continually surveyed and watched what he was doing, was taken to be the superego. However, it is plain from the material in these cases and the discussion that we have already undertaken, that it is relatively limiting to consider the introjective pathology simply in terms of superego functions.

If it is true that paranoid patients tend to project part of the inner persecutory introjects to the external realm and respond to it as threatened and helpless victims, it is also true that the paranoid patient can project the introjective content of victimized helplessness to the external world and relate to it in terms of his more powerful and dangerously destructive introspective potential. As we shall see in more detail later in our discussion, the introjects are susceptible to projection regardless of their content.

If we regard the internal structure of the paranoid as being compounded of a severely destructive and powerful superego with a weak, helpless, and victimized ego, we may miss some important aspects of the paranoid dynamics. If it is true that the paranoid ego is weak and vulnerable, it is also true that it is powerful and destructive. There is no question in this regard that the superego is harsh and particularly severe. It manifests its capacity for destructive impact particularly in the depressive phase of the paranoid illness.

But the determination of the projective content is not a function of the inclusion of introjective content in either superego or ego, but rather is a reflection of the dynamics of the introjects as such. The question of which set of introjective attitudes and contents are subject to projection is determined by other factors. The other question has to do with the alignment of respective introjective contents with ego and superego, as the case may be. I do not think that one can make any hard and fast conclusions about this. The introjects represent quasi-autonomous presences in the psychic economy and they function in terms of quasi-independent, instinctually driven forces. Thus it would seem to me that they can be assimilated to ego functions or to superego functions, as may be dictated by the state of intrapsychic organization.

It has often been said that parental introjects, particularly those derived from the Oedipal situation, are the basis for the formation of the superego as a split-off part of the ego. There is no need to question or deny the process, but it is clear from the foregoing patient material that parental introjects can also be assimilated in a variety of other ways. In the depressive position it seems arguable that the respective introjects line up in clearly delineable ego and superego contexts, the ego being the object of the attack from a destructive and persecutory superego. The question of superego versus ego introjects does not seem to me to be of major moment. But it is clear that the ramifications and implications of the introjective process extend beyond concerns of superego formation, and are intimately and in complex ways also involved in the development of the ego.

Relation to Self

I would like to point out at this juncture in the consideration of introjective processes that the organization of introjects is closely involved with the setting up of the self. The concept of the self is one that has had a recent history in psychoanalytic reflection. I raise the question of the relationship between introjective processes and the formation of the self, since it seems to me that it forms a necessary component of the understanding of the paranoid process.

There is considerable divergence in point of view about the actual content and the intrapsychic function of the self. I will begin by basing the present consideration on the excellent analysis of the self provided by Levin (1969), to which I will append some of my own thinking on the question. I will also rely on Kohut's recent extensive discussion of clinical aspects of the self (1971). It is clear to begin with that, however one conceives of the self in the psychic economy, the notion of it does not function at the same level of abstraction or constituent functioning as the structural agencies which constitute the psychic apparatus—specifically the id, ego, and superego. As Kohut phrases it, the structural entities are experience-distant abstractions by which the psychic apparatus is conceived to be formed. The self, however, is conceptualized in a comparatively low-level and experience-near form of abstraction, rather as a content of the mental apparatus than as a constituent part of it. Kohut goes on to say:

> While it is thus not an agency of the mind, it is a structure within since (a) it is cathected with instintual energy and (b) it has continuity in time, i.e., it is enduring. Being a psychic structure, the self has, furthermore, also a psychic location. To be more specific, various—and frequently inconsistent—self representations are present not only in the id, the ego and the superego, but also within a single agency of the mind. There may, for example, exist contradictory conscious and preconscious self representations—e.g., of grandiosity and inferiority—side by side, occupying either delimited loci within the realm of

the ego or sectorial positions of that realm of the psyche in which id and ego form a continuum. The self, then, quite analogous to the representations of objects, is a content of the mental apparatus but is not one of the constituents, i.e., not one of the agencies of the mind (1971, p. xv).

That description of the self has a certain viability, specifically insofar as it serves the ends of Kohut's purposes in dealing with the vicissitudes of narcissism. But the status of a mental entity, which is at once structural yet not constitutive, provides some puzzlement. As I have suggested elsewhere (1971b, 1972), the meaning of the self cannot be regarded in simply representational terms—but rather the self reflects a structural component of the personality.

Ego and Self

The analysis of the self was given a setting and an impetus by the observation of Heinz Hartmann (1950), in his observation that the essential element in narcissism must be a libidinal cathexis of the self rather than of the ego. The essential opposition between narcissism and object love in this view was not between ego and objects, but rather between self and objects. Freud had originally regarded the ego as the repository of narcissistic libido, but it was also clear that the ego as the repository of narcissism was difficult to reconcile with the picture of the ego as the systematic organization of functions by which internal regulation and control was organized and directed.

The ego was the executor of psychic energies, by which the direction of libido and its attachment to objects, or to the self, could not be easily reconciled with the previous view of the ego as a reservoir of narcissism. However, according to Hartmann's formulation, the quota of libido was stored in the self, as opposed to the ego. It was from the narcissism of the self that the ego was able to derive and direct energy to objects. The ego thus remains a system of functions, specialized and autonomous organ of adaptation, the centralized controlling and regulating agency of the personality structure.

These two aspects of the personality—ego and self—can be seen as following quite different developmental courses. Thus Levin (1969) can envision one course of development of the self and its relations to the object out of primary narcissism, and the second course of development of the organized system of ego functions out of an undifferentiated state of ego-id constituents. The child's narcissism is gradually differentiated into what Kohut (1966) has described as the narcissistic self along with the idealized parent imago. This forms the earliest stage of attachment of narcissistic libido to the primary object. The further course of development involves an increasing control of ego functions over the narcissistic self, so that the latter becomes gradually transformed into a self whose functions center on object relations. Levin comments, quoting Kohut:

The two different paths of development come closer and closer together with the increasing attainment of a dominance of ego functions over the narcissistic self. We can say that the capability of the ego to manage, to tame and to transform these narcissistic energies of the self is at least one measure of ego strength. We do not believe that the task is ever complete. "The ego's mastery over the narcissistic self, the final control of the rider over the horse, is not achieved without a long struggle, and may after all have been decisively assisted by the fact that the horse, too, has grown old" (Kohut, 1966; Levin, 1969, p. 43).

It must be remembered that introjection brings about a structural modification of the self. As we have already noted, it is difficult at times to locate specifically that structural modification in terms of the specific intrapsychic agencies. It is also clear that the self forms an intersystemic referent system which has specific relationships to the constituencies. Thus, if we speak of self-representations, these undoubtedly reflect the content of all of the intrapsychic agencies in combination. Thus the self-representations embrace id, ego and superego contents, expressing them in an objectified frame of reference. The self thus expresses in a form of intersystemic organization the reality of the intersystemic relations of the constituent agencies as placed over and against the object world. Thus it can be said that the introjects provide the content and the points of reference of the self-system—to use a Sullivanian term for the moment.

Role in Self-formation

The specifics of the metapsychology of the self remains to be spelled out, particularly in the area of the relationship between the self-system and the constitutive agencies of the psychic apparatus. What is clear at this point is that the self functions as an intersystemic referent for the psychic agencies, serves to represent and express their content and relations, and is intimately connected with the vicissitudes of narcissism. The point that we are concerned with, however, at the present juncture, is the influence of the introjective components on the formation of the self. It seems reasonable to assume from the evidence that we have already examined that the introjective processes in these paranoid patients throw a particular light on the dynamics of the self and its emergence. We will have more to say about the introjective aspects of the self in our consideration of the genetic aspects of the paranoid process. But at this point it may be useful to point out the ways in which the defensive implementation of introjection influences the formation of a self-image and a self-system within these patients.

Our emphasis on this point is limited to the appreciation that introjection is an essential dimension of the process of self-formation. Here again the understanding of both introjection and the self-system itself are matters of central moment. From one point of view introjection can be discussed in terms of its representational implications; that is to say that one can think of introjection in terms of the translations of object-representations or aspects of these into self-representations. But it seems to me that the representational view leaves out of consideration the structural reality of the self-system itself and substitutes a consequence of a formation of such a system for the system itself. Consequently introjection cannot simply mean the translation of representations, but must imply something which involves a structural effect on the internal psychic organization.

False Self-organization

A useful concept which I wish to introduce at this point is the notion of "false self," as proposed by Winnicott (1965). The latter relates his distinction between the true self-system and the false self-system to the Freudian division of self into a part that is central and intrinsically related to instinctual drives, and a pair that is turned toward and related to the external world. The false self has a defensive nature basically; its function is to hide and protect the true self.

Winnicott sets up a series of levels of false self-organization. At one extreme, false self is presented as the real personality, and would be taken as the real person by extrinsic observers. The false self fails in meaningful human relationships, however, particularly situations in which some wholeness or integrity of the personality is expected. In less extreme situations, the false self acts to defend the true self. The true self carries on a secret life, but the false self carries on with the positive aim of preserving the individual in spite of abnormal environmental circumstances.

On a somewhat healthier level, the false self concerns itself with searching out the conditions which would make it possible for the true self to survive. If such a defensive reorganization cannot be established, then the clinical result, according to Winnicott, is suicide. Suicide thus becomes the destruction of the total self to avoid the threatened annihilation of the true self. It is the false self that organizes and executes the suicide. At a still healthier level, the false self is based on the integration of introjections. And at a still healthier level—a quite normal level of adjustment—the false self represents the organization of polite and socialized attitudes which enable the individual to surrender infantile ominpotence, with the gain of shaping a place in the social order which could never be maintained by the true self alone.

The concept of the false self is important because it raises some difficult clinical and theoretical questions about the whole question of identity formation—in what way and by what processes is the formation of identity authentic, in the sense that it gives birth to a true self, and in what sense is it inauthentic, as giving birth to a false self-system. Looking at the patients we have studied heretofore, it seems that the pathology of the false self is a very striking aspect of the clinical picture in all of these cases.

In some of these cases the false self-system seems to take over and predominate the organization of the personality. It seems to me that this was most striking and vivid in the case of Bob B. Through the years of his childhood Bob had shaped a false self which embraced his childish conformity to the wishes of his parents, his desperate attempts to live up to and measure up to his father's manly expectations, his attempts to conform and embrace his mother's dictates as to what it meant to be a "good Jewish boy," his dedication to a profession, etc. The interesting thing of course is that the entire complex which constituted this false self-facade was in tune with the ideals of a competitive and highly ambitious cultural framework with which we are all fairly familiar. To all external observation Bob was a bright, ambitious, successful young surgeon. He had every promise of worldly success and reward.

Furthermore, it was at the point at which the realization of the false-self ideals were to be finally grasped and achieved that Bob began to decompensate. The choice was a radical one for him. Was he going to live up to and live out the false self-ideal—something that meant submission and conformity to his parent's expectations, to the expectations of society, to the wishes of people around him who, it seemed, were interested in his success not out of any concern for him or any real love for him, but out of a selfish and narcissistic concern for what gratifications and glorifications his success would bring them.

His psychosis was a desperate attempt to break out of this false self-trap. The situation was desperate. If he were to take up the trappings of his false self, with its ambitions and demands on him, it would mean setting himself on an inexorable path that led only to death. To move was life, and to be alive was to be on the way to death. To move was to move toward death. His was an "ontological insecurity." As Guntrip (1969) has written so eloquently:

> "Ontological insecurity" means insecurity as to one's essential being and existence as a person, insecurity about one's ego-identity, the feelings of a basic inadequacy in coping with life, an inability to maintain one's self as in any sense an equal in relationships with other people. It involves therefore urgent needs for support but at the same time a great fear of too close relationships which are felt as a threat to one's own status as an individual. The schizoid person, to whatever degree he is schizoid, hovers between *two opposite fears, the fear of isolation in independence with loss of his ego in a vacuum of experience, and the fear of bondage to, of imprisonment or absorption in the personality of whomsoever he rushes to for protection* (1969, p. 291, italics in original).

Caught in this profound and ontological insecurity, Bob could do little but cling to the isolated rock of his psychosis. We might ask ourselves where his true self was. It seems to me that it was almost totally displaced by a false self, and what was left was so fragmentary, so overwhelmed and immersed in the false self, that it was what confronted us at the extremities of his psychosis and in the depths of his depression.

There are other patients, however, for whom the organization of the false self, based on specific introjective contents, serves an explicitly defensive function. In some of these patients there was available a rudimentary sense of self which could be authentically autonomous and creatively spontaneous. I think for example of Clare, who forms a fascinating case study, particuarly from the point of view of the therapeutic process. It is apparent in retrospect, that the striking success which she enjoyed in therapy was due to the fact that she was able to in some ways abandon the false self-system and allow herself room for real growth which gave space to the expression of her true self. A similar situation—although not as striking or dramatic as was the case of Clare—obtained for Don D. It was only by small steps in various areas of testing out his capacity for independent initiative and self-expression that he was able, little by little, to chip away at the fragments of false self which he had been struggling with for most of his life. It is fascinating in looking at these patients in terms of the varying degrees and levels of organization of the false self-system that the false self can present an extremely pathological facade, but it can also present an apparently well-functioning and well-organized facade, which fulfills all of the expectations and requirements of an adequate personality in behavioral and cultural terms. But, as we are all too well aware, even if the false self presents an apparently strong and capable facade, it is also capable of rapid regression and dissolution, even to the level of psychotic disorganization. Where there is a false self without any development of a true self this propensity is all the more marked and all the more dangerous. An unfortunately not uncommon experience for psychoanalysts is to put an apparently healthy and reasonably neurotic analyzand on the couch—and begin to find, under analytic regression, that the false self begins to fail and the patient begins to look more primitive and infantile.

Introjection and the False Self-system

The point that I am making here on a theoretical level is that the false self-system, which can be clinically and phenomenologically described, is organized around and built out of introjects. The false self-system becomes the bearer of the content of the pathology in these patients in very striking and specific ways. The content of the introjects may be split and opposed, as we have seen clearly in the introjective content of the victim as against the victimizer. Often the false self-system would tend to be organized around one or the other of these introjective contents, not to the exclusion of other aspects, since the organization may take place at other times in relationship specifically to those other contents.

But typically, when the content of the false self-system is organized around one introjective pole, the residual introjective content is projected. Consequently, it does not seem to function as an operative part of the false self-system at that point in time. However, as we have seen clearly—either under the influence of situational stress, activation of conflicts, intensification of anxiety, or for other defensive reasons—the introjective alignment can shift and the pattern of introjection and projection can be altered, with an accompanying alternation in the false self-system. Even in the case of Bob B., for whom a false self-system seemed to maintain a consistency over time, we are well aware that the appearance of ambition, successful attainment, professional standing, etc., was broken at innumerable points by a reorganization of the self-system in terms of his weakness, impotency, inadequacy, etc.

Another interesting facet, which is very striking in the case of both Jim J. and Karen K., is that the false self-system becomes organized, persists, carries out its function, and gives rise to the sorts of neurotic disturbance that we have seen in these patients—but that nonetheless the patient is able to carry on a level of authentic development and meaningful and autonomous self-expression which reflects the operations of a true self. But somehow or other, the functioning of the true self fades into the background and is overridden by the fantasy content which is related to the false self-system. Thus in the case of Karen K., it was clinically striking that, despite her fears of vulnerability, there was no question of her capacity to function under situations of considerable stress and her ability to tolerate anxiety, and to perform on a high level of responsibility. A similar thing was true of Jimmy J., despite his conviction, linked inexorably with his false self-system, of his own defectiveness and impotence.

Thus it seems clear that the introjective process, modeled after Freud's original ideas pertaining to narcissistic identification, forms a modification of the self-system which provides a meaningful structural referent within the organization of the psyche and which bears rather complex and as yet poorly understood relationships to both the true self and the structural components of the psychic apparatus—specifically ego and superego. This takes us back to the question raised earlier regarding the location of specific introjective contents in either ego or superego. It is clear at this point that the problem cannot be adequately understood until we have settled the issues that are related to the complexities of the self. I do not wish at this point to undertake an investigation of the theoretical aspects of the metapsychology of these processes, but the importance of their understanding cannot be underestimated.

Moreover, it seems to me that the progression toward a better understanding of them must lie in the direction of understanding the processes which underlie the development of a false self-system, which is phenomenologically available to us on the level of clinical observation. An important aspect of this process is the whole problem of introjection and the manner in which internalized objects are integrated into our inner world. It is the operative presumption in this consideration and in the further theoretical considerations that we will undertake that introjection is closely related to the dynamics of self, and it will be our attempt here to specify the terms under which introjection and identification relate to the derivatives of the false and true self-systems. I would want to say at this point that the true self is derived from the functioning of what I have called authentic ego-identifications. These are clearly distinguished from introjections and function at a quite distinct level of metapsychological integration. I have attempted to differentiate these functions on more specifically theoretical grounds elsewhere (1971b, 1972).

CHAPTER 18

Paranoid Mechanisms: Projection

We have already had occasion in our preliminary discussion of paranoid mechanisms to delineate some of the formal aspects of projection. We emphasized in that discussion some of the basic functions and the nature of projection, particularly emphasizing its correlative relationship with the mechanism of introjection. One of the characteristic dimensions of introjects is their susceptibility and availability for projection.

We have made the point already—but it bears repeating—that projection has often been taken as the hallmark of paranoia. However, it is clear on clinical grounds that one cannot identify projective mechanisms with paranoia, as well as its being abundantly clear that projection plays a role in other diagnostic categories. Our shift in emphasis has been from the diagnosis of paranoia to a consideration of the paranoid process. But even here, it must be said that the paranoid process is a more complex phenomenon than would be implied if it were to be regarded reductively simply in terms of projection. We will have occasion to amplify this point of view later on. But our present concern is to specify the notion of projection, to clarify our conception of how it relates to, and is involved in, the paranoid process, and envision the extent, variety, and ultimately the connotations of its expression.

Delusional Projection

The first task in this endeavor to gain theoretical precision and depth is to clarify, for our own understanding, the patterns of projection which manifest themselves in the clinical material we have been considering. I think this is particularly important, since it is often thought that projection is the basis of the paranoid delusional system. It is clear that all of our patients have been very much caught up in the process of projecting, but it is also clear that not all of them can in any way be said to have had a developed paranoid delusional system. There is in fact considerable variation in the patterns of projection.

In several of our patients we can point to a frank delusional system as such. For Ann it was the delusional belief that she was the object of a world-wide Communist conspiracy which was meant to undercut and destroy her. For Bob B., on the other hand, the delusional system which marked the acute phase of his illness centered around his belief that he belonged to a race of superhuman, godlike beings who were immune from injury and death and who were relatively omniscient and omnipotent. The persecutory aspect of Ann's delusional system is directly expressed. For Bob, however, it can only be inferred insofar as the grandiose position of power and invulnerability would seem to serve defensive intents against the implied and potential threat of attack or death.

Moreover, for Ann the delusional belief remained a more or less fixed aspect of her pathology, even though it was not always explicit. At no point did she surrender the belief, and would repeatedly return to it at points of intensified stress. For Bob the belief was episodic and, when the psychotic process had been more or less compensated, the delusional belief was dissipated—such that he could regard it as a set of crazy ideas which were part of his psychosis and which he regarded as somehow ego-distant and alien. For Ann the projection, then, seemed to be quite direct, based on the introjection of the sadistic and persecuting mother. Consequently we can look on Ann's delusional system as a re-creation on another level of an important relationship with her mother. For Bob on the other hand what is projected is the narcissistic and defensively grandiose self-image. What stands out is the intense and delusional grandiose wish, and the threatening and persecutory aspects fade into the background, so that they are not explicitly presented.

For several of our other patients—and here I would include Clare, Don, Ellen, Gloria, and Henry—what we see is not so much a delusional system, as a vague conviction that people are out to get them, that they are the object of evil intentions of people around them, that they must be fearful and on guard toward hostile attacks, etc. Quite clearly in these cases the quality of the ideation is markedly paranoid and forms a relatively predominant aspect of their pathology, but the projections do not have an organized and formulated quality which would lend them to a systematic delusion. Moreover, at points of stress or decompensation, these patients do not produce systematic delusions, but rather have a marked intensification of their paranoid fears and anxieties. This is true even where the level of the patient's decompensation is clearly psychotic.

The outcome for these patients is varied: for some it is the unleashing of aggressive and destructive attacks against themselves in the form of acute depression and suicidal attempts—this was the case for Clare, Don, and Henry particularly. But for others, like Ellen, there is a launching of a terrified and desperate counterattack which is intended to fight off and destroy the persecuting enemies. Moreover, in these cases we can clearly trace the basis for the projected attitudes. We can recognize that the destructive quality of the introjects is based primarily and in part on the sadistic, destructive, undercutting, undermining, and devaluing elements which were built into the highly ambivalent relationship with one or other or both parents. Thus for Gloria, the persecutory dread which she experienced in her most phobic and paranoid states was clearly a reflection of the sadistic, infantalizing, devaluing, and controlling aspects of her father, although the rejecting and unloving aspects of her cold and ungiving mother also played into this paranoid picture.

Diffuse Projections

If we look at the projective elements in Fred's case, however, we are struck by the fact that again there is no systematic delusion, but that it is more a question of displacement of the projective elements into social institutions and the general social fabric of his life and experience. It is in that area that he carries out the struggle with the introjected elements which constitute his inner pathology. In his case particularly, then, it is quite difficult to draw the line between projected elements and real ones, which were embedded in the social realities to which he addressed himself and against which he reacted so violently.

Again if we look at the healthiest patients in this series, we are struck by the fact that there are no delusions—let alone systematic delusions—but that there is a definite paranoid flavor to the patient's quality of interaction with the significant figures in his environment. For Jim J., the projective element took the form of a constant expectation that he would be attacked, criticized, put down, humiliated, embarrassed—a whole catalogue of attitudes and threats that he encapsulated in his fear of being "shot down" or "fucked over." It seemed quite clear that the predominant elements in this pervasive and anxiety-provoking disposition stemmed from the intrusive, controlling, critical, and infantilizing attitude of his mother, reinforced and intensified by the rather sadistic, demeaning, and destructive attitude of his older brother. The total impact of this set of attitudes and expectations was to preserve his position as the defective, weak, and failure-doomed baby of the family.

For Karen, on the other hand, it was quite clear that her pervasive expectation was that she would be taken advantage of, that people would criticize and devalue her, that they would not value her for her strengths and capacities—particularly for her highly masculinized intellectual capacities—and that somehow or other she would be subjugated and imposed upon. All of this had the overtones of degrading and humiliating submission which she attached so strongly to the victimized "martyr" position that was so strongly evidenced in her mother. It was against this inner core of feminine weakness and vulnerability that she reacted so strongly with aggressive and highly intellectualized defenses. But in both of these cases the projected elements did not operate in terms of a specifiable delusional content, but rather manifested themselves in a generalized characterological attitude or disposition which generated certain projective expectancies.

Thus, if we examine the spectrum of projective contents which are

manifested in these cases in various ways, it becomes evident that projection is far from being a monolithic or simple mechanism, as it has so
often been conceptualized or regarded. Rather it must be regarded as a complex set of mental attitudes which both reflects and serves to reinforce the inner introjective elements of the personality organization. It is quite clear,
however, despite the variety of contents and forms in which the projections
are expressed, that in each case the projective content is on the one hand
derived from introjective elements, but on the other seems to play off
against and reinforce, by a kind of extrinsic confirmation, the internal alignment of introjective elements. Thus for our analytic patient Jim J., it seems
quite clear that his constant anxiety and his expectations of hostility and
destructive criticism in all areas of his experience and endeavor serve to confirm and consolidate his own inner view of himself as somehow weak, defective, and destined to failure.

Freud and Projection

We now wish to examine more carefully the nature of the mental operations which constitute the projective process as well as some of its specific
functions and implications.

We can do no better in our assessment of projection itself than to return
to the most important text which Freud has provided us in which he discusses the mechanisms of projection. We have had occasion to discuss the
development of Freud's ideas on projection in our preliminary consideration of the Schreber case. But we can concentrate most usefully at this point
on the important third section, in which he specifically focuses on and discusses the mechanism of paranoia.

The discussion is particularly one of projection. Freud was obviously
more secure in his grasp on the formalities and functions of projection,
rather than on the mechanism itself. He approached the consideration of
projection by dividing the discussion into a consideration of the mechanism
by which the symptoms are formed and the mechanism by which repression
is brought about. Projection is thus the mechanism of symptom formation.
Freud leads us, as it were, to the threshold—but no further. He wrote:

> The most striking characteristic of symptom-formation in paranoia is the
> process which deserves the name of *projection*. An internal perception is sup-
> pressed, and, instead, its content after undergoing a certain kind of distor-
> tion, enters consciousness in the form of an external perception. In delusions
> of persecution the distortion consists in a transformation of affect: what
> should have been felt internally as love is perceived externally as hate. We
> should feel tempted to regard this remarkable process as the most important
> element in paranoia and as being absolutely pathognomonic for it, if we were
> not opportunely reminded of two things. In the first place, projection does
> not play the same part in all forms of paranoia; and in the second place, it
> makes its appearance not only in paranoia but under other psychological con-

ditions as well, and in fact it has a regular share assigned to it in our attitude toward the external world. For when we refer the causes of certain sensations to the external world, instead of looking for them (as we do in the case of others) inside ourselves, this normal proceeding, too, deserves to be called projection (1911, p. 66).

Having brought us thus far, Freud promises us a further benefit which is in fact never delivered.

Having thus been made aware that more general psychological problems are involved in the question of the nature of projection, let us make up our minds to postpone the investigation of it (and with it that of the mechanisms of paranoic symptom formation in general) until some other occasion; and let us now turn to what ideas we can collect on the subject of the mechanism of repression in paranoia. I should like to say at once, in justification of this temporary renunciation, that we shall find that the manner in which the process of repression occurs is far more intimately connected with the developmental history of the libido and with the disposition to which it gives rise than is the manner in which symptoms are formed (*Ibid.*).

The editor of the *Standard Edition* goes on to note that there was no trace of any such promised discussion—although Freud may have had in mind his subsequent metapsychological papers, some of which have never been discovered.

It is clear, then, that Freud's effort to analyze the mechanism of projection passes quickly on to a related analysis of repression in the genesis of paranoia. He was apparently anxious to demonstrate that the theory of libido and repression, which he had derived from his study of neurotic and, particularly, hysterical states, was applicable to the material of the Schreber case. Thus the emphasis shifts quickly from less familiar to more familiar ground—to our loss—in the attempt to understand paranoia and projective processes.

Freud was fairly clear about the function of projection. He determined that the basic core of Schreber's illness was a homosexual impulse directed toward his father. That impulse had subsequently been transferred to his doctor, Flechsig. The principal mechanisms were a "reversal into the opposite" by which the loving impulse was transformed into an impulse of hate and the homosexual wish replaced by a delusion of sexual persecution which was expressed in the vivid emasculation fantasy. The figure of Flechsig is replaced by the higher and more powerful figure of God, thus transforming the emasculation fantasy into one which made Schreber himself a feminine redeemer.

Related to this is the delusion of the end of the world as a projection of Schreber's own internal catastrophe, the end of his own inner, subjective world which has come to an end by reason of the withdrawal of love—as Freud would see it. The function of the projection at this point is clear: it is a reconstruction, a restitution. Freud wrote:

And the paranoic builds it again, not more splendid it is true, but at least so he can once again live in it. He builds it up by the work of his delusions. The delusional formation, which we take to be the pathological product, is in reality an attempt at recovery, a process of reconstruction. Such a reconstruction after the catastrophe is successful to a greater or lesser extent, but never wholly so; in Schreber's words, there has been a "profound internal change" in the world. But the human subject has recaptured a relation, and often a very intense one, to the people and things in the world, even though the relation is a hostile one, where formerly it was hopefully affectionate. We may say, then, that the process of repression proper consists in a detachment of the libido from people—and things—that were previously loved. It happens silently; we receive no intelligence of it, but can only infer it from subsequent events. What forces itself so noisily upon our attention is the process of recovery, which undoes the work of repression, brings back the libido again onto the people it had abandoned. In paranoia this process is carried out by the method of projection. It was incorrect to say that the perception that was repressed internally is projected outwards; the truth is rather, as we now see, that what was abolished internally returns from without (1911, p. 71).

Thus the redeemer aspect of his delusional system gave a context of meaning, a purpose and a relatedness to the world of objects and things that he otherwise could not feel. The redeemer fantasy also affected a reconciliation (he becomes reconciled to his persecution) and allowed the expression of his feminine voluptuous wishes, which were intolerable toward Flechsig, but were a sign of grandiose glorification in relationship to the godhead. Emasculation was no longer a humiliation and a disgrace, but became part of a great cosmic chain of events which was ordered to the re-creation of humanity. The feminine wish became acceptable in the context of Schreber's megalomania. The reconciliation was then, in effect, one with Schreber's father. Freud noted that the persecutory figure is split between the figure of Flechsig on the one hand and God on the other. The dual projection expresses the basic ambivalence of Schreber's relationship to his father, who was both a physician like Flechsig and a figure of godlike distance and reverence.

However, despite this important insight, Freud does not elucidate the mechanisms of projection any further. His preoccupation is with the establishment of the sexual etiology of paranoia. He thus exposes the erotic component and connects it to the basically homosexual and narcissistic phase of object-choice. The subsequent analysis of repression and regression is obviously a point at which Freud is considerably more comfortable. The process of symptom formation, however, creates difficulties, since the projection seems to undo the work of repression by restoring it from without. Freud thus successfully avoids an explanation of projection, although he succeeds in delimiting its boundaries.

It is worth noting in passing that Freud's treatment of projection in this context also raises the interesting problem of the relationship between projection and the mythopoeic capacity of man. He hints in the postscript to the Schreber case at the implications of our understanding of projection for understanding the generation of belief systems and the generation of mythologies. The whole subject of the genesis of belief systems, as we have noted repeatedly, is intimately connected with the workings of the paranoid process. But our understanding of that aspect of the process must wait upon our better understanding of projection itself, along with its related functions.

If we reassess the Schreber case in the context of our previous formulations, it seems reasonable to conceptualize Schreber's experience in terms of the introjection of the sadomasochistic relationship between his powerful, controlling, autocratic, and sadistically rigid father and his submissive and probably depressed mother by contrast. The drama of victimizer and victim was spelled out with considerable clarity in the Schreber household. The dynamics of this constellation clearly parallels those that we have found in our own cases. The case of Bob B. comes immediately to mind, with his impotent struggles to satisfy and gain the begrudging acknowledgment and approval of his harsh, cold, distant, tough, and domineering father. The fascinating element in his story is, of course, that when he comes to the point of fulfilling the father's wishes in becoming the accomplished surgeon, he breaks down and plunges himself into a paranoid delusional system. The parallels to Schreber are obvious, for Schreber too decompensated at points at which he was confronted with an apparent achievement in his life.

Projection and Externalization

Our concern for the moment, however, is to gain some greater clarity in our understanding of the mechanisms underlying the phenomenon of projection. Projection itself must be understood in relation to the broader process of externalization. While the terms are used in varying relation, our intent in this discussion will be that projection is regarded as a form of externalization—understanding externalization in the broader sense of an attribution of inner phenomena to the outer world. Thus Freud's notion of projection as related to causal thinking fits more broadly under the rubric of externalization. In this vein he wrote to Fliess in 1895, "Whenever an internal change occurs, we have the choice of assuming either an external or internal cause. If something deters us from the internal derivation, we shall naturally seize upon the external one" (1950 [1892-1899] p. 201).

It is well to recall at this point that projection is not a simple or unequivocal phenomena. We should remind ourselves that Freud himself had seen that projection was an essential process that was involved in the early development of the self and the differentiation between self and object in the infant's experience. Subsequent to the influence of Melanie Klein, of course, the importance of the interaction between introjective and projective mechanisms in the early development of the child has received considerable attention. In the Schreber case, Freud seems to have explicitly differentiated a type of projection that had to do with change of subject from the projection of drive impulses. By means of a change of subject from "I (a man) love him" to "It is not I who loves the man—she loves him"—the whole process was thrown outside of the self and became a matter of external perception. His most consistent use of the notion of projection was that—also as described in the Schreber case—of the paranoid defense against homosexuality as involving a projection of unconscious hate. Thus "I hate him" is transformed into the more conscious and tolerable thought, "He hates me." Thus drive projection was explicitly linked with the defense against ambivalent conflict. And hence the paranoid fear of a girl that she would be killed by her mother is the result of drive projection of her own hostile and destructive wishes.

The point that we would consider basic to this sort of clarification is that even such simple examples involve more than just drive projection. It is clear from the data in our case studies and the fuller understanding of what is involved in the projection, that what might pass for drive projection involves a complex process which is related to an internal state based on prior introjective elements. Thus, for example, Gloria G., who experienced the paranoid and terrifying fear that her mother would kill her, was expressing a rather malignant and destructive introject which represented the image of the internalized victim and at the same time expressed the introjective aspects of the sadistic and destructive victimizer which she had internalized from both parental figures. As we shall see in the subsequent discussion, perhaps the only case where drive projection as such is at issue is in the area of phobias, but even there the case is neither clear-cut nor decisive.

Projection and Generalization

There are some important discriminations that need to be made in focusing on the projective mechanism. One important discrimination is that between projection and generalization. Novick and Hurry (1969) observe that after the stage of self-object differentiation, the child's view of the external world and the objects around him will be determined in large measure by what he knows of himself. Thus with the dawning awareness of his own wishes to devour the object, for example, the child naturally ascribes similar wishes to the object itself. They comment: "This process is not projection proper; the conscious awareness of his own wish continues to exist. We would term this process 'generalization.' The process of generalization remains the child's major mode of apprehending the unknown and persists to some extent throughout life. Examples are legion; the infantile sexual theories, for instance, provide clear illustrations" (p. 5). They go on to observe that the assumption that Freud saw projection as central in the process of superego formation is inaccurate, since Freud ascribed the severity of the superego not to projection of aggressive wishes onto the introjected object, but to other factors, including the natural assumption on the part of the child that he and the father had similar aggressive wishes toward each other.

It seems to me that the distinction between generalization and projection can be clearly drawn. Generalization is a learning phenomenon and is presumably based on the data provided by reality. Thus one can infer on the basis of external clues that someone else has feelings similar to what one experiences within oneself. But one would not expect that the generalization of itself would be extended in the face of contradictory or nonsupportive evidence.

The point at issue, it seems to me, in the mechanism of projection, is that the child's perception of destructive and hostile aggression in the parent is maintained not only without proportional supportive evidence, but in the face even of contradictory evidence. Or to put it in other terms, that the child's perception of the parent is maintained without adequately supporting evidence—that is, that the parent may indeed have hostile impulses toward the child, but that the child's perception of this magnifies the destructive element out of proportion. This cannot be simply generalization, as a relatively normal learning phenomenon relatively removed from conflictual and defensive involvement, but would seem more appropriately to be ascribable to the operation of projective mechanisms. This seems to me to be the point of Freud's discussion of the origins of superego aggression in *Civilization and Its Discontents.*

Moreover it cannot be simply said that projection serves as a defense against an object-directed drive derivative, but rather that projection serves as a defense against self-directed destructive impulses. The inner force, which overrides the experience of reality and interferes with the processes of learning and generalization, involves a more complex process by which the subject relates to the object in question. In the child's relationship to the father, for example, there is apparently an originating introjection which is based on and reflects the more or less moderated and realistic degrees of ambivalence that are inherent in the gratifying and prohibiting aspects of the real relationship. Once the introject is drawn within the inner world, however, it becomes susceptible to attribution of more intense and aggressive components which remain relatively unneutralized in the child's psychic economy. The reprojection of this aggressivized introject then colors the child's interaction with the real object and tends to magnify and distort the aggressive aspects of the parent-child relationship.

This interaction of projection and introjection would seem to underlie and build a foundation for the subsequent fear of the object—in the case of the male child, that of the father, most clearly, as an internal organization which underlies the subsequent castration threat and anxiety. Thus, to return to the example cited by Novick and Hurry (1969), the obsessive-compulsive child undoubtedly was highly conflicted about aggression, but his paranoid fear that his therapist was going to attack and kill him would seem to me to involve more than simple generalization. The fear was generated not simply by external evidences nor simply in the face of a lack of such supportive evidences, but arose in the face of contrary evidences from a presumably sympathetic and reassuring therapist, even to the point of total unmanageability and the necessity for referral for intensive treatment.

I do not mean to imply, in the discussion of generalization, that this does not play a significant role in the genesis of paranoid states. Part of what we have been attempting to focus on in the analysis of our own cases has been that the child is exposed to a series of persecutory contexts and experiences, which extend from earliest childhood even to the period of the patient's adult illness. The persecutions may take the more subtle form of an attempt by parental objects to subjugate and deprive the patient of autonomy and the opportunity for adult assertiveness and independence, so that such a repeated "learning" experience can underlie the generalization, which might tell the patient to expect persecution from other objects in his experience. But at the point where projection is introduced into this process, the process becomes resistant to extinction as well as to the effects of corrective learning experiences. Thus I would not wish to rule out the phenomenon of generalization as pertinent and relevant to the understanding of paranoia, but it seems to me that one should not mistake it for the influences coming from the defensive process of projection.

Benign Projection

It should be noted that projection is not limited to the externalization of destructive impulses onto a malignant persecutor. Not only is the projection of loving impulses possible, it is an important part of the evolution of the positive object relation, developmentally between child and parent, and therapeutically between patient and therapist. But another frequent pattern of projection is the denial of aggressive wishes or impulses in oneself, together with a displacement of such wishes to extrinsic social agencies or institutions. Thus the state, the police, the armed forces, or other social agencies are permitted the expression of aggression that the individual denies himself. The individual can then see the external agency as victimizing himself, or can protect himself by allying himself with or identifying with the aggressive agency (A. Freud, 1972).

Characterological Externalization

It is worth noting that projective mechanisms can function not only at delusional and psychotic levels, but also at the level of characterological defects which are manifestly nonpsychotic, but which form important parameters of the analytic experience. Giovacchini (1967), for example, has described patients who maintain a more or less distorted perception of the environment, such that the patient re-creates in the transference an environment based on the externalization of aspects of his inner world along with projected affects, impulses and attitudes. The structuring of his environment through such projections leads to inevitable frustration. The patient seems to have a need to construct a painful reality and attributes the trauma he experiences to his inability to cope with the external world. His environment is seen as complex, impossible to deal with by available adaptive techniques. The patient feels helpless and vulnerable and weak—a helpless baby cast into a harsh environment he is totally incapable of dealing with. I am reminded, in reading Giovacchini's description of his patients, of both Karen and Jim in the present series. For both of them it was the weak, vulnerable, and helpless little child that was the source of fear and which lay at the core of their fantasies about themselves—issuing in phobic anxieties in one case and in excessively rigid and severe coping reactions in another. Yet in less specific and often more severe ways, the same perception permeates the case material of the other and sicker patients as well.

Such patients tend to identify their universal experience in terms of a level of childhood involvement with early and predominantly primary objects. Giovacchini writes, in this regard,

> To feel secure in one's identity, one has to know where he stands in his universe. The self-image contains numerous introjects, so one perceives the self in the same way as the external objects that have been introjected. So external objects are among the first representations of reality. So one's sense of identity, if it is firm and coherent, corresponds to the environment that contributes to its formation. The early environment of patients with ego defects is different from that experienced by persons with a relatively good psychic organization. The ego of the person with the character disorder is not in resonance with any reality that differs radically from the one he knew in early childhood. The degree of difference determines how well he can master external stimuli and perceive himself as a meaningful person in an acceptable world (1967, p. 576).

The patient's attempt to structure the treatment situation in terms of an environment, embedded in the childhood past, can be seen as a repetition compulsion. The analyst who refuses to frustrate the patient by verifying his projection ends up frustrating him anyway. With my patient Jim, this situation in the analysis was described as a no-win situation—as he put it, "If I win, I lose; if I lose, I lose." We can remind ourselves of the "no-win" situation that we have seen in some of our paranoid families, most strikingly in the G. family. The patient's externalization structures reality in such a way that it becomes a frustrating reality.

Giovacchini (1967) hesitates to call this projection, since it is not the attribution of hostile wishes to a persecuting figure, but rather represents a mode of adjustment which makes interaction between self and the outer world possible. He prefers to label this externalization, although the latter, it seems, is built upon projection, since the construction of reality necessarily involves the attributing of unacceptable and particularly hostile impulses to external objects. The clinical situation which Giovacchini describes is readily verifiable, but it may not be helpful to describe the situation merely in terms of externalization. It is not clear how the externalization specifically differs from projection.

It is nonetheless clear that such patients with characterological defects do indeed project, and that they construct reality to support and verify the projections. We will deal with this aspect of the paranoid process later in terms of the paranoid construction. What is at issue is the patient's need to fail. He must create an environment, both in the external world and in the analysis, in which he can feel frustrated and defeated.

Degrees of Externalization

Let us focus for a moment on the notion of externalization. Externalization is a correlative of internalization. The notion of externalization can best be seen in the context of the idea of "degrees of internalization." Loewald (1962) had presented the idea in the following terms: "The concept of degrees of internalization is advanced. This implies shifting distances of internalized material from the ego core and shifting distances within the ego-superego system, as well as transformations in the character of the introjects according to the respective degrees of internalization" (p. 503). Thinking of specific introjects in terms of degrees of internalization, then, we can regard the superego introjects as elements which may, under certain circumstances, be further internalized into the ego core, or in the opposite direction, may be externalized in the direction of object-representations.

Thus at the highest degree of internalization, a well-established identification is capable of resisting regressive pulls toward the introject type of inner experience, and lies closest to the intentionally realized core of the ego. Where a greater degree of externalization exists, there may be a relative increase of passivity in the subjective experience of the introject. Thus Schafer has observed:

> ... It must always be borne in mind that internalization is a matter of degree; the degree to which external regulations have been taken over by the subject and stamped with his self-representations; the degree of influence ex-

erted by the internalizations; and the degree of stability in the internalizations, that is, their resistiveness to being regressively abandoned and restored to the environment or lost altogether in systemic de-differentiations that involve primitive mergings of self and object representations (1968a, pp. 14-15).

Consequently, if there are degrees of internalization, there are, correlatively, degrees of externalization. As I have written elsewhere:

Rather than use the concept of externalization as a modification of projection, it seems more exact to formulate it as the reverse of internalization. Thus externalization would refer to a process of transformation by which elements of the structure of the personality that function in more immediate relation to the core of the ego become less immediately related to the ego core, and are modified in the direction of independently functioning personality structures or, with increasing degrees of externalization in the direction of object-representations. Thus projections can be regarded as a special case of externalization in which externalized elements are transformed into object-representations and so perceived (1971b, p. 280).

Projection and Introjection

If the correlative of internalization is externalization, then it seems reasonable to consider the correlative of introjection to be projection. Projection, therefore, comes to refer to a process in which attributes which are derived from the inner world of the subject are attributed to and attached to real objects (object-representations), so that the object, as perceived and experienced, comes to be constituted of qualities which are derived from both the environment and the inner modification of the subject's self. Thus the object-representation as modified by projection has the quality of a transitional object representation.

It is important to realize that the interplay of projection and introjection has important implications for the development of object-relations as well as for the organization of inner psychic structure. At the most archaic and primitive levels, the ego attempts to purify itself of unpleasant or painful elements, as Freud suggested (1915), by projecting the almost purely oral-sadistic elements to the exterior, thus leaving the purified pleasure ego intact. The subsequent history of introjective and projective processes makes the developmental sequence more complex. Internal structure becomes gradually organized around successive introjective modifications so that there is an increasing capacity to bind, neutralize, or even tolerate in terms of utilization of aggressive impulses in signal discharges. Correlative to this internal development, the quality of projection becomes modified in the direction of more muted and balanced ambivalence.

Destructive projective elements become modified as constituents of transitional objects in proportion to the apparent qualities of the object itself. Thus sadistic projections can be modified by an adequate maternal object in the direction of ambivalence. The subsequent introject, therefore, is less malevolent and its corresponding projection less destructive and/or hostile. The modifications in the interactions of introjection and projection along with the increasing capacity for binding and channeling of destructive aggressive energies leads to a gradual increase and stabilization of inner structure along with a more mature capacity for object-relationships. Projection, therefore, as derived from and correlative to internal introjects, can serve important defensive functions in the economy and mastery of instinctual drives. While they remain essentially defensive functions, they can become less susceptible to instinctual influences with the gradual emergence of structure and its increasing strengthening. Thus both introjection and projection are modified in more realistic directions during a relatively normal course of ego development.

The vital interplay of introjection and projection was grasped and articulated in a succinct fashion by Anna Freud in her discussion of "identification with the aggressor" (1936). The latter can be regarded as a special case of the interaction of introjection and projection. As Ms. Freud observes, when the external criticism has not been introjected, the threat of the punishment and the offense have not yet been connected in the patient's mind, so that, as soon as the criticism is internalized, the offense is externalized. Thus the introjection of aggression is supplemented by the projection of guilt. The ego is then able to project prohibited impulses to the outside. It learns to blame as a means of protecting itself from unpleasant self-criticism. Indignation thus increases automatically when one's own guilt begins to be felt. This form of introjection is a stage in superego development and forms a preliminary phase of morality. As Ms. Freud observes, true morality begins when the internalized criticism which is embodied in the superego standard coincides with the ego's perception of its own fault. The severity of the superego is turned inward rather than outward and the ego has to endure the unpleasure of self-criticism and guilt. Consequently, "identification with the aggressor" represents a preliminary phase of superego development on one hand, and an intermediate stage in the development of paranoia on the other. It looks in two directions, then, one as a result of its introjective elements, and the other as a result of its projective reaction.

Mechanism of Projection

Some of Anna Freud's comments about projection can serve as a useful jumping off point for some specific reflections about the mechanisms of projection, which Freud, as you remember, left us wondering about. Ms. Freud writes:

> The effect of the mechanism of projection is to break the connection between the ideational representatives of dangerous instinctual impulses and the ego.

> In this it resembles most closely the process of repression. Other defensive processes, such as displacement, reversal or turning around upon the self, affect the instinctual process itself; repression and projection merely prevent its being perceived. In repression the objectionable idea is thrust back into the id, while in projection it is displaced into the outside world. Another point at which projection resembles repression is that it is not associated with any particular anxiety situation, but may be motivated equally by objective anxiety, superego anxiety, and instinctual anxiety (1936, p. 122).

The comparison with repression seems useful in the context of reflection on the defensive functions of projection. We can presume that both defensive maneuvers, repression and projection, serve to alleviate the ego from the threat of internal danger. The hysterical patient represses the instinctual content back into the unconscious; the paranoid displaces it to the outside world.

The immediate question, which such an observation prompts is, "What is it that determines whether or not an ego's defensive response to threat should follow the path of repression or that of projection?" We find ourselves stumped for a reply. Although there does not seem to be any conclusive or decisive response to the query, certain pieces of an answer come to mind. We can think for a moment of the tiny infant who follows the primitive dictates of the pleasure principle and purifies his experience by "projecting" what is unpleasant or disagreeable to the outside. If there is any reality or validity to the principle, then at best we are dealing with primitive precursors of projection rather than with a developed mechanism.

The basic principle that the infant avoids what is unpleasant and seeks to incorporate what is pleasant seems inviolable. The basic model for this may be primarily oral, in terms of spitting out or vomiting out what is unpleasant or repulsive, or it may be based on primarily anal components—the anal expulsion of powerful and poisonous fecal content. But the notion of attributing to objects what is internally sensed as painful or repugnant requires some further degree of development, at least to the point where some separation begins to take place between the inchoate self and the first glimmerings of objects. At this level, if we can begin to speak of precursors of projection, it would seem that we are dealing with the basic tendency of the organism to minimize pain by referring the pain to an outside source, rather than by holding it within.

I am reminded at this point of the first glimmerings of the reality principle, as Freud described it. With regard to the inner yield of pleasure, the infant ego learns gradually that the adequate satisfaction depends on an external source for the attainment of pleasure. But that gratification cannot be immediate and must tolerate a certain degree of frustration and pain in waiting on the response of the reality. Thus, in even its early stages of development, the infantile ego learns to delay gratification and to tolerate pain in the service of gaining a more satisfactory real gratification from the real object; it must also learn in the same developmental course that the external object is the source of the frustration and pain and denial of its wishes. Thus the external object becomes the focus and object for ambivalence.

Inner Danger

We must presume at this point that there is also something embedded in the inner workings of the organism that tells it that somehow external danger is preferable to internal danger. As Rochlin puts it, the child "finds it more manageable to cope with a monster of his own making than to carry about within himself his own menace" (1973, p. 176). Presumably the internal danger is based upon the destructive and malignant introject, which has taken its place in the inner world and works its evil magic there (Schafer, 1968b). In the face of that inner presence the ego feels itself to be relatively passive and helpless. The sense of inner destructiveness and evil must be gotten rid of, must be escaped. The ego readily exchanges the sense of inner power and destructiveness for the position of victimhood. Thus the destructive content can be detached from the self-representation and reattached or displaced to the object-representation. In this way the ego creates for itself an enemy, which it can deal with as an external force, rather than as an inner destructiveness.

There is a considerable need in a young child to minimize and deny the intensity of aggressive impulses. As Rochlin (1973) has observed:

> Beginning to deny one's own inclinations does not require that they must first be precisely defined. How great a gap there is between repudiating one's aggressive impulses and attributing them to others, and in the course of it to develop fears of being attacked or menaced, may not handily be stated. But it is characteristically displayed by a child of 3 years. This mental process, "projection" as it is called, is one of the child's earliest and most effective defenses to lighten the burden one's aggressive wishes may create. And it is not readily relinquished in adult life (p. 16).

In early childhood the inner resistance to aggressive impulses stems primarily from anxiety and the fear of consequences. The child's natural inclination is to attribute his own inclinations and wishes to all sorts of objects and persons in his environment. Quite typically his aggression comes back to haunt him at bedtime when he faces the fear of darkness and the monstrous and vicious animals which populate it. He is in fact the victim of his own violence. The night terrors and nightmares tend to diminish when the regulating influence of conscience is established. As the inner rule of law is established, there is less need to fear the unconscious destructive wishes.

The law which seems to assert itself in these circumstances is that aggressive impulses are tolerated best and with least conflict when we believe we are the victims of another's hostility. The denial of hostile reactions and the defensive use of projection are a well-known syndrome, and are quite characteristic of ordinary childhood experiences. The objective is not merely to escape from the stigma of destructive impulses, but it aims also at a recovery of the self-esteem whose loss lies at the root of the destructive wish. The destructive impulses are too threatening and serve only to diminish self-esteem. They must be rejected, projected, divorced from all connection with the self. Little Hans could not tolerate his hostility toward his father, but could escape it by imagining himself to be a victim—fear was more tolerable than aggression. Rochlin's (1973) comments are again to the point:

> The unconscious use of "projection" together with a "denial" of destructiveness are among the most developed of early childhood defenses. They are the unconscious means, beginning in childhood and carried forward into adult life, by which we may disengage ourselves from being concerned over wishes and impulses which are a source of conflict. To attribute disquieting aims to others and thus unwittingly deny one's egocentric wishes and the aggressive inclinations that issue to support them affords a measure of relief. Under these conditions a child's fear of what might happen to him, a blameless victim of circumstances, are apt to become prominent. Fears, phobias, and nightmares then frequently appear (p. 165).

Motivational Aspects

I am not sure at this point that I find myself in full agreement with the statement of Anna Freud, quoted above, that projection, like repression, may be motivated indifferently by objective anxiety, superego anxiety, and instinctual anxiety. It seems to me that there is no point to projection in reference to objective anxiety, unless it be to paradoxically intensify the anxiety. This may not be true, as we will see of externalization. Nor is it clear to me that projective defense would in any preferential way be exercised against instinctual dread. Nor is it clear to me, in reviewing the patient material that we have been discussing, that the paranoid defense operates with any specificity against superego anxiety or guilt. The question is what serves as the signal affect for the projective defense. It seems to me that it is more likely that the specific signal affect for projection is depression. The depressive position may manifest itself in a variety of ways, including a sense of inner inadequacy, vulnerability, shame, or powerlessness. It does not even seem adequate to express the depressive affect in terms of sadness or sorrow. Rather than a sense of loss, what seems more at issue is a form of narcissistic mortification.

We will have more to say of this in our discussion of the defense aspects of the paranoid process, including both projective and introjective elements. As has recently been reemphasized in Jaffe's (1968) excellent discussion, the essence of the notion of projection involves not merely the conflictual and defensive aspects of projection, but also its function in the preservation of object ties. This was initially indicated by Freud's view of the reconstitutive aspect of projections. Along with the repression of subjective elements of self-reproach, there is also an attempt to preserve or restore object ties. Thus, in the Schreber case, there is a defense against homosexual impulses, as well as an attempt to reestablish important object ties with the substitute for the glorified father through projective devices.

It seems apparent, in the cases we have described, that the projective defense carries with it a number of significant implications. If the projective effort is motivated by the need for defense, it nonetheless has embedded in it other specific functions which also express motivational aspects. It seems quite clear, for example, that the projection of persecutory elements has the secondary effect of reinforcing and confirming the introject of the suffering victim. In a number of our male subjects, the result of course is to reinforce primarily the sense of identification with the depressed and victimized mother, not to rule out contributing elements from the father. Consequently, there is a defensive advantage not merely in expelling to the outside and placing blame upon the evil persecutors, but there is also a gain in preserving and intensifying the internalized relationship to the relatively unavailable, depressed, and victimized mother.

Another aspect of the projective dimension is that it serves to relate the self significantly to a projective system. We will have more to say about the notion of a projective system in our discussion of the paranoid construction. The point I wish to emphasize here is that the projection works to establish a meaningful context to which and within which the introject can be related. As we have suggested previously, the introject itself provides a focus for the internal organization of the self-system. The correlative function of projection is to provide a context within which that self-system can be regarded as relevant, and in terms of which it is provided a context of meaningful belongingness. This aspect of the interplay of introjection and projection will be most relevant in our discussion of the organization of belief and value systems and their relationship to the integration and stabilization of identity. In this context, then, the connection between projection and object ties becomes more general and more diffuse. The projective system may involve signficant objects, but its implications are broader and more extensive than the limited perspective of immediate object-relations.

Compliance and Rebellion

If it is true that object ties can be consolidated by the reciprocal reinforcement of introjects, as I have suggested above, it is also true that the recourse to projection also serves to preserve the relationship of the subject to the persecuting object as such. From one point of view, the relationship to the persecuting object is the opposite face of the reciprocal reinforcement of the introject, as well as the dynamic substratum for the formation and preservation of the false self-system. In our series of patients it seems quite clear that the outcome, in behavioral terms, of this dual aspect of the projective mechanism—confirming the introject and preserving the relationship to the object—is that the patients are compelled to adopt a position of compliance or rebellion, or that they find themselves alternating between the two, often in a somewhat unpredictable and chaotic fashion. Thus, for Bob B., the pattern of compliance became a characteristic of his false self-system, but at the critical point he turned to a violent rebellion in the form of his psychotic decompensation. Similarly Ann A. preserved a smoldering facade of compliance in the face of her mother's sadistic attacks, but periodically would break forth in an outburst of violent and panicked paranoid rebellion.

In the cases in which an acute psychotic decompensation seems to occur, most often this can be seen in terms of a violent rebellion against the pattern of enforced compliance. Whatever the other external terms of the compliance may be—whether of specific or general expectations of reward or punishment—there also seems to be important internal motivational aspects. The compliance becomes the price of the preservation of the relationship to the persecuting object, on the one hand, as well as the duty that the patient pays for preserving the inner relationship to the introjected object on the other hand.

In any case the issues of compliance and rebellion are pervasive elements in the inner life and experience of these patients, undoubtedly correlative to the threatened and fragile status of their sense of inner autonomy. Often enough the external demands and the need to comply are functioning at a relatively unconscious level. One of the important parameters of treatment of such patients is the increasing bringing to awareness of the issues of compliance and/or rebellion in their relationship not only with significant objects, but in the broader contexts of their experience. As Freud once commented, "You cannot exaggerate the intensity of people's inner lack of resolution and craving for authority" (1910, p. 146).

It becomes quickly apparent that the issue of compliance is a delicate and important one for the analytic situation. There seems little doubt that some degree of compliance is essential to it. The question that remains open, however, is whether analysts tend to mistake compliance for therapeutic alliance. Schafer draws a distinction at this point between the technical preferences of the analyst and personal preferences. He writes,

> The analyst attempts to convey only technical preferences to his patient, and not personal ones. His *technical* preferences are for free association, frankness, introspection, verbalization, keeping appointments, maintaining

the recumbent position, and paying bills. It is generally recognized, however, that the analyst's *personal* preferences are represented in his analytic behavior: they are implied in his style of work, and in the seepage of his specific counter-transference reactions (1968a, pp. 35-36).

Consciously or unconsciously the patient responds to these dictates of the analytic situation, whether explicit or implicit. The patient's compliance may take the form of positive transference, productivity, production of useful free associations, and a whole host of other "good patient" behaviors. The patient's rebellion may take the place of negative transference, various forms of resistance and other patterns of obstructive and negative behavior. It is often very difficult to judge analytically whether what one is seeing is a pattern of compliance or rebelliousness, which is associated with the operation of the paranoid process, or whether what one is seeing is either authentic collaboration or autonomous and healthily independent behavior. My only point at this juncture is that these issues are alive for the paranoid patient and must also be alive for his therapist.

CHAPTER 19

Paranoid Mechanisms: Phobic States and Nightmares

PHOBIC STATES

I would like at this point to return to a consideration of the problem of phobias. The interest in phobias is prompted by the general phenomena in the case histories we have been studying of persistent phobias in childhood among these patients. For almost all of these patients childhood phobias form a fairly intense symptomatic aspect of their early experience. In addition the phobic element seems to form a prominent part of the adult pattern of illness. It would be useful at this point to consider the relationship between phobic symptoms and phobic states to the paranoid process. The question also seems to me to be of some utility in concretizing and specifying some of the connections between externalization and projection as such.

Factors in Phobias

A relatively extensive treatment of phobic states has been provided recently by Marks (1969, 1970). He notes a number of important elements in phobias which can usefully be taken into account. He notes, for example, that certain classes of stimuli have a certain prepotency to involvement in phobic reactions. Thus phobias of going into open spaces or traveling by train or plane are relatively common, whereas phobias of traveling by car are relatively rare, despite the frequency of these situations in everyday experience. Moreover certain classes of stimuli are more likely to trigger phobic responses at particular ages and not at others. Loud noises or sudden movements easily trigger the response of fear in young infants: stranger anxiety is commonly seen in older infants of about 8 months, and animal phobias are common in children of preschool age. Yet the fear of open spaces or of social situations, while rare in childhood, seems to increase in incidence between adolescence and middle age.

This is partly due to maturational factors, but experiential factors are also an important determinant. These phase-determining incidences, however, are also involved in the emergence of specific dynamic patterns which can underlie the specific fears that are generated. Thus separation anxiety is a more common fear for infants, while animal phobias may be more in evidence in Oedipal age children. The influence of intrinsic and extrinsic factors varies with age. In preschool children, either trivial incidents or none at all can be associated with the origins of animal phobias, while in adults such phobias are usually associated with a definite fright or trauma involving the feared animal. Exposure to the feared situation is also obviously an important factor in school phobias, also in job phobias, and similarly, in later adult life, disease phobias of heart trouble or cancer or even death.

It is interesting that in general the phobic patients have personalities which are described as timid, shy, dependent, and immature. This obviously does not mean that the development of phobias is restricted to such personalities, although a relatively immature and dependent personality organization seems to form a more appropriate matrix for phobic symptoms to take hold. Similarly phobias can frequently run in families and are quite susceptible to cultural and social influences (Marks, 1970). Phobias may be relatively limited when they follow a simple physical trauma, as for example, fears of dogs after being bitten, or a phobia of heights after a fall, or a fear of driving after a car accident. Fears of horses are relatively common after being thrown by a horse.

Psychological trauma is usually more subtle and involves a phobic result when it touches on or produces severe anxiety, or guilt, or impotent resentment. Phobias may also be triggered by more general life disturbances without specific links between the disturbing situation and the subsequent phobia. Thus agoraphobia may start shortly after traumatic events, like bereavement, marital separation or divorce, accidents, or even severe physical life-threatening illness. The onset of phobic symptoms may not be associated with any major environmental change, and in these instances the change seems to be more within the patient than without. Thus the spontaneous appearance of animal phobias in preschool children may often be related to no specific extrinsic situations or events, but may have internal links to dynamic and instinctual sources of anxiety. Phobias may also serve as a defense against depressive states.

Disease Phobias

It seems worth noting at this point that a number of the relatively frequently reported and studied phobic states show strong coincidence with factors which we have delineated in some of our paranoid patients. The disease phobias are generally statistically dominated by cancerphobia. These patients seem to manifest a subvariant of hypochondriasis. Their fear is persistent and unfounded and their doubts about it remain despite detailed examination and medical reassurances. Several of our patients have manifested this form of phobic anxiety. Such patients usually exhibit an excess of guilt, and prior to the onset of the phobia are more prone to the inhibition of anger, to excessive bodily concern, and to low self-esteem. As children they were often weak, sickly, and overprotected. The pattern of frequent family illness and maternal overprotectiveness and oversolicitude seems to be prominent in their background. Their tolerance of pain is low, and they have a deeply ingrained sense of personal vulnerability. The pattern has by now become a familiar one in this study.

Job Phobias

A recent study of job phobias reveals that patients experience extreme difficulty in getting to work, as well as frequent bouts of anxiety, depressive episodes, and multiple somatic complaints connected with employment. These patients tend to be conscientious and relatively perfectionistic in the performance of their work tasks. Their work, however, never measures up to their own standards, and they continually resort to self-criticism and a feeling of failure. Such patients are sensitive to any reproach from authority figures with whom they may be in conflict and are constantly in fear of losing their job—even though the standard of job performance is generally good (Radin, 1972). This same pattern is identifiable in several of our patients, particularly Jimmy J., on the level of the anxious and neurotic commitment to failure, and in Bob B., on the level of psychotic paralysis and avoidance of career commitment.

The fear of vocational success is a not uncommon phobic condition, particularly in highly competitive and achievement-oriented culture like ours. The essential feature in such cases is the inhibition of aggression. The inhibition has its origin in the rivalries between child and parent or between child and siblings. The rivalries are experienced unconsciously as murderous attacks, and where the competition is intense, the pattern of interaction tends to reinforce the symbolic equation of aggression or assertion and violence. The patient becomes inhibited and withdraws from all forms of competition out of a fear of murderous retaliation. At times these fears take the form of more explicitly paranoid concerns over homosexual assault (Ovesey, 1962). The picture seen so often in these patients was reproduced in a very characteristic fashion in Jim J. His commitment to failure was in part a retreat from competitive confrontation of both the Oedipal father and the intensely rivalrous sibling. But it was also based to a considerable extent on other pregenital determinants as well.

Spider Phobias

The projective elements can be seen somewhat more clearly in the case of spider phobias. The basic conflicts seem to involve fears of phallic castration by an aggressive mother. Such patients reveal transference fantasies in which symbolic equivalences are drawn between the silent, watchful, hidden and waiting spider and the analyst who sits silently and watchfully behind the couch. Little (1967) presents evidence from several cases to indicate that the patient's fears are related to both oral and phallic fantasies, the oral fears stemming from the fear of losing the penis by its being swallowed by the orally aggressive mother. Such patients tend to feel trapped in the therapeutic situation, or feel that they must placate the therapist in some way lest the therapist pounce on them and devour them. These fantasies may be related to beating fantasies. Similar fears were patently manifested in both the analytic patients described—Jimmy J. and Karen K.—but also formed a significant aspect of the treatment situation in the patients treated psychotherapeutically. It is clear in these cases that the phobic anxiety approaches close to, if it does not cross, the border into the area of explicitly paranoid anxieties. Melitta Sperling's (1971) study of spider symbolism indicates that the important genetic factors involved are pregenital, and specifically involve anal fixations and unresolved preoedipal attachments to the mother. Spider symbolism is usually associated with severe sleep disturbances and phobias. Separation conflicts and a high degree of ambivalence seem to underlie the symptomatology. She notes that the personalities of these patients and of their mothers seem to reveal a marked paranoid quality.

Animal Phobias

Other animal phobias have been reported even in very young children, even in the second (Sperling, 1952) and third (Bornstein, 1935) years of life. Such phobias involve the mechanisms of projection of a relatively intolerable inner danger based on oral or anal-sadistic impulses, which are thus transformed into an outer danger, the fear of biting animals.

The animal phobias have been perhaps more extensively studied than any of the phobic states. The classic and original case, of course, was Freud's analysis of Little Hans (Freud, 1909). Hans' presenting symptom was his fear of going out in the street because he might be bitten by a horse. Freud's analysis revealed that the phobia was based on a conflict between Little Hans' instinctual urges and the demands of his ego. The conflict was an Oedipal one, and involved a strong hostility to his father. This gave rise to fears of punishment in the form of castration fears, which he then transformed into a phobic anxiety of being bitten by a horse. Thus the internal danger was changed into an external danger, and the fear of the father was displaced onto a more remote substitute. It seems easier to avoid biting horses than castrating fathers. The death wishes against the father and the castration fears as a reprisal for such violent wishes were repressed in view of the fact that Hans' conscious feelings toward his father were also strong and loving and positive.

The choice of the horse as the substitute object was not at all accidental. Hans had previously shown a considerable interest in horses. He observed that they had large "widdlers," that is, penises. The possession of a large widdler established the association with his father. Little Hans' sexual feelings toward his mother were not immediately manifested in the phobic symptom, but nonetheless provided in part the motivation of his fear of punishment and castration from the father.

The unconscious fear of castration was a direct result of his romantic attachment to his mother, but this does not explain the severity of the phobia of attack and mutilation. As Rochlin (1973) has astutely observed, Hans began as an aggressor and ended as a victim—and herein lies the key to the understanding of the phobia.

In his nightmare, Hans saw himself as a helpless victim. Huge animals frightened him because he expected them to turn on him and do him violence. This was associated with his parents, as we have seen, particularly with his father. All of this expresses Hans' apprehensiveness over his own smallness and weakness, since in any comparison with such big animals as his parents or even horses he must have come out very much the loser.

Hans was able nonetheless to take measures to counter these terrifying anxieties. In his play he would imagine that he was a horse, and would bite his father and try to threaten him. He would also play the horsemaster, beating the horses and showing them, as well as himself, that he had nothing to fear from them. Such aggressive wishes, particularly when they take the form of wishes to harm or attack or injure important figures, become severely threatening. The aggressive "wish-turned-threat" expresses itself in phobic reactions in which the patient sees himself as a helpless victim of potential attack. The phobia is in fact an expression of the dread of carrying out the destructive wishes. It also serves to spare and preserve the object of attack. In both his daytime phobias and his nighttime nightmares, Hans became the victim; the aggression he felt toward those whom he loved became turned against himself. The defensive process was one of victimizing himself and thus effectively inhibiting any expression of aggression toward the loved object. The aggressive impulses, however, found more direct expression in his play. The compensation for his Oedipal disappointment was countered by his playing out his father's aggressive role, just as his anxieties based on a sense of his own smallness and vulnerability were countered by his playing out the role of the aggressor. It is only when the Oedipal ambition is relinquished along with its attendant rivalry, that the threat diminishes and need for the phobic defenses can be resolved.

Phobias and the Paranoid Process

Our purpose at this juncture is to gain some insight into the relationship between phobic and paranoid manifestations both in terms of the relationship of phobic anxieties to the paranoid process and in genetic terms of the relationship between phobic mechanisms and paranoid mechanisms. The relevant question in this context is whether phobic symptoms are simply the result of externalization or whether they involve projective mechanisms. In the usage we are following in this study, projection is regarded as the correlate of introjection, so that an appeal to projective mechanisms depends in part on our ability to show that the content of the projection, which is displaced to the external world, is based on an introjected content from the inner world. Thus the basic issue in the consideration of phobias is whether the projected fears and their content can be shown to be related to internal introjects.

Externalization, on the other hand, has a broader significance in that it deals with the displacement to the outside world of any intrapsychic aspects or components. Thus the childhood phobias can be regarded in general as reflecting the influence of externalization, since it is clear that what is defended against and displaced onto the external world is the child's aggressive and destructive impulses, whether they can be specified as oral or anal or not. The question of projection, then, would seem to hinge on the further organization and elaboration of such destructive impulses in relation to introjective content derived from specific object relations.

It is of interest in this regard that Melanie Klein, in discussing the origins of early childhood phobias (1932), relates the anxiety connected with such phobias to the early stages of superego formation. She views the phobic elements as consisting of fears of violent objects which are both external and introjected. Such objects are seen as devouring, cutting, castrating, etc., reflecting both oral and anal-sadistic elements. She observes that the difficulties of small children in eating are closely connected with early anxiety situations and reflect paranoid origins. Food is symbolically related with the father's penis or the mother's breast and is responded to with love, hatred, or fear, as are these part objects. Thus food gives rise to a multitude of fears of being poisoned or internally destroyed, which relates to the internalized objects or excrements in these early anxiety situations. She describes animal phobias in the following terms:

> Infantile animal phobias are an expression of early anxiety of this kind. They are based on the ejection of the terrifying super-ego which is characteristic of the earlier anal stage, and thus represent a process, made up of several moves, whereby the child modifies its fear of its terrifying super-ego and id. The first move is to thrust out those two institutions into the external world and assimilate the super-ego to the real object. The second move is familiar to us as the displacement onto an animal of the fear felt of the real father (1932, p. 220).

Thus she established a connection between superego, object-relationship, and animal phobias.

Klein places at the heart of the phobic mechanism the interaction of projection and introjection. It is thus a more complex phenomenon than the mere defensive substitution of one external danger for another, of a mere distortion of the fear of castration by the father into a fear of being bitten by a horse or a wolf. The castration fear is related to the more basic fear of superego aggression. For Little Hans, the castration fears were mixed with positive affection and love for his parents, and his environment was generally positive. His oral and anal sadism was not severe enough to prevent his reaching a normal phallic stage, and apparently his phobia was quickly dissipated by a relatively short and superficial analytic intervention. The aggression in the case of the Wolf-Man, by way of contrast, seems to be more primitive and destructive, and reflects the still active influence of the oral sadistic instincts. It gives rise to fears of a dangerous, devouring beast which he equates with his father's penis. As Klein comments, "The Wolf-Man did not overcome this early anxiety. His fear of the wolf, which stood for his fear of his father, showed that he had retained the image of his father as a devouring wolf in subsequent years. For, as we know, he rediscovered this wolf in his later father-images, and his whole development was governed by that overwhelming fear" (1932, p. 223).

The operation of such excessively strong and destructive sadism, which had not been successfully modified and which had been manifested in excessive anxiety in the early stages of life, results often in the production of severe obsessional and paranoid traits. This view would seem to gain some support from the development in later life of the Wolf-Man's paranoia (Gardner, 1971). Thus Klein's discussion indicates the possibility of an interconnection between such early phobic symptoms of childhood and the later emergence of paranoid manifestations. As I have already made clear in discussing Klein's contributions, I am not at all convinced that her explanation of the origins of such phobias has general validity. Even though such complex animal phobias can be identified in children in the second and third years of life, it is not clear that we are dealing with specifically superego introjects or projections, but it seems safer to assume that we are dealing with a more primitive level of the interplay of introjection and projection, which has more to do with the overall context of intrapsychic development.

School Phobias

Another important area of childhood phobias is the so-called school type. In her excellent review of school phobias, Melitta Sperling (1967) indicates that such phobias lie midway between obsessive-compulsive and hysterical neurosis, and that they involve mechanisms closer to the obsessive, namely, displacement, isolation, and projection. Separation anxiety in these cases is a central issue. Acute school phobias are often related to traumatic events which usually represent a danger to the child's ability to control reality, particularly a loss of control over a given situation or a particular object, especially the mother. The fear of the illness or death of the parent represents an acute separation threat. This is usually related to fixations at an anal-sadistic level and reflects itself in the ambivalent object-relationship and persistence of narcissistic fixations and magical thinking by which the child equates unconscious death wishes with reality.

These traumatic phobias are usually related to precipitating events which unconsciously signify the traumatic loss. The induced school phobia, however, usually manifests itself in the absence of such a precipitating event, and reflects instead a less dramatic, but more insidious, traumatization of the child on account of a more pathological parent-child relationship. Such children usually show a history of phobic behavior prior to coming to school. Thus the school phobias seem to form a complex set of reactions in which the actual phobic symptomatology forms a sort of common pathway for the expression of a variety of mechanisms. The role of separation anxiety must be taken into account, since it is a prominent feature of such phobias, and in any number of early animal phobias, as for example with Bornstein's two-and-a-half-year-old child, where the threat may involve the loss of a significant object. We will have occasion to return to the role of separation anxiety and its relationship to the paranoid process later on.

"Elementary Neurosis"

In any case, it seems reasonable to presume that such phobic states in early childhood are related to the intolerable ambivalence in early object-relationships. There seems to be good reason to understand the mechanisms of such early animal phobias as involving an interplay of introjection and projection. Thus the image of the feared father is introjected, and once within the inner world becomes the focus for inner destructive and sadistic tendencies. It is this introjective content that is then reprojected as a dangerous and threatening animal. Thus the child can be seen to be employing projective and basically paranoid mechanisms in the service of defense and in the production of a childhood neurotic state.

We are well advised to remind ourselves of Freud's thoughts about this matter. In discussing the phobia of Little Hans, he commented:

> When, however, an adult neurotic patient comes to us for psycho-analytic treatment (and let us assume that his illness has only become manifest after he has reached maturity), we find regularly that his neurosis has as its point of departure an infantile anxiety such as we have been discussing, and is in fact a continuation of it; so that, as it were, a continuous and undisturbed thread of psychical activity, taking its start from the conflicts of his childhood, has been spun through his life (1909, p. 143).

To this we can add a quotation from the minutes of the Vienna Psychoanalytic Society for November 17, 1909, from the same year in which the study of Little Hans was published. This is quoted by Jones (1955):

> We expect it would turn out that the severe neuroses all have their prototypes in childhood life, so that we should find the kernels of the later neurosis in the disturbances of development in childhood .... It is a question whether everybody has not passed through a kind of elementary neurosis in childhood years, and whether the inter-relationship be not still closer than we imagine, so that not only the elements but the very prototype itself originates in childhood. The later neurosis may well be only a magnification of a product, which one can only call a neurosis, of the later or middle years of childhood. In that event we should have a clear view of the source of neurosis and should have to interpolate the "elementary neurosis" as an intermediate stage between the nuclear complex (i.e., the oedipus complex) and the subsequent severe neurosis (pp. 443-444).

NIGHTMARES

We have had occasion in discussing the above cases, to note that in nearly all of these patients, there has been a pattern of recurring childhood nightmares, as well as frequent adult nightmares. We can now inquire into the significance of this recurring phenomenon in the life experience of our patients, and explore its potential relationship to the paranoid pathology. The study of dreams, beginning with Freud's ingenious explorations, has shown that unconscious wishes of the dreaming subject may be embodied in the dream content in representations of other persons.

Dream Projection

Thus the dreamer's own wishes, particularly those that are unacceptable to him in his waking experience, are expressed by means of projection onto these other dream figures, which are separated from the self. The dream figure becomes a displaced object for the projected wishes of the dreamer's self, an inner self based on and constructed in terms of specific prototype for the functioning of projective mechanisms in relationship to objects, whether the latter be figments of the dream life or real objects in the patient's waking experience.

The whole subject of nightmares has a special fascination in this regard. It is an area of relatively common experience in which many of the mechanisms and dynamics which we have been discussing in this study come into vivid and dramatic play. Our purpose at this juncture is to examine the phenomenon of the nightmare and to relate it to the clinical experience we have been investigating. The basic argument that we are advancing here is that the nightmare is a prototypical expression of the paranoid process, which employs the same basic mechanisms, deals with the same basic conflicts and fears, serves the same basic functions and psychic intentions. It is an expression of the common lot of mankind which reaches into the realms of pathology, but also is an expression of basic and important human processes which mobilize man's creative capacities in the service of preserving and establishing his own identity and his relatedness to the human context. John Mack, in his recent excellent study of nightmares, writes:

> Of the experiences that terrify mankind and invite our humility, nightmares are perhaps the most widespread and characteristic, for human beings are the only creatures so fully aware of the precariousness of their existence. It is precisely this sense of vulnerability that is the most essential feature of these dreams. The nightmare is the prototype of man's terror. The common feature of helplessness in confrontation with forces that threaten to be overwhelming has led to the application of the word *nightmare* to any psychological horror or external catastrophe over which the persons involved have little or no control and which makes them feel gravely imperiled. No group of human beings seems to escape at least the sporadic occurrence of these terrifying dreams. Very small children and adults of all ages, emotionally ill and relatively healthy persons, primitive peoples as well as members of the most highly civilized societies—all may have nightmares. Any theory which attempts to offer a general explanation of this type of dream must take into account this universality (1970, p. vii).

As Mack notes, the understanding of the nightmare must embrace a number of significant points. It must account for the fact that nightmares occur at all ages, even in children of only about a year. It must explain the fact of nightmares in emotionally disturbed psychotic patients as well as relatively normal and healthy people. It must explain the occurrence of nightmares in all cultures, even primitive cultures. And it must explain the fundamental emotional facts of the nightmare—the feelings of helplessness and powerlessness, the severe and threatening danger, the overwhelming anxiety, and the imminent threat within the dream of violence and destructiveness. The suggestion that we are advancing here is that these many facets of the nightmare experience can be encompassed by understanding the nightmare phenomenon as an expression of the paranoid process.

Helplessness

We have been confronted at many points in the present study with the sense of vulnerability and helplessness and powerlessness that is so characteristic of all of these patients. The experience of vulnerability seems also to be a central one in the nightmare. There is a nameless terror, a sense of helplessness, persecution by monstrous and uncontrollable threatening forces, violence, and even a lapping over of such fearful experiences into waking life that characterizes the nightmare, whether it is the night terror of a child or the terrifying dream of the adult. It provides this community of experience within the nightmare, the experience of helplessness and powerlessness, convincing proof that the archaic fears and conflicts of early childhood persist throughout the course of life.

They express themselves in vivid and dramatic form in the nightmare experience. The child is confronted with his own weakness and vulnerability. He is confronted with the fear that loved ones can really disappear and die. It is no wonder that the child experiences terror of the nightmare, particularly when his wishes toward the important objects, upon whom he depends and whom he loves, have been overloaded with aggressive and destructive tendencies. The earliest helplessness in human experience—a feeling that seems to underlie the anxiety of the nightmare at whatever age—is that of the helplessness of the small child who feels powerless to keep the mothering person, upon whom he depends so intently, with him and to prevent her from leaving him. It is this feeling of powerlessness and the anxiety that accompanies it which are renewed every time the child faces a new task, until he attains the skills and the sense of mastery and control which enables him to both tolerate and diminish the anxiety. Mack comments:

> Nightmares are often a sensitive indicator of the presence of anxiety and may reflect this feeling of helplessness that occurs when major new tasks are undertaken before the motor skills, cognitive capacities, defenses, or other ego functions necessary for such mastery have developed. The content of the dreams may be of the usual "raw-head-and-bloody-bones" variety, but the ego factor of powerlessness, which makes the dreamer feel subject to danger and attack, may be of greater importance than the instinctual elements that are suggested by the dreamer's content (1970, p. 214).

Levels of Anxiety

We can remind ourselves at this point of Little Hans' anxiety dream which preceded the outbreak of his phobic state by just a few days. He had dreamt that his mother had gone away, and Freud interprets this as a punishment dream expressing Hans' fear of retaliation for his forbidden Oedipal wishes. But the Oedipal fear clearly expresses a more primitive anxiety, namely, the loss of the mother. We can also recall that the Wolf-Man's famous dream of the wolves in the walnut tree was a fairly typical nightmare for the four-year-old child. While Freud again appealed to castration fears, he also pointed to the anal-homosexual preoccupations it expressed, as well as the primitive oral-sadistic fears of being eaten or bitten. The Wolf-Man's experience in dreaming seems to have been the more primitive and the more terrifying.

One of the fascinating questions concerning nightmares is the variation in levels and intensity of the anxiety. Some valuable information has been added by the researches of Charles Fisher and his co-workers (Fisher, 1965). Fisher has distinguished on a number of grounds severe anxiety dreams, which occur during the REM phase of the sleep cycle, from nightmares, which are found to occur in the non-REM phase of the sleep cycle. The

The Paranoid Process

severe anxiety dream contains threats of violence which are more elaborate and often disguised. The anxiety experienced is intense, but the subjects are relatively lucid and dream activity can generally be recalled (Broughton, 1968).

The nightmare occurring in a non-REM phase, however, is usually accompanied with considerable motility, even to the point of violent body movement. The subject may sit up or stand up and move about and often is found screaming. The content is violent and persecutory, usually with intense sadistic oral-aggressive and destructive features. The anxiety is severe to the point of panic, and the subject is disoriented, confused and often hallucinating immediately after arousal. Frequently, there is a general amnesia for the whole nightmare experience. Similarly, differences have been described between the nightmare attacks of children and night terror attacks of pavor nocturnus (Mack, 1970).

Thus there are identifiable neurophysiological states which may parallel the degrees of experienced anxiety and terror in the nightmare. Obviously a theory of the nightmare must also take into account this diversity of patterns of neurophysiological activation, which distinguish anxiety dreams from the more disruptive and terrifying nightmare experience. We can note in this connection that there seems to be a qualitative difference in the dream experience of our patients. The anxiety dreams experienced by Jimmy J., for example, certainly have a persecutory aspect, but the organization is more complex: there is usually an evolved plot element in the dream sequence, and the attack takes a modified and less violent form of being chased by police or even a fear of being attacked. Nowhere in his dream content was there a direct violent and destructive attack—at most, there was only the apprehension over the possibility of attack. However, in the dreams reported by Bob B. or Fred F., there was a marked destructive and murderous aspect to the persecutory content. These latter patients were certainly much less healthy, and the quality of their nightmare experience was much more primitive and much more in the line of the typical nightmare experience, with an extreme degree of panic and terror, a sense of helplessness and vulnerability, often as a sense of paralysis, and inability to breath or move, which the patients found to be quite terrifying.

The primitive quality of the fears expressed in the nightmare has been frequently noted. In the nightmares of children, the anxieties and conflicts expressed in the content of the nightmares were related to anxieties relating to earlier levels of development which were elicited by the regressive conditions of sleep. Under the sleep conditions, various ego functions undergo regression with a resulting impairment of reality testing and a failure of defensive configurations. There is a return to more concrete and symbolic forms of thoughts.

Under the force of this regression and the relative helplessness that is associated with it, earlier conflicts and anxieties are aroused, typically the fears of devouring and being devoured, or even a primitive terror concerning the loss of the mother or a fear of abandonment and loss of love. This regressive content is frequently quite oral in character. The quality of children's nightmares is frequently highly aggressive, with a devouring oral element. The child fears being eaten up or devoured by huge monsters or machines. Or the dream content will express impulses of oral-sadism or aggression by biting or devouring someone else. Often, even in older children, these same regressive oral conflicts over devouring and being devoured are reactivated (Mack, 1965).

Parental Anxiety

One of the important aspects of the whole phenomenon of nightmares in children is the manner in which parental anxieties are communicated to children and are manifested in the content of nightmares. Nagera (1966) has pointed to the influence of maternal conflicts and fears in the production of the child's sleeping difficulties. There is much yet to be understood about this aspect of the involvement of parental fears, but an important part of it seems to be the unconscious reinforcement of the validity of the child's fears by the parents' incapacity to deal with the same source of fear in their own experience (Mack, 1970).

This is a particularly important aspect of the developmental experience in paranoid families. There the reinforcement of the child's fears by the parent is a much more widespread response, and we will have occasion to look at it more closely in regard to its developmental influence. But it is nonetheless fascinating to discover that the paranoid fears and anxieties of the child are in fact reflected in the inner concerns and fantasy life of the parent. Thus, for example, the paranoid anxieties of Gloria G., that she would be murderously attacked on the streets, was transparently a reflection of her father's view that the world was filled with "creeps and weirdos" who attacked, murdered, and raped innocent victims on the streets. It is little wonder, then, that Gloria's dreams were filled with episodes of attack, murder, death, and violence. Nor is it any wonder that her waking experience carried within it the same fears and anxious terrors.

Part of the interaction with the parents which tends to undermine the child's position and contribute to the reinforcement of fears is the attack upon the child's self-esteem. Gloria was always in a position of having to protect herself from unwarranted hostility, devaluing criticism, and a sense of rejection from her parents. She saw herself as a victim of the demands and failures of those around her. She was an unloved and unwanted child. The resentment and angry hurt associated with this narcissistic injury and deprivation found expression in her recurrent and violent nightmares. In all of these dreams she was the object of injury and attack, a victim who was threatened by death and physical harm. She was never the aggressor, but it was always others who attacked and violated her.

Introjects in Nightmares

The projective content of the nightmare can be seen to be derived from the introjects which are the product of various levels of the patient's experience. Under the regressive pull of the sleep state, it is the threatening figures and the angry voices from the past, related to introjects acquired in the earliest years of childhood, that come alive in the dream and turn upon the dreamer to attack him—often decades later, when the child has become an adult. For the child, of course, it would seem that the availability of loved objects during the daytime serves as a buffer for these regressive anxieties. But sleep inevitably involves a separation from parents or other loved objects. Frequently enough, it is the threat of abandonment or the separation from loved objects that triggers the anxiety which results in the production of nightmares in which the subject feels abandoned and unprotected. Frequently enough the nightmare results in a reestablishing of contact with these important figures, as for example when the child is taken into the parents' bedroom or even into the parents' bed to be quieted and comforted. Mack even suggests that this secondary gain is not only a help in enabling the child to master the dream anxiety, but that it also has the secondary gain of restoring contact with the loved object.

The content of the nightmare experience itself would seem to be reflective of the level of regression to which the dream is drawn. The dream objects reflect the influence of the developmental period in which the introjection took place. Generally, the introjects prior to the age of two are represented as threatening aspects of other persons or as menacing machines or animals. From two to five it is simple monsters and animals that predominate, while more sophisticated monsters, machines, and human figures are found in the nightmares of older children and even adults. A given nightmare, however, can resurrect dream images which relate to introjects from any or all of these levels of development. Parents are often represented not as they are currently seen by the individual, but rather as they are perceived in the pregenital period in terms of highly ambivalent attitudes which are considerably overloaded with primitive oral and anal aggressiveness. Thus the dream regression reflects the intense projection of the child's own destructive impulses onto the parental images.

We can suggest that the persistence of these introjective contents, so highly colored with infantile ambivalences, is one of the clues to the primitive organization of the inner world of our own patients. It is the relative fixation of these highly ambivalent introjective contents, which fail somehow to be modified or metabolized by later internalizations that forms the basis for the paranoid distortion. Such paranoid elements, indeed, may also emerge under the regressive conditions of the dream, particularly when the adult waking experience is accompanied by particular stresses or anxieties. Thus Mack notes:

> Regression in nightmares may also affect portions of the personality that have seemed to function independently from the original objects. Personality structures that were formed from the internalization of object representations that have been built into apparently stable ego identifications temporarily undergo regressive transformations. Regression in this situation results in a kind of segregation or re-segregation, in which structures such as the superego, which have come to function automatically within the personality, seem to become fragmented. The early object representations, especially hostile ones, then confront other portions of the ego in the dream in their original elemental form as an angry voice, noise, or other threatening or accusatory image (1970, p. 66).

Aggression in Nightmares

One of the primary elements in the nightmare is projection of intense hostility or destructiveness into the persecuting objects. Actually, hostility or hatred of loved objects is one of the most intensely threatening things to the human child. It poses for him the threat of object loss, the loss of love, abandonment, or even destructive retaliation. The earliest nightmares in childhood seem to be related to the child's primitive struggles with the aggression arising within himself or as it is perceived coming from the world around him. Certainly after the differentiation of self and object has been achieved—probably in the second year—aggressive behavior becomes a significant aspect of the developing relationships.

This is particularly true where childish needs have been denied. Such denials, whether from advertence or parental anxieties or parental narcissism, is equivalent to a demeaning or a devaluing of the child. The aggressive wishes that are mobilized in the interest of preserving and restoring self-esteem cannot be allowed expression. The intensity of the rage, the violent fantasies and nightmares which such children experience, serves neither to promote narcissistic recovery nor to enhance the diminished self-esteem. As criticism for aggressive impulses from one's self increases, the expectation of such devaluation and criticism from others also enlarges. As Rochlin has commented (1973), self-esteem is in greater jeopardy as the need for it intensifies.

The interplay of introjective and projective mechanisms comes more explicitly into play, so that the interplay of these elements is often seen in the content of nightmares and anxiety dreams. This is related to the process of identification with the aggressor as we have previously observed. In fact, the mastery of such intense and destructive aggression is one of the major developmental tasks of the small child. In the conflicts between aggression and loss of the loved and needed objects or abandonment, the child must mobilize primitive defenses, particularly displacement, projection, denial, and various forms of introjection. Thus these mechanisms can also come to serve important developmental functions.

For the child, in the internal drama of the dream, the inner struggles over aggression and its consequences take on a greatly intensified and magnified significance. It is remarkable in these dream experiences of small children that they are almost always portrayed as the victims of malicious and destructive attacks, and almost never the aggressor. This would seem to reflect the fact that the aggressive feelings are totally unacceptable and intolerable, particularly in view of the threat that such feelings pose to loved objects. Thus, if murderous and destructive wishes and impulses are directed toward the dreamer as the victim, it seems likely that such a projective defense serves to protect himself from an even more threatening experience, namely, assuming responsibility for the murderous impulses toward important and loved objects upon whom the child is physically and emotionally dependent.

The striking resignation of aggression and reassignment of it to external objects, which takes place in the nightmare experience, effectively denies and dissociates the dreamer from hostile wishes and impulses particularly when directed against loved objects. This process takes place very early in the child's experience. When the child's wishes for gratification or affection are not met, he experiences this as a loss of affection with a concomitant diminution of his own sense of value. Aggression rushes in to redeem the loss of self-esteem, and the hostility generated expresses itself in anxiety.

Consequently, the child carries into his dreaming experience the same mechanism for dealing with aggression and injured narcissism that he evolves in his waking experience. The hostility toward others is feared from them by reason of projection, so that aggression is transformed into self-destructiveness. In the nightmare experience the dreamer is threatened, humiliated, victimized, or killed. His experience is that of helplessness and weakness. He is unable to offer resistance or to struggle effectively. All activity, power, aggressive potentiality, and intention are given over to the threatening figure. This pattern of victimization is characteristic not only of childhood nightmares, but is one we have become familiar with in the experience of our patients. The nightmare experience, then, seems to be a unique expression of the paranoid process, one in which the paranoid mechanisms involve and capture the dreaming process so that the motifs of vulnerability, narcissistic injury, denied destructiveness, and victimization are played out on the dream stage.

Nightmares and Paranoia

A relevant question in regard to the problem of nightmares is whether there is any intrinsic relationship between the nightmare experience as such and the development of paranoid mechanisms (Mack, 1969). In his meta-psychological supplement to the theory of dreams, Freud (1917) commented on the resemblance of projection in dreams to paranoid projection. Certainly a case in point is the Wolf-Man, whose childhood nightmare we have discussed and who later developed a paranoid psychosis. Six years after he had completed his analysis with Freud, the Wolf-Man resumed treatment because of a paranoid psychosis with acute delusions of persecution (Brunswick, 1928; Gardner, 1971). Both the content and structure of his psychosis were related to the childhood nightmare. The psychosis seemed to have resulted from an unresolved homosexual transference to Freud, so that similar conflicts to those that were expressed in childhood dream permeated his awareness and diminished his capacity to test reality. The nightmare may well have been a form of infantile psychosis.

One is indeed struck by the phenomenological similarity between nightmares and acute psychotic states. The terror is striking. The individual feels himself to be weak, helpless, and totally vulnerable to the attack of powerful external forces, which strive to destroy or annihiliate him. Characteristically, the danger in the nightmare reflects more immediately the world of childhood fears and dangers—biting animals, snakes, monsters, spiders, or creatures of the child's world of fantasy or storybook or even television characters. Persecuting figures in a paranoid psychosis, however, are more likely to be either the subject's personal enemies or elements drawn from the patient's world of experience.

In both states, the dreamer or the psychotic feels helpless and vulnerable to the violent attack that he feels is directed against him. The nightmare victim loses his grasp on reality not only in the dream but also sometimes even for a short period afterward. The reality testing of the psychotic also fails him during the period of his acute decompensation. The underlying conflicts and particularly the use of projective mechanisms are quite similar in both states.

It is striking, in this regard, that some patients find it difficult to draw the line between the persecutory and threatening experiences of the nightmares and their experiences in the waking state. Thus, little Fred F. was terrified by the rabid foxes of his nightmares, but also developed a severe phobic state in which he fantasied rabid foxes under his bed and prowling the woods where he played, ready to pounce on him and to bite him. Similarly Gloria G. lived in a dream world, in which she was constantly under attack from malicious forces and murderous individuals who attack and kill her. But her living and waking world was filled with the same fears and threats. It was as if the dream and reality for her were one.

The vital difference, however, between the nightmare and a psychotic state is that one can awaken from the nightmare and leave its terrors in the land of dreams, but for the decompensated psychotic the nightmare becomes a dream from which he does not awaken. Discussing this striking similarity, Mack writes as follows:

> For the nightmare victim and the psychosis-prone individual, the immediate precipitating factors have re-evoked painful memories of abandonment by infantile love objects and conflicts over annihilation, oral incorporation, and destructiveness. Both the nightmare and the acute psychosis reflect the ego's efforts to deal with these early anxieties and conflicts through the construction of a primitive symbolic structure whose content is derived from the interweaving of the residues of day time experience and regressively revived early memories. This regressive re-evoking of fantasies of violent attack is of particular importance in the dramatic intensification of anxiety that occurs in both nightmares and acute psychosis (1970, p. 173).

Thus the nightmares and night terrors of childhood may serve as precursors of later paranoid manifestations. One of the striking findings in the case material that we have presented is that persistent early nightmares were a predominant feature of their childhood histories. The themes and content are frequently the same: conflicts over passivity, over helplessness and vulnerability, conflicts over intense ambivalence and the yearning for love accompanied by a terror of rejection and repulsion, and the tendency to resort to projective defenses. The conflicts are rooted in intense, dependent oral longings and wishes for fusion with the parent, along with destructive hatred that is projected onto the menacing persecutor. In the dream the madness is reversible, and it can be escaped by a flight into consciousness.

And, in addition, an important aspect of the whole process—one which Mack has taken particular note of—is the manner in which the parents respond to the nightmare experience. In our case histories, and particularly in the family studies, there is apparent an inability on the part of the parents to deal with the child's anxieties in a comforting, reassuring, supportive and loving manner. It is too often in these cases as though the inner world of the parent himself were peopled with threatening objects and dangerous eventualities. What the parent communicates to these troubled children is a sense of his own insecurity and threatenedness and anxiety. What the child internalizes is the threatening and threatened aspects of the parents' inner world, around which these anxieties cluster and feed. One can at least speculate in this context that the parent's failure to assist the child to learn to discriminate between the dream and reality, between the world of fantasy and the world of real things that surrounds him, contributes significantly to the impairment in reality testing that is so frequently seen in such patients.

Nightmares and the Paranoid Process

In the light of these observations we can reach a conclusion that has some relevance for our considerations of the paranoid process. The experience of nightmares is one which is a quite common—if not general—human experience. It occurs in all cultures, at all ages, and is particularly a marked experience of childhood. Obviously the nightmare experience varies considerably in intensity and frequency. Not all children suffer from the forms of intense and persistent nightmares that we have identified in our patients. However, if the nightmare experience bears a consistent relationship to paranoid manifestations—as it does on so many of the parameters we have suggested—then it seems reasonable that we regard it as a manifestation of the operation of paranoid mechanisms which are quite general in the population, and that these same mechanisms operate with varying degrees of intensity and disruptiveness.

What we are led to conclude, then, is not that paranoid mechanisms are restricted to the relatively severe instances of the operation of these mechanisms, but that they are in fact a widespread and common experience in human kind. The difference between the Wolf-Men of this world—such as the patients we have been investigating here—and the normal run of men is precisely that the basic conflicts are deeper, more strongly and deeply embedded in ambivalent conflicts, and reflect more primitive levels of psychic organization and aggressive intensity. If we join the evidence based on nightmares with the evidence derived from childhood phobias, we are faced with the fact that such fears of vulnerability and conflicts over aggression and the use of projective defenses are indeed widespread and quite general.

Our conclusion, then, is that these paranoid manifestations reflect the operation of paranoid processes at large, as a fundamental and unavoidable dimension of human experience, and that they eventuate in psychotic processes or paranoid syndromes only under certain conditions of development and stress, which intensify the basic conflicts and undermine the adaptive and interpretive capacities of the ego. It remains that we try to integrate this basic perception into our more general understanding of the paranoid process and the various aspects of its functioning.

CHAPTER 20

Paranoid Construction

Functions

In the theoretical appraisal of the paranoid process, which we are attempting here, the notion of paranoid construction occupies a central position. It is intended to describe the central cognitive organization which both characterizes and derives from the paranoid process. However, it is also that aspect of the paranoid process which, perhaps more than any other, establishes its links and lines of continuity with other realms of human experience.

In our previous description of paranoid construction, I described it as a cognitive process, by which incoming impressions are organized into a pattern of meaning which is primarily validated by reference to subjective needs rather than objective evidence or consensual agreement. I would specify in addition that another important parameter of the paranoid construction is that it involves an intrinsic reference to the individual's self-system.

The paranoid construction, then, serves the very important function of providing a context of meaningful interaction and experience which provides a framework for the meaningful definition of self, as well as a setting in which the self is enabled to achieve a sense of congruence and belonging. Seeing the paranoid construction in this light makes it obvious, in addition, that the paranoid construction serves important functions relevant to the maintenance of self-esteem. Our objective at this point in our discussion is to establish the links of the paranoid construction to other basic aspects of human cognition, as well as to specify its role in the functioning of human personality.

Manifestations

If we look at the experience of the patients whom we have described, we can begin to appreciate the extent to which the paranoid construction forms a central aspect of their pathology. For all of them it forms a view of the world and of themselves which gives a specific quality to their experience. The manifestations of it vary, as might be expected. For Bob, the paranoid construction expressed itself most vividly in his acute delusional system. But that certainly seemed to have been an acute and exacerbated and highly defensively organized view of his world and his place in it. The delusional quality of this construction, as well as its defensive purposes, are not difficult to see. This is particularly true since almost every point in Bob's delusional system answered to an underlying need or defect that he felt in himself. Moreover the interpretive and constructional aspect of this cognitive organization is quite apparent. The grandiose delusional notion of belonging to an undying and powerful race of gods has obvious compensatory and restitutional components.

However, more subtle, as well as more chronic and difficult to assess, is the paranoid construction which characterized most of his premorbid experience and adjustment. In this aspect he saw himself as weak, defective, impotent, and as a victim of forces and persons which surrounded him and constantly took advantage of and in various ways diminished him. As we have already seen, this particular organization of his experience answered to several important influences generated within his family life and particularly related to the patterns of internalization which we have described. What I wish to emphasize at this point is that this aspect of Bob's experience formed a cognitive synthesis in which these various elements were combined to provide an interpretive schema, within which he was able to define his own sense of self, as well as to elaborate a schema by which he was able to interpret the world around him and its relevance and impact upon himself.

In other patients as well, the paranoid construction manifests itself in characteristic ways. For Ann, the paranoid construction, in its most flamboyant and pathological form, expressed itself as an elaborate and highly developed Communist plot—worldwide in its implications and extension—which was directed toward her humiliation and destruction. For Ann, this particular construction, delusional as it obviously was, expressed only an intensified and elaborated form of the underlying construction which permeated her whole life's experience, namely, her sense of worthlessness and humiliation and victimization, particularly at the hands of her pathogenic mother.

For Jim, who was able to function at a much higher level of personality organization and whose pathology was solidly stabilized at much higher neurotic levels, the perception of himself as weak, defective, special, inadequate, doomed forever to be a failure in life, seen in its cognitive perspective, forms an elaborate representation of himself and his relationship to the world, and conversely of the world and its relationship to himself, which served to stabilize his own fragile sense of self and to preserve a meaningful context of interaction with that world. The meaningfulness of this interaction was determined at many levels since it provided a persistent interpretive framework in which he could relate himself to other individuals around him and to other forces in his experience, but also functioned at a highly unconscious level to preserve a meaningful context of infantile relationships by which he defined and sustained his relationship with his parents.

Similarly, if we look at the experience of Karen, it seems quite clear that her view of herself as susceptible and vulnerable was part of an elaborate cognitive schema which allowed her to relate to the world of her experience. The pattern which that construction assumed was highly overdetermined by multiple influences, particularly those derived from her relationships with her primary objects. But the construction worked in such a way that it permitted her to not only define her relationship to the world, but to preserve within that definition aspects of the definition of herself that had emerged in the context of her infantile relationships with parental figures.

It should be apparent that what we are describing in these patients is not something that clinicians, who deal with psychopathology on a day to day basis, have not been quite familiar with. What I am emphasizing here is the cognitive and constructional aspects of these clinical phenomena. What I have described in Jim or Karen, for example, is content which is quite familiar in our understanding of the neuroses, but I am describing it here in terms of the paranoid construction for particular purposes of this analysis. The same material can be looked at in terms of fantasy formation, or in terms of Oedipal displacements, or in a variety of other ways. The point here, however, is that the patient derives an interpretive construction, which is based primarily on internal needs and pressures and which denies or selectively distorts available evidences in reality to support the internal formulation. My purpose in describing this process in these terms is to emphasize its continuity not only with severe forms of pathological distortion, but also with relatively normal and healthy cognitive processes which characterize every human being.

Cognitive Reconstruction

In fact it should be noted that the essential elements in the description of paranoid construction were pointed to and emphasized by Freud in his thinking about paranoia. In *Totem and Taboo*, for example, he related the constructional aspects of not only paranoia but several neurotic syndromes to the work of secondary revision in dreams. He wrote:

> The secondary revision of the product of the dream-work is an admirable example of the nature and pretentions of a system. There is an intellectual function in us that demands unity, connection and intelligibility from any material, whether of perception or thought, that comes within its grasp; and if, as a result of special circumstances, it is unable to establish a true connection, it does not hesitate to fabricate a false one. Systems constructed in this way are known to us not only from dreams, but also from phobias, from obsessive thinking and from delusions. The construction of systems is seen most strikingly in delusional disorders (in paranoia), where it dominates the symptomatic picture; but its occurrence in other forms of neuro-psychosis must not be overlooked (1913b, p. 95).

Nor was Freud unaware of the restitutional and motivational aspects of this reconstruction. In commenting on Schreber's delusional system, Freud makes the point that the delusional formation is precisely a process of reconstruction. Freud quotes a passage from Faust having to do with the destruction of the world, and then he adds—

> and the paranoic builds it again, not more splendid, it is true, but at least so that he can once more live in it. He builds it up by the work of his delusions. *The delusional formation, which we take to be the pathological product, is in reality an attempt at recovery, a process of reconstruction.* Such a reconstruction after the catastrophe is successful to a greater or lesser extent, but never wholly so. In Schreber's words, there has been a "profound internal change" in the world. But the human subject has recaptured a relation, and often a very intense one, to the people and things in the world. Even though the relation is a hostile one now, where formerly it was hopefully affectionate (1911, pp. 70-71).

It is basically this insight which we are at pains to elaborate here. But it is our intention not simply to understand the function of the paranoid construction in relationship to paranoid symptomatology, but to see it in much broader terms as related to basic processes which are at work in human adaptation and personality development.

Perception and Cognitive Style

We can consider in the first instance the matter of perception. As we have already observed, the paranoid construction is largely a matter of interpretation of input data. We might ask ourselves to what extent this process operates on the perceptual level. We know, first of all, that the paranoid disorder is not specifically a disorder of sensory physiology. In fact the available evidence suggests the opposite—that paranoid sensory functions are as acute, if not more acute, than normal. Silverman's (1964) study of perceptual control of stimulus intensities in matched groups of schizophrenic patients showed that, while nonparanoid schizophrenics showed a marked reduction in kinesthetic figural aftereffects, the paranoid group showed no such pattern. The small degree of perceptual modulation in the interests of defense was minimal, and consequently that the perceptual process was relatively intact.

In this connection also Witkin (1954) has noted that paranoid patients have a predominantly articulated cognitive style, as opposed to a more undifferentiated global cognitive style. When patients who possess a relatively articulated cognitive style which is highly differentiated begin to break down, they tend to show delusions, expansive and euphoric ideas of grandeur, externally directed aggression, intellectualization and a continuing struggle for identity maintenance. Witkin goes on to say:

> . . . in patients in whom paranoid reactions are central in the symptom picture . . . an articulated cognitive style is frequently found. Projection, a characteristic defense of the paranoid, is quite specialized, in comparison to such

generalized tension-reducing techniques as eating and drinking. The paranoid projects his own system of ideas upon the world, and does so in a highly selective fashion—particular people, particular situations may be especially implicated. Such selectivity requires that experience of the world be articulated. In this connection, the paranoid is noted for his detailed, articulated system of ideas. As an attempt at a preservation of the self, projection contrasts with the alcoholic's preferred way of dealing with stress, which in extreme cases results in the dissolution of the self in drink. The use of projection as a device for self-preservation, however bizarre, presupposes a self that has achieved some degree of differentiation (1965, pp. 395-396).

If the paranoid perceptual experience is in fact a sensorially intact and articulated experience, it is nonetheless an experience that is significantly distorted by the interpretation imposed from within. It is at this level that the paranoid construction begins to have effect. It is only in fact in recent years that we have become increasingly aware of the influence of motivational factors on perceptual experience (Klein, 1970). Related to this, of course, is the whole concept of cognitive controls and cognitive styles. In commenting on the study of the clusters of cognitive attitudes, Klein remarks that in the 1959 study, which he and others conducted dealing with cognitive controls, they observed certain clusters of scanning behavior:

> In one of these clusters, scanning appeared with *sharpening, narrow equivalence range in categorizing*, and *constricted response to ambiguity*. A distinctive cognitive style characterized the scanning subjects in the attitudinal context. The dominant impression that this group gave was of intense control and inhibition, with very pronounced intellectualizing tendencies and pervasive experiences of ambivalence, mistrust, and expectations of being hurt. They regarded the world as a source of malevolence and danger and were generally pessimistic about the present and the future. They seemed preoccupied with issues of mastery, and they were intensely self-absorbed (for example, they made an unusually large number of references to body parts on the Rorschach). They felt guilty and dissatisfied with their achievements, and their contacts with objects and people were darkened by aggression. At the same time, they were intensely absorbed in the rejecting and threatening world of people and things (1970, p. 227).

Scanning in this context refers specifically to the broad and intensive deployment of attention to the environment, so that the scanner becomes acutely aware of the background qualities of a stimulus field, and a rather indiscriminate peripheral sensitivity that makes many aspects of the field available to conscious recall. It is this cognitive attitude which seems to be closely aligned with what Shapiro (1965) has referred to as "rigid intentionality." The cognitive description which Klein gives of the particular group of scanning subjects comes very close to a cognitive description of paranoid pathology.

We can conclude, then, that the influence of the paranoid construction may extend beyond the mere question of the interpretation of sensory input data as a matter of content analysis. It seems in addition that one must take into account the influence of the paranoid construction on the formalities of cognitive style and the implementation of cognitive controls.

Motivational Organization

But the phenomenon of motivational impact upon perceptual processes has been a part of our standard lore of psychological thinking for some years. The role of motivations and their influence on perceptual processes and the importance of understanding and studying individual differences in perceptual processes was clearly stated in Gardner Murphy's classic text over a quarter of a century ago (Murphy, 1947). And as Murphy noted so well, the primacy must lie with the internal needs and dispositions. In a famous paragraph, he wrote:

> It must, however, be borne in mind that the *existence* of needs precedes their expression in perception. Needs are present before one opens his eyes, before a voice strikes the ear. Needs determine how the incoming energies are to be put into structured form. Perception, then, is not something that is first registered objectively, then "distorted." Rather, as the need pattern shifts, the stage is set, minute by minute, for quasi-automatic structure-giving tendencies that make the percept suit the need. The need pattern predisposes to one rather than another manner of anchoring the percept around one's needs. *Needs keep ahead of percepts* (pp. 377-378).

In fact, the general principle of the influence of motivational states on cognitive states has been well documented. The influence has pertinence at almost all levels of cognitive organization. The influence of motivational states on perception has been experimentally validated from the early experiments of Postman and Bruner and others on the influence of values and need states on perceptual behavior (Postman and Bruner, 1948; Bruner and Goodman, 1947; Bruner and Postman, 1947ab, 1948; Bruner, Postman, and McGinnies, 1948). The understanding of the impact of motivational and dynamic factors on perceptual systems and their cognitive integration has reached highly sophisticated levels of conceptualization and experimentation (Klein, 1970).

The whole area of the influences determining selective attention has recognized the strong influence of motivational elements (Norman, 1968, 1970). The role of such selective factors both in selective preservation of memory elements and in phenomena of distortion in memory and repression of memory elements was amply documented by the work of David Rapaport (1942) and even earlier, if implicitly, in the classic work of Bartlett. The role of need states and internal motivational forces has also been recognized in forms of pathological functioning of learning and memory systems (Talland, 1968; Talland and Waugh, 1969). And even more graphically the role of such motivational states has been traced in higher forms of conceptual and theoretical thinking (Bruner, Goodnow, and Austin, 1956).

In a highly suggestive, if heuristic, presentation, Henle (1955) has delineated a variety of ways in which need states and attitudes come to influence cognitive processes—at whatever level they may occur. Need states may operate as vector forces, pointing attention in one direction rather than another, so that aspects of perceptual field may be brought into awareness that otherwise might not. They may serve to organize and structure the perceptual or cognitive field, to a certain extent within the limits of conscious experience, but also taking place quite obviously on unconscious levels. This may also lead to the perception of other relations not previously grasped. The arousal of needs or attitudes may function as a selective factor among a variety of possibilities presented. Or they may supply a context for meaningful integration.

The organization of contexts can decisively influence the experience of specific cognitive items so that changing patterns of interpretation of elements of experience can be a result. The functions of needs and attitudes as temporally extended organizations can arouse memory traces relevant to these organizational patterns. Thus previous experience has a determining effect on cognitive processes, such as the establishing and contributing of meanings, the establishing of judgmental norms or adaptation levels, or the shifting of levels of significance of experienced items—either rendering it commonplace, so that it is overlooked, or increasing its significance in the cognitive field. Thus previous experience, shaped and aroused by motivational elements, can serve as a strong selective factor which favors certain possibilities and minimizes or rejects others.

Motivational influences or needs may likewise arouse expectations which have an influence on the determination of cognitive sets. They may even lead an individual to withdraw from cognitive interaction and discourage a desire to understand or ask questions or consider relevant evidences. They can also be a source of distortion by interfering with our capacity to discriminate differences and make distinctions or to minimize or magnify contrasts. And last, but not least, motivational aspects may lead us to intensify or diminish the degree of effort which we bring to the performance of cognitive tasks.

All of these variations in the play of motivational and need states upon cognitive processes have their role in the paranoid process. But as much of our analysis here has indicated, the play of motivational states does not take place in a vacuum. Rather it takes place in a highly organized internal milieu, which is given its shape and its structure by the clustering of motivational influences around certain meaningful patterns of organization which we have described as introjects. Consequently the motivational states, which we are discussing and describing here, differ from the experimentally based and laboratory-induced forms of deprivation which are often used to study motivational influences in an experimental context. Rather they are embedded in and derived from interpersonal contexts, in which the processes of introjection and projection play themselves out.

Symbolization

In this context we are reminded of Felix Deutsch's notions of objective symbolization and the conversion process. Deutsch envisioned this process as a central element in the production of psychosomatic symptomatology. Deutsch based his notion on Freud's idea that a sense of reality originates from a projection of sensory perceptions of one's own body or body parts onto objects outside of it, and in which the external objects are perceived as if somehow severed from the body and lost. This basic separation is accompanied by a continuing wish to restore the lost part and thus a sense of bodily integrity.

In the *Interpretation of Dreams* (1900), Freud mentions that we become aware of living objects around us by way of perception complexes which derive from those objects, but which are fused with memories of similar perceptions of our own bodies. Thus the sensory memories are associatively connected with reactive movements once experienced in the body. Objects are recognized perceptually through recollections which are rooted in sensory perceptions of the body itself. The response to the sensory signal is in part an instinctual one, and represents a tending toward or away from the object. Deutsch goes on to say:

> Thus these feelings are derived from a sensory perception which serves as a warning signal against a wish toward a symbolized object. The desired object is always closely connected with a series of sensory perceptions. The wish has become repressed but is continually reawakened by sensory stimuli. Originally, sensory perception was directed toward the own body only, and there *sensu strictori* was without an object. When primary sensory perceptions become libidinized, they gradually spread over the objects, keeping them and their perceiver in continuous contact with past and present reality. At the same time, they become the mediators for the symbolized objects (1959, p. 89).

As Deutsch would see it, then, the symbolized object is a composite of early cathected sense perceptions which were formed into a body ego. These sensory configurations had been fused through partial identification with the perceived parts of other objects. They are the earliest perceived objects with which the child has the most intense and perduring sensory contact, which carry the significant meanings related to these objects. Consequently, the loss of these objects and their attendant meaning signifies and is equivalent to a bodily loss.

We are not so much concerned at this point with the contribution to the understanding of conversion, but rather we are concerned with the cognitive implications for the perceptual process resident in Deutsch's ideas. What he is describing in terms of projection and reintrojection is an interplay of introjective and projective mechanisms by which perceptual contents contribute to the organization of internal objects, and the projection of introjective content onto external objects provides the context of meaning within which the conversion process takes place. Thus conversion is specifically understood in terms of the projection of bodily significances related to the organization of introjects onto the respective objects. The cognitive implications of this, however, are that the perceptual process involves an interplay and a derivation from the correlative processes of introjection and projection. Consequently the symbolic aspect of the perceptual level of experience is tied in with the history of object relations experienced by a given individual, as bound up in the internal organization of his introjects.

It is apparent, then, that the perceptual process is from the beginning caught up in the dynamic interaction and interplay of projective and introjective mechanisms. There are unquestionably complex issues involved in this that require closer inspection. For example, we are clearly faced with a problem as to the extent and nature of the influence of projective and introjective processes on perceptual processes and their interplay in the context of understanding the nature of development, as well as the nature of perception itself. There is little doubt that there is a significant area for investigation here, but at this point there is little we can say about it. To focus on only one aspect of the problem, we need to better understand in psychoanalytic terms the nature of object-representations and their derivation and dependence upon perceptual processes. It is clear that they cannot be identified, but at the same time it is clear that they cannot be separated.

Perceptual Readiness

Then, of course, related to the whole question of capacity to form object representations, is the whole question of reality testing. Consequently, while it is reasonable to say that the paranoid construction operates on an interpretative level, the specifics of what this means and its implications for various related processes, as well as an understanding of how these processes reciprocally interact and influence each other in the complexities of cognitive awareness, remains a task for further study. What is useful in all this for our present argument, however, is that perceptual processes are in no sense immune from the influence of inner dynamic configurations and that the integration of external input with inner configurations of force and meaning cannot take place without a cognitive construction which gives them shape and meaning and relevance. It is in this aspect of the process that the paranoid construction becomes relevant.

This view of perceptual processes was given definitive shape by Bruner in his classic article on perceptual readiness (1957). As Bruner views the perceptual process, it depends upon the construction of a set of organized categories in terms of which stimulus inputs can be sorted, given identity, and given a more elaborate connotative meaning. The categories are formed in such a way as to allow for the inference of object identity on the basis of a selection of cues or "clues." Identity in this perceptual context, then, represents the range of inferences having to do with properties, uses, and consequences of objects which are predictable on the basis of specific criterial clues. Perceptual readiness, therefore, has to do with the relative accessibility of these categories to afferent stimulus input. If a category is relatively accessible, the stimulus input, which would be required for sorting the stimuli in terms of the category, is much less. Category accessibility can be determined by the probability of occurrence of events, usually in redundant sequences which have been learned in the course of experience, and by the internal requirements of environmental search which may be demanded by need states or by the need to carry out habitual activities.

In paranoid states, analogizing Bruner's description of perceptual readiness to the paranoid construction as we have described it, the accessibility of the category can be determined either by the adaptability of external input to the requirements of the category, as a result of the configuration of stimulus clues or as a result of selected patterns of attention and denial motivated by inner need states. Or on the other hand, accessibility can be dictated from the internal side by the intensity of need states to fit input data into the category format. The interaction can be seen as well in terms of Piaget's concepts of accommodation and assimilation. The fit of the paranoid construction with external sensory input can be accomplished either by accommodation of the data to the category, or conversely by an assimilation of the category to fit the data. In reality, both processes take place simultaneously in complex interaction.

Bruner goes on to observe that the failure to achieve a state of perceptual readiness, which is attuned to the probabilities of external events, can be dealt with either by relearning categories and expectancies, or by a constant close inspection of events and objects. This former alternative is relatively less available to the pathological paranoid individual, but the latter alternative is one which he must put to use. This has the decided disadvantage of losing the advantage of a real perceptual readiness—in the sense of a preadapted set of categories which permit adequate adjustment to changing patterns of stimulus input—and, in consequence, the paranoid is caught under the pressure of continual stimulus input to adopt a stance of hypervigilance, hyperattentiveness, and continual suspiciousness and guardedness.

Influence of Inner Need States

The interplay of extrinsic input and the derivation of perceptual and cognitive categories from internal need states is a matter of considerable complexity and interest. It seems that the maintenance of perceptual categories requires a minimum of continual stimulus input for them to function in a normal and reality-oriented fashion. This has to do with the whole issue of stimulus nutriment which Piaget discussed. In the absence of such nutriment, perceptual processes tend to become disorganized and cognitive processes seem to become dominated by internal influences.

Rapaport (1958), in discussing the question of autonomy, cited some experiments of Hebb and his students (Bexton, Heron, and Scott, 1954; Heron, Doane, and Scott, 1956; Heron, 1957) in which subjects were subjected to conditions of sensory deprivation, including auditory, visual, sensorimotor, tactile, and kinesthetic isolation. Two important observations were made. First, that the subjects experienced autistic fantasies in the sensorially deprived condition and that their ability to pursue ordered thought sequences was diminished. Second, when repetitive verbal information was given to the subjects in the condition of stimulus deprivation, this material was taken by some of the subjects and experienced as though it were the truth. This experience approached delusional intensity and apparently persisted for several weeks.

Rapaport understands this phenomenon in terms of the relative autonomy from reality influences in a stimulus-deprived context, with a corresponding diminution of autonomy from inner drive influences. There is undoubtedly some validity in this formulation of the phenomenon observed, but I would like to suggest that an alternate interpretation, although not exclusive of the preceding, is that the human mind functions in such a way as to provide consistency, organization, meaning, and relevance to whatever experience is available to it, regardless of the amount of sensory informational input. The same phenomenon is at work in these experiments as underlies the factor of perceptual readiness described by Bruner.

In the reported experiments, it is reasonable to presume that the effects of sensory deprivation were to induce a state of cognitive regression in the subjects. In such a regressed state, the judgmental capability of the mind is more susceptible and responsive to the determining influences of inner need states, and correspondingly less responsive and oriented toward the determining influence of extrinsic stimuli. This is not quite the same as what has been traditionally described in terms of a regression from secondary to primary process. In fact, the secondary process organization of mental operations remains intact, but the determining influence, which gives the particular mental operations their apparent truth value, is shifted from objective and verifiable real events to the level of subjective and internal need states. And in fact, this configuration is quite characteristic of the paranoid mentality. It is quite characteristic of the paranoid to maintain high standards for logical integration and secondary process functioning, but the basic truth-motivation of his cognitive orientation is somehow divorced from the available real evidence.

Negation

If we choose to parallel Rapaport's argument about relative autonomy from both external reality and from internal drives, we can see that there are cognitive influences which parallel and derive from each of these conditions. Freud had called attention to the relationship between negation and repression. He wrote:

> Since to affirm or negate the content of thoughts is the task of the function of intellectual judgment, what we have just been saying has led us to the psychological origin of that function. To negate something in a judgement is, at bottom, to say: "This is something which I should prefer to repress." The negative judgement is the intellectual substitute for repression; it's "No" is the hall-mark of repression, a certification of origin—like, let us say, "Made in Germany." With the help of the symbol of negation, thinking frees itself from the restrictions of repression and enriches itself with material that is indispensable for its proper functioning (1925, p. 236).

Negation, however, can also operate in the direction of external reality. Here it is more akin to the mechanism of denial. In relation to external reality, however, the paranoid construction is capable of utilizing negation, denial, selective attention, isolation, and even distortion. At times the distortion is even primarily a perceptual form of distortion. Negation can serve in any of these processes as a means of declaring what is not consistent with the paranoid construction to not exist, regardless of its reality status. From this point of view the paranoid construction is transparently in the service of defense, and functions in this respect as determined by id derivatives. In this respect it represents an impairment of reality testing.

But in another respect it serves as the instrument of the latter. Reality testing in this sense is never a matter of totally objective and impartial evaluation of extrinsic evidences according to rational and logical secondary process criteria. There is always a place and function in the cognitive scheme for the subjective activity of the knowing observer. As Bruner's analysis of perceptual readiness suggests, and as we shall see more at length in a moment, our cognitive contact with reality is never total, never complete, never without its gaps and lacunae, never grasps totally, without the accompanying processing of input information by a series of cognitive schemata and categories which organize and construct the world of inner meanings. Such internally constructed schemata cannot escape the influence of internal forces and motivations.

Cognitive Closure

Moreover, we can postulate an internal drive in human cognitive apparatus toward cognitive closure. Such a cognitive dynamism pushes us in the direction of the achievement and realization of truth and meaning, even when the external supports are lacking. Thus, truth and meaning tend to run ahead of proof. Ideas tend to outrun facts. Theories tend to accelerate beyond the range of data. The theoretical hare is always ready and willing to outdistance the empirical tortoise. And depending on the intensity of inner needs to achieve meaning and relevance, cognitive organization and closure become increasingly premature and increasingly resistant to alteration in the face of even convincing and opposing evidences. All of this, however, is quite familiar to us from the study of paranoid pathologies.

However, such a basic tendency for thought to outrun reality is a fundamental dimension of the workings of human intelligence. Even at the level of basic perceptual processes, as we have seen, part of the process is the learning of the properties of a class of functionally equivalent objects, which we then use as a basis for inferring whether a newly encountered object belongs to that particular class or not. The range and flexibility of this process are truly remarkable. As Bruner has noted, both a speck on the horizon accompanied by a plume of smoke and the towering bulk of a transatlantic liner moored at its docks are both categorized under the equivalent class of ship.

Coding System

That classification, however, can be made on the basis of the most minimal clues. Essentially the minimal clues and the small amount of information they provide are located in a more generic coding system which provides additional information about the utility and function of the object. Bruner's discussion of such coding systems (1975) points to several conditions for the acquisition of such systems. The first important condition is the set or attitude which can determine what and how something is learned. Instructions serve as a means of producing sets which can bring different forms of coding into play. Bruner points out that the principal source of instruction and corresponding sets or attitudes is the individual's own past history. While the setting function of situational instruction is obviously transient, the influence of past experience tends to be a more perduring determination. From the point of view of the application in the present context, the past experience reflects a history of object relationships which is embedded in the organization of introjects.

Bruner also relates, as a second condition for acquisition of coding systems, the need of the organism. He proposes that the generality of the coding system, in relation to which newly acquired information can be organized, depends on the presence of an optimal motivational state. Conditions of high or very low drive or motivation tend to increase the concreteness of cognition. Thus under conditions of high drive, if a path to a goal is learned it is as a concrete path, namely, *this* path to *this* specific goal. The experimental animal under conditions of high drive does not evolve a generic coding system that permits him to pass beyond that level of training and to transfer the training to similar situations. Thus under conditions of high drive or need, cognitive adaptability or flexibility is lost and conditions of narrowness and rigidity are reinforced.

From the point of view of our consideration here, the paranoid patient can be seen as operating under a condition of high need or drive. The paranoid construction is a form of coding which allows him to systematize and organize and give meaning and relevance to his experience. In his driven need state, the paranoid patient is under a strong compulsion to maintain the paranoid construction with a high degree of rigidity and a low degree of adaptability or flexibility. The construction enables him to go beyond the available information, but the drivenness of his inner need state prevents him from adapting the construction to new informational input and thus prevents him from going beyond the paranoid construction. Consequently, any new input data must be reduced to the terms of the paranoid construction or eliminated by selectivity or denial.

Thus it can be seen that much of the cognitive activity that we engage in is caught up in an active and dynamic process of continual categorizing and forming of hypotheses, as well as a continuing process of modifying, reshaping, and remaking such categorizations and hypotheses. In its cognitive perspective, this is what human adaptation and adjustment are all about. Piaget's instinct was unerring when he spoke of the need for the interplay of accommodation and assimilation in all of human cognitive functioning. It can also be seen, whether at the level of the simplest perceptual organization, or at the level of highly sophisticated and complex scientific theorizing, that the cognitive process involves a continual organization and synthesis of cognitive functions in the service of interpreting and making sense out of cognitive elements. It is at this point, in fact, that the potential for creative cognition enters, along with the potential for the radical breakdown of cognitive processes.

The paranoid construction is specifically such an organization of categorizations and an elaborate process of hypothesis formation. The constructive element enters into the organization of experience and available information in such a way as to give coherency and meaning and sense to what is experienced. When the paranoid process is operating, the primary determinants of the construction are internal need states and attitudes. The organization of such need states and attitudes depends to a powerful degree on the history of past experience and particularly the history of object relations which has characterized the individual's life experience. Thus what is experienced, how it is experienced, and how the experience is interpreted are influenced in significant ways by the organization, content, and defensive functioning of internal objects.

Relation to Projection

A word of caution is advisable here. The paranoid construction is not identical with the organization of introjects, nor can it be identified with the content of projections. The paranoid construction is specifically a cognitive integration and formation. It accompanies and incorporates specific projections, and derives its motivating force from its relation to the underlying introjective system. It is a complex cognitive organization which is elaborated on the basis of not only projections, but also other sources of informational input derived both internally and externally.

Thus the paranoid construction can have a profoundly distorting effect on experience and reality testing without necessarily involving projection. As, for example, in the case of Bob B., who was profoundly and persistently convinced that he was impotent, in the face of an indeterminant string of pregnancies and abortions related to his sexual activity. The inner conviction clearly related to the introjective aspects of his experience in which he felt himself to be defective, inadequate, and impotent. The clearly contrary indications in reality had to be negated and denied.

Similarly Jimmy's need to see himself as a weak, dependent, and failure-doomed child allowed him to see the world in terms of threatening or defeating or overwhelming or even hostile and persecutory objects. But there are many aspects of his experience that countered this view, specifically in his capacity to function at a relatively high level of capacity. Similarly Karen's perception of herself as vulnerable and susceptible, such that she could easily be taken advantage of by others, particularly by the men of her acquaintance, blindly overlooked and ignored the obvious capacities and strengths that she did in fact possess.

But in none of these instances can it be said that the complete understanding of what was at issue could be encapsulated in the term "projection." Unquestionably there were often projective elements involved, but what was more to the issue was the fact that these individuals had constructed an interpretive set of categories and system of hypotheses by which they interpreted their experience and evaluated their own position and place within that experience. Thus the paranoid construction becomes a kind of internal and private belief system by which they guide themselves and through which they can evaluate what passes in their experience.

Besides its continuity with normal and basically human cognitive processes, one of the important characteristics of the paranoid construction is that it has an immediate reference to the individual's self-concept. The organization and structuring of experience which it provides offers a context within which the specific introjects can function. The paranoid construction, therefore, serves partly defensively and partly adaptively the inner need to sustain and support the alignment of introjects. The motivation for the paranoid construction stems partly from the cognitive dynamism toward integration and coherency of meaning, but also in important ways stems from the need to preserve the introjects. In part, therefore, the paranoid construction derives from the same basic motivations that inhere in the formation of the introjects to begin with. The introjects form the basis for the perception of the self which the paranoid construction complements by building a view of reality and of input information, which is congruent with that perception of self and gives it a meaningful matrix by which it can be related to significant objects. In other words, the patient must see the world in terms that allow him to persist in the belief about himself which is based upon the relevant introjects. The persistence and resistance to change which characterize the paranoid construction are correlative with the pressure to retain the introjects and the defensive need which underlies that pressure.

CHAPTER 21

Defensive Aspects: Narcissism

ON THE BORDERS OF PATHOLOGY

In our consideration of the paranoid process to this point, our focus has been primarily on the pathological aspects of the process. Even in the consideration of pathology, however, it becomes increasingly clear that we are dealing with a fundamental process in the human psyche that has ramifications and applications beyond the realm of mere pathological distortion. It becomes increasingly clear that what we are conceptualizing has definite lines of continuity and implication, which extend into the realm of relatively healthy and normal human psychological functioning.

We can begin at this point, then, to turn away from the clinical and the pathological and begin to focus on some of the broader implications of the paranoid process. The line that separates the normal from the abnormal cannot be clearly drawn. It is a fuzzy, wavering, broken line. In our consideration particularly of the paranoid mechanisms above, we have seen at a number of points that the line that separates the operation of such mechanisms from normal psychic processes, both emotional and cognitive, is not easily determined. If introjection can be delineated as a process by which pathology is instituted and maintained, it can also be regarded as an essential part of the normal psychic development through which every human being must pass. If projection can be seen to be a form of defense which saves the inner world from the torment of intolerable or destructive affects, it can also be seen to be not only an important element in psychic development, but a pattern of experience which is the common stuff of childhood and becomes an important component of human experience more generally. If the paranoid construction can be articulated in its pathological dimensions as an essential aspect of the cognitive formation of paranoid states, it likewise can be seen to operate with relative efficacy in a wide spectrum of human cognitive endeavors.

Perhaps it is simply a problem of categorization. What the clinical psychiatrist classifies as pathological or abnormal, may in common human experience and the transactions of everyday life pass for normal and adaptive functioning. Perhaps we psychiatrists see too much pathology—or perhaps others see too little. Perhaps such thinking can only serve to confuse the normal and the abnormal. Some may see in this approach a form of psychiatric reductionism whereby the range of normal and higher human capacities are explained in terms of psychopathology. Some may object that there is an inherent danger in such an attitude of mind which studies the normal from the perspective of the abnormal, namely, that what is seen is only that aspect of the normal which reveals its parallels or continuities with the abnormal.

I would assume these all to be justifiable questions. But I would also remind myself, as we enter this new phase of our study, that a continual question that I must present to myself—and I would hope the reader would present to himself—is why it is that of these processes, which are so similar and continuous in organization and function, we choose to regard some as normal and adaptive and we choose to regard others as pathological and maladaptive.

DEFENSIVE ASPECTS

We begin our extrapolation of the paranoid process with a consideration of its defensive functioning. While the consideration of defensive functioning is rooted in the pathology of the process, it nonetheless provides an important transitional consideration. It is not simply that the defensive aspects of the process are such that no human being escapes them. It is also that the reflection on defensive functions points the way to and illumines our consideration of later developmental and adaptive aspects of the process.

The perspective of a consideration of the defensive aspects of the paranoid process must be primarily intrapsychic. The process functions essentially in the service of narcissism. We want to focus on this relationship, particularly bringing into conjunction the functioning of the process in relation to injured or deprived narcissism. The particular pathological manifestations which we are to focus on are depression, shame, and envy.

Related to this whole question of narcissism is the other essential element in paranoid manifestations, namely, that of aggression. Aggression plays an important role in the paranoid process, particularly in the service of salvaging and redeeming narcissistic deficits. But what becomes quickly apparent in this transitional consideration of defensive aspects is that the same processes operate in important and significant ways in sustaining and promoting normal processes of development and adaptation. It is only in the deeper consideration of the defensive functions that we can begin to bring into focus some of these more constructive and productive aspects of the process.

THE RELATION TO NARCISSISM

The Tyranny of Narcissism

One inescapable impression which quickly arises in reflecting on the patients we have studied, is that the whole course of their pathology and treatment is shot through with narcissistic concerns. All of our patients are victims of an injured narcissism. They are all victims of the tyranny of narcissism. They are all caught up in the inexorable process of struggling to salvage and preserve whatever remnants of narcissism are available to them. In fact, quite simply, the workings of the paranoid process in each of our patients can be seen quite directly as a manifestation of this narcissistic conflict and torment.

The manifestations of this are protean. They include Jimmy's infantile and neurotic wish to remain the special, protected, weak, and defective child. They include Karen's hidden conviction that she was a special and privileged person so that love and consideration and deference should be paid to her regardless of the cost to others. They include Bob's and Fred's grandiose delusions that they were powerful and invincible godlike figures. They include Ann's and Ellen's embattled and hostile confrontation with the world in which they saw themselves as constantly watched, surveyed, so that countless people were taken up with the important project of working some evil effect on them. They include Gloria's intense clinging to a position of infantile dependence, in the continually frustrated demand and expectation that she would gain the love and caring affection that she felt was her due. They include Clare's continual rage at her parents for not having given her what she always expected and continued to expect from them.

It is interesting to compare these last two cases. Both persons were deeply immersed in a malignant and destructive form of pathology. However, it was only when Clare began to surrender and modify some of her narcissistic expectations that her treatment took a turn for the better and she was able to set her foot on the road to a happier and healthier life. Gloria was not able to do this. She remained immersed in her infantile dependence and her outraged and unremitting narcissistic demands.

In all of these patients there is an underlying substratum of lethal narcissism which lies at the root of their pathology. Often the narcissistic core is well concealed and well guarded. Therapeutically, it lies for all practical purposes at the core of the disorder. It takes long periods of intense therapeutic effort to work one's way through the layers of defense to the narcissism which lies at the heart of it and for the protection of which all the rest is stoutly maintained and preserved. This narcissistic core is expressed in a basic conviction that life should not have been as it was or is, that the world should treat them with greater consideration and kindness, that their parents and family should be held accountable for what they were deprived of and prevented from having. Along with this basic sentiment there is a sense of outrage, of resentment, of bitter disillusionment and frustration. These patients are all victims of the inexhaustible tyranny of narcissism, with its unending and uncompromising demands and expectations. Theirs is a narcissism that has been traumatized and brutalized, deprived and dishonored. The pathology which we have witnessed and described is an elaborate attempt to redress and redeem this sense of loss and deprivation.

The Preservation of Self

While the pathology of narcissism can be so graphically illustrated in these cases, we should not allow ourselves to be deceived into thinking that the concerns over narcissism are limited to such pathological manifestations. Rather they form a fundamental human concern from the cradle to the grave. Human psychology is a constant struggle to preserve narcissism. From earliest childhood to the last gasp of dying breath, human beings are caught up in the preservation of a sense of self-esteem which remains highly vulnerable and fragile and open to attack. Whatever threatens our status in life, whatever throws into question our accomplishments and attainments, whatever threatens us or limits us, or prevents us from attaining the object of our desires, all these and more are forthright assaults on our narcissism. All this brings our self-esteem into question and makes us feel vulnerable and defeated and humiliated. We must struggle to find ways to protect ourselves, to sustain a threatened sense of selfhood within us, to preserve and support in whatever way possible the diminished sense of self-esteem which accompanies such attacks. All of us are the possessors of an embattled narcissism.

From the very beginning of his experience, the child is dependent on his relationship with significant others for the building and maintaining of the sense of self. The child's ontological security rests on a fundamental commitment to others, along with a basically sensed and realized commitment of others to him. Whatever the subsequent developmental history of such relationships, we nonetheless cling to them as to a taproot of our existence. As Rochlin has commented so well:

> To lose them would mean to give up our demands for imperishable relationships, and to acknowledge the transience of all things and therefore of ourselves. It would signify too a willingness to forego denials of vulnerability and thereby relinquish our religious beliefs, renounce our expectation of altering reality, and thus in consequence abandon wishes for fulfillment. We would also forego a sense of the future toward which we strive and would remain confined to the limits of a present dissociated from the past. There is nothing in the human condition to indicate that we are likely to follow such a course (1973, p. 3).

The force that opposes any such relinquishment is the power of narcissism. Any separation from the things or the objects which we value is poorly tolerated. One way in which the child clings defensively and desperately to his objects is through the process of introjection. The loss of the loved object inflicts a deprivation upon our narcissism so that self-esteem is placed in jeopardy. Patients with narcissistic personality disorders are highly susceptible to the fear of loss of objects, of love, or of the symbolic losses of castration anxiety. But in the narcissistic disorders, the fear of the loss of the object takes first place (Kohut, 1971). A narcissistic investment of self in objects sets the stage for the susceptibility to loss. The result is a narcissistic disequilibrium which disrupts the sense of self-cohesiveness and self-esteem which has come to depend on the presence, the approval, or other narcissistic gratifications derived from the object. The diminution of self-esteem is a major parameter and signpost of narcissistic injury.

Vicissitudes of Narcissism

According to Kohut's (1971) schema the disturbance of the original narcissistic equilibrium, produced by the unavoidable defects in maternal care, leads to replacing the original narcissism by establishing a grandiose and exhibitionistic self-image, the grandiose self, or alternatively, by attributing the narcissistic perfection to an omnipotent object, the idealized parent imago. These antithetical and basic narcissistic configurations serve to preserve a part of the original experience of narcissistic perfection. Optimally the exhibitionism and pomposity of the grandiose self can be gradually contained and integrated into a more mature personality structure and thus come to supply the narcissistic basis for an emerging sense of healthy self-esteem. The idealized parent imago can be similarly integrated by way of introjection as the ego ideal or the idealized aspect of superego. Under the burden of narcissistic disappointment, however, the archaic narcissistic self retains its grandiosity and the idealized imago remains unaltered and unintegrated as an unassimilated introject which is required for narcissistic homeostasis. These relatively stable configurations can become highly cathected with narcissistic libido and can thus contribute to a degree of cathectic constancy toward particular objects. Such stable configurations, when attached to the analyst, can become the basis for narcissistic transference.

Certainly one of the most significant disappointments and humiliations that a child suffers comes with the termination of the Oedipal period. His expectations come to naught, and the experience of failure of his Oedipal wishes serves as a template for subsequent losses and disappointments. The depression which follows upon subsequent losses in life reflects unconsciously back to the loss suffered in failure of Oedipal ambitions. As Rochlin (1973) points out, there is no reason to suppose that when longings or wishes are thwarted that the result is ever resignation or abandonment of these wishes. The Oedipal situation is accompanied by a painful disappointment and is brought to a close with a serious loss of self-esteem. This condition provides the stimulus for the recovery of lost narcissism. The child is thrust into a latency period of development, in which the heroes of myths and fairy tales serve as a means of retrieving some sense of power and high-minded worthiness. Similarly, the child's immersing himself in the rigors of learning and attainments, both mental and physical, serves to channel his energies toward the restitution of the narcissistic injury he has suffered.

Not the least of the narcissistic assaults that all men must subject themselves to is the threat of death. The struggle between the realization and acceptance of the fact of death and the wish to repudiate and overcome it is lifelong. Facing the remorselessness and inevitability of death leaves us with a sense of helplessness and ultimate vulnerability. Primitive man turned to magic, more contemporary man turns to religious beliefs which find their most profound motivation in restitutive attempts to overcome this fundamental narcissistic assault. Man can also turn to less realistic and more pathological forms of restitution as well, particularly fantasies of omnipotence and invulnerability. We can recall here our patient Bob, whose pathological and grandiose delusion included his being a member of a race of godlike beings, one of whose properties was that they would never die. We have seen in other respects how his delusional system and the construction that supported it served to deny and counterphobically transmute all of those elements in his experience and the reality that surrounded him and served to undermine and assault his basic narcissism. Similarly, his fear of death played a major role in the pattern in which his pathology expressed itself during the subsequent course of his illness. For him to feel, to live, to act, to make a decision and carry it out, were in part to move closer to the inevitability of death—a narcissistic affront which he could not tolerate and against which he could only rage with impotent bitterness.

Primary Narcissism

Freud originally postulated a state of primary narcissism which was gradually altered in the course of development as the infant becomes aware of significant figures around him and becomes attached to them. This dependent and infantile attachment to significant others is never completely satisfying and is always discolored by human limitations. The greater the dissatisfaction and the less the infant's demands are met, the more he will cling to his original narcissism and its attendant egocentricity. Further failures, in the form of losses or disappointments, serve to further injure the sense of self. Such narcissistic defeats only serve to turn the infant back towards his self-contained primary egocentricity. Such deprivations are experienced as a loss of self-esteem. Rochlin writes:

> The paradox is that the indulged child tolerates any deprivation poorly and is affected by it even more severely than one who has been less generously cared

for. The more narcissism is indiscriminately satisfied, the less strain it bears. As the egocentric character of early childhood is extended through excessive gratification, it shows as an unconscious resistance to change with less and less effort to accommodation to others. The ordinary search for satisfaction or pleasure is not necessarily toward a further indulgence, although that may be present, as it is a hardening lack of compromise (1973, p. 50).

It is this disturbance in the equilibrium of primary narcissism produced by the shortcomings of maternal care and its associated disappointments and deprivations that leads the child in the direction of establishing the exhibitionistic grandiose self or to attributing the previous perfection to an omnipotent self-object, the idealized parent imago (Kohut, 1971). From the earliest moment of infantile existence throughout the rest of life, our unfulfilled needs and wishes compel us to relieve the sense of deprivation. The experience of deprivation, moreover, is intimately linked with the demeaning of self-esteem. The child's reach inevitably exceeds his grasp. His limited and feeble powers are impotent against the powers that oppose him. His feeble efforts to enforce his will and the frustration in not getting what he wants leave him both unsatisfied and threatened.

These are significant blows to the developing child's sense of self-esteem. It is only when he begins to attach himself to another person and to invest that other with interests and importance that the primary state of narcissism begins to be eroded. Should this process fail, should it meet with obstacles and inhibitions, should it stumble upon frustrations and deprivation, narcissism suffers. Frustrated narcissism responds not with resignation, but with an intensification and obstinate clinging to its infantile and self-centered demands. The experience of Gloria can be taken as a stunning paradigm of this paradox of narcissism. The more frustrated and denied and deprived she was in her experience of her relationship with her parents the more stubbornly and obstinately did she cling to her narcissistic expectations. The more she was deprived, the more intently did she seem committed to her pain and suffering, and the more unwilling or unable she was to extricate herself from it.

Narcissism and Reality

As the growing child comes to know reality, his narcissism is inevitably and profoundly affected by it. He is forced on countless fronts to accept limitation, to give in to the insistence and convictions of others. The child must learn that his capacities are limited, that his existence is finite, that choice and determination are fraught with anxiety and uncertainty. Through all of his painful learning experience, there runs the thread of the child's continuing sense of helplessness and weakness: that he is in fact dependent on the whim and the will of those more powerful caretaking creatures who surround him. Children manage to transcend the real world and its limitations by the force of imagination, active and vivid fantasy, a belief in magical power and omnipotence, and a capacity for imitation and assimilation to the powerful figures around them. The young child's tendency to identify with the aggressor, which Anna Freud describes so vividly, is a striking example. It is through such devices that the child gradually turns from the precarious weakness of passivity and victimhood, to the relative activity and striving for mastery which is dependent on psychic growth.

This pressure toward redeeming a diminished self-esteem leads inevitably to an expression of aggressive feelings of competition and rivalry, particularly within the family context. This sometimes serves to contribute to and continue the sense of inadequacy and inferiority, since in the continuing competition with parents and older siblings particularly, the child is inevitably and inexorably the loser. This was so graphically and poignantly one of the important lessons to be drawn from the case of Jim. His childishly ambitious and aggressive attempts to salvage his damaged narcissism served only to merit him the benignly knowing smiles of his elders who thought that his attempts were "cute." Consequently, his attempts to redeem and salvage his injured narcissism served only to confirm and reimpress upon him his weakness and comparative incapacity.

There are elements of narcissism which are basic to its understanding. Narcissism is incapable of self-sustaining action. It is by its nature uncompromising and continually requires fresh gratification. It is not self-limiting. It has no inherent stability, and has a quality of insatiability. Pathological narcissism can allow no allies. It can tolerate only enemies. The narcissistic image must be endlessly restored. The struggle with reality convinces the child, undoubtedly quite correctly, that but for reality he would not be deprived and would have what he wished. The very nature of his wishes precludes their realization, and it is this that is at the basis of his deprivation. It is in this regard, then, that we can begin to grasp the inner links which forge the tie between narcissism and the paranoid process. The paranoid process is thrown into the service of narcissism. It seeks to separate and divide; it seeks to find and establish enemies. It is uniquely the process by which deprived and threatened narcissism is sustained and restored. And we must not forget that the operation of the paranoid process has as its purpose the defense and preservation of the self.

THE PATHOLOGY OF NARCISSISM

Depression

Depression is par excellence the clinical expression of pathological narcissism (Rochlin, 1961, 1965). We have already considered the relationship between clinical depression and the forms of paranoid pathology. We have also discussed at various points the underlying mechanisms of these clinical states, particularly the mutually determining involvement in introjective and projective mechanisms.

Narcissistic Identification

The basic insight into the nature of depressive states was provided by Freud in his *Mourning and Melancholia* (1917 [1915]). The bases of the pathology in Freud's formulation lie in the narcissistic (introjective) identification by which the ambivalently regarded object was internalized. With the shift in libidinal cathexis from an exterior to an interior direction, there was a redirection of aggressive and destructive energies. Consequently, the resentment and hateful components of the original ambivalence came to be directed against the patient's self. The emphasis in Freud's approach fell upon the redirection of aggressive impulses, but nonetheless the involvement and derivation from a basically narcissistic libidinal distribution were an evident and primary part of the pathology. The introjective mechanisms were later adapted by Freud to his concept of superego formation, so that the superego came to provide the basis for understanding unconscious guilt mechanisms and also became the vehicle for the understanding of depressive states.

Diminution of Self-esteem

The understanding of depressive phenomena and their intimate involvement in narcissistic dynamics was clarified by Edward Bibring (1953). Bibring pointed to the common theme in a variety of depressive states of the undermining or diminution of self-esteem. In depressive states, patients felt helpless in the face of superior forces, or in the grip of organic diseases. Or on a more psychological plane they felt incapable of controlling or directing an inescapable fate—of loneliness, isolation, a lack of love and affection, or other apparent evidences of weakness, inferiority, or failure. They were without hope; they were helpless and powerless. Bibring consequently defined depression as ". . . the emotional expression (indication) of a state of helplessness and powerlessness of the ego, irrespective of what may have caused the breakdown of the mechanisms which established his self-esteem" (1953, p. 24).

Paradoxically, in the face of such feelings of helplessness these patients tend to maintain strongly a set of goals and objectives which are highly narcissistically determined and pertinent to the individual's self-esteem. The depressive patient aspires to be worthy, to be strong and powerful, to be loved or appreciated, to be valued and esteemed by those around him, to be thought superior or talented or especially gifted. They wish to be felt good and loving; they wish not to be thought hateful or destructive. It is the disparity between these highly charged narcissistic aspirations and the acute awareness of the ego's helplessness and inability to meet them or attain them that lies at the heart of the depression. There is a haunting fear of failure, and whenever the fear of inferiority or defectiveness comes into play, the patient begins to feel hopeless. He feels that he is doomed to be a victim in the face of overwhelming powers that confront him, or he feels himself to be hateful and evil in the face of his latent aggressive tendencies. We have seen both of these affective states amply demonstrated in our patients.

Whatever the narcissistic aspiration, whatever shape or direction it takes, the resulting mechanism of the depression seems to follow a final common path. It is, in Bibring's terms, "the emotional correlate of a partial or complete collapse of the self-esteem of the ego, since it feels unable to live up to its aspirations (ego ideal, superego) while they are strongly maintained" (1953, p. 26). As long as the ego maintains its investment in and longing for the narcissistically invested object, and as long as the circumstances persist in which it is confronted with its inability or inadequacy to obtain the object or to undo the loss, the conditions of the depression persist. Thus depression must be regarded as an affective state which is characterized primarily by a diminution of self-esteem, along with a more or less intensely felt state of helplessness and/or hopelessness.

In Bibring's view, then, the basic mechanism of depression, namely the ego's awareness of its helplessness in relation to excessive or unattainable aspirations, represented the core of the depressive state whether the depressive response took place in a normal, neurotic, or even psychotic level. Bibring felt that the tendency to depression was thus related to early childhood fixation of the ego to the state of helplessness, and that this original state was regressively reactivated in situations of later frustration of narcissistic wishes. The depressive reaction to narcissistic frustration was thus seen to be independent of the aggressive component, rather than directly a function of internally directed aggression as in Freud's formulation. This does not mean, however, that aggression does not play an important role in not only depressive states but in the paranoid process as well. Bibring summed up and specified the relationship to narcissism in the following words:

> In general, one may say that everything that lowers or paralyzes the ego's self-esteem without changing the narcissistically important aims represents a condition of depression. External or internal, actual or symbolic factors, may consciously or unconsciously refute the denial of weakness or defeat or danger, may dispel systems of self-deception, may destroy hope, may reveal lack of affection or respect or prove the existence to one's self of undesirable impulses or thoughts or attitudes, or offer evidence that dormant or neutralized fears are actually "justified" and so forth; the subsequent results would do the same: the individual will regressively react with the feelings of

powerlessness and helplessness with regard to his loneliness, isolation, weakness, inferiority, evilness, or guilt. Whatever the external or internal objects or representations of the narcissistically important strivings may be, the mechanism of depression will be the same. The narcissistic shock may be mild or severe, focal or extensive, partial or complete, depending on whatever peripheral or central narcissistic aspirations are involved. These factors will contribute to the extent and intensity of the depression as well as the possibilities, the means or the tempo of recovery (1953, pp. 42-43).

Nor must the claims of narcissism on us be restricted to a more or less pathological concept of orally fixated and infantile narcissism. Rather the claims of narcissism are universal, and its demands for satisfaction are inescapable. As Rochlin has recently observed in telling fashion—

Neither the beloved child nor the fabled heroes of legend, any more than a people chosen by God, are spared outrageous trials. The flaw and the virtue in all is in the peril to self-esteem. Its defense may bring the highest honors and justify the lowest violence. But its loss risks our extinction (1973, p. 216).

He coined the excellent phrase "the tyranny of narcissism." It is a tyranny because the demands of narcissism are unconquerable and inexorable. Narcissistic fixation in the form of the grandiose self, usually as a consequence of pathogenic experiences of enmeshment with a narcissistic mother and a consequent traumatic disappointment, leaves the exhibitionistic and grandiose fantasies isolated and disavowed, or repressed, and consequently inaccessible to the more realistic and adaptively functioning ego. The persistence of the grandiose self carries with it a damming up of primitive narcissistic-exhibitionistic libido which can be symptomatically manifested in an intensification of hypochondriacal concerns, or of self-consciousness to the point of shame and embarrassment.

Grandiose Fantasies

Reich (1960) relates the problem of narcissistic fixation to conditions of quantitative cathectic imbalance, i.e., when the balance between object-cathexis and self-cathexis has been disturbed in the direction of excessive self-cathexis, or to the persistence of infantile forms of narcissism in which self-cathexis is fixed at a level of incomplete ego differentiation and self-object differentiation. Such fixation often results in the resort to magical devices to achieve satisfaction of needs or to attain some degree of mastery of reality. However, the growing ego is always confronted with its own weakness and limitation and continually challenged to accept these limitations. The persistent infantile wish to attain the impossible thus reveals a lack of ability to face both inner and outer reality. The injury to self-esteem is compensated often by narcissistic self-inflation and grandiosity. When this attempt at compensation fails, however, it may result in severe symptoms.

In our patients, where the failure of highly narcissistic convictions and ambitions—most acutely and extremely in the form of psychotic delusional systems—occurs, the patient is inevitably plunged into a severe depressive state. Often when such compensatory mechanisms become undermined, forms of self-consciousness and hypochondriacal anxiety manifest themselves. Thus Jim's recurrent hypochondriacal concerns or Bob's delusions of impotence which were so resistant to modification by reality. Such states of mind along with depression form the primary aspects of pathological narcissism. The persistence of grandiose fantasies is described further by Reich (1960) as forms of primitive ego-ideals related to primitive identifications (introjections). The degree of pathology depends on the capacity of the ego to function adequately on a realistic level and on the availability of or capacity for sublimation in the service of partially realizing or transposing the fantasy ambitions into realistic attainments. Often the grandiose fantasy is over-cathected due to the intensity of inner needs and the distinction between wish and reality becomes obscure.

Such unsublimated and relatively grandiose fantasies easily shift to feelings of utter dejection, worthlessness, or to hypochondriacal anxieties. Often the narcissistic affliction takes the form of extreme and violent os-cillations of self-esteem. Periods of elation and self-infatuation are followed almost cyclically by feelings of total dejection and worthlessness. The infan-tile value system knows only absolute perfection and attainment or com-plete destruction and worthlessness. The shift can be precipitated by the most insignificant disappointment or experience of failure. A patient like Jim does not suffer from a slight muscle spasm; he suffers from some form of cancer. He does not merely have a cough, but suffers from lung cancer. He could paralyze himself in indecision over a simple telephone call because of the potential for disappointment which his narcissism translated into total defeat and failure and loss of career. In the logic of such extremes, there are no degrees of shadings. The situation is all or nothing, black or white, all good or all bad, omnipotent or impotent. Any shortcoming or failure to attain absolute perfection is translated into terms of absolute failure.

The narcissistic and exhibitionistic urges seek to overcome feelings of inadequacy by seeking attention and admiration from those around them. But their failure to attain this leads to the feeling that the attention they receive is more negative than positive. They fear that others will see through the facade they present and will recognize the inferiority and defectiveness within. There is defensive contempt for those whose admiration is nonethe-less sought. Contempt turns to self-contempt and is experienced often as shame. These patients feel themselves constantly to be evaluated or judged by outside observers who in effect play the role of the reexternalized superego. The narcissistic defense, therefore, is in the form of projection. Consequently, the sense of self-consciousness and shame or embarrassment provides a first step toward a more frankly paranoid orientation.

Pathological Organization

As Kernberg (1970) pointed out in the pathology of narcissistic personalities, the grandiose and coldly controlling behavior of such patients can often be seen as a defense against the projection of basically oral rage which forms a central component of the psychopathology. This aspect of narcissistic pathology points to the primarily introjective component with its primitive, destructive, and depressive aspects. This is reflected in the clinical dialectic of introjection and projection, and in the sometimes difficult-to-detect distortion in object-relations. Where the introjective aspects come to dominate the inner realm of the patient's experience, there are often strong conscious feelings of inadequacy and inferiority.

These feelings (as has been noted), caught up as they are in the narcissistic polarization of extremes, may alternate with grandiose and omnipotent fantasies. Frequently enough the omnipotence and narcissistic grandiosity of such self-demeaning patients is long and laborious in coming to the surface. The pathological organization of such personalities may often approach a borderline constellation. They may often resort regressively to primitive defense mechanisms of splitting, denial, projection, omnipotence and idealization. Usually they are able to preserve areas of adequate social functioning, often to the point of being able to mask the underlying pathology quite effectively. In addition they often demonstrate a remarkable capacity for consistent and effective work in some areas of their life which provides them with significant amounts of narcissistic reward and gratification.

Such personality organization by no means excludes creative capacity in professional fields of endeavor. They are often outstanding leaders in areas of professional and academic life and may be distinguished performers in the arts. Moreover, more often than not, their insistence on living at the extremes and the depressive impact of failure to live up to and meet the demands of their narcissistic expectations serve as a greater impediment to their professional and artistic attainment. There is a failure to integrate ego-ideal percursors and idealized self-images; consequently, the grandiose self on one hand and the unmodified and primitive aggressive aspects of the superego on the other are left relatively intact. These structures are left at a primary introjective level of integration with the result that primitive elements of aggression, both oral and anal, are highly susceptible to reprojection in the form of paranoid projections.

While such individuals may show a pattern of authoritarian conformity, they nonetheless see themselves as getting away with something. It is often out of this context of narcissistic grandiosity and its attendant unleashing of primitive aggressive impulses and their correlative projection to the outer world that the antisocial tendencies and conflicts with authority arise. The narcissism in such cases may take the form of the demand that recognition and reward be given them without the necessity of having to work for it or earn it, along with the resentment at the failure of the world to respond to this demand, which may then take the further form of resentment and resistance to all forms of external control. This was, for example, the difficulty with our young student radical Fred. Behind his wish to destroy contemporary institutions was the intense resentment and bitter hatred of his father. But behind both of these, there was the insatiable and demanding narcissism which dictated the terms of his disappointment and bitterness toward both of these unresponsive and uncaring institutions.

The "Exceptions"

A particularly interesting manifestation of paranoid pathology is the process of narcissistic fixation in connection with bodily defects. Physical deformity can become a significantly pathogenic element in the formation and preservation of narcissistic disturbances. In discussing character types, Freud (1916) described what he called the "exceptions." These were patients in whom congenital anomalies or physical malformations had occurred early in life and who consequently refused to accept the regulation or limitation imposed by reality. These defects were often minor or hidden imperfections, but they became the vehicle for the expression of often intense narcissism. Such patients often manifest the residues of an unresolved narcissistic injury (Bing and Marburg, 1962). The unresolved narcissistic injury may result in compensatory narcissistic grandiosity or increased aggression, often expressed in temper tantrums or outbursts of rage. Such patients frequently entertain fantasies of revenge along with fantasies of birth and rebirth. The themes of omnipotence and immortality are often woven through the fabric of such fantasies. Patients will cling to a fantasy of invulnerability and invincibility with a persistence and tenacity which assume almost delusional intensity. This characteristic is often found in creative or artistic personalities who attribute to their creative activities a quality of great significance or timelessness (Niederland, 1965).

Often the defect is cloaked with a secrecy and a context of magical connotations and may be concealed in the course of analysis until the second year or even later. As we have noted, this area of the patient's traumatized narcissism is often shrouded in secrecy and hidden from the attention or inquiry of the analyst. There is often a linkage of secrets and a keeping of secrets to this secret defect. This, as we can recall, was a significant aspect of the pathology in our patient Jim. The heart defect, for which he was operated on at the age of five, was kept as a terrible and powerful—even magical—secret, which formed a special bond between himself and his mother. As a child, and even later into his young adult years, the emphasis on secrets and the significance of secrets as a vehicle of maintaining his contact with his mother and the sense of narcissistic investment he derived from her were significant aspects of his family involvement. The secrets inevitably had to do with the ultimate secret of his defectiveness and the link that it established to his specialness as her defective baby who needed to be cared for and protected. While there were Oedipal elements in this yearning for closeness and special relationship with his mother, the determinants were to a significant degree also pregenital. His inner defect became a special focus and highly cathected core of his narcissistic disorder. Beyond the defect, there was the hidden aspect of things that were powerful and magical and overburdened with sadistic destructiveness. The anal implications of such material were transparent. To keep the defect a secret, as to hide his feces, represented a narcissistic empowerment to Jimmy, and represented the grandiose and fantasied power which lay behind and was cloaked by the special magical quality of his defectiveness. Thus the narcissistic trauma was magically undone.

As was evident in Jimmy's case—as also to a certain extent in Bob's where the defect was a more specifically genital defect—the narcissistic fixation and related trauma were significantly involved with the mother's pathology. This aspect of the pathology of narcissistic traumata in defective children has been focused on by Lax (1972). During pregnancy there is a marked shift of libidinal concentration on the self within the mother, so that her expanding self-representation is more intensely cathected with narcissism. This established a more or less symbiotic bond between herself and the infant-to-be. The symbiosis, nonetheless, continues after birth so that the child, even though he comes to be regarded as an object now separated from the mother's body, is nonetheless cathected with a fusion of narcissistic and object libido.

When the child turns out to be somehow defective, the mother's worst fears during pregnancy of the child being misshapen or retarded or otherwise undeveloped are realized. The effect is a severe narcissistic trauma. The intensity and pathogenicity of this result depend on the degree of narcissistic distortion present in the mother. Since the child is a split-off portion of the mother's self, a defective child profoundly affects the mother's self-image. The impairment of the mother's self-image is followed by a sense of devaluation and feelings of evilness and worthlessness.

These feelings are intensified to the extent that the child may come to represent a compensation for the earlier narcissistic wound involved in the little girl's lack of a penis. The more intense, therefore, the element of penis envy in such mothers, the more debilitating is the narcissistic affront. The birth of a defective child rekindles these latent, unconscious conflicts and their related resentments. The child comes to represent the mother's unconscious and infantile-damaged and deprived self. The mother is often overwhelmed with a sense of hopelessness and failure. The assault on the mother's self-esteem, and her sense of helplessness, hopelessness, and defectiveness set the stage for the operation of the mechanism of depression. The highly cathected narcissistic aspiration for the compensating and wished-for baby is confronted by the ego's disappointment, and its realization of its helplessness to achieve the object of its aspiration. The disparity between the hoped-for ideal and the reality evokes a narcissistic mortification, a depletion and impairment of the self-representation. Depression follows due to the shift in narcissistic equilibrium.

An important element in this constellation of narcissistic vicissitudes is that the magnitude or obviousness of the child's defect has little to do with the severity of the depressive reaction (Niederland, 1965). The severity of the depression depends to the extent to which the mother sees the child as an externalization of her own defective self. We can judge, for example, from the obsessional concern and preoccupation demonstrated by Bob's mother over his undescended testicle and from the anxious and concerned worry and preoccupation evinced by Jimmy's mother over his patent ductus, that the physical anatomy became quickly overburdened by the weight of the mother's projection of defectiveness and inferiority onto the child. In both cases the projection reflected the underlying narcissistic deprivation that persisted in the mother's own self-image. In both cases the impact of the child's own emerging sense of self was considerable and could hardly have had any other effect but to diminish and deplete the child's own sense of narcissistic fulfillment.

Patterns of interaction between such mothers and their defective children can span a wide spectrum from hypersolicitude to complete rejection. Such mothers can completely deny the child's handicap, or they can excessively emphasize and magnify the defect. Often the mother's own narcissistic vulnerability cannot tolerate the mortification derived from the impaired child figure. The child is rejected, consequently, due to its incapacity to gratify and fulfill the mother's narcissistic needs. Often in such cases the overly protective and solicitous and concerned mother overcomes her wishes to neglect and even destroy the impaired child. Such attitudes would seem to reflect unconscious inner feelings of self-hatred and self-contempt, which are projected onto the child as the representative of the mother's own self-image.

While these dynamics are dramatically displayed in the mothers of defective children, one might wonder the role that they might play in the birth of female children. To the mother who devalues herself as a woman, the birth of a female child must in some way represent something analogous to the birth of a defective child. The child does not coincide with the mother's image of the narcissistically invested, hoped-for infant. The projection of this defective self-image onto the female child may therefore form the basis of a fundamental introjection, which serves to distort the child's emerging sense of self-awareness. Thus the chain of narcissistic disappointment can be handed down from generation to generation. Solnit and Stark have also described this process in terms of a mourning process (1961). The process is easily identifiable in each of our female patients.

Psychoanalytic View of Shame

Narcissistic Mortification

The point of view that is emerging in the course of this study, takes the affect of shame to lie close to the dynamic heart of the paranoid process. Shame is, in this view, the direct affective expression of the underlying narcissistic deprivation or mortification. In all of the patients we have discussed, we have found significant elements of shame. Often this aspect of their inner state has remained relatively concealed through significant periods of the therapy. It is an area which carries the burden of sensitivity and guardedness, as though it were a sensitive pain center which the patient needed to keep hidden and concealed at all costs. While the affective shame could be frequently attached to certain past actions or characteristics or behaviors, more frequently the focus of the feeling of shame was directed toward the self. These patients are by-and-large ashamed of what they have come to be.

The extent to which this whole area of shameful feeling can be preserved over long periods of time is sometimes astounding. Perhaps the best example of this was Gloria. Through all the nearly five years of psychotherapy which she and I carried out together, the pattern of her response was one of constant blocking and obfuscation. Whenever we would get close to any area of significant emotional involvement for her, her mental processes would seem to fragment and become disorganized before my eyes. She would forget statements she had made minutes before. Her memory would become a blank. She would literally be unable to put together two consecutive sentences. The blocking was massive and sometimes almost total. On rare occasions—very rare occasions—by dint of some effortful digging on my part, we were able to get at some of what she was feeling. Inevitably it came out to be a feeling of confusion and shame, a general state of feeling that she described as "embarrassment." At such points in the therapy it seemed that we had come close to, if not touched upon, areas of self-concern and self-contempt which generated a feeling of deep and pervasive shame in Gloria. It should be added that I was never able to break through this stubborn barrier. It inevitably stalled and frustrated any progress in her therapy.

But similar attitudes and feelings, in varying degrees of intensity and dimension, were recognizable in all our patients. In Jimmy, for example, there was no question that he felt an abiding sense of inferiority and shamefulness about himself. It expressed itself in his profound and utter conviction of failure. For him it was very precisely and specifically a defense against his underlying narcissistic and exhibitionistic wishes. Any occasions on which we were able to break through this feeling of shameful inferiority, were labeled by him as "showing off." It was only by dint of long and laborious and repeated clarifications that it became clear to him that he was unable to see the difference between showing himself with whatever talents and capacities he might realistically possess, and exhibitionistically "showing off."

Often the patient's resistance, which seems so intense and belabored, finally yields up a relatively trivial fantasy to which the feeling of shame is attached. Often this terrible secret is shared with the analyst as a privileged communication. It becomes a communication which is enshrined with special importance and significance within the patient's inner world. The analyst or therapist may experience a sense of disappointment, a letdown which does not measure up to the echoes of power and importance that the experience has in the patient's perspective. As Kohut (1971) has pointed out, the patient's shame is related to the discharge of relatively crude and unneutralized narcissistic exhibitionistic libido. His concern is inevitably associated with his fear of ridicule and humiliation.

Psychoanalytic View of Shame

The concept of shame does not have a significant history in psychoanalytic thinking. In the older literature it was generally discussed under the rubric of inferiority feelings. In Alexander's treatment, rather typically the discussion of shame was related to that of guilt, both being regarded as affective states related to superego functioning. Alexander defined guilt as a fearful expectation of deserved suffering for commitment of certain acts which results in inhibiting the discharge of forbidden impulses, usually of a destructive nature. The punishment is deserved because the aggression is unjustified. In contrast, inferiority feelings are based on making of comparisons in which one is regarded as a failure (Alexander, 1938). Alexander pointed out that while guilt was relatively inhibitory of hostile, aggressive impulses, the sense of shame often stimulated an aggressive response. The overcoming of guilt required atonement and repression, while the overcoming of shame required an increase in ambition and competitive behavior. Thus he felt that inferiority feelings stemmed from deeper or earlier conflicts.

Some years later, Piers and Singer (1953) sought to distinguish between shame and guilt on the basis of their respective relations to the functioning of ego-ideal, while guilt arises out of the tension between ego and superego. Linked with shame was the fear of contempt and rejection, and on a deeper level abandonment (Spiegel, 1966). To this was contrasted the fear of castration that was linked to a sense of guilt.

The link between shame and narcissism was established through the ego-ideal, which was the psychic representative of the child's original narcissism. The ego-ideal is constructed out of positive identifications with the parents, and thus contains a core of narcissistic omnipotence. Later identifications, particularly those which are significant in determining social role, are also included in the ego-ideal. Another significant portion concerned certain goals of the ego which relate to the concept of mastery, such that the successful expression of the drive to mastery and its accompanying accomplishment in accordance with the demands of the ego-ideal is a source of significant narcissistic gratification of the ego. Thus guilt is the penalty of transgression; shame is the penalty of failure.

The connection with aggression, however, forms one of the more significant aspects of the dynamics of shame. Over a decade ago Eidelberg pointed out the connection between narcissistic mortification, with its components of humiliation and helplessness, and its connection with revenge as a means of undoing what has happened. Aggression is mobilized and the individual seeks to inflict narcissistic mortification on the object (Bing and Marburg, 1962). However, as Ross was quick to indicate in the same symposium, the feeling of helplessness related to the narcissistic mortification does not necessarily lead to a need for revenge. He commented that, at least on the levels of neurotic adjustment, the accomplishment associated with a sense of mastery might be sufficient to compensate for the narcissistic mortification. Eidelberg's reply was significant for the present discussion, since he observed that narcissistic mortification is ubiquitous in all neurosis, and that the motivation of revenge was not simply limited to paranoid psychopathology. The argument, of course, which we are proposing in this study, is that the rudiments of shame and its associated narcissistic deprivation or mortification are inherent not only in psychopathology, whether explicitly paranoid or more generally neurotic, but that they are fundamental aspects of all human experience. This important point in our argument has been amply substantiated by Rochlin's recent contribution (1973), but this consideration has more specific application in connection with the dynamics of aggression.

Shame as Signal Affect

In following Freud's suggestion that shame, along with disgust, was one of the important inhibitory forces opposing the excessive expression of the sexual instinct, Levin (1967) has suggested that shame can function as a signal affect. Thus it has the important function of preventing overexposure to trauma—in Levin's terms the trauma of rejection. However, in terms of the present discussion, shame serves as a protection from narcissistic trauma. Shame is effective in controlling the degree of self-exposure as well as the direction of such exposure, in order that one is not needlessly subjected to the possibilities of trauma. Trauma can take the shape of ridicule, scorn, abandonment, rejection, etc. (Rochlin, 1961; Spiegel, 1966). It thus stands in opposition to the wished-for acceptance or respect which is a component of self-esteem.

Shame is thus the signal affect for feelings of humiliation, inferiority, or narcissistic mortification. It can easily be seen that shame can function quite directly in relation to the projective economy, since the self-exposure involved in shame must involve a perception of others perceiving the self as a failure, or as regarding him with some form of devaluation or contempt. In a derivative sense as well, it serves as a painful affect which can in a secondary way serve to stimulate signal anxiety, which arouses the ego to defend against the shame affect by repression or other defensive maneuvers.

Shaming

Although shame may arise in the course of development as a basic inner regulator of libido, its function is primarily a reflection of injured narcissism. The susceptibility to shame is undoubtedly influenced by the tendency of parents to utilize it in the socialization of the child. Such shaming from the parents can again serve as a narcissistic trauma. The traumatic effects of parental shaming obviously are mitigated by a larger context of parent-child interaction and the extent to which parental shaming reflects a basically positive affection for the child.

The infantile response to parental shaming is usually in the direction of inhibition or repression. It is on this basis that some of the basic repressions which are reflected in adulthood become established. Thus the influence of parental shaming on the development of character and the subsequent history of the child's capacity to reach out and express are sometimes profound. Lichtenstein has in fact related the impact of parental shaming to the acquisition of the child's identity (1961). Quite frequently in patients with paranoid propensities there is a certain distance from others around them as a means of self-protection and as a way of avoiding the intense shame they experience under conditions of self-exposure. In many such patients, any attention from others is experienced as shameful. Even when the response of others is one of admiration or praise, these patients react with feelings of shame.

Such individuals are often acutely attuned to the potentialities of criticism from others. Frequently when such critical attitudes are not forthcoming as expected, they then become guarded and suspicious, with the presumption that even more dreadful criticism is being kept concealed. Such patients tend to become very guarded and often secretive. The same sorts of reaction, when generated at a slightly greater degree of intensity of shame, can easily issue into frank paranoid symptoms of ideas of reference, or a feeling that one's mind is being read, etc.

The motif of shame and its connection with these attitudes are brought sharply to mind by my experience with another patient not reported in the cases. This was a young woman of about 30 who came to analysis for a rather severe depression, which involved a severe impairment of self-esteem. Her chronic and recurrent expectation was that she would be criticized for whatever she did. These feelings could easily be traced to her hypercritical mother, in whose eyes this girl could do nothing right and could do nothing to demonstrate any worthwhileness. These expectations were transposed to the transference and expressed themselves in her conviction that I would be critical of her, that I would tell her she was a worthless patient who did not deserve to be analyzed. Her conviction was that I was sitting, waiting and watching her, letting the analytic material build up so I could then turn on her and show her how worthless and evil she was. She even felt at times that I was reading the perverse and degenerate thoughts that came into her mind and that I could only feel contempt and disgust at what I must be seeing in her. The whole of this material was underlaid quite extensively and intensively with shameful feelings.

Dynamics of Shame

Levin has referred to two levels of shame. The first and deeper level is that of primary shame, which attaches to thoughts, feelings, and impulses which in consequence tend to be inhibited or suppressed. On a more superficial level, secondary shame is experienced as a response to the primary shame affect. The patient is in a sense ashamed of shame. On the secondary level, however, there may be efforts to conceal shame and its related inhibitions. Individuals may be led to conform with peer group expectations as a result of secondary shame. Thus students may indulge in sexual activity or take drugs as a way of avoiding the criticism or ridicule of fellow students. The avoidance of such shaming attitudes of others may be unconsciously motivated by previous shaming experiences on an infantile level. Moreover, the lack of shame is regarded in many subcultural settings as a sign of strength or capacity, so that concealment of such shame responses becomes a necessity. This process may at times take the form of counterphobic maneuvers or attempts at excessive exposure to shame-inducing experiences.

It has been observed that shame and guilt are often associated in the patient's experience. Piers and Singer (1953) refer to such complex reactions as "guilt-shame cycles." Shame is related to the frustration of narcissistic aspirations, but depends for the most part on the perception of such failure on the part of others. Such attitudes can be internalized, but often the experience of shame still requires the external exposure. The intense experience of shame can lead to the disturbance of the libidinal economy so that diffusion ensues and destructive energies are thus deneutralized and may be channeled via the superego against the self. When this happens it is experienced by the subject as guilt. In such cases, the narcissistic defense takes the introjective route and gives rise to a depressive position. However, the deneutralized energy can also be directed exteriorly in the form of a blaming response. This is more typically associated with projected elements and is more characteristic of a paranoid response. The blaming operation has the advantage of helping to support and restore narcissistic equilibrium. The depressive alternative is less satisfactory in this regard.

The presumption on which much of the discussion of shame rests, namely, that the affect of shame is related to the tension between ego and ego-ideal and reflects a failure on the part of the ego to live up to ego-ideal aspirations, has been challenged in passing by Kohut (1971). He agrees that shame signals do play a role in restoring and maintaining homeostatic narcissistic equilibrium. But he rejects the notion that shame is a reaction of the ego to failure in fulfilling ego-ideal expectations. He observes that many shame-prone individuals do not have strong ideals, but that for the most part they are exhibitionistic people driven by ambition. The economic imbalance which is experienced as shame is rather due to a flooding of the ego by unneutralized exhibitionism rather than to a comparative ego-weakness in relationship to the ego-ideal.

Narcissistic defeats for such individuals are experienced as shame, but then, more often than not, the experience of shame is followed by envy. This combined state of shame and envy may be followed by self-destructive impulses and a feeling of guilt. But Kohut understands these not as superego attacks, but as attempts by the ego to do away with the disappointing reality of failure. Self-destructive impulses are an expression of narcissistic rage. Kohut cautions in this connection that the attempt to deal with shame-prone patients therapeutically by diminishing the power of the ideal system is frequently a technical error, but that success is more frequently founded on the basis of a shift in narcissism from investment in the grandiose self to the ego-ideal system. His approach is based on the strengthening of the ego-ideal rather than on attempting to diminish it.

It must be confessed that the resolution and integration of the patient's shame experience can provide one of the stickiest and most difficult areas in the therapy of patients with paranoid elements. The cases, which may be regarded as therapeutically least successful in our series of patients, are those in which there was a central shame-enshrined core which the patient was either unable to share with the therapist or in which the therapy had not progressed to the point where the intensity of the shame had been mitigated to any significant degree. In the case of Gloria, the intensity in the area of shame seemed to cover a wide area of her inner experience of herself.

Enuresis

We have taken note in passing of the prominence of enuretic symptoms in a number of these patients and of its role in their developmental experience. In all of these cases it is apparent that the parents used shaming as a form of disciplinary regulation. Thus the shaming experience based on persistent enuresis and its regressive determinants became a focus for the emerging sense of self as shameful and defective that played such a prominent role in the pathology of these patients. Enuresis is not significant in this development, except as a focus by which the shaming tendencies of the parents could be expressed and by which the child could elicit and channel the parent's shaming tendency.

It is well known in general that enuresis is a not uncommon and highly multidetermined symptom. Often it is associated with situations which induce regression in the child—such as disappointments, rejections, abandonments, losses, birth of siblings, etc. The regressive loss of control over bladder functions offers the potentiality for shameful experience. But the pathogenic impact of it depends on the manner of the parent's shaming attack on the child, as well as upon the extent to which the child is forced to resort to the eliciting of shame in the context of interaction with the parents. What is apparent is not merely that the shaming inflicts a narcissistic injury on the child, but the latter in many ways invests himself in eliciting such injury. There is often a defiant quality to this, something to which Winnicott (1958) has called attention in terms of the "nuisance value of the symptoms."

The important points that need to be made at this juncture are the following: first, that the enuresis serves to elicit a shaming response from the parents; second, that the shaming activity on the part of the parent carries the potentiality for narcissistic injury; third, that the pathogenic impact of the shaming is a function of the extent to which the enuresis carries the connotation of parental failure or ineptitude which serves to make it a narcissistic defeat for the parents; fourth, that the effects of shaming are complexly related to aspects of parental psychopathology, often involving narcissistically susceptible areas of the parents' own personalities, which are projected onto the child and condemned and devalued and shamed in him; fifth, the shame experience together with the context of parental projection, often sets off a chain of contextual responses by which the child internalized the parental shaming attitude and sets about achieving a verification of the parental shaming attitude by prolonging the shame-inducing situation or by substituting other shame-producing symptoms or behaviors.

Finally, it should be noted that shaming is a variant of blaming which we have identified as so closely involved in the paranoid process. We have already noted the role of blaming in setting the cognitive style as well as the defensive style in the family context. We will have more to say about this later, but the relationship of shaming to blaming should not be allowed to pass unnoticed. We will return to this subject later in connection with the development of delinquency or antisocial tendencies.

Envy

Relation to Narcissism

We have already given adequate consideration to the pathology of envy and its relation to the paranoid process (see above pp.). There would be little point in recasting that discussion at this point, except to underline the intimate connection between envy and jealousy as pathological states of mind, or pathological affect states, and the vicissitudes of narcissism.

On a clinical level, it must be said that envy has a marked component in the psychological makeup of all our patients. The component of envy is in each of them intimately tied up in the feelings of shamefulness and the correlative tendency to projection and blaming which characterized their pathological adjustment. To a man (or a woman) they all felt themselves to be deprived, cheated, unfortunates. In one way or another, they felt strongly and bitterly that life had somehow deprived them of something that was their due.

Such envious feelings are frequently identifiable in narcissistic patients. The paradigm is that offered by Freud, namely that of the "exceptions" (1916). In these cases, as we have noted, the physical malformation serves as a narcissistic injury which allows the individual to feel deprived and correspondingly entitled to compensatory recognition or acceptance, or entitled to special considerations and benefits and benefits that others who have not suffered such deprivations are in no way entitled to. Such individuals feel they should not have to earn recognition, but it should be accorded them automatically. They feel resentful that they must work to support themselves, feeling the world somehow owes it to them to support them without such strenuous efforts on their own part. They have an abiding sense of unfairness at having to face, acknowledge, and submit themselves to the restraints and limitations of an unfeeling and forbidding reality (Jacobson, 1959).

Such feelings of deprivation and resentful entitlement are often bound in with penis envy in certain female patients (Freud, 1916; Jacobson, 1959). But if we were to allow ourselves to consider only the genital implications and relation to castration concerns, we would miss the essential narcissistic dimension of this basic envy state. These feelings also can play a role in the transference. This was particularly true in one of my female patients whose narcissism was quite strongly fixated at an infantile level. At the birth of her two years younger brother, she felt herself deprived and cheated, particularly since she felt she was no longer the center of her parents' affection and attention, and she was forced to take a second place to her brother.

The narcissistic loss and the resulting envy drove her to focus all her resentment on her brother's penis—the only obvious difference between herself and him upon which she could attach her attempts to understand why he had become more important than herself. Penis envy became a pervasive aspect of her neurotic adjustment and led to highly competitive and narcissistic ambitions which drove her to seek high academic accomplishments. When her efforts did not measure up to the level of her aspirations, she inevitably felt herself to be a failure, and plunged once again into the depressive trough. Her state of mind was overshadowed by the overwhelming conviction that anyone who did not have a penis was not worth anything and could never be in a position to achieve anything significant in life.

In the transference relationship, she carried the conviction that she could only improve her situation by depending on me and keeping in my good favor. This was a direct reflection of her childhood conviction that the only way she could maintain any importance or any value in her parents' eyes was by a continual attempt to please her father and keep in his good favor. She did not have a penis.

Only late in the analysis was this patient able to express and work through some of her intense envious feelings of me. She saw me as a strong, capable, helping person and came to feel she could rely on and trust me. But beyond this capacity for trust and her therapeutic compliance, there was the conviction that she had to depend on, please, and comply with my wishes, since it was only by clinging to a powerful penis-bearing object that she could have any hope of gaining strength for herself and stabilizing her sense of self-worth. Embedded in this was a deep and abiding sense of envy. This envy was focused on the issue of penis-power, but at a deeper primitive level, it cloaked the primitive oral rage at having been deprived of the pleasures of mother's breast and the accompanying infantile attention and adulation.

Envy and Paranoia

Something similar can be identified in the paranoid patients we have been discussing. The envy is often difficult to get at and along with the associated shame is often long in coming to the surface. However, since the envy is so closely related to these patients' tendencies to blame and to project, the most superficial levels of enviousness are relatively more available than the levels of shame. The problem often is that envy quickly activates the patient's underlying shame and stimulates the defensive retreat and guarded suspiciousness and secretiveness that one so often sees in such patients.

Enviousness of this sort can often be an impediment to treatment. This element has been recently suggested by Modell (1971). He points out that, while Freud had originally assumed the content of unconscious guilt feelings was responsible for the negative therapeutic reaction, specifically the incestuous and rivalrous impulses, his own experience indicates that the guilt associated with negative therapeutic reaction is related to the conviction that one does not have a right to the better life that might follow as a consequence of the success of the analytic process. The essential element here is that of envy. Such individuals seem to suffer from a conviction that they do not have a right to such improvement and therapeutic success. Modell points out a common fantasy shared by these patients, namely, that if they were to possess something good, this would mean that they were depriving someone else of this same improvement. Modell comments, "These individuals seemed to suffer from a particularly intense form of envy and greed, i.e., they wished to take away all that others possessed. So that in an additional sense the negative therapeutic reaction could be understood as a wish to deprive the analyst of the 'good' that he possessed by virtue of his therapeutic skill" (1971, p. 340). A similar point, based on somewhat different theoretical presumptions, was made by Melanie Klein (1957), who interpreted envy as one of the primary contributing factors to negative therapeutic reactions.

The Logic of Narcissism

The presumption which Modell underlines is basically embedded in a narcissistic logic. The logic of narcissism states originally that if the subject is without a certain good, then everyone else must be in possession of it, so that the subject is therefore inferior. The postulate, true to the dynamics of narcissism, is unwilling to consider the proposition in any but absolute terms. That is, if the patient is deprived to any degree, the deprivation is seen as absolute. Consequently, if the patient feels himself to be so deprived, he sees himself as having nothing and others around him having everything. Herein lies the root of the jealousy. If the proposition can be converted, however, it would come to mean that when the patient comes to acquire some good others would thereby be deprived—and that the acquisition and deprivation had to be seen in absolute terms. Herein lies the root of a possible negative therapeutic response.

The same process of envious possessiveness and blaming and the logic of absolutes can be seen in our patients. For Jimmy, whatever was possessed or attained by his brothers in any degree was thereby proscribed and prohibited for him. If his oldest brother was able to achieve academic success and recognition, this inevitably meant, by the inexorable logic of his narcissism, that Jimmy was foredoomed to academic failure and ineptitude. A similar process takes place in the process of blaming, which tends to gravitate toward the excessive extremes of the absolute. It is extremely difficult for such patients to accept and recognize that the course of real events and experiences through which they have passed may have been due to responsibilities and failures that could be shared by those around them as well as themselves.

It is very difficult for them to understand that responsibility as well as blame can be distributed in degrees and in proportions. There is a tendency to want to escape any onus of blame and discharge it from the self by projecting it onto others around them, particularly the parents. The logic of narcissistic injury dictates that if blame is to be accepted, then it must be accepted totally and absolutely. Similarly, if blame is to be charged against someone else, the charge must be total and absolute. Thus it was fascinating, in the course of Karen's treatment, to watch her vacillate back and forth between these two alternatives—either by accepting blame for what she had experienced and for her bitter anger and resentment about it, thus completely absolving and exonerating her parents and others who had disappointed her, or by discharging blame totally on them and seeing herself completely and rather paranoidally as a victim, helpless and vulnerable.

The other interesting part about the dynamics of envy, which also contributes in part to the negative therapeutic response in these patients, is the persistence with which they adhere to their enviousness and the attendant resentment. This was particularly striking in Gloria's case, as we have noted in other respects elsewhere. This state of mind with its intense and perduring envy allows no room for forgiving or forgetting. For one very dramatic moment in the course of her therapy, Gloria stated flatly and unequivocally—as well as angrily and provocatively—that she had no intention of making any efforts to improve her lot or to help herself get better, that she had no intention of cooperating with the process of therapy any more than was minimally required. She expressed the intense feeling that she had been deprived, cheated, treated unfairly by her parents, and that it was up to them to do something about it. She said, "I'll be Goddamned if I'm going to budge a single inch! It's up to them to make up for what they did to me, and I'm not going to do anything to make it easier for them!" The statement was vehement, angry, bitter, stubborn, and unyielding. It reflected the intensity with which Gloria was clinging to her position of narcissistic affront, and the demand that it carried with it of the recompense that she felt was due to her. She would exact the price no matter what it cost her!

It is plain that, in addition to the narcissistic mortification that lies behind such feelings, there is a great deal of aggression mobilized. We will focus more explicitly on the role of aggression in the following section, but at this point it is important that the aggressive component and its mobilization be seen in relation to the underlying narcissistic issues. The aggression in such paranoid states of mind is not a blind resentment or lashing out. It is rather a motivated response which has specific entanglements with the underlying narcissistic deprivations and traumata. This is of particular importance in the understanding of paranoid processes since what is often primarily the content of projective mechanisms is the derivative of aggressive impulses. But this brings us more immediately to the threshold of the consideration of aggression in the paranoid process.

CHAPTER 22

Defensive Aspects: Aggression

AGGRESSION IN PARANOIA

It would be difficult, indeed, to miss the strong aggressive component in paranoid manifestations. Even though Freud's treatment of Schreber's paranoia was so taken up with libidinal emphases that Freud did not explicitly develop the role of aggression in Schreber's illness, as we have seen, Freud was well aware of the destructive and aggressive impact of paranoid delusions. Whether we are dealing with fantasies of world destruction à la Schreber or whether we are dealing with sensitive apprehensions of being "dumped on" or "put down," the content of the paranoid projection is inevitably aggressive in tone—even though the degree of aggression expressed can vary across a very wide spectrum indeed. From this point of view there are few of us who from time to time do not experience moments of paranoid apprehension and uneasiness.

Consequently it is no great labor to discern the elements of aggression in the patients we have described. The intensity of their projected aggression varies over the full extent of the spectrum. It ranges from fears of murderous intent on the part of others to mildly phobic and anxious tension and apprehension over the devaluing and critical attitudes of significant figures around them. Within the psychoanalytic setting as well, the spectrum of such paranoid feelings runs from a level of intense persecutory anxiety and near panic to a much more muted and chronic level of mild tension and discomfort.

There is certainly something very fatalistic and pessimistic about an instinctual theory of aggression simply stated as such. There is much in Freud's own writings, particularly with reference to the "death instinct," that suggests that his own instinctual theories carried with them this pessimistic and highly deterministic conviction. In an era in which war and violence are matters of general human concern, and in which the potential for human destructiveness has reached nuclear proportions, the ominousness of such theory is powerful and quite overwhelming.

Such an attitude sees aggression as an inexorable natural force and its destructive consequences as being somehow inevitable and uncontrollable. It would seem to me an unavoidable consequence that such a conviction about the nature of aggression could carry with it only sentiments of fright and powerlessness, which can find their sole solace in resignation and submission to these ineluctable forces of nature. Thus, if we all perish as a result of the overwhelming capacity for destructiveness buried in human nature, at least we will have the consolation that this tragedy was forced upon us by our natures and that we had no control over it. But, I would suggest that such an attitude bears the stamp of paranoid thinking—particularly in that it elicits a response of masochistic submissiveness to powerful and uncontrollable forces, which exercise their malignant intent upon us without any capacity within ourselves to alter their tragic outcome.

Ictal Destructiveness

There are of course some data, as we have already indicated, which suggest that the impulse of destructiveness may in some cases be relatively uncontrollable and may have destructive outcomes. But the number of patients in whom ictal aggression can be linked to specific epileptic focuses in the amygdala and temporal lobe structures is quite restricted. In such individuals, the concept of a spontaneous outburst of compulsively destructive aggression, propelled by the discharge of electrical impulses in these abnormally functioning parts of the brain, cannot serve as a sufficient basis for an understanding of the nature and function of aggression. It does, however, help us to define one polar expression of the aggressive spectrum (Mark and Ervin, 1970).

Even in these selected cases where epileptic focuses can be specifically linked with outbursts of destructive behavior, the appearance of the dysrhythmia is not entirely autonomous and may reflect complex interactions with other physiological and motivational barriers. And also, it cannot be said that the relationship between aggression and the occurrence of psychomotor seizures is a direct relationship. Specific instances of ictal aggression are difficult to demonstrate and even some of the patients reported by Mark and Ervin (1970) have shown improvement in aggressive behavior as a result of stereotactic amygdalotomy, but their psychomotor seizures have not abated. A recent study, moreover, has suggested that as a general rule psychomotor seizures are not associated with aggressive or destructive behavior, but that if the patient is physically restrained during a confusional state he might react in a defensive manner that might be interpreted as aggressive assault. However, if the patient is left to his own devices during the seizure episode, his behavior is generally limited to somewhat confused and aimless automatic behavior.

Certainly the connection between limbic system structures and aggressive behavior has been well established in animals, and probably can also be reasonably presumed to be involved in human aggressive behavior as well. While psychomotor seizures are known to originate from sites within the limbic system, there may be other mechanisms that underlie specifically aggressive acting-out. But we can, at this point of our knowledge, by no means state unequivocally that the epileptic discharge in such specific brain centers as the amygdala are unequivocally associated with aggressive behaviors as a direct effect of the brain discharge without other complicating and modifying motivational or situational factors which may serve to channel the basically physiologically impulse into forms of destructive expression (Rodin, 1973). Consequently even in this narrowly selected category of aggressive behavior, we cannot conclude that man is constantly driven by a bombardment of aggressive impulses which are somehow struggling for expression.

Certainly we must ask ourselves what are the conditions under which excessive and destructive violence can be unleashed. The answers are complex and varied. Rollo May, for example, appeals to "powerlessness" as the underlying motivational circumstance which unleashes violent reaction (May, 1972). Related to this, is Fromm's notion of boredom (1973). Fromm sees boredom as not due to external circumstances, in terms of absence of excitation or stimulation, but as a subjective factor within the personality which reflects an inability to respond to objects in the environment with any real sense of interest. Boredom thus resembles the patterns of apathetic and lethargic disinterest so often seen in depressed states. There is a lack of appetite, a lack of interest or responsiveness to events or persons, and a feeling of powerlessness and incapacity which leads only to a sense of doleful resignation. Often such individuals in milder states of boredom, usually unconscious, are constantly seeking new stimulation, new excitement.

This attitude is so widely distributed that it seems almost a chronic and universal symptom of contemporary industrial society. There is an almost compulsive consumption of sex, liquor, drugs, travel, and the toys and trinkets that modern advertising and industrial productiveness dangle before our eyes. There is a chronic addiction to use and consumption, and the seeking of new and different experiences, things, people, and places. But, as Fromm points out, one of the important ways of dealing with boredom and escaping from it is through aggression—even to the point of violence and destructiveness. The expression of violence and destructiveness can provide an immediate outlet and relief from boredom, particularly for those who have not the resources, either financial, educational, or personal, to seek out other more constructive and productive means for relieving such inner boredom.

Such an escape into excitement has been thought to be related to the development of juvenile delinquency as well. Many adolescents who have resorted to forms of delinquent behavior seem to have undertaken criminal acts for the purpose, in part at least, of relieving and overcoming a sense of boredom. Even in cases of murderous assault, such delinquents often describe a feeling of intense excitement, of feeling once and for all recognized and responded to, of finding recognition in the anguished and fear-ridden face of the victim. Such feelings have also been described in cases of sexual assault.

There are perhaps good reasons to be concerned about the role of boredom and powerlessness and their relationship to aggressive behavior in contemporary society. The increase of boredom can be seen in relation to routinization of job tasks and the proliferation of mass production techniques. Most manual work is extremely monotonous and repetitive, and, consequently, is boring. Even white collar work tends to be boring in nature, because of the elaborate bureaucratic structure of managerial organizations, which leaves little room for responsibility or initiative to the individual functioning within the structure. It can certainly be suggested at this point, that in the syndrome of boredom we can recognize an aspect of the depressive component which relates to the operation of the paranoid process.

Antisocial Tendencies

One of the important forms of aggressive behavior is manifested in antisocial tendencies, including delinquency. Such antisocial tendencies have definite links to the paranoid process, as we shall see. This presents another area, as others we have seen, where the workings of the paranoid process interdigitate with social and environmental factors to produce complex patterns of behavior. Delinquents in general tend to be concentrated in large population centers, and particularly to be drawn from areas where social disorganization, poverty, and economic deprivation are observable. Underprivileged classes, whether social classes or racial groups, are highly overrepresented.

In general, the families of delinquents tend to be larger and more conflictual and disrupted, with more frequent changes of living place and a higher degree of disharmony than controlled homes. In such families there tends to be a higher incidence of criminal conduct and ill-defined standards of behavior and values. Delinquents generally show poor school achievement, a high rate of truancy, and their working histories are often more erratic and unstable (Glueck and Glueck, 1950; Robins, 1966). Within certain underprivileged and deprived groups and within certain areas of social disorganization in urban centers, there appear to be certain groups where individuals seem to be at high risk for delinquency. Even certain streets, particular areas, and within these areas certain families have a higher rate of delinquency. Consequently, such antisocial tendencies do not seem to be attributable only to environmental factors. It appears that the parents of the delinquents with a high rate of recidivism were in their own formative years exposed to a similar damaging family environment as the one they created for their own children. The problem can be traced back at least two generations. The same family difficulties and inadequacies that tend to produce delinquent personalities in the slums, have a similar result in middle- and upper-class families (Roth, 1972).

Such delinquent individuals exhibit a definable syndrome, a combination of immature egotism and aggressiveness that would tend to bring such individuals into conflict with any community that required cooperation and social responsibility for its functioning. In Robins' (1966) studies of delinquents in St. Louis, there was a high arrest rate and a tendency to heavy drinking. The terms "sociopath" and "psychopath" were merely reference points along a continuum of degrees of severity of pathology. Individuals given these diagnostic labels proved almost without exception to have a poor work history, to be financially dependent on social welfare, and to suffer from significant degrees of marital difficulty. The histories were replete with impulsivity, sexual promiscuity, vagrancy, etc. The individuals were described as belligerent, delinquent in paying debts, and socially alienated. Mortality was markedly higher than the normal population.

In general, the younger people who tend to have criminal charges brought against them on repeated occasions share a number of features with cases of attempted suicide, drug addiction, or severe alcoholism. They are all related to patterns of impulsive and violent behavior that often constitute a threat to life. Social and familial backgrounds are similar, along with patterns of maladjustment during certain stages of the life cycle. They also share in common a tendency to antisocial, aggressive, and self-destructive acts. The incidence peaks at the 15-24 age range and usually tends to burn out as middle age approaches. Usually in each of these deviant groups males predominate, with the exception of self-poisoning. Moreover, all of them, including delinquency, crime, attempted suicide, and drug dependence, have shown a precipitious increase in prevalence in industrial societies. And their influence has tended to spread through all levels of society, affecting younger age groups and all levels of the social hierarchy—both underprivileged and privileged.

The heart of the difficulty seems to lie in the family circumstances and particularly the quality of the relationship between the parents. Personality development reveals intense sexual, emotional, or identity difficulties in the adolescent periods, and a tendency to impairment of educational and social attainment. The utilization of drugs, which promote oblivion or increase confidence or both, is a marked aspect of their behavior. All these groups in varying degrees use alcohol, sedative or narcotic drugs, and amphetamine-like substances to a fairly significant degree. The incidence of experimentation among younger people, either with antisocial acts or in seeking out drug experiences of various kinds, is relatively high.

But a considerable mass of evidence bears testimony to the significant dichotomy between the casual experimenters and the persistent hard-core delinquents. There are significant differences in family history, in predictable course, in definable hazards, in mortality rates, and in the presence of anxiety, immaturity, hostility, impulsiveness, and low frustration tolerance. The expression of aggression in these groups has been called "frustrative-impulsive" by Roth (1972). We can suggest at this point that such patterns of impulsive aggressiveness and destructiveness are significantly related to the developmental and specifically the introjective history of such individuals. The exposure to parental and familial patterns of destructive aggression undoubtedly influences the quality of internalized aggression and the capacity for constructive utilization. This relates specifically to the question of the development of internal destructiveness, which we have seen is such a prominent aspect of the paranoid pathology.

Psychosocial Context of Delinquency

From this it is readily seen that the operation of the paranoid process cannot be easily divorced from broader psychosocial influences. In a very useful study, Kaplan (1972) has pulled together and synthesized a considerable body of evidence. He has combined these into a general statement of the bases of psychosocial deviance—particularly in relationship to the genesis of antisocial tendencies for the expression of aggressive and destructive behavior. The conclusions he reaches are readily placed in conjunction with our own findings regarding the paranoid process, particularly in terms of the relationship between paranoid manifestations and their function in preserving injured narcissism and maintaining the integrity and sense of esteem of the self.

Kaplan's model postulates that among the motivational goals of any individual are the maintenance, restoration, or attainment of positive attitudes toward the self, specifically self-esteem, as well as the avoidance of negative self-attitudes. A considerable body of empirical support is offered to this point of view by the consistent observation of associations between negative self-attitudes and specific indices of subjective distress, such as anxiety, depression, or other psychopathological responses.

Within the psychosocial framework, Kaplan denominates three areas of antecedents of such self-attitudes. The first has to do with attitudes of other people toward the subject. The degree to which such attitudes influence self-evaluations appears to be a function of factors such as the discrepancy of self and other evaluations, the actual communication of such evaluations to the subject, and finally the importance of self-evaluating persons to the subject. Secondly, the nature of the individual self-attitudes seems to be a function of the subject's possession of certain ascribed or achieved qualities, or his success in the performance of particular behaviors where such qualities or performances are highly valued. Thirdly, the subject's self-attitude seems to be influenced by his ability to utilize controls and defenses, which serve to enhance his capacity, and to define events which may be filled with negative consequences or implications in a way that will not detract from his own sense of worth, ability, or power. Effective use of denial, avoidance and rationalization, devaluation of circumstances or objects, selectivity or standards and behaviors, or selectivity in choice of personal relationships, all may be used effectively in this regard.

Selection and the use of particular mechanisms or patterns of defense and their utilization in the service of preserving self-esteem seems to be a function of early childhood experiences, the range of available options in the current situation, the degree to which the situation is relatively unstructured, and the availability of social supports and reinforcements for particular defensive patterns. Thus the model suggests that individuals who have negative self-attitudes will be more likely to adopt deviant behavior patterns than individuals who have developed positive self-attitudes.

Other factors contribute to this expectation. If an individual attributes the causes of his impaired sense of self-esteem to environmental influences, or if he is unable to perceive or pursue the available alternative patterns of action, which may be socially approved and may offer a reasonably high subjective probability of resulting in improvement of his self-esteem, or if he perceives alternative deviant patterns as more available or as offering a relatively higher degree of subjective probability in improving self-attitudes, the likelihood of his adopting deviant patterns of behavior increases. Deviant patterns may function to decrease the level of self-rejection in a number of ways: by the distortion of reality in the service of increasing self-approval of one's behaviors or achievements or characteristics; by attacking the validity of social norms and expectations of the system within which the individual has failed; by the avoidance of potentially self diminishing experiences; or by the assimilation or creation of new standards which the individual is capable of attaining and which thus offer him the possibility of gaining approval of others who may share the same or similar standards. The operation of such influences can be regarded as operating in a wide spectrum of deviant behaviors, including cheating, delinquency, drug addiction, alcoholism, or even suicide.

An implicit expectation in the adoption of such deviant patterns is the proposition that the adoption and persistence in particular patterns of structured psychosocial deviance will be attended by a more satisfying sense of self-esteem and self-attitudes than were effective prior to the adoption of such patterns. To the extent that the deviant pattern results in the sustaining of self-esteem, such a pattern would be correspondingly resistant to change unless its effectiveness in maintaining self-esteem should be diminished or unless the pattern itself becomes the occasion for further devaluing experiences, such as contempt, shaming, rejection by significant others, etc.

In applying the consideration specifically to juvenile delinquency, it can be assumed that the individual who adopts the normative standards of the adolescent delinquent subculture does so as a result of his failure to obtain positive self-evaluation according to the standards of the conventional adult culture. The more closely the delinquent identifies with the standards of the delinquent subculture, the less relevant will the conventional standards become for his own self-evaluation. This perception can be supported by data which suggest that delinquents, who identify strongly with the delinquent subculture, tend to manifest higher degrees of self-evaluation than delinquents who identify less intensely with the subcultural norms and values.

Turning to the relationship between social deviance and forms of aggressive behavior, Kaplan observes that the literature on aggression seems to be consistent with the view that overt expression of aggression, even in forms of physical violence and destructiveness, shares with other modes of psychosocial deviance the characteristic of serving as a response to a preexisting history of more or less intense self-devaluation. Such aggression also serves important functions in reducing the severity of self-rejecting attitudes. The backgrounds of individuals who characteristically employ aggressive patterns of behavior suggest that, regardless of the cultural context or mode of aggressive response, such individuals are more likely to have previously experienced self-devaluing circumstances than individuals who are not prone to the use of such destructive patterns.

Thus the suggested model of psychosocial deviance indicates that aggressive response patterns are more or less functional in reducing the severity of self-rejecting attitudes as well as the subjective distress associated with them. Data in support of such a conclusion can be found in studies of criminal assault, preschizophrenic aggression, urban revolt, school rebelliousness and even aggressive responses in clinically normal subjects. In regard to urban revolt, for example, civil disorder may become the vehicle for increasing self-esteem and self-acceptance. Even when such destructive outbursts are precipitated in the name of moral objectives such as the civil rights movements, many of those who are caught up in the intensity of the destructive outburst have no moral conviction and their involvement seems to serve primarily personal psychodynamic frustrations. Their need may be to destroy, to rebel, to seek punishment, to join themselves to a particular group, or to secure attention, or even to satisfy their own need to be victimized and martyred by injury or imprisonment. Destructive behavior thus may be seen as a form of acting-out regardless of the objectives of the cause with which it is associated—whether it be civil rights action, attaining of basic human rights, or even fanatical patriotism.

Whether the intention of such individuals is to satisfy moral convictions or to satisfy inner needs, they share the common motive to gain greater self-acceptance either by avoiding the self-undermining circumstances, or by identifying with acceptable and worthy values, thereby gaining some sense of worth for themselves, or by attacking a social structure or organization to which they attribute the basis for their self-devaluing and rejecting attitudes. Thus the participation in mob violence by blacks or students may provide them with a sense of power which serves to minimize their feelings of lack of worth and provide them a basis for increasing self-acceptance.

Kaplan also points to important cultural determinants of the tendency to adopt aggressive response patterns. Thus individuals who have been raised in cultural or subcultural settings, in which the external expression of aggression is either tolerated or encouraged, may be more likely to manifest aggressive responses under stress than other individuals who may have been reared in other cultural settings in which such expression is disapproved or prohibited. The contrast between black and Jewish subcultures in the United States has been described in this regard. The black culture is a relatively dispersive and aggression-tolerating culture, which is characterized by the encouragement of more independent and aggressive assertion and a pervasive belief in the natural aggressiveness and undependability of other persons. In parts of the black community the expression of hostility and even actual assault is a frequent part of daily experience. In the Jewish culture, by way of contrast, there is a more cohesive and aggression-inhibiting quality, which is characterized by a strong emphasis on group life and participation, mutual aid and support, family rituals and closeness among groups of relatives. There is also a strong prohibition against physical aggression.

Thus, to the extent that a culture positively sanctions the external expression of aggression, the effect is to legitimize the expression of such aggressive impulses for the individual. In consequence of such legitimization, the external expression of aggression is more highly probable. Such cultural attitudes are often transmitted within the family context. If cultural attitudes endorsing the expression of aggression are transmitted to the child in the course of early parent-child interactions, they are more likely to find expression than if they are not so transmitted. Thus the frequent association between aggressive behavior and familial contexts which tolerate a high degree of aggression can be more readily understood.

Another important determinant of the tendency to aggressive display has to do with social position. Individuals are more likely to express aggression if they occupy social roles in which such aggression is socially endorsed.

652 The Paranoid Process

An individual may occupy a number of social roles whose expectations may either reinforce or modify the propensity for aggressive expression. One such important social role is that related to sex. Social sexual roles are frequently associated with prescriptions and expectations for the expression of aggressive behavior. Certainly in Western societies aggressive behavior is regarded as more appropriate to the male than to the female role. Aggressive behavior in female children is often punished disproportionately. The socially endorsed view that aggressive behavior is more appropriate in males is learned early in the developmental process so that the suppression of overt aggressive responses is more frequently found in girls than in boys.

Religious status is another important social role which may have an inhibitory effect on the expression of aggression. This conflict is frequently found in the attitudes of militant blacks. Religiosity and militancy tend to be inversely related in black groups. This seems to obtain regardless of educational level, age, geographic region, sex, or religious denomination. A religious rationale frequently offers support to the relatively passive acceptance of the status quo. Thus refraining from militant action may be a way of submitting oneself to God's will. The religious perspective also offers recompense to the downtrodden by the promises of the afterlife and thus tends to undercut the necessity for seeking self-assertion or rebelliousness in this life. These religious alternatives may serve as more available channels for the enhancing of self-esteem than the more militant and destructive alternatives.

However, even when aggressive behavior may be sanctioned by a particular culture or the expectations of particular social roles, such behavior may not be perceived as appropriate in a particular social context. Thus the expression of male aggressiveness may be appropriate in cultural terms, but it may not be appropriate in the immediate context of interaction with a woman. Aggression is more likely to be expressed when the behavior is perceived as appropriate to the context of the immediate social relationship. The perception of relative power within such a relationship may also play a role. Aggression is more likely in a social relationship in which one party does not perceive himself as dependent on the other for need satisfaction. It could also be the case if he perceived himself as possessing relatively greater power in the relation, or if he perceived the other party as being incapable or unwilling to retaliate. The tendency to act aggressively can be strongly influenced by the probability of retaliation. Consequently, the masochistic tendency to react to aggressive onslaughts by a pattern of defeat and submission can contribute to the probability of further attack by the aggressor. The need to victimize thus can be fed and encouraged by the availability of the victim.

Altruistic Aggression

If we broaden our perspective slightly on the subject of aggression we are immediately confronted with a problem. If aggression in many respects can be regarded as destructive and antisocial, it is also true that in the perspective of history it is also regarded as constructive and entirely social in intention. Wars, crusades, and revolutions are the stuff out of which history is made. Young men even in our own times are taught to kill without compunction and even to relish the pleasure of killing for the sake of defense of their country. War and combat can provide a legitimated outlet for the expression of violent impulses. During periods of great wars and revolutionary upheavals it has often been documented that suicide rates decline. It is as though the release of aggression and violence in support of a national cause provides protection against the self-directed destructive impulses expressed in suicide. Such periods are also periods of increased social cooperation and sense of purposeful interaction, so that motives and behaviors are brought into significant congruence with other individuals. The decline of suicidal impulses is noted not only in those who are engaged in combat, but also in those who are pledged in the service of an altruistic cause, whether serving in the lines or behind them. Similar patterns of group behavior have been noted in connection with dissent, protest, civil wars, revolution, all of which exhibit their portion of violence and cruelty along with dedication and altruistic surrender.

We thus find ourselves confronted with contrasting patterns of aggressive and violent behavior. Frustrated-impulsive aggression tends to be manifested in the phenomena of delinquency and crime and other forms of antisocial activity. But another form of aggression is also expressed in political, ideological, and religious movements and has thrived during wars, revolutions, civil strife, and religious conflict. Even the latter forms of altruistic aggression can express itself in suicidal acts which are deliberately intended. Suicide can be employed to expiate dishonor in certain cultures, or in forms of ritual suicide, or even the dramatic gestures of self-incineration which have been undertaken, particularly on the Vietnam scene, as a form of political protest. Self-flagellation and self-injury have for centuries been associated with certain forms of religious fanaticism.

The frustrative-impulsive form of aggression is characteristically associated with unstable or psychopathic (antisocial) personalities, and therefore has been regarded clinically as a form of psychopathology. But altruistic forms of aggression are frequently sanctioned by large segments of the community and can be carried out by large groups of people, who are presumably to be judged as normal from a psychiatric point of view. However, it is clear historically that mass movements have often been led by decidedly psychopathic leaders and have raised themselves on the foundation of severe psychopathology. One can hardly think of the Hitler phenomenon in any but pathological terms. In the name of idealized purposes and noble attainments, unspeakable cruelties may be tolerated or passively agreed to by large segments of society. Such tacit approval to the most heinous crimes may even be given by respectable citizens who are regarded as exemplars of domestic virtue and civil responsibility. This is perhaps one of the most painful and repugnant lessons to be learned from recent history. If we judge history by the degree of death and misery, criminal violence must certainly take second place to violence that has been perpetrated in the name of good conscience. As Roth has noted so well:

> Crime in the broad sense, and the disorders linked with it, have close affinities with disease and may be regarded as undesired and dispensable manifestations to be gradually eliminated as knowledge grows. On the other hand, altruism in the sense employed, is a uniquely human quality, indispensable for social cooperation, and in some of its achievements are among the noblest works of man. Our problem today is to harness altruistic aggression to non-violent means (1972, p. 1052).

Paranoid Process

The burden of the problem for our purposes in this present study is that both of these forms of aggression are specifically manifestations of the paranoid process. In fact, the interplay of the pathological and the altruistic can be seen very clearly in the case of Fred. It is quite clear in such cases that, if a valid distinction can be drawn between anger and hostility or destructiveness, these patients are incapable of making the distinction or find it extremely troublesome (Rothenberg, 1971). As was the case with my patient Fred, it was quite clear that many of the situations to which he reacted so strongly and with such paranoid feelings were situations which involved perhaps reasonable circumstances for anger. But his anger could not be kept within the limits of constructive reaction and appropriate dissent. Instead the paranoid process quickly took over and pushed his reaction in the direction of destructive hostility. Instead of anger, therefore, serving as an alerting phenomenon, which provided the basis for mobilization of effective resources and for the communication of intents and purposes with others who were similarly angered by the situations he was dealing with, Fred's rage quickly assumed a degree of intensity and hostility which left no room for corrective action, but which went directly to the inexorable extreme of wishing to completely destroy and obliterate the object of his aggression.

What clearly motivated this shift from a level of anger to a level of hostile destructiveness was the influence of the paranoid ideation which saw the object of aggression as powerful, destructive, hostile, and capable of coldly and malevolently crushing Fred and the other helpless and powerless victims with whom he associated himself. Consequently moderation and compromise were incapable of dealing with the causes of his anger since they allowed for the persistence and existence of the powerful persecutor. Thus the destructive impulse flows out of the feeling of anxiousness and helplessness and powerlessness, rather than out of the feelings of anger themselves. The normal person is able to feel and exploit anger in the interests of obtaining objectives or in righting wrongs. But where the operation of the paranoid process becomes too overwhelming, the need to lash out blindly and destroy the enemy becomes overpowering.

Violence in War

A similar expression of the wish to violence has been studied in a recent paper by Gault (1971). He analyzed his experience in interviewing a number of young Vietnam veterans who had in one way or another participated in slaughter during their Vietnam tours of duty. The circumstances under which such a propensity to slaughter other human beings can be mobilized and activated in otherwise relatively normal young men were somewhat complex and related to the peculiar nature of the Vietnam conflict. In the first place, there was a great deal of uncertainty about who the enemy was and where he was. United States combat troops in Vietnam perceived intense hatred and physical threat from nearly every quarter. The combat soldier cannot distinguish farmer from terrorist, innocent youth from Vietcong spy. He begins to perceive his entire environment as hostile and trying to murder him.

In such a situation of pervasive hostility, the young soldier forms a desperate trust and loyalty to his own immediate combat unit and rigidly regards everything else in his environment, no matter what age or sex or condition, as part of the ubiquitous, murderous enemy.

Secondly, the enemy is dehumanized in various ways. The degradation of the enemy is essential to the psychology of any combat team from whom homicide is expected. The enemy were regarded as "Gooks." They were regarded as strange, inscrutable, profoundly different, and incomprehensible to Western notions. Killing the enemy, consequently, was not like killing real human beings. There was also a tendency toward dissolution of responsibility which tended to remove the combat soldier from the direct situation of deliberately killing another human being. Moreover, technology places a considerable distance between the killer and the killed. The respective roles of executioner and bombardier are psychologically very different indeed.

Moreover the conditions of jungle warfare increase the level of anxiety and the feeling of helplessness and vulnerability. The enemy is often unseen. Comrades are shot down without a visible enemy to shoot back at. Mines can often explode and kill or maim with no enemy to serve as the object of retaliation. The rage and the wish to revenge such outrages become intolerable. Gault reports one young sergeant who said matter-of-factly after the wanton devastation of a small village, "We took too many casualties. Somebody had to pay."

In the dehumanizing context of warfare in general, and particularly in the stressful context of the Vietnam conflict, civilized conventions and the inner prohibitions are often suspended. In the face of the pressure to kill or be killed, the civilized virtues of trust, gentleness, restraint, and decency have little utility. In such a situation the psychopathic tendencies are easily unleashed, and the psychopathic character becomes the natural leader in the expression of aggression. The psychopath finds himself at last in a world that is suited to his inner propensities. He is ready for the expression of violence without the burdens of empathy or compassion that inhibit others. His conduct is often selfless, heroic, exemplary.

If we reflect for a moment on these dimensions of the phenomenon of slaughter, it becomes clear that they are manifestations of the operation of the paranoid process. The inner sense of threat and helplessness sets up a situation in which the persecuting enemy is universalized and is seen as increasingly destructive and malignant. The paranoid dynamics operate in such a way as to dictate that such an enemy is to be blindly and wantonly destroyed. It is the universal paradigm for the expression of violence.

DEVELOPMENTAL ASPECTS

In approaching the relationship of aggression to the paranoid process, it is well to keep Anna Freud's recent cautions in mind (1972). She comments on the tendency to transfer the basic paradigm developed in relations to libidinal impulses to the realm of aggressive impulses. In the beginning of life, both libidinal and aggressive processes take the mother as their primary target. The cathexis of both drives can be regarded as anaclitic, as reflecting the satisfying and/or frustrating functions of the mother in response to the infant's needs. But as development progresses, the lines of sexual and aggressive development begin to diverge.

Libidinal development progresses toward an increasing independence of needs and tensions in the direction of object constancy. Consequently libidinal development tends toward a more or less permanent loving attachment, which is rooted in the total personality of the subject and directed toward the total personality of the object. But the aggressive drive tends to remain anaclitic more consistently and thoroughly in that it is more closely tied to the dimensions of pleasure-pain, and satisfaction-frustration. There is no tendency in the development of aggression toward object-constancy.

Rather the activation and attachment to the object of aggression tend to be intermittent and transient. As Anna Freud observes:

> We call a "good lover" one who is faithful to his objects, i.e. constant in cathecting them. In contrast, the "good hater" is promiscuous, i.e. he has free aggression at his disposal and is ready to cathect with it on a non-permanent basis any object who, either by his actions or his characteristics, offers adequate provocation (1972, p. 166).

The interesting exception to this tendency for aggressive expression is the paranoid state, in which the hatred of the paranoid patient is relatively permanently attached to the figure of the persecutor. Ms. Freud, however, is unwilling to allow even this exception, since she regards the pathological fixation in paranoia as a vicissitude of libido rather than expression of the aggressive drive. In the view presented here, the fixity of the paranoid aggression is related to its derivation from the introject. As we have discussed it, this is clearly related to Ms. Freud's description of the "identification with the aggressor." The fixity of the projection is ultimately rooted in the persistency of the introject and its organization of internal aggressive impulses. Obviously the vicissitudes of both libido and aggression are tied up in this aspect of the paranoid economy, along with the masochism which serves as its internal counterpart.

The quality of the internal aggression and the capacity to direct it effectively is a function of the child's developmental history and the emerging capacity to bind aggression. The infant's aggressive response to the restricting, confining, or impinging aspects of the mothering situation are at first diffusely directed but gradually become attached to the primary object. By the end of the first year, both libidinal and aggressive impulses are directed toward the mothering object. The binding of aggression in the subsequent phases of development constitutes a major step forward. The child learns to master his aggressive impulses in a variety of ways, but perhaps the most decisive influences are the binding of aggressive impulses with the help of the libidinal investment in the object. In part this constitutes what Melanie Klein has described as the "depressive position" but from another point of view it is a reflection of a successful developmental course which allows for the gradual integration and neutralization of aggressive impulses.

A significant amount of neutralization is achieved in very gratifying and pleasurable ways during what Mahler (1968) describes as the "practicing period." The child's interaction with the environment becomes highly charged with aggression and in the mastery of his environment the child learns to employ successfully and productively his aggressive impulses. Aggression plays a role not only in the demolishing and manipulating of playthings, but reflects itself also in the wish to master the loved object and to focus and fix the mother's affection in the first instance, and increasingly also the father's. Aggression has its place in this aspect of mastery as well (Frijling-Schreuder, 1972). We will have more to say about these developmental vicissitudes of aggression later on.

Introjection of Aggression

As is quite evident in our own patients, difficulties with aggression begin in the earliest phases of their life histories. The problem brings into focus the origins and influences on the basic introjective and projective processes by which the child's emerging personality is shaped. These influences are closely related to the patterns of gratification and frustration which emerge from the parent-child interaction. The mothering figures around the child, usually the mother herself, are the primarily responsible agents for satisfying essential needs. Gratifying the child's needs undoubtedly conveys a certain degree of pleasure, but inevitably the frustration and delay that must be encountered in the interface between mother and child introduces an element of frustration. This frustration and denial of gratification become a source of unpleasure for the child and stirs his aggression.

This interplay of maternal responsiveness and frustration serves as the basis for an emerging dialectic of love and hate. In the first instance, the mother becomes the object of love insofar as she is a gratifying object, and she becomes the object of hate insofar as she is the cause of the infant's discomfort and the feeling of helplessness due to his inability to relieve his own pain. The frustrating mother then undermines the child's sense of narcissistic omnipotence. The child cannot help but feel his helplessness. The child's narcissistic rage rushes to the aid of his threatened omnipotence. Thus even from the earliest phases of his experience the child's aggression is stirred, even though it cannot be clearly differentiated from discomfort or distress.

As the child's internal capacity develops, he gradually establishes a dichotomy between good and bad objects, by means particularly of the interplay of introjection and projection. In the beginning the self and the world of objects are poorly differentiated, so that the shifting of hostility from self to objects and objects to self is rather fluid. As self-object differentiation progresses, the child attempts to rid himself of the hostile elements by projecting them onto the bad object. The good object does not withhold or deny gratification, but the bad object often does. As Bychowski (1966) observes:

> The infant must resort to overpowering violence in order to force gratification and response from the stronger, bad objects. The demands of omnipotence require that the gratification be unconditional. The child's sense of weakness and vulnerability set up the conditions for the introjection of the

bad object, equivalent to the process of identification with the aggressor. The intense ambivalence and the necessity of splitting form the basis of the introjection of the bad introject and impede the process of positive integration both of object representations and ultimately internal structures.

The results of such processes at their pathological worst are seen in psychotic patients, and are quite dramatically presented in paranoid pathology. This is quite apparent in our own psychotic patients, in whom the persistent and unintegrated bad object persists as a malignant and horribly destructive introject, which serves as the basis for the paranoid projection. The primitive and archaic characteristics of the bad objects are thus preserved. Consequently, primitive and highly destructive oral and anal rage has a tendency to persist without significant degrees of neutralization. The primitive and destructive character of this rage can be identified in childhood nightmares and in the pathological projections of some of our patients. The patient in dreams may see himself as the victim of horrible monsters which pursue him with the intention of torturing and destroying him. But when the projective defense is not operating, the patient may feel himself to be a horribly destructive and sadistic monster. As Bychowski puts it, "The archaic image of the self and the archaic images of the original love-hate objects undergo a process of interpenetration as a result of early projections and introjections." (1966, p. 176). He goes on to describe this process in the following terms:

> This interpenetration of hostility contributes to the formation of archaic object representations, which become an important depository of primitive destructive hostility. In a predisposed psychic organization distorted representations of the original love-hate objects remain split off and isolated from the rest of the ego, and therefore may at some future time become the source of serious psychopathology. In such formations hostility is externalized and projected onto the original love-hate objects or their derivatives, which then assume the status of an arch enemy and persecutor (1966, pp. 190-91).

One of the major vicissitudes of such hostility is the turning of anger against the self. The primitive superego releases against the self the hostility and destructiveness which cannot be discharged either toward the original hate objects or their substitutes. The patient makes himself the object of his own destructive, narcissistic wrath. The turning of aggression inward is not the whole story, however, since the process involves a dual identification—both with the sadistic and hostile aggressor and with the passive and vulnerable victim.

The Process of Separation
The conflict between activity and passivity is central in this process. When the child's rage against the parental figure is aroused, this becomes a

situation of danger for him. The murderous wrath raises the potentiality for destruction of the needed object upon which the child is so dependent. The parent is still the source of the gratification of the child's needs, the object of the child's dependence, and the source of loving care. Destruction of the object carries with it the implications of loss of love and abandonment. This conflict is particularly intense at the stage when the child begins to show signs of independence from the parents and may begin to undermine and deny the parent's own narcissism by its attempts to be self-assertive and independent.

The child's capacity to separate from the maternal narcissism depends to a considerable degree on the position of the father. If the father responds with excessive hostility to the child's attempts at independent self-expression, castration anxiety is unavoidably intensified, and the child is driven back into a closer dependence on the mother for protection and love. The child may opt for feminine passivity and may attempt to avoid or deny masculine aggression. This was clearly the case in the childhood experience of both Bob and Jim. As latency children both boys were relatively passive and unaggressive. But clearly Bob was the more passive and phobic, like the Wolf-Man in comparison to Little Hans, and this indeed would seem to serve as a harbinger of his future pathology.

In the normal course of development, ambivalence is neither so intense nor so destructive that it interferes with the basic sense of relatedness to the mother and with the good enough quality of her mothering. From such a relationship the child internalizes a sufficiently good and integrated object that serves as the nucleus for his own emerging self-esteem. If this core of his personality is allowed to take root and grow, in later life, even when he meets with rejection and failure, he carries something within himself that gives him an inner sense of security and a sense of his own lovableness. This is substantially the good introject, at first a maternal introject, but later also embracing the elements introjected from the strength and the firmness of the father. If the mothering has been "good enough," and if the object relationship with the mother has been sufficiently good, the infant internalizes a resource which buffers and absorbs the impact of the inevitable frustration and lack of gratification that is involved in his relationship to the mother.

If the good internalized object, the maternal introject, is sufficiently stabilized it can resist the intense and frustrated rage that is unleashed by the injury to infantile narcissism. Just as in relationships between adults, frustration and anger do not necessarily wipe out and destroy the basic love one feels for another person. In fact aggression, hostility, and even destructiveness can be tolerated when there is sufficient quotient of persistent love in the relationship. Without the cushion of self-esteem which derives ultimately from the acquisition and elaboration of a good internal object, the individual remains vulnerable to failure, rejection, disappointment, or abandonment. He will be unable to tolerate anger, either in those around him or in himself. He will find it especially difficult to tolerate hostility from those whom he loves and upon whom he depends.

Particularly difficult in these circumstances are any impulses toward independence of parental figures, so that the process of separation and individuation becomes precarious and problematic. In part the child will continue to seek out and yearn for that measure of love the mother was unable to give him, and in part he will be unable to express the natural self-assertive and aggressive drive that is necessary to enable him to separate himself from his mother. This results inevitably in a clinging to the mother which often has the appearance of devotion and loving affection to the mother, as it often did in the case of Jimmy for example; but in fact what underlies this behavior is a fundamental uncertainty of her affection for the child and of the child's affection for the mother. The child has equivalently been unable to internalize the mother's love and carry it with him into new relationships with other people in the broader spheres of the school and the outside world.

THE SCHIZOID ADJUSTMENT

The persistence of the bad object can express itself in a variety of forms of adult psychopathology. One of the basic defenses against the sense of inner destructiveness and hostility is the schizoid defense. Schizoid individuals find their greatest conflicts in the area of loving and being loved, such that the deep distrust of themselves and others leads them to feel that any intimate relation with another human being is fraught with considerable dangers. The schizoid defense, therefore, constitutes a withdrawal from human contact which isolates them not only against love, but against hate as well.

There are many aspects of the schizoid personality that reflect the influence of the paranoid process. Quite typical of schizoid individuals is a strong desire for power and superiority, along with an inner feeling of vulnerability and weakness. We have seen this constellation of factors in a number of our own patients. Schizoid individuals may indeed attain power, but they do not thereby shed the inner vulnerability that they feel so intensely, nor is it possible for them to establish more intimate relations with other people. If they do not achieve power in reality, they often lead a secret inner life of fantasy in which their wishes for power and invincibility are gratified. In the breakdown of the schizoid defenses and acute schizophrenic decompensation, the fantasies burst forth into grandiose delusions of power, privilege, and magical omnipotence. This pattern of response is clearly manifested in several of our patients. In Ann, for example, the inner sense of weakness and vulnerability was compensated for by a variety of highly erotic fantasies. In Bob and Don and Fred, the inner fantasy life, which was so highly narcissistically determined, burst forth in the acute psychotic phases in bizarre delusions of grandeur and omnipotence.

For the schizoid mentality, love is equivalently a humiliation. He remains desperately in need of affection and exquisitely vulnerable to its withdrawal. Love is terribly conflicted and dangerous because it can be lost, and the schizoid individual lies in the perpetual fear of potential rejection. The horns of the dilemma are clearly drawn. The alternatives he provides himself are either to deny the needs for love and affection and accept complete isolation, or to accept love and thereby place himself in a position of humiliating dependence, in which he feels himself to be weak and submissive and vulnerable. Consequently schizoids perceive the affection of those from whom they receive love as powerful, but also potentially destructive and hostile. This is precisely the psychology of the victim which we have seen so elaborately displayed in all of our patients. Their own hostile feelings are either internalized so that the pathology is primarily depressive, or externalized so that the pathology takes on a more paranoid flavor. When they are the objects of any aggression from the environment, they retire into icy detachment and isolation, terrified not only of the destructive power of others but also of their own inner hostility. The inner hostility is intense and often terrifying. They are exquisitely sensitive to any narcissistic affront and, in the face of any narcissistic disappointment, their rage is intense and vindictive. Any narcissistic affront, however minor, is interpreted as a profound humiliation and degradation.

PSYCHOPATHIC PERSONALITIES

Another important pathological group, in which hostility is a particular problem, are the antisocial personalities. The problem of hostility in this group is particularly significant since these individuals have a strong propensity to act out their hostility in destructive ways. We have already discussed some of the aspects of the aberrant physiology often found in antisocial disorders, but we are focusing here on the psychological aberration and particularly on the conflicts over hostility. The antisocial individual is characterized by an abnormal ruthlessness and disregard for the feelings of other human beings. He tends to be egotistical, selfish, and impulsive. The tendency to impulsive acting-out, together with a disregard for consequences, often leads to antisocial and criminal behavior. Such an individual does not hesitate to use violence to gain his objectives. Often these persons are found to be pathological liars, presumably because of the failure to form any sort of mutual relationship with other people which would incur the obligation for respecting normal human conventions.

Psychopathic personalities rarely feel any sense of guilt or depression, but rather their hostility tends to be exteriorly directed. The psychopath uses projection as a basic defense and has a strong tendency to blame other individuals or external circumstances for the difficulties he gets himself into. But the sense of fear and vulnerability, which we have found so characteristic of our paranoid patients, is singularly lacking in the psychopath. It is not clear whether such inner fear is entirely lacking or whether it is simply deeply buried, so that we have little evidence of it. The psychopath remains strikingly unafraid of his own destructiveness or of destructiveness that might be directed toward himself. Such persons have a relative disregard of danger and of the possibilities of danger. The circumstances often make them capable of feats of bravery and daring that other individuals would shrink from in terror. These individuals then become the heroes in wartime, whose heroic deeds win them admiration and esteem and medals. Their ruthlessness and destructiveness are placed in the service of defense of their country and gain them a considerable amount of gratification, largely narcissistic. They often act in the face of danger as though they were omnipotently immune from any injury.

While the antisocial pathology is in many aspects similar to paranoid pathology, there are clear differences which separate them. Psychopathic violence has little revengefulness about it, and is usually quite general in its direction. Psychopaths do not focus on particular individuals or groups as the objects of their hostility in the manner so characteristic of paranoid individuals. Their resentment is more general and diffuse.

PARANOID HOSTILITY

While the schizoid and psychopathic varieties of hostility are relatively infrequent, there is good reason to suggest that the paranoid variety of hostility is far more broadly distributed in the population. I would like to cite at this juncture a paragraph or two from the pen of Anthony Storr, which are entirely congruent with the focus and direction not only of this chapter but of this entire study. He writes:

> Although most obvious in the insane, the capacity for paranoid projection is, regrettably, not confined to them. Indeed, we must assume that the whole of mankind possesses some underlying paranoid potential. When discussing depression, it is indicated that most people, at least in our culture, know what it is to be depressed. But depression is, in nearly every instance, a transient condition from which, whether mild or severe, the majority of persons recover. The tendency toward paranoid projection, though more deeply buried in

"normal" people, is far less intermittent and even more ubiquitous than the tendency toward depression (1968, p. 96) . . .

He goes on, then, to add some of his own evidence, which must be compiled with the evidence presented in this study. He says:

It will, no doubt, seem offensive and incredible to suggest that ordinary people have hidden paranoid tendencies and a proclivity for brutality. Yet the evidence is there. Public executions are still exciting spectacles to which mothers take their children in parts of the so-called civilized world; and it is not so long since, in our own country, traitors were dragged through the streets and publically castrated before the executioner finally dispatched them. It is a mistake to believe the ordinary man is not capable of the extremes of cruelty. We would like to believe that guards in the German concentration camps can be classified as abnormal, but many seem to have been ordinary men whose taste for cruelty had only to be reinforced by training and example for them to become accustomed to the daily, wanton infliction of abominable pain and humiliation . . . but the catalogue of human cruelty is so long and the practice of torture so ubiquitous, that it is impossible to believe sadism is confined to a few abnormals. Indeed, any writer who dwells upon the details of man's cruelty to man, is likely to be accused of merely seeking the widest public for his work rather than making a serious contribution to understanding, a fact that demonstrates the universality of public interest in the subject. We have to face the fact that man's proclivity for cruelty is rooted in his biological peculiarities, in common with his capacity for conceptual, for speech, and for creative achievement (1968, pp. 98-99).

AGGRESSION AND NARCISSISM

The problem of aggression in the paranoid process is not simply a problem of the expression of aggressive instincts. Rather it is a question of aggression which is rooted in and derived from the basic vicissitudes of narcissism. We have already discussed the vicissitudes of narcissism and particularly what Rochlin calls the "tyranny of narcissism" (1973). The question is not so much one of how is it that paranoid content is overloaded with aggressive and destructive elements, but more specifically the question is what is it that makes the individuals concerned feel so vulnerable and fragile and humiliated. It is in this shameful sense of humiliation that the roots of paranoid aggression and violence must be identified.

As we have seen, narcissism is closely linked with the necessity of preserving a sense of the self. When self-esteem is injured, narcissism is injured and the result is experienced as a sense of humiliation or shame. The sense of self is always precarious, always in jeopardy, always at risk of being diminished and damaged. The birth of a sibling, a parental disapproval or the withdrawal of parental affection, an illness, a disappointment, an impairment of sphincters are all experiences which put the sense of self at risk. The sense of self is also in jeopardy whenever the reach exceeds the grasp, or whenever ungovernable chance and forces beyond our control direct the course of events. In the fact of such devaluations and assaults on self-esteem, self-esteem must be restored and salvaged. It is at this point that aggression enters the scene. Its role may be destructive and revengeful—or it may be employed in the interests of creative efforts (Rochlin, 1973).

But the vicissitudes of narcissism and aggression do not display themselves only within the confines of the individual psyche. As Kohut (1973) has pointed out, some of the most dreadful and destructive displays of aggression in the history of modern civilization have been based on the proclamation that their destructive deeds were performed in the service of nature. The Nazi rationale for extermination was based on a vulgar Darwinism which proclaimed the inherent right of the stronger to destroy the weak in the interests of the preservation of the purity of the race. But the horror of the Nazi phenomenon cannot simply be regarded as a disgusting regression to sadistic barbarism. It was an expression of a basically human process, an integral part of the human condition, "a strand in the web of the complex pattern which makes up the human situation." Kohut writes with telling accuracy:

> Human aggression is most dangerous when it is attached to the two great ab-
> solutarian psychological constellations: the grandiose self and the archaic
> omnipotent object. And the most gruesome human destructiveness is en-
> countered not in the form of wild, regressive, and primitive behavior, but in
> the form of orderly and organized activities in which the perpetrators'
> destructiveness is alloyed with absolutarian convictions about their greatness
> and with their devotion to archaic omnipotent figures (1973, p. 378).

Unquestionably the vicissitudes of narcissism during the course of development are complex, but almost unavoidably they are tied up with the narcissism of the parent. In addition to innate determinants, the specific interplay between child and the parental figures, in the beginning, the mother, either furthers or hinders the development of a cohesive self and the formation of idealized psychic structures. In varying degrees and in shifting patterns, the parents relate at times to the child with a narcissistic attitude that sees a child as an extension of their own highly libidinal cathected selves. But at other times they respond to the child as somehow independent and are consequently able to invest him with object-libido.

The child may find itself as having to accede to the narcissistic wishes of the parent, thus arresting and disturbing the process of narcissistic gratification. Such a child needs desperately to please, so that libidinal ties are intensified in the interests of protecting against the underlying rage. The combined need to please and to possess the parent plays a decisive role in the organization of introjects. This is particularly true in relationship to the mother. As Rochlin comments:

But when she (the mother) is herself too childishly self-serving, a serious conflict arises in the child. The child's own narcissism is opposed by the mother's;
the child adopts (through identification) the mother's attitude. It means to
become as narcissistic as she. And also as intolerant of it in others as she. The
internal or unconscious struggle in the child is the conflict between self-
concern coupled with aggression to assert it, and the strong self-
condemnation of it (1973, p. 47).

The constellation is frequently enough at the root of clinical depressions
since the child's aggression cannot be directed against the maternal object,
for to do so would be to destroy the object that is loved and desperately
needed. The likely outcome is the turning inward of aggression against the
self and the resulting depressive constellation.

A particularly crucial area in which narcissism is put at risk is in working through the Oedipal situation. Without question the Oedipal involvements on both sides are a dangerous and risky undertaking, whose outcome
inevitably is the failure and humiliation of the child. As we have seen with
all of our patients the Oedipal involvements are intense and pathologically
distorted. The Oedipal outcome in all of these cases was pathological.
Rather than a resolution of the Oedipal difficulties, these patients experience the emergence from the Oedipal situation as a defeat (Rochlin,
1973). The result was to provide them with a defective sense of self.

This whole topic is closely related to the sense of inferiority that
children feel about the size of their genitals. The little boy feels inferior when
he compares his small genital with that of his father, and the little girl feels
inadequacy by reason of lack of such a visible organ. Sensitivity about genitals reaches its peak during the phallic-Oedipal phase so that, in Kohut's
terms (1973), the genital region during this phase becomes the leading zone
of the child's narcissism. The intense narcissistic cathexis of the genitals,
along with the relatively unneutralized exhibitionist component of the infantile narcissism, provides the substratum for the significance of penis envy. Thus the sense of genital shame is closely related to whatever it is that
the child has to show in the service of his exhibitionistic wish. It is thus of
small consolation to the little boy that his penis will grow, and of even less
consolation to a little girl to know that she carries within her the invisible
machinery for making babies. We can remember particularly here the pervasive notion in young Jimmy's mind that he was forever doomed to be an
inferior, small, weak child without any room in his fantasy for the possibility of growth to some more mature and adult level of capacity and potentiality.

When our wishes are denied or blocked, or if we are deprived of that
which we have set ourselves to possess, the narcissistic demand by no means
abates or diminishes. On the contrary, it persists stubbornly and engages
our aggressive drive in its service. Narcissism demands that when reality

places impediments or limitations in our path, we identify our efforts to defeat and overcome them. In the face of all the pressures and forces which propel the child toward growing up, he tends to cling to his primary wishes and resists any attempt to force him to resign these. But he is an unwilling subject. His feeble powers can do little against the forces opposed to him. He is inevitably deprived of the gratification he demands, and he is left frustrated and threatened. These are all powerful blows to the developing sense of self-esteem. Aggression is thus mobilized in the interest of protecting his precarious sense of self. It is at this stage that nightmares and phobic reactions are so frequently observed.

Identification with the Aggressor

Often enough, to escape the web of entangling limitations and frustrations which his growing-up experience provides him, the child retreats to a relatively unconscious and natural belief in magic. He retreats to the consolation of powerful fantasies and wishes rather than remain entangled in the reality of his weakness and dependence. While these fantasy wishes are disturbing, he cannot easily divest himself of them except by magically projecting these hostile and destructive wishes particularly to the outside world. He thus creates a world full of hazards and dangers of his own creation, but against which he must defend himself.

The child fears the magical power of his own aggressiveness. One major means of protecting himself from the resultant threatening hostility and the sense of victimhood that accompanies it is the identification with aggressive figures in the environment. Such an identification provides a buffering against the fears of vulnerability and the sense of being a victim, while it also provides an incentive for aggressive outlet as well as the wish to victimize others. Identification with the aggressor, consequently, does not diminish the conflicts over aggression, but merely reincarnates them on another level. The phenomenon of identification with the aggressor is writ large across all of our above case histories. In the case of Bob, for example, the identification with the harsh, remote, and domineering father was reenacted in Bob's sadistic treatment of the women in his life. He was driven by the unconscious wish to deny his own weakness and inadequacy, while at the same time expressing the sadistic wish to domineer and subjugate women, particularly sexually.

Identification with the aggressor, therefore, serves as a powerful defense against victimhood. But its greatest importance is in the role it plays in the overcoming of threats to fragile narcissism. As the aggression of the aggressor is introjected, it enables the child to fend off fears and the uncertainties of everyday life. One possible outcome, of course, is the enhancement of self-esteem. The child may thereby gain a capacity for self-assertion and of aggressive competitiveness which contribute to the building up of self-esteem. The resulting achievements can serve as narcissistic rewards which preserve self-esteem and reflect a shift in the direction of aggression from destructive intent to constructive enterprises involving the acquisition of skills and the mastery of tasks. As Rochlin observes:

> The gain in identification with the aggressor serves, in the course of becoming aggressive oneself, to enhance self-esteem. Aggression thus commences in early childhood to assume a major role essential to the protection of narcissism. In fact, in its relation to narcissism, aggression gets its clearest definition of function. In the formation of emotional defenses, in achieving skills and mastery, in adaptation to the environment, aggression performs a role in all aspects of daily life. Employed in the permanent service of restitution of our narcissism, which the conditions of everyday life tend to erode, aggression becomes its indispensable arm. When it fails, narcissism suffers (1973, pp. 213-214).

To this it must be added, following Kohut (1973), that the identification with the aggressor is also related to the need to convert a passive experience into an active one. Rather than experiencing himself as the passive victim of the sadistic hostility of others, the child is thus enabled to become the sadistic aggressor himself. Thus shame-prone individuals reveal a readiness to react to a potentially shame-provoking situation by inflicting on others the narcissistic injuries which they feel most themselves.

However, as we have previously observed, it must be remembered that if the identification with an aggressor serves to protect from a sense of vulnerability and victimhood, it is inevitably accompanied by the underlying and accompanying identification with the victim. Thus the victim introjection can function not only as a precondition but also as a consequence of identification with the aggressor. The child assumes the attributes of and imitates the aggressive object and thus transforms himself from the person threatened into the one who makes the threat. The child thus takes upon himself the characteristics of the parental objects. The process precipitates the child into an irresolvable dilemma. At the same time, he fashions within himself a self-governing agent which is opposed to aggression, while at the same time he strives to become like the aggressive figures, whom he perceives as powerful and aggressive. The predicament, consequently, is that one has to disclaim within oneself that which is the source of aggression, and at the same time claim for oneself that which is the source of aggression.

Identification with the Victim

The resolution is effected by projecting the inner source of aggressive impulses to the outside. This results in a world which unconsciously assumes the aspect of a hostile and threatening place. The process can be self-generating and self-enhancing. Insofar as malevolent intent is ascribed to others, the defenses against such fantasized threats need to be reinforced. Thus violence is increasingly justified and identification with the aggressor intensified (Rochlin, 1973). Quite obviously, in addition to the projection of the undesirable aggressive impulses and intentions, the identification with the victim provides a further internal buffer against the expression of destructive impulses. Thus the narcissistic conflict remains unresolved. The demands of narcissism are confronted by the demands of narcissism. Insofar as we flee from narcissistic mortification to an identification with the threatening aggressor, we must also deny and escape that monstrous identification by retreating to the protection of victimhood and narcissistic vulnerability.

Narcissistic Rage

The rage which finds its expression in the paranoid dynamics bears the stamp of its narcissistic origins. It frequently bears the stamp of the wish for revenge, for the intent of righting a wrong or undoing a hurt. It tends to be deeply anchored, persistent, and unrelenting in the pursuit of these aims. Moreover, such narcissistic rage knows few limits. The shame-prone individual is prepared to experience any setback as a narcissistic injury and to respond with an insatiable rage. He cannot recognize an opponent as somehow an independent focus of initiative, which happens to be in cross purposes to his own. He does not wish merely to defeat the enemy that blocks his way. He cannot rest until he has blotted out the persecutor or offender who has dared to attack, oppose, disagree, or outdo him. Typically there is an utter disregard for any limitations and an almost unlimited wish to undo an injury and obtain revenge. As Kohut puts it:

> The enemy, however, who calls forth the archaic rage of the narcissistically vulnerable is seen by him not as an autonomous source of impulsions, but as a *flaw in a narcissistically perceived reality*. He is a recalcitrant part of an expanded self over which he expects to exercise full control and whose mere independence or other-ness is an offense (1973, pp. 385-386).

Narcissistic injury and the resulting narcissistic rage can be experienced at all degrees of intensity. At the upper end of the spectrum narcissistic injury may be reacted to with embarrassment or shame and anger. But at the lower level of the spectrum, where the intensity of the shame and the violence of the narcissistic rage are overwhelming, the individuals so affected find indispensable for the maintenance of self-esteem a sense of absolute control over an archaic environment and of the self.

Narcissism of the "Exception"

The elements of shame in connection with narcissistic rage are sometimes seen in those particular cases of narcissistic impairment which have become familiar to us as the "exceptions." In such cases the child's archaic narcissism, which is primarily invested in the child's body-self, fails to undergo the transformation that takes place through the approving and accepting responsiveness of the mother. Such children with their physical malformations or defects become affronts to the mother's own narcissism. This puts the child's narcissism in conflict with the mother's narcissism, as we have already seen. The area of defect becomes invested with an intense narcissistic cathexis which remains unaltered so its grandiosity and essential exhibitionism cannot be transformed or integrated with the rest of the psychic organization. This investment of narcissistic libido becomes split off or repressed, and from time to time breaks through the defenses of the ego and floods it with unneutralized narcissistic cathexis which is experienced by the ego with intense shame and consequent narcissistic rage (Kohut, 1973).

Our focus at this juncture is on the narcissistic rage and destructiveness which flows out of such exceptional narcissism. This is in fact the essential point in Freud's selection of Richard III as the typical exception. Richard feels himself exempt from all moral constraints or all moral laws—particularly the incest taboo and the law against patricide. His archaic, narcissistic, and destructive passion is revealed in his inability to love women. He felt himself to be hated and despised by his own mother, and the narcissistic injury resulting from this, related to and focused on his deformity, becomes the vehicle for murderous revenge.

His narcissism can be satisfied only by power and the fulfillment of his devouring ambition. His ruthless and apparently guiltless ambition is fed on brutal crimes. He becomes the rebel against his own conscience and is constantly forced to mock the power of conscience and the weakness of human love and pity—even though it is conscience that haunts his repose with terrible nightmares. As Jacobson points out (1959), Richard's murderous actions are equivalently a sadomasochistic provocation of fate, so that his final defeat and punishment become inevitable. Richard thus becomes the architect of his own ruin, and the destructive urges ultimately turn upon himself. At the end of the play (Act V, Scene III), he cries out in an anguished voice:

> My conscience hath a thousand several tongues,
> And every tongue brings in a several tale,
> And every tale condemns me for a villain.
> Perjury, perjury, in the high'st degree:
> Murder, stern murder, in the dir'st degree;
> All several sins, all us'd in each degree.
> Throng to the bar, crying all, 'Guilty! guilty!'
> I shall despair. There is no creature loves me;
> And if I die, no soul will pity me:
> Nay, wherefore should they, since that I myself
> Find in myself no pity to myself?

The masochistic need for punishment seems to be present not only in the variety of "exceptions," but seems also to be consistently manifested in the patients we have been discussing. The masochistic wish may be warded off by a rebellious attitude and a scorn for the laws which others are forced to obey as was so clear in the case of Fred in his antisocial rebelliousness, as well as in the highly phallic and rebellious fantasies of Jim. Or, conversely, the masochistic wish may itself serve as a defense against rebellious rage and thus find an expression in conscious terms in a belief that one is chosen in some special way to suffer. We have seen this form of intensely masochistic and narcissistic wish expressed by several of our patients, more particularly, it might be noted, by female patients.

In his original study of the exceptions, Freud brings his consideration to a close by reflecting that the conclusions regarding the exceptions may have some application to the psychology of women who often base their claims for privilege on a narcissistic injury, namely, their castration (Freud, 1916). Freud seems to have regarded the lack of a penis as a physical defect or detriment, an attitude which contributed heavily to his thinking of the psychology of women. He seems to have felt, on the basis of the real castration, that a woman's object-relations were generally more narcissistic than that of man, and that she lacks the same incentives as the male for overcoming Oedipal fixations and hence emerges from the Oedipal constellation with certain superego defects. Jacobson has extended this consideration to the character of a certain class of women of exceptional physical beauty (1959). This forms a counterpoise to the narcissism of physical affliction or deformity. As Jacobson observes, "If the physically damaged feel unjustly blamed and punished, and thereby are moved to rebel, the beautiful feel unjustly praised and rewarded, and therefore tempted to challenge the world and to sin" (1959, p. 153).

The Masochistic Defense

These considerations bring us close to a consideration of the relationship between narcisisstic injury and rage and the masochistic defense. Some years ago, Bak (1946) had stressed that the main paranoid defense against destructive drives was to convert the aggression into masochism. The paranoid aspiration to eliminate evil completely prompts him to try to rid the world of destruction in all its forms. This must of course begin with the repudiation of his own destructiveness. It is when he meets destruction and aggression in others that the conflict becomes intensified. If he submits to their violence, he will be destroyed. If he struggles against their violence, however, he must use violence himself. As we have seen, both aspects and both sides of the conflict have their place in the paranoid dynamics.

The link between these elements and feminine sexuality has been recently explored in a provocative article by Green (1972). One of the basic feminine fears, which is amply demonstrated by psychoanalytic studies, is the fear of penetration. The penis is commonly symbolized as a knife or spear or other penetrating object. The woman's fear is a double fear: fear for the penis and a fear of the penis. It is a fear of somehow damaging or castrating the penis, but at the same time a fear that the penis itself might penetrate and destroy the internal genitalia or even the abdomen itself.

Even in my own analytic patients, the fantasy is relatively common that there is somehow a communication between the genitals and the abdominal cavity, so that the penis might be incorporated or swallowed up and internally retained. This is obviously related to pregnancy fantasies. Green has related such fantasies to the rather Kleinian early fantasies of oral sadism related to fears of destroying the mother's breast or of attacking and destroying her abdomen and it contents. This anxiety consequently is not merely a fear of destroying, but also a wish to destroy. Consequently a woman must face a combination of fantasies—the fantasy of destroying as well as the fantasy of being destroyed by the object that is both intensely desired and intensely feared. In this aspect of feminine psychology, therefore, there is operative a dual identification: an identification with the damaged victim as well as with the aggressor. Thus the woman must be able to reach a compromise between the fear of object loss and its consequent mourning (hysterical depression), and the threatening incorporation which serves as the basis for persecutory anxiety and fear.

In the transference relationship, such women often respond with a form of masochistic submissiveness which tends to place the analyst in a position of strength and power. At the same time the power which these women attribute to him is feared and the reintrojection of the projected strength is stoutly resisted. The analyst is sometimes overidealized in this fashion, so that the woman is unable to effectively separate from him, give him up, and endure the mourning process which is required for an effective termination. Something similar is often seen in male patients with marked feminine tendencies. I have often found this to be the case in women who retreat to a highly masochistic defensive position. It was also strikingly the case for young Jim, for whom the closing stages of his analysis were almost exclusively taken up with his clinging to a passive, masochistic postion and his reluctance to enter upon a self-assertive, masculinely aggressive and successful style of life. Equivalently it meant surrendering his feminine identification, renouncing his wishes for passive homosexual surrender to his father, and giving up the highly gratifying and narcissistically cathected position of special and defective child of his mother.

In his early considerations of sadomasochism, Freud related the process primarily to libidinal vicissitudes. He emphasized physical pain as a means to achieving sexual discharge. Masochism thus came to mean the need for physical pain as a prerequisite for orgasm. In his *Three Essays* (1905), Freud saw sadism as ranging from violence toward the sexual object to the dependence of sexual satisfaction on the humiliation and mistreatment of the sexual subject. He also regarded masochism as ranging from passivity to the sexual object to the extreme state of sexual satisfaction being dependent on actual physical suffering or mental torment. He also saw the sadistic and the masochistic impulses as related. Masochism was merely the turning of the sadistic impulse against the self. The impulse to inflict pain upon the object was inhibited because of a sense of guilt and thus was changed into a masochistic, self-directed and self-punishing mechanism for the aggressive impulse against the object. Similarly sadism may be put to the service of defending against masochistic wishes, as we have seen in the case of identification with the aggressor. In a sadomasochistic sexual relationship, therefore, the sexual experience is turned into a struggle between a victim and an aggressor.

By 1924, when he wrote his famous paper on *The Economic Problem of Masochism*, Freud had arrived at his theory of the death instinct and applied it to the phenomenon of masochism. He described a primary masochism which was directly related to the operation of the death instinct, specifically that part that was not directed externally in an aggressive or destructive form. The secondary forms of masochism were described as "feminine masochism," the supposedly feminine tendency to place oneself in the position of being dominated or castrated, and "moral masochism" in which a priority of value is placed on suffering itself exclusive of its more sexual connotations. Thus, as Freud conceived it, the masochistic wishes were the result of the subject's guilt feelings about prohibited sexual wishes, so that the suffering becomes the price that the masochist pays for sexual pleasure. The pain is suffered willingly because of the conviction that one cannot have pleasure without paying the price. Consequently the masochist is able to put pain in the service of pleasure.

In a sense, it can be said that patients with this sadomasochistic inclination are enacting as an internal psychic drama a version of the child's perception of parental intercourse. Quite frequently in such patients one finds a history of exposure to the primal scene which is inevitably seen by the child as an act of physical aggression and violence. But the determinants are not simply this. More frequently the whole issue of such sadistic and masochistic propensities is a question of the general quality of the relationships not only between parents, but also among members of the family. Such families are dominated by the conflicts over aggression and victimhood. Family relationships are seen in terms of aggressive struggles in which the issue is always winning and losing and in which human relationships are impossible except in terms of someone winning and someone losing, or someone dominating and others submitting. It is hardly necessary to recall the frequency with which such intensely sadomasochistic relations are found to characterize marital relationships. The tendency for masochists to seek out and become intensely involved with sadists, and vice versa, is a well-known clinical phenomenon.

It is altogether typical of such patients, when they are operating from the position of masochistic fixation, that they idealize or regard as extremely powerful the parental figure. Often such patients have experienced a relationship with a mother, who is characteristically unloving, exploitative, and critical, and is seen by the child as extremely powerful and influential. We have seen this interaction as a characteristic part of the early-life experience of all our female patients. The typical fantasy, which governs the child's, and later the masochistically inclined patient's view of reality, is that others, particularly influential persons upon whom they in any way depend, are seen as superior beings who are possessed with great power. It is the view of the weak, helpless, and dependent child of his omnipotent and powerful parents. The patient remains in his own eyes an inferior, inadequate, helpless, impotent, and defective creature.

Masochism and Paranoia

The relationship between the masochistic character and paranoid traits has been discussed in some detail by Nydes (1963). In his view the masochistic character renounces power for the sake of love, while the paranoid renounces love for the sake of power. In delusional paranoia, for example, the patient becomes God or some equivalently powerful figure; but the masochist projects his omnipotent wish to an outside figure and renounces his own power for the sake of love of the powerful object. The paranoid defense consequently is an alternate defense to the underlying sadistic and aggressive wishes. However, the paranoid identification with the victim which is so central to his pathology and which enables him to provoke and elicit attacks from the persecutor, lies very close to the position of the masochist. The masochist renounces power for the sake of love, but the love which is in question is a love based on weakness, subjugation, castration, and homosexual degradation.

The paranoid and the masochist share a common failure to identify in a healthy manner with the parent of the same sex. The Oedipal wish is to eliminate the parent of the same sex and to possess the parent of the opposite sex. Both carry with them a dread of retaliation and castration anxiety. For both, any opportunity for self-assertion or for the achievement of real success is fraught with anxiety and threat, since it is unconsciously associated as effectively a defiance of and transgression against a powerful authority figure. Success means both incestuous conquest of and possession of the parent of the opposite sex, as well as the elimination and murderous destruction of the parent of the same sex. Any competition implies a combat which is penetrated through and through with destructive impulses. Both the paranoid and the masochist project these infantile destructive impulses. The paranoid is often tormented by them and becomes their anguished victim, while the masochist often submits to them more willingly.

For these and any other reasons the paranoid character has particular difficulty with any situation in which individuals must function in a more or less autonomous manner. The independence of other individuals is extremely threatening. Any power which others possess, even if it is merely the power of self-possession and personal initiative and independence, tends to be distorted into a hostile and destructive power which is interpreted as intending the subjugation and humiliation of the self.

This understanding of the dynamics of masochism makes it clear that the underlying constellation of factors involved in masochism lie very close to those we have already identified in depressive states. At the root of both forms of pathology, there is the victim introject. There is also involved, however, as a correlative aspect of the pathology, the aggressor introject. It is difficult clinically—if not theoretically—to draw any clear lines between either side of this set of defensive dichotomies. The line between depression and masochism is often difficult to determine, just as the line between paranoia and sadism is often not easy to delineate. It is my impression generally that clinically the sadomasochistic vicissitudes often show a more intense determination of sexual conflicts, consistent with the original description and discussion of sadomasochism provided by Freud.

The vicissitudes of the paranoid-depressive continuum, on the other hand, seem more directly related to offended narcissism and aggression. Thus in my own limited analytic experience, patients who present with depression and a strong bent toward masochism often can be shown to have a strong sadistic component in their personality organization. But they tend not to manifest paranoid attitudes. Nydes (1963) has attempted to distinguish between sadistic and paranoid aggression. Sadistic aggression is based on an identification with the aggressor and the rage is accompanied by a sense of malicious triumph. The motive for the aggression is simply to hurt the victim who is unable to fight back and the aggression thus works to achieve an intimidation or domination over the victim. The paranoid aggression, however, is seen as derived essentially from an identification with the victim and functioning as a more or less hostile defense against anticipated attack. The rage is accompanied by a sense of self-righteousness. Moreover, the apparent motive of the aggression is to protect against the anticipated attack of the persecutor. But the effect of the aggression is often to provoke further punishment, thus gratifying the regressed wish for humiliation and victimization. To this it must be added that the paranoid defense is essentially based on the underlying narcissistic trauma. Thus the narcissistic rage has a quality of revenge that simple sadism does not. Moreover the narcissistic injury and the deprivation associated with it, along with the signal affects of shame or envy, do not leave any room for the form of sexual gratification so frequently found in the masochistic position.

Another interesting facet to the problem of masochism is its relationship to fantasies of being beaten. Freud originally described a stage in the psychosexual development of females in which the girl fantasies herself as being beaten on the buttocks by her father. There is a parallel fantasy among boys of the mother similarly beating him. Freud interpreted the fantasies in psychosexual terms as representing the child's wish for sexual assault on the part of the parent of the opposite sex, in which the attack was displaced from the genitals to the buttock. The essential aspect of the fantasy is that an aggressive wish is used in the defense against erotic wishes. The experience of spankings or face-slappings or shaming or other humiliations are by no means unusual in the experience of children. Being spanked on the bare buttocks often can produce erotic overtones, which may frequently be related to sexual and seductive elements in the parent-child interaction.

Rather than seeing such beating fantasies in the context of abnormal sadomasochistic development, recent trends have seen the role of the beating fantasy evolving within a context of a normal development phase. This reflects the frequency with which children interpret the act of intercourse as physical beating (Rubinfine, 1965). In the course of normal development the fantasy seems to lose its cathexis, whereas in more sadomasochistic channels of development the fantasy maintains a special psychosexual importance. Rubinfine has advanced the hypothesis that it is the effects of parental surrender to the child's aggression or withdrawal from it which result in the intensification of infantile sadism, that is related to the persistence of beating fantasies. In his cases it was the failure of obsessional mechanisms to adequately guarantee the safety of the child's good objects, which set the stage for the formation of beating fantasies as a means of protecting both the object and the self against the destructive sadism.

The beating fantasy can consequently be looked at as a subvariant of a projective defense, by which aggressive or sadistic impulses are externalized with corresponding development of a phobic state. Such fantasies can be fixed at a genital level so that the attitudes toward sexuality became tinged with elements of sadomasochism. In Freud's later writings, beating fantasies came to represent not only Oedipal wishes but also a punishment for masturbation, castration, copulation, or giving birth. Later work has increasingly amplified the number of determinants and functions of beating fantasies, with an increasing shift toward the emphasis on preoedipal rather than Oedipal determinants.

It seems that the beating wish may be regarded as an instinctual manifestation, which may be conscious or unconscious and may be variously defended against, sublimated, or displaced. The beating fantasy itself thus becomes a sexualized fulfillment of the underlying wish. The manifestations of such wishes have been found in a broad spectrum of childhood behaviors spanning the range from quite normal to relatively severely disturbed (Novick and Novick, 1972). The beating wish and its connection with the expression of aggression in forms of hitting and being hit is sexualized in terms of the sadistic theory of intercourse. The hitting and chasing among both boys and girls during the phallic stages takes on an aspect of intense sexual excitement. In these games the active and the passive roles are alternated, along with the roles of attacker and victim.

In this phase of phallic development the beating comes to represent parental intercourse and consequently carries with it the connotations of castration and passive femininity. Boys find themselves struggling against passivity and the wish to be beaten. Girls, however, who may have difficulty in accepting the lack of a penis, would either give up the beating games and regress to anality, or conversely deny the lack of penis and adopt a more active role in the beating games. Thus the beating wish, the sadistic intercourse theory, and phallic beating games are seen in some form or other in most young children. Follow-up studies of such children in adolescence found no excessive masochism in the girls and what seemed to be adequate sublimation of the beating wish into appropriate feminine passivity. They conclude that the beating fantasy and the Oedipal wish to be beaten are a normal, phase-specific, transitional component and may be relatively common. In more severely disturbed children, however, the beating fantasy may become fixed and develop as a relatively permanent part of the child's psychosexual experience.

It can be added in terms of our own case material that it is not only beating fantasies which may serve similar developmental functions, but also memories of beatings or, as in the case with Karen, being slapped in the face particularly by the father, which can serve in the experience of girls as a focus for the Oedipal wish to be beaten. The process involved and the vicissitudes of the aggressive components displayed in the sadomasochistic aspects of the wish to be beaten again reflect the relatively common status of the processes by which instinctual components, particularly aggressive and sadistically destructive ones, are defended against. The beating fantasies or the fixations on beating memories seems to be another aspect of the projective management of internal aggressive impulses in the interest both of preserving self from the destructive aggressiveness as well as the needed and loved objects. The mechanism, consequently, is quite close to what we have discussed in connection with nightmares and phobias.

CHAPTER 23

Genetic Aspects

THE DEVELOPMENTAL PROCESS

We can now turn our attention to the developmental aspects of the paranoid process. In so doing, we need to remind ourselves that we are beginning a consideration of development itself specifically as a process—that is, involving a certain organized sequence, following a more or less epigenetic pattern in which prior attainments are continued and extended in later portions of the developmental sequence and become the determining basis for later developmental attainments.

Maturation and Environment

We must also remind ourselves that the developmental process is an · extremely complex phenomenon which reflects the influence of many determinants—some of which remain obscure and relatively unanalyzed. We need also to remind ourselves that the developmental process involves not merely intrinsic maturational factors, but that it also involves a complex process of environmental stimulation and interaction. The critical locus for such stimulation and interaction is the developmental matrix provided by the parent-child relationship, and in the earliest phases of development most significantly the mother-child relationship.

From the side of the infant, there seems little doubt that the child brings to the developmental process a certain set of innate givens and constitutional factors, and that these behavioral and physical characteristics play a significant role in influencing the emergence of the mother-child interaction. Such constitutional or congenital factors have been designated as inherited physical characteristics, anomalies deriving either from genetic or birth trauma influences or the vicissitudes of pregnancy, patterns of neonatal motility, emotional responsivity, or even sensitivity to stimuli.

Congenital Activity Patterns

Thus over a score of years ago, Fries and Woolf (1953) studied the patterns of activity in neonatal infants and described a series of "congenital activity types" ranging from extremely active to relatively quiet patterns. These congenital patterns were based on the observations of the amount, tempo, rhythm, and intensity of bodily movements observed in the first months of life, which seem to become organized into unique and stable patterns of activity. These congenital patterns of activity provide the basis of the child's contribution to the interaction with the parent and contribute to influencing parental attitudes and modes of responding within the interaction. Thus a relatively hyperactive infant can create considerable anxiety in a compulsive, controlled, and controlling mother for whom such behavior becomes relatively destructive. These patterns can also be involved in the infant's experience of reality and his capacity to master reality. Thus the excessively hypoactive child with an obsessive mother may find his needs closely attended to and even anticipated. As Fries and Woolf point out, these innate activity patterns may also have an influence on the development of defenses and in shaping the forms of later psychopathology. Thus a very quiet activity type may be associated in later development with a higher degree of withdrawal and the development of schizoid traits.

Along similar lines, Mittelmann (1954) described unique patterns of the expression of motility which seemed to be related to other functions in the growing child, particularly mastery and testing of the environment, impulse control, emotional expression, and the sense of self-evaluation. Here too the inappropriate coordination of parental responses to the child's motoric activity can serve as the basis for the formation of psychopathology. Thus sustained restrictions of motility, particularly when the urge to motoric activity is at its highest during the second year, can result in anxiety reactions and compensatory hyperactivity.

Similarly, patterns of sensitivity, motility, and drive-endowment observed in the first years of life have been examined in relationship to the development of psychopathology by Chess and her co-workers (1963, 1967). They have described temperamental styles which are defined as inborn behavioral patterns which can be identified early in life and persist through childhood, and involve such parameters as activity level, mood, rhythmicity, approach, withdrawal, adaptability, intensity of reaction, and sensory threshold. They describe symptom patterns which can be classified as either "active" or "passive." The premorbid temperamental style of children with active symptoms can be contrasted with those presenting passive symptoms. Thus from even the third month of life, children with active symptomatic styles show a significantly higher degree of irregularity, nonadaptability, intensity of reaction, and negative mood.

Another approach which has been taken to the question of innate levels of responsiveness has been to focus on variations in sensitivity to stimulations. In this regard, Bergman and Escalona (1949) reported on a sample of five children who demonstrated atypical sensitivities to a variety of stimuli in the first year of life and who subsequently developed psychotic manifestations. They found atypical reactions to vary quantitatively in terms of stimulus intensity or also in terms of stimulus quality. Referring to Freud's concept of the stimulus barrier, they conceptualize the atypical patterns of reaction in terms of these children having been born with an excessively thin stimulus barrier (hyperexcitable) or an excessively thick stimulus barrier (hypoexcitable).

In either case, without an appropriately modulated and adapted response on the part of caretakers in suitably modifying the stimulus environment, this would result in the development of premature ego-functions to enable the child to manage his inborn incoordination with the available stimulus. Such premature ego-functions and defenses are relatively fragile and easily disintegrate under the pressure of more complex stimulus configurations and stresses which emerge in later development. The result is a psychotic disintegration of ego-functioning. Along a similar vein, Brazelton (1962) applied the concept of stimulus barrier to account for the variability in the capacity of infants to defend against and minimize excessive stimulation.

To these considerations there can be added the earlier formulations of Greenacre (1952) on predispositions to anxiety. The irritability, which she associated with the tendency to an anxiety response, can be specified in terms of the innate parameters we have been discussing. Greenacre also suggests, however, that where there is such an increase in early anxiety, there is also an increase in narcissism. We can infer, then, that a disproportion or imbalance between the stimulus characteristics and response pattern of the caretaking environment on the one hand, and the innate capacities to regulate and integrate stimulus reception and responsiveness within the infant on the other, play a significant role in the emergence and handling of anxiety and in the developmental vicissitudes of narcissism.

Adaptation

Thus the elaboration of a relatively normal developmental progression requires that the process operate within the constraints of a given range of adaptability. The growing organism must phase itself in with and fit into the environment in terms of a series of average and expectable behavioral organizations. In normal development, these behavioral patternings more or less match and fit in with environmental expectations, limitations, and potentialities. The environmental nontext of development likewise presents the individual with an evolving series of average acceptable stimulus contexts in which the available stimulation is more or less adapted to the sensing and responding apparatuses of the developing organism.

It should be noted that the formulations of the adaptive hypothesis, which are so central to psychoanalytic thinking and were stated primarily by Hartmann and Rapaport in the interests of developing a generalized ego psychology, tended to deal with the problem of adaptation in general biological terms—that is, in terms of average expectable environment and in terms of biologically preadapted apparatuses within the developing organism. But the match between organism and experience is never carried out on such generalized terms. In the first place, the match is never perfect so that the individual organism must be continually changing and modifying its responses and expectations. There is also a certain flux within the process of adaptation whereby particular behavior systems and structural components are more ready or available within that period, the pattern of development will presumably begin to follow a deviant line of response.

Moreover, the environment plays a role in determining which behaviors at a given time are adaptive. Stimulation that may be average and expectable and adaptive in one context may become atypical in another context. Thus the adaptive response of the individual organism in one situation may come to represent a developmental failure in another.

Finally, the developmental process, not only in human organisms but in animals as well, never takes place simply in terms of the average and expectable. Rather it is elaborated out of the context of specific and individualized relationship in which the particular innate configuration of drives and stimulus sensitivities and response thresholds characteristic of an individual infant must be met and responded to by the highly individualized traits, inner needs, sensitivities, and response capacities of a particular mothering figure. Thus in discussing the vicissitudes of object relationships, we are concerned more with highly individualized and personalized dynamic interactions and responsiveness, rather than with general biological principles of adaptation.

Development and the Paranoid Process

In discussing the developmental aspects of the paranoid process, we have a dual perspective that must be taken into consideration. We are concerned first of all with understanding the developmental influences which come to bear on and modify the emergence and functioning of the paranoid process. From another perspective, conversely, the paranoid process itself has a reciprocal influence on the process of development. Thus our discussion must embrace not only the experiences and developmental vicissitudes that influence and shape the emerging aspects of the paranoid process we have been considering, but it must also articulate the manner in which the economy of introjection and projection along with the accompanying phenomena of cognitive integration (paranoid construction) enjoy their influence on the emerging personality. As we have suggested in a number of places, the mechanisms of introjection and projection play a vital role at many levels of the developmental sequence, particularly in giving shape to and defining the boundaries between the realm of inner experience and external reality, and in qualitatively shaping the organization of the child's experience.

An attempt to bring into focus this latter aspect of the role of the paranoid process in development brings into much clearer articulation the whole issue of the discrimination between more normal developmental patterns and those which are determinably pathological. We are dealing with the situation in which our understanding of the developmental process must allow for the elaboration of basic mechanisms, both in the service of defense and in the service of self-definition and internal structuralization. If the fundamental insight to be formulated from this perspective is that paranoid mechanisms and the paranoid process play a vital and integral role in the formation and development of even normal personality, we must obtain a finer degree of discrimination in our understanding of what determinants come into play when the paranoid process can be seen to follow deviant developmental lines, as opposed to those influences which determine the outcome to be along more normal developmental lines.

Development and Defense

The larger question, of course, has to do more specifically with the relationship between the emergence of patterns of defense and the developmental vicissitudes as such. The question is of general significance for the understanding of personality dynamics. As Zetzel (1970) has observed, the role of anxiety and the capacity of the ego to tolerate anxiety and to exploit and master it in the interest of development is one of the most essential stimuli to ego-development. The ego's capacity to mobilize defenses, which can then be integrated into psychic structure and become functional aspects of ego-organization (Hartmann's "change of function"), is a central aspect of the developmental process. More specifically, in terms of the crucial internalizations which we have been at pains to elaborate in this study, introjection may arise quite specifically in the service of developmental objectives in contributing to the differentiation of self and object, or it may arise more specifically in response to defensive needs. Thus the developmental and defensive objects can overlap, often to a considerable degree, but in deviant forms of pathology the defensive employment of introjection seems to override developmental potentialities. It is important, then, in terms of our understanding of the paranoid process to be able to discriminate between these aspects and to determine those contexts and patterns of influence under which the defensive needs come to undermine the developmental objectives.

Similarly, we understand the role of introjections in the formation of superego as frequently originating in the service of defense against Oedipal impulses, but we also need to understand the process by which such introjective components are integrated into maturer and more constructive superego functioning rather than becoming fixated or undergoing more defensive deviation into aberrant forms of superego development. Ultimately it is only by means of a grasp on the nature and function of these fundamental processes that we will be able to effectively formulate and understand the role of elements of the paranoid process, not only in the organization and sustaining of personality functioning as such, but also on the larger scale of the organization and maintenance of social processes and belief systems. Consequently, in discussing the developmental aspects of the paranoid process, we are dealing with a series of gradations of developmental phenomena which include in their implementation the extreme deviance of the most severe forms of paranoid disorganization and psychopathology and, at the opposite extreme, the constituents of normal, healthy, and adaptive psychic organization and functioning.

Perhaps one useful way to conceptualize this overlap and confluence of the pathological and the relatively normal is to put it in terms of the interplay between the specific mechanisms which we have been discussing and the background of conflict against which they display themselves. It is in the area of this interweaving of conflict and mechanism that the developmental process works itself out and the patterning of personality is pressured in a relatively constructive and adaptive direction, or in a more deviant and pathological direction. The degree to which the mechanisms are taken up in the service of resolving conflicts, and correspondingly the extent to which conflicts influence the functioning of paranoid mechanisms, must therefore be a constant preoccupation throughout this discussion.

SEPARATION—INDIVIDUATION AND THE PARANOID PROCESS

Dependence

I would like to begin this discussion of development and the paranoid process from the starting point of dependence, following the general insights provided by Winnicott (1965). In this perspective, the infant begins his developmental course in a state of absolute dependence which is correlated with the caretaking aspects of the maternal environment. Winnicott refers to this originating environment as "holding." As the infant emerges from the context of absolute dependence on this holding environment, his developmental course can be traced in terms of a progression of gradually increasing independence and diminishing dependence. The child gradually becomes aware of the mother as a need-satisfying object and increasingly acquires the means for divesting himself of his intense need for the object and his unremitting reliance on it for the assuagement of basic tensions and need-states.

Impingement

As this development progresses, the earliest rudiments of the ego begin to take shape. As these first integrations give rise to the beginnings of psychic structure, they also provide the basis for a potential for anxiety. Such emergent integrations do not take place without the concurrent risk of disintegration, just as the latter differentiation of self and object in the infant's experience concurrently gives rise to the threatening potential for object-loss. The function of the holding maternal environment and the emerging context of object-relatedness is to buffer the infant's emerging experience from such anxieties. Under the continuing protection of the holding environment or of properly attuned and emphatic responsiveness on the part of the caretaking mother, the progression toward increasing integration can be successfully accomplished. In Winnicott's view, the continuity of integrative processes can be interrupted by what he calls "impingements" (Winnicott, 1958). He defines the concept of impingement in relationship to his treatment of the development of the self. He writes:

> Another phenomenon that needs consideration at this phase is the hiding of the core of the personality. Let us examine the concept of a central or true self. The central self could be said to be the inherited potential which is experiencing a continuity of being, and acquiring in its own way and at its own speed a personal psychic reality and a personal body-scheme. It seems necessary to allow for the concept of this isolation of this central self as a characteristic of health. Any threat to this isolation of the true self constitutes a major anxiety at this early stage, and defenses of earliest infancy appear in relation to failures on the part of the mother (or in maternal care) to ward off impingements which might disturb this isolation (p. 46).

Thus the notion of impingement assumes a very central role in Winnicott's notion of the development of psychopathology. In fact, he is quite explicit in linking it to the notion of paranoia. In discussing Greenacre's (1952) articles on the predisposition to anxiety, he suggests that certain cases demonstrate such a marked propensity to ideas of persecution that it is unlikely that the origin lies in an elaboration of oral sadism as suggested by Melanie Klein. Rather, he suggests that it may rather be a traumatic birth experience which sets the pattern of expected persecution. Thus in certain cases of latent paranoia the analysis, which seeks to recover the full extent of oral sadism, does not succeed in bringing a complete resolution of the anxiety about since there is also required a reliving and working through of the traumatic birth experience. The traumatic event is related to the infantile expectation of interference with basic "being."

We need not follow the details of Winnicott's argument, except to note that he postulates a basic continuity of the infant's inner experience which provides the beginnings of an experience of self. This sense of continuity of

self-experience is periodically interrupted by phases of reaction to impingement. The reaction to impingement remains relatively nontraumatic as long
as the level of stimulation does not exceed that for which the infant is already prepared.

A basic question in the infant's developmental experience has to do
with the balance between the basic experiences of continuity of the emerging
self, specifically, and particularly in relationship to the holding maternal environment, and the impingements which constitute the residue of the experience. The impingements are thus constituted by those stimulus
parameters which exceed the receptive capacity and readiness of the infant's inner organization. The reactions to such impingements can be ag-
gravated and integrated independently of the sense of inner continuity and
thus come to form rudiments of what Winnicott has described in terms of
the "false self." The same impingements, serving to disrupt the inner continuity of the emerging self, can set up a pattern of expected persecution
"which can serve as both an expression and a fundament of further elaborations of the paranoid process."

Winnicott's schema makes it abundantly clear and explicit that the
developmental process cannot simply be conceived in terms of maturational elaborations, but that the emerging growth potential of the infant is inte-
grally connected with and dependent on a complex interaction that takes
place between the child's emerging needs and capacities and the reciprocal
nurturing, receptivity, and responsiveness of the mothering or caretaking
figure. Our first considerations of infant development consequently are cast
in terms of the continuity of the coordinated bond between mother and
child. Impingements come to represent those elements and influences which
come to create discontinuity in that bond, thus creating an intrusion of
other aspects of reality upon this mother-child unity. The same developmental exigencies are articulated in Mahler's (1968) theory of separation
and individuation. Development is thus conceived in terms of the infant's
emergence from the absolute dependence on the mother-child unit through
stages of increasing separation and individuation, and thus progressing toward and enlarging capacity for independence.

Autism

Mahler's views are well-known and can be schematically presented
here. As she views the process, the infant is born into a consideration of normal autism in which mother and child are caught up in an indifferentiated
unity of function, in which need satisfaction is a function of this omnipotent
autistic orbit, rather than of discriminable agents. The infant's experience is
centered on the continuing need to achieve homeostasis as a means of
modifying physiological tension-states, and thus reducing disruptive

stimulation which may exceed the infant's capacity to absorb it. The mother's need-reducing functions are not differentiated from the infant's own physiological tension-reducing activities. This stage of normal autism is marked by absolute primary narcissism which is still oblivious to any differentiation or discrimination between the mothering agent and the infant's own homeostatic regulatory mechanisms.

Symbiosis

Gradually, somewhere in the course of the second month, the infant begins to acquire a dim awareness of the mother as need-satisfying object, a progression which marks the emergence into a phase of normal symbiosis. Within this primitive differentiation, primary narcissism is still operative insofar as satisfaction is recognized as coming from the need-satisfying object, but this object remains within the omnipotent orbit of the child's symbiotic unity with the mothering agent. Within this state of undifferentiated fusion with the mother, the differentiation between self and external objects has not yet been achieved, and the discriminations between inside and outside are only beginning to be sensed. Unpleasurable perceptions, whether derived from external or internal sources, must be projected beyond the common boundary of the symbiotic unit.

The progression from the autistic to the symbiotic phase is accompanied by a cathectic shift from the predominantly proprioceptive-enteroceptive focus towards a sensoriperceptive cathexis of the body periphery. Parallel to this is the projective elimination of destructive unneutralized aggression beyond the body-self boundaries. The infant's inner sensations provide a core awareness of self around which the emerging sense of identity takes shape. Correlatively, it is the mother's maintenance of a holding environment which stabilizes and organizes this symbiotic structure.

In the hallucinatory omnipotence of the autistic phase, the mother's breast or any of her nurturing activities were undifferentiated from the infant's global sense of self. But in the symbiotic phase, the object begins to be perceived as an unspecific yet need-satisfying object (A. Freud, 1965). Thus, with the emergence into the symbiotic phase, the autistic shell which has served to keep external stimuli out begins to crack and is replaced by a protective stimulus shield—functioning at the sensoriperceptive periphery—which serves both receptive and selective functions. This stimulus shield envelops the symbiotic unity of the mother-child matrix. We should remember in terms of previous observations that the symbiotic stimulus-barrier is susceptible to varying degrees of thickness and stimulus sensitivity. The effects and delineation of impingements are in part a function of the characteristics of the symbiotic matrix.

Within the symbiotic matrix important developmental processes are at play. Not only does the differentiation of self from need-satisfying object begin to take place within this matrix, but the infant's sense of self also begins to take shape and emerge. Within the symbiotic orbit, in terms of the interaction between mother and child there is indelibly impressed on the infant a complex pattern of internal integration which Lichtenstein (1961) has referred to as "imprinting an identity" upon the infant.

This raises the critical question of what is to be derived from the symbiotic relationship, and therefore what is brought to the symbiotic relationship by the participating parties. If the mother brings to the symbiotic relationship a firm sense of identity and autonomous self, the imprinting process can serve to provide the infant with the rudiments of an autonomous and integrated sense of self. Within the symbiotic matrix, important internalizations take place which significantly help determine some of the more central parameters of the infant's internal development. Searles has said so convincingly:

> I believe that the more successfully the infant and young child internalizes as the foundation of his personal identity a symbiotic relationship with a predominantly loving mother, the more accessible is his symbiotic level of existence, in all of its infinite richness, through the more structured aspects of identity which develop; which develop not primarily as imposed restraints upon him, but as structures that facilitate the release of his energies and capacities in creative relatedness with the outer world. Such a symbiosis-based identity serves as one's most sensitive and reliable organ for perceiving the world, not merely by mirroring a world set at some distance, but through processes of introjection-and-projection, literally sampling, literally mingling with—in manageable increments—the world through which, moment by changing moment, one lives (1966-67, p. 529).

Thus a positive symbiotic relatedness is a developmental achievement. Within this matrix significant internalizations are elaborated primarily in terms of the interplay of introjection and projection.

As Winnicott (1965) suggests, the basic anxiety in this early stage of mother-child unity is the threat of annihilation. The mother's function in the symbiotic unity is to reduce to a minimum those impingements which threaten the symbiotic ties. From this perspective the impingements would threaten the integrity of the symbiotic unit and thus raise the specter of annihilation. Viewed intrapsychically, as Angel (1967) has pointed out, symbiosis refers to the intrapsychic relationship between self- and object-representations. In the symbiotic state, self- and object-representations remain merged so that the fundamental issue behind the threat is not specifically separation, since sufficient individuation has not yet occurred. The symbiotic panic of annihilation consequently is relatively more overwhelming than the milder separation anxiety.

There is a corresponding wish to merge with the omnipotent invulnerable object, along with a simultaneous fear of such merging or of being devoured by the bad symbiotic object. Thus the symbiotic phase precedes any sufficient differentiation of self and object and adequate development of object constancy to allow for separation anxiety in a more restrictive sense. Patients who have fixated at the symbiotic level are preoccupied with control of the mother. The fear is not loss of the object, but loss of omnipotence which is equivalent to becoming nothing. This occurs either by abandonment of the omnipotent object or by merging with the devouring object (Angel, 1972).

Thus the symbiotic phase can serve important developmental functions, but it can also serve as the point for significant pathological deviation. Mahler (1968) has discussed the notion of the symbiotic psychosis. The psychosis represents a defect in the child's utilization of the mother during the symbiotic phase, resulting in an inability to internalize the representation of the mothering object. Thus the child is unable to differentiate his self from the symbiotic phase, resulting in an inability to internalize the representation of the mothering object. Thus the child is unable to differentiate his self from the symbiotic unity and individuation is correspondingly impaired. Mutual caring and responsiveness are essential ingredients of the normal symbiotic phase. An important function of the symbiotic buffering is the absorption and protection from the child's own unneutralized aggression.

As the mother emerges as a need-satisfying object, she also emerges more clearly as a need-frustrating object. The other aspect of the child's experience of his interaction with the mother opens the way for often intensely aggressive responses. The successful symbiotic unit serves to minimize this aggressive disruption and to preserve the child's sense of unruffled omnipotence. To the extent that the mother's nurturing and buffering capacities are exceeded, or to the extent that she contributes punitive and destructive elements to the symbiotic confluence, the child will begin to experience these destructive elements as a part of his own emerging sense of self. Here the complex mechanisms of introjection and projection are at work, constantly playing off between the contributions made from the infant's own internal processes and the gradually differentiating and distancing aspects of the mother's own destructive potential. The mother's capacity to remain nurturing and loving in the face of the infant's aggression can have a buffering and modulating effect on the intensity of his aggression. If the mother's own aggressive propensitites, however, respond to and reciprocate with the infant's own projected destructive impulses, we have the setting for the emergence of more pathological forms of symbiotic progression.

Differentiation

It is out of the symbiotic matrix provided by the mother-child interaction that the child must begin to differentiate himself as an individual.
Along about the fifth month a gradual shift in cathexis begins to take place
which is associated with a shift of the infant's attention increasingly toward
the outer world. Within the symbiotic orbit, the child's symbiotic partner
has protected the infant from the necessity for having to prematurely
develop his own resources for mastering external stimulation. We have discussed this function, particularly in relationship to dealing with impingements on the symbiotic unity.

The more optimally that function is performed, the more is the infant
enabled to begin what Mahler calls the "hatching process." If the infant has
a secure symbiotic base, he is better able to begin the process of separating
himself from the relatively undifferentiated symbiotic matrix in a smoother
and more positively constructive manner. The process of gradually differentiating and establishing his own self-representations and separating them
from the gradually emerging and consolidating representations of objects
can then proceed apace. The whole process involves a continual give-and-
take between mother and child, a mutual selection of cues which indicate
from moment to moment the state of needs, tension, pleasure, and states of
threat and anxiety. The mother responds selectively to the cues emitted by
the child, and the child in turn modifies his behavior to adapt to the
mother's selective responsiveness. The same process of mutual responsiveness, which provided the basis for a sense of the child's emerging sense
of self within the symbiotic orbit, now becomes the process which regulates
and directs the gradual emergence from the symbiosis and the progressive
and gradual establishment of the child as an individuated self.

Mahler refers to the first subphase of the separation-individuation
process as the phase of *differentiation*. The assurance of a safe and secure
haven within the symbiotic relationship allows the child to begin to divert
his attention to the outside world and by increasing degrees to expand his
awareness beyond the boundaries of the symbiotic unit. The process is undoubtedly connected with maturational developments within the perceptual
and central nervous systems. The child becomes increasingly attentive to external stimuli during the gradually increasing periods of wakefulness.

Then the systems begin to take form which provide a basis for internalized experience which is gradually differentiated from present external experience. Little by little the infant begins to break away from the passive
babyhood that characterized the symbiotic stage. The child begins to
physically separate himself from the mother's body not only to get a better
look at her, but also at the world around him. Even so, he does not stray far
from the safe haven of mother's body. Children, for whom the symbiotic
phase has been optimal and who have achieved a sense of confident expec-

tation (Benedek, 1938) or basic trust (Erikson, 1963) are able to meet the external world with a sense of curiosity and wonder, even in their inspection of strangers.

Children for whom the symbiotic phase has been less than optimal and for whom the symbiotic envelopment has not adequately neutralized the aggressive elements or has not adequately protected them from threatening impingements, tend to face the external world with a sense of anxiety and insecurity which can interfere with the otherwise pleasurable inspection of the surrounding world. This can take the form of stranger anxiety or a more generalized reluctance to explore the external world and to separate from the protectiveness of the symbiotic orbit.

As Mahler (1972) has pointed out, even these first steps in the separation process involve the risk of loss of the object, so that the process of separation and gradual emergence of the child's individuality also involves a process of mourning of the partially lost object. The threat of loss and the necessity for resignation of the attachment to the object are inherent in every step of the developmental process. Whatever the pressures toward increasing individuality and whatever the inherent gains in the process, it must constantly work itself out in the face of the threat of loss. The basic anxiety, therefore, against which the developmental process must work is a separation anxiety. At later stages of maturity and greater capacity for psychic functioning, the same dialectic is elaborated in terms of restitution and loss—the warp and woof of the fabric of human experience.

Separation

These early differentiations lead to a period which follows and in fact overlaps the earlier period and which Mahler (1968) refers to as the *"practicing period."* The child begins to achieve a sense of separate functioning, even though the achievement still requires the presence and emotional availability of the mother. The process is permeated with tension between the pleasure involved in separate functioning as over against the continuing threat of separation and object loss. The infant is at first able to physically separate himself from the mother, and then with the acquisition of upright locomotion he is able to experiment with the process of distancing himself from his mother's body and presence.

A critical aspect of this phase is the emergence and integration of autonomous ego apparatuses. The fact that this emergent autonomy is so critically related to the child's attachment and dependence on the mother and that his emerging autonomy inevitably confronts the mother with a whole new constellation of interactional difficulties, makes this phase a critical one for the shaping of the child's basic autonomy. In terms of the paranoid process, we have been at pains to indicate the extent to which fragile autonomy plays a critical role in the deviant forms of its expression.

Consequently, this period is one of particular relevance to the understanding of the genesis of paranoid pathology. The culmination of the practicing period comes in the middle of the second year and is marked by the child's belief in his own magical omnipotence, an omnipotence which is yet dependent on his sense of sharing in the magical power and strength of the mother (Mahler, 1968).

The gradual distancing increasingly allows the exploring child freedom to begin to investigate the outside world, now at a physical distance from the mother. Nonetheless, mother continues to be a necessary base to which the child can return for "emotional refueling." The child gradually builds a reservoir of internal security which allows him to tolerate increasing distance and separation from the mother, as long as when he begins to approach the limits of that security credit he can once again return to the basic source of confidence and reestablish the internal security which is still linked to the need-satisfying and protective object. As Mahler observes:

> As the child through the maturation of his locomotor apparatus, begins to venture farther and farther away from the mother's feet, he is often so absorbed in his own activities that for long periods of time he appears to be oblivious to the mother's presence. However, he returns periodically to the mother, seeming to need her physical proximity and refueling from time to time (1972a, p. 336).

It is not difficult to see in this context that the mother's attitudes toward the child's emerging autonomy can play a significant role in the success or failure of his venture into the world. If the mother anxiously pushes the child, increasing the distance between herself and him prematurely and excessively, she forces the child into a position of having to rely on his own resources prematurely. On the other hand, if she is overly protective and sheltering, she can create an excessive dependence in the child that inhibits his capacity to separate from the symbiotic orbit and to establish appropriate areas of autonomous functioning. In either case, whether the mother binds the child excessively to the symbiotic dependence or thrusts him prematurely into premature autonomy and thus deprives him of the security and support of symbiotic protection, the development toward autonomy and appropriate independence is interfered with.

Some toddlers consequently will cling to the mother in an intense anxiety due to the threat of separation. Yet at the same time they must struggle against the threat of reengulfment due to the reactive concern of the mother. The negativistic phase of the toddler, usually seen in the second year, is a relatively normal aspect of this prospect of disengagement from the mother-child symbiosis. The newly achieved and fragile differentiation, however, is threatened by a fear of reengulfment and must be defended against. The child's negativism consequently is a reaction to such a fear and constitutes an attempt on the part of the child to preserve his fragile sense of autonomy and independence. The more ambivalent the symbiotic relationship has been, and the more clinging the symbiotic ties, the greater will be the threat of reengulfment and the more will be the negativistic reaction.

Separateness

If the practicing period achieves a sense of thrill in the exercise of autonomous function, complemented by the toddler's feeling of his own magical omnipotence—a state which Joffe and Sandler (1965) refer to as "the ideal state of self"—it is inevitably followed by a period of retrenchment in which this ideal state is modified by the child's increasing experience of and contact with reality. The phase of rapprochement which follows on the practicing phase thus becomes a period of relative vulnerability in which the child's self-esteem may be at stake. The basic question is whether the child can surrender and modify some of his narcissistic overestimation of his powers without suffering an excessive sense of depletion or defeat.

He begins to learn that there are obstacles that stand in the way of his omnipotent domination of the world. In the face of frustration and pain and limitation, his need for the protective and powerful mother increases, and along with it, his separation anxiety becomes more intense. His behavior is increasingly characterized by an attitude of active approach and increasing concern with the whereabouts of the mother. There is an increased need for the mother to share each new acquisition and each new experience. The earlier "refueling" is replaced by a constant seeking of interaction with the mother, and also at this stage increasingly with the father and other significant adults.

The contact is more and more cast in progressively higher levels of organization of function and symbolization. Physical contact is increasingly replaced by the use of language and other communications. The toddler is essentially confronted with the fact that the world is not his to have on his own terms, but that he must come to cope with it increasingly on his own and increasingly without support and protective intervention of his parents. He begins to feel a sense of smallness and relative helplessness and to become aware of the limitations of his strength and his fragile capacities (Mahler, 1972b).

Separateness from the powerful protecting figures is thus a more critical issue in this phase, and the child exercises himself to resist it. The realization becomes increasingly relevant that the objects of his love and dependence are indeed separate individuals, even as he himself has increasingly become a separate individual. The woeful struggles which the child engages in with both parents have very much to do with not only the stabilization of autonomy and a resistance to reengulfment, but have also to do with the child's unwillingness to recognize and tolerate the individuality of his parents. The threat in this phase, then, is not simply that of object loss, but more specifically that of loss of object love. The child experiences this state of separation and the periods of maternal absence or unavailability as rejections (A. Freud, 1970). The child's separation anxiety at this stage reflects the underlying sense of impotence and vulnerability as well as the sense of continuing dependence on the powerful yet separate parents.

Mother-Child Interaction

An additional perspective is contributed to our understanding of this basic developmental process by the work of Sander (1962, 1964, 1969). Sander and his group have undertaken detailed observations of mother-child pairs, particularly during the first eighteen months of life. Through a comparison of sequences and trends in the observational material across a sample of such pairs, they have been able to describe a sequence of adaptations which were found to be common in all of the different mother-infant pairs, but were carried out in a highly individual manner within each pair. It was essentially an epigenetic process in which at each stage of the process a new equilibrium and balance in the interaction had to be achieved.

In the view that emerges from these studies, mother and child are caught up from the very beginning of their experience of each other in a continuing process of interaction which can be described and defined in terms of certain sets of negotiations which take place within the interaction. Thus Sander describes a series of issues around which these negotiations focus, and which provide the stable configurations of mother-child interaction.

The first issue is negotiated particularly during the first three months of life. This is the issue of *initial regulation*—that is the achievement of a stable regulation of basic biological processes which are related to feeding, sleeping, elimination, etc. The negotiation between mother and child normally settles down to a relatively predictable routine, in which the mother begins to feel a sense of confidence in her ability to know and respond to her baby's needs. The affective tone in their interactions is basically pleasant and positive, particularly with the onset of the smiling response.

The subsequent issue is that of *reciprocal exchange*. This is negotiated in the second three-month period. The present pattern of smiling exchanges becomes elaborated and extended to more motor and vocal involvement in spontaneously affective exchanges. The pattern of spontaneous play emerge which both mother and child participate in with delight and increasing expressions of pleasure. Increasingly the primary caretaking activities such as diapering, dressing, or spoon-feeding are accomplished more and more easily through a reciprocal coordination between mother and child.

The next trimester is taken up with the issue of *initiative*. The infant begins to express his own initiative with increasing vigor in his bids for attention, social exchange, and other exploratory or manipulative activities. He begins to express his own special preferences and the mother becomes more attentive to and more responsive to these activities. There is also an increasing element of acknowledgment of the unique and individual quality of the infant's initiatives. The question here is the degree to which the child can begin to experience success in the exercise of these initiatives as opposed to the failure of them. The mother's response to the initiatives is critical insofar as her own ambivalence toward these newly emerging capacities may lead to interference with or reinforcement of them.

The next issue, which occupies the latter portion of the first year of life, is the issue of *focalization*. With the onset of locomotive capacity and the increased capacity for voluntary activity and the expression of the child's specific intentions, he can begin to negotiate the question of the extent to which he can bring it about that the mother is available to him. Mothers differ considerably in their reactions to the child's effort to have their attention attention and activity focused around the child's needs. All the reciprocal exchange of information and adaptation between mother and child builds on the earlier achievements of reciprocity which were accomplished in previous phases of interaction.

Some mothers are gratified by this focusing from the child and take some satisfaction in their capacity to reply to it. Others, however, experience the child's more intent and specific demands as threatening. Their response is either escape from or defense against the child's wishes. The mother's limited or ambivalent availability may now become quite apparent as limits begin to be set. The pressure upon the child to focus the mother's responses varies with the mother's ambivalence in making the response. If her response is relatively assured and he can have some degree of confidence in it, it is possible for him to turn his attention more easily to extrinsic interests. If her response is to withdraw and become less available, the level of his demand increases. If her response tends to be aggressively controlling or intrusive, he may seek to elicit her attack.

Individuation

The final issue which Sander defines becomes the central preoccupation for the following six months (approximately the fourteenth through twentieth). One begins to see a marked capacity in the child for *self-assertion* and for widening the range of his initiatives to determine and select the directions of his activity. The critical question has to do with the degree to which he can maintain his own initiative and self-assertion in the face of and in opposition to the mother's wishes and the rules which she has established.

The child's initiative is not completely directed in a manner contrary to the mother's wishes, but is mixed with positive bids for reciprocal interaction with her. This in a way is a continuation of the focusing pattern of interaction which was established in the previous phase. The infant gains a new sense of gratification and apparent success when it becomes evident that he is able to maintain his own aims even when they are in opposition to the other's. Prior to this achievement, separation was reacted to as a distressing and threatening event, but now separation, both in a physical and psychological sense, can begin to be the object of the child's initiative. This links up with the familiar period of negativism which we have previously discussed.

Within this developmental interaction, basic processes of initiation, reciprocation, and regulation are worked out at various levels between mother and child. The essential questions are concerned with the levels at which the infant is capable of initiating activity and the relative degree of reciprocal coordination which is then achieved in the interaction with the mother and her caretaking activity. The essential processes are mutual regulation and reciprocal response. As Sander notes, these processes inevitably contribute to the increasing differentiation—and we would add, therefore, individuation—between child and mother. He comments:

> Those activities initiated by the infant which become incorporated into this reciprocal coordination become differentiated from those which do not. That this should be so becomes even more reasonable as it is appreciated that stability of regulation for the infant, as the months pass, depends on this increasingly differentiated reciprocal exchange. The advanced levels include newly coordinated elements as well as features of old behavior whose coordination has already been established at an earlier level. To put the same thing into the language of adaptation: as new capacities for activity appear in the infant's behavior, as he advances chronologically, fitting together or adaptation is reachieved between infant and mother at each new level (1969, pp. 197-198).

Sander's descriptive schema of patterns of mother-child interaction shows considerable overlap with the separation-individuation schema provided by Mahler. Thus the period of reciprocal exchange would correspond roughly to that of differentiation, while the period of growing initiative and focalization relate roughly to the practicing subphase. The added perspective which Sander's data bring to the separation-individuation process is that the basic mechanisms by which the process is carried out, while based on innate potentials in the child and dependent on the biologically determined emergence of certain ego capacities and functions, are nonetheless basically interactional, and in a direct and intimate way involve the eliciting of certain behaviors out of the matrix of the child's developmental potentialities by the stimulations and appropriate responsiveness of the mother. It also makes it quite clear that, looking at the relationship in terms of its reciprocity, the child plays a major role and is a significant contributor to the patterning and the course of the interaction which takes place between himself and the caretaking figure.

Internalizations

At this point in the consideration of these overlapping developmental contexts, we would like to add an additional developmental consideration of some significance. The burden of our investigation is not only that the child's course of development is determined by the vicissitudes of separation and individuation, not only that the patterns of development are powerfully influenced by the sequences of interaction and mutual regulation which emerge within the matrix of the mother-child interaction, but that there is also an internal process, which has to do with the organization of self-representations and object-representations, which reflects, is partially derived from, and powerfully influences the patterns of relationships with objects and the direction of the developmental sequence. It is at this point, then, that our discussion of the paranoid process can be focused on in its reciprocal influence on the process of development.

As Angel (1967, 1972) has made clear, the symbiotic phase, as well as the subsequent process of separation-and-individuation, is less a matter of relationship and interaction than a matter of internal differentiation and organization. This has reference particularly to the differentiation and organization of both self- and object-representations. In this sense separation and individuation are mutually linked processes.

The successful separation from the symbiotic orbit is not only accomplished by significant cathectic shifts to the periphery as we have noted, but also is accompanied and sustained by significant internalizations. The basic mechanism which contributes to these important developmental progressions is that of introjection. Where the titer of separation anxiety runs high, the quality of introjection is shifted toward a more global, total, and undifferentiated state. Consequently the introjection is placed at the service of relatively intense defensive needs and constitutes a prolonging and extension of the symbiotic orbit.

As Mahler has pointed out (1968) where the symbiotic involvement allows no choice or possibility for the experimentation which prepares the infant for the gradual process of separation, the more normal process of partial and more differentiated introjection of the mother is impeded. In such cases the separation panic, which is equivalent to a fear of annihilation, becomes so great that the child is driven back toward the symbiotic involvement. Thus the more primitive introjection serves as a counterbalancing defense to the severe separation panic which threatens the child's fragile and inchoate ego. In its more severe forms this process results in symbiotic psychosis. This global and undifferentiated introjection of the mother destroys her function as mediating the reality to the child. The differentiation between object- and self-representation is obscured with the result that object choice and object finding are significantly impaired.

Separation Anxiety

If we ask what it is within the symbiotic orbit which is responsible for this extreme degree of separation anxiety, the best reply we can offer is that it must have something to do with the degree of unneutralized aggression which is resident within the mother-child union. As the child begins to distance himself and separate himself from the symbiotic environment, the aggression which is latent in the fundamental ambivalence toward the symbiotic object becomes mobilized and expressed in the form of annihilation anxiety.

Here again the degree of anxiety and the intensity of unneutralized aggression is related to the successful degree of adaptation which obtains in the mother-child relationship and on the successful negotiation of these earliest developmental phases. Where there is imbalance in these processes or failure in the successful negotiation between mother and child, there begins to appear a discontinuity in the organization of the child's experience of self and other, which allows for the stimulus of destructive responses or what Winnicott has referred to as "impingements." Where the regulatory balance has been achieved and the secure symbiotic base laid down which not only tolerates but supports further developmental steps, the separation can be made from the mother's symbiotic influence in a gradual and appropriate manner. Separation anxiety consequently is within manageable limits. As a result, the introjection does not carry within it an excessive degree of destructive and ambivalent energies. Consequently, the introjection rather than serving as a defensive regression to a symbiotic level, becomes a focus for the increasing differentiation of the infant's self-integration and self-representation and his increasing differentiation from external objects and representations.

Introjection and Projection

In the inner dialectic which leads to the progressive definition and delineation of the self, the gradual definition of self is achieved not only by a building up of self-representations, but also by the gradually increasing separation from the mother, and later from both parental figures. Gradual definition of self is achieved by the interacting processes of introjection and projection which continue to be rehearsed at each stage of the separation-individuation process. The introjective content which is gradually built up in successive stages is at each phase again reprojected onto the parental figures. The displacement of content from self-representation to object-representation and the reintrojection of the continually reconstituted object serves as the basis for the gradual delineation and differentiation between self and object.

The quality of this interaction is determined in part by the elements projected from the child's inner world, but these must be placed into a complex interaction with the contribution to the child's developmental experience that is made by the parents and other significant adults around him. In the early stages of the child's negotiations with the parents, particularly at points where the expression of the child's initiatives becomes an issue, the mother's capacity to tolerate and respond constructively to the child's aggressive impulses contributes in a significant way to the gradual modulation of the child's destructiveness and in increasing neutralization of aggression.

Where the child's aggression, however, does not meet the protective tolerance and absorptive capacity of the mother, but rather meets a contrary destructiveness or lack of protective stability in the interaction with the mother, the destructive aspect of the aggression tends to be reinforced by the subsequent reintrojection derived from the maternal object. The child's initiative can be threatened and made precarious by the parent's repressive or intrusive response. His capacity to leave or separate himself as an independent and self-directing (willing) individual is undermined and impeded. Thus the child's emerging autonomy does not achieve the status of a secure attainment, but is constantly threatened by the potential destructiveness of an external persecutor. This is the essence of what has become known as the "bad mother."

It should be noted that every mother, and by way of implication every parent, is a bad mother or a bad parent. The mother particularly, and in the first instance, is both the nurturer and protector as well as the withholder. The child's narcissism is boundless and cannot be satisfied with less than everything, so that it is inevitably fated to be disappointed. The parents further set themselves against the child's omnipotence in their functions of training, disciplining, and punishing the child. We are reminded of Freud's remark to the effect that the germ of paranoia was to be found in the restrictions which the physical care of the child made necessary (Freud, 1939 [1929]).

The child's rage at his sense of deprivation and the incursions upon his cherished omnipotence are projected and reintrojected. They provide the basis for an internalized introjective economy which is permeated with significant degrees of unneutralized aggression and ambivalence. Consequently the child's capacity for autonomous functioning and his capacity for progressing in autonomous development are undermined. Any attempt to function more autonomously, to become more independent and to move in the direction of greater individuation, poses a severe threat. Self-assertion consequently becomes tenuous and dangerous.

Thus the essential development of separation-individuation rests internally on the dialectic of introjection and projection. In the normal course of development these mechanisms result in a progressive differentiation and delineation of self and object-representations. They serve as the focal points around which the internal integration of self takes place. The same processes, however, can be caught up in the service of defensive needs and subjected to defensive pressures. The process of autonomous growth to greater independence and individuation is thereby undermined.

PARENTAL INVOLVEMENT

Mother-Infant Relationship

Our discussion of the earliest phases of development and their relationship to the paranoid process has focused on the earliest stages of the parent-child relationship. Our emphasis is on the elements of reciprocal interaction and mutual regulation which govern the parent-child interaction through the full extent of its course, from the earliest moments of neonatal existence through the last stages of the child's separation and individuation of himself from his parents.

In the very beginning the entire interaction is dominated by the quasi-automatic correlation between the infant and the mother's caring responsiveness. The ways in which the maternal ego comes to supplement, support, and nourish the child's latent ego and provide the context which enables it to grow have been matters of considerable study and argument. As we shall see, and as we have seen in all of the cases we have been considering in this study, one cannot underestimate the child's contribution to the emerging pattern of interaction. But for the moment we are content to focus our attention on the parental contribution.

Good-Enough Mothering

Referring to "good-enough mothering" Winnicott has observed that mothers who are able to provide such good-enough care can be supported and sustained in their efforts to do so, but that those mothers who do not have it in them to provide such care cannot be extrinsically provided with it. In a sense, then, the mother's capacity to hold and to intuitively respond to the infant's initiatives is not a matter of training or instruction, but is a matter of intuitive responsiveness. As Winnicott observes:

> Holding includes especially the physical holding of the infant, which is a form of loving. It is perhaps the only way in which a mother can show the infant

her love. There are those who can hold an infant and those who cannot; the latter quickly produce in the infant a sense of insecurity, and distressed crying. All this leads right up to, includes, and co-exists with the establishment of the infant's first object relationships and his first experiences of instinctual gratification (1965, p. 49)

It is within this close-bound matrix of mother-child responsiveness that the essential negotiations take place around which the developmental experiences cluster. When the infant is responded to and is the recipient of adequate maternal care, it begins to build up an inner experience of self and a personal existence which serves as the basis for the gradual emergence of the infant ego. If such maternal care is not adequate, then the coming to existence is correlatively impaired. Instead the personality is organized on the basis of reactions to disruptions in the continuity of care or holding, which Winnicott refers to as environmental impingements. As in other human affairs, when things go smoothly and needs are being responded to and tensions and levels of stimulation adequately encompassed and buffered, the process tends to work itself out without drawing much attention or concern. But when things do not go well, the infant becomes aware of a discontinuity in his experience of care, and is forced to react to an impinging stimulus which escapes the inherent integrative capacities of his own emerging resources, conjoined to and abetted by the protective resourcefulness of the mother.

The conditions of the maintenance of continuity and adequacy of maternal care provide the matrix for essential internalizations that begin to take place and play a significant role in the shaping of the infant's internal environment. These earliest internalized assimilations have been variously described in terms of "basic trust" by Erikson, or of "confident expectation" by Benedek. When the conditions which underlie such a developmental matrix are disrupted, the resulting pattern of internalizations is similarly affected. At the earliest level of experience they raise the specter of annihilation anxiety, and, at somewhat later stages, separation anxiety and its variants.

The question we must focus on at this juncture of our investigation has to do specifically with those factors which impair and interfere with the parental capacity to maintain the developmental matrix and to respond in phase-appropriate fashion to the emerging individuality of the infant and the developing child. We will consider these disruptive factors under the dual headings of parental narcissism and parental destructiveness.

Parental Narcissism

The effects of parental narcissism are matters of common, everyday observation. But the varieties of vicissitudes of such parental narcissistic investment are matters of psychoanalytic investigation. The parental narcissism so commonly described is affected by the projection onto the child of a portion of the parent's own self-image. By reason of this investment in the child, the latter becomes the vehicle for parental aspirations and hopes, for the regaining of parental failures and disappointments, and for the filling up of internally sensed, if unacknowledged defects in the parent's own inner sense of self.

Making Up Parental Deficits

The parents may as a result relive segments of their own developmental conflicts through the child. If the latter to a sufficient degree gratifies these aspirations and fulfills these often unstated expectations—although they may frequently as well be relatively conscious and explicit—the child contributes to the parent's own development, to the filling-out and complementing of their personalities, to the deepening and enhancing of their own sense of identity and of the meaning and purposefulness of the parents' relationship to each other. Thus the transactional processes that work themselves out between parents and child create a matrix of interactions which is calculated to sustain and develop the participating identities of each of the actors (Benedek, 1970). Such triadic configurations form the basic structural pattern of organization within the family system, and the family organization can be broken down into a series of overlapping and interacting, but significantly different, triangular units which exercise a mutual and reciprocal influence within the family system (Bowen, 1960).

From this point of view it seems likely that in mother-infant interactions, in which the process of differentiation from the symbiotic union is impeded, an important contribution from the side of the mother may be that the symbiotic relationship provides her with a sense of fulfillment and purposeful relatedness which satisfies an inner sense of deficiency and need in her. At least transiently, then, and in terms of the symbiotic matrix, the profound unity she experiences with the child may serve to fill out and stabilize her own sense of identity.

However, the issue of the potential contribution which the child makes to the parent's own inner integrity and sense of identity remains a significant developmental issue through the entire extent of the developmental process. Searles (1966-67) has noted the significance for the child's developing self-esteem of the contribution he is able to make to the respective identities of the parental figures. Time and again, in the details of the case histories we have examined, it becomes evident that these patients, in the course of their earliest years, became drawn into the process of being put at the service of parental needs. It somehow became their responsibility to bring it about that through them the parents should derive a certain degree of satisfaction, gratification, fulfillment of aspirations, and unsatisfied needs of a variety of kinds. And it is also noteworthy that inevitably these children failed to fulfill the aspirations or to measure up to the expectations.

Often they are caught up in an effort to "cure" a deeply disturbed narcissistic psychopathology in the parent. We will have more to say about the developmental impact of this circumstance on the child later on, but our concern at the moment is with the parental aspect of the involvement. However, it is this narcissistic investment on the part of the parent which lays the motivational basis for the important caretaking and nurturing aspects of the parent-child relationship. At the same time the narcissistic involvement of a loving parent places a demand on the child to reciprocally support the parent's own self-esteem and the integrity of that self-system by responding to the implicit expectations of the parental projections.

As long as the child is symbiotically joined within the maternal orbit and as long as the child is congenially responsive and adherent to parental expectations, the child's response enhances the parent's sense of worth and the perception of the parental self as the good, loving, and nurturing parent. The child's separation and independence, particularly when the pattern of self-initiated behavior is divergent from or incongruent with parental expectations, can then pose a threat to parental self-esteem. Such negativistic or independent behavior serves to separate the child from the parental self-system so that the child now can become the object of projected elements of the parental self-system which are relatively repressed or split off. The projection of these negative and defective aspects of the parental self sets the stage so that the angry parent now introjects the angry child. Thus the child can inflict by its independence and negativism a narcissistic injury on the parent which serves to elicit the parent's aggressive response in an effort to redeem the narcissistic loss. The regressive reintrojection of the projected parental aggression further serves to undermine and threaten the integrity of the parental self. The regressive reactivation of such old introjects may again serve as the basis for projection onto the child so that the child is now responded to in nearly delusional terms according to the pattern of response to the parent's own aggressive and hostilely destructive parent.

Effects on Child

The effects of this complex interaction on the child are variable. If he senses the parent's incompleteness, as well as the latter's inner need and destructiveness, the child may begin to feel guilt for his part in eliciting and precipitating this condition. It was after all his spontaneous promptings toward self-assertion, initiative, and relative independence that set the terms for this outcome. The child may then begin to feel guilt for his bid for independence and may find himself assuming the responsibility for parental well-being. This essentially takes the form of wanting to fill up the incompleteness that the child senses in the parent. The need that thus arises

can take a variety of forms including adherence to parental demands and expectations, fulfillment of parental needs of a variety of kinds, feeling responsible for parental happiness, accepting a position of submissive obedience
and unquestioning loyalty to parental attitudes and values, all capped and
made definitive through the internalization of the parent figure.

Moreover, the child's own narcissistic demands urge him to seek the
completeness of the parental figures. The introjection of the essential incompleteness of the respective parental figure leaves the child feeling un-
whole and internally deprived. As Searles puts it:

> These parents, the internalized images of whom have formed the foundation
> of his own sense of identity, are revealed as unwhole, incomplete; the very
> building-blocks of his own identity are revealed as fragmentary. His need for
> each of his parents to become whole—a need which springs from undifferen-
> tiated "selfish" and "altruistic" motives—now places him under pressure to
> somehow fill, himself, the incompleteness in their respective identities (1966-
> 67, p. 520).

Similarly, the child's needs to idealize the parent facilitate the parent's
own identification with the child and also reactivate in the parent the
relatively omnipotent fantasies of his own childhood. The parent thus comes
to accept the omnipotence attributed to him by the child's fantasies and thus
reactivates aspects of the parent's own infantile and rather omnipotent ego-
ideal. The parent comes to identify with the omnipotence of his own parents
as he might have wished to do in his own childhood fantasies. Thus the narcissistic stimulus and gratification provided by the child allows the parents
to build a sense of themselves specifically as good, and perhaps even better
than their own parents had been.

In important ways the child's dependence or relative independence can
serve to enhance or to traumatize parental narcissism. Thus clearly the
emerging existence of the child as a potential individual, separate and distinct and increasingly independent from the mother, can serve to undermine
her sense of identity, whether that identity is sustained defensively by a symbiotic involvement or by other and more differentiated narcissistic investments in the child. In this circumstance of narcissistic jeopardy, the
mother may react as though the developing individuality of the child were
directed against her own narcissistic (omnipotent), relationship-dependent
(symbiotic), identity. The child's individuality may thus become a matter of
malevolent intent to destroy the integrity of her sense of self. It hardly seems
necessary to point out the paranoid nature of this process.

Separation and Mourning

The process of separation-individuation thus involves a continual
dialectic between impending object-loss and the gains in object-relatedness
to an increasingly individuated love object. At each stage of the progression,

the mother must be prepared to sustain the mourning involved in the loss of a particular quality of closeness of the child's dependence within the relationship, and be ready to adapt to the requirements of a new phase of object relatedness in which the child assumes an increasing independence and separateness and his progressive individuation create a pressure on the mother's capacity to passively sustain loss and tolerate the depressive dimension of the loss, and correlatively to actively adapt to and master the requirements of a new quality of relationship.

The capacity of any given mother to work through this process may not be homogeneous, but may differ qualitatively from stage to stage of the interaction process. Some mothers function best in the symbiotic phases and find increasing difficulty as the child strives toward greater and greater autonomy and separateness. Others, however, may find the total dependence of the symbiotic child difficult and perplexing, and find themselves increasingly comfortable in dealing with the child as he becomes more differentiated and more capable of signaling his needs and desires with explicit cues.

Thus the mother must experience over and over again in the process of separation-individuation the conflicting tensions of loss of ties to the object as opposed to gains in object relationship with the individuating child (Mahler et al., 1970). Such difficulties, however, may reflect the developmental vicissitudes experienced in the parents' own course of development. Parents who have experienced a traumatic symbiotic phase in their own development are relatively unable to relate to a child who has achieved a measure of autonomy and separateness. As Giovacchini (1970) has noted, the histories of parents who have had difficulties in resolving symbiotic attachments with their own children feel intensely inadequate when trying to respond to the more individualistic needs and demands of their children. Such parents seem to

> encompass their children as narcissistic extensions that are part of their amorphous selves. To see their children as individuals in their own right is a massive threat because they lack the differentiated ego mechanisms required to adapt to a complex and sensitive person. Even though the overt technique involved in taking care of a neonate and a somewhat older child may not be radically different, the interpersonal qualities of the latter relationship require considerable flexibility and maturity. Parenthood is traumatic because these patients lack the synthesis and differentiation to relate to a distinct external object (1970, p. 534).

The Defective Child

A particularly important consideration relevant to the influence of parental narcissism is the narcissistic trauma, both for mother and father, in the birth of a defective child. The psychology of narcissism in this situation is focused for us in cases of actual physical (congenital) defect. This calls into play the entire psychology of the "exceptions" which Freud (1916) described so brilliantly—as we have seen. But as is clear from the study of the foregoing cases, the defectiveness need not be a matter of physical or congenital defect, but has more to do with the congruence between the narcissistic parental expectations and the child's fulfillment of them.

During the process of pregnancy, the mother's libidinal concentration on the self occurs, so that the increasingly invested self-representation also encompasses the growing child within the mother's body. Pregnancy daydreams and fantasies contribute to the shaping of the mother's narcissistic expectations and reflect her own inner needs, wishes and ego-ideals. The symbiosis, with its fusion of narcissistic and object libido, continues during the symbiotic phase of the child's infancy. Thus conscious and unconscious expectations are generated and consequent to them anxious thoughts and doubts that something would happen to adversely affect the pregnancy so that the child would be born deformed, or retarded or otherwise defective. Consequently the birth of the truly defective child can constitute a narcissistic trauma and undermining of the mother's self-esteem. The mother's reaction can be one of profound self-devaluation and deep feelings of worthlessness (Lax, 1972).

A critical question in this regard has to do with the whole matter of the birth of a girl baby and the relative narcissistic injury that may be connected with this to the mother. As we have noted, the question of defectiveness is a relative one, relative, that is, to the mother's narcissistic expectations and projected ideals. If the mother tends to devalue her own femininity and harbors a defective sense of self because of it, the birth of a girl must carry the significance to the mother of the birth of a defective child.

The dynamics of penis envy and the compensatory wish for a penis from the father presumably play a role in the mother's pregnancy wishes and her compensatory narcissistic fantasies. If it is true that the birth of a defective baby rekindles the mother's unconscious conflicts, because it represents the mother's unconscious sense of her own infantile and damaged self, the birth of a girl baby which presumably relates to the same unconscious complex—however well mastered in the mother's own functioning —will unavoidably activate the same unconscious conflicts and serve to undermine the mother's sense of self-esteem.

The more fragile and precarious that sense of self-esteem in the mother is, the more of an impact will the birth of such a child have upon the mother's narcissism and the more intensely will the trauma be felt. The effect is to make such women feel helpless, hopeless, inferior, and weak. It serves us well to remember at this juncture, that this particular process was observable and definable in all of the patients we examined in the study. In every case the mothers entertained a devalued and impaired image of themselves and of their femininity as weak, inadequate, victimized, and castrated. In each case—with varying degrees of intensity and correlative to the degree of pathology involved—this image was projected onto the daughters and correspondingly internalized to become a central nidus for the organization of the paranoid pathology. The mechanism is definable even in the most pathologically affected cases, such as Gloria, but also is clearly operative in the healthier and better-functioning patients such as Karen.

Moreover as Lax (1972) notes in her excellent discussion of this problem, what is in question is not the degree of impairment in the child, but rather the extent to which the mother perceives the child in an unconscious manner as an externalization of her own defective self. Thus the degree of impairment of the child does not serve as an adequate basis for prediction of the degree of subsequent depression in the mother. Rather what seems to be in question is the degree of narcissistic insult as measured by the disparity between the maternal fantasied expectations and the real impairment of the child. From the mother's side, the level of narcissistic expectation would seem to be determined by the degree of self-devaluation and impaired self-esteem which underlies the mother's compensatory narcissistic fantasies. Thus, as a general rule, the degree to which the child fails to measure up to and satisfy parental narcissistic expectations dictates the basis on which, and the degree to which, parental destructiveness may be mobilized within the developmental interaction. We will want to turn at this point to a more explicit consideration of parental destructiveness.

Parental Destructiveness
Relation to Narcissism

I would like to focus the problem of parental destructiveness specifically in terms of the paranoid process. The phenomenon of parental destructiveness can be seen in broader terms as a reflection of a very general and human tendency to strive to preserve intact the rudiments and structures, which preserve and sustain narcissistic investments, and to see as hostile and opposed any sources or agencies which tend to undermine or stand in opposition to such narcissistic bases. To the extent that the child does not support, sustain, and nourish parental narcissism, he becomes an enemy against whom the defensive and protective aggressive energies must be directed. The preservation of the parent's own sense of self either accepts the child as an extension of and a sustaining support for that basic narcissism, or must confront the child as standing in opposition to and thereby threatening that narcissism.

More basically, the either-or of such a dynamic is rarely witnessed. Rather what is the more common stuff of parent-child relationships is that the child is seen in some part as a support and extension of parental narcissism, and simultaneously in some part as deviant and threatening to it. Both sides of this dynamic play themselves out in the common run of parent-child interactions. This tension which underlies the basic ambivalence of the parent-child interactions is embedded in the relationship from the very first, but becomes more explicit and more differentiated as the child enters on the progressive stages of separation and individuation.

The initiation of self-directed activity on the part of the child—whether in relative independence of parental support or in direct opposition to parental wishes—creates a crisis in the evolution of parental narcissism. The child's independence and the inability of the parent to control or direct the child's self-generated activity places parental narcissism in jeopardy. The child then becomes equivalently an enemy.

It must be recalled that this basic process, by which narcissistic dynamics operate to define the limits of what is to be aggregated to the self and what is to be assigned to the other, is the basic process which underlies the establishment of human groups. The process of assimilation and inclusion and affiliation to the self serves to define and establish the ingroup, while the process of exclusion and separation operates to establish the limits of outgroups. The process is a basic aspect of the paranoid process, and we can note here that the same process operates in the establishment of a wide variety of social groupings and the formation of social structures.

The basic question in this framework of parent-child interactions is whether the internal resources of the parent can withstand the narcissistic onslaught which is provoked by the increasing separation and independence of the child. Consonant with our basic thesis in this study that the paranoid process is in fact a general manifestation of basic human motives and the mechanisms, the developmental vicissitudes reflect the basic operation of the paranoid process both in the progeny and in the parents. These processes call up and rely on basic mechanisms of introjection and projection which underlie the definition of narcissistic limits and work defensively to redeem narcissistic loss.

It is important as well to keep in perspective that the paranoid process works on all sides of the parent-child triad. We will have to consider maternal destructiveness as a primary phenomenon, since it is within the mother-child matrix that some of the most basic and fundamental aspects of development are elaborated. We must not lose sight of the fact, however, that parental destructiveness plays an important role, not only indirectly through its effects on the mother-child interaction, but also in terms of the father's own interaction with the child. The data of this study would suggest that this is particularly pertinent in the development of forms of paranoid pathology in male children.

Maternal Destructiveness

Nature. The interaction between mother and child, viewed from the aspect of the mother's attitude and responsiveness to the child, is a mixture of influences which affect and facilitate the healthy development of the child along with influences which bring that development into jeopardy or actually impair it in various ways. The latter aspect of this interaction, which exercises a generally negative influence on the child's emerging self, is what we have in mind by the notion of maternal destructiveness. What is in question, then, is not of the order of malevolent intentions on the part of the mother or explicit destructive impulses which reach the level of conscious awareness. Such impulses are frequently enough consciously available, but in the common run of mothering experience such impulses more frequently remain at an unconscious and repressed level, even though their expression is detectable by careful clinical evaluation.

The evidence regarding maternal destructiveness has been summarized and evaluated by Rheingold (1967). He comments:

> There is both a negative and a positive mechanism of destructiveness: deprivation and threat. Deprivation refers to failure to provide adequate sustenance and protection and to the absence of maternal warmth and optimal stimulation. The positive pathogenic influence refers not just to rejection, cruelty, and reaction formations but to unconscious attitudes and impulses which may co-exist with genuine motherliness (p. 152).

However, maternal destructiveness does not seem to me to be a primary quality of the maternal response to the child, but rather it emerges as an essentially reactive phenomenon, responding to the underlying narcissistic vicissitudes. The relationship between the emergence of aggression and destructiveness—both directed toward external objects and against the self—in relationship to underlying narcissistic dynamics and vicissitudes has been amply documented in Rochlin's careful clinical analysis (1973). We have already discussed this fundamental point in the treatment of the defensive functions of the paranoid process. Thus maternal destructiveness must be seen as an explicit expression of the operation of the paranoid process in the context of mother-child interaction and as an expressly defensive reaction to the underlying narcissistic loss and impairment.

The whole problem of maternal destructiveness is one which has emerged in repeated contexts in the course of this present study, particularly in relationship to the female children. We are reminded again of Freud's comments regarding the role of maternal destructiveness in the genesis of paranoia in female children (Freud, 1931). The role of maternal destructiveness can be documented in all of the cases of our study, not merely in those where the pathogenic influence is most extreme and destructive, as for example Ann or Ellen or Gloria, but even those where the paranoid process operates with considerably less destructive effect, but nonetheless carries a decisive influence on the character organization of the patient.

Thus Karen's experience of her relationship to her mother was one of constant intrusion and control, developing in later aspects of her experience as a constant undermining attack directed against her by her mother. As we have seen, the narcissistic underpinnings of such destructive attacks are relatively clear. We have seen repeatedly how the child becomes the victim of the mother's destructive attacks and correlatively introjects that victimized aspect of the mother, which is attacked as a consequence of its projection onto the child by the mother. The mother equivalently attacks in the child that displaced aspect of her own defective, weak, victimized, and helpless self, which she hates in herself and which provides a constant inherent flaw and nidus of narcissistic impairment and loss within the integrity of her own sense of self. The degree of internal defect and sense of narcissistic injury related to it determine the intensity and the destructiveness of the maternal attack on the child.

Rejection. Maternal destructiveness can express itself in a wide variety of ways, which are often quite subtle and expressed in nuanced and indirect ways. The mother's unconscious and automatic response is to attempt to rid herself or to do away with the narcissistically offending object. Maternal rejection, therefore, is one of the basic channels through which maternal destructiveness may be expressed. Commenting on the rejection of defective children, Lax has observed:

> Rejection of various degrees, culminating in the actual giving away of the child, is a reflection of the mother's need to emphasize her separateness from the child who symbolically represents her unconscious defective self. This type of mother, because of her narcissistic vulnerability, cannot tolerate the continuous mortification caused by an impaired child. Further, the defective child in these cases has to be rejected since it cannot serve as a narcissistically gratifying object choice or as a fulfillment of narcissistic needs (1972, p. 341).

However, Anna Freud (1970) has correctly pointed out that rejection is a relatively imprecise notion which requires considerable specification. Rejection can occur in many ways and for many reasons—some good and some not so good. Some mothers do not take on the role of motherhood willingly or voluntarily, but have it forced on them. Their unwillingness may relate to external circumstances of their lives, financial, social, etc., or may relate to the unsatisfactory emotional climate in the family or the state of the affective relationship with the child's father. Many women are unsatisfied and humiliated at the implicit confrontation with their own femininity and consequently waver between rejection and acceptance of the maternal role. Mothers who are affected by schizoid withdrawal or even schizophrenic impairment cannot communicate the warmth and acceptance to the child which would be required for establishing a relatively normal symbiotic involvement. Such children are unavoidably brought up in a situation of relative rejection.

Similarly physical separations from the mother, as when the mother goes on trips or must go to the hospital for an operation or delivery or other separation, for whatever reason, is inevitably experienced by the child as rejection. Even temporary separations can have a severe impact on the child (Bowlby, 1951). Even without physical separation, however, rejection can be experienced by the child in the face of significant variations in the libidinal attachment of the mother to the child.

Such fluctations or libidinal retreats may be experienced by the child as rejection. However, such libidinal withdrawals are part of the inevitable flux of experience in the course of the mother's own life. Other claims on her emotional investment will be made by other children, by her husband, and by other significant persons in the mother's life. Significant libidinal shifts are unavoidably attached to the coming of a new infant in the family in which the mother's libidinal attachment to the new infant inevitably implies a degree of withdrawal of libidinal attachment to the older siblings. Perhaps more devastating than any is the withdrawal of libidinal attachment due to the mother's depression. We have seen in a number of our cases the devastating effects of maternal depression on the child, who feels not only rejected and abandoned, but also feels somehow responsible for his mother's pain and for her abandonment of him. Such a dynamic unquestionably contributes to and reinforces the child's introjection of the victimized mother.

Overprotection. Another and well-documented channel for the expression of maternal destructiveness is overprotection. Frequently such overprotection masks a strong rejection and serves as a compensation for such destructive feelings. Thus the overprotective and oversolicitous attitude toward the child serves as the opposite to the neglectful and indifferent attitude by which mothers may attempt to cope with the destructive and frequently murderous impulses toward their infants. These defensive postures nonetheless reflect unconscious feelings of self-hatred which are projected onto the child. The child then comes to represent the unconscious, negatively protected self-representation of the mother.

The intensification of such attitudes is frequently elicited by illness or accident or deformity in the child. Such mothers tend to favor the weaker or more dependent children in the family. The mother's protectiveness expresses itself in excessive closeness to the child and a continuing of infantilization which results in impairment of the child's attempts to establish greater separateness and more independent behavior. Such guilt-driven compensatory protectiveness may take the form of giving in to the infantile demands of the child so that the latter's sense of infantile omnipotence is allowed to expand in an unmodified fashion.

Other mothers may exercise their oversolicitousness by preserving the child's dependency and maintaining themselves in the dominating position in the relationship. Such maternal overprotection involves an excessive constriction of the sense of infantile competence rather than its excessive expansion. Thus maternal indulgence can foster infantile omnipotence and maternal domination can foster infantile dependence and submissiveness. In either case the normal growth to autonomy in the child is subverted. The mother's compulsion to motherliness is dictated by the elements of her own ego-ideal. Her basic narcissism and the preservation of self-esteem demand that she live up to the dictates of the ego-ideal and thus respond compulsively to the implicit superego demand presented by the child (Levy, 1970).

These patterns of maternal destructiveness unquestionably reflect attempts of the mother to resolve her own inner conflicts relative to the child. From the point of view of the children, however, what seems to be most decisive is not the mother's external behavior, but the unconscious attitude toward the child which underlies the behavior. The mother's unconscious regard toward the child has the most powerful influence on the organization of the child's feelings and attitudes about himself. The earliest symbiotic dependency of the child on the mother provides the context for assimilating the subliminal clues, which reflect the mother's inner attitudes and feelings and which have a fundamental bearing on the child's emerging sense of self. Though the child does not experience his mother's unconscious attitude in terms of total and unconditional acceptance, he introjects that attitude as part of the unconscious nucleus of his own attitudes toward himself. These form the basis of a negative self-image which may continue to function as a residual nidus of psychopathology even into adult life.

Relation to Projection-Introjection. Any disparity between maternal expectations, so narcissistically determined as we have suggested, and the extent to which the child provides a suitable object for the reception of the mother's projection of the denied and hated parts of her own self, creates the matrix within which maternal destructiveness can operate. In the present study we have seen repeatedly the manner in which maternal depression has operated as an important component of the child's developmental matrix. Such depression sets the stage for and determines the child's identification with the devalued, victimized, vulnerable, and masochistically invested mother.

The dynamics of this complex circumstance of the child's development have been concisely articulated by Lax:

The mutually satisfying mother-child interaction is interfered with by the extent to which mother's unrealistic wishes become a source of her disappointment in the baby, to which she therefore cannot respond as narcissistically gratifying. Her depression, a reaction of varying magnitude and duration, affects the mothering pattern and is expressed by the degree to which she finds the baby consciously or unconsciously unacceptable. All these factors, which are reflected in the earliest interplay between mother and child, invariably must affect the child's self-feelings and thus influence the forming kernel of his self-awareness. To the extent to which mother's attitude will be depressive and non-accepting, reflecting mother's injury caused by the unfulfilling qualities the child has for her, the child's early self-representation will be negatively cathected (1972, p. 343).

We have had occasion previously in the course of this study to call attention to the significance of beating fantasies, as often expressed in the form of screen memories or even dream fantasies. These often hold a prominent position in the psychopathology of female patients who demonstrate either a depressive or a paranoid form of psychopathology. The beating fantasy is essentially related to and reflects the underlying masochistic dynamics. It derives essentially from an unconscious wish located on one level in the phallic phase, but possibly also, we have already discussed, reflecting the earlier pregenital and particularly anal determinants. The Oedipally motivated unconscious fantasy of being beaten by the father is usually subject to repression and comes to light only in the analytic reconstruction.

A useful analysis of this phenomenon and its relevance to the developmental context has been provided by Brody (1970). Following the assumption of Freud's classic paper on the beating fantasy, in which that fantasy is taken to reflect the childhood perception of the primal scene as one of violent beating, Brody proposes that the major aspects of maternal attitudes and dynamics are determined by the unconscious wish to be beaten by the father. The resolution of the unconscious wish can take place in a variety of forms. Some women have a greater capacity to sublimate the wish and by way of reaction-formation change the wish into a need to be loved and accepted. Thus the passive wish is changed into an active one by regarding the needs of the child as greater than her own.

While the wish to be beaten may be changed to a wish to have demands placed upon her, the acceptance may approach masochistic surrender unless the passive role of the beaten child is also changed by assuming active charge in superego-consistent ways. Other mothers may use greater degrees of repression in congruence with other defense mechanisms—often denial or projection. Such women are occasionally vulnerable to anxiety connected with the masochistic wish to be beaten or the sadistic counterpart to beat. Other women find the primary defense against the unconscious beating fantasy and wish in an identification with the aggressor. Thus the baby's passive position helps to support the mother's defensive level of activity. Usually the repression of such passive aims is less successful and such a mother is often the victim of ambivalent impulses which led her to both approve and support the infant's activity and aggression on the one hand, but also bring her to rebel against his demands upon her on the other hand.

For some of these women the defensive introjection is so intense that any passivity that might be connected with the carrying out of maternal obligations quickly evokes a countering posture of activity or control. Consequently the feelings of badness and passivity are projected onto the infant. When the sadism does break through, she is able to justify her own punitive harshness which she rationalizes as having been provoked by the child. Not unexpectedly the depressive variant is also a common enough clinical picture, in which the wish to be beaten is basically turned against the self. Such mothers are more disposed to follow a pattern of avoiding maternal caretaking activities, causing them to feel burdened, guilty, inadequate, and beaten down.

The depression in such women may be related to the introjection of the hated, beating, devaluing father, which is sometimes again reprojected, in an attempt to rid themselves of the hated introject, onto the "bad" or unmanageable baby. Thus, for example, the postpartum depression, which can range in the intensity of its disturbance from mild and transient states of depression to severe psychotic episodes, is an expression of the introjection of the beating father which gives way to a subsequent projection which can terminate in abusive or murderous treatment of the infant.

Abusing Parents. The dynamic constellation which characterizes parents who abuse children can be taken as in many respects paradigmatic for the problems in the parent-child interaction which contribute to the emergence of paranoid psychopathology. Such parents are almost universally in one degree or other depressed. They share a basic attitude toward infants which holds that children exist for the purpose of gratification of parental expectations and for the satisfaction of parental needs. This often is more unconscious than conscious. It dictates that infants who fail to live up to this expectation are deserving of punishment to insure that they fulfill this function. The need and expectation is operative from very early in the infant's life. The corollary of this unconscious conviction, as we have already observed, is that the infant's own needs, wishes, and urges assume a secondary position to the needs and wishes of the parent. Consequently the delicate balance of mutual regulation and reciprocal responsiveness which are so central to the maintenance of a holding environment, in Winnicott's terms, is placed in severe jeopardy. To reverse Anna Freud's concept, the child must become a need-satisfying object for the parent.

Such abusing parents sometimes have experienced a similar pattern of upbringing in relation to their own parents, whether or not the family environment was one which characteristically involved physical abuse or not. These patients recount the feeling that their parents placed upon them severe demands for submission and proper obedience. At the same time they expressed the intense feeling that their own feelings, desires, and wishes were to a large extent disregarded, belittled, or simply did not count at all. These patients feel that they were never able to measure up, never able to fulfill parental expectations and standards, never able to gain approval and acceptance from their parents.

Thus the rule of motherhood for many of these women is one which becomes equivalently an attempt to bid for approval and acceptance from their own mothers by becoming a good mother according to their own mother's lights. Their behavior is motivated by a continued deep yearning for understanding, sympathy, and approval from the mother—a yearning which is constantly doomed to frustration and failure. They are rewarded with disappointment, disillusionment, diminished self-esteem, and frustrated rage. Quite typically such patients have made vain attempts to redeem something from this frustrating context by idealizing their fathers and seeking to gain approval and acceptance from them, only to meet further disappointment since the fathers too were unable to meet the child's emotional needs adequately. Such patients rarely if ever are able to disagree openly with their own parents or to rebel against them, but have to resign themselves to a pattern of passive submission to parental judgment and criticism. The feelings of anger and resentment toward the parents were often intense, but tended to be expressed in internalized ways rather than through direct expression toward the parental objects.

Underlying the abusive attitude on the part of such parents toward the child, there is the projection of the parent's own view of himself as a bad child. The projection is directly related to the underlying introjection which is embedded in the parent's personality structure and which derives from the relationship between the parent and his own parent of the previous generation. Along with this there is a pervasive conviction that anyone from whom one seeks need-satisfaction will inevitably and correspondingly fail to respond to the need. The parent has derived this firm conviction from his childhood experiences with his own parents. Thus the abused child is inevitably seen as a need-satisfying object which is unrewarding and unresponsive to the intensely felt inner needs of the parent.

In describing this situation Steele (1970) has commented:

> The abusing parent's ideas of people being unhelpful and attacking can in some instances become so pervasive and intense that they have a paranoid-like quality. The mechanism of projection, however, is not involved. Rather

> there is a widespread expression of feelings that originated toward the parents in early childhood. Whenever there is a need for love and understanding, the object becomes dangerous, a direct transference reaction. This lack of confidence is a most important element in the pattern of abuse. When spouse, family, friends, and neighbors cannot be looked to for aid in time of difficulty, the abusing parent has nowhere to turn except to his own infant for this comfort (p. 461).

Despite Steele's disclaimer, the basic mechanism involved in this process is essentially projection, derived from and expressing the internal configuration of introjects that lies at the basis of a substantially paranoid form of psychopathology. Here again the pattern of destructiveness and its relationship to underlying narcissistic needs reflects and expresses the paranoid process.

Steele goes on to describe this dynamic in quite vivid terms. It is specifically in the more violent forms of abusive attack that the full flavor of the psychopathology expresses itself.

> Usually the mother approaches the caretaking tasks with the good intention of doing well for the baby, both because she wants to and because she thinks it is her duty. She is handicapped, however, by her own lifelong, unsatisfied need to be loved and cared for and her conviction that she is basically unable to do well enough at anything expected of her. If, previous to her caretaking activity, she has been criticized, misunderstood, or deserted by spouse, family, or any other important figure, she feels especially inferior and lonely, her needs for loving approval are increased, so she turns as an unloved child herself to the only available object, her baby, to get this desperate need satisfied. If the baby happens to respond well, cooperates, and seems happily satisfied by her efforts, all goes well. If the baby continues to cry in spite of what she does, however, or if the baby in any way interferes with what she is trying to do, she becomes increasingly frustrated and feels criticized and unloved (1970, p. 471).

The introjected patterns which underlie such mechanisms of parental abuse or murderous obsessions can be varied. They may relate to a hated parent or sibling—and we can recall here the vicissitudes of unconscious beating fantasies—or it may take the form of an identification with the aggressor. In either case all of the fear, guilt, shame, and rage that was experienced in the original object relationship is again activated in the context of the mother-child interaction (Anthony and Kreitman, 1970). The importance and the impact of such murderous elements in the parent-child interaction cannot be overestimated. As Searles (1966-67) has noted the intrusion of such intense and unassimilable murderousness into the mother-infant relationship during the symbiotic phase, before the child is able to differentiate himself from the mother as a separate person, leads to the direst consequences for the emergence of the child's sense of self and his sense of inchoate identity. Searles comments:

> In healthy development the mother and infant become aware of murderous feelings in manageable increments and the child's murderous feelings become one of his most powerful assets in the struggle for fashioning an identity, a weapon wielded in a workmanlike, ruthless when necessary, way to psychologically dissect each parent, carve from him or her that which is valuable and make it his own and discard the rest, with recognition on both their parts, however unformulated, that this process is not actually destroying the parent as a person in outer reality (pp. 520-521).

Where such dissection and differentiation fails to take place in an appropriate and phase-specific manner, the residuals of destructiveness and their toxic potential permeate each phase of the individuation process by which the child strives toward the attainment of a sense of his own independence and identity.

Paternal Destructiveness

Sadomasochism. While we have had ample evidence of the manifestations of maternal destructiveness and even murderousness in our case studies, we have also seen the expression of paternal destructiveness. The destructiveness of the father in the basic triadic relationship may function either in terms of the father's relationship with the mother, or may function more directly in terms of the father's relationship with the child. These father-mother relationships have a distinctly sadomasochistic quality.

The intensity of the sadomasochism is more marked in the more severe forms of paranoid pathology. But the influence of paternal destructiveness is most marked in the relationship between fathers and their paranoid sons. Inevitably the relationship is one of distance and coldness and remoteness. These fathers generally reject their sons in whom they see a reflection of the weak, inadequate, and dependent aspect of themselves with regard to which they feel shame and revulsion.

It seems quite likely that the dynamics in this destructive pattern of father-child interaction are quite similar to those described in the case of mother-child interactions. These sons present themselves to the father as having failed to measure up to the masculine ideal of strength and aggression which operates in the father as a defense against his own inner sense of weakness and inadequacy. Thus the son becomes the bearer of the repressed and reviled part of the father's own self and consequently becomes the focus for a narcissistic affront to the father's sense of masculine pride. Conversely, for these male children, to violate the projected image derived from the father is to run the risk of aggressive confrontation and competitive struggle with the father. The risk is twofold—either defeat and shameful humiliation at the hands of the father or victory and murderous destruction of the father.

Thus children become the victims of parental fantasies and wishes and needs which dictate the pattern and course of their developmental experience. Parental fantasies, largely unconsciously derived, provide the matrix within which the belief systems around which the family is organized are generated. It is in terms of this mythology that the basic techniques of resolving ambivalence, perceiving reality, and understanding the world of objects and relationships around the child must be achieved. The fantasies are derived from both parents, the maternal fantasies having an earlier and more direct influence than paternal ones, but both come to exercise a powerful influence in highly specific and complex ways.

Unresolved Ambivalence. Such fantasies can be either life-sustaining and promoting or destructive. The child's earliest growth to psychological life is dependent on and promoted by the symbiotic matrix within which the mother can see the child as a good part of herself which is fed and loved. The extent to which the baby is seen as associated with mother's own sense of herself as bad and destructive, contributes to the degree of basic ambivalence embedded in the symbiotic relationship. The mother's narcissistic fantasy of symbiotic union serves to defend against such hostile and destructive wishes and may emerge into a pattern of oversolicitousness and overprotection. But the underlying destructiveness carries through the reactive defense so that the burden of the mother's love and care is the frustration of the child's own need for self-assertion and initiative.

The effect of such intense and unneutralized aggression within the symbiotic context can be seen relatively clearly in the effect of severely disturbed mothers—either psychotic or borderline—on their children. Such women are angrier, needier, more depressed, and less able to acknowledge their children as separate individuals, and consequently less able to respond to their developmental needs. The intensely symbiotic union with the child serves to defend against the intense hostility which is projected into the relationship from the mother's relationship with her own mother. As soon as the child begins to separate from these symbiotic ties, the mother experiences anxiety and distress and struggles to frustrate the child's separative impulse and to maintain the symbiotic ties. Where the intensity of the ambivalence is overriding, the mother will see the child as a rejecting and persecuting object.

The child thus becomes the object of negative destructive fantasies and is readily subjected to abuse and murderousness on the part of the mother, since she is unable to separate the child as an individuated entity from her own negative and destructive fantasies and projections. Thus Newman and San Martino (1971, 1973) report the experience of six-year-old Stefanie in her relationship with a guilt-ridden and somewhat depressed borderline mother. Stefanie was afraid of being destroyed by her mother, a response to mother's own fantasy of herself as poisonous and destructive. The child not only reacts to the mother's fantasy, but identifies with its destructive potential, and consequently becomes a child whose own aggression is highly charged and difficult to contain and who feels herself to be a destructive and poisonous agent. Thus the capacity for projection that can be mobilized by a relatively compensated borderline mother may operate to protect the mother from the destructiveness of her own aggression, but it functions at the expense of the child. Thus the mother's own paranoia induces a paranoid response and a paranoid organization within the child's own inner world.

Basic to this whole consideration, however, is the realization that ambivalence and hate are normal components of every parent-child relationship and interaction. The essential question, which will determine the developmental outcome for the child, is first of all the extent to which the parent can tolerate such aggression in himself or herself and not find it necessary to allow his own internal destructiveness to issue into forms of defensiveness—particularly the forms of projection we have been discussing here, which work their evil potential upon the developmental experience of the child. As Winnicott puts it:

> A mother has to be able to tolerate hating her baby without doing anything about it. She cannot express it to him. If, for fear of what she may do, she cannot hate appropriately when hurt by her child, she must fall back on masochism, and I think that it is this that gives rise to the false theory of a natural masochism in women. The most remarkable thing about a mother is her ability to be hurt so much by her baby and to hate so much, without paying the child out, and her ability to wait for rewards that may or may not come at a later date (1958, p. 202).

The good parent must not only be able to tolerate and sustain his own hatred and destructiveness, and the anxiety which it creates within him, but must be able to absorb and respond constructively with toleration and consideration for the aggression of the child, particularly that aggression and hatred which must be expressed in forms of separation from the sustaining dependence on the parental figures. Thus the process of separation-individuation, far from being a developmental experience isolated within the child, must become also a developmental experience within the parent. It is a process by which both of them surrender infantile needs and dependencies and come to function in more adaptive and mature ways. And as we shall see further, it is a process by which both of them are enabled to formulate a more mature and functional sense of self which sustains a growing and more integrated sense of personal autonomy and adaptive capacity.

CHAPTER 24

Narcissistic Development

THE VICISSITUDES OF NARCISSISM

We have already considered some of the substantial aspects of the problem of narcissism in relationship to the defensive functions of the paranoid process. We would like to turn our attention at this point to a consideration of the vicissitudes of narcissistic development, particularly in view of the fact that the dynamics of the paranoid process as they function in the course of development have a particular bearing on the narcissistic aspects of developmental experience. As we have seen in countless instances in this study, the paranoid process functions in the service of narcissistic needs and defenses. We can turn at this point to a specification of the operation of the paranoid process and its relation to narcissistic needs in the developmental process.

The narcissistic aspects of early developmental vicissitudes have been spelled out with considerable insight and clarity by Brodey (1964). The narcissistic relationship depends upon an externalized image of the narcissistic self. Such externalization is essentially a defense derived from the early narcissistic, pre-object period of development. It makes it possible to sustain relationships with unseparated but distanced aspects of the self. The projection which underlies the narcissistic relationship requires validation. The validation is accomplished by an intense searching only for that which is expected, so that with each validation the unquestionable and unquestioned conclusion is reinforced.

Moreover, the reality as perceived has been experienced as though it were the total reality. The narcissistic person must learn to manipulate reality to conform with the expectations implicit in his own projection. Consequently, the externalization consists in a projection which is matched by a manipulation of reality which serves to verify the projection. Any reality that cannot be placed in the service of the projection and thereby verify it is denied.

Within a family matrix, and particularly within the central triad which we have described as basic to these unconscious affective configurations, the only information transmitted within the system is that which is useful in validating the projective system. Reality testing and consensual validation within the family is thus placed in the service of this process. This pattern of interlocking of externalizations and projections provides the developmental matrix within the family within which the budding narcissism of the child begins to work through the initial stages of the process of differentiating self from other and formulating the rudiments of his own inner sense of self.

The differentiation from the objectless symbiotic matrix takes place in gradual steps. The first one is a step of tension in which cathectic forces can be differentiated only in terms of affective states of being, either pleasant or unpleasant. This is the initial stage of mutual negotiation between mother and child which Sander (1964, 1969) has described in terms of initial regulation. The rhythms of physiological experience are regularized through the collaboration and correlation between infant needs and maternal caretaking and tension-relieving activities. At the same time, the rudiments of differentiation and the beginnings of a sense of separation in terms of bodily areas are established. The distancing of fingers from mouth, for example, begins to provide a sense of distance in the infant's experience.

The second phase of differentiated aim finds the basic cathexes differentiated now in terms of aim, but not yet in terms of object. Thus, for example, the focus is on the experience of feeding, but not on the feeding object. Here distancing begins to occur without separation as a first manifestation of externalization. Thus the mother's nipple is gradually experienced as distanced from the mouth but not yet separated. Nor does the infant at this stage attach the specific gratification of being fed with an object. Satisfaction is a function of the present nipple and dissatisfaction of the absent nipple. There is no awareness of the mother's existence or activities outside the range of this immediate aim.

It is only in the next stage that the differentiation of objects takes place and that the distancing begins to give way to separation between self and other. These first steps of separation, by which the differentiation between self and object is first experienced, takes place by the distancing of an "as-if" separate self. Thus distancing precedes true separation. The image of the nipple must become discontinuous, before it is possible that the infant should have the experience of being fed by a separate object. It is only in the context of such separation and as a function of it that the infant can experience the feeding now not as a function of his own narcissistic orbit but as a function of a separating and differentiated object. In this fashion the infant begins to separate himself out of the narcissistically omnipotent orbit of the symbiotic attachment.

Projective Expectations

Important cognitive advancements take place in this pattern of emerging experience. As a function of separation the infant begins to learn the mode of reality testing which serves as an aspect of real object-relationship and can be called the "object mode." It stands in opposition to the "image mode" which characterizes the earlier and more narcissistically embedded phases. The image mode, however, is more closely attached to the externalizing aspect of the infant's separation experience in which external reality is experienced in terms of and through a split-off image of the self which is projected to the outside.

The regulation of this cognitive emergence is in part attributable to the interactions between the mother and the child. At this critical stage of separation and individuation, the mother's response to the child's attempts to distance and separate become a critical variable. Brody (1964) writes:

> The mother who knows her child is able to titrate the experience of their separation, conforming with his wish just enough to allow the distancing of his wish to neutralize his fear of abandonment. This conforming is more than just satisfying—it is more than meeting his expectation. It is a part of teaching him to learn. She gauges his tension level so that overwhelming unpleasure will not interfere with the tender growth of investment in a separate outside world (p. 176).

Within a family matrix which operates in terms of this narcissistically determined cognitive mold, the parents have not succeeded in resolving their own earliest fears of abandonment and have not been able to proceed beyond the stage of inner narcissistic development which would allow them to experience and respond to the child as a separate other. Their perception of the child is limited to cathecting the child as a distanced part of themselves according to the image mode of experience. Thus the child exists only as a relocation of a part of the parental self. Consequently, the child is responded to only as an "as if" child, that is, he is responded to only when and to the extent to which he validates the parental projection. The child is thus what Kohut (1971) refers to as a "self-object."

Thus the child is mobilized in the service of parental narcissistic needs and serves to sustain and support the parent's fragile sense of self. The child must then conform to parental expectations in order to prevent psychological decompensation of the parent. This tends to reinforce the dual polarity of narcissistic involvement which we have seen in so many of our patients. On the one hand the child has the sense of fragile vulnerability as the victim of parental expectations, yet at the same time he nourishes an inner sense of power and omnipotence. The child in fact does hold power by reason of his capacity to validate or not validate parental projections. From the child's side of the relationship it is his capacity to manipulate the parents by reason of this power which contributes to the form of the pathology. The child is essentially invested in drawing upon himself parental intrusiveness and control, both to reinforce the child's own sense of weakness and vulnerability, and at the same time to sustain his more repressed and hidden sense of omnipotent control and power.

PSEUDOIDENTITY

During the gradual movement of this differentiation and separation, the child begins to fashion a pseudopersonality which is organized as a response to parental expectations and which serves to match either negatively or positively parental projections. Other aspects of the child's activity and energy which are irrelevant to this acknowledged portion on the part of the mother remain extrinsic to this pseudoidentity. Thus the child is forced into a mode of reality which is based on this conformity to parental expectation. An identity begins to take shape that has no support from the inner sources of natural impulse within the infant himself.

This pseudoidentity is further consolidated and verified by its utility in focalizing the responsiveness of the parent. The reciprocally reinforcing and selectively verifying interaction that is thus set up between mother and child serves to prolong the earlier symbiotic attachments and becomes impervious from both sides of the relationship to the inroads of other forms of reality testing. As Brody (1964) observes:

> Even when the mother is more able to use the object mode of relationship to her child, she will not be acknowledged: the child has learned to attend only to that which fits the earlier projected explanations. Ego energy exists only in the service of validating the expected tautology. Inertia in a closed system is high. Ego libido does not become object libido. Instead, it invades the object world, working to keep the [mother's-child's] unbounded megalomanic or hypochondriacal delusions appropriately verified. This becomes the work of the ego that has no true object relations. The ego operations become hyper-cathected to a preoccupation—in a hypochondriacal way (p. 187).

Thus the rudiments of narcissistic development are rooted in the essentially narcissistic nature of the relationship which obtains between mother and child. Moreover, the narcissistic aspect of that relationship is sustained and reinforced by the pattern of narcissistic relationships which obtain between the mother and the other elements of the family matrix, particularly the father. Such relationships reflect a basically reciprocal imaging process between two or more people who collaborate in externalizing and verifying each other's projections. They are fostered and sustained by reason of the gratification of narcissistic needs involved in the conformity of the object to projected expectations. The family system in such contexts becomes a narcissistic system of multiple pseudorelationships within which mutuality is virtually impossible and relationship is sustained only at the cost of responding to severely narcissistic expectations by excessive degrees of pseudoresponsiveness and conformity.

Need to Be Special

The effect of such a developmental experience upon the child is seen in a variety of forms of narcissistic fixation and entitlement. One striking example of the impact of such processes on the developing child has been described in terms of the "need to be special" (Lomas, 1962). Such "special cases" are not infrequent in the experience of any practicing psychiatrist or any hospital setting. Such patients usually bring it about that those who are responsible for them come to regard them as unique cases for which the ordinary practices, whether in the office or in the hospital, are inappropriate. Consequently, these patients receive special privileges and attention, but somehow these efforts inevitably prove valueless.

These patients acquire a special status which elicits extraordinary efforts on the parts of physicians and staff to affect their treatment, but their efforte are inevitably frustrated and they become exhausted in the process of trying to meet these patients' needs. Inevitably all efforts to alleviate their suffering are frustrated and the caretaking persons become failures. Lomas suggests that the original trauma in the developmental experience of such patients is a failure on the part of the mother to recognize and respond appropriately to the patient's individuality. The patient is thus left with an unsatisfied craving for recognition and a resulting clinging to the special and exclusive relationship with the mother, in which the child feels valuable only in terms of their relationship.

The complement to this close and quasi-symbiotic relationship with the mother is a rather paranoid view of the rest of the world. The fear arises that other agents will come between the child and the mother and will disrupt the relationship with her. The families of such patients tend to become close-binding and tend to protectively narrow the focus of relationships. The implicit mythology that permeates the family relationships is that one can find acceptance and protection within the family, and that any relationships outside it are to be held suspect and a source of trouble and persecuting attacks. Thus while the need to be special manifests itself most strikingly in narcissistic terms, it can be readily seen that it becomes the vehicle for substantially paranoid concerns. Perhaps more clearly than in other cases, we have seen this same set of dynamics operating in the case of Karen.

Role of Introjection-Projection

The essentially narcissistic and imagining character of object relations has also been identified in the psychopathology of borderline children (Fast and Chethik, 1972). In such children neither the self-representations nor the object-representations have been adequately integrated into stable and coherent wholes. Such children are caught up in the continual interaction between projective and introjective processes. These processes are fixated at an often primitive and highly defensive level and reflect a failure to achieve the transition out of narcissistic modes of relating into more mature and object-directed forms of cathexis. The failure of these primitive self- and object-representations to adequately differentiate provides the basis of splitting which is so characteristic of borderline pathology. As Modell (1963) has noted in this description of borderline relationships, the borderline patient establishes relationships to persons actually separate from themselves, but the object is then invested with qualities which almost entirely emanate from the self.

Within this developmental perspective, then, we can begin to grasp the significance of the correlated processes of projection and introjection for the preservation of pathological narcissism. Introjection functions as a process of internalizing from the need-satisfying object or from the sustaining and powerfully omnipotent object what is required to maintain and preserve the residues of infantile narcissism. At the most primitive levels of development, where the earliest separations from the symbiotic partner threaten the infant's narcissistic omnipotence, introjection is equivalently a survival mechanism, since it fends off and serves as a defense against the impending annihilation.

At later phases of the developmental sequence, however, introjection serves as a basic defense against separation anxiety and preserves the nascent ego from the destructive effects of the loss of omnipotent control. At each phase of separation and individuation, therefore, the child must resolve the threat of an implicit narcissistic trauma by salvaging something from the separated object by way of introjection.

Projection functions in a reciprocal relationship with the underlying introjections. The infant's sense of narcissistic wholeness is threatened by unresolved and unneutralized aggressive impulses. The projection of these onto the idealized or omnipotent object can serve in part to neutralize and modify the intensity of these destructive impulses. However they also pose a threat to the dependent relationship and consequently the projection of such impulses may be displaced to other objects in a paranoid fashion. This is the typical pattern that we have been able to identify in the phobic anxieties of younger children and also in the frequently witnessed nightmare experiences.

Moreover, an important developmental impact of the interplay of introjection and projection is that by a process of continuing introjection, the child builds up a sense of internalized possession which becomes the nucleus of his emerging sense of self and the point of articulation for his sense of identity. Correspondingly, it is through the mechanism of projection that the differentiation between his own self and the selves of others is gradually defined and articulated. Consequently within this developmental context and in reference to the developmental process the interacting and correlated processes of introjection and projection play an essential role in providing the inner mechanisms by which the processes of separation and individuation become psychologically possible. Moreover they contribute in central and essential ways to the vicissitudes of object relationships. We have spoken at length in this analysis of the role of the self in the developmental process and particularly of its relationships to aspects of the paranoid process. It is to this central and illuminating point that we would wish to turn now.

THE DEVELOPMENT OF THE SELF

Relation to Narcissism

The first important point to make is that the development of the self is intrinsically related to and inherently dependent on the vicissitudes of narcissism. The relationship between the psychoanalytic notion of "self" and narcissism was first stated decisively by Hartmann. Freud's own usage had been somewhat ambiguous, but the general tenor of psychoanalytic thinking had been to establish a loose equivalence between narcissism and the libidinal cathexes to the ego. Hartmann's statement, however, made the essential clarification:

> But actually, in using the term narcissism, two different sets of opposites often seem to be fused into one. The one refers to the self (one's own person) in contradistinction to the object, the second to the ego (as a psychic system) in contradistinction to other substructures of personality. However, the opposite of object cathexis is not ego cathexis, but cathexis of one's own person, that is, self-cathexis; in speaking of self-cathexis we do not imply whether this cathexis is situated in the id, ego or superego. This formulation takes into account that we actually do find "narcissism" in all three psychic systems; but in all of these cases there is opposition to (and reciprocity with) object cathexis. It therefore will be clarifying if we define narcissism as the libidinal cathexis not of the ego but of the self (1964, p. 127).

The establishing of a link between narcissism and the notion of the self cleared the ground for a consideration of the relationship between the development of the self and the vicissitudes of narcissism, which has not yet been adequately examined by psychoanalytic theorists. Hartmann's formulation not only establishes this connection, but also postulates that the vicissitudes of narcissism are related to all of the parts of the tripartite intrapsychic structure. By inference, then, the notion of the self has a parallel if derivative relationship to these same substructural entities.

Nature of Self

A variety of views have arisen about the nature of the self as so conceived. These vary from a merely representational view, according to which the self is conceived of restrictively in terms of self-representations and functions as a form of cognitive framework in relation to specific ego capacities. Others, however, envision the self as an alternative psychic structural entity in the tripartite theory. One difficulty is that the respective concepts lie at different levels of cognitive derivation and organization. The notion of self lies at a much more specifically phenomenological and experience-based level than do the notions of id, ego, and superego. The latter function more specifically as theoretical constructs which serve to organize certain clinical observations and which express groupings of functions, each of which has a differentiated character and a specifiable role in the psychic economy.

Without entering exhaustively into the murky metapsychological waters at this point, the view of self which is operative in these pages is that it is equivalently the sum total of the tripartite substructures as representable and phenomenally experienceable as a coherent and integral internal possession. We will return later to a specification of the relationship between the self as so conceived and the structural entities of ego and superego. For the moment I would like to turn to the developmental influence of the important internalization processes on the formation of the self.

Internalization and the Self

Let us look at the role of introjection in development first. The notion of introjection, as we are discussing it here, is intrinsically related to and correlated with projection. Introjections are in varying degrees defensively motivated and begin their operation from the very beginning of the infant's experience. It is through the reciprocal functioning of introjective and projective mechanisms that the self is gradually established and differentiated from objects outside of it.

In the very beginning of the infant's experience the process of introjection functions at a most primitive, inchoate, global, undifferentiated, and unselective fashion. In the earliest stages of development, in the context of the symbiotic relationship, such introjective processes are at work to preserve the rudiments of infantile narcissism and symbiotic omnipotence. As maturation progresses, however, the ground on which the child's narcissism is buffered and protected gradually shifts. The narcissism serves as the protective shell which guards against the destructive impact of unneutralized aggression within the symbiotic context. To the extent to which the dialectic interaction of introjections and projections in relationship to the caretaking figures fails to modify the aggressive element, the child will cling to the narcissistic protection. This has important implications for the emerging sense of self that the child acquires, since the inability—for the varieties of reasons we have been discussing in terms of the significant interactions with caretaking figures—to modify aggressive elements leaves him progressively with an impaired and deleterious sense of self.

Under these circumstances the process of separation-individuation is impaired and the child must resort to and increasingly rely on defensive resources. Thus in the normal course of development the processes of introjection and projection become modified in the direction of constructive influences, which elicit the growth potential of the child to the degree that they successively operate to mitigate and minimize the destructiveness of the inherent aggression. The critical element in this, of course, as we have already seen, is the extent to which the child, during the course of this process, is introjecting elements of unneutralized and unsublimated parental aggressiveness. Here the interdigitation of the child's introjections with corresponding parental projections becomes a vital matter.

The outcome of these developmental vicissitudes can be varied. Where the titer of maternal destructiveness is too intense or the buffering capacity of the symbiotic narcissism insufficient, the child can be driven to a premature and precipitous separation of his self from the symbiotic matrix. Searles has commented on this matter as follows:

> On the other hand, one sees patients who, to keep from being swallowed up in a chaotic symbiotic relatedness with a less differentiated, larger area of the parent's personality, cling compulsively to a defensive ego-identity founded upon identification with some part aspect of either mother or father. But if this person is to achieve in the course of analysis a much deeper and larger identity, the maelstrom which comprises both the vast bulk of the mother's "insides" and his own true potential self must, despite his fear of the "craziness" of regressive ego-disorganization, be braved and explored (1966-67, p. 511).

Such a precipitously formed self serves defensive motivations against the overwhelming fear of engulfment in the threatening symbiosis. Such a sense of self is indeed a fragile one which must be riddled with intense ambivalence, since, while it provides a protection against threatening engulfment, it also serves as an inherent limitation on the individual's developmental potentiality.

The quality of the child's introjections, then, is a function of not only the projections which underlie and correlate with them, but is also strongly influenced by and reflects the quality of the child's object-relatedness to the significant figures in his environment. The child's introjective development is thus a matter of what the parents bring to the relationship with the child as modified and contaminated by the child's own inner projections. The introjective process is mirrored in the translation of object-representations into self-representations. I do not mean, as many authors seem to imply, that the introjection is simply a matter of such translation, but that the introjective process is reflected in such representational shifts.

The introjection is thus in the first instance a modification of the self. And it is around these progressively modified introjections that the self takes shape and undergoes its developmental progression. The introjections and their correlative projections have a primary reference to the self, rather than to the rest of the structural organization. This way of conceptualizing the relationship between introjective processes and the development of the self bypasses the language of ego-as-opposed-to-superego introjects. Introjections are essentially neither, but are applied to and have reference to the organization of the self as such.

Furthermore, introjections are always in some degree defensively motivated. By that I mean that they are concerned with the building up and maintaining of the self. This motivational concern is rooted in the child's basic narcissism, as it is equivalently rooted in the narcissism of the adult counterpart. Thus the workings of internalization through introjection are motivated by a need to sustain and build the substance of the self, just as the functions of projection at all levels of development and defense are calculated similarly to preserve and sustain the self. Consequently the motivational bases for processes of introjection and projection must be inherently narcissistic.

But what, we may ask, about identification? As I have indicated at length elsewhere (1971b, 1972), identifications and introjections must be regarded as quite different and distinct, although intimately related, processes which have their play in the organization of internal structure. The primary frame of reference for identifications as such is not the self in the first instance, but rather the psychic structure. Identification is an internal synthesizing process which may relate to the development of ego or superego or both in combination. Relative to the developmental phase in which it operates, identification functions more or less autonomously in the building up of internal psychic structure.

The nature of such internal organizations is basically derivative from the quality of the infant's object-related experience and the rudiments of structural organization on which the identification process bases itself. Thus at the very beginning of the child's experience, which is essentially global and undifferentiated, identification processes have a very rudimentary aspect which would have to do more with the building up within the child of a sense of internal comfort and goodness which has been variously described, but which is closely related to what Erikson has described in terms of "basic trust." This statement does not imply an identity, but rather a relationship between such emergent trust and primitive identifications. The element of trust as Erikson analyzes it has more direct reference to the organization of an emerging sense of self, but the ego integrations which take place alongside it must not be lost sight of.

This interdigitating of introjective and identification processes plays itself out throughout the whole course of development and the shaping of the human personality. Although identificatory processes can be elicited in other ways than through introjections—as for example immediately in terms of object-representations themselves—the interplay between introjective and identificative mechanisms provides the primary channel by which identificative processes are activated and elicited. Moreover, introjects have a varied capacity to induce or inhibit consequent identifications. In general, those introjections which carry within them significant amounts of un-neutralized and destructive aggression tend to impede and distort the more autonomously functioning and selectively internalizing identifications. However, those introjections in which such ambivalent elements are significantly modified or sublimated have a significant eliciting potential on the identificative processes, which consequently contribute to the building up and strengthening of ego and superego resources.

The elements which are inherent in the model, which the parent brings to the parent-child relationship, can have tremendous significance in the implementation, or conversely, the impairment, of the child's capacity for identification. Thus, Searles has pointed to the significance of:

> processes of the developing child's identification with the parent's individuality, or perhaps better described, his identification with the parent's courage-to-be-an-individual—and at the same time his acceptance of the fact that each of these parents has an individuality, an identity, which he cannot otherwise possess (except through identification) (1966-67, p. 518).

Thus the child's introjection of the parent's self-trusting autonomy serves to elicit identificative processes which model themselves after the parental image and which thus contribute to the building up of trust and autonomy in the child's inner world. The elements of trust and autonomy that the child acquires in the first instance through introjection become an internalized possession and a consolidated ego-attribute through the consequent identification. It is also important to add that this internalized possession is not simply attributable to the ego, but becomes a shared property, in diverse and differentiated ways, of both ego and superego. Thus, in terms of the mature integration of ego and superego functions, the building up of an autonomously functioning psyche is a function of both ego and superego autonomy in different ways and with different perspectives.

Contribution of Aggression

It is specifically in this context that the contribution to the development of the self on the part of aggression can be best formulated. Aggression arises in the context of the need to defend the self from threatening impingement. If instinctual satisfactions and gratification create a feeling of goodness in the child, so that he becomes filled with a sense of trusting confidence and benign expectation, it is through the eliciting of aggression that he begins to feel within him a sense of what is bad or destructive. The mobilization of aggression in the service of the defense of the self, as has been clearly delineated in Rochlin's (1973) discussion, is a dynamic process that is continually elaborated throughout the course of the life cycle. Before the baby has differentiated his emerging sense of self from the world outside him, the language of self is not yet proper; we must speak rather in terms of discontinuities or impingements or (vaguely) threats to the symbiotic unity.

The arousal of aggression in the service of the defense of the self creates certain internal problems. The aggression does not inherently become a problem until it begins to outstrip the reserves of narcissistic and structural buffering, which are available both within the internal organization of the child's psyche and in conjunction with the interactional resources provided by the parental interactions. To the degree that this aroused destructiveness exceeds the buffering capacity of these internal resources, the aggression becomes threatening and destructive and must be dealt with by a variety of defense mechanisms. The primary defense mechanism, as we have seen, is that of projection.

Beginning with these first rudimentary projections, we have the beginnings of a separation within the child's inner world. Thus the origin of paranoid anxieties in their most primitive and undifferentiated form, lie intertwined with the roots of separation and individuation. If such primitively projected destructiveness is not successfully buffered—either internally or in the maternal interaction—and is reintrojected, it begins to serve as the nidus for emerging pathology. Winnicott (1958) has described this phenomenon in the following terms:

> In respect of the total environment-individual set-up the integration activity produces an individual in a raw state, a potential paranoiac. The persecutors in the new phenomenon, the outside, become neutralized in ordinary healthy development by the fact of the mother's loving care, which physically (as in holding) and psychologically (as in understanding or empathy, enabling sensitive adaptation), makes the individual's primary isolation a fact. Environmental failure just here starts the individual off with a paranoid potential (p. 226).

PATHOLOGICAL DEVELOPMENT

False Self-System

The course of pathological development whose rudiments we have been sketching here leads inevitably in the direction of the "false self." The notion of the false self was initially contributed by Winnicott (1958, 1965). When I began to study the clinical material with an eye to specific theoretical formulation, I felt sure that the material pertaining to the paranoid process would relate neatly and rather snugly to the notion of the false self as Winnicott has described and analyzed it. The more carefully I thought about it, however, the less sure I became, until at this point it is quite clear to me that the notion of the false self as it is employed in this study has considerable overlap with Winnicott's notion, but that they are not simply identical. The false self, as conceived here, describes a configuration of experienceable and representable elements which form themselves around the pathological introjects as we have been describing them. While I have found that Winnicott's formulations regarding the false self resonate with my own clinical experience, I am not confident that his formulations regarding the relationships between the true and the false self are consonant with my own experience or my own thinking on these matters.

Nonetheless, the false self organizes itself around those introjects which are responsive to and determined by the projections that are imposed on the child by parents and other significant figures and which operate at large within the family emotional system. These projections are correlated with patterns of interaction and behavior which are mutually reinforcing, and which shape the infant's place and role and sense of self as he comes to maturity under the influence of these dynamic and emotional forces. The projections and their correlated introjections on all sides are in the service of pathological narcissism. Thus the system of projections and their reciprocal derivation from inner introjects on the parental side serve to sustain and preserve parental narcissism, while within the child they serve specific defensive needs in the interests of preserving infantile strata of narcissistic investment.

Consequently the pathology of introjects and their correlated projections is specifically one of narcissism. The basic principle in terms of which introjections are correlated with projections, is the conformity to narcissistic expectations. Consequently, for the child, compliance with parental expectations and preservation of narcissistic dependence are essential for the preservation of a relationship of some kind to significant figures in the family. Further they are the necessary touchstone and price of bondage by which the child is maintained as a psychological component of the family system. It is the price that must be paid in order for the child to be the child of this parent. If the child does not comply with and respond to the parent's narcissistic projections and expectations, he is denied recognition as belonging to this parent and/or this family.

Autonomy vs. Compliance

The true and false self are essentially discriminable in terms of their relative autonomy and compliance. In the first instance this autonomy and compliance has to do with the framework of parental demands and expectations. Later in the course of development the context of such autonomy vs. compliance is considerably broadened. Thus it does not seem to me that the true and false self can be organized into independently existing psychic subentities, but rather what we are dealing with is the self-system as characterized by relative degrees of compliance and autonomy. Thus compliance and autonomy can be conceived of in terms of a continuum of states reaching from the most compliant and dependent extreme to the opposite extreme of fully developed and authentic autonomy.

The sense of autonomy in this context is akin to that proposed by Erikson (1959)—that is, a sense of self-control without loss of self-esteem, and a capacity for self-assertion and self-reliance without shame or doubt. That hyperautonomy which translates itself into stubborn self-willedness and willfulness and unrelenting independence is not in question here. The more autonomous is the function and organization of the sense of self, the more does it set the conditions whereby independent inner ego and superego development are elicited and subsequently more autonomously integrated ego and superego functioning promoted. However, insofar as the sense of self is false, that is, that it is based upon compliance, particularly the essential compliance which is involved in conformity to parental expectations and projections, the more symbiotically and defensively must the organization of the false self be, and consequently, the greater impediment does it provide to the second-order induction of growth potential in the underlying structures.

Such a false self-organization tends to impede structural development and to supplant it to a certain degree. Thus the extreme forms of false self-organization which we have seen in some of our patients—particularly the patients in whom the dismemberment of the false self gave way to a psychotic process—the false self came to serve as the substance of the functioning personality. Such a self can be conceived of as drawing into its service functionally less autonomous ego and superego functions which operate correlatively to the underlying defensive organization and needs which the false self-system serves. At its extreme this quality of the inner psychic organization serves to undermine autonomy all along the line. Where the organization of the self-system is more autonomous and consequently less defensive, the self-system not only elicits the growth potential of ego and superego but functions more congruently with their autonomous capacity to function in more conflict-free and authentically independent ways.

Thus in the healthy and relatively autonomously functioning psyche, one has a sense of the congruence and integration between the self-system and the other functioning structural systems. Under conditions of false self-organization, however, one senses a disparity between ego-superego and the self-system. This contributes to the fragmentation and splitting which is so often seen in what we refer to as defective egos. Thus the fragmentation of the schizophrenic process would seem to reach a level of specifically ego and superego disorganization. In more borderline types of psychopathology, what one sees is a splitting of the self-organization, reflecting the intolerance of ambiguity and the incapacity for resolving it, but only transient disorganization of ego-superego systems. Along this line of thinking, Winnicott (1965) has described a classification of the false self-organization, which extends from the extreme condition in which the false self functions and is regarded as taking the place of the real personality, through varying degrees of split between the false and true self, to a healthier state of false self-organization in which the false self expresses itself in the individual's polite and mannered compliance with social attitudes and behavioral expectations.

Thus the internal autonomy becomes the touchstone of the integration of the personality. Moreover, it is a significant integrating force in healthy personality development. When the developmental context, and, specifically, the interactional process which takes place between the child and his parents acts in such a way to inhibit the strivings toward autonomous development, then the developmental course is diverted into structurally damaging and undermining channels. The basic issue between parent and child—as between more mature adults as well—is the extent to which the price of instinctual gratification is the surrender of autonomous strivings. Too often the demand for compliance is attached to the rewards and gratifications that adults are willing to offer to children, as well as to other adults. Such an emphasis on compliance can only lead to the substitution of needs for achievement and approval for authentic autonomy. In this way the avoidance of feeling of impotence and helplessness is accomplished by fostering a need for power.

Consequently I would not see the true self as an isolated and protected core of the personality which never enters into communication with the world of objects around it. The self as we are considering it here is that part of the inner psychic organization which is particularly in communication with the reality around it. It not only organizes itself in terms of internalizations from that surrounding environment, but it is also constantly interacting with it and subject to a wide variety of influences from it. Thus the notion of self which we are developing here is much more akin to Erikson's sense of the self (identity) as a socially and culturally related psychic organization than to that part of Winnicott's formulations which see it as uncommunicable and uncommunicated. The latter author, for example, remarks:

> I suggest that in health there is a core to the personality that corresponds to the true self of the split personality; I suggest that this core never com-municates with the world of perceived objects, and that the individual person knows that it must never be communicated with or be influenced by external reality. . . . Although healthy persons communicate and enjoy com-municating, the other fact is equally true, that each individual is an isolate, permanently non-communicating, permanently unknown, in fact unfound (1965, p. 187).

It seems to me that Winnicott's isolationist formulations regarding the true self may have greater relevance to the ego, although his own attempts to link the concept of the self with tripartite substructures are ambiguous, at times linking it to the ego, at other times to the id.

Functions of Self

We can ask ourselves what the functions of this self-organization may be. From an internal perspective the organization of the self answers to the need to have a coherent and integral internal organization. Thus the self-organization becomes a kind of "holding" operation. In this sense Winni-cott's notions on the holding function of the false self are quite similar to the present formulation. But it is not simply the false self which serves the func-tion of contributing internal cohesion and unification. The function is served in both pathological and normal developmental contexts. The ex-treme disruption and intense overwhelming anxiety that are experienced when this function is not achieved can be quite impressive. When the self-organization begins to fragment, as in certain cases of pyschotic regression, the resulting sense of overwhelming panic can be terrifying in the extreme.

Moreover, if the self-organization serves important inner defensive needs, it must also be seen in an adaptational perspective. The sense of self serves as the link between the individual and the community of objects which surround him. The link to specific and significant objects early on in the child's experience takes particular precedence, but in the later stages of development and in adult life, the network of significant object relations can be quite broad. An essential issue in such contexts of object relatedness is that the individual have a sense of communion and belonging, which adheres in the very notion of object-relations, but which has much broader implications than the mere notion of object-relation itself. The individual seeks a sense of having others somehow matter to him and having it such that he matters to others.

The self-system offers a dual aspect in this regard. In one sense as the nidus of individuation, it provides a sense of internal self-possession and integrity which serves to set the individual off from and to separate him from objects around him. At the same time the self becomes the vehicle of providing a sense of belonging and communication. Thus the self-system at one and the same time serves to separate and to communicate. These dual functions reflect the dynamic influence of the underlying processes of introjection and projection which are constantly at work in defining, sustaining, organizing, and delineating the self. It is specifically the work of projection to delineate and separate. As we shall see later, these processes function not only at an individual level, but have pertinence at the level of group and social processes as well.

These comments have pertinence not merely for the more autonomous organization of the self-system, but apply specifically to the false self-organization as well. It is our contention in this study that the interaction of projection and introjection serves to provide the basis for the organization of a false self which serves the equivalent functions of internal organization and cohesiveness, as well as external belonging and communion. In pathological paranoid states, the false self is organized around and derived from the specific pathogenic introjects. Thus based on the conditions of narcissistic compliance which we have described in the developmental context, the introjects serve to lend internal integration and to serve specific narcissistic needs and defenses. By means of the correlative projections, moreover, the self is both separated out over against the surrounding context, as well as placed into significant communication with it. In the pathological state of a paranoid delusion, the fragile and vulnerable self is placed in significant communication with the persecuting agents which surround him. Thus a meaningful relationship is restored and maintained, sometimes with specific persecutory objects, but in more advanced and elaborate delusional systems with a large complex of conspiratorial and persecutory forces. Such projected elements can then be elaborated upon and articulated within a more complex cognitive framework which is provided by way of the paranoid construction. In this way the paranoid mentality can elaborate complex ideological or belief systems to sustain the false self and the paranoid system to which it relates.

Within this perspective it can be seen that the development of the false self spans a spectrum of developmental variants, including at the further reaches of deviation frank paranoid psychopathology. However it can also be seen that the organization of the false self utilizes the same mechanisms and processes that are inherent in the development of a true self and which are in fact inherent in and part and parcel of the developmental process itself. Moreover it can also be seen that both the development of the false self and the more constructive organization of the true self are placed in the service of the same functional ends. We are forced to conclude, then, that the forms of paranoid pathology that we have been studying are not the manifestations of abnormal or qualitatively different processes than we are familiar with in the more normal and adaptive ranges of human development and functioning. Rather they are the same process, which functions in a variety of conditions of defensive need and developmental vicissitude.

CHAPTER 25

The Paranoid Process
in Early Development

The basic element in the process of individuation is the increasing capacity of the child to define himself as an individual and to effectively separate himself out from the individuality of the significant figures in his environment on whom he is particularly dependent and attached. We have seen in sufficient detail the manner in which the elements of the paranoid process interact with this progressive elaboration of both individuation and separation in the earliest phases of differentiation out of the primal symbiotic matrix. An important contribution to the successful individuation of the child and in the progressive elaboration and stabilization of a sense of self and identity is the emerging and enlarging capacity to tolerate the separateness of significant objects. Our attempt in the present section is to specify the contribution of the paranoid process to specific levels of developmental experience and particularly to the specific phase-appropriate tasks that are accomplished at each of those levels.

THE OEDIPAL PERIOD

Preoedipal Determinants

Let us turn our attention first to the vicissitudes of Oedipal development. The Oedipal child emerges from the period of heightened negativism and the anally determined struggles over establishing the limits and scope of his burgeoning autonomy into a configuration of specific emotional involvements with the parental figures.

In terms of the scope and complexity of object relationships, the child emerges from a level of relatively divergent one-to-one relationships with each of his respective parents into a more complex configuration which is essentially triadic. It must be seen immediately that the quality of the triadic configuration must necessarily be a function of the history of significant introjections and projections which have qualified the child's relationship with both the mother and the father. Moreover, the quality of those introjective and projective processes will usually carry a differential emphasis with respect to each of the parents, so that the reorganization of introjections and projections as the child emerges into the Oedipal situation will be correspondingly subject to varying modifications and emphases.

The child's maturation into a phase of libidinal genital organization is not simply a matter of the enactment of a genetically determined maturational timetable. It is in part that, but it is also responded to in significant ways by the parents, again in a specifically differentiated fashion. If the little boy's Oedipal interest in his mother becomes specifically genitalized and erotized, it is also reciprocally true that the mother's interest in the little boy becomes correspondingly erotized and sexualized. The seduction becomes an integral part of the sensualized gravitation which is a normal part of the mother's pleasure in and stimulus by the child's loving affection and interest in her, and is an important contributing factor to the development of a meaningful Oedipal involvement which can serve as the launching point for important developmental attainments. Similarly, if the little girl's growing interest in her father is increasingly erotized and genitalized, the father's reciprocating interest in and responsiveness to the daughter begin to carry an increasingly erotic and genitalized libidinal component. There is a normal range of experience within which this libidinal experience connected with Oedipal involvements serves as a motive-making power which serves to drive the developmental process in appropriate directions.

We are familiar in general with the alignments within the Oedipal configuration and specifically with both the positive and negative alignments which inhere in every Oedipal involvement. As Freud was insistent in pointing out, the child's Oedipal involvement featured not only a loving attachment to the mother and a rivalrous hatred for the father, but conversely also involved a negative and hostile feeling toward the mother and a loving attachment and yearning for closeness to the father. However, the balance of these attitudes in the child's achievement of an Oedipal equilibrium reflects the quality of the child's object-relations with respect to the parents in the pregenital levels of development.

For example, where the child's attachment to and dependence on the mother have been excessive, and where the maternal anxieties have contributed to this excessive attachment and correspondingly undermined the child's nascent attempts to separate and become more autonomous, we can expect the same dynamics to carry over into the more specifically genitalized relationships of the Oedipal period, so that the child continues to be excessively dependent on the mother and more closely attached. This would serve to increase the pressure of Oedipal wishes toward the mother as well as to intensify the titer of ambivalence within the Oedipal relationship to the mother. It would also serve to affect the relationship to the father, since the latter could be expected to become a more forbidding and hostilely perceived figure, in part due to the child's need to project aggressive impulses toward the father in order to preserve the closeness and dependence on the mother. Moreover, the underlying contribution of persistent separation anxiety would contribute to more specifically genitalized castration fears.

None of this, however, takes place in a vacuum of relationships with the father. The child's response to the father is not only motivated and propelled by significant contributions from the side of the persistent elements of the relationship with the mother, but also reflects a continuing contribution that has evolved through the history of the child's relationship with the father through the stages of infantile and pregenital development. Thus if the father in the early stages of the child's experience has remained aloof or has responded in ways which serve to reinforce or sustain the child's projected destructive and aggressive impulses, the Oedipal involvements will consequently be colored by an increased titer of aggression, so that castration fears will be intensified and the mechanisms propelling the child in the direction of a more pathogenic identification with the aggressor will be reinforced. This configuration in fact has been quite readily identifiable in any number of our patients, in whom the excessive closeness and anxiously preoccupied dependence on the mother have been complemented by a relatively distant and unavailable or even sadistically hostile relationship with the father.

Role of Paranoid Process

It should be immediately apparent that the emphases of libidinal and aggressive involvements which take shape within the Oedipal triangle reflect the vicissitudes of earlier processes of introjection and projection that have taken shape in the child's earlier experiences with the parents. I would like to carry the argument a step further to say that the processes of interlocking introjection and projection make a significant contribution to the setting up of, and organization of, the Oedipal situation. I would also like to make the point that the operation of the paranoid process through the mechanisms of projection and introjection makes a significant contribution to the individuation and differentiation which characterize the child's Oedipal involvement, specifically as a developmental achievement.

If we start with the assumption that the child's relationship to both parents are characterized by ambivalence of some degree—and, as we have noted, the degree of ambivalence is correlated with the emergent pathogenicity of such relationships—we can recognize that one of the developmental problems that the child faces in his experience with these significant objects is specifically the management of such ambivalence. At the most pathogenic levels of the intensity of ambivalence, the child resorts to rudimentary mechanisms of splitting and projection which have been characterized in various ways (Klein, 1932, 1964; Kernberg, 1966, 1967). Thus the intensity of the ambivalence and the intolerance for it require the mechanisms of introjection and projection to be relatively isolated and attempts to rid the psyche of destructive hostility become more global and inclusive.

However, at less pathogenic levels of ambivalence, the operations of introjection and projection are less driven by the intensity of defensive needs and the quality of the underlying anxiety is less destructive and total. Consequently, the tolerance for greater degrees of ambivalence is correspondingly increased. It is increasingly possible, therefore, for the infant's psyche to resolve the difficulties in the management of ambivalence by resorting to mechanisms of repressive defense rather than the more primitive and pathogenic defenses of splitting. Correspondingly the use of projection is more modified and the resulting relationship with the object of projection is less distorted and essentially less paranoid. Thus both the integrity of the emerging self and the stability of the relationhips with significant objects can be correspondingly preserved.

We can also note at this juncture that at less pathogenic levels of ambivalence—and, therefore, at these pathogenic levels of unneutralized aggression—levels of anxiety are less toxic and overwhelming. The ego, in consequence, is in a much more effective position to integrate the anxiety as a signal function in the service of promoting developmental objectives (Zetzel, 1970). The emergent capacity of the child's ego to tolerate anxiety is correspondingly reinforced and basic ego strengths are enlarged and supported. This is particularly relevant at this level of development to the toleration of separation anxiety, since this capacity is an important achievement which allows for the setting up and involvement in Oedipal relationships. Both separation and castration anxiety become more relevant in the resolution of Oedipal attachments.

In broad perspective, then, the management of such ambivalence, at whatever level of intensity it is involved, is a basic aspect of the vicissitudes of instinctual involvement and emerging object relationships. The necessity of resolving ambivalence on both sides of the parental involvement requires that mechanisms of projection and introjection be brought into play. The suggestion we are making here is that the operation of these respective mechanisms in dealing with the vicissitudes of ambivalence leads the child's gradually individuating psyche inexorably in the direction of an evolving Oedipal involvement. As the child projects and introjects in the context of an ongoing interaction and relatedness with both parents, there evolves that configuration of loving attachments and fears of punitive rejection which we have come to characterize as the Oedipal involvement.

Again we must emphasize the complexity and integrity of these relationships. If, for the sake of analysis and understanding, we can at times isolate aspects of the Oedipal involvement—as, for example, the problem of castration anxiety—we must continually remind ourselves that such partial aspects of the total configuration take place within a broader and more complex developmental situation. If the dynamics underlying castration anxiety can be related to the projection of aggressive and destructive impulses to the father figure, they must be complemented both by the correlative introjection of aggressive components, as a part of the identification with the aggressor, as well as the loving and positively constructive aspects of the relationship with the father, which contribute to more positive identifications that relate to the developing sense of mastery and competence in both sexes.

In the course of normal and healthy psychic development, the intertwining and balancing of the projections and introjections, which play themselves out within the Oedipal situation, tend to resolve the more intensely ambivalent components of the relationships to both parents and allow the child to achieve a new level in the management of object-relationships, which not only tolerates but is enriched by the triadic involvement, as opposed to the relatively restricted and exclusive involvement with single objects as characterized by earlier developmental attainments.

The developmental failure to achieve this level of complex object involvement is reflected in common experience with borderline or more primitive patients, in whom the capacity to resolve ambivalence is significantly less, and who find it necessary to vacillate back and forth between relatively segregated and isolated object contexts in which the ambivalence is sustained and resolution of it becomes less possible. We can recall the situation with Gloria, for example, in which the alternation in her feeling states in regard to her mother and father followed this extreme pattern. She would alternately totally attached to and dependent on her mother at one point in time, feeling that her mother was the only one who really loved her and cared about her, and totally rejecting and hating her father, seeing him as the destructive persecutor in the most extreme and dire terms. Yet at another time, the situation would be diametrically reversed so that her father was seen as the only loving and saving figure in her environment and her mother correspondingly seen in terms of the direct destructiveness and hatefulness. The vacillation between these polar positions characterized her course of treatment over the course of years and showed little or no sign of modification or abatement. One could say that Gloria vacillated between extremely polar variants of both positive and negative Oedipal configurations, and that her inability to resolve any of this ambivalence was contributed to not only by her own internal developmental deficits, but by the ongoing pattern of destructive interaction that obtained within the Oedipal configuration.

Emerging Individuation

The point that should be stressed is that the child's Oedipal experience not only introduces him to a new level in the management of complex object relationships, but also serves to advance the process of individuation and separation. The child moves from a level of infantile dependence on each of the parental figures in characteristically unique ways to a new level of involvement in which his dependence is cast more specifically in terms of the larger social unit of the family, and in which his own sense of autonomous individuation in relation to the family unit becomes more specifically established. The increasing sense of individuation, which is related to the Oedipal attainment, is both a result of the continuing process of introjection, which builds up the sense of emerging self and its correlative autonomy, as well as the ongoing sense of separation which the child attains in relationship to both parental figures.

The emergence from a level of infantile dependence to a level of triadic dependence requires that the child achieve a more developed sense of separation from the individual parental figures and an increasing capacity to relate to them in more developed and socialized terms. While analysts have focused primarily on the genital aspect of this developmental phase, presumably because of the instinctual emphasis within psychoanalytic thinking, the social and object relations aspects of it should not be disregarded. Thus the Oedipal configuration provides the significant first step in the child's socialization, in the broader sense of his emerging capacity to relate to other human beings in terms of group constellations, such that elements of communal sharing take on increased emphasis.

The important emphasis that we would like to make here is that these processes of individuation and separation are linked to the continuing working of projection and introjection. The child's capacity to introject continues to build up his sense of self, particularly the sense of self in relationship to others around him. Similarly, the process of projection serves to underline the sense of otherness and of separateness from objects around the child.

Thus we are talking here about a continuing process of self-object differentiation which extends the basic mechanisms which were at work in the child's first delineations of self from the surrounding environment. It is an inherent aspect of the process of projection that what is separated off from the self and attributed to the outside world is thus conceived of as separated from the self and inherent in the other as other. There is consequently an increasing awareness of and tolerance for the separation of the significant objects.

The very fact that the child attains a level of complex social interaction within the triadic context implies that in some degree his tolerance for the separateness and individuality of the respective parental figures has to that degree been significantly increased. But that tolerance itself is correlative to the child's own emerging sense of individuality and his sense of autonomy as an independently existing person. It is important in this regard to remember that separation does not mean isolation. If the child achieves a new degree of a sense of separation and individuation, it is important to remember that the sense of individuation is related to and built into a context of continuing object relatedness which serves to sustain his newfound and newly achieved individuality. The child's sense of individuality or identity is related to and sustained by his continuing involvement with parental figures—not in the same form as had been achieved at a pregenital level, but in a new form which is dictated by the larger social involvement of the family unit. Thus the Oedipal involvement carries with it a sense of belonging and participation which is linked to and responsive to the child's newly emerging sense of identity. The projective aspect of the Oedipal involvement can be seen to serve not only to successively separate the child from significant figures, but also to preserve significant object ties in more appropriate and adaptive fashion consistent with the developmental progression.

Castration Anxiety

Before leaving considerations of the Oedipal developmental phase, it may be useful to briefly consider some of the pathological aspects of Oedipal involvements. Both castration anxiety and penis envy are specific manifestations of the pathology of Oedipal relationships. Both of these, however, can be brought into focus as specific manifestations of the paranoid process in this pathological expression.

As we have already observed, castration anxiety reflects not only the hostile projections from one aspect of the child's Oedipal involvement, but also reflects his sense of vulnerability and weakness as a part of his own sense of emerging self. Thus the emergence of castration anxiety in the young boy is a result not only of a projective elaboration of the aggressive and destructive rivalry with the father, but also to a significant degree reflects the introjection of the vulnerability and victimized (castrated) weakness of the mother. The child's sense of potential identification with the mother is thus an integral part of his castration fears.

As we have already noted in our earlier discussion, the emergence of castration anxiety is thus quite closely linked to the parameters of separation anxiety that had adhered in earlier developmental levels. The degree to which the mother projects upon the child her own sense of vulnerability and victimization contributes to the pattern of introjection which underlies the child's emerging sense of susceptibility, and thus contributes to the degree of castration anxiety. It is important to keep this introjective element in focus, since the more traditional approach to castration anxiety has focused on projective elements of the child's relationship to the father. It also suggests that the phenomenon of castration anxiety is considerably more complex than is suggested by an appeal to motivations of simple Oedipal guilt.

When we turn to castration anxiety in the female and its inherent relationship to penis envy, it is apparent that we move to a new and significant level of discourse. It becomes quickly apparent that a fundamental aspect of the phenomenon of both castration anxiety and penis envy is their relationship to narcissism. Both castration anxiety and penis envy represent a severe compromise in the child's residual sense of narcissistic omnipotence and entitlement. While the mutilative and aggressive aspects of these states have been amply demonstrated and considered in the literature, less than adequate attention has been paid to these states as reflections of underlying narcissistic trauma.

From this point of view castration anxiety is a reflection of the child's loss of a sense of omnipotence and the correlative emergence of a sense of vulnerability. In this regard castration anxiety can be regarded as a reflection of the child's unwillingness to surrender this sense of potency. For the male child, for example, to accept the smallness and inadequacy and impotency of his genitals in comparison to his father's, is to accept his inadequacy within the context of Oedipal wishes and desires.

Castration anxiety in a sense, then, is an attempt to salvage the wish for more mature sexual potency and to avoid the narcissistic injury that would be connected with accepting the child's relative impotency. Thus, if the father is in fantasy intent upon punishing the child for his genital wishes, the fantasies associated with castration anxiety must serve to preserve the illusion of genital capacity. The set of projections which underlie and support the castration fears can be seen as a narcissistic defense which serves to preserve the underlying narcissism and the intactness of the child's sense of self in the face of the admission of real inadequacy.

Furthermore, the little boy's small genitals must be compared with the large and potent ones of his father, so that part of the child's castration anxiety complex must include an element of penis envy. The narcissistic affront involved in this is based on the underlying entitlement, which requires that whatever someone else has should also belong to the individual by right. This aspect of the Oedipal involvement was clearly stated in the case of Jimmy, for whom his own sense of genital inadequacy provided a severe narcissistic trauma from which he could protect himself only by a set of pathological defenses. Thus castration anxiety can serve not only as a punishment for Oedipal genital wishes, but also serves in a less obvious way as a means of preserving the underlying narcissistic wish by means of the projective defense. We have seen this aspect of the projective defense in other areas of paranoid pathology as well.

Penis Envy

Similarly in the case of penis envy in little girls, the phenomenon develops not only within a context in which the sense of having been castrated and deprived dominates the set of fantasies, but also in which the underlying introjection of the victimized and disadvantaged mother figure serves as the basis on which the feelings of penis envy are elaborated. Thus genital differences between the parents can become the focus for the child's understanding of other distortions in the parents' sadomasochistic relationship. Consequently, while penis envy is related to and attached to basic biological differences, it nonetheless reflects underlying introjective dynamics which are considerably more significant in the understanding and in the vicissitudes of such envy. This became quite clear, for example, in the analysis of Karen, for whom the violent and intense feelings about the whole issue of penis envy, displayed at large in her relationships to men and displayed in particularly intense and vivid ways within the analysis, reflected in a very basic sense Karen's underlying sense of identification with her vulnerable and victimized mother. Thus both castration anxiety and penis envy are reflections of the pathological operation of the paranoid process.

The question which this, of course, raises is whether such pathological manifestations of Oedipal involvements are not indeed universal as expressions of such involvement and do not form important motivating aspects of the later developmental vicissitudes. Once again we are unavoidably confronted with the question of the overlapping and interdigitating of processes which can be regarded as pathological, but yet seem inexorably to be drawn into the vicissitudes of even normal development.

Clearly in the course of normal development the issues of castration anxiety or penis envy are readily assimilated into a fuller context of significant and supportive object relationships which provide other buffers to the narcissistic trauma and provide other resources by which the child is enabled to sustain and elaborate a sense of self-esteem. It is the child's continuing introjection of paternal strengths and his positive object involvement with his father that provides the basis of an assurance against castrative loss and offers the promise through identification of the achievement of greater potency and masculine power. Consequently, it is in this aspect of the Oedipal involvement that the narcissistic injury can be redressed and the bases for more realistic sustaining of the child's emergent self-esteem can be achieved.

Hence it can be seen that the Oedipal period, as a central and critical stage in infantile development, is a vital phase for the working through of the paranoid process. But not only that, insofar as the paranoid process operates in critical ways to establish the psychological parameters along which the Oedipal attainment takes shape and builds itself. It is not only in the pathological deviations that we are able to identify the workings of the paranoid process, but in the very central and significant dimensions of the developmental process itself are the workings of the paranoid mechanisms to be discovered.

THE LATENCY PERIOD

Resolution of Oedipal Situation

In the transition to the latency period from the Oedipal situation, the most significant task facing the developing child is the resolution of the Oedipal attachments. The child must resolve the intense erotic and conflictual involvements with both parents in the interest of establishing less ambivalent and less threatening relationships which can provide the basis for future developmental elaboration.

Our interest here is not in rehashing the details of latency development, but in bringing into focus the relevant role of the paranoid process in this development. The classic theory enunciates that the Oedipal erotization of the little boy's attachment to his mother gives rise within the triangular context to fears of castration from the father as retaliation for his incestuous urges. Under the pressure of castration anxiety, the little boy is motivated to renounce these dangerous wishes and thus to surrender the Oedipal attachments to the mother. Correspondingly, the little girl follows a somewhat different path. Her infantile attachment to the mother is contaminated by her discovery at the threshold of the Oedipal situation of phallic differences. Her resentment against the mother for having sent her into the world "scarce half made up," with inferior genital equipment, drives her to seek compensation from attachment to the penis-bearing father. Her disappointment from the father leads her to renounce her wishes and attachment to the father.

Simply stated the theory is correct as far as it goes. The Oedipal renunciation results in profoundly meaningful internalizations which classically are regarded as forming the core of the superego. The superego is thus the central acquisition of the Oedipal resolution and the subsequent developmental task of the latency period is the consolidation and integration of these fundamental superego introjects.

Introjection-Projection

If we can center our attention on the processes of introjection and projection, we have already seen the role they play in the Oedipal involvements. The same processes play themselves out in the developmental vicissitudes of the latency period. The process is reinforced and in part motivated by the effects of maturational changes in developing ego-functions. Thus in the normal course of Oedipal resolution, the modifications of Oedipal ambivalence taking place through interlocking projections and introjections lead in the direction of modulating instinctual attachments and gradually building up a sense of individuated and increasingly competent self. This latter aspect is a vital element in latency development, since the maturation and integration of executive, motoric and interpretive capacities places an internal demand for higher-order organization and synthetic integration. This is normally provided by higher-order and more autonomous introjections and identifications.

To be more specific, the workings of the paranoid process in the Oedipal boy normally draw him in the direction of decreasing ambivalence toward both parents. Castration anxieties are thus diminished and fall within the range of manageable anxiety and within the scope of the developing ego's capacity to constructively integrate its experience. Such modified levels of anxiety serve as stimuli to the development of ego resources. This is equivalent to the emergence of signal anxiety at the Oedipal level of development as a specific developmental achievement (Zetzel, 1970; Zetzel and Meissner, 1973). As a consequence the fragile ego does not need to cling to defensive postures to preserve its emerging integrity. As a result, the father emerges as a less threatening figure, with whom the child can establish a more meaningful and satisfying relationship. The father thus becomes an object for more autonomous identification and less an object for defensive introjection. The critical introjections that embody the Oedipal resolution are less conflictual and follow more in the direction of internalization of the father's real strengths and capacities to master than in the direction of an identification with the aggressor-father. As a byproduct of these less ambivalent internalizations, the child begins to see himself increasingly in terms of the availability of masculine strengths and capacities, and thus as potentially growing up in the image of his father. This opens the way to increasingly solid and positive masculine identification and the attendant potentiality of establishing meaningful relations with a woman like his mother.

The resolution of ambivalence toward the mother opens the way to a more stable and less instinctually driven relationship with her as well. The child's modified hostility lessens the need for defensively motivated erotic attachment and the clinging to infantile dependence. The relative sexual unavailability of the mother becomes less threatening and less narcissistically traumatic in view of the supports to masculine identity derived from the relationship and identification with the father. It is precisely the emergence and consolidation of the child's masculine identity—such a vital and central aspect of the latency identity formation—that provide the basis on which the Oedipal attachments to the mother can effectively be renounced. The child becomes more capable of real sexual potency and likeness to the father, and is thereby released from the nongratifying, fantasied, and threateningly incestuous ties to the mother.

Under these circumstances, he is freed to establish a more productive and less threatening relationship with the mother as well. In this manner, the

Oedipal resolution for the little boy does not become a narcissistic defeat with the resulting loss of self-esteem that may result from more pathogenic attachments. The child is thus free to renounce his intense Oedipal attachments to both parents. Likewise, his renunciation sets the stage for less conflictual and more autonomous identifications with both parents.

The situation is quite similar for the little girl. The interlocking of projections and introjections serves to modify the intensity of ambivalence toward both parental figures. The diminishing of ambivalence toward the mother allows for more positive and constructive introjections and thus identifications with her. The child's emerging sense of feminine identity brings further resolution to the relationship with the father so that the intensity of Oedipal erotic attachments is lessened and more appropriate forms of affection and interaction are sustained.

It is important to remember that these crucial internalizations take place in a complex and interactive manner. The influences are overlapping and mutually modifying. The successful resolution of Oedipal attachments is thus contingent on multiple factors—genetic, maturational, experiential, interactional, etc. The factors which contribute to the distortion or impairment of the working through of reciprocal introjections and projections will contribute similarly to a pathological outcome. There seems to be good evidence to suggest, as Sarnoff (1972) has indicated, that there is a further progression detectable in the modification of introjective and projective processes as the course of latency development unfolds and verges into early adolescence.

With regard to superego formations at this stage, the emergence of the superego in the context of the Oedipal resolution is an established conclusion. However, as our previous examination of introjection suggests, the postoedipal introjections are not simply limited to superego formation. They have a much broader influence on intrapsychic organization. Similarly, it is not altogether satisfactory to account for superego formation itself simply in terms of these postoedipal introjections. There are also significant identifications as well as other significant introjections involved. This is not to minimize the significance of the role of these postoedipal internalizations, but to underline their complexity and richness.

Increasing Autonomy

At this point, we shall confine ourselves to the consideration that a primary aspect of this latency development is the articulation and consolidation of a richer and more autonomous sense of self. The formation of the self is accomplished through the further elaborations provided by the mechanisms of the paranoid process. It is accompanied by significant degrees of increasing separation and individuation, particularly in the renunciation of Oedipal attachments and in the establishing of more independent and autonomous object-relationships with parental and other figures.

The latency period is generally regarded as one of marked diminution of drive components. This aspect of the shift from Oedipal involvements to latency manifestations has been stressed by Anna Freud (1965). She writes:

> The manner in which drive and ego progression either cures or causes the developmental disturbances is displayed most convincingly at those transition points between phases where not only the quality but also the quantity of drive activity undergoes a change. An example is the extreme castration fear, the death fears and wishes, together with the defenses against them, which dominate the scene at the height of the phallic-oedipal phase, and which create the well-known inhibitions, masculine overcompensations, passive and regressive moves of this period. This cluster of symptoms disappears as if by magic as soon as the child takes the first step into the latency period, that is, as an immediate reaction to the biologically determined lessening of drive activity. Compared with the oedipal child, the latency child seems definitely less beset by problems (p. 163).

Some of the modifications in the internal economy which transpire in the transition to the latency period are thus contributed to by the diminution of drive components which correspondingly limits the intensity of the child's ambivalent involvement with the parental figures.

Other developmental factors are the emergence of ego structures which contribute to the capacity for tolerance of anxiety and for the mastery of greater degrees of both aggressive and libidinal instinctual impulses. Moreover the significant and relatively nonambivalent postoedipal internalizations serve to both bolster and organize inner structure—both ego and superego—and provide the capacity for increased neutralization and constructive exploitation of instinctual drives. Rather than being caught up in the intensity of instinctual impulses and the defenses against them, the child's ego is left relatively free to begin to explore the outside world, the world beyond the boundaries of the family, the world beyond the limits of his immediate experience. The child's capacity for dealing with disruptive instinctual impulses is greatly expanded and the repertoire of defensive resources is correspondingly amplified. The effect of these developing resources is to take the pressure off the basic maneuvers of projection and introjection as major defensive resources. Thus both projections and introjections become less overloaded with instinctual contaminants and can be increasingly enlisted in the constructive effort of internal psychic organization and structuralization.

In his discussion of latency development of ego structures, Sarnoff (1971) divides the period into two phases: the early phase, from six to eight years, and the later phase, from eight to twelve. The early phase is predominated by the child's preoccupation with himself. It is marked by inhibition of masturbatory activity, superego strictness and rigidity, unavailability of objects as drive outlets, and fantasies which contain amorphous and threatening monsters. The use of fantasy dominates the child's defensive posture, while reality is used only in a derivative manner as a guarantee of secondary autonomous functions. In the later phase, the availability of objects in the outside world increases considerably as a means of gratification. The fantasies become more human; instead of monsters and dragons, they are peopled with witches and robbers. Superego rigidity and strictness is modified so that the child becomes increasingly able to accept and integrate his instinctual urges and becomes more aware of his relationship to the world, his place in it, and the potentialities for future development.

Narcissistic Vulnerability

It should also be noted that the child's emergence into the broader world of increasing experience and development of skills and knowledge often provides a considerable buffering for the child's narcissistic vulnerability. To the extent that this obtains in a given case, the need for the narcissistic defenses—specifically introjection and projection—will be correspondingly modified. However, the child's experience, particularly in the face of regressive responses to instinctual pressures or in the face of disappointments or frustrations in the school situation, may expose the child to considerable self-doubt and shaming which serve to undermine his emerging self-esteem and to pose the threat of narcissistic injury. In such cases the need for narcissistic defense can be increased so that the normal and expectable modifying influence of introjective and projective development will be distorted in ways which increase their pathogenic potential. Thus in complex ways there is an interactional effect of the vicissitudes of ego development on the workings of the paranoid process, in addition to the reciprocal influence of paranoid mechanisms on the pattern and quality of emerging ego consolidation.

As a result of this process, the ego undergoes a certain consolidation, so that it increases its capacity to resist regressive pulls of various kinds. Parental approval and support become increasingly less important for the maintenance of the child's sense of worth and self-esteem. Rather his self-esteem increasingly derives from his own sense of mastery and capacity for achievement which provides him with a certain amount of object recognition and social approval. Thus the child's inner sense of resourcefulness and mastery become the primary regulators of self-esteem.

In parallel with these aspects of development, and closely coordinated with them, the ego functions of perception, learning, memory, and thought become increasingly well established and achieve greater levels of functional capacity. They are thus increasingly available as resources which the ego is able to employ in dealing with both intrinsic and extrinsic stimuli. These functions also achieve an increasing degree of autonomy, with the result that they are less subject to instinctual influences and more able to operate effectively in given areas of conflict-free functioning.

Superego Modification

The higher functions of ego and superego thus become increasingly autonomous and operate more in the secondary process modality and less in primary process ones as a result of regressive instinctual influences. This emergence and consolidation of relatively more autonomous ego functions is attributable to the progressive consolidation and integration due to positive identificatory processes which affect the organization and the structuring of the ego itself, as well as its gradual integration with superego elements as a result of these same processes.

We might add a word about superego development in this period. We have already noted the frequently seen transition in quality of superego activity from a relatively rigid and primitively strict superego to an increasingly flexible and more realistic superego in the progression from early to late latency (Sarnoff, 1971). The internalization of the superego provides the child with an internal resource which was in large measure lacking during the Oedipal period. Superego internalization is based on the renunciation of parental attachments and is a necessary consequence of the cathectic shifts and structuralizing processes which bring the Oedipal situation to its resolution. As we have already noted, the resolution of Oedipal attachments is not a magical process and does not occur in instantaneous fashion. The quality of the early latency superego is in fact determined by the residual influence of Oedipal instinctual attachments and defenses against them.

Part of the internalization of parental imagos and a significant contribution to resolution of the real Oedipal attachments is the turning of aggression inward and its internalization in the form of superego pressures. The internalization is directed primarily to parental superego attitudes, so that the internalized possession of these parental controls provides the child with a resource for regulation of Oedipal instinctual attachments and consequently contributes to the modification of drive intensity and the severity of ambivalent involvements.

The gradual modification of superego severity, however, is part of the continuing work of latency development. It is accomplished intrinsically by the continued working of paranoid processes in the continuing process of modification by means of reciprocally interlocking projections and introjections. As the child expands the limits of his latency experience, the availability of a variety of significant objects to assist him in this process becomes a marked feature of his developmental experience. Not only does the process of projection and introjection continue to be worked through in relationship to parental objects, but the child's involvement with other adult figures, particularly teachers, also serves to modify the configuration of introjects and their corresponding projections. To a certain extent I believe that the process also involves the child's relationships with other children with whom he becomes more closely and extensively involved. Some of these projected elements are worked through in the context of play activity with other children, but other significant contributions come from sharing of experiences, and broadening of the child's awareness of the varieties of experience provided by other children. Thus a significant contributing force to the modification of the child's superego intensity comes by way of vicarious experiences.

In summary, then, the latency period emerges as a phase of significant internalizations, which serve to resolve and modify the intensity of Oedipal attachments, and second, as a period of significant amplification of the child's inner resources and of consolidation and continuing modification of emergent ego and superego structures. The important developmental attainments that the child realizes during this period serve not only as an important basis for his future role and functioning in the world around him, but particularly serve as an important resource for the sustaining and stabilizing of self-esteem. To the extent that this acquisition becomes a permanent one, and one which is relatively immune from instinctual regression, the child derives a continuing source of narcissistic resourcefulness which will stand him in good stead in confronting the inevitable regression of the adolescent period.

CHAPTER 26

The Paranoid Process
in Adolescent Development

THE TRANSITION TO ADOLESCENCE

The transition to the adolescent phase of development is marked by some of the most significant processes which contribute to the definition of individual personality. If the latency period can be aptly described as a period of relatively instinctual quiescence, the transition to adolescence must be described as a period of recrudescence of instinctual pressures. A variety of developmental changes are thus instigated which open up areas of basic conflict which remain as residuals of earlier levels of development and offer the opportunity for a reworking of those conflicts and their fashioning into a new and emergent sense of identity. The emphasis that I would like to make in the present discussion is that this regressive moment in the adolescent developmental process serves to reactivate and intensify the functioning of basic mechanisms of introjection and projection. These are in large measure responsible for the reworking of personality configurations which characterizes this period. Thus the paranoid process has a particular and special role to play in the working through and elaboration of the vicissitudes of adolescence.

The shift specifically in the use of projection from latency to early adolescent phases has been described by Sarnoff (1972). He describes this as a shift from projection associated with repression in the earlier phase to a use of projection associated with denial in the later phase. Sarnoff particularly notes that the latter form of projection, namely that associated with denial, is equivalent to the form of projection and displacement frequently involved in paranoid conditions. On the contrary, projection associated with repression, which is characteristically found in latency manifestations, follows more closely the pattern of phobia formation. We have previously discussed the relationship between paranoid mechanisms and formation of phobias. But Sarnoff's analysis makes it clear that the progression to early adolescent developments marks a definite shift more explicitly in the direction of a characteristic paranoid style of defensive projection.

This shift in projection parallels a transition of the primary role of defense from fantasy and symptom formation to a role in the testing of fantasy against reality in establishing object-relations, along with the partial dissolution and opening up of the superego to cultural influences. In other terms there is identifiable a shift from id projections to superego projections. As Sarnoff (1972) notes:

> Through projection the superego is externalized. The child who attributes her formerly internalized commands to a peer or teacher stands the chance of acquiring an externalized ego ideal, with characteristics of the ego ideal of the new object. With reinternalization of the ego ideal (the projection-rein-ternalization is a dynamic, ongoing series of events) modifications of the superego takes place (p. 521).

The transition to adolescence is marked by changes in bodily growth and an upsurge of hormonal influences. The onset of such changes is associated with an upsurge of instinctual pressures, so that adolescence is characterized by a reopening and a reworking of earlier developmental conflicts and fixations. The more marked upheaval of adolescence is to a certain degree anticipated in the closing stages of the latency period by more subtle and transient cathectic shifts. The preadolescent typically forms close and somewhat idealized friendships with same-sex peers. This reflects an intensification of already established latency patterns. The capacity, which is often developed in the latency period, for sustaining sublimated interests and work habits seems to become more fluid and variable. There is a confused and somewhat conflicted searching for different interests, goals, and sources of involvement, which reflects an underlying sense of dissatisfaction. These transitional shifts signal the onset of a developmental phase which promises to be considerably more active and tumultuous than the relative quiescence of the latency period (Blos, 1962).

The upsurge of instinctual drive-intensity at the onset of adolescence obviously presents the ego with a problem. Mastery of these instinctual drives and their derivatives is one of the major developmental tasks of adolescence. As a result of these increased drive pressures, there is induced a regression in ego-functioning which serves to reactivate basic unresolved conflicts from earlier developmental levels. The developing ego is thus presented with the necessity and the opportunity of reworking some of these underlying conflicts in a more thoroughgoing and definite way. There is thus the opportunity to undo earlier developmental defects and consequently remodel the psychic apparatus in more effective and positively constructive ways. Thus adolescence opens up the opportunity for new and more meaningful identifications which can provide a major direction and organization for these remodeling processes.

IDENTITY FORMATION

Second Individuation

Increasingly in recent years, the attitude toward the adolescent period has shifted from seeing it as a period of upheaval or developmental disorganization to viewing it more in terms of a normative crisis. The view that adolescence is a normal growth experience which is marked not only by conflict and regression but also a remarkable growth potential, is one that has received increasing acceptability. Thus infantile conflicts and fixations can be reworked in ways which give rise to a new organization of the personality. The reworking is accomplished by an exposure to and a complex interaction with social and cultural influences stemming from the larger society, into which the adolescent is gradually introduced and in terms of which he must seek a definitive place. The resolution of these basic conflicts has a twofold potentiality. They may be resolved in terms of more effective forms of structural and characterological organization—or conversely they may be resolved in terms of a solidification into more stable symptom patterns of characterological defects.

A significant part of the adolescent development is what Peter Blos (1967) refers to in terms of "second individuation." The first individuation, as we have already discussed above, is one which takes place in the first two years of life in the achievement of self-object differentiation. The individuation of adolescence, however, is considerably more complex and leads ultimately to the establishment of a sense of identity. The adolescent process is one of increasing self-definition. In this connection it is important to note that the same processes which we have already identified as pertinent to the definition and delineation of self are also at play in critical and important ways in the adolescent stage of development. The adolescent must search for and experiment with his identity. The relationship between self and identity and their relationships to problems of adolescent development are discussed in Marcus (1973) and Wolf et al. (1972).

Adolescent self-awareness is at first fragmented and disjointed. The person must struggle to achieve some sense of self by opposition to what he or she wishes not to be. Thus the rejecting, opposing, contradicting, resisting and rebelling of the adolescent are driven by this underlying need. Thus the issue of separation along with the companion issue of individuation is a primary concern of the adolescent vicissitudes. The adolescent must also test himself in a variety of roles and functions—often finding it necessary to push experimentation to the limits of excess in order to clarify his sense of inner confusion and uncertainty. These strivings and testing of the limits have a positive value in making a contribution to the adolescent's emerging sense of self-awareness and self-definition. The negative delineation of self, however, fosters an essential individuation that is required for the building of a more mature sense of identity and at the same time contributes to the adolescent's increasing sense of relative autonomy.

The working through of such a process of individuation is subject to multiple difficulties. Becoming more of an individual by way of separation from significant objects places the adolescent more and more at risk. He may be overwhelmed by feelings of isolation, loneliness and confusion. He may be confronted with the futility and the unreality of childhood (narcissistic) dreams and fantasies. He becomes increasingly aware of his own inherent limits as well as of the need for more mature involvements and commitments. He is faced with the inevitability and the decisive finality of the end of childhood. He must increasingly surrender his dependence on significant adults and gradually assume responsibility for himself and the direction of his life. It is no surprise consequently that many adolescents find the vicissitudes of development threatening and seek to find ways to prolong the adolescent posture by clinging to more regressed and dependent positions.

Object-Relations

One of the primary adjustment problems of the adolescent period has to do with object-relations. In the child's earlier experience his development was closely linked as we have seen with objects. In the earliest stages there was the crucial capacity for self-object differentiation. His optimal development in the first two years of life depended vitally on the quality of his relationship with his mother—on his trusting reliance on her mothering activities and on his emerging capacity to tolerate her absence for increasing periods of time. Object-relations for the preoedipal child are concerned with establishing meaningful and mutually rewarding relationships on a one-to-one basis with both parents. If the child has been able to accomplish these adaptive goals in the preoedipal years, when he comes to the triangular Oedipal involvements in which he must relate to both parents simultaneously in the Oedipal situation, his capacity to resolve these relationships and their accompanying conflicts is correspondingly improved. He can establish less threatening and more comfortable relationships with both parents by reason of a patterning of identifications based on the relative strengths of both parents. Even through the preoedipal and latency years the parents remain the predominant objects in the child's life—although the broadening of the child's object-relation involvement has begun even there. Teachers and other significant adult objects begin to play a significant role in the child's development.

When the child enters adolescence, however, object-choice and object-involvement take a decisive turn away from the parental objects. The major developmental task of adolescence is the establishment of a capacity for heterosexual object-choice on a genital level. An essential part of this process is the renunciation of the primary objects—the parents or parental substitutes. The child must surrender the parents as its love objects. The changes in the quality of parental relationships which were brought about in the resolution of the Oedipal situation and the subsequent modifications of the latency involvement with parents must give way to a decisive renunciation. The necessary relinquishing of these important objects leaves the adolescent with a marked object-hunger. The abandonment of parental objects and the seeking of new and appropriate objects gives rise to important inner shifts of cathexis which strongly influence both object-representations and the representation of the self. There arises an inner lability of cathexis which makes the adolescent's sense of self all the more uncertain and confused. The adolescent's capacity to carry through his important developmental step rests on the extent to which he is capable of tolerating the insecurity and loss that is implicit in the separation from and renunciation of the parents as love objects. That capacity reflects previous developmental achievements.

During adolescence the libidinal economy becomes organized around genital impulses. Preoedipal and Oedipal attachments to parental objects are replaced by nonincestuous attachments to heterosexual objects. The transition from one phase to the other is attended by other shifts in instinctual alignments. The quality of object-relations shifts subtly and gradually from a need to be loved and taken care of to a progressively manifest need to love and take care of. The child's dependence on parental objects and relative passivity is gradually translated into relatively more independent self-direction and activity. The polarity of activity and passivity which was elaborated in earlier interactions with the parents reemerges in adolescence as one of the crucial issues that must be decisively resolved. The struggles over renunciation and finding objects as well as the crisis of activity and passivity provoke a recrudescence of ambivalence. The adolescent becomes overly sensitive to the currents of love and hate that are stirred up within him, and he may often vacillate confusingly and confusedly back and forth between them. He does this both with his relationships with his parents whom he both rejects and clings to and with his new found objects whom he both hungers for and reviles. The resolution of these conflicts culminates in the normal course of development in relatively nonambivalent object-relations and in an ego-syntonic balance of activity and passivity which consolidates into a characteristic pattern.

The intensification and reactivation of basic ambivalences regressively activate defensive processes for managing these conflicting impulses. Thus basic processes of projection and introjection come into play, and are potentially brought into the service of reworking the emerging sense of adolescent identity. This developmental potentiality, however, is both progressive and regressive. These defensively motivated operations of the paranoid process may be pulled by the intensity of defensive needs and the underlying conflicts into more regressive forms of resolution which leave the resulting identity more susceptible to Oedipal and preoedipal instinctual pressures.

Narcissistic Regression

The renunciation of parental objects and the attendant loss of object-libido have a number of important consequences. The loss of parental objects leads to a transitional narcissistic phase which is intermediate between the attachment to parents and a more definitive heterosexual object-involvement. Libido is withdrawn not simply from the external parent or parental object-representations but from the internalized parent as well. The superego, as we have seen, arises from the internalization of parental representations in the resolution of the Oedipal situation. The superego, together with the ego-ideal, thus becomes the primary agency for intrapsychic regulation and for the maintenance of self-esteem. The shifts in cathexis bring about a weakening of superego. In renouncing the parents, the adolescent also withdraws from the internalized parental equivalents which reside in the moral evaluative standards of the superego. This has its risks for future development and for the adolescent's adaptation to the world around him, but as Erikson has pointed out so clearly these inner developmental shifts provide the continuing potential for reformulation and revivification of the values and beliefs not only of youth, but of the community at large.

The adolescent's withdrawal from the familiar objects of childhood leads to a narcissistic overvaluation of self. The adolescent becomes increasingly aware of his inner processes. He becomes self-absorbed, self-centered, and self-concerned. This may lead to a narcissistic withdrawal and disturbance of reality-testing. The adolescent often resorts to narcissistic defenses to defend against the disappointment and disillusionment of his meager position in reality. He may find it difficult to give up the gratifying parent on whom he has come to depend—especially if the parent has been overly protective and solicitous—and face his own limitations and inadequacies. He may be afraid to take responsibility for his own abilities and their consequences—as well as unwilling to face the demands of adult responsibility.

With the induced narcissistic regression, the intensity of narcissistic needs is heightened. This leaves the adolescent self more susceptible to narcissistic injury and disillusionment. This provides another important source of the mobilization of introjection-projection, specifically as narcissistic defenses. Thus introjection and projection come into operation in specific ways to sustain the threatened sense of self and preserve its threatened integrity. The regressive activation of introjection-projection tends to regressively intensify cathexis of and attachment to parental objects.

In this way adolescent conflicts can be prolonged for a considerable time. It becomes easily understandable that the reluctance to renounce dependence on and love of parents often is not simply an adolescent issue, but that it has its roots in the child's previous developmental history. The process of detachment from parental objects or their substitutes can go on for a very long time—and even in the normal course of development continues on through adolescence into the postadolescent period. Only when the individual enters upon and can accept responsibility for adult tasks and commitments is the relationship to the primary objects finally decided and resolved.

Emerging Identity

The withdrawal of libido from parental objects disqualifies the parents as sources of libidinal gratification and the adolescent is beset with a hunger for objects. This hunger is reflected in the marked adolescent propensity for shifting, labile, superficial, and transient attachments and identifications. This is the adolescent's way of preserving his ties to the outside world and avoiding a complete libidinal withdrawal. The lability of this internal situation makes the ego susceptible to regressive pulls. The relatively stable identifications acquired in the preceding developmental phases lose their stability and consolidation to a certain extent. They are subject to regressive influences and the pattern of relationship to parental objects becomes a matter of more primitive forms of internalization. The relations to the parents are based on the interactions of introjection and projection. As has been the case in earlier levels of development, the real parents become confused with "good" and "bad" introjects. The pattern of adolescent vacillation between rejecting and clinging to parents reflects the influence of these introjective components in the relationships. The introjects have been more or less dormant during the latency period but are revivified in the adolescent regression. The attachment to new objects serves a twofold purpose in this regard. It facilitates the decathexis of the old introjects, and at the same time—particularly in regard to the "bad" introjects—it offers the possibility of modifying and neutralizing these potentially toxic introjects by the acquisition of new "good" introjects. Ultimately these inner vicissitudes of the infantile introjects must be resolved through a definitive identification—preferably with the parent of the same sex.

The adolescent's capacity to turn to appropriate heterosexual objects and to establish meaningful nonincestuous relations is linked to his emerging sense of sexual identity. The resolution of the Oedipal complex carries with it the residues of both positive and negative Oedipal strivings. The resulting identifications are composite integrations of identifications with both parents. Little boys carry away with them residues of feminine identification and feminine strivings. The polarity of masculine and feminine roles is fixed, however, in the adolescent synthesis. The adolescent boy experiences an upsurge of homosexual libido and feminine strivings which he must relinquish in order to reach a more definitively masculine position.

The girl must relinquish her masculine striving and its underlying component of penis envy in order to achieve her full potential as a woman—and further as a mother. The onset of menarche polarizes and confirms this development. The success of the development to feminine sexual identity depends on the girl's successful renunciation of maternal dependency—but at the same time on her successful identification with the mother as a reproductive and sex-role model. These developmental contingencies are in turn dependent on the quality of previous identifications with the mother. If such identifications are contaminated by hostility, the girl will not be able to accept her own heterosexual desires and maternal sense of identity without anxiety and conflict. The emergence of a healthy and mature sense of sexual identity for both sexes is thus based in part on the establishment of a secure sense of sexual identity and the capacity to accept adult sexual roles without anxiety. Identification with the same-sex parent is a crucial aspect of this process. Obviously, when the parents do not provide the child with adequate models of masculinity or femininity the child's adjustment in this regard becomes more precarious.

Identity Formation

The critical achievement of adolescent development is the sense of identity. The definition of self which emerges in late adolescence is a work of synthetic processes in the ego. Erikson has described the establishment of a sense of identity as a phase-specific achievement which involves the formation of a qualitatively new psychic formation. The formation of a sense of identity is more than a sum of childhood identifications. As Erikson describes it:

> The sense of ego identity, then, is the accrued confidence that one's ability to maintain inner sameness and continuity (one's ego in the psychological sense) is matched by the sameness and continuity of one's meaning for others. Thus, self-esteem, confirmed at the end of each major crisis, grows to be a conviction that one is learning effective steps toward a tangible future, that one is developing a defined personality within a social reality which one understands (1959, p. 89).

Identity develops out of a gradual integration of identifications, but the resulting whole forms an integrated totality that exceeds the mere sum of its parts. Childhood identifications are subjected to a new integration in the adolescent remodeling which issues in a more final self-definition and to irreversible role-patterns which set the young person on his life course.

In the elaboration of these inner processes, it is essential that the emerging adolescent self be recognized and responded to in meaningful ways by the adult community into which he is growing and within which he seeks a place. Such a reciprocal response—an extrapolation of the mutual regulation or earlier phases of development—offers the emergent self of the adolescent a necessary support to enable him to sustain vital defenses in the face of the growing intensity of instinctual impulses, to consolidate areas of growing capacity and achievement with social roles and work opportunities, and finally to reorganize earlier patterns of identification in a consistent fashion and to integrate the new configuration with the patterns of role and value available within the society. Erikson has stated this complex aspect of adolescent development in lucid terms.

> *Identity formation*, finally, begins where the usefulness of identification ends. It arises from the selective repudiation and mutual assimilation of childhood identifications, and their absorption in a new configuration, which in turn, is dependent on the process by which a *society* (often through subsocieties) *identifies the young individual*, recognizing him as somebody who had to become the way he is, and who, being the way he is, is taken for granted. The community, often not without some initial mistrust, gives such recognition with a (more or less institutionalized) display of surprise and pleasure in making the acquaintance of a newly emerging individual. For the community, in turn, feels "recognized" by the individual who cares to ask for recognition; it can by the same token, feel deeply—and vengefully—rejected by the individual who does not seem to care (1959, p. 113).

In summary, adolescent development marks an advance in instinctual drive organization toward genital heterosexual position. The genital position becomes relatively definitive and irreversible. The libido is directed outward and the ego gains a new investment in objects. The turning to new love objects reactivates Oedipal fixations which must be renounced and resolved. The adolescent is thereby enabled to elaborate more mature and adult positions of masculinity and femininity. The ego gains in its capacity to organize more effective defenses and sublimations, to reach restitutive solutions and adaptive accommodations. These become aligned in highly individual and unique patterns which are gradually consolidated into an emerging character structure. Thus adolescent development translates the idiosyncratic constellation of drives and conflicts into more unified and integrated patterns of personality organization. The normal developmental process of adolescence arrives at a final integration in which the emerging pattern is subjectively grasped and more or less accepted as belonging to an inherently identifiable sense of self.

The Sense of Identity

The formation of a sense of identity is a significant developmental achievement. It provides the developing personality with a coherent sense of its own individuality and a sense of both what it is in itself and in its relationships with the significant objects in the world around it. It is obvious that in a sense the issue of identity pervades all phases of the developmental process—specifically in terms of its relationship to the emergence and shaping of the self. But, as Erikson has so clearly articulated, the issue of identity rises to a characteristic crescendo in the adolescent period. This is understandable insofar as it is specifically within the adolescent context that the individual must define and delineate his identity now in broader and more complex terms which reach out to the broader stage of social interaction and cultural involvement. It is through his emergent sense of identity, then, that the adolescent individual achieves a sense of belonging and participating and sharing in the concerns and directions of the human community of which he is a responsible and responsive part.

Such an emergence and stabilization of the sense of identity has a twofold component in it. The first is the shaping and stabilizing of the internal psychic resources which lend a sense of inner organization and stability of inner states. It is through the inner vacillation and cathectic shifts that are so characteristic of adolescence that increasingly the young individual must define a sense of persistent and coherent self-identity, which allows him to both sense himself and to present himself with some consistency and continuity to the world around him. But there is also another significant component. The sustaining of a sense of identity also requires that the individual identifies himself as a member of the community and in terms of which the community reciprocally identifies him as belonging to it and as having been accepted by and integrated in the community as such.

In this connection, Searles (1966-67) has brought this issue into focus in terms of the sense of identity regarded as a perceptual organ. Searles observes:

> In the light of the foregoing concepts, one's sense of identity emerges as being, in a tangible and thoroughly dynamic sense, one's most valuable organ for perceiving the world. When this essential function of the sense of identity is grasped it becomes understandable why the fashioning of an identity seems to us so endlessly fascinating and significant. The struggle for identity is no mere narcissistic interest but, is rather—among its other fundamental significances—a struggle to fashion and ceaselessly perfect one's potentially most sensitive and reliable instrument for psychologically grasping the outer world. Man's identity enables him to perceive the world not merely by mirroring it, but, at a symbiotic level of relatedness, by literally sampling it through processes of introjection-and-projection (p. 526).

Thus it is true in terms of a sense of identity that the individual achieves a feeling of belonging and participating in the world around him—particularly the world of significant human objects. Derivatively and by extension, however, the sense of identity is equivalently an organ by which the individual perceives and articulates himself within the broader contexts of social and cultural interaction.

Identity and the World of Objects

It is important to see that this function of identity is one that serves to both shape and sustain the normal and adaptive functioning of human personality. But the function in question is not merely supported by the internal shaping of and delineation of a sense of self. There must go along with it and evolve in reciprocal interaction with the emerging sense of identity a perception of the meaningful world of objects to which the individual relates himself by way of his emerging sense of identity. The point of view we are developing in this study would suggest that there is a complex cognitive function, which is carried on in conjunction with the elaboration of an identity which has to do with the cognitive structuring, selecting, organizing, and integrating of these elements in the outside world into a coherent system of meaningful relationships, which provides the reciprocal context within which the emerging sense of identity articulates itself.

Thus the individual literally builds for himself a community which is reciprocally related to his own inner sense of emerging identity and which provides the context of relatedness within which the sense of identity articulates itself and provides itself with a context of meaningful participation. In more rudimentary and less elaborate ways, this process plays itself out throughout the developmental experience. From the very first, while the child is fashioning a sense of self through the interaction with significant objects, as we have discussed it here, he is also correlatively fashioning a world of objects and experiences and relationships within which he can comfortably find his place and achieve a sense of belonging.

If in the earliest phases of development that context of belonging in a most rudimentary sense means no more than the symbiotic relationship to the mother, it is nonetheless quickly broadened to include other significant figures who in the first instance achieve their significance through their relationships with the caretaking mother, but quickly assume an independent relevance and place within the child's experience. The construction then becomes increasingly complex and the borders of its extension are rapidly expanded. The transition from Oedipal involvements, where the limits of such significant belonging are relatively narrow, to the latency experience, where there is a rapid and broad expansion of such a sense of belonging—certainly to the context of the child's school experience and also possibly to the experience of neighborhood and even town—call for important reconstructions in the child's cognitive schema which allow him to place himself in relationship to these expanded horizons.

Paranoid Construction

In the reworking of adolescent adjustments and relationships, however, the construction takes on new richer and considerably broader implications. This aspect of the shaping and sustaining of a sense of identity is what we have referred to as the "paranoid construction." We emphasize here that it is a necessary and integral part of the emergence of a sense of identity which assumes particular and significant dimensions in the adolescent experience. In significant ways, then, the paranoid construction provides a context within which the residual projections which are elaborated within the adolescent phase can be absorbed and integrated to provide the psychological context within which the emerging sense of identity can function and to which it can relate itself in meaningful ways. From this point of view we must conclude that not only the paranoid construction but the workings of projection itself serve a significant function in the overall elaboration of a sense of identity which emerges in the adolescent reworkings of the personality.

ADOLESCENT PARANOIA

Tolerance for Separation

If the sense of identity requires and builds itself in relationship to a sense of communion and belonging with both significant objects and a context of belonging, as we have suggested, it is also true that an important element in the maintaining and functioning of the sense of identity is its capacity to tolerate a separation from the same significant objects. Modell (1968) has discussed this important developmental attainment in the following terms:

> That a loving parent has been internalized and become part of the self, so that one is able to love oneself, has been described as an aspect of narcissism. . . . I am suggesting that the awareness of the self as a discrete and beloved entity (the narcissistic gratification of self-love) may enable the individual to accept the fact that objects in the external world are separate and can be lost and destroyed. . . . Whether or not this assumption is correct, it is a fact that those individuals who have the capacity to accept the separateness of objects are those that have a distinct, at least in part, beloved sense of self. If one can be a loving parent to oneself, one can more readily accept the separateness of objects. This is a momentous step in psychic development (p. 59).

We have already touched in our discussion on the developmental aspects of the capacity to tolerate anxiety, frustration, and disappointment. The capacity to tolerate separation of significant objects is a correlative of the capacity to tolerate painful reality. It is only on this basis that a mature capacity for realistic object-relations can be established and sustained. The mature sense of self, the fully developed sense of identity, then, is correlated with the capacity to recognize and accept the identity of others and the ability to come to terms with and acknowledge the separateness and the autonomy of those others. Where there is an intolerance for such separateness, there develops an inner need to both incorporate the object within the limits of one's own self or to extend the orbit of the self to encompass that object. This incorporating or extending is accomplished through defensively toned uses of projection and introjection. When a relationship is contaminated with introjective components, the object begins to be regarded as somehow belonging to the self—the sort of self-objects to which Kohut's (1971) considerations of narcissism address themselves.

It can be quickly seen that in these terms we are dealing with an extension of the basic concerns of individuation and separation that have been an integral part of the developmental process from the beginning of the child's experience. But we need to go a step further. It is our contention here that development and maintenance of the sense of identity require not only a capacity for the toleration of the separateness of objects, but that an integral part of the process is the active separation out from and over against such objects. We are bringing into focus consequently the obverse of the concerns for relatedness and belonging which we have been discussing. If the processes which underlie and build a sense of inner integrity and belonging can be seen in terms of their contribution to the process of identity formation, they must also be seen as functioning in reciprocal interaction with other processes, which serve to separate the emerging identity out from and to place it over against other objects and contexts—literally defining the emerging sense of identity in terms of such opposition. We are talking here substantially about the need for an enemy.

The Need for an Enemy

The subject of a need for an enemy is one which I find rather distressing. It is painful to me to reckon with the possibility that the very mechanisms, which we have been at pains to define as substantially contributing to and sustaining the sense of identity, are also intrinsically related to a process which serves to separate that identity out from others and to set it over against them in basic opposition. But I find myself forced to this consideration. The basic dilemma and the difficult task which is imposed upon the adolescent by the exigencies of development is that he articulate a sense of himself and integrate that sense of self with a specifically defined social unit, a community which organizes itself and expresses itself in terms of specifically defined limits and internally generated and specific criteria of belonging and sharing values.

However, as Erikson (1959) was quick to point out, the integration is a function of mutual recognition and acceptance. The community may feel recognized by the emerging individual who is ready to seek recognition and acceptance. It can also feel rejected by those more alienated individuals who reject it, rebel against it, or simply seem not to care. If the community responds to the former with acceptance—thus promoting participation and integration—it can withhold its acceptance from the latter. This creates a paranoid impasse—a standoff of mutual rejection. The individual and the community become enemies. The paranoid process requires the individual to seek affiliation with other groupings—often countercultural subgroupings—or failing that, to construct a more decisively pathological paranoid system.

The Self and the Ingroup

Thus the defining of self and the articulating of its relationship—both under conditions of mutual rejection and under conditions of acceptance—are achieved in part through a setting of the self over against other communities, other groupings, other contexts of belonging which are defined in terms of their exclusiveness from the initial social grouping and in terms of their opposition in beliefs, values, attitudes, etc.

Thus the community which the adolescent shapes about himself is one which is built around a core of inherent values and attitudes, but which is likewise set in opposition to other such groupings. The adolescent in our society delineates and articulates his sense of identity as participating in certain specific groupings. He envisions himself as sharing certain common affiliations with different groupings. Thus he envisions himself as an American citizen, or as Jewish, or as Republican, or in terms of professional affiliations as a psychiatrist, or perhaps as a psychologist, or perhaps as a carpenter, or perhaps as a truck driver.

The important point that I am stressing is that such paranoid propensities make a significant contribution to the forming of ingroups, which provide the context for significant adherences within which the sense of identity can articulate itself and significantly maintain contexts of belonging and sharing which serve to sustain and confirm the inner sense of individual identity. The important tasks which confront the adolescent have to do precisely with his articulating his sense of self in terms of these complex social groupings—that is to say, that an integral part of the forming of an identity is the acquiring of a sense of belonging to certain specified ingroups, thereby defining oneself as opposed to and separated out from other social and cultural groupings which constitute the body of the outgroupings.

The phenomenon is applicable in terms of social and cultural groupings, but it also has relevance in terms of the very personalized and individualized articulation of the sense of self as separate from and over against other selves. Thus in a certain necessary sense, an important task of adolescent development is that the adolescent set himself apart from, separate himself from, and posit himself in opposition to his parents or other significant caretaking figures. The adolescent revolt against parental restrictions cannot be seen simply in pathological terms but must also be seen as a way of making a significant contribution to the adolescent attainment of identity. This also applies to the adolescent exigency to revolt against all forms of authority.

Paranoid Mechanisms

Thus these considerations lead in the direction of suggesting what can be denominated as a process of "adolescent paranoia." I am suggesting that such an adolescent paranoia is based on the working out of the specifically paranoid mechanisms we have been discussing—projection, introjection, and the paranoid construction—and that it provides an essential and integral part in the process of achieving a sense of identity which is so characteristically a developmental task of the adolescent period. I am suggesting further that even though these mechanisms are a continuation and a further expression of developmental vicissitudes, in the adolescent period they assume a specifically paranoid quality—more akin to the paranoid manifestations that we are more familiar with in the context of clinical psychopathology.

The adolescent unavoidably sees himself in some sense as the victim of parental restraints and restrictions. He must also to some extent see himself as the victim of social pressures and cultural constraints which require him to integrate himself with the society around him in terms of certain standards of behavior and values. It is the working of this adolescent paranoid process and its attendant persecutory anxieties which contribute significantly to the tumultuousness, the anxieties and rebellious turmoil that we have come to associate with adolescent concerns. It is terribly important, however, not to lose sight of the fact that such deviant and rebellious expressions—marked by the usual accompaniments of paranoid distortions such as extreme narcissism, defensiveness, rebelliousness, hostility, and destructive potentiality—are at the same time an expression of important developmental functions which are operating in the service of establishing and consolidating a sense of identity.

NEGATIVE IDENTITY

Definition

The phenomenon of negative identity was first clearly denominated and described by Erikson (1959). As he saw it, it often expressed itself in a rather scornful or snobbish hostility to the roles and values which were offered to the individual as appropriate for his family or community context. This might concern any aspect of the context of social belonging, whether masculine or feminine roles, or class membership, or nationality, or religious affiliation, or whatever. The young individual reacts with contempt and disdain for the values and attitudes and beliefs that are embedded in such contexts. We have seen such manifestations of negative identity in all our patients—as for example the attitudes of Bob and Karen toward their Jewishness, or the attitudes of most of the females toward their femininity, or quite strikingly the attitudes of Fred toward a broad spectrum of social and cultural institutions involved in our own society. The issues of separation and opposition are often quite effectively displayed in such forms of pathology.

As Erikson acutely and correctly notes, this resolution of the identity crisis has buried in it a powerful death wish against the parents, which expresses itself in explicitly paranoid form. But the estrangement from origins and affiliations rarely takes the form of a complete denial of identity or a total immersion of identity diffusion. Rather it finds a more subtle expression in the choice of a negative identity. Erikson (1959) defines negative identity as "perversely based on all those identifications and roles which, at critical stages of development, had been presented to the individual as most undesirable or dangerous, and yet also as most real" (p. 131).

The Role of Projection/Introjection

The presentation, however, as we have been at pains to ariculate here, is not merely a matter of explicit designation or inference. It has to do more with the interlocking of projections and introjections which provide the psychological context within which the individual adolescent elaborates his emerging sense of identity. Erikson provides the example of a mother who, in her unconscious ambivalence toward an alcoholic brother, responds selectively only to those traits in her son which seem to flow in the direction of a repetition of the brother's fate. In such a case, the emerging negative identity elicited in response to the mother's implicit projections may begin to take on more reality for the son than any of his other attempts to establish his own sense of inner integrity and external acceptance.

The classic expression of this in the clinical literature is the so-called "superego lacunae" described by Johnson and others (Johnson and Szurek, 1952; Giffin, et al., 1954) in the explanation of antisocial acting-out and delinquency. The phenomenon is particularly identifiable in the adolescent phase. In fact, the child acts out and expresses in his rebellious confrontation with expressed parental values the inner impulses and antisocial wishes which remain latent and hidden in the parents. From our perspective here, such an outcome is the result of the child's responding to the implicit projection which comes from the parent and which equivalently sets the terms on which the child not only introjects and forms the nucleus of his emerging sense of self, but also sets the conditions for the child's acceptance and belonging in the relationship with the parents. Thus the patient can form a negative identity which in varying degrees is set in opposition to expressed parental values and wishes, but at the same time can be responsive to unexpressed parental needs.

But such a negative identity is often an expression of an underlying struggle with the introject (Greenson, 1954). This situation is particularly identifiable in the case of Karen, whose more or less delinquent sexual acting-out was directly an expression of her struggle against an underlying introjection of the maternal imago. Karen in effect set herself up to oppose, fight off, and destroy her mother's implicit values, but the necessity for the struggle was internally based on the fact that Karen had in fact internalized those very values. With regard to such a choice of negative identity, Erikson comments:

> Such vindictive choices of a negative identity represent, of course, a desperate attempt at regaining some mastery in a situation in which the available positive identity elements cancel each other out. The history of such a choice reveals a set of conditions in which it is easier to derive a sense of identity out of a *total* identification with that which one is *least* supposed to be than to struggle for a feeling of reality in acceptable roles which are unattainable with the patient's inner means. . . . At any rate, many a late adolescent, if faced with continuing diffusion, would rather be nobody or somebody bad, or indeed, dead—and this totally, and by free choice—than be not-quite-somebody (1959, p. 132).

Thus there is an inner developmental compulsion to achieve and articulate a sense of identity—even if that identity need be a negative identity. But even that negative identity must be based on the necessary correlates of any acceptable sense of identity. It must be based on the dual elements of need for an enemy which the negative components of the identity complex often express in striking and dramatic terms, but also it needs the sustaining and reinforcing embeddedness in a context of meaningful belonging. Thus the negative identity in our alienated youth often seeks to confirm and support itself by an affiliation to rebellious outgroupings which constitute a counterculture often embracing deviant values and attitudes and defining itself by way of opposition to the prevailing social milieu and cultural context.

Relation to False Self

At this point, it may be useful to relate these considerations regarding a negative identity to what we have already formulated regarding the false self. I would regard the negative identity as one modality of expression of the false self. The false self may cast itself in such deviant and oppositional terms, but need not. In fact, more often than not, the false self shapes itself along the lines of the demands for conformity and submission of expectations. Indeed the negative identity may emerge at critical phases of the individual's developmental experience as a rebellion against and defensive alignment over against such a false self. The retreat from the false self may express itself in forms of psychotic disorganization, as we saw in the case of Bob B., but it may also play itself out in terms of the conflict and tension of opposite tendencies. Thus for Jim, the omnipotent fantasies of powerful exploitation served to counterbalance his underlying convictions of weakness and inadequacy, but the sense of false self that was embedded in both of these contexts did not express the true self potential that was ultimately revealed through the workings of his analysis.

Similarly with Karen, the oppositional dialectic that was set up between her sense of feminine vulnerability and her need to be hyperdefended and aggressively castrating expressed her struggle with the dimensions of her own false self. Her rushing to a polarized form of hyperaggressive defensiveness gave expression to a form of negative identity that served to defend her against the sense of susceptibility and weak vulnerability that inhered in her sense of self—a sense that was essentially false and had to be undone by means of the analytic work. In both cases, when the attachment to the basic introjects was finally resolved through the analysis, the potential for an authentic and maturely operative sense of self was unleashed and was enabled to find its expression.

In discussing the antisocial tendency, Winnicott (1958) has called attention to the essentially redeeming quality of the antisocial behavior, as well as its potentiality for recovery, as a means of effecting a cure of underlying deprivation or defect. From the point of view of our discussion in this study, we can suppose that the same processes which are an expression of the potential for growth and for inner integration of the self, as well as its articulation in a context of relatedness to the environment around it, underlie both the establishment of a true self and its attendant sense of relatedness and belonging, as well as these pathological deviations. Thus the emergence of a false sense of self, as well as the formation of a negative sense of identity, can be seen as direct expressions of the same needs for internal organization and external embeddedness which are basic expressions of the inherent growth potential of the individual psyche.

Context of Relatedness

A point that has been touched on previously, but bears reemphasis at this juncture, is that such deviant expressions of these important processes which contribute to the formation of identity also carry with them the exigency for articulating that sense of identity—however deviant—within a context of belonging and relatedness. This basic contribution to, and sustaining component of, the self finds its expression and its application even in the most deviant forms of paranoid pathology. From this point of view, the formation of the false self is as we have seen partially a response to the implicit demands placed by significant objects surrounding the individual. The false self thus becomes a response to those demands and provides a fulfillment of both the inner needs for coherency and organization of the sense of self and the extrinsically directed needs for affiliation and acceptance. As we have seen, the individual thus constructs a context of belonging within which his false self can remain functional and operative. The most extreme form of this expression is the paranoid delusional system within which the pathologically formed sense of self sustains itself in relation to those objects through the modality of helpless victimization with its reciprocal projective components of persecutory involvement.

Thus the affiliative needs inherent in these mechanisms can find a variety of expressions—either positive or negative—as an expression of the underlying ambivalences. Where the negative aspects predominate, however, as they do in the forms of pathological paranoia and negative identity, it must be seen that the persecutory context or the more muted oppositional contexts of negative identity serve to provide such a matrix of involvement and relatedness. Thus the affiliative need may find an important form of expression—however unsatisfactory and undesirable from other points of view—in the need for an enemy. Thus, in the resolution of such pressures, which are resolved through the formation of a negative identity, it is far more preferable to be related to others as enemies, or to be treated as bad and undesirable, than the more painful and more desperate alternatives of being unrecognized, unrelated, uninvolved—a nobody or even a not-quite-somebody.

ALIENATION

One of the interesting spin-offs of this consideration is the role that these processes play in the antisocial tendencies that express themselves in delinquency or criminal tendencies and in the more general phenomenon of alienation. Delinquency is in effect a form of negative identity which sets itself over against the standards and expectations of the society at large and responds to the social pressures involved by criminal or delinquent forms of acting-out. Thus it seems to me that delinquent behavior must be set in the larger context of the alienation that takes place between the emerging younger generation and the older and more established segments of the society within which the younger generation seeks to establish and integrate itself. The delinquent becomes identified through his antisocial acting-out, but his turning to a negative identity and his rebellion against social mores is only one form of less-than-optimal resolution of a larger and more significant question that relates to the issue of alienation.

Conflict over Values

A central element of the alienation syndrome is the rejection of, or the conflict over, social values. The alienation syndrome, as we have already noted, lies at the interface between the person and social processes. The feature raises a problem in differential diagnosis. Psychiatrists have tended to see the clinical manifestations of the alienation syndrome more in terms of the parameters of inner psychic dysfunction and less in terms of the social parameters. Thus the alienation syndrome is usually described in terms of some form of character pathology, or in terms of its narcissistic aspects, or in terms of its depressive aspects.

But the associated estrangement reflects a more basic rejection of values which the society embodies and implicitly requires that they accept. Their rejection of these values may leave them in a relatively valueless vacuum, or they may actively foster divergent values which they oppose to those prevailing in the culture around them. Or there may arise an inner conflict between partially accepted values of the general culture and partially accepted values of a divergent nature. The alienation syndrome adds specifically to those other well-known clinical pictures the aspect of value conflict and a tendency to reject the accepted cultural value system of one's own society.

The rebellious expression of the alienation syndrome is characterized by the formulation or acceptance of a divergent set of values. Often this takes place in conjunction with a group of like-minded individuals who can share the same set of deviant values. It should be noted that the term "deviant" in this context does not have the connotation of better or worse, but simply emphasizes that the values of the subgroup stand somehow in opposition to the general culture. Such value-oriented subgroupings are alienated from the larger social group, but may be quite unified within themselves. This allows the alienated individual to achieve a compensatory sense of belonging. This compensatory aspect of group formation is a significant part of the motivation behind adolescent gangs and the youth movement in general. The value deviance can be focused and expressed in almost any aspect of behavior—clothing, hairstyles, sexual mores, languages, expression of values, attitudes, beliefs, etc.

The important dimension of this value divergence is not so much the formation of new and constructive and meaningful values; but the emphasis in the alienation syndrome falls on the rejection, and, in the rebellious extreme, the overthrow of preexisting values. Divergent alienated groups seize on any ideology or any formulation of divergent attitudes to express their rejection. Often in the service of frustrated and impotent rage, the objective seems to be to find the most extreme form of articulation of values that might fly in the face of prevailing social values. Thus rebellious groups spout the most extreme Socialist and Communist rhetoric: the thoughts of Chairman Mao are preferred in many quarters. There is also a need to question and challenge and confront social institutions and practices on all levels.

One of the basic questions I wish to raise in this discussion is concerned with the formation of divergent values. The capacity to reformulate and revitalize values is essential to the continuing flexibility, strength, and vitality of any social system. The formation of divergent or deviant values can have a constructive impact on the social system, or it can have a decidedly destructive impact. Thus there is an inherent ambiguity about alienation. Is it an expression of psychopathology, or does it carry the potential for growth and revitalization of social values? Are the elements of the alienation syndrome, as I have described them, a form of pathological failure to mature, or the product of inner conflicts; or are they a necessary by-product of a dialectic of deviance and revolt that the reformulation of social values requires? It is not so easy to disentangle these elements. They may be closely intertwined and one has to examine each individual case carefully in order to gain some approach to resolution. The extremes of rebellious alienation are rarely met. Rarely does one see the naked wish to overthrow and destroy, without an accompanying ideology and a wish to replace what is rejected by something better. The dimensions of this dramatic struggle between the potential for the emergence of new values and the potential for revolutionary destructiveness was displayed quite clearly in Fred's inner conflict.

Adolescent Alienation

Alienation is a frequent and familiar part of the picture presented by adolescents in our culture. Adolescence is a developmental period of regressive disorganization hopefully followed by a progressive reorganization of the personality. This developmental progression allows the child to pass through the physical and inner psychic changes that are required for him to begin to approach his definitive role and position in adult society. But the adolescent is not really a part of that society; he is only potentially a part. He will only be able to integrate himself with the adult by forming himself to fit adult roles and by demonstrating to the adult community that he is ready and capable of fulfilling them. Only then can the adult community recognize and receive him. During the period of adolescent development, however, he remains outside looking in. There is a sense of estrangement which is embedded in the adolescent experience in our culture (Berman, 1970). It is an expression of what I have already described as "adolescent paranoia."

Helene Deutsch (1967) has pointed out the frequency of depressive affects in many adolescents. For many adolescents, the period is a traumatic one in their lives. They are confronted by the demands of reality, by performance standards, by adult competition for positions, awards, etc., which is often intense, and by an increasing realization of their own limitations. A crucial aspect of the child's capacity to adapt is related to the issue of narcissism. Promising children often come to the adolescent challenge with narcissistic dreams of accomplishment and glory, dreams that may have been fostered and prolonged by their parents, most often mother. Thus the infantile narcissism with its dreams and expectations and sense of entitlement is often prolonged into adolescence, and the inevitable disappointment becomes traumatic. An increase of narcissism is quite characteristic of adolescence anyway, but these particularly narcissistic adolescents were raised in an atmosphere of expectation generated by their mothers' excessive investment in them, in the hope that they would one day compensate for the mothers' own sense of disappointment and frustration.

To this basically narcissistic picture, alienated adolescents show an added feature. The narcissistic investment from the mother tends to undermine the position of the father as a model for identification. The mother's disappointment is often intensified and magnified by the failure of the father to measure up to her standards. The father is thus devalued. The child who is caught up in this process must therefore devalue the father in order to share the mother's dream and to gain her approval. He, too, devalues and rejects the father, and this devaluation is intensified during the adolescent period. The father is seen as weak, debased, worthless, insignificant, inconsequential. At a deeper level, the adolescent boy's resentment against the father is often due to the fact that the father was too weak to protect him from an often ambivalent dependency on his mother, as well as from an incestuous involvement with her. This underlying devaluation of the father often erupts in adolescence, even though it may have been there since earliest childhood. It becomes extended to the entire world of adults, including their standards and institutions. The adolescent rage against society and its values and its institutions can be rooted in a rage against the devalued father and all he stands for.

Thus the adolescent boy stands on the threshold of a world of adult standards and expectations. But it is his father's world. The devaluation of the father and the struggle against identification with the father leads to a rejection of all social commitments, all social values, all conventional roles, all responsibilities, and many of the forms of emotional relatedness with others that form the normal fabric of society. A similar problem confronts the adolescent girl. If she idealizes her father excessively, she runs the risk of devaluing and despising her mother, with an intensification of her penis envy and an impairment of a meaningful and constructive identification with her mother. She thus tends to reject and rebel against any conventional forms of feminine role or status, and strives for more masculine competitiveness and forms of accomplishment. The rebellious expression of these aspects is eloquently expressed in some of the Women's Lib phenomena.

Adaptive Alienation

It is useful to realize that in large measure the process of alienation may serve some important developmental functions. One of the questions that the apparent increase in manifest alienation raises is the extent to which social and cultural conditions require that the forms of alienation take the patterns of expression that they do. Alienation is a feature of all adolescent development, but the reorganization of inner structures, defenses, values, and patterns of identification can be pressured into maladaptive and even pathological molds. This developmental perspective is expressed by Berman in the following terms:

> The process of identification facilitates adaptation during childhood. Its characteristics will determine how the adolescent will cope with change. When adolescence is reached, childhood identifications must undergo radical revision because of the strength of the sexual drive and the need to master it. Alienation is a mental process serving to achieve this necessary physical and psychic distance from parents and society. It is a defense against painful ideas and affects associated with the disruption of cathexis to the past relationships. The process also supports the establishment of genital primacy, new object relations, and a firm sense of self (1970, p. 250).

In the normal course of things, such adaptive alienation is not extreme and is resolved into new and functional adult patterns of identification and role-functioning. The extremes of alienation, however, distort the growth process and make adaptive resolutions less possible and more precarious.

Deutsch (1967) has noted that many of these alienated adolescents come from upper-middle-class families. The idealized world of academic or professional success is often held up to children in such families, but it is in the form of the idealized accomplishments of the parents' dream. The alienated adolescent rejects and protests specifically against that world. To realize the dream, to achieve success, to join the establishment, is to become like his parents, to embrace and endorse what he feels he must reject and devalue. The alienated adolescent thus becomes a paradox of our society—often brilliant, talented, sensitive, perceptive, and imaginative, but also emotionally empty, isolated, lonely, and estranged.

Such feelings can be seen in their more flamboyant and extreme forms in many public expressions, but they are also the common coin of many apparently well-adjusted and well-functioning adolescents. Feelings of loneliness and isolation are endemic among adolescents. The more narcissistic adolescent may seek others out in order to gain their admiration—the alienated adolescent prefers to isolate himself and often rejects attempts to interfere with his isolation. Many adolescents seek relief from these feelings in group activities. Participation in such activities is motivated by a need for group acceptance and approval—so-called "peer-group pressures." Pot-smoking has this quality almost universally; it is a minor form of escape, but it also has the connotations of sharing a group experience and gaining transient relief from the intolerable feelings of loneliness. It also symbolizes a shared antiestablishment, anticultural position—a rejection of what the adult world holds up as a standard of acceptability.

Alienation and Violence

The problem and the paradox of alienation are acutely focused in the use of social protest and frankly revolutionary violence. Revolution and the use of violence in the service of revolution are obviously nothing new, but it has taken on new social implications in our own time. The threat of violence has become a familiar refrain from all sorts of disaffected and dissatisfied subcultural groups. We hear it from student revolutionaries and radicals, from black radicals and militants, and even from Women's Lib extremists.

The first important consideration is that we live in a culture that sanctions violence as a means of conflict resolution. We approve of some forms of violence and disapprove of others. Our best heroes are those who are the toughest and who are capable of the greatest violence. Of course, we rationalize the violence of our heroes; they are violent only in the service of justice and the protection of the weak and innocent. As a nation, we use a similar rationale for our participation in the paroxysms of violence and destruction that are the staples of war. The violence of the enemy is evil and without justice, while our own violence is found to be just and good. The psychology of legitimate violence requires our being able to attribute to the bad guys or the enemy evil intentions and motives. Because they are violent, we are forced to be violent also, and because their violence is evil, our violence must be good. The inevitable conclusion is that if I can find a justification, if I can convince myself that what I oppose is unjust or evil, I am thereby justified in using violence to destroy it. This is precisely the rhetoric and the rationale of the use of violence among student radicals and black militants.

We must be clear about the role of protest and dissent in social processes. The process of dissent, protest, challenge, and innovation is an essential part of human progress at all levels. It is an essential aspect of individual human psychological development, it is inherent in many forms of intellectual and scientific progress, and it is a necessary channel by which social structures correct intrinsic defects and adapt to changing conditions of social life. The principle of dissent is an essential part of the democratic process politically. The democratic principle is based not only on the right of the minority to have a point of view different from that of the majority, but it includes both the freedom and the political necessity that the minority make an effort to persuade the majority to accept its point of view. There are two important elements necessary to preserve this basic aspect of the democratic process. There must be the willingness and the courage on the part of those who dissent to express their view and to persuade others to accept it. It is also necessary, however, that the majority make it possible for the minority to express its view and that they safeguard the means by which effective dissent can be expressed. Both the minority and the majority have an interest in the expression and effective channeling of dissent.

CHAPTER 27

Family Processes
in the Genesis of Paranoid Ideation

Paranoia in the Family

There are several preliminary comments that can be made in turning to a consideration of family interaction in the genesis of paranoia. The first is that we are turning to a somewhat different level of analysis. Up to this point, we have been focusing on primarily intrapsychic and interpersonal factors to illumine the developmental process that lies behind paranoid processes. We are now turning to a level of intrafamilial analysis which is more social in focus than interpersonal. The emphasis on group processes and interactions, however, does not prescind from complex interpersonal processes and from the intrapsychic implications and impacts of group interactions. The processes at each level are mutually responsive to processes at other levels, but it is important to recognize that analysis of family group processes contributes a distinctly different dimension to our understanding.

It was Sullivan (1956) who pointed out that the tendency to use transference of blame, which he regarded as the core of the paranoid process, was closely related to the degree to which paranoid attitudes and techniques had been current and accepted in the home environment. But he noted that even in families where paranoid activity was prominent, the impact on the child could be mitigated by the presence of someone in the family who calmly and reasonably questioned such projective maneuvers. Such an influence can have beneficial preventive effects on the absorption of morbidity. Other mitigating influences on the morbid impact of a paranoid parent can exercise significant effect. The presence of siblings can serve to alter the impact of the paranoid process. In one family in our experience, the oldest daughter was affected by the paranoid process in the family in such a way as to provide a protective and preventive influence for the second daughter who was not affected. A third daughter, however, in the same family was also affected by the family pathology (Meissner, 1970e). Sullivan also points out that extrafamilial experiences can have a corrective effect on the intrafamilial process and serve to modify the tendency to transfer blame. Extrafamilial experiences, however, can reinforce pathological patterns acquired in the family.

Influences on Self-esteem and Autonomy

We have pointed out that influences which undercut the child's sense of self-esteem and autonomy are closely related to the genesis of paranoia. Allport (1958) reviewed studies of the development of prejudice which, as we have seen, is a subvariant of the paranoid process. He concluded that the manner of a child's upbringing had a significant impact on the development of prejudice. Mothers of prejudiced children far more frequently express authoritarian and repressive attitudes, emphasizing the importance of obedience, compliance to parental demands, and repression of the child's spontaneous activity. Such mothers are more likely to punish the child for masturbation, while mothers of unprejudiced children tend to ignore it. The family atmosphere is suppressive, harsh, and critical. The parent's word is law.

Allport concludes that the effect on the child is to put him on guard against his own impulses. Because of them he suffers both punishment and withdrawal of love—leaving him alone, exposed, and desolate. The child learns that the parents have the power to withhold love so that their power and will become decisive influences on him. The balance in his object-relations is shifted to a base in power and authority and away from trust and tolerance. The child comes to mistrust his own inner impulses, to mistrust himself and the evil in him, and by projection to fear the evil impulses in others. The world becomes threatening and not to be trusted. The incidence of prejudicial attitudes is related to rejective, neglectful, or inconsistent styles of training. Family backgrounds marked by quarreling, violence, or divorce are frequent. Rejection of the child by one or both parents is the rule. Anti-Semitic attitudes, for example, are not taught specifically by parents but seem to be taken in by the child from the infected family atmosphere (Allport, 1958).

Conversely, tolerant children seem to come from homes in which there is a calm and permissive atmosphere. They feel welcome, accepted and loved, whether they are good or bad. Punishment is neither harsh nor inconsistent, so that the child does not have to be constantly on guard against evil impulses. Strategies of control using threat are relatively missing, so that the atmosphere which surrounds the child is one of security and acceptance. Consequently, the child is better able to accept himself and his impulses and to maintain a sense of his own value. Self-esteem is a by-product of parental acceptance and comfort with the child's impulsiveness and spontaneous expression of feelings. Since the parents do not feel the need to repress and control the child, the issues of his upbringing are not power or obedience rigidly enforced. There is room for the child to develop a sense of self-control without shame or doubt, and the sense of autonomy can follow its normal developmental course.

While these issues of power-relations, control, and autonomy are often writ large in families of paranoid patients, the same issues can also be brought to bear in subtle and insidious ways that can only be illumined by careful examination of the patterns of interaction in families. This makes the problem all the more difficult to analyze and to treat. It is interesting, for example, that the series of family studies offered by Laing and Esterson (1964) contains material from eleven families—and ten of these show clearcut patterns of paranoid dynamics. Here again even though the diagnostic focus is on schizophrenia, the mechanisms at work seem to be relevant to the paranoid process in the family. In each of these families, mechanisms are at work constantly to undercut, devalue, and repress the autonomous functioning and independence of the affected member. Laing (1965) identifies the process as "mystification," by which he means the process by which the family interaction confuses, befuddles and masks the real nature of whatever is the real issue in the family negotiation. Similar phenomena have been described in terms of double-binds (Bateson et al., 1956) or pseudomutuality (Wynne et al., 1958). All of these mechanisms have the effect of confusing and muddling thought processes and limiting the capacity for those caught up in them to adequately test reality. Their influence is therefore growth inhibiting. But I would like to emphasize that in addition, or perhaps correlatively, they serve very effectively to inhibit the differentiation between the child's emerging self and the parents' selves. There is a tendency for symbiotic modes of interaction in which repressed impulses are communicated and shared so that the child participates in the parents' anxiety over issues of control and the feeling of threat and destructive evil that becomes attached to such impulses. The mechanisms of dealing with such problems operate to effectively convince the child of his inner evilness and lack of worth and impair his growth to autonomous independence and self-government.

Such patterns of interaction apparently reach across cultural boundaries. Tseng (1969) has recently reported a Taiwan family in which eight members of the family were involved in a paranoid delusional system—a striking case of folie à famille. The family atmosphere was characterized by frequent conflicts, inhibition of anger and an inability to express angry feelings, a constant tendency for family members to blame others within and without the family as responsible for their difficulties, rigidity, argumentativeness, lack of insight, self-assertiveness and a marked fondness for preaching to others in a relentless attempt to persuade or convince them to change their perceptions. The father used what is described as a "brainwashing" technique to break down his son's resistance to the psychosis. This terribly sick and disruptively fragmented family achieved an increased sense of cohesiveness from their sharing in the delusional system. These same

mechanisms of blaming and relentless convincing we have also seen in some
of our clinical cases, although often the process is neither so blatant nor so
generally effective as in the Taiwan family.

An interesting cross-cultural study was reported several years ago by
Hitson and Funkenstein (1959). They studied the relationships between
types of family patterns, types of personality disposition, and types of mental illness in two divergent social structures. They studied differences in
depressed and paranoid patients in Boston and Burma. In Boston, they
found that the dominant parent (usually the father) of the depressed patient
tended to put responsibility on the child and punished him because he
"ought" to have done something or known what was expected of him. But
in paranoid families, there was no "ought." The child was expected simply
to follow the often inconsistent rules laid down by the dominant parent
without question or complaint. They conclude that depressed patients learn
the moral imperative early in life, but that the paranoid as a child learns to
protect himself from a hostile and unpredictable environment by denying
his own responsibility and throwing the blame elsewhere. In Burma, similarly, fathers are dominant and children submissive, but "ought" is not involved. Misbehavior is justified on the grounds that children are not responsible. Correlatively, the Burmese show a strong paranoid cast and tend to
see their environment as potentially harmful. Paranoid forms of illness
predominate over depressive and there is a high homicidal rate. This kind of
information is consistent with our previous conclusions regarding paranoid
and depressive states. But it becomes apparent that patterns of child-rearing
and family interaction can have significant influences on the development of
these states.

Social Interaction

Our analysis is focusing on the family as the unit of organization and
action. We can view the family in terms of group processes and structures,
rather than in terms of the interactions between individual persons. While
we can speak of patterns of interaction within the family, we should keep in
mind that the processes we are dealing with at this level are properly
processes of the family itself. The family can be viewed as a system of social
interaction. Processes go on in the family which determine the roles and
functions which each participating individual assumes. One of the important processes which organize the definition of the family situation and the
individual's place in it is what Goffman (1969) calls collusion. The family
can form "collusive nets" or "collusive alignments," a coalition between
two or more persons which is aimed at control of another person by
manipulation of his definition of the situation. The collusion involves a certain hiddenness of communication which keeps the excolluded person in an
unstable position. If the colluders were to reveal what they know and sus-

pend their management of the situation, the excolluded person's definition of the situation would be discredited. If, in addition, he were to discover the collusion, his relationship to both parties would be undercut. Collusions are a normal part of social interaction and often are carried on in subtly implicit and unconscious ways.

Such collusive definitions are important aspects of the individual's participation in the system. Virtual definitions are attributed to the individual by the conduct and expectations of other agents. There is also a definition of the individual which he himself enacts, and in some sense the external and internal definitions are mutually related and influencing. One defines the person in terms of his external influence and the response of others in the social system to him. The other defines the person in terms of his perception of himself and his projection of his self from within. The interaction between them defines his personality or character. As Goffman puts it:

> The individual stakes out a self, comments on his having done so, and comments on his commenting, even while the others are taking the whole process into consideration in coming to their assessment of him, which considerations he then takes into consideration in revising his view of himself (1969, p. 361).

The complex process by which an individual defines himself, even as the social system defines personal place and function, has to do with rules of conduct by which activities are allocated to individuals and are accepted by him as obligations or expectations. Thus the individual comes to make assumptions about himself which are correlative to his socialization in the group. By his behavior and social interaction the individual communicates these inner assumptions, thereby confirming or disconfirming their expectations and notifying them that he may or may not acknowledge and accept the place they have defined for him.

Social Control

Thus the individual's socialization and participation in group processes involve him in systems of social control. Insofar as the individual internalizes social codes and normative standards, he comes to accept them as right and develops a sense of obligation to observe and support them. Failure to do so provokes remorse and guilt and sets in operation reparative mechanisms which reinstitute the norms as valued and himself as one who respects and observes them. This is a form of social control which is personal and entirely internal. Social control may be exercised in more external and formal ways, however, by agents designated by the society for such purposes: police, courts, prisons, etc. Social systems also exercise control by corrective feedback which in less formal and more continuous ways lets the individual know that he is getting out of line and that persistence in his behavior will meet with disapproval or deprivation. One of the most effective forms of informal control is withdrawal from dealings with the offender. But social controls, of whatever kind, may not be effective. Negative sanctions and deprivations may serve only to further alienate the deviant and commit him further to the offensive course. The offender cannot be effectively outlawed nor isolated; he remains as a source of offense and outrage in the system.

The relation between processes of social exclusion and paranoid symptoms was studied by Lemert (1962) in patients whose difficulties seemed to arise in the job situation. Each case seemed to have suffered a severe loss or threat of loss which could not be compensated. The individual responds by declining to exercise inner personal control and by resisting the informal control attempted by others. He begins to intrude on subordinates and makes improper demands. He breaks the pattern of communication with equals, leaving them uncertain and insecure in their relations with him. He becomes insulting and arrogant and fails to show the expected tact and consideration for others. He assumes informal privileges which are marks of status that do not belong to him. His behavior becomes disruptive for his associates, undermining their sense of consensus regarding the definition and allotment of each one's social place. These concerns, after all, are important in that they determine patterns of work activity and contribute to each individual's assumptions about himself.

The offender's co-workers respond by excluding mechanisms, avoiding him physically and excluding him from joint decision processes and activities. In face-to-face interaction they employ a humoring, pacifying, and noncommital style which damps the interaction but tries to give minimal cause for complaint. To cope with his disruptive maneuvers, they might spy on him in subtle ways, or share their reactions to his most recent move behind his back as it were, and in general reinforce the special solidarity that has formed around their response to his disruption. In his exclusion, the offender is deprived of corrective feedback and may find it necessary to reach violent levels to break through the wall that has been built around him. The others have formed a collusive net which defines the offender as deviant. Tact and secrecy, utilized in the interest of preserving social structure, can form the basis of a real excluding community which provides a counterpart of the paranoid community. The individual's disruptive reaction to loss can lead to a failure of control mechanisms which operate to exclude the patient and set the conditions for a paranoid response. The disruptive effect continues until the patient is hospitalized or until his reputation becomes established so that no one takes him seriously. This latter form of encapsulation is frequent in large organizations with the result that the system is redefined, the patient is effectively excluded and his disruptive effect neutralized, and his pathology is sustained.

Belonging and the Definition of Self

The complex interplay of assumptions about oneself and others and the expectations of oneself and others takes place in families and forms a critical aspect of their inner life. The perduring character or personality of any one of the family members is seen in terms of his or her typical style of participation in and support for family patterns of activity and family relationships—his acknowledgement and acceptance of his place in the family (Goffman, 1969). Any change in this pattern is identified as a change in character. Any change in the pattern of interaction and response changes the inner homeostasis within the family system. The quiet disorders—the depressions and withdrawals—disturb the inner functioning of the family, but the family can often effectively conceal these disorders and carry on its external functioning more or less conventionally. But the development of paranoid delusions and grandiosity can have severely disruptive effects on family functioning. Paranoia, along with mania, forms a radical disavowal of the patient's place within the family relationships. The efforts of others, so often seen in families of paranoids, to argue with the patient, to disprove his suspicions and paranoid convictions, to bring him back to reason and his behavior back to reasonable limits are ways in which the family responds to the estrangement from their expectations and tries to bring the patient back into his appropriate place.

These patterns and their mutual adjustment are of the utmost importance, since they are not only involved in responses to deviant behavior in one of the family members, but they are also involved in determining the preparanoid's place and position within the family. Goffman (1969) refers to the self as a code that makes sense out of almost all the individual's activities and provides a basis for giving them meaning. The code is read by interpreting his place in socially organized activity as expressed in his behavior. When the individual fails to express a workable definition of himself and his place, one that others in the same system can accord him, this becomes threatening to them. Their own selves are organized in part in response to him and the definitions and assumptions he gives them. He changes and becomes a stranger to them, and their own definitions of themselves are put in jeopardy. Collusive mechanisms come into play which only feed the paranoid's suspicions and reinforce his conviction of a secret plot against him. Subtle patterns of excollusion evolve which may end in the patient's separation from the family and his hospitalization. The family finds a new place for the deviant member and appoints him to the status of "patient" or the position of sickness. The family must achieve this clarification, and even to gain from the patient an admission of his sickness and patienthood, in order to reassure themselves that their assumptions and definition of the situation have been above reproach.

It is important to realize that such mechanisms of social organization are at work in all families and that they define a place for each individual in which his own inner definition of self corresponds. The family, in a sense, provides the preparanoid with a place and definition of himself against which he is regarded as and feels himself to be inadequate, without rights or privilege, not counting in any meaningful or real sense, not being able to measure up to the expectations of those around him, not having a sense of his own valuedness in the eyes of others or of his own inner value. An integral part of this process of self-definition and promulgation of assumptions about others is a pattern of style of family interaction which influences the individual styles of response and reaction of family members. The family in that sense shapes the pattern of responsiveness by which individuals learn to adapt to a variety of pressures within the family and to respond to sources of stimuli and to moderate elicited anxiety. It has frequently been noted that paranoid patients show traits and attitudes that are shared by other supposedly nonparanoid members of their families. Will (1961a) had noted such peculiarities in his paranoid patient which seemed to reflect aspects of the patient's family culture. The entire family, including the parents and several siblings, seemed to share attitudes of suspiciousness, competitiveness, feelings of social inadequacy and estrangement, envy, jealousy, and a general expectation of mistreatment at the hands of others.

One of the important dimensions of the interaction within families are the patterns and strategies of control that members exercise on each other. These processes have been rather intensively studied by Mishler and Waxler (1968). They have found that normal families use a variety of person- and attention-control strategies and that these strategies are more likely to be used even by the low-status members, i.e., children, than they are in schizophrenic families. This is true even though the distribution of power and authority in normal families is relatively clear-cut. In schizophrenic families, however, the distribution of power deviates from normative role prescriptions (mother-father, parents-children), and the exercise of power through control strategies becomes impersonal and indirect. Moreover, the significant differences between the patterns of exercising control seem to show up most acutely in situations in which the patient is present. This suggests that the issues of power and control, who has it, who exercises it, and who submits to it, are particularly mobilized by the interaction which is set up around the patient. There is good evidence to suggest that such strategies have a growth-inhibiting potential which is related to schizophrenic development. But it may also be that the same strategies may set a pattern of influencing others which contributes to the development of a paranoid style in the family and, correlatively, in the preparanoid family member. One of the basic elements of the paranoid constellation is the dual conviction that others can exercise control over oneself and that oneself has no control or rights of control over the others.

Introjection and Projection

One of the basic insights that has derived from the intensive study of families is that in the course of development individuals internalize something from the family structure. This has been conceptualized as internalization of a family-role structure or superego. Certain aspects of the transactional networks in families can be introjected and thus contribute to the organization and functioning of the individual personality. The issue of autonomy, which is so crucial in many ways to the understanding of paranoid dynamics, cannot be divorced from homeostatic balancing of autonomous functioning within the family system. The observation of an increase in autonomous functioning in one family member being paralleled by a decrease in autonomous functioning in one or another family member is commonplace. When the "sick" member improves, decompensation and pathology may break out elsewhere in the family. It is as though the autonomous functioning of some family members can be sustained only in terms of the nonautonomous functioning of others. Moreover, unconscious, if not conscious, efforts are brought to bear to keep the nonautonomous members in that place and position. One is reminded of Harold Searles' (1965) observations and analysis of what he calls the effort to drive the other person crazy. The effort is often motivated unconsciously by the inner need of the one driving to preserve his own precarious self-esteem and autonomy.

Another pattern that is closely related to the balance of autonomy is the tendency for families to assign good and bad roles. This is the well-known mechanism of scapegoating (Vogel and Bell, 1967). It is usually accompanied by a complementary idealization of other family members. The process brings mechanisms of projection and introjection into play. Fantasies become shared and mutually reinforcing. Family transactions become rigidly fixed in terms of these assigned roles and the affected members are deprived of all flexibility or initiative. The member who is assigned the bad role (scapegoat) is deprived of any opportunity to test out or clarify his position or to assert himself in appropriately aggressive or autonomous ways. It should be emphasized that it is not only the external relationships and interactions that undermine the affected member, but that aspects of the family structure are introjected and thus oppose any autonomous tendency from within (Boszormenyi-Nagy, 1965).

We have only begun to realize that the inner psychological reality of families has to do with the complex interplay of projections and introjections. To the extent that family members are caught up in the emotional matrix of the family (Meissner, 1964, 1970e), they are involved in the process of projection and introjection, they contribute to the projective elaborations which play upon all the involved family members and they internalize the projective matrix that is set up and sustained by the family interaction. What is introjected, and thereby becomes part of the inner world of each member, is the complex of interpersonal projections and introjections—the stuff of psychoanalytic personality formation which is based on and derived from object-relations. That does not exhaust the introjective context of the family, even if one takes into account all of the family members, including siblings. There is a sense in which the family system, taken as a whole, is introjected, with its patterns of emotional expressivity, codes, rules of interpretation, cognitive and expressive styles, patterns of organization of experience and handling of anxiety (Framo, 1965). Bowen (1965) has employed the term "family projection process" to describe the process by which the family arrives at a family projection which can then be put on a member. The affected member can then accept the projection by introjection, and thus verifies the projection. He describes three steps in the process: in the process of projecting the sick role on one family member, for example, the process involves (1) thinking of the member as sick, (2) diagnosing the member and designating him as "patient," and (3) treating the patient as a sick person. The process is complementary to the previously described patterns of family interaction involving family assumptions and definition of self. The family projective process, however, brings into play unconscious and repressed aspects of family functioning which derive specifically from the inner world. The contents of parental projections, which have the major determinative force, derive from their respective introjective patterns gained from their own families of origin.

The child, then, during the course of his development, is reacted to in large measure in terms of the parental projections. He becomes, in a sense, a projective reincarnation of the ghosts of the past—the introjects that derive from the parents' own childhood. As a consequence, he is called on to fulfill certain rigidly projected roles which leave little room for him to grow up in the experience of himself as a unique human individual or as experiencing the sense of change that goes with the process of development. The child is left in a psychological vacuum without appropriate objects with which he can relate and through which he can gain some sense of homeostatic control over inner impulses. The parents hate his projected identity and fear his developing self, so that he too comes to hate and fear his own inner self along with the magical powers that his parents ascribe to him and which he neither understands nor feels are within his capacity to control. He becomes convinced that he is the malevolent cause of the misfortunes and suffering that befall the family and is the responsible agent. The rest of the family may unconsciously reinforce this conviction by a variety of conscious and unconscious blaming and scapegoating mechanisms (Searles, 1965).

Family Projective System

The invasiveness of such parents is a major factor in the developmental experience of the preparanoid parent. While one can often denominate such invasive or controlling parents, the mechanisms are often more subtle and have to do more with the projective system in the family. The entire family may be involved in unconsciously shaping the projective system and in directing it to the preparanoid member. The unconscious processes are paralleled and bridged into family interaction by collusive nets and alignments which define a place or position for the preparanoid member. The process is completed by his introjection of the projective assumptions and acceptance of the defined place in the family. He comes to regard the introjected content and the place affiliated with it as defining his own self, and he comes to experience himself in these terms. It only remains that he complete the picture by enacting these presumptions and completing the feedback to the family which will verify their projections and assumptions. Thus the growing child is prevented from coming to know any genuine reality either outside himself or within himself. The "reality" he does come to know and to hate is the reality derived from the pathogenic projective process with the family, the symbiosis-derived pseudo-reality of the family projective system.

The impact of this pattern of family interaction is considerable. The interplay of projection and introjection fixes him in an unfortunate position in which the opportunities for growth and change are minimized. He comes to accept his appointed place and feels himself to be valueless, deficient, unlovable and unloved, working good to no one, not even himself. Moreover, if he makes attempts to break out of this system or to advance to some level of greater autonomy or individuation, this is regarded as an attack by the rest of the family. They must resist any such change vigorously and convince the "deviant" member of the evil of his ways. He can only break out of this bind by open rebellion if he is capable of that, or by the more pathological alternatives of denial and the paranoid construction. It is of importance that we keep in mind that the family communicates more to the preparanoid than a definition of place and self. There is additionally and implicitly a style of enacting and reacting, styles of communicating and organizing attention and meaning, and overall patterns of family structure by which anxiety-provoking feelings and events are managed (Morris and Wynne, 1965). The stimulating studies of Wynne and Singer (1963a, b) have shown that projective test material of schizophrenic patients reflects certain patterns of thought organization that can be related to patterns of family interaction.

Two general patterns of family relatedness that Wynne has described are pseudomutuality (Wynne et al., 1958) and pseudohostility (Wynne, 1961). These are both forms of family organization which enable the family group to ward off threatening or anxiety-producing experiences when the individual coping mechanisms and defenses of the family members have failed. Pseudomutuality is often seen in the families of schizophrenics. It is a mode of relatedness which insists on a superficial harmony and accord as shared efforts to mask the underlying feelings of emptiness, meaningfulness and frustration, fears of rejection, loneliness, hostility and murderous rage—all common currency in schizophrenic families. These feelings are denied or only vaguely perceived by reason of a pseudomutual collusive denial of their reality. Similarly pseudohostility maintains a surface interaction of strife and hatred which is directed to warding off the anxiety and expected humiliation that would result from expression of positive effects of tenderness and intimacy. Pseudohostility is often related to paranoid styles of interaction. One is reminded of Searles' (1965) emphasis on the role of repressed positive effects in the relationship between the schizophrenic and his parents.

Paranoid Style
We have tried to bring into focus some of the aspects of family functioning which have a bearing on the genesis of paranoia. Many of these mechanisms and patterns of interaction can be seen at their intensive best in schizophrenic families, but they also operate, often in more subtle and more modulated ways, in families in which the level of pathology is considerably less. At more pathological levels, these mechanisms can have disastrous consequences for the ego-development of the affected family members. But at less pathological levels, the consequences may be spelled out less in terms of deficits in growth potential and more in terms of styles of interaction and functioning. The paranoid style, therefore, can persist in the family structure without the emergence of frank clinical paranoia. There may be little more than an atmosphere of guardedness and suspicion which serves to more or less isolate the family and its members but which does not interfere with their capacity to function adequately in their life context.

The paranoid style may in fact be expressed in ways which are more or less socially acceptable. Patterns of jealousy, envy, or prejudice are by and large generated within the family. As Allport (1958) remarked, prejudice is not *taught* by parents to the child, it is *caught* by the child from an atmosphere of prejudice in the family. But such paranoid aspects of family and individual functioning are well within the limits of acceptable and normal behavior. No one regards prejudice as pathological although it embodies many aspects of the paranoid style. Even further, paranoid elements can be displayed in the organization of belief systems, as we have suggested. The paranoid style within the family may be expressed in a form of religious conviction which may vary from intense and hate-filled bigotry to more or less rigid religious adherence. It is to this kind of stylistic expression and its dynamic underpinnings—within which the crucial intrapsychic mechanisms of projection and introjection are at work—that we must look for a better understanding of how paranoid responsiveness is generated. In this light, it is not difficult to see that a conjunction of influences may impinge upon the child in a family context which gives every appearance of reasonable and even successful adjustment, but which has the twofold effect of undermining his inner sense of security, worth and autonomy, and shaping his patterns of responsiveness—whether cognitive or affective or defensive—into a style of functioning which under the appropriate precipitating conditions may express itself in a clinically paranoid form.

CHAPTER 28

The Paranoid Process in Adaptation

ADAPTIVE ASPECTS OF THE PARANOID PROCESS

General Hypothesis

Our discussion to this point has led us through a consideration of the pathology of paranoid states to an examination of the paranoid process itself. We have seen that not only does the paranoid process function in specific aspects of defense, but that it plays an essential and critical role in the workings of the developmental process itself. In the course of our journey, the appreciation of the more positive and constructive contributions that the mechanisms of the paranoid process make to the building up and sustaining of the human personality and its functions has grown apace. At this point we can move our considerations to a new level. We can shift to an explicit consideration of the more adaptive functions of the paranoid process, particularly emphasizing the role that they play in the broader reaches of human social and cultural experience.

The general hypothesis that I am proposing here is that when we examine the clinical manifestations of the paranoid process—that is, in their specifically pathological forms which make a presentation at the clinical level—we are seeing what is essentially the tip of the paranoid iceberg. As we have seen clearly in our examination of a substantial spectrum of clinical cases, we can find identifiable paranoid mechanisms operating in a broad spectrum of psychopathologies. Further reflection, however, makes it obvious that the pathologically distorting operation of these same mechanisms is identifiable in broad segments of the population, manifested as we have already discussed in more commonly evidenced clinical states of envy, jealousy, prejudice, etc. Quite obviously large segments of the population are afflicted with such basically paranoid attitudes without ever coming to clinical attention. In fact, our social fabric is such that we entertain a high degree of tolerance of such attitudes without feeling it necessary to regard them or react to them as forms of pathology.

However, further reflection on the nature and operation of the paranoid mechanisms yields a further realization. We have found, for example, that these same mechanisms can have a significant role to play in the normal workings of the developmental progression that can lead in the direction of the forming and sustaining of a healthy and productive sense of identity. Thus the paranoid iceberg is definable not merely in terms of realms of identifiable pathology which remains socially acceptable and is generally regarded as nonclinical, but also has relevance to wide areas of not merely socially acceptable, but constructive and adaptive processes that serve to sustain the functioning of human personality on one level, but which on another level make significant contributions to the development and functioning of social processes and institutions.

Our basic argument, then, is that not only does the paranoid process operate intrapsychically and developmentally as we have already discussed, but that the social organism find ways in which it can exploit the potentialities of the paranoid process in the interest of forming social groupings and institutionalized patternings. Such social structures both serve to sustain the fabric and functioning of society and provide a matrix, within which the individual personalities which constitute the social grouping can find support for maintaining a sense of identity and a responsive and integrative context within which such identities can function in meaningful and productive ways.

Quite obviously in proposing such a hypothesis, we are taking leave of the level of clinical analysis with its rooting in clinical experience. The argument becomes enlarged and extrapolated to levels at which the clinical experience has little or no relevance. Consequently, I am acutely aware that the argument being presented here is one that cannot be regarded as supported by the evidence presented, but rather must be regarded as an hypothesis seeking confirmation. The confirmation and the seeking of the supportive evidence is an effort that exceeds the limits of the present study and its immediate intentions. It is a work that will have to wait for another time and another place.

Clinical Implications

But its implications nonetheless do have important ramifications that affect even the more clinical level of understanding with which we have been dealing. What it enunciates is the realization that even the most extreme psychopathological expressions of the paranoid process do not take place in a vacuum. Rather they emerge out of an extremely rich and complex social, cultural, and familial matrix which can have powerful determining influences on the emergence and expression of the paranoid process. Thus, for example, in considering the vicissitudes of an individual case of paranoid pathology, we are faced with the possibility that the identifiable levels of distortion in terms of the patient's developmental experience may be strongly influenced by paranoid attitudes, which permeate the family system in which the child grows up.

However, such attitudes do not always reach the level of acknowledgeable psychopathology in other family members, particularly the parents. In several of our own case studies, this pattern seems to be quite clear. In the case of Clare, it seems quite likely that her father carried a certain paranoid disposition, but its manifestations were by no means clinical and he was able to integrate this basically paranoid disposition into a pattern of life and work that enabled him to maintain himself without any significant dysfunction. Similarly in the case of Gloria, her father's attitudes were quite explicitly paranoid, but the expression of his paranoia seems to have been limited more or less to the family context and seems not to have affected significantly other areas of his life and work. However, such attitudes may not even be identifiable as pathological at all.

Social Processes

The question we wish to raise here is whether social processes do not organize themselves in such a way as to absorb significant degrees of paranoid potential and employ them in more constructive ways in the service of implementing important social functions. Thus the pathologically affected and clinically identifiable paranoid personality may be in fact reflecting a variety of paranoid influences that swirl around him and may have contributed in significant ways to his own paranoid disposition, yet the paranoid influences in themselves may fall within quite acceptable areas of social attitudes and propensities which we would otherwise hesitate to designate as pathological.

Indeed, they may in many instances be quite consonant with the expectations and demands of the surrounding society. They may, even further, serve important adaptive functions within the social fabric so that they are encouraged and supported by social processes and fulfill important identity-sustaining needs of the individuals who participate in them. At the same time, while they are caught up in the service of these adaptive functions, they may be concurrently contributing to the fostering and shaping of clinically paranoid attitudes in susceptible individuals around them.

One of the most basic aspects of the functioning of social processes is the formation of groups. The forming of social groupings is in part a shaping of an ingroup, to which are aggregated the aspects of value and belonging which provide the matrix of support for individual identities. As we have already seen, a basic aspect of the process of identity formation has to do with the delineation and affiliation with such specific ingroups, within which the individual can define himself as a participating member with a sense of belonging and purposive participation. However, the defining of the ingroup is in part accomplished by setting it apart from and in opposition to the variety of outgroupings, which represent divergent or oppositional sets of values to those adhered to by the ingroup.

Resolution of Ambivalence

If we can recall at this point our discussion of the influence of paranoid mechanisms in the Oedipal period, we can recall that the Oedipal involvement provides for the young child the initial point of a more complex level of social involvement. It is in terms of the Oedipal situation and his involvement in it that the child begins to grapple with the complexities of relating to individuals in terms of more complex social relationships, rather than in terms of one-to-one situations which characterized earlier developmental experiences. We have also seen the manner and the extent to which paranoid mechanisms are called into play in the service of resolving the inherent ambivalence of such involvements.

The Oedipal situation itself is an expression of such mechanisms and is to that extent brought into being by the workings of the mechanisms of introjection and projection. The need to resolve ambivalence and the manner of its accomplishment suggest that the loved object can only be protected from destructive impulses by the diversion of such impulses to alternate objects which are then assigned a negative status. The conflict which is inherent in all ambivalence, namely the impulse to destroy what one loves and wishes to preserve, can be resolved to the extent that the conflicting impulses can be distributed between different objects. Thus the use of the familiar mechanisms of splitting and projection to resolve ambivalence leads to a situation in which the loved object is preserved by projecting destructive impulses to a relatively devalued object, thus leaving the preserved object relatively idealized.

Where the object of the displaced destructive impulses is a part of one's self, the outcome is potentially toxic and self-destructive. This is the course that is followed in many forms of depressive illness, in which the value of the ambivalently held object is sustained by means of the devaluation of the self (Rochlin, 1965). We have already examined the implications of this depressive alternative to a paranoid resolution. However, as Pinderhughes (1970, 1971) points out, the destructive impulses are ultimately a part of the self and can only successfully be gotten rid of and projected insofar as they are linked associatively with those components of one's own person which lend themselves readily to devaluation and expulsion. Thus the object of destructive impulses must be linked to representations of expendable body parts or products so that it can be successfully utilized as an object for projection. Thus a variety of processes of riddance of devalued body products can come into play as the symbolic equivalents of the projective displacement of negative and destructive attitudes. The most striking and powerful of such bodily processes of devaluation and riddance is obviously the anal one. Pinderhughes comments:

> Mental representations associated with excreted body products are invested with a denigrating false belief system as they are ejected, projected upon, and attacked. Mental representations of persons or groups may be invested with denigrating false belief systems, often by linkages with excreted body products through relationships in the body image. Idealized persons, groups, and body parts are invested with an aggrandizing false belief system. Both patterns are employed normally and consistently in the resolution of ambivalence by a non-pathological but nevertheless paranoid mechanism which projects negative components of ambivalent feelings toward a renounced outside object, and positive components toward an object one associates with oneself. Each individual achieves thereby an outward expression of destructive aggression without endangering any acknowledged parts of the self (1971, pp. 680-681).

Thus as we have seen in the context of Oedipal relationships the ambivalence in the relationship with each parent is thus reduced by distributing ambivalent feelings between them. Classically, in the positive resolution of the Oedipal constellation, it is the opposite-sex parent who is consciously idealized and sought after, while the same-sex parent becomes the object of aggressive and negative impulses. However, in the negative resolution of the Oedipal configuration, the opposite tendency obtains—namely, that the same-sex parent becomes the object of positive and idealized strivings while the opposite-sex parent becomes the recipient of negative projections. Thus the libidinal bond with the one parent and the aggressive bond with the other serves to protect from the threat of psychic loss of these significant objects which is involved in the destructive components of the underlying ambivalence. Thus the protection from the threat of loss and separation is dependent on the success with which this process can be worked through and the paranoid mechanisms successfully employed in the interests of resolving ambivalence. The paranoid mechanisms thus serve to divert destructive feelings and to resolve ambivalence. They accomplish this by the use of displacements, projections, introjections, and the institution of a form of false belief system in which one object is relatively idealized and the other devalued (the paranoid construction).

Group Formation

The resolution of ambivalence in the Oedipal context serves as a paradigm for the use of paranoid mechanisms in the resolution of ambivalence more generally. In the organization of groups and the working out of group behavior, protection from the sense of loss and separation is accomplished by idealizing and libidinizing the values and attitudes and beliefs of one's own group while, at the same time, devaluing, rejecting, and opposing the values and attitudes of what does not belong to one's own group. Many aspects of these forms of group-related paranoid mechanisms act to insure that group members will direct positive feelings toward one another and toward their own group and negative feelings toward outsiders. The process serves to resolve the inherent ambivalence in any such group relationship and provides a greater constancy and stability of psychic relationships. It is a form of normal delusion formation which serves to aggrandize one object or set of objects and conversely denigrates and devalues all other objects.

This can take place at a family level, as we have clearly seen in our case studies. A pervasive attitude in many of these families is that safety, security, acceptance, and approval can be expected only within the bosom of the family, and conversely what one can expect to receive from the outside world is rejection, hostility, undermining attacks, and destructive hostility. Clearly at this level the mechanisms of ingroup formation, based on introjection and separation from the outgroup in terms of hostile and destructive projection, are fully operative. But the concept can be applied readily to the broader field of social relationships and can provide us a basic insight into the nature of social processes, the formation of social groups, and the problems of social conflict. Thus the hypothesis which Pinderhughes had formulated and which is quite congruent with the point of view in the present study, can be given as follows:

> One relates by introjection to representatives of groups of which one feels a part, and one relates by projection to representatives of groups which one perceives as different from one's own. Thus, a group or its constituents are perceived and related to as if they were a single object. One is inclined to join or leave, to swallow or spit out, to accept or reject, and to associate pleasure or discomfort with social groups insofar as they are perceived as similar to one's own or different from one's own (Pinderhughes, 1971, p. 685).

Thus the operation of paranoid mechanisms can be seen to serve highly adaptive functions in the elaboration of social groupings and in the working out of social processes. One of the primary adaptive functions in the mobilization of paranoid mechanisms is the avoidance of loss and the resolution of ambivalence. Where the levels of ambivalence are not excessively intense, and where the susceptibility to loss is not catastrophic or overwhelming, and where sufficient ego-resources have been allowed to emerge by way of significantly constructive introjections and internalizations, there will be a sufficient capacity for trust to enable an individual to form social bonds with other individuals and to align their paranoid responses with those of others to permit the development of such nonpathological and group-related paranoid systems. Thus they can become members of an ingroup and share a certain set of values, attitudes, positions, belief systems, or ideologies, etc., with other like-minded individuals.

Such individuals are able to respond to and satisfy the needs which underlie the paranoid process and thus achieve a sense of belonging and acceptance which mitigates the basic ambivalence that threatens both their internal sense of self and their sense of participation and belonging extrinsically. Thus the paranoid mechanisms are placed in the service of important adaptive ends. However, where individuals are unable to form such social bonds, they become vulnerable to increasingly idiosyncratic belief systems, and the workings of the paranoid process must then begin to verge toward the pathological.

Consequently the nonpathological group-related paranoias operate to idealize by projection the groups with which an individual affiliates himself and with which he identifies, and they correspondingly serve to denigrate by means of projection the groups from which the individual disassociates himself. Thus the forming of such groups can provide a buffer against the loss of significant relationship and belonging within one's own group, but at the same time it provides a potent source for intergroup conflict.

Reciprocally, of course, the group process provides a support and context within which the individual paranoia can assert itself and sustain itself. Given the mutual support and reinforcement for the false belief system shared by the group, the belief system then becomes for the group a matter of principle, an ideology, or a dogma, for which group members are willing to contend, fight, and even in certain extreme situations surrender their lives. In reflecting on the paranoid process, consequently, it is important to remember that the system of delusional belief which characterized the paranoid distortion is driven by strong internal defensive and adaptive needs. It is motivated by the need to resolve intolerable ambivalence and to avoid the pain of loss—most poignantly and pressingly the pain of narcissistic loss and deprivation. Thus the individual psyche resorts to any devices which offer it the promise of sustaining narcissistic impairment and integrating a sense of self and identity, which is both internally consistent and coherent and articulated within a context of acceptance and belonging. It is precisely this aspect of the pressure toward identity which the group formation most acutely responds to.

Clinical Paranoia

The clinically paranoid patient is from this point of view precisely the individual for whom the embedding of paranoid mechanisms in this social matrix proves inadequate to satisfy the intensity of the inner needs and drives. Where the level of ambivalence is too intense, or the sensitivity to narcissistic loss and compromise too powerful for the individual to be able to sustain an adequate sense of self in interaction with such a social matrix, the powerful pressures continue to operate in such a way that the individual must resolve the defensive needs by resorting to a more idiosyncratic and divergent paranoid system.

Where the sense of self is more profoundly threatened by unresolved ambivalences, the need for an enemy becomes a predominant influence in the shaping and sustaining of a sense of self. We can recognize in this aspect of the process the workings of unresolved narcissistic needs. Primitive and unresolved narcissism, with its tendency to unremitting and exclusive demands, leaves little room for sharing or alliance, and sees external objects as generally threatening to its need for omnipotence and omnivorous possessiveness. Such pathogenic narcissism carries within itself the potentiality and the need for enemies.

As long as the individual sense of self remains congruent and adaptive in the functioning social matrix, we do not tend to regard the sense of self as pathological. Where the individual's relationships to the group are pervaded by a sense of conformity, we may recognize a certain impairment of the individuality of that identity and may be able to recognize the lineaments of what is essentially a false self, but we nonetheless regard this as falling within the relatively normal range of socially acceptable adaptation. Where the individual cannot join himself to these forms of group-related paranoia and where the internal pressures override the resources of these processes to absorb the intensity of destructive and ambivalent impulses, the individual must resort to a delusional system within which the false sense of self overwhelms the intrapsychic configuration and in which that false sense of self seeks its pathological relatedness to a persecutory environment.

Nonpathological Paranoia

The burden of these conclusions is obvious, since it points us in the direction of resolving broad areas of social conflict in terms of the underlying paranoid mechanisms. As Pinderhughes (1970), in a lucid discussion of these issues, has observed:

> Nonpathological paranoia well might be viewed as a pervasive, even universal, process stimulated by and dealing with conflicting psychic impulses. Such a concept is consistent with the vast scale on which we find conflict, exploitation, discrimination, and destruction taking place between human beings.
>
> One of the reasons why we have made so little progress in curbing and eliminating discrimination, exploitation, violence and war lies in our refusal to recognize and acknowledge that all human beings depend heavily upon paranoid processes throughout their lives. Most persons are too narcissistic to conceptualize themselves as primitive or irrational in thinking and behavior. They prefer instead to view themselves as intelligent and rational, while failing to observe that their intelligence and reason are impaired in the service of paranoid processes which aggrandize those with whom they identify and denigrate those they project upon. Intellect and reason are employed unconsciously to maintain and advance the position, benefits, and comforts of some persons at the expense of others (p. 608).

In the perspective which is being proposed in the present study, however, we wish to emphasize the adaptive aspects of the paranoid process. It is our conviction that only when we can envision and appreciate the positive and constructive and adaptive role of paranoid mechanisms, both in the organization and sustaining of individual personalities and in the formation and function of broader social groupings and processes, will we be able to come to terms effectively either with the pathological distortions which affect individual personalities or the patterns of social distortion and conflict which afflict the broader ranges of social experience.

We would like to turn at this juncture to more specific areas of sociocultural adaptation and to specify, if possible, the ways in which paranoid mechanisms serve the process of social adaptation in these respective orders. I must remind my readers that in this connection our purpose here is no more than to suggest the direction of further exploration and thinking and to sketch the portrait of the modality of paranoid expressions in the broadest and unfortunately most impressionistic terms. It can be hoped, however, that these observations may have some heuristic value.

SOCIOPOLITICAL ADAPTATION

The Political Order

Political Paranoia
The realities of the political order find their expression at multiple levels, extending from the immediate political involvements of the local neighborhood and community, through the broader reaches of city, county and state governments, to the higher levels of national organization, and finally that of international relationships. It should be immediately evident that the study of the operation of the paranoid process at each and all of these many levels introduces a complex patterning of causes, functions, and influences which derive from multiple levels of the social organization. We can only begin here to hint at the complexity and the dimensions of the problem.

It is not difficult to discern the operations of paranoid mechanisms in the political order. In fact, the evidence of paranoid influences is too dramatic and too overwhelming. There is a tendency to overlook the adaptive function of such political mechanisms, particularly where they are so transparently open to the distorting influences of pathologically determined paranoid mechanisms. This opens the way, indeed, to an examination of the psychology of political processes—a vast and relatively uncharted area in fact.

I am quite aware, nonetheless, that the territory is not entirely virgin, but that some pioneering pathways have been broken into the wilderness by such intrepid thinkers as Lasswell and Hofstadter and many others. As is so often the case, the lessons of history are also lessons that we need to learn again and again. They are the lessons that are taught us in terms of our own personal daily experience; they are also the lessons that we need to learn again and again in the endless variety and repetition of their motifs and patternings from the multiple contexts of our clinical experience. We can only come to terms with the pathological distortions and fixations which inhere in clinical psychopathology, when we are able to see our way through to the constructive and adaptive potential of such seemingly pathological distortions. A similar truth obtains, it seems to me, in the larger issues and grander scale of the political order. We cannot find our way through the thicket of hateful divisiveness and often destructive counterbalancing of forces until we can also see through to the adaptive and sustaining functions served by these same political processes.

Adaptive Aspects

While the paranoid aspects of these situations are relatively transparent and easily identifiable, we want to keep in focus the adaptive aspects which also serve in important ways to sustain these processes. In this regard we must remind ourselves that there is a twofold aspect to the formation of any social grouping. The first is the rewards which accrue to the individual by reason of his affiliation to the group. There is a sense of acceptance and belonging: there is an affiliation to a certain set of values which are esteemed and accorded regard within the community. By assimilating and adopting as well as internalizing these values, therefore, the individual aggregates himself to the community and thus assimilates to himself some of the esteem and sense of value that are derived from and inherent in the community.

But this is apparently not enough. There is another aspect of group formation which must not be lost sight of. And that is that the sustaining of the integrity and strength of the group requires in some part that it set itself over against an enemy. This is specifically where the paranoid mechanisms come into play. In a sense the group needs an enemy in order to bolster its own inner resources and to maintain its own inner sense of value and purposiveness. One sees this often in the clinical setting with patients who alternate between a sense of superiority and depressive inferiority—something that we have seen frequently in our own paranoid patients. It is as though one sustains a meaningful sense of self in some part by putting down and devaluating others around oneself. A similar mechanism operates at the group level. There the group helps to sustain itself by idealizing its own values and setting them over against and in conflict with the lesser and denigrated values of other groups. Furthermore, the dynamics of the situation will not tolerate a mere appraisal in terms of greater-or-lesser or more-or-less, but the narcissistic basis on which the process operates demands a logic of extremes, in which there is a tendency for all value to be inherent in the ingroup and no value or negative value to be inherent elsewhere. The natural extension of this logic is to set the respective value systems in opposition and to regard them as mutually exclusive and destructive. Thus what is in question here is not merely differences in degree but narcissistically derived need for enemies.

The existence of the enemy and the threat he poses has an indirect but beneficial effect within the ingroup. The threat posed by the enemy forces the members of the ingroup to value all the more intently and fanatically what the group stands for and to commit themselves all the more convincingly to the purposes and values to which it directs itself. Thus the more strongly the enemy confronts and attempts to undermine the group, the more powerful is the inner impulse to defend and cherish and adhere to what the group represents. This is an applicable principle in analogous ways at all levels of the human experience of social and political groupings. It applies just as truly in labor-management negotiations, where the attempts of management representatives to undermine and put the union at risk in some manner, calls for a countering impulse within the ranks of the union to adhere all the more desperately and fanatically to their purposes and intents.

The more the Arab states pose a threat to the existence of Israel, the more intense is the need for Israeli adherents to promote with fanatical and unremitting and uncompromising zeal the rights and prerogatives of the Israeli state. From this point of view, with regard to the Israeli situation, one might even think that the fanatical opposition of the Arab states to the existence of the state of Israel may in fact do Israel a great service. It calls forth a fanatical dedication and resolve, not only on the part of Israelis, who live and hold citizenship in the embattled state, but also in Jewish adherents whose numbers count in the many millions spread over the face of the globe. The mobilization of resources in the face of such adversity is a spin-off of the paranoid process at work.

The Need for Enemies

Interestingly enough, shrewd leaders know this and make use of it. Much of Stalin's ruthless modernization of the Russian economy was made possible by the generation of paranoid fears of attack and violation by the Western powers. The fact that there were historical precedents for such fears served only to validate and intensify the paranoid delusional context which permitted such incredible demands and toleration of murderous destructiveness on the part of the Russian people at the hands of their paranoid

leader. Similarly the mobilization of paranoid fears relative to the Jews served Hitler very well in gaining political support for his own regime. He was
even able to use the paranoid rationalization of an international Jewish conspiracy as one of the important props for his rationalizing of German
militarism and aggression.

One wonders at the comparative success of Communist-inspired subversive activities on many fronts of the world—whether in Southeast Asia or
in South America or other parts of the globe. The answer is in part the success with which the Communist ideology nourishes and exploits the
paranoid processes in the service of facilitating political and economic goals.
The process is self-nourishing and self-abetting. Paranoid convictions lead
to a necessity for destructive and subversive acts which in turn elicit the retaliation of capitalistic or authoritarian regimes, which then verifies and
validates the paranoid fears of Communist subversives and serves to consolidate and intensify their basic motivations. This again is the sort of complex interaction, in which paranoid responses on one side of the situation of
conflict serve to reinforce and sustain the paranoid distortions on the other
side.

Once we are in a position to grasp the significance of the sustaining of
the values and perspectives of the ingroup, we can also begin to appreciate
the important dynamics which are brought into the service of such needs,
particularly in terms of the need for an enemy in sustaining and reinforcing
the integrity and cohesiveness of the group. A striking phenomenon during
periods of war mobilization in our own country was the sense of purposefulness and meaningful participation by many segments of the population,
which in times of peace find themselves without a meaningful or productive
role in society. Whatever one thinks of the morality of war and killing, the
mobilization of masses of men in the armed services in the time of war,
serves an important psychic function. These men now become valued participants in an important national effort. They are allowed to wear a uniform,
are trained in the skills of warfare, and are accorded honor and praise as
heroes who go forth to do battle in defense of their country. Other individuals on the homefront find productive places in the intense mobilization of the war effort, which bring them a sense of satisfaction and sharing
in an enterprise of great meaning and purpose. Consequently, rates of
alcoholism and crime in such periods of mobilization decrease.

One can suggest that the participation in such massively paranoid un-
dertakings has an important function in terms of the adjustment capacity
for such individuals. The mobilization of the war effort seems to absorb
significant amounts of paranoid potentiality, so that instead of resorting to
deviant forms of antisocial behavior, they are enabled to share in a communal effort in the defense of shared values and convictions. These individuals are thus accepted into a transient grouping, which provides them

with a context of usefulness and meaningful belonging and participation serving to sustain and consolidate their fragile or fragmented sense of identity. It is clear that the parameters of the paranoid process, as we have been developing them here, play a central and significant role in such manifestations. They serve to undercut the elements of self-devaluation and self-rejection which play such a central role in psychosocial deviance (Kaplan, 1972). At the same time, they provide the context of meaningful participation and group belonging which contributes powerfully to the maintenance of self-esteem.

Social Structures and Processes

Paranoid and Social Processes

Our basic hypothesis with respect to the organization of society is that social processes organize themselves in such a way as to provide appropriate contexts within which the paranoid process comes into play, so as to preserve certain specific adaptive functions within the society and to provide the appropriate context within which individuals may find a sense of appropriate belonging and useful participation. The achievement of these goals is intimately linked to the sustaining of a sense of identity, as we have already discussed it. We are dealing with an area here in which the links between the intrapsychic organization of the self and the social participation and embeddedness of the self are intimately intertwined and connected. Thus society provides structures and contexts within which the basic mechanisms of the paranoid process can be turned to adaptive and useful purposes.

The implications of this intertwining of social and paranoid processes are multiple. From our point of view it suggests that the organization of social processes and institutions has a significant psychological impact, in that it draws the operation of paranoid mechanisms into more adaptive and self-sustaining contexts. At the same time, these same processes, operating in broader and less pathological human contexts, can be seen in terms of their relevance to the genesis of paranoid psychopathology. If the system of social processes and institutions builds on and provides a context for the operation of paranoid mechanisms, we are equivalently saying that the organization of such social processes and groupings provides a matrix, which at the same time sustains and serves to elaborate these same basic paranoid mechanisms. Consequently the organization of social processes provides a fundamental matrix, within which paranoid mechanisms are allowed to elaborate themselves.

When we inquire into a causal context out of which paranoid pathology arises, we are unavoidably led to consider the relevance of this essentially paranoid matrix which permeates the whole of our social fabric and which serves adaptively to sustain both social and intrapsychic objectives. The point of view that we are advancing here suggests, then, that the process by which the paranoid disposition is formed takes its origins in part from this matrix and is influenced by other social and group processes, which take place around it and which can contribute important influences to the shaping of the paranoid disposition in a given pathologically affected individual.

We have suggested at a number of points and have identified unequivocally in the study of the above group of patients that the immediate matrix within which this broader social and cultural influence is brought to bear is that of the family. Thus the whole range of family dynamics and family patterns of interaction form a middle group between the realm of intrapsychic dynamics, which we have been at pains to discuss in considerable detail, and the present realm of social and cultural processes, which we are presently able to delineate only in the broadest terms. Thus we can conclude that the paranoid process and its associated mechanisms play themselves out in complex and interrelated ways at all levels of the integration of the social organism, from the basic social unit of the socially involved and embedded individual in the immediate transactional context of the family system to the broadest units of social and political organization.

Social Structures and Groupings

Social structure takes the form of the organization of multiple social subgroupings, which provide the varied and overlapping context within which the individual person defines and articulates his sense of social self. The catalogue of such groupings is large and varied indeed. The multiple groupings into which society organizes itself articulate themselves around a wide variety of differences, each of which can serve as the rationale of grouping and for the division and opposition between groups. A given individual living within this social ambivalence may affiliate himself in varying degrees with many such groupings, most of which have a degree of nonexclusiveness, but among which certain tensions are possible. Thus a man can be Republican, a musician, a Protestant, a Rotarian, a stamp collector, and married. But he cannot be female, nor can he concurrently be a Democrat, nor can he be Jewish. Thus while certain membership potentialities are not mutually exclusive, others are.

Yet, even within such nonexclusive groupings, tension and potential contradictions can arise. Thus if an individual were Democratic and Catholic, tension may arise between the political platform which calls for the repeal of the abortion statutes and the espoused position of the Church, which regards abortion as sinful and opposes the liberalizing of abortion laws. Similarly, a Jewish politician might find himself in conflict if his political party espoused a position condemning Israeli attacks as aggression and supporting Arab demands in Middle East negotiations. While such nonexclusive groupings can be a source of conflict and tension, they are usually not the arena in which the paranoid mechanisms generally come into play.

The paranoid mechanisms are much more likely to find expression in the context of exclusive group membership. We can often easily identify such mechanisms at work. On the contemporary scene, the radical Women's Lib Movement seems to lend itself to such manifestations. The standoff between male chauvinism and the Women's Liberation Movement, particularly in its more extreme and abrasive forms, seems to take on a somewhat paranoid cast.

Paranoid Process and Social Adaptation

In all of these instances and many more that we cannot take the occasion to discuss here, society organizes itself into a variety of groupings and structures which are based on and organized around discriminable differences and which bring into play the operations of the paranoid process. The paranoid process functions not only to define and consolidate such groupings, but to provide the basic psychic conditions in terms of which the group processes work themselves out and through which the interaction between groups on various levels is determined and qualified. Thus the functioning of the paranoid process in its various manifestations becomes an essential dimension in the organization and maintenance of such social groupings.

If, as we have been at pains to point out, such social organization serves the interests of sustaining and integrating individual identities, we must also not lose sight of the fact that such groupings and the working through of social processes have an important role to play in the maintaining of social order and in the working out of social adaptations. Social processes are by no means fixed or static in nature. They are rather processes of dynamic tension and change, in which progressive social adaptations and structural modifications are continually being elaborated and worked through by means of the oppositional tension created between relevant social groupings. In the context of a dynamic and changing social structure, a reasonable and manageable degree of confrontation and social struggle is not only avoidable, but is indeed a necessary and optimal condition for the functioning of social processes.

The functioning of the paranoid process within such a social system provides the dynamic underpinning and motivating force which maintains social processes in a state of continual tension and dynamic opposition. The dynamic operation of such processes and their contribution to the working through of social problems can be seen perhaps most vividly in our own time in the civil rights confrontations of the last decade. The operation of paranoid mechanisms not only serves to promote and sustain a sense of black identity and purposeful striving, which makes a significant contribution to the elevation of black self-esteem, but it also brings into meaningful conflict the tension of rights and values which is a much broader and significant social issue that the body of society must face, work through, and resolve. Thus the working of these mechanisms makes a significant contribution to the continuing process of social adaptation.

The danger as always in the operation of such paranoid mechanisms is that the same mechanisms which can be seen to serve such adaptive purposes can also be turned to the uses of destructive interference with the working of social structures. Thus the working of such processes in the political and social orders can lead to revolution, which may serve the purposes of destruction rather than adaptation. However, even here, one must ask the question as to whether the revolutionary outcome itself is destructive or not. Such a question is not always easily answered. Certainly one could in historical retrospect feel that the American Revolution was in large part an adaptive expression of the functioning of these mechanisms. But what should one say about the French Revolution, or the Russian Revolution, or even in our own time the Chinese Revolution?

One could argue, it seems to me, that in some degree in each of these instances important adaptive functions were served even by the revolutionary outcome. In any case, in all of these instances, we have ample evidence of the operation of the paranoid process. In the case of the revolutionary outcomes, what is most striking is that such an outcome is the product not only of the operation of paranoid mechanisms on the side of those perpetrating the revolution, but it is met by and responded to by equally distorting and destructive manifestations of the operation of the paranoid process on the part of the established regime. It is in the clash of these paranoid propensities that the emergence of potential destructiveness is realized.

CULTURAL ADAPTATION

Religious Belief Systems

There is probably no more significant or telling area in which the operation of the paranoid process can be identified than in the development of religious belief systems. We have already had occasion in our previous discussion to suggest the role of the paranoid process in respect to such belief systems, particularly in regard to the cognitive elaboration which is reflected in the paranoid construction. Similarly there is probably no other area in which the adaptive capacities of paranoid mechanisms are more apparent.

Conflict among Belief Systems

If we cast an eye over the long history of religion, we are provided with a rich mine for the study of the operation of the paranoid process. The history of religion as far back as we are able to trace it in the dark glimmerings of Mesopotamian origins and the stirrings of man's religious impulses, even in the prehistoric era, is a history of conflict and struggle. Adherence to religious belief systems is paralleled at every point with the setting of one such system against others, and the placing of them in conflictual opposition. The pages of the Old Testament redound with the constantly reiterated theme of the struggles of the chosen people and their monotheistic system of belief, set in dire and desperate opposition to the malicious and threatening menace of the pagan nations which surrounded them. Those who worshipped pagan gods, those who worshiped at the shrines of the Ba'al, were the enemies of Israel. One can turn to almost any segment of the Old Testament, and the sparks of paranoid antagonism and the rhetoric of paranoid aggression can be found. The constant prayer to Yahweh was that he save his chosen people from their enemies. The very notion of a "chosen people" set in opposition to its "enemies" provides us with a classic paradigm of the paranoid system.

If we turn to the more modern context of the New Testament, the very rise of Christianity was such as to take its origins in persecution. The very roots of Christian tradition, consequently, must be seen as taking their origin out of a paranoid matrix. The blood of martyrs became the seed of Christians. The early history of the Christian Church was a history of persecution and struggle against the enemies of Christianity. In the first instance it was the Jews, but with the advance of the Church and the progression of time it became the Roman Empire. The Acts of the Christian Martyrs stand as a testimonial to the persecutory life of the Church in those early centuries. But the early centuries of persecution were not without great benefit to the nascent Christian Church. It provided the Church with a sense of mission, of purposeful striving and struggle. The experience of the early Church rehearses the constantly reiterated tale of any persecution—that persecution serves only to intensify the purpose and resolve of the persecuted. It provides them with a sense of meaning and useful striving that otherwise might not be so readily or so intensely available. The Church not only survived, but thrived on such persecution.

The church has always had her enemies. We can even wonder whether it would be fair to say that the Church has always needed her enemies. In the Middle Ages, the organization of Christianity took on a more explicitly political reality in the form of Caesaropapism. The Church's struggle for autonomy and survival took the form of resistance against the incursions of the growing influence of nationalism and monarchical power. In the light of the necessity for struggling for such religious autonomy, the medieval involvements of the Church in secular and political and even military struggles is perhaps understandable. But from our perspective it provides a striking example of the implementation of paranoid mechanisms and the bringing into conflictual opposition of paranoid tendencies in the service of the working through and resolution of social and political tensions.

Maintenance of Belief

The question that this raises in my mind is whether or not the persistence of religious groups in some sense requires the opposition of enemies in order to sustain and support itself. Like the process of formation of individual identity and a sense of self, as we have discussed it in terms of its developmental vicissitudes, a significant variable in regard to the maintenance of religious groupings and religious belief systems has to do with the extent to which such systems are sustained by the operation of paranoid mechanisms as opposed to more constructive and positive mechanisms. I have in mind here the discrimination between introjective mechanisms, as mobilized in the service of defense, and identificatory mechanisms, which are mobilized in the organization of personality in relatively more autonomous and less defensive ways. The ultimate mechanisms which affect the organization not only of religious belief systems, but also social processes in general, as we have suggested, lie in the realm of the internal psychic processes. The critical question, then, in this regard is whether individual adherents of the religious belief system have internalized the belief system of the group and its correlative value system in predominantly introjective terms, or whether the internalization has been able to organize itself on the basis of more autonomous identifications. It seems to me that at this point we can begin to glimpse with considerable impact the continuity that extends from the most basic levels of intrapsychic organization and the formation of structure to the broadest and richest realms of social and cultural development.

Paranoid Process and Faith

A question that we can only touch on here, but which I think is of extreme importance and significance, is the question of the relationship between such paranoid processes and religious faith. Certainly religious belief, as we have already seen, provides the motivation for adherence to the belief system, but it is an adherence that is not based on objective evidence or evaluations, nor is it insistent on such forms of verification. Rather it is derived from and impelled by inner needs to which the belief system as a cognitive structure responds in meaningful and supportive ways. In the face of the greatest and most overwhelming uncertainties of life—particularly those that have to do with the meaning and purpose of human life and the inevitability of death—religious systems provide the context within which hope can be sustained and the ultimate despair mitigated. The ultimately narcissistic motivation consequently is quite clear.

In terms of the paranoid process, it raises the question as to the extent to which such paranoid mechanisms, particularly the elements of introjection, projection, and paranoid construction, enter into and form an essential part of the faith process. Is religious faith, then, in the sense of the motivated adherence to a religious belief system, an expression of essentially paranoid dynamics? Can a religious faith consequently be regarded as another adaptive manifestation of the paranoid process—one which is consequently subject to the pressure of narcissistic demands and can readily be distorted in the direction of religious fanaticism as a more pathological expression of the same mechanisms?

The question, it seems to me, is quite parallel to the problem of ideologies, which form the more or less secularized belief systems that are built into political and social systems. The ideology is a cognitive system which can serve as a principal guide for the action of the social group, but can also become the radicalized and fanaticized creed, which becomes the vehicle of the more distorting and pathological paranoid influences within the group. In these instances, as in all forms of social organization and group formation, the paranoid mechanisms operate to develop a paranoid construction which serves as a mythology, an ideology, or a belief system, and which serves to articulate certain basic values and attitudes and criteria of adherence which guide the group's life and which dictate the course of its decisions and actions.

In any form of social organization, therefore, where the motivating forces which dictate and reinforce the belief system are mitigated, we must seriously take into account the effects on the life and vitality of the group. This applies not merely to religious belief systems as we have suggested, but to all forms of social organization and their respective forms of belief. The conflicting ideologies of capitalism and communism are a ready case in point. The extent to which mutually exclusive and antagonistic paranoid attitudes must be reciprocally generated within each group as a means of sustaining and reinforcing their respective ideologies is a real and problematic question.

The Problem of Values and the Paranoid Process

Values and Belonging
In bringing this attempt to formulate some of the implications and elaborations of the paranoid process in the wide spectrum of social and cultural phenomena to a close, I would like to call particular attention to a pressing yet relatively unexplored area of psychological thinking which is

becoming a focus of increasing psychiatric concern. I refer to the whole question of the formation and function of value systems. It can be immediately seen that the whole question of ideologies and belief systems is closely intertwined with, and to a considerable degree overlaps, the question of value systems. It is also apparent that value systems hold a special and extremely significant place in the formation and adaptive organization of social groupings. It has been in fact maintained that the cultural life of the group is equivalently the vehicle through which the value system of the group is expressed and sustained (Parsons and Shils, 1962).

From the perspective of the participating member of the group, membership and the sense of participative belonging associated with it is in part a reflection of the internalization of group values. The member's affiliation and commitment to the group is a function, therefore, of the internalization of group values in such a way that they become incorporated with and assimilated to the inner frame of reference and structural organization which serves as the basis for the individual's sense of identity and selfhood. It is through this articulation and assimilation of values, then, that the individual attains a sense of self as belonging to, recognizing, participating in, and as acknowledged and accepted by the group. The group recognizes its members by reason of their adherence to its shared and communicated values. Consequently the mechanisms of sharing of values and their internalization serves as an essential component of the formation of and persistence of a sense of identity.

Values and Identity

To approach the question from a slightly different orientation, the notion of identity has achieved prominence in psychoanalytic parlance through the work of Erik Erikson. It is the contention in this study that the parameters of identity as described and defined in Erikson's work are value-embedded terms. The terms of trust, autonomy, initiative, industry, identity, intimacy, generativity, and integrity are all terms which derive from a structure of values and which express those values in concrete ways. Erikson (1964) himself has traced the explicit link between the elements of identity and what he refers to as a "schedule of virtues." "Virtues" are specifically ethically related and determined concepts.

Erikson goes on to spell out the specific ethical dimensions of some of those concepts in terms of the ethical implications for the cycle of generations and in terms of his own characteristic version of the Golden Rule. The important theoretical concept of identity and its component parts cannot be simply accredited to the ego as such. They must involve important aspects of superego functioning and even must involve characteristic alignments between structural components and aspects of id functioning. The consideration of the problems of identity and identity formation, then, introduces us into the important realms of value theory—an area which has only begun to be explored in psychiatric and psychoanalytic terms.

The consideration of value systems in relationship to the patterns of individual identity cannot be understood or formulated in exclusion from an understanding of the role of and function of values on the social and cultural levels. It is clear that the formation of values is one of the primary aspects of group processes, that in many respects one of the primary functions of social groupings is precisely the articulation and maintenance of such value systems (Meissner, 1971c). The link to the formation and sustaining of parameters of individual identity through the forming and sharing of value systems in an integrated manner involving both individual psychic formations and group processes lies at the heart of such an understanding.

Values and Paranoid Process

The impact of these considerations is that the reflection on values leads us back again to a consideration of the workings of the paranoid process. If we combine these considerations with what we have already had to say about the relevance of the process to identity formation and to the adaptive aspects of group organization and functioning, we find it difficult to avoid the conclusion that the process is intimately and deeply involved in the processes of value formation and integration. We have already seen at considerable length and in considerable detail the role which introjective and projective processes play in the formation of groups and in their significant contribution to the forming of identity intrapsychically. An important area of concern vis-à-vis the understanding of values is the role which these processes play in the formation and sustaining of value systems.

Internalization of Values

An examination of the significant areas of reflection, it seems to me, would bear upon the relative role which introjections and identifications play in the internalization and integration of value systems within the inner psychic world. But this is not the exclusive area of consideration. Just as the pathology of paranoid states cannot be understood in terms of either introjective or projective processes in isolation, but can only be grasped substantially by a fuller understanding of the interplay of both introjective and projective mechanisms, so in the consideration of the complex phenomena of value systems, such an integrative approach is essential to any further progress in understanding. We must, therefore, envision that the role of projection and its correlative cognitive elaborations which we have characterized as the paranoid construction, have an important role to play in the development of such value systems. Like the belief system which inheres in religious structures, the value system represents in part a cognitive elaboration which is organized in such a way as to build upon and integrate central projective elements which ultimately derive from the internal frame of reference.

A value system, taken in terms of its reference to the formation of identity and within the framework of the inner world of the subject's experience, must be based on the internal structural configurations which derive from specific introjections and identifications. At this point it is not clear how such internalizing processes work to build and maintain value systems. Part of the resolution of the problem lies in the understanding of how such internalizing processes contribute in specific and varied ways to the organization of ego and superego functions. Undoubtedly the formation of the internal value system relates to the establishing of such components of psychic structure in complex and variable ways. Other complex issues, however, are involved in the manner in which values are formed in the broader scale of group processes—at whatever level of complex group cultural experience or process this takes place.

This suggestion can only be made with a certain amount of trepidation, since we are treading upon thin ice and in a situation of darkness and obscurity, where any given step can be a false one. We are proposing here that the basic analysis which we have undertaken in the understanding of paranoid mechanisms and their relationship to the paranoid process provides an important conceptual vehicle that may be able to contribute to the illumination and clarification of these problems. It may also be hoped in a reciprocal fashion that further exploration of these unchartered ways in the understanding of value formation and value theory will provide us with a further purchase on the clinical problems which relate to the paranoid process. Progress in the understanding of human behavior and experience is never linear but rather is epicyclic or dialectic, turning back upon itself illuminating glimmers which shed new light and bring new complexity and ever-increasing deepening to our understanding of complex human motivations and capacities. Reflection on values, in an even more telling and dramatic fashion, impresses us once again with the important lesson of the continuity of human experience and its complex transactional intertwining at all levels of human organization and functioning, from the level of individual intrapsychic dynamics to the most complex and variable functionings of the great masses of mankind. But we must leave this dark continent for another expedition.

Epilogue—A Psychoanalytic Postscript

We have come to the end of a perilous journey. What began as an inquiry into paths that seemed well-marked and well-trodden turned into an exploration of complex thickets and hidden areas of obscurity and complexity that we could hardly have anticipated. We began with the first rough paths hewn into the darkness by Freud himself, particularly in the classic analysis of the Schreber case. Our subsequent excursions and particularly our immersion in the complex detail of a number of clinical case studies told us that matters were hardly as concisely formulable as they seemed in Freud's deft and masterful handling of the Schreber material. Rather we entered a difficult and complex area in which the richness of the material and the far-reaching impact of the processes involved served only to tantalize the more the further we went, and seemed to offer the possibility of little or no resolution.

From an evaluation of states of clinical pathology, this study has become an investigation of the paranoid process. We have come to recognize that process as not merely a pathological expression of deviant and distorted psychic functions, but rather as a complex process which is endemic to human psychological functioning and which forms an integral and essential aspect of human psychological development and functional capacity.

We have seen further that the process reaches out to broad levels of human interaction and the integration of human activities in terms of broad social groupings and levels of cultural functioning. It is here that important bridges—I will not say have been established—have been at least sketched out as potential channels of communication and interchange between the understanding of the organization of intrapsychic functioning and the broader and more complex levels of social and cultural transaction. The burden of the argument is that there is a link and a line of continuity that runs between the psychoanalytic couch and the rest of the broad realms of human experience and activity.

This is no new or revolutionary insight. It is the problem that Freud appreciated from his earliest years and which he struggled with through his lifelong endeavors to understand the complexities of the human mind. It is a problem that others have pursued with great vigor and ingenious diligence through the subsequent years, and the enterprise is by no means finished. Our attempt here in bridging from the level of clinical analysis to broader sociocultural extrapolations has been an attempt to broaden the implications of specific and concrete mechanisms and to envision their mode of operation in specific and complexly intertwined ways at many levels of their functioning. The enterprise is not without risks, nor do we entertain any delusion in bringing this present study to a close that the objectives have been accomplished. Rather such an attempt at enlarging a focus and extrapolating of concepts derived from a clinical perspective runs severe risks and can expect to do little more than to serve as a basis of stimulation for further research. Reflection on the level of social and cultural processes demands deeper reflection and investigation.

But in attempting such a development of thinking, the wheel turns and the cycle completes itself. One of the important implications of the present study has a particular clinical referent. We are proposing an attempt to substantiate the argument that embellishments and adaptive expressions of the paranoid process, on the levels of broad social and political and religious involvement that we have discussed, are not without relevance and implications for the understanding of clinical paranoia.

Our proposition is that such socially embedded manifestations of the paranoid process provide a context and a generative matrix out of which states of clinically paranoid pathology emerge. In countless ways the developmental matrix out of which our patients have emerged was permeated with paranoid attitudes and defensive alignments. Such paranoid sentiments were often deeply embedded in the family context, and often formed latent and unsuspected elements of parental personality organization and functioning. For particular individuals and family structures, such paranoid alignments serve as the habitual and relatively adaptive mode of organization which permits such structures to persist in a reasonably effective and relatively nonpathological fashion.

Moreover, it is our contention that the organization of social structures functions in such a way as frequently enough to absorb and channel and sustain such basically paranoid configurations. In an ultimate sense, then, the extrapolations to broader levels of human organization and social functioning cannot be divorced from the level of clinical analysis and of specific clinical implications.

Not only does this fundamental appreciation condition our understanding of individual patients and their pathology, but it dictates important parameters of our approach to the clinical management and treatment of such forms of pathology. If the patient comes to the psychiatrist's office as an individual and if the psychotherapeutic or psychoanalytic process deals in the first instance with his intrapsychic dynamics as an individual and isolated phenomenon, we must also remember that, to regard him as in a psychological sense an isolate, or as a phenomenon which arises independently of or in isolation from the multiple and complex influences we have discussed, truncates our understanding of the patient, his understanding of himself, and our effectiveness in helping him to find his way out of the situation of clinical discomfort and pain in which he finds himself.

Consequently, the implications of this orientation for the treatment not only of specifically paranoid patients but also, as our study richly implies, of a broad range of patients in whom the manifestations of the paranoid process operate, must be correspondingly modified and adapted. Here again is a broad area for serious investigation and reflection which we cannot undertake here. It would seem to be a most significant area of application in which those intrepid souls who have persevered through this long exploration may find some useful therapeutic emendations and applications within their own clinical experience.

My own experience in dealing with a wide variety of patients of both neurotic and psychotic levels of personality integration has taught me that a capacity to discern and read the operations of the paranoid process in such patients has led to extremely fruitful and clinically productive lines of work with them. I can only hope that further efforts in extending the borders of this exploration will come to a fuller and more explicit development of the themes and implications that can be only hinted at and inferred in the present context.

REFERENCES

Abraham, K. (1954) *Selected Papers of Karl Abraham*. New York: Basic Books.

Abroms, G. M., Taintor, Z. C., and Lhamon, W. T. (1966) Percept assimilation and paranoid severity. *Archives of General Psychiatry*, 14: 491-496.

Adorno, T. W., Frenkel-Brunswik, E., Levinson, D. J., and Sanford, R. N. (1950) *The Authoritarian Personality*. New York: Harper.

Alexander, F. (1938) Remarks about the relations of inferiority feelings to guilt feelings. *International Journal of Psychoanalysis*, 19: 41-49.

Allen, T. E. (1967) Suicidal impulse in depression and paranoia. *International Journal of Psychoanalysis*, 48: 433-438.

Allport, G. W. (1958) *The Nature of Prejudice*. Garden City, New York: Doubleday.

Angel, K. (1967) On symbiosis and pseudosymbiosis. *Journal of the American Psychoanalytic Association*, 15: 294-316.

Angel, K. (1972) The role of internal object and external object in object relationships, separation anxiety, object constancy and symbiosis. *International Journal of Psychoanalysis*, 53: 541-546.

Anthony, E. J., and Kreitman, N. (1970) Murderous obsessions in mothers toward their children. In Anthony, E. J., and Benedek, T. (eds.) *Parenthood: Its Psychology and Psychopathology*. Boston: Little, Brown, 479-498.

Arieti, S. (1961) Introductory notes on the psychoanalytic therapy of schizophrenics. In Burton, A. (ed.) *Psychotherapy of the Psychoses*. New York: Basic Books, 68-89.

Arieti, S., and Meth, J. M. (1959) Rare, unclassified, collective, and exotic psychotic syndromes. In Arieti, S. (ed.) *American Handbook of Psychiatry*, I: 546-563. New York: Basic Books.

Aronson, M. L. (1964). A study of the Freudian theory of paranoia by means of the Rorschach Test. In Reed, C. F., Alexander, I. E., and Tomkins, S. S. (eds.). *Psychopathology: A Source Book*. New York: Wiley, 370-387.

Artiss, K. L., and Bullard, D. M. (1966). Paranoid thinking in everyday life. *Archives of General Psychiatry*, 14: 89-93.

Bach-y-Rita, G., Lion, J. R., Climent, C. E., and Ervin, F. R. (1971). Episodic dyscontrol: A study of 130 violent patients. *American Journal of Psychiatry*, 127: 1473-1478.

Bak, R. (1946). Masochism in paranoia. *Psychoanalytic Quarterly*, 15: 285-301.

Baker, H. J. (1969). Transsexualism—problems in treatment. *American Journal of Psychiatry*, 125: 1412-1418.

Barchilon, J. (1971). A study of Camus' mythopoeic tale *The Fall* with some comments about the origin of esthetic feelings. *Journal of American Psychoanalytic Association*, 19: 193-240.

Bateson, G., Jackson, D., Haley, J., and Weakland, J. (1956). Toward a theory of schizophrenia. *Behavioral Science*, 1: 251-264.

Beitner, M. (1961). Word meaning and sexual identification in paranoid schizophrenics and anxiety neurotics. *Journal of Abnormal and Social Psychology*, 63: 283-293.

Benedek, T. (1938). Adaptation to reality in early infancy. *Psychoanalytic Quarterly*, 7: 200-215.

Benedek, T. (1970). The family as a psychologic field. In Anthony, E. J., and Benedek, T. (eds.). *Parenthood: Its Psychology and Psychopathology.* Boston: Little, Brown, 109-136.

Bergman, P., and Escalona, S. K. (1949). Unusual sensitivities in very young children. *Psychoanalytic Study of the Child,* 3/4: 333-352.

Berlyne, N. (1972). Confabulation. *British Journal of Psychiatry,* 120: 31-39.

Berman, S. (1970). Alienation: An essential process of the psychology of adolescence. *Journal of the Academy of Child Psychiatry,* 9: 233-250.

Bernhardson, G., and Gunne, L-M. (1972). Forty-six cases of pyschosis in Cannabis abusers. *International Journal of Addictions,* 7:9-16.

Bexton, W. H., Heron, W., and Scott, T. H. (1954). Effects of decreased variation in the sensory environment. *Canadian Journal of Psychology,* 8: 70-76.

Bianchi, G. N. (1971). Origins of disease phobia. *Australian and New Zealand Journal of Psychiatry,* 5: 241-257.

Bibring, E. (1953). The mechanism of depression. In Greenacre, P. (ed.), *Affective Disorders: Psychoanalytic Contribution to Their Study.* New York: International Universities Press, 13-48.

Bing, J. F., and Marburg, R. O. (1962). Narcissism. *Journal of the American Psychoanalytic Association,* 10: 593-605.

Bleuler, E. (1950). *Dementia Praecox or the Group of Schizophrenias.* New York: International Universities Press.

Blos, P. (1960). Comments on the psychological consequences of cryptorchism: A clinical study. *Psychoanalytic Study of the Child,* 15: 395-429.

Blos, P. (1962). *On Adolescence: A Psychoanalytic Interpretation.* New York: Free Press.

Blos, P. (1967). The second individuation process of adolescence. *Psychoanalytic Study of the Child,* 22: 162-186.

Blum, H. P. (1970). Maternal psychopathology and nocturnal enuresis. *Psycho-analytic Quarterly,* 39: 609-619.

Bonner, H. (1950). Sociological aspects of paranoia. *American Journal of Sociology,* 56: 255-262.

Bornstein, B. (1935). Phobia in a two-and-a-half year old child. *Psychoanalytic Quarterly,* 4: 93-119.

Boszormenyi-Nagy, I. (1965). A theory of relationships: Experience and transaction. In Boszormenyi-Nagy, I., and Framo, J. L. (eds.), *Intensive Family Therapy.* New York: Harper and Row, 33-86.

Boszormenyi-Nagy, I., and Framo, J. L. (eds.), (1965). *Intensive Family Therapy.* New York: Harper and Row.

Bowen, M. (1960). A family concept of schizophrenia. In Jackson, D. D. (ed.), *The Etiology of Schizophrenia.* New York: Basic Books, 346-372.

Bowen, M. (1965). Family psychotherapy with schizophrenia in the hospital and in private practice. In Boszormenyi-Nagy, I., and Framo, J. L. (eds.), *Intensive Family Therapy.* New York: Harper and Row, 213-243.

Bowlby, J. (1951). *Maternal Care and Mental Health.* Geneva: World Health Organization.

Brazelton, T. B. (1962). Observations of the neonate. *Journal of the American Academy of Child Psychiatry,* 1, 38-58.

Brigham, J. C. 1971. Ethnic stereotypes. *Psychological Bulletin,* 76:15-38.

Brodey, W. M. (1964). On the dynamics of narcissism. I. Externalization and early ego development. *Psychoanalytic Study of the Child,* 19:165-193.

Brody, S. (1970). A mother is being beaten: An instinctual derivative and infant care. In Anthony, E. J., and Benedek, T. (eds.), *Parenthood: Its Psychology and Psychopathology*. Boston: Little, Brown, 427-447.

Broughton, R.J. (1968). Sleep disorders: Disorders of arousal? *Science*, 159:1070-1078.

Bruch, H. (1967). Mass murder: The Wagner case. *American Journal of Psychiatry*, 124:693-698.

Bruner, J. S. (1957a). On going beyond the information given. In *Contemporary Approaches to Cognition*. Cambridge: Harvard University Press, 41-69.

Bruner, J. S. (1957b). On perceptual readiness. *Psychological Review*, 64:123-152.

Bruner, J. S. and Goodman, C. (1947). Value and need as organizing factors in perception. *Journal of Abnormal and Social Psychology*, 42:33-44.

Bruner, J. S., Goodnow, J. J., and Austin, G. A. (1962). *A Study of Thinking*. New York: Science Editions.

Bruner, J. S., and Postman, L. (1947a). Emotional selectivity in perception and reaction. *Journal of Personality*, 16:69-77.

Bruner, J. S., and Postman, L. (1947b). Tension and tension release as organizing factors in perception. *Journal of Personality*, 15:300-308.

Bruner, J. S., and Postman, L. (1948). Symbolic value as an organizing factor in perception. *Journal of Social Psychology*, 27:203-208.

Bruner, J. S., Postman, L., and McGinnies, E. (1948). Personal values as selective factors in perception. *Journal of Abnormal and Social Psychology*, 43:142-154.

Brunswick, R. M. (1928). A supplement to Freud's *History of an Infantile Neurosis*. *International Journal of Psycho-Analysis*, 9:439-476.

Bullard, D. M. (1960). Psychotherapy of paranoid patients. *Archives of General Psychiatry*, 2:137-141.

Bunney, Jr., W. E., Goodwin, F. K., and Murphy, D. L. (1972). The "switch process" in manic-depressive illness. III. Theoretical implications. *Archives of General Psychiatry*, 27:312-317.

Bunney, Jr., W. E., Goodwin, F. K., Murphy, D. L., House, K. M., and Gordon, E. K. (1972). The "switch process" in manic-depressive illness. II. Relationship to catecholamines, REM sleep, and drugs. *Archives of General Psychiatry*, 27:304-309.

Bunney, Jr., W. E., Murphy, D. L., Goodwin, F. K., and Borge, G. F. (1972). The "switch process" in manic-depressive illness. I. A systematic study of sequential behaviorial changes. *Archives of General Psychiatry*, 27:295-302.

Bychowski, G. (1966). Patterns of anger. *Psychoanalytic Study of the Child*, 21:172-192.

Bychowski, G. (1967). The archaic object and alienation. *International Journal of Psychoanalysis*, 48:384-393.

Caine, T. M. (1960). The expression of hostility in melancholic and paranoid women. *Journal of Consulting Psychology*, 24:18-22.

Cameron, N. (1959). Paranoid conditions and paranoia. In Arieti, S. (ed.), *American Handbook of Psychiatry*, I:508-539. New York: Basic Books.

Camus, A. (1946). *The Stranger*. New York: Knopf.

Carlin, A. S., and Post, R. D. (1971). Patterns of drug use among marihuana smokers. *JAMA*, 218:867-868.

Carlson, G. A., and Goodwin, F. K. (1973). The stages of mania: A longitudinal analysis of the manic episode. *Archives of General Psychiatry*, 28:221-228.

Carr, A. C. (1963). Observations on paranoia and their relationships to the Schreber case. *International Journal of Psycho-Analysis*, 44:195-200.

Cassirer, E. (1955). *The Philosophy of Symbolic Forms. Vol. II. Mythical Thought.* New Haven: Yale University Press.

Cauthen, N. R., Robinson, I. E., and Krauss, H. H. (1971). Stereotypes: A review of the literature 1926-1968. *Journal of Social Psychology.* 84:103-125.

Chapman, A. H. (1954). Paranoid psychoses associated with amphetamine usage: A clinical note. *American Journal of Psychiatry*, 111:43-45.

Chess, S., Rutter, M., Thomas, A., and Birch, H. G. (1963). Interaction of temperament and the environment in the production of behavioral disturbances in children. *American Journal of Psychiatry*, 120:142-147.

Chess, S., Thomas, A., and Birch, H. G. (1967). Behavior problems revisited: Findings of an anterospective study. *Journal of the American Academy of Child Psychiatry*, 6:321-331.

Cleckley, H. M. (1959). Psychopathic states. In Arieti, S. (ed.), *American Handbook of Psychiatry*, I:567-588. New York: Basic Books.

Committee on Alcoholism and Addiction and Council on Mental Health. (1966). Dependence on amphetamines and other stimulant drugs. *JAMA*, 197:1023-1027.

Connell, P. H. (1958). *Amphetamine Psychosis.* London: Oxford University Press.

Crumley, F. E., and Blumenthal, R. S. (1973). Children's reactions to temporary loss of the father. *American Journal of Psychiatry*, 130:778-782.

Dalman, C. J. (1955). Criminal behavior as a pathologic ego defense. *Archives of Criminal Psychodynamics*, 1:555-563.

Daston, P., King, G., and Armitage, S. (1953). Distortion in paranoid schizophrenics. *Journal of Consulting Psychology*, 17:50-53.

de Busscher, J., (1963). Le thème de l'inceste dans les psychoses paranoides. *Acta Neurologica et Psychiatrica Belgica*, 63:862-891.

Deutsch, F. (1959). Symbolization as a formative stage of the conversion process. In Deutsch, F. (ed.), *On the Mysterious Leap from the Mind to the Body.* New York: International Universities Press, 75-97.

Deutsch, H. (1958). Trust and suspicion. *Journal of Conflict Resolution*, 4:265-279.

Deutsch, H. (1962). Cooperation and trust: Some theoretical notes. *Nebraska Symposium on Motivation*, 10:275-320.

Deutsch, H. (1965). *Neuroses and Character Types.* New York: International Universities Press.

Deutsch, H. (1967). *Selected Problems of Adolescence.* New York: International Universities Press.

Diagnostic and Statistical Manual of Mental Disorders (DSM-II). (1968). Washington, D. C.: American Psychiatric Association.

Dias Cordeiro, J. (1970). Les idées délirantes de préjudice. *Annales Médico-Psychologiques*, 1:719-734.

Dongier, S. (1959). Statistical study of clinical and electroencephalographic manifestations of 536 psychotic episodes occurring in 516 epileptics between clinical seizures. *Epilepsia*, 1:117-142.

Duncan, G. M., Frazier, S. H., Litin, E. M., et al. (1958). Etiological factors in first degree murder. *JAMA*, 168:1755-1758.

Duncan, J. W., and Duncan, G. M., (1971). Murder in the family: A study of some homicidal adolescents. *American Journal of Psychiatry*, 127:1498-1502.

DuPont, Jr., R. L. and Grunebaum, H. (1968). Willing victims: The husbands of paranoid women. *American Journal of Psychiatry*, 125:151-159.

Ebaugh, F. G., and Tiffany, Jr., W. J. (1959). Infective-exhaustive psychoses. In Arieti, S. (ed.), *American Handbook of Psychiatry*, II:1231-1247. New York: Basic Books.

Ehrenwald, J. (1960). The symbiotic matrix of paranoid delusions and the homosexual alternative. *American Journal of Psychoanalysis*, 20:49-65.

Ellinwood, E. H. (1969). Amphetamine psychosis: A multi-dimensional process. *Seminars in Psychiatry*, 1:208-226.

Ellinwood, E. H. (1971). Assault and homicide associated with amphetamine abuse. *American Journal of Psychiatry*, 127:1170-1175.

Ellinwood, E. H., Sudilovsky, A., and Nelson, L. M. (1973). Evolving behavior in the clinical and experimental amphetamine (model) psychosis. *American Journal of Psychiatry*, 130:1088-1093.

Erikson, E. H. (1959). *Identity and the Life Cycle.* New York: International Universities Press.

Erikson, E. H. (1962). *Young Man Luther.* New York: Norton.

Erikson, E. H. (1963). *Childhood and Society.* New York: Norton.

Erikson, E. H. (1964). *Insight and Responsibility.* New York: Norton.

Ervin, F. R. (1967). Brain disorders. IV. Associated with convulsions. In Freedman, A. M. and Kaplan, H. I. (eds.), *Comprehensive Textbook of Psychiatry.* Baltimore: Williams and Wilkins.

Fast, I., and Chethik, M. (1972). Some aspects of object relationships in borderline children. *International Journal of Psycho-Analysis,* 53:479-485.

Fenichel, O. (1945). *The Psychoanalytic Theory of Neurosis.* New York: Norton.

Fisher, C. (1965). Psychoanalytic implications of recent research on sleep and dreaming. *Journal of the American Psychoanalytic Association*, 18:747-782.

Fisher, C., Byrne, J., Edwards, A., and Kahn, E. (1970a). A psychophysiological study of nightmares. *Journal of the American Psychoanalytic Association*, 18:747-782.

Fisher, C., Byrne, J., Edwards, A., and Kahn, E. (1970b). REM and NREM nightmares. In Hartmann, E. (ed.), *Sleep and Dreaming.* Boston: Little, Brown, 183-187.

Fitzgerald, R. G. (1970). Reactions to blindness: An exploratory study of adults with recent loss of sight. *Archives of General Psychiatry.* 22:370-379.

Framo, J. L. (1965). Rationale and techniques of intensive family therapy. In Boszormenyi-Nagy, I., and Framo, J. L. (eds.), *Intensive Family Therapy.* New York: Harper and Row, 143-212.

Frederick, C. J. (1972). Drug abuse as self-destructive behavior. *Drug Therapy*, March, 49-68.

Freeman, T. (1971). Observations on mania. *International Journal of Psycho-Analysis*, 52:479-486.

Freud, A. (1923). The relation of beating-phantasies to a day-dream. *International Journal of Psycho-Analysis*, 4:89-102.

Freud, A. (1936). *The Ego and the Mechanisms of Defense.* Revised edition. New York: International Universities Press, 1966.

Freud, A. (1965). *Normality and Pathology in Childhood: Assessments of Development.* International Universities Press.

Freud, A. (1970). The concept of the rejecting mother. In Anthony, E. J., and Benedek, T. (eds.), *Parenthood: Its Psychology and Psychopathology.* Boston: Little, Brown, 376-386.

Freud, A. (1971). Foreword. In Gardiner, M. (ed.), *The Wolf-Man by the Wolf-Man*. New York: Basic Books, ix-xii.

Freud, A. (1972). Comments on aggression. *International Journal of Psycho-Analysis*, 53:163-171.

Freud, S. (1887-1902). *The Origins of Psychoanalysis: Letters, Drafts and Notes to Wilhelm Fleiss.* Garden City, New York: Doubleday, 1957.

Freud, S. (1950 [1892-1899]). Extracts from the Fliess papers. *Standard Edition*, 1:173-280. London: Hogarth, 1966.

Freud, S. (1896). Further remarks on the neuropsychoses of defence. *Standard Edition*, 3:157-185. London: Hogarth, 1962.

Freud, S. (1900). The interpretation of dreams. *Standard Edition*, 4 and 5. London: Hogarth, 1953.

Freud, S. (1905a). Fragment of an analysis of a case of hysteria. *Standard Edition*, 7:3-122. London: Hogarth, 1953.

Freud, S. (1905b). Three essays on the theory of sexuality. *Standard Edition*, 7:123-245. London: Hogarth, 1957.

Freud, S. (1908). Hysterical phantasies and their relation to bisexuality. *Standard Edition*, 9:155-166. London: Hogarth, 1959.

Freud, S. (1909). Analysis of phobia in a five-year-old boy. *Standard Edition*, 10:1-149. London: Hogarth, 1955.

Freud, S. (1910). The future prospects of psycho-analytic therapy. *Standard Edition*, 11:139-151. London: Hogarth, 1957.

Freud, S. (1911). Psycho-analytic notes on an autobiographic account of a case of paranoia (dementia paranoides). *Standard Edition*, 12:1-82. London: Hogarth, 1958.

Freud, S. (1913a). Observations and examples from analytic practice. *Standard Edition*, 13:191-198. London: Hogarth, 1955.

Freud, S. (1913b). Totem and taboo. *Standard Edition*, 13:1-162. London: Hogarth, 1955.

Freud, S. (1914). On narcissism: An introduction. *Standard Edition*, 14:67-102. London: Hogarth, 1957.

Freud, S. (1915). Instincts and their vicissitudes. *Standard Edition*, 14:109-140. London: Hogarth, 1957.

Freud, S. (1917[1915]). A metaphysiological supplement to the theory of dreams. *Standard Edition*, 14:222-235. London: Hogarth, 1957.

Freud, S. (1916). Some analytic character-types met in psycho-analytic work. *Standard Edition*, 14:309-333. London: Hogarth, 1957.

Freud, S. (1916-17). Introductory lectures on psycho-analysis. *Standard Edition*, 15 and 16. London: Hogarth, 1963.

Freud, S. (1917). Mourning and melancholia. *Standard Edition*, 14:237-258. London: Hogarth, 1957.

Freud, S. (1919). A child is being beaten. *Standard Edition*, 17:175-204. London: Hogarth, 1957.

Freud, S. (1922). Some neurotic mechanisms in jealousy, paranoia and homosexuality. *Standard Edition*, 18:221-232. London: Hogarth, 1955.

Freud, S. (1923 [1922]). A seventeenth-century demonological neurosis. *Standard Edition*, 19:67-105. London: Hogarth, 1961.

Freud, S. (1923). The ego and the id. *Standard Edition*, 19:1-66. London: Hogarth, 1961.

Freud, S. (1924). The economic problem of masochism. *Standard Edition*, 19:155-170. London: Hogarth, 1961.

Freud, S. (1925). Negation. *Standard Edition*,19:233-239. London: Hogarth, 1961.

Freud, S. (1927). The future of an illusion. *Standard Edition*, 21:1-56. London: Hogarth, 1961.

Freud, S. (1930 [1929]). Civilization and its discontents. *Standard Edition*, 21:57-145. London: Hogarth, 1961.

Freud, S. (1931). Female sexuality. *Standard Edition*, 21:221-243. London: Hogarth, 1961.

Freud, S. (1933 [1932]). New introductory lectures on psycho-analysis. *Standard Edition*, 22:1-182. London: Hogarth, 1964.

Freud, S. (1937). Constructions in analysis. *Standard Edition*, 22:255-269. London: Hogarth, 1964.

Freud, S. (1940 [1938]). An outline of psycho-analysis. *Standard Edition*, 23:139-207. London: Hogarth, 1964.

Friedman, I. (1957). Characteristics of TAT heroes of normals, psychoneurotics, and paranoid schizophrenic subjects. *Journal of Projective Techniques*, 21:372-376.

Friedman, M., Glasser, M., Laufer, E., Laufer, M., and Wohl, M. (1972). Attempted suicide and self-mutilation in adolescence: Some observations from a psychoanalytic research project. *International Journal of Psycho-Analysis*, 53:179-183.

Fries, M. E., and Woolf, P. J. (1953). Some hypotheses on the role of the congenital activity type in personality development. *Psychoanalytic Study of the Child*, 8:48-62.

Frijling-Schreuder, E. C. M. (1972). The vicissitudes of aggression in normal development, in childhood neurosis and in childhood psychosis. *International Journal of Psycho-Analysis*, 53:185-190.

Fromm, E. (1941). *Escape from Freedom.* New York: Holt, Rinehart and Winston.

Fromm, E. (1973). *The Anatomy of Human Destructiveness.* New York: Holt, Rinehart and Winston.

Frosch, J. (1967). Delusional fixity, sense of conviction, and the psychotic conflict. *International Journal of Psycho-Analysis*, 48:475-495.

Frost, J. B. (1969). Paraphrenia and paranoid schizophrenia. *Psychiatric Clinics*, 2:129-138.

Gardiner, M. (ed.), (1971). *The Wolf-Man by the Wolf-Man.* New York: Basic Books.

Gardner, G. (1931). Evidences of homosexuality in one hundred and twenty unanalyzed cases with paranoid content. *Psychoanalytic Review*, 18:57-61.

Gardner, R., Holzman, P. S., Klein, G. S., Linton, H., and Spence, D. P. (1959). *Cognitive Control: A Study of Individual Consistences in Cognitive Behavior.* New York: International Universities Press.

Gault, W. B. (1971). Some remarks on slaughter. *American Journal of Psychiatry*,128:450-454.

Giffin, M. E., Johnson, A. M., and Litin, E. M. (1954). Specific factors determining antisocial acting-out. *American Journal of Orthopsychiatry*,24:668-684.

Giovacchini, P. (1967). Frustration and externalization. *Psychoanalytic Quarterly*, 36:571-583.

Giovacchini, P. (1970). Effects of adaptive and disruptive aspects of early object relationships upon later parental functioning. In Anthony, E. J., and Benedek, T. (eds.), *Parenthood: Its Psychology and Psychopathology.* Boston: Little, Brown, 525-537.

Glover, E. (1956). *On the Early Development of the Mind.* London: Imago.

Glueck, S., and Glueck, E. T. (1950). *Unraveling Juvenile Delinquency.* New York: Commonwealth Fund.

Goffman, E. (1969). The insanity of place. *Psychiatry,* 32:357-388.

Goldberg, G. J. (1965). Obsessional paranoid syndromes. *Psychiatric Quarterly,* 39:43-63.

Goldstein, A., and Carr, A. (1956). The attitude of mothers of male catatonic and paranoid schizophrenics toward child behavior. *Journal of Consulting Psychology,* 20:190.

Gonen, J. Y. (1971). Negative identity in homosexuals. *Psychoanalytic Review,* 58:345-352.

Goodman, I. Z. (1968). Influence of parental figures on schizophrenic patients. *Journal of Abnormal and Social Psychology,* 73:503-512.

Grauer, D. (1954). Homosexuality in paranoid schizophrenics as revealed by the Rorschach test. *Journal of Consulting Psychology,* 18:459-462.

Green, A. (1972). Aggression, femininity, paranoia and reality. *International Journal of Psycho-Analysis,* 53:205-211.

Green, R., Newman, L. E., and Stoller, R. J. (1972). Treatment of boyhood "transsexualism." *Archives of General Psychiatry,* 26:213-217.

Greenacre, P. (1952). *Trauma, Growth and Personality.* New York: International Universities Press.

Greenacre, P. (1970). Youth, growth and violence. *Psychoanalytic Study of the Child,* 25:340-359.

Greenberg, R., and Pearlman, C. (1967). Delirium tremens and dreaming. *American Journal of Psychiatry,* 124:133-142.

Greenson, R. (1954). The struggle against identification. *Journal of the American Psychoanalytic Association,* 2:200-217.

Greenson, R. 1967. *The Technique and Practice of Psychoanalysis.* Vol I. New York: International Universities Press.

Griffith, J. D., Cavanaugh, J. H., Held, J., et al. (1970). Experimental psychosis induced by the administration of *d*-amphetamine. In Costa, E., and Garattini, S. (eds.), *Amphetamines and Related Compounds.* New York: Raven Press, 897-904.

Griffith, J. D., Cavanaugh, J., Held, J., and Oates, J. A. (1972). Dextroamphetamine: Evaluation of psychomimetic properties in man. *Archives of General Psychiatry,* 26:97-100.

Grinspoon, L., and Hedblom, P. (1972). Amphetamine abuse. *Drug Therapy,* Jan., 83-99.

Guntrip, H. (1969). *Schizoid Phenomena, Object Relations and the Self.* New York: International Universities Press.

Hader, M. (1965). Persistent enuresis: The incidence of a history of persistent enuresis in offenders attending an outpatient psychiatric clinic. *Archives of General Psychiatry,* 13:296-298.

Halleck, S. (1967). *Psychiatry and the Dilemmas of Crime.* New York: Harper and Row.

Harford, T., and Solomon, L. (1969). Effects of a "reformed sinner" and a "lapsed saint" strategy upon trust formation in paranoid and nonparanoid schizophrenic patients. *Journal of Abnormal Psychology,* 74:498-504.

Harmatz, J. S., Shader, R. I., and Salzman, C. (1972). Marihuana users and nonusers. *Archives of General Psychiatry,* 26:108-112.

Hartmann, E. (1970). A note on the nightmare. In Hartmann, E. (ed.), *Sleep and Dreaming.* Boston: Little, Brown, 192-197.

Hartmann, H. (1950). Comments on the psychoanalytic theory of the ego. *Psychoanalytic Study of the Child*, 5:74-96. Reprinted in Hartmann, H. (1964).

Hartmann, H. (1964). *Essays on Ego Psychology*. New York: International Universities Press.

Havener, P., and Izard, C. (1962). Unrealistic self-enhancement in paranoid schizophrenics. *Journal of Consulting Psychology*, 26:65-68.

Hellman, D. S., and Blackman, N. (1966). Enuresis, firesetting and cruelty to animals: A triad predictive of adult crime. *American Journal of Psychiatry*, 122:1431-1435.

Henle, M. (1955). Some effects of motivational processes on cognition. *Psychological Review*, 62:423-452.

Herbert, M. E., and Jacobson, S. (1967). Late paraphrenia. *British Journal of Psychiatry*, 113:461-469.

Heron, W. (1957). The pathology of boredom. *Scientific American*, 196:52-56.

Heron, W., Doane, B. K., and Scott, T. H. (1956). Visual disturbances after prolonged perceptual isolation. *Canadian Journal of Psychology*, 10:13-18.

Hesselbach, C. F. (1962). Superego regression in paranoia. *Psychoanalytic Quarterly*, 31:341-350.

Hitson, H. M., and Funkenstein, D. H. (1959). Family patterns and paranoidal personality structure in Boston and Burma. *International Journal of Social Psychiatry*, 5:182-190.

Hoch, P. H. (1959). Pharmacologically induced psychoses In Arieti, S., (ed.), *American Handbook of Psychiatry*, II:1697-1708. New York: Basic Books.

Hollister, L. (1971). Marihuana in man: Three years later. *Science*, 172:21-28.

Horner, M. S. (1970). Femininity and successful achievement: A basic inconsistency. In Horner, M. S., *Feminine Personality and Conflict*. Belmont, California: Brooks/Cole, 45-74.

Horney, K. (1950). *Neurosis and Human Growth*. New York: Norton.

Izard, C. E. (1959). Paranoid schizophrenic perception of photos of human faces. *Journal of Consulting Psychology*, 23:119-124.

Jacobson, E. (1957). Denial and repression. *Journal of the American Psychoanalytic Association*, 5:61-92.

Jacobson, E. (1959). The "exceptions": An elaboration of Freud's character study. *Psychoanalytic Study of the Child*, 14:135-154.

Jacobson, E. (1964). *The Self and the Object World*. New York: International Universities Press.

Jaensch, E. R. (1938). *Der Gegentypus*. Leipzig: Barth.

Jaffe, D. S. (1968). The mechanism of projection: Its dual role in object relations. *International Journal of Psycho-Analysis*, 49:662-677.

Jaffe, D. S. (1971a). Postscript to the analysis of a case of hysteria. *International Journal of Psycho-Analysis*, 52:395-399.

Jaffe, D. S., (1971b). The role of ego modification and the task of structural change in the analysis of a case of hysteria. *International Journal of Psycho-Analysis*, 52:375-393.

Joffe, W. G. (1969). A critical review of the status of the envy concept. *International Journal of Psycho-Analysis*, 50:533-545.

Joffe, W. G., and Sandler, J. (1965). Notes on pain, depression and individuation. *Psychoanalytic Study of the Child*. 20:394-424.

Johnson, A. M. and Szurek, S. A. (1952). The genesis of antisocial acting out in children and adults. *Psychoanalytic Quarterly*, 21:323-343.

Jones, E. (1929). Jealousy. In *Papers on Psycho-Analysis*. Boston: Beacon Press, 1961, 325-340.

Jones, E. (1955). *Sigmund Freud: Life and Work. Vol II*. New York: Basic Books.

Kalogerakis, M. G. (1971). The assaultive psychiatric patient. *Psychiatric Quarterly*, 45:372-381.

Kaplan, H. B. (1972). Toward a general theory of psychosocial deviance: The case of aggressive behavior. *Social Science and Medicine*, 6:593-617.

Katan, A. (1946). Experience with enuretics. *Psychoanalytic Study of the Child.*2:241-255.

Katan, M. (1950a). Schreber's hallucinations about the "little men." *International Journal of Psycho-Analysis*, 31:32-35.

Katan, M. (1950b). Structural aspects of a case of schizophrenia. *Psychoanalytic Study of the Child*, 5:175-211.

Katan, M. (1952). Further remarks about Schreber's hallucinations. *International Journal of Psycho-Analysis*, 33:429-432.

Katan, M. (1953). Schreber's prepsychotic phase. *International Journal of Psycho-Analysis*, 34:43-51.

Katan, M. (1969). A psychoanalytic approach to the diagnosis of paranoia. *Psychoanalytic Study of the Child*, 24:328-357.

Kee, H. W., and Knox, R. E. (1970). Conceptual and methodological considerations in the study of trust and suspicion. *Journal of Conflict Resolution*, 14:357-366.

Keniston, K. (1965). *The Uncommitted: Alienated Youth in American Society*. New York: Harcourt, Brace Jovanovich.

Kernberg, O. (1966). Structural derivatives of object relationships. *International Journal of Psycho-Analysis*, 47:236-253.

Kernberg, O. (1967). Borderline personality organization. *Journal of the American Psychoanalytic Association*, 15:641-685.

Kernberg, O. (1969). A contribution of the ego-psychological critique of the Kleinian school. *International Journal of Psycho-Analysis*, 50:317-333.

Kernberg, O. (1970). Factors in the psychoanalytic treatment of narcissistic personalities. *Journal of the American Psychoanalytic Association*, 18:51-85.

Keup, W. (1970). Psychotic symptoms due to cannabis abuse. *Diseases of the Nervous System*, 31:119-126.

Kinzel, A. F. (1970). Body-buffer zone in violent prisoners. *American Journal of Psychiatry*, 127:59-64.

Klaf, F. S. and Davis, C. A. (1960). Homosexuality and paranoid schizophrenia: A survey of 150 cases and controls. *American Journal of Psychiatry*, 116:1070-1075.

Klein, E. B., and Solomon, L. (1966). Agreement response tendency and behavioral submission in schizophrenia. *Psychological Reports*, 18:499-509.

Klein, G. S. (1970). *Perception, Motives, and Personality*. New York: Knopf.

Klein, H., and Horowitz, W. (1949). Psychosexual factors in the paranoid phenomenon. *American Journal of Psychiatry*, 105:697-701.

Klein, M. (1932). *The Psycho-Analysis of Children*. New York: Grove Press, 1960.

Klein, M. (1957). *Envy and Gratitude.*London: Tavistock.

Klein, M. (1964). *Contributions to Psycho-Analysis: 1920-1945*. New York: McGraw-Hill.

Knight, R. P. (1940). The relationship of latent homosexuality to the mechanism of paranoid delusions. *Bulletin of the Menninger Clinic*, 4:149-159.

Kohut, H. (1966). Forms and transformations of narcissism. *Journal of the American Psychoanalytic Association*, 14:243-272.

Kohut, H. (1968). The psychoanalytic treatment of narcissistic personality disorders. *Psychoanalytic Study of the Child*, 23:86-113.

Kohut, H. (1971). *The Analysis of the Self: A Systematic Approach to the Psychoanalytic Treatment of Narcissistic Personality Disorders*. New York: International Universities Press.

Kohut, H. (1972). Thoughts on narcissism and narcissistic rage. *Psychoanalytic Study of the Child*, 27:360-400

Kolansky, H., and Moore, W. T. (1971). Effects of marihuana on adolescents and young adults. *JAMA*, 216:486-492.

Kovar, L. (1966). A reconsideration of paranoia. *Psychiatry*, 29:289-305.

Kramer, J. C., Fischman, V. S. and Littlefield, D. C. (1967). Amphetamine abuse. *JAMA*, 201:305-309.

Laing, R. D. (1965a). *The Divided Self: An Existential Study in Sanity and Madness*. Baltimore: Penguin.

Laing, R. D. (1965b). Mystification, confusion and conflict. In Boszormenyi-Nagy, I. and Framo, J. L. (eds.), *Intensive Family Therapy*. New York: Harper and Row, 343-363.

Laing, R. D., and Esterson, A. (1964). *Sanity, Madness and the Family. Vol I. Families of Schizophrenics*. New York: Basic Books.

Lanzkron, J. (1961). Murder as a reaction to paranoid delusions in involutional psychosis and its prevention. *American Journal of Psychiatry*, 118:426-427.

Lanzkron, J. (1963). Murder and insanity: A survey. *American Journal of Psychiatry*, 119:754-758.

Lax, R. F. (1972). Some aspects of the interaction between mother and impaired child: Mother's narcissistic trauma. *International Journal of Psycho-Analysis*, 53:339-344.

Lemert, E. M. (1962). Paranoia and the dynamics of exclusion. *Sociometry*, 25:2-20.

Levin, D. C. (1969). The self: A contribution to its place in theory and technique. *International Journal of Psycho-Analysis*, 50:41-51.

Levin, S. (1967). Some metapsychological considerations on the differentiation between shame and guilt. *International Journal of Psycho-Analysis*, 48:267-276.

Levy, D. M. (1970). The concept of maternal overprotection. In Anthony, E. J., and Benedek, T. (eds.), *Parenthood: Its Psychology and Psychopathology*. Boston: Little, Brown, 387-409.

Lewis, A. (1970). Paranoia and paranoid: A historical perspective. *Psychological Medicine*, 1:2-12.

Lichtenstein, H. (1961). Identity and sexuality: A study of their interrelationship in man. *Journal of the American Psychoanalytic Association*, 9:179-260.

Lidz, T., Fleck, S., and Cornelison, A. R. (1965). *Schizophrenia and the Family*. New York: International Universities Press.

Lion, J. R., Bach-y-Rita, G., and Ervin, F. R. (1969). Violent patients in the emergency room. *American Journal of Psychiatry*, 125:1706-1711.

Little, R. B. (1967). Spider phobias. *Psychoanalytic Quarterly*, 36:51-60.

Loewald, H. W. (1962). Internalization, separation, mourning, and the superego. *Psychoanalytic Quarterly*, 31:483-504.

Lomas, P. (1962). The origin of the need to be special. *British Journal of Medical Psychology*, 35:339-346.

Lowenfeld, H., and Lowenfeld, Y. (1970). Permissive society and the superego: Some current thoughts about Freud's cultural concepts. *Psychiatric Quarterly*, 39:590-608.

Lynn, E. J. (1971). Amphetamine abuse: A "speed" trap. *Psychiatric Quarterly*, 45:92-101.

MacAlpine, I., and Hunter, R. A. (1953). The Schreber case. A contribution to schizophrenia, hypochondria, and psychosomatic symptom-formation. *Psychoanalytic Quarterly*, 22:328-371.

MacAlpine, I., and Hunter, R. A. (1956). *Schizophrenia 1677*. London: Dawson and Sons.

Macdonald, J. M. (1963). The threat to kill. *American Journal of Psychiatry*, 120:125-130.

Macdonald, J. M. (1967). Homicidal threats. *American Journal of Psychiatry*, 124:475-482.

Mack, J. E. (1965). Nightmares, conflict, and ego development in childhood. *International Journal of Psycho-Analysis*, 46:403-428.

Mack, J. E. (1969). Dreams and psychosis. *Journal of the American Psychoanalytic Association*, 17:206-221.

Mack, J. E. (1970). *Nightmares and Human Conflict*. Boston: Little, Brown.

Mahler, M. S. (1968). *On Human Symbiosis and the Vicissitudes of Individuation. Vol. I. Infantile Psychosis*. New York: International Universities Press.

Mahler, M. S. (1972a). On the first three subphases of the separation-individuation process. *International Journal of Psycho-Analysis*. 53:333-338.

Mahler, M. S. (1972b). Rapprochement subphase of the separation-individuation process. *Psychoanalytic Quarterly*, 41:487-506.

Mahler, M. S., Pine, F., and Bergman, A. (1970). The mother's reaction to her toddler's drive for individuation. In Anthony, E. J., and Benedek, T. (eds.), *Parenthood: Its Psychology and Psychopathology*. Boston: Little, Brown, 257-274.

Malinowski, B. (1955). *Magic, Science and Religion and Other Essays*. Garden City, New York: Doubleday.

Malmquist, C. P. (1971). Premonitory signs of homicidal aggression in juveniles. *American Journal of Psychiatry*, 128:461-465.

Marcus, I. M. (1973). The experience of separation-individuation in infancy and its reverberations through the course of life: 2. Adolescence and maturity. *Journal of the American Psychoanalytic Association*, 21:155-167.

Mark, V. H., and Ervin, F. R. (1970). *Violence and the Brain*. New York: Harper and Row.

Marks, I. M. (1969). *Fears and Phobias*. New York: Academic Press.

Marks, I. M. (1970). The origins of phobic states. *American Journal of Psychotherapy*, 24:652-676.

May, R. (1970). Paranoia and power anxiety. *Journal of Projective Techniques and Personality Assessment*, 34:412-418.

May, R. (1972). *Power and Innocence*. New York: Norton.

May, R., Angel, E., and Ellenberger, H. F. (eds.), (1958). *Existence: A New Dimension in Psychiatry and Psychology*. New York: Simon and Schuster.

McCawley, A. (1971). Paranoia and homosexuality: Schreber reconsidered. *New York State Journal of Medicine*, 71:1506-1513.

McCord, W., and McCord, J. (1956). *Psychopathy and Delinquency*. New York: Grune.

McKeton, B., Griffith, R., Taylor, V., and Wiedeman, J. (1962). Rorschach homosexual signs in paranoid schizophrenics. *Journal of Abnormal and Social Psychology*, 65:280-284.

McReynolds, P. (1960). Anxiety, perception and schizophrenia. In Jackson, D. D. (ed.), *The Etiology of Schizophrenia.* New York: Basic Books, 248-292.

Mehlman, R. D. (1961). The Puerto Rican syndrome. *American Journal of Psychiatry,* 118:328-332.

Meissner, S. J., W. W. (1964). Thinking about the family—psychiatric aspects. *Family Process,* 3:1-40.

Meissner, S. J., W. W. (1966). Hippocampal functions in learning. *Journal of Psychiatric Research,* 4:235-304.

Meissner, S. J., W. W. (1970a). *The Assault on Authority—Dialogue or Dilemma?* New York: Orbis.

Meissner, S. J., W. W. (1970b). Erickson's truth: The search for ethical identity. *Theological Studies,* 31:310-319.

Meissner, S. J., W. W. (1970c). Notes toward a theory of values: The place of values. *Journal of Religion and Health,* 9:123-137.

Meissner, S. J., W. W. (1970d). Notes toward a theory of values: Values as psychological. *Journal of Religion and Health,* 9:233-249.

Meissner, S. J., W. W. (1970e). Sibling relations in the schizophrenic family. *Family Process,* 9:1-25.

Meissner, S. J., W. W. (1971a). Freud's methodology. *Journal of the American Psychoanalytic Association,* 19:265-309.

Meissner, S. J., W. W. (1971b). Notes on identification. II. Clarification of related concepts. *Psychoanalytic Quarterly,* 40:277-302.

Meissner, S. J., W. W. (1971c). Notes toward a theory of values: Values as cultural. *Journal of Religion and Health,* 10:77-97.

Meissner, S. J., W. W. (1972). Notes on identification. III. The concept of identification. *Psychoanalytic Quarterly,* 41:224-260.

Melon, J. (1970). Psychopathologie de la transplantation. *Les Feuillets Psychiatriques de Liège,* 3:386-412.

Melon, J., and Timsit, M. (1971). Etude statistique sur la psychopathologie des immigrès. *Acta Psychiatrica Belgica,* 7(2):98-120.

Merton, R. K. (1957). *Social Theory and Social Structure.* New York: Free Press.

Miller, C. (1941). The paranoid syndrome. *Archives of Neurology and Psychiatry,* 45:953-963.

Mishler, E. G., and Waxler, N. E. (1966). Family interaction processes and schizophrenia: A review of current theories. *International Journal of Psychiatry,* 2:375-413.

Mishler, E. G., and Waxler, N. E. (1968). *Interaction in Families: An Experimental Study of Family Processes and Schizophrenia.* New York: Wiley.

Mittelman, B. (1954). Motility in infants, children and adults: Patterning and psychodynamics. *Psychoanalytic Study of the Child,* 9:142-177.

Modell, A. H. (1963). Primitive object relations and the predisposition to schizophrenia. *International Journal of Psycho-Analysis,* 44:282-292.

Modell, A. H. (1968). *Object Love and Reality.* New York: International Universities Press.

Modell, A. H. (1971). The origin of certain forms of pre-oedipal guilt and the implications for a psychoanalytic theory of affects. *International Journal of Psycho-Analysis,* 52:337-346.

Modlin, H. C. (1963). Psychodynamics and management of paranoid states in women. *Archives of General Psychiatry,* 8:262-268.

Money-Kyrle, R. E. (1960). On prejudice: A psychoanalytic approach. *British Journal of Medical Psychology,* 33:205-209.

Money-Kyrle, R. E. (1968). Cognitive development. *International Journal of Psycho-Analysis*, 49:691-698.

Moore, B. E., and Fine, B. D. (1967). *A Glossary of Psychoanalytic Terms and Concepts*. New York: American Psychoanalytic Association.

Morris, G. O., and Wynne, L. C. (1965). Schizophrenic offspring and parental styles of communication. *Psychiatry*, 28:19-44.

Murphy, G. (1947). *Personality: A Biosocial Approach to Origins and Structure*. New York: Basic Books.

Murray, J. M. (1964). Narcissism and the ego-ideal. *Journal of the American Psychoanalytic Association*, 12:477-511.

Nagera, H. (1966). Sleep and its disturbances approached developmentally. *Psychoanalytic Study of the Child*, 21:393-447.

Newman, M. B. and San Martino, M. (1971). The child and the seriously disturbed parent: Patterns of adaption to parental psychosis. *Journal of the American Academy of Child Psychiatry*, 10:358-374.

Newman, M. B., and San Martino, M. (1973). The child and the seriously disturbed parent: Treatment issues. *Journal of the American Academy of Child Psychiatry*, 12:162-181.

Nicholi, A. M. (1970). Campus disorders: A problem of adult leadership. *American Journal of Psychiatry*, 127:424-429.

Niederland, W. G. (1951). Three notes on the Schreber case. *Psychoanalytic Quarterly*, 20:579-591.

Niederland, W. G. (1959). Schreber: Father and son. *Psychoanalytic Quarterly*, 28:151-169.

Niederland, W. G. (1960). The miracled-up world of Schreber's childhood. *Psychoanalytic Quarterly*, 29:301-304.

Niederland, W. G. (1963). Further data and memorabilia pertaining to the Schreber case. *International Journal of Psycho-Analysis*, 44:201-207.

Niederland, W. G. (1965). Narcissistic ego impairment in patients with early physical malformations. *Psychiatric Study of the Child*, 20: 18-534.

Niederland, W. G. (1968). Schreber and Flechsig: A further contribution to the "kernel of truth in Schreber's delusional system." *Journal of the American Psychoanalytical Association*, 16:740-749.

Norman, D. A. (1968). Toward a theory of memory and attention. *Psychological Review*, 75:522-536.

Norman, D. A. (1970). *Memory and Attention*. New York: Wiley.

Northrup, G. (1959). Transsexualism: A case report. *Archives of General Psychiatry*, 1:332-337.

Novick, J., and Hurry, A. (1969).Projection and externalization. *Journal of Child Psychotherapy*, 2(3):5-20.

Novick, J., and Novick, K. K (1972). Beating fantasies in children. *International Journal of Psycho-Analysis*. 53:237-242.

Nunberg, H. (1952). Discussion of M. Katan's paper on Schreber's hallucinations. *International Journal of Psycho-Analysis*, 33:454-456.

Nunberg, H. (1955). *Principles of Psychoanalysis*. New York: International Universities Press.

Nydes, J. (1963). The paranoid-masochistic character. *Psychoanalytic Review*, 50:215-251.

Orbach, C. E., and Bieber, I. (1957). Depressive and paranoid reactions: Application of adaptational principles to their understanding. *Archives of Neurology and Psychiatry*, 78:301-311.

Ovesey, L. (1954). The homosexual conflict: An adaptational analysis. *Psychiatry*, 17:243-250.

Ovesey, L. (1955a). The pseudohomosexual anxiety. *Psychiatry*, 17:17-25.

Ovesey, L. (1955b). Pseudohomosexuality, the paranoid mechanism and paranoia. *Psychiatry*, 18:163-173.

Ovesey, L. (1962). Fear of vocational success: A phobic extension of the paranoid reaction. *Archives of General Psychiatry*, 7:82-92.

Pao, Ping-Nie. (1969). Pathological jealousy. *Psychoanalytic Quarterly*, 38:616-638.

Parsons, T., and Shils, E. A. (1962). Values, motives and systems of action. In *Toward a General Theory of Action*. New York: Harper and Row, 47-275.

Pauly, I. B. (1965). Male psychosexual inversion: Transsexualism: A review of 100 cases. *Archives of General Psychiatry*, 13:172-181.

Piers, G., and Singer, M. B. (1953). *Shame and Guilt: A Psychoanalytic and a Cultural Study*. Springfield, Ill.: Thomas.

Pillard, R. C. (1970). Marihuana. *New England Journal of Medicine*, 283:294-303.

Pinderhughes, C. A. (1969). Understanding black power: Processes and proposals. *American Journal of Psychiatry*, 125: 1552-1557.

Pinderhughes, C. A. (1970). The universal resolution of ambivalence by paranoia with an example in black and white. *American Journal of Psychotherapy*, 24:597-610.

Pinderhughes, C. A. (1971). Somatic, psychic and social sequelae of loss. *Journal of the American Psychoanalytic Association*, 19:670-696.

Planansky, K., and Johnston, R. (1962). Incidence and relationship of homosexual and paranoid features in schizophrenia. *Journal of Mental Science*, 108:604-615.

Postman, L., and Bruner, J. S. (1948). Perception under stress. *Psychological Review*, 55:314-323.

Prange, Jr., A. J. (1959). An interpretation of cultural isolation and alien's paranoid reaction. *International Journal of Social Psychiatry*, 4:254-263.

Radin, S. S. (1972). Job phobia: School phobia revisited. *Comprehensive Psychiatry*, 13:251-257.

Rapaport, D. (1944). The scientific methodology of psychoanalysis. In Gill, M. M. (ed.), *The Collected Papers of David Rapaport*. New York: Basic Books, 1967, 165-220.

Rapaport, D. (1952). Projective techniques and the theory of thinking. In Gill, M. M. (ed.), *The Collected Papers of David Rapaport*. New York: Basic Books, 1967, 461-469.

Rapaport, D. (1958). The theory of ego autonomy: A generalization. In Gill, M. M. (ed.), *The Collected Papers of David Rapaport*. New York: Basic Books, 1967, 722-744.

Rapaport, D. (1961). *Emotions and Memory*. New York: Science Editions.

Raybin, J. B. (1971). Aggression, mythology and the college student. *American Journal of Psychiatry*, 128:466-472.

Reich, A. (1960). Pathologic forms of self-esteem regulation. *Psychoanalytic Study of the Child*.15:215-232.

Retterstl, N. (1968). Paranoid psychoses associated with unpatriotic conduct during World War II. *Acta Psychiatrica Scandinavica*, 44:261-279.

Rheingold, J. C. (1967). *The Mother, Anxiety, and Death: The Catastrophic Death Complex*. Boston: Little, Brown.

Rickles, N. K. (1971). The angry woman syndrome. *Archives of General Psychiatry*, 24:91-94.

Riesman, D. (1950). *The Lonely Crowd.* New Haven: Yale University Press.

Riviere, J. (1932). Jealousy as a mechanism of defence. *International Journal of Psycho-Analysis,* 13:414-424.

Robbins, E., Robbins, L., Frosch, W. A., and Stern, M. (1970). College student drug use. *American Journal of Psychiatry,* 126:1743-1751.

Robins, L. N. (1966). *Deviant Children Grow Up.* New York: Williams and Wilkins.

Rochlin, G. (1961). The dread of abandonment: A contribution to the etiology of the loss complex and to depression. *Psychoanalytic Study of the Child,* 16:451-470.

Rochlin, G. (1965). *Griefs and Discontents: The Forces of Change.* Boston: Little, Brown.

Rochlin, G. (1973). *Man's Aggression: The Defense of the Self.* Boston: Gambit.

Rodin, E. A. (1973). Psychomotor epilepsy and aggressive behavior. *Archives of General Psychiatry,* 28:210-213.

Rokeach, M. (1960). *The Open and Closed Mind.* New York: Basic Books.

Roth M. (1972). Human violence as viewed from the psychiatric clinic. *American Journal of Psychiatry,* 128:1043-1056.

Roth, S. (1972). The seemingly ubiquitous depression following acute schizophrenic episodes, a neglected area of clinical discussion. *American Journal of Psychiatry,* 127:51-58.

Rothenberg, A. (1971). On anger. *Journal of Psychiatry,* 128:454-460.

Rubin, B. (1972). Prediction of dangerousness in mentally ill criminals. *Archives of General Psychiatry,* 27:397-407.

Rubinfine, D. L. (1965). On beating fantasies. *International Journal of Psycho-Analysis,* 46:315-322.

Rycroft, C. (1960). The analysis of a paranoid personality. *International Journal of Psycho-Analysis,* 41:59-69.

Rylander, G. (1972). Psychoses and the punding and choreiform syndromes in addiction to central stimulant drugs. *Psychiatrica, Neurologia, Neurochirurgia,* 75:203-212.

Salzman, L. (1960). Paranoid state: Theory and therapy. *Archives of General Psychiatry,* 2:679-693.

Sander, L. W. (1962). Issues in early mother-child interaction. *Journal of the American Academy of Child Psychiatry,* 1:141-166.

Sander, L. W. (1964). Adaptive relationships in early mother-child interaction. *Journal of the American Academy of Child Psychiatry,* 3:231-264.

Sander, L. W. (1969). The longitudinal course of early mother-child inter-action—Cross-case comparison in a sample of mother-child pairs. In Foss, B. M. (ed.), *Determinants of Infant Behavior IV.* London: Methuen, 189-227.

Sarnoff, C. A. (1971). Ego structure in latency. *Psychoanalytic Quarterly,* 40:387-414.

Sarnoff, C. A. (1972). The vicissitudes of projection during an analysis encompassing late latency to early adolescence. *International Journal of Psycho-Analysis,* 53:515-522.

Sarvis, M. A. (1962). Paranoid reactions: Perceptual distortion as an etiological agent. *Archives of General Psychiatry,* 6:157-162.

Satten, J., Menninger, K., Rosen, I., et al. (1960). Murder without apparent motive. *American Journal of Psychiatry,* 117:48-53.

Schafer, R. (1960). The loving and beloved superego in Freud's structural theory. *Psychoanalytic Study of the Child,* 15:163-188.

Schafer, R. (1968a). *Aspects of Internalization.* New York: International Universities Press.

Schafer, R. (1968b). The mechanisms of defense. *International Journal of Psycho-Analysis*, 49:59-62.

Schmideberg, M. (1931). A contribution to the psychology of persecuting ideas and delusions. *International Journal of Psycho-Analysis,*12:331-367.

Schreber, D. P. (1955). *Memoirs of My Nervous Illness.* Translated and edited by MacAlpine, I., and Hunter, R. A. Cambridge, Mass: Bentley.

Schwartz, D. A. (1963) A review of the "paranoid" concept. *Archives of General Psychiatry*, 8:349-361.

Schwartz, D. A. (1964). The paranoid-depressive existential continuum. *Psychiatric Quarterly*, 38:690-706.

Searles, H. F. (1965). *Collected Papers on Schizophrenia and Related Subjects.* NewYork: International Universities Press.

Searles, H. F. (1966-67). Concerning the development of an identity. *Psychoanalytic Review*, 53(4):507-530.

Shakespeare, W. (1945). *The Complete Works of William Shakespeare.* London: Oxford University Press.

Shapiro, D. (1965). *Neurotic Styles.* New York: Basic Books.

Shobe, F. O., and Brion, P. (1971). Long-term prognosis in manic-depressive illness: A follow-up investigation of 111 patients. *Archives of General Psychiatry*, 24:334-337.

Siegel, R. K. (1971). Marihuana and psychedelics: Some aspects of social use. *Drug Therapy.* June: 43-51.

Silver, L. B., Dublin, C. C., and Lourie, R. S. (1969). Does violence breed violence? Contributions from a study of the child abuse syndrome. *American Journal of Psychiatry*, 126:404-407.

Silverman, J. (1964). Perceptual control of stimulus intensity in paranoid and nonparanoid schizophrenia. *Journal of Nervous and Mental Disease*, 139:545-549.

Singer, M. T. and Wynne, L. C. (1965a). Thought disorder and family relations of schizophrenics. III. Methodology using projective techniques. *Archives of General Psychiatry,* 12:187-200.

Singer, M. T. and Wynne. L. C. (1965b). Thought disorder and family relations of schizophrenics, IV. Results and Implications. *Archives of General Psychiatry, 12:201-212.*

Sletten, I., and Ballous, S. (1967). The selection of delusional persecutors. *Canadian Psychiatric Association Journal*, 12:327-331.

Snyder, S. H. (1972). Catecholamines in the brain as mediators of amphetamine psychosis. *Archives of General Psychiatry*, 27:169-179.

Snyder, S. H. (1973). Amphetamine psychosis: A "model" schizophrenia mediated by catecholamines. *American Journal of Psychiatry*, 130(1):61-67.

Socarides, C. W. (1966). On vengeance: The desire to "get even." *Journal of the American Psychoanalytic Association*, 14:356-375.

Socarides, C. W. (1969). The desire for sexual transformation: A psychiatric evaluation of transsexualism. *American Journal of Psychiatry*, 125:1419-1425.

Solnit, A. J., and Stark, M. H. (1961). Mourning and the birth of a defective child. *Psychoanalytic Study of the Child*, 16:523-537.

Sperling, M.(1952). Animal phobias in a two-year-old child. *Psychoanalytic Study of the Child*, 7:115-125.

Sperling, M. (1967). School phobias: Classification, dynamics and treatment. *Psychoanalytic Study of the Child,* 22:375-401.

Sperling, M. (1971). Spider phobias and spider fantasies. *Journal of the American Psychoanalytic Association*, 19:472-498.

Spiegel, L. A. (1966). Affects in relation to self and object: A model for the derivation of desire, longing, pain, anxiety, humiliation, and shame. *Psychoanalytic Study of the Child*, 21:69-92.

Spielman, P. M. (1971). Envy and Jealousy: An attempt at clarification. *Psychoanalytic Quarterly*, 40:59-82.

Steele, B. F. (1970). Parental abuse of infants and small children. In Anthony, E. J., and Benedek, T. (eds.), *Parenthood: Its Psychology and Psychopathology*. Boston: Little, Brown, 449-477.

Stenback, A. (1964). Hypochondria and paranoia. *Acta Psychiatrica Scandinavica*, 49:379-385.

Stevens, J. R. (1966). Psychiatric implications of psychomotor epilepsy. *Archives of General Psychiatry*, 14:461-471.

Steyn, R. W. (1972). Medical implications of polyglottism. *Archives of General Psychiatry*, 27:245-247.

Stoller, R. J. (1968) *Sex and Gender: On the Development of Masculinity and Femininity.* New York: Jason Aronson, Inc.

Storr, A. (1968). *Human Aggression.* New York: Atheneum.

Sullivan, H. S. (1953a). *Conceptions of Modern Psychiatry.* New York: Norton.

Sullivan, H. S. (1953b). *The Interpersonal Theory of Psychiatry.* New York: Norton.

Sullivan, H. S. (1956). *Clinical Studies in Psychiatry.* New York: Norton.

Swanson, D. W., Bohnert, P. J., and Smith, J. A. (1970). *The Paranoid.* Boston: Little, Brown.

Tajfel, H. (1969). Cognitive aspects of prejudice. *Journal of Social Issues*, 25(4):79-97.

Talbott, J. A., and Teague, J. W., (1969). Marihuana psychosis: Acute toxic psychosis associated with the use of *Cannabis* derivatives. *JAMA*, 210:299-302.

Talland, G. A. (1968). *Disorders of Memory and Learning.* Baltimore: Penguin.

Talland, G. A., and Waugh, N. C. (1969). *The Pathology of Memory.* New York: Academic Press.

Tamarin, J. S., and Mendelson, J. H. (1969). The psychodynamics of chronic inebriation: Observations of alcoholics during the process of drinking in an experimental group setting. *American Journal of Psychiatry*, 125:886-889.

Teoh, Jr., I. (1972). The changing psychopathology of amok. *Psychiatry*, 35:345-351.

Thompson, G. N., (1959). Acute and chronic alcoholic conditions. In Arieti, S. (ed.), *American Handbook of Psychiatry*. II:1203-1221. New York: Basic Books.

Tseng, W. S. (1969). A paranoid family in Taiwan. *Archives of General Psychiatry*. 21: 55-63.

Tuovinen, M. (1970). Crime as an attempt to save one's integrity. *Dynamische Psychiatrie*, 3:99-105.

Umphress, A., Murphy, S., Nickols, J., and Hammar, S. (1970). Adolescent enuresis: A sociological study of family interaction. *Archives of General Psychiatry*, 22:237-244.

van den Aardweg, G. J. M. (1972). A grief theory of homosexuality. *American Journal of Psychotherapy*, 26:52-68.

Vogel, E. F., and Bell, N. W. (1967). The emotionally disturbed child as the family scapegoat. In Handel, G. (ed.), *The Psychosocial Interior of the Family*. Chicago: Aldine, 424-442.

Waelder, R. (1951). The structure of paranoid ideas. *International Journal of Psycho-Analysis*, 32:167-177.

Wallace, A. F. C., and Fogelson, R. D. (1965). The identity struggle. In Boszormenyi-Nagy, I., and Framo, J. R. (eds.), *Intensive Family Therapy*. New York: Harper and Row, 365-406.

Walters, O. S. (1955). A methodological critique of Freud's Schreber analysis. *Psychoanalytic Review*, 42:321-342.

Weidman, H. H., and Sussex, J. N. (1971). Cultural values and ego functioning in relation to the atypical culture-bound reactive syndromes. *International Journal of Social Psychiatry*, 17:83-100.

Weil, A. T., Zinberg, N. E., and Nelson, J. M. (1968). Clinical and psychological effects of marihuana in man. *Science*, 162:1234-1242.

Westermeyer, J. (1972). A comparison of amok and other homicide in Laos. *American Journal of Psychiatry*, 129:703-709.

White, R. B. (1961). The mother conflict in Schreber's psychosis. *International Journal of Psycho-Analysis*, 43:55-73.

White, R. B. (1963). The Schreber case reconsidered in the light of psychosocial concepts. *International Journal of Psycho-Analysis*, 44:213-221.

Will, O. A. (1961a). Paranoid development and the concept of the self: Psychotherapeutic intervention. *Psychiatry*, 24, (Suppl.):74-86.

Will, O. A. (1961b). Process, psychotherapy and schzophrenia. In Burton, A. (ed.), *Psychotherapy of the Psychoses*. New York: Basic Books, 10-42.

Williams, F. S. (1970). Alienation of youth as reflected in the hippie movement. *Journal of the American Academy of Child Psychiatry*, 9:251-263.

Winnicott, D. W. (1958). *Collected Papers: Through Paediatrics to Psycho-Analysis*. New York: Basic Books.

Winnicott, D. W. (1960). Ego distortion in terms of true and false self. In *The Maturational Process and the Facilitating Environment*. New York: International Universities Press, 1965, 140-152.

Winnicott, D. W. (1965). *The Maturational Processes and the Facilitating Environment*. New York: International Universities Press.

Winnicott, D. W. (1969). *The Child, the Family, and the Outside World*. Baltimore: Penguin.

Witkin, H. A. (1965). Psychological differentiation and forms of pathology. *Journal of Abnormal Psychology*, 70:317-336. Reprinted in Warr, P. B. (ed.), *Thought and Personality*. Baltimore: Penguin, 1970, 391-411.

Witkin, H. A., Lewis, H. B., Hertzman, M., Machover, K., Meissner, P. B., and Wapner, S. (1954). *Personality Through Perception*. New York: Harper and Row.

Wixen, B. N. (1971). Grudges: A psychoanalytic study. *Psychoanalytic Review*, 58:333-344.

Wolf, E. S., Gedo, J. E., and Terman, D., M. (1972). On the adolescent process as a transformation of self. *Journal of Youth and Adolescence*, 1:257-272.

Wolowitz, H. (1965). Attraction and aversion to power. *American Journal of Psychology*, 70:360-370.

Wolowitz, H. (1971). The validity of the psychoanalytic theory of paranoid dynamics: Evaluated from available experimental evidence. *Psychiatry*, 34:358-377.

Wolowitz, H., and Shorkey, C. (1966). Power themes in TAT stories of paranoid schizophrenic males. *Journal of Projective Techniques and Personality Assessment*, 30:591-596.

Wolowitz, H., and Shorkey, C. (1969). Power motivation in male paranoid children. *Psychiatry*, 32:459-466.

Woods, S. M. (1972).   Violence: Psychotherapy of pseudohomosexual panic. *Archives of General Psychiatry*, 27:255-258.

Worden, F., and Marsh, J. (1955). Psychological factors in men seeking sex transformation: A preliminary report. *JAMA*, 157:1292-1298.

Wynne, L. C. (1961). The study of intrafamilial alignments and splits in exploratory family therapy. In Ackerman, N. E., Beatman, F., and Sherman, S. N. (eds.), *Exploring the Base for Family Therapy*. New York: Family Service Association of America, 95-115.

Wynne, L., Ryckoff, I., Day, J., and Hirsch, S. (1958). Pseudo-mutuality in the family relations of schizophrenics. *Psychiatry*, 21:205-220.

Wynne, L. C., and Singer, M. T. (1963a). Thought disorder and family relations of schizophrenics. I. A research strategy. *Archives of General Psychiatry*, 9:191-198.

Wynne, L. C., and Singer, M. T. (1963b). Thought disorder and family relations of schizophrenics. II. A classification of forms of thinking. *Archives of General Psychiatry*, 9:199-206.

Zetzel, E. R. (1956). An approach to the relation between concept and content in psychoanalytic theory. *Psychoanalytic Study of the Child*, 11:99-121.

Zetzel, E. R. (1968). The so-called good hysteric. *International Journal of Psychoanalysis*, 49:256-260. Reprinted in Zetzel (1970).

Zetzel, E. R. (1970). *The Capacity for Emotional Growth*. New York: International Universities Press.

Zetzel, E. R., and Meissner, W. W. (1973). *Basic Concepts of Psychoanalytic Psychiatry*. New York: Basic Books.

NAME INDEX